# Twentieth-Century Literary Criticism

## Topics Volume

# Guide to Gale Literary Criticism Series

| For criticism on | Consult these Gale series |
|---|---|
| Authors now living or who died after December 31, 1959 | *CONTEMPORARY LITERARY CRITICISM (CLC)* |
| Authors who died between 1900 and 1959 | *TWENTIETH-CENTURY LITERARY CRITICISM (TCLC)* |
| Authors who died between 1800 and 1899 | *NINETEENTH-CENTURY LITERATURE CRITICISM (NCLC)* |
| Authors who died between 1400 and 1799 | *LITERATURE CRITICISM FROM 1400 TO 1800 (LC)* <br><br> *SHAKESPEAREAN CRITICISM (SC)* |
| Authors who died before 1400 | *CLASSICAL AND MEDIEVAL LITERATURE CRITICISM (CMLC)* |
| Authors of books for children and young adults | *CHILDREN'S LITERATURE REVIEW (CLR)* |
| Dramatists | *DRAMA CRITICISM (DC)* |
| Poets | *POETRY CRITICISM (PC)* |
| Short story writers | *SHORT STORY CRITICISM (SSC)* |
| Black writers of the past two hundred years | *BLACK LITERATURE CRITICISM (BLC)* |
| Hispanic writers of the late nineteenth and twentieth centuries | *HISPANIC LITERATURE CRITICISM (HLC)* |
| Native North American writers and orators of the eighteenth, nineteenth, and twentieth centuries | *NATIVE NORTH AMERICAN LITERATURE (NNAL)* |
| Major authors from the Renaissance to the present | *WORLD LITERATURE CRITICISM, 1500 TO THE PRESENT (WLC)* |

ISSN 0276-8178

Volume 94

# Twentieth-Century Literary Criticism

## Topics Volume

**Excerpts from Criticism of Various Topics
in Twentieth-Century Literature, including Literary
and Critical Movements, Prominent Themes and
Genres, Anniversary Celebrations, and Surveys
of National Literatures**

**Jennifer Baise**
*Editor*

**Thomas Ligotti**
*Associate Editor*

GALE GROUP

*Detroit*
*New York*
*San Francisco*
*London*
*Boston*
*Woodbridge, CT*

## STAFF

Jennifer Baise, *Editor*

Thomas Ligotti, *Associate Editor*

Maria Franklin, *Permissions Manager*
Kimberly F. Smilay, *Permissions Specialist*
Kelly A. Quin, *Permissions Associates*
Sandy Gore, *Permissions Assistant*

Victoria B. Cariappa, *Research Manager*
Andrew Guy Malonis, Barbara McNeil, Gary J. Oudersluys, Maureen Richards,
Cheryl L. Warnock, *Research Specialists*
Patricia T. Ballard, Tamara C. Nott, Tracie A. Richardson, *Research Associates*
Phyllis Blackman, Timothy Lehnerer, *Research Assistant*

Mary Beth Trimper, *Production Director*
Stacy Melson, *Buyer*

Michael Logusz, *Graphic Artist*
Randy Bassett, *Image Database Supervisor*
Robert Duncan, *Imaging Specialists*
Pamela Reed, *Imaging Coordinator*

Library of Congress Catalog Card Number 76-46132
ISBN 0-7876-2751-8
ISSN 0276-8178

Printed in the United States of America
10 9 8 7 6 5 4 3 2 1

# Contents

Preface   vii

Acknowledgments   xi

# Preface

Since its inception more than fifteen years ago, *Twentieth-Century Literary Criticism* has been purchased and used by nearly 10,000 school, public, and college or university libraries. *TCLC* has covered more than 500 authors, representing 58 nationalities, and over 25,000 titles. No other reference source has surveyed the critical response to twentieth-century authors and literature as thoroughly as *TCLC*. In the words of one reviewer, "there is nothing comparable available." *TCLC* "is a gold mine of information—dates, pseudonyms, biographical information, and criticism from books and periodicals—which many libraries would have difficulty assembling on their own."

## Scope of the Series

*TCLC* is designed to serve as an introduction to authors who died between 1900 and 1960 and to the most significant interpretations of these author's works. The great poets, novelists, short story writers, playwrights, and philosophers of this period are frequently studied in high school and college literature courses. In organizing and reprinting the vast amount of critical material written on these authors, *TCLC* helps students develop valuable insight into literary history, promotes a better understanding of the texts, and sparks ideas for papers and assignments. Each entry in *TCLC* presents a comprehensive survey of an author's career or an individual work of literature and provides the user with a multiplicity of interpretations and assessments. Such variety allows students to pursue their own interests; furthermore, it fosters an awareness that literature is dynamic and responsive to many different opinions.

Every fourth volume of *TCLC* is devoted to literary topics. These topic entries widen the focus of the series from individual authors to such broader subjects as literary movements, prominent themes in twentieth-century literature, literary reaction to political and historical events, significant eras in literary history, prominent literary anniversaries, and the literatures of cultures that are often overlooked by English-speaking readers.

*TCLC* is designed as a companion series to Gale's *Contemporary Literary Criticism,* which reprints commentary on authors now living or who have died since 1960. Because of the different periods under consideration, there is no duplication of material between *CLC* and *TCLC*. For additional information about *CLC* and Gale's other criticism titles, users should consult the Guide to Gale Literary Criticism Series preceding the title page in this volume.

## Coverage

Each volume of *TCLC* is carefully compiled to present:

- criticism of authors, or literary topics, representing a variety of genres and nationalities

- both major and lesser-known writers and literary works of the period

- 6-12 authors or 3-6 topics per volume

- individual entries that survey critical response to each author's work or each topic in literary history, including early criticism to reflect initial reactions; later criticism to represent any rise or decline in reputation; and current retrospective analyses.

## Organization of This Book

An author entry consists of the following elements: author heading, biographical and critical introduction, list of principal works, reprints of criticism (each preceded by an annotation and a bibliographic citation), and a bibliography of further reading.

- The **Author Heading** consists of the name under which the author most commonly wrote, followed by birth and death dates. If an author wrote consistently under a pseudonym, the pseudonym will be listed in the author heading and the real name given in parentheses on the first line of the biographical and critical introduction. Also located at the beginning of the introduction to the author entry are any name variations under which an author wrote, including transliterated forms for authors whose languages use nonroman alphabets.

- The **Biographical and Critical Introduction** outlines the author's life and career, as well as the critical issues surrounding his or her work. References to past volumes of *TCLC* are provided at the beginning of the introduction. Additional sources of information in other biographical and critical reference series published by Gale, including *Short Story Criticism, Children's Literature Review, Contemporary Authors, Dictionary of Literary Biography,* and *Something about the Author,* are listed in a box at the end of the entry.

- Some *TCLC* entries include **Portraits** of the author. Entries also may contain reproductions of materials pertinent to an author's career, including manuscript pages, title pages, dust jackets, letters, and drawings, as well as photographs of important people, places, and events in an author's life.

- The **List of Principal Works** is chronological by date of first book publication and identifies the genre of each work. In the case of foreign authors with both foreign-language publications and English translations, the title and date of the first English-language edition are given in brackets. Unless otherwise indicated, dramas are dated by first performance, not first publication.

- Critical essays are prefaced by **Annotations** providing the reader with information about both the critic and the criticism that follows. Included are the critic's reputation, individual approach to literary criticism, and particular expertise in an author's works. Also noted are the relative importance of a work of criticism, the scope of the essay, and the growth of critical controversy or changes in critical trends regarding an author. In some cases, these annotations cross-reference essays by critics who discuss each other's commentary.

- A complete **Bibliographic Citation** designed to facilitate location of the original essay or book precedes each piece of criticism.

- Criticism is arranged chronologically in each author entry to provide a perspective on changes in critical evaluation over the years. All titles of works by the author featured in the entry are printed in boldface type to enable the user to easily locate discussion of particular works. Also for purposes of easier identification, the critic's name and the publication date of the essay are given at the beginning of each piece of criticism. Unsigned criticism is preceded by the title of the journal in which it appeared. Some of the essays in *TCLC* also contain translated material. Unless otherwise noted, translations in brackets are by the editors; translations in parentheses or continuous with the text are by the critic. Publication information (such as footnotes or page and line references to specific editions of works) have been deleted at the editor's discretion to provide smoother reading of the text.

- An annotated list of **Further Reading** appearing at the end of each author entry suggests secondary sources on the author. In some cases it includes essays for which the editors could not obtain reprint rights.

# Cumulative Indexes

- Each volume of *TCLC* contains a cumulative **Author Index** listing all authors who have appeared in Gale's Literary Criticism Series, along with cross references to such biographical series as *Contemporary Authors* and *Dictionary of Literary Biography*. For readers' convenience, a complete list of Gale titles included appears on the first page of the author index. Useful for locating authors within the various series, this index is particularly valuable for those authors who are identified by a certain period but who, because of their death dates, are placed in another, or for those authors whose careers span two periods. For example, F. Scott Fitzgerald is found in *TCLC,* yet a writer often associated with him, Ernest Hemingway, is found in *CLC.*

- Each *TCLC* volume includes a cumulative **Nationality Index** which lists all authors who have appeared in *TCLC* volumes, arranged alphabetically under their respective nationalities, as well as Topics volume entries devoted to particular national literatures.

- Each new volume in Gale's Literary Criticism Series includes a cumulative **Topic Index,** which lists all literary topics treated in *NCLC, TCLC, LC 1400-1800,* and the *CLC* yearbook.

- Each new volume of *TCLC,* with the exception of the Topics volumes, includes a **Title Index** listing the titles of all literary works discussed in the volume. In response to numerous suggestions from librarians, Gale has also produced a **Special Paperbound Edition** of the *TCLC* title index. This annual cumulation lists all titles discussed in the series since its inception and is issued with the first volume of *TCLC* published each year. Additional copies of the index are available on request. Librarians and patrons will welcome this separate index; it saves shelf space, is easy to use, and is recyclable upon receipt of the following year's cumulation. Titles discussed in the Topics volume entries are not included *TCLC* cumulative index.

# Citing Twentieth-Century Literary Criticism

When writing papers, students who quote directly from any volume in Gale's literary Criticism Series may use the following general forms to footnote reprinted criticism. The first example pertains to materials drawn from periodicals, the second to material reprinted from books.

[1]William H. Slavick, "Going to School to DuBose Heyward," *The Harlem Renaissance Re-examined,* (AMS Press, 1987); reprinted in *Twentieth-Century Literary Criticism,* Vol. 59, ed. Jennifer Gariepy (Detroit: Gale Research, 1995), pp. 94-105.

[2]George Orwell, "Reflections on Gandhi," *Partisan Review,* 6 (Winter 1949), pp. 85-92; reprinted in *Twentieth-Century Literary Criticism,* Vol. 59, ed. Jennifer Gariepy (Detroit: Gale Research, 1995), pp. 40-3.

# Suggestions Are Welcome

In response to suggestions, several features have been added to *TCLC* since the series began, including annotations to critical essays, a cumulative index to authors in all Gale literary criticism series, entries devoted to criticism on a single work by a major author, more extensive illustrations, and a title index listing all literary works discussed in the series since its inception.

Readers who wish to suggest authors or topics to appear in future volumes, or who have other suggestions, are cordially invited to write the editors.

# Acknowledgments

The editors wish to thank the copyright holders of the criticism included in this volume and the permissions managers of many book and magazine publishing companies for assisting us in securing reproduction rights. We are also grateful to the staffs of the Detroit Public Library, the Library of Congress, the University of Detroit Mercy Library, Wayne State University Purdy/Kresge Library Complex, and the University of Michigan Libraries for making their resources available to us. Following is a list of the copyright holders who have granted us permission to reproduce material in this volume of *TCLC*. Every effort has been made to trace copyright, but if omissions have been made, please let us know.

## COPYRIGHTED ESSAYS IN *TCLC*, VOLUME 94, WERE REPRODUCED FROM THE FOLLOWING PERIODICALS:

*American Literature*, v. 52, January, 1981. Copyright © 1981 Duke University Press, Durham, NC. Reproduced by permission.—*Books Abroad*, v. 46, Spring, 1972. Copyright 1972 by the University of Oklahoma Press. Reproduced by permission.—*Canadian Literature*, n. 62, Autumn, 1974 for "Women in Canadian Literature" by Isobel McKenna. Reproduced by permission of the author.—*Chicago Review*, v. 19, 1967. Copyright © 1967 by Chicago Review. Reproduced by permission.—*CLA Journal*, v. XIX, June, 1976; v. XX, June, 1977; v. XXVIII, March, 1985;. Copyright, 1976, 1977, 1985 by The College Language Association. Both are used by permission of The College Language Association.—*Commentary*, v. 65, January, 1978 for "New Israeli Writing" by Alan Mintz. Copyright © 1978 by the American Jewish Committee. All rights reserved. Reproduced by permission of the publisher and the author.—*Contemporary Literature*, v. 9, Spring, 1968; v. 28, Fall, 1987. © 1968, 1987 by the Board of Regents of the University of Wisconsin. Both reproduced by permission of The University of Wisconsin Press.—*Critique: Studies in Modern Fiction*, v. XVI, 1975. Copyright © 1975 Helen Dwight Reid Educational Foundation. Reproduced with permission of the Helen Dwight Reid Educational Foundation, published by Heldref Publications, 119 18th Street, N. W., Washington, DC 20036-1802.—*Cross Currents*, Dobbs Ferry, v. XXXIX, Summer, 1989. Copyright 1989 by Cross Currents Inc. Reproduced by permission.—*Hebrew Annual Review*, v. 9, 1985 for "The Evolution of the Israeli Attitude Toward the Holocaust as Reflected in Modern Hebrew Drama" by Ilan Avisar. Reproduced by permission of the author.—*The Jerusalem Quarterly*, Fall, 1980. Reproduced by permission.—*Judaism: A Quarterly Journal*, v. 33, Winter, 1984. Copyright © 1984 by the American Jewish Congress. Reproduced by permission.—*The Literary Review*, v. 26, Summer, 1983 for "Kafka's Traffic in Women: Gender, Power, and Sexuality" by Evelyn Torton Beck; v. 26, Winter, 1983 for "The Violence of Collision: Hebrew Poetry Today" by Gabriel Levin. Copyright © 1983 by Fairleigh Dickinson University. Reproduced by permission of the authors—*Literature and Psychology*, v. XXXI, 1981. © Editor 1981. Reproduced by permission.—*Massachusetts Review*, v. XX, Autumn, 1979; v. XXIII, Summer, 1982.. © 1979, 1982. Both reproduced from *The Massachusetts Review*, The Massachusetts Review, Inc. by permission.—*Michigan Quarterly Review*, v. XXI, Spring, 1982 for "The Image of the Arab in Modern Hebrew Literature" by Edna Amir Coffin. Copyright © The University of Michigan, 1982. All rights reserved. Reproduced by permission of the author —*The Midwest Quarterly*, v. XVII, 1976[ v. XXII, Winter, 1981; v. XXVI, Summer, 1985. Copyright © 1976, 1981, 1985 by The Midwest Quarterly, Pittsburgh State University. All reproduced by permission.—*Modern Drama*, v. XIV, December, 1971; v. XXI, September, 1978; v. XXIII, January, 1981. Copyright © 1971, 1978, 1981 University of Toronto, Graduate Centre for Study of Drama. All reproduced by permission.—*Modern Fiction Studies*, v. 38, Autumn, 1992. Copyright © 1992 by Purdue Research Foundation, West Lafayette, IN 47907. All rights reserved. Reproduced by permission of The Johns Hopkins University.—*Modern Language Studies*, v. XXIV, Fall, 1994 for "The Holocaust and the Bible in Israeli Poetry" by David C. Jacobson. Copyright, Northeast Modern Language Association 1994. Reproduced by permission of the publisher and author.— *The Nation*, New York, v. 222, February 21, 1976. © 1976 The Nation magazine/ The Nation Company, Inc. Reproduced by permission. *Nineteenth-Century Fiction*, v. 32, March, 1978 for "Conrad's Women" by Gordon W. Thompson. © 1978 by The Regents of the University of California. Reproduced by permission of the publisher and the author.—*Partisan Review*, v. 54, Fall, 1987 for "Anti-War Poetry in Israel" by James E. Young. Copyright © 1987 by Partisan Review. Reproduced by permission of the author.—Poetics Today, v. 7, 1986. © The Porter Institute for Poetics and Semiotics. Reproduced by permission of Duke University Today.—*Prooftexts: A Journal of Jewish Literary History*, v. 6, May, 1986; v. 10, Summer, 1990. ©1986, 1990. Both reproduced by permission of The Johns Hopkins University Press.—*Salmagundi*, v. 82-83, Spring/Summer, 1989. Copyright © 1989 by Skidmore College. Reproduced by permission.—*The Sewanee Review*, v. LXXXV, Fall, 1977; v. C, April-June, 1992. Copyright © 1977, 1992 by The University of the South. Both reproduced with permission of the editor—*South Atlantic Quarterly*, v. 78, Winter, 1979; v. 82, Summer, 1983. Copyright © 1979, 1983 by Duke University Press, Durham, NC. Both reproduced by permission.—*Studies in the Literary Imagination*, v. 16, Fall, 1983. Copyright 1983 Department of English, Georgia State University. Reproduced by permission.—*Studies in the Novel*, v. 16, Fall, 1984. Copyright 1984 by North Texas State University. Reproduced by permission.—*Texas Quarterly*, v. 21, Winter, 1989. © 1989

# Israeli Literature

## INTRODUCTION

The creation of the modern Israeli state in 1948 marked the beginning of a new era in Hebrew literature. While Hebrew writers had long been active in the eastern Mediterranean region that was formerly known as Palestine, the establishment of Israel as the culmination of the Zionist movement proved decisive in reaffirming the vital language and culture of Hebrew-speakers. Locked in conflict with surrounding Arab nations, the state of Israel has struggled to define itself through its literature. Combining the concerns of Middle Eastern and European Jews—the latter having suffered near total destruction during the Nazi Holocaust—Israeli literature represents the unique expression of a nation and a people seeking to express a new collective identity. Critics have generally divided Israeli literature of the twentieth century into three periods. Works of the first period are labeled "Palmach" literature, a term derived from the Israeli military. The Palmach authors, who are sometimes called the generation of 1948, flourished in the late 1940s and the 1950s. Their works of drama, poetry, and fiction reflect a social realist aesthetic, and frequently express themes related to Israelis as a group: political issues, the war of independence, the Israeli army, the *kibbutz,* or collective farm settlement, and the assimilation of immigrants to the region. By the 1960s and 1970s the so-called New Wave of Israeli literature had began. While national concerns were still prominent, an individual and universal emphasis characterizes the literature of this period. While addressing subjects of vital interest to Israelis, writers of the New Wave endeavored to reproduce the interior lives of individuals and offered a historical contextualization of Israeli life and its past origins in their works, reflecting a move to universal themes. In the 1970s, the voices of women were heard increasingly among Israeli writers, and Israeli poetry and drama developed considerably. The state of Israeli literature in the 1980s and 1990s generally reflects modern attitudes of innovation and experimentalism and has demonstrated a need to more fully confront the subject of Arab-Jewish relations in Israel. Since 1948 Israel has in large part been defined by the brutality of this ancient ethnic conflict. By the close of the century, however, expressions of diversity and dissent are more often heard as the nation struggles to define the meaning and values of its evolving democracy.

## REPRESENTATIVE WORKS

Shmuel Yosef Agnon
  *Selected Stories of S. Y. Agnon* (short stories) 1970

Nissim Aloni
  *Most Cruel the King* (drama) 1954
Yehuda Amichai
  *Lo me'-akhshav, lo mi-kan* [*Not of This Time, Not of This Place*] (novel) 1964
  *Selected Poems* (poetry) 1968
Aharon Appelfeld
  *Masot beguf ri'shon* [*Essays in First Person*] (essays) 1979
  *Badenhaim, ir nofesh* [*Badenheim, 1939*] (novella) 1980
Hanoch Bartov
  *Shesh kenafayim le-ehad* [*Each Had Six Wings*] (novel) 1954
  *Pitse bagrut* [*The Brigade*] (novel) 1968
  *Ha'abady* [*The Dissembler*] (novel) 1975
Yitzhak Ben-Ner
  *Aharei ha-geshem* [*After the Rain*] (short stories) 1979
H. N. Bialik
  *Selected Poems* (poetry) 1965
Yosef Haim Brenner
  *Schokol we-Kishalon* [*Breakdown and Bereavement*] (novel) 1971
T. Carmi
  *The Brass Serpent: Poems* (poetry) 1964
  *The Penguin Book of Hebrew Verse* [editor and translator] (poetry) 1981
Amir Gilboa
  *The Light of Lost Sons: Selected Poems of Amir Gilboa* (poetry) 1979
Leah Goldberg
  *Ba'alat ha'armon* [*Lady of the Castle*] (drama) 1954
Haim Gouri
  *Iskat ha-shokolad* [*The Chocolate Deal*] (novel) 1964
  *Hasseper hammeshugga'* [*The Crazy Book*] (novel) 1971
David Grossman
  *Hiyukh hagedi* [*The Smile of the Lamb*] (novel) 1983
  *Ayen erekh ahavah* [*See Under: Love*] (novel) 1986
Shulamith Hareven
  *Ir yamim rabim* [*City of Many Days*] (novel) 1972
Amalia Kahana-Carmon
  *Ve-yareah be-emek Ayalon* [*And Moon in the Valley of Ajalon*] (novel) 1984
Yoram Kaniuk
  *Ha-yored l'ma'alah* [*The Acrophile*] (novel) 1961
  *Himo melekh yerushalayim* [*Himo, King of Jerusalem*] (novel) 1966
  *'Aravi tov* [*A Good Arab*] (novel) 1984
Shulamit Lapid
  *Gei Oni* (novel) 1982
Hanoch Levin
  *Malkat haambatyah* [*Queen of the Bathtub*] (drama) 1970
Aharon Megged
  *Hannah Senesh* (drama) 1958
  *Ha-hai 'al ha-meth* [*The Living and the Dead*] (novel) 1965
Sammy Michael
  *Hasut* [*Refuge*] (novel) 1977

Yitshak Orpaz
  *Bayit le-adam ehad* [*A House for One*] (novel) 1974
  *Ha-gevirah* [*The Mistress*] (novel) 1983
Amos Oz
  *Makom aher* [*Elsewhere Perhaps*] (novel) 1966
  *Mikhael sheli* [*My Michael*] (novel) 1968
  *La-gaat ba-mayim, la-gaat ba-ruah* [*Touch the Water, Touch the Wind*] (novel) 1973
  *Har haetsah haraah* [*The Hill of Evil Counsel*] (novellas) 1976
Dan Pagis
  *Poems* (poetry) 1972
Dahlia Ravikovitch
  *Ahavat tapuah ha-zahav, shirim Daliyah Ravikovits* (poetry) 1958
Pinhas Sadeh
  *Ha-hayyim ke-mashal* [*Life as a Parable*] (novel) 1958
Yaakov Shabtai
  *Zikhron dvarim* [*Past Continuous*] (novel) 1977
Natan Shaham
  *Heshbon hadash* [*A New Reckoning*] (drama) 1953
Moshe Shamir
  *Melekh basar wa-dam* [*The King of Flesh and Blood*] (novel) 1954
  *Hayyai 'im Yishma'el* [*My Life with Ishmael*] (novel) 1970
Anton Shammas
  *Arabeskot* [*Arabesques*] (novel) 1986
Dennis Silk
  *The Punished Land* (poetry) 1980
Yehoshua Sobol
  *Geto* [*Ghetto*] (drama) 1984
Benjamin Tammuz
  *Be-sof maarav* [*Castle in Spain*] (novel) 1966
  *Ha-pardes* [*The Orchard*] (novel) 1971
  *Mishle bakbukim* [*Bottle Parables*] (novel) 1975
Avraham B. Yehoshua
  *Mul ha-ye'arot* [*Three Days and a Child and Other Stories*] (short stories) 1970
  *Bi-tehilat kayits 1970* [*Early in the Summer of 1970*] (short stories) 1971
  *Gerushim meuharim* [*A Late Divorce*] (novel) 1982
  *Mar maniy* [*Mr. Mani*] (novel) 1990
S. Yizhar
  "Hashavuy" ["The Prisoner"] (short story) 1948
  *Yemei tsiklag* [*The Days of Ziklag*] (novel) 1958
Natan Zach
  *Kol hechalav vehadvash* [*All the Milk and Honey*] (poetry) 1964
  *Anti-mehikon* [*Hard to Remember*] (poetry) 1984

---

# OVERVIEWS

**Robert Alter**

SOURCE: "Afterword: A Problem of Horizons," in *TriQuarterly*, No. 39, Spring, 1977, pp. 326-38.

[*In the following essay, Alter views the tension between home and horizon—between the limits of the Israeli state and the expanse of the world—in contemporary Israeli literature.*]

It seems to me often that life in this tiny country is a powerful stimulant but that only the devout are satisfied with what they can obtain within Israel's borders. The Israelis are great travellers. They need the world.

—Saul Bellow, *To Jerusalem and Back: A Personal Account*

One of the most striking qualities of Israeli literature since the beginning of the 1960s and, increasingly, into the 1970s, is that it remains intensely, almost obsessively, national in its concerns while constantly pressing to address itself to universal issues and situations, perhaps to an international audience as well. This dialectic is inherently unstable, and of course its operation will be felt differently in different writers, or in poetry and prose. Nevertheless, one can detect in most contemporary Hebrew writers a high-pitched vibration of nervousness about the national setting which is the principal locus of their imaginative work; and if we can understand the peculiar nature of that nervousness, we may be able to see more clearly why the Israeli literary imagination has adopted certain characteristic modes and even certain characteristic constellations of plot and dramatic setting.

The nervousness I have in mind is not about the specific problems that confront the state of Israel, grave or abundant as they may be, but rather, to put it bluntly, about the simple fact of being in Israel. I do not mean to suggest, as some observers outside Israel would no doubt like to think, that Israeli writers tend to be covert anti-Zionists. On the contrary, what particularly characterizes most serious writers in Israel is their surprising combination of chronic disaffection and unswerving commitment. Whatever radical doubts they may, on occasion, raise in their writing, they are notable for their unwillingness to drop out of, or rebel against, the troubled national enterprise. Whether high school teachers, university instructors, kibbutzniks, or journalists by profession, they tend politically to gravitate toward small, ineffectual groups of the responsible opposition (usually on the Left). They seem ever ready to lecture to popular audiences, to join in symposiums with Arab intellectuals, to sign manifestos, to deliver scathing statements on current controversies to the daily press, or to picket the office of the prime minister, as the case may require. But it is one thing to be an engaged intellectual and quite another to be an imaginative writer in a constantly beleaguered nation-state the size of Rhode Island, and it is the pressures and constrictions of the latter problematic condition that repeatedly make themselves felt in contemporary Hebrew literature.

In a sense, this tension of attitudes is part of the legacy of classical Zionism and of the antecedent Hebrew literature which flourished in Central and Eastern Europe in the nineteenth and early twentieth centuries. Modern

Hebrew literature was born out of the German Enlightenment, with a vision of progressive cosmopolitanism, the dream of a new brotherhood of man in which a renascent Hebrew culture within the European sphere would be accorded the opportunity to play its rightful role. By the end of the nineteenth century—the old cosmopolitan optimism having collapsed under the pressures of a new European era of fierce particularism—the early Zionists nevertheless argued for a nationalism which would somehow be universal in scope. A resurgent Jewish commonwealth, they hoped, would not be a new kind of ghetto on a national scale or simply a "Bulgaria in the Middle East," but a vital center for all world Jewry and, with intricate links both to the best modern culture and to the Jewish past, a small but precious beacon for mankind. One might conceivably argue from the complex facts of Israeli actuality in the seventies that the visionary notions of the Zionist founders were not entirely off the mark; yet the discrepancy between vision and reality is obviously enormous, and it is out of the pained consciousness of this discrepancy that Israeli writers tend to shape their work.

When your whole cultural tradition tells you that you should be a universalist, though with a proud particularist base, and when, in this tension of expectations, you find yourself part of a tiny linguistic pocket hemmed in at the eastern end of the Mediterranean by enemy guns and a wall of nonrecognition, striving to maintain connections that sometimes must seem tenuous with the "great world" thousands of miles away—you are quite likely to experience flashes of claustrophobia. The only dependable antidote to this collective sense of cultural entrapment is a strong dose of messianism. For if you believe that the future of mankind rides with the ebb and flow of your nation's destiny, then no political or geocultural encirclement, however constricting, can ever cut you off from a realm of larger significance. Old-fashioned messianism, however, is not much in evidence these days among serious writers in Israel. In fact, the only convincing example that comes to mind is the poet Uri Zvi Greenberg, now in his eighties, whose fierce, mystic nationalism has produced poetic moments of awesome power but who has not inspired any literary emulators. The overwhelming majority of Israeli writers, for whom national identity is an incontestable fact and not an incandescent faith, must settle for scrutinizing the surfaces and depths of their national reality while sometimes secretly longing for a larger world to embrace—perhaps even feeling, in some corner of awareness, the persistent needle of doubt as to whether, if it were only possible, life might not be more fully livable somewhere else.

*Somewhere Else,* in fact, is the symptomatic title of Amos Oz's first novel, published in 1966 (the English translation is entitled *Elsewhere Perhaps*). It is one of several books of the early and mid-sixties that could be taken as points of departure for the so-called New Wave in Israeli fiction. Shimon Sandbank is surely right in proposing a new uncertainty about values as one of the distinguishing traits of the last decade and a half of Israeli writing. Viewing the transition from another angle, however, I

would suggest that the difference is also essentially the difference in the imaginative horizons of the fiction and poetry. I am not using the word "horizons" in any metaphorical sense; what I am referring to, as I shall try to illustrate through some specific instances of Israeli writing, are the actual geographical limits that define the imagined world of the literary work.

The novelists of the generation of 1948—writers like S. Yizhar, Moshe Shamir, Natan Shaham, Aharon Megged—created fictional worlds focused on distinctive Israeli social realities like the army, the kibbutz, and the socialist youth movement, with horizons that never visibly extended beyond Israel. In these works Europe appeared, if at all, as a bad memory, and America was simply not a presence. The writers may have been, like writers elsewhere, acutely unhappy with what they saw, but they never seemed to imagine or seriously muse over any arena of existence other than this newly independent national one in which they were struggling to articulate an authentic identity.

*Somewhere Else* is, like earlier books by Shaham, Shamir, and others of the older generation, a novel of kibbutz life (Oz in fact has remained a kibbutz member since adolescence). Yet it is profoundly different from Hebrew fiction of the forties and fifties, not only because of its pronounced symbolism and its plangently lyric style but, more crucially, because its imagined horizons are different, as the very title declares. Oz's kibbutz is not simply an assumed institutional framework within which certain social and moral problems may be explored. Sitting in the shadow of ominous mountains and enemy guns, huddled within the perimeter of its own fences, it becomes a parable of claustrophobic collective existence. All the action takes place within the kibbutz, but all the urgent *pressure* on the action originates "somewhere else"—whether in the dark beyond the Syrian border, where jackals howl and primordial forces lurk, or in the moral quagmire of postwar Germany, which, through the agency of a sinister visitor, penetrates the kibbutz. The novel's oppositions between here and elsewhere tend to be too simple and sometimes melodramatic—Oz was scarcely twenty-six when he completed the book—but the schematism has the effect of making the symptomatic aspect of the novel vividly clear. Whatever "somewhere else" may actually be, it embodies a disturbing, and alluring, depth, complexity, ambiguity that go beyond the rationalist, optimistic commitment to the salubrious collective endeavor of Israel's tight little island.

Recent Israeli literature, I would contend, galvanized by these claustrophobic flashes, has tended to swing in rapid oscillation between two poles: on the one hand, an imaginative leap outward to Europe and the West; on the other hand, a return to roots, an attempt to recapitulate the Israeli self in all its distinctiveness by imaginatively recovering the world of the writer's childhood. Let me offer a variety of examples of this dialectic movement in Israeli fiction of the sixties and seventies. Haim Gouri, an established poet of the 1948 generation, set his first novel, *The Chocolate Deal* (1964), in postwar Germany. This fable of the moral ambiguities of Jewish survival was followed by a work written in a totally different vein, *The Crazy Book* (1972), an affectionate evocation of Palestinian life in the Mandatory period when Gouri was growing up. Hanoch Bartov, a contemporary of Gouri, returned to his own childhood in *Whose Are You, Son?* (1970), a subtly convincing re-creation of a boy's experience in the town of Petah-Tikvah during the 1930s. On the other hand, his most recent novel, *The Dissembler* (1975), is set mainly in England and deals with a mysterious accident victim who turns out to have three national identities—German, French, and Israeli—and with them three different, internally coherent personal histories. The plot of *The Dissembler* is actually a brilliant focusing of the whole problem of horizons—Israel collapsing into France and Germany, or vice versa, until the entire structure of national identities seems like a house of cards—but Bartov's rendering of the psychological dimension of his situation, as the "serious" conclusion to his whodunit scheme, is unfortunately lame.

There is often, it seems to me, some problem of artistic authenticity in Israeli fiction set in another country. The simple and obvious reason is that no Israeli writer can ever know, in all their nuanced variety, the foreign milieus he chooses to evoke. French people in Hebrew novels show a propensity to eat nothing but pâté de fois gras; Englishmen repeatedly consume tea and scones; and so forth. This effect of straining after a European horizon is transparently illustrated by Rachel Eytan's recent book, *The Pleasures of Man* (1974). In its first half this is a competent, more or less feminist novel of conjugal distress and social satire, focused on what passes for the glittering circles of Tel Aviv society, but it noticeably loses credibility at precisely the point where the heroine runs off to the south of France with a French lover. The general rule of thumb seems to be that when a Hebrew novelist moves dialectically in his work between fictions of Israeli origins and fictions of foreign horizons, the realm of origins is the one that is most consistently handled with authority and conviction.

Amos Oz, whose first novel gave us our point of departure for defining this whole problem, provides an instructive instance of how a gifted writer can variously work with the geocultural tensions we have been observing. All his early fiction—the volume of stories *Jackal Country* (1965) as well as *Somewhere Else*—is obsessed with a claustrophobic sense of constriction. The penned-in kibbutz, its recurrent symbol, is in turn converted into an image of the human condition, hedged in and menaced (as Oz conceives it to be) by vast and inimical forces that man, through his self-deceiving schemes of rational order, vainly hopes to subdue. This essentially symbolic conflict in the early fiction forms the base for Oz's more probing psychological portraits, beginning in the later sixties, of deeply troubled protagonists whose mental disturbances mirror certain distinctive focuses of neurosis in Israeli life. After one remarkable novel in this manner, *My Michael* (1968), and a striking novella, *Late Love*

(1970), Oz was for once seduced by the beckoning expanses of "somewhere else." In *Touch the Water, Touch the Wind* (1973), he tried to put together a novel that would embrace past and present, Poland, Russia, Israel, the Western world at large, even time and infinity. The result is unpersuasive, especially when compared with the genuinely hallucinated intensity of his best writing. Finally, in his most recent collection of novellas, *The Hill of Evil Counsel* (1976), Oz has gone back, in his brooding fashion, to his Jerusalem boyhood, just as Bartov, Gouri, Kaniuk, and others have turned to the Mandatory Palestine of their formative years. In these three utterly compelling stories, set in the last years before the establishment of the Jewish state, Oz manages to enjoy the imaginative benefits of Zionist messianism without having actually to believe in it himself. In each novella, there is at least one central character obsessed with the apocalyptic vision of a "Judea reborn in blood and fire." These prophetic delusions of the extreme Zionist Right have a profound subterranean appeal for Oz, an antimilitant man of the Zionist Left. By re-creating such messianism in his characters, the writer partly suspends disbelief and momentarily transforms a minutely particularized Jerusalem setting into a landscape of ultimate significance—just as U. Z. Greenberg, with no such ventriloquistic obliquity, does in his poetry. In these fictions, then, set on the threshold of Jewish statehood, there are no inviting horizons to distract attention from the portentous fullness of this time and place.

The nervous shuttling between home and horizon in Israeli writing is also perceptible in the new prominence it has given to the role of the expatriate. Again, in order to keep biographical and literary facts properly sorted, we should remember that scarcely a single Israeli writer of any consequence has actually emigrated, although most of the writers find repeated occasions to spend a year or more in England, on the Continent, or, most frequently, in America. Expatriation, in fact, never seems to solve anything for the spiritually displaced personae that populate this literature. Nevertheless, the expatriate is now a figure who has to be contended with, empathically explored, because he tries to follow to the end a personal way out of Israel's landlocked location in history. Hebrew, one should note, has no comfortable neutral way of saying "expatriate." The usual term for an emigrant from Israel is *yored,* which literally means "one who goes down," and which has at least some of the pejorative force (depending on who is using the word) of "turncoat" or "renegade" in English. In recent years, writers have tried to see what light this conventionally deplored figure could throw on the perplexities of the Israeli condition in the second generation of national independence.

The earliest Hebrew novel I can recall that focuses on an expatriate is Yoram Kaniuk's *The Acrophile* (1961), which in Hebrew is called, much more pointedly, *Ha-Yored L'Ma'alah*—"the upward *yored,*" or "he who goes down upward." Kaniuk himself had been living in New York for some time when he wrote this first novel, which deals with the marital and spiritual confusions of an ex-Israeli teaching at a university in New York. Kaniuk's subsequent novels, like their author, have returned to the Israeli scene. The terrific tension between home and abroad then became the explicit subject of *Rockinghorse* (1973), a wildly uneven novel about an expatriate who, out of a sense of radical disorientation, returns from New York to Tel Aviv to try to make contact with his earliest origins. Kaniuk's latest book, and in many ways his most appealing, is *The Story of Big Aunt Shlomtziyon* (1976). Like the novels we noted by Bartov and Gouri, this is an affectionate, imaginative engagement in personal history—working back anecdotally, through the outrageously domineering figure of Aunt Shlomtziyon, to family beginnings in the pre-Mandatory period. Finally, Kaniuk's story "They've Moved the House," included in this volume, swings once more to the other pole of the dialectic, following the farcical and pathetic odyssey of two expatriate Israelis through California and Central America in search of a kind of El Dorado—deeply uneasy in a world where houses roll along on trailer frames instead of sitting on permanent foundations. (A story by Amalia Kahana-Karmon, "To Build a House in the Land of Shinar," provides a neatly complementary opposite to Kaniuk's fable of the moving house. Her model Israeli household in a new town, visited by a foreign home economist, is a quietly claustrophobic setting of stale domesticity. The ironic epic overtones of the title—no national symbolism is intended—alluding to the builders of the tower of Babel in Genesis, imply that this is not a house which will stand.)

Elsewhere, the *yored* stands at the center of Yehuda Amichai's farcical extravaganza, *Hotel in the Wilderness* (1971), a novel about an Israeli residing permanently in New York. He works for a Zionist agency propagandizing Israelis in America to return to Israel (!), and eventually finds an outlet for his dormant powers as a long-silent poet in writing advertising copy for ladies' underpants. Bartov's *The Dissembler,* of course, takes as its subject the intriguing impossibility of a man who is simultaneously an *oleh* (immigrant to Israel, "one who goes up") and a *yored,* at once a rooted Israeli and a rootless cosmopolitan. Still more recently, in a collection of poems which the quarterly *Siman-Kriyah* began publishing in installments with its Spring 1976 issue, a gifted new poet (in fact an important figure in literary-academic circles in Israel) adopts the persona of "Gabi Daniel"—a Russian-born Israeli living in Amsterdam. In experimental Hebrew verse of Mandelstamian formal intricacy, he ponders the role of his peculiar language and culture in the vast arena of human languages and cultural perspectives. In the dramatic setting of these poems, as in much contemporary Hebrew fiction, the figure of the expatriate is used to test some of the fundamental assumptions of the Israeli national enterprise.

Finally, the value-challenging idea of the *yored* is given an ultimate turn of the screw in a chapter of a novel-in-progress by A. B. Yehoshua, published in this volume. Here the expatriate Israeli, having returned to his homeland chiefly to look after a legacy, finds himself caught in the deadly meshes of the October 1973 war. Seeking,

like a number of his fictional counterparts, a way out, he finds it paradoxically through a way in: disguising himself as an ultra-orthodox Jew, he slips away from the Sinai front to one of the old quarters of Jerusalem; there, in the beard, sidelocks, and black kaftan of a pre-modern, pre-Zionist Jew, he is for the moment exempt from duty, exempt from history.

In Hebrew poetry contemporaneous with the New Wave in fiction, the problem of horizons is not usually so transparently evident—except where, as in the case of "Gabi Daniel," there is an elaborated dramatic or narrative context for the poems. The simple reason is that a lyric poem is not under the same obligation as a novel to articulate an imagined geography or a set of characters moving within or against cultural limits. Nevertheless, I would argue that the oscillations we have been observing in Israeli fiction are present in a good deal of recent Israeli poetry—sometimes on the level of explicit theme, sometimes in the formal shaping of the poem's world.

The situation in Israeli poetry today stands in marked contrast to that of the Israeli novel. Although there has been abundant and at times highly interesting activity among younger poets, no new creative figure has emerged to rival in stature the leading poets who achieved prominence after 1948, like Yehuda Amichai, Natan Zach, Amir Gilboa, and, just a few years later, Dan Pagis. Given this circumstance, shifts in the literary fashionability of the various established poets become revealing.

The poet par excellence of the so-called Palmach Generation (the war generation of 1948) was Haim Gouri. Although he is still very much alive and still writing, his plain-spoken style, his frequent focus on group experience, his nostalgic impulse, and his pervasive Israeli-ness now seem out of date, and his poetry attracts little attention in serious literary circles. Yehuda Amichai, in my view the finest poet of this generation, combines a colloquial sense of place with rich imagery, inventive allusiveness, and an easy movement between disparate cultural worlds. He has managed to remain a perennial favorite, even though at various moments his preeminence has been partly eclipsed by the very different modernist idioms of Natan Zach and Amir Gilboa. In the last few years, some younger literary intellectuals seem to have fixed particularly on the poetry of Dan Pagis, and Pagis' popularity, though well deserved on the genuine merits of the poems, is instructive. This is a poetry that visibly, in terms of its optic perspectives, shrinks the Israeli landscape to one dot out of many on an imagined global scene. Local allusions are relatively rare, and the language is for the most part meticulously clinical, manifestly a distancing medium. Beginning with his 1970 volume, Transformation, Pagis has frequently favored science-fiction situations (using verse for many of the same ends that Italo Calvino has used prose) in which terrestrial space and time are seen at an enormous telescopic remove—either from the other end of evolution, long after a global holocaust, or from the observation post of a spaceship or alien planet. This peculiar distanced mode is an authentic development within Pagis' poetry. It clearly gives him a means of confronting historical horror with artistic restraint and intellectual lucidity (he himself was a concentration camp prisoner as a child, and demons of disaster haunt his work); but I suspect that the gift of globality which the poetry offers is at least one important reason for the attraction it now holds for Israeli readers.

At the other end of Pagis' high-powered telescope, and on the opposite side of this geocultural dialectic, one discovers a poet like Dahlia Ravikovitch, whose imagination has virtually a fixed focus on a palpable Israeli geography that repeatedly becomes a screen for the projection of her personal anguish. A sense of entrapment and a dream of escape are recurrent presences in Ravikovitch's poetry, and although hers is a very private claustral distress, she manages to give it a local place and habitation in her encircled native land. One of her best known poems, "The Blue West," is in fact an archetypal expression of the problem of horizons that figures so importantly in the Israeli literary imagination. The poem begins (I shall quote from Chana Bloch's fine translation) with an image of ruins which is a distinctive piece of local landscape: "If there was just a road there / the ruins of workshops / one fallen minaret / and some carcasses of machines, / why couldn't I / come to the heart of the field?" But there is an opaque impenetrability at the heart of the field, at the heart of the native landscape, so that the attempt to penetrate it only reinforces the poet's sense of desperate entrapment. She then turns, at the Mediterranean shore, to a "blue west" which is not real like the landscape around her, but a visionary gleam that can only be imagined on another temporal plane, at the end of days. First, she conjures up a kind of surrealistic extension of Israel's actual beleaguered situation, a desolate coast with unvisited harbors: "If only we could reach / all the cities beyond the sea— / And here is another sorrow: a seashore where there are no ships." Then, in the two concluding stanzas of the poem, she shifts into prophetic style, mingling the grandeur of biblical eschatology with the naive fantasy of a fairy tale:

> On one of the days to come
> the eye of the sea will darken
> with the multitude of ships.
> In that hour all the mass of the earth
> will be spread as a cloth.
>
> And a sun will shine for us blue as the sea,
> a sun will shine for us warm as an eye,
> will wait until we climb up
> as it heads for the blue west.

It would be simplistic, I think, to draw direct political inferences from this underlying tension between homeland and horizon in Israeli literature. What the tension reflects most profoundly is the key psychological paradox of an imaginative literature that feels itself to be a full participant in modern culture at large, and yet is boxed into a tiny corner of geography, linguistically limited to at most a scant two million readers. In this regard, contemporary Hebrew literature provides a vivid if extreme paradigm for the difficult fate of all small cultures in an age of vast linguistic-cultural blocs and of global communications. In order to define the outlines of the paradigm, I have been stressing points of resemblance in distinctly different novelists and poets, although the points of divergence among them are at least as prominent, and in any case writers may do remarkably different things with the same set of oppositions. Most Israeli writers, it seems to me, tend to cluster at the end of the spectrum we have been concentrating on, where the imaginative confrontation of here and elsewhere is felt as a continual distress of creative consciousness. To avoid any misleading schematism, however, I would like to offer one final example from the other end of the spectrum—the poetry of Yehuda Amichai.

For Amichai, the West has not been a blue vision calling to him from beyond the shore, but a variegated, concretely perceived intellectual and emotional legacy. His German childhood reverberates through his poetry. Rilke and Auden are as natural sources for his poetic idiom as are Israeli speech and the Bible; and the various American and European scenes he has passed through as an adult are evoked with little sense that they present a challenging or alluring alternative to the Israeli setting in which he has taken root. Indeed, some of Amichai's finest poems over the past ten years, beginning with the remarkable cycle, "Jerusalem 1967," have been imaginative realizations of distinctive Israeli cityscapes and landscapes, where topography, architecture, cultural history, politics, and the record of age-old vision are so extraordinarily interfused.

Amichai is surely as aware as any other Israeli writer of the pull of the great world and of the exiguous dimensions of his national sphere (as his novel, *Hotel in the Wilderness,* makes clear). Yet the peculiar acerbic, playful, and at times visionary intimacy with the local scene which he has cultivated in his poems tends to keep the problem of horizons outside them. It may be that the messianic perspective, which makes one little state an everywhere, still remains, despite the prosaic logic of intellectual history, more available to Hebrew writers than I have allowed. In Amos Oz, we observed a ventriloquistic messianism which might reflect the writer's half-willingness to believe, or rather to surrender to, a fiery doctrine of national redemption that he would reject on the grounds of sane political principle. In Amichai, one sees instead a wryly nostalgic messianism that reflects an affectionate, self-ironic longing for the flashes of transcendental vision that in the past so repeatedly illuminated the Jerusalem landscape in which he lives. The nostalgia does not dissolve into sentimentality because his attraction to Jerusalem as the seedbed of prophecy is always articulated through an unblinking perception of the terrestrial Jerusalem—in all its hodgepodge of noise, stench, dirt, color, and piquant incongruity, and always rendered through the flaunted inventiveness of an imagery that constantly yokes feelings and spiritual entities with the most earthy of mechanical accouterments of the workaday world. These characteristics can be observed in lively and significant play in the following untitled poem from *Behind All This a Great Happiness Is Hiding* (1974), Amichai's most recent volume of poetry. (My translation must unfortunately surrender much of the verbal wit and sound-play of the original.)

The only real horizon of the poem's Jerusalem, at once a city of the seventies and of the ages, is, in defiance of geography and optics, an absolute vertical above the city; the switch in diction in the last two lines to a virtual nursery lisp expresses, not a wish of simple escape, as in Ravikovitch, but a fantasy of assumption in the theological sense. For three faiths, Jerusalem has been the locus of ascent, the "navel," as rabbinic tradition has it, joining heaven and earth; and even an ironic modern poet cannot put that fact of the spirit's history out of his mind as he muses over the city. It is this awareness that makes the poem intensely local—yet, like other Hebrew writings that have come out of Jerusalem, a prism of meaning that focuses a universal dream:

> All these stones, all this sadness, all
> the light, shards of night-hours and noon-dust,
> all the twisted pipework of sanctity,
> wall and towers and rusty halos,
> all the prophecies that couldn't hold in like old men,
> all the sweaty angel-wings
> all the stinking candles, all the peg-legged tourism,
> dung of deliverance, gladness and gonads
> refuse of nothingness bomb and time,
> all the dust, all these bones
> in the course of resurrection and in the course of the
>      wind,
> all this love, all
> these stones, all this sadness.
>
> To fill with them the valleys around her
> so Jerusalem will be a level place
> for my sweet airplane
> that will come to take me on high.

**Adam Gillon**

SOURCE: "Contemporary Israeli Literature: A New Stance," in *Books Abroad*, Vol. 46, No. 2, Spring, 1972, pp. 192-9.

[*In the following essay, Gillon surveys Israeli literature of the mid twentieth-century, focusing on the poetry of Yehuda Amichai and T. Carmi, and the short fiction and drama of Avraham B. Yehoshua.*]

During the fifties and sixties Israeli poetry produced more original talent than the novel and drama. While some of the outstanding older poets still continued to do significant work (like Uri Tzvi Greenberg, Avraham Shlonsky, Nathan Alterman, Jonathan Ratosh), the chorus of younger poets rose to "sing and speak . . . in many sorts of music": lyrical, elegiac, intellectual, sardonic, melancholy, obsessed with the Holocaust, fiercely existentialist or absurdist, experimental, traditional, delicate, robust, anarchic, and precise—indeed a veritable explosion

of poetic creativity. The list of poets is too long for the scope of this article, which precludes a systematic survey of contemporary Israeli literature. Some of the names must be mentioned, if only as brief guideline for the uninitiated reader: Yehuda Amichai, T. Carmi, Amir Gilboa, Hayyim Guri, Binyamin Galai, Omer Hillel, David Rokeah, Nathan Zach, Dan Pagis, David Avidan, Dalia Rabikovitz, Avraham Hus, Yitzhak Shalev, Moshe Dor, Yaoz-Kesset, Ya'akov Besser, Hayyim Be'er, Shlomo Tanny, Miriam Oren, Tuvia Rübner, Ozer Rabin, Eytan Eytan, Avner Trainin, Hanokh Levin, Malakhi Beit-Arieh, Esther Rab, Aharon Amir, Zelda (Mishkovsky), Miriam Shneid, Abba Kovner, Matityahu Shoham, Esther Rab, Anadad Eldan.

Given this profusion of poetic expression, the critic has a choice of either offering a few discursive comments or attempting a brief discussion of one or two poets. In electing the latter alternative, I must caution the reader that my selection reflects a personal preference and does not imply that the poets (and novelists) studied here are more important than those who could not be included.

Although not all Hebrew writers in Western or Eastern Europe (or the U.S.) were Zionists, it is fair to say that the theme of the Return to Zion was central to modern Hebrew literature. Upon the establishment of the State of Israel, the main motifs of Hebrew literature shifted from a depiction of Jewish life in the Diaspora to a portrayal of life in the land of Israel. The European Holocaust provided another major preoccupation.

As the early Hebrew writers probed the essential duality of the Jewish condition (the hope for salvation and the tragic destruction of the faith, without which salvation is impossible—as in the works of S. Y. Agnon, for example), so some native Israeli writers, or those who came to Israel at an early age, examine the problems of survival before and after the War of Independence among a people that can no longer embrace a messianic faith nor is free from the heritage of the past. The centuries of persecution and discrimination exact a costly toll from the Israeli writer who chooses to write of war—a permanent condition of Israel's existence. In book after book we discover an introvert hero who knows that he must win but refuses to accept himself as a victor, for he will not tolerate injustice even against his own enemy. Thus, the moral predicament and the old theme of exile loom large in the manifold trends of contemporary Israeli literature.

Although poets like Uri Tzvi Greenberg and Nathan Alterman often sound the "prophetic" tones of Hayyim N. Bialik, most of the important recent writers shun patriotic themes and the descriptions of social and political topicalities to which the earlier generation of writers was attracted; and when they do write of social and political problems, they invariably present the hero trying to reconcile the past with the present, the religious with the secular.

A typical example of this attempt to bridge the gap between the past and the present is the poet and novelist

Yehuda Amichai, who was born in Germany in 1924 but came to Israel as a child. The Hebrew name he adopted means: "My people lives." Two of his major works, the first collection of poems and a recent novel, harp on the word *akshav* (now). His first volume *Now and in the Other Days* (1965) was followed by *Poems* (1948-62), *Now in the Noise: Poems* (1963-68), and a novel *Lo' Me'-Akhshav, Lo Mi'khan* (Not of Now, Not of Here), published under the English title of *Not of This Time, Not of This Place* (translated by Shlomo Katz, Harper & Row, New York, 1968). The "nows" of Amichai's work are inextricably linked with the past; upon closer scrutiny a "now" is merely another perception of the past which weighs heavily upon the author. Thus, in "Autobiography in the Year 1952," he gives an account of his debt to his father and mother and the impact of certain years upon him:

> And in the year '51 the motion of my life
> Was like that of many slaves rowing a ship,
> And my father's face like a lantern of a receding
>      train . . .
> But *now* in the spring of '52,
> I see that more birds returned than had left last
>      winter.
> And I come back along the slope of the hill to my
>      house
> And in my room the woman whose body is heavy
> And full of *time*.

Memories of childhood, the dream and the reality of life, the intimate details of love and hate juxtaposed humorously with depictions of armed conflict, the blending of the heroic and mock-heroic stance, these are the basic threads of Amichai's poetic tapestry that is woven with great delicacy and a superb sense of irony. Time is indeed a key word if not a central image in Amichai's work, for it enables him to achieve an artistic distance from which he can view himself, Israel, and the world.

Amichai's work reflects his personal problem. When at the age of fifteen he lost his faith, he felt he had rejected not only God but also his beloved father and, in a larger symbolic way, the Jewish people which survived by dint of its faith. He writes of his father and the lost faith quite often, and one of his sonnets is entitled "My Father." It is an interesting illustration of Amichai's versatility; while the octet follows the Shakespearean form, the sestet rimes aba ccb. His use of meter indicates a further departure from the strictness of the sonnet form; he uses everyday language, enjambments, assonant rhymes, and some hexameters.

The freedom with which the poet assimilates older European literary forms with those of the Bible and Hebrew literature in general, accounts in some measure for the freshness of his style. Some critics attribute his fondness for the rhythms and idioms of daily speech to his being a latecomer to the Hebrew language. But the use of ostensibly simple language is deceptive, for Amichai can be a most profound writer who regards the poet as a very special person dwelling in two worlds without belonging in either. In "Of Three or Four in a Room," he shows this

ambiguity of the poet as an ironic intermediary. The poem presents the contrast between men of ancient days who prophet-like went out into the waterless lands, their hearts full of the life-giving waters of faith, and the faithless men of our own day who cannot read the "large stones" (the tablets of God), for they had set out without true hope. In a sense this poem reminds us of Frost's concluding lines in "Desert Places": "I have it in me so much nearer home / To scare myself with my own desert places." Amichai suggests that a man can be swallowed up by the desert outside but also by the desert within.

Another personal problem—a divorce—is handled without a trace of sentimentality although it is obviously a traumatic experience. In a poem about his American tour "Holy Days in New York" Amichai begins on a note of irony since the title in Hebrew contains an untranslatable pun, being, literally "Terrible Days" or "Days of Awe."

> I came because they told me:
> New York is a good country for a man to
>      disespouse
> himself, I could get a divorce from the one I used
>      to be.
> Movement is fast here, courts
> are fast, and forgetfulness fastest of all.

Everything in the poet's experience is grist to his artistic mill; and wherever he goes, he still feels apart, identified with Cain or the Wandering Jew, bearing the burden of his parents upon his shoulders, condemned to the lonely but also exalted task of singing his verses in an astounding variety of forms, the sonnet, the quatrain, the elegy, the lyric, the poetic short story, the rubaiyat, and finally the novel.

In "The Two of Us Together, Each of Us Alone" the poet mockingly twists a legal phrase borrowed from a lease contract to comment on the lost Eden of his childhood and the transition from peace to war. In a state of general conflagration how can two people survive if each remains a separate entity? The poet offers little consolation in his final two lines: "Accept me. We have no redeeming angel. / For two of us together. Each of us alone."

Love can redeem man but it is a fleeting redemption. Time alone remains the constant, as the destroyer of life and of civilizations—this is the message of "Half of the People in the World." Love and the breath of a spring song, as in "Now, as the Waters Press with Force" which describes the transition from the past to the present of flaming jet planes; *now* that the great dangers hover above in the skies, "How much more it is necessary / To fill all the empty vessels / And the clocks which ceased to mark time, / And how much breath, / Storm of a breath / to sing the small song of spring." In "Now in the Noise" the poet further comments on the significance of *now:*

> I am sitting here now with my father's eyes
> And with the greying hair of my mother on my head,
>      in a house
> That belonged to an Arab who bought it

From an Englishman who took it over from a
 German,
Who hewed it out of the rocks of Jerusalem which
 is my town . . .
My hands are stretched towards a *past* that isn't
 mine
and to a *future* that isn't: It is hard to love,
hard to close an embrace with such hands.

Or again in "Criminal Law and Ashes" which is a view of
the past from the poet's *now:*

Every ninth of *Ab* my mother rummages
Among the photos of her dead and those not dead
 yet
The ruins of my life.

Ashes and criminal law. Titus did not intend
To burn the Temple. He only wanted
To peek, to lift the heavy curtain of the Ark,
Like an adolescent boy: only to peek.
But the frightened priests began to sing
The songs of death and Halleluja, and he was scared
And he burned the City like a madman.
Ashes. Criminal law.

In his last collection of poems *And Not in Order to Remember* (1971), Time is still the hero (or villain) of
Amichai's drama—a remembrance of things past with a
feeling of nostalgia and world-weariness. A sense of profound sadness has crept into his work, I think, and it is
indicated by a number of poems which deal with death
and suicide, the loss of love of faith, with corresponding
images of cemeteries, graves, deadly elements, stones,
fog, and rain. Yet as if to balance these expressions of
nostalgia and anguish, the poet also displays a delightful,
wry sense of humor with his early lyrical tones, especially in his love poems.

Life is like death.
(The same water, water, water.)

My life is a chessboard.

One must go *now*
If I still believed in God
I would know that one should go *now,*
But *now* is time.

It is hard to understand your death in London
In a fog; as it is hard for me
To understand my life *here* in the brightness.

Some of the poems are travel vignettes, like the "Songs
of Buenos-Aires"; there are also "Biblical Contempla-
tions." Again and again the poet returns to his *now*, the
present seen in terms of the past:

I live in Jerusalem *now.*
We're forgetting whence we have come. Our
 Jewish
names from Exile reveal us
Evoke the memory of flowers, fruit, medieval
 cities . . .
What are we doing *here* returning with this pain.

Amichai is a natural poet and when he turns to fiction, he
still remains a poet and still harps on his familiar themes,
as in the story "The Times My Father Died," where the
father image is also that of God who is a blessing as
well as a burden. The novel *Not of This Time, Not of
This Place* (1968—shortened English version) portrays
a schizophrenic hero who appears in two locales:
Jerusalem and Weinburg, Germany. He is not the
early, somewhat stereotyped hero of Israel reborn, but
a man who is like the heroes of Kafka and Conrad, a
betrayer. Amichai explores the compelling theme of a
divided soul, using an involved and not entirely successful technique of parallel narratives in the first and third
person—both from his non-hero's point of view. Yet
the tale is an authentic and forceful comment on the
spiritual ambivalence of a Jew who is both an Israeli
and a European. Moreover, the nostalgic memory of his
childhood makes it impossible for Joel, the protagonist, to become an avenger. "My vengeance was like a
wax sword. A great sadness descended upon me because
I was empty of vengeance." Thus the remembrance of a
lost childhood and the return to it are the devices that
enable him to overcome the trauma of the Holocaust: "I
came here to take vengeance and to know the truth, but
the more I examined the men who committed all these
atrocities and the places of horror the more I sank down
into the knowledge of my own self."

Like Amichai, T. Carmi (Carmi Tcharney) was born outside Israel (in 1925 in the U.S.), but Hebrew was his
native language. His work is also a synthesis between
Hebrew, Jewish, European, and American traditions. An
acknowledged translator for the Hebrew theater (of
works by Shakespeare, Sophocles, Fry, Albee, B. Behan,
Brecht, Osborne, Lillian Hellman, Michel De Ghelderode,
Edgar Lee Masters, André Obey, Tom Stoppard) Carmi
brings to his poetry a cosmopolitan touch, without
Amichai's conflict between the past and the present.
Rather, he is a detached observer of man's manifold
moods which he renders in an intellectually disciplined
manner, drawing his images from the physical landscapes
of Israel or the literary landscapes of world literature,
especially the Bible.

Having lived in France for some time (where he worked
in refugee orphanages in 1946), Carmi translated this
experience into "René's Songs" which appear in his first
volume *There Are No Black Flowers*. These are moving
poems in rhymed but irregular stanzas, full of compassion for the orphaned children's plight.

Blood lurks for each cough, brothers,
With each loaf of bread the mouth kisses anguish.
Tomorrow, father, the spring will fly up to you.
Mother, tomorrow my charmed voice will be lost.

. . . . .

Mother, o my mother!
I burst into the Spring's heart like an almond tree,
Into the Spring's heart with sonorous pipes—
 There are no black flowers!

One of the several volumes of Carmi's poems was translated by Dom Moraes (*The Brass Serpent,* Ohio University Press, 1964), aptly capturing the poet's free, contemporary idiom, his Biblical motifs, and the delicate lyricism.

> The moon like a squinting lizard bobs at me.
> I am tired, very tired. My bride, how shall we fly
> Upon the belly of our frayed love: by
> What miracle? And how can we be free
> If we do not dare lift our eyes to the power
> That stands in the heart of the sky, serpent and
>   flower?
>
>                         (From "Vigils")

But Carmi can also combine an intensely personal poem with a Biblical allusion, as in the powerful "Dream" in which the poet uses the symbolic refrain: "Last night I dreamt my son did not return." Paradoxically, however, the son comes to his father and reminds him that when he was small he wouldn't be told the story of Isaac "to frighten me with knife fire and ram." He ends with the following stanza:

> Last night I dreamt my son did not return.
> I expected him back from school
> and he was slow in coming.
> Then, when I told her
> she put her hand over me
> and I saw all the voices he had seen.

This poem is from a charming little collection *The Unicorn Looks in the Mirror* (1967) of many moods, reflective, whimsical, or lyrical. In "Songs Without a Name" Carmi comes close to Amichai's tone of tender mockery and use of ordinary language of prose as he prefaces the brief two and three-liners or quatrains with: "I write these words in prose / For they were started and finished a long time ago; / If I knew their end, / I would write them in verse." The frame of reference in Carmi's volume is universal—although there are allusions to Jewish or Biblical motifs, his chief interest is in the existential moment: love, friendship, pain, joy, sadness, and a sense of wonder. Some of the poems have the simplicity and economy of the Japanese haiku: "A white bird over a green river; two; / then three. / One telegraph-pole; two; / three bushes." (From "Landscapes"). The last poem is from a most recent collection of 28 poems translated into English by Stephen Mitchell (André Deutsch, London, 1971). As in the earlier English volume, the serpent image is in evidence as well as an uncompromising view of the alienated poet revealing himself through a series of self-analytical, descriptive or sensual love poems. Like Amichai, Carmi is an acute observer and a confirmed voyager who gives us varied landscapes of Israel and, more specifically, of Jerusalem, instructing and often entertaining the reader with a controlled humorous touch, as in "Those Who go on Voyages," where an unholy traveler climbs a dream ladder:

> He descended and ascended and descended,
> He bumped and he shoved and he thumped
> all the angels he met.

Then he stopped on the way:
> All at once he opened his years
> like an antique spice-box,
> and filled them with the strange fragrance.

Contemporary Israeli novelists also descended and ascended their dream ladder. The older writers, like S. Y. Agnon and H. Hazaz, regarded Israel as part of the Jewish world, placing the emphasis on the destruction of the religious tradition in the Diaspora. To the new "native" writers, on the other hand, the Diaspora was only an aspect of the reborn, secular Israel. It is little wonder that the national theme, and especially the social values of Socialist Zionism dominated the so-called Palmah Generation of the forties and early fifties, e.g. M. Shamir, S. Yizhar, H. Bartov, N. Shaham, A. Megged, and Y. Mossinson. Their works were evaluated mostly in terms of their contribution to and understanding of the problems of the nascent Israeli culture. And some of these writers, notably Shamir and Yizhar, occasionally issued their own artistic "manifestoes" at writers' conferences, protesting their commitment to a set of values, the former to a modified form of socialist realism, the latter to a more existential view of a personal commitment to moral values.

During the late fifties and sixties, however, Israeli literature underwent a radical "sea change." The literature of the War of Independence was primarily concerned with the collective "we"—now it moved in the direction of the writer's singular "I". The cult of egalitarianism, the kibbutz ethic, the conquest of Arab lands, the brutalization and horror caused by war, the anguish of an individual's conscience, the sacred cows of Zionism and its rhetoric—these were some of the themes the writers tackled, without the former reverence or romantic idealism.

The recent trend in Israeli fiction is towards a withdrawal of the hero into his personal world and a critical view of present reality.

Four other writers illustrate the drastic departure from the literature of the forties: Amos Oz, Binyamin Tammuz, Yitzhak Orpaz and Avraham B. Yehoshua, all celebrating the non-conformist, the outsider, the non-hero. The most controversial young writer of the "new Wave" of Israeli literature is Avraham B. Yehoshua (b. 1936) whose stories and drama elicited much discussion. His collection of short stories (novellas, really) *Opposite the Forests* (1968; English version by Miriam Arad, with another story "Flood Tide," 1971, published by Doubleday under the title *Three Days and a Child*) is a *tour de force,* manifesting an original, sparse prose style and an uncanny ability to convey allegorical meanings in ostensibly realistic narratives. The influence of Kafka can be detected immediately because Yehoshua's concrete settings are recognizable but they impart a dreamlike, or rather a nightmarish, kind of reality. Yet, unlike Kafka's *The Trial* and *The Castle,* Yehoshua's stories are not the quest for the incommensurable Court, Judge, or any Higher Authority in a Divine or human Castle; nor do they suggest an absurdist, comic view of the universe and the tragic disparity between the divine and the human. Instead, they paint a bleak canvas of contemporary Israel, whose heroes are completely estranged in the midst of their familiar landscapes.

A scout entrusted with the security of the national forests doubts their very existence (in the title story)—they are merely artificial bureaucratic forests of public relations between the foreign donors and the Israelis. The Israeli scout is thus an ironic conqueror of a land in which he does not truly belong. "An Evening in Yatir Village" is an Israeli version of Anthony Burgess' *A Clockwork Orange*—a story of a boy and a girl who cause a terrible railroad accident for their own amusement, to release the pent-up violence within them, with a sexual orgy thrown in for good measure. In "The Long Continuing Silence of the Poet," the hero is a morbid, sterile intellectual, whose dull-witted son carries out his father's secret wishes, as the father destroys himself through his son. Similarly, the hero of "A Long Hot Day, His Despair, His Wife and His Daughter," is a father sexually rejected by his wife, unable to control his daughter, find employment, or inner peace. In "Three Days and a Child" there is another father who repeatedly attempts to kill his son, finally destroying himself. Here we have a stylized parable on the theme of Isaac's sacrifice, quite different though from the subtle inference of Carmi's "Dream." The names of the characters (*Dov*, meaning bear; *Ze'ev*—wolf; *Tzvi*—gazelle) give the story the appearance of a parody of an Aesop tale—a parody because there is no moral lesson to be gained from it.

Yehoshua's vision is bitter. It is an unrelenting satire on the dream that has come true. But like any satirical vision, stark and convincing though it is, it is limited in scope, for it must exaggerate and thus ignore many positive aspects of Israeli reality. His recent play *A Night in May* was greeted by Mendel Kohansky, Israel's leading drama critic, as a major Israeli play. In it seven characters under one roof of a Jerusalem house reveal their sundry psychological problems—on the eve of the Six Day War. Kohansky finds a heavy indebtedness to Albee's *Who's Afraid of Virginia Woolf* in the play's "general tenor of emotional cannibalism." Like the stories, the play is a dark, disturbing view of contemporary life.

Baruch Kurzweil, an eminent Israeli critic, fears that Yehoshua's work may be "the most authentic artistic expression of [our] self-destruction." I think this is not the case. Yehoshua merely expresses the sense of alienation and restriction that reflects the tensions of people living in a garrison state. If he typifies the present malaise of the younger generation, he does not thereby typify or suggest a total rejection of Israeli reality by the Israelis, certainly not by the youth who have repeatedly expressed (in an overwhelming majority) their endorsement of the national ideal and their leaders. Paradoxically, despite the perpetual state of war, life in Israel goes on normally, even joyfully or placidly. But the writer is always the conscience of his country, and the sensitive

Israeli artist is no longer satisfied with the task of being an "engaged" didactic servant of the Zionist Establishment. The new wave of Israeli literature suggests, in my view, a growing spiritual maturity, the necessary pangs attendant upon any serious quest for identity.

The prophets of old, after all, did not exactly indulge in sycophantic praise of the Kings of Israel. They scolded, complained, and bemoaned the many evils that had fallen upon their nation. Perhaps it is fitting that in this new-old Land of Israel the writers are not smug or easily deceived by political rhetoric. The fact that they can show all kinds of *awareness*, seek out the grotesque, the ridiculous as well as the sublime in the Israeli experience is ample testimony to the vitality of their utterance and to the intellectual freedom in a country beset by many problems, not the least of which is that of physical survival.

If one wanted to hazard a general summation of the present character of Israeli literature, one could say that its drama is still a fledgling being (although the theater is alive and doing well); that its fiction is, with a few exceptions, derivative in narrative techniques, and that the poetry is dynamic, innovative, blending the old and the new forms successfully; but all of it conveys the anguish of conscience and is animated by a pervasive sense of humanism.

## Gila Ramras-Rauch

SOURCE: "Cultural Nationalism in Israeli Literature," in *The Cry of Home: Cultural Nationalism and the Modern Writer,* edited by H. Ernest Lewald, The University of Tennessee Press, 1972, pp. 334-49.

*[In the following essay, Ramras-Rauch considers the trends and subject matter of Israeli literature.]*

### INTRODUCTION: THE PROBLEMS OF ISRAELI LITERATURE

In speaking of Israeli literature we refer to a secular literature written in a sanctified language, a modern literature using a language which is ancient. It is a modern, secular literature in the sense of voicing current moods, in contemporary modes of expression, but it must use a language laden with religious and historic meaning. This is the dilemma going to the heart of Israeli literature. As a result, the creative framework of the Israeli writer is problem-laden, involving his relation not only to the language to whose use he is born, but also to the land in which he is born. These factors of language and land manifest themselves as problems of time (past or present) and space. It is in relation to these problems that the Israeli writer must constantly define himself. If his existence is completely secular, so that the religious and historic connotations of, e.g., the word "Israel," are entirely outside his spiritual sphere, then the Israeli writer must ask himself what sort of meaning he is to attach to the here-and-now, to a place and a time which, in their deepest significance, transcend their secular actuality. Is the

Wailing Wall, for example, a symbol of destruction and exile, of promise and return? Or is it merely an archeological artifact of general interest? Is Mount Sinai the site of the Revelation and the Covenant? Or is it merely a geological entity? These are problems about the land; there are corresponding problems connected with the use of language—which we shall touch upon in due course.

The problematic condition of the Israeli writer begins prior to his time, in the last quarter of the nineteenth century, which was marked by the return of the European Jew (as writer) to the land or to the language of his forefathers. It is a return which is problematic, even paradoxical, since the return is secular, not apocalyptic, whereas the land and language to which he comes are anything but secular. In the nineteenth century, this paradox is immanent in the future development of Israeli literature, raising questions which persist into the present. These are questions pertaining to the very nature of one's existence as an Israeli and to one's *raison d'être* as a writer:

1. What is the relation between the rebirth of the nation and the rebirth and regeneration of man?

2. What is the meaning of the nation? the land? the return?

3. Is the return to the land also a return to one's sources in the past, or is it the secular founding of a modern nation?

4. What are to be the boundaries (physical and spiritual) of Israel? Philosophically (i.e., in formal terms), these are all one question: What is the relation between the here-and-now and eternity? Only in literature (i.e., in terms of content) can we display the differences between these questions.

### HEBREW VS. ISRAELI LITERATURE

One fundamental distinction to be made is the distinction between Hebrew and Israeli literature. The distinction begins in a simple way and proceeds to complex and profound differences. The term "Hebrew literature" refers to writers in Hebrew whose mother tongue was either Yiddish (a variant of German) or some other language. The term "Israeli literature" refers to writers whose mother tongue is Hebrew (either because they were born in Israel or came to Israel as small children, prior to or during the Second World War).

This simple distinction regarding the writer's mother tongue involves a many-sided connection to different cultural, social, and religious circumstances. If, for example, the writer of Hebrew literature (in the original generation living in the spiritual as well as geographic Diaspora of late-nineteenth-century Europe) secularized the sacred language as a return to cultural sources, the return to the land was at first only an aspiration for him, and *then* a reality. The modern writer of Israeli literature, on the other hand, is connected to his land as something immediate; he is born to the language. Thus,

the disconnection or connection of the language to the land—and the part played by the land in the respective literatures—provide one of the primary bases for the distinction between the Hebrew and the Israeli literatures, and for the characterization of the latter.

The writers covered by the rubric "Hebrew literature" were born and raised in eastern Europe (mainly in Poland or Russia). Their childhood landscape is essentially European, i.e., immersed in the life of the small hamlet (or *"shtetl,"* in Yiddish). They were brought up to define themselves as Jews and as participants in the Jewish tradition. Even though their knowledge of Hebrew was deep and was part of their self-definition as Jews, they were brought up not to use Hebrew as a daily language, but reserved it for prayer and religious study. There was no delineation of the self apart from one's membership in the Jewish world and its heritage. (This is the phenomenon of the "collective mentality"—which we shall discuss later.)

The fact that these writers turned to the Hebrew language, rather than confining themselves to Yiddish (or to Russian or Polish), and that they used the holy language to express themselves in a secular manner provides some indication of the many-sided ambiguity of the individual's relation to his tradition. They looked to a return to the language as a spiritual, cultural, and national renewal. Their turn to the secular use of Hebrew may therefore be considered something of a Renaissance.

Under the complex heading of "Hebrew literature" are writers such as Mendele Mocher Sefarim (1836-1917), Mordecai Zeev Feierberg (1874-1899), Uri Nissan Gnessin (1879-1913), and Micha Yosef Berdichevsky (1865-1921), who never lived in Israel; Yosef Chaim Brenner (1881-1921), Chaim Nachman Bialik (1873-1934), and Saul Tchernikovsky (1875-1943), who were born in Europe but who lived and died in Israel. And then there are writers such as Shmuel Yosef Agnon (1888-1970), Gershon Shoffman (1880- ), and Haim Hazaz (1898- ), who lived most of their creative lives in Israel. This is the generation of the Renaissance.

In addition, a younger generation of Hebrew literature, the generation of the Realization, also Europe-born, has been, in some complex ways, more open to what might be called "modern" European influences: Uri Zvi Greenberg (1895- ), Abraham Shlonsky (1900- ), Yitzhak Shenhar (1907-1957), and Nathan Alterman (1910-1970). Needless to say, there are many other highly significant writers whom we have not mentioned at this point.

The writers covered by the rubric "Israeli literature" were born or raised in Israel, a secular state. The language in which they write is that of their everyday speech, rather than that of the Book. Their version of the "collective mentality" is more national than cultural or religious. Their self-definition is as Israelis more than as Jews. They have a stronger affiliation to the land than to the faith. The main figures are: S. Yizhar (1916- ), Moshe

Shamir (1921- ), Aharon Megged (1920- ), Haim Gouri (1923- ), Hanoch Bartov (1926- ), Yehuda Amichai (1924- ), Nissim Aloni (1926- ), Aharon Appelfeld (1932- ), Avraham B. Yehoshua (1937- ).

Accordingly, one can say that there are three generations of writers now living and working in Israel: (1) the older generation of Hebrew literature—the "Renaissance," e.g., Shoffman and Hazaz; (2) the newer generation of Hebrew literature—the "Realization," e.g., Greenberg, Shlonsky, Alterman; and (3) the current generation of Israeli literature, whose work began to appear in the 1940s.

### THE PROBLEM OF SECULARIZATION

In the Diaspora (the dispersion of the Jewish people in Europe, from which the Hebrew Renaissance emerged in the late nineteenth century), Judaism's unifying attitude was the hope of redemption and return. Three times daily, prayers were said facing in the direction of Jerusalem. The prayers as constant reiterations of that hope were therefore reminders of the unrootedness of a people.

The existence of that people is thoroughly time-oriented. From the very beginning, its view is that time is the plane on which God manifests His will, and that God's central act is the selection of *this* people as the people to whom He will impart His law. All time is sanctified: every moment of every day is referred to God's will, and to man's interpretation of that will. Finally, God's will is expected to redeem His people and to restore it to Jerusalem, to a condition that will complete and transcend history.

The process of secularization, by which the writers of the Renaissance turned to the secular use of the sacred language, involved the writer's withdrawal from the "collective mentality"—in such a way that the writer severed his connections with the sense of continuity but retained his connections with the present. Accordingly, these writers can be characterized as moving in the direction of greater individualism and yet utilizing the temporal *Weltanschauung* in expressing this individualism. One of the finest examples of this standpoint is Feierberg's short novel *Whither?*[1] This is a novel of a tormented young man who has lost faith in the traditional way as a way to redemption. His inability to find satisfaction in the tradition leaves him with himself alone, a being immersed in a rootless time. His problem is representative of the generation which could neither continue in the tradition of millennia, nor break the bonds with that tradition, nor find a meaningful synthesis between the Judaic and the Western worlds. He cannot go back to the God of his people. Time is no longer redemptive for him. And yet his continued search is a search within a temporal framework, i.e., a search for a meaning which will transcend time.

Whereas Hebrew literature can be characterized by its temporal framework, Israeli literature can be characterized by a spatial aspect. The latter's emphasis is on the here-and-now, without reference to a collective memory; it is an emphasis on the relation between the individual and his environment, the individual set against his landscape. Whereas the sources of Hebrew literature are in the tension between the individual and the collective experience,[2] the Israeli writer is not imbued with a sense of history. His sources are mainly autobiographical—there being for him no problem of defining himself as an individual *vis-à-vis* a historical and spiritual environment. Yet although his outlook regarding his environment is more national than cultural, his persisting problem is that of finding a balance between his national and cultural loyalties.

During and immediately after the War of Independence, in 1948, the writer's concern was solely with the "we" in the present and with Israel's national aspirations—but not at all with the sources of those aspirations in the past. More recently, however, one can detect a trend toward the incorporation of the past into the present. That past includes Israel's broader history as a nation as well as the more proximate experience of the Holocaust (the influence of which we shall discuss below).

The spatial aspect, which may be said to characterize Israeli literature, gives a special importance to the landscape. The land is itself saturated with religious-historic meaning, but the problems of building a modern nation and of giving voice to its national consciousness also tend to stress the relation of the individual to the land. Conceivably, therefore, there could be two sources (religious and secular) of the emphasis on the land in modern Israeli literature. But for the Israeli writer, the land is no longer a redemptive goal in the remote future, but rather a present possession. And yet, paradoxically, that possession derives at least part of its justification from the redemptive (time-oriented) hopes of the past.

The return to the land in our time therefore creates a tension between time and space, as literary elements: the individual writer's relation to historical time and heritage will eventually dictate his relation to site and space. To the individual who is not filled with the sense of time in Israel, the landscape inevitably loses its historic value.

The time-oriented aspect of Hebrew literature has its source in the fact that for the biblical man, the present gets its meaning from the past and the future. Even much later, the traditional Jew is essentially a man-in-the-middle, a link between generations, imparting the meaning of the past to the future—this being an interpretation of time and history in the direction of a unifying heritage and not in the direction of the isolated individual. For the modern Jew, however, a separation is made: one can belong to the Jewish people, yet not serve as bearer of the tradition.[3] His stance is as a part of a didactic continuity, i.e., he is aware of his successive position in the chain of history, but he rejects his position as hander-on of received values.

This in some way illuminates the ambiguous position of the Israeli writer: he is not tied to a continuation of tradition, yet he continues the national existence of his forefathers—by living in the land of his forefathers. Thus, the emphasis on one's connection to the land serves the purpose of cutting one's connection with the redemptive-temporal dimension and of asserting the national dimension! And in this we have the complex phenomenon of a nationalism which ties itself to the most remote past of the people as a nation, but not to the intermediate past with is religious expression.

ISRAEL AND THE DIASPORA

The new generation of Israeli writers, having experienced the creation of a new bond between man and land, considers itself a "genesis-generation." The older generation of Hebrew writers, having experienced the Diaspora, when Israel was merely a hope based on biblical promise, might be called the "memory-generation." The confrontation between these generations is given expression in their respective literatures; and this repeated confrontation provides the basis for national self-definition in literature. In this process, one question which is constantly being explored is whether the "genesis-generation" has experienced a real national genesis or merely a revival or continuation.

Aharon Megged's short story "The Name" describes touchingly a confrontation between a grandfather—raised in the Diaspora and steeped in memories—and his Israeli-born, genesis-oriented grandchildren.[4] The old man wants their newborn son to be named for a grandson of his who perished in the Holocaust. The baby's mother rejects the suggestion: the name is a ghetto name, ugly and horrible; she would prefer to forget the dreadful past. The baby's father rejects the name because it is suggestive of the Diaspora, an era to which he feels no connection. To the time-haunted old man, "Ties are remembrance," and the attitude of his grandchildren means the cutting of those ties, total death in a very real way. The old man cannot rid himself of bitterness about the past, about the many who were lost. If the child is not to be named for the dead grandson, there will be no memorial, no continuation. He ignores the child, and when the mother leaves with the baby she feels that it is in need of pity, as though it were an orphan.

The Israeli story may be said to evolve out of a problematic incident—as in the story just described. The outlook of the Israeli writer is shaped by a changing reality outside him. He brings with him no fixed ideas, or fixed feelings, about the past. The Hebrew writer, on the other hand, brings with him an already problematic set of convictions and attitudes—framed by his sense of time—and when reality clashes with those convictions, reality becomes even more problematic. It is therefore the Hebrew writer who indulges in ideological self-examination, and this stems from the fact that the present reality which is Israel must be viewed by him in the light of convictions and attitudes acquired in a pre-Israeli (Diaspora) experience.

In "The Sermon," a short story by the Hebrew writer Haim Hazaz, the protagonist addresses his comrades in a *kibbutz,* or Israeli communal farm.[5] In a meeting devoted to local problems, this pathetically inarticulate individual speaks about the meaning and quintessence of existence in the land of Israel. He maintains that Zionism begins with the wrecking of Judaism, namely, that it is not a direct continuation of Judaism. He regards the history of the Diaspora as a history of suffering and ignominy. But it is easy to understand his disquiet about the new way of life: If a people is shaped by exile, could not the end of exile destroy that people? Here in this treatment of the relation between Diaspora and Homeland, it is the issue and not the incident that takes precedence.

In the writing of S. Y. Agnon, winner of the Nobel Prize for Literature, the use of the particular incident and didactic argument (as literary devices) gives way to an emphasis on complexity and process. [Editor's note: Agnon died in 1970 after this article was completed. According to the author, the power and influence of Agnon in Hebrew and Israeli literature are without equal.] He re-created, in artistic terms, the fullness of Jewish existence in the past as well as the Judaic trauma in the present. One finds in his work the contrasting themes of faith and doubt, destruction and redemption, the literal and the symbolic, innocence and irony, exegesis and the occult, identification and alienation, concealment and disclosure, yearning and repulsion, entrapment and release, fiction and fact, past and present, the holy and the profane—as well as the contrast between Israel and the Diaspora, combining all these themes in a synoptic vision. In present-day Israel, where one's language indicates one's generation and one's primary identification, Agnon utilized every layer of language from the Pentateuch to the present. This makes it possible for us to read his work on the simplest as well as the most complex levels.

The young Israeli can relate to the Diaspora only extrinsically, and in a remote way—either as history or as the experience of his forefathers. Thus, when an Israeli writer looks to the past for subject-matter, he may even focus on the pre-Diaspora era, e.g., the first century B.C., as in Moshe Shamir's novel *King of Flesh and Blood.*

For Agnon, the relation to the Diaspora is far deeper, involving all the themes—literal as well as symbolic—mentioned above. His relation to the Diaspora allows him, therefore, to go beyond it, to universal themes: the home is broken, the key is lost, and man is naked and maimed. Man is driven out of the Eden of faith, into the macabre annihilating reality. Agnon shows us the Diaspora, spiritual as well as physical, as an exile from grace.

THE WAR OF INDEPENDENCE: 1948

The State of Israel (which was established in 1948) is physically, demologically, and spiritually in the process of becoming. The first generation of Israeli writers, the generation which matured during the war period, is sometimes referred to as the Palmach generation (the word *palmach* refers to underground military brigades operating during the time of the British Mandate). They grew up in the land of Israel in its pre-state days. In addition to their affiliations to language and land, another factor in their growing-up is the youth movement, which provided the ideological framework for their eventual *Weltanschauung.* Despite their various political standpoints, the different factions of the youth movement instilled values common to Zionist, Socialist, and liberalist ideologies. The young were expected to realize and materialize these ideals by joining a *kibbutz*—a collective agricultural settlement.

In 1948, the young generation was called upon to translate national aspirations and national yearnings into reality. Regrettably, the establishment of the state was met by war. This led to a situation in which, for the young, prior values and present reality were not in full accord: the shared experience of the "we"—which was cultivated in the youth movement and implied a mentality of collectivity and belonging—was challenged by the experience of the "I," the experience of fighting as an individual. The war threw the individual back onto his personal responsibility; his sense of belonging to the collectivity was confronted by war, bloodshed, and horror.

One writer who gave voice to the discord between self and reality is S. Yizhar.[6] His typical protagonist is a captive of his sensitivity and his sensibility. He is passive—because activity involves preference, choice, commitment, and irrevocability. Decisiveness and absolute certainty are foreign to him. The time of bliss for Yizhar's protagonist—as for many another Israeli writer—is therefore the period of childhood, before the initiation into adulthood and war. In that period, the landscape and the child are seen to be in complete accord, with open vistas suggesting a world without boundaries. Initiation into reality meant a moment of personal call and ultimately a reassessment of the sense of the belonging of man to land and land to man.

The war raised issues of personal morality: What is to be one's relation to the enemy? to the prisoner? What is to be considered a genuine act of faith and what *mauvaise foi?* Where does justice lie: with one's personal convictions or with collective national need? Yizhar's protagonist does not pass judgment, nor does he undergo an essential change of outlook; the situation is only a stage for his perennial interior monologue, a monologue studded with self-mockery. He tries to escape time and his consciousness. He realizes the irony and ambiguity in reality. Further, he is perpetually aware of his "otherness" in the tension between his self-searching sensitivity and the actions of the others.

Yet this standpoint is by no means the view of all Israeli writers. Moshe Shamir, for example, rejects the separation of the "I" from the "we"—either in literature or in life.[7] Recognizing the tension between the collectivity and the individual as a recurring theme in Israeli literature, he emphasizes the shared experience as a key motif. His protagonists of twenty years ago reflect these feelings: self-assertion rather than self-doubt, action rather than contemplation. They are at one with the call of their time.

Thus, the War of Independence provided for most Israeli writers an initiation into reality and a more complex relation to the land. It also meant the making of history, together with certain ramifications which were problematic for some, but not for others. To most writers it meant an increased self-consciousness as an individual, although not all writers were led to a sense of isolation as a result. In any event, it may be said with some certainty that the experiences of the War of Independence and the subsequent establishment of the State of Israel (two types of event not necessarily connected with any particular literary effect in other literatures) served as the formative crucible for the first generation of Israeli writers.

### THE HOLOCAUST

The two major events of Jewish life in the twentieth century are a positive one and a negative one: the establishment of the State of Israel and the Holocaust.

The theme of the Holocaust has been coming up in recent Israeli prose—in such a way as to raise questions about the individual Israeli's personal relation to Germany and the Germans (past and present) as well as questions of national self-definition. But there are even deeper existential questions, both national and individual. Not enough time has passed to permit the observer to state with certainty the reasons for this phenomenon. A short survey, however, of the various trends and treatments of the subject may shed light on this phenomenon.

There are Israeli writers who experienced the Holocaust at first hand, and for whom it has been the key motif of their entire output.[8] Aharon Appelfeld, in his short stories, creates a symbolic vision of the eternal journey, the endless snowy vista and the delayed spring.[9] His hollow people are in a no-exit state of being. They are the messengers and bearers of an apocalyptic horror.

Writers such as Amichai and Ben Amotz share a similar personal background, without having experienced the Holocaust. This theme did not appear in their work, either explicitly or implicitly, until quite recently. Now in their forties, they have returned to the problem of their interrupted youth in Europe: their protagonists return, belatedly, to the landscapes of their childhoods.

Yehuda Amichai, in his novel *Not of This Time, Not of This Place,* portrays an Israeli archeologist who, in his life, reaches the crossroads of self-questioning.[10] Further, the author resorts to the fictional device of splitting the protagonist's existence, so that he lives and experiences simultaneously in Jerusalem and in Germany. He lives in outer and inner time, in a patchwork of imagination and reality, fantasy and presence.

Dahn Ben Amotz, in his novel *To Remember and Forget,* treats this theme in a still bolder manner, more realistic, explicit and naked.[11] Written in the first person, the novel depicts a young Israeli architect, Uri Lam (né Hirsch Lampel), who returns to Frankfurt, the town of his birth, to collect his German reparations. While despising himself for his lack of integrity and for returning, he rediscovers his lost home in his love for a German girl. This brings forth an identity crisis. His self-questioning (am I a Jew or an Israeli?) and the haunting presence of the past are terminated in his return to Jerusalem with his German wife.

Both novels seem to maintain that a complete self-realization in understanding is impossible without the lost chapter of childhood. It is only a restored contact with the lost landscape of suppressed memories that can complete one's self-portrait—even if these memories are the most painful one can evoke.

A contrasting approach is to evoke, as a deliberate enterprise, one's experiences in the Second World War, as in Hanoch Bartov's novel *The Brigade.*[12] This book deals with the Jewish Brigade of the British army. Specifically, it describes the encounters of a young volunteer with two groups: the desolate Jews and the defeated Germans. This double confrontation leaves the protagonist (and the reader) with an awareness of the limitations of love and hate. Many problems arise: How does the individual avenge the crime committed against others? Can the individual wage a private war? Is the brigade an army of salvation or of retribution? And the answers are shown to have opposed consequences in action. The only certainty is the ineradicable memory of the Holocaust and the frustration of arrested reaction.

There is, in addition, another group of writers concerned with the Holocaust, namely, those who did not experience it directly. Haim Gouri's novel *The Chocolate Deal* is an effort to perceive and understand the Holocaust from this more remote vantage point, i.e., lacking the direct childhood recollection.[13] In the novel, two Jewish refugees return to the scene of their prewar existence in an unnamed city. To one of them, Mordi, the destruction of all remnants of the past means the destruction of the future. Time is at a standstill for him, since it brings no change or continuity. He aspires only to death, as a last act of will. Serenely he withdraws into himself, and death redeems him from a senseless existence. To the other, Rubi, only the world of fantasy can provide a bridge between himself and the present. In a reality devoid of meaning, existence may be possible only outside consciousness, outside reason. Gouri avoids the historical treatment, like many of the other writers in this group. The protagonists are, therefore, the existential and symbolic representatives of the Holocaust.

Earlier, we suggested that it was too early to state the reasons for the rise of the Holocaust as a theme in contemporary Israeli prose. The personal experiences of the writers can account for it only in part. In any case, the present interest in areas beyond autobiographical boundaries may point to a quest for a wider historical framework within which to regard the Jew, i.e., for a wider temporal and geographic frame of reference for the Jewish experience.

### TRANSITION TO INDIVIDUALISM

The individualistic trend in contemporary Israeli prose has come to the fore only since the early 1960s. The writers of the 1940s and the early 1950s were mainly engulfed in a combination of personal and national ethical problems, a trend which lent a somewhat didactic flavor to their writing. This was an inevitable outcome of their life situation, namely, the proximity of personal to national existence. Thus, their *raison d'être,* both personal and literary, was in a way imposed upon them by the time. Their typical protagonist exists usually against a collective background. His dialogue with this background, expressed in the tension between his being and his action, forms the artistic fabric in which he is revealed. The problem of one's identification as Israeli or Jew was one of the primary concerns of those writers.

Contemporary Israeli writers such as, among others, Avraham B. Yehoshua (b. 1937) and Amos Oz (b. 1939) face problems altogether different from those just described. In a recent interview, Yehoshua has said, "The question of Jewish existence occupied us many years ago, but today it doesn't bother us anymore—as Israelis. We aren't searching for our Jewish identity." Dalia Rabikovitz, a young poetess, says, "The question of belonging [to the Jewish people] doesn't raise any problems. I have no doubt I'm a Jewess. Moreover, here in Israel the Jewish heritage doesn't carry any sense of humiliation as perhaps it still does for Jews abroad. What bothers one more is the Israeli heritage."[14]

The search for roots is a prominent feature in Israeli literature. The question is where to search: In the biblical time? Or in the 2,000-year Diaspora? In the nation when it resides in the land? Or in the nation when it only dreams of residing in the land? Must a nation define itself only in reference to land?[15] More pressingly, must an individual identify himself in this way as well?

It is clear that it is the present rather than the past that will dictate the shape taken by the process of self-definition. The recent concern with the Holocaust as literary material may, perhaps, be seen as an effort to widen the Israeli writer's frame of reference, beyond his immediate time and place, in his quest for self-definition.

Whatever that quest might be, it is accompanied by the young writer's search for self-determination and a noncollective "privacy." Writers now in their thirties lived vicariously through the Second World War, the Holocaust, and the subsequent Ingathering, and experienced directly three wars in Israel, those of 1948, 1956, and 1967. Thus, personal and collective experiences are closely connected. At the same time, the young writer considers himself a man of the twentieth century, open to European and American trends in art, literature, and philosophy. As a result, it is possible to detect a tendency to widen the gap between one's past experience and the here-and-now. This leads to a quest for a deeper and more personal perception of reality. The result is expressed in the symbolism of the personal dream-world— this being one of the means, among others, for the expression of the individual vision.

Nissim Aloni (b. 1926), who shifted from prose to drama, uses motifs of fairy-tale and myth to create a vision of the absurd. An early play of his, *Cruelest of All Is the King*, draws on biblical material and is perhaps the finest Israeli drama of recent times. Yet the world view Aloni seeks is one going beyond the Hebraic or Judaic, approaching the universal.

Amos Oz, in his novel *My Michael*, utilizes the stream-of-consciousness technique, as well as dream and fantasy, to depict a world devoid of any objective correlative.[16] It is an allegorization of reality—of such a kind that to portray its incongruities reveals a depth of vision entirely personal and removed from all collective awareness.

Simultaneously, a bold attempt is being made to face the complexity of reality in the writing of the novella and the short story. A. B. Yehoshua, one of the most prominent of young Israeli writers, has been powerfully influenced by Kafka and Agnon and is emerging as a writer with a distinct personal idiom. His latest collection of short stories makes use of all the themes and techniques just mentioned: biblical motifs, existential symbol, and even the use of the land as a protagonist.[17]

## CONCLUSION

The Israeli writer—like his contemporaries in other cultures—is faced by the twentieth-century verbal crisis regarding the uncertainties of literary form and content. Yet his primary problem comes from his ancient language and his modern land.

Over the millennia, the language has left deposits, like archeological strata, in which are embedded the cultural history of the people. Most of the young writers are acquainted with these sources (especially the Bible), so that the use of a certain word or phrase immediately relates their expression to a certain era in the long history of the national consciousness. Moreover, certain archetypes, symbols, images, motifs, and stories are part of their upbringing and present make-up.

Some of the contemporary writing fuses personal experience with the imagery of the past. Any evocation of the language of the past points simultaneously to the extended national consciousness as well as to an ironic reduction of the sanctified to a personal everyday level. Thus, their language serves to express their ties to and their discontinuities with the past.

Quite different problems are presented to the writer by the fact of his living in modern Israel, where life means change—and this is more often revolutionary than evolutionary, e.g., in the growth and change of population, in the alteration of geographical boundaries. One cannot, in Israel, talk of a totality or reality which is the result of slow, organic growth. This has affected literature, the subject matter as well as the writer's relation toward it.

Basic to the writer's *Weltanschauung* are his belonging to the nation, to the land, and to its language. His relation to Jewish history as a whole and to the Jews in the world is more complex; its outcome is in the hand of time.

NOTES

[1] Mordecai Zeev Feierberg, *Whither?*, trans. Ira Eisenstein (New York, 1959).

[2] See Baruch Kurzweil, *Our Contemporary Literature: Continuity or Revolution?* (published in Hebrew by Schocken Publishing House, Tel-Aviv, 1965), 110.

[3] This view is expressed by Nathan Rotenstreich of the Hebrew University, Jerusalem, in an article in Hebrew, "Historical Consciousness and Jewish Historical Reality," in *Ma'ariv*, 22 April 1969.

[4] Aharon Megged, "The Name," in *Israeli Stories*, ed. Joel Blocker (New York, 1966). All the stories in this anthology are translated into English.

[5] Haim Hazaz, "The Sermon," in *Israeli Stories*.

[6] S. Yizhar, "The Dead and the Living," in *A Whole Loaf*, ed. S. J. Kahn (New York, 1963). An anthology, in English, of stories from Israel. See also S. Yizhar, "The Prisoner," in *Israeli Stories*.

[7] In a symposium in *Ma'ariv*, Oct.-Nov. 1968.

[8] Mention must be made of Elie Wiesel, an Israeli who writes in French.

[9] Aharon Appelfeld, *In the Wilderness*, short stories translated from the Hebrew by T. Sandbank, S. Berg, and J. Sloane (Jerusalem, 1965).

[10] Yehuda Amichai, *Not of This Time, Not of This Place*, translated from the Hebrew by Shlomo Katz (New York, 1968).

[11] Dahn Ben Amotz, *To Remember and Forget* (published in Hebrew by Amikam, Tel-Aviv, 1968).

[12] Hanoch Bartov, *The Brigade*, translated from the Hebrew by S. Segal (New York, 1968).

[13] Haim Gouri, *The Chocolate Deal*, translated from the Hebrew by Seymour Simckes (New York, 1968).

[14] Both interviews are cited in *Jerusalem Post Weekly*, 3 Feb. 1969. They are part of a collection of 25 interviews with as many Israeli writers, entitled *It's All There in the Book*, ed. Y. Bezalel (published in Hebrew by Hakibbutz Hameuchad, Israel, 1969).

[15] According to the small and marginal "Canaanites"—a cultural movement which arose in the early 1950s—land and language are the only genuine sources of identification; they therefore advocate going back to pre-biblical times! Its spokesmen distinguish between the "Hebrew" and the Jew: the former identified with the land, and the latter with the Diaspora. They stress the present and reject completely the idea of the nation as Jewish. The brilliant poetry of J. Ratosh, one of their main figures, evokes pagan myth and the lore indigenous to the region of the Fertile Crescent.

[16] Amos Oz, *My Michael* (published in Hebrew by Am Oved, Tel-Aviv, 1967).

[17] Avraham B. Yehoshua, *Over Against the Woods* (published in Hebrew by Hakibbutz Hameuchad, Israel, 1968).

---

## ISRAELI FICTION

**Robert Alter**

SOURCE: "Fiction in a Stage of Siege," in *Defenses of the Imagination: Jewish Writers and Modern Historical Crisis,* The Jewish Publication Society of America, 1977, pp. 213-31.

[*In the following essay, Alter studies the fiction of Amos Oz and Avraham B. Yehoshua.*]

> One should present the great and simple things, like desire and death.
>
> —Amos Oz

Something new has clearly been happening in Israeli fiction. Literary generations of course never really correspond to those symmetric schemes in which writers are seen marching past the review-stand of criticism in neat rows two decades apart; but now that twenty years have elapsed since the emergence of the first generation of native Israeli writers, one becomes increasingly aware of new Hebrew writers who have grown up with the accomplished fact of Jewish sovereignty in a state of seige, and whose attitudes toward language and literary tradition, as well as toward the social realities around them, are often strikingly different from those of their predecessors.

The writers who first came to prominence in the later forties are generally referred to in Hebrew criticism as the Generation of '48, sometimes even as the Palmach

Generation, and there is a certain justice in the fact that their literary effort should be linked in this way with a historical event and a national—necessarily, military—institution. Historical trauma was a first fact of manhood for many of them; public events had irrupted into their lives with all the imperiousness, the ugly violence, and the moral ambiguity that such events can assume in a time of war, against a background of ideological stridencies. The act of writing fiction, then, was frequently the direct critical response of a troubled individual consciousness to the political and social realities that impinged upon it, pained it, threatened its integrity. Consequently, the most common mode of Hebrew fiction throughout the fifties and early sixties was social realism, usually of a drably conventional sort, however strong the moral impulse behind it. Such writing was often primarily an examination of the problematics of self-definition through a repeated sifting of the various social, political, and ideological materials that were the particular circumstances of the Israeli self at a fixed point in time. Thus, the nature of the kibbutz, the army, the youth movement, the new urban milieus, was sometimes almost as much the "subject" of this fiction as the lives of the characters, or, at any rate, individual lives were conceived in terms of their entanglement in these social spheres, and the social setting in turn was implicated in the destiny of the nation.

Such characterizations of whole generations, to be sure, easily lapse into caricature and in fact one can find a few exceptions to my generalization among books written by members of the Generation of '48, but the broad orientation of the group toward social realism seems to me undeniable. On the other hand, there were a few writers old enough to have fought in the War of Independence whose cultural background, personal experience, or sensibility set them quite apart from this group; who have been attracted to symbolic, parabolic, or expressionist modes of fiction; and whose writing looks beyond the historical situation to trans-historical questions about human nature, value, existence itself.

Perhaps the earliest and most peculiar Israeli book of this sort is Pinhas Sadeh's *Life as a Parable* (1958), the autobiographical record of a Rimbaud-like spiritual quest beyond the limits of conventional morality. One might also mention Yehuda Amichai's first volume of experimental stories, *In This Terrible Wind* (1961), his remarkable symbolic novel, *Not of This Time, Not of This Place* (1963),[1] and Yoram Kaniuk's Agnonesque first novel, *The Acrophile* (1961). Kaniuk's second novel, *Himmo, King of Jerusalem* (1966),[2] is an especially clear illustration of the distance between this middle group of writers and the Generation of '48 because, like many of the earlier Israeli novels, it is set in the War of Independence, but with a startlingly different perspective. (It might be noted that both Kaniuk and Sadeh are in their late thirties, while the typical Palmach Generation writers are now in their late forties or early fifties.) The substantive action of the Kaniuk novel—the eery, ambiguous love of an Israeli army nurse for a hideously mutilated casualty—could have taken place in any war, at any time. The novel is actually a kind of clinical investigation into the extreme limits of human love, into the moral ambiguities underlying our ultimate categories of life and death.

Pinhas Sadeh's second prose work—he published poetry earlier—provides an even more dramatic antithesis to the fiction of the Generation of '48. The first volume of a projected longer novel, it is called, apparently without either irony or allusion to Malraux, *On the Human Condition* (1967). Deploying its characters in a recognizable Jerusalem setting, often with persuasive fidelity to details of milieu, the novel and its protagonists conjure with such terms as the image of God and the image of man, divine jest and cosmic dread, infinity and finiteness, loneliness, lust, the hunger for beauty, and their dialectic interrelation. Sadeh's radically antinomian religious vision—both Sabbatai Zevi and Joseph Frank are invoked in the argument of his novel—is admittedly rather special, perhaps finally private, but his explicit insistence on using the medium of fiction as a means of confronting nothing less than "the human condition" is shared by the two most original and highly regarded of the new Israeli writers, Amos Oz (who is just twenty-nine) and Avraham B. Yehoshua (who is now thirty-two). Like Sadeh, like Amichai and Kaniuk, both Oz and Yehoshua are capable of precise observation of Israeli actualities, but their real interests, too, lie far beyond or below the particular structures of Israeli society.

At first thought, it may seem a little odd that Hebrew writers should permit themselves the "luxury" of contemplating man as a moral, spiritual, or even metaphysical entity rather than as a social-political agent at the very moment when the vise of historical necessity has gripped Israel's national existence more tightly than ever before. On reflection, though, one can see a kind of logic in this whole shift of perspective. For Israelis who have grown up with the State, harsh historical necessity has lost the upsetting impact of traumatic surprise. Statehood and armed confrontation with the Arabs are basic facts of existence, no longer new crises that throw into question the whole moral and political vocabulary with which one has been raised.

There is even a sense, I would argue, in which Israel's continuing existence as a sophisticated technological society and parliamentary democracy in a state of siege becomes a sharply focused image of the general conditions of life in the second half of the twentieth century. Israelis live with a full sense—at times even a buoyant sense—of realized "normalcy," committing their constructive energies to the continuing development of a civilized order of existence, while the contradictory awareness of the menace of the abyss on the other side of the border has itself become a part of normalcy. The insistent presence of the Palestinian landscape, moreover, with its startling topographical contrasts and its complex web of historical associations, amplifies and complicates this sense of looming oppositions in the Israeli situation.

For Amos Oz, and in a more restricted way for A. B. Yehoshua, there is something uncannily semantic about Israeli reality. Topographical, architectural, even institutional actualities allude to things beyond themselves, and though both writers have been guilty on occasion of symbolic contrivance (Oz much more glaringly), one gets some sense that their cultural predicament has made symbolists out of them. One of Yehoshua's narrators in fact comments on the temptations of symbolism which the setting offers: "For everyone here is addicted to symbols. With all their passion for symbolism the Jerusalemites imagine that they themselves are symbols. As a result they speak in symbolic fashion with a symbolic language, they walk symbolically and meet each other in symbolic style. Sometimes, when they lose their grip a little, they imagine that the sun, the wind, the sky above their city, are all merely symbols that need looking into." There is, patently, an acerbic ironic perspective here on the excesses of symbol-hunting and symbol-making; the ironic intelligence points to the admirable artistic restraint with which Yehoshua, in his second volume of fiction, *Opposite the Forests* (1968),[3] develops a distinctive mode of symbolism that is quietly suggestive and for the most part not obtrusive.

Perhaps the best way to see what Yehoshua and Oz do with their local surroundings is to observe an instance of their treatment of Jerusalem. For Jerusalem, as the passage quoted from Yehoshua suggests, is the most portentously "symbolic" of Israeli realities, its streets and skyline and natural setting a crazy-quilt pattern of all the profound antinomies of Israeli life—modernity and antiquity intermingled; brisk Western energies amid the slow, patient rhythms of the Orient; incessant building on a landscape that remains fiercely unbuilt, or somehow in ruins; the seat of Jewish sovereignty hard against the presence of the Arab antagonist. Here is Yehoshua, in as long a descriptive passage as the taut surface of his writing will permit: "Apartment buildings all around, bared rocks, crimson soil. Half city, half ruin. Jerusalem in her sadness, her unending destruction. No matter how much they build, there will always be within her a remembrance of the destruction." And here is Oz, with somewhat untypical conciseness, reflecting on the same setting in a novel where the presence of the city dominates the action: "On winter nights the buildings of Jerusalem seem like mirages of coagulated gray on a black screen. A landscape of suppressed violence. Jerusalem knows how to be an abstract city: stones, pine trees, and rusting iron." Or, later on in the same novel, when political boundaries—they are those of the period before June 1967—give a special resonance to the symbolism of the landscape: "Through the defiles of the streets in Jerusalem at dusk one can see the mountains growing in obscurity as though waiting for the darkness in order to fall on the drawn-in city."

The opposition between Yehoshua and Oz is roughly that between daytime and night world. Though Yehoshua's first volume of stories, *The Death of the Old Man* (1962), draws frequently on fantasy, with signs of influence from both Kafka and Agnon, his world is characteristically one of bright Mediterranean daylight, and it is instructive that the principal action in three of the four novellas grouped together in *Opposite the Forests* takes place during a *khamsin,* when the pitiless summer sunlight gives an astringent definition to surfaces, contours, colors, people. The swift staccato phrases quoted on the paradox of Jerusalem occur in the first-person narration of an aging, long-silent poet who has just come to leave his retarded son as an apprentice with a Jerusalem bookbinder. The city quite naturally becomes a voice in the frustrated poet's disheartened meditations on the futility of all creative activity, the ambiguity of speech, the eternal dead ground of silence from which language arises and in which it is absorbed again. The harsh peculiarities of the local landscape are a means of giving shape and solidity to the harsh contradictions of being a man, a speaking creature in a universe that cares nothing for speech.

Oz's vision of Jerusalem is also seen through the eyes of a first-person narrator, in this case a young married woman obsessed with death, the passage of time, the threat of violence, and dreams of sexual debasement. The perspective he tries to establish, however, for all his fiction is ultimately not clinical but mythic: Jerusalem the city surrounded by ancient mountains and enemy forces, as it is mediated through the consciousness of his protagonist, becomes the flimsy structure of human civilization perched on the lid of a volcano of chthonic powers, and so the "true" city emerges in the developing solution of darkness as a coagulated mirage, while the sinister darkling mountains all around prepare to pounce, to destroy.

The work of both Oz and Yehoshua raises an interesting question about Israel's peculiar cultural situation. Their concerns, as I have already intimated, are if not quite apolitical then metapolitical, seeking to come to grips with the ultimate facts about human nature and social existence which issue in political events, institutions, and conflicts. But given the explosively charged nature of Israel's political situation, it is not surprising that a good many readers should see directly political, even "subversive," implications in this new kind of Hebrew fiction. Oz's books and the response they have elicited are especially instructive in this connection because his imagination has been powerfully attracted to visions of Dionysiac release which he has repeatedly translated into local social situations and political terms.

The plot of his first novel, *Somewhere Else* (1966)[4] is a writhing tangle of adulterous and quasi-incestuous relationships in a kibbutz near the Syrian border. (Oz himself has been a member of Kibbutz Hulda near the old Jordanian border since 1957.) Some reviewers, reading Oz's novel as though it were one of the novels of kibbutz life of the preceding generation, denounced him for sensationalistic distortion, even accused him of attempting to discredit Israel's noblest social experiment. The real function, however, of the kibbutz for Oz is as a focused, dramatically tractable image of the fragile and precarious nature of all civilized order. His fictitious kibbutz sits

under the shadow of enemy guns, with the murky realm beyond the border almost a kabbalistic Other Side, or, to use the animal imagery in which Oz delights, a howling, primeval "jackal country"—the title of his first book, a collection of short stories issued in 1965—that both entices and disturbs those who dwell within the tight geometric boundaries of the kibbutz.

The collective settlement, then, is more a convenient microcosm than the "representation" of an actual institution: a small, rationally ordered society, explicitly idealistic in its purposes, where roles and relations are sharply defined, and where forced proximity can serve as a social pressure-cooker for petty jealousies and instinctual urges, the kibbutz becomes in Oz a kind of schematic recapitulation of civilization, its self-delusions and discontents. The Israeli critic Gershon Shaked has stated this same point succinctly in a cogent argument against the conception of Oz as a tendentious social realist: "His kibbutzim are human islands in a 'jackal country' that breaks into the islands and destroys them from within." This process of the symbolic transmutation of the political may become clearer through example. Here is a description of night on the kibbutz, in fact part of a short chapter devoted solely to such description, which occurs about halfway through *Somewhere Else:*

> Now the crickets. The crickets exchange secret signals. The distant motor of the freezer-shed slips in among their voices. The swish of the sprinklers tricks you and falls into the camp of the crickets. The crickets are discovering your hidden places, giving away your fear in sound-signals to their friends who listen to them from the enemy fields.
>
> And what is in the howling of the dogs? There is a dark nightmare in the howling of the dogs. One must not trust the dogs. The howling of the dogs goes whoring after the mountains.
>
> The mountains are unseen but their presence weighs on the valley. The mountains are there. Wanton gulleys descend and charge against this place. Somber masses of rock hang by a thread on the heights. Their connection with the mountain range is suspect. A kind of muted stirring, a restrained patient murmur, glides down from somewhere beyond. The mountains are there. In absolute stillness they are there. In a position of twisted pillars they are there, as though an act of burning lust had taken place among the eternal elements and in the very moment of heat it had petrified and hardened.

This remarkable piece of disquieting prose catches up most of the important elements of Oz's distinctive world. One notes a strange interplay between descriptive specification and looming vagueness, between massive solidity and wraithlike elusive substance and sound. The stately, repetitive, almost incantatory movement of the prose points toward the revelation of some dimly impending cataclysm, prefigured here in the violent image of the last sentence. Oz is a poet of fluid and disruptive energies, and for him the solidity of the "real" world—

whether natural scene or man-made object and order or human nature—is illusory, merely the temporary hardening of volcanic lava that seeks to become molten again, or, as in his vision of Jerusalem, merely a mirage of "coagulated gray on a black screen." Significantly, the violent forces locked up in nature are linked with wild sexuality: the gulleys storming down on the kibbutz are "wanton," the contorted forms of rock are testimony to a primordial past of vast orgiastic dimensions. Correspondingly, in the action of the novels and short stories, it is chiefly through his sexuality that man answers the call of the darkness "out there." The howling dogs of this passage are a dramatic model of the human response to the darkness within. In proper biblical language, their cry "goes whoring after the mountains," for one assumes it is an answer to the howl of their untamed cousins, the jackals, out beyond the pale, where human restraint and discipline are unknown, where every instinct to raven and destroy, to sate all appetites, is, quite literally, unleashed.

The scene, of course, has a direct relation to recognizable political realities. The mountains are forbidding not only because of their ontological otherness from man but because they are in Syrian territory, and they hide an armed human enemy waiting for the chance to attack the kibbutz. What should be noted, however, is the way in which the Arab military adversary has been completely assimilated into the mythic landscape, interfused with it. As a matter of fact, actual Arab antagonists do not appear in this passage at all (though they do frequently elsewhere in Oz), but nature here has itself become the invading threat—the spy network of crickets, the treacherous dogs howling up to the mountains—and the Arabs when they are imagined directly are merely extensions, embodiments, of an inimical yet seductive nature. Oz's imaginative rendering of the state of siege, in terms of its origins in his private world of neurosis, is an Israeli's nightmare of life in a garrison-state, but as a component of a realized artistic whole, it has very little to do with the actual conditions of the state of siege, whether political, moral, or even psychological.

All this needs to be clearly stated in order to see in proper perspective Oz's most fully realized book to date, *My Michael* (1968).[4] The novel, which was a spectacular best-seller in Israel in 1969—over 30,000 copies sold in a country where the Hebrew-reading public can scarcely number a million—has enjoyed the peculiar fate of being at once a *succès de scandale* and a *succès d'estime*. The critical esteem seems to me warranted because *My Michael* is an arresting novel in itself and represents an impressive advance in artistic control over its author's two earlier books. For Oz's brooding lyric prose, as one might infer even from the passage just quoted, is often in danger of breaking out into purple patches; and his intense desire to connect characters with elemental forces sometimes leads him into blatant melodrama or painfully contrived symbolism. (Some of the early fiction makes one think of the most sophomoric things in D. H. Lawrence, like "Nomads and Viper," the story of a kibbutz girl who, repelled, frightened, and attracted by a

dusky, potent bedouin, imagines she has been touched by him and is racked with physical revulsion, then is bitten by an all-too-phallic snake and dies in sweet waves of ecstasy.) In his latest book, Oz demonstrates a new sureness of touch in arranging a suggestive dialectic between fantasy and outer reality through the language of his first-person narrator.

Hannah Gonen, the protagonist, the wife of a graduate student in geology at the Hebrew University, is, as at least two reviewers have observed, a Madame Bovary of the interior world. Trapped in the flat bourgeois existence of a Jerusalem hausfrau, her isolation ironically reinforced by the good-natured devotion of her systematic, practical-minded, "achievement-oriented," hopelessly unimaginative husband, she escapes into an inner realm of fantasy, compounded of early memories, juvenile literature, and suppressed desires, where she can reign as a splendid queen and abandon herself to lovers who exist solely in a subterranean sphere of the imagination. What Oz has done in this novel is to find a fully-justified location within character for that chthonic world to which his own imagination is drawn. As Hannah Gonen's narrative shuttles between outer and inner worlds, the quality of the prose itself oscillates—on the one hand, a parade of brief, factual, elliptic sentences whose flat rhythms and direct unqualified statements precisely define the deadness of the external world for Hannah; on the other hand, in her interior monologues, a haunting florescence of language, highly colored with emotive adjectives and vivid sensory imagery, run-on sentences spilling from fantasy to fantasy through underground caverns out of Jules Verne. It is precisely because Michael, her husband, has no access to this private world, is incapable even of imagining its existence, that conjugal sex itself is finally adulterous for Hannah. She clings to her husband's body in fear and desperation, as Emma Bovary grasped at Rodolphe and Leon, but he cannot release her from the prison of her isolation even when he gives her ecstasy. Thus, after a pyrotechnic description of the heights and depths of orgasm with Michael, Hannah tells us, "And yet I evaded him. I related only to his body: muscles, arms, hair. In my heart I knew that I was betraying him, over and over. With his body."

Hannah's maddening desire to break loose from the trap of her own existence is, like the dark urges of the characters in Oz's previous novel, a response to the basic condition of civilization, but it is presented in a familiar social context, and this is what has given the book a certain degree of notoriety in Israel. For the Israeli, Jerusalem is the political center, the key historical symbol, and since June 1967, the chief non-negotiable fact, of national existence. (One notes that the draft of the novel was completed just weeks before the war broke out.) In *My Michael,* however, Jerusalem, the illusory, unknowable city of congealed nightmare and suppressed violence, is the principal symbol for the protagonist's state of alienation. The single moment in the novel when she can pronounce the words, "I belonged," is during a visit to a kibbutz in the Galilee, where "Jerusalem was far away and could no longer pursue." But a glimpse of Arab shepherds on an opposite slope is enough to remind her of her lack of connection with the world around her, and at once a vision of the somber, forbidding Jerusalem of her fears rises before her again.

Oz thus puts the materials of the Israeli scene to darkly suggestive use in a mythic drama, but it is clear why some readers should feel at least uneasy with what he has done. Such uneasiness becomes acute in the response to his treatment of Arab terrorism in *My Michael.* Hannah Gonen remembers a pair of Arab twins, Halil and Aziz, with whom she used to play as a child in Jerusalem during the period before 1948. Halil and Aziz return now in her fantasies to break into her house and violate her, and it is evident that she is far more fascinated than frightened by them. She imagines them as having become terrorists, and it is in this guise that they appear in the climactic fantasy of destruction which concludes the novel, and which more than one reviewer quoted in outrage: Hannah sees Halil and Aziz gliding across the Judean Desert toward their objective within Israel, daggers in hand, submachine guns and explosive devices on their backs, so thoroughly part of the natural setting that their movements are pure feline grace and fluidity, and, like the crickets in *Somewhere Else,* their communication an exchange of guttural "sound signals," not human language. The alluring alien twins are in some way an uncanny and piquant doubling of the male principle for Hannah; she imagines both their animal grace and their capacity for violence in erotic terms: "Theirs is a language of simple symbols—gentle touches, a muted murmur, like a man and woman who are lovers. A finger on the shoulder. A hand on the nape. Birdcall. Secret whistle. High thorns in the gulley. The shadow of old olive trees. Silently the earth gives herself." Thus there is an almost exhilarating feeling of release in the explosion that culminates this fantasy, and the chill silence that afterward descends on the land, in the final sentence of the novel, brings with it a curious sense of relief for the protagonist.

Now, it is obvious that this dream of terrorists flowing across the desert in perfect catlike motion "that is a caress full of yearning" corresponds faithfully only to Hannah Gonen's fantasy world, not to the actual motley collection of unstable, deluded, and generally inept types that have tried to carry out the fundamentally ineffectual program of Al Fatah. As some of the response to the novel indicates, Oz is playing with explosive material in more than one sense by pulling these political actualities into the warp of a mythic confrontation. What should be noted is the peculiar double edge of his whole literary enterprise. In one sense, it can legitimately be conceived as a document, and a very troubling one, of Israel's state of seige; but at the same time, paradoxically, it bears witness to the complete freedom of consciousness of the Israeli writer, who does not feel compelled to treat the conflict with the Arabs in a context of political "responsibility" but may reshape it into an image of human existence quite beyond politics.

Avraham B. Yehoshua writes a much cooler, more understated kind of fiction than Oz, sometimes arranging his narrative materials in generalizing designs that place them almost at the distance of parable from the reader; but there are certain affinities in theme between the two writers. Several of Yehoshua's protagonists, like those of Oz, bear within them a deep sexual wound that humiliates them, drives them to acts of hostility. Without a trace of Oz's mythopoeic imagination or his interest in an erotic underworld, Yehoshua also often sees lurking animal instincts beneath the façade of the civilized self; his educated, ostensibly pacific, ineffectual personages frequently harbor a murderous impulse to destroy whatever stands in their way or whatever is associated with those who have given them pain. "Three Days and a Child," the last story in *Opposite the Forests,* is the account of a bachelor who agrees to take care of his former mistress's son and then struggles—in quiet ambivalence, never melodramatically—with the desire to do away with the child as an act of vengeance against its mother, who has dared to prefer another man.

Peculiarly, but most appropriately, this tersely-reported first-person narrative proves to be a kind of submerged animal fable. If we translate the rather common Hebrew names of the protagonists—all of them are graduate students at the Hebrew University and none is overtly "animalistic"—we find that Wolf the father brings his small son (whose garbled name remains a puzzle) to Bear, his wife's former lover. Bear has a new mistress, Gazelle, a naturalist devoted to the collection of thorns, and he shares with her an odd friend, a gentle, slightly daft herpetologist named Hart, who gets bitten by one of his snakes during the course of events because he refuses to crush it when it slithers away. Near the end of the novella, Bear tells the child a story about a bear, a fox, a wolf, a hart, and their wives who go off to the forest where they carry on "cruel wars." The boy is especially moved by the little wolves that are drowned in the river; and at the end of the tale, when the teller decides to destroy every living creature, leaving only one little wolf-cub, we infer that an ambiguous reconciliation has been effected between the man and the child he thought of killing: Bear (is he also the ravening fox of his tale?) identifies with his rival's son, the wolfling, out of self-pity, and so allows him to live, in story and in fact. The scheme of the animal fable here may suggest how Yehoshua deftly defines an intricate constellation of ambiguous motives and relations with great economy of means.

Also like Oz is Yehoshua's fascination with destruction for its own sake, the desires civilization breeds in people to escape its imposed order and rational framework. Yehoshua treated one variant of this condition in an early story, "The Tropville Evening Express," about a quiet little town that is pitifully *de trop* in a world of vast wars and so its citizens conspire to cause a train wreck simply to make something happen in the dead air of their empty existence. More memorably, this time using materials from Israel's political situation, Yehoshua deals with the same problem in the title story of *Opposite the Forests.*

A quick summary will reveal the direct thematic connection with Oz. The protagonist, a badly-blocked graduate student in history, has taken a job as a fire watchman at a Jewish National Fund forest so that he can have the uninterrupted solitude to write an essay on the Crusades. (In order to see the full point of the story, one must keep in mind the comparison between Israelis and Crusaders frequently drawn in Arab propaganda.) The man-made forest has grown up over the site of an Arab village that was razed in the fighting of 1948. One of the villagers, however, an old mute, remains as caretaker of the ranger's station together with an enigmatic little girl who seems to look after him. At first the new ranger strains every nerve watching day and night for a sign of fire in order to call in the alarm, but imperceptibly it becomes clear to him and to us that he really wants the fire to break out, and when the Arab mute finally puts the forest to the torch, the watchman is a passive accomplice, exhilarated by the all-consuming flame and by the vision of the long-destroyed village he sees rising in the tongues of smoke and fire.

The political application of the story is transparent, and for anyone accustomed to thinking of Israel in official Zionist terms, it may seem more comprehensively "subversive" than anything in Oz. Yehoshua, let me emphasize, is unswervingly committed to Israel's survival and to the constructive development of Israeli society—he is, of all things, Dean of Students at Haifa University—and the story must properly be seen as an unflinching exploration of the shadowy underside of ambivalence in Israeli consciousness within the state of siege. A more general human ambivalence is also implied in the story's use of the local situation; as we move in a typical Yehoshua pattern from the frustrations of impotence—here, the unwritten paper—to the thirst for destruction, we get a sense of the balked consciousness of civilized man secretly longing for the cataclysm that will raze all the artificial hedging structures of human culture. The steadily generalizing perspective of all Yehoshua's fiction is clear from the opening sentences of "Opposite the Forests":

> The last winter, too, was lost in fog. As usual he did nothing. He put off his exams, and the papers, of course, remained unwritten. Yes, he had long since finished hearing everything, that is, all his lectures. A chain of signatures in his dog-eared registration book certified that everyone had fulfilled his obligation toward him and had disappeared in silence, and now the obligation was left in his hands alone, his slack hands. But words make him tired; even his own words, and certainly the words of others. In the world around him he drifts from one apartment to another, without roots or a steady job.

The unnamed graduate student at once becomes an exemplar of contemporary futility, purposelessness, deracination, but with none of the self-conscious reaching for the effects of a Kafka parable that one finds in some of Yehoshua's earlier stories. The language is unpretentious, the diction largely colloquial, the references to the

details of student life factually precise yet formulated to make their paradigmatic implications evident. The first sentences of the story introduce us immediately to the characteristic Yehoshua world, which is, in a word, a world of incompletions. Characters undertake all kinds of projects which they are incapable of seeing to an end—a thesis, a poem, a love affair, the building of a dam in Africa. As this protagonist's fatigue with language suggests, the individual is confirmed in his radical loneliness because the instruments of communication seem so pathetically inadequate, or futile. "Is it still possible to say anything?" asks another Yehoshua protagonist at the end of his disillusioning experiences. Most of Yehoshua's stories are models of the difficulties of communication; as we have seen, he delights in juxtaposing mutually incomprehensible figures—an Israeli student and an old Arab mute, a poet father and a retarded son, a bachelor and a three-year-old, and, in the fourth story of this volume, an Israeli engineer and a hostile, mocking African doctor. In each of these cases, communication of sorts does take place, but it is generally an ambiguous, troubling communication, sometimes with ominous results, destruction becoming the final language. I alluded earlier to Yehoshua's ironic intelligence; one is especially aware of its presence in the wryly comic effects of poignant farce through which he frequently conveys the breakdown of communication, the failure of human relation. An ultimate act of derisively inadequate communication is the visit paid to the fire-watcher in his lonely station by a former mistress, the wife of a friend:

> Only toward sunset does he succeed in stripping her. The binoculars are still hanging on his chest, squeezed between them. From time to time he coolly interrupts his kisses and embraces, lifts his binoculars to his eyes, and peers into the forest.
>
> "Duty," he whispers in apology, with a strange smile, to the naked, embarrassed woman. Everything intermingles in the illumination of the far-off, reddish sun. The blue of the sea in the distance, the silent trees, the drops of blood on his bruised lips, the despair, the insipidness, the loneliness of naked flesh. Unintentionally her hand touches his bared skull, and recoils.

Such a bleak view of humanity as this would be utterly depressing were it not articulated with a quality of imaginative wit, as a critique of mankind's inadequacies, a sort of ultimate satire, that is finally moral in purpose. If, as I have suggested, there is some relationship to Kafka in the earlier Yehoshua, he stands at about the same distance from the German writer as Isaac Rosenfeld. Like Rosenfeld, he offers us in place of Kafka's neurotic visionary intensity a critical shrewdness in the manipulation of narrative, a certain muted intellectual verve, an ironic perspective in which sympathy for the characters and their predicaments is continuous with rigorous judgment of them. Because of this effect of broad critical overview in his fiction, Yehoshua is able at times to project with the greatest naturalness a general image of human existence out of the particular tensions, strains, fears, and ambiguities of life in an Israel surrounded by enemies. The suggestive connection between particular and universal is especially clear in a story called "The Last Commander," which is included in *The Death of the Old Man*. This is how the story begins:

> Since the end of the war we have been sitting in gloomy offices, gripping pencils and sending each other chilly notes on matters we regard as important. Had we lost, we would now be cursed. Called to account for murder, for theft, for our dead comrades. Having won, we brought redemption, but they must keep us busy with something; if not, who would get down from the swift, murderous jeeps, piled high with their machine guns and bands of bullets.

At once we are presented with a world that is based on Israeli reality but not a direct representation of it. Reflections and refractions of particular facts of Israeli existence glimmer through the story: the veterans are called on annual reserve duty to maneuvers in a blistering desert where two or three of the enemy, "wrapped in black," are occasionally glimpsed disappearing into the distant hills; a staff officer descends in a helicopter from the pitiless desert sky to supervise the reservists; even the transition indicated in the opening sentence from military service to bureaucracy is an especially characteristic fact of Israeli life. However, only one place name, presumably Arab, is given in the entire story, the few names of characters offered have no clear national identity, and the war that has been fought is not specifically the war of 1948-49 but an archetypal "seven year's war" with an anonymous enemy who remains completely faceless.

The story finally is not "about" Israel's security situation but about human effort, will, and the strain of maintaining the disciplines of civilization in an utterly indifferent cosmos. The veterans are deposited in a completely isolated desert campsite where they find themselves under the command of an enigmatic officer named Yagnon who promptly sprawls out on the ground and goes to sleep, very quickly inducing his men to follow his example. Long undifferentiated days of languid stupor under the hot desert sun are finally interrupted by the airborne arrival of the company commander, who at once begins to put the men through their paces—setting up tents, building latrines, erecting a flagpole, charging, crawling, scrambling in full battle gear across the sun-baked terrain hour after hour in mock pursuit of an imaginary enemy, even forced to bellow out old battle songs around the campfire at night. Six days the commander works the men, and on the seventh day he allows them to rest while briefing them on a week-long forced march across the desert that he has devised for them. But on the morning of the eighth day the helicopter descends out of the empty sky to take the commander back to the base, and in a single impulse, the men wreck the latrines, overturn the tents, pull down the flagpole, throw off their battle gear, and fling themselves onto the ground, to return to their previous state of numbed somnolence. "Seven days he was with us," the narrator comments, "and every day

he engraved with white-hot iron. He wanted to make order, and what he brought was fear."

If one tried to restrict the story to a purely political frame of reference, it would emerge as a parable of encounter with a fascist ethos. The writer, however, offers a number of important indications that the meaning of the events demands a broader and more complex perspective. We are made significantly aware of the presence of the elemental desert over against the sky, described at the very end as "the stretches of whitish glare called the heavens"; we note equally the descent of the commander out of the fierce blue like an implacable god, and the six days of creation through which the soldiers labor on their exhausting and futile tasks. The story might usefully be viewed as an ironic inversion of the great desert myth of modern Hebrew literature, Bialik's *Desert Dead*. In the Bialik poem, the titanic figures who sought to rebel against the Lord of Hosts lie struck to stone, massive granite forms cast by the divine wrath out of the stream of time. In "The Last Commander," rebellion expresses itself not as in Bialik by an assertion of clenched will but in a slackening, a lapse into lassitude. The bodies stretched out on the desert sands represent an ironic victory over the divine imperative in having escaped from the agonizing and abrasive effort of life in history— the seven days of creation—to an unending antisabbath of leaden slumber. The story maintains a fine balance of perspective to the end; the narrator makes us feel the voluptuous attraction of sleep, and more sleep, for the exhausted men, but we are also led to see that this orgy of indolence signifies moral and physical paralysis, is finally a sour parody of death.

Both Yehoshua and Oz, then, achieve the widest reverberations of meaning not when they attempt self-consciously to be universal but precisely when they use their fiction as an instrument to probe the most troubling implications of their own cultural and political reality. One is tempted to see them as a kind of Faulkner-Hemingway polarity of talents, Oz having the greater range—in resources of style, in realization of character, in sheer mimetic ability—and Yehoshua a greater degree of poise, efficiency, artistic cunning. Either of them, I believe, would be an exciting writer in any national literature. Their appearance on the Hebrew literary scene bears witness to the ability of Israeli society to maintain under the shadow of the sword a complex culture that is both a medium of self-knowledge and an authentic voice in the larger culture of men.

NOTES

[1] English translation, Harper & Row, 1968.

[2] English translation, Atheneum, 1968.

[3] An English translation was published under the title, *Three Days and a Child* (Doubleday & Co., 1971). All translations of Yehoshua and Oz cited here are my own.—R.A.

⁴ An English translation called *Elsewhere Perhaps* was published by Harcourt Brace Jovanovich, Inc., in 1973.

⁴ An English version was published by Alfred A. Knopf, Inc., in 1972.

**Nurith Gertz**

SOURCE: "Israeli Novelists," in the *Jerusalem Quarterly*, No. 17, Fall, 1980, pp. 66-77.

[*In the following essay, Gertz compares the fiction of the Palmah authors of the 1940s and '50s with that of the new generation of Israeli writers in the 1960s and '70s.*]

In Amos Kenan's *Holocaust II* (1975), written in part before, but completed after the Yom Kippur war, the refugees of a devastated Tel-Aviv live in an immense camp in a tropical region without sky, where there is no day or night, no bird or tree or nature, neither past nor future.

Yitzhak Ben-Ner's story 'After the Rain', which was published in the daily *ha-Aretz* (1977), also describes Tel-Aviv after destruction—a lawless city where roaming street gangs rule, while frightened solitary people wander through the streets because they are afraid to stay at home, for there, too, fear lurks. All hope for a sudden miracle—the discovery of oil in the desert, a diplomatic breakthrough with China—anything to end the nightmare, to bathe them in a light that will suddenly beam on them all.

A. B. Yehoshua's novel, *The Lover* (1977) is not about destruction. It concerns a young Israeli garage owner who has lost his capacity to function in a normal human way: Arabs work for him, others go to war for him, he needs someone to love his wife for him, someone to dream for him, to hope for him, while the real dreams in the story are those of an Arab boy who works in his garage.

Amos Oz's last story, 'The Hill of Evil Counsel' (1976), does not contain a terrifying apocalyptic vision either, but it does portray the destruction of a family in Jerusalem prior to statehood in 1948. The account of this family's disintegration is also a description of the shattering of dreams about the establishment of the state, even before these began to be realized.

From the looks of it, it appears that Israeli literature is reflecting the fear of a new holocaust, or another trauma more devastating than the Yom Kippur War. What is the source of this sense of imminent disaster?

The ready explanation is that it was indeed the Yom Kippur War that shocked the Israeli consciousness out of its sense of inviolability. But this does not apply to the literary consciousness, for in the six-year period between the last two wars, and even previously, when morale was at its peak, Israeli literature constantly dwelt on terror and destruction.

Until recent years this theme was either kept below the surface, treated metaphorically, or relegated to sub-plots. When it did appear undisguised, it was not recognized by critics or readers.

What could be clearer or more explicit than the story of the Israeli student who helps an Arab watchman set fire to a young forest in order to discover beneath it the ruins of a destroyed village ('Facing the Forests' by A. B. Yehoshua, 1972). Or the story of a strange old man who goes from *kibbutz* to *kibbutz* warning the Jews of the Russian threat because he fears that the State of Israel stands on too flimsy foundations, like a cardboard stage set, surrounded by hostile forces ('Late Love' by Amos Oz, 1971)? Could there be a clearer socio-political measure than that of an aging Bible teacher who, after the death of his soldier son, awakens to hopes for renewal, by discovering his son's faiths and beliefs as a source of meaning for his own existence?

These and other stories were seen to be not political but psychological studies in political settings. When the politics could not be attributed to the psychology of the heroes the stories were criticized for resembling reality too closely (as, for example, Amos Oz's 'Late Love').

In fact, then, it is precisely when Israel was strongest that its literature dealt with the fears of the persecuted Jew still without refuge, even in his homeland—either because past destruction and disaster must inevitably be repeated (Aaron Apelfeld), or because in Israel past and future belong not to the Jew but to the Arab (A. B. Yehoshua), or because 'this evil land' and its inhabitants, the jackals and the Arabs, are hostile to the Jews (Amos Oz), or because the threat of war is ever present.

Few stories deal with these things explicitly, but rather only allude to them, as in Amalia Cahana-Carmon's *The Moon in the Valley of Ayalon* (1971).¹ In the early sixties Israeli literature began to evince two new traits: an attempt to avoid political involvement and the use of a symbolic allegorical style. This writing was influenced by Kafka and Agnon and came as a reaction to the political-social writing of the *Palmah* authors.²

Nevertheless, writers such as Amos Oz, A. B. Yehoshua, Yitzhak Orpaz, David Shahar, and Yehuda Amichai, most of whom were involved in Israel's political life (taking leftist positions), did not avoid grappling with national and social problems. In most cases their social meanings are conveyed by way of symbolic structures, images, allegory or by a world view realized in personal situations weighted with social significance (drawing on leftist Zionist ideology).³ According to the world vision of those years all the trans-individual values with which the hero seeks to link up (another person, nature, divine mystical forces which govern the world arbitrarily, etc.)

can in fact be attained, but only through the destruction of both himself and his object. This formula is used in the story of a solitary, forsaken and estranged hero who tries (or, more accurately, is pushed, for these heroes are invariably passive) to establish contact with a woman, or man, or nature or mystical forces. As the plot progresses towards the moment of contact or fulfillment, it becomes apparent (more to the reader than to the hero) that the world with which the hero is trying to establish contact is a deformed one, that the hero himself is either warped or lacks the moral fibre to take a stand. Thus, the moment of attaining the goal is one of unleashed passion, destruction and disaster, in which the hero destroys either himself, the other or both. It is for this reason that the myth evoked by this writing is the sacrifice of Isaac and the story of Jephtah. In modern dress this myth takes the form of the sacrifice or destruction of the son's lives for the parents' dubious goals.

This structure is found in its purest form in the early stories of Orpaz, Oz and Yehoshua. A good example is a story by the latter, 'Night Convoy to Yatir' (1972). It tells of an isolated mountain village whose inhabitants decide to establish contact with the world by derailing an express train that speeds past them twice a day. The insane decision is reached and acted upon without objection; neither from the station-master, who is likened to God, nor the hero who, although he feels that the act is evil, is attracted to the woman who proposed it. The train is derailed. By torchlight and amidst the screams of the dying and wounded the village reaches a moment of true spiritual elevation, the villagers achieve human contact and the hero lies with his love 'on the twisted rocky ground of a beloved country'.

In the early sixties the political content of this type of writing is not yet apparent. The problems are human and personal but even then they are laced with political meanings that will become more dominant later. The quest is for human contact, or contact with nature; symbolic allusions and secondary plots give this quest a national dimension, in which fulfillment can only be achieved through social destruction, i.e., war.

In this writing we may find an indication of trends which took place in Western literature in the twentieth century. In the sixties, writers were influenced by Kafka and the existentialists. Thus, for example, the futility of trying to make contact with an indifferent and alien nature here assumes national significance: nature is alien to a people who have not managed to become part of an alien land. Life appears to be a series of unrelated moments, the meaningless extension of a perpetual present, not only because of 'the dark wind blowing from the future' (in the language of Camus' *The Stranger*), but also because according to these writers past and future in Israel do not belong to them. The heroes move through their world alone and detached from each other not only because one must die alone but because there is no hope of contact between people who lack a common social past; they have no way of building a common future. The terror is not only the existential one of having been thrown into the world, but of finding oneself in a strange, rejecting land.

On the other hand, while the existentialist hero, on which the Israeli hero is based, discovers the possibility of union with nature through total renunciation and solitude (*The Stranger*), or through a common but hopeless social struggle (*The Plague*), the Israeli literary hero, influenced by Zionism's long and bitter struggle, achieves the longed-for union in destruction and war.

A vivid example of this mixture of existential and national themes, of social-political and personal-human situations, is Amos Kenan's *Holocaust II.*

The action is set in a camp, after the destruction of the world. This setting is described in existential terms, in Israeli political terms and in universal social terms. For example, there is a daily execution in the camp. But since neither the condemned man nor his friends know who the victim will be, every day may be one's last. As the hero puts it: 'The truth is that I know that every minute is the last minute of my life. That's a strong physical feeling'. This is the definition of an existential situation, in this case in a political-social setting: national holocaust. Moreover, since every moment is the final one, time is Bergsonian—a series of present moments without past or future. There are no hopes in the camp, but memory too is confounded. The hero repeatedly tries to recall the beautiful Tel-Aviv he knew, but his recollections give way to memories of death and destruction. He tries to remember the golden sands but instead recalls the zealots' last stand at Massada. He wants to picture a camel caravan but remembers the Ninth of *Av* (the day of the destruction of the Temple in Jerusalem) and the Spanish Inquisition and Expulsion. Where there is no hope, there is no memory, but that of death. The assumption is familiar although here a Jewish political variant has been added. The death of the individual represents national destruction (also worldwide destruction, for the Israeli holocaust is but part of a world ecological holocaust).

There is no escape through time or space. Dreams of distant, exotic places become thoughts of Massada; memories of pine forests, blue skies and snow-covered landscapes lead to visions of the transports to the death camps. It is almost like the Midas myth twisted so that everything turns not to gold but to blood, war and death. Even the moment of love becomes the moment of execution: a shapely woman opening a door, slipping off a shoe or a silk stocking, is transformed into a naked woman taking her last steps towards the extermination chamber. It is hardly surprising, then, that the intimate dialogue of a tryst is placed in the context of death. For example, the hero meets a pretty girl and asks her, 'Is this your first time?' The conversation ends with her angry reply: 'You men are all the same'. The conversation is not about love but about execution, which this young woman has carried out.

In other words, the concentration camp is a focus of various themes: the human condition, Israel's present and future political reality, and the world political situation. To bind them together, the author employs a mixture of styles: journalistic, to describe Israeli life in almost documentary fashion; poetic, to add metaphorical meaning to the reportage; and fantastic, to heighten the imaginary reality of the story. This imaginary reality is itself composed of several imaginations: that of the author, who envisions the concentration camp of the future and that of the heroes, who envision their own enchanted worlds—two people who dreamed of building a new world, a magician who builds a golden city for children in the forest filled with dwarfs and fairies, people who build a *kibbutz* with plowed fields and thick woods. The author apprehends these dreams at the moment of their collapse. The imagined *kibbutz* is slowly sinking into the mud, the two who dreamed of a new world become maimed, the magician's forest is surrounded by tanks and the procession of fairies, children, princes and gnomes begins to march towards death. The combination of poetic and journalistic prose tries to convey both a specific Israeli reality and its general universal significance as well as the connection between present and future and between legend and dreams, clashing with reality and shattering it.

Other authors achieve this blending of themes by attaching diverse meanings to metaphorical situations. Thus, the hero of A. B. Yehoshua's 'Facing the Forest' who is sent to guard a national forest, has his private dreams of human warmth and light. These dreams are reflected in his attraction to fire. When he discovers that beneath the young forest are the ruins of an Arab village, the fire acquires a social meaning: the need to set the forest ablaze in order to discover the true past buried beneath it.

Israeli writing reflects Western literary trends in another way. The change it has undergone within two generations corresponds to developments in Western literature since the nineteenth century. When this transformation takes place over a relatively short time, as in Israel, the social factors that have influenced it are fairly easy to trace.

Israeli writers in the late forties and early fifties, referred to as the *Palmaḥ* generation, were influenced primarily by socialist realism and in their own way emulated American action literature of the twenties. Their heroes are not isolated individuals, but members of society—usually a *kibbutz*—and they believe with their fellows in a common social national purpose. The dilemma is how to integrate two ideals—collective fulfillment (in society, work, war) and personal fulfillment (in artistic creation, love, the family). These two goals sometimes clash and the hero is often compelled to sacrifice his individual world for society, for the collective. But even such sacrifice represents a correct value choice, if only partially.

An example of this is Moshe Shamir's story 'Until Dawn', in the collection *Women Wait Outside* (1952). The hero, who is in charge of giving out work assignments on his *kibbutz,* is so totally immersed in this task that he forgets himself and his family. His wife leaves the *kibbutz* because it does not give her the freedom to find artistic fulfillment by teaching piano to the *kibbutz* children—and because her family life is crumbling under the burden of work. After some serious introspection the hero sees his error and goes to the city to regain his wife. A similar course of events, with some variations, can be found in many of Shamir's stories (in *Women Wait Outside*), in his novel *He Walked in the Fields* (1947), and in many stories by Aharon Meged (1957), Nathan Shaham (1960), Yigal Mosinzon (1946), Ḥanoch Bartov (1962) and others.

Other stories of this period deal with external not internal conflict, in which the enemy comes from without. The hero of these stories (Moshe Shamir's 'With His Own Hands', for example) is a combination of Wild West courage and *sabra* doggedness. The plot formula is standard: a tremendous challenge is presented, which the hero meets with valour and resourcefulness. The threat to the *kibbutz,* the woman, the nation, is averted.

The world view that emerges from these stories is analogous to that of the *Palmaḥ* generation, namely that the social Zionist dream, and perhaps all other dreams, can be realized by war, struggle and work. Ten years were to elapse before major Israeli authors considered the price paid for the fulfillment of this dream.

The poetics of this literature matches its world view and sets it apart from the poetics of later writers. In these stories, the narrator is always reliable, and he is always in harmony with his hero; his attitudes are stated clearly and explicitly. There is no missing his meaning. At most, he is sidetracked by internal conflicts or by external obstacles placed in his path. In *He Walked in the Fields,* Uri, the first-born son of the *kibbutz,* knows that he can fulfill himself in love, in building a family, in work on the *kibbutz,* and if necessary in war. Only because of a weakness of which he is aware, and troubled by the stigma of his parents' failings (his father volunteers for the British army and his mother has an affair with another man), he is incapable of forming a loving relationship with a woman and indirectly this leads to his death in a military training exercise. Uri erred and failed. The work ethic prevails, personified by the parents who are finally reconciled, both with each other and with the *kibbutz.*

A hero of this sort is inconceivable to the next generation of writers. In stories by Oz, Yehoshua, and Orpaz the heroes prevaricate to a degree that leaves the reader unsure where reality ends and distortion begins, and what, if any, is the moral position—either of the author or his characters. In Amos Oz's *My Michael* (1968, 1972) the heroine, who dreams of romantic love in faraway places, with strange men, does not know what she loves. For her, love means domination, violence and hatred. This has been her experience in the past, and is the subject of her present fantasies, which include a pair of Arab twins, her childhood playmates. It governs her relations with her husband, a young neighbour and others. But there is no judging her for blocking out a reality which is unrelentingly miserable, empty and bourgeois, killing all. There is no figure in the work who represents a sane alternative.

Since the values of the *Palmah* generation are clear and easily translated into action, the plot in these stories develops with evident causality. The hero faces problems, takes action to solve them, successfully or not, which accordingly creates a new set of problems, and so on. Such a pattern cannot occur in the following generation, where the stories are merely a succession of eruptions of inner passion and external disaster. The passive hero understands neither himself nor his world, and is propelled by fatal external forces and uncontrollable inner ones. The narrative, therefore, is not constructed as a series of causal events but of recurrent outbursts of violence until the final eruption, at the climax of the narrative (especially in the stories of Amos Oz), or as an unlikely devolution of a destructive idea nearing realization (especially in the works of A. B. Yehoshua).

Even the landscape takes on an altogether different aspect in the two generations. In the earlier generation it is beloved and familiar, the hero feels at home in it and the narrator describes it in colourful detail. In the later generation, the landscape becomes ominous, filled with threatening mountains where jackals, Arabs and other untamed forces lurk. Not surprisingly, this landscape is bare of concrete detail, serving primarily as a metaphor for savage forces operating beyond it.

The generation that fought to end the British mandate and gain independence, created a literature in which the protagonist maintains a tie with the world. This tie is severed in the subsequent generation, when confidence in Zionist values and their fulfillment are in question. It would seem that a complete reversal of world view and literary poetics occurred over the last two generations. In fact, however, signs of this reversal could already be discerned in the earlier generation.

The outstanding example of this is S. Yizhar, considered one of the major writers of the *Palmah* generation. Yizhar's hero is not the valiant *sabra* who plants himself firmly in the landscape of his homeland. On the contrary, his is passive, out of place in the toiling or fighting group (although he generally accepts its values). Unlike the heroes of Shamir, Megged, Mosinzon and others, the medium of this type of hero is not action but the lyrical interior monologue. The accepted hero of that generation, the dauntless fighter, is here a secondary figure. He is often described with mocking disdain by the narrating hero, who wants to be part of the group, to be active like the others but whose longings for love, nature, and home set him apart. He expresses the author's beliefs and doubts in the contemporary style: describing the struggle between two sets of values—the public-collective and the private-personal. But there is one small difference: both the hero and the author, rather than feeling any ties with the values of the real world, long for contact with a strange land, of open spaces and undisturbed nature.

They feel estranged from their group. It is hardly surprising that Yizhar had the greatest influence of any of his contemporaries on the writers of the subsequent generation. His two political stories, Ḥirbet Ḥiz'ah' and 'The Prisoner' sparked countless debates in intellectual and non-intellectual circles alike.

Ḥirbet Ḥiz'ah' describes one day at the end of the war when the narrating hero and his fellows are ordered to burn and blow up an Arab village and to expel its inhabitants. Of the two groups—the tough Israeli soldiers inured to the suffering of the Arabs, and the victims who do not comprehend the cruel fate that has suddenly been thrust on them—the narrator identifies with the latter. For him (especially at the end of the story) it is the Arabs, not his own peers, who have the values on which he was nurtured.

The progress of Israeli literature of the sixties is actually the story of the consequences of Ḥirbet Ḥiz'ah'. There, in Yizhar's village, those who fought the War of Independence severed all meaningful ties with essential values. The open spaces of this country, the eternal cycle of sowing and harvest, memories of a meaningful historical past, the biblical God who commands his prophets to foretell comfort or destruction, the traditional Jewish values of justice and morality—all these and not only the narrator's sympathy, pass over to the expelled Arab villagers. At the end of the story the narrator goes searching among the assembled Arabs.

> I passed among them all, among those crying aloud and those gnashing their teeth in silence, regarding themselves and their possessions, among those fighting their fate and those submitting to it mutely, among those shamed by themselves and their disgrace, and among those already making plans to get by somehow. Among those weeping over fields that will be laid waste and among those silenced by weariness, gnawed at by hunger and fright. I wanted to find out whether among all these there wasn't also one somber and blazing Jeremiah, forging a rage here within his heart, calling in a choked voice to an old God from the waggons of exile . . .

Small wonder, then, that the Israeli writer of the next generation wakes up on the morning after Ḥirbet Ḥiz'ah' to discover that lo and behold everything that matters has moved to the other side: history, space, nature, meaningful time, social morality and divine force—all are now in the mountains, with the Arabs and the jackals, waiting for revenge.

However, while Yizhar's hero lives in the world of the social Zionist values and his writing accords with the contemporary style, an anti-establishment political group known as *Cana'anites*[4] was using an altogether different type of writing (with modernistic forms, some of which were to be adopted by the subsequent generation) to give expression to a marginal and oppositional vision of the world.

The central vehicle of this literature is parody, attacking the stereotypes of the period by presenting the exploits, the heroes, the poems and the songs of that generation in a ridiculous light.

For example, in a story by Eitan Notev, 'The Battle of Fort Williams' (1950), a skirmish that had actually taken place in the War of Independence is compared to all the great heroic battles in which the hero participated as a child. 'From the Jewish revolt against the Romans to Genghis Khan's invasion of Europe, from the Hundred-Year War to the Chmielnicki uprising, from the conquest of the Wild West to the war between the North and the South'. Clearly, when compared to all these historic battles the skirmish in the War of Independence is minor and paltry and even the hero's possible death in this war is only an unnecessary addition to his most staggering defeat by 'more serious' enemies: the Indians.

This story was in advance of the next generation in that for the first time it shattered the illusion of literary reality. This reality, which was so secure among Notev's contemporaries, here becomes a mere game, a fantasy. It was before its time also in its parodic treatment of the invincible *Palmah* hero, and in its dealing with a theme that only later would become central in Israeli consciousness and literature: the war with the Arabs as a battle with the ghosts and phantoms of the national memory, peopled by generations of enemies whose sole purpose is to destroy the Jewish people ('Late Love' by Amos Oz).

Another way this marginal group challenged accepted literary conventions was by breaking chronological causal time relations. In contrast to the narrative of the *Palmah* writers in which past actions influence the present, and present actions determine the future, the writing of the contributors to *Alef* (a journal published by the *Cana'anite* group) plays arbitrarily with time. Amos Kenan's story, 'His Big Brother' (1950), is a short monologue about a big brother who has left for distant places with a rifle over his shoulder. The monologue confounds three temporalities until it becomes unclear whether the big brother really existed, whether he exists now or whether he is tomorrow's daydream. This amalgamation of times breaks the reality of which the *Palmah* generation was so confident, even more than the following generation will be prepared to do.

In this regard the differences between the three types of writing are clear enough. The *Palmah* writers begin their stories in the heart of the action. The hero is presented to us in the present. Immediately thereafter the narrative goes back in time and presents the problem he will confront. Once that is done the hero begins to grapple with the problem and sets out to solve it. The following generation shatters this kind of plot structure and employs an assemblage of analogous situations or a circular plot in which the beginning is the end and everything that the hero does merely brings him back to his point of departure. The *Cana'anite* authors break time—and plot—structures (as well as the figure of the hero) much more

radically, which is perhaps why to this day this type of writing has not been admitted to the center of Israel's literary world.

Amos Kenan's story 'In the Station' is in fact an anti-story with an anti-hero in an anti-plot. The plot cannot develop because every moment of the present is used by the protagonist to build some kind of dream for the future, but before this dream is transported into the present by being made real it immediately becomes the past. In such a transformation of time nothing has real existence, everything disappears before it happens. For example, in a railway station stretching as far as the eye can see the narrator is heard saying: 'I take a drag on the cigarette. Wait. Something will happen. I think I may fall in love.' In the second paragraph the beloved appears and the hero begins to dream of love: 'We will go together to the riverbank, at dusk. The birds are chirping, the sun is setting, a big red moon will appear above a dense forest.' In the course of the description the dream becomes reality, the future becomes present but immediately thereafter becomes the past: 'You remember that day at the station? he asks'. As the times change so do the protagonists. The woman he loved becomes an old woman sweeping the platform, to be crushed under the wheels of the locomotive. The memories shift from that day of love to a day of disaster. The hero is transformed into an analogous figure, an old man on the other side of the tracks. In all these transformations the only thing that persists is the train that passes and crushes, like the violent destructive voyage through time and space. What sets this book apart from other writing of the sixties is its total disdain of plot, character and literary illusion. While other heroes dream of love and try or are compelled to fulfill their dreams through destruction, with Amos Kenan there simply is no story. As soon as the dream is born it is transformed into destructive action; hopes immediately become memories. Behind all this is the political vision of an author who fought in the War of Independence, but already then viewed events with a sharply critical eye.

At the end of the sixties, in *Holocaust II,* the social ideology that was latent in the time structure of 'In the Station' reaches full expression. The story of a man and a woman and a dream of love becomes a story of two men and the dream of a state: 'When we grow older, Habakkuk and I', says the narrator, a soldier in a trench in the middle of the war, 'we will build a new country, where people do only what they like'. The dream of a new country is a dream of life without pain, without laws, in cottages dotting the mountain slopes, in a country where death comes gently, and everyone loves his fellow man and hates only one thing—the past. But the dream gradually and imperceptibly becomes a vision of the wounded and dead who will be rehabilitated: 'There they will be made whole again and what can be reattached will be sewn back on. And then they will be taught to speak, to walk, to remember and to piss as they like and also to live again a family life without too much crying out in the night.' The great hope and dream were not distorted in reality but were transformed while they were still only a dream.

In various forms, especially since the last two wars, which made Israeli literature more realistic and its political base more apparent, this sensibility has been expressed by most of Israel's major writers. The protagonists set out towards a lofty goal, to their Jerusalem, and on the way the goal is perverted, their humaneness thwarted, their inner world laid waste and the external world destroyed (Amos Oz, 'Until Death'). They remain alone, beneath empty silent skies.

Since Pascal, of course, the sky has been silent for all mankind, Israelis and non-Israelis alike. Nevertheless, the difference between Israel and, say, the United States, is that in Israel the existential problem is a political one. To be or not to be is not a personal dilemma, but a national one. Israeli writers treat national problems not because they have decided that the writer must be involved, but because their most fundamental existential problems are shared by all Israelis. The personal biography of an Israeli writer is also a social-historical biography.

### NOTES

[1] Amalia Cahana-Carmon is a writer who by age belongs to the *Palmaḥ* generation but was received enthusiastically by the generation that followed because of her unique style and syntax, the richness of her images and her individual-universal subject matter—love stories in which her heroes give meaning and significance to their lives.

[2] The *Palmaḥ* was a military arm of the Zionist establishment's defence force, the *Hagganah.* It had a socialist orientation and its members combined military training with agricultural work on the *kibbutzim.*

[3] Interestingly, for the previous generation that fought the War of Independence the Arab is a political problem to be solved by war or by some kind of accommodation. For the subsequent generation, whose basic experience is not the struggle for independence but its realization and consequences—the expulsion of Arabs and also a state of siege in a hostile region—the Arab becomes a threatening, in some instances metaphysical, figure, a symbol of non-acceptance of Israel's existence.

[4] The *Cana'anites* were a political group active in the forties who advocated that the Jewish *yishuv* in Israel cut itself off from Diaspora Jews and its culture, and that a new Hebrew nation be created in *Eretz Yisrael.* They maintained that this new nation, to be composed of the local Arab inhabitants and the new Hebrews, should revive the ancient Hebrew culture that had prevailed in the region before the Exile. Among the writers who were associated with the group are Yoram Kaniuk, Aharon Amir, Amos Kenan and Benjamin Tammuz.

## Alan Mintz

SOURCE: "New Israeli Writing," in *Commentary,* Vol. 65, No. 1, January, 1978, pp. 64-7.

[*In the following essay, Mintz evaluates the "dual urge toward nostalgia and apocalypse" in contemporary Israeli fiction.*]

The state of Israel was conceived by force of a messianic vision, but its existence has been maintained by order, sacrifice, and the rational setting of priorities—and this in the face of another, more ominous vision held by its neighbors. Life under such mixed conditions of ordinariness and dread might well seem cribbed and predetermined, and it is understandable that Israelis would search for various ways of becoming released from it. In Israel's literature, that search has often taken one of two forms, a looking back to happier times, and a reaching forward toward some new vision of an end, either individual or collective, in which the anxieties of history will be dissolved. Indeed, ever since the pioneer period, one of the chief functions of Israel's literature, especially its prose literature, has been to represent and also to criticize this dual urge toward nostalgia and apocalypse in Israeli consciousness.

A recent spate of translations gives the English reader a chance to observe at first hand this tendency in Israeli writing. Of particular interest are two new anthologies. One, *Contemporary Israeli Literature,* which began as a special number of the journal *TriQuarterly,* is quite substantial, containing ten short stories and the work of twenty-three poets, and featuring an introduction by Shimon Sandbank and an afterword by Robert Alter, both extremely useful. The second anthology, *New Writing in Israel,* is a more modest and uneven affair, with an abbreviated poetry section and no introduction. And one should also mention a new novel by Shulamith Hareven, *City of Many Days,* and a collection of short stories by A. B. Yehoshua, *Early in the Summer of 1970.*

In recent Israeli fiction, the period returned to most often as an object of nostalgia is that of the British Mandate, a period when the conflict that was to become the Jewish state's lot after 1948 seemed neither inevitable nor irremediable. Jerusalem between the two world wars is the setting of Shulamith Hareven's *City of Many Days,* a novel whose ostensible focus is the history of a specific Sephardi family but whose real subject is Jerusalem itself, bodied forth in the book through a polyglot cast of eccentrics who make their way through the city's bewildering array of sights and smells. Miss Hareven's Jerusalem catalogue (gorgeously rendered in English by Hillel Halkin) is meant to suggest the idyll of possibility which somehow was allowed to flourish in the years before the rise of intensive nationalism in Palestine. Relations between Arabs and Jews during the early Mandate are depicted as amicable, if standoffish. The British presence is exemplified by an army officer so fascinated by his "colonial" subjects that he throws in his lot with them. And then there is the most vital element of all, the Jews themselves, the half-pious, half-worldly Sephardim whose luxuriant openness becomes all the more precious a quality as it is seen to be eclipsed by the gathering of historical forces.

Unfortunately, the charm of Miss Hareven's picture of Jerusalem—there is no question of the beauty of her evocation—is purchased through her excluding from it anything which is *not* charming. Miss Hareven's characters are innocent of history, and their innocence attenuates their charm until it threatens to become mere idealization. The Sephardi community has, it is true, been underrepresented in modern Hebrew fiction, but Miss Hareven tends to err in the opposite direction. There is scarcely a trace here of the large numbers of Eastern European Jews, the pioneers and the socialists, who during these same years were changing the face of the Jewish settlement in Palestine and preparing the greater transformation to come. Lacking a dialectical view, which could comprehend what was being created as well as what was being destroyed, *City of Many Days* remains an exquisite piece of literary nostalgia rather than a full evocation of a historical moment that might instruct as much as it delights.

The Mandate setting is put to a much different purpose in David Shahar's story "Louidor Louidor," which is included in *Contemporary Israeli Literature*. For Shahar (two of whose books have already appeared in English, a collection of short stories, *News from Jerusalem*, and a novel, *The Palace of Shattered Vessels*), Palestine of those years is also a landscape of eccentrics, as it is for Miss Hareven, but his eccentrics are driven by the contradictions of history rather than by private idiosyncracies. Louidor, for example, is a distracted Tolstoyan intellectual who comes to Palestine to realize his rationalist-pacifist principles in a Jewish homeland. Shocked to find the country filled with Arabs, he converts to Islam in order to have the moral right to appeal to his new "brethren" to leave Palestine for the "blessed lands of Arabia." Louidor's eventual fate—he is beaten up and dismembered by an Arab gang—is for Shahar a way of suggesting that imported visions will always be rejected by a land so pocked by historical ironies and crossed national destinies.

Though the tone of Shahar's story is elegiac and nostalgic, what motivates his hero is rather an apocalyptic (and almost psychotic) passion for redemption, a yearning for an impossible future in which all obstacles to moral purity will have finally disappeared. Something of the same passion motivates Joseph della Reina, the hero of a fine story by Dan Tsalka included in *New Writing in Israel*. The story is based on a kabbalistic legend about a 15th-century mystic who attempted to bring about the messianic age by capturing Satan, but who failed under terrifying circumstances and ended his days as Satan's ally and as the lover of Lilith, the arch-female demon of Jewish folklore. In Tsalka's retelling, the legend takes an eerily modern turn by the addition of an existential context, with della Reina's passion understood psychologically as that familiar kind of moral zeal in which the unacknowledged element of self-aggrandizement insures future corruption and failure.

If messianism, even misplaced messianism, is the "positive" paradigm of Jewish apocalypse, the Holocaust, both as event and as symbol, is its negative pole. Among Hebrew writers of fiction, Aharon Appelfeld is the one who has most unequivocally taken the Holocaust as a field of imaginative activity. Appelfeld, whose work deserves to be better known in English, is a master of obliqueness; rather than describing atrocity directly, he focuses instead on the historical moments just before and just after the Holocaust, and speaks through them of what is in itself unspeakable.

Appelfeld's story, "Badenheim 1939," included in both *Contemporary Israeli Literature* and *New Writing in Israel,* is an ingenious and ornate parable about the fall of German-speaking Jewry. The locale is an Austrian resort town whose inhabitants reveal themselves to each other in the course of the story as they are forced to register with the local authorities as Jews. Instead of being panicked and cowed, the Jews assume a kind of calm gaiety. As the registration proceeds and the routine of the resort breaks down, there is an immense sense of relief at being able to confess the deep and troublesome burden of Jewishness, "as if they were talking about a chronic disease which there was no longer any reason to hide." With the resort finally closed and the transports waiting, the Jews, who believe they are being returned to the simpler life of their ancestral home in Poland, express appreciation to the authorities and look forward to their "repatriation." It is characteristic of Appelfeld's laconic and perverse brilliance that the story ends here, with no further comment or elaboration.

Like the state of Israel itself, that ambitious social experiment, the kibbutz, came into being in large part through a messianic drive, and it, too, paradoxically, has been maintained through the anti-messianic values of order, rationality, and institutionalization. As setting and theme, the kibbutz has undoubtedly been overworked in Hebrew literature, but it still retains a rich potential for fictional treatment. The isolation and self-sufficiency of the kibbutz offer exactly the kind of manageable and self-contained world that is so desirable to fiction, and the situation of the kibbutz suggests a microcosm of the larger situation of Israel as nation and society. Among recent Israeli writers, the novelist Amos Oz has in fact used the kibbutz in just this way (as in his 1966 novel *Elsewhere, Perhaps*); he is represented in *Contemporary Israeli Literature* by a kibbutz story from the '60s. *New Writing in Israel* also contains a story with a kibbutz setting, this one by Yitzhak Ben Ner. Both stories are examinations of the price paid by kibbutz members for, precisely, the rationality of kibbutz existence.

Ben Ner's "A Village Death" is a wonderfully told monologue, whose narrator, a forty-three-year-old member of a collective village, has assumed the responsibilities of undertaker and mourner of the dead in order to expiate an affair he had twenty years earlier with the wife of another member. His death-in-life represents one way of dealing with the persistence of two antagonistic forms of feeling: lust for what is alien and dangerous, and love for one's native ground.

Oz's "A Hollow Stone" concerns the honored memory of a kibbutz founder whose brand of romantic socialism led him to his death in the Spanish Civil War. His wife has been left behind to play the role of a sainted widow of the revolution—a role the kibbutz despises. "Martyrdoms, Mediterranean tragedies, emotional arabesques," remarks the anonymous narrator who represents the community's conventional wisdom, "were irreconcilable with the principles by which we guided our lives."

To escape a life hedged in by principles and responsibilities, a life symbolized in miniature by the kibbutz but characteristic as well of Israel's entire national situation, Israelis flee to zones of imagined freedom like the United States, a country where there is seemingly no limit to the romance of individual achievement and where a man has room to pursue private dreams of experience, money, sex. The fragility of such dreams is suggested by the novelist Yoram Kaniuk in "They've Moved the House," one of a pair of stories with an American setting that are included in *Contemporary Israeli Literature*. With enormous linguistic energy Kaniuk evokes the mixture of wide-eyed naiveté and grandiose ambition that marks his two Israeli *schlemiels* as they untiringly conceive new money-making schemes.

In "The Orgy," an amusing and cerebral story by the well-known poet, Yehuda Amichai, America likewise serves as a symbol of liberation from the disciplines of history and holiness that are the conditions of life in Israel, but it is a symbol heavily charged with irony. Amichai's first-person narrator is an Israeli student, worn down by his doctoral studies, who comes to New York in search of a new source of transcendence. He finds it in sex, something America has abundantly to offer and a commodity which in Amichai's rendering assumes a kind of Sabbatian appropriateness as the supreme value in a transvalued world, a world in which the orgy has become the means of reconstructing the rituals of collective experience. Amichai's story ends with a jocular account of a road show formed by the narrator and his friends to expound and practice their new Torah.

Nostalgia for an idealized past, the frenzied search for a transcendent future—it is one of the marks of A. B. Yehoshua's achievement as a writer that he refuses to give way to either of these temptations. In his new collection, *Early in the Summer of 1970,* as in a previous collection, *Three Days and a Child,* Yehoshua sticks resolutely to the harrowing confines of the present, even though, within those confines, he often works with the touch not of a realist but of a fabulist. The stories in the new collection take place in the period between 1967 and 1973, a time of wearying stalemate between Israel and its Arab neighbors, punctuated by random, sporadic death. In Yehoshua's imaginative reconstruction of this period, the larger collective purposes of the national existence have lost their clarity; his characters struggle on, but the struggle discloses no meaning to them. If there is any heroism in Yehoshua's world, it consists in the courage to face facts as they are and still proceed with the business of life.

The nameless hero of "Missile Base 612" cannot muster such courage. Rather, he persists in demanding some revelation that will explain the disorientation of his existence. Like the aimless fighting between Israel and Egypt along the Suez Canal, his life has become a permanent battle fought from fixed positions: though he and his wife share the same house and the same child, they squabble or ignore each other, and at the university where he works, his career has bogged down. Thus, when he is asked to spend a day lecturing in the Sinai to army troops, he is grateful for the chance to break out of his isolation. Yet he who has come to lecture is actually the one in need of enlightenment. The army is full of people who have adapted to the conditions of uncertainty and attrition, and his fumbling and grandiloquent overtures to the men are met by stupefaction or bemused skepticism.

Finally, he steals a close look at the missiles on the base and is electrified by the spectacle they present of impersonal, erotic power. But he characteristically fails to grasp the nature of this power. Searching for an epiphany that will explain, and release him from, the deadlock of his own life, he cannot understand that the purpose of the missiles is *not* to be fired, that they are there to prevent an apocalypse by remaining in check.

Loss of meaning, and the baffled search for a way to overcome that loss, is similarly at the center of the title story, "Early in the Summer of 1970," Yehoshua's brilliant recasting of the motif of the sacrifice of Isaac. (This story was first published in English in *Commentary,* March 1973.) The father here is an aging high-school teacher who has stubbornly refused to retire, to accept the fact that his life is over. He looks to his son, a university lecturer who has recently returned from abroad with a young American wife, for the enunciation of some new message, the banner of a new generation. But the son is remote and ungiving. Then one day, while teaching in school, he is suddenly informed that this son, who is on reserve duty, in the Jordan Valley, has been killed.

When he goes to identify the body, however, it develops that there has been an administrative error: the dead man is not his son after all. There follows a frantic journey to the outpost where the son's unit is on maneuvers, and a face-to-face encounter in which the son shows himself to be completely unresponsive to the ordeal his father has undergone; all he can do is mutter bitterly about his military experience, "such a loss of time . . . so pointless."

The story is told with an obsessive, almost painful, allegiance to the point of view of the father, who returns constantly in his mind to the moment when he was given the news of his son's "death." With each repetition, it becomes clearer that instead of reliving a moment of pain, the father is actually reliving a moment in which his son's life, and his own, seem finally to have taken on meaning. He sees himself, guilty and bereft, but somehow heroic, offering up his son on the altar of national existence, and he sees his son as a willing martyr in the same cause. As in the biblical tale, however, the son is allowed to live. But whereas in Abraham's case it was trust in God that was being tested and revealed, in the case of Yehoshua's story what is being tested is only the father's desperate and misplaced faith in a deliverance wrought by others. And whereas in the biblical story, ordeal is followed by covenant, by the striking of a new redemptive relation between God and His chosen ones, "Early in the Summer of 1970" ends back in unillusioned reality: the ordeal will simply continue.

Yehoshua's stories sound grim and severe when stripped to their moral burden, but as works of art they are marvelously accomplished, rich and precise in language and startlingly inventive in their use of non-realistic modes of narration. As a moralist, Yehoshua is relentless, and he shows his characters no quarter. Conspicuously absent from his work is just that element of sympathy toward the yearning for deliverance which runs like a scarlet thread through so much serious Jewish writing in this century—and not only in this century.

Still, what Yeshoshua does share with almost all Hebrew writers of the modern period, and with many contemporary Israeli writers in particular, is a highly charged sense of obligation toward his material, an obligation not only to depict faithfully but also to evaluate and comment upon the twists and turns of the national consciousness as they reveal themselves in character and incident. That so many Israeli writers have been able to transform this sense of obligation into successful works of the imagination is a remarkable achievement, and in its own way a tribute to the vigor of the Jewish national spirit.

# ISRAELI POETRY

### David C. Jacobson

SOURCE: "The Holocaust and the Bible in Israeli Poetry," in *Modern Language Studies*, Vol. XXIV, No. 4, Fall, 1994, pp. 63-77.

*[In the following essay, Jacobson examines biblical allusions in Israeli Holocaust poetry.]*

Although the destruction of European Jewry in World War II took place outside of the Land of Israel, Israeli culture has been greatly preoccupied by this historical event. Zionism was a movement founded in Europe with the purpose of saving the Jews of the Diaspora from gentile anti-Semitism. For Jews engaged in the Zionist enterprise in the Land of Israel during and immediately after World War II, Hitler's genocidal attack on the Jews of Europe grimly confirmed their conviction that Diaspora Jewry was doomed and that the only viable alternative for Jews was the development of the Land of Israel into a sovereign Jewish state. As Dina Porat observes, the events of the beginning of the War were already enough to confirm this Zionist conviction:

> The suffering of Polish Jews, the largest community in Europe, in the ghettos appeared to the Zionists as proof confirming their predictions that diaspora Jewish life would end catastrophically. The contrast between the destruction of European Jewry and the constructive efforts in Palestine to build a homeland seemed ample confirmation of Zionist assumptions. Tragically, it was a far stronger confirmation than the Zionist movement had wanted or needed.[1]

At the same time, as Tom Segev has noted, even if the Zionists were powerless to stop the Nazis' program of genocide, the destruction of European Jewry put Zionism in a position of defeat, for "the Zionists were unable to convince the majority of the world's Jews to come to Palestine before the war, while that was still an option."[2] This failure of Zionism was experienced on a particularly painful level by the many Jews who had emigrated from Europe to the Land of Israel before the War and had to come to terms with the fact that their grandparents, parents, siblings, cousins, aunts, uncles, and friends were among the victims of the Holocaust. For those mourning such personal losses the issue was how to live with a sense of guilt for having saved themselves in time by emigrating to the Land of Israel and having failed to influence or help their loved ones to do the same.

The Jews living in the Land of Israel in the years since the end of the War have related to the Holocaust not only as an historical event of the past. Living representatives of that period, the survivors, flooded the Land of Israel in the years immediately before and after the establishment of the State in 1948. From 1946 until 1951, so many Holocaust survivors emigrated from Europe to the Land of Israel that almost one quarter of the population of Israel in 1951 were Holocaust survivors.[3] Eventually, Israel became the country with the highest percentage of Holocaust survivors relative to the Jewish population.[4] The living legacy of the Holocaust survivors has continued with the birth of a second and third generation of descendants of the survivors, who are personally affected by their forebears' sufferings.

Those Jews who were in the Land of Israel during World War II, as well as those born after the War, initially had an uneasy relationship with the survivors of the Holocaust. As Tom Segev observes, the Jews of the pre-State Zionist settlement period had developed an image of the fighting, native-born sabra as the ideal to replace the Jew of the Diaspora, who was seen as weak and defenseless, and the survivors of the Holocaust were viewed as seriously falling short of that ideal. Not only were the survivors viewed as flawed, but their very presence was seen as a threat to the Zionist program to liberate the Jews from what Zionism saw as the negative qualities of Diaspora Jewish life:

> The sabra represented a national ideal, and the Holocaust survivor its reverse. Moreover, the survivors threatened that ideal at a time when sabras were still fighting their parents' generation for preeminence in Israeli society. The country fostered the sabra image, seeing in it the fulfillment of the Zionist and labor movement dreams of national renewal and return to a "healthy" social structure. Yet most people could not live up to this ideal. They had not lived long in the country, and many had not yet rid themselves of their "Diaspora mentality." Holocaust survivors imposed on earlier immigrants a past that many had not yet succeeded in putting aside, and their disdain of the survivors often reflected a desire to distance themselves, to deny what they themselves were. The survivors forced the Israelis to realize that the vision of the "new man" was not to be. Most came as refugees, not as visionary Zionists.[5]

Segev quotes the account of Yoel Palgi, who when he returned to the Land of Israel in 1945 from a paratrooper mission in Hungary found that his fellow Jews viewed the victims of the Holocaust in derogatory terms:

> Everywhere I turned . . . the question was fired at me: why did they go like lambs to the slaughter? Suddenly I realized that we were ashamed of those who were tortured, shot, burned. There is a kind of general agreement that the Holocaust dead were worthless people. Unconsciously, we have accepted the Nazi view that the Jews were subhuman.[6]

In his collection of essays *Masot beguf ri'shon* (*Essays in First Person*) the Israeli survivor novelist Aharon Appelfeld (1932-) conveys his painful sense on arriving in his early teens in the Land of Israel in 1946 that the survivors had been fit into a national myth that called into question their political sagacity, as well as their moral character.

> The days of the eve of the War of Independence were days of great excitement. Modest words and lofty words were mixed together. Expressions and slogans were created without much thought: the expression "destruction and revival" was festively adopted, and connected with it were notions of cause and effect, rebuke and justification, mourning followed by celebration. In short, it is practically a law, the slogan proclaimed, that on the ashes of one period will rise another period. The application of the interpretation swooped down on us and without mercy established parallels: exile—redemption, Zionism versus assimilation, the guilty as opposed to the blameless, the wise as opposed to the naive. There was a terrible transparency to these analogies.[7]

As Dina Porat puts it, the survivors were suspected of having engaged in morally compromising acts to save their lives during the War:

> Slowly, the suspicion developed [among Jews who had not experienced the Holocaust] that those who survived had perhaps managed to do so because they had been unwilling to sacrifice themselves in the struggle against the Nazis. . . . Comparisons were often made between the Zionist image of a productive person, imbued with universalistic humanistic values, who worked for the common good, and the survivors, who seemed, at first sight, to be the polar opposites of that ideal type.[8]

One kibbutz Passover Haggadah went so far as to blame the deaths of the victims on their passivity:

> Hitler alone is not responsible for the death of the six million—but all of us and above all the six million. If they had known that the Jew has power, they would not have all been butchered . . . the lack of faith, the ghettoish-exilic self-denigration . . . contributed its share to this great butchery.[9]

Even though, as Porat notes, the heroism of the survivors in their role of courageous illegal immigrants and soldiers in the Israeli army often belied their image as "the polar opposites" of the ideal Zionist type, Israelis who had not experienced the Holocaust continued to have a problematic relationship with that period. This difficulty of connecting the experience of national rebirth in the establishment of the State of Israel with the experience of defeat in the Holocaust apparently was one reason why in the early years of the State the Holocaust played a very small role in the consciousness of Israelis. Porat writes that during this period,

> it seems as if all talk of the Holocaust and its survivors disappeared from the Israeli scene. The Holocaust was not taught in schools, nor was it a topic of research at the Hebrew University (the only one in Israel at the time). In drama and theater, the Holocaust was hardly mentioned; and when it was, it was mostly as part of the background. In both poetry and fiction, other topics shaped the agenda.[10]

Aharon Appelfeld describes this period of public avoidance of the Holocaust in Israel as one in which both the survivors and those who had not been in Europe during World War II tacitly agreed to refrain from talking about an historical event that seemed to be too horrible to contemplate:

> And just as the [survivor] witness could not continue to stand in the space of this terror, neither could the Jew who had not experienced it. A kind of secret covenant was created between the survivor witness and the one to whom, as it were, this testimony was directed, a covenant of silence. . . . [11]

As many scholars have noted, the trial of the Nazi war criminal Adolf Eichmann in Jerusalem in 1961-62 made an important contribution to Israeli identification with all

Holocaust survivors and victims, whether or not they participated in armed struggle. The opportunity the survivors had to tell their stories to the nation when they testified in the trial broke what Appelfeld has characterized as "the covenant of silence" between the survivors and Israelis who did not experience the Holocaust.[12] In an article that appeared in the Israeli daily *Ma'ariv* at the time of the Eichmann trial, two native-born Israeli writers, the prose writer Moshe Shamir (1921-) and the poet Dalia Ravikovitch (1936-), made revealing comments indicating how deeply affected they were by the Holocaust on a personal level. In his comments Shamir notes that his relationship to the Holocaust is most problematic precisely because his "normal" life and that of his fellow Israelis is so radically different from that of the evil years of World War II:

> But when the Eichmann trial took place in the early 1960s—there was the great, dramatic, and shocking contrast between the world that this trial evoked and the experience of our lives today, when people traveled to hear the trial in their private Volkswagens, with German gasoline—this contrast, for me at least, made concrete for the first time in an actual personal experience the fact of the great distance between my life and that conflagration. The power of the testimonies of death in the trial in the context of our life of *dolce vita* caused me, more than anything else, to feel for the first time the subject of the Holocaust as my personal problem.[13]

In her comments Ravikovitch asserts that the suffering of the Holocaust has strongly influenced all Israeli writers, even a writer like herself who as a third-generation resident of the Land of Israel did not have any first-hand experience with that tragic event:

> The Holocaust gave us a feeling of disintegration, even if this disintegration gave a new color to our literature. The Holocaust is like a hand grenade that exploded and each of us received his personal piece of it in his body. And this piece is hidden also in most of our poems. Unconsciously, therefore, the subject of the Holocaust is the central subject in our literature, even to the point that love poems become horror poems and children's poems cannot distract them from unfortunate maturity.[14]

It has been a central tenet of Zionism that the establishment of Jewish sovereignty in the Land of Israel in the twentieth century constitutes a restoration of the sovereign existence of the ancient Israelites in the Land of Israel in biblical times. This tenet has often led Israelis to see themselves as reenacting the Bible. In the context of this close identification with the Bible it is not surprising that Israeli poets have so frequently published poems that allude extensively to the Bible. These poems assume the likelihood of discerning analogous relationships between contemporary Israeli and ancient Israelite events. Among those Israeli poets who have identified with the destruction of European Jewry in World War II, several have written poems about the Holocaust with extensive allusions to the Bible. In these poems biblical expressions and images serve as emotionally powerful vehicles to express the poets' visions of the Holocaust and its aftermath. The effect of such poems is to assimilate the Holocaust experience to the Bible and thereby establish for the poets and their readers a more direct connection with the destruction of European Jewry in World War II. In so doing, they follow a trend in Jewish Holocaust literature noted by Sidra Dekoven Ezrahi:

> It can be said, then, that even though both internal and external forces had eroded the links between Yiddish and Hebrew literature and the literary and religious traditions which had reflected and shaped collective responses to catastrophe over the centuries, most of the writers who have appropriated the subject have also appropriated the classical forms, as if these provided access to an otherwise unintelligible and inarticulable experience.[15]

Even as Israeli poets appropriate biblical imagery to write about the Holocaust, however, the very gap that they sense between their world and that of the Holocaust is paralleled by the gap that they sense between what the Bible teaches about reality and the reality of the Holocaust. This drives them to the effort characterized by Robert Alter as "stand[ing] the [biblical] sources on their heads, borrowing images, symbols, and situations for the expressive needs of a very different kind of poetic voice."[16]

### A HOLOCAUST VICTIM IN ISRAEL; AN ISRAELI IN THE HOLOCAUST

The poet Amir Gilboa (1917-1984) emigrated from Eastern Europe to the Land of Israel at the age of twenty, two years before the outbreak of World War II. His parents, two brothers, and four sisters all died in the Holocaust. His situation as an emigrant to the Land of Israel who lost family members in the Holocaust was, as we have seen, not unique. In many European Jewish families it was members of the younger generation in their late teens and twenties who were adventuresome enough to move to the Land of Israel, often leaving behind their parents and siblings in Europe. By the time they became fully aware of the Nazi threat to their families, those who had emigrated to the Land of Israel were powerless to help them.

Two poems by Gilboa based on biblical allusions reflect the ways that life in the Land of Israel feels so distant from life in the Holocaust. Despite that distance Gilboa, who mourns the death of his immediate family in World War II, is driven to imagine in one poem that the spirit of a member of his family visits him in Israel, and he is driven in another poem to imagine himself in Europe at the time of the War, possibly capable of changing the course of history.

In his poem *"Penei Yehoshua'"* ("The Face of Joshua")[17] the speaker imagines seeing the face of his dead brother Joshua in the moon.[18] Consideration of Gilboa's relationship with his brother may shed light on the significance of this poem. In her monograph on Gilboa, Eda Zoritte notes that Gilboa had been very close to his brother Joshua. The image of the brother Joshua able to follow the speaker to Israel has added poignancy when we consider that the brothers shared a strong commitment to Zionism in their youth. Together with another friend the two brothers established the local branch of a Zionist youth group in their town. As the older brother, Joshua acceded to their father's pressure to abandon his Zionist activities and learn the family trade of tailoring. Gilboa, in contrast, defied their father and insisted on emigrating to the Land of Israel in order to fulfill his desire to be a Hebrew writer in Zion.[19]

Western folk belief has often contained the image of the restless ghost of a person who was murdered before his or her time or whose life work was unfinished. The best known literary expression of this image is in the first act of *Hamlet,* in which Hamlet's father's ghost appears to him to reveal to him that he was murdered.[20] Having been dealt an untimely and unjust death by the Nazis, the speaker's brother Joshua appears to him in the form of the face people often discern in a full moon. In this case the face that the speaker sees is that of the biblical hero Joshua. Gilboa has apparently drawn on an expression that appears in a talmudic interpretation of a passage describing the beginning of the transition of power from Moses to his successor Joshua. In that passage God commands Moses, "Give him [Joshua] some of your authority (*mehodkha*) . . ." (Numbers 27:20). According to the talmudic interpretation the reason the biblical passage reads "some of your authority," and not "all of your authority" is that Joshua was less honored than his predecessor Moses, to such an extent that the elders of the generation in which the transition took place made use of the contrast in strength between moonlight and sunlight to state, "The face of Moses was like the face of the sun; the face of Joshua was like the face of the moon" (Baba Batra 75a).[21] In an analogous way, as he appears in Israel the speaker's brother's honor would be considered by other Israelis to be tarnished, for he did not fight during World War II in the Zionist spirit of armed self-defense:

> And Joshua above looks at my face. His face of gold
> beaten. Cold dream. Embalmed dream.
> And at my feet the sea strikes eternities on the shore.
> I am sick of longing for him. It seems I am about
>     to die.
> But I must, I must wait alive
> forever.
> My brother above, his face rising in a cloud
> To recount my footsteps in the washed away sand.
> The sea strikes and withdraws. Strikes and
>     withdraws.
> Warring forces of nature conditioned by law.
> I. In the wind. Another. Flee. Far.
> Joshua too now rests from wars.
> That he gave in inheritance to his people,
> but a grave he did not dig for himself
> in the mountains of Ephraim.
> So night after night he goes out
> to meditate in the heavens.
> And I am sick, it seems about to die
> barefoot in the sand of a cold moon
> at the edge of the water
> and roaring in me, roaring in me the end

> striking my death at my feet
> wave after wave—
>
> upon much life
> it will be extolled and glorified.

The association of the moon with Joshua's face is significant, as Hillel Weiss suggests, in terms of the image of the moon's symbolic death and renewal in the monthly cycle of waning and waxing, which parallels the rhythmic coming and going of the waves of the sea.[22] Like the moon, the dead brother Joshua is regularly resurrected and continually returns to haunt the speaker. As the speaker stands on the shore of the Mediterranean Sea, he compares his brother Joshua to Joshua of the Bible. The life and death of his brother, the Holocaust victim, stands in marked contrast to the life and death of the biblical Joshua. Joshua led the ancient Israelites in many battles with the residents of Canaan, and their victories gave him the power to divide the land of Canaan, granting an inheritance (*hahalah*) to each tribe. When he died, the Bible recounts, Joshua was buried in the mountains of Ephraim (Joshua 24:30). The speaker's brother Joshua also experienced war, not as a victorious fighter, but rather as a defeated victim. The rest granted him after his defeat as a young victim of the Nazis was very different from that of the biblical Joshua, who was buried at the age of one hundred ten after a long and successful life. The speaker's brother did not have the benefit of being buried in the Land of Israel, and because he lacks the sense of personal completion that the speaker feels as a resident of Israel, "night after night he goes out / to mediate (*lasuah*) in the heavens," a description reminiscent of Isaac, who "went out to meditate (*lasuah*) in the field" (Genesis 24:63) in the period between his near sacrifice by his father Abraham and his marriage to Rebecca. Joshua is an actual victim, without the sense of divine purpose that accompanied the binding of Isaac, nor is he about to experience the blessings of marriage that Isaac eventually was granted. What is left from the speaker's brother Joshua's life is the memory of the struggle for Jewish survival in Europe in World War II, and what has followed his life is the continuing struggle for the survival of Israel in which the speaker participates.

There is a particular irony in the speaker using expressions that play on references to the Song of Songs. As Arieh Sachs notes, the original Hebrew for "I am sick of longing for him" (*'ani holeh nehiyyato*) is based on the expression "sick with love" (*holat 'ahavah*) in Song of Songs 2:5; 5:8, and the original Hebrew for "much life" (*hayyim rabbim*) in the context of the sea water imagery in the poem alludes to the expression "many waters (*mayim rabbim*) cannot quench love" in Song of Songs 8:7.[23] The pain of the speaker is reinforced by the ironic contrast between the unbridgeable gap separating him from his dead beloved brother and the celebration of union in love that is so central to the Song of Songs.

The speaker's longing for his unjustly murdered brother evokes in him a nearly overwhelming preoccupation with his own mortality. The poem is largely about the tension between his sense of the arbitrary cruelty of humanity's mortal condition and his acceptance of this reality. Indeed, the victimization of his brother and the mortal limitations of humanity stand in marked contrast to the sense of control of their fate that Israelis have felt they share with the victorious Joshua. There are, the speaker suggests, natural and historical forces that set limits to the possibility of human accomplishments. The lines "The sea strikes and withdraws. Strikes and withdraws. / Warring forces of nature conditioned by law" connect the reality of the Holocaust and the forces of nature and contrast them with the heady self-confidence of Israelis identifying with Joshua's conquest of Canaan. The Hebrew terms used to refer to striking and withdrawing (*makeh venasog*) have military associations. The waves of the sea reflect a static, eternal rhythm of aggression and acquiescence in which the Holocaust victims were caught. As an Israeli who believes in his country's ability to assert power and who feels uncomfortable facing the necessity at times to acquiesce when his country cannot successfully assert power, the speaker must come to terms with this alternative reality of the defeat of the Holocaust victims at the hands of forces beyond their control.

The speaker can only accept human mortality when he is able to see the death of his brother and his own ultimate death as events that cannot be changed. By associating this healing acceptance of reality with the Joshua story, Gilboa points to the larger national question of how to make peace with the past limitations on Jewish power in Europe and the present limitations on Jewish power in Israel. At the end of the poem the speaker internalizes the wave-like reality of his mortality, and just as the believing Jew confirms the reality of God's power in the traditional Jewish memorial prayer, the Kaddish, so the speaker makes use of words from that prayer, "it will be extolled and glorified" (*yitromam veyitgaddal*) to declare his acceptance of the ultimate victory of death.

A person in the position of Gilboa undoubtedly experienced a tremendous sense of frustration at not being able to save his family from destruction at the hands of the Nazis. Gilboa captures that sense of frustration in his poem *"Bamatsor"* ("Under Siege").[24] In the poem the poet's desire to bridge the geographical and chronological gap between his existence in the Land of Israel and the European Holocaust is represented by the speaker travelling back in time to the period of the destruction of the First Temple by the Babylonians. The use of a biblical scene to represent the Holocaust is in keeping with the trend among Israeli poets to assimilate the Holocaust experience to the Bible as a way to connect more directly with that experience.

In the beginning of the poem the suffering of the people is captured by selected concrete images of hand-to-hand combat, walls crumbling, and a little girl scurrying about, but holding back any cry of fear. When the speaker sees the horrifying image of a man who has been blinded screaming he calls out, like a viewer of a suspenseful movie, to one of the central characters of the period, the prophet Jeremiah, to do something to prevent the disaster: he requests that Jeremiah assassinate Nebuchadnezzar, the King of Babylonia, before that enemy of Judea can be victorious:

> The hand of each man is against his neighbor
> and wall after wall crumbles.
> Little Daliah scurries about,
> no one is with her
> and she doesn't cry.
> Who's this facing the sun
> screaming.
> Aie, already not eyes in
> his burning sockets.
> Jeremiah, Jeremiah
> take what I have been saving
> the pistol
> and for God's sake
> a small bullet
> in Nebuchadnezzar's heart
> will be praised.

The speaker's decision to call out to Jeremiah is significant. In the period leading up to the destruction of the First Temple, Judea, under the leadership of King Zedekiah, rebelled against the rule of the Babylonians. Jeremiah opposed the rebellion, because he believed that the Babylonians had been sent by God to punish the people of Judea. He advised the king to submit to Babylonian rule, for rebellion against Babylonia was counter to the will of God and therefore would not succeed (Jeremiah 27). Jeremiah's position that the people could not succeed in militarily overthrowing their rulers represents in the poem the relative weakness of the Jews in their confrontation with the genocidal Nazis. The prophet's approach is problematic for an Israeli when applied to the Holocaust because it suggests divine sanction for the power of the Nazis and because it eliminates the possibility of military victory over one's enemy.

The image of the blinded man alludes to the biblical account of the fate of King Zedekiah following the failure of the rebellion against Babylonia. Nebuchadnezzar executed Zedekiah's sons in front of him, then blinded him and sent him off to captivity in Babylonia (Jeremiah 39). This image of children being killed before their parents can be seen as a reflection of the Holocaust experience. It is this scene that arouses the speaker to urge Jeremiah to reject his passive response to evil and to undertake the only violent response that could stop the disaster. The speaker tries to hand Jeremiah a pistol so that the prophet can assassinate Nebuchadnezzar. Since the readers know that such an event did not take place, just as efforts to assassinate Hitler failed, they conclude that this is a futile cry, the cry of frustration of the poet who was in effect as far from the Holocaust in Europe as he was from the period of the Bible. The readers must conclude that neither the theological justification of evil that leads to acceptance of the victims' fates nor the drive to overcome one's enemies by means of violence could work when applied to the Holocaust.

THE HOLOCAUST SURVIVOR AND "NORMAL" EXISTENCE

Dan Pagis (1930-1986), who actually experienced the Holocaust as a child, approaches the gap between the world of the Holocaust and the world of "normal" existence following the Holocaust from a perspective different from that of Gilboa. Pagis is preoccupied with his own sense that the world he lived in during World War II and the world he has lived in since the war are radically different. The transition of the survivors from one world to the next after the war is captured in Pagis's poem *"Ararat"* ("Ararat"),[25] in which he portrays the Holocaust as analogous to the Flood in the days of Noah (Genesis 6-9):

> When all the survivors of the Ark burst onto dry land
> And in the muddled joy
> chattered, roared, shouted for prey
> cried to be fruitful and multiply,
> and above their heads the rainbow hints
> there'll never be another end—the end came
> for the fish with no worries that lived
> off the disaster like flexible profiteers:
> now on the surface of congealing earth
> with unruly fins they were caught
> with mouths wide open, they drowned in the air.

The world of the Holocaust is presented as analogous to the destructive waters of the Flood, which provided an unnatural atmosphere in which human beings could not survive for long. Those who are fortunate enough to survive the Holocaust leave their refuge enthusiastically, driven to resume a normal physical life of eating and sexual reproduction. In the biblical Flood story the only animals to survive were the fish, who could swim in the water. Similarly, a kind of corrupt humanity emerged in the Holocaust, perhaps a reference to the Nazis themselves, to their collaborators, or to others who profited monetarily from the war. As long as the flood-like, corrupt world of the Holocaust persisted, those people thrived. Once the dry land of rational morality emerges, like fish who are deprived of water, this corrupt humanity cannot survive, and so they die "drowning in air."

Pagis's use of the Flood story to represent the transition from the Holocaust world to the post-Holocaust world is significant in terms of what he has omitted from the Bible. After this Holocaust Flood there is no covenant between God and humanity. The rainbow, which was the sign of God's solemn promise after the Flood never to destroy the world again, now only "hints / there'll never be another end," and yet the deaths of the fish contradict that hint. People are essentially on their own after the Holocaust, with no divine help. Those irrevocably corrupted by the war cannot survive in the post-Holocaust world, while those who resisted corruption at least can return to fulfilling the physical drives of food and sex, although it is not clear they can go much beyond that into the realm of the spiritual.

In two poems, *"Edut"* ("Testimony") and *"Edut 'aheret"* ("Another Testimony"),[26] Pagis explores the ways that

the events of the Holocaust radically undermine basic assumptions about the nature of humanity underlying the account of Creation in Genesis 1. In the testimony in the first poem the speaker focuses on the biblical statement that God created humanity "in the image of God" (Genesis 1:27). For the speaker the gap between the characteristics and fate of the Nazi victimizers and those of the Jewish victims of the Nazis was so great that it is difficult to conceive of both types of human beings as created by the same God. The speaker begins by rejecting the commonly held assumption that the Nazis had moved beyond the bounds of normal human behavior and had somehow turned themselves into amoral monsters:

> No no: they definitely were
> human beings: uniforms, boots.
> How to explain? They were created
> in the image.

Ironically, the speaker is forced to conclude that if the Nazis were human beings, then he and his fellow victims were of a different category of humanity:

> I was a shade.
> A different creator made me.
>
> And he in his mercy left nothing of me that would
>    die.
> And I fled to him, floated up weightless, blue,
> forgiving—I would even say: apologizing—
> smoke to omnipotent smoke
> that has no face or image.

The victory of the Nazis over the victims suggests that the former were created and protected by a demonic God who gave them power and the capacity for great cruelty. They were the human beings who, according to the Bible, were created "in the image of God" (*betselem 'elohim*, Genesis 1:27). A different God must have created the victim in His image, which the speaker considers to be as substantial as "shade" (*tsel,* a Hebrew word made up of two out of three letters of the Hebrew word for image, *tselem*). The God of those whose bodies were turned into smoke in the crematoria did not help them, presumably because He too is no more powerful or substantial than smoke. Sadly, the victim is so degraded by his experience that he somehow feels the need to apologize to this powerless God who did not save him.

In the second poem it is not the speaker who offers the testimony. The speaker begins the poem by turning to God, who although He is eternal appears to share humanity's inability to comprehend the injustices of the Holocaust. According to Deuteronomy, when the local communities in ancient Israel found a legal case to be too difficult to resolve, they were supposed to turn to the central legal authorities:

> If a judgment be too wondrous for you to decide
>    between blood and blood, between law and law,
>    or between blow and blow—quarrels in your
>    gates—you shall rise and go up to the place which

the Lord your God will have chosen and come to
the levitical priests, or the judge of that time. . . .
(Deuteronomy 17:8-9)

Now that after the Holocaust God is as confused as humanity, His only recourse, the speaker asserts, is to pay closer attention than He had before to the suffering of the Holocaust victim:

> You are the first and you remain the last.
> If a judgment be too wondrous for you between
>  law and law
> between blood and blood,
> listen to my heart hardened in the law, see my
>  affliction.

God, according to the speaker, must not only face the suffering of humanity during the Holocaust. He must also face the testimony of His partners in creation, the archangels Michael and Gabriel, who confess that it is God and the angels who are guilty for having created human beings capable of the evil of genocide:

> Your collaborators in creation, Michael, Gabriel,
> stand and confess
> that you said: Let us make man,
> and they said: Amen.

### DIVINE PROVIDENCE AND THE HOLOCAUST

Avner Treinin (1928-), a native-born Israeli writer who did not experience the Holocaust directly, looks at the gap between the Holocaust and the "normal" world of existence in a more abstract way not colored by Gilboa's mourning for his family and Pagis's traumatic experiences during World War II. In his poem *"Ketonet 'ish hamahanot"* ("The Coat of the Man of the Camps")[27] Treinin explores that gap by creating a contrast between the Holocaust and the original story of Joseph in the Bible (Genesis 37-50). In the Joseph story, what appears to begin as a tale of tragic conflict between siblings is seen by the end of the narrative as a part of God's plan to save Jacob and his family from famine by having Joseph rise to power in Egypt. The speaker, however, can discern no meaningful divine plan in the events of World War II, and so the Joseph story must be retold in a radically new way:

> And the brothers were not jealous
> of the coat of stripes,
> in which they too were dressed
> when lowered from the tracks.
>
> And he did not dream and he did not interpret
> and from the sheaf he did not rise,
> and no kid was missing
> when it was dipped in blood.
>
> And their father did not recognize it,
> for he had many sons of old age,
> and he merely mumbled, "A wild beast"
> and to see them he did not return.

In the Holocaust there were no special heroes like Joseph: all Jews, regardless of social status, were reduced to the same fate of annihilation in the concentration camps. The special "coat of many colors" (*ketonet hapassim*) by which Jacob singled out Joseph has been transformed into the "coat of stripes" (also called *ketonet hapassim* in the poem) that was the uniform of the Jews imprisoned in the Nazi concentration camps. Joseph's coat of many colors that was dipped in the blood of a kid to cover up his brothers' crime of selling him into slavery has become the millions of Jewish victims' prison uniforms stained by their own human blood. This Holocaust world overwhelmed by the shedding of human blood could find no one to decipher the mysteries of human fate, as Joseph had done when he interpreted the dreams of his fellow prisoners and of Pharaoh. God Himself is portrayed as even more overwhelmed and helpless than Jacob was in the Joseph story. Jacob recognized Joseph's bloody coat when the brothers showed it to him and concluded that a "wild beast" (*hayyah ra'ah*) had devoured his beloved son. God, in contrast, cannot recognize the special qualities of any individual Jew: too many have been killed. The Nazi "wild beast" (*hayyah ra'ah*) is beyond God's control, and so unlike Jacob who was eventually reunited with his beloved son Joseph, God will never again see the victims who were killed.

The poets whose works I have discussed push biblical analogies to the Holocaust as far as they can go. Each time they do so, there is a disjunction between the biblical world view and the reality of the Holocaust. Joshua, the Holocaust victim, is the opposite of Joshua, the victorious warrior, with whom Israelis have identified. The faith in God's providence that underlies the prophecies of Jeremiah and the story of Joseph is not applicable to the Holocaust. The destruction of the Holocaust is radically different from the destruction of the Flood in Noah's time. Unlike the Flood in Noah's time, the Holocaust cannot be seen as a justified act of divine punishment. There is no rainbow covenant after the Holocaust to reassure the survivors that such destruction will never happen again, and it is unclear that the victims and those who actually profited from World War II can possibly live in the same world. The very concept of humanity embodied in the biblical story of Creation is difficult to accept in the aftermath of such extreme crimes against humanity committed by the Nazis. Nevertheless, despite this disjunction between the biblical world view and the Holocaust, when writing poems about the Holocaust these poets are drawn to make use of biblical allusions as important sources of images that can help them to articulate that which cannot be adequately said in the language of everyday speech.

### NOTES

[1] Dina Porat, "Attitudes of the Young State of Israel toward the Holocaust and Its Survivors: A Debate over Identity and Values" in Laurence J. Silberstein, ed., *New Perspectives on Israeli History: The Early Years of the State* (New York and London: New York University Press, 1991) 158-159.

[2] Tom Segev, *The Seventh Million: The Israelis and the Holocaust,* trans. Haim Watzman (New York: Hill and Wang, 1993) 514.

[3] Dina Porat, "Attitudes of the Young State of Israel" 166.

[4] Arye Carmon, "Holocaust Teaching in Israel," *Shoah: A Journal of Resources on the Holocaust* 3. 2-3 (1982-83): 22.

[5] Tom Segev, *The Seventh Million* 180.

[6] ibid. 183.

[7] Aharon Appelfeld, *Masot beguf ri'shon* (Jerusalem: World Zionist Organization, 1979) 88-89. Appelfeld portrayed this experience in his novel *Mikhvat ha'or* (Tel Aviv: Hakibbutz Hameuchad, 1980). For a more detailed discussion of the issues Appelfeld had to deal with as a Holocaust survivor writer see David C. Jacobson, "Kill Your Ordinary Common Sense and Maybe You'll Begin to Understand': Aharon Appelfeld and the Holocaust," *AJS Review* 13 (1988): 129-152.

[8] Dina Porat, "Attitudes of the Young State of Israel" 162.

[9] Quoted in Charles S. Liebman and Eliezer Don-Yehiya, *Civil Religion in Israel: Traditional Judaism and Political Culture in the Jewish State* (Berkeley, Los Angeles, London: University of California Press, 1983) 102.

[10] Dina Porat, "Attitudes of the Young State of Israel" 166.

[11] Aharon Appelfeld, *Masot beguf ri'shon* 20.

[12] Aryeh Carmon, "Holocaust Teaching in Israel" 23. See also Alan Mintz, *Hurban: Responses to Catastrophe in Hebrew Literature* (New York: Columbia University Press, 1984) 239-241; Tom Segev, *The Seventh Million* 11.

[13] Quoted in Jacob Robinson, *He'aqov lemishur: yehudei 'eiropah befnei hasho'ah le'or ha'emet hahistorit umishpat Eichmann byrushalayim lefi 'hanohag habenle'umi,* trans. Zevi Bar-Meir and Aryeh Mor (Jerusalem: Mosad Bialik, 1965) 126.

[14] ibid. 127.

[15] Sidra DeKoven Ezrahi, *By Words Alone: The Holocaust in Literature* (Chicago and London: The University of Chicago Press, 1980) 106.

[16] Robert Alter, "A Poet of the Holocaust," *Commentary* (November, 1973): 60. For my analysis of other Israeli Holocaust poems not included in this essay that draw on biblical imagery see David C. Jacobson, *Modern Midrash: The Retelling of Traditional Jewish Narratives by Twentieth-Century Hebrew Writers* (Albany: State University of New York Press, 1987), chapter 6. The poems analyzed there are by Amir Gilboa, Abba Kovner, and Dan Pagis.

[17] Amir Gilboa, *Kehullim va'adummim* (1963; reprint, Tel Aviv: Am Oved, 1971) 344. The English translation is mine.

[18] Arieh Sachs, in an interpretation of the poem, points out that "the dedicatory note to the volume [*Kehullim va'adummim*] reads: 'With me are my father and mother Haim and Frieda and my brothers and sisters Bella and Joshua and Brunia, Moses and Sara and Esther' (slaughtered members of his family who appear in many of the poems and often in terms of their biblical namesakes)." See Stanley Burnshaw, T. Carmi, Ezra Spicehandler, ed., *The Modern Hebrew Poem Itself* (New York, Chicago, San Francisco: Holt, Rinehart and Winston, 1965) 143.

[19] Eda Zoritte, *Hahayyim, ha'atsilut: peraqim biyografiyyim ve'iyyunim bamarkivim haqabaliyyim-hahasidiyyim shel shirat 'Amir Gilboa'* (Tel Aviv: Hakibbutz Hameuchad, 1988) 37-42.

[20] See the interpretation by Arieh Sachs in Stanley Burnshaw, T. Carmi, Ezra Spicehandler, ed., *The Modern Hebrew Poem Itself* 144.

[21] ibid. 143.

[22] Hillel Barzel, *'Amir Gilboa': monografyah* (Tel Aviv: Sifriat Poalim, 1984) 118-119.

[23] Stanley Burnshaw, T. Carmi, Ezra Spicehandler, ed., *The Modern Hebrew Poem Itself* 143, 144.

[24] Amir Gilboa, *Kehullim va'adummim* 217. The translation by Stephen Mitchell is from *Ariel* 33-34 (1973): 6.

[25] Dan Pagis, *Shahut me'uheret* (Merhavia: Sifriat Poalim, 1964) 44. The translation is mine.

[26] Dan Pagis, *Gilgul* (Ramat Gan: Massada, 1970) 24-25. The translation of *"Edut"* by Stephen Mitchell is from Dan Pagis, *Points of Departure* (Philadelphia: The Jewish Publication Society of America, 1981) 25. The translation of *"Edut'aheret"* is mine.

[27] Avner Treinin, *Har vezetim* (Jerusalem: Agudat "Shalem," 1969) 52. The translation is mine.

**Gabriel Levin**

SOURCE: "The Violence of Collision: Hebrew Poetry Today," in the *Literary Review,* Vol. 26, No. 2, Winter, 1983, pp. 196-210.

[*In the following essay, Levin explores theme, subject matter, and style in modern Hebrew poetry.*]

The recent publication of the *Penguin Book of Hebrew Verse* (edited by T. Carmi) will both delight the English-speaking reader with its storehouse of ancient and modern poetry and serve to dispel a number of preconceptions concerning the practice of Hebrew poetry throughout the ages. We have been led to believe, for example, that Hebrew as a living language was miraculously revived toward the end of the nineteenth century as political and cultural Zionism gained momentum in Europe. Some will point to such figures as Ahad Ha'am, Bialik, and a host of Jewish writers and intellectuals who gathered in Odessa in the 1880s and not only spoke and wrote in Hebrew but argued heatedly in its accents. Others will point to the indefatigable Eliezar Ben-Yehuda, who, at the turn of the century, compiled in Jerusalem the first modern Hebrew dictionary, and who demanded that his household speak nothing but Hebrew.

Such instances, dating back to the late nineteenth century, have been heretofore understood as the first glimmerings of the revival of Hebrew as a spoken, secular language. Until that time the use of Hebrew was limited to the reading and studying of the Bible and to the reciting of the *piyutim*—liturgical songs. At least this is what we have come to believe. The *Penguin Book of Hebrew Verse* shows otherwise: Hebrew poetry, both religious and secular (and most frequently a marriage of the two) has flourished throughout the ages and in a wide diversity of lands.

Although the Bible remained the gravitational center of all Hebrew writing, Jewish migrations and settlements across North Africa and Europe enabled Hebrew writers to come into contact with a rich and diverse range of poetic styles. In medieval Spain Hebrew poets adapted the festive tones of Arabic poetry to their verse; in Provence poets came under the influence of the troubador poets; and in Italy the sonnet was introduced into Hebrew verse as early as 1300. In effect, Hebrew has always been steeped in two cultures, one clinging to the Hebrew of The Book and of Rabbinical writings, and the other attentive to the language and culture of its adopted country. Such a dual identity has had its effects upon the texture of Hebrew poetry. As one astute critic has put it: "it loves the hybrid and the mongrel; because to write Hebrew now (whenever its "now") is to slap together two worlds; it prizes the violence of the collision."

The "violence of the collision" has persisted right up to modern times, including that period in which Israel gained statehood; or, perhaps I should say *especially* during and after that period in which Israel gained statehood. It is therefore with much poignant insight that the contemporary Hebrew poet Harold Schimmel (himself American-born) has—in his long poetic sequence, *Ar'a*— a certain character named Symkin, a *chalutz,* or pioneer, exhibiting some flair and just a touch of truancy, scrawl in bold (Hebrew) letters on the wall of a settlement town, in the year 1890:

> God's a wiz
> 　　　look
> even the crows on the shingles
> craw-craw:
> 　　　"what sort of different things
> 　　　　　　come together?" And—

"What
　　will become of us from now on?"

Symkin's graffiti is but the dawning of a notion that if the *Yishuv* (as pre-state Israel was fondly called) was to have a soul it would certainly be a soul of many parts: part old country, part agrarian, part cosmopolitan, part Yiddishkeit and part Levantine, to name only a few of the constituent elements of the *Yishuv* at the turn of the century.

For the most part Hebrew poets lingered on in Europe, loitering about such centers as Odessa, Vienna, and Paris before finally descending upon the Levant in the 1920s. Half a dozen men of letters then trickled into Palestine. Some, like H. N. Bialik and Shaul Tchernikhovsky were already poets of no mean repute. (Bialik was by then fifty-one years old and had composed all of his major poems.) Others, like U. Z. Greenberg and S. Y. Agnon, the Nobel Prize winner, shuttled between Europe and Palestine over a number of years before finally settling in the latter for good.

Poets writing between the World Wars were literally stirred by the land under their feet. They had come, as one song put it, to build and be rebuilt. It was during these early years in Palestine that written Hebrew hesitantly approached the fresh rhythms and tonal modulations of spoken, *chalutz* Hebrew. Such a rapprochement was not a simple matter; the collision of two opposing sensibilities was keenly felt. On the one hand there was the very urgency of registering all that the eye and ear could possibly pick up in new surroundings; and on the other hand there remained in the poets of the second and third *Aliya* (the waves of immigration into Palestine in 1904 and 1920) a strong nostalgia for Europe, for its northern climate and, particularly, for its literature. Thus the major poets of the third *Aliya,* Natan Alterman and Avraham Shlonsky adapted into Hebrew the literary techniques of Russian and French modernism.

There were of course exceptions. U. Z. Greenberg, attacked in his writings both Gentile Europe and secular Jewish Palestine. In the early forties Yonatan Ratosh founded the "Canaanite" movement, which rejected Judaism as it had developed in Europe and embraced a new identity grounded in pre-biblical, Canaanite mythologies.

Midway, perhaps, between Greenberg's prophetic dithyrambs and Ratosh's proddings into the fertile Canaanite soil stands the poetry of Avoth Yeshurun. Born in Poland in 1904, Yeshurun arrived in Palestine in 1925 and forthwith plunged into the Mediterranean melée, a far cry from the atmosphere of the Hassidic home of his grandparents in Poland where he had spent most of his childhood. During these early years in Palestine, Yeshurun roamed through the country, becoming acquainted with its Jewish-Arab villages and scraping together a living as laborer, fruit-picker, building-hand, swamp-dredger, and watchman. Out of such vagabondage Yeshurun gradually developed—or perhaps a better word would be agglutinated—a distinct poetic style: the Hebrew which Alterman and Shlonsky sought to purify was in Yeshurun's hands battered and hammered into a babel of dialects; Yiddish, Arab, and English phrases slide in and out of the poems, as do startling portmanteau words; the syntax is purposively roughened and incomplete; archaisms appear alongside the easy vernacular of the street. Such a style was slow in emerging. Yeshurun's first collection of poems appeared in 1942, when he was 38 years old. His second volume appeared in 1961. Since the early sixties, however, Yeshurun has published several volumes of poetry, including his major work, *The Syrian-African Rift.*

Yeshurun, the last remaining poet of the *Yishuv,* and now in his late seventies, may very well be to this day one of Israel's most innovative poets. His style is characterized by his methodical violence to the Hebrew tongue, a technique adopted, often with far less success, by a host of younger poets; and there is in Yeshurun's poems something fiercely local. Perhaps it comes from—to borrow a phrase from Louis Zukofsky—his "cold physical eye"—and his crunching embrace of the land, whether desert wadis, city rubble, or the teeming souk. "In everything multiple-eyes," writes Yeshurun.

A number of poets who fought as young men and women in the Israeli War of Independence and wrote their first poems in the war's aftermath developed a poetic style which ran counter to Yeshurun's linguistic torsions. Following the lead of Natan Zach and Yehuda Amichai, these poets adopted a lean, bare-bones style. The poetry disengaged itself from broad, national concerns and in their stead spoke in ironic tones of the self's daily labors and loves. All action became understand. Measured cadences and fixed stanzaic forms were replaced by shifting line lengths and—for the most part—internal rhymes. Biblical allusions were either treated in mock-heroic tones, such as in Amichai's poem, "King Saul And I":

> They gave him a finger, but he took the whole hand.
> They gave me the whole hand, I didn't even take
>    the little finger.
> While my heart
> was weight-lifting its first feelings
> he rehearsed the tearing of oxen.

or were replaced by a growing lexicon picked up in the new, urban environment. Hebrew verse became increasingly concerned not with a Hebrew of the Book, but with a Hebrew of the street and, most significantly, with a Hebrew as seen and heard from the child's knee-high perspective.

Thus, poets such as Amir Gilboa, Natan Zach, and Yehuda Amichai early on in their verse wrote, albeit with searing irony, in the pure tones and nostalgias of childhood. In "Death Comes to the Rocking Horse Michael," for example, one of Natan Zach's major poems, a typical refrain jingles with the wide-eyed simplicity of a children's bedtime song:

> Rocking horse Michael, rocking horse Michael.
> There is he that craves and he that weighs,

> he that sinks and he that falls,
> come along, come along, rocking horse Michael.

And again, in "Dantès, No," Zach fools his reader by hiding the true identity of the speaker. Identifying the speaker requires of the reader to shift from adult literature (mistakingly identifying Dantès with Dante Alighieri) to boyhood adventure stories. For the "true" speaker in the poem is Edward Dantès, the character created by Alexander Dumas and commonly known as the Count of Monte Cristo. The ruse is significant. A nineteenth-century action-packed adventure story, where all comes to a good end, is now transformed into its near opposite: life, in the end is "not pitch darkness yet certainly not light." What was taken for a boyhood reverie is cast in the shadows of disillusionment and confinement. It is moreover a disillusionment which may be read as bearing not only upon a single life but perhaps also upon that of a people dreaming of Zion.

Zach was not alone in deploying childhood props, often for darker ends. In one of Amir Gilboa's most well-known poems, the speaker is the child Isaac as he walks with his father in the forest. Again, note the child-like perceptions and tone and the poem's sudden exposure to violence:

> Towards morning the sun walked through the forest
> together with me and my father,
> my right hand in his left.
>
> like lightning a knife flashed between the trees.
> I was afraid for my eyes seeing the blood on the
>    leaves.
>
>         (from: "Isaac," trans. by A. C. Jacobs)

Gilboa, a near contemporary of Yeshurun's, and a poet who shares with the latter a certain *Yishuv* toughness, is master of the dreamlike interior landscape. Individual and historical memory are fused in the poems' surreal texture. The vision is severe. What is seen by the child or the soft-eyed gazelle in Gilboa's poems is more often than not a beauty or an innocence bordering upon terror. Language explodes on a field torn by ancient and recent warfare.

The present selection begins with a generation of poets whose works appeared close to the time that Israel achieved statehood. Most were born in Europe and emigrated to Palestine in their early youth. (The major exception is Gabriel Preil, who was born in Russia and has lived in New York City for the greater part of his life.) This generation set the tone—lean, understated, and nostalgic—in which poetry would be written well into the sixties and up to the early seventies. It is a tone indebted to Rilke (both Amichai and Zach were born in Germany) and to Auden and T. S. Eliot.

In 1952 a number of these poets joined forces and formed a literary movement, called *L'krat* (Toward), which set out to create a new poetics as well as to debunk the old. Natan Zach was its leading figure, both as poet and as critic. His vitriolic attack against the poetry of Natan Alterman—the leading poet of the period before statehood—reflects the role of the new *avant-garde.* Speaking of Alterman, Zach writes: "There has not yet been in modern Hebrew poetry a major poet in whom the music of his poetry is so far from the rhythms of the spoken tongue." And again, more devastatingly, Zach writes: "Something essential is impaired in him as a poet—impaired are the means of feeling open to the world of people and things. Impaired (in Alterman) is the ability to be a human being participating in the world and to give expression to this."

Poets were quick to rally to Zach's call for "openness" and "participation." And the poet who did this best was certainly Yehuda Amichai. Having always been a "big-game hunter of feelings," Amichai touches upon anything and everything. His language is immediate, concrete, yet startling in the twists and turns of its similes. Hebrew simply had never been used *on the page* in such a fashion.

Hebrew, it must be remembered, was and is to this day in a state of constant flux; new words have been coined and slapped into life almost daily. The pre-statehood poets were certainly conscious of their role in reviving the Hebrew tongue, yet they did so largely to revive the language of the Bible. Words and phrases which for centuries were read or chanted in school or synagogue were now thrown into a new, secular context. In a sense, the metaphysical edge of the Hebrew tongue now hovered between two worlds, the one biblical and timeless, and the second historical and earthbound. S. Y. Agnon, for example, mastered a literary style which straddled both worlds, and as such the writing is at once ancient and contemporary. The writer dipped his pen into a wide linguistic pool of biblical phraseology, Mishnaic syntax, and Rabbinic lore, then put it to use in his cautious explorations into the modern, secular world of Europe, Palestine, and—in his later writings—modern-day Israel.

The writers and poets of this period embodied, in fact, in letter and spirit, Eliot's dictum to "procure the consciousness of the past" in the present. It is particularly a sense of the past which grew out of Jewish religious tradition. Biblical and Rabbinic writings have always imposed upon the reader a literary discipline which is primarily exegetical—a text inevitably begs interpretation and commentary; it also begs the reader to pay due respect to his historical predecessors.

What would come into effect, though, with the revival of the Hebrew language in Israel was the increasing impingement of the present upon the past. Thus when Natan Zach attacked Alterman for not being open to the world, his criticism was undoubtedly aimed at Alterman's inability to keep pace with the rapid developments and changes in the way in which Hebrew was daily spoken. Conversely, Amichai's verbal combustions occur in the light of his juxtapositions of the new—the *brand* new—and the old. Humdrum objects of everyday life and their seemingly flat, banal vocabulary enter the poem and mix with objects from the near and distant past. Thus fig, telephone, and vine commingle in an early poem:

> The man under his fig tree telephoned the man
> under his vine:
> "Tonight they definitely might come.
> Armor-plate the leaves. Secure the tree.
> Call the dead home, and make ready!"

> (from: "Sort of Apocalypse" trans. by
> H. Schimmel)

Thirty years have elapsed since the members of *L'krat* banded together. We offer here only a sampling of the most recent writings of this group of poets—poems published in the late sixties and, for the most part, on through the seventies. The direction which some of these poets have taken in their verse is significant.

Avoth Yeshurun's poetry came into full maturity in the aftermath of the Yom Kippur War. As a frequenter of the small, lively cafes which line the streets of Tel-Aviv, his poems now endlessly crisscross the sprawling metropolis, meandering along its streets, and stopping only to count losses. In "Prelude on the Demise of the Mulberry Tree" it is the cypresses who "died standing," and the margosa and mulberry trees; elsewhere it is the sound of sledge hammers, "blow after blow" which Yeshurun notes, or "the little windows in the puddle, just off Dizengoff Center."

"The evening mixed remembering and forgetting like my mother/mixing hot and cold water in the bath," writes Amichai in "Second Meeting with a Father," and indeed, his poems written in the past ten years are steeped in nostalgia. Amichai's tone is now quieter, less varied, and a shade darker. As it stands, however fervent his attachment to the land, particularly to Jerusalem, Amichai has remained the eternal emigré within *Eretz Yisrael.*

Finally, there is Natan Zach, who, following the publication of *All the Milk and Honey* in 1966, stopped publishing for more than a decade, residing during that time in England. Zach returned to Israel in 1978 and a year later published *North Easterly.* A large number of poems in this collection were written in and about England. It is their very "Englishness," I believe, which contributes to the change in tone: once seemingly effortless in its musical phrasing,

> Restlessness on all sides and angels. And agitation
> they are always agitating in their ceaseless
> motion: they are always moving about
> and moving others from place to place, rousing
> themselves as though to prove they are alive and
> now
> restlessness on all sides and angels.

> (from: "Restlessness on All Sides and Angels")

the poetry is now hesitant and restrained:

> Grass scorched land sloping or falling
> toward the water, cut inlets unfurling waves,

a shore where even the Atlantic laps
its chasm in measured waves, obedient

(from: "Wessex")

Another sign of the poetry's "Englishness"—one which
brings to mind Hardy and Auden—is Zach's conscious
efforts to embrace both a private and public self. The
tone, grave and elegiac, comes from Ecclesiastes (see
"The Countries We Live In"); the genre is English pastoral.

Can one speak of a shared style or tone in the poetry
of the late sixties and early seventies? The present
anthology's inclusion of poets who began publishing in
the late sixties, loosely identified as the "Tel-Aviv poets," may answer the question in part.

How to identify such a band of poets? The bulk have
lived in Tel-Aviv, Israel's sprawling coastal city, a hybrid of
the Orient and the West. As Menachem Ben writes:

> Tel Aviv at dawn
> like a herd of black jaguars, scalped, surrounded
> by wonderful fields
> but what human neglect
> inside!
> What human nakedness!

(from "The Sea Transparent Slices")

The bulk are also poets born in Israel, and if they have
a second tongue then it is clearly a "foreign tongue,"
acquired in school. The older living Hebrew poets whom
they most admire and publish in their literary review,
*Siman Kri'a,* are Avoth Yeshurun and Gabriel Preil. The
latter writes out of New York City, in a clear, modern
Hebrew, delicate tales spun out of memory and fantasy:

> I saw a monk from Siam, thin and ascetic as a reed,
> sitting on the wellspring of oblivion—
> like him I was punished by scorpions of memory
> and in pale waters I made myself clean.

(from: "A Summing Up")

The foreign poets whom they admire are American: Ezra
Pound, William Carlos Williams, Robert Lowell, and
John Berryman. The leading figures of this group are
Meir Wieseltier, Yair Hurvitz, and Yona Wollack; *Achshav*
and *Siman Kri'a* are the two literary reviews which did
most to publish and promote their verse, and to this day
the "Tel-Aviv poets" have gathered round the latter.

What brings these poets together is their open rejection
of the lean, understated language of Zach's generation
(Meir Wieseltier would attack Zach for not being "engaged" in reality, only a decade after Zach's own accusations against Alterman), accepting in its stead "a more
luxuriant language," in the words of the Israeli critic
Shimon Sandbank.

The first signs and testimonies of such verbal expansive-
ness appear in the early poetry of David Avidan, the
gadfly and provocateur of the Israeli literary scene.
Avidan's language is playful, self-mocking and—in sharp
contrast to his elders—it is *garrulous.* Reminiscent somewhat of Frank O'Hara's urban chatter, Avidan's poetry is
studded with urban accessories and the technical and
advertising jargon of hyped-up city life.

Alongside such sheer verbal excesses there developed in
this "younger" group of poets a closer attentiveness to
their immediate surroundings, that is, to the objective and
local. Nostalgia and the criss-crossing of identities is
practically absent, and in its place appears a thirst for
tangible realities: Yeshurun's "multiple-eyes" and "bits
of nickel, chrome, iron"; Meir Wieseltier's lurid urban
snapshots; Geldman's painterly depiction of Tel-Aviv
beach boys, an aestheticism which is close in spirit to
Baudelaire's *Les Fleurs du Mal,* ("With long hooks that
moved in the fog / that moved in unfeeling water / they
dredged his corpse from the river"), and, at its extreme,
Aharon Shabtai's catalogue poems:

> a radish, also, lies
> there
>
> (in a cardboard box
> slightly damp)
>
> and on the floor
> ants and bread crumbs

The poetry works primarily on a pictorial plane rather
than a literary one: a tall order considering the Hebrew
poet's literary heritage, a heritage which was used by
such poets as Zach and Amichai ironically, or, as Dan
Laor has called it, as "a vehicle of parody." Parody occasionally surfaces in the poetry of the "Tel-Aviv poets"
though their preference is for a nonliterary "natural"
style. And naturalism now means a hard-hitting directness—
living, in Meir Wieseltier's words, "close to the senses."

For Yona Wollach, living close to the senses has meant
writing almost exclusively of the ruthlessness of feeling.
In her poems, the speaking voice is often that of the
child, yet Wollach's child-poems have little in common
with those of an earlier generation: androgynous, victimizers, often greedy, sinful ("O Bonnie look at my sins all
of them / like endless children they'll go they're all
sweet"), these are children who share with Rimbaud a
great pleasure in turning their backs on the grown-up,
adult world. In "Jonathan," child-play rapidly gives way
to a wild unleashing of violence:

> I run on the bridge
> and the children after me
> Jonathan
> Jonathan they call
> a little blood
> just a little blood to wipe up the honey

There is here a double allusion with its own cutting edge.
First: the biblical story of Jonathan, Saul's son, who defies
(though in the Bible it is an unknowing transgression) his

father's order not to taste of the honey of the Philistines. In Wollach's poem, however, the admission of guilt—*'I did but taste a little honey with the end of the rod that was in mine hand, and, lo, I must die'*—is transformed into a nightmarish stripping bare of the emotions: unlike the biblical story, greed is avenged by blood-retribution and the persecutor is not the father but the children themselves. Secondly, the poem's edge is whetted by its reference—immediately recognizable to an Israeli reader—to a popular nursery rhyme: Jonathan, as every Israeli child knows, is also the little rascal who climbs a tree instead of going to nursery school and tears a hole in his pants.

By the late '70s, with the publication of Yona Wollach's *Collected Poems,* black humor, direct confrontation, and emotions veering close to madness would strike a familiar chord in a large segment of the Israeli public. Its cutting language seemed to speak to a generation of readers who, like Wollach, were born and raised in Israel and who saw in her demonic, half-crazed figures (more often than not female and Christian, with names such as Cordelia, Teresa, Christina, and Lola) a sort of shattered defiance of the self in a country caught in a *cri de conscience* in the aftermath of the Yom Kippur War.

The ground was prepared for such a confessional mode by Dahlia Ravicovitch, a contemporary of David Avidan, who published her first book of poems, *The Love of an Orange,* in 1959. More than those of any other contemporary poet, Ravicovitch's poems manage to fuse the personal and the descriptive mode. Early on in her writing, Ravicovitch constructed carefully metered and rhymed poems. In recent years, however, her style has loosened in a direction which brings to mind the poetry of Lowell and Plath, two poets who share her thematic preoccupations: loneliness, unfulfilled love, and a tremulous sensuality. Such themes are never aggrandized but are given expression through lingering notations of the plainest of daily acts, actions which in Ravicovitch's poetry are transformed into instances of ablution:

> Some ants found half a dead fly
> and it wasn't easy for them
> to drag it off the grass.
> Their little sides nearly burst with the effort.
> Just then the grass bristled
> all at once, like a barley field.
> What madness, that the grass
> should think itself a barley field.

> (from: "Two Songs of the Garden")

There exists, moreover, another side to Ravicovitch's poetry, a side displaying a lively, tropical imagination. Her thoughts appear to push toward extremes, and long for the exotic and miraculous—Chad and Cameroon, Hong Kong, Australia, Ghana, Zanzibar: all are evoked in her poems, evoked only to be suddenly revoked by the intrusion of reality, "like sand that crumbles."

The thirst for the exotic may very well have become by now a shared quest for a growing number of poets—a byproduct, perhaps, of Israel's admixture of East and West. In Yair Hurvitz's poetry it is primarily a kind of *alchimie du verbe,* a weaving of mood and dream. Its musical Arabesques and aural evocations make the poetry especially difficult to translate.

Israel Pincas and Menachem Ben are two more poets in whom the voyage out—in search of splendor and the exotic—is blended with the soul's inner voyage into the unknown. The former poet's classical learning and latter-day Hellenism are rendered on the page in the clear, spoken rhythms of the "lean" school of poetry. Most of Pincas's poems take place in an imaginary Italian landscape and are filled with quiet moments of contemplation which border on religious adoration. The poet's repeated evocations of "the gods" may be understood as an aesthetic ideal. It is the Platonic Eros, the rapt contemplation of beauty, apprehended, though only momentarily, and in its evanescence, lacking the fixed, imperturbable quality of art in the Hellenic world:

> When love was here, for her regal visit,
> she brought such splendor,
> until many, as though operated, from within,
> sensed its presence,
> till it vanished, like mist, completely.

> (from: "Script")

Israel Pincas's moments of briefly apprehended beauty, his solicitude of the still-points within the fluidity of life, his being seized and consumed by the sensible world— "the drunken magic square"—may serve as a modest foil to the dominating thrust of contemporary Hebrew verse, which is predominantly kinetic and speaks in the language of struggle and becoming. Such tensions reflect the tensions of a country in the throes of rebuilding itself, though it also seems possible that such a dynamism reflects at a deeper level qualities of being inherent to Hebraic thought.

The poetry of Menachem Ben, with its unleashed energy and playful collisions, is no longer between two worlds but rather between two states of mind—the real and the surreal. There is a great deal of Avidan in Ben's disjunctive, agitated talk, edging away from the comprehensible, yet always impassioned; and perhaps also some of Amichai in the quick display of imagery. Yet unlike these poets, Ben's geographic explorations are inner voyages (in a later edition of his selected poems, Ben changed the title of the poem "The Sea Transparent Slices" to "Chronicle of One L.S.D. Trip"). Ben mixes the psychedelic with the sensuous and the ordinary. Thus the Mediterranean shivers in his mind's eye:

> What wonderful pineapples!
> Tennis fields and showers.
>
> Everything in the morning.
> Everything.
>
> The sea—transparent slices of a longing
> shivering chunks of green

a lot of green
in the fingers of morning
in the polite
the gorgeous
the refined
the unagitated
fingers of pleasure.

One may conclude from the sampling of poets under discussion that recent Hebrew poetry has increasingly embraced, both in tone and subject matter, the off-beat and exotic. The drama of reason, which in Zach's generation was enacted under the somber shadow of Europe, is now enacted under the full light of the Mediterranean. Touched, in one manner or other, by the Orient, the drama is transformed into a pageant; reason is subordinated to feeling; and the self, once ironically detached, is now submerged in a world of sense-impressions. I am thinking in particular of such poets as Yair Hurvitz, Aharon Shabtai (in his most recent verse), Maya Bejerano, Zali Gurevitch, and Ronnie Someck—the last three being poets who began publishing in the late '70s.

Bejerano's poetry is the most colorful and whimsical of the lot. Narrative, especially in her "Data Processing" poems, gives way to a lively pastiche of sense and nonsense; the self is barely identifiable, surfacing for quick cameo appearances in the midst of the poems' layering of details. Bejerano's enmeshing in the fantastic ("crushed, I was pressed to the trunk of a poppy") is certainly new to Hebrew verse. Her only competition in this may be David Avidan, whose poems in recent years have skyrocketed into the world of computer and sci-fi talk.

But has the self—the carrier of romantic feeling—been completely submerged? Poets such as Gurevitch, Galili, Miriam, and Someck attest to the contrary. In as much as the style touches upon the dreamlike, and, particularly in Gurevitch's case, is attentive to the mind's sifting of experience, it is also a poetry with a definite speaking voice, sharing with previous generations of poets writing in Israel a sense of unrest and impending threat—unrest which alternatively is sung with bitter irony, or brought up "close to the senses," or, finally, which shimmers in the near-distance like a *fata morgana,* as in Ronnie Someck's pop mythologies:

A Bedouin who croaked from desert cancer
    flashes through my thoughts
like a white Mercedes.
They say that after he died "phantasia-shots" were
    fired in the air.

A final word before turning to the poets themselves. I was surprised, in reading through our selection, by the underlying current of emotion shared by many of the poets. Loss and the hesitant, antiphonal voice of reparation seemed the dominant mode of feeling. It is apparent in Avoth Yeshurun's voyage-cum-operation; Amir Gilboa's poem, "This Isn't What I Want To Write I" is no less severe in its pared down vision. Zach, Amichai, Pagis, and Carmi deal with equally painful feelings, albeit ironically.

Thus Zach has God mourning for "his sweet servant Job," Carmi transforms a plane ride into the shadowy pursuit between lovers, and Pagis, metamorphosed into a "lost gold coin," has himself picked up, rubbed "between thumb and finger," struck, bitten, and finally spent at will. These are all, in short, poems of loss, buoyed by the poets' wit and pleasure in noting their predicament.

The Tel-Aviv poets, with their demand for direct confrontation, speak almost obsessively of the wrenching of relationships, and in its extreme case, as in Wollach's poetry, not merely of loss, but of loss of mind. This "younger" band of poets, moreover, are gripped by an aesthetics which borders on the decadent. Take Mordechai Geldman's "Fat Boy" and Hurvitz's "Darkness Will Sweeten," two poems in which beauty and death are closely aligned. Certainly the conflation of beauty and loss and decay appears in Dahlia Ravicovitch's poetry. Can it be that aesthetic detachment has replaced the previous generation's use of irony as the primary means of bracing itself against loss? It is now the poet's *eye,* its cautious notations, which counterpoints the poem's pain. And as such it is the eye which contributes to the poem's quiet, hesitant, reparative work. Meir Wieseltier's short poem "Fruit" is an instance in which aesthetic precision raises the poem several notches above its otherwise resigned tone:

A burning cigarette flipped into the tree
(at 5 a.m.)
blossoms a moment in red splendor between the
    leaves.

After all it's fruit of the tree
(tobacco, paper), indeed a different
tree, but why be exacting.
The fruit glows, the fruit is extinguished,

a man is replete a moment and isn't.

There are, of course, other examples: Israel Pincas's refined aestheticism, reminiscent of the Alexandrian poet, C. P. Cavafy; or Harold Schimmel's *collagist* poetry, particularly in his book-length poem, *Ar'a,* a modern-day *vade mecum* of Israel; Menachem Ben "visions" in "The Sea Transparent Slices"; and Aharon Shabtai's paganism in his "House Poem." These are all poets who seemed to have turned to beauty out of a strong feeling for the radiating, life-giving image.

Thus the movement from loss and mourning and the uncertainty of the present have been turned into a newfound aestheticism in which, to paraphrase one reviewer's description of Mordechai Geldman's poetry, the poet turns to beauty on the very threshold of pain.


**Gila Ramras-Rauch**

SOURCE: "Modern Hebrew Verse," in *World Literature Today,* Vol. 60, No. 2, Spring, 1986, pp. 229-33.

[*In the following essay, Ramras-Rauch comments on the varied character of modern Hebrew poetry and principally considers the verse of Yehuda Amichai, Natan Zach, and Avot Yeshuruh.*]

What characterizes modern Hebrew poetry as a whole is the absence of a common characteristic (other than the basic fact of its being written in Hebrew). Among its practitioners are writers born in Europe and others born in Israel; there are poets who have been influenced by traditionally Jewish or biblical themes, and others whose work was shaped by Russian, French, or English literary elements, as well as those who have partaken of both worlds; and there are those who have sought a continuity with the styles and motifs of the past, and others who have set out on paths of their own, seeking their individual voices. The rubric "modern Hebrew poet" must be applied first to figures such as Nathan Alterman (1910-71), Abraham Shlonsky (1900-73), Uri Zvi Greenberg (1895-1981), and Leah Goldberg (1911-70). They were the first to identify themselves as modernists, they wrote manifestos on modernism, and they gave Hebrew poetry its modern voice.

Most articles and anthologies begin the "modern" category with Haim Nahman Bialik (1873-1934), undoubtedly the greatest Hebrew poet in the modern era, yet his status as a "modern" is open to conjecture. He released Hebrew from the shackles of nineteenth-century neoclassicism, expanding the boundaries of poetic expression beyond the stilted imitation of quasi-biblical verse. Without him, modern Hebrew poetry would not be what it is. In Bialik's own lifetime, however, Shlonsky and Greenberg had rejected him for being a classicist, not a "modern" poet. (It is of some significance that several of the youngest poets of the "postmodern" era have turned to Bialik with renewed interest.)

Obviously, a poet can be living in the modern age and not be truly modern. Shimon Halkin (b. 1898), thoroughly acquainted with the entire range of poetry in English, has written as though it ended with Keats and as though Eliot and Pound never existed. At a still further extreme, Yonathan Ratosh (1908-81) sought inspiration in *pre*-Hebraic civilization and is thus identified with the "Canaanite" movement in Hebrew poetry. Among the older generation there are other interesting anomalies: Zelda (1914-84) did not publish her first collection of poetry until 1967; Gabriel Preil (b. 1911 in Estonia) has lived in New York since 1922 and qualifies as a modern Hebrew poet because he writes in that language; Amir Gilboa (1917-84) began writing Hebrew poetry in the Ukraine before he came to Palestine in 1937; and Avot Yeshurun (b. 1904), who settled in Palestine in 1925, has expressed a sensitivity to the Arab milieu quite unusual in the Hebrew poetry of his time.

In more recent years there has been a large and impressive group of poets who began their creative activity at a time nearer to 1948, the year of Israel's founding as a state: Haim Guri (b. 1922), Nathan Yonathan (b. 1923),

Tuvia Rivner (b. 1924), Yehuda Amichai (b. 1924), T. Carmi (b. 1925), Avner Treinin (b. 1928), Dan Pagis (b. 1930), Natan Zach (b. 1930), Moshe Dor (b. 1932), and others. In addition, there is a still-younger generation of active and interesting poets such as Daliah Rabikovitch (b. 1936), Asher Reich (b. 1937), Aharon Shabtai (b. 1939), Yair Hurvitz (b. 1941), Meir Wieseltier (b. 1941), and Yona Wallach (1944-85). These poets vary as widely as can be imagined in their linguistic innovation, in the range of their subject matter, and in their individual poetic outlooks.[1]

Modern Hebrew poetry is thus a heterogeneous totality—if it is a "totality" at all, there being no one "school" prevailing, let alone a uniform mode or mood. Predominant, however, is the element of modernity: verbal embellishments are not to be found, any more than soulful longing or other romantic trappings. Ranging from the direct statement to the allusive, from the explicit to the implicit, or from the colloquial to the elliptic, contemporary Hebrew poets will strive for simplicity: adopting a personal idiom yet recasting everything in a recognizably modern mold.

In order to understand modern Hebrew poetry, there are two facts about it that one must keep in view: a) as modern poetry it participates in everything that can be said to characterize modern Western poetry; and b) it is written in the language of the Bible, a text that can be read with comprehension by any seven-year-old child in Israel. These two facts constitute the armature of contemporary Hebrew verse. Its language is loaded with allusion, laid down through the centuries like geological strata, and it therefore provides the poet with a wide array of motifs and diction immediately recognizable by the reading public as linked to the tradition, although the modern struggle for poetic voice and form is (as elsewhere) linked to modern experience, which is global.

All the phases and movements of twentieth-century poetry are to be found in Hebrew verse, from futuristic attempts to shatter all symbols of culture, to imagism, acmeism, symbolism, surrealism, and every other movement that has come and gone in Europe and America. Among the older poets, Uri Zvi Greenberg was powerfully influenced by German expressionism, Nathan Alterman by French poetry, Abraham Shlonsky by Russian symbolism, and Shimon Halkin by English romanticism. In later generations there are those who follow and those who reject those key figures. Haim Guri and Nathan Yonathan have been heavily influenced by them, especially by Alterman, assimilating in their own work the rhythms and other poetic elements deflected from languages they themselves do not know (e.g., Russian). Each generation is rocked by waves that originate elsewhere in the world. A huge mass of contemporary fiction and poetry is steadily being translated into Hebrew, and Israeli poets are frequent travelers abroad, so that exposure to heterogeneous experience contributes to the many-sided nature of contemporary Hebrew poetry.

It is significant also that many of the major poets who have shaped modern Hebrew verse were not born in Palestine or Israel and had to adopt Hebrew as a second language. The older generation (Alterman, Shlonsky, Uri Zvi Greenberg, Leah Goldberg) were all born in Eastern Europe (Warsaw, the Ukraine, Austria-Poland, and Lithuania, respectively), and much the same is to be said for Yeshurun, Preil, and Gilboa, as we have seen. It is also true for Amichai (Germany), Rivner (Czechoslovakia), Carmi (New York), Pagis (Romania), Zach (Berlin), and Wieseltier (Moscow), and of course there have been subsequent influences derived from concrete experience with other languages: Amichai, whose native language was German, came to Palestine in 1936 and served in the British army in World War II. Undoubtedly, it was this experience that provided the English component of his poetic language, and he has been influenced by poets as different as Eliot, Auden, and Ted Hughes.

Modern Hebrew poetry can also be seen as a struggle between "fathers" and "sons": Bialik was attacked by Shlonsky and Greenberg, as noted, Alterman was attacked by Zach, and Zach's poetry and his poetics have been attacked in turn by the generation of Wieseltier. The older generation, coming to prominence between the two world wars, continued to write into the 1970s. The generation associated with 1948 had been nurtured by the "fathers" yet found its own way and in the last three decades has taken broad steps in new directions. One of the main reasons was the separation of the earlier poetry from the ideological dimension. Indeed, it is only in the 1980s, with the continuing war in Lebanon, that Hebrew poets—formerly remote from political issues—have begun to voice their political attitudes in poetry. This is not to say that their ideological tenets have issued in anything like propaganda verse. On the contrary, it has been a poetry of personal revelation of new landscapes.

. . . . .

In the last three decades of modern Hebrew poetry, the two major figures have been Yehuda Amichai and Natan Zach. Amichai has created a new rhythm, introducing a new mood born of his ironic outlook toward himself and his world. He expresses this as the clash between the way things seem and the way they are. By means of a figurative language, he enters into his private vision to escape the mundane, yet he escapes even the reader's expectations in regard to the figurative. In constantly remapping his life, he strips it of myth. There are repeated images, however, arranged in a cycle of changes that expand and extend verbal limits. His own existence is a source of wonderment to him; and in the unending dialogue he conducts with his existence, he weaves and unravels in turn the essences that constitute his "life."

I have referred to Amichai's attempt to strip away the element of myth; actually, his poetry aims at a metaphorization of reality. Existence itself is verbalized, but only by dint of his irony and a deep sense of the incongruous in existence. Since the late 1970s, his poetry has taken on a mellower tone: the speaker is beset by a sense of time, the prison of an aging body, the joint tyrannies of memory and death. Despite the muted tones and his singing in a minor key, he does not entirely surrender the volatile voice of his young persona. In *Amen* (1977) he tells us:

> Once a great love cut my life in two.
> The first part goes on twisting
> at some other place like a snake cut in two.
>
> The passing years have calmed me
> and brought healing to my heart and rest to my
>         eyes.
>
> And I'm like someone standing in
> the Judean desert, looking at a sign:
> "Sea Level."
> He cannot see the sea, but he knows.
>
> Thus I remember your face everywhere
> at your "face level."[2]

As indicated earlier, Amichai's ironic outlook is directed toward himself as much as toward his world, but it is also directed at his own way of reporting. What had been a voracious perception of God, world, love, Jerusalem, or his parents is now more focused, less omnivorous. He continues to map the stations in the life-journey of his speaker, who is in constant search of the right metaphor, yet he avoids the obscure, the elliptic, the opaque expression beyond communication. His poetry of the 1980s retains its process of dialogue. In *Great Tranquility* (1983) he states:

> People in the painfully bright hall
> Spoke about religion
> In the life of modern man
> And about God's place in it.
>
> People spoke in excited voices
> Like at airports.
> I left them:
> I opened an iron door over which was written
> "Emergency" and I entered into
> A great tranquility: questions and answers.[3]

As a philosopher philosophizes, so Amichai's speaker poeticizes as his poems unfold. The poet's voice of the last decade is more wry, subdued, less boisterous, as though the challenges raised by the earlier voice were left unanswered. As the poet ages, so does the speaker, and tones of resignation become more evident. Still, there is no major change to be detected. Occasionally he refers to twilight experiences, where the implicit would be expected, but inevitably he returns to the mundane, despite his efforts to escape it, and responds to it with a mature whimsicality.

Amichai is a poet of images, a noncerebral poet whose metaphors are vehicles for his states of mind. Time (the title of one of his collections) is an ever-present mystery, although it is measured by observed changes in the poet's life. In his late poetry he indulges in linguistic playfulness. There is a diminished need to tame his recalcitrant experience or to go beyond experience itself. Now the aged speaker sees the world as a series of incongruities. He will take up single events or sights to weave into a new verbal constellation, sometimes as part of a language game, at other times as part of a new verbalized experience. Through random, even marginal utterances, Amichai will try to reach a more significant statement—not by speculative means but rather through metaphor. His poetry is essentially visual, his eyes giving situations their significance or vacuity. The ironic tone emphasizes his role as a craftsman working with words, as he dons the garb of Everyman. The irony works toward demythification and a sense of the absurd, the Everyman garb toward sensitivity, alertness.

A typical Amichai poem will seem to dwindle toward its closure, after having opened with a charge. There is no point in looking for the objective correlative in his verse; the raw material is the poem itself, inviting the reader to partake of the poet's revelation of the process of *poesis* itself. His private album, his private cosmos, or his natural voice—all address the reader. The pictoriality of his poetry, the sense of immediate presence and the absence of the merely implicit states of being, all put one in mind of an epic quality. The subsidence of the earlier bravura can be attributed to the changing function of irony: from a rhetorical device of an innovative sort, to a weltanschauung pointing to the absurd in existence. In sum, his poetic work, now reaching its fourth decade, combines the personal voice with an epic dimension.

. . . . .

Zach shares with Amichai the fact of having been born in Germany; but whereas Amichai came to Palestine as a twelve-year-old, Zach arrived there at the age of five. In his mature work Zach undertook no less a project than the reshaping of Hebrew verse. He sought to diminish the importance of such founding poets as Alterman and Shlonsky, attacking them for their poetic excesses. He also devoted much time and effort to promoting poets whose work had been considered "marginal"—e.g., David Vogel (1891-1944) and Jacob Steinberg (1887-1947)—but who have lately been receiving new critical acclaim for their subtle personal voice. Like Amichai, Zach was deeply influenced by the work of Pound, Eliot, and Auden, and he therefore worked for a hard and undiffuse poetry without soft undulations. Strong emotions are restrained by irony, as in Amichai; and for somewhat the same reasons, Zach is interested in the poem per se, in its forms and deviations more than in its "subject matter." What he has sought to do, and has succeeded in doing, is to write a poem which is nonmimetic and anything but surface-emotive.

The differences between the two poets, however, is decisive: whereas Amichai is a highly metaphoric poet, combining the mundane and the fantastic in a richly visual world, Zach is inclined to limit his diction in a rather conscious way, using simple words, repetition, and understatement in an effort to arrive at a deep emotive level. Further, whereas Amichai, in his earlier work, had made use of biblical allusion, Zach deliberately avoids it. On the rare occasion when he does resort to such allusion, it is to a biblical echo that has been absorbed into spoken Hebrew, and thus it is to the spoken language that the poem refers.

What characterizes Zach as one of the most prominent and characteristically "modern" of modern Hebrew poets is the austerity of his language, the deceptively barren simplicity of his images—qualities that have marked his thirty years of poetic production. Moreover, he has scrupulously avoided using the collective "I" as the voice of his persona, and there is a sense of indeterminacy and hesitation throughout his writing. His self-restraint and understatement reflect a tremendous intensity, only slightly mitigated by his intellectualism and wit. One sometimes feels inclined to erase a statement of his as too bold, and there is none of the booming sonority of Shlonsky, nothing of the complex layers of Alterman.

In his attack, Zach saw Alterman as a magician tossing off words while hiding behind numerous masks, in a poetry refraining from any active rapport with the world of people and things and instead veiling itself under the foliage of figurative devices. As a result, Zach argued, Alterman's work lacked inner tension and movement. Zach not only insists on a contact with reality, but he also rejects excessive musicality and rhyme. (The fact is, however, that Alterman is still regarded as a central figure in modern Hebrew poetry, and his work has continued to draw the attention of readers and critics. In recent decades there have been more books devoted to Alterman's poetry than to the work of any other modern poet, living or dead.)

Zach's critical articles of the 1950s and early 1960s culminated in *Zeman Veritmus Etzel Bergson Ubashirah Hamodernit* (Time and Rhythm in Henri Bergson and Modern Poetry; 1966). Here he attempted to set up a new poetics of Hebrew verse and to assess the fundamental position of the poet in the making of poetry. The effect of Zach's poetics and verse on the young generation of poets has been immense. What characterizes the lyric work of Bialik, Alterman, Shlonsky, and Greenberg is the centrality of the speaker. Irony has now deemphasized that centrality, and in recent Hebrew poetry we see the speaker as neither a witness nor a commentator. The self is depicted as a process, without a mediator, and this is typical of the post-Zach period. As a "practitioner" of poetry, Zach avoids all reference to the acknowledged "giants," and unlike them, he limits his poetic lexicon. His poetic "self" does not seek self-expression, and what he aims for is understatement and depersonalization. As an example, the influence of Eliot is evident in *Against Parting* (1967).

How is it that
one star, alone,
dares. How does he dare;

for heaven's sake.
One star alone. I
would not dare. And I
am, as a matter
of fact, not alone.[4]

In his early poems Zach attempts to speak colloquially, to touch the reader through the language of his own time, avoiding all embellishment and metaphor (with rare exceptions). Where Amichai aims at a broadening of the linguistic framework, Zach aims at minimalism. This Spartan self-restraint is all the more startling against the background of the opulent allusiveness of the Hebrew language itself, with its millennia of stratified associations. Thus his words are neither a mirror nor a lamp; they are an entity *an sich*. As a modern writer, Zach knows that the attempt to arrest the eternal through the transitory no longer rings true as a poetic enterprise. In *Kol Hechalav Vehadvash* (All the Milk and Honey; 1964) three lines from "The Right Poem" read: "when the emotion dwindles, the right poem speaks. / Till then the emotions spoke, the other poem. / Now the time has come for the right poem to speak" (my translation). The word for "right" here has connotations of "correct" or "true."

Zach's latest collection of poems bears the title *Anti-Mechikon,* which translates as "Hard to Remember" (1984). Its various cycles reveal facets of Zach's autobiographical persona hitherto unknown. A return to Haifa evokes memories of a child who had come from Germany as well as the tragedy of German Jews in the 1930s and 1940s: "a thirteen-year-old German-speaking highbrow; the best way to get into trouble." In this collection Zach has introduced the personal narrative, something that had hardly been suggested in his prior work. His youthful memories as a refugee child coexist with sensitive poems about age, love, and the death of his mother, and there are poems as well about the war in Lebanon.

. . . . .

The new wave of contemporary Hebrew poetry is thus self-reflective, even solipsistic, stemming from the fact that the craftsman understands his tools by means of his products, so that the poem is both a process and a test: the poetic process itself becomes the primary subject of that process. In addition, the dialectic of the generations continues. I remarked earlier that Shlonsky attacked Bialik, and as Zach attacked Shlonsky's generation, so Meir Wieseltier has attacked Zach. To be sure, Wieseltier's attack is milder, an effort to show the proximity of rather than the gap between Zach and Alterman. Wieseltier's work is multifaceted and adds the element of violence in an attempt to penetrate his own thematic structure. In similar fashion, Yair Hurvitz attempts to break through the essence of substance, to create an anatomy of objects and thus escape from language. In an early poem Zach had written: "I to myself I sing. / I saw a leaf falling yesterday." Wieseltier sees this—the poet singing to himself—as coquettish, hackneyed, defeatist, an attempt to evade the world. Instead, Wieseltier, in his Hebrew collection titled "Take" (1973), urges the reader:

Take poems, and don't read
do violence to this book:
Spit on it, squash it
kick it, pinch it.

Throw this book into the sea
to see if it knows how to swim.[5]

The poet Yona Wallach, who died in 1985 at the age of forty-one, joined Wieseltier and Hurvitz as one of the new voices of the 1960s, breaking all taboos, linguistic and thematic, and relating to the word as nature, not invention. Her poetry touched on the erotic-confessional, on the one hand, and on the religious-elliptic on the other. The array of gifted young poets is startling in its variety: there is Asher Reich, who is daring in subject matter and highly metaphorical; there is Aharon Shabtai, who has attempted to shatter the boundary between mimesis and praxis.

I have chosen, however, to conclude this article by going back to an earlier generation, to discuss Avot Yeshurun, who was born in 1904, came to Palestine in 1925, and is still one of the most interesting figures on the poetic scene in Israel. He builds his poetry out of broken fragments. One of his collections is titled *The Syrian-African Rift* (1974; Eng. 1980), echoing the Hebrew name for the Great Rift Valley formed by plate tectonics and extending some three thousand miles from East Africa through the Red Sea, the Dead Sea, and the Jordan and Al Biqa valleys. The rift can therefore be seen as a human metaphor: its destructiveness opens fresh possibilities. In this light, Yeshurun's freedom with language is refreshing; he creates neologisms, alters existing words, uses Arabic and Yiddish words and Hebrew slang, and gleefully breaks the laws of syntax. In a prose piece he says:

> You ask how does one become Avot Yeshurun?
> The answer is through breakage. I broke my mother
> and my father. I broke the house for them. I broke
> their peaceful nights. I broke their holidays and
> I broke their sabbaths. I broke their own self-
> esteem. . . . I broke their language. I rejected
> their Yiddish; and their Holy Language I took
> for everyday.[6]

He is haunted by his breaking away from his home in Europe and the death of his family in the Holocaust. The broken language refers also to the broken state of man. The colloquial language is a reflection of the way people speak who were uprooted and were thrown into the Hebrew language (and the shock of using the Holy Language for everyday purposes). In his unfinished sentences, his broken verse, Yeshurun is indirectly rejecting earlier contemporaries such as Alterman and Shlonsky, who courted the language. However that may be, he, as poet, is compelled to shape his final product by means of the distortion of language and the abandonment of what the language once was.

Most of the key figures in the early and middle generations of Hebrew poets were (as I have said) not born in the Land of Israel, and this is perhaps the most significant single fact binding them together. Many were, like

Leah Goldberg, poets of two landscapes. Every one of these poets, even those who had had previous schooling in the Hebrew language, had to acquire Hebrew as a spoken tongue and to master it as spoken. This need to master the language can perhaps be seen as a compensation for not being native-born. Many of the major poets now in their forties or fifties have foreign accents—German, Polish, Russian—which makes their achievements in Hebrew poetry all the more impressive.

From the time Avot Yeshurun came to Palestine in 1925, at the age of twenty-one, he insisted on pronouncing words as they were commonly heard. In Hebrew the word for "Poland" is *Polin,* yet he will pronounce it "Poilin," as Yiddish-speaking Jews do, thus maintaining the ring of the spoken language which is being inexorably devoured by modern spoken Hebrew. With his planted "mistakes" and neologisms, he aims at expressing the ephemeral sound; and along with his use of Yiddish and Arabic, this signifies not only his breaking away from home but also the breakup of the Tel Aviv he had known and loved. He is not a master of the language in the sense that Shlonsky and Alterman were: his language is not musical, its syntax is often faulty, and he even misspells words (as an Arabic or Yiddish speaker might do in using Hebrew).

The unevenness of mode, tone, manner, matter is only multiplied in the new collections of poetry now appearing in Israel. Holocaust poetry, more and more poetry by women, poetry by young Arabs writing in Hebrew—all are interesting fields calling for separate discussion. Recent Hebrew verse is marked by its variety and vitality, a burgeoning field.

### NOTES

[1] Among the many *BA/WLT* essays on Israeli poetry and on individual Israeli poets who are mentioned in this article, the reader is referred especially to the entries by Gillon, Silberschlag, Lewis, Mazor, and Riggan in this issue's "Selected Bibliography of Articles on Near Eastern Literature." I would also point out the following four anthologies, the first three of which are bilingual editions: *The Modern Hebrew Poem Itself,* S. Burnshaw, T. Carmi, E. Spicehandler, eds., New York, Holt, Rinehart & Winston, 1965; *The Penguin Book of Hebrew Verse,* T. Carmi, ed., Harmondsworth, Penguin, 1981; *Modern Hebrew Poetry,* R. Finer Mintz, ed., Berkeley, University of California Press, 1966; *Modern Hebrew Poetry,* Iowa City, University of Iowa Press, 1980.

[2] Yehuda Amichai, *Amen,* New York, Harper & Row, 1977, p. 46. The translation is by Amichai himself.

[3] Yehuda Amichai, *Great Tranquility: Questions and Answers,* Glenda Abramson and Tudor Parfitt, trs., New York, Harper & Row, 1983, p. 90. Other available collections by the poet include: *Selected Poems,* London, Cape Goliard, 1968; *Poems,* Harper & Row, 1969; *Songs of Jerusalem and Myself,* Harper & Row, 1973; *Time,* Harper & Row, 1979; and *Love Poems,* Harper & Row, 1981.

[4] Natan Zach, *Against Parting,* John Silkin, tr., Newcastle upon Tyne, Northern House, 1967, p. 16. Also available in English is *The Static Element,* Peter Everwine and Shulamit Yasny-Starkman, trs., New York, Atheneum, 1982.

[5] Meir Wieseltier, *Kach* (Take), Tel Aviv, University Publishers, 1973. The translation is my own.

[6] Avot Yeshurun, *The Syrian-African Rift and Other Poems,* Harold Schimmel, tr., Philadelphia, Jewish Publication Society, 1980. This edition does not contain the passage cited, and the translation is my own.

### Ruth Whitman

SOURCE: "Motor Car, Bomb, God: Israeli Poetry in Translation," in *Massachusetts Review,* Vol. XXIII, No. 2, Summer, 1982, pp. 309-28.

[*In the following essay, Whitman discusses Israeli poetry in English translation.*]

Israeli poets live in a world of extremes, of constant military threat and political uncertainty, in a country where centuries of religious conflict have been concentrated in an area not much larger than Rhode Island, an area no bigger on the map than the paring of a fingernail. Throughout the history of Hebrew poetry, biblical Hebrew has been its chief foundation. In every period and place, during the past twenty-three hundred years, Hebrew poetry picked up local influences, but the language remained unified because, since the beginning of the Diaspora, Hebrew was not spoken. It was kept apart from ordinary life as a written language only. But since the end of the nineteenth century, with the resettlement of Jewish pioneers in Palestine, Hebrew has been revived as a spoken language.

This means that the Hebrew of the Old Testament must suddenly be stretched and reinvented to fit the circumstances of the contemporary world, that the language of twentieth-century Israeli poetry has been transformed into a demotic tongue. The poets of Israel must build a linguistic bridge between the orthodox imagery of their heritage and the secular passion of their present. Yehuda Amichai writes in his poem, "National Thoughts":

> To speak now, in this tired language
> torn from its sleep in the Bible—
> blinded it lurches from mouth to mouth—
> the language which described God and the
>     Miracle
> says:
> Motor car, bomb, God.

Many of these poets have come from the Diaspora—from Europe or America—to join the new state of Israel, created thirty-five years ago. Some of them witnessed its creation. All of them brought along at least one other language, and in addition were faced immediately with the task of writing in a new/old tongue that was malleable in the present, but resonant with the past. Jewish tradition has always regarded the word as a living entity: Yiddish poets have written love songs to their language. The nine Hebrew poets described here often seem to feel a possessiveness and tenderness about their tongue, a deep sense of its ontology as both newborn and ancient. In addition, they must make a constant attempt to reconcile their former life with their present one; their present with the unimaginable future.

Yehuda Amichai was the first Israeli poet to win notice among American poets and readers of poetry. His *Selected Poems,* published in 1968 by Harper and Row, was received with an enthusiasm that has steadily increased during the past fifteen years and has made it possible for him to make an annual trip to give readings in the United States—an enviable achievement for any foreign poet. Amichai's innovative handling of the Hebrew language, his use of words with biblical overtones for secular, even sexual, subjects, yet always having a tender piety, is apparent even in English translation. Tender is the right word for him. His early poems, astonishing and fresh, present a portrait of a man human, faulty, easy with himself in an apocalyptic world.

From the beginning Amichai has regarded himself—his pain and his loves—with a humor sometimes gentle and sometimes black. He is awry poet, always thinking of himself in the context of his biblical past, as in "King Saul and I":

> He is a dead king.
> I am a tired man.

Amichai writes too out of his more recent personal history—his transition from the Diaspora to Israel. Like most of the other poets considered here, he was first born into another language and another country—in his case, Wurzburg, Germany. He came to what was then Palestine at the age of fourteen, fought in the Second World War with the British Army, then later the War of Independence in Israel and subsequent wars. He tries to bring the two halves of his life together, his faraway childhood and his marred and fragile present:

> The town I was born in was destroyed by shells.
> The ship in which I sailed to the land of Israel was
>   drowned later in the war. . . .
>
> The bridge at Ismailia, which I crossed to and
>   from on
> the eve of my loves,
> has been torn to pieces. . . .
> The girl from my childhood was killed and my father
>   is dead.
>
> That's why you should never choose me
> to be a lover or a son, or a bridge-crosser
> or a citizen or a tenant.
> ("Patriotic Songs")

He often views the human being as a child, a metaphor for his own sense of vulnerability. It is also an aspect of his personality—he is affectionate, needy, childlike himself. He thinks of the soldier as a child:

> a soldier is filling bags with soft sand
> in which he once played. . . .
> ("Patriotic Songs")

and draws an image from his experience both as child and as father:

> But leave
> a little love burning, always
> as in a sleeping baby's room a little bulb,
> without it knowing what the light is
> and where it comes from. . . .
> ("Seven Laments for the Fallen in the War")

In *Amen* (1977), there is a slight loosening of the energy that charged the earlier poems. It may be partly the fault of the translator. Reading over the selections in the Penguin edition of 1971, I again find Amichai's brilliance and invention stunning. In this book, however, there is a relaxation of language that sometimes approaches the banal:

> Ruth, what is happiness? We should have
> talked about it, but we didn't.
> The efforts we make to look happy
> takes our strength, as from tired soil.
> ("Ruth, What Is Happiness?")

The flatness of plain conversational rhetoric can be disarming, even charming, but it always runs the risk of sounding like colorless prose. When it works it becomes the backdrop for those flashes of imagery that mark Amichai's best work. Here, in another poem, he suddenly flings an image like a lightning bolt and the old power, elemental and erotic, is back:

> Now I'm like a Trojan horse
> filled with terrible loves:
> Each night they break out and run amok
> and at dawn they come back
> into my dark belly.
> ("Love Song")

Ted Hughes, the translator, declares in his introduction to *Amen* that he has left the author's own translations generally rough and uncorrected, no doubt in an attempt to convey the quality of Amichai's "primitivism," which Hughes finds attractive. But Hughes would have done the poet a far better service to correct all the "intrusive oddities and errors of grammar and usage." Amichai's Hebrew is correct and it is misleading to hear a transposition like "fill up with them all the valleys around . . ." or a gaucherie like "I'm happy so" or "such a man you are" or "As even the most victorious army / Always leaves itself a retreat open." Amichai's primitivism does not lie in awkward or incorrect grammar. These are not "Yehuda Amichai's own English poems," as Hughes describes them. One longs for the beautiful translations of Amichai's first translator, Assia Gutmann, or for his later translators, Harold Schimmel, Stephen Mitchell, Ruth Nevo.

In Amichai's recent book, *Time* (1979), the problem of translation is further compounded. The book is raw Amichai. He has translated the poems himself, and Ted Hughes, after reading the English, suggested that Amichai publish without revision. Again, it is a disservice to Amichai to allow inversions, incorrect grammar and idiosyncratic usage to mar many beautiful poems. Amichai's lack of critical judgment about his own work has led him to include some poems that seem to be no more than loose prosaic jottings. Nevertheless, there are still enough superb poems here to justify his continuing reputation as the most popular Israeli poet in both Israel and America.

The poet's experience as lover, father, citizen, patriot, tired man, caught in the inexorable processes of decaying, aging, dying, is expressed most poignantly in such poems a "I passed a house where I once lived," "To my love, while combing her hair," "The diameter of the bomb was thirty centimeters," "A song, a psalm, on Independence Day," and "My son, in whose face there is already a sign."

The complete poem, "When my head got banged on the door, I screamed," demonstrates the simplicity, directness, and natural tenderness that have become the trademark of an Amichai poem:

> When my head got banged on the door, I
>     screamed,
> "My head, my head." And I screamed "Door,
>     door."
> And I did not scream, "Mother," and not "God. . . . "
>
> When you stroked my head I whispered,
> "My head, my head," and I whispered, "Your
>     hand, your
>  hand,"
> And I did not whisper "Mother," and not "God . . . "
>
> Whatever I scream and speak and whisper is
> to comfort myself: my head, my head.
> Door, door. Your hand, your hand.

Stephen Mitchell is the translator of the double volume published by Penguin in its series of Modern European Poets, *The Selected Poems of T. Carmi and Dan Pagis*. To juxtapose these two poets in one volume might suggest a stylistic community between them, as M. L. Rosenthal rightly notes in his introduction, but I can't think of two more different poets: Carmi, lyrical and metaphysical; Pagis, surrealistic and colloquial. There are times, however, when the two poets take on each other's qualities. Carmi's most recent poems (especially "Examination of Conscience Before Going to Sleep," which is dedicated to Pagis) have moved towards Pagis' contemporary idiomatic style; and Pagis, who writes out of his personal encounter with the Holocaust and his ironic view of man's span from the creation of the world to the twenty-first century, has written a metaphysical sequence with a purity reminiscent of Carmi, called "Twelve Faces of the Emerald."

T. Carmi was born in New York and studied at Yeshiva University and Columbia before emigrating to Palestine in 1947. There is little in Carmi's early poems to suggest that the young poet from the Bronx who made bombs in the 1948 War of Independence wrote out of a sense of political urgency. He is primarily a poet of erotic experience, of relationships with lover, wife, child, friend, and his early poems emerge out of an abstract metaphysical world. This is not to say that they are not beautifully made. His language is spare, his imagery brightly visual.

The poems selected from his last book, *Somebody Like You* (1971) have a new immediacy and irony that relates to his earlier work like a chemical acting on a developing photograph: his early shadowy world slowly takes on the outlines of the real world of Jerusalem. He is now a poet with a place and a history.

There is a haunting new poem about seeing a man fall out of a tree as the poet passes by in a train:

> All this I saw
> from the window of a train,
> after a green meadow
> and before a team of horses.
> I note only the fact
> of his falling.
> I didn't hear
> the scream.
>
> ("Landscapes")

Brought up reading and writing Hebrew, Carmi thinks continually about the relation between language and reality. This thinking is different from Amichai's, who has come more recently to Hebrew. But they both share in common with other Hebrew poets a feeling for the Word, for language, regarding it as a dynamic entity in itself, almost a personification with a soul. It is an attitude that is part of the Jewish tradition. It occurs in ancient Talmudic writing, in the Kabbala, in Yiddish poetry. Carmi writes:

> First I'll sing. Afterwards, perhaps I'll talk.
> I'll return to the words I said
>
> like a man rehearsing his face at dawn.
>
> ("Condition")

In a poem about the Mahane Jehuda explosion in 1969, when a terrorist bomb went off in the Jewish marketplace, he writes:

> The mine is a name.
> The raid is a door.
> The trap is a part.
> There is no thing
> that does not compel its opposite.
>
> A grammar of fears.
> The rules—extremely sudden,
> and it's hard to talk.
>
> ("A View of Jerusalem")

Carmi was for a time the editor of the prestigious journal *Ariel,* and it is interesting to see how he combines the professional language of his one-time trade with his traditional sense of language as metaphor:

We discussed the margins and the typeface.
I too like precision,
and many dates are written in my notebook.
On other pages are:
a shorthand account of night-birds,
and terrifying voices at noon;
syllables of panic,
and silences, in a first draft.

                   ("Memorial Day, 1969")

Carmi is a poet who has moved from the abstract and metaphysical to a precise contemporary imagery. He is always intense, always lyrical, achieving a purity of form by working with an austere and exacting technique. He has solved the duality of language—the marriage of old and new Hebrew—with a seamless lyric mastery.

Carmi's most recent achievement is the publication of *The Penguin Book of Hebrew Verse,* which he has edited and translated into English. It includes a range of selections from "The Song of Deborah" in 3000 B.C. to poems by Dalia Ravikovitch, born in Israel in 1936. It spans poetry written in Palestine (which remained the center of Hebrew poetry until the eleventh century) and in the Diaspora—in Spain, Italy, Africa, Germany, Greece, Holland, France—from the ninth century until the present. Out of such a huge body of diverse and recently discovered texts, it requires great courage and superlative poetic taste and judgment to make a comprehensive and comprehensible anthology. Carmi has done this.

His translations are in literal prose, the English side by side with the Hebrew, a valuable aid for those who may feel moved to master the Hebrew or to make more finished verse translations. What is surprising is how poetic his renditions are, even though they are written in prose paragraphs. It is a reflection of the elegance and sensitivity of Carmi's own poetic language.

Despite the monumental scope of Carmi's undertaking, he has been careful to maintain a consistently high quality in his selections. If I have any complaint, it is that in his contemporary section, which of necessity must be short in proportion to the centuries represented, he has omitted his own poetry. Even among a most limited group of Israeli poets, Carmi ranks as a poet of major stature. The omission of his own work in his anthology—unlike the practice of countless contemporary anthologists—is a measure of Carmi's modesty as a poet and strength as an editor.

Some critics and historians believe that the best literary comment on the Jewish Holocaust is silence. A gathering volume of prose and poetry strives to grapple with the event, and Dan Pagis is a living rebuttal of the view that silence is the most appropriate response to it.

Born in Bukovina, he was in a concentration camp for several years during the Second World War. He emigrated to Palestine in 1946, learned Hebrew, and received a Ph.D. from Hebrew University, where he is now a professor of Medieval Hebrew Literature. Because he has entirely confronted the implications of his own personal history, as well as the homicidal history of mankind, he is able to write:

Where to begin?
I don't even know how to ask.
Too many tongues are mixed in my mouth. But
at the crossing of these winds,
very diligent, I immerse myself
in the laws of heavenly grammar: I am learning
the declensions and ascension of
silence.

                   ("Footprints")

Out of a remarkable spiritual strength, this shy humble man prepares himself to speak about the unspeakable. In "Encounters" he says:

You're ready for the encounter, rise and break
    open
        the door
and climb down the cellar stairs and introduce
    yourself
        to the wall.

It is worth the search, and the torment of the search, to be able to create a testimony as succinct and chilling as this tiny "Written in Pencil in the Sealed Railway Car":

here in this carload
i am eve
with abel my son
if you see my other son
cain son of man
tell him i

In this minimal poem, primitive as a wall painting, we see the whole Jewish people, in fact all the sufferers and victims of the civilized world, stifling in the sealed railway car on its way to Auschwitz, the whole of mankind personified in grieving mother Eve. Not silence, but the body of traditional literature, beginning with Genesis, speaks for Pagis. Yet he is a totally contemporary poet, in many ways more modern than any other Israeli poet in his use of imagery from the scientific world and from the world of invention and space exploration. He speaks of a post-nuclear holocaust world in "A Lesson in Observation":

Pay close attention: the world that appears now
at zero-point-zero-one degrees
was, as far as is known,
the only one
that burst out of the silence. . . .

         . . . outside there were
clouds, screams, air-to-air missiles,
fire in the fields, memory.
Far beneath these, there were houses, children.
    What else?

In "Spaceship" he imagines he is one of the last beings left on earth:

Now to take off.
There is not time left.

I am preparing myself
to hover over the face of the non-abyss
into my body and onwards.

Here are some excerpts from his long poem, "The Brain":

> . . . the brain is
> the organ of time. A dog from which the cerebrum
>     has
> been removed is still able to live for a time, but only
> in the present. All the doggish past vanishes
>     instantly,
> and the doggish future already does not exist . . .
> But brain has learned to defend himself
> from such attacks.
> He gives a sign: Let there be darkness!
> And at once
> the fingers shut the encyclopedia.

Whether Pagis writes of the world during the Jewish Holocaust or of the world after the final nuclear holocaust, his poems are apocalyptic, terrifying. His is the duality not only of the Diaspora and Israel, of the old Hebrew and the new, but of the Holocaust and post-Holocaust experience.

Abba Kovner is also a survivor of the Holocaust. During the Second World War he was one of the commanders of the Vilna Ghetto uprising, and after it fell, he was leader of a company of partisans in the Vilna forests. But while Pagis' language is colloquial, Kovner's is transcendent. He conveys his terror and pain by indirection, allegory, mystery.

His long poem, "My Little Sister," takes place in a dreamlike world. She is both his real little sister, who perished young, and the "little sister with no breasts" from The Song of Songs. The little sister of the poem is hidden in a convent among Christian nuns:

> They came as far as a wall.
> On the seventh night into the dawn
> heard from the wall the drowning in the snow
> not seeing the marchers' faces
> in the white wind. . . .
>
> My sister's eyes search the wall of the convent
> for a scarlet thread. A candle trembles
> in the nuns' hands.
> Nine holy Sisters look at my sister
> seeing—ashes that speak. . . .
>
> In seventy-seven funerals we circled the wall
> and the wall stood.
> From the promised land I called you,
> I looked for you
> among heaps of small shoes. . . .

The wall has now become the Wall of Jerusalem. We have moved from the Holocaust of the Diaspora to the promised land of Israel.

> . . . In the unrepenting street of the city
> the shorn head of my sister
> breaks out of a wall.

The poem is full of multiple symbols: the little sister, who is also a personification of the Jewish people; the wall which is the wall of the convent, the wall of imprisonment, and the Wall of Jerusalem. The shorn head is the head of the bride that is shaved for her wedding—in this case, a wedding with death—and also the shorn heads of the women in the concentration camps.

Kovner's other major poem, "A Canopy in the Desert," is also full of multiple reverberations and allusions. The canopy is a bridal canopy, a *chupa,* and the poet is journeying towards his bride, the desert; but the marriage never takes place.

> Proud. My desert is
> too proud to answer.

Kovner draws on traditional liturgy and *piyyutim* (hymns of praise), but is free and inventive in his playing with form, the use of truncated phrases and imagery bordering on surrealism:

> . . . Almost
> like Hebrew grammar like
> guttural letters and the rule
> when the throat is full of hard words
> that are exceptions to the rule. But how to
>     pronounce it
> so it will be clear
> with the right intonation in an open vowel
> not in a strange accent.
>                                              ("Ninth Gate: 52")

He too is relying on the Jewish tradition of the Word, the sense of its sacredness and power. He is fortunate in having Shirley Kaufman as his translator. A distinguished poet herself, she has worked hard to match the form and sound of his words, even at their most original and untranslatable. Here is an excellent example of her achievement:

> There is a hive for bees for snakes a season
> a way for eagles a map for the sea and none
> for me   for dreams recurring   no meaning no
> reason   only the curse       and
> whoever yearns to read will come   I look
> above me   a sea of silence     I speak to
> myself   I speak and speak       I'll return
> I'll return here   alive
>                                              ("Twelfth Gate: 96")

In translating Amir Gilboa, however, Shirley Kaufman's problem is quite different, as the describes it: "It is almost impossible to render into English his fragmented thought, unusual word relationships, the ways in which a line works backward and forward at the same time . . . the enjambment, the silences, the leaps."

Born in Poland in 1917, Gilboa emigrated to Eretz Israel in 1937. This book of selections in English represents his work from 1946 to 1974. Although he came from the Diaspora and lost his family in the Holocaust, Gilboa has an underlying current of joy, stronger in his earlier work, but nevertheless present, even when he writes out of sadness, a sense of the loss of innocence, of the memories of childhood and of man before the Holocaust. He says, "In Very Ancient Days":

> In very ancient days
> everything was sun

and the title of these selected poems, *The Light of Lost Suns,* comes from this passage:

> And all this? And from here I'll see
> distant craters beyond me where
> suns were shattered distant craters
> oiled by the light of lost suns
> and all this and nothing else.
>
>                 ("And All This")

Notice the lack of punctuation in this passage. It is part of a staccato style, betokening disorientation, nervous energy, grief. There is also a use of childhood experience and deceptively innocent statements redolent of Theodore Roethke, especially in Gilboa's famous poem, "Isaac," about the sacrifice of Isaac, where the victim turns out to be Abraham himself:

> Early in the morning the sun took a walk in the
>      woods
> with me and my father
> my right hand in his left
>
> Father father come quick and save Isaac
> so no one will be missing at lunchtime.
>
> It's I who am butchered, my son,
> my blood's already on the leaves.
> And father's voice was choked.
> And his face pale . . .
>
> And my right hand was drained of blood.

The language of the poem casts a backward look at the traditional biblical account and at the same time a forward look at the imagery of the Holocaust.

Nevertheless, Gilboa demonstrates an inclination towards joy that few other Israeli poets evince. Even in his more recent metaphysical lamentations there is a tendency to rejoice:

> The whole land is mine asleep and awake I see
> one long dream electric spirits making
> flocks of swallows hover in branches of the tree
>      weaving the window
> and my bones and flesh in a dizzy wind over a
>     huge land
> all mine
>
>               ("The Whole Land Is Mine")

Even in his fear of nihilism—and to Gilboa, the opposite of joy is nothingness—still, he has hope, as expressed in the last poem in this volume, that he will

> go toward the source of the sunrise
> when it burns again, scarlet. . . .
>
>             ("He'll Take You with Him")

I consider Robert Friend an Israeli poet, although he grew up in the United States, moved to Israel after the War of Independence, and writes in English. Well known for his excellent work as an editor and translator, his own poetry has been undeservedly neglected. An urbane, graceful poet, in the tradition of Auden, he often conceals his seriousness beneath a technique so artful that one tends to overlook its profundity. He is a modern master of the epigram. His poem "The Practice of Absence," the title poem of an earlier book and now collected in his *Selected Poems* (1975), is a love poem based on C. S. Lewis's remark, "If we cannot 'practice the presence of God,' it is something to practice the absence of God."

> Therefore do I faithfully
> practice Your absence
>
> listening for the silence
> in the water's voices
>
> seeking a face
> in the teeming mirror
>
> reaching to touch
> in the veined body
>
> of woman or pebble
> the body of the dark.

Friend's duality of linguistic allegiance makes his sensitivity to language, the problems of semantics and ontology, particularly acute. In "The Test" he writes:

> But was the language alive?
> Bialik wished he knew,
> thoughtfully slapped a child.
> Was the pain Hebrew?

He grapples with another aspect of the problem in his poem "Identity":

> . . . I have come to read my name
> where even the birds are Jewish
> and the cats yowl
> in the holy language,
>
> whose mystery I master,
> its stubborn consonants
> and its warm vowels,
> but not that mystery
>
> I shroud in English.
> Robert, I say,
> pronouncing who I am
> in the cold syllables
>
> of the tongue I love.

Friend has lived in Jerusalem for a quarter of a century. There could hardly be a better or more moving statement of the dual allegiance to two languages.

Robert Friend's excellence as a poet is reflected in his translations of the *Selected Poems* of Leah Goldberg. The poems were published after her death of cancer in 1971.

Goldberg, like Friend, is a classic poet who writes lyrics of love, of separation, of exile. Born in the Diaspora, she tries, in her early poem, "In the Jerusalem Hills," to reconcile the duality of her life:

> A stone among stones, I do not know
> the ancientness of my life
> or who will yet come
> and with a kick
> send me rolling down the slope. . . .

and later:

> All the things
> outside love
> come to me now:
> this landscape with its old man's understanding
> begging to live
> one more year, one more year,
> one generation more,
> one more eternity.

Friend's translations are careful and technically accurate, allowing the delicacy of Goldberg's voice to come through to us. Friend has arranged the sequence of poems sensitively, leading us into the poet's life both before and after her knowledge of her own impending death. Her poems become stronger, more intense, more laconic as the end draws closer:

> The day has turned away—
> a day like no other.
> The day has turned its back on me.
> My night's a candle for the dead.
> Now the poems will come
> mercilessly.
>
> ("At a Small Station")

And finally, a hair-raising simplicity:

> I can almost forget, but always each day sends
> one hour of all its hours to murder me.
> Slit throat, slit throat, and a hen screeching.
> And now it falls. And silence again descends.
> All, all is destined. Truth and faith.
> Wake me. I have not been sleeping.
>
> ("Nightmare")

Dalia Ravikovitch stands apart from this group of poets in several respects. She is a Sabra. She was born in Ramat Gan, educated in a kibbutz, and studied at Hebrew University. She therefore writes from a single experience, the experience of an Israeli who comes out of one locality and one language. She is, however, intensely aware of the duality of the Hebrew language itself—its biblical sources and it contemporary rebirth.

She has been called the Israeli Sylvia Plath, principally because she writes in a state of extreme personal vulnerability. Listening to her read in a bookshop in Jerusalem several years ago, I could sense her almost unbearable aura of psychic fragility. At the same time she possesses a verbal power that transcends the pain: she has an exotic imagination that allows her to find refuge in fantasy and surreal imagery. Writing out of frustration and a sense of abandonment, she depends on the reverberations of a simple and economic vocabulary to carry the weight of the poem.

Her lament for her father, who was killed in a road accident ("And even though I was his eldest daughter / He cannot tell me one word of love") seems to be the archetype for a series of abandonments:

> Again I was like one of those little girls
> who sail in one night around the whole world
> and sail to the land of Cathay
> and Madagascar,
>
> and who smash plates and saucers
> from so much love,
> so much love,
> so much love.
>
> ("Time Caught in a Net")

Her poem "The Horns of Hittin" and her interest in reliving a historical moment is reminiscent of Cavafy; like him she casts herself in the role of loser, together with all the losers of the past. But her role of victim goes beyond the merely erotic; it is the world, really, that deceives her:

> I am not in Hong Kong
> and Hong Kong is not in the world.
> Where Hong Kong used to be
> there's a reddish stain
> half in the water and half in the sky.
>
> ("How Hong Kong Was Destroyed")

Her "dress of fire" is the burning dress that Medea gave to Jason's new wife:

> But the dress, she said, the dress is on fire.
> What are you saying, I shouted,
> what are you saying?
> I'm not wearing a dress at all,
> what's burning is me.
>
> ("A Dress of Fire")

This is the title poem ("A Dress of Fire") from the volume reprinted and reedited from the earlier collection published in 1976 by the Menard Press in London. The translations have been improved and fifteen new poems have been added. They tend to reinforce Ravikovitch's constant use of biblical allusion, although *allusion* is too academic a word to describe what for her is inherent in the flesh and bones of her language. In "Deep Calleth Unto Deep" she says:

> Alone, in somebody's house,
> I lifted my eyes to the hills
> to see if help would come. . . .
>
> And my longings drenched me
> and sawed in my head like a cricket
> and swarmed like wasps inside me
> I was that lost.

The comparison with Sylvia Plath is apt, not only in Ravikovitch's sense of being a constant victim, but in her ability to transform her life into myth.

Like Robert Friend, Dennis Silk is an Israeli poet who writes in English. And like many other Israelis, he has a dual allegiance, a dual background. Born in London, in 1928, he speaks of his birthplace in deprecating terms. He feels like an alien in the land of his birth. Traveling across the channel on a visit home, he writes:

> I lean over the rail
> and read with persistence
> the map, mother of distance.
>
> ("Laissez-Passer")

He describes his coming to Israel:

> I knew it was my country I felt so various,
> felt I was geography.
> The mines said
> you too, you too, are a crack of a man.
>
> ("Watch Out!")

> I've phantasmal army boots
> and a khaki Bible
> and a heart of Hebrew.
>
> ("Basic Training")

and his effort to link the two identities:

> My voice here,
> hoarseness assuaged,
> enlaces
> London and here.
>
> ("Ein Karem")

His earlier book, *Retrievals,* a collection of passages in prose and poetry about Jerusalem from ancient and modern sources, likely and unlikely, is the most stimulating and eccentric anthology I have had the pleasure to read. The title of his new book of poetry, *The Punished Land,* refers of course to the biblical Promised Land.

He has a wide variety of styles. He can be epigrammatic, surrealistic (as in his "Blue" poems), lyric, prosaic. As a writer of puppet plays, he includes some songs for plays, including "Masowka, a Japanese doll, travels to the Death Camps":

> All the mothers are in the carriage.
> It is so stuffy and they ask,
> When will we reach the railhead?
> At each wayside halt they ask,
> Why don't you sing, Masowka?

The last section of the book, "Guide to Jerusalem (Second Edition)" includes prose poems, epigrams, aphorisms, lyrics. He perceives Jerusalem as the most ineffable and magical of places:

### SCALE MODEL

> I observe a model of the Second Temple
> expounded by an old religious woman.
> She walks among the ample measurements,
> Jerusalem big as a box.

> It is a toy lying in a box.
> Now it is limp as a gollywog
> but could lash out like a jack-in-the-box.

Silk is essentially a poet of the absurd. He uses many devices: rhyme, gnomic sayings, surrealism, prose, fragments, parts of plays, songs, to describe his sights and insights, to portray the duality of his life in and out of the Punished Land.

Historical continuity, political emergency, and linguistic duality—these three realities work in both Sabra and immigrant to produce a poetry of crisis and eloquence. In addition to the poets described here (and these are by no means all the major writers), Zerubavel Gilead, Avner Treinen, Tuvia Ruebner, Meir Wieseltier, and Natan Zach, among others, are poets worthy of international attention.

The most complete anthologies of contemporary Israeli poetry in English are the Israeli issue of *Modern Poetry in Translation,* published in 1974, edited by Robert Friend; and *Fourteen Israeli Poets,* edited by Dennis Silk and published in 1976. Silk's anthology ought to be reprinted in paperback in the United States. An anthology of both prose and poetry is the Triquarterly issue of *Contemporary Israeli Literature* (Jewish Publication Society), with the poetry edited by Robert Friend. In 1982 The Jewish Publication Society brought out a bilingual edition of selected poems by Dan Pagis, one in a projected series of bilingual volumes of the work of major Israeli poets.

WORKS CITED

The books discussed in this essay are:

Yehuda Amichai, *Amen* (tr. by the author and Ted Hughes), Harper & Row, 1977; *Time* (tr. by the author), Harper & Row, 1979.

T. Carmi, *The Penguin Book of Hebrew Verse* (edited and translated, with an introduction by T. Carmi), Viking, Penguin, 1981.

T. Carmi and Dan Pagis, *Selected Poems* (tr. by Stephen Mitchell), Penguin, 1976.

Robert Friend, *Selected Poems* (The Seahorse Press, 1975).

Amir Gilboa, *The Light of Lost Suns* (tr. by Shirley Kaufman), Persea, 1979.

Leah Goldberg, *Selected Poems* (tr. by Robert Friend), Menard Press, 1976.

Abba Kovner, *A Canopy in the Desert* (tr. by Shirley Kaufman), University of Pittsburgh Press, 1973.

Dalia Ravikovitch, *A Dress of Fire* (tr. by Chana Bloch), Sheep Meadow Press, 1978.

Dennis Silk, *The Punished Land,* Penguin, 1980.

**James E. Young**

SOURCE: "Anti-War Poetry in Israel," in *Partisan Review,* Vol. 54, No. 4, Fall, 1987, pp. 594-602.

[*In the following essay, Young analyzes the place of the Holocaust in modern Israeli anti-war poetry.*]

Of the centuries of historical archetypes for suffering accumulated in Hebrew, those generated during the period of the Holocaust have begun to overwhelm all others. Even the names for this era in Hebrew and Yiddish, *Sho'ah* and *Churbn,* which previously designated other catastrophes, are in themselves now reinformed by the last and greatest disaster. Due partly to the sheer enormity of events, partly to the great proportion of Holocaust survivors in Israel (nearly half the population in 1948), and partly to the central place of the Holocaust in Zionist ideology, images and figures from the *Sho'ah* have all but displaced their historical precedents. Not only has the *Sho'ah* begun to represent retroactively all pre-Holocaust catastrophes—lending them a significance they would not otherwise have had—but it has also become the standard in Jewish literature by which all kinds of post-Holocaust calamities, Jewish or not, are now measured. Thus, whether Israeli writers turn around to represent other victims' suffering or their own, their remembrance of past suffering necessarily informs both their language and figures. In the reflections on Arab-Israeli wars by soldiers and in recent poems and plays by Tzvi Atzmon, Efraim Sidon, Dalia Ravikovitch, Natan Zach, Alex Lee, and Hanoch Levine, among others, it is rarely a matter of the soldier-poets finding concrete historical correspondences between their Arab enemies and the Nazis, or between Palestinians and Jews. Rather, these Israeli writers draw automatically from their own lexicon of suffering to represent the present.

In reflections of writers and soldiers at Kibbutz Ein Hahoresh after the Six Day War in 1967, Israelis explored the extremely complicated relationship between collective Holocaust memory, their reasons for fighting in the War, and their understanding of the enemy. Twenty-two years after World War II, their proud Zionist education notwithstanding, Israeli soldiers came inevitably to see themselves as little more than another generation of Jews on the brink of a second great massacre—and responded in battle as if the life of an entire people depended on every firefight. As Muki Tzur describes waiting for the beginning of this war, in fact, it grows clear that his inherited memory of the Holocaust constituted his primary reason for fighting, the impetus driving him and his comrades—all now identifying figuratively with the generation of survivors preceding them:

> We tend to forget those days before the war, and perhaps rightly so—yet those were the days in which we came closest to that Jewish fate from which we have run like haunted beings all these years. Suddenly everyone was talking about Munich, about the holocaust, about the Jewish people being left to its own fate.[1]

Questioned later by a slightly incredulous Abba Kovner, who led the Vilna partisans during the Holocaust and came to Israel with the Zionist belief that by definition, Israel made the possibility of another Holocaust "unthinkable," another soldier revealed that not only was it thinkable, but it was in fact the *governing* thought underlying his very *raison d'être* as a soldier:

> It's true that people believed that we would be exterminated if we lost the war. They were afraid. We got this idea—or inherited it—from the concentration camps. It's a concrete idea for anyone who has grown up in Israel, even if he personally didn't experience Hitler's persecution, but only heard or read about it.
>
> . . . Did you really get the feeling that extermination could happen here? [asks Kovner].
>
> . . . Yes, certainly. I think it's an idea that everyone in Israel lived with.

This is the great irony of the Israelis' grasp of their predicament. On the one hand, only a people fighting another Holocaust will survive with Israel's tenacity. On the other hand, the *sabra* has been educated to believe that Israel is the only safe haven for Jews in the world, the only guarantee against another Jewish Holocaust, and that the "holocausts" happen only in the Diaspora. Thus, the soldier is compelled to fight by the memory of what happened in the Diaspora, precisely and paradoxically because it could also happen in Israel. But this is not the only paradox. Of more serious consequence is that expressed by Muki Tzur at the end of his opening meditation:

> We know the meaning of genocide, both those of us who saw the holocaust and those who were born later. Perhaps this is why the world will never understand us, will never understand our courage, or comprehend the doubts and the qualms of conscience we knew during and after the war. Those who survived the holocaust, those who see pictures of a father and a mother, who hear the cries that disturb the dreams of those close to them, those who have listened to stories—know that no other people carries with it such haunting visions. *And it is these visions which compel us to fight and yet make us ashamed of our fighting. . . .* [my emphasis] . . . We carry in our hearts an oath which binds us never to return to the Europe of the holocaust; but at the same time we do not wish to lose that Jewish sense of identity with the victims.

This movement between past and present persecution, between the compulsion to fight and the shame of fighting, exemplifies Israel's own ambivalent need to remember the Holocaust and to forget it: it is simultaneously the reason for the Jews' life in Israel—for the state itself—and that which incites empathy in them for their new, defeated enemies. The consequences of these figures can only be speculated upon: at what point does this memory, and the subsequent empathy it generates for a defeated enemy weaken the resolve to fight further, and at what point does it make Israel stronger? Always struggling with this dilemma, Israel found in 1982 a renewed tension in it, represented now by her soldier-poets in their anti-war poetry.

Thus, when Prime Minister Menachem Begin responded to a reporter's questions about Israel's bombing of Beirut, he reflexively asked, "And if Hitler himself was hiding in a building with twenty innocent citizens, you still wouldn't bomb the building?" The Prime Minister was immediately challenged by Holocaust historians Yehuda Bauer and Ze'ev Mankowitz and by novelist Amos Oz, among others, who answered, "No, Mr. Prime Minister, your example is not an equivalent. . . . "[2] In fact, one of the distinguishing characteristics of the anti-war poetry flowing from Lebanon during and after the war was precisely this repudiation of Holocaust imagery as justification for the war, even as the poets simultaneously embraced such imagery as the primary means for representing victims of this war—especially the children.

During this protracted war and even after the Israeli withdrawal from Lebanon, poetry and essays, handbills and posters thus appeared throughout Israel responding to the war with both explicit and oblique references to the Holocaust. Two collections, in particular, *Border Crossing: Poems from the Lebanon War* and *Fighting and Killing without End: Political Poetry in the Lebanon War,*[3] illustrate the sheer impossibility of representing or reading about contemporary destruction and suffering without recourse to both the most traditional figures in the liturgy as well as to those more recently acquired during the Holocaust. But as dominant as the Holocaust had been before 1982 as an image of survival, it was now handled ironically in reference to the Israelis' situation in Lebanon. For the first time, Jewish suffering was not the principal object of Israel's war poetry. Instead of recalling traditional Jewish archetypes to represent the deaths of Israeli soldiers or the condition of bereaved families at home, Israel's poets used such imagery more often than not to depict the death and suffering of others, especially that of Arab children. The Holocaust was now being used not as an image for Jewish suffering, but as an anti-trope for it.

In a poem that was distributed widely during the war, Efraim Sidon thus conjures remembrance of the Holocaust explicitly to discard it as justification for the war in Lebanon. He begins with a mock pronouncement of guilt on the heads of the children for their own fate:

> I accuse the children in Sidon and Tyre
> Whose numbers are still uncounted
> Three-year olds, seven-year olds, and others of all
>     ages,
> Of the crime of residing in the vicinity of
>     terrorists.
> If you hadn't lived near them, children,
> You could have been students today.
> Now you will be punished.
>
> (from *Fighting and Killing*)

He then continues by accusing the women and mothers who lived near the terrorists, as well as the houses that sheltered terrorists, and ends by blaming everyone in Lebanon for the Holocaust itself, for which all there will be punished:

> I accuse the residents of Lebanon—all of them.
> For the Nazis' mistreatment of us in the World War.
> Because in every generation, one must see himself
> As if he were destroying Hitler
> Always, always
> And that is what Begin is doing.
>
> I accuse you all!
> Naturally.
> Because I am always, always the victim.

By literalizing the figure of the Holocaust here, stretching the linkage to the Holocaust as argument for the war to its breaking point, the poet seeks to invalidate this figure as a basis for military action.

Just before their afterword to *Fighting and Killing without End,* the editors have reproduced a poster in which Chaim Nachman Bialik's "Upon the Slaughter" is printed in Arabic and Hebrew, side by side, overlaid on an Israeli map of Beirut. In this graphic way, the poster forces the reader quite literally to read the map of Sabra and Shatila between and through the lines of Bialik, the national poet. It also literally re-figures Jewish experience in Arabic, with its own pool of references, allusions, and tropes—even as it incorporates into Bialik's lines the suffering of Palestinians. For once "Upon the Slaughter" is used to represent another pain (as it was by writers in the Vilna and Warsaw ghettos), it not only organizes the pain of others, but also absorbs—and thereby remembers—it, as well.

As the greatest test for Abraham's faith had been his aborted sacrifice of Isaac, the least bearable kind of suffering in Jewish tradition seems always to have been that of children. Almost every figurative allusion to the Holocaust in recent Israeli anti-war poetry begins with an image of suffering children. At some level, it seems to have been just this unprecedented prospect of having both to fight children and find them massacred in Sabra and Shatilla that broke Israel's resolve in this war and turned so many soldiers against it. For we find once again that even as the memory of Jewish children murdered in the Holocaust compelled Israelis to fight, it seems also to have paralyzed them as soldiers sympathetic to suffering children.

Thus, Tzvi Atzmon recites one Jewish calamity after another in his poem "Yizkor" before ending the litany with slaughtered Arab children. Although the *Yizkor* blessing is recited on neither of the ritual days of remembrance (*Yom Hasho'ah* and *Tisha Be'av*) recalling national catastrophes, it has come through custom to be associated with the dead of the Holocaust, primarily as an engraved icon on Holocaust memorials and monuments. *Yizkor* ([God] will remember) and *Zachor* (Remember!)

have both become liturgical words for remembering not just the dead, but by extension the era and circumstances in which loved ones have died. In his poetic transfiguration of the *Yizkor* blessing, Tzvi Atzmon expands this latter sense to include not the individual names of deceased loved ones (as would be the tradition), but the larger, collective death of a people—and then it's not just to remember the dead, or even that they have died, but specifically how they died.

> In Eretz Israel arose the Jewish people
> Who were dispersed . . .
> Pursued and tortured and sold into slavery, and
>    expelled from France, Portugal, from England . . .
> Raped, beaten, sacrificed . . . , drowned . . .
> Murdered in broad daylight, in the crusades, in the
>    black
> plague, in the revolutions of the cossacks, and in
>    the darkness of the inquisition.
> Kidnapped, incarcerated, massacred, stoned
> And defiled in pogroms, and cursed for murdering
>    God
> And for drinking children's blood.

And then, it is the death of children—the point of departure for the other poets—that stops the poet's voice, which makes him recall here again Bialik's lines, "Vengeance for the spilt blood of a child, / the devil has not yet compiled." He catches himself, stutters and repeats:

> And the revenge upon every small child will cry out.
> And suddenly
> He wakes up in the morning, sees
> He wakes up in the morning, sees
> Children who were shot when the sun rose
> And real blood, it's not just a libel.
> Arab children, without pity.

The murdered children simultaneously oppress the poet and inspire him to remember them in the *Yizkor* prayer. That they are killed by Christians may, in fact, only exacerbate the figure's memory of traditional anti-Jewish persecution. But this is real blood, not a blood libel as it had been traditionally and as Begin had described the accusations against Israel, and these were real Arab babies now slaughtered.

Of the many references to children, the most haunting and explicit come in the poems of Dalia Ravikovitch. Although Ravikovitch does not explicitly refer to the Holocaust, it remains difficult to read three of her poems, in particular, without the associations created for us by the Holocaust. In "Exit from Beirut," the speaker commands the refugees to:

> Take the rucksacks
> And the household bric-a-brac
> And the books of the Koran . . .
> And the children scurrying like chickens in the
>    village.

At which point, she interjects:

> How many children do you have?
> How many children did you have?
> It's hard to watch over kids in a situation like
>    this. . . .
> Put into sacks whatever isn't fragile,
> Clothes and blankets and bedding
> And something as a souvenir
> Perhaps a shiny artillery shell
> Or any utensil that comes in handy
> And the rheumy-eyed babies
> And the R.P.G. kids.

And then in a language that is both forever corrupted by its application to the Jews in Nazi Germany and laden with Jewish memory of expulsion with no known destination, the poet simultaneously recalls and creates a new "voyage of the damned," leaving little doubt as to the source of her figures:

> We want to see you sail in the water, sail
>    aimlessly
> Not to any harbor or shore
> They will not receive you anywhere
> You are banished human beings
> You are people who don't count
> You are people who are superfluous
> You are nothing but a handful of lice
> Stinging and itching
> To madness.

Speaking on behalf of all Israelis in this ironic inversion, the poet would thus avenge the Jews' past suffering by condemning their present enemy-refugees to suffer *as* Jews.

Finally, in "One Cannot Kill a Baby Twice," Ravikovitch overlays imagery drawn almost directly from Bialik with language infused by the Holocaust; and again, children provide both the essential locus of horror and motivation for the poem:

> Upon sewage puddles in Sabra and Shatilla
> There you transferred masses of people
> Great masses
> From the world of the living to the world of the
>    dead.
>
> Night after night.
> First they shot
> After that they hung
> Finally they slaughtered with knives.
> Terrified women appeared in haste
> Above a dust hillock:
> "There they slaughter us,
> In Shatilla."
>
> A delicate tail of a new moon was hung
> Above the camps.
> Our soldiers illuminated the place with flares
> Like daylight.
> "Return to the camp, march!" the soldier
>    commanded
> The screaming women from Sabra and Shatilla.
> He had orders to follow.
> And the children were already laid in filthy puddles
> Their mouths wide open

Calm.
Nobody will hurt them anymore.
One cannot kill a baby twice. . . .

The soldiers are only "following orders," and it happens if not in broad daylight, then beneath the light of the soldiers' own flares. One cannot kill a baby twice, it turns out, except in memory and its resonance in contemporary experiences; in this way, the children in Bialik's poem and those remembered from the Holocaust die again and again in every subsequent child's murder.

Occasionally, references seem to come only in the reader's own specific knowledge of events, in projections of Holocaust memory onto more general suffering. But in fact, it is partly in memory of events that analogy and metaphor are created in the first place; an expression like "we didn't see and we didn't know" is so burdened with past violence, for example, that it becomes impossible to recite it innocently in Israel: it can only be repeated ironically.

To this day, it seems that the rest of the world has confused genuine Israeli empathy for the victims of the Sabra and Shatilla massacres with culpability in the killing itself. When 400,000 Israelis marched in Tel Aviv to protest the killings, the world mistook a profound expression of sympathy for the victims and outrage at the killers for a demonstration of guilt. In its craving for the facile symmetry of persecuted turned persecutor, the world seems to have ignored the capacity of one people to feel—if only figuratively—the pain of another. The world has not understood that an outpouring of grief like this might have been spawned as much by the memory of past Jewish suffering as it was by the massacre itself of Palestinians by Christians.

For memory of the past is not merely passed down *mi dor le dor*—from generation to generation—but it is necessarily regenerated in the images that transport it from one era to the next. The past is thus recalled in present figures no less than contemporary events are experienced in light of past events. In this exchange between past and present, every generation simultaneously inherits and transmits memory—which now becomes in itself a series of analogues linking events to one another. Rather than attempting to legislate the inevitable framing of present crises in the figures of the past, we might recognize that historical memory itself may be invigorated by this framing. Reimagining contemporary and past historical crises—each in terms of the other—may ultimately be the only way we remember them.

### NOTES

[1] *The Seventh Day: Soldiers' Talk About the Six-Day War,* recorded and edited by a group of young Kibbutz members. Middlesex. Penguin Books, 1971, p. 38.

[2] Amos Oz, "Hitler kvar met, adoni rosh ha-memshala" [Hitler is Already Dead, Mr. Prime Minister], in *Chatziat*

*Gevul: Shirim Mimilchemet Lebanon* [Border Crossing: Poems from the Lebanon War] Tel Aviv: Sifriat Poalim, 1983, p. 71, in Hebrew. This translation as well as others from the Hebrew are mine unless noted otherwise.

Also see Yehuda Bauer, "Fruits of Fear," *Jerusalem Post,* 3 June 1982, p. 8; and Ze'ev Mankowitz, "Beirut is not Berlin," *Jerusalem Post,* 4 August 1982, p. 8.

[3] *Ve'eyn tichla lakeravot velahereg: Shirah politit bemilchemet Levanon* [Fighting and Killing without End: Political Poetry in the Lebanon War], edited with an Afterword by Hannan Hever and Moshe Ron. Tel Aviv: Hakibbutz Hame'uchad, 1984.

---

# ISRAELI DRAMA

## Shosh Avigal

SOURCE: "Patterns and Trends in Israeli Drama and Theater, 1948 to Present," in *Theater in Israel,* edited by Linda Ben-Zvi, The University of Michigan Press, 1996, pp. 9-50.

[*In the following excerpt, Avigal surveys developments in Israeli theater from the beginning of statehood in 1948 to the mid-1990s.*]

### IN OTHER PLACES PEOPLE DIE OF STROKES

One evening in 1985, about three years after the Lebanon War, I sat in the Rovina Hall of the Habima National Theater and witnessed a revolution, revolutionary only in Israeli terms, since what seemed so unusual here would have been routine for a Broadway or West End stage. For the very first time in Israeli theater a Yuppie couple, the same age as the playwright and I, dealt with entirely personal problems: the breakdown of a marriage, midlife crisis, personal fulfillment, and self-analysis. Traditionally, Israeli drama had concerned itself with themes of national identity. Individual problems were seen as only a reflection of collective values, too petty and unimportant for a national theater to present.

The play, Hillel Mittelpunkt's *Temporary Separation,*[1] presents a couple in their late thirties who spend a weekend at a beachside hotel trying to rehabilitate their shaky relationship. The husband is a playwright, the wife a university lecturer dedicated to the Palestinian issue. She brings with her to the hotel the reels she recorded on the West Bank, regarding Palestinian hardships, perhaps as refuge from the heart-to-heart talks she is expecting to hold with her husband. In response to her indifference about visiting his friend in the hospital, he chides her: "Take your tape recorder when you go on Sunday. You can find two or three Hebronites in the oncology ward, too. It isn't just the occupation that's killing them, sometimes it's the liver or the spleen . . . or the expectation" (11).

I attended the play with a friend, a former Israeli, who had left the country on a Palestinian passport in 1947, before the state was founded. On hearing the dramatic text he was surprised and whispered: "Funny, in Europe, in a similar situation, they would have said the exact opposite, that there are places where people don't just die of strokes, cancer, or liver problems, but of wars, oppression, occupation."

An outsider, unfamiliar with the Israeli experience, would find it difficult to understand this quirk of Israeli drama, prevailing even in autobiographical-realistic plays. What seems ordinary from the local Israeli point of view seems extraordinary from the outside, and vice versa. It is private life that is considered shocking fodder for theater; the political is the norm. Israeli theater treats the anomaly of Israeli existence as accepted material and uses it to produce realistic dramas, bourgeois plays and entertainment. And even exceptional human situations, of the kind portrayed in the stylized classical tragedies, can be perceived, through analogy, as mimetic reflections of current reality.[2]

### FROM THEATER OF VALUES TO PRODUCTION-VALUE THEATER

All theater is a reflection of society, and the Israeli theater expresses this to an extreme degree: it not only reflects the sociocultural and political developments in Israel but also participates, quite actively and articulately, in their shaping. The not-too-long history of the Israeli theater offers a reflection of the tumultuous story of the Zionistic ideology in contemporary Israel: a painful process of secularization, turning from a sacred-mythological era of ideological visionaries to a secular reality of disillusionment and ennui. The Hebrew theater, from its beginnings in 1917 in Moscow with the Habima, perceived itself as being ideologically committed to the Jewish national movement and to the growth of a new national and cultural identity, and it bore this weighty national message.[3] Until recently, it had never been considered "just entertainment" or "merely an aesthetic experience." Each opening of a new theater became cause for a national celebration, and until the 1960s theater reviews referred almost exclusively to the ideological content or to the moral and national message of the plays. Aesthetics and theatrical craftsmanship came last, if at all. Adherence to reality and reference to the here and now were ideological imperatives that, over the years, acquired formal-aesthetic values. Theatergoers referred to plays whose content conformed with their expectations as "good theater."

Plays written in Israel after the War of Independence tended to copy bourgeois realism, paying tribute to the solid national consensus. This was the apprenticeship stage of a young theater, not yet familiar with the tools of the trade. Thereafter, in the 1950s and 1960s, the

"promotion of original drama," in the sense of Hebrew plays treating local themes, became a national value in its own right. Original plays enjoyed state subsidies and were praised for their adherence to reality—even when they could not meet artistic standards. Up until the 1970s, most of the repertoire played in Israeli theater consisted of translated European classics or modern Western plays. In the 1970s, when the theatrical tools had improved, Hebrew drama no longer needed artificial encouragement. It awakened and began to flourish in its own right, discovered the here and now along with self-criticism, in the form of documentary, journalistic drama. In fact, only at this point did Israeli drama assume the role expected of theater as an art in a civilized society: it became society's watchdog as well as its prophet of doom.

The 1970s were years of awakening. Israeli theater started to express doubts about the Zionist dream and the means of its realization. These were the sobering years of self-awareness, both for the arts and for Israeli society as a whole. It was in this period that the dreams of the romantic founding fathers faded away, albeit slowly. The wars, the continuous bloodshed, financial and economic difficulties, and day-to-day worries took over. Instead of classic Zionism, Israelis adopted a local version of the American dream, a myth of individual success in an efficient technologically oriented consumer society. This new myth triumphed over the old collective dreams.

Early in the 1980s the Lebanon War broke out, and the national consensus was shattered. For the first time many Israelis spoke of the lack of justification for war and saw that there could be another way. This crack in the national consensus was immediately expressed in the theater, both in original drama and in local interpretations of classic and translated plays. The early 1980s, the time following Lebanon, were characterized by protest theater, with a good deal of self-flagellation. It was a theater of disillusionment, with a strong undercurrent of nostalgic eulogizing of the Zionist dream and its demise. But all too soon the hue and cry quieted down, and it was back to business as usual. The switch was, in fact, not too sharp, since alongside the "relevant" plays, such as Yehoshua Sobol's *Ghetto* and *The Palestinian Woman,* there were the plays of Neil Simon, Henrik Ibsen, and Arthur Miller, which still formed the main part of the repertoire. Political plays as well as others that "enjoyed" censorship scandals, simply enjoyed a greater portion of the public attention.[4]

The time that has passed since then has proved the "revolution" to have been an elusive, pale imitation of the drama of the late 1960s in Europe and the United States. And yet there was a unique authentic Israeli aspect to this theater, which moves theater critics and aficionados to remember it with nostalgic fondness—despite all its faults. Content often overshadowed form and quality. Occasionally it was the very adherence to reality and the immediacy of reaction that precluded aesthetic perspectives and undermined theatrical achievement. After the short wave of the post–Lebanon War protest drama declined, the Israeli theater began to concentrate on form and artistic matters as well as on marketing and the box office. Establishment theater productions—and since the mid 1980s this comprises the majority of theatrical activity in Israel—began to strive for technical professionalism, taking over where the aesthetic quest, in the sense of experimental theater, had left off.

In less provincial countries, having a more developed theatrical tradition, this is known as the development of "production values"—to wit—proper professional performances and forget about the content. Original drama began to recede from political and social relevance and limited itself to individual problems of the Israeli society, especially since the beginning of the Intifada (1987), developing various mechanisms for the denial of reality. While the Likud government was busily paving roads to circumvent the Arab villages on the West Bank and make them invisible, an escapist attitude of "It's all right" and "It'll soon pass" developed in the theatrical arena. Established theater became a production line and marketing mechanism for conservative subscribers, who came to the theater in order to get their dose of entertainment and denial. . . .

Israeli drama went all the way from an ideological theater, committed to a general cause—through different phases of confusion and disillusion—to a new illusion of faked normality. It ran the course, from a theater of values to a production-value theater.[5]

### CENTRAL THEMES IN ISRAELI DRAMA

Israeli theater is preoccupied by a number of central themes, recurring in the writing of local playwrights, as well as in local interpretations of translated material. These themes undergo a metamorphosis concurrently with the transformation of the attitude of Israeli theater as a whole, from the collective approach to the personal-individual point of view related to Jewish/Israeli identity and the unique circumstances of Israeli existence.

### From National Resurrection of Self-Fulfillment

Early Israeli drama, written before and immediately after the War of Independence, was dominated by a genre of realistic "settlement" plays, which dealt with the Zionist dream. The individual in these plays was a mere tool for the realization of the collective dream, which included the establishment of a state, conquest of lands, rural and urban settlement, kibbutz life, coping with setting up the groundwork for the state-to-be, absorption of Aliya, and the making of a melting pot of Jewish immigrants.[6] During the 1950s and 1960s this theme was translated into an existentialist context: the myth of national fulfillment became a myth of existential fulfillment, under the clear stylistic inspiration of the European Theater of the Absurd. The settlement play reemerged during the 1970s with a twist. Now it evoked the problem of the individual versus the collective, questioning the sacrifices and compromises the individual has to make for the sake of the society.

### Survival Dilemmas

Many Israeli plays deal with the price of survival, in terms of the Jewish people's Massada complex: What are the limits of sacrifice an individual or a nation should make for a cause, while its very existence is endangered? What is the lesser evil—heroic suicide, which zealously maintains the national identity while forsaking physical well-being, or compromise and survival? A more personal version of this dilemma places the individual's happiness and unique identity in contrast to the common benefit of the national collective. Throughout the years the historical circumstances vary, but the dilemma remains intact. The enemy changes from era to era: from the Romans, during the fall of the Second Temple (Sobol's *The Jerusalem Syndrome*), through the Germans, during the Holocaust (Aharon Meged's *Hanna Senesh* or Sobol's *Ghetto*), including the mythical Arab foe (Yigal Mossinsohn's *In the Plains of the Negev*, Natan Shacham's *They'll Arrive Tomorrow*, and most of the plays written during the War of Independence).

The survival theme is a subtheme of the plays dealing with identity, the early version, in the 1940s and 1950s, concerned with the survival of collective existence, threatened by an external menace and commending the sacrifice of individual life and privacy in favor of the supreme value—the life of the people. After 1967 these values were questioned, and a new motif emerges: the idea that war is negative and that survival and peace are paramount. The value of self-sacrifice began to be doubted and the value of life itself was finally acknowledged. From here the way was paved for playwrights to discuss not only life itself but also the quality of individual life.

### Plays of Doubt and Questioning

Doubt, in Israeli drama, is mostly connected to the norms accepted by the collective, the values of preceding decades, or national myths. Such plays are the flip side of the resurrection plays, which dealt with the realization of the Zionistic dream, bemoaning the shattered dreams. Israeli playwrights touched upon this theme in historical and documentary plays, beginning with Nissim Aloni's *Most Cruel the King* in 1954, through Sobol's social-historical epics, the satires of Sobol, Hillel Mittelpunkt and Hanoch Levin, and, at the end of the 1980s and the beginning of the 1990s in a new genre of historical nihilistic parodies, such as Eldad Ziv's *Laisse-moi t'aimer* and *Lucas the Coward* and Yonatan Gefen's *Lullabye to My Valley*. This last variety of play looks back upon the recent past with an ironical sweet-and-sour gaze and deromanticizes the very content and symbols that were so heroically portrayed during the drama of the Palmach decade.[7]

### Holocaust: Commemoration and Memorial or Eerie Analogy?

The Holocaust theme permeates almost all other themes dealt with in Israeli drama. This is the ultimate trauma of the Jewish people, according to which all other themes are measured, as against a severe existential ruler. Israeli theater never portrays the Holocaust directly and probably never can. Nevertheless, Israeli and Jewish playwrights everywhere are obsessed by this difficult subject. The attitude of theater toward the Holocaust reflects the changing attitudes of Israeli society to the problem of the Holocaust in general but also to related existential themes, such as the ethical dilemmas of survival, the Massada complex, and the problem of identity. The first plays to have broached the Holocaust generally expressed the need to emphasize the heroism of the survivors and to commemorate the horror (Meged's *Hanna Senesh* or Yisrael Hameiri's *Ashrei Hagafrur*). Other plays considered various aspects of guilt: the guilt of the survivors themselves, for having survived (Ben-Zion Tomer's *Children of the Shadow*), as well as the confusion and embarrassment of the Eretz-Yisrael population, at the lamblike acceptance of the slaughter by the victims themselves; the very denial of the Holocaust, as part of the "new Israeli Jew's" denial of the Diaspora culture; and the problem of financial compensation made by Germany to survivors (Moshe Shamir's *The Heir* and Aharon Meged's *The Burning Season*). . . .

During the 1970s, when Israeli theater started reexamining all value systems of Israeli society, the Holocaust theme became the ultimate metaphor for doubts and existential questions, in their new form. Collaboration with the Nazis in order to save a few Jewish lives was no longer regarded as mortal sin, as life came to be considered the supreme value, explored in Sobol's *Ghetto* and Motti Lerner's *Kastner*.

While the Israeli Philharmonic Orchestra, considered a national cultural icon, still bans the music of Wagner (at this writing), Israeli theater has long since broken the taboo on Holocaust symbols. Swastikas, SS uniforms, yellow Stars of David, or the anti-Semitic Sturmer-style caricature of a Jew appeared here and there on the Israeli stage, although they were mostly in translated plays such as Robert D. McDonald's *Summit Meeting,* produced in 1982 by the Beersheva Municipal Theater, in which Hitler's and Mussolini's mistresses met against the background of a giant swastika, and Martin Sherman's *Bent,* in the Haifa Theater, which includes scenes from a concentration camp.

These symbols were sometimes used in the context of a disturbing analogy between the post-1967 Israeli conqueror and the Nazi fascist. This reversal of roles—of the victim becoming the persecutor, an extreme protest against the state of conquest—caused a great deal of anger in the Israeli public. This analogy was in fashion mainly in plays inspired by the Lebanon War (Hanoch Levin's *The Patriot;* Michael Kahane's *The Last Dance of Genghis Cohn,* after Romain Gary's novel; Yosef Mundy's *The Merry Days of Frankfurt;* Shmuel Hasfari's *Kiddush;* and some stage interpretations of translated plays, such as Holk Freitag's *The Trojan Women,* by Euripides.) Two extraordinary performances by the Akko

Theater, directed by Dudi Ma'ayan, employ the Holocaust as an expression of collective spiritual reckoning of the Israeli identity. These two group works, targeted at a limited audience, deal with the Holocaust and with Jewish history from the personal point of view of young Israelis, who were educated in Israeli schools, where they absorbed the Holocaust mythology as part and parcel of history lessons. Ma'ayan's *Second Generation's Memories in the Old City* and *Arbeit Macht Frei* are, at this writing, the two most complex and difficult expressions of the way the Israeli consciousness copes with the memory of the Holocaust. They also combine the thematic struggle with a search for new and daring theatrical language.

### Coexistence in a Heterogeneous Society

Under this heading are plays that relate to varied conflicts, resulting from the heterogeneous nature of Israeli society, which contains Jews of various ethnic extraction as well as Christian, Muslim, and Druse Palestinian Arabs, some of whom are Israeli citizens and some of whom live under military occupation. Conflicts of coexistence persist both within the Jewish society and at the binational level of the Jewish-Arabic conflict. Both levels reflect a gradual shift from the collective stereotypical treatment to the more recent personal, individual approach. An example of plays of the first type, within Jewish society, is Ephraim Kishon's *His Name Precedes Him* (1953), Yigal Mossinsohn's *Kazablan* (1954), and *Eldorado* (1955), Hanoch Bar-Tov's *Six Wings for One* (1958), Judith Handel's *The Alley of Stairs* (1958), and *The Neighborhood* (1956), and Gavriel Ben-Simshon's *Moroccan King* (1984). Examples of plays relating to the Jewish-Arabic conflict are enumerated in Dan Urian's essay, in this volume.[8]

### Universal and Existential Issues from a Daily Perspective

As noted, the subject that has received the least attention from Israeli dramatists, until recent years, is that of the common person's day-to-day routine, in its psychological, social, and financial aspects. Romantic comedies and melodramatic love stories are hard to find in Israeli drama.[9] Hanoch Levin deals extensively with the antihero, within the framework of the family and neighborhood (in plays such as *Hefetz, Krum, Ya'akobi and Leidental, The Suitcase Packers,* and *The Craft of Life*), but he does it in his unique poetic style, which is very hard to translate, in its use of both Hebrew and theatrical language (see the essays by Yaari and Brown, in this volume).[10]

Beginning in the 1970s and thereafter, playwrights tended to relate the private, personal level of their stories with social, national, and even political considerations. This relationship is expressed through a network of symbols, which emerges from the realistic texture of the play, such as in novelist A. B. Yehoshua's plays, *A Night in May, Objects, Late Divorce,* and the recent

*Night Babies,* and in the plays of Yosef Bar-Yosef: *Difficult People, Elka, Butche, The Orchard,* and *Winter Ceremony.* Another instance of such a combination is expressed in the apparent family dramas by Shulamit Lapid, *Deserted Property* and *His Life's Work,* and in Shmuel Hasfari's *Kiddush.*

. . . . .

### YOU AND ME AND THE NEXT WAR: THE MAIN PHASES OF ISRAELI THEATER

Hanoch Levin, who was once the black sheep of Israeli theater and is currently one of the best-known Israeli playwrights, wrote a satirical cabaret called *You and Me and the Next War* (1969), a title that has become an idiom in modern Hebrew. Israelis tend to organize their collective memory according to the wars. When trying to describe the main trends in Israeli theater since the war of 1948, it is almost impossible to avoid grouping them according to the six wars in Israel's history, as each war represents a new phase in the Israeli dynamic of shattering old myths, and another step in constructing the multifaceted Israeli reality.

Each of the Israeli wars carries a nickname—sometimes receiving more than one name—each embodying the ambivalence toward these wars: 1948, the War of Independence, or Sovereignty (Komemiyut), the foundation of the State of Israel; 1956, the Sinai War, or the "Kadesh" (lit. sanctify) Operation, although not seen as a "real war," since it did not endanger the existence of the state and did not leave behind a specific cultural residue; 1967, the Six Day War, which actually lasted much longer, followed by the War of Attrition; 1973, the Yom Kippur War, or the Day of Atonement War because of the day on which the war began; 1981, the Lebanon War, or, by its official name (which, ironically, binds war with peace) "the Peace for the Galilee Operation," the first war which most of the Israeli public felt was not a necessity for survival; 1987, the Intifada, the Palestinian popular uprising in the Occupied Territories, which for some reason is known as neither a war nor an "operation," since Israelis are unused to a prolonged state of battle, which becomes an existential dilemma and can be solved not by force but only by political resolution; 1991, the Gulf War, which, like the Sinai War, is not considered a "real" war, since there was no danger to Israel's very existence and the army did not take active part.

The first period is that of the 1950s (1948-56), the years when the great dream of the founding generation was at its best. In the 1960s (1956-67) came the years of awakening. Sobriety following the 1967 euphoria and facing reality from a new vantage point characterized the country in the 1970s (1967-73) until the 1973 war ushered in doubts, negations, and new perspectives seen in protests during and immediately after the Lebanon War. This period (1981-91), from the Lebanon War through the Intifada, years of middle-class comfort, produced a theater that was detached but professionally competent, es-

capist entertainment seeking to evade reality. In the early 1990s, we have seen the new political upheaval that brought the Labor Alignment back into power. It is the end of an era and the beginning of a new cycle. The theater is returning to historical, social, and political issues, from a sober but not necessarily bitter vantage point of a young generation, unburdened by nostalgia for the early Palmach years.[11]

The division of theatrical periods according to wars is convenient in terms of overviews and titles, but is not, of course, precise. Israeli theater reflects reality and often foresees processes before they occur. Thus, for example, Hanoch Levin wrote satires against the Military Government and Israel's new army of masters while he still was a student at the Tel Aviv University, in the mid-1960s, before the Six Day War. In 1970 he wrote *Queen of the Bathtub,* a bitter satire about the empire and bereavement, wherein he first dared question the myth and necessity of self-sacrifice. The play was written in 1970, three years before the Yom Kippur War. It caused a public outcry, mainly due to the scene in which a bereaved father stands on the fresh grave of his son, fallen in the war, and is reproached by the dead young man:

> Father dear, when you stand at my grave,
> Old and tired and very alone [ . . . ]
> Do not stand so proud,
> Don't lift up your head, father
> We are left flesh to flesh
> And now is the time to weep, father.

During one of the performances at the Cameri Theater, the well-known and respected Cameri actor, Yosef Yadin (whose brother, Yigal Yadin, discovered the Dead Sea Scrolls and was leading archaeologist at Massada, also a former chief of staff of the army), stood up and protested. In 1984, fourteen years later and only two years after the Lebanon War, the very same Yosef Yadin appeared in the Akko Fringe Festival, cast as a bereaved father in a play entitled *Akeda* (Sacrifice of the Son). The play questioned the need for sacrificing young lives in preventable wars but not as harshly as in Levin's play. This time not one member of the audience protested. Some may have shed a private tear.

### The 1950s: "Oh, What a Lovely War"—The Dream

The 1950s were the first years after establishment of the state. All social, political, and cultural frameworks were in their first stages of organization, as was the theater. Playwrights wrote mainly current, sociorealistic, amateurish, stereotyping plays. They were photographing, via the theater, a heroic victory album, in a theatrical language that was only just beginning to make its way upon the stage and had little or no theatrical heritage (Shoham 19). The primary playwrights were Moshe Shamir (*He Walked in the Fields* [1949]), Yigal Mossinsohn (*In the Plains of the Negev* [1949]), Natan Shacham (*They'll Arrive Tomorrow* [1949]), Nissim Aloni (*Most Cruel the King* [1954]), Aharon Meged (*Hedva and I* [1954]), and

Ephraim Kishon (*His Name Precedes Him* [1953]). Most of them were of the same age group, most grew up with a socialist pioneer background (Chalutzim), with a liberal-socialist orientation, served in the Palmach and Hagana military undergrounds before the establishment of the state, and fought in the War of Independence. Although some of the playwrights have turned rightwing over the years (e.g., Shamir and Kishon), they still draw from the same ideological background and employ a similar imagery (Shoham 19). Because most of the plays were written and directed in a realistic style and made much use of the current slang idiom, they dated very quickly. They now have a primarily historical value, as their dramatic and theatrical value is negligible. Most playwrights of the period abandoned theatrical writing over the years and focused on prose. Occasionally, they would write a play or have others adapt their works to the theater, but of all playwrights of the time only Nissim Aloni remained first and foremost a theatrical artist.

In these plays Arab characters are entirely missing. An Arab figure shimmers into Shacham's *They'll Arrive Tomorrow* as an anonymous, faceless enemy, whose life is entirely worthless. During this period there was no satire at all and almost no open criticism of the establishment and accepted values. Conversely, deviations and misfits were denigrated. The exception to this rule is *Most Cruel the King,* Aloni's first great play, which was the most interesting of a series of historical plays, written employing a historical perspective and analogies in order to refer to the present (Shoham 160-200; Ofrat 48-58). Theaters of the period produced many translated plays; original plays were by far the minority.[12]

## The 1960s: The Period of Original Drama

In the second decade of its existence the new state stabilized and discovered a daily routine. The short Sinai Operation, which erupted in 1956, had no significant impact on this routine. These were years for settling down and a relative improvement in material comforts, a tendency for "provincial" imitation of American and European fashions, in all facets of life, a tendency expressed in the theater by an eclectic imitation of formal models of Western cultures, without internalization of the spiritual and thematic contexts that engendered such forms. Imitation served as a useful exercise for artistic expression and accelerated the local process of becoming acquainted with the theatrical medium. One of the strongest influences was that of Bertolt Brecht, mostly in the Haifa Theater, whose head, Yosef Milo, mounted Brecht's *Caucasian Chalk Circle,* with Chaim Topol in the leading role and a set by Brecht's original designer, Theo Otto.[13] This was a time of enthusiastic experimentation and apprenticeship, of absorbing important models to the verge of imitation, be it by translating and producing foreign plays or through the writing of local dramatists. Besides the Brechtian model, Israeli drama at the time was influenced by Pirandello's play-within-a-play structure as well as its French counterpart, as in the plays of Giraudoux and Anouilh, and the theatrical expression

of European existentialism, as expressed in what is called the Theater of the Absurd: Beckett, Ionesco, and Genet. This last philosophical trend was very influential on the writing of Nissim Aloni as well as on the writings of other dramatists of the period.[14] Aloni linked the existential search for the self, hiding behind a variety of misleading masks, with the public and social identity and developed an ironic and detached outlook on Israel: "Small country in Africa, on its way to independence. Very fanatic. Lots of folklore." (*The American Princess,* 12).

The importing of culture also had ideological significance. In this period, with Israeli industry and culture still in their infancy, anything "foreign" was considered perforce better than the local equivalent. "Homegrown" needed a sales promotion. In this way the struggle for "promotion of original plays" took on a local aspect: defending the national patriotic values.

This struggle was a direct continuation of the value-laden patterns that prevailed during the establishment of the state, when the cultural, political, and geographical separation of Israel led to a unique idealization of all things foreign. The concept of "the outside world" in the 1960s became the idiom for an unreachable dream. It is difficult to grasp the sense of isolation and enclosure of Israel at the time, surrounded by seven enemy Arab countries and without even television broadcasting to connect it to the Western world. Trips abroad were a great luxury; the idealized concept of "abroad" became a submyth of the Israeli unattainable dream, a contrasting mythology to the ideal of settlement and national reestablishment of the Jewish homeland in Eretz-Yisrael. Whereas the first years after the establishment of the state were characterized by an attempt to create an authentic Israeli culture that would turn its back on the ghetto psychology and negate it, in later years Israeli artists, who were mainly the product of Western culture, sought means to break the boundaries of the cultural isolation that had developed. They found themselves virtually imprisoned in an ambivalent island of Western culture within the Middle East, physically rooted in the East while spiritually focused on the West. The cultural import brought about new styles and themes in the theater. The more theater was exposed to external forms, the more it absorbed the systems of values expressed by these foreign, formal patterns.

Israeli theater gradually departed from the Habima and Cameri's original naturalistic tradition, and the stylistic and formal changes were accompanied by a metamorphosis of values as well. Gone was the committed ideological basis, on which the Habima had been founded. It was no longer considered shameful to concentrate upon the artistic aspect in its own right; art was admitted to have a right of existence beyond serving the ideal of national renaissance (Ofrat 185-88).

The Israeli theatrical scene of the period was a hectic field of creation. It was even called "the Explosion of the Sixties" by the *Jerusalem Post*'s theater critic, Mendel Kohansky. Many small theaters, some old and some new, worked beside the large institutionalized theaters. They were considered avant-garde and daring. Along with Do-Re-Mi, Zuta, and Zavit, founded in the 1950s, Theatron Haonot was established, with Nissim Aloni as its central figure; the Actor's Stage, with Oded Kotler and a group of actors; and Yaakov Agmon's Bimot. The innovations introduced in the small theaters began to be reflected by the larger institutions. Writing and translating for the theater were considered to be highly respected professions, and some of Israel's greatest poets, writers, and playwrights took to translating plays, thus creating a new reservoir of world drama, both classic and modern, in Hebrew. In this manner they added an additional dimension to the process of cultural rebirth and to the development of modern Hebrew, binding it to the sources of Western culture. Among the translators were poets Avraham Shlonsky and Natan Alterman as well as Natan Zach, Yaakov Orland, Raphael Eliaz, Yaakov Shabtai, T. Karmi, Nissim Aloni, and others, who translated Shakespeare, Molière and Chekhov.

### The 1970s: Facing Reality

The Six Day War (1967) was the most critical turning point in Israeli history to date, and it brought about a great change in the country, not only a wave of nationalistic fervor and a euphoria of victory (which died down all too soon, during the long and difficult War of Attrition), but also television broadcasting, thus opening the Israeli ghetto to the world. Until the 1970s, Israel was traditionally a few years behind European and American fashions. As playwright Eldad Ziv put it about the preceding decade: "The 1960s reached our country shortly before their formal demise in Europe. Here and there we'd hear about long hair, miniskirts and elephant pants. Israel collected photos of IDF [Israel Defense Forces] generals in uniform, General Bar-Lev continued to build his lines" (*Laisse moi t'aimer* [1991]). The time gap began to close only after the Israeli Television Broadcasting Service was established and television sets became widely available, during the 1970s.

Unlike the escapist drama of the 1960s, dreaming of other worlds, in the years following the Six Day War theater woke up to the immediate Israeli society, to naturalistic styles, and even to satire. It seemed to return to documenting reality and the style that characterized the first decade after the War of Independence. Actually, it used a similar style to achieve different aims. This was not heroic drama, meant to glorify reality, but, rather, here-and-now drama, seeking means to cope with the complex dilemmas of the Israeli people and with the heavy price the society must pay for its existence, a price stated in terms of the number of casualties in the 1967 and 1973 wars. These were the young sons of the former Palmach fighters, who had created the state and now sacrificed their sons on the altar of national survival and continued wars. A modern version of the national myth, the myth of sacrificing the first-born sons (*akeda*), was brought forth as the penalty paid for survival despite doubts engendered by pain and bereavement.

Bitter doubt first surfaced in intellectuals and artists, and the theater was a leading voice in legitimizing this doubt. Sacrificing the life of the individual for the collective, which was an absolute value not subject to discussion during the formative years of the state—as expressed in Shamir's *He Walked in the Fields*—lost its absolute status. In 1969, only two years after the war, still within the euphoric period, Hanoch Levin produced his poignant satirical revue, against war and establishment. *You and Me and the Next War* was largely seen to be spitting in the eye of the nation, but it happened in a fringe theater, the student Bar-Barim jazz bar, in southern Tel Aviv. In 1970 Hanoch Levin dared to cope with the sacrifice myth in the institutional Cameri Theater, with *Queen of the Bathtub*, arousing a national outcry that forced the Cameri to close down the play.[15]

After 1973 the doubt that Levin was audacious enough to express, shared only by a minority after 1967, became a powerful and legitimate sentiment, shared by many.[16] The 1973 war was the antidote to the Six Day War euphoria. It was perceived as an inevitable retribution for the hubristic faith in the concept of power as an omnipotent guarantee of existence. This mythical shield of "security" was cracked, and many Israelis began to cultivate another solution. The results of this war gave rise to protest movements, including Peace Now, which eventually brought down Golda Meir's Labor government, put the Likud into power in 1977, and soon thereafter led to a peace agreement with Egypt.

Ideologically speaking, this decade is characterized by crisis and soul-searching by a generation that still clung to the old value systems but no longer found existential justification therein. The Yom Kippur War, and the feeling of near extermination, dramatically raised the level of skepticism of Israeli theater regarding the solid value systems typical of the state's formative years. Israeli society and theater in the mid-1970s were preoccupied by soul searching. The means of theatrical expression became more sophisticated, due to imitation of artistic models from previous periods, enriching the theater's capacity to cope with the new complexity of local reality.

Original drama flourished in the many styles exercised during the previous decade. Two primary trends characterized the dramatic writing of this period: a direct response to the current scene via the naturalistic docudrama of Nola Chilton of the Haifa Municipal Theater, and a more aesthetically ambitious personal poetic response by Nissim Aloni and Hanoch Levin. These were the years of Aloni's spectacular tragicomedies, in Habima, and of Levin's comparatively intimate family neighborhood, in the Haifa Theater and later in the Cameri. Hanoch Levin was the man people loved to hate: critics praised him, the conservative audience was ideologically appalled and disgusted by his dirty language, and the attacks launched against him by right-wing politicians served to advance his fame or at least his notoriety.

Levin's plays of the period paint a grotesque portrait of the Israeli society of the fat years before the Yom Kippur War. It is an absurd tragicomic universe, populated by a repulsive Jewish-Israeli family, with a spineless father devoid of values, a monstrous, powerful mother, a selfish materialistic daughter—all racist, fascist, and living off the war. If they happen to have a son, he would usually be a shlimazel, or "loser," as are all other young men—creatures having no chance whatsoever to achieve anything in their lives but to be potential mates for the daughters. The mates are destined to be killed in wars, the lovers never to realize their passion. It is a cynical, materialistic world, in which people's strength is measured only in terms of their financial worth, in petit bourgeois terms of the old Jewish shtetl and by their capacity to realize the dream of traveling abroad. Levin created a closed system of social hierarchy, a chain of the weak pecking the even weaker beneath them, all sharing the same dreams, which are destined never to be realized.[17]

Some other dramatists and adaptors of the period coped with the contemporary scene in stylized, indirect forms, thus developing a poetic-realistic drama, which crossed the boundaries of the realistic convention and borrowed from the Theater of the Absurd as well as from symbolistic and expressionistic European theater. Playwright Yosef Mundy, for example, directed his political satire *The Governor of Jericho* in the Cameri, in 1975, using techniques from European models, but his topics were drawn from the immediate reality and portrayed the new Israeli soldier as a fascist tyrant. The play caused a great deal of anger and was closed after thirty-seven nights. Amos Kenan, who followed the French Theater of the Absurd in the 1960s, razed the heroic mythology of the Palmach generation and ironically lamented the murder of the dream of the early period of the state in his bitter satires (*Maybe an Earthquake* [1970], *Friends Discuss Jesus* [1972], and *As I Still Believe in You* [1974]). Playwright Danny Horowitz examined the myth of the Sabra in *Cherli Ka Cherli* (1977); Yosef Bar-Yosef did so in *The Wedding* (1974); and playwright Avraham Raz in *Mr. Shefi's Night of Independence* (1972), each developing his own personal style of poetical realism.

The theater that contributed most to the takeover of local drama was the Haifa Municipal Theater, in the period from 1975 to 1980, under the management of Oded Kotler and the social and artistic leadership of director Nola Chilton. . . . American-born Chilton, known first as an excellent actors' coach, found her place in the Haifa theater and began to edit, adapt, and direct plays on social and political issues, beginning in 1970. Most of the plays had no literary value and were based on texts borrowed directly from everyday life. Many critics were not enthusiastic about the artistic aspect of this kind of theater, with its excessive proximity to the daily scene and the lack of aesthetic distance; and they referred to it sarcastically as "the tape recorder theater."

The Haifa Theater of the time legitimized the far reaches of Israeli life. This was the first appearance on stage of characters from "the other Israel": Oriental Jews, Arabs, residents of development towns, the underdogs whose frustration would bring about the political upheaval of 1977, which overthrew the Labor administration and put the right-wing national camp in power for fifteen years. Nola Chilton brought her former students, from her acting studio and the theater department of Tel Aviv University, to the Haifa Theater. The students, devoted to her method, joined her in group work projects that involved live-in research in deprived communities, which resulted in docudramas. These documentaries, which started on the second experimental stage of the Haifa Theater, gradually found their way to the main stage and aroused disapproval among the local conservative and bourgeois subscribers and led to an exodus of the artistic leadership of the theater, back to Tel Aviv, where they tried to found another pioneering project in Neve Tzedek. Yet, the work of Chilton at the Haifa Theater gave rise to a whole school of new writers and actors, such as Yehoshua Sobol, Itzik Weingarten, and Hillel Mittelpunkt as well as Hanoch Levin and Yosef Bar-Yosef. Apart from semidocumentary dramas, such as *Sylvester '72* (1974), *The Joker* (1975), and *Cold Turkey* (1976), Sobol, at the time virtually apprenticed to Chilton, wrote one of his most important plays, *The Night of the Twentieth.*

The Haifa Theater was not alone in dealing with sociopolitical issues. Some other playwrights in the Tel Aviv theaters also touched upon delicate topics, and especially the subject of Jewish-Arabic coexistence. These were not docudramas. Such plays are Miriam Kainy's *The Homecoming* (1972), Arab playwright Rateb Av'auda's *A Sub-tenant* (1978), and Gavriel Ben-Simshon's *A Moroccan King* (1984), a poetical-musical eulogy for the Jewish community of Morocco.

The 1980s—From a Peace-War to a War for Peace

The 1980s started with a bang: the Lebanon War broke out and the national consensus broke down. The process that had taken form in the 1970s was vindicated historically. For the first time in Israel people spoke openly of an unjustified war and acknowledged other options. The war split Israeli society into two opposite camps: the right-wing camp, which saw itself as "the National Camp," and the left-wing camp, which defined itself as "the Peace Camp." A giant demonstration held in a central piazza in Tel Aviv in the midst of the war, an unprecedented event in the history of Israeli wars, protested the army's shut-eye policy during the slaughter of Palestinian refugees in the Sabra and Shatila camps in Lebanon. This crack in general agreement was immediately expressed in the theater, both in original drama and in local interpretations of translated classics (such as *The Trojan Women,* Jean-Paul Sartre's adaptation of Euripides, directed by Holk Freitag in Habima and Yehoshua Sobol's adaptation of *The Trojan War Will Not Take Place,* by Jean Giraudoux). Censorship attempts to block presentation of Hanoch Levin's antiwar satire, *The Patriot,* at Neve Tzedek were met by active support for the play from theater groups and intellectuals, unlike the position taken by the very same public during the presentation of *Queen of the Bathtub* in 1970.

The theater of the first part of the decade, in the years following the Lebanon War, was a theater of protest, with a generous amount of self-flagellation. It was a theater of disillusionment, with a strong undercurrent of nostalgic eulogizing of the Zionist dream and its demise. Such plays as Shmuel Hasfari's *Tashmad,* on a Jewish terrorist underground of suicidal fanatics in Samaria, and Ira Dvir's *The Sacrifice,* which dealt with bereaved parents who lost their faith in the justification for their sons' deaths, found their place in the new framework of the Akko Festival of Fringe Theater, which was initiated by Oded Kotler in 1980. Before long the Akko Festival became the showcase for young Israeli theater and a fine sensor of the mood in Israeli theater at the time.

As of 1985, all public repertory theaters were managed by Israeli-born directors, who more or less shared a world view. The Haifa Theater, under Noam Semel, Gedalia Besser, and Yehoshua Sobol—who took over after Kotler's demise—was still the leader, in its preoccupation with such delicate subjects as the Holocaust, orthodox versus secular tensions, and the Jewish-Arabic conflict. Arab actors found their way into this theater, expressing their conflict of identities in plays such as Fugard's *The Island,* produced both in Hebrew and Arabic versions (1983), *Waiting for Godot,* in a joint Arabic and Hebrew version (1984); *The Optimist,* by Palestinian writer Emil Habibi (1986); and Sobol's *The Palestinian Woman* (1985).

This was the heyday of the Haifa Theater. Under the new management the theater continued the docurealistic drama, with Yossi Hadar's *Shell Shock,* and became entangled in censorship by the orthodox establishment with Martin Sherman's *Messiah* (1983) and with the Board of Censorship over Yosef Mundy's *The Gay Nights of Frankfurt* and Yitzchak Laor's *Ephraim Returns to the Army* (1985), a play that was entirely rejected by the censors. Both plays suggested an analogy between Israelis and Nazis. The Haifa Theater also won international acclaim, with Sobol's historical epic dramas, which dealt with the moral and ideological issues of the survival of the Jewish people.

But all too soon the hue and cry quieted down. The emotional after-effect of the Lebanon War was as intensive as it was short-lived, and it actually started dying out as early as the mid-1980s. Sobol's famous international hits *Soul of a Jew,* on Otto Weininger (1982), *Ghetto* (1984), and *The Palestinian Woman* (1985) were already produced, although not consciously or intentionally, with an eye for the larger audience and for export. They were understood in different ways in Israel and abroad. What had locally been interpreted as a critique of Israeli identity, the need to choose between Judaism and Israeli-ism, and the evaluation of the moral price of survival were understood abroad as a historical

monument for the Holocaust (*Ghetto*) or a tribute to the early days of Zionism in Vienna at the turn of the century (*Soul of a Jew*).[18] The Holocaust theme was also employed metaphorically by other playwrights. Motti Lerner's *Kastner* (1985) and Shmuel Hasfari's *Kiddush* (1988) were not actually meant to be dramatic monuments to the Jewish tragedy of the Holocaust but, rather, to give voice to the very here-and-now ideological confusion and split identity of the new Israeli.[19]

On 9 January 1988, during the celebrations in honor of the fortieth anniversary of the state, Sobol and Besser presented *The Jerusalem Syndrome,* their swan song as managers of the Haifa Theater. Sobol had long since become a negative political symbol for the extreme right wing, which was not at all interested in the artistic theatrical merit of the play. What was meant to become a festive theatrical event at Habima became a nightmare. *The Jerusalem Syndrome,* which blamed the fall of the Second Temple upon the Jewish zealots of the period, aroused the wrath of the right wing even before it opened. The audience that arrived at the festive occasion was greeted by a violent right-wing demonstrating mob, who picketed the Habima entrance bearing banners with hostile slogans, terming Sobol and his colleagues "anti-Semites." Several dozen picketers found their way into the performance and disrupted the play with noisy protest and firecrackers. The show could not go on.

I was present at the Habima hall on that evening, and this was an event I will not forget. It was terrifying. The prevalent feeling was that the fascists had won and that we had lost our membership in the community of civilized nations. The performance made front-page headlines in the following day's press. The Israeli media unanimously condemned the intolerance and the violent attempt to curtail the freedom of expression. Unfortunately, the critics condemned the play's artistic merit as well. Sobol and Besser, who confused their personal professional frustration with ideological and social disappointment, resigned from management of the Haifa Theater, and that act was the official end of the period of protest in the 1980s.

The end of the Sobol-Besser era also marked the end of involved theater in Israel and the beginning of the business-as-usual phase. Sobol and Besser liked to portray this change as a result of their resignation, but it was actually the peak of a process that had begun much earlier. The unfortunate events at the premiere of *The Jerusalem Syndrome* were the last nail in the coffin of experimentation, which started after 1973, reached its peak during the Lebanon War, and came to a close in the mid-1980s. Both the audience and the artists were tired of protesting in vain. Visionary Hanoch Levin aptly expressed this mood in the title of his 1985 play, *Everybody Wants to Live.*

In July 1987 the Cameri Theater of Tel Aviv presented the glitzy musical *Les Miserables* after the London model. In December 1987 the Intifada broke out. A month later, while the Haifa Theater cast of *The Jerusalem Syndrome* stood onstage in horrified silence, the Tel Aviv audience in the Cameri was already applauding the new wave of glittering musicals and professionalism and quality productions for their own sake. Within a period of six months, July 1987 to January 1988, Israeli theater switched directions. It turned its back on the embarrassing political situation and voted for song and dance. This tendency had been felt in Israeli theater for a few years; *The Jerusalem Syndrome* was actually an anachronistic relic of the theater of the early 1980s. Israeli society now sunk into the escapist attitude of the first Intifada years.

*Les Miserables* marked a turning point in the annals of Israeli theater. The extravaganza was produced according to European standards, using highly sophisticated lighting and sound equipment, formerly unseen and unheard of in Israel. Financially and technically, such a production would have been more appropriate to a private commercial producer, but in Israel at the time, only a government-subsidized theater could handle an investment so huge. Each night, when the two sections of the set mechanically rolled toward each other from the two sides of the stage, in time with the music—and actually fit—the audience brought the house down. For the first time, audiences and critics alike applauded the technical achievement of the production in its own right, thus applauding what was termed by Michael Handelsaltz, the theater critic for the daily *Haaretz,* as "production value." Technical smoothness took priority over thematic content, in contrast to the traditional Hebrew theater since its infancy. *Les Miserables* was the first production in Israel so enthusiastically accepted for its sheer professionalism, though it bore no social message and was completely detached from the local scene. Critics who praised it in the Cameri applied the very opposite criteria from those they used when appreciating the committed here-and-now theater of the 1970s, which was far from meeting the professional standards of advanced theatrical technology.

This change of climate had constructive as well as disturbing aspects. It did mark the technical maturation of Israeli theater. Once this high professional standard was obtained neither audience nor critics were willing to tolerate amateurism. At the same time, good intentions and an important ideological message were no longer enough, and repertory theaters began to produce more and more entertainment and commercially oriented plays. Among these were musicals, which until then had posed too great a professional challenge and required too many professionally grounded actors. *Les Miserables* was not only the most expensive production in Israeli history, it was also one of its greatest box office successes. The public repertory theater, which tried to repeat this success in order to meet the audience's demand, was drawn into the "entertainment loop." The public theater became more and more populistic, both in its repertory choices and in staging concept, increasingly compromising artistic considerations for box office receipts. Commercial theatrical

entrepreneurship shrank and almost disappeared. The subsidized professional public theater took its place.

The left wing, and with it the theater, which had been largely identified with the Peace camp, took a few years of siesta. Peace Now demonstrations became as rare as protest plays. Playwright Hillel Mittelpunkt, who made an unusual attempt to present an almost-protest play (*Mami*), did it in the Tzavta Club, which is fringe theater identified with the Left rather than the mainstream, and did so within the genre of a rock musical, coating the ideological message with both a musical and tempting rock hits to appeal to the young audience. This was one of the only means of feeding the indifferent audience with a portion of criticism against racism, discrimination, and military occupation.

Yosef Mundy, the eternal rebel, wrote an impressionistic drama about eccentric characters in a Tel Aviv pub (*Closing the Night* [1989]). Controversial Hanoch Levin repeated himself, and even he tended more and more toward light entertainment, returning to humoristic entertainment cabaret (*The Gigolo from Congo* [1989]). These productions were played on the Cameri's second stage. The main stage was reserved for well-made West End and Broadway hits. All the public theaters tried to balance their budgets with imported "moneymakers," detached from Israeli reality. Even the daring Akko Festival began to become commercialized. Artists working within it used it mainly as a launching pad to the establishment and not as a testing ground for audacious artistic experimentation. Young acting school graduates, recruited to established theaters straight from school, first asked how much they would be paid. This may sound perfectly reasonable and normal in any Western country, but in Israel it reflected new standards. Where theatrical work had previously been considered a privileged pioneering mission, this new opportunistic and self-centered approach seemed odd.

Many people began to find the theater boring and stopped attending it, particularly the younger audiences. Israeli drama went all the way from an ideological theater, committed to a general cause—through different phases of confusion and disillusion—to a new illusion of faked normality.

### The 1990s—Back to History

In June 1992 a political upheaval occurred: the Likud was voted out of government, and the Labor Alignment took its place. As always in Israel, the theater sensed the changes before they were expressed in the polls.

Not unexpectedly, the change was first felt in the fringe theater, rather than in the well-oiled institutional theater. At the eleventh Akko Festival in October 1990, the first prize was awarded to the play *Reulim* (Masked-Faced Terrorists), the first play by the young playwright Ilan Hatzor. This was the first Israeli play to deal entirely with the Intifada. The play tells the story of three

Palestinian brothers in a village on the West Bank. One brother is suspected of having cooperated with Israeli authorities, another is a wanted terrorist, living as an outlaw in hiding, and the third is an innocent young boy. Three Jewish actors were cast as three Palestinians in a realistic play, not experimental in any respect, but simply well done, maintaining a high level of tension and emotional intensity throughout. The play's special power and its ideological impact were derived directly from its artistic achievement: the Jewish spectator simply could not help but relate to the three dramatic characters, on an emotional and human level. This was theater at its best, as it enabled not only actors but also the audience to empathize with the "other," whose existence they preferred to deny. But in order to achieve such a level of realistic and nonstereotypic character design, Israeli theater had to undergo all the apprenticeship processes and development it had gone through over the years. Ilan Hatzor, a twenty-six-year-old freshman at the Tel Aviv University Theater Department, had been born into a theater whose professional standards were taken for granted.

*Reulim* was immediately embraced by the theatrical establishment and was performed for two years on the second stage of the Cameri Theater, as part of its subscribers' program. In other words, the play and its subject were given an instant legitimation from the bourgeois Tel Aviv subscriber, who was probably fed up with the populistic menu set before it and was ripe for a change.

Following the success of *Reulim,* the repertory of the Cameri Theater offered to its subscribers more and more plays based on immediate topical subjects or the recent historical past. Its greatest success to the present has been Hillel Mittelpunkt's *Gorodish,* more a séance than a dramatic work, which presented traumatic scenes from the collective Israeli memory of the 1967 and 1973 wars. Demythologizing General Gorodish became cathartic theater, and it was soon followed by other topical plays, with much less success and power: *Fleisher* by Yigal Even-Or (1993), *Shaindele* by Rami Danon and Amnon Levy (1993), and *Pollard* by Motti Lerner (1995).

The 1990 Akko Festival offered some other signals of the forthcoming change. A marathon of documentary theatrical readings was held, presenting the minutes of the Givati Corp trials (some Givati soldiers were tried for inappropriate conduct against civilians in the Occupied Territories during the Intifada). The reading went on continuously throughout the festival. This was a dubious documentary theatrical manifestation but a straightforward political statement that went to the core of a national wound, in a style reminiscent of the theater of the 1970s and early 1980s. In another performance Arab actor Haled Abu-Ali, a member of the regular Akko Theater Company, devised a one-man show that dealt with his own confused identity, as a Palestinian Israeli. These shows were performed with no undue disturbance, no special demonstrations of support or dismay, no censorship. It seemed that the audience was ripe for something new.

In the winter of 1991 the Gulf War broke out. It heightened the sense of the absurd and helplessness of Israelis regarding their individual existence, within an impossible political context that was no longer under control. This may have had an effect on a certain style of humor and outlook: the world as we knew it turned upside down. In this war, unlike the previous ones, it was the civilians who were endangered; the army did not fight, and holding fire was considered a great achievement and an act of maturity. This war did not produce any victory albums or protest plays; its main artistic products were in the form of ironic graphic expressions. The Gulf War took away what was left of the myth of Israeli power and heroism. It added to the sense of disgust with empty nationalistic slogans. In the long run it may have contributed to the process that gave rise to the political upheaval of June 1992 and to the peace process.

In the twelfth Akko Festival, held in 1991, plays drawn from Jewish and Israeli history reappeared. They discussed problems of essence and identity, but not in the documentary epic style of Sobol or Lerner. Young theater people returned to difficult and painful subjects—Israeli and Jewish identity, the effect of the Holocaust and the Arab-Israeli conflict on this identity, the here and now—but from a somewhat detached point of view: stylized, careful, without committing themselves to a clear statement, and with many external gimmicks. The most important show in the 1991 Akko Festival was undoubtedly *Arbeit Macht Frei in Teutland Europa,* the five-and-a-half-hour show by the Akko Theater Company, directed by Dudi Ma'ayan.

During the early 1990s Israeli movement theater and modern dance joined the theater in dealing with social ideological issues. This was mostly evident in the repertoire of the Kibbutz Dance Company, which devoted an entire program to the story of a reserve soldier during the Intifada; in the work of choreographers such as Arye Burstein and Nir Ben Gall and Liat Dror, and in abstract creations of Ohad Naharin, with the Batsheva company; as well as movement-theater directors such as Ruth Ziv-Eyal and Nava Zuckerman, dealing with images of Zionist mythology and the broken dreams. What Pina Bausch does in abstract-existential images becomes localized and politicized in Israel.

A new genre of theater, actually bordering on stand-up comedy, has become popular in the 1990s. It does what political satire does: present topical situations using zany anarchistic comedy laced with black humor and nonsense jokes. Estevan von Gottfried, in *Ziona Halo Tishali* (Ziona, Won't You Ask?), wrote a crazy parody on anti-Semitism and the cynical rhetorical use made of it for nationalistic purposes. In terms of genre and style this directly followed from *The Gospel According to Christine,* a play he created for the 1990 Akko Festival, which stingingly attacked the matters of compulsory orthodox tyranny and its influence on the Israeli identity. In his 1991 play he plants a fictional Third Temple Israel in Uruguay. Here the Jews nostalgically reminisce about how "every day, in civic studies, we'd go out and kill a Palestinian," missing the times they were persecuted victims, and the persecutions added flavor to their lives and helped them forge their Jewish identity. In *The Last Game of Ping-Pong,* by young playwrights Tal Friedman and Moshe Frester (who held a long-running success in student clubs in Tel Aviv, two years previously, with their nonsense play *The Tales of Moshe in the Big City*), one can see a form of ironic nostalgia for the Israel of the 1970s, actually a parody of nostalgia for the Palmach generation dream. What blunted the sting of these satires was their tendency toward light entertainment, sometimes quite vulgar, and their lack of commitment to an alternative system of values.[20]

These new "relevant" plays were nonrealistic. They applied a variety of theatrical means of expression, with a special stress on the visual aspect, on design and movement. For instance, in *Dancing Tonight,* a dance and movement theater and a poetic eulogy by Sinai Peter, directed by Yigal Ezrati and choreographer Gabi Eldor, echoes of the Intifada join the Gulf War. This play portrays, in movement and music, the history of a Yaffo coffeehouse, over eight stops along the history of Israel between 1919 and 1991, beginning with the onset of the British mandate to the Gulf War. The years dance by, each period in its own dance. As the play continues, its message becomes more political and clearer. There is no need for words in order to understand the significance of the time bomb that explodes at the end.

One of the strongest scenes in the play is the one showing the night of the declaration of the Jewish state, in 1948. Everyone is excitedly huddled around the radio set, and only the Arab and his daughter, when they realize what is happening, bow their heads, and with their bundles on their shoulders make their way into exile. At the end a Schwarzkopf-like U.S. general in uniform stands on the bar, in a macho stance of the new master. They all dance for him like remote-controlled mechanical puppets who have lost their volition. The cycle is complete.

A few months before the June 1992 elections, a wave of stand-up comedy swept over the fringe theaters of Tel Aviv, appealing mainly to younger audiences. Stand-up had long since become an accepted form of entertainment for young audiences, thus taking the place once held by satire, which had all but disappeared. Young stand-up artists generally abstained from making direct political statements about the situation in Israel and preferred to deal with personal situations, drawn from everyday life. One month before the elections, in the small Tzavta-2 fringe club, the "How It Really Works" trio presented a parody of two yuppies who are sick and tired of the Likud regime and decide to liquidate Prime Minister Shamir. They open their diaries and go over them, day by day, but are unable to find the time to realize this plan— one's daughter has a dance class, another simply cannot give up an appointment with a shrink—until the year is over and the elections have come and gone. "This sort of humor does not overturn a government," I wrote at the

time, after an investigation into the stand-up scene of Tel Aviv. Indeed, but it may be a small step toward normalcy, which would finally lead to some peace. Then it would finally be possible to spend an afternoon at the shrink's with a clear conscience, without having to feel guilty for not sacrificing one's individuality for the collective needs, and quietly to snore in front of a television showing soap commercials instead of air raid announcements.

In November 1991 I published an article in *Politica,* referring to the new trends apparent in the Israeli atmosphere, as expressed in the 1991 Akko Festival. I wrote then:

> If my intuition is correct, and the 91 Akko Festival reflects the beginning of a change of attitude towards reality, maybe something is about to change in Israeli reality itself. The Israeli theater has been known for an almost frightening prophetic power and if it has risen from its pleasantly drowsy illusion of normality, maybe our fossilized social and political establishment is finally about to wake up, as well. Let me remind you: If the theater is the mirror of society, the Akko Festival is the seismograph of Israeli theater.[21]

The 1991 Akko Fringe Festival was probably the last time for some years that Israeli theater preceded reality; in the 1992 Festival the two merged. In June 1992 elections were held in Israel. The fifteen-year-old Likud regime was replaced by a new labor government headed by Yitzchak Rabin, and Israel entered a new era—the era of the peacemaking process. The 1992 Akko Festival held in October already reflected the ripeness of Israeli society for the changes that were taking place in secretive diplomatic channels. For the first time in the thirteen-year history of the festival, one could sense the crumbling of the unseen barrier that had stood between the local Arab population of this old Arab city and the young and exuberant Jewish Israeli theater-goers who attended the Festival. Also for the first time some plays were performed in Arabic by Arab actors, which attracted Arab audiences. *Um Rubabika,* a one-woman play performed by Bushra Qaraman, was written by the famous Palestinian author Emil Habibi, who later that year was awarded the Israel Prize for Literature, the first Israeli Arab to receive the distinguished medal that the state reserves for its best talents in all fields. Such an award could never have happened in the previous administration.

The female presence was also strongly felt in 1992, linked to a new, more liberal approach to minorities in general (see my essay on "The Liberated Woman on the Israeli Stage," in this volume). Another major theme in the Festival was, not surprisingly, Jewish-Palestinian coexistence. One of the most interesting plays—which also won a special prize—was *The Coexistence Bus* by Pablo Salzmann and the Akko Theater Center, which took place in an actual bus as it traveled along a guided "tour" of Arab villages in the Lower Galilee, overseen by Jewish and Palestinian actors, some of whom were authentic inhabitants of the villages visited. Hagit Yaari's play

*Abir* represented the most successful merger between the two themes: women's emancipation and Palestinian identity. Five Jewish actors play five Palestinian women during the Intifada, struggling for both female and national independence.

If theater and reality merged in 1992, at the 1993 Akko Festival reality outstripped theater. The Festival, held a month after the unforgettable handshake on the White House lawn, caught Akko with its pants down. In light of the Oslo Agreement most plays presented that year seemed anachronistic or irrelevant. The most outdated productions were the ones that protested against Israeli occupation and portrayed images of corrupted Israeli soldiers, themes that had been regarded as poignant and daring only a few months earlier. Political events had occurred so fast that what had seemed like science fiction the day before—Israelis and Palestinians signing a peace agreement—had become history, leaving Israeli theater for once lagging behind the reality of the times.

One example of a play that had become instantly outdated was Sinai Peter's adaptation of *Poets Will Not Write Poems,* based on a book by Roli Rosen and Ilana Hammerman documenting testimonies of the moral dissolution of IDF reserve soldiers on duty during the Intifada. Seen even two months earlier, that very play would have been moving: seen two years later it could have provided a historical reminder of what had been and should not be forgotten. In autumn 1993 the play seemed an aesthetic and intellectual regurgitation of the already known.

In general the 1993 Akko Festival revealed the danger of a too-close documentary style. In the past it had fostered plays about self-assessment of the Israeli situation during the Intifada but had not offered a "futuristic" depiction of what the next step might be: not more of the same, as in the above plays, but perhaps a possibility of dialogue between two peace partners in an actual exchange. Instead there were a growing number of works on personal relations and problems of the individual self, perhaps a reaction to the years when the political situation was the primary topic.

The 1994 Akko Festival presented a theater in a state of embarrassment, still not able to catch up with the changing world around it. Plays dealt more than before with down-to-earth topics that now did not stand for a fake normality but represented a legitimate orientation of a younger and perhaps healthier generation than Mittelpunkt's *Temporary Separation* couple who were unable to have a juicy family fight without dragging the Palestinian problem into the matrimonial bed. Topics such as feminism (*Heidi, Daughter of a Bitch* by Ayelet Ron) and ecology were presented; experiments in form and language for their own sake were staged (*Hanoch,* an environmental event, and the Jerusalem Zik group performance of fire and water); and materials were taken either from famous Israeli authors (Agnon, A. B. Yehoshua, and David Grossman) or from international writers (Gabriel García Márquez, Jean Genet, or Eugene Ionesco). The

Palestinian El-Hakawati theater, which resumed work in East Jerusalem and made its comeback in the 1994 Festival (after having spent most of the Intifada in Europe), presented a confused play about an Intifada hero who comes back home to Jericho from an Israeli prison and does not find his place in the new reality of "autonomy."

In a way, what happened to Israeli theater at Akko in 1994 was similar to the situation in the Russian theater right after Perestroika when there was no longer censorship that could be used to justify symbolic revolt and subversive theatrical language. Despite the poetically euphoric words with which the mayor of Akko greeted the crowds who attended, the general euphoria that accompanied the first months after the basic peace agreement had started fading away. Both Israelis and Palestinians realized that peace was going to be a long, tiresome, and sometimes painful process, and the theater had no way to cope with such undramatic, unexciting, and slow-paced material that it found in the political interim reality. So theater chose to turn its back on politics and mind its own business. Israeli theater, which had been for more than two decades a restless ideological battlefield, relaxed at last and prepared itself for a less exciting and perhaps more ordinary "new" normality, where—like everywhere else—people die naturally of strokes and not of wars.

NOTES

[1] The play premiered in 1985 in Habima, directed by the playwright, with Natan Datner and Yona Elian in the leading roles. Published by Or-Am, Tel Aviv 1985 (Hebrew).

[2] See S. Avigal and S. Weitz, "Cultural and Ideological Variables in Audience Response: The Case of *The Trojan Women,*" *Assaph* 3 (1986): 7-42.

[3] For a general historical introduction to the Israeli theater see "Israel," by H. Nagid, in *World Encyclopedia of Contemporary Theater* (London: Routledge, 1994).

[4] Ever since the British mandate over Israel, censorship of plays and movies has been enforced due to an old colonial regulation. The censorship committee, officially known as "the council for critique of films and plays" has often served to block the freedom of expression and as an ideological and political means to silence unwanted ideas, but very few plays were actually censored in their entirety. After a long struggle against censorship, the council was temporarily disbanded for two years and finally canceled in 1991. The fight against film censorship still continues. A security-based censorship is held separately and does not deal with the dramatic stage.

During the Likud administration, especially in 1980-85, the censorship board had been exceptionally active and often made the headlines. In 1985 it banned poet Yitzchak Laor's play *Ephraim Returns to the Army,* which caricatured the occupation, entirely, under the pretext that the play offends the IDF and distorts reality. The prolonged struggle of the playwright, who appealed to the highest court, and the trial that followed Levin's *The Patriot* (presented in Neve Tzedek in the midst of the Lebanon War) were the last two blows to the censorship and became the legal precedents that led to its annulment. The censorship committee initially vetoed Levin's play and later agreed to a compromise: the offending passages would be cut. The actors found a way to circumvent this intervention and read the forbidden passages to the audience, with the lights on. For this act they were tried and convicted.

[5] See A. B. Yehoshua's collection of essays *In Favor of Normality* (Jerusalem: Schocken, 1980) (Hebrew).

[6] See Chaim Shoham, *Challenge and Reality in Israeli Drama* (Ramat Gan: Bar Ilan University, 1975), 9-24 (Hebrew); Gideon Ofrat, *Israeli Drama* (Jerusalem: Tcherikover and Hebrew University, 1975), 26-83 (Hebrew). See also Gideon Ofrat, *Earth, Man, Blood—The Myth of the Pioneer and the Ritual of Earth in Eretz-Israel Settlement Drama* (Tel Aviv: Tcherikover, 1980) (Hebrew). All other references will appear in the text.

[7] See David Alexander, *The Jester and the King: Political Satire in Israel, 1948-1984* (Tel Aviv: Sifriat Hapoalim, 1985) (Hebrew).

[8] Also see S. Avigal, "Moroccan Dybbuk?" *Jerusalem Quarterly* 21 (Fall 1981): 48-54.

[9] In spring 1994 the Khan theater of Jerusalem presented Shakespeare's *Romeo and Juliet* with Jewish and Arab actors, as an analogy of the Jewish-Palestinian problem. The theme of a woman struggling for status and recognition within the family and the society is first legitimized in the Jewish-Arabic political context in Sobol's *Palestinian Woman* and, only ten year later, in a realistic play that deals with an Israeli woman as a private case, in Miriam Kainy's *The End of the Dream Season* (see my essay on "Liberated Women in Israeli Theater" and my interview with Kainy, in this volume).

[10] See S. Avigal, "Hanoch Levin, Enfant Terrible of the Israeli Theater," *Ariel* 63 (1986): 38-57. See also M. Handelsaltz, "The Game of Humiliation in Hanoch Levin's Theater," *Theatron* 75-76: 28-30.

. . . . .

[11] See S. Avigal, "Returning to History", *Politica* 41 (November 1991): 57-58.

[12] A detailed repertoire of Habima's productions of the period may be found in *Habima: The First Seventy Years,* ed. Shlomo Shva (Tel Aviv: Keter and the Friends of Habima, 1987) (Hebrew), as well as in Emanuel Levi's *The National Theater of Habima* (Tel Aviv: Eked, 1981) (Hebrew). A similar list may be found for the Cameri in *Forty Years of the Cameri Theater* (Tel Aviv: Cameri, 1984) (Hebrew). Details on the

repertoire of other theaters may be found in the archives of individual Israeli theaters and the Israeli Documentation Center for the Performing Arts, Tel Aviv University.

[13] In 1992 Milo again directed this historical production at the Haifa Theater, with Topol and a young company. For more material on the period of Haifa Theater in the 1960s, see *Ha Theatron,* a theater periodical that was published by the theater during its early years.

[14] See Ben-Ami Feingold, "Pirandello and Israeli Drama," *Bamah* (1991): 49-61. See also references to Amos Kenan in Martin Esslin, *The Theater of the Absurd* (New York: Anchor Books, 1961), 190-91. In later editions of this book Kenan was omitted.

[15] Interesting details of the affair, including spectators' letters, may be found in David Alexander's book *The Jester and the King.*

[16] See Freddie Rokem, "Archetypical Patterns in Israeli Drama," *Theatre Research International* 13, 2 (1988): 122-31, which deals with the changes to the myth of sacrificing the sons as reflecting the changing attitude toward the values of Zionism in plays such as An-Ski's *The Dyybuk;* Shamir's *He Walked in the Fields;* and Hanoch Levin's *Shitz.*

[17] See Avigal, "Hanoch Levin."

[18] See S. Avigal, "Judaism vs. Zionism, on Sobol's *Soul of a Jew,*" *Spectrum* (October 1984): 9-32.

[19] See S. Avigal, "The Myth of Suicide," *Spectrum* (December 1985): 22-23.

[20] See S. Avigal on stand-up comedy and satire (*Hadashot,* 24 April 1992) (Hebrew).

[21] See *Politica* 41: 57-58 (Hebrew).

## Ilan Avisar

SOURCE: "The Evolution of the Israeli Attitude Toward the Holocaust as Reflected in Modern Hebrew Drama," in *Hebrew Annual Review,* Vol. 9, 1985, pp. 31-52.

[*In the following essay, Avisar studies the treatment of the Holocaust in Israeli drama of the 1950s and 1960s.*]

The appropriation of the Holocaust into the Israeli national consciousness has always been problematic and painful. Following the realization of the Jewish state in 1948, the quest for cultural identity prompted only a reserved and diffident identification with Jewish history. Most Israelis viewed themselves as being the antithesis of the perennially homeless and persecuted Diaspora Jews. In particular, it was difficult to overcome their sense of massive victimization during World War II and reconcile it with the pride and assertiveness that followed the impressive triumphs and accomplishments of the young Jewish state.

To be sure, the catastrophe of European Jewry and the building of a homeland in the land of Israel constitute two parallel courses in modern Jewish history, the former being the cataclysmic harvest of millennia of antisemitism whereas the latter was the culmination of a national revival inspired by the rise of modern western nationalism. The creation of Israel had little to do with the effects of the Holocaust. The temporal proximity of these two crucial events might invite metaphysical conjectures about their combined meaning, but historians usually agree that there was no significant causal linkage between the Nazi atrocities and Jewish independence.[1] The popular misconception of Israel as having arisen out of the ashes of Auschwitz has no historical grounds and is not shared by most Israelis. But the country has gone through some dramatic changes in its attitude toward the historical trauma, ranging from complete rejection to an identification of contemporary situations with the past predicament. In addition, specific events and developments, such as the involvement of the Yishuv in the war efforts, the survivors' presence in Israel, the Eichmann trial, and the developing relationships with postwar Germany have established direct and indirect connections with the Holocaust and its implications, thereby compelling citizens and artists to define their attitude toward the past and to reflect on the place of the tragedy in Israeli culture.

Our study will examine the developing attitudes toward the Holocaust in the first two decades of the Jewish state as they are manifested and implied in Hebrew dramas on the subject. The focus on Hebrew drama provides a particularly revealing perspective, for in Israel dramatic literature is closely tied to its social milieu. The playwrights often gravitate toward controversial issues which supply intriguing conflicts and an opportunity to assert the author's social involvement and to state his or her ideological attitudes. Very often the playwrights' responses to current social problems and political situations turn the theatre into a public arena where typical characters and topical standpoints are analyzed and evaluated. Indeed, critics Haim Gamzo and Gershon Shaked observed once that the subjects of most Israeli plays correspond directly to the contemporary issues discussed in the daily newspapers.[2]

Our study will deal with six plays that treat the subject of the Holocaust from the perspective of Israeli reality—remarkably, there were no Hebrew dramas set within the world of the concentration camp, for the Israeli theatre usually shunned realistic subjects which were not part of its immediate environment.[3] We exclude from our discussion plays or playlets which never gained considerable public recognition and focus on those works which were written by prominent Israeli authors and performed by the major theatre companies. The plays are: Nathan Shaham's *A New Reckoning* (*Ḥešbôn ḥādāš,* 1953), Leah Goldberg's *Lady of the Castle* (*Ba'alat hā'armon,* 1954), Aharon Megged's *Ḥannāh Seneš* (1958), Ben-Zion Tomer's *Children of the Shadow* (*Yaldê haṣṣēl,* 1963), Moshe Shamir's *The Heir* (*Hayyôreš,* 1963), and Aharon Megged's *The Burning Season* (*Hā'ônā Habbô'eret,* 1967).

Shaham's *A New Reckoning* takes place in Sodom during the early years of the reborn Jewish state. The dramatic action is triggered when Ammi, an ardent young idealist, is led to suspect that Dr. Auerbach, the local director, was a Kapo in Auschwitz. Indignant that a former collaborator with the Nazis remains free and unpunished, Ammi decides to take the law into his own hands. His scheme is to extort a confession from Auerbach and then kill the survivor, for the latter cannot be legally prosecuted. In the climactic scene Auerbach admits his past position as a Kapo, but then we learn that he was also a member of the resistance movement. Realizing that it is impossible to judge the actions of those who lived in the camps, Ammi does not pull the trigger.[4]

While the drama's ending is somewhat ambivalent, suggesting that the Holocaust kingdom is beyond the comprehension or reprehension of the victims, the characterization of the dramatic agents reveals unambiguous sympathies and antipathies. Nathan Shaham draws sharp contrasts between the Holocaust survivors and young Israelis. Doctor Auerbach, his wife Helen, Pomeranz, and Veksler have conspicuously foreign names, denoting their estrangement from the biblical land. On the other hand, the protagonist's name "'Ammî" means "my people," and that of his companion, "Srulik," is the nickname for Israel, so that the combined meaning is "my people Israel." The two handsome young veterans and kibbutz members are characterized by their idealism and devotion to hard pioneering labor. In contrast, Veksler constantly complains about the hardships; Pomeranz is "like a manager" avoiding difficult jobs; and Auerbach is the chief director living comfortably in an air-conditioned house. These survivors, burdened by the immoral behavior of their shadowy past, came to Sodom in order to escape and to forget the Holocaust trauma. Auerbach's wife, Helen, allegedly spent the war years living in comfort and luxury with a wealthy Jew! Note that she lived with a Jew, not a Gentile, so that this fantastic tale illustrates the play's negative attitudes toward the survivors. The author's view is that they must have sinned greatly in order to avoid the fate of the others, for, as Pomeranz cynically declares, good people like Ammi were the first to perish in the camps.

The juxtaposition of the Sabras with the survivors also yields alternative meanings with respect to the setting. For the Israelis, Sodom, because of its barren soil, difficult climate, and location by the Dead Sea, is a special challenge to pioneering aspiration. But in light of the survivors' presence there, the setting comes to be associated with the biblical Sodom, the city of human malice that is traditionally conceived of as being the incarnation of hell on earth. In other words, for these people, Sodom is a place giving expression to their ethical degeneration during the war which, in the present, can give them the opportunity to atone for their sins, should they wish to rehabilitate themselves and become like other Israelis.

*A New Reckoning* reflects an early attitude prevalent in Israel of insensitivity toward and impatience with the victims of the Nazis. The survivors are viewed as an alien or even infected element in need of rehabilitation. While Ammi's extreme idealism is somewhat tamed by the incomprehensibility of the concentration camp universe, he still represents an outstanding innocence, perhaps signifying a more general national purity on the part of the newly-born state that is threatened to be spoiled by those who came from the Nazi hell. Shaham's exaltation of Zionist achievements versus the survivors' world was excessive and untenable. Artistically, the play is a poor derivative of Ibsen's *The Wild Duck*—Ammi being a version of Gregor Verla—but with a heavy-handed action and a lack of artistic refinement. The Kameri production was a failure, closing after less than two dozen performances.

The confrontation between the Zionist accomplishments and the conduct of European Jewry during the war is also the central concern of Aharon Megged's *Ḥannāh Seneš,* a homage to the heroism of the young woman, often referred to as the Israeli Joan of Arc. The Hungarian-born Hannah Senesh was sent from Palestine to parachute into Europe on a spying mission for the British army and thereafter to organize the rescue of Hungarian Jews from the Final Solution. She was captured shortly after her landing. In prison she exhibited extraordinary courage and defiance, which made her a modern Jewish martyr and a national Israeli hero. Megged, who knew Hannah Senesh personally—they were both members of the same kibbutz—wrote a semi-documentary play, based on Hannah's diaries, her mother's accounts of her childhood years, and his own research on Hannah's fate and conduct in the Hungarian prison. However, given the unabashed sympathies toward his heroine, Megged created a moving melodrama loaded with ideological content eulogizing everything Hannah stood for.

The play's action is set in the Hungarian prison after Hannah was caught and revolves around the preparation for her trial and the efforts to save her life. The dramatic action, sustained by the tension stemming from the proceedings toward the execution, focuses on a study of the central character in this edge situation. However, Megged sees Hannah's entire career, especially her Zionist identity, as the key to understanding the significance of her life and death, and thus a number of flashback scenes unravel Hannah's past, presenting the crucial moments in her decision to go to Palestine and her activities in the kibbutz.

Megged's play is a mixture of documentary theatre and unrealistic sequences—the latter include Hannah's dreams, fantasies, and memories. These scenes are designed to portray Hannah as a sensitive young person whose great spirit and determination never made her larger than life; rather we see her as being vulnerable, fallible and ultimately movingly humane. There is, however, a tendency toward mythicizing the central character, which is implicit in Megged's adoption of the formal principles of martyrology to organize the dramatic material. As in most martyrologies of ancient Jewish and Christian traditions, the action revolves around the protagonist's trial, which becomes an opportune setting to express and elaborate on the conflicting viewpoints and arguments. The hero's physical death is not a tragic ending but a gesture of willful sacrifice, signifying the spiritual triumph of the martyr's ideals. In addition to these narrative elements, Megged explicitly compares Hannah in the text with such classical martyrs from the European Christian tradition as John Huss, John Wyckliffe, and Galileo, as well as Jewish martyrs like Hannah and her seven sons.

Unlike the old Jewish martyrologies, however, Hannah's sacrifice brings vindication not to all the Jews but only to a small group of the nation, namely, the Zionists. Despite the fact that, of all the Hebrew Holocaust plays, *Ḥannāh Seneš* is the only one set amidst the war reality, Megged features the sharp contrasts between two modes of Jewish existence, the negative one in the Diaspora and the positive in Israel. Hannah Senesh returns to her birthplace to save fellow Jews as an essentially Israeli character. She insists on calling herself *Ḥannāh,* with the Jewish Hebrew sounds, and not Anna, as indeed the other characters in Hungary call out to her. As a brave army officer, Hannah is an admirable representative of the "new Jew" developing in Eretz Israel. The former winner of a poetry competition and the daughter of a distinguished Hungarian author, she decided to give up a promising career and her respectable social status because she felt the best place for her as a Jew was in the land of Israel. In the context of the Holocaust turmoil, her idealistic act is reinforced as being the only course of Jewish salvation. But Zionist ideals do not merely constitute a program to save Jews from the threats of the Diaspora existence. They manifest such supreme values as hard labor, productivity, socialism, and comradeship, values which became fully realized in the model society of the kibbutz. On the other hand, the Jews in Europe are sharply criticized for their fearfulness, passivity, and expedient self-interest. The moment which most forcefully shows the discrepancy between the two Jewish worlds occurs during the meeting between Hannah and her lawyer. The lawyer tries to persuade Hannah to save her life and the lives of many other Jews by disclosing the broadcasting code to her interrogators. For Hannah the idea is appalling—she will never violate her loyalty, nor will she ever make any deals with murderers. The lawyer attempts to use a rational argument by claiming that Hannah's act may save the lives of many. He calls it a beneficial reckoning. Hannah replies:

> A reckoning? I know another reckoning, a bigger reckoning than that, lawyer Dverechi. I know that a position of honor can save a whole nation, and that fear and capitulation kill it. (p. 77)

The real shock comes at the end of the scene; Hannah angrily asks who stands behind this offer and is answered: Jews. On top of the effect of this startling revelation, the emphasis here on the concept of "reckoning," which of course also recalls the title of Shaham's play, indicates the assessment and negative judgment upon the world of those values represented by the Diaspora Jews, in contrast with the positive ethical considerations and admirable values embraced by Hannah and the pioneers in Israel.

The Zionist achievements in Israel carry an additional significance as an alternative option to the entire European tradition that, after all, was the womb of the genocide. The encounters between Hannah and Janush, the old Christian jailer, convey the differences between two opposite mentalities. Janush turns out to be a comic figure because Hannah's stories about Eretz Israel throw him off balance—in his words, "my head turns like a wheel" (p. 72). His European values of respect for authority, recognition of social status, stereotypical views of Jews, and traditional conservative attitudes toward women cannot come to terms with the facts of this talented girl from a distinguished family who is an officer in the army, yet who shares equally the labor burden on a collective farm; he also cannot grasp how a young Jewish girl can display so much heroism against the ruthless repression of those whom he is forced to serve. He seems to understand when Hannah explains that she came from the holy land, which is for him the land of saints and miracles. As a prototype of the traditional Christian attitude, Janush, despite his benevolence and good nature, represents the failure or refusal of many Europeans to acknowledge the reality of Jews returning to their homeland and rebuilding the holy land.

The Habima production of *Ḥannāh Seneš* was a major contribution to the idolization of the modern Jewish martyr. Compared with Shaham's attempts to touch on complex ethical issues, Megged creates a homage to the heroism of a noble spirit struggling against the oppression of great evil. Unfortunately, in exalting Hannah's life and death, Megged tended to overpopularize the subject, occasionally lapsing to near trivialization. Thus, the ending avoids a final note of defeat or loss because Megged concluded the drama with a dream sequence of Hannah's ghost appearing to comfort her mother. The heroine's physical stage appearance belies the sombre effect of the execution and, along with the overall exaltation of Hannah's fate, spoils any sense of tragedy. In summary, *Ḥannāh Seneš* is a well written popular drama commemorating an extraordinary character and a fascinating life. However, it is loaded with a simplistic and single-minded ideology, postulating an unjustified dichotomy between the Diaspora Jews and the Zionists in Israel, and implying an attitude that lacks compassion for the Nazis' victims; these shortcomings make the play somewhat outdated for contemporary audiences.

The differences between the reality of the Jewish state and the values of the old European continent constitute the basis for the dramatic conflict in Leah Goldberg's *Lady of the Castle*. Michael Sand and Doctor Dora Ringel are two emissaries from the holy land in search of relics from the Holocaust. Sand tries to recover rare books and manuscripts and Dora, a motherly figure, looks for orphans and lost children. Stormy weather forces them to spend the night in a remote castle in central Europe. Their host, Zabrodsky, formerly a count and owner of the place and currently an officially appointed custodian of the castle-turned-into-museum, reluctantly allows them to stay. When they prepare to sleep, the clock strikes ten, and from a hidden door a beautiful young girl appears. She is Lena, who was sheltered by the count during the war but continues to live in hiding because he never told her that the war was over. The play's second part focuses on their attempts to persuade Lena to go to Israel and leave behind the castle and the count. Lena is torn between her attachment to her savior and his castle and the promise of a new life in Israel which offers drastic change and challenges. After torturous deliberations and painful changes of mind, she decides to join Dora and Sand in going to the Jewish state.

The central thematic conflict in the play is delivered through the characters of Dora and Zabrodsky, the two main rivals struggling over Lena's future. In addition to the narrative clash, Goldberg characterizes each one with well defined alternative world views, charging the play with an intriguing measure of ideological and cultural contrasts. Even before Lena appears, Dora and Zabrodsky can hardly conceal their mutual dislike. Dora finds Zabrodsky's aloofness and ceremoniality to be archaic gestures of cultural pretensions that must give way to the pressing needs of modern times, which are to her mind best served by technological progress. Zabrodsky is appalled by Dora's pragmatism and her expressed defiance of the cult of beauty. For Dora, castles are pretty but not to be lived in, whereas Zabrodsky inveighs against the "modern boxes," i.e., the massive new apartment buildings, and the rise of industrial and vulgar culture. Goldberg also uses the two rivals to present additional differences, more directly pertaining to the Holocaust and its aftermath. After all, Zabrodsky is not only the obstacle to be overcome in the struggle to liberate the imprisoned girl, but he is also a devout Christian and a European aristocrat and, as such, a representative of the Christian European culture that attempted to destroy the Jewish people. Thus, the count and Dora represent for Lena a whole series of choices regarding life-style and values: imprisonment versus liberation, the old versus the new, Christianity versus Judaism and, ultimately, Europe's diaspora versus Israel. Lena's final choice is a testimony to the triumph of Jewish nationalism.

While the triumph of Zionist promises recalls the thematic concerns of Megged's *Ḥannāh Seneš*, there is still a significant difference in the attitudes of these two plays. First, Hannah Senesh is a highly motivated character firmly believing in the righteousness of her ideals, which in the course of the play's action are demonstrated as being superior to both the diaspora's life and the gentile mentality. By contrast, Leah Goldberg does not present a clash between clear-cut positive and negative forces. Lena's predicament is a genuine one, for she must choose between two options, both of which are equally attractive to her. Her attachment to the count was not achieved merely through deception. Zabrodsky is indeed a fascinating character. He lost his aristocratic status and property but continues to exhibit a nobility of spirit. He is deeply in love with Lena, and her departure would ruin his last source of happiness. During the war he courageously subverted the Nazis who were based in his castle and risked his life to shelter Lena. His pathetic fate and dignified character caused Gershon Shaked, the eminent Israeli critic, to consider him to be the truly tragic hero of the play while viewing Dora as the opposite expression of vulgarity and crudeness.[5] But Shaked, in my opinion, misinterpreted Dora's role, for she, too, is a highly complex character. After all, Dora, like Hannah Senesh, grew up in a respectable European family, and she declares that she has a firsthand knowledge of the count's world. Her rejection from a position of familiarity adds authenticity and power to her attitude (whereas Sand's fascination with the count's life is a typically plebeian reaction to the presence of magnificent wealth and external dignity). Dora's current preoccupation with finding surviving children has caused her to develop a new scale of values, so that her tough-minded pragmatism and her impatience with Zabrodsky's romantic indulgences look quite understandable, if not quite justified. Dora is equally realistic about life in Israel. She explains to Lena that it is not perfect and will involve struggles and painful experiences, but she also promises the vitality of freedom and new opportunities while avoiding any ideological indoctrination.

Leah Goldberg, in her poetry as well as in her dramas, presents an outstanding attitude toward the Holocaust with respect to the future of Hebrew culture. Unlike poets such as Uri Zvi Greenberg, she refuses to view Israel as the antithesis of the gentile world that was the progenitor of Nazism. Nor is she willing to view World War II as being evidence of the bankruptcy of western civilization. In the play the Nazis are referred to as a bunch of beasts and the enemies of culture. Throughout her career as an artist, critic, translator, and teacher, Goldberg sought to create a balance between the classic treasures of western culture, Jewish tradition, and the national rebirth in the land of Israel. In *Lady of the Castle* she deals with the problematics of cultural identity and successfully avoids any expression of ultranationalism or propagandism—the choice of Zionism is a serious one, but it does not mean the complete rejection of its alternatives, specifically, the Jewish Diaspora and the gentile world; rather it involves a careful process of their appropriation.

*Lady of the Castle* amalgamates the principles of the well made play—a development of clear action revolving around a few well defined characters—with such motifs of gothic romances as the remote castle, the stormy night, secret doors, the mysterious beauty, the weird count, and more. Goldberg has used these popular elements to create a finely written drama whose mood is symbolic-expressionistic, while its thematic concerns address political issues against the backdrop of existential decisions. *Lady of the Castle* is to my mind one of the best Hebrew plays; its combination of artistic talent, popular motifs, and an ideological view that had a certain appeal to many Israelis made it a special favorite for Israeli audiences.

Ben Zion Tomer's *Children of the Shadow* presents a more personal account of the conflicts that underlie Goldberg's drama. The protagonist, Yoram, is a twenty-eight-year-old man in search of self-identity. At the age of fourteen he was transported out of Nazi-occupied Europe to Palestine through Teheran (Tomer himself was one of the "Teheran children", and he clearly identifies with his hero). The main dramatic conflict is basically internal, involving the protagonist's assessment of his past *vis-à-vis* the present, while the symmetrical temporal division of his life—half of it in Europe and half of it in Israel—signifies the equal force of each side.

When Yoram came to Israel he enthusiastically adopted the Israeli identity and tried to realize it by working in the kibbutz, serving in the army, and changing his name from the traditionally Jewish "Yossele" to the more Hebrew-sounding "Yoram". His endeavors to identify completely with the new environment never succeeded, as we learn from Nurit, who tells him, "you never managed to be Yoram to the end" (p. 48).

Yoram's main problem is rooted in his uncritical determination to become an Israeli character while renouncing his links with the past. His parents, for example, have always reminded him of a shameful past, a "miserably poor" family in "a dirty little town" (p. 47) in Poland—a succinct summary of a prevalent Israeli attitude toward the *štetl* life. In addition to his shame, Yoram suffers from guilt feelings, the burden and curse of every survivor, which were in his case caused by the discrepancy between his relatively secure position and success in Israel and the horrors that his family had to endure in Europe. His attempts to forget his parents lead him to tell his wife that they perished. A letter announcing their coming impels Yoram to confront the reality of their existence. At the end of the first act he dreams that their ship sank, and he wakes up terrified by the recognition that this was a wishful dream. At this moment he realizes the futility and the moral degradation of his attitudes, and he then confesses the truth to Nurit as well as to himself.

*Children of the Shadow* signifies the transition of Israeli drama between the first and the second decades of the Jewish state. In its references to the War of Independence, the problems of soldiers adjusting to civilian life, the arrival of Holocaust survivors, and the issue of leaving the kibbutz, the play reflects the major themes of the Israeli theatre of the fifties. But Tomer's work expresses the cultural crisis that swept Israel in the sixties, sparking a revision of the previous national assertiveness and the dismissal of the Jewish past. The crisis occurred primarily as a result of the apparent gap between, on the one hand, the development of a fairly common western society such as Israel had become and, on the other, the earlier idealistic expectations and semi-utopian visions. In particular the critics lamented the decline of the spirit of the 1948 generation, specifically the change from those ideals of pioneerism, devotion to the collective nation, and readiness for sacrifice, to what they perceived as being a manifest hedonism and growing materialism. (The critics of the young generation proved to be too harsh—they acknowledged it in the Six Day War.) Tomer presents a grotesque celebration of Independence Day, replete with uncontrolled drunkenness and shallow revelry, in order to illustrate the current drifting and decadence. In addition, Dubi, the Sabra who once courted Nurit, is the embodiment of this social and national decline. Nurit points out that, despite Yoram's efforts, Dubi was always more truly an Israeli than Yoram. In the present, however, Dubi is attracted by foreign influences—represented in the play by jazz and jeans—and prefers to spend most of his time outside Israel, in places like Paris.

While Dubi's character signifies the vanity of Yoram's quest to be totally immersed in Israeli reality, Yoram's attempts to reclaim his personal past force him to revise his attitudes toward the Holocaust experience. The core of Tomer's drama focuses on these attitudes, which are consolidated and recognized through Yoram's complex relationship with Sigmund. Doctor Sigmund Rabinowitz was married to Yoram's sister, who perished during the war. Through his membership in the Judenrat and his collaboration with the Nazis, Sigmund was able to save himself. (It is characteristic that for the Israeli author the Judenrat is a clear symbol of betrayal and cowardice. As a matter of fact, many Judenrat members fought bravely for their Jewish brothers.) Sigmund was imprisoned at the end of the war; now he roams the streets of Tel Aviv, tortured to the point of insanity by guilt feelings.

The dramatic action is triggered when Sigmund accidentally sees Yoram and recognizes him as his brother-in-law, while Yoram begins to plan revenge and punishment against the old man. It is interesting to note that the character of Dr. Sigmund is almost identical to Dr. Auerbach's role in Shaham's *A New Reckoning*. In terms of their personal and historical backgrounds, both Sigmund and Auerbach are patriarchal figures and representatives of the old generation (in the Habimah production of Tomer's play, Aharon Meskin played the role of Sigmund, while Yoram's role was played by his son Amnon Meskin). The generation gap and the father figure are common themes and motifs in modern Hebrew literature, conveying the full weight of a burdensome past on the young Israelis. But the crucial difference between the two plays is that Shaham's young protagonist is driven by what resembles an Oedipal rage—Auerbach's control over Lisa underscores the Oedipal theme—whereas Tomer's hero relates to the haunted survivor as his alter-ego, and Sigmund indeed represents many of Yoram's anxieties and obsessions, his own roots and past traumas. Nevertheless, the concluding sequence in *Children of the Shadow* is almost identical to the climax of Shaham's *A New Reckoning*. In the crucial encounter with Sigmund, Yoram feels he must punish the former collaborator. Aware of the fact that his hatred toward the man is also an outlet for his own frustrations and guilt feelings, Yoram is torn between the quest for vengeance and Nurit's advice to forgive and forget. Sigmund's reflective statements on the Holocaust only deepen his confusion in their lucid ideas and terrifying images. Tomer's approach to the subject is expressed in the following account of a conversation between Sigmund and a Nazi officer who had once studied Humanism with Sigmund at the University of Heidelberg. Sigmund recalls their exchange:

> In the end you'll be burnt to death. I told him, we'll consume you yet. No one will consume us, he said to me, we will leave behind us a world so stripped clean of everything that there won't be a rag of an ideal to cover the nakedness with . . . And he was right . . . (after a pause). He mustn't be right! He mustn't be! (p. 88)

In contrast to Goldberg's reluctance to view Nazism as being an evidence of cultural bankruptcy, Tomer sees little hope for idealistic progress after Auschwitz. The playwright refrains from radical nihilism by having Sigmund crying that it mustn't be like this. He makes Yoram deliver the key words: "To ask. That's the most that can be. Never to understand" (p. 88).

The chief problem in Tomer's play is that what had to be the premise of his work became its conclusion. He touches on many issues, actually on too many, but he fails to explore them, to feature a dramatic action that presents a dialectical development, or to create any meaningful resolution. In other words, Yoram's confusion is the author's confusion. Tomer attempts to identify Yoram with Hamlet through numerous references to Shakespeare's hero. However, the analogy is forced by the dialogue and has no validity beyond the direct references. The playwright, in fact, tries to use many other myths in a similarly unfounded fashion. Characters are associated with Faust (Sigmund), Orpheus (Yoram), and Ophelia (Nurit) in one or two sentences in the text with no narrative justification. The play, as a whole, is the embittered protest of a young Israeli poet in the early sixties revealing the contemporary critical mood on such issues as cultural decadence, the reevaluation of attitudes toward Jewish history, and, in particular, the enormous difficulties, both emotional and rational, of integrating the Holocaust into the Israeli consciousness.

Tomer's play features realistic characters, topical ideological problems and a recognizable social environment, but it is actually dominated by the style of poetic expressionism. The dramatic structure is based on numerous short episodes which are not connected by linear narrative development but, rather, constitute critical moments in the inner lives of the characters. The dialogues elaborate upon Yoram's torments and Sigmund's obsessions, which induce the latter's bizarre performance. The work is richly embellished with poetic images, symbols, songs, dream sequences, and Sigmund's gothic appearance. The playwright, however, failed to accomplish an intense and gripping action; nor did he develop the supporting characters fully; and he often resorted to simplistic symbols and gratuitous references to Shakespeare's Hamlet. Nonetheless, the play's honest treatment of profound themes and serious issues won it a respectful reception.[6] One critic praised the play "as an expression of something exceedingly personal, yet it serves as a biography of a generation bearing in the very fact of its existence the possibilities of great drama."[7]

In addition to the plights of the survivors in Israel and the dramatic encounters between the Sabras and the Jewish refugees, there were other political developments that compelled the Israelis to confront the reality of World War II. One outstanding dilemma involved the relationships with post-war Germany. A few events highlight some of the important stages of this process. In the early fifties, the decision to allow West Germany to pay reparations money for those directly affected by the Nazi persecution stirred one of the most serious controversies in Israel's history. (Menachem Begin, as leader of the opposition party, fiercely objected and delivered a number of inflammatory tirades against the proposed agreements.) Then came the Eichmann trial of 1961 that served as a catalyst to remind and inform the whole world of the Jewish genocide. And finally, in the mid-sixties Israel decided to undertake full diplomatic relations with West Germany, following a period of fairly extensive commercial connections. Israeli playwrights found material for dramatic conflicts and tensions in the apparent incongruity between the enormity of Germany's past crimes and Israel's normal connections with the German state in the present.

Shamir's *The Heir* was a satirical black comedy accusing the Israelis of being too eager to turn a profit from the Holocaust. The death of an Auschwitz survivor gives a young impostor the opportunity to claim compensations from the Germans. The claim eventually escapes the protagonist's control after his greedy lawyer relentlessly explores the past and makes the Germans pay a huge fortune. When the commercial empire purchased by this fortune reaches gigantic dimensions, the impostor breaks and admits his big lie. But his lawyer and secretary refuse to expose the scheme and prefer to declare him insane and take over his property. In the end his mother and girlfriend do not assist him in his efforts to prove his sanity and true identity, and he is faced with the choice of being taken to an asylum or going to jail. His fall ends with a desperate cry: "Who am I . . . who am I. . . . " (p. 47).

The protagonist's final question reveals Shamir's concern with the national identity crisis in Israel at the time (the play was written in the same year as Tomer's *Children of the Shadow*). The hero, Wolf Cohen, is the Israeli prototype—among other things, he is the son of an Oriental Jew and an Ashkenazi woman. He eventually changes his name to Yigal Barnes, meaning "deliverance" and "miracle," two notions associated with Israel's birth. The

play was written in the wake of the Eichmann trial, which is also the background for some of the action. It focuses on an apparent contradiction between the trial of the Nazi war criminal and the reparations agreement with West Germany. The playwright used this doubtful charge to unleash a wild attack on the Israeli society as a whole. Like Tomer, Shamir condemns the loss of pioneerism and idealism; he wishes to shock his audience through the portrayal of social hypocrisy, cynical exploitation, hedonism and limitless materialism. However, his attack was so extreme that it lost its legitimacy, for the lack of any redeeming elements made the work a sheer fantasy with an irreconcilable gap between the grotesque show and the reality it intended to address. In addition, the play's extremely negative characterization undermines its dramatic power. With all the major characters, including the protagonist, being grotesque caricatures, the hero's final pathetic predicament and his profound crisis are totally unconvincing.

The most disturbing aspect of Shamir's work is the attempt to create a funny satire with material taken from the Holocaust experience and its aftermath. For the most part, the comic style ranges from bad taste to reprehensible insensitivity. For example, when Wolf Cohen goes to meet a former Auschwitz doctor in her clinic, he is asked about his number, "the hand . . . a blue number" (p. 44). This is supposed to be a comic moment of misunderstanding stemming from the confusion between an ordinary visit number and the notorious camp tatoos. Here Shamir is not better than those he condemns for exploiting the Holocaust for extrinsic profits. Even if he was motivated by a genuine discomfort over the disparity between the grim events of the genocide and what he termed the Israeli "circus," his satire is in the final account a product of the "circus" and a symptom of it rather than its repudiation. *The Heir* understandably stirred a public scandal. Most critics deplored its excessiveness, while few found much merit or truth value in its critical vision. Remarkably, this highly offensive play never met any calls for censorship. After all, *The Heir* was the comic complement to Tomer's *Children of the Shadow*, insofar as both plays reflect the sense of cultural crisis that prevailed among the Israeli intellectuals in the early sixties.

In the same mood, Aharon Megged wrote *The Burning Season,* an allegorical drama based on the story of Job. The names and the main action recall the biblical setting, but the play is set in present times. The plot begins after the central character, Job, has recovered completely from his great disaster. Job's current prosperity is evident from the intense activities that take place during the "burning season," which actually means the high season of agricultural production. However, the past is revived when Hadad, Job's arch-enemy, who engineered the catastrophe, is suspected of illegal actions, and his investigation leads to the reopening of Job's case. After Job decides to avenge his tragedy by providing crucial evidence against Hadad, he finds out that for many years his foreman, Knaz, had been developing extensive commercial connections with his foe Hadad, who, it turned out, was instrumental in regenerating Job's wealth. Job's embarrassment and his denials of any knowledge of these relationships encounter disbelief and suspicion. His workers, who were always hostile to the man whom they considered a foreigner in their land, erupt in an orgy of derision and destruction, finally setting the house on fire.

*The Burning Season* was allegedly written in response to the growing relationship between Israel and Germany culminating in 1966 with the opening of the German embassy in the Jewish state. In the play, Hadad stands for the role of Germany during the Nazi era and after the war, and Job and Knaz represent Israel and the Jewish people. Despite these analogies the political problem at the background, i.e., the German-Israeli relationship, is not resolved in terms of formulating a clear and definite attitude. On the contrary, the attempt to elicit specific analogous interpretations between Megged's story and the present political situation results in obscure and confusing conclusions. Why should Megged find potentially catastrophic consequences in the new relationships with Germany? Is Job the Israeli prototype, or is he the representative of the recovering Jew in the Diaspora? And what is the law that seeks to punish the perpetrators? These questions and more remain unanswered. Actually, this finely written drama possesses a special power, because it transcends immediate political concerns in addressing some more profound aspects of Jewish existence. Megged's choice of Job's story as the underlying myth for his allegorical play allows him to project a vision of the Jewish predicament in all times and places, while the implied references to the Holocaust render the genocide as the most awesome manifestation of this predicament.

Megged's feelings about Israel's place in the framework of Jewish fate, and about the desirable ethical stance of the nation toward historical realities of threats and opportunities, disasters and recoveries, are expressed through the characters of Job, Knaz, and Job's two daughters, Yemima and Keziah. These four characters are carefully balanced against each other. Knaz's relentless pragmatism is motivated by the will to ensure recovery and actual strength. Job feels that Knaz is heartless and immoral; however, his own self-esteem as a paragon of virtue was facilitated by Knaz's activities. Moreover, Job's professed benevolence is the product of self-delusion and a repression of justified grievances against his enemies. Keziah belongs to Knaz's camp by virtue of her efforts to conduct normal relationships with her society—she plans to marry the gentile lawyer's son. Yemima maintains an uncompromising aloofness; unable to forget the past and always believing in the workers' unchanging hatred toward her family, she presses her father to leave the place. Compared with Yemima, Keziah is unsophisticated and almost vulgar, although she is actually a lively girl exhibiting healthy and charming vitality. On the other hand, Yemima's noble aloofness is fascinating and at times even admirable; however, in insisting on the reopening of the case against Hadad and her quest for revenge, she plays an instrumental role in bringing about the second disaster.

*The Burning Season* abounds with critical references to such contemporary ills in Israeli society as excessive materialism, ignoring the past, and the seemingly mindless renewal of relationships with Germany. Yet the play avoids providing a clear message, or an analysis of the problem with specific ideas for remedy, because the author tries to reflect the complexity of Israel's existence, a complexity that defies clear-cut conclusions or solutions. This approach is nowhere more evident than in the assessment of the central character. While the biblical Job owned flocks and cattle, Megged's Job specializes in growing vineyards, and the text explicitly points out that he once did own cattle but has changed his occupation. Gideon Ofrat finds in this detail "an echo to the image of the new Jew: the Diaspora's professions—the merchant, the doctor, etc.—were converted to new professions connected with working the soil."[8] At the same time the playwright implies that in the past Job's life was spiritually superior. One of the characters comments that Job used to have many books: "He was a rich man and a philosopher. Now—a rich man" (p. 11). However, unlike Tomer's critical indulgences and Shamir's extreme social assault, Megged succeeds in touching more profound nerves of the national psyche, elevating his drama from a specific social commentary to an intriguing vision of the essential Jewish predicament *vis-à-vis* the gentile world and its threats of pogroms and genocide. The evocation of the Job myth as potentially analogous to the Holocaust reinforces the historical fate of the Jews, who have had to endure from one fire to another. Megged's naturalistic treatment of the biblical allegory is actually dominated by the expressive images of blood, heat, intoxication and ominous signs of the inevitable and imminent doom. The frantic gathering of the grapes in the high season, the act which gives the play its title, is a major symbol of Jewish life on the edge, culminating in the final great fire. The play's artistic quality and its rigorous treatment of fundamental problems in Israeli life led to its success when it was staged on Habimah in 1967.

In conclusion, the Israeli playwrights never attempt to confront directly the Holocaust horrors, probably because of their concern with problems of their immediate reality and because of the enormity of the subject matter. With respect to the latter point much has been said about the difficulty of reconciling art and the actual atrocities. Here I would like to recall Peter Brook's admission that, after trying to create a theatrical expression of the concentration camp universe, he realized that the most effective way to convey whatever there is to be said would be to leave the Auschwitz gates open to conscientious visitors.[9]

The Israeli plays that deal with the subject of the Holocaust do so in examining the past trauma *vis-à-vis* current realities in the Jewish state. Moreover, they usually feature a dramatic conflict juxtaposing the Holocaust against Israel. Usually, the characters' names, either Hebrew or foreign, give away their background and affiliation. At times a change of name indicates an attempt to move from one group to another, as in the case of Hannah Senesh, who insists on the Hebrew pronunciation of her name, or

Tomer's hero, who states: "Whoever wants to change his biography in this country, changes his name" (p. 28).

The most disturbing aspect of these Israeli plays is their palpable insensitivity to the historical tragedy. Whereas *The Heir* is an outstandingly obscene example, in most other works the authors fail to provide an adequate picture of the horrors of the Final Solution. There are many platitudes, like that of Shaham's Auerbach, "We were millions of Jews, and each one faced death in solitude" (p. 35), or unconvincing and almost cliched references to the killing of children in *Ḥannāh Seneš*. In that play Megged features Fruma, a mother who lost her daughter. Unfortunately, the dramatic presentation is so superfluous that neither the character nor her story possesses any vividness or poignancy. In order to underscore the pathos involved in the killing of children, Megged puts the following statement in Fruma's mouth: "They kill them all. I saw with my own eyes how they shot a kid who was running in the street after his father" (p. 60). This is a needless redundancy, as if her own personal tragedy may not have been sufficiently moving to make the point. Then there is an additional odd contradiction. Fruma, the bereaved mother, declares that she no longer feels anything; yet, when she sees Hannah's writing of "Shalom" on the wall, the stage directions indicate that she recognizes the meaning with great excitement (p. 61). Leah Goldberg also displays a similar failure to appreciate the monumental sufferings of the victims. The growing compassion for the Count's predicament culminates with Sand's statement: "I think he's the most unfortunate man I've met in all these years" (p. 66)—a rather odd observation by a Jew about a Christian in post-war Europe.

The Israeli plays also demonstrate harsh criticism of the victims' behavior. They project the image of the European Jews killed like slaughtered sheep. Explicit references to the notion of "sheep to the slaughter" appear in *Ḥannāh Seneš* (p. 77). Further, in the same play the Jews plan a disgraceful bargain with the Nazis. The incident of collaboration is often mentioned. Lena suspects the Israeli emissaries because she knows that "there are Jews who work for them" (p. 43). Auerbach and Sigmund are two examples of such collaboration. Shamir goes so far as to hint at another kind of Jewish complicity in the genocide through the "ironic" information that Wolf Cohen's father-in-law was the owner of gas factories in Germany. Usually the survivors command little respect or compassion. The recurrent theme is that a moral degradation was necessary to avoid death. Pomerantz often teases the idealistic protagonist of *A New Reckoning* by saying that people like Ammi would not have had a chance to survive the camps, and in Shamir's *The Heir* the same sentiment is echoed: "Dutch and German women died first: they were not ready. . . . They did not understand that you get dirty in the war, cheat the enemy, steal, pretend. . . " (p. 44).

Having set the action by contrasting the Holocaust with Israel, the playwrights do acknowledge that the conflict is not a clash between mutually exclusive and contradictory forces. The linkage between the two worlds is manifested by the presence of a pathetic young woman who shares the values of both worlds and is torn in the middle during the unfolding of the dramatic crisis. This clearly is the underlying structure of *Lady of the Castle,* and in each of the other plays there is a similar role. In *A New Reckoning,* Lisa, Dr. Auerbach's daughter, is the goal of her father's possessive attitudes and of Ammi's passion. Lisa survived the war by hiding in a monastery, but she can also qualify as an Israeli because of her youthfulness, purity, and her belief in pioneering. She is tied to her father, but she is also moved by Ammi's fresh love. The play's ending, which shows her in a dream-like scene with Ammi, suggests the latter's implicit triumph. In *Children of the Shadow,* Nurit is "purely" Israeli, yet she is unhappy with her environment, and she displays great sympathy for Yoram's problems and for his family. Nurit is desired by both Dubi and Yosselle-Yoram, but she loves Yoram because, as she puts it, he always remained Yossele. In *The Heir,* the protagonist's beloved, Hannah, is the only non-grotesque character of the play. She follows her father to Argentina, an act that draws her into the Diaspora world, but she then decides to return to the homeland. She loves Zeev-Wolf, but she is appalled by his vanity and finally leaves him. Thus, the presence of the young heroine—a curious parallel to the character of the pathetic Jewish female in Christian literature—is another key to the drama's ideological tendencies. Hannah Senesh demonstrates a triumphant Zionism, Lena's hesitations reflect Goldberg's cultural dilemmas, and Nurit's social criticism expresses Tomer's own revision.

A diachronic view of the six works reveals a remarkable difference between the three plays written in the fifties, *A New Reckoning, Lady of the Castle,* and *Ḥannāh Seneš,* and the plays written in the sixties, *Children of the Shadow, The Burning Season,* and *The Heir.* In the earlier works the Holocaust is conceived of as being a bad dream, or a terrible experience which ought to evaporate or be exorcised in the new entity of Israel. Israel's actuality is confronted with European tradition and culture in Goldberg's work; Hannah Senesh is an example of a heroic and idealistic Zionist, in contrast with the passive Jews who accept the expected death without any resistance; and the immorality of Shaham's survivors is contrasted with the idealism of the young kibbutz members. All these plays express the belief that the horrors of the Holocaust may be overcome in the new existence in Israel through a transformation of spirit and values. Clearly, that is a symptom of the great sense of exaltation in the early years of the state, when the realization of a two thousand-year-old dream ignited a belief in the visionary mission of the reborn Jewish homeland.

Disillusionment was gradual and inevitable. The forward-looking optimism gave way to an introspective contemplation of the past. The negative attitude toward the Holocaust was replaced by a search for roots and a reconciliation with the experience of the past. Practically, the plays of the sixties simply criticize the previous approach. Ben-Zion Tomer suffers precisely because in the early years of the state he was given, under tremendous pressure, to cast away his past identity for the sake of a new one. He realizes that each one is equally important for him, that he is both a new immigrant and a young pioneer, a survivor of the persecutions and a soldier fighting for his own country. In *The Burning Season,* Aharon Megged criticizes the ignorance and forgetfulness of the lessons of the past. The survivors close their eyes before another potential catastrophe, and the Israelis do not hesitate to turn a profit by signing a new contract with the devil. The apocalyptic tone of *The Burning Season* is replaced by bitter irony and black humor in *The Heir.* In Shamir's play the Isrealis take advantage of the guilty German conscience, and the survivors themselves mindlessly suppress the trauma of the past. The surviving members of the Auschwitz orchestra now make their living by playing in night clubs, and they plan their joyful reunion in order to make money from an extraordinary public performance. In a way, they recovered too much. In conclusion, the plays of the sixties undermine the nationalistic assurance of the preceding works. Rather than viewing the Holocaust as being an obstacle to the full realization of the new ideals, they find the concept of national identity itself to be confusing and problematic.

The Israeli self-examination is characterized by an extraordinary rigor. Despite the significant achievements of Zionism in the twentieth century, there is a strong tendency among most Israeli intellectuals to concentrate on negative points which must be changed or improved. This critical spirit often leads to the inflation of minor problems into major crises and the aggrandizement of imperfections into unbearable flaws. (Some feel this is an admirable atavistic attitude originating with the classical biblical prophets; others regard it as a regrettable Jewish compulsion to be unrealistically obsessed with perfect justice and morality under any circumstances.) In the case of the Israeli experience, there is an additional dimension that accounts for some misjudgment of the significance of historical developments: it is precisely the very intimate involvement with crucial events that tends to obscure the proper perspective.

The Israeli author finds himself in a paradoxical position in which his critical stance and vision compel him to be at once the judge, the witness, and the judged. In addition, he or she is often encumbered by the mundane details of civic responsibilities, annoying bureaucracy, and partisan politics, all of which frustrate the inclination to appreciate great historic moments and extraordinary predicaments. Thus, the failure to recognize the Holocaust's uniqueness and its crucial implications for the Jewish state was symptomatic of a national drama that lacks the necessary distance or the will to mythologize familiar events. In the seventies, however, after the shock of the Yom Kippur war and a recognition of Israel's new predicament in the international scene, Hebrew literature manifested a growing identification with the Holocaust Jew. Although no significant play on the subject has emerged from this mood, the Israeli theatres staged numerous productions on the Holocaust,

based on international dramas and local projects.[10] Of the authors mentioned in this study (with the exception of Goldberg, who died in 1970), each has demonstrated in his literary creation or personal politics the acceptance of the past trauma as an integral part of the national psyche.[11] The final note of Mintz's recent book is the following statement: "The long estrangement between contemporary Zionist enterprise and the full Jewish past is ready to be lessened. The encounter is just beginning" (1984, p. 269). This phenomenon undoubtedly deserves another serious study, for this encounter is part of a broader process, which is the growing acceptance by the Israelis of their identity as a Jewish state in terms of the national and historical fate of the Jewish people throughout the ages. The gestation of this attitude in the sixties and its culmination in the seventies and eighties is in sharp contrast to the Yishuv tendency to view itself as being the antithesis of the last two thousand years of Jewish history. The integration of the Jewish past involves the glorious days of biblical times and the cultural peaks of post-biblical periods as well as the great calamities of Diaspora persecutions, including the Holocaust. Thus even though there is no causal connection between the Nazi genocide and the creation of Israel, the two events must be considered as crucial moments in the history of the Jewish people, and so they must be contemplated in relation to each other. The pattern reflected in the Israeli Holocaust plays is that of the gradual abandonment of the Yishuv mentality, which is being replaced by the development of a national identity in the context of the entire Jewish history. We began our discussion with the dichotomous presentation of Shaham's *A New Reckoning* and concluded with Megged's *The Burning Season,* which addresses contemporary issues relating to the Holocaust while blurring the distinctions between the Diaspora Jew and the Israeli, or between biblical trials and modern predicaments. Ultimately the course of Hebrew drama is bound by an umbilical cord to the complexities of modern Jewish history. And this is why Peter Brook once made the following statement in a radio interview: The Israelis, according to the British director, don't have to write great drama—they actually live it.

### NOTES

[1] Yehuda Bauer (1982, p. 348) wrote: "The state of Israel did not result from the Holocaust; in fact, had the Holocaust not occurred, it is more than likely that Israel may have risen quicker, and better and more securely."

[2] See Shoham (1975, pp. 20-21).

[3] This essay deals only with the Israeli drama in the fifties and sixties. In recent years a number of remarkable works have been produced on the Holocaust, including Yehushua Sobol's *Ghetto* and plays on such figures as Anne Frank, Korczak, and Kastner. The causes for this new interest in the past catastrophe should be the subject of another essay.

[4] Shaham's plot was undoubtedly inspired by the Kastner trial which preoccupied the entire country in the early fifties.

[5] See Shaked (1958). Shaked is usually a highly perceptive reader. He wrote the review of Goldberg's play many years ago, and I suspect that his uncritical fascination with the Count's figure and his world are symptomatic of the contemporary Israeli feelings toward the Diaspora; i.e., for the young Israeli critic, the Count represented a fascinating and respectable European dignity which was the opposite of the rejected shtetl misery.

[6] Lewis Funke, the *New York Times* critic, observed the play's weaknesses but praised its thematic concerns and its effectiveness. In his review of the Habimah production in New York, he wrote: "Conceived somewhat more in terms of the novel than the stage, episodic at times and sprawling, it nevertheless carries an impact that thrusts deep into the heart and chokes the throat. Weak at times in motivation, awkward in its meanderings, it encompasses the inescapable inner drama of its subject—the problem of building a new life in a new country by those who have known the terrors of the Nazi holocaust, the ever-present haunting past of those who in the time of the bloodletting and the crematoriums chose collaboration and life in preference to revolt and death" (February 27, 1964).

[7] See Abramson (1979, pp. 132-133). Abramson's book on modern Hebrew drama includes a section entitled "the plays of the Holocaust." Less interest in the topic itself, the critic considers the treatment of the Holocaust as a subgenre and examines its place in the general evolution of Israeli drama. Abramson however discusses the dramatic themes in *Lady of the Castle* (which she calls *The Chatelaine*), *Children of the Shadow*, *The Heir*, and *Ḥannāh Seneš* in that order. This order, which is not chronological, reflects the author's judgment on the relative importance of each work in the development of Israeli drama.

[8] See Ofrat (1975, p. 163).

[9] See Naveh (1977, p. 9).

[10] See also Ramras-Rauch (1978) and Oren (1983).

[11] The most dramatic example of political reversal is the case of Moshe Shamir, who has changed from a leftist socialist to a member of a right-wing, nationalist party.

BIBLIOGRAPHY

Abramson, Glenda. 1979. *Modern Hebrew Drama*. London.

Bauer, Yehuda. 1982. *A History of the Holocaust*. New York.

Goldberg, Leah. 1974. *Lady of the Castle*. Trans. by T. Carmi. Tel Aviv.

Megged, Aharon. 1958. *Ḥannāh Seneš*. Tel Aviv.

———. 1967. *Ha'ona habbo'eret.* Tel Aviv.

Mintz, Alan. 1984. *Hurban: Responses to Catastrophe in Hebrew Literature*. New York.

Naveh, Edith. 1977. "Dramaturgical Problems in Plays with the Theme of the Nazi Holocaust." Ph.D. Dissertation, University of Pittsburgh.

Ofrat, Gideon. 1975. *Haddrāmā hayyisre'ēlît*. Tel Aviv.

Oren, Yosef. 1983. *Hahitpakkeḥût bassipōret hayyisre'ēlît.* Tel Aviv.

Ramras-Rauch, Gila. 1978. "The Re-Emergence of the Jew in the Israeli Fiction of the 1970's." *Hebrew Annual Review* 2:131-144.

Shaham, Nathan. 1954. *Ḥesbôn ḥādāš. Māsāk* 1:5-37.

Shaked, Gershon. 1958. *"Hā'armôn vehehāmôn." Moznayim* 3:186-190.

———. 1971. *Gal ḥādāš bassipōret ha'ibrît*. Tel Aviv.

Shamir, Moshe. 1963. *Hayyôrēš. Te'aṭrôn* 9:27-47.

Shoham, Haim. 1975. *'Etgār umeṣî'ût baddrāmā hayyisre'ēlît*. Ramat Gan.

Tomer, Ben-Zion. 1982. *Children of the Shadow*. Trans. by Hillel Halkin. Tel Aviv.

## Emanuel Rubin

SOURCE: "Israel's Theatre of Confrontation," in *World Literature Today*, Vol. 60, No. 2, Spring, 1986, pp. 239-244.

[*In the following essay, Rubin describes the sociopolitical role of contemporary Israeli theater.*]

Israel, as an open, democratic society existing in a state of siege, is a country in which all the measures of artistic and individual expression are daily put to the test of whether they do—or should—serve the nation's interests. In those circumstances Israeli theatre, especially in the past few years, has moved into the vanguard of the arts in taking a didactic tack that has often brought it into outright confrontation with the public. That approach is hardly an Israeli invention, but it does represent a departure from the mainstream of Western theatre, recently dominated by a focus on self-discovery and the relationship of individuals rather than ethical or cultural values. In this article the Israeli stage is examined as a forum for expression of the artist's vision of a higher law, the roots of that attitude are traced, and its implications explored.

Theatre attendance is very high in Israel, with some three million tickets reliably estimated to have been sold in 1980, a number equal to the total population of the country.[1] That gives Israel the highest per capita theatre attendance in the world, about eight times that of the United States. Nor is attendance class-related. It cuts across all social and economic lines, making the stage a truly demotic forum for ideas: "In Israel . . . bringing the blue-collar worker and lower classes to the theatre was never a problem" (Levy, 40). Then too, the country is small enough that almost everyone knows almost everyone else in the professional world, and because of its strong egalitarian outlook there is more offstage fraternization between actors and their audiences than one finds in most Western countries. Being so deeply entwined in the society, actors, playwrights, and directors have always been unusually sensitive to national moods. It would come as no surprise, then, to see the present depression and frustration reflected on the stage. What does strike an observer as unusual is to find professional theatre acting as a brutal goad rather than a sympathetic nurse. Where one might expect to find solace, Israeli theatre doses its public with wormwood and gall. Sartre's *Trojan Women,* for example, was set in a refugee camp with the guards wearing Israeli uniforms and carrying Israeli weapons. This was not a random choice for dramatic updating, but was staged during the turmoil that followed charges of Israeli negligence in permitting Phalangist massacres in Lebanon's Sabra and Shatila refugee camps. "It was very hard to take, but it had some truth in it," said actor Misha Asherov.[2] To make a play of the past come to grips with the present is hardly a new idea; but methodically to create a setting with the intent of affronting the audience is not simply "relevant," to use a word with hackneyed overtones; it is provocative. It is a theatre of confrontation.

Such a stance produces practical, not just theoretical, problems in the politics of art. When poet Yitzchak Laor, seething with anger, wrote a poem for the literary journal *Siman Kri'ah* that included the phrase, "and in our *matzot* the blood of Palestinian youths," he enlisted two thousand years of blood libel against the Jews as a powerful yet extremely offensive ally in opposition to the government's internal policies. The potency of burning Israel's sacred Torah onstage, as was done in the play *Tashmad,* cannot be denied; but must any society stand by and watch its most cherished symbols desecrated, its history flogged, and its recent wounds torn open publicly in the name of "Art"?

The answer, of course, is clear if one lives in Switzerland, Denmark, or the United States. There society is strong enough and the freedom great enough to withstand such attacks. The long-range value to the culture far outweighs the shock to community delicacy, and the principle of untrammeled artistic expression is of greater import than any temporary discomfort. In more stringently regulated countries such as the Soviet Union or Chile, the question is moot. Whether by consensus or fiat, those societies have subscribed to the Platonic vision of art regulated in support of a prescribed political vision. Violation of that aim, however courageous, is viewed as a thoughtless or selfish aberration, like someone who insists on driving through red lights or absconding with his neighbor's goods, and is treated accordingly.

Israel presents a more problematic situation. Maintaining the ideal of an open society, it is beset by external enemies and internal tensions that threaten imminent destruction in very real terms. Those who widen existing fissures or diverge from the common purpose can easily be viewed as insurgents or dangers to the integrity of the body politic. One need only think of the treatment accorded to American Vietnam protesters of the sixties and seventies under much less stringent circumstances to imagine the situation. This is further complicated by the fact that the performing arts are publicly subsidized in Israel, with all that implies, from government intervention in their content and presentation to the right of the artist to bite the hand that feeds him.

During a brief return of several weeks to Israel I spoke about this to a number of people in the theatre and uncovered not a festering sore, as I had expected, but a pot boiling with philosophical currents and crosscurrents, arguments and convictions on every side of the issue. In a country where 26 percent of the population are theatregoers,[3] the events of the 1983-84 season outline the main themes of that debate, as the arts, with theatre in the vanguard, attempt to delineate the ethical and moral center of the country's national life. Israeli theatre sees itself as a voice of opposition, probing at national ideals from the stage in an abrasive way that is uniquely and aggressively Israeli. Art in the public market has once again become a vehicle for reform, as it had been in an earlier Jewish commonwealth for Jeremiah, Ezekiel, and Hosea.

Some fundamental assumptions about theatre's place in modern society were made and questioned in such presentations as Moshe Shamir's *Judith of the Lepers,* a 1968 play based on the biblical story of Judith and Holofernes. Shamir's *Judith* was not simply a Bible story. It carried a bitter message that there is no morality in war or international relations. "For Jews, even fanatical ones," laments Uri Rapp in his review, "the play is a rejection of whatever they believed in."[4] The content may have been about characters from the Bible, but the subject was today's world, and an unpleasant view of it at that.

This is not to say that the entire season is an unrelieved succession of head-on collisions between the theatrical establishment and its public. *Much Ado about Nothing* was on the boards at the Haifa Municipal Theatre, and the national theatre, the Habimah, presented the Neapolitan farce *Caviar and Lentils* in Tel Aviv along with a setting of *Hamlet* as "re-adapted" by David Avidom and directed by Dino Cernescu. *Mephisto* was imported, based on Klaus Mann's novel by Ariane Minouchkine, founder of the Théâtre de Soleil in Paris, and for local color, *Behind the Fence,* an adaptation of a Bialik love story by Avi Koren, was presented. Those only served, though, to make the Israeli plays of confrontation and the controversies surrounding them stand out in bolder relief.

Nola Chilton, 1972 winner of the Tel Aviv Prize for directing and developing Israeli drama and twice winner of the "David's Harp" Award (1974, 1982), staged a play by Yehoshua Sobol, *The Seamen's Mutiny,* dealing with a scandal from the early days of the state in which many felt that the ideals of Zionism were sacrificed to the exigencies of politics. Motti Barhav's *Sanjer* dealt with drug addiction and Haim Marin's *Bunker* with the unpleasant but ever-present topic of war. A new play called *Ali the Galilean* by François Abu Salem, a Palestinian theatre director living in Jerusalem, was produced. In spite of many trials, at the end Ali is still an Arab and not "a hollow man calling himself Eli and trying to pass for a Jew."[5]

> The message of the play for an Arab audience is . . . keep your chins up and hang on to your culture. . . . The message for a Jewish audience is: Here's what you look like to the people who clean your streets and bake your bread. (Grossman, 17)

Hanoch Levin's cynical and scatological play *The Patriot* was excoriated by the government censorship board, which sued to have it banned. *The Patriot* rubbed Israeli sensibilities the wrong way. The protagonist is a cynic who, unwilling to participate in the spiritual or physical defense of the country, falls back on Johnson's "last refuge of a scoundrel" to profiteer from his fellow citizens' plight. Another committee of the same government, though, awarded the author the Leah Porat Prize for Literature only a few months later, confusing the issue still further.

In December 1983 Haim Druckman, a conservative member of the Knesset, had had enough and initiated a parliamentary debate on the "offence to the basic values of Judaism, the nation and the state in theatre productions."[6] That, in turn, sparked a March 1984 meeting of two hundred Israeli writers, artists, and academics in Tel Aviv's Tzavta Theatre, where a resolution was unanimously adopted establishing a watch-dog committee to "defend freedom of expression in the arts." In fact, the Israeli arts in general have come under increasing fire from the country's conservative elements. Deputy Minister of Education and Culture Miriam Ta'asa-Glaser referred to poet Yona Wallach as a "beast in heat" in an interview for the now-defunct newspaper *Rehov Rashi.* The remark was made in reference to a poem published in the monthly literary magazine *Iton 77* entitled "T'fillin," in which "the phylacteries of the title are used to embellish sexual intercourse" (Pomerantz, 12). Tel Aviv University suspended support of the literary review *Siman Kri'ah* when it printed an offensive political poem by Yitzchak Laor. "Liturgica," an international festival of religious music held annually in Jerusalem, had a performance of Bach's *Passion According to St. John* disrupted by an organized demonstration of students from one of the yeshivas.[7]

The case of *The Patriot,* which engendered angry censorship on the one hand and inspired a national award on the other, was just one of a series of contradictions. Another play, *The Soul of a Jew,* by Yehoshua Sobel (directed by Gedalia Besser), had a run at the Riverside in London and was a hit at the 1983 Edinburgh Festival, where "the audience gave it a rapturous reception."[8] Theatre critic John Clifford, writing in *The Scotsman,* praised it as "intellectually enthralling and very deeply moving . . . it is easy to understand its impact in Israel, given its intense relevance to the country's current crisis of ideals and identity." In Israel, though, the play met with a mixed reception, to say the least. Performances were disrupted by zealous demonstrators, and even erstwhile supporters occasionally walked out of the theatre in distaste. Professionals and audiences alike were divided in their opinion of the play, which may be as it should be, for the work deals, in explosive language, with a Jewish protagonist living in Europe at the end of the nineteenth century who represents an assault on every value held dear to the Israeli: a sexist, self-hating, homosexual nihilist who finally commits suicide.

A speech in Martin Sherman's *Messiah,* given at the Haifa Municipal Theatre, resulted in threatening letters and two bomb scares at the theatre. The play is about Shabetai Zvi, the sixteenth-century poseur and false messiah, and the particular lines cited as so offensive are those of a young woman who, in an intense dialogue with God, cries out, "Cursed be You, God Almighty," then "You do not exist" and "I hate you." The embattled government and the religious establishment did not take this lightly. Moshe Blimenthal, head of the three-member United Religious Front of the Haifa City Council, filed a complaint with the city police, who finally decided that there were insufficient grounds on which to act.

The artistic director and playwright, of course, stood firm on leaving the lines in. At that point, in this already overheated atmosphere, Shlomo Lorincz, an Orthodox rabbi, member of Agudat Yisrael (a right-wing religious-political party), and chairman of the Knesset Finance Committee, threatened to withhold some two billion shekels in government funds owed to the city unless mayor Arieh Gurel forced the theatre to remove the lines. The issue was finally resolved with the lines' being stricken, but the intervention of Israel's president, Chaim Herzog, was required. Without having seen the play, Herzog asked that those lines be deleted "in the spirit of tolerance and mutual respect."[9] The president's polite request, however, did not neglect to bring up the matter of a little-used 1973 law that could be used to impose a one-year jail sentence for any person who "offends in speech or writing the religious faith and feelings of others." Israeli political scientist Allan Shapiro explains:

> Offending religious sensibilities was a punishable offense under the Ottoman code, and was perpetuated in British-ruled Palestine even before the formal inception of Mandatory rule. In independent Israel it has been evoked to protect Christian sensibilities,

as in the banning of Amos Kenan's play, *Friends Tell about Jesus* in 1972, which resulted in a high court decision referred to . . . by president Chaim Herzog in the matter of the Haifa production of *The Messiah.*[10]

In reaction to Herzog's plea, the author Aharon Megged, president of the Israeli branch of PEN, released a statement attacking the president for his interference with free speech.

Somewhere in this mixed bag of provocations and responses one can sense a confused search for a principle that would harmonize the heritage of open-mindedness with the fears of a religious-political establishment that feels beset from within the country as well as from without. What is taking place is something more complex than a descent down the dreary path of repression already trod by so many nations. Having inherited censorship laws from both Turkish and British administrations together with a centuries-old tradition of individualism and the free exchange of ideas, Israel is wrestling anew with the question of the mutual responsibilities of the artist and society. Time-honored arguments over the purpose of art have become pressing, practical issues in Israel today, perhaps more so than anywhere else, and the answers are making headlines and lawsuits on the eastern edge of the Mediterranean.

For every attempt to quash the confrontational nature of Israeli theatre there has been a counterploy to support it. The parliamentary debate on theatre as an "offense to the basic values of Judaism" was met by another motion opposing any intervention whatsoever in the country's artistic, creative, and intellectual life. Given the complex structure and party discipline of Israeli politics, it is heartening to note that even though it was defeated, the countermotion proposed by M.K. Yossi Sarid received forty-seven votes, whereas the floor had been opened to the original debate on a vote of only fifty.[11]

The theatre critic Uri Rapp wrote, quite reasonably, in *The Jerusalem Post:*

> The girl [in Martin Sherman's *Messiah*] who curses God and denies his existence in one breath . . . is an ardent believer. Only a deeply religious person could give vent to such disillusionment. . . . The offending sentences are part of a very intimate relationship with God.
>
> There are few other forums [besides theatre, in Israel] where issues can be thrashed out publicly. Thus constant vigilance is imperative against any attempt to silence the debate. Art is not a matter of consensus but of controversy, at least in a pluralistic society. A play like Martin Sherman's *Messiah* could have been a case in point . . . but no genuine debate materialized for two reasons. First *Messiah* is simply a bad play . . . [but] this is not the first time that artists and intellectuals have had to fight over a piece of little artistic value all for the sake of freedom of expression. The

second problem was the attempt to get the play taken off the stage, or at least to get the theatre to delete a passage which "offended" the kind of people who don't go to the theatre anyway.[12]

What is taking place in this pragmatic pressure cooker appears to be a gradual redefinition of theatre's sociopolitical role in the country. Aharon Megged, who had castigated President Herzog for his attack on free speech, also said, following the protest meeting at the Tzavta Theatre in Tel Aviv: "Someone coming to the Tzavta meeting from the outside might have thought this was Chile. We don't have to act as if we're in a fascist regime."[13] The Haifa police found no cause to close the municipal theatre over Martin Sherman's *Messiah,* and the fuss, as might be imagined, contributed greatly to the financial success of the play, as it had for Levin's *Patriot.*

Is it possible for a government that holds the purse strings of the arts and carries a public censorship law on its books to maintain even a façade of freedom of expression? Most in the West would answer no. It can only lead, one would think, to state control of the arts, a horror that seems to follow logically from state support of the arts, at least in American eyes. It is also clear, though, that official attempts at repression have put no appreciable brake on the assault emanating from the state-subsidized stage, and that until the issue is finally resolved, it will bear close observation.

That all this should be coming to the fore now is no accident. A national culture grows out of the weaving of threads into a fabric that becomes a cloth of assumptions against which value judgments can be projected by members of the society. The Israeli stage has a history of political awareness dating back to the birth of the Habimah in Moscow during the second decade of the century as a Hebrew theatre-in-exile. From the earliest days of its existence, "Most of the idea-elements in the *Habimah* ideology, artistic and nonartistic, were based primarily on moral and ethical, rather than aesthetic, considerations."[14]

The establishment of a national theatre was an early priority to the founding fathers of the state. That meant more than simply creating a paid troupe of actors with a performance venue; it meant developing the language and creating new plays relevant to the culture expressed in modern Hebrew as well as transmitting the heritage of the past. At the same time that new literature came into being in a revived Hebrew, Haim Nahman Bialik translated *Don Quixote* and Saul Tchernikovsky brought out the *Iliad,* the *Odyssey,* and the *Kalevala* in Hebrew as part of the earliest stages of revitalizing the national language and culture.

The Habimah was performing in Hebrew in Moscow by 1918 and established itself in Tel Aviv by 1926. Its first production, opening on 18 October 1918, was the Hebrew-language composite *Neshef Bereshit* (An Evening of Beginning), composed of *The Eldest Sister* by S. Asch,

*The Hot Sun* by I. Katznelson, *The Fire* by I. L. Peretz, and *The Bone* by I. D. Berkowitz. The balance between theatre as national expression and theatre as world art has seesawed back and forth since then, but "The topic of the play, i.e., Jewish or non-Jewish, did not in itself guarantee a successful or popular production. . . . What accounted for the popularity of these plays was not their topic or ideas, but their artistic level" (*H,* 48-49).

By 1948, when the nation gained official recognition, state support of theatre was well established. The theatre had played a significant role in setting the standard of a reconstituted Hebrew language as well as disseminating Zionist ideals of the collective future of the land, the value of physical labor, and aspirations to intellectual achievement. In the next twenty years Israeli theatre grew in a climate of financial and intellectual expansion, developing new performance venues throughout the country and strengthening an already solid popular base.

Emanuel Levy, in his 1980 study of the Habimah, concluded that Israeli theatre has been, from its outset, internationally oriented, with artistic quality being the most important factor in establishing a play's success (*H,* 48-49). He also noted a high proportion of new native plays produced by the country's four major theatres, remarking as an aside to the main thrust of his interest, "Indeed, most of the Hebrew-Israeli plays were topical and realistic . . . for their subject matter they drew upon current events and issues" (*H,* 43). His point was that an affinity for "imported" culture exists in Israel as a manifestation of opposition to ethnocentrism and that Israeli theatre strives for universality in repertoire and outlook, downplaying parochial interests and local playwrights.

There has been a change in the mood of the country, though, in reaction to the situation in Lebanon, and in response, confrontational theatre has come to play a more important role in Israel within the last few years than in the period covered by Levy's study. Productions that "draw upon current events and issues" have promoted the sense of social commitment, always an important secondary role in Hebrew drama, into a frothing, cudgel-swinging main character prowling the forestage. There are two principal reasons for this. The first is based on the particular social and financial circumstances in which the theatre establishment finds itself today; the second, and more far-reaching, grows naturally out of the traditional mission of theatre within the Zionist enterprise.

To understand the first of those reasons, it is necessary to recall as background that until 1969 all the theatres in Israel were cooperatives, with actors and professional staff enjoying a beneficent system that virtually assured tenure. A few years of work guaranteed, if not assignments, then at least a low-pressure sinecure followed by a comfortable pension. It took a fortunately-timed financial and administrative crisis in the government to impose belt-tightening, which resulted in the present structure of public corporations. Those corporate theatres were provided with substantial subsidies jointly from the central government and their local municipalities in order to maintain what was perceived as a central role for theatre in Israeli cultural life. While standards have risen in the permanent repertory troupes, the division of responsibilities and loyalties has produced an administrative ambiguity that has, in effect, given artistic directors greater independence than they might have enjoyed under the earlier system.

The second reason is far more compelling, for it grows out of the reactions of artists themselves to frustration with their society and its loss of innocence. Zionism, whatever else it may have been, was based on a unique mélange of political and spiritual ideology envisioning the reentry of a people into the realities of history after a two-thousand-year hiatus. That reentry, though, was to have been on a basis that would establish new societal standards for humanitarian and egalitarian behavior among nations as well as among its own citizens. The facts of the matter have resisted that idealization. The triumph of the 1967 "Six-Day War" may have done more damage to the values of Zionism than any other single event. Culturally, it was a pyrrhic victory. "It killed us." said sixty-year-old Misha Asherov.

> You can't even imagine what happened. . . . I was in Chicago the day it happened [6 June 1967] and I couldn't come [home]. And when I arrived it was four days after the war was finished. When I arrived I took a Jeep with a friend to the Golan Heights, and when I came there and saw the things, the defeated [Syrian] army . . . all of a sudden I felt myself like—no use! I felt, maybe, like Alexander the Great when he is in his prime. And if you are not sane, at that moment you start to become the megalomaniac. . . . With the inflation we had and the boom we had, everyone [thought] we could buy America!

A great euphoria, almost akin to megalomania, swept the country. At that moment many of the younger generation of Israeli artists began to see their homeland not as the conquering lion of Judah portrayed in the world press, but as a defector from the social ideal toward which all their history had aspired. The stage was set for a generation of socially-oriented artists to charge their elders with living up to their teachings. Nola Chilton put together her emotionally charged "docudrama," *Soldiers Talk,* a powerful series of dialogues assembled from interviews with young Israelis still hot from the battlefield. A generation of artists looked at what had been foisted on them by friends as much as by enemies and were dissatisfied. What they saw was a country aspiring to wealth, power, and material values, not to freedom and justice. Israel was to have become a "light unto the nations," but it appeared to be only one more country on the map, no different than the others.

Actors and directors took every opportunity to express their opinion of the wrong turn they saw the country taking. Asherov recounts a typical story describing the forms that expression took.

You know that I played in *Who's Afraid of Virginia Woolf?* . . . We planned this play as a political play, a social/political play. We planned the subject of false belief, that they believed that they had a child. We planned it for Israel to [relate to] the actual life that we have here now. What's the actual life that we are living and dreaming? That we are big, that we are rich, that we can afford everything. Then all of a sudden, all the banks are down and all the economy is down: the child is dead. That's the thing we turned into the play. You see, it depends what drives you to give the interpretation.

Prodded as to whether such an interpretation was legitimate for a group of actors to take upon themselves, he responded, "Yes, especially now." It wasn't, he explained, that they favored this or that political party as much as it was that artists needed to be on guard against government itself.

Look, from one side it doesn't matter if it is Russia or the way it was in the Nazi time; they wanted that the artist will serve the regime. Artists here say that we have to serve the ideas that we believe are right. As I told you about *The Trojan Women,* if you play it in Athens or Troy in that time, what do you care about it? But if things [are represented], actual things that happen to you now, and you have to give the answers now, it turns the theatre . . . the theatre becomes a live theatre. You see, we have to say what we have to say because . . . I don't know how it is in America . . . maybe what happened now with the Marines. . . . My dear friend, two hundred and some people killed in Lebanon. Isn't it your relative, isn't it your neighbor, isn't it an American? Why did people not ask [in 1982], "What are Americans doing in Lebanon?"

Viewed in this way, every play becomes more than a theatre event. It becomes, as well, a tool for the artist to shape society. In Haifa, at the Municipal Theatre, manager Noam Semel and artistic director Omri Nitzan have developed a policy in which they see each new Israeli play as "another point in a sort of connect-the-dots game: it's our self-portrait. With local material, by necessity, we make more mistakes. But point by point we begin to see ourselves."[15] That approach carries through even in the choice and staging of foreign plays. *The Island,* for instance, was not set in South Africa with prisoners of Soweto, but in Israel, and was performed by two Arab actors—in Arabic.

It is clear that the recent theatre seasons were not simply an aberration of dirty words, offensive phrases, and anti-government sentiments, as may appear at first glance. They were the fruits of a scenario that had its roots in the earliest principles of public theatre in Israel, then grew to maturity in the atmosphere of disgust with a '67 victory that smacked of too much triumph and despair at the '73 victory that tasted too much of defeat. The disastrous Lebanon adventure, a divisive and perhaps pointless exercise, ground an additional sense of bitter disillusionment into Israeli idealists.

Conventional wisdom has it that, to the extent that art remains pure, it better serves the muse. "The arts as a political weapon proved impotent,"[16] wrote Robert Corrigan, who found that politics proved "deaestheticizing" to American theatre of the sixties. It has certainly been true that for every *Guernica* there have been hundreds of polemical works that have not survived their immediate political point. There is no reason, though, to believe that a work's subject matter must necessarily weaken its artistic thrust. Corrigan's concern, and thus his conclusion, was less with the uses of theatre than with its form; but theatre has been a didactic art since its beginnings. In all its rituals and expressions it has served the purposes of education, propaganda, and public morality from time immemorial. Whether demonstrating the fate of Oedipus, the prayer of the *Pattukaran,* or the postadolescent problems of Laverne and Shirley, a principal impetus for theatre through most of its history has been the transmission and explication of culture.

The theatrical establishment in Israel is imbued with a fierce sense of mission. Only in a brief period toward the end of the Vietnam War did American theatre attempt to serve as the country's political conscience, and as important as that effort may have been as a political gesture, its impact on either history or theatre in the United States was infinitesimal. Israeli writers, though, have taken the tough stance of biblical prophets with their audience and have touched off a predictably heated reaction. Hardly a single new play has appeared in the last few years that did not have some such component, and many productions of traditional and foreign works gained a dimension in their direction and staging that put them into just such a posture. Seen from that perspective, the recent swirl of conflict takes on a pattern that reflects a view of theatre as a sociocritical voice actively creating and maintaining the values of a cultural system.

#### NOTES

[1] Emanuel Levy, "National and Imported Culture in Israel," *Sociological Focus,* 13 (January 1980), p. 40.

[2] Misha Asherov was a student of Stanislavsky and has been a member of the Habimah's staff in Tel Aviv since 1946. The direct quotes from him in this paper are taken from a personal interview which I conducted with him at his home in Tel Aviv on 3 January 1984.

[3] Augustine Zycher, "Israeli Theatre Is Now Developing Its Own Character," *New York Times,* 3 December 1978, pp. 6 ff.

[4] Uri Rapp, "Kill or Be Killed," *Jerusalem Post* (International Edition), 22-28 January 1984, p. 18.

[5] Ed Grossman, "A Palestinian's Message," *Jerusalem Post* (International Edition), 3-9 October 1984, p. 17.

[6] Marsha Pomerantz, "Muzzling the Muses," *Jerusalem Post* (International Edition), 15-21 April 1984, p. 12.

[7] Exception was taken to specific anti-Jewish sentiments expressed in St. John's account of the Passion, not to the work as a whole or its other theological content. Berlioz's setting of the Te Deum, for example, met no objections when it was performed in that same series, because the text conveyed no such offense.

[8] "Israeli Play Is Edinburgh Hit," *Jerusalem Post* (International Edition), 28 August-3 September 1983, p. 16.

[9] "Herzog in Flap over Haifa Play's 'Blasphemous Line,'" *Jerusalem Post* (International Edition), 5-11 February 1984, p. 9.

[10] Allen E. Shapiro, "A Question of Blasphemy," *Jerusalem Post* (International Edition), 12-18 February 1984, p. 14.

[11] There are a total of 120 members in the Israeli Knesset or Parliament. Members are designated, in English, by the letters M.K. ("Member of the Knesset") preceding their name, or sometimes by H.K. ("Haver Knesset," Hebrew for the same).

[12] Uri Rapp, "A Challenge Missed," *Jerusalem Post* (International Edition), 12-18 February 1984, p. 17.

[13] Pomerantz, p. 12.

[14] Emanuel Levy, *The Habimah: Israel's National Theatre,* 1917-77, 1980, p. 27. Subsequent citations use the abbreviation *H.* For a review, see *WLT* 54:3 (Spring 1980), p. 482.

[15] Marsha Pomerantz, "Shakespeare and the Jewish Question," *Jerusalem Post* (International Edition), 6-12 November 1983, p. 19.

[16] Robert Corrigan, "The Search for New Endings: The Theatre in Search of a Fix, Part III," *Theatre Journal,* 36:2 (May 1984), p. 153.

---

# WOMEN AND ISRAELI LITERATURE

### Dror Abend

SOURCE: "Solipsism in Israeli Feminist Poetry: The Great Male Writer, Toni Morrison," in *World Literature Today,* Vol. 68, No. 3, Summer, 1994, pp. 505-08.

[*In the following essay, Abend assesses the influence of American literature and culture on Israeli feminist poetry.*]

Individualism, a distinctly Western ideal, is a concept one often associates with personal freedom, privacy, and control over one's life choices. But within the consumer-oriented structures of the West, individualism is also a solipsism, as one is often more interested in one's own wishes and sentiments than in the greater issues of society. In the exportation of this ideal to the cultural provinces of the United States, one wonders which of its two facets will prevail: that of individual freedom—supposedly freedom for all—or that of social solipsism. In the case of feminist writings and practices, the interpretation of individualism is significant. An earlier call for women's rights by privileged women in the United States in the 1970s and 1980s was well received by other privileged women in different parts of the world. Current association of the plight of women with that of American minorities, and even that of unprivileged people in the Third World, may pose a problem to women in countries that practice various forms of social injustice.

A look at the development of a feminist tradition within Israeli poetry in the last forty years provides an opportunity to realize the extent to which cultural provinces of the United States are influenced by American ideas and ideologies. In this respect, poets such as Emily Dickinson, Anne Sexton, and Sylvia Plath are presented as cultural role models who, much like the movie stars of the 1940s and 1950s, serve as ambassadors of American culture. It is important to realize, however, that it is not only the projection of ideals that is examined here, but also the willingness of the receiver to be influenced by certain messages, as well as the receiver's unwillingness to be influenced by others. In the poetry of Israeli women, the concept of the individual and her right to personal happiness was easily received by a society that imitates the consumer-oriented mechanisms of American economics. Feminism, as a result, was translated into the idea of the individual woman's right to the pursuit of happiness in terms of education, life opportunities, and equal pay—that is, so long as she lives in a Tel Aviv suburb. In a country that limits one's choice of food—not to mention the choice of Palestinian children to become Palestinian adults—the values of freedom and equality, under the assumption that they are applicable to all, certainly constitute a weaker message. Moreover, in the political reality of Israel, feminist poetry not only failed to protest the shortcomings of society, but was actually the bandwagon of solipsism for male poets who could no longer deal with the social reality. Certainly the recent announcement on Israeli national radio that the famous *male* writer Toni Morrison had won the Nobel Prize in Literature reflects on the Israeli image of feminist writings, as it tends to eliminate facts and notions that may stretch beyond one's own realms of individualism.

In its political, economic, and cultural aspects, Israeli society was first intended as a socialist structure, modeled after the turn-of-the-century ideals of Eastern Europe. Hebrew poetry in Palestine, and later in Israel, was, accordingly, highly prophetic, society-oriented, and considered the individual only in relation to his—and seldom, her—role in society. Despite certain influences of European romanticism, highly significant in turn-of-the-century Hebrew poetry, and early translations of modern

American poetry, available in Yiddish as early as 1927,[1] the main influences on Hebrew poetry until the 1950s were largely those of such Russian writers as Chekhov and Tolstoy and the poet Pushkin, who helped win the hearts of many young women when properly read on dark Oriental nights. The 1950s, characterized by such American symbols as James Dean, Coca-Cola bottles, and, finally, the shutdown of the Israeli embassy in Moscow in 1952—only four years after the official declaration of the State of Israel—unleashed a group of young poets who, well beyond the bounds of rhyme and meter, swept through the streets of Tel Aviv with what would then be considered subversive poetry, speaking of individualism, hedonism, love, and sex. David Avidan's poem "Apropos the Wretched Love of J. Alfred Prufrock," in which he attributes little or no advantage to old age, is part of a poetic revolution that preferred the individualism of young poets in the culture of a new world to the authority and tradition of national poetry. Certainly the political reality of Israel did not change overnight. Nevertheless, the poetry of the 1950s and 1960s offered a haven from the national effort and encouraged the reader to consider aspects of life beyond the common values of society.

The history of individualism in women's poetry begins much earlier, for, as Lily Ratok of Tel Aviv University claims in her article "The Portrait of Woman as an Israeli Poet," the development of a feminine tradition within Hebrew poetry is a development by default. The highly moral and authoritarian tone of male writers, claims Ratok, left women to a discussion of intimacy, silence, and a concentration on the individual and her seemingly mundane world.[2] For example, the turn-of-the-century poet Rachel Bluwstein entitled one of her poems "Only of Myself I Knew How to Tell." In a different poem she addresses the homeland: "Indeed, very wretched is the gift of thy daughter." In her 1988 article Ratok takes Elaine Showalter's concept of women's culture in "Feminist Criticism in the Wilderness" as the wild zone of women's experience, a territory that lies beyond the reach of patriarchal dominance, and views it as an appropriate characterization of the culture of Israeli feminism.[3] Certainly the inability of women to define themselves within a prior "heroic" or even prophetic tradition of Hebrew poetry has led to what Ratok defines as a binary choice of subject matter. In opposition to a masculine, heroic tradition, women had to create a different poetry that is more intimate, with a greater concentration on the individual and possessing little or no pathos.[4] The retreat into less authoritarian, more reflexive themes and subject matter added up to what Julia Kristeva names in *Revolution in Poetic Language* as the generation of new significance within society. The initial discourse within the poems has finally developed into a more coherent, at times explicit tradition of poetry that not only excludes itself from a "heroic" and "prophetic" mainstream but is finally able to refer to and even criticize the mainstream and its hierarchical implications.[5]

There is little wonder, then, that the nineteenth-century poet Emily Dickinson served as an important influence on Israeli women poets even before her wider publication in the 1950s and 1960s. Dickinson, whose poetic method is described by Adrienne Rich in "Vesuvius at Home" as a resistance to patriarchal laws and taboos, was certainly helpful to poets who tried to define themselves beyond the mainstream of authority and absolute statement.[6] One example of this influence is provided by the comparison of Dickinson's poem 289 with the poem "The Old House" by the Israeli poet Zelda. Zelda—usually referred to by her first name alone—is a descendant of the famous Rabbi Shneerson from Lubavitch. Born in 1914, first published in 1967, and buried in 1984, she is, like Dickinson, a unique poet who served as a major influence on modern poetry in general and women's poetry in particular. Also like Dickinson, Zelda did not confine herself to the authority of a strong patriarchal household and tradition; both her attending a secular institution of higher learning and her writing of poetry were, according to her family tradition, unbecoming of men and women alike.[7] In fact, after her death, Zelda's relatives attained a court order which forbids any form of public access to her files. Also, as in Dickinson's case, the publication of Zelda's poems was delayed for many years, and her voice, talking of loneliness and of unsatisfactory communication with the world, carries little or no authority in poems that speak of individual bewilderment and limitations. In "The Old House" Zelda inserts the traditional symbol of the house—a symbol of a family, its honor and hierarchy—and uses it as a synecdoche for the predicament of a lonely individual within a spiritual desolation. She writes:

> There, beyond the house,
> On the horizon,
> Their silent lives
> The hemstitched mountains live, wearing
> Their gray scarf secrets,
> And under the floor of the house
> Its enigmatic life,
> Its special life, lives
> The dirt,
> And all that is buried within—
> Seeds, roots, streams . . .

Dickinson also places the house in a physical and psychological wilderness: "I know some lonely Houses off the Road / A Robber'd like the look of— / Wooden barred, / And Windows hanging low, / Inviting to— / A Portico." Certainly, for both Dickinson and Zelda, the house is an ambivalent symbol, as both poets wish to free themselves from the authority and artistic silence imposed by family, tradition, and anonymity while simultaneously wishing to enjoy their protection.[8] The issues of publication, communication, and love in these poems, as well as in others, became a popular theme in the poetry of Israeli women, who largely ignored social and national themes. Moreover, the choice of short, enigmatic poems pertaining to such themes became the trademark of women's poetry, which, unlike the male poetry of the 1950s, did not have to preach its individualism; for within the heroic tradition of the 1930s and 1940s the individualism of women was a given and, in fact, a must.

It is difficult, of course, to prove that Zelda actually read Dickinson. The research conducted for this article in the summer of 1993[9] leads to the conclusion that Dickinson's influence is possible and even probable. Dickinson was available, translated, and highly praised at a very early stage, and Zelda, a studious reader of world literature—an admirer, for example, of William Faulkner—quite likely read this "new" American poet. Moreover, little documentation is available in regard to the influences on modern women poets such as Leah Goldberg, Yocheved Bat Miriam, and Zelda in the 1930s and 1940s. However, if Dickinson's poetry was not an absolute influence, it certainly was not an isolated phenomenon as far as Israeli poets are concerned. Yona Wallach, possibly the most significant woman poet since the 1960s, is the author of "Absalom," a poem that discusses abortion and the special relationship of the would-be mother to her dead fetus. "Absalom" is certainly influenced by a tradition of abortion poems such as Sylvia Plath's "Morning Song," "The Mother" by Gwendolyn Brooks, and Adrienne Rich's "Night-Pieces: For a Child." In the 1970s a poem by Rachel Chalfi entitled "A Witch Without a Coven" reminds one of Anne Sexton's "Her Kind." Tzipy Shachrur, a contemporary poet, published in 1987 a poem called "Grudge," a blunt accusation directed against the heroine's father and clearly influenced by Sylvia Plath's "Daddy," a poem directed against a father, fatherhood, and patriarchal hierarchy in general.

Interestingly, the title of the collection in which Shachrur's poem appears is *Common Language,* recalling the title of Adrienne Rich's book *Dream of a Common Language.* Certainly the influences of American women poets contributed to the formation of a common language, at least within an international community of women, when the individual as a woman, and the woman as an autonomous individual, became a subject well preferred over earlier themes of national strife and Zionist revival. This tendency, as mentioned before, was actually followed by male poets who, after the westernization of the 1950s, and the gradual development of Israel from a pioneering society to a relatively prosperous economic entity, searched for new themes and poetic instruments beyond the national tradition and the heritage of Russian poetry. Poets such as David Avidan and Nathan Zach, and later Yair Horowitz and Meir Viziltir, presented the individual as an outsider, indifferent or even hostile to his environment. Verse that dealt with the economic scene, the political predicament, and the reality of war was, and still is, considered naïve, unesthetic, and unfitting within the canon of modern and postmodern poetry.

Certainly one must consider exceptions, such as Dalia Rabikovitz, a woman poet who has been well accepted into the canon since the 1950s. Over the last decade Rabikovitz has published many poems protesting the political scene in Israel and the West Bank and has actually identified her predicament as a woman with that of social and racial injustices. Of course, these are not the poems which won Rabikovitz her popularity in the 1950s. Her earlier verse addresses certain women's issues but

does not view them in relation to other social and political realities in the Middle East. Another example is Yehuda Amichai, who, although better received in other countries than in his own land, has certainly been able to express himself on subjects connected with the reality of Israeli life.

Another necessary disclaimer, to be sure, is that feminist discourse and the theme of individualism are in themselves political stands of undeniable value. However, as Kristeva suggests, the displacement of "socially established signifying practices" does not necessarily equal a revolution.[10] Within the deplorable reality of Israeli society, poetry has failed to pick up on a second lesson in American feminism, a lesson taught by the later works of Adrienne Rich as well as by poets such as Audre Lorde, Marlene Nourbeze Philips, and Ntozake Shange and by novelists such as Alice Walker and Toni Morrison. Not that every American writer is a conscious feminist. American poetry has its own share of solipsistic writers. Nevertheless, this essay deals with the reception of a particular message, which, best put by Rich in "Blood, Bread and Poetry," is that the predicament of the individual, or even of a particular group, is tied to the predicament of others and can only be helped through a general resistance of power systems in society.[11]

In order to appreciate the lack of multicultural and socially critical influences on Israeli women's poetry, it is necessary to recognize the prior influences of American poetry on a tradition that held no significant place for women poets. In the 1950s and 1960s a number of themes were made available through poems on women's issues such as abortion, rape, parenthood, and sexual and social deviation from female stereotypes. Such themes not only legitimized women's poetry but actually placed it in a leading position within a modernist celebration of individualism. Dalia Rabikovitz's poem from the 1950s, "Vanilla," is a declaration on behalf of a heroine who yearns for vanilla ice cream. This call for individualism can be traced back to a number of sources, but ice cream, one must remember, is an American symbol as well. It stands not only for simple hedonism but also for an ideology that allows free choice of purpose, occupation, and flavor of ice cream. However, Israeli women did not retain their leadership position as social innovators. Their poetry, which was finally acknowledged after a long period of silence, was naturally reluctant to embrace new voices of racial, cultural, social, and economic plights that might be denied acceptance by both the public and literary circles. The refusal of women's poetry in Israel to go beyond a certain ideological step well served a literature that embarked on an idea of individualism that is solipsistic and stationary.

One also needs to consider that, unlike the movies and poems of the 1950s, the influence of contemporary American culture is no longer as direct and certainly not as univocal as it once was. Peace and prosperity, presented in the movies of the 1950s, turned American cultural heroes into role models admired all over the world, and the image of white, urban, well-to-do America presented in those movies, as well as within the recent context of upper-middle-class feminism, is a projection that is well delivered and well received. Here not only does the colonizer wish to bestow an ideology, but the colonized are eager to be bestowed upon. Individualism, in such a context, is perceived as one's liberation from the ideologies of one's society rather than one's obligation to the liberty of other individuals. Such a reception is more difficult in the case of works such as the novels of Toni Morrison or even television programs such as "Roseanne," which tell certain unpleasant truths about the United States. In countries surrounded by war and economic catastrophes, one has to believe in the existence of a rich, universally literate, universally employed America. The reference to "the great male writer, Toni Morrison" is certainly a part of the tendency to resist new and, to some, unexplained phenomena in the United States such as the recognition of African American women writers.

Such changes in the image of the United States, as well as Israel's own political reality, provide additional difficulties for women poets, who must decline a second revolution in Israeli poetry. For although American benefits such as individualism and vanilla ice cream were easily adopted forty years ago by a society eager to embark on an American myth, contemporary themes such as the painful consideration of social inequality and actual criticism of the American dream are, at this stage, rather difficult to accept.

### NOTES

[1] Michel Licht, "Modern American Poetry" (a series of translations), in *Our Book,* vol. 2, 1927.

[2] Lily Ratok, "The Portrait of Woman as an Israeli Poet," *Moznaim,* 2-3 (May-June 1988), p. 58.

[3] Elaine Showalter, "Feminist Criticism in the Wilderness," in *Modern Criticism and Theory,* David Lodge, ed., New York, Longman, 1988, p. 347.

[4] Ratok, p. 59.

[5] Julia Kristeva, *Revolution in Poetic Language,* Margaret Waller, tr., New York, Columbia University Press, 1984, p. 13.

[6] Barbara Charlesworth Gelpi and Albert Gelpi, *Adrienne Rich's Poetry and Prose,* New York, Norton, 1993, p. 195.

[7] Hamutal Bar-Yosef, *On Zelda's Poetry,* Tel Aviv, Hakibbutz Hameuchad, 1988, p. 15; Yedidya Zhaki, "Zelda's Poems in Vast Retrospect," *Iton 77 Literary Monthly,* May-June 1985, p. 14.

[8] For further discussion of the house as an ambivalent symbol of confinement and protection, see Gaston Bachelard, *The Poetics of Space,* Maria Jolas, tr., Boston,

Beacon, 1969; and C. G. Jung, *The Collected Works of C. G. Jung,* Sir Herbert Read, ed., Princeton, N.J., Princeton University Press, 1968. See also Cynthia Griffin Wolff, *Emily Dickinson,* Christopher L. Carduff, ed., New York, Addison-Wesley, 1988, pp. 127, 130, 386, and 524 for further discussion of Dickinson's relationship to her father's house as a relationship of resistance and as a usurpation of patriarchal authority.

[9] See Reuben Avinoam, *A Hebrew Anthology of American Verse,* Tel Aviv, Am Oved, 1953; Michel Licht, "Modern American Poetry" (preface to a series of translations), in *Our Book,* vol. 1, 1927, p. 1519; Michel Licht, "Modern American Poetry," in *Our Book,* vol. 2; N. B. Minkow, "Introduction," in *Modern American Poetry,* Michel Licht, ed. & tr., Buenos Aires, 1954, p. 913.

[10] Kristeva, p. 16.

[11] Gelpi and Gelpi, p. 249.

## Yael S. Feldman

SOURCE: "Feminism under Siege: The Vicarious Selves of Israeli Women Writers," in *Prooftexts: A Journal of Jewish Literary History,* Vol. 10, No. 3, Summer, 1990, pp. 493-514.

[*In the following essay, Feldman explores feminist themes in Shulamith Hareven's* A City of Many Days *and Shulamit Lapid's* Gei Oni.]

> I live on the top floors now, she summed it up to herself, where there is a constant commotion, workrooms, children's rooms, the kitchen, the living room, all kinds of things. [Only] the cellar is locked, and I don't even know where the key is [any more]. Perhaps one should not know.
>
> *A City of Many Days,* Shulamith Hareven, 1972

The imagery underlying this self-examination is age-old, almost a stock metaphor—the house as the image of its tenant and vice versa. Yet what gives this particular metaphor an added twist is its specific psychological edge, one that is implied by the vertical division of this human house: the upper floors full of movement and light in contrast to the locked cellar—a clear analogue to Freud's topographic model of the human psyche. However, the female voice using this metaphor seems to question the very foundation of the Freudian quest: Does one *have to* unlock the inaccessible, unconscious if you will, underground room?

This questioning grows out of the experience of Sarah Amarillo, the protagonist of the novel *A City of Many Days* (1972),[1] in which Shulamith Hareven reconstructs life in Jerusalem under the British mandate, before and during World War II. Although the impulse for self-knowledge is quite palpable here, it clearly stops short of breaking into the locked psychological "cellar." Introspection is thus displaced to externally observable facts, and a potentially psychological exploration turns into a socio-cultural inquiry.

Situated as it is a few pages before the end of the narrative (p. 184; 199), this arrested introspection functions as an interpreting sign, almost as a closure. It highlights retrospectively the cultural code underlying this novel—the uneasy co-existence of modern psychology within a society of collective persuasion.

This inherent tension is not unique to Hareven's narrative. Rather, it is characteristic of a whole range of contemporary Israeli novels that come very close to introspection and self-analysis but exhibit ambivalence when approaching the "forbidden zone." This is particularly true of a modality that I have elsewhere called "the arrested autobiography in Israeli fiction."[2] As a rule, these novels are the products of writers in mid-career who try to make sense of their life and art by constructing a real or fictive "self" whose life-story they tell in retrospect, as viewed from the vantage point of the present (e.g., novels by Shahar, Bartov, Tamuz and Oz). Yet a close look at this group of narratives unravels an additional common feature: In these personal stories—all authored by *male* writers—psychological introspection is checked (or "arrested") by the pressure of socio-political realities, usually condensed into particular historical moments. While this pressure, which often takes the shape of an ideological crisis, is the moving force behind the need to construct a "self" and fix it in language, it also undermines any attempt to live up to the ideals of the (male) "subject" as conceived in classical western thought—autonomy, privacy and psychological individualism.[3]

If this observation is correct, then these Israeli life-stories may add a new dimension to the contemporary debate over the construction of the "subject," and especially to the question of gender distinction: To the extent that they collapse the conventional oppositions between the individual and the communal, the private and the public, the psychological and the ideological, they seem to undermine some of our most cherished concepts about subjectivity and gender. If we remember in particular that for certain gender psychologists it is the *female* subject who is relational rather than autonomous, her identity—in life and on paper—is generally conceived as mediated through "others," and her "self" is viewed as communal and collective rather than purely individual—then the Israeli corpus could cast grave doubts on *essentialist* definitions of gender. In fact, it should encourage culturalist approaches, as it unambiguously demonstrates how gender boundaries may be crossed given the pressure of similar socio-cultural conditions.[4]

Yet this is not the whole picture. If features of female selfhood may be found in male subjects, one should rightly ask if the reverse is also true: Do Israeli *women* writers create cross-gender subjects in their life-stories? To what extent are they free to imbue their imagined selves with "male" features, to cross traditional gender boundaries?

The answer to this set of questions is not readily available. First of all, because contemporary Israeli women seem to shy away from telling their life-stories directly.[5] This absence is doubly surprising in view of the intimately autobiographical Hebrew prose written by women at the beginning of the century.[6] In this they did not differ, of course, from their sister autobiographers in English, and perhaps the world over.[7] But this resemblance is only superficial, pertaining to non-canonic texts. For unlike the English tradition, the Hebrew canon has featured a long list of women poets but no women novelists. Until the last decade Hebrew prose was mostly the domain of male writers. The few women who excelled in fiction mostly wrote short stories and novellas, mainly in the lyrical-impressionistic mode (e.g., Devorah Baron, 1887-1956).

Does this mean that we have come full circle to bedrock gender differences? I suspect not. Rather, as early as the turn of the century women were cast in a well defined role by the arbiters of the renaissance of Hebrew: "Only women are capable of reviving Hebrew—this old, forgotten, dry and hard language—by permeating it with emotion, tenderness, suppleness and subtlety." This generous, as well as limiting, evaluation was offered in 1897 by Eliezer Ben-Yehuda, the first propagator of spoken Hebrew; and it is not easy to determine today which was more effective: the encouragement or the limitation. For although a number of women graced Ben-Yehuda's journals (including his wife, who was actually trained in chemistry!), not one of them left her mark on the canon of Hebrew literature. Predictably, the breakthrough of women into the canon took place—two decades later—in poetry, where it was easier to accommodate the stereotypic ideal cut out for them by their male patrons.[8]

It took more than half a century for the old barriers to begin crumbling. And it was only in the last two decades that a number of women made the shift from short stories to novels, some of which are of almost epic proportions. Until very recently, however, none of these narratives came close to the fictional autobiography, even in its "arrested" form, as found among Israeli male writers. I would nevertheless argue that it is in these novels that one is to look for the (indirect) representation of the "self" of the Israeli female author. Moreover: As we shall soon see, the generic choice is neither accidental nor arbitrary; for these quasi-historical novels camouflage a contemporary *feminist* consciousness and express, in different degrees of displacement, their authors' struggles with questions of female subjectivity and gender boundaries. That they do this "under siege," in a society that is fundamentally inimical to their quest, is part of the explanation of their literary choices, but also part of the paradox. For it is precisely those very pressures, which have rendered Israeli male subjectivity *different* from its western counterparts, that have also prevented the direct expression of Israeli female subjectivity. For contemporary women, issues of selfhood and gender definition are inextricably bound up with feminism; as such they automatically become politicized, a process the American scene clearly bears witness to. But in Israel such an agenda would per force collide with the larger political issues that are always at the center of attention. Israeli women writers are therefore trapped in a double bind: Unwilling to relegate themselves to the marginalized "women's journalism" and "female thematics," they are obliged to enter the mainstream "in disguise," registering their critique vicariously via their presumably historical protagonists.

I first suspected that this was the case when I saw the term "feminist" on the jacket of *Gei oni,* a "historical" novel published in 1982, whose narrated time is the early 1880s.[9] The transparent anachronism of the usage set me on the detective trail. (In the Oxford Dictionary, composed between 1884 and 1928, "feminism" gets the briefest treatment of all female-related entries—"The qualities of females"—and it is accompanied by the qualifier "Rare" . . . ) I soon discovered a pattern: In several recent novels by Israeli women, contemporary concerns are projected into "liberated" heroines of another time or another place. In fact, one can point to a process of regression in the choice of historical settings, from Jerusalem of the 1920s and '30s in *A City of Many Days* (1972, quoted in our epigraph)—a period the author, Shulamith Hareven, could not have experienced directly, since she arrived in Palestine as a child only in 1940)—through Palestine of 1882 in Shulamit Lapid's *Gei oni* (1982), to the vaguely and poetically defined European past (17th century) in Amalia Kahana-Carmon's novella "The Bridge of the Green Duck" (in *Up on Montifer,* 1984).[10] However, this regression is counterbalanced by a diametrically opposite *progression* in the "feminist" consciousness of the protagonists of these novels. As a group, they move from traditional gender roles in a patriarchal society to a utopian new womanhood, paradoxically projected back into the historico-mythical past.

If this analysis is correct, then Hebrew literature is still at the stage that Carolyn Heilbrun charted out about a decade ago. in *Reinventing Womanhood:* "Women are only recently taking up autobiography in the attempt to show themselves . . . (though the autobiographies are often in the form of novels)."[11] But why should this be so? Why should contemporary Israeli women be incapable of facing their personal selves directly? Moreover, why can't they, to quote Heilbrun again, "imagine women characters with even the autonomy they themselves have achieved" (p. 71)? Why isn't one of these *Bildungsromane* cast in the mold of the *Künstlerroman?* And why isn't there even one "portrait of an artist" among these novels of development? Is it because of the precariousness of their writers' self-image as "artists"? Or is it because this aspect of their recently gained autonomy is subsumed by more communal—and perhaps more basic—concerns and achievements?

The answer is "yes," I am afraid, to both questions. The first will take us back to woman's problematic place in the Jewish tradition, which by-and-large excludes her from participating in man's public roles.[12] The second "yes," on the other hand, will highlight the *cross-gender* correspondence apparent in the Israeli corpus: For just like their male counterparts, these novels of development are motivated by socio-political pressures and organized around major historical events. And although the latter function as the pivotal moments in the heroines' "voyages in," they also embed their subjective experience within a larger, collective order. It is precisely this embeddedness, however, that is at odds with any feminist aspiration; and it is the slow and vicarious realization of this unavoidable conflict that is the subject of the following analysis.

For Sarah Amarillo, the protagonist of *A City of Many Days,* the pivotal historical moment is the breakdown of the Jewish-Arab equilibrium in Jerusalem of World War II. As the tension heightens, the narrative is permeated by a sense of an ending: "Something was ending, and something was about to begin" (p. 136; 146; cf. p. 75; 77). The oriental design which Jerusalem had been—and which the novel recapitulates in its lyrical impressionism—is doomed to oblivion, except in the literary reconstructions of its mourners (David Shahar, Hayyim Be'er, and, to some extent Amos Oz).[13] Jerusalem's polyphony of voices will be replaced by the "first person plural" of the next generation, as the male protagonists wistfully observe:

> "All these men will be coming home from war now," said Professor Barzel. "They'll all have learned to fight. The country will change again. Everything will become more professional, the fighting too. The individual won't count any more—only the stupid plural. The plural is always stupid."
>
> [ . . . ]
>
> "And what will be then, Elias?" asked Hulda worriedly. "We will be then," said Elias, so quietly that they couldn't be sure they had heard right. "For better or worse, we will be." (pp. 182; 197-98)

This is the notorious "we" of the Palmach ("We are everywhere the first / we, we, the Palmach" as their song proudly announced), which has been the object of nostalgia since the fifties and the subject of debunking since the early eighties.[14] Hareven walks the middle way, having her characters grieve this loss of the first person singular, while rationalizing it as the unavoidable result of the political situation. Her ambivalence is further demonstrated by her treatment of Sarah's interior monologue (quoted in our epigraph): On one hand, she allows Sarah a measure of self-awareness, the admission that she lives "on the top floors." But then she lets her state flatly, without any change of tone, that "the cellar is locked, and I don't even know where the key is any more" (pp. 184; 199). Moreover, the attentive reader may note not only what is marked as "locked" but also what is marked by its absence: the curious omission of a bedroom from the list of rooms on the top floor, which is passed unnoticed.

Apparently, in order to join the war effort, Sarah must, like Professor Barzel before her, "skip over her own self" (ibid.; cf. pp. 122; 130): Barzel, the German-born physician who had trained her as a nurse in her youth, now insists that she help him prepare paramedics for the insecure, threatening future. It would seem that in this society under siege male and female share the same lot. But not quite: It is Sarah and not Professor Barzel who registers the loss in psychological rather than social or intellectual terms. While he is reported to "have lost the key" to his hobbies and philosophical ideas (pp. 122; 130), Sarah is aware that what she misses is nothing less than the key to her own "underground room," to the cellar of her *psychic* apparatus (pp. 184; 199).

Her metaphoric language barely camouflages a Freudian insight; "repression" is of course unnamable in the discourse of this narrative.[15] Yet this insight does not lead to any action. Neither the protagonist nor the authorial voice shows any signs of rebellion ("Perhaps one should not know"). On the contrary: Despite the great losses, the novel closes on a poetic note of mystical transcendence:

> a silent presence, the whole city spread at her feet, and [she] looked at the lambswool light out over the mountains, over the houses drowning in radiance, as if once this city, long, long ago, soon after Creation, had burst from some great rock and its truth flown molten and shiny over the hills. She could feel the moment to the quick. Now this is me, she told herself, now this is me, here on this hill, with this feeling of great peace [reconciliation] that will never last, or standing in the street, people know [recognize] me: I have three sons and so little time. Now this is me in this moment of hers. Tomorrow I'll be gone and the street will be gone. Or another street and another time. And always, forever, this fleecy pile of light, that rock tumbled halfway down the hill to a lonely stop, a terraced alley, a dripping cypress tree, a caper plant in a wall. A place to walk slowly. A place to touch the sky: now it is close. To breathe in mountain-and-light. Now.

It is hard to exaggerate the contrast between this reconciled woman and the spunky girl that she once was. Described by herself and by others as a chip off the strong and feisty (mostly male) Amarillos, those who "are always quarreling with life" (pp. 36, 113; 36, 119), this "big" emancipated woman now takes a turn towards submission, "lying low in realities, the wick trimmed all the way down" (pp. 179; 194). The woman who prided herself on her sharp tongue and unabashed "meanness," is now beginning to wax emotional over her motherly duties (ibid.). And the daughter who as a young girl vented her rage against her absent father by screaming "No father! No mother! No grandpa! No grandma! No nothing" (pp. 16; 14), is now processing *poetically* her discovery of his helpless insanity: "I went down into a garden of nut trees [to see the fruits of the valley]. Down down down. To the

rock-bottom beauty of madness" (pp. 187; 202. Cf. Song of Songs 6:11). Again, the anguish is camouflaged by the indirection of metaphor. And again both protagonist and narrator stop on the brink of the abyss: "Sarah looked at him for a long while, the great question that had haunted her for so long, now a spent little answer, cast mindlessly before her" (ibid.).

This is all Hareven grants her protagonist by way of self scrutiny. Staged as it is two pages before the end of the novel, this encounter loses its potential force as an all-embracing psychological explanation. The "haunting question" is allowed to enter into language only when it has lost its power and turned into a "spent little answer." For despite the intimation of Freudian depths, this is no novel of psychological motivation. In its laconic, pointillistic style, its skimpy descriptions and its quick shifts of centers of consciousness, the narration hovers above and around the characters, empathically engaging them and ironically disengaging itself, but never aiming at rendering fully rounded psychological portraits.

Even Sarah, whose "education" is at the core of the plot, is rendered by brief surface brushstrokes. Moreover, she does not occupy center stage by herself; as the lyrical fusion of her last narrated monologue makes clear, she shares it with another female, the city of the title of the book. It is Jerusalem who is the strongest presence in this novel, because, ironically, it is "she" ("city"—as well as land, country, state—are conveniently genderized as feminine in Hebrew) who embodies the powers of history ("This city abides no one's decision about who they are. It [she] decides for them, it [she] makes them, with the pressure of stones and infinite time. It teaches humility." pp. 121; 129). In the final analysis, it is history rather than psychology that circumscribes human action in this novel, subsuming both anguish and pleasure under its impersonal workings.

What place is there for the female subject in this kind of narrative? To begin with, there is the closing statement of the poetic coda: Despite the constant effort of the authorial voice to decentralize its focalization, to multiply its points of view, Sarah emerges as the central consciousness of the narration. The more the rich mosaic of the past disintegrates, the more her introspective voice usurps that of the ironic narrator, culminating in the final monologue we have read. Should we hear there the beginning of a direct self-representation?

If we do we do so at our own peril. For Shulamith Hareven has not followed the lead she herself suggested. She never adopted the autobiographic modality in her writing, and except for one collection of stories partially addressing women issues (*Loneliness,* 1980), she has shunned female protagonists altogether. *A City of Many Days* stands alone in her oeuvre, written after two books of poetry and two collections of stories (1962-1970), and followed by more collections of poems, essays, short stories and two (allegorical?) novellas whose narrated time is the biblical past.[16] Moreover, Hareven is notorious for her refusal to participate in any forum dedicated to "women's literature"; she does not believe in Women Writers as a category; and she has often claimed that a writer is a writer, never mind her (his?) gender. At the same time, she is politically active, voicing her ideological positions in her oral pronouncements and excellent essays (which are, by the way, among the best written in Hebrew today).[17] But when critics tried to read her political convictions into her latest "biblical" novellas, she vehemently protested: Art is art and should not be confused with one's worldly preoccupation.[18]

In other words, the woman behind the novel is an engaged person of clearly drawn convictions and priorities. "Feminism," however, is not among them, as *A City of Many Days* complexly demonstrates. Why complexly?— Because, on the one hand, cross-gender equality as a realistic possibility is an unquestioned premise of this novel. Without this premise the characterization of Sarah would be totally spurious. In fact, in her independence of spirit, intolerance of weakness and provocative sexual freedom she is almost a parody of the typical male adolescent. It is almost as if she was naturally born to all those "privileges," never having to fight for them. Indeed Sarah, as we have seen, *was* free, easily brushing aside— with no separation anxiety, it would seem—the "weak" maternal tradition of her Sephardi stock (mother, paternal grandmother and sister). On the other hand, by equipping her with a weak father (he is easy prey for false female charms *and* a victim of mental illness) and a "strong" paternal aunt (the colorful, single but happy Victoria[!]), Hareven seems to give the lie to the feminist cliché of "transcending gender roles."

Sarah *starts* from a non-genderized dichotomy, unproblematically rejecting one model and adopting another. Structurally, she functions somewhat like Jo of *Little Women,* a single strong presence in a female household. But unlike Louisa May Alcott, Hareven accompanies her heroine into matrimony. Here is the moment of truth, the real test of this "new female" (the aunt, we recall, has never married): How would this male-modelled, autonomous woman function as a wife and mother? Superbly, of course, but at a "cost."

After giving birth to her first son, Sarah for the first time allows "weakness" to penetrate her hitherto armoured psyche. The self-centered, *un*relational ego restructures itself, but reacts with a sense of loss and fear: "Help me, Grandpa," she prays from her maternity bed, "because a frightening vulnerability has opened up in me today" . . . (p. 111. Although the contemporary connotation of the word used in Hebrew, *turpah,* is generalized, on the order of "Achilles' heel," the context no doubt activates the word's original denotation [in Rabbinic Hebrew] of 'nakedness', 'private parts'; and we need not elaborate the sexual connotation of the use of the verb "open" in this connection—all of which is missing from Halkin's bland translation, "I've never felt so defenseless before," p. 118). But if we think that motherhood is the end of "androgyny," we are mistaken, at least as far as

this novel is concerned. It is the father, not the mother, who verbalizes the effect of parenthood on the self: "The first child forces you to define yourself. When the second comes you are already defined. Not just as a parent. Whatever you are and aren't, you can be sure that's what your child will learn to demand from you" (pp. 112; 119). At this point of the narrative we are just past the midpoint of the story, and the myth of androgyny is still holding sway. But not for long. In the following pages we witness the deterioration of Arab-Jewish relations and the palpable echoes of World War II. Life is disrupted; individual destinies get farcically and hopelessly entangled in plots they do not comprehend (Miraculo, Zion). The dichotomy of weak/strong, so hopefully deconstructed in the human sphere, ominously sneaks back into people's political discourse (see particularly Professor Barzel, one of the first victims of Arab atrocities). Against this background, Sarah slowly emerges to her *difference* only to realize that *under the circumstances* she cannot take this difference anywhere.

The motive power behind her emergence is, predictably, a chance rekindling of a youthful love. But just as predictably, this emotional reawakening is painfully cut off, undermined by the historical moment—the underground activities and military voluntarism of men at war. All that she has left is "acceptance" of her "locked cellar," *amor fati.* So that when her self-conscious "I" is finally vocalized, it is only to be defined in terms of others: "They recognize me: I have three sons and so little time. . . . " The irony could not be any greater: Sarah Amarillo, the paradigm of the "new," Jerusalem-born, Jewess (echoes of the social-Zionist ethos of the "new man/Jew" are not unintentional here!), falls back on the most traditional and often maligned Jewish definition of womanhood. Like the biblical Sarah, she gains status through motherhood and more significantly, through the recognition of others. In the Hebrew phrase *makirim oti,* she is clearly the passive receptor of the action.

Inadvertently, Hareven offers a Lacanian insight: Reflected in the gaze of others, the subject of necessity perceives herself as an object ("me," *le moi*). But does this mean that the subject is *in principle* alienated from her/his own selfhood, as Lacan would have it?—Not quite. For unlike Lacan (and the Jewish tradition as well!) Hareven optimistically harbors a contextual rather than ontological "explanation" of the structure she has created. Subjecthood, female or otherwise, is suspended when the cannons are roaring. The celebration of the self, feminist or not, is *temporarily* compromised under the historical circumstances dramatized in this novel. The socio-political conditions that have given rise to the ideology of "we," the "stupid first person plural," have also dictated the suppression of the Freudian quest and the throwing away of the key to the psychic underground room. But all this is historically, not universally or essentially, determined.[19] And if the female subject of this narrative cannot be privileged with a fully autobiographic voice, she is allowed the empowerment of existential transcendence: Stretching from Genesis to eternity, it is the big *female* Other, Jerusalem, that offers a moment of ecstasy, of metonymic submersion:

> Now this is me, she told herself, now this is me . . .
> with this feeling of great peace [reconciliation]. [ . . . ]
> Now this is me in this moment of hers. [ . . . ] A
> place to touch the sky: now it is close. To breathe
> in mountain-and-light. Now.

The uniqueness of Hareven's position on feminism (among Israeli writers), is paralleled by the splendid isolation of her heroine among Israeli female protagonists. In no other novel had the gap between lofty ideals (both authorial and Zionist, both intratextual and contextual) and the limitations of reality been so sensitively (but also ambivalently) dramatized. In some sense, this novel was ahead of its time. In the early seventies the horizon of expectations was not yet ripe for a literary discussion of feminism, even in its moderate, selective form. Female victimization was convincingly evoked by the early work of Kahana-Carmon, but it would take her more than a decade to get to a stage of protest and action. In poetry, one could hear some revolutionary tones in Yona Wallach's verse, but not too many were willing to listen. It is not surprising, then, that *A City of Many Days* was received as another nostalgic tale about Jerusalem, "lacking highly significant themes and conceptual contents."[20] That the issues of gender and female subjectivity, as well as their conflict with the historical constraints, are central to the novel—this passed totally unnoticed. It goes without saying that the potential critique of Zionist ideology implied by this material was not even surmised.

It would take a whole decade for the next attempts to materialize, and this not without the impact of the Yom Kippur War (1973) and its aftermath: the protest movements, Lesley Hazelton's demythologization of "the realities behind the myth" (*Israeli Women,* 1977) and the first report of a Knesset commission on the status of women (1978).[21] This report, says Dafna Sharfman, a political scientist at Haifa University, "publicly revealed and described in detail the real situation of the women in Israel, and the discrimination to which they are subject" (p. 14). But in the early seventies, when Hareven was writing, the topic was still dormant. Although Shulamit Aloni's treatise on woman's deplorable status within the Israeli legal system, *Women as Human Beings,* appeared in 1973, nothing changed in the view that "their contribution to society was marginal and supportive by nature . . . a reflection of their political status and the inclination of the Labour Movement elite to view them as voters but not as decision makers" (ibid.).

As for Shulamith Hareven, raised as she was outside the ranks of the Labor movement (in fact, well to the right of it) but with a strong faith in "human Zionism" (which eventually has moved her left), she was no doubt torn between her political critique and her intuitive "selective" feminism (her terminology).[22] This is why, I believe, the ideological underpinning of her characterization of Sarah is totally suppressed, thereby giving the

impression of "inadequate motivation," as critic Gershon Shaked has put it.[23] Displacing the gender codes *theoretically* adumbrated by the Zionist movement and the Palmach generation (which will be confronted head on only in the next decade by Netiva Ben Yehuda, 1981) to a different ethnic setting (where they hardly belong), Hareven created in Sarah a vicarious self that released her from the risk of personal exposure, while giving her the liberty to explore her own ambivalence. If we add that Hareven served as a paramedic in the besieged Jerusalem of 1947-48 and that she likes to trace her maternal lineage to the fifteenth century Spanish exiles, the parallels as well as the disguises become transparent.

The distance travelled by Hebrew readers in the seventies can be readily measured by the openness in which *Gei oni* (1982), a highly popular historical novel, tackled the very issues upon which Hareven had circumspectly touched a decade earlier. Here we do not find metaphoric indirection and nuanced play of voices. On the contrary. In a rather coarse realistic style, crowded with dialogues and interior monologues that are stylistically indistinguishable, the third person narration weaves its way through a maze of "relationships" that would easily rival those of any Hollywood or TV romantic melodrama. Nothing is implied here, not even the characters' most intimate reflections. Thoughts, emotions, ideology and popular psychology are all evenly spread out as if illuminated by the bright Israeli sun.

Yet despite its limitations (and perhaps because of them—the book is often classified as a novel for young readers), *Gei oni* caught the imagination of Israeli readership in an unprecedented manner. In the first place, it played right into the wave of nostalgia that swept the country in the eighties, when the first centenary of the earliest Jewish Aliya (immigration) to Palestine was celebrated. Indeed, Shulamit Lapid—until then a rather obscure short story writer,[24] but since then a prolific novelist and dramatist—wrote her first novel *in anticipation* of 1982. In that year the Galilean settlement Rosh Pinah, whose earlier name had been Gei Oni, celebrated one hundred years of its existence. Judging by the reception the book enjoyed, the timing was right; readers exhibited great hunger for the richly documented panorama of that distant past filtered through a fictional prism.

This was not the only reason. Readers were no doubt responding to the novelty of being introduced to a "serious" historical reconstruction through the eyes and mind of Fanya, a young Russian immigrant who joins Gei Oni in the opening scene, and remains the central consciousness through which the narrative is focalized throughout the novel.

But why should this be considered such a novelty? Wasn't the pioneer movement, indeed the Zionist ethos in general, supposed to have promoted the equality of women? In fact, wasn't "the woman question" one of the basic issues debated—and deemed solved—by the early communes and kibbutzim?[25] The answer is, of course, "yes" to all of the above; but only as long as we remember to add the qualifier—"in theory." For what recent research has shown is that in practice, neither the early settlers nor the second wave of immigrants at the turn of the century had transcended the patriarchal norms of their home communities in Europe.[26] And as Shulamit Lapid herself has recounted, she could find no historical model for her heroine in the archival records of Gei Oni—later named Rosh Pinah.[27]

As the jacket of the book states, the names of those "giant women" who were part and parcel of the early settlement wave "are absent from history books because the records of the saviors of the motherland list only men." Even among the figures of the second aliyah, Lapid could make use only of one exceptional personality, Manya Shochat (1879-1959).[28] Fanya had to be invented; here is a woman who "did not know she was a feminist," but whom the contemporary reader recognizes as such, as the jacket of the book clearly attests.

We are in a better position now to appreciate the source of the great appeal that *Gei oni* exerted on its readership. The book was a bold attempt to do justice to the founding mothers, to rectify by fiction the wrongs of (male-dominated) historiography. And it was no small challenge. For how does one create a narrative frame that would authentically preserve the patriarchal way of life of the 1880s, while at the same time accommodate a fictive protagonist whose own norms would satisfy contemporary "feminist" expectations?

The solution came in the form of a collage, piecing together two novelistic genres: the settler epic and the romantic melodrama. On one level, *Gei oni* is a typical settlement drama, almost a western ("The Wild East," as one of its reviewers labelled it[29]), realistically depicting the struggles against all odds of the small Galilean group in the early 1880s. The chief antagonist of this plot is nature itself, the mythic mother-earth. In this story she is no welcoming bride; as we join the narrative she has been holding back her gifts for two consecutive years. Severe draught has chased away most of the pioneers, leaving behind just a few tenacious and idealistic families, including that of Yehi'el, the male protagonist of the novel.

On another level, this is a typically euphoric "heroine's text," as defined by Nancy Miller.[30] It is a predictable love story whose models are not only the canonic texts adored by the protagonist (*Anna Karenina,* which had just "arrived" from Russia, and the novels of Jane Austen, Fanya's favorite; see p. 161), but also popular romances à-la Rudolf Valentino which Shulamit Lapid herself ridiculed in one of her journalistic forays.[31] Despite her ridicule, Lapid utilizes the popular genre with great dexterity: Fanya is the self-conscious budding young woman, who struggles to preserve her independent spirit while falling in love with her enigmatic "dark prince." The latter, for his part, is "handsome like the Prince of Wales" (pp. 34, 69, 85), "wise like king Solomon" (p. 117), and the envy of all women. Predict-

ably, he is also proud, reticent and distant, the very qualities Lapid has enumerated in her brief article ("preferably, a widow / divorcé /bachelor, thirty-year-old, tanned, dark hair, a sneering look . . .")—which means, of course, that although he falls in love with Fanya's looks the moment he sees her, he keeps the secret to himself. Since neither the reader nor Fanya gets to know the truth before half the story is over, a chain of romantic misunderstandings and jealousies constitute the better part of the plot. To add insult to injury, there are echoes of Daphne du Maurier's *Rebecca:* Fanya is "welcomed" to her "prince's" abode by the picture of his deceased wife, whose two sisters are conveniently present to evoke her beauty and otherworldly qualities whenever they can. All this naturally makes the denouement that much sweeter.

But before we get there, a question arises: Haven't we wandered too far afield from "founding mothers" and "inadvertent feminism," as I have elsewhere called it?[32] Can the conventions of the romance, of the heroine's euphoric text, which Lapid herself declared "obsolete," indulge a fighting, independent spirit à la Manya Shochat? Hardly, of course, Lapid could not have sustained her model *and* satisfied her feminist quest had she kept the model intact. Nor could she write a true historical novel (fully omniscient narration, authorial perspective into general historical processes) while staying as close to Fanya's consciousness as she did (more about this below). She resolved this problem, however, by splicing the two models together just at their respective points of cracking. In other words, the meeting ground between them is that of deviation, where their generic conventions are violated. As we shall soon see, it is from this intersection that a new model emerges, one that generously accommodates contemporary expectations.

To begin with, Fanya's romance deviates from its imputed model in one crucial detail: its denouement does not coincide with the closure of the novel. Nor does it lead to a proposal or an engagement. For all this typical "heroine's text" takes place *within* the boundaries of a marriage. And our two protagonists are *a*typical as well: Fanya is not only an orphan, as suggested by Lapid in the above-quoted piece ("an English orphan, preferably penniless . . ."); she is a 16-year-old survivor of a Russian pogrom (the infamous Ukrainian pogroms of 1881-82 that are credited with inspiring the first wave of immigration to Palestine), who finds refuge in the Promised Land, accompanied by an old uncle, a deranged brother, and a baby—the initially unwanted fruit of her rape in that pogrom. Yehi'el, who happens to see her upon her arrival in Jaffa, is a 26-year-old widower and a father of two, one of the few courageous souls still left in the nearly desolate Gei Oni.

As the narrative opens, we are privileged to hear Fanya's reflections after a hasty betrothal in Jaffa. While Yehi'el's motives are not disclosed, it soon becomes clear that for Fanya this is not just a marriage of convenience but also a marriage of appearances. Upon arrival in Gei Oni she insists on separate sleeping arrangements, a rather unexpected turn within the conventions of the romance but a perfectly plausible step for a psychologically conceived character who is still smarting from her traumatic past. The attentive reader, however, will notice a structural and symbolic analogy in this otherwise realistically motivated action. It is not only the human bride who denies her husband her favors; with the draught continuing, the fertilization of mother earth is also prevented.

There is a perfect symmetry, then, between the two plots: the psychological and the mythic, the romantic and the historical. In both the male principle is initially defeated and no consummation is possible. This symmetry does not escape Yehi'el himself, who, unaware of Fanya's trauma, reacts to her refusal by saying: "When you change your mind, let me know. I ask for favors only from the land (= earth)" (p. 45). To get the story rolling again both female protagonists must give in; it is against the background of the long-awaited rains (pp. 117, 121, 123)—a pioneers' version of the notorious Romantic storm?—that the passionate (and confessional) reunion between Fanya and Yehi'el finally takes place (pp. 119-28), and the euphoric plot seems to have reached its happy ending.

But not quite. For in the second part of the narrative, the settlement plot comes back with a vengeance, leaning down heavily on the delicate balance of the new romantic attachment. Not unlike Hareven's Jerusalem, the Galilee, or mother earth (or perhaps the pioneering quest itself) exerts pressure on the human subjects of this story, limiting their freedom of choice and forcing them into its mold. But unlike Hareven, Lapid seems less willing to accept the verdict of the historical moment, of the Zionist "dream of redemption, burning like fire in the bones" (pp. 103-4, 144, 175). She does not have Fanya "skip over her own self," as did Sarah in *A City of Many Days,* but rather lets her develop her female subjectivity despite and against the pressures of the collective vision, with all its tragic consequences. By so doing, Lapid has unwittingly blended her two models into a third one, a *Bildungsroman* which may be rather fanciful for the 1880s but totally satisfying to readers one hundred years later.

I have elsewhere suggested naming this new model after Erich Neumann's Jungian analysis of the legend of *Amor and Psyche,* namely, "The Psychic Development of the Feminine."[33] The heuristic convenience of this choice stems from the story's origins, as Neumann brilliantly shows, in the myth of the "Great Mother," the archetypal mother-earth. It is this archetype that has nourished all myths—old and young—of a return to the motherland, Zionism not excluded. And it is this nexus of images and metaphors that has been recently questioned in the attempt to explain the problematic place of woman in the Zionist ethos.

Only a few years before the publication of *Gei oni,* psychologist Lesley Hazelton deconstructed the familiar Zionist image of sons-lovers returning to mother-land/earth

"to build and be rebuilt in her" (notice again the effect of Hebrew's genderized grammar!). She did this by a literal, almost *ad absurdum* analysis of the psychoanalytic ramifications of this language:

> But while Zion played Jocasta to the male pioneers' Oedipus, where was the Agamemnon to the women pioneers' Electra? What value could all this libidinous attraction have for them? What archetypal images could it arouse in a woman's mind? What role was there for women in this scenario of sons and fathers fertilizing the motherland?[34]

As startling as this query is on first reading, it loses some of its persuasive power once we recognize one small oversight: Except in songs, has Zion ever played Jocasta to her returning sons? *Was* she a welcoming bride? Or was she mostly an earlier Jungian archetype: "The Great Mother"?

The difference is crucial: In the primitive myth the female figure had not yet undergone what Neumann calls "the process of secondary personalization"; she had not yet functioned as a human representation, but as an "impersonal blind principle of fertility."[35] In fact, this is the *negative* aspect of the "great mother," the scary "Terrible Mother" that Neumann has unearthed in the ancient myths and fertility rituals. In these myths the male had more to lose than to gain, for the impregnation of the female principle was achieved only through the perennial death of her "consort," her son/lover/savior, later incarnated in the myths of Tamuz, Osiris and Dionysus.

We can now return to the plot of *Gei oni* and discern that this scenario does not support Hazelton's feminist worries. Here it is not "Electra" who is excluded from the game but rather "Oedipus." The deep structure of the settlement plot is therefore not a Freudian triade, but an earlier, Neumannesque diade, that of the Terrible Mother and her doomed consort. In Yehi'el's failure to conquer mother-earth (he eventually dies of malaria), primitive fertility myths play themselves out once more. The essence of myth, we are reminded, is endless repetition. Standing alone, then, the settlement script would have come to an impasse if not for its dynamic intersection with the second plot, the heroine's text.

In this text, Yehi'el is a "passive accomplice" in Fanya's long and often bewildered search for her own identity as a woman and an autonomous individuum. As in the story of Amor and Psyche, the main psychological thrust of the novel is the liberation of the female protagonist from the yoke of the social norms imposed on her by Aphrodite-like representatives of the community. "Psyche's act of rebellion," says Neumann in *Amor and Psyche,* "signals the end of the mythic era. . . . From now on it is the era of human love, when the human soul knowingly undertakes all fateful decisions for its own life."[36]

It is interesting to note that Neumann speaks about the maturity of the human soul in general. That this process is symbolized for him precisely in the process of individuation of the feminine principle, should come as no surprise. After all, it is the latter that has to liberate itself from the blind collective principle of fertility and veer toward the "light"—the archetypal symbol of masculine consciousness in Neumann's (and others') conceptual system. Although this genderized reading has its problems, particularly for feminist critics,[37] it can readily accommodate the *Bildung* plot of our story. Fanya "develops" from a scathed teenager who acts under duress and runs away at her first experience of pain and frustration, to a mature woman who stays on out of conscious choice to realize the pioneering dream of her dead husband-lover.

Predictably, Fanya achieves her independence by a process of individuation in which she transcends the norms dictated to her by mother-figures who try to teach her "her natural place" (pp. 117, 144, 175, 234). Like Psyche, she reaches maturity after a series of tasks which she undertakes in order to save her husband and home from the devastation wrought by mother nature. We find her breaking into the male-dominated world of commerce, political discussion, even armed self-defense. At the same time, she does not deny her femininity (cf. Psyche's care to preserve her beauty), her *difference* from the male world surrounding her: the fun of light-hearted chat, of good romantic novels, of some childlike pranks (pp. 104, 144, 175). Her personal code is defined, then, as the freedom to choose the best of the two worlds, to move freely from one to the other. More than her predecessor in Hareven's novel, this heroine fully embodies cross-gender equality as she shuttles between home and "world," Gei Oni and Jaffa, taking care of husband and children—and trading. Yehi'el turns out to be just as exceptional. Although he does not fully approve of Fanya's "androgynous" tendencies, he does not stand in her way, which is more than can be said of any of his peers (pp. 109, 172-73, 188, 236). The result is a virtual reversal of conventional gender-roles (with Yehi'el staying close to home and Fanya going into the world), and more importantly—the transformation of Fanya from a child-bride into a mature wife-companion, fully aware of her choices, sexual as well as social.

It is only natural, then, that as the novel comes to a close and Yehi'el succumbs to exhaustion and malaria, the reader is ready to embrace Fanya's *Bildung* as a necessary training for her ultimate task: the perpetuation of the mythical male quest. But in an ironic twist on Hazelton's critique, Fanya, though ready to undertake the role, perceives it as something alien, not her own script:

> Shall she sell their home? Driving Yehi'el out of his dream? This home and this land were the purpose of his life. Once again fate has decreed that she realize others' dreams. Has she ever had her own dreams? But perhaps everyone is like this? Everyone realizes someone else's dream? (p. 256)

Is this a "feminist" protest lamenting the lot of women in general? Or is this a specific charge against the androcentric Zionist dream? And who is the "everyone" of the final questions: Women? All people? The lines seem to blur here, leaving the reader with a sense of an unfocused grievance. For what is read throughout the novel as a critique of a male-engendered ideology ("Her father's dream of rebirth has turned into sacred madness which now consumes her youthful years, her life," p. 102; and cf. 142, 194, 202-3, 226), is now taking on an existential turn, possibly hiding behind "the human condition."

We may be witnessing here an attempt (prevalent in women's life writing, as recently demonstrated by Carolyn Heilbrun[38]) to rationalize away the justified rage against the social system, which, in the guise of a new ideology, has reinscribed traditional double standards toward women. More often than not Fanya's feelings remain unexpressed. Typically, her frustration and hurt are reported to the reader ("Fanya wanted to scream: And I? And I?, but she kept silent," p. 176, and cf. 105, 144, 164, 187, 217), but they always remain confined within the seething turmoil of her narrated inner monologues. When they are actually verbalized, it is only in the framework of private female discourse. Fanya may have penetrated male praxis, but not its public discourse. The prevailing ideology remains uncontaminated by her feminist critique. In the final analysis, Fanya's quest for selfhood inscribes itself only as a comment on the margins of an androcentric system.

We should not be surprised, then, that Lapid does not give her heroine the chance to try and make it on her own. In the last page, the plot of the romance prevails. Sasha, an old acquaintance, himself a survivor of the Ukrainian pogroms, reappears, asking permission "to help and be helped" (cf. the Zionist quest "to build and be rebuilt"). With this new beginning, the novel reverts to its original two models: the historical and the romantic. Subjective experience is embedded again in Jewish collectivity, symbolized throughout the story by the legendary Phoenix ("This is what we Jews do. Start all over again. Again. And again. And again."), only to be taken over by an old/new romance closure:

> "I need you, Fanya! Will you allow me to help you?"
>
> Fanya looked at him wondering. Then she thought that if he hugged her, her head would barely reach his shoulder. And then her eyes filled with tears. (p. 266)

What right do we have to claim this quasi-historical, quasi-feminist romance set a century ago as a vicarious representation of the contemporary author's self? The answer lies in the transparency of the authorial intention, which is hardly camouflaged by the historical displacement. This intention grows suspiciously palpable when we consider a peculiar technical aspect of the novel. Although it is told in a straightforward third-person narration, information is mostly limited to that which is available to the heroine. Fanya is not only the protagonist of the action but also its point of focalization. Her inner world is too close to that of the narrator (to the exclusion of all other figural perspectives), to do justice to the narration of a *historical* novel. This lack of distance (ironic or other), as well as the narrator's narrow point of view, undermines the work's claim to be a historical novel. It generates the impression that the development of the historical heroine represents the concerns and expectations of a contemporary consciousness which Israeli present-day reality cannot satisfy. In some sense, *Gei oni* is a feminist *Bildungsroman* masquerading as a more acceptable genre: the historical novel. Lapid had obviously felt that Israeli society of the early 1980s would accept a "feminist" identity as a historical projection but would find it difficult to digest as a realistic proposition for the here and now.

This impression is further reinforced by the (unmistakenly contemporary) feminist protest of one of Lapid's earliest stories, "The Order of the Garter,"[39] and by the totally female orientation of her oeuvre in the last few years. Although, like Hareven, she does not consider herself a feminist, she has been limiting herself, by her own confession, "to women's thematics" and perceives herself as "small, delicate, and becoming more and more aggressive" at the "ripe age of 54."[40]

While her play *Abandoned Property* (1987) explored the psychological dynamics between mother and daughters in a broken family on the margins of the social system (and her forthcoming play is entitled "Surrogate Mother"), her recent novel, *Local Paper*,[41] features a lower middle-class woman journalist in a contemporary provincial town (Beer Sheva). Thirty years old and single, Lisa is not a descendant of Hareven's aunt Victoria, but rather a throwback to the turn-of-the-century detective spinster of English literature. In this popular quasi-detective story Lapid does what she has not dared to do in *Gei oni;* she imagines a female character more common in contemporary America than in Israel: an unmarried woman who is proud of her work ethic, of her "professionalism," and whose priorities are "working" and "being in love." (This seems like a rather wry commentary on Freud's notorious definition of [male?] mental health which stipulated the ability to work and love! Similarly, the novel's final question, repeated twice, "What do you want, Lisi?" reads like a parody on Freud's famous question, "What does woman want?") Yet despite this daring move, Lapid's penchant for romance, for the euphoric heroine's text, is operative here as well (although from a more ironic perspective). For if matrimony has totally lost its appeal ("I have seen my sisters," Lisa explains), the romantic attachment has not. Like Fanya, Lisa gets her reward in the form of a "dark prince," updated for the 1980s: a tawny, handsome, rich and worldly divorcé, whose timely offered "information" rescues Lisa from the imminent danger of losing her job.

Working within the conventions of the popular romance, Lapid (who is herself a happily married mother and a former Chair of the Israeli Writers Association) has created female subjects whose identity seems to be much more seamless and unconflicted than those created by Hareven (or other women writers, such as Kahana-Carmon and Ruth Almog). While Hareven, for example, consciously questions the place of individual autonomy, gender difference and psychological determinism in a society under siege, Lapid uses the historical and ideological materials as a setting against which her protagonists reach toward their optimal development. By the same token, she does not subject her own premises about gender to a serious scrutiny ("motherhood," for example, is never really problematized: Lisa rejects it out of hand and Fanya just weaves it into her busy schedule, although it is never clear how); nor does she indulge in a true psychological exploration of her characters. In a curious way, the wealth of information we accumulate about them, even about their past, does not allow for any meaningful conceptualization. Lapid is content to follow their present entanglements to their happy endings without delving into the larger questions posed by the issues she has dramatized.

The exploration of some of these issues (not least among them the question of women as representing the "other" in general[42]) is carried out in the latest work of two other writers, Amalia Kahana-Carmon and Ruth Almog.[43] Although highly different in almost every aspect of their artistic conception, these two narratives share a common impulse—the attempt to overcome the state of siege so convincingly dramatized by Hareven and Lapid. While the first is still couched in the language of the "historical" romance, breaking out of captivity and reaching the feminist quest only in its last page (more as a promise for the extratextual future), the latter has successfully transcended the limitations of this tradition, testing feminism in the here and now of contemporary reality. That by so doing it uncovers a new set of limitations and perhaps another kind of "siege" (psychological or existential rather than historical) is an inevitably ironic chapter, to be told elsewhere.[44]

NOTES

Work on this essay was made possible by an NEH Fellowship for summer 1989.

[1] Shulamith Hareven, *'Ir yamim rabim* (Tel Aviv, 1972), p. 184. Subsequent references appear in the body of the text. The second page number refers to the English version, *A City of Many Days* (New York, 1977), translated by Hillel Halkin.

[2] Yael Feldman, "Living on the Top Floor: The Arrested Autobiography in Contemporary Israeli Fiction," *Modern Hebrew Literature* 1 (Fall/Winter 1988): 72-77.

[3] The only exception to this generalization, Pinhas Sadeh's *Haḥayim kemashal* (Tel Aviv, 1958) [Life as a Parable] (London, 1972), stands alone in Israeli literature in its blatant denial of the national collective with all its trimmings. Despite its belated popular appeal, particularly among young readers, Sadeh's example of solipsism, mysticism and (Christian?) confessionalism was not followed by any of his fellow writers, nor by the younger generation (at least not before the eighties).

The literature on the construction of the subject in Western literature is too vast to be enumerated here. For a recent monograph see Paul Smith, *Discerning the Subject* (Minneapolis, 1988).

[4] I develop this idea in my article "Gender In/Difference in Contemporary Hebrew Fictional Autobiographies," *Biography* 11:3 (Summer 1988): 189-209; reprinted in *Sex, Love and Signs: European Journal for Semiotic Studies* 1 (1989): 435-56.

[5] This is not to say that women do not use autobiographic materials—e.g., Naomi Fraenkel, Rachel Eitan, Amalia Kahana-Carmon, Dahlia Ravikovitch, Hedda Boshes, Yehudit Hendel—but rather that their narratives generally do not take the *shape* of autobiographic retrospection. (On the obvious exception, Netiva Ben Yehuda's *Bein hasfirot* [Between the Calendars, 1981], see my article [n. 4].)

[6] See Yaffa Berlowitz, ed., *Sippurei nashim* [Stories by Women of the First Immigration] (Tel Aviv, 1984).

[7] See, for example, Shari Benstock, ed., *The Private Self* (Chapel Hill and London, 1988).

[8] It was also easier to write verse without the training in classical Hebrew traditionally reserved only for males. It is no coincidence that the first modern Hebrew prose writer, Devorah Baron, had been raised "as a son," that is—instructed in the sacred sources—by her father who was a rabbi.

On the emergence of women's poetry see most recently Dan Miron, "Founding Mothers, Step Sisters" [Hebrew], *Alpayim* 1 (June, 1989): 29-58.

[9] Shulamit Lapid, *Gei oni* (Tel Aviv, 1982). All further references will appear in the body of the text, translated by the author of this essay.

[10] Amalia Kahana-Carmon, *Lema'lah bemontifer* [Up on Montifer] (Tel Aviv, 1984), pp. 59-184.

[11] Carolyn G. Heilbrun, *Reinventing Womanhood* (New York, 1979), p. 134.

[12] See, for example, Susannah Heschel, ed., *On Being a Jewish Feminist* (New York, 1983).

[13] And see on this point Gershon Shaked, "Imbued with the Love of Jerusalem" in *Gal ahar gal* [Wave after Wave in Hebrew Narrative Fiction] (Jerusalem, 1985), pp. 15-23.

[14] See in particular Netiva Ben Yehuda, *Between the Calendars,* 1981.

[15] Although the precarious position of Freudian psychology is most palpable in the language and plot of this narrative, it is not easy to determine whether it derives from the historical materials themselves (the 1930s-40s), or from the personal ambivalence of the author, who expressed her contempt of classical Freudian psychology in her conversation with me (August 16, 1989). The problematic reception of psychoanalysis in Hebrew literature is the subject of my *Freudianism and Its Discontents* (work in progress), and is partially presented in "Back to Vienna: Zionism on the Literary Coach," in *Vision Confronts Reality,* eds. Sidorsky et al. (Rutherford, 1989), pp. 310-35.

[16] *Sone' hanissim* (Jerusalem and Tel Aviv, 1983) was published in English as *The Miracle Hater,* trans. Hillel Halkin (North Point, 1988); *Navi'* [A Prophet] (Jerusalem and Tel Aviv, 1988) was also translated by Halkin (Worth Point, 1990).

[17] *Tismonet Dulcenea* [The Dulcenea Syndrome] (Jerusalem, 1981).

[18] See, for example, her essay "The First Forty Years," *The Jerusalem Quarterly* 48 (Fall 1988): 3-28, esp. 25-26; and more recently, an interview with Helit Bloom in *Bamahaneh,* March 1, 1989.

[19] See on this point the succint analysis of Noami Chazan, "Gender Equality? Not in a War Zone!" *Israeli Democracy* (Summer 1989): 4-7.

[20] Shaked, p. 23.

[21] See Dafna Sharfman, "The Status of Women in Israel—Facts and Myth," *Israeli Democracy* (Summer 1989): 12-14.

[22] Private communication, August 16, 1989.

[23] Shaked, p. 20.

[24] Shulamit Lapid, *Mazal dagim* [Pisces] (Tel Aviv, 1969); *Shalvat shotim* [Fools' Paradise] (Tel Aviv, 1974); *Kadahat* [Malaria] (Tel Aviv, 1979).

[25] See, for example, Elkana Margalit, *Hashomer hatsa'ir: me'adat ne'urim lemarksizm mahapkhani* [From Youth Movement to Revolutionary Marxism] (Tel Aviv, 1971).

[26] See Dafna Izraeli, "The Labor Women Movement in Palestine from Its Inception to 1929" [Hebrew], *Cathedra* 32 (1984): 109-40; and Devorah Bernstein, "The Status and Organization of Urban Working Women in the 20s and 30s," [Hebrew] *Cathedra* 34 (1985): 115-44.

[27] Private communication, 1984. Literature does not score much higher on this point, the few exceptions [e.g., Rivka Alper's *Hamitnahalim bahar,* and Moshe Shamir's *Hinumat kalah*] notwithstanding. Israeli literature has been good in inscribing women's victimization, as shown by Esther Fuchs in her *Israeli Mythogynies* (Albany, 1987), although I am not sure I share her enthusiasm for this project.

[28] Shochat's fascinating biography, *Before Golda,* told by Rachel Yanait Ben-Zvi, was recently released in English, translated by Sandra Shurin (New York, 1988), as was a documentary film based on it. See also Shulamit Reinharz, "Toward a Model of Female Political Action: The Case of Manya Shohat, Founder of the First Kibbutz," *Women's Studies Int. Forum* 7:4 (1984): 275-87.

[29] Yehudit Oryan, *Yedi'ot aharonot* (April 16, 1982): 22, 26. See also Shlomo Har'el, "Around the Settlement—between Myth and Historicism," in *Bein historya lesifrut* (Tel Aviv, 1983). pp. 134-50.

[30] Nancy Miller, *The Heroine's Text* (New York, 1980).

[31] Shulamit Lapid, "The Romantic Popular Novel" [Hebrew], *Ma'ariv* (Oct. 17, 1975).

[32] "Inadvertent Feminism: The Image of Frontier Women in Contemporary Israeli Literature," *Modern Hebrew Literature* 10 (Spring/Summer, 1985): 34-37.

[33] Erich Neumann, *Amor and Psyche: The Psychic Development of the Feminine* (Princeton, 1952). And see my essay, "An Historical Novel or Masqueraded Autobiography?" *Siman qri'ah* 18 (March 1986): 208-13.

[34] Lesley Hazleton, *Israeli Women: The Reality behind the Myth* (New York, 1977), p. 93.

[35] See Erich Neumann, *The Origins and History of Consciousness* (Princeton, 1973), p. 50 et passim.

[36] Neumann, *Amor and Psyche.* pp. 55, 60, 68.

[37] For a summary of the debate see Mary Ann Ferguson, "The Female Novel of Development and the Myth of Psyche," in *The Voyage In: Fictions of Female Development,* eds. Elizabeth Abel, Marianne Hirsch, and Elizabeth Langland (Hanover and London, 1983), pp. 228-43.

[38] Carolyn G. Heilbrun, *Writing a Woman's Life* (New York, 1988).

[39] In *Mazal dagim,* 1969.

[40] See an interview with her in *Lilith* (Summer, 1989): 20. [The same issue also includes a translation of one of her new "aggressive" stories, "The Bed."]

[41] Shulamit Lapid, *Meqomon* [Local Paper] (Jerusalem, 1989).

[42] See my "The 'Other Within' in Contemporary Israeli Fiction," *Middle East Review* 22:1 (Fall, 1989): 47-53.

[43] Ruth Almog, *Shorshei avir* [Dangling Roots] (Jerusalem, 1987). For Kahana-Carmon see note 10.

[44] See my forthcoming "Inventing a Life for Oneself, or: Taking Feminism to the Streets in Israeli Literature."

## Esther Fuchs

SOURCE: "Images of Love and War in Contemporary Israeli Fiction: A Feminist Re-vision," in *Arms and the Woman: War, Gender, and Literary Representation,* Helen M. Cooper, Adrienne Auslander Munich, Susan Merrill Squier, eds., The University of North Carolina Press, 1989, pp. 268-82.

[*In the following essay, Fuchs observes the identification of women with destruction in Israeli fiction of the 1960s and 1970s.*]

In an essay on the new Israeli story, Baruch Kurzweil argues that since the early 1960s, Israeli fiction has demonstrated an increasing obsession with the subject of Eros. He refers to Eros not in its Freudian sense of the life instinct but in the sense of "the temptations of woman," and as such he uses it as a term of opprobrium: "But this special conspicuousness of Eros, which is so characteristic of so many Israeli stories, testifies to the lack of a real goal in life. This mania for Eros in the Hebrew story is not a sign of effervescent vitality, but of something sick. It signifies an escape from the emptiness of life."[1] Kurzweil goes on to interpret the proliferation of the stories about the sexual "temptations of woman" not only as a manifestation of existential nausea, but also as an expression of self-hatred, an attempt to flee from Jewish identity, a suicidal pursuit of false Western idols. Although he calls attention to an important development in what came to be known as the literature of the New Wave (which emerged in the late 1950s and early 1960s in reaction to the confined realism and socialist Zionist ideology of their predecessors), Kurzweil ignores the fact that Eros (in his sense) is often linked to Thanatos, the human desire to die. By failing to note the punitive element in the association in the literature of the 1960s and 1970s of "the temptations of woman" with the motif of death, Kurzweil implicitly endorses the androcentric vision which couples woman's sexuality with destruction. It is this tendency in the new Israeli story, to couple woman with destruction, that I would like to examine here.

The thematic relationship between heterosexual love and national war has pervaded Israeli fiction since its inception in the late 1940s. Yet the presentation of this relationship has undergone radical structural transformations from its bipolar appearance in the works of S. Yizhar and Moshe Shamir to its interdependent presentation in the works of Yitzhak Ben Ner, Ya'akov Buchan, and David Schütz. Whereas in the Palmah fiction romantic love and national war appear as dichotomously opposed indices of happiness and anguish, hope and despair, peace and violence, life and death, in the fiction of the generation of the state, the boundaries between the thematic poles seem to have dissolved: love and war are not only inextricably intertwined, but, in terms of their ideational function, virtually reversed. Heterosexual love is exposed as a power struggle, a relentless war leading to atrophy, to psychical and even physical death; whereas military confrontation emerges as a kind of refuge. The female character, previously symbolic of peace and love, turns into a pernicious victimizer. Romantic love—previously idealized as the loftiest human drive—is translated into lifeless, exploitative, and mechanical sex, degrading and debilitating for both man and woman. Perhaps the most dramatic expression of the thematic complementarity of love and war in Israeli narrative fiction can be found in war-related stories, in which the horror of war is both highlighted and counterbalanced by a subplot revolving around romantic love. In addition, most stories about romantic heterosexual love contain war-related subplots and/or war-related thematic kernels. Another common feature in this context is the identification of national war with male characters, and the complementary identification of love and sex with female characters—a tendency which, in view of the active involvement of women in Israel's military history, should not be taken for granted. The agenda of this study is then threefold: first, to illustrate the dialectical relationship of love and war in stories by the most prominent writers of the 1960s and 1970s; secondly, to analyze the implications of the results within the context of sexual politics; and thirdly, to suggest some general explanations for the most common configurations observed in our examples.

The transformation of woman from an icon of peace and romantic love (e.g., in Yizhar's *Yemei Tsiklag* [The days of Ziklag, 1959]) into one of death is illustrated in Yoram Kanyuk's *Himo melekh yerushalayim* (Himo king of Jerusalem, 1966). The novel revolves around the peculiar love of Hamutal Hurvitz, a young and beautiful nurse, for Himo, a casualty of the 1948 War of Independence. The only unmutilated remainder of what used to be a dashing young officer is Himo's lips, which convulsively and incessantly mumble, "Shoot me! Shoot me." The rest of his body, including, most significantly, his genitals, have been irreparably damaged. Undeterred by Himo's ghastly physique, Hamutal showers all her love and devotion upon him, to the astonishment and envy of the other wounded soldiers in the hospital. Finally, however, Hamutal gives up and decides to poison Himo in order to put an end to his agony. Ironically, Himo undergoes a strange transformation just as Hamutal is preparing the fatal injection. He is shown suddenly to recover his long-extinct desire to live: "He is pleading for his life. His mutilated body is writhing now, he tried to stretch out his hands imploringly; he pleaded like a starving dog, but he could no more say a word."[2] The juxtaposition of the upright stature of the beautiful nurse, gripping boldly the poisonous injector, determined and all but immune to the dramatic reversal of events, and the victimized man writhing helplessly at her feet, dramatizes the reversal in traditional power relations between male and female that are often occasioned by war.[3] I would like to suggest that the transformation of Hamutal from an icon of love to an angel of death reveals a male fear of the radical transition that wars in patriarchal societies tend to bring about in the status of women, changing them overnight from passive dependents to active participants in the economy and in leadership roles on both the civilian and military fronts. While wars are likely to empower the "weak" sex, they also tend to emasculate the "strong" sex. War casualties find themselves at the mercy of female nurses, and even male survivors discover their dependency on female services and nurturance. Himo, who used to be the epitome of virility, is not only sexually emasculated and physically incapacitated, but also emotionally dependent on Hamutal.

By ending with a calm and collected Hamutal stopping at a coffee shop several years later, only to remember the tragic incident in passing, Kanyuk's novel subverts the romantic image of woman in the Palmah literature as protective mother/lover, as well as that of the perennial mourner.[4] It is true that Hamutal's love for Himo supplies the motivation for the larger part of the novel, but the ironic denouement challenges the impression heretofore created. Hamutal's decision to kill Himo turns out to be just as irrational and unpredictable as her unyielding love for him: neither one serves the desires and needs of the male victim. Woman's proverbial selflessness and concern for the male war victim are here exposed as irrational and transient.[5] Even her deepest identification with the male victim, even the most passionate love, is shown to have its limits. At best, woman is an outsider in war. At worst, she is a dangerous enemy under the guise of a caring, nurturing female role model.[6]

In Amos Oz's novel, *Michael sheli* (*My Michael*), the symbolic representation of woman as Thanatos in the guise of Eros becomes even more explicit. Although this novel also presents the man, Michael, as victim, and the woman, Hana, as victimizer, the novel celebrates the male victim's quiet victory over his destructive enemy. Despite Hana's refusal to cooperate with Michael either as wife or as mother, and despite her exploitative and humiliating treatment of him, it is she who finally degenerates through successive stages of boredom, passivity, and physical sickness into psychosis, while Michael succeeds in launching a brilliant academic career, moving progressively toward greater professional accomplishment and economic stability. Hana's perverse attitude toward her husband is most eloquently dramatized in her sexual exploitation of him: "I would wake up my husband, crawl under his blanket, cling to his body with all my might. . . . Nevertheless, I ignored him; I made contact only with his body: muscles, arms, hair. In my heart I knew that I betrayed him over and over again with his body."[7] Hana's sexual abuse of her husband is a perversion and prevarication of Eros. Using Michael as a sex object (the traditional literary role of the female), she turns what constitutes the ultimate symbolic expression of love into a ritualistic enactment of war.[8] Having failed to vitiate her husband's virility by other means, she attempts to castrate him by exhausting him sexually. Sexual relations in *Michael sheli* become a metaphor for the power relations between man and woman, and it is a woman who is blatantly responsible for this perverse reversal. Hana is incapable of and uninterested in love; what she seeks is sadomasochistic titillation, a luxury her dedicated husband does not afford her. She therefore resorts to erotic fantasies in which she is both the commander and the victim of Halil and Aziz, her Palestinian childhood playmates, who she imagines have become terrorists. It is significant that Hana first starts to fantasize about Halil and Aziz when Michael is drafted during the war of 1956. The analogy between the husband, who is fighting the Egyptians in the Sinai Peninsula, and the wife, who indulges in erotic fantasies about the Arab twins, dramatizes not only Hana's infidelity, but also her national disloyalty.[9] This becomes even more pronounced at the end of the novel as Hana imagines herself sending her Palestinian lovers/servants on an anti-Israeli terrorist mission: "I will set them on. . . . A box of explosives, detonators, fuses, ammunition, hand grenades, glittering knives."[10]

The presentation of woman as conjugal and national enemy reveals, among other things, a deep-seated suspicion of woman's allegedly passive role in wartime. The notion that married women stay home, secure and relatively invulnerable, while men sacrifice their lives to defend them has powerful implications for relations between the sexes in a country constantly threatened by war. It must be remembered that despite the compulsory draft in Israel, only 50 percent of draftable women actually join the armed forces. Religious, illiterate, married, and pregnant women are exempted from the draft. Furthermore, the law bars women from combat duties; consequently, the majority of women serve in auxiliary jobs (e.g., as secretaries, clerks, teachers, drivers, wireless operators, parachute folders).[11] These circumstances create the impression that women are not really involved in the war effort, that their suffering and sacrifices are negligible compared to the price paid by male fighters. This impression is shared by both men and women in Israel. Two factors are all too often forgotten in this context: first, that women were not consulted when, in 1948, as the War of Independence was underway, it was decided to pull them out of the front and confine them to noncombat duties;[12] and secondly, that war takes a heavy psychological toll on Israeli mothers and wives, especially *because* of their inability to contribute to the war effort more substantially. This imposed impotence results in anxiety, guilt, alienation from the national scene, and a loss of self-esteem.[13] While in reality war ends up damaging the status of women both inside and outside the army, mythical thinking, which often serves as grist for literary creativity, tends to envision women as protected and secure, and perceive men as vulnerable and victimized by war.[14] Mythical thinking, to which Amos Oz, like other New Wave writers, is especially susceptible, ignores social, economic, and legal constraints, and tends to perceive the human world *sub speciae aeternitatis*.[15] A literature inspired by mythical thinking will construe a social situation not as the outcome of external constraints, but as the product of human nature. From this perspective, woman stays home because she is inherently passive, confined, indifferent to war. In the volatile political context of Israel, a country continually on the brink of military conflagration, willful passivity entails treachery or, worse, a perverse subconscious love for the enemy: Eros bound with Thanatos, Thanatos in the guise of Eros. Fostered on the one hand by the archetypal association of treachery with female sexuality, and on the other by the Freudian theory concerning woman's alleged masochism, this vision spawns an image very much like that of Hana Gonen, a woman who indulges in orgiastic fantasies of rape by Palestinian terrorists while her husband fights for the common weal.[16]

If the implicitly incriminating portrait of Hana Gonen derives from the subconscious mistrust of the homebound passive woman, Ben Ner's "Nicole" (1976) is inspired by the apparently opposite distrust of the active army woman. While Hana's passivity and unsociability are essentially excoriated by the standards of socialist Zionism, Nicole's participation in the army is criticized by the traditional Judeo-Christian endorsement of woman's place in the home. Like Hamutal and Hana, Nicole is beautiful and sexy; like Hana, Nicole wields her sexuality as a weapon in her eternal contest with men she wants to subdue. Unlike Hana, however, Nicole is not content with fantasies of self-destruction. In order to satisfy her sado-masochistic proclivities, she joins the army and ends up destroying others. What attracts Nicole to a career in the army is not patriotism or even a professional interest, but the vulnerability of the sex-starved soldiers, the perfect potential victims for her narcissism and nymphomania. The story focuses on Nicole's sexual campaigns and conquests, especially after her affair with Lt. Col. Baruch Adar, or Barko, whom she seduces away from his lawful wife, as she has done with all her previous lovers. On the eve of the fateful Yom Kippur of 1973, she convinces Barko to spend the night with her in a hotel whose location remains undisclosed to their brigade. When the war breaks out, the soldiers are unable to contact Lieutenant Colonel Barko, which results in confusion, disorientation, and ultimately defeat. Although Barko blames himself for the tragic blow to his brigade, the story implies that the military defeat is the product of Nicole's wiles. The aetiological linkage of one of the most traumatic wars in Israel's military history with woman's role in the army reveals a deep-seated distrust of women soldiers, especially those endowed with authoritative status and power. When allowed to affect the public scene, woman evolves from a personal to a national enemy; her vampiric bite affects not only the individual man, but the entire army.

In addition to the distrust of women in power—who endanger the traditional power-structured status quo between the sexes—the story reveals a deeper discontent with woman's encroachment into what appears to be an exclusively male domain. The next monologue, in which Amiram castigates Nicole for her neglect and irresponsibility, reveals not only contempt for women in power, but also a vision of woman as an outsider who is incapable of comprehending even the most basic facts about the army: "Look madame, this is the army. This is an army at war for life or death. In such a war, things must be decided like that, sharply, this or that way. You have been among us long enough to understand this, haven't you?"[17] Amiram implies that despite Nicole's status and experience, she remains a woman, a "you," an outsider, against "us," the male insiders. The hostility toward military women corresponds to a masculinist insecurity rooted in the identification of virility with military prowess. In a patriarchal and militarized culture, successful military women may compromise the self-image of men as fighters and defenders of the civilian population, namely helpless women and children.[18] Furthermore, a military woman constitutes a threat to male bonding, of which the army is one of the remaining socially sanctioned mainstays.[19] Finally, symbolically identified with sex, gentleness, pleasure, and sensuality, woman embodies all the values that threaten the military ethos, which thrives on coarseness, vulgarity, toughness, and the suppression of Eros.[20] In a military context, woman is reduced to a sex object, and sex to a mechanical activity, intended to relieve physiological tensions rather than gratify emotional needs. Because it is necessary not to give in to normal human needs for love and intimacy, women and sex become the subjects of vulgar jokes, and objects whose importance must be defied in order to sustain the psychic balance necessary for military efficiency.[21]

Like Hamutal Hurvitz and Hana Gonen, Nicole is an epitome of the castrating bitch who, under the guise of love, emasculates her male victims: "She is so glad to know that he [Barko] is afraid. At last. He should be afraid. She wants him to be afraid."[22] Like Hana Gonen, Nicole sadistically tortures her man in an attempt to vanquish his male pride and subject him to her will. Realizing how guilty Barko feels about his brigade's defeat, she calls him up, pretending to be a widow of one of his dead soldiers. But in this battle between the sexes, Nicole, like Hana, cannot win. With resentment and exasperation, Nicole admits her defeat: "But, damn it, he does not crawl, break down, quiver, cry, scream, writhe helplessly; he keeps rising from his downfalls."[23] Once again, man is victimized not by national but by sexual war—the real enemy is not the Arab across the border, but the Israeli woman inside the hospital, the home, the camp. The most fatal blows come not from firearms, but from the "loving" arms of woman. Death lurks not in violence, but in sexuality; love is not the opposite, but the motivating principle of war.

Although the interdependence of Eros and Thanatos is conspicuous in Israeli literature, it pervades other literature as well. The motif of man's fatal entrapment by a sexually irresistible woman has deep roots in the Western literary tradition; from Samson and Delilah, to Holofernes and Judith and to John the Baptist and Salomé, from the Sirens and the Sphinx to the Lorelei, woman serves as the composite symbol of Eros and Thanatos. Karen Horney suggests that this ubiquitous phenomenon derives from man's castration anxiety, which is related to his realization of the difference between his genitalia and that of the female, and from man's dread of physical flaccidity/weakness/death after coitus.[24] To conceal his anxiety and dread, man either glorifies woman, putting her on an unreachable pedestal, or objectifies her as evil and dreadful, thus rationalizing and justifying his

dread. "'It is not,' he says 'that I dread her; it is that she herself is malignant, capable of any crime, a beast of prey, a vampire, a witch, insatiable in her desires. She is the very personification of what is sinister.'"[25] This psychoanalytic explanation has a political dimension that Horney does not go into. Since men have been the primary producers of canonic religion, art, literature, and culture until fairly recently, their representations of women have become a hegemonic perspective through which both men and women perceive themselves. The representation of woman as the embodiment of Eros and Thanatos then serves as an important weapon in the hands of patriarchal hegemony; by wielding this image, the patriarchal system succeeds in both fostering man's distrust of woman as well as in keeping woman in her proper place.[26] One can conclude, then, that war and love appear together so frequently because love, as perceived in Western culture, is a kind of war.[27] Romantic love in Western society perpetuates the power imbalance between the sexes; rather than drawing them together, as it often purports to do, it intensifies the enmity between them.[28]

To return to our specific case study, it is clear that contemporary Israeli literature has not invented the thematic and compositional interdependence of Eros and Thanatos; as an essentially Western literature, it has inherited this vocabulary of images and concepts. Nevertheless it is unique in its quantitative and qualitative use of this vocabulary. Here Eros and Thanatos are usually polarized and then welded together as, respectively, sex and war. Eros is usually represented not as a love or life instinct, but rather as a sexual drive; Thanatos is normally associated with violent death—usually war. In this context, man is the victim of woman, who is out to destroy both his virility and his life.

Israel's protracted war with its surrounding neighbors, a war whose inevitability and complexity began to emerge in Israel's national consciousness after the war of 1956, has created what Marcuse calls "a repressive society," a society in which death is either feared as constant threat, glorified as supreme sacrifice, or accepted as inescapable fate.[29] In a repressive culture, Eros is feared as a distracting, energy-consuming principle. Instead of allowing human sexuality to sublimate itself into Eros—a life-giving social order—a repressive system suppresses it by trivializing it, reducing it to a biological need and presenting it as potentially dangerous. Under repressive circumstances, especially in the context of war, which sanctions and often sanctifies the destruction of life, sex, symbolically represented as woman, is depicted as life-threatening. The cultural acceptance of Thanatos brings about a reversal where woman, the giver of life and the principle of Eros, is depicted as a deathly victimizer, while man, who does the killing, is perceived as the victim. On a less abstract level, Israel's protracted war and the sexual division of labor within the army produce a suspicion of women who seem not to do quite their share, despite their traditional nurturant and protective roles as wives and mothers outside the army, or nurses and auxiliary soldiers within it. On the other hand, the constant threat of war and continuous political instability create a strong need for security within the private sphere, a need that is often translated into a nostalgic and regressive move back to traditional—namely patriarchal—patterns of intersexual and marital relations. In this context, women who seem to defy traditional power relations inspire anxiety and distrust.

Contemporary Israeli literature reflects not only the effects of war and siege; to a large extent, it is also what Yosef Oren calls a literature of disillusionment.[30] The disenchantment with both Israel's political and military constraints and with the gradual transformation of what used to be a pioneer society—dedicated to utopian and idealistic visions—into an organized, bureaucratized state that often sacrifices ideals for pragmatic considerations, is sharply registered in Israel's canonic literature. The internecine relations between husband and wife and the degeneration of love into mutually destructive sexual relations serve as metaphors for what Israeli writers perceive as Israel's ideological disorientation and social disintegration. As Oren points out, "The writers of the new generation dramatize an extreme scene that has not yet been established in Israeli reality, and [they] ask us to accept it as an authentic testimony to the reality of our lives."[31] Identified with the family (the fundamental unit of society), woman came to signify the stultifying and corrupt society from which the Israeli male hero constantly flees, often right into the arms of war. Thus the romanticized nurturant mother/lover of the Palmah generation—often the symbol of civilian life—became the vampiric bitch in the literature of the 1960s and 1970s, just as the idealistic, victorious, and admirable male fighter turned into a pathetic victim.[32] In so far as private relations serve as allegorical constructs signifying a national reality, the vampiric woman reflects not only the exasperated society, but also the devouring country with its insatiable demand for sacrifices, with its endless hunger for male corpses. The land of Israel is often symbolically portrayed as a female principle, a conception with deep biblical roots.[33] Just as in Hebrew-Palestinian utopian literature, this country is often depicted as a loving mother/wife waiting for her son/lover to return to her; in contemporary Israeli literature, it appears as a deathly woman exacting endless sacrifices from her male lover.

Baruch Kurzweil was right in observing the increasing prevalence of what he calls Eros in Israeli literature, but his interpretation of this development can only be accepted if we consider its full range. It is not merely the increasing preponderance of women (especially in the capacity of sexual agents) that conveys a sense of disorientation and existential nausea. It is rather the presentation of women as symbolic of death that may perhaps signal an expression of despair, disorientation, and demoralization in Israeli fiction. It is the pervasive combination of Eros with Thanatos that may convey what Kurzweil sees as the flight from affirming values to self-hatred and self-destruction.

NOTES

I would like to thank the editors of this volume and John Bormanis for their editorial assistance in the preparation of this article, which also appeared (in a modified version) in *Modern Judaism* 6 (1986): 189-96. See also Fuchs, *Israeli Mythogynies.*

[1] Kurzweil, *Hipus hasifrut hayisraelit,* 67. This and all the following quotations from Hebrew sources are based upon my own translations.

[2] Kanyuk, *Himo melekh yerushalayim,* 170-71.

[3] In her article on British literature during and after World War I, Sandra M. Gilbert notes that "the unmanning terrors of combat lead not just to a generalized sexual anxiety but also to a sexual anger directed specifically against the female, as if the Great War itself were primarily a climactic episode in some battle of the sexes that had already been raging for years" (Gilbert, "Soldier's Heart," 424).

[4] Yigal Mossinsohn appears to be the exception in the overall tendency of the writers of the late 1940s and 1950s to portray woman as a symbol of peace and normal civilian life. His portrayal of women as adulterous traitors suggests that it is man's failure to assert himself, rather than woman's innate power, that is the true cause of his defeat.

[5] Although this is not one of the major themes of the novel, Hanoch Bartov's *Pitsei bagrut* (Acne, 1965) offers an analogous example of woman's transient commitment to the male warrior. Likewise, Benjamin Galai, in "Al haholkhim" (On the travelers who will not return), writes, "For not forever will your girl cry, and not forever cast down her eyes" (313-15).

[6] Woman also appears as outsider in Yitzhak Orpaz's *Masa daniel* (The voyage of Daniel, 1969).

[7] Oz, *Michael sheli,* 178.

[8] Yitzhak Orpaz's *Nemalim* (Ants) offers an analogous description of internecine relations between husband and wife.

[9] An allegory of the political situation of Israel as a state in siege, Orpaz's *Nemalim* also presents woman as a potential national threat.

[10] Oz, *Michael sheli,* 197.

[11] On the status of women in Zahal, the Israeli Defence Force, see Yuval-Davis, "The Israeli Example," 73-78; Hazelton, *Israeli Women,* 112-61; Rein, *Daughters of Rachel,* 44-54; Lahav, "The Status of Women," 107-29; and Padan-Eisenstark, "Are Israeli Women Really Equal?" 538-45.

[12] Women protested indignantly against the decision to exclude them from combat duties. See Rein, *Daughters of Rachel,* 46-7; Yehuda, *1948—Bein hasefirot,* 277-81.

[13] Only recently have Israeli women begun to give expression to their frustrations in wartime. See Sharron, "Women and War," 8.

[14] In Amos Oz's "Minzar hashatkanim" (The Trappist monastery, 1965), the male protagonist sets out on a reprisal mission against an Arab village while his girlfriend stays at the army base. A. B. Yehoshua also casts his male heroes as victims and his female characters as passive outsiders who are, in the final analysis, the enemies of their male counterparts. See his "Besis tilim 612" (Missile base 612, 1975) and Shamai Golan's *Moto shel uri peled* (The death of Uri Peled, 1971), where woman appears not only as passive, indifferent, and treacherous, but also as the perpetrator of her husband's death.

[15] The New Wave emphasized the universal and unchanging patterns of human behavior, rather than the peculiarities of the Israeli situation, and hence its frequent use of allegory, archetype, and myth. See Shaked, *Gal hadash basiporet haivrit.*

[16] The association of woman, and especially female sexuality, with treachery has a long tradition in Western culture and literature; see Hays, *The Dangerous Sex;* Rogers, *The Troublesome Helpmate.* For a critique of Freud's theories on female masochism, see Horney, *Feminine Psychology,* 214-33. For a more general revision of Freudian theories on female sexuality and psychology, see Chodorow, *The Reproduction of Mothering,* 141-58.

[17] Ner, "Nicole," 170.

[18] Natalie Rein, *Daughters of Rachel,* 47, suggests that the reluctance to credit women for their contribution to the underground groups of Etsel and Lehi, as well as to the Palmah, manifests the unwillingness of male Jews, who have come from generations of emasculated manhood, to share with women the experience of asserting their newfound virility. The reluctance to acknowledge women's military contribution is a rather common phenomenon. Despite their participation in Europe's modern armies, mostly in service jobs, women are barely mentioned in most military histories; see Hacker, "Women and Military Institutions," 643-71.

[19] According to Lionel Tiger, for example, women are by nature incapable of bonding, and as such threaten male bonding, which he sees as one of the major forces of social cohesiveness (see Tiger, *Men in Groups*). On the hostile responses to integrating women into regular combat forces in modern armies, see Rogan, *Mixed Company.*

[20] Amos Elon notes that the continuous and repeated periods of war and military tensions in Israel have produced a cult of toughness. On the effect of this cult on intersexual relations, he points out, "The letters written by young Israelis to their sweethearts are notoriously dry, unimaginative, and frequently, oddly impersonal. They are often so skimpy in exclamations of love, devotion, or longing—indeed of any feeling whatsoever—that a reader may suspect a near total lack of sensitivity and refinement. Or else he may suspect that the young writers, if they have feelings, are so frightened by them—or so ashamed and embarrassed—that they have apparently resolved to keep them permanently concealed. One does not talk of feelings, one rarely admits that they exist" (Elon, *The Israelis,* 238).

[21] See Fetterley (*The Resisting Reader,* 51) on the analogous attitude toward women and sexuality in Hemingway's *A Farewell to Arms.*

[22] Ner, "Nicole," 179.

[23] Ibid., 180.

[24] Horney, *Feminine Psychology,* 107-18; 131-46.

[25] Ibid., 135. Horney also points out that Freud himself objectifies the male dread of woman when ascribing this fear to woman's actual hostility toward the male, a hostility that is allegedly generated by the pain and discomfort of defloration. See Freud, "The Taboo of Virginity," 70-86.

[26] On the political dimension of male-authored literature describing women and intersexual relations, see Millett, *Sexual Politics,* 3-31; 331-505.

[27] See Rougemont, *Love in the Western World.*

[28] For a political analysis of romantic love in Western culture, see Firestone, *The Dialectic of Sex,* esp. 126-45.

[29] Marcuse, *Eros and Civilization,* 222-36.

[30] See Oren, *Hahitpakhut.*

[31] Oren, *Hahitpakhut,* 24.

[32] This is only one aspect of the parodic treatment of the Palmah literature by the New Wave. For further analysis, see Gertz, "Haparodia," 272-77.

[33] The words referring to the concept or object of the land of Israel are all of the feminine gender in Hebrew. For example, "erets" (country), "adama" (earth), "moledet" (homeland), "medina" (state). Biblical literature, notably prophetic writings, and later Jewish traditional literature often identify the land of Zion as an abandoned wife or a widow. The symbolic presentation of the land as female has had an enormous impact on modern Hebrew literature, as well as on contemporary Israeli writers. In a recent treatise on Zionism, A. B. Yehoshua identifies the land of Israel as the long-neglected symbolic mother of the Jewish people. See Yehoshua, *Bizkhut hanormaliut,* 55-62.

WORKS CITED

Ben-Yehuda, Netiva. *1948—Bein hasefirot* (1948—Between the calendars). Jerusalem: Keter, 1981.

Chodorow, Nancy. *The Reproduction of Mothering.* Berkeley: University of California Press, 1978.

Elon, Amos. *The Israelis.* New York: Rinehart & Winston, 1971.

Fetterley, Judith. *The Resisting Reader: A Feminist Approach to American Fiction.* Bloomington: Indiana University Press, 1971.

Firestone, Shulamith. *The Dialectic of Sex.* 2d ed. New York: Bantam Books, 1979.

Freud, Sigmund. "The Taboo of Virginity." In *Sexuality and the Psychology of Love,* 70-86. 2d ed. New York: Macmillan Co., 1974.

Fuchs, Esther. *Israeli Mythogynies: Women in Contemporary Hebrew Fiction.* Albany: State University of New York Press, 1987.

Galai, Benjamin. "Al haholkhim shelo yashuvu" (On the travelers who will not return). In *Modern Hebrew Poetry,* edited and translated by Ruth Fein-Mintz, 313-15. Berkeley: University of California Press, 1966.

Gertz, Nurith. "Haparodia behilufei hadorot basifrut ha'ivrit" (Parody in generational transitions in Hebrew literature). *Siman keriah* 12-13 (1981): 272-77.

Gilbert, Sandra M. "Soldier's Heart: Literary Men, Literary Women, and the Great War." *Signs* 8, no. 3 (Spring 1983): 422-50.

Hacker, Barton C. "Women and Military Institutions in Early Modern Europe: A Reconnaissance." *Signs* 6 (1981): 643-71.

Hays, H. R. *The Dangerous Sex: The Myth of Feminine Evil.* New York: G. P. Putnam's Sons, 1964.

Hazelton, Lesley. *Israeli Women: The Reality behind the Myth.* New York: Simon & Schuster, 1977.

Horney, Karen. *Feminine Psychology.* New York: Norton, 1967.

Kanyuk, Yoram. *Himo melekh yerushalayim* (Himo king of Jerusalem). Tel Aviv: Am Oved, 1966.

Kurzweil, Baruch. *Hipus hasifrut hayisraelit* (In search of Israeli literature). Ramat Gan: Bar Ilan University, 1982.

Lahav, Pnina. "The Status of Women in Israel: Myth and Reality," *The American Journal of Comparative Law* 22 (1974): 107-29.

Marcuse, Herbert. *Eros and Civilization.* Boston: Beacon Press, 1966.

Millett, Kate. *Sexual Politics.* New York: Ballantine Books, 1970.

Ner, Yitzhak Ben. "Nicole." In *Shkiah kafrit* (Rustic sunset). Tel Aviv: Am Oved, 1976.

Oren, Yosef. *Hahitpakhut basiporet hayisraelit* (The disillusionment in Israeli narrative fiction). Tel Aviv: Yachad, 1983.

Orpaz, Yitzhak. *Masa daniel* (Daniel's Voyage). Tel Aviv: Am Oved, 1969.

———. *Nemalim* (Ants). Tel Aviv: Am Oved, 1968.

Oz, Amos. *Michael sheli* (My Michael). Tel Aviv: Am Oved, 1968.

———. "Minzar hashatkanim" (The Trappist Monastery). In *Artsot hatan* (Lands of the Jackal). Tel Aviv, 1965.

Padan-Eisenstark, Dorit D. "Are Israeli Women Really Equal? Trends and Patterns of Israeli Women's Labor Force Participation: A Comparative Analysis." *Journal of Marriage and the Family* 35 (1973): 538-45.

Rein, Natalie. *Daughters of Rachel: Women in Israel.* New York: Penguin Books, 1979.

Rogan, Helen. *Mixed Company: Women in the Modern Army.* New York: G. P. Putnam's Sons, 1981.

Rogers, Katherine M. *The Troublesome Helpmate: A History of Misogyny in Literature.* Seattle: University of Washington Press, 1966.

Rougemont, Denis de. *Love in the Western World.* Translated by M. Belgion. 2d ed. Princeton, N.J.: Princeton University Press, 1983.

Shaked, Gershon. *Gal hadash basiporet haivrit* (A new wave in Israeli fiction). 2d ed. Tel Aviv: Poalim, 1974.

Sharron, Nomi. "Women and War." *The Jerusalem Post: International Edition,* November 7-13, 1982, 18.

Tiger, Lionel. *Men in Groups.* New York: Random House, 1969.

Yehoshua, A. B. "Besis tilim 612" (Missile Base 612). In *Ad Horef* (Till Winter). Tel Aviv: Hakibbutz Hameuchad, 1975.

———. *Bizkhut hanormaliut* (The right of normalcy). Tel Aviv: Schocken Books, 1980.

Yuval-Davis, Nira. "The Israeli Example." In *Loaded Questions: Women in the Military,* edited by W. Chapkis, 73-78. Amsterdam: Transnational Institute, 1981.

## ARAB CHARACTERS IN ISRAELI LITERATURE

**Edna Amir Coffin**

SOURCE: "The Image of the Arab in Modern Hebrew Literature," in *Michigan Quarterly Review,* Vol. XXI, No. 2, Spring, 1982, pp. 319-41.

[*In the following essay, Coffin discusses representations of Arabs and Arab-Jewish relations in Israeli literature.*]

> *The encounter between the Arab residents and the Jewish settlers does not resemble an epic or a western, but is, perhaps, closest to a Greek tragedy. That is to say, the clash between justice and justice . . . and like ancient tragedies, there is no hope for happy reconciliation on the basis of some magic formula.*

This vision of the conflict between Jews and Arabs in Israel is that of Amos Oz, one of Israel's leading fiction writers and, like many of its writers and intellectuals, a political activist as well. While writers may not have a significant effect on political life in Israel, they have for the most part been outspoken social critics and have fulfilled an important role in reflecting the central concerns of the society. Even writers who have tried to disengage themselves from national politics and focus on more general aspects of the human condition have been unable to avoid the immediate moral issues resulting from the Arab-Jewish confrontations. Israeli literature has always expressed a great yearning for coexistence; at the same time it has evidenced a growing frustration and sense of pessimism. After three decades, the "magic formula" Oz refers to seems more illusive than ever.

While not the only major theme claiming the attention of Modern Hebrew writers, the Arab-Jewish encounter occupies an important position even in the earliest literary expressions of the Jewish community in Eretz Yisrael. Modern Hebrew literature had its beginnings in the late eighteenth century in Central Europe; it is, however, almost entirely a literature of this century, written for the most part in the Near East. It can be divided into four major phases characterized both by shifting moral concerns and changing modes of literary expression. These modulations of emphasis and style can be seen in the treatment of the Arab presence. The idealized portrayal of Arabs as romantic or exotic Oriental figures early in this century is succeeded by a scarcely less sentimental treatment in the social-realist fiction of the 1940s and early 1950s. Writers of the 1950s and 1960s replace or supplement this approach by a parabolic mode in which profound feelings of guilt and hostility find expression in symbolic narratives. After the 1973 war newer works tried to give even fuller representation to Arabs, both as individuals and as members of various communities, as if the art of description could effect the sympathetic understanding each side has found so elusive. A closer look at sample texts from each historical phase will suggest the somber evolution of this crucial motif.

### I. BEFORE 1948

Jewish authors exhibit divergent attitudes in their early portrayals of Arabs: on the one hand, a strong attraction to the exotic strangers, and on the other, misgivings about the injustice manifest in their semi-feudal society. Traditional customs, often tribally based, provide insights into an attractively different culture for both fictionists and folklorists, but writers find it difficult to accept the systematic violations of what they perceive to be individual rights. They see the common man, the Arab *fellah* ("farmer") exploited by a class of landlords, the Arab woman denied the freedom to determine her own fate, and the children robbed of their childhood and made to join the labor force at an early age. The preoccupation with various aspects of the local scene follows not only from observation but also from major concerns of early Jewish settlers: the need to reestablish connections with the ancient biblical past and with the land, and the desire to build a new society based on the principles of equality and justice—a desire that prompted identification with the oppressed.

Moshe Smilansky (1874-1953), while a minor figure in Modern Hebrew literature, is nonetheless well known for his fictional treatment of interactions between early Jewish settlers and their Arab neighbors. Smilansky was a farmer as well as a writer; he employed Arab as well as Jewish laborers on his land, learned to speak Arabic well, and familiarized himself with Arab customs and traditions. Under the pen name of Hawaja Musa (Mister Musa), the name by which he was known to Arab friends and neighbors as well as to his laborers, he published short stories depicting episodes of forbidden love, tragedies of arranged marriage, the heroism of young Bedouins, and tribal feuds involving blood vengeance as well as the conflict of generations. While exposing the Jewish reader to Arab culture, as Smilansky came to know it, the stories also highlight the problems to which later writers would return.

Smilansky addressed himself, in a more realistic vein, to encounters between Arabs and Jews at the beginning of this century, drawing on his own daily experience. One such encounter is described in "Latifa." The young Arab girl Latifa works in the fields of the narrator, a young Jewish farmer. She yearns for a life of her own, for closer contact with the young farmer, but is bound by tradition to marry a man she does not love, chosen by her father. She is destined to live in misery and servitude, like many women in her society whose marriages were arranged by their families. Latifa and the narrator are attracted to each other; they react both as individuals and as representatives of their respective cultures. Latifa is endowed by Smilansky with romantic and exotic attributes. She evokes the biblical image of women drawing water at the well, chief among them the matriarch Rebecca.

If you never saw Latifa's eyes—you don't know how beautiful eyes can be. . . . A young girl of fourteen, upright and agile, in a blue dress. One end of a white kerchief covered her head, while the other end fell on her shoulders. . . . Her eyes were lovely—large, black, flaming. The pupils sparkled with happiness. . . . Once I was riding to the field on my small grey ass. At the well I met Latifa, a pitcher of water on her head.

While Latifa comes to represent all that is attractive about Arab culture, her father, Sheikh Surbaji, represents rejectionist attitudes. A meeting between the narrator and the Sheikh reveals the intolerance and hostility toward Jews of Arabs who refuse to acknowledge any possibility for coexistence.

He was an old man with a fine white beard, a tall tarbush on his head, riding on a spirited white mare that pranced and curveted beneath him—he gave greetings to the laborers, who on their side all bowed to him with great humility and became silent. At me he threw an ill-tempered look, and he greeted me with a snarl in his voice. . . . There was no love lost between the Colony [the Jewish settlement] and the Sheikh, who bore a fanatic hatred toward Jews.

Latifa's miserable fate, and that of her Arab sisters, derive from Arab traditions that contrast to the narrator's humane values. An intimate conversation between the two young people reveals these differences.

—My father wants to give me to the Sheikh of Agar's son.

—And you?

—Sooner would I die. . . . Hawaja, is it true that your folk take but one?

—But one, Latifa.

—And your folk do not beat their women?

—No. How shall one beat the woman whom he loves and who loves him?

—Among you the girls take those they love?

—Assuredly.

—While us they sell like beasts of burden. . . .

Latifa is forced to marry Sheikh Agar's son, "a small and ugly fellow," as one of the Arab workers in the story describes him.

The story ends with an encounter between Latifa and the narrator years later. Latifa's spirit has been broken, but though "she has grown old. . . . her eyes still retained traces of their former brightness." The understated final lines speak to the sadness of her condition.

—Hawaja Musa has taken a wife?

—Yes, Latifa. . . .

I called my wife out. Latifa looked at her for a long time. There were tears in her eyes. . . .

I have not seen Latifa since then.

Sheikh Surbaji has triumphed, and with him the aspects of Arab society which accentuate the differences between the two cultures. In "Latifa" Smilansky not only mourns the fate of an individual woman, but also the failure of two societies to find a common ground.

Among other writers of pre-State days, Yitzhaq Shami (1889-1949) and Yehuda Burla (1886-1969), both of whom were native born and had full command of Arabic, included interesting portrayals of Arabs in their stories. Both Shami and Burla represented in their works many of the local Oriental communities, including Arabic- and Ladino-speaking Jews as well as Arabs. They thus were able to give important insights to the growing Hebrew reading population of European background and helped bridge gaps among various sectors of the population.

The absence of serious treatment of this subject in the fiction of the two major authors of the pre-State period, S. J. Agnon (1888-1972) and J. H. Brenner (1881-1921) is notable and at the same time understandable. Their concern was mainly with the Jewish community itself. Agnon was preoccupied with providing continuity for Hebrew literature, addressing himself mainly to traditional Jewish themes. Brenner's principal concern was with Jewish struggles toward the realization of the early Zionist dream and its socialist aspirations. Neither could speak Arabic and quite likely neither felt that he could effectively portray Arabs as major figures in works of fiction. Brenner, who was killed by Arabs in 1921, left an interesting account of an encounter with local Arabs shortly before his death. "We Are Brothers" is colored by Brenner's socialist ideals. Though he was rebuffed by some segments of Arab society, he felt a strong sense of kinship and brotherhood with what he perceived to be the oppressed classes of Arab society. While it seemed that there was no way of achieving a dialogue between the two national groups, Brenner, like many other socialist ideologists, preferred to believe that class bonds could bridge the gap. Jewish laborers, rather than all Jews, would eventually find common ground with Arab laborers, rather than all Arabs; shared class interests would overcome national concerns.

In "We Are Brothers" Brenner tells of walking through orange groves near Jaffa and passing a group of Arabs seated on a front porch. The group was composed of "an *effendi* in the company of two elderly neighbors and a young fellow of about twenty with a cap. . . . I greeted them; they did not answer. So I went on. As I happened to glance back I noticed by their look that their silence was a purposeful and mean one. The young fellow had already stretched himself upon the ground and cast about a triumphant expression, as if to say: We didn't answer that *yahud* ["Jew" in Arabic]." Later he meets with a young Arab worker, "only a lad of thirteen years." His sympathy for the worker, similar to Smilansky's for Latifa, is partly a response to the boy's friendly greeting; it also reflects a feeling that the two of them share a common adversary—the cadre of Arab landlords and their representatives symbolized in this essay by the group on the front porch. Though Brenner does not know much Arabic and the young worker knows no Hebrew, the two manage to interact, overcoming language barriers. Able to elicit basic information from the young man about himself, Brenner is distressed that he is unable to communicate his sense that the young Arab is being exploited by the *effendis.*

> Just then I reproached myself, rather severely, for not having learned to speak Arabic. Oh, if I could have only conversed with you better—my orphan worker! My young comrade, whether it is true or not what the scholars say about your being my blood relation, I feel responsible for you. I should have opened your eyes and let you enjoy some human kindness!

In his closing lines Brenner expresses longingly the aspirations which have been reiterated by many writers since: "We want only a soulful relationship . . . today . . . for centuries to come . . . for many, many days . . . with the meaning of being brothers, comrades."

Brenner saw not just an Arab-Jewish conflict, but a society ripe for changes to be brought about by Jews and Arabs alike. He was aware how profoundly his interpretation of local matters differed from the one probably held by Arab workers. He allowed that these workers may not share his views of the future and that he could have been wrong in including them in his future dreams. He concluded his essay by admitting that "maybe this"—the socio-economic conditions of the Arab population and their internal political system—"isn't even any of our business."

## II. 1948 AND AFTER

The political conflict between Arabs and Jews came to a head with the 1948 War of Independence, which followed the Second World War so closely that the survival of the Jewish population seemed at stake. The war presented, however, not only problems of survival, but also major moral questions: the Jewish community for the first time found itself in the position of being a major participant in a war, and therefore vulnerable to genuine guilt for its consequences. Most of the writers of the Generation of 1948, in their early twenties, had taken part in the war and the establishment of the new state, but they were not accustomed to the new role in which history had cast them. Though it was perceived as a just war, this perception did not minimize the fact that as in any war, just or unjust, defensive or offensive, human lives were taken and civilian populations were victimized. Raised on national as well as humanistic values, these writers, of a generation seen as heroic, felt ambivalence rather than heroism. Benjamin Tammuz, a member of that generation, summarized these reactions discursively.

> . . . in the absence of answers a certain vague and undefined ambivalent attitude prevailed, yet typified by a single feature: deep pangs of guilt.
>
> —We are guilty because, for two thousand years, we have tolerated the ignominy of hatred and persecution in the Diaspora.
>
> —We are guilty, because we reacted either as lambs brought to the slaughter or, through assimilation, renounced our identity in return for economic or social profit.
>
> —We are guilty, because we returned to the land of our forefathers though we lost their Faith.
>
> —We are guilty, because we expel the Muslim Fellah who has been tilling his land.

These lines demonstrate not only the intensity of this guilt but also the contradictions embodied in it. On the one hand, the guilt has been generated by two thousand years of being victims, accentuated by the events of the Holocaust: this situation made it imperative to take one's fate into one's own hands and fight for survival. On the other hand, the military victory put the Jewish community in the new position of perceiving itself not only as intended victims, but also as potential victimizers; defending itself, but also expelling civilian populations from villages and homesteads. As Tammuz points out,

> In 1948, at the close of a year of heavy sacrifices when, out of the country's Jewish community of six hundred and thirty thousand, the death toll was ten thousand, the weight of guilt in Hebrew literature reached its climax.

This sense of guilt provides the context of early literary responses to the war. There is little interest in Arabs as aggressors, as active participants in the armed conflict; rather the concern which finds expression in literature involves the Arabs who suffered the consequences of the war, captives of ambivalent captors.

The best-known expositor of this theme is S. Yizhar (born 1918), by no coincidence the nephew of Moshe Smilansky. Yizhar wrote a number of short stories as well as a long novel on the subject of the war. His stories "The Prisoner" and "Hirbet Hiz'ah" (1948-49) remain controversial even today. Speaking at a time of heavy losses for the Jewish community, Yizhar forced his readers to examine the war and all its ramifications not only from a national point of view, but from a human point of view as well. The Arabs in these didactic stories are often depicted in a rather shallow, stereotyped manner; the intent being to summarize, to sketch, and to generalize. They are not presented realistically but one-dimensionally, to sharpen Yizhar's point. The Israelis too are flat figures, often no more than caricatures.

"The Prisoner" was written in 1948 and first published in *Molad,* a monthly sponsored by Mapai, the leading Labor party; time and place of publication are significant as an index to the openness of political discussion. Such literature of radical self-criticism was not only allowed, but was actually expected. "The Prisoner" tells of an Israeli army unit taking an Arab shepherd captive during the 1948 War. Yizhar opens the story with an idyllic description of Arab shepherds and their flocks. The scene ironically recalls the Jewish patriarchs:

> On the plains and in the valleys flocks of sheep were wandering; on the hilltops, dim, human forms, one here and one there, in the shade of olive trees. . . . In the midst of the distant fields shepherds were calmly leading their flocks with the tranquil peace of fields and mountains and a kind of easy unconcern—the unconcern of good days when there was yet no evil in the world to forewarn of other evil things to come. In the distance quiet flocks were grazing, flocks from the days of Abraham, Isaac, and Jacob.

The Israelis in contrast are portrayed as a group of outsiders, not only as a military presence intruding on the pastoral world, but also as an urban presence, inherently evil, encroaching on the creative world of the past. The narrator finds before him "the kind of world that fills you with peace, while a lust for good, fertile earth urged one to return to back-bending work." Yet the innocent spirit of place, a shepherd, is placed under arrest.

More than a story of an Arab victimized by circumstances, "The Prisoner" surveys a gamut of Israeli reactions toward the encounter. Jews are cast in the role of hunters; the role of the hunted now belongs to the Arab. A new dimension has entered the Israeli construct of reality, and it is here tested in the most extreme of fictional situations. At one point the captive is portrayed as an object of pity: one against many, caught because there was a need for "something concrete to point to", a simple, unthreatening figure of "A man about forty, with a moustache drooping at the corners of his mouth, a silly nose, slightly gaping lips, and eyes . . . but these were bound with his *kaffiyah* [Arab headdress] so that he could not see, although what he might have seen I don't know." On the way to the military post, for a moment, the captive is described as having become part of the group.

> Two corporals and a sergeant came, . . . took the prisoner, and led him away. Unable to see, he innocently leaned on the arm which the corporal had just as innocently extended in support. He even spoke a few words to guide the prisoner's groping steps. And there was a moment when it seemed as if both of them were laboring together peacefully to overcome the things that hindered their way and help each other as if they went together, a man and another man close together.

The interrogation scene that follows is described with little sympathy for the military. The soldiers threaten the shepherd with a beating unless he cooperates. In their eyes he becomes the symbol of an intransigent enemy. Unable to get information out of the prisoner, the soldiers send him off to headquarters, with the narrator as sentry holding the official order. At this point in the story Yizhar's narrator becomes a split consciousness, engaging in internal dialogue, raising questions not only about the nature of the "enemy" and his ultimate fate, but also about his own responsibilities.

> This man here at your feet, his life, his well-being, his home, three souls, the whole fabric of life, have somehow found their way into the hollow of your hand. . . . The abducted man, the stolen sheep, those souls in the mountain village . . . suddenly, you are the master of their fate. . . . Stop the jeep and let him go, and the verdict will be changed.

The sentry is faced with a choice: he could free the prisoner, or follow the order given to him.

> This time you can't escape behind "I'm a soldier" or "It's an order" or "If they catch me, what will they do?" . . . You are naked now, facing your duty, and it is only yours.

Another voice answers:

> I can't. I'm nothing but a messenger. What's more, there's a war, and this man is from the other side. Perhaps he is a victim of the intrigues of his people, but after all, I am forbidden and have not the power to free him. What would happen if we all started to set prisoners free? Who knows, maybe he really knows something important and only puts on that silly face?

The story of this encounter of two human lives, on two sides of the fence, ends with a set of questions which remain unanswered.

> And yet behind us . . . in the misty evening coming over the mountains, there, maybe, there is a different feeling, a gnawing sadness, the sadness of the "who-knows?" of shameful impotence, the "who-knows?" that is in the heart of a waiting woman, the "who-knows?" of fate, a single, very personal "who-knows?" and still another "who-knows?" belonging to us all, which will remain here among us, unanswered, long after the sun has set.

The controversy over Yizhar's story "Hirbet Hiz'ah" was renewed in the late 1970s when it was adapted by Israeli television. In this fictional account of a captured Arab village whose civilian population is being evacuated, Yizhar once more places a uniformed narrator in a moral dilemma. Unlike the other men in his unit, who are preoccupied with carrying out the evacuation of the population of the captured village, the narrator steps aside and is able to identify with the plight of the evacuees, the civilian victims of war. As the narrator observes the parade of humanity making its way to the trucks, he sees them not only as a collective being but as individuals.

> At the end of the line came the women. . . . Two old men passed in front of me muttering as they went. . . . After them, thinking they were going

the right way, came others, dragging their feet through water. . . . I do not know why it seemed so degrading to me. Like cattle, I thought, like cattle.

Yizhar singles out a woman to serve as an image of the individual who keeps her human dignity:

> She looked strong, self-controlled, taut in her grief. . . . Suddenly we saw that this was the only woman who knew exactly what was happening to her, so that I felt ashamed in front of her and lowered my eyes. . . . We saw also how she was too proud to pay us even a morsel of attention. We understood that she was strong-headed, and saw that the furrows of restraint and the will to suffer heroically had hardened the lines of her face, and how, when her world had perished—she did not want to break before our eyes.

If we compare this Arab woman with Smilansky's heroine, Latifa, a structural affinity emerges at once. Latifa's affection for the Jewish narrator is alienated by an oppressive Arab father, whereas the figure of authority in 1948 is a Jewish narrator himself. The biblical setting further complicates the reader's response: is the tribal nature of Arab families reminiscent of the Old Testament kinship systems? Is the military prowess of the Israeli army a modern version of the victories in Exodus? In the second phase, the Israeli writer must mediate two cultural traditions at once, fused as they are by the Zionist movement: the modern (which seems so obviously appealing in "Latifa"), and the biblical.

### III. THE NEW WAVE

The guilt that characterizes much of the Israeli war literature produced by the Generation of 1948, as well as the self-critical examination of social and moral values, continues in the literature of the 1950s and 1960s, which has come to be known as "The New Wave." Many of the writers of this period consciously attempted to free themselves from total engagement in national concerns, but none has fully succeeded in doing so. However, many Israeli-born writers made serious attempts to focus their attention on basic existential problems similar to those which preoccupied European and American writers of that period. A leading Israeli literary critic, Gershon Shaked, remarked that these writers found their way into the mainstream of literature "through many windows and side entrances" acting "all together and each one alone." The focus on the individual gave rise to fiction with a psychological orientation: social reality is important primarily as it affects the individual. Time and place now often take on metaphorical dimensions and self-consciousness, a descriptive tool in the hands of Yizhar, becomes a truly inventive device in the best modernist manner. These developments affect the way authors incorporate Arab characters into their fiction, particularly the best-known New Wave authors, Amos Oz and A. B. Yehoshua.

Amos Oz, who was born in Jerusalem and makes his home at Kibbutz Hulda, often uses both landscapes and populations as his theatres of action for the fantasy world of his characters. External conflicts are used to display inner tensions, to illustrate conflicting psychological forces within an individual. Oz's protagonists lead a dual existence, divided often between the worlds of day and night. Oz is attracted to the darker aspects of the soul, primary urges and sexual drives, as well as vitality and artistic creativity. These are portrayed in many of his stories through demonic and animalistic images, dominating the world of his heroes and bringing them dangerously close to madness.

In his novel *My Michael* (1967), a pair of Arab twins, Aziz and Halil haunt its heroine, Chana. This story of a young Jerusalemite woman is narrated in the first person: the reader is given direct entry to Chana's innermost thoughts. Chana, in typical Oz fashion, shifts constantly from the world of everyday life to the fantasy world of the night. As the story progresses, the balance between dream and reality is disturbed, and the dream world begins to invade daytime existence. The dream-figures come from the world of fiction as well as from Chana's childhood; Captain Nemo and Michael Strogoff from Jules Verne's fiction exist alongside of Chana's childhood playmates Halil and Aziz. The twins function as inseparable parts of the heroine, reminiscent in their double identity of Jeremiah and Arthur in Kafka's *The Castle* and of Dürrenmatt's mirror-image twin couples in *The Visit of the Old Lady*. They assume a political role as well. They become an embodiment of her fears and violent wishes in contrast to her husband, Michael, who in her eyes lacks their vitality and force and whose existence belongs to the world of restrained desire, devoid of ecstasy and fire. Not surprisingly, they appear as a stereotypical composite of Palestinian guerillas, as in this dream sequence.

> Dreams.
>
> Hard things plot against me every night. The twins practice throwing grenades before dawn among the ravines of the Judaean Desert southeast of Jericho. Their twin bodies move in unison. Submachine guns on their shoulders. Worn commando uniforms stained with grease. A blue vein stands out of Halil's forehead. Aziz crouches, hurls his body forward. Halil drops his head. Aziz uncurls and throws. The dry shimmer of explosion. The hills echo and re-echo, the Dead Sea glows pale behind them like a lake of burning oil.

Oz, in an interview given shortly after *My Michael* appeared, conceded that the twins are drawn from what might be called a "psychopolitical construct": political realities have merged inseparably with other, more intimate realities. Speaking of stereotypes of the "enemy" in both cultures, Oz tries to define the center of the conflict.

> I feel that it is fundamentally a struggle not over territories or over symbols and the emotions they raise. I think that both sides in the conflict overlook the actual enemy. . . . Now for the Palestinian Arab, we are not Jews but a mere extension of the

arrogant, white European oppressor. . . . Both parties regard their enemy as an extension of their traumatic experience. Both Israelis and Arabs are fighting against the shadows of their own past.

Oz's comment helps explain the function of the Arab twins. The author feels the need to exorcize the demons within him and to expose hidden fears. Through his works of fiction he can involve his readers in a similar experience, helping them as well as himself deal with inescapable traumas. The threatening Arab presence serves as a metaphor but also as precisely the kind of daily pressure upon the Israeli psyche most conducive to recurrent neurosis.

Symbolism and allegory dominate much of the early fiction of A. B. Yehoshua, another Jerusalem-born author who came to prominence in the 1960s. In his early stories Yehoshua seeks to dissociate himself from the Israeli landscape, and to deal with concerns of the human condition. The conflict between life forces and death yearnings, the rebellion against the absurdity of a life which lacks meaning, the loss of faith, the alienation of people in a mechanized society, the loss of hope and innocence of youth: these are some of the themes in his short stories. *The Death of the Old Man* (1962), his first collection, is permeated by pessimism and hopelessness.

In Yehoshua's second collection of stories, *Facing the Forests, which* appeared in 1968, a new development becomes apparent. While he continues to pursue earlier themes, his use of time and place exhibits a marked change: the earlier unidentifiable symbolic landscapes metamorphose into the Israeli landscape of the 1960s. The characters, too, are no longer identified by initials or by names reflecting only generic societal roles; they now assume national and ethnic identities as well as generational affiliations. These developments do not signal a change in Yehoshua's basic preoccupations, but rather give force and added complexity to his fictions. Rebellion against social norms and conventions, against boredom and routine, takes the shape of rebellion against the symbols and rituals of Israeli society. The feelings of guilt, anxiety, and entrapment which haunt his heroes appear in forms recognizable in a specifically Israeli context.

The title story, "Facing the Forests," concerns two characters, an aging Israeli graduate student turned fire-watcher in a Jewish National Fund forest and an elderly Arab, survivor of a village destroyed in the 1948 war and buried beneath the forest. Each moves from his own vantage point toward their common goal, destruction of the forest. Each understands the forest differently: for the fire-watcher it embodies the ideals of the generation of the fathers, the accepted rituals and values of the founders, the aging hopes of the Zionist dream, while for the old Arab it represents the invasion of his village by foreigners. The student carries on the age-old conflict of the generations, while the Arab's burden is a political one. Both characters are marginal members of their own

societies. The student, who is approaching middle age, is both unable to work on his research on the Crusades (a suggestive topic in the context of the Arab-Israeli conflict) and unable to assume his place in adult society, while his contemporaries have settled down, pursued careers and gained status in society. The Arab also lives in isolation; he no longer has a village to which he belongs. He lives in the forest with his young granddaughter, on the ruins of the old village, waiting for an opportune moment to take revenge.

Yehoshua provides the reader with little description of the old Arab, who never materializes in the story as a full flesh and blood figure. He simply embodies the consequences of the war: "The Arab turned out to be old and mute. His tongue was cut out during the war. By one of them or one of us? Does it matter?" The Arab's muteness emphasizes the lack of communication between the Arab and Jew and contributes to his one-dimensional shadowy character. The reader cannot identify with or fully understand the old Arab. But he fulfills one, all-important function: lacking the ambivalence of the main protagonist, the old Arab can and does carry out the act of destruction. The indecisive hero needs his Arab companion to do the job, for he himself is rendered impotent by his inner conflicts and cannot translate his desire into action.

The Arab and the Jew in this story are united by much more than their common goal. If the story were essentially a political piece, aspects of this union would seem arbitrary and unconvincing. However, the story is more of a psychological essay; the two characters are not separable but add up to one identity. The old Arab personifies the "other" of the student. Representing but one force in a complex subconscious world, the Arab can act unequivocally, while the student, psychologically constrained, is inactive. The fusion of the two figures into one is clearest near the end of the story, where Yehoshua describes the two in the forest after they have reached an agreement, through non-verbal communication, to set the forest on fire.

> Together, in silence, they return to the forest, their empire, theirs alone. The fire-watcher strides ahead and the Arab tramples on his footsteps. . . . He leads the Arab over roads that are the same roads always. Barefoot he walks, the Arab, and so quietly. Round and round he is led, roundabout and to his hideout, among chiseled stone and silence.

The ruined village has a special meaning for the student as well as for the Arab. As in Yizhar's stories, village life represents the focus of romantic yearnings for a past which no longer exists, for earlier times when innocence and youthful vision as well as hope were available. The act of violence which destroys the forest gives the student a momentary glimpse of the dream which preceded it.

> He turns his gaze to the fire-smoking hills, frowns—there, out of the smoke and haze, the ruined village appears before his eyes, born anew in its basic outline, as an abstract drawing of all things past and buried.

The aftermath of the destruction leaves the student disillusioned and without hope, having descended to a further level of desperation. The mythologized past in which Arab and Jew might have lived together as Semitic kin is no longer accessible to either side, certainly not by means of the mutual destruction each group finds so tempting as a final solution.

### IV. SINCE 1973

The 1973 War had a strong psychological impact on Israeli society, which no longer saw itself as invincible. In literature the change is manifested in a return to immediate social and political concerns. The fictional works of writers like Yitzhaq Ben-Ner and Sami Michael deal with Israeli reality, and A. B. Yehoshua's novel *The Lover* (1979) explores directly the impact of the war on its participants. Yehoshua presents one of the most interesting and well-developed Arab characters in Israeli fiction. The scene is clearly identified politically and socially: the months before and after the 1973 war. Of the cast of six principal characters in search of love and lovers, the most interesting is Na'im, an adolescent Arab. When *The Lover* was adapted for the stage Na'im became, even more clearly, the central figure, and the play took his name for its title.

Far from being a stereotype, Na'im is revealed to the reader as a complex individual, who grows and attains identity and maturity as the story progresses. His role as a lover does not end when the story ends but gives promise of continuing. Unlike the old Arab in "Facing the Forests," Na'im not only has the power of speech but speaks in the first person. The reader gets to know his innermost thoughts, and is offered an interesting and convincing view of the Arab presence in Israeli society. Though a villager, Na'im works in Haifa, in a garage owned by Jews, and is thus part of the world where Jews and Arabs interact. When the war breaks out, he finds himself, like other Israeli-Arabs, entangled in ethnic and national conflicts of identity. Yehoshua attempts to understand his difficult position as the enemy within.

> They are getting themselves killed again and when they get themselves killed we have to shrink and lower our voices and mind not to laugh even at some joke that's got nothing to do with them. This morning on the bus when the news was coming over the radio Issam was talking in a loud voice and laughing and the Jews in the front of the bus turned around and gave us a dry sort of look.
>
> Knowing where to draw the line, that's what matters, and whoever doesn't want to know had better stay in the village and laugh alone in the fields or sit in the orchard and curse the Jews as long as he likes. Those of us who are with them all day have to be careful. No, they don't hate us. Anyone who thinks they hate us is completely wrong. We're beyond hatred, for them we're like shadows. Take, fetch, hold, clean, lift, sweep, unload, move. That's the way they think of us.

Adolescent diffidence and villager distance from city life: these factors shape Na'im's words but the complexity of his position transcends them.

There are six narrating voices in *The Lover;* the major characters speak in turn about each other and events involving them. Thus Yehoshua not only looks at his world through Arab eyes, but also at the Arab world through Jewish eyes. Adam, who employs many Arab workers in his garage, reflects on "The Arab Question" with an informed resistance to usual formulations. Describing a get-together with friends, he expresses irritation with the usual generalizations which bring Jews no closer to understanding.

> One of those Friday night debates. . . . when they start on that political crap about the Arabs, the Arab character, the Arab mentality and all the rest of it, I get irritable, start grumbling, lately I've lost patience with these debates. "What do you really know about them? I employ perhaps thirty Arabs in my garage and believe me, every day I become less of an expert on Arabs."
>
> "But those Arabs are different."
>
> "Different from what?"

Na'im is not a product of traditional Arab society alone, but has also been shaped by the Israeli society around him. His ambivalence and confusion concerning his identity are viewed by Yehoshua as giving reason for both hope and despair. The influences on Na'im are many, putting before him several models for behavior and action. For example, one of his brothers, unable to fit into Israeli society, with its limited opportunities for Arabs, turns to terrorism. Others prefer to work with the system, but remain separate and aloof.

Yehoshua successfully allows his characters to move in a psychopolitical arena; they gain an added dimension of strength from the political reality around them. While love rather than war becomes the center of the conflict, like war it remains unresolved. Na'im is at the center of these interchanges, a threatening yet deeply attractive figure for the Jews around him. As Adam states at the end of the story, when he discovers that Na'im has become his daughter's lover: "What's he thinking? He's a stranger really, another world, and I thought he was close to me." Adam is paralyzed by the whole complex of events surrounding the war. Na'im, however, comes into his own both as an Israeli-Arab who acknowledges that "It's possible to love them and hurt them too," and as a young man with an uncertain future. In the last line of the novel, he says of himself: "The people [in my village] will wonder what's happened to Na'im that he's suddenly so full of hope." There is little hope expressed by Adam for himself and for his generation; that is left to his daughter Dafi, and more so, to Na'im. No realistic portrayal, this novel is perhaps as one Israeli critic writes, "distant, perplexing, irrational and absurd—almost like life."

Another novel of Haifa in the 1973 War offers a more hopeful view of Israeli society but at the same time a more pessimistic view of Arab-Israeli relations in Israel. Sami Michael's *Hasut* ("Refuge") (1977) describes a broad sample of Arab figures and their interactions with part of Israeli society. The novel ends where a more optimistic narrative would have begun: "He was just an Arab and she was just a Jew." No closer relationship is promised or deemed possible; rather, the story describes growing distance and manifold tensions between the two groups. *Hasut* focuses on the personal, political and social problems among members of a binational Communist organization in Haifa. It traces the deterioration of co-existence as the ideological common ground for the two groups, which sufficed in prewar days, breaks down during the '73 War. Arab and Jewish members are polarized. Even though all are revolutionaries and wish to see fundamental changes in the existing structure of society, such common values cannot bridge the deep differences which separate them into two distinct groups.

The city of Haifa provides an obvious locale for the activities of the organization. It is the northern capital for both Jews and Arabs and contains within it some of the elements which earlier earned it the name of "Red Haifa." The organization is on the edge of both Jewish and Arab societies. Among its members are old-time Communists, accustomed to accepting discipline without questions, and young idealists who believe that Communism offers a way for true cooperation between the two national groups. The loss of this belief is one of the major focuses of the novel. The Jewish protagonists have to acknowledge that the realization of Arab national-territorial aspirations stands in direct opposition to similar needs in Jewish society. While they demonstrate sympathy for the complicated position of Israeli-Arabs, who feel like strangers in their own land and like second-class citizens, they cannot accept the dissolution of the Jewish national entity as the price for redressing Arab grievances.

As the title *Hasut* suggests, the story is about giving refuge and shelter to those who need it in times of emergency. The need for refuge is examined in two parallel situations. The first is recounted in a flashback and concerns refuge given to Mardukh, an Iraqi-Jew (with a background suggestive of that of the author) while he was an active Communist in Iraq. The second involves the shelter given to Fathi, an Arab-Israeli poet, in Mardukh's Israeli home. Both Mardukh and Fathi perceive themselves as revolutionaries escaping the authorities, although the similarity of their situations is only superficial. Mardukh, fleeing from Iraqi authorities, fears for his life. He is indeed captured by the authorities and jailed. Mardukh tells of the cruelty of his jailers, who "do not believe in using only psychological means [of persuasion]," who live in a culture which "used and still uses today physical means only." Although Mardukh is reflecting about the past in Iraq, it is clear that Michael here intends these words to serve as a clear warning for the present as well. Mardukh is eventually driven out of Iraq by the same revolutionaries at whose side he fought;

he is driven out merely because he is Jewish, and eventually finds himself in Israel, as a place of last resort. "He did not come to Israel as a tourist, nor as a new immigrant. He did not want to come here at all . . . but they did not want him . . . they told him that only Israel would accept him . . . and here he found work, and even freedom to continue to curse everything that comes to his mind . . . this country gave him refuge." Israel, refuge, and home have become synonymous not only for Mardukh as an individual, but for Jews in general.

The Israeli-Arab poet Fathi, on the other hand, has different motives for seeking refuge. He is not running away from a well-defined physical danger. The motives for his running can be found in his own needs; he must see himself as a pursued person in order to maintain the illusion that he is taking an active part in the Arab struggle against the Jewish population in Israel. Mardukh's wife, Shula, gives him shelter in her home, while her husband is fighting at the front. For Shula and Mardukh the act of granting refuge has become a holy value. Those around him see Fathi's hiding as a way of running from reality; Fathi is the only one who entirely believes that he is in need of shelter. When he comes to believe that victory for the Arab armies is at hand, Fathi offers Shula and her son refuge with Arab friends. Shula refuses the offer because Israel and shelter are identical, not just for Shula and her son but for the entire nation. Jews have no real refuge except in their own home, and an offer of a stranger's home is unreliable.

While Fathi is the most complex character in the novel, the real tragic character, evoking the full sympathy of the reader, is Fuad. A revolutionary ideologist, he is searching for the golden path of mutual coexistence. He continually rejects violence and military conflict as the only solutions, in spite of the fact that he feels pride as an Arab whenever he hears of an Arab military victory. Obstinately, without hope or illusion, Fuad continues in the political struggle for both social and national justice. The national tragedy which affects his people is also expressed on a personal level. He is married to a Jewish woman from a family with deep Zionist roots. Fuad, his wife and their three sons do not find their place in either Jewish or Arab society, with grave consequences for the sons, who lack both national and personal identities. Fuad sees Fathi as an Arab devoid of national pride who is hiding not from Israeli authorities but from his own problems. "As an Arab," says Fuad to Fathi, "you are a man with the soul of a pursued animal." It is mainly the characterization of Arabs in Fathi's poetry that angers Fuad.

> "What does this guy know about Arabs? He knows nothing about the past of his people, and one searches his poetry in vain for the proud fighting Arab. He portrays exactly the Arab in the minds of Tel Aviv females, . . . a character which he portrays well himself. It wins him another fuck. A desperate, pursued, landless miserable Arab, afraid and trembling with fearful nightmares, and so he longs for the pity of some female who will play to the neglected child in him."

The contemporary assimilationist solution to the problem of the Israeli-Arab, with the attendant loss of all Arab characteristics, is also described by Michael in negative terms. Emil and Amalia, another mixed Arab-Jewish couple who are members of the leftist organization, have solved their problems at the cost of Emil's loss of Arab identity. "Emil is now pasteurized and homogenized . . . he is brainwashed . . . he is not an Arab anymore . . . he has lost his identity as an Arab. His Arab friends do not dare express everything openly, but they say that he is no longer a man," remarks Fuad's Jewish wife.

The main question facing the Jewish members of the group is that of physical and national survival. They are confronted with a war situation, and in spite of their ties to the binational leftist group, there is no question of their ultimate allegiance. The war clarifies ambiguities for the Jewish participants, just as it multiplies them for the Israeli-Arabs. Mardukh asks himself the relevant question when the war breaks out, and is able to provide an answer for it. The question is put in the following words: "If Israel ceases to exist, what will later generations remember?" He answer thus: "Only two things, . . . a fantastic agriculture in an arid region and the defeat of the Arabs. I have no part in either." However, by the end of the novel he has some stake in both, since by his participation in the 1973 war he both defends the agriculture and takes part in defeating the Arabs.

Defeating the Arabs. Being defeated by the Arabs. Coexisting with the Arabs. History has provided Israeli writers with the same inescapable options as the nation at large. There can be few literary circles which feel so closely monitored by their reading public as in Israel, for every narrative turn and counter-turn is tantamount to a political manifesto. To tread the fine line between wish and reality—the dream of conciliation, the fact of armed resistance—has been the art of Israeli fiction. The evolution surveyed here has not been in the direction of amelioration and community. In spite of hopes for closer ties through better understanding there is a growing pessimism in recent writing. The tensions between the two groups have in many ways increased. However, Israeli writers continue to speak, knowing that openness in discussing even the most painful issues is necessary. It is appropriate to conclude this essay with a recent poem by Yehuda Amichai, one of the leading poets of Israel, which expresses the ever-present hope for a new beginning.

An Arab Shepherd Searches for a Lamb
on Mount Zion

An Arab shepherd searches for a lamb on Mount
   Zion,
And on the hill across I search for my little son,
An Arab shepherd and a Jewish father
In their temporary failure.
Our voices meet over
the Sultan's pool in the middle of the valley.
We both want the son and the lamb
to never enter the process
of the terrible machine of "Chad Gadya".*

Later we found them in the bushes,
and our voices returned to us crying and laughing
   inside

The search for a lamb and for a son
was always
the beginning of a new religion in these hills.

                    (free translation by EAC)

* *Chad Gadya* ("One Little Lamb") is a traditional poem recited during the Passover Seder, in which the lamb, bought by the father for his children, is devoured, starting a chain of similar events, which are climaxed by a divine intervention (cf. This is the House that Jack Built).

## Gilead Morahg

SOURCE: "New Images of Arabs in Israeli Fiction," in *Prooftexts: A Journal of Jewish Literary History,* Vol. 6, No. 2, May, 1986, pp. 147-62.

[*In the following essay, Morahg investigates the trend toward the depiction of Arabs in contemporary Israeli fiction as individuals rather than as abstractions.*]

Israeli fiction has been increasingly preoccupied with the implications of the Jewish response to the Arab presence in the land. Yet it has been habitually oblivious to the complex implications of the *Arab response* to the corresponding Jewish presence. This fact may well account for the general paucity and marginality of representations of Arabs in the fiction of several generations of Israeli writers, whose works form an illuminating backdrop for a new phenomenon: a body of narrative literature in which Arab characters figure in ways that are radically different from the functions traditionally assigned to them.

The corpus of narrative literature written during the first four decades of Jewish settlement in Israel addresses many aspects of this historic transition. It captures much of its drama and explores a wide range of personal, cultural and ideological problems experienced by the Jewish settlers in their encounter with the realities of the new land. But there remains an almost absolute disassociation between the works of the better writers of this period and the actualities of Arab presence in the land in which their fiction is set. Works by such writers as Brenner, Agnon and Hazaz that deal with the experiences of the Jewish settlers contain virtually no instances in which the Arab inhabitants are regarded as a significant element of the new reality and a constitutive factor in the experiences it entailed.

Recognition of the Arab presence and attempts to incorporate it into works of narrative fiction appear only in a few works by such minor writers as Yitzhak Shami[1] and Yehuda Burla[2] and in the fiction of even lesser writers such as Moshe Smilansky, Nahum Yerushalmi, Yaakov Rabinowitz, Moshe Stavi and Yaakov Hurgin. The characterizations of Arabs in the works of these writers are largely shaped by the preconceived constructs made up of conventional European notions of the Orient combined with the ideological convictions of the Jewish settlers. Although many of the writers share a romantic fascination with the mystique of Arab primitivism and a genuine curiosity about the customs and traditions of Arab society, their works are informed by an overriding sense of innate separateness between Jews and Arabs. As a result, the literature of this period is remarkably oblivious to the growing Arab antagonism towards the Jewish presence in the land. It shows little awareness of the gathering forces that would bring about conflict and conflagration.

Later Israeli fiction reflects greater recognition of the Arab-Jewish encounter. As awareness increases, however, the scope of Arab representations in the literature decreases. Although the concern with the consequences of the Arab-Israeli conflict moves to the thematic foreground of the later fiction, the use of Arab characters as a means of engaging this concern is greatly diminished.

This fact is reflected in the literary criticism of the period. Discussions of the image of the Arab in the works of the Palmach Generation writers during the 1940s and '50s usually draw their examples from the same three short stories dealing with the wartime experiences of young Israeli soldiers: S. Yizhar's *Hashavuy* ("The Prisoner," 1948) and "Hirbet Hiza'h" (1949) and Benjamin Tammuz's *Taharut sehiyah* ("The Swimming Race," 1953).[3] The story is not much different when we move up in time to the fiction of the 1960s and early '70s. Here is an equally spare cluster of three works containing peripheral Arab characters: A. B. Yehoshua's *Mul haya'arot* ("Facing the Forests," 1963) in which the nameless protagonist establishes a nihilistic relationship with a mute Arab and his always silent daughter; Amos Oz's *Navadim vetsefa* ("Nomad and Viper," 1964) in which Geula, a frustrated kibbutz member experiences a brief but unsettling encounter with a barely articulate Arab shepherd; and Oz's novel *Mikhael sheli* (*My Michael*, 1968) in which dream images of the symbolically stylized Arab twins, Halil and Aziz, make occasional appearances in the fantasies of the novel's protagonist, Hanna Gonnen.[4]

Critical studies of the Arab theme in Israeli fiction have taken a diachronic approach. They have sought to correlate the changing representations of the Arab with the changing nature of Israeli history by establishing clear typological distinctions between the images of Arabs that appear in the fiction written during each period. There is a large measure of agreement among these typologies. In the settlement period the image of the Arab is seen as an idealized correlative to the yearnings of the Jewish settlers to discard the enervating heritage of the diaspora and create a vigorous new identity. The repeated characterizations of the Arab as a true native, deeply rooted in the land and fully at ease in its recalcitrant terrain signify a desirable antithesis to the uprooted, urbanized Jewish settlers who struggled to overcome their sense of loneliness, alienation and overwhelming inadequacy. "For the Jew of the Palestinian Mandate," says Warren Bargad, the Arab represented "wishful possibilities of his own self-renewal as a deghettoized, liberated, natural human being."[5] In the works of the Palmach Generation, Arab characters are routinely regarded as reflectors of the unsettling guilt and moral confusion experienced by this first generation of modern Jewish warriors and conquerors. For them, writes Robert Alter, fiction "turned into a seismograph of moral shock" in which images of Arabs are incorporated into an overall "schematization of the materials of history in the interest of conscience."[6] In a more recent discussion of the fiction of this period, Shimon Levi confirms the notion of Jewish guilt as a shaping factor in the representation of Arab characters who are designed "to measure the morality and humanity of the Israeli in times of military strife, mortal danger and fierce combat."[7]

These typologies of Arab characters are also in agreement as to the fundamental shift that came next. The transition from a state of war to a state of siege is reflected in the transformation of Arab characters from realistic signifiers of national moral choices to symbolic embodiments of universal existential concerns. Representations of Arabs in the fiction written between 1960 and the late 1970s are seen as the product of a new literary trend in which "the conflict is not a moral trauma but an existential condition that lends itself to symbolic developments beyond political or moral concerns."[8] Within these works, says Ehud Ben Ezer, "the Arab no longer constitutes a moral question for the Israeli. He becomes the Israeli's nightmare." The Arab is represented not as an individual but as a "symbol of the existential dread that engulfs the Israeli protagonist and prevents him from living his life as he would have wished to live it. The image of the Arab is a projection of the internal anxieties of the Israeli characters."[9] No matter what correlation is found between the image of the Arab and the given historical period, the *mode of Arab characterization* remains virtually the same. What Risa Domb says of the settlement era is just as true of the late periods: "Our writers do not depict the Arab as an individual either in his physical appearance or in his mental makeup. Regardless of the different literary genres employed, the result is stereotyped."[10] From Moshe Smilansky's *Children of Arabia* (1911) to Amos Oz's *My Michael* (1968) most Arab characters in Israeli fiction are abstractions whose characterization is limited to superficial externals. They are depersonalized figures who serve as schematic catalysts for the internal dilemmas of their Jewish counterparts, and it is only these Jewish characters whose inner worlds are much more deeply penetrated and extensively portrayed. This disproportion between the levels of depth and complexity in the representations of Arab and Jewish characters reflects a broad *thematic* synchronicity no matter where the works are located along the diachronic continuum.

Thematic development in fiction is usually generated by a dynamic opposition between equally weighted and fully articulated narrative forces. It is therefore important to note that despite the growing preoccupation of Israeli fiction with the various implications of the Arab-Israeli conflict, the conflict itself is rarely to be found at the generating center of thematic development. There are no significant works that address this conflict directly by counterbalancing the Jewish perspective with an equally powerful representation of the Arab side of the conflict. The thematic orientation of the fiction is consistently unilateral. It is not directed towards the complex generating factors of the conflict between Arabs and Jews but rather towards the equally complex but radically different aspects of the Jewish reaction to the *consequences* of this conflict.

The fiction of the first seven decades of the Arab-Jewish encounter constitutes a hermetic body of works whose energies and concerns are consistently directed inwards. The focus is on the drama of internal Jewish experiences in which Arabs play a very minor role, and rarely that of a true antagonist. Although the encounter with the Arabs is generally recognized as having affected the changing nature of the Jewish experience in Israel, neither Arab individuals nor the Arab community as a whole are regarded as an integral part of this experience. Arabs are regarded as an external force impinging upon the central drama and are depicted as an abstracted human presence that must be reacted to but not accounted for.

There are signs, however, that this configuration may be loosening. Recent literary reactions to the circumstances created in the wake of the Six Day War indicate that a growing number of writers associate this new stage in the Israeli experience with the need for a new perspective on Arab-Israeli relations. This is reflected in a radical reorientation of the role they assign to the Arab characters in their works. We may well be witnessing the emergence of a significant body of narrative works that are no longer bound by the constraints of the unilateral approach to the Arab-Jewish encounter. Since 1977 there have been at least six novels that manifest this reorientation: Sammy Michael, *Ḥasut* (*Refuge*, 1977); A. B. Yehoshua, *Hame'ahev* (*The Lover*, 1977); Shimon Balas, *Ḥeder na'ul* (*A Locked Room*, 1980); Hadara Lazar, *Mikan vahal'ah* (*From Now On*, 1983); David Grossman, *Ḥiyukh hagedi* (*The Smile of the Lamb*, 1983); Yosef Sherara [Yoram Kaniuk], *'Aravi tov*, (*A Good Arab*, 1984). Although each of these novels is unique, they are bound together by a conviction that the destinies of the Arab and Jewish communities in Israel can no longer be regarded as separate because these communities have become inextricably intertwined in a relationship that is damaging to both sides. One of the Arab characters in *Refuge* articulates the painful nature of this interdependence in a crude but compelling image:

> I'm sure you have seen two dogs who got stuck while copulating in the street. They writhe and they shriek but they are unable to separate one from the agony of the other. So they keep on squirming and pulling—each in a different direction.

These are the Jews and the Arabs caught in their foul trap . . . and there are always some feeble-minded people who stand around enjoying the disgusting spectacle.[11]

A determination to explore the human implications of this reluctant binding of conflicting national destinies underlies the narrative development of all six novels.

The result has been a relocation of the concern with the Arab side of the conflict from the periphery to the center. This thematic shift has created a new set of structural imperatives, principally a *bilateral* narrative matrix that would provide for authentic representation of both sides of the national divide. All of the new novels aspire to this bilateral mode by creating a fictional context that enables significant interactions between equally realized Jewish and Arab characters. These new Arab characters are no longer static and stereotypical points of moral reference for a central Jewish protagonist; rather they are sharply differentiated individuals whose development in the course of the narrative is integral to its thematic signification.

Some critical recognition has already been given to the achievements of Arab representation in several of the new novels. Nilli Sadan-Loebenstein regards Yehoshua's characterization of Naim, the young Arab villager transplanted into the Jewish milieu of *The Lover*, as a tour de force of authentic representation of a protagonist who is also "the author's harshest instrument of social criticism."[12] Amnon Navot considers the character of Hilmi, the enigmatic Arab hermit in *The Smile of the Lamb*, as "an enormous achievement" in Grossman's attempt" to break through, to create real and powerful contact with characters and contexts that Hebrew fiction has continuously failed to attain."[13] But these are not isolated literary incidents. They are manifestations of a considerably larger pattern. The same measure of authentic representation and thematic signification can be found in the figures of Fathi, the Communist Palestinian poet and his friend, Faud, in *Refuge;* Sa'id, the young Arab intellectual who narrates *A Locked Room;* John Khouri, the self-exiled Arab lawyer in *From Now On* and Yosef Sherara, the tormented offspring of a Jewish mother and an Arab father, who is the fictional author and protagonist of *A Good Arab*. The internal and external worlds of all of these Arab characters are deeply penetrated and fully portrayed. Each is allowed a powerful voice as his personality, loyalties and values are put to the test of critical circumstances that involve significant interactions between equally realized Jewish and Arab characters.

The change in characterization is related to a distinct generic transformation. Although there are several novels of the settlement period that are devoted to depictions of Arab life, the tendency to regard the Arabs as being marginal to the Israeli experience is reflected in the way Arab characters are subsequently relegated to works of shorter fiction, primarily the short story. The short story is a natural vehicle for an approach which attributes disproportionate values to Jewish and Arab experiences. It tends to concentrate on the consciousness and development of a single protagonist, and during the first thirty years of Israeli statehood there were no notable works in which this protagonist is an Arab. The short story allowed for the foregrounding of complex Jewish characters against a background of schematically represented Arab figures. The new fiction of the Arab-Israeli encounter is marked by a growing number of longer narratives, and this fact suggests that the thematic implications of its bilateral orientation predicate a generic shift from the short story to the novel. For it is only within the broader scope of the novel, which allows for a multiplicity of fully developed characters, that the complexities and adversities of Arab-Jewish relations can be authentically depicted and explored.

One of the most striking formal changes affects the narrative point of view. Prior to 1977 fictional depictions of the Arab-Israeli encounter were habitually presented from the point of view of a first-person Jewish narrator, which inevitably oriented the reader towards an emotional and perceptual validation of the Jewish perspective. None of the recent novels, however, is developed through the perceiving consciousness of a first-person Jewish narrator. Each involves an empathic effort by a Jewish author to imagine and portray the inner and outer world of an authentically realized Arab character whose consciousness serves as a strong orienting force and a major means of thematic definition. *A Locked Room* and *A Good Arab,* are oriented by the singular point of view of their respective Arab and half-Arab first-person narrators. The handling of point of view in the other four novels is more varied and complex. But in each case it is effectively designed to distribute the reader's empathy among Arab and Jewish protagonists by creating a shifting emotional and perceptual focus. This is most evident in *The Lover* and *The Smile of the Lamb.* Both novels are narrated through a series of intertwined interior monologues in which the inner worlds and personal voices of the Jewish narrators are counterpointed with the equally individualized narrations of Naim and Hilmi, whose perspectives are distinctly Arab. Unlike Yehoshua and Grossman, Sammy Michael and Hadara Lazar do not relinquish the prerogatives of the authorial voice. The broad range of Michael's omniscient narration brings life to the many characters populating *Refuge* and provides ample scope to the conflicting perspectives of the novel's main antagonists. The inner and outer worlds of Shula, a young Jewish housewife with increasingly tenuous ties to the Israeli Communist party, and Fathi, the Arab poet who seeks refuge in her home during the first days of the Yom Kippur War, are deeply penetrated and fully portrayed. Their personal histories, changing perceptions and ongoing interactions serve as major vehicles of Michael's ambitious exploration of Arab and Jewish identity. The narrating voice in Lazar's *From Now On* is also omniscient, but it is selectively focused on the brooding inner world of Gabbi, a wealthy Israeli suburbanite, as she charts her way through an affair with John Khouri, the self-exiled Palestinian lawyer. But the candid

conversations Gabbi has with John, coupled with the rich shadings and complex tonalities of his characterization, capture John's complex stance towards his land and his people and track the critical junctures of his gradual development and change.

Like many of their literary antecedents, the new narratives embody a desire to infuse the Jewish experience in Israel with a viable moral stance towards the problems created by the Arab-Israeli encounter. The thematic orientation and narrative modalities of the new novels reflect a shared conviction that the moral dimensions of the Jewish experience may be clearly defined and honestly addressed only in the context of the related moral, psychological and political aspects of the Arab experience in Israel. Although they are different from each other in many ways, the Arab characters in the new novels express a remarkable consensus as to the essential features of this experience. And these perceptions often stand in ironic opposition to the notions informing the earlier fiction. Risa Domb regards Moshe Smilansky as representative of the writers of the settlement period in that "he upholds and propagates the Zionist theory, which is that the Arabs ought to be grateful for the coming of the Jews to Palestine because they introduce progress and advancement into the Middle East."[14] Summing up her discussion of relations between Arabs and Jews in the fiction of this period, she observes that "the writers maintain that the Arabs derive economic and technical advantages from the arrival of the Jews, but this is clearly only as the Jews see the situation. They do not give the Arab viewpoint."[15] This is a viewpoint that is aspired to in the new fiction and it is consistently represented as having little appreciation for the benefits of the powerful Israeli presence in the land.

"We explain, and it is the truth," says one of the Arab characters in *Refuge,* "that the Jews dispossess the Arabs of all they have. They take an Arab and strip him naked They even steal the land from under his feet, destroy his house, put a staff in his hand and order him to start walking" (*R,* p. 87). None of the new novelists embraces this simplistic view of Arab-Jewish relations. But their portrayals of Arab characters reflect a shared belief that such views must be recognized as authentic representations of the prevailing Arab perspective, which regards life under Israeli rule as fraught with humiliation, alienation and despair.

Encounters with callous and abusive Israeli authorities are repeatedly depicted as a major cause of an overriding sense of aggrieved humiliation. Yosef's confrontation with the Israeli police at the time of the Arab "Earth Day" demonstrations (in which he takes no part) is typical:

> I was stopped and searched. They pushed me, beat me, mocked me. I told them I was on my way to visit a friend and they said, "Today is the day of the stolen Arab land, eh, little Arab? The holy Arab land, eh?" I said to them, "A good Arab is a dead Arab;" and they answered, "You said it."[16]

Other novels recount the embittering effects of similar instances: Sa'id's violent interrogation and "administrative" incarceration in a foul jail cell continue to haunt him long after his release.[17] John Khouri cannot disassociate his feelings towards the country and its people from the humiliation of the rude strip-searches and exhaustive questioning to which he must submit every time he comes to Israel for a visit.[18] Fuad, who is required to report regularly to the police, feels condemned to a futile existence of humiliation and outrage. "Don't forget," he tells Tuviah, one of Shula's Jewish neighbors,

> that before you took over this country I tasted a different kind of life. Then, for years, I needed a permit to travel from my village to Haifa. Today every time I get on a bus I'm considered suspicious. I am a stranger in the land of my fathers. Sometimes I feel like putting you all on one hand and squashing and squashing with the other. (*R*, p. 314)

Naim's brother, Adnan, attributes his despair, radicalization and suicidal violence to the arbitrary refusal of the Israeli authorities to grant him entry to the university.[19]

The account of harsh conduct given Hilmi, the reclusive Arab protagonist of *The Smile of the Lamb*, coheres with the general Arab view of life under Israeli rule.

> And he told me all that I did not wish to know. That which I had been evading all my life. One of our boys, the son of Araf the oil merchant, was injured in a demonstration, his head was split open with a club and he never regained his senses. And one thirteen-year-old girl, from the girls' school in Junni, was arrested and interrogated by men for a whole night, and her mother was not allowed to be in the room with her. And houses were blown up in Nablus and in Arikha and in Beit Sekhur, and pastures and wheat fields were expropriated—and that means that they were stolen for money—and families were broken apart, and people were banished across the river, and others were forbidden to leave their houses.[20]

Such realities force Hilmi out of the world of protective fantasy he has created for himself and undermine the vision of ultimate Arab triumph through passivity and patience he has been nourishing in the isolation of his hermitage. Compelled to venture into the town of Junni in order to arrange the release of his son Yazdi, who was arrested for subversive activities along with several other youths, Hilmi sees for the first time "the army camps, the soldiers at the roadblocks, the girl soldiers and the tanks along the way." Absorbing these sights, Hilmi finds himself agreeing in his heart with the words of one of the released boys who says that "our youth is tired of humiliation and is rejecting the notion of patient suffering which is nothing but an elaborate excuse for cowardliness" (*SL*, p. 214).

At this point Hilmi still regards the boy's words about "vengeance, . . . the duty of rebellion, . . . armed resistance . . . and symbolic deeds that must be done" as being "barbed and empty" (*SL*, p. 214). But in the aftermath of Yazdi's death in a violent encounter with Israeli soldiers, Hilmi concludes that his dream of a natural and peaceful resolution of the conflict is misconceived, and that he himself must resort to a symbolic act of armed resistance. In an analogous reenactment of the Binding of Isaac, Hilmi holds Uri, and Israeli soldier who befriended him and soon became his beloved disciple and surrogate son, as a hostage at gunpoint. He then delivers a poignant ultimatum: "Don't be mad, Uri. All I ask is this, that by sunrise tomorrow all your military forces will get out of our lands that they conquered in the war" (*SL*, p. 120). To Uri's question, "And what will happen if they won't do it?" Hilmi replies simply: "Then I will kill you" (*SL*, p. 121).

The pathos of Hilmi's act of sacrificial defiance provides an ironic counterpoint to what Shimon Levi has aptly defined as the recurrent "prisoner motif" in the fiction of the Palmach Generation. Levi demonstrates that in the fiction of that generation the Arab is usually presented as a helpless prisoner whose fate is given over to the hands of his victorious Jewish captors. He concludes that the image of the Arab as a prisoner serves as a metaphoric means of expressing "the Israeli drive to resolve difficult dilemmas: how to remain an idealist, a pioneering Zionist, a Socialist and a humane person and, at the same time, a conqueror and a captor."[21] Seen from the perspective of the Arab characters in the new novels, this earnest call for a moral stance that would mitigate the brutalizing consequences of military conquest has been largely unheeded.

For Fathi, for example, the prevailing Israeli attitude towards the Arabs is exemplified in an overheard conversation between two Jewish men who refer to Arabs as "garbage" and discuss the most effective ways to "finish them off." "We are playing democracy with them," says one of the men. "What do they know of such nonsense. They need whips. Before we came everybody whipped them and all was well in the world" (*R*, p. 322). Yosef regards the true Jewish stance towards the Arabs as "a sophisticated mechanism of hostility wrapped in the benevolent smile of an innocent nature lover" (*GA*, p. 108). *The Smile of the Lamb* pits the innocence of Uri, who still upholds a humanistic vision of Arab-Jewish relations, against the ruthlessness of his commanding officer, Katzman, a tormented Holocaust survivor who feels these values slipping away from him and creating a moral vacuum that is rapidly filled with brutal contempt for the Arabs he must govern: "I have nothing but contempt for them, do you hear, for this million, maybe million and a half people that live under a rule which they do not want and still keep silent" (*SL*, p. 278). This, to a large extent, is an expression of self-contempt for the parallel experience of Jewish docility in the face of subjugating power that continues to haunt Katzman.

The extent to which Jewish attitudes towards the Arabs have been shaped by the lingering effects of a Jewish history of being relentlessly persecuted is a recurrent preoccupation in the new novels. It adds yet another dimension to the perception of the parallel destinies of the two nations. This perception is evident in the manner in which *The Smile of the Lamb* reintroduces the "prisoner motif" with an ironic twist that shifts the burden of resolving the moral dilemma from Jew to Arab. For now it is the Jewish protagonists, Uri and Katzman, who have come to negotiate Uri's release, who are held prisoner by an Arab who in turn must decide their fate. But there is no resolution in this novel, only tragic action. The brutalizing effects of the conflict between Arab and Jew are apparent in the reactions of both Hilmi and Uri. The harsh realities of the conflict that have encroached upon Hilmi's dream world now drive this visionary proponent of compassion to an act of senseless violence. Choosing to spare Uri, Hilmi shoots Katzman. But the man who is spared is no longer the man Hilmi has come to love. A moment before his death Katzman sees that "all the features of Uri's face are still there, and all the features of his smile are still etched on his face, but it is no longer the smile of the lamb. It is a cunning, evil mask, a silent curse that Uri is casting at him, for lack of strength to say the words" (*SL*, p. 280).

It is important to note that the new novels do not portray acts of physical violence against Arabs as being characteristic of Israeli society. Rather they are presented as deviations from the accepted norms of a society that is largely indifferent to the personal and national identity of Arabs. "They don't hate us," says Naim. "Anyone who thinks they hate us is completely wrong. We are beyond hatred. For them we are like shadows. Take, fetch, hold, clean, lift, sweep, unload, move. That's the way they think of us" (*TL*, p. 153). The Arab protagonists of all the other novels also regard themselves as victims of the Jewish failure to recognize their individuality and essential humanity. Their perceptions suggest a strong causal relationship between the tendency of the earlier fiction to represent Arabs as stereotypical abstractions and the actual attitudes of Israeli Jews towards their Arab counterparts. They also serve to indicate that this depersonalizing, and ultimately dehumanizing, tendency is a mutual process affecting both sides of the national divide. The Arab characters in the new novels are equally inclined to regard the Jews they encounter as stereotypical reflections of their own grievances. When Tuviah, who is the voice of pragmatic reason in *Refuge*, accuses Fuad of not understanding what it means to be a Jew, the reply is categorical: "And I do not wish to understand so long as I am treated as an inferior native in this land" (*R*, pp. 342-43).

In the new fiction of the Arab-Israeli encounter the potential for mutual recognition and authentic personal relations between Arab and Jew is repeatedly subverted by the practice of regarding each other as national stereotypes. Fathi's view of his relations with Jewish women is one of many examples of this perceptual and emotional configuration. He bemoans the fact that in the eyes of most Jewish women with whom he had relations he was always an outsider, a visitor; little more than a pleasing object of passing fancy. He recalls the few who "wept

with real tears . . . because they had the misfortune of falling in love with an Arab." This, he concludes, "was the worst of all. The tears were real, but the irony in them scorched his soul. None of them ever considered paying attention to his own anguish" (*R*, p. 276). But Fathi is no less oblivious to the humanity and individuality of the Jewish women he encounters. He thinks of them disparagingly as "the blondes of Tel Aviv" (*R*, p. 40) and pursues his romantic conquests as a means of validating his faltering dignity as a man and as an Arab. Shula recognizes this when she observes that Fathi desires her not as a person but as "a representative of a guilty nation" (*R*, p. 354).

Fathi is not alone in regarding Jewish women as objects of personal gratification and national vindication. Yosef describes this as a prevalent attitude among young Arab radicals who go out with Jewish women with the vindictive intent of "cracking the sacred wombs" that are so dear to the Jewish fathers who are responsible for Arab dispossession and humiliation (*GA*, p. 81). The Arab characters' view of Jewish men is similarly stereotypical, and Yosef's portrayal of his Jewish friend, Rammi, captures the essence of this stereotype as an ironic antithesis to the cherished self-image of the Israeli soldier as a moral warrior and benevolent conqueror. In Yosef's eyes Rammi is "a model soldier who always responds to injustice but does what he is told to do, agonizes and shoots, . . . who follows orders with the countenance of a rebel, who defends the homeland and is full of remorse, who loves his enemies and shoots them with great efficiency, who believes in a dream that has been misinterpreted for him" (*GA*, p. 21). Perhaps the most telling expression of the Arab perception of the conquering Jew is articulated by Hilmi who, from the vantage point of his isolated village regards the Israeli occupiers as an incomprehensible presence whose aloofness and disdain undermine the foundations of Arab dignity and vitality:

> New colors and new sounds. And the glint of the sunglasses on the officers' eyes, and the soft words they speak. . . . And their aloofness towards us. Not hatred. Not fear: aloofness. No body touching body. No eye to eye. . . . What kind of conquerors are these who have not touched our women, and have not executed even one village leader, or even one man from the roving gangs, and why do they despise us so much that they walk about the village alone or in pairs, practically unarmed, and what happened to us that this contempt of theirs grinds us to the dust and their cool arrogance envelopes us like a sticky, mocking web, and all of us walk around like the living dead, and our movements before them are like the movements of puppets; and gradually we stop arguing among ourselves, and slowly we stop talking politics, a little out of fear and a little because the things are beyond us. How did all this happen, and what is happening to us that young men of thirty have suddenly become old. (*SL*, p. 137)

Representations of the enervating effects of Jewish domination on Arab life are central to all the new novels being discussed, and they add yet another dimension to the difference between these novels and their predecessors. The fiction of the settlement period, as we have seen, often upheld the Arab, with his native affinity with the land, inherent sense of tribal identity and natural self-sufficiency, as an idealized object of emulation for the Jewish settlers who were seeking to overcome their alienation and redefine their identity along similar lines. The new novels are unanimous in their perception that in the course of pursuing their own national redemption Israeli Jews have undermined the old foundations of Arab rootedness and identity by afflicting them with the same existential burdens the Jewish settlers were so determined to discard.

The Arab perspectives in all six novels represent an Israeli society in which Jewish domination has resulted in a growing alienation of Arab individuals from the land and from their communities. Typical is Yosef's gradual realization of the impossibility of attaining his desperately desired affinity with the land and its people. "Acco is in me," he says, "and Germany is in me and the Land of Israel and Palestine, and I am in all of these yet I am nowhere" (*GA*, p. 46). In his case, as in the cases of Sa'id and John Khouri, the agony of alienation ultimately leads to an uprooted life of self-imposed exile. "I don't live in any real place," he writes from his hiding place in Europe. "I merely exist, a stranger to myself and to all those around me" (*GA*, p. 103). Sa'id's unspoken words to his father during a brief visit to his native village convey a similar sense of estrangement: "I have no home—I said to him in my heart. I am a wanderer in strange countries, uprooted, spewed out by the land . . . I am a visitor here, my father. A visitor, not a son returning to his domain" (*LR*, p. 195). John Khouri, who was born in Haifa but chose to make his home in Geneva, away from the land he can no longer consider his own, feels incapable of sharing his people's nationalist aspirations. "I am not there," he tells Gabbi when she visits him in Switzerland. "I just go to visit. I go because I have to see what else has happened in the meantime: what other street has had its name changed . . . what other houses have been torn down, who else has left, what else has been diminished" (*FNO*, p. 165). As John and Gabbi's love for each other grows, they grope towards a relationship between Arab and Jew that would transcend the mystique of the land that both binds and separates their respective nations. This is far more difficult for John because the existing situation in which "you [Gabbi] are here [in Israel] and here you have a home and I am only coming to visit" is intolerable to him (*FNO*, p. 179).

The Arabs who remain in the land fare no better. Trapped by the paradoxical necessity of being both an Arab and an Israeli, they repeatedly find themselves in the painful position of being neither. This is reflected in Sammy Michael's portrayal of Fathi which, although disdainful of the young poet's weaknesses of character and intellect, is unrelenting in its depiction of his corrosive predicament as an Israeli Arab. While Fathi's integrity may be questionable, his pain is real. The agony of alienation follows him wherever he goes. "I am a stranger in Moscow and in Tel Aviv," Fathi confides to an acquaintance. "I am also a stranger in my own village. I . . . am a stranger in my own land" (*R*, p. 64). Fathi's venture into the towns and camps of the West Bank is an attempt to restore his vitiated sense of personal and national identity, to "find his way as an Arab whose soul has been burdened with so many Israeli layers" (*R*, p. 117). But the attempt fails: "He came to find his roots and step by step discovered how much of a stranger he was in this place" (*R*, p. 107). Fathi's anguish is compounded by the fact that the inhabitants of the West Bank often mistake him for a Jew. Even when they are corrected they insist on regarding him as an Israeli, not an Arab.

As the demarcations of national identity become blurred, the sense of personal identity becomes increasingly tenuous. Naim, who like Fathi is often mistaken for a Jew, feels this as he becomes assimilated into the Jewish environment of Haifa. "I have been noticing," he says, "that I am no longer recognized as an Arab. Not by the Jews. Only the Arabs still hesitate about me. Has something changed in me? Am I no longer exactly myself?" (*TL*, p. 301). There are times when Naim actually regrets being an Arab and dreams of becoming a Jew (*TL*, pp. 234, 284). Sa'id, the intellectual, is more cognizant of the contrary forces that have brought about the fracturing of Arab identity. "A portrait of a Palestinian as an Israeli citizen!" he exclaims. "This is a very peculiar portrait with a built-in contradiction. And this is me. A person with a double identity, buffeted between two gravitational poles. Torn" (*LR*, p. 153). Born of a Jewish mother and an Arab father, Yosef regards himself as "a victim of two opposing histories" (*GA*, p. 45). His character embodies the internal agonies and detrimental personal implications of the tragic encounter between Arabs and Jews.

The fictional world of *A Good Arab*, is a densely constructed metaphor for a reality in which Jews and Arabs are welded together in a shared fate of doomed relationships and impassable emotional barriers. The novel traces the failure of Yosef's efforts to establish an identity for himself, first as a prototypical Israeli Jew and, later, as a militant Palestinian Arab. It exposes the anguish of his futile attempts to reconcile these opposing elements within himself. The narrative action confirms Yosef's observation that "the enormous desire to belong has a price" (*GA*, p. 120) and shows him paying this price without ever attaining the object of his desire. Unable to align himself with either side and convinced that the struggle between them will be perpetuated into future generations, Yosef, much like Sa'id and John Khouri, has little recourse but to remove himself from the arena. In the self-imposed solitude of his Paris hideaway Yosef writes his story, covering the paper with tears and uttering curses on both his houses (*GA*, p. 46).

The portrait of the Arab as an alienated expatriate relegated to the fringes of history is one of the many ironic correspondences between long-standing Jewish experiences and present Arab realities that emerge from the new fiction of the Arab-Israeli encounter. A full discussion of this subject is beyond the scope of this essay. But it should be noted that this multi-faceted parallelism of national destinies may appear at times to lend credence to the caustic observation that the Arabs in Israel have become "the Jews of the Jews" (*GA,* pp. 17, 122). Such neat formulations entail the obvious danger of substituting one set of national steroetypes for another. That this does not happen in the new novels is due to the fact that each of these narratives is constructed in a manner that pits the rigidity of stereotypical preconceptions against the flow of human interactions between Arab and Jewish characters.

The confrontation between national conventions and personal relations invariably yields moments of mutual recognition in which the stereotypical constructs of both Arabs and Jews give way to a confirmation of each other's essential humanity and unique individuality. "What a wonderful man, this Hilmi," says Uri of the Arab who has come to love him as a son. "If someone would have told me that they have such people I would not have believed it. How we don't know them. And how we have buried them under our disdain" (*SL,* p. 120). This exclamation of dismayed wonder by a Jewish character is no less typical than Naim's realization that Adam, his Jewish employer, is "a good man, a good tired man" (*TL,* p. 435). It is this realization that leads Naim to extend his confirming recognition to the Israeli Jews in general and to conclude *The Lover* on a resounding note of affirmation: "It is possible to love them and hurt them too— . . . The people will wonder what happened to Naim that he is suddenly so full of hope" (*TL,* p. 435).

All of the novels explore the potential power of the capacity for mutual recognition to effect a positive change in the existing patterns of Arab-Jewish relations, but none of the other five shares the apparent optimism of *The Lover.* Sammy Michael's *Refuge* represents the opposite extreme. In the forced proximity of their shared apartment Shula and Fathi struggle with their national and ideological biases amidst a growing feeling of physical and emotional attraction to each other. But the conclusion of the novel leaves little doubt as to its perception of the inviolability of national differences. "Do you hate me?" asks Shula as Fathi prepares to terminate his stay in her apartment.

> He got up and his dry lips sought her mouth in the dark. Her face drew back and he felt the chill, as if a wall, cold as death, had risen up between them. At that moment they ceased being a man and a woman. He was just an Arab and she just a Jew. (*R,* p. 372)

The remaining novels are less resolute in their final stance. Their open-ended conclusions mix varying measures of hope and despair. They reflect a shared sorrow at the great losses incurred by both sides of a tragic conflict, but offer no answers as to the possibility of its ever being resolved. Yet the empathic attempts of all six writers to provide a deep penetration and authentic representation of the Arab perspective serve to better define the true contours of the reality that must be engaged if such answers are to be earnestly sought.

## NOTES

[1] Yitzhak Shami, "Bein ḥolot hayeshimon" [Amidst Desert Sands] *Moledet,* 2/5 (Jaffa, 1913): 359-68; *Nikmat ha'avot* [Vengeance of the Fathers] (Jerusalem, 1928); "Juma'ah alhabal" [Jumah the Fool] *Moznayim,* 5 (1937): 37-58. The above stories were reprinted in *Sippurei Yitzḥak Shami,* ed. A. Barash (Tel Aviv, 1951).

[2] Yehuda Burla, *Beli kokhav* [Without a Star] (Jerusalem, 1922); *Naftulei adam* [Man's Struggles] (Tel Aviv, 1929); "Bein shivtei 'arav" [Among the Arabian Tribes] in *'Al hasaf* (1929); *Hameranenet* [The songstress] (Tel Aviv, 1930).

[3] See, for example, Robert Alter, "Images of the Arab in Israeli Fiction," *Hebrew Studies* 18 (1977): 61-65; Warren Bargad, "The Image of the Arab in Israeli Literature," *Hebrew Annual Review* 1 (1977): 57-59; Edna Amir Coffin, "The Image of the Arab in Modern Hebrew Literature," *Michigan Quarterly Review* (Spring, 1982): 326-30; Shimon Levi, "Prisoners of Fantasy: The Arabs in Modern Hebrew Fiction" [Hebrew], *Moznayim* 57 (October-November, 1983): 71-73; Gershon Shaked, "The Arab in Israeli Fiction," *Ariel* 54 (1983): 74-85.

[4] See, for example, Alter, pp. 66-68; Bargad, pp. 59-65; Coffin, pp. 330-34; Levi, p. 73; Shaked, pp. 76, 83-84.

[5] Bargad, p. 56. For further examples of the same conception see: Alter, p. 61; Ehud Ben Ezer, "Between Romanticism and the Bitterness of Reality: The Arab Question in Our Literature" [Hebrew], *Shdemot* 46 (Spring, 1972): 12; Risa Domb, *The Arab in Hebrew Prose: 1911-1948* (London, 1982), pp. 146-47; Jacob Kabakoff, "The Arab Image in Hebrew Fiction Between World War I and World War II," *Hebrew Studies* 18 (1977): 50-54; Levi, pp. 70-71; Shaked, pp. 80-83.

[6] Alter, pp. 62, 64.

[7] Levi, p. 72. For further examples of this view see: Bargad, pp. 57-59; Ben Ezer, p. 12; Coffin, pp. 325-30; Shaked, pp. 83-84; Leon Yudkin, *Escape into Siege* (London, 1974), pp. 108-9.

[8] Alter, p. 65.

[9] Ben Ezer, pp. 12-13. For further examples see: Alter, pp. 66-68; Bargad, pp. 59-60; Coffin, pp. 330-34; Levi, p. 73; Yudkin, pp. 108-9, 113-14.

[10] Domb, p. 108.

[11] Sammy Michael, *Ḥasut* [Refuge] (Tel Aviv, 1977), p. 237. All subsequent references to this book, hereafter cited as *R,* are in the text. The translations are mine.

[12] Nilli Sadan-Loebenstein, *A. B. Yehoshua* [Hebrew] (Tel Aviv, 1981), p. 201.

[13] Amnon Navot, "A Lamb in Literary Milk" [Hebrew], *Ma'ariv,* 7.22.83.

[14] Domb, p. 143.

[15] Domb, p. 152.

[16] Yosef Sherara [Yoram Kaniuk], *'Aravi tov,* [A Good Arab,] (Tel Aviv, 1984), p. 145. All subsequent references to this book, hereafter cited as *GA,* are in the text. The translations are mine.

[17] Shimon Balas, *Heder na'ul* [A Locked Room] (Tel Aviv, 1980), pp. 52-55, 179-85. All subsequent references to this book, hereafter cited as *LR,* are in the text. The translations are mine.

[18] Hadara Lazar, *Mikan vahal'ah* [From Now On] (Tel Aviv, 1983), pp. 178-79. All subsequent references to this book, hereafter cited as *FNO,* are in the text. The translations are mine.

[19] A. B. Yehoshua, *Hame'ahev* [The Lover] (Tel Aviv, 1977), pp. 187-89, 191-94. All subsequent references to this book, hereafter ciṭed as *TL,* are in the text. The translations are mine.

[20] David Grossman, *Ḥiyukh hagedi* [The Smile of the Lamb] (Tel Aviv, 1983), p. 209. All subsequent references to this book, hereafter cited as *SL,* are in the text. The translations are mine.

[21] Levi, p. 73.

**Menakhem Perry**

SOURCE: "The Israeli-Palestinian Conflict as a Metaphor in Recent Israeli Fiction," in *Poetics Today,* Vol. 7, No. 4, 1986, pp. 603-19.

[*In the following essay, Perry notes the tension between Arabs and Israelis reflected in the fiction of Amos Oz, Avraham B. Yehoshua, and David Grossman.*]

Just prior to the Six Day War, a popular song writer, Naomi Shemer, wrote a song that quickly turned into a hit and included the following lines:

> How dry are the water cisterns,
> How empty is the marketplace
> No one visits the Holy Mount
> In the Old City [ . . . ]
> No one goes down to the Dead Sea
> On the Jericho Road.

Right after the war, she changed these lines:

> We have returned to the water cisterns
> To the marketplace and square
> A shofar calls on the Holy Mount

> In the Old City [ . . . ]
> Once more we go down to the Dead Sea
> On the Jericho Road.
>
>          ("Yerushalayim shel Zahav"—
>            Jerusalem the Golden)

It was only the new contrasting version that drew attention to the precise content of the old one and Naomi Shemer was attacked repeatedly in intellectual circles for her chauvinistic view of the marketplace and the road to the Dead Sea as empty territories prior to the Israeli Occupation.

But Naomi Shemer's text is not typical of Hebrew literature. The question of whether the Founders of Zionism related to Palestine as empty territory may be open to argument, but there can be no doubt that, in Hebrew literature of the last eighty years, awareness of an Arab presence in the area has played an important role.

Nevertheless, there is an interesting contradiction: Hebrew fiction has persistently exposed the immoral actions of Jews against Arabs, has protested against repression and eviction, has questioned—in recent years—the legitimacy of war and has raised doubts about Zionist ideology and its future. Whenever the Arab *problem* is the issue, Hebrew literature has acted as an opposition to the conservative national consensus. When, on the other hand, we examine the concepts involved in the characterization of the *Arab himself,* sometimes by the very same authors, we can only be amazed by the preconceptions derived from nineteenth century European romantic colonialism. Most Arab characters in Hebrew literature are synthetic stereotypes, nٰot individual, "full" people, based on real observation.

The main conceptions of the Arab in Hebrew literature in this century can be structured in a binary system with two columns of predicates. Within each column, there is some equivalence and the columns themselves are opposed to each other. One column reflects a positive evaluation, the other negative. Indeed, the overall attitude toward the Arab—as abstracted from many texts—is ambivalent and not separable from the tension between contradictory elements in Zionist ideology. The Arab is always perceived as the opposite of Europe but, for Zionism, Europe itself involves a contradiction. Negation of the East-European Jewish small town, the *shtetl,* and the desire to build a healthy life in the Middle East are linked with two opposing attitudes toward Europe. On the one hand, there is the desire to detach oneself from sick, tired and decadent Europe. On the other hand, detachment from the *shtetl* does not necessarily mean a break with Europe. On the contrary, the Zionist enterprise can be founded on bringing European progress to the backward Orient.

In the positive column, based on a romantic idealization of the East, the Arab was perceived not only as exotic but also as close to nature and to healthy "roots," as someone living harmoniously with his environment and as the possessor of primeval simplicity and vitality. One should learn from him, copy his customs and dress, adopt elements of his music and food. He was a link with the biblical past and maintained the ways of our forefathers. Abraham was also a sort of Bedouin with camels. The Arab was actually our true "self" from which we had been exiled and to which we were now returning.

At the turn of the century, a popular idea was that the Palestinian Fellahim not only resembled the ancient Hebrews but were in fact ancient Hebrews who had been forced to convert to Islam.

After the establishment of the State of Israel, the Arabs were associated in Hebrew literature with a different notion of "roots" and with more recent nostalgia: They became the representatives of the writer's childhood environment in the agricultural settlements of Mandatory Palestine—an innocent world, lost with the hasty erection of ugly housing projects and the developments of the early years of the State.

The characteristics of the Arab in the positive column are, thus, variants of "beginnings" or "origins." The link between the Arab and "nature," "past," "forefathers," "childhood," etc., can evoke a sense of closeness but it can also be an alienating factor arising from our own position of inferiority: the Arab is a natural element well-integrated into this land, whereas we are a foreign element disturbing the landscape. Even in "the land of our forefathers," we are in exile. This theme was repeatedly developed in Brenner's prose during the second decade of the century.

This alienation can also be viewed from a position of superiority. Several of the characteristics in the negative column are inverted variants of those in the first. Here, "simple" and "natural" become "primitive" and "backward." The Arab is strange and frightening, destructive and dangerous, cunning and cruel, dirty and decadent and associated with disease and madness. He must either be advanced or removed. His attachment to the land is to a sick land that must be dried of swamps and freed of malaria. Because of passivity, laziness and inefficient farming methods, the land decayed and was devastated. Arab goats defoliated the forests. Like the Jews in the Diaspora, so the land itself was "in exile" and in need of *redemption.* There was not much difference between the Fellah and the Bedouin: one had depleted farm land, the other had desert. In contrast to the variants of *"beginnings"* (in the other column), this column presents variants of *"decay," "end"* and *"death."*

## 2

These columns are constructed from a synoptic view of a great number of texts. Up to the 1960s, no effort was made within any single literary text to deal with the entire system and with the tension between the mutually exclusive conceptions.

In the early sixties, major Israeli writers began writing stories exploiting that tension between the opposing conceptions and incorporating much of the entire system. In these works, the attitude toward the Arab is not the central theme. They are focused upon a completely different subject with no causal connection with the Arab issue. The central figure in the story is concerned with personal-psychological matters. In some of the stories, the Arab can be removed without disturbing the general run of the plot. The main function of the Arab is as a metaphor or analogue for an aspect of the central character, an aspect that is shadowy and alien to his everyday conscious life. In other words, the Arab, who is *contiguous* to the main character, is, at one and the same time, in strong *opposition* to him as well as a *metaphor* of his unconscious. The encounter with him is an encounter with another area of the self. These stories are either told by their central characters or are focalized upon a central character. This provides a motivation for the stereotypic presentation of the Arab. He is merely a projection of the main character and hence closer to the "natives" in Conrad's *Heart of Darkness* than to any Arab in reality.

In such texts, the Arab can be linked with a most basic, intrinsic and intimate essence and yet be strange and unknown; vital but also passive; associated with life-sources—dissociation from him is a dangerous death-in-life—yet cooperation with him also leads to destruction and death. The entire system can be activated. The Arab is equivalent to several absences: silence, darkness, lack of words, passivity, enigma, desert—and on the other hand, he is equivalent to several intense presences, such as wild-singing, flowing and over-flowing, heat and fire. He is lustful and dangerous, hard to control yet dangerous to ignore; he is linked to disorder, dream and hallucination; he is surprising and unpredictable and relations with him are relations with "real life." It is unnecessary to complete the list. A whole tradition of romantic terms transformed into Freudian ones and placed in the historical situations of modern Israel is at work here: the Arab is the repressed in the Jew.

## 3

A prominent and complex novel which belongs to this trend is *My Michael* by Amos Oz. However, within the limited framework of this paper, this trend will be illustrated by "The Nomads and the Viper," an earlier and simpler story, written by Oz in 1963.

During a drought year, the Bedouins leave the desert and wander northward, reaching the vicinity of the narrator's Kibbutz. Their arrival is rendered in metaphors of water and flowing: "They seep through the dusty tracks," they are "a stubborn current, twisting and turning in channels hidden from the sight of house-dwellers" and so on. The Bedouins are "secretive," trying hard not to be seen, and they are "dark like pieces of basalt." "The darkness is an accomplice to their crimes" and they are linked with madness: The voice of their dogs drove the best dog in the Kibbutz mad and it had to be shot—"Every normal person would justify the action." The Bedouins are accused of petty thievery, of damaging the irrigation pipes and of bringing Foot-and-Mouth Disease ("from the desert came the disease"). Their speech is incomprehensible ("a barbarous single syllable"). They are characterized more by singing than by speech: "A sort of wild, unintelligible howl" rises from their tents and blends with the sounds of the night, a song of "a single note" together with the attractive, muffled sound of drums: "The sounds permeate the paths of the Kibbutz and enrich our nights with something like an enigmatic heaviness"—but this distant, incomprehensible sound is also internal and intimate: the distant drum is like a heartbeat. There is also fire: nimbly they whip out gilded lighters igniting little flames.

Indeed there are sufficient indications in the story that the accusations of the Kibbutz-members, at least in part, are not reliable. In fact, the description of the Bedouins and the attitudes toward them are rendered through internal-focalization, representing the stereotypic manner in which the Kibbutzniks view them rather than any objective viewpoint supported by the story. This is the first step on the path to subjectivization of the Arab's image. The conception of "the wild man of the desert" as a stereotype ironically illuminated by the story is typical of Hebrew literature of the 1960s. In these works, the reliability of those Arab characteristics, taken seriously by earlier generations of writers, is challenged. But on the other hand, these stories do not suggest an alternative characterization. It is not a particular "truth" about the Arabs that interests them but rather some psychological "truth."

The Kibbutz secretariat is to meet to reject the proposal of the young kibbutzniks "to one night go and teach those savages an object lesson." Only at this stage, more than a third of the way into the story, does the central character appear—one of the secretariat members, Geula: a poetess, single, 29 years old, who spends most of her time dealing with the social and cultural life of the Kibbutz. (Her name is not incidental—Geula means redemption.) Before the meeting, Geula slips through a hole in the fence into the dusky garden adjoining the Kibbutz where she meets a Bedouin shepherd with whom she exchanges several words and who offers her a cigarette. To her, the Bedouin seems "endowed with a repulsive beauty." Externally, nothing takes place between them. But from her reactions to marginal "irrelevant" details (a passing airplane, the Arab's lighter, the way the Arab looks after one of the goats, etc.), it is clear that this meeting is an encounter with her repressed desires. The Arab is frightened by her and she herself is filled with terror and nausea.

While taking a shower, upon her return to the Kibbutz, trembling with disgust, she imagines her report to the secretariat meeting of how she was raped by the fierce young man. But she doesn't get to the meeting. Vomiting and weeping, she lies among the shrubs of the Kibbutz garden and is bitten by a snake. As the young kibbutzniks, armed with clubs, set out for the nomads, she is actually dying, experiencing intense erotic excitement. She listens to the sweet *wave* penetrating her body and intoxicating her.

If we wish to weave together the various episodes of the story (including marginal ones like making coffee or smashing a bottle) into a unified causal chain, we have to interpret Geula's responses to her surroundings as responses to external correlates of her psyche. Without being conscious of it, she responds to her environment as to a series of metaphors, including the attractive-frightening Arab. In stories of this period, not only is the conflict with the Arab an internal one but the contact with the "Arab" within is an outburst of life resulting in death or disaster.

4

Active initiation of a catastrophe or destruction for the purpose of making contact with the vital elements of life is a permanent theme in A. B. Yehoshua's writing. His story, "Over Against the Forest," was written in the same year as Amoz Oz's story and the Arab in it fulfills a similar function.

The main character in the story is a "rootless" student in a state of weary listlessness, bored into a sort of death-in-life. The solution he is offered is to become a fire-ranger in a national forest. At the beginning of the summer, he leaves for the forest, taking some foreign books, with Latin quotations, to write a research paper on the Crusades hoping "to re-acquaint himself with the words" which presently exhaust him.

In the distant and isolated forest there is another worker—an Arab, whose tongue was cut off during the war, it is not clear by whom, and so he is wordless like the silence of the forest. The Arab lives on the *ground* floor with his daughter who has a dress as red as fire.

The research is not progressing. "The text is difficult, the words distant." "Strange words from other worlds"; "If only he could skip the words and reach the main point." Instead of the research which is abandoned, the student is increasingly gripped by a joyous obsession to burn down the forest. He gradually discovers that the forest covers a ruined Arab village. The Arab, who was born in that village now buried under the trees, collects and hides small tin cans full of gasoline. At the end of the summer, the Arab burns down the entire forest with the complete cooperation of the student.

For the student, the burning of the forest is a wonderful outburst of vitality and mad freedom. "The earth is freed from its bonds" and what is buried is revealed. Out of the smoke, "the little village emerges before him," "it is reborn . . . like all the sunken past." The arson and destruction are acts of communication and contact, of a "full" voice (opposed to the empty words). The wordless Arab seems to speak too:

> The flames rise *madly* over the treetops, *crying out* to the lighted skies. Pines crack with a *joyous sound* and collapse. A profound excitement sweeps him. He is happy. Where is the Arab now? The Arab is *talking* to him in fire, he is trying to say everything and at once. Will he understand?

The next day, the Arab is taken for police questioning. The investigation is seen as analogous to the abandoned research ("A real labour of research was taking place before him") and the burnt forest "gives off a putrid odour as if there was a gigantic, stinking carcass around them." The student returns to his decaying life in the city.

The network of details in the story is far more sophisticated than is possible or necessary to present here. Most significant is the order of events: The notion of setting fire to the forest begins to take shape in the student's mind *before* he knows about the Arab village and before he discovers that the Arab has a similar idea. As far as the fire-ranger is concerned, the notion is not the result of any moral decision or intention to take revenge for what was inflicted on the Arab village but rather his own destructive self-realization and a creation of a link with what is buried in him. The covered village, the buried past and the fire are not the opposite of the Zionist enterprise, but of books, masking words, culture and the conscious. The Arab's considerations are secondary, his cunning destructiveness is mainly metaphorical. In the story, he functions as a double of the main character and his problem *as an Arab* is not the subject of any moral struggle. One could say that the student would have set fire to the forest even without the Arab in the story. It is the Arab's *hatred* that finds an echo in his heart and attracts him, not a desire for justice. The Arab is linked to his Id and not to his Super-ego.

## 5

The "internalization" of the Arab and of the conflict with him goes both ways. Ostensibly, the link with the other is tightened. His alienation is only apparent, in fact he is in close proximity with the most intimate regions. The Arab and his problem move to the existential center; cooperation between Jew and Arab or their common fate is brought to light. The Arab is linked to a problem whose repression leads to an incomplete life.

In fact, however, in such stories, approaching what the Arab signifies also involves destruction. Moreover, the other is not a real other but a projection; there is no real Arab problem but a psychological problem; it is irrelevant to ask who the Arab "really" is or to ask moral questions about the real political conflict. Turning the conflict into a psychological one leads to its "universalization." It becomes an ordinary, "normal" phenomenon, typical of cultured people everywhere and at all times, rather than an anomaly peculiar to the Middle East.

## 6

In his essay, "Individual and Society in a Prolonged Conflict," A. B. Yehoshua refers to the *repression* of the Israeli-Palestinian conflict, which characterized Israeli society after the Six Day War, as one cause of the profound crisis that overtook Israel after the Yom Kippur War. Prior to the Yom Kippur War, Israel lived a divided life. "During the War of Attrition, when its end

was nowhere in sight, an attempt was made to maintain simultaneously a system of normal life and all that goes with it. The soldiers themselves, fighting on the front lines, would repeatedly say, we are fighting here so that life in Tel Aviv can continue as if nothing is happening here."

Indeed, only in the last decade is there a growing awareness of the link between the continuing conflict and other aspects of life in Israel, including phenomena with no direct connection with the conflict. I do not only mean awareness of the relevance of the conflict to economics, agriculture, land settlement, religious thought or culture, but also its relevance to interpersonal relations among Jews or relations between the authorities and the Jewish citizen. Right after the Six Day War, when Professor Yeshayahu Leibowitz said that the Occupation would corrupt Israeli society, he was considered an eccentric. But today, the sentence, "He who today acts in this way toward an Arab will tomorrow act in the same way toward a Jew," is almost a cliché in journalism, in speeches and among intellectuals. There is no doubt that the consciousness of the conflict as a central factor in our mode of existence has increased.

This fact, it seems, is not irrelevant in describing the shift in the position of the conflict in Hebrew literature in recent years. In major stories and novels of the last decade, Palestinians and the conflict with them still appear as analogous to subjects far removed from the conflict but some changes have occurred in comparison with the literature of the 1960s.

1) The Palestinian in recent literature is not an analogue to a limited part of the mind of the central figure in the work, hence the conflict with him is also not an analogue to an internal conflict. The *Palestinian* now becomes an analogue to the whole character, functioning as a prism that reflects and defines the essence of his total mode of existence. Accordingly, the Israeli-Palestinian *conflict* is an analogue to the interpersonal relations in the novel— either man-woman relations or relations between one human being and another.

2) In the stories of the 1960s, it is the *reader,* in the process of textual understanding, who reconstructs the Arab as a metaphor. The central figure does certainly *respond* to the Arab as analogous to an aspect of his mind but *he is not conscious* of doing so and does not understand the meaning of his responses. On the other hand, in recent fiction, not only is the analogy more total, it is also brought to light. The analogy is made consciously by the central figure himself and hence he can also deal actively with self-characterization by looking at the Palestinian and even by asking his Palestinian analogue questions about his own life. In some stories, the Arab, on his part, is also conscious of the analogy and of the role he plays in the life of the central character.

3) In the stories of the 1960s, the stereotypic perception of the Arab is ironically illuminated as reflecting the

projection of the central figure and with no pretensions to reliability. Hence, the analogue characterizes the central figure, the Israeli, but the analogy will neither lead to new insights into the Palestinian nor into the conflict with him. More recent stories do tend to supply new insights into the behavior of the Palestinian in the conflict. The metaphor is becoming bidirectional.

7

Several characteristics of this new approach can be seen by juxtaposing A. B. Yehoshua's "Over Against the Forest" with his recent novel, *A Late Divorce*. At first glance, it seems strange to choose this novel: There are no Palestinians in it, except for an episodic appearance of an Arab waiter in a restaurant. However, I would claim that the Israeli-Palestinian conflict is a total metaphor hovering in the background of the novel, which the reader is directed to reconstruct. The novel assumes, therefore, a reading public for whom the conflict is a central awareness, able to fill the gaps on suitable presentation of cues in the text.

Most of the novel consists of Faulknerian interior-monologues, through which the reader has to reconstruct the events.

Yehuda Kaminka is an aging Israeli emigrant in the United States. He is presently awaiting the birth of a baby and has returned to his family in Israel (a married daughter and son; two grandchildren and an unmarried son) to divorce his wife, who is institutionalized in an insane asylum, that has a view of the superb landscape of the Haifa Bay. Their long marriage was a period of fighting and hostility and the wife, Naomi, was institutionalized after an insane attempt to thrust a knife into her husband's heart. He shows the scar over and over again to the family as he retells the story. Israel Kedmi, his son-in-law, a rather unsuccessful lawyer, is supposed to arrange the divorce and the property settlement. During the couple's first meeting in the asylum, it appears at first "as if he had come to ask not for a divorce but for a reconciliation." The meeting ends without results. The wife has changed her mind and refuses to sign the agreement—she now opposes the property division, demanding the whole house. Furiously, Kaminka rips up the agreement and one of the sons, Asa, has a fit of madness. In the following days, Kaminka relinquishes one thing after another and, in the end, the divorce takes place. But a few hours before his departure from Israel, he sneaks into the asylum through a hole in the fence, ostensibly because he regrets giving up his property. Now, with the divorce documents in his hand, he intends to steal the agreement and get back half the property. However, the "visit" is in fact more complex. Kaminka is suddenly drawn to put on his wife's dress and lie in her bed. Instead of a severance of the tie, there is full identification. Dressed in his wife's clothes, he tries to escape through the hole in the fence but does not succeed. The tie which cannot be severed ends in death: an insane giant who has appeared repeatedly throughout the novel is working near the fence; he grows furious when he discovers that the person in the dress is not Naomi but the husband Kaminka and murders him with a pitchfork. The texture of the text indicates that the murder comes not only from "outside" but also from "within" and is, in a sense, a suicide.

During the week-long visit, the members of the family incite the couple against one another. In a certain respect, not only is the husband not interested in the divorce but neither are the other members of the family. Asa, the son, in his fit of insanity claims that, for his parents, "there is a joy in this endless struggle. In the knife, the sickness, the pretense, there is a hidden pleasure . . ." but he also smites himself, to the delight of the mad people around him, and "joy is trembling in me, such lust, I am caught up in the rhythm."

The central topic of the novel is an anatomy of a conflict. A synopsis of the plot cannot bring out the richness of meaning and links constructed in the story through the texture of reality and language. I can give only a simple exposition of them here.

The cast of characters can be divided into the "sane" *vs.* the "insane"; the "parental couple" *vs.* their "children"; "blood kinship" (with perhaps genetic insanity) *vs.* "non-kin."

However, the novel points not to the opposition but to the essential analogy between these sub-groups. The analogy is "woven" by the novel through dozens of minute marginal details, which recur in almost the same way in various characters and which signal the analogy. The characters unwittingly use the same verbal metaphors and terms in their interior-monologues and this is another way of directing the reader to the parallels between them.

I will present just one cluster of details: The old mother in the asylum is working in the garden and watering the *shrubs* with a *hose* and "pours unlimited quantities of water on whatever she sees. It is lucky that the hose isn't long enough, otherwise she would try and water the sea." At the end of the novel, the threatening giant with the pitchfork in his hand is standing by the fence and tending the shrubs, the rubber hose lying near him on the ground. The son, Zvi, whose relationship problems and homosexuality are perceived as a type of distancing from "life sources," tells his psychologist a dream about a hostel by a lake surrounded by distant mountains. There is a thicket of shrubs and an earthen-colored hose is sticking out of the thicket. Suddenly the flow of water ceases as if somebody twisted the hose to stop it. (In the novel—water, including the Haifa Bay, becomes a metaphor of vitality.) The grandfather, arriving in Israel and seeing his seven year old grandson, Gadi, says: "You have raised a real *giant*. A *giant* he said and not a fat kid." In one of Gadi's drawings, there is a *house* and a *fence* and a man is standing near the fence holding a child. By adding a beard to the child, he turns him into a man and he then makes the first man into a woman. There is a scene where he waits in ambush for a friend near a *fence* with an iron bar in his hand to hit him. In another instance, he brings a bent *iron pipe* for the same purpose. In one of the scenes, the grandfather and grandson are giving the granddaughter a bath. The grandfather cannot *untie the knot* in the string of her undershirt and he cuts it with a knife. The water fills with blood. After a moment of fear it is evident that he has wounded himself and not the child. Blood and injury next to water-and-a-hose also appear when Asa pommels himself in the asylum: "I notice spots of blood on my hand . . . there is a faucet near the path, but a long hose is attached to it . . . I clean off the blood, licking it."

During the week-long visit, the opposition between the members of the family and the inmates of the asylum increasingly becomes an essential similarity. The epigraph for the last monologue (from Montale), "Whether separate or apart we are one thing," refers both to the relations between Kaminka and his wife and to all the characters in the novel.

The starting point of the various characters is a state of distance from a genuine tie to raw life and feelings. The father moved to America, and in Israel (because of jetlag) he is living "outside time." Dina, Asa's Orthodox wife, remains a virgin and is afraid to have sexual contact with him and Asa has a similar problem. Zvi's homosexuality is perceived as the ceasing of the flow in the water pipe. He cannot create real links but only those that can easily be untied. Most of the characters deal in meta-life. Kedmi, the lawyer son-in-law, is constantly writing in his mind the books he will one day publish about his "successes" as a lawyer. Asa is a lecturer in history who turns his back on the present. His wife, Dina, walks around with a notebook and is constantly writing a story which transforms the details of what is happening around her. Instead of living, she writes in bed, among other places, as a sort of substitute for sex, and her writing is filled with distancing figurative language "as if you are afraid to touch distress." The epigraph for her monologue is from a poem by Yona Wallach: "The gaze is protected by the imagination, and viewing art as an act protects all life." A comical resumé of this theme is the scene in which Gadi changes his baby sister's filthy, stinking diaper and protects himself: He wears a raincoat, puts a wool hat on his head, wears leather gloves, covers his mouth with a handkerchief and pulls off the diaper with sugar-tongs.

The anarchy caused by the grandfather's visit becomes a contact with dangerous life sources. The family is reborn. The insane link between Kaminka and his wife is a vital love-hate relationship; it is as impossible to live without as to live with. Key terms in the story and a central opposition in it are "freedom" *vs.* "bondage." But "free" also means "detached" and "bound" is also "attached." The only place where there are both "bond" and "freedom," both "law" and "anarchy" is in madness and in the insane link—an attachment maintained through loss of control, maximum closeness to life and detachment from reality. The climax of the contact with life leads to death. The choice is between death-in-life and life-that-leads-to-catastrophe. It should not surprise us

that the wild monologue of the insane woman takes place on the eve of Passover, "The Night of the Seder" ("Night of Order").

How is the Israeli-Palestinian conflict activated in the background of the book? First, through details of language. The old father is called Yehuda, his son-in-law is called Israel. The allusion is to a Jew (Yehudi = Jew) *vs.* an Israeli. The link between the name of Israel and the State of Israel is strengthened when he explains why everyone calls him by his last name and not his first name: "One Israel is enough." But "One Israel"—outside the novel—is also the slogan of those who oppose repartition of the country. Israel's last name is "Kedmi" which means "of the east." The name of the insane giant is "Mussa." The name of the baby born in America is "Moses."

The events of the novel are repeatedly described by the characters in terminology characteristic of the national conflict. The words *boundary* or *borders* (which are the same in Hebrew) are very common. The state of insanity of various characters or the collapse of the family is a state of open *borders* ("the boundaries are overrun"; "the boundaries are dissolved") and the freedom of divorce is perceived as the obliteration of borders. A "border" is an imaginary line and Kaminka thinks about the half-apartment that he will get back—about "the imaginary line cutting across the apartment." Relinquishing the apartment is perceived in terms of returning territory. No wonder Kaminka earlier looks at a map of Israel without marked borders. "My Homeland, why didn't you know how to be a homeland?" asks Kaminka referring to his wife. The separation from Israel and the separation from his wife are equated.

During the negotiations for the divorce, the son-in-law, the lawyer Kedmi, repeatedly imagines himself—certainly as a joke—as Kissinger conducting negotiations between Israel and the Arab states: "Kissinger dines before a delicate mission"; "Kissinger sits on the banks of the Nile and explains the *Separation* of Forces agreement"; "Kissinger reports to the Israeli Government" etc.

Here and there the characters digress on political issues but the context always points to the analogy with the personal story. For example: "Israel has lost control," says the father. "Don't forget, this is only a partial peace and people don't really believe," says the son's homosexual lover to the father concerning peace with Egypt. "This country is a little beyond our powers," he adds, but this is also how he feels about his relations with Zvi. "A nervous country. He gave up his share in the house with such ease" is a sentence in the father's monologue. When the father is due to depart from the country and leave the family with the insane mother, his son-in-law says to him: "In a little while you will fly off into the distance . . . and you are leaving us here alone with Begin. . . ." And when the family celebrates the divorce in a restaurant, after the entire house has been given to the mother, an Arab waiter comes to them, convinced they are celebrating a birthday. Kedmi explains that this is a divorce party and adds:

"Grandpa is leaving the country. Are you happy? One less. . . ." The waiter smiles: "Why should he leave Israel, what's wrong with it?" And Kedmi replies: "For you, maybe. You are the masters of the land." For a moment the desire is stirred in Kaminka to open his shirt and show the waiter the scar from the attempted murder.

Asa, the historian, does not deal with the Middle East conflict but the subjects of his lectures are relevant. He treats the moral justification of terrorism in the nineteenth century with respect and admiration for the young terrorists (Karl Heinsen's article "Murder"); he wishes to break the code of Historical Necessity; and, during the visit to the asylum, he reflects on the attempt made by the Anglo-Saxons in Rhodesia to struggle against historical laws. They begin with something rational—the desire to protect their prosperous farms—but they gradually lock themselves into a stubborn, mad belief that they can twist history's arm. There are only two hundred thousand of them but they are convinced that they can control six million blacks in the heart of Africa. They believe they have a mission, they turn their piece of land into a holy land, they lose faith in the world that condemns them and when the world has begun getting used to their insanity—they weary and are driven from compromise to compromise, until they lead to their own domination by the worst of their enemies. The analogy with the father is clear, as is the analogy with the State of Israel.

The father says of his son's historical "investigations": "You will not convince me that everything is ideology, I always look for the personal story." After he succeeds in stealing the agreement from his wife he says, ironically, to himself: "Does history enclose? Indeed it does *not* enclose, my boy. One can evade it." In the next page of the novel, it becomes clear that it is impossible to evade it.

*A Late Divorce* is not an allegory of the Israeli-Palestinian conflict, which is only a hyperbolic metaphor hovering in the background of the personal story. It is certainly a surprising metaphor which requires mutual adjustment of the two frames to be understood. As such, it can be bi-directional. Is the national conflict also a type of insane link, full of vitality and destruction, a link it is impossible to get away from—by the partition the country—but also a link that is impossible to live with? The analogy with the Israeli-Palestinian conflict is, in fragments, consciously made by the *characters* but does the *novel* support it? If so, then instead of two justifiable but irreconcilable viewpoints, the two possible alternatives are of distortion and death: the conflict on the one hand, divorce on the other. The lack of a positive alternative characterizes recent Hebrew literature that touches upon the conflict.

As a good Leftist, A. B. Yehoshua would not venture to write these things in an essay. At the same time as *A Late Divorce* appeared, he published a book of political essays titled *For Normalcy*. But throughout this book, ideas that deal with the positive experiential vitality of the abnormal state also creep in. The Israeli-Palestinian conflict produces a deep relationship with the landscape; it is a powerful catalyst which unites society; it stirs energy from hidden sources; it rouses the imagination and the creative force. Without it, Israel would sink into a passive slumber and powerful energy would be wasted.

Despite all this, A. B. Yehoshua's essay explicitly favors a sane solution. Even the novel demonstrates the heavy price of insanity. But it suggests something else—if indeed it does—that the normal solution is not possible.

8

In A. B. Yehoshua's novel, there is an Israeli-Palestinian problem but it lacks concrete Palestinians. David Grossman, the young author of the novel *The Smile of the Lamb* (1983), spent a great deal of time in the West Bank before writing his book. His novel is rich in the concrete details of everyday life in the West Bank and has a variety of Palestinian characters, folkloristic anecdotes and even a detailed "semiotics" of plants that are unknown to the Israeli reader and called by their Arab names. The text is interspersed with Arabic phrases. Hilmi—the central figure on the Arab side—has no fewer interior-monologues in the novel than the Israeli characters.

The analogies in the novel are constructed, first and foremost, by the characters themselves. Most of their time is devoted to a detailed attempt to define themselves through juxtaposition with the other and, through the other and his way of life, to find an answer to a disturbing question about themselves. Hilmi is an important junction in the novel. The similarity he himself constructs between Uri—the central character—and Yazdi—his adopted son killed in the service of the P.L.O.—is a central factor in moving the action forward. Uri runs to him because, among other things, he sees in Hilmi's way of life an analogue to his own state. He willingly surrenders to him because he is captivated by his personality.

The Israeli-Palestinian conflict in itself is not a topic of this novel which is concerned, rather, with *alternative modes of conduct* within the conflict. These are perceived as analogues or negative-analogues to the individual life styles of the various characters or to their interpersonal relations. Concepts like "truth" *vs.* "lie" and "justice *vs.* "injustice" once again become central (as in the literature of the 1950s) because they are the issue in the personal lives of the characters. The Palestinian issue, despite functioning as a metaphor for a different issue, becomes an equivalent sub-issue in the novel. Personal life and West Bank problems are inseparable. There is an integral Israeli-Palestinian totality reflecting a single set of tendencies. The mutual metaphoric relations between the Palestinian and the Israeli domains in the novel cover them both entirely. What appears in one domain as metaphors and similes in the language of a character's monologue is basic reality in the other domain and vice versa. Each is, therefore, the realization of the other.

Most of the novel consists of interior-monologues of various characters during one night and the following day. In contrast to A. B. Yehoshua's monologues, which mainly follow external events, the interior-monologues of Grossman's characters are mostly analyses of the self and the other. What they express appears to the character as true at the time of the monologue but it changes in the next one. The information the reader receives is, therefore, subjective and temporary. External events can be reconstructed only with great effort and, right up to the end, it is not exactly clear what really happened. The fact that several characters are involved in weaving a network of lies—including lying to themselves—or a network of fantasies, adds to the difficulty. This also explains why the Faulknerian narrative technique of the novel is so essential to it.

Uri is an assistant to a military governor in the West Bank. He is an innocent young man—"God's idiot," as he is called—caught between his wife Shosh and his close friend Katzman, the military governor. Shosh is a psychologist. Mordi is a boy she treated and whose treatment was considered a success but was really a failure. She failed to lead the boy to discover his unconscious truth. She "fantasized" another boy and lied to herself and to her superiors. At the peak of the "success," the boy committed suicide. Behind her husband's back Shosh has an affair with Katzman and three days before the novel begins, Shosh reveals the "truth" to her husband. It is not clear what she told Uri; apparently she lied this time too and combined the two stories: she told him that she had slept with Mordi and that was why the boy committed suicide.

Shosh's monologues are ostensibly her attempt to tape an analysis of her life. In the end, it grows clear that she was not speaking but only thinking and the tape never recorded anything. She attempts to peel off one layer of lies after another in a desperate effort to find the kernel of truth of her life—to find "who it is in her that says 'I' without uttering a big lie." Her life is revealed to her as a masking web of deceitful words. Her lies are the only thing in the world that is really hers.

Katzman is a child of the Holocaust. During the Second World War, he hid in a pit with his parents who went insane. Since then, he is an alienated man afraid of feeling, who hates the world and wants to destroy everything around him. His life is an experiment aimed at verifying the assumption that no one speaks the truth and no one is just. He chose Uri as his assistant in the West Bank to destroy his innocence. Only toward the end of the novel does he understand that his "experiments" were to examine how far one could go, in the hope that life would *stop him* and, in fact, what impels him is the fear of real feelings. His fear is his only real possession.

Uri, who comes to the West Bank an enthusiastic idealist, having in mind development projects, is astounded to discover what is going on there. After learning of Shosh's lie, he loses his temper because of the behavior of some soldiers during a house search. As a result of his behavior, he is imprisoned. He feels that those around him, as

he saw them, were only fantasies. "I invented them all." He does not understand the lies or the betrayals nor does he understand what is happening in the West Bank. He escapes from prison in Katzman's car, running to Hilmi. This is where the novel begins.

Hilmi is an old, half-blind, half-crazy Arab, who lives in a cave. He is exciting and exceptional among Arab characters in Hebrew literature. Nevertheless, it seems impossible to avoid stereotypes in describing the other. In Grossman too, Hilmi the Arab is close to nature, speechless, occupied with fantasies and day-dreams, passive and insane.

In opposition to the deceitful *words* of the Israelis, which have a "deathly cold" about them and on which "a weary foot cannot be set"—Hilmi is an absence of words. He did not speak until the age of fifteen and, even now, he uses words rarely. He too lives in a world of lies and fiction and invents characters endlessly. He spends his days fabricating events for characters he may have invented himself. He lives near the village of Andal but, in his imagination, he creates another, detailed Andal where everything happens according to his wishes. Fathers bring him their pregnant daughters and pay him to marry them. He pretends to believe that the children are his. Over the years he has had 22 bastard children. The women and children have abandoned him and he raised only the last one—Yazdi—as an "idiot of God." He tried to shape his character without words but "the world stole him." The retarded Yazdi joined the P.L.O., where he was fed on ideological words and slogans. In Hilmi's opinion, hatred turns people into stuffed animals and he terms the P.L.O. "declamatory organizations." Just as Shosh created her own Mordi, he created his own Yazdi. After Yazdi left, he continued to correspond with Hilmi—not in words but through plants he would leave for him in hidden spots. Once Yazdi began to write letters in words, Hilmi knew that he had lost him, that Yazdi changed from an "Uri" to a "Katzman." To Yazdi, Hilmi is a day-dreamer in a period when fighting is needed. But Hilmi fights differently, his war is "to be weaker than a feather" and his weapons are "stubbornness and patience and endless weakness. They won't be able to cope with it." "My land which I dreamed up will never be conquered by anyone else," he says.

Uri's escape to Hilmi is meant to tell him that Yazdi has been killed (to Hilmi, Yazdi has already been "lost" for some time); and to tell him about Shosh whom he is trying to "erase"; and also to learn from him "how to deceive lie itself." Hilmi sees Uri as his last bastard, a version of Yazdi. He wants to prevent Uri-Yazdi from being taken from him. He wishes to bring him into his fictitious world, to teach him how to tread lightly, how to touch without touching, to embroider him invisibly into his own pattern. To keep him as "matter for reflection," he must kill him.

Uri, who cooperates with him, transmits Hilmi's message on his two-way radio: if the Israeli Army doesn't withdraw from the occupied land by morning, Uri will be killed with the gun Hilmi stole from Yazdi. Although Uri can escape he does not. He lies over the radio, saying that he has been kidnapped by several Palestinians. Katzman goes up to the cave to liberate him and gets killed by Hilmi although he could have avoided it. Hilmi is caught.

To cooperate with Hilmi's world, Uri is forced to *lie* and Hilmi must take an active line just like the P.L.O. he hates. Hilmi's fiction up to this point was different from the lies of other characters. In a lie, one person knows the truth and the other does not: it is a manipulation of someone else. The fabricated stories are something positive, a journey several people take together, of their own free will, to a "better world." But Hilmi's last deed resembles the lies of others. In a desperate attempt to preserve his own world he must act according to the rule opposed to his world.

The conclusion is that all lines of response—both personal and political—have collapsed. The only tangible things left are the lies. In spite of the fact that in political articles Israeli authors usually suggest a solution in terms of an independent Palestinian state, their literary works seem to suggest that there is no tangible solution.

---

# FURTHER READING

## Anthologies

Anderson, Elliott, and R. Friends, eds. *Contemporary Israeli Literature: An Anthology*. Philadelphia: Jewish Publication Society of America, 1977, 342 p.

> Retrospective anthology that features the prose of Aharon Appelfeld, David Shahar, A. B. Yehoshua, and Yehuda Amichai along with a cross-section of contemporary Israeli poetry.

Ramras-Rauch, Gila, and Joseph Michman-Melkman, eds. *Facing the Holocaust: Selected Israeli Fiction*. Philadelphia: Jewish Publication Society of America, 1985, 292 p.

> Collection of short stories and novel excerpts on the subject of the Holocaust.

Spicehandler, E., and C. Aronson, eds. *New Writing in Israel*. New York: Schocken, 1976, 225 p.

> Contains five short stories from S. Y. Agnon, Aharon Appelfeld, Yitzhak Ben-Ner, and others, as well as selected poems from Don Pagis, Zelda, Amir Gilboa, and Yehuda Amichai.

Taub, Michael, ed. *Israeli Holocaust Drama*. New York: Syracuse University Press, 1996, 332 p.

> Features a critical introduction to the Holocaust in Israeli theater, and reprints several plays including Leah Goldberg's *Lady of the Castle*, Aharon Megged's *Hanna Senesh*, and Yehoshua Sobol's *Adam*.

## Secondary Sources

Alter, Robert. *After the Tradition: Essays on Modern Jewish Writing*. New York: E. P. Dutton & Co., 1969, 256 p.

> Offers essays on the Israeli novel, S. Yizhar's *The Days of Ziklag*, poetry in Israel, and literary interpretations of the Holocaust.

Ben-Yehuda, Nachman. "Sociological Reflections on the History of Science Fiction in Israel." *Science Fiction Studies* 13, Part 1, No. 38 (March 1986): 64-78.

> Explores the vicissitudes of science fiction's acceptance by Israeli readers.

Ben-Zvi, Linda. *Theater in Israel*. Ann Arbor: University of Michigan Press, 1996, 450 p.

> Includes essays on historical, cultural, and thematic issues related to Israeli drama, as well as critical evaluations of and interviews with significant Israeli playwrights.

Cohen, Joseph. *Voices of Israel: Essays on and Interviews with Yehuda Amichai, A. B. Yehoshua, T. Carmi, Aharon Appelfeld, and Amos Oz*. Albany: State University of New York Press, 1990, 231 p.

> Examines the work of five major figures among the New Wave of Israeli writers, combining interviews and critical analysis.

Ezrahi, Sidra Dekoven. "Revisioning the Past: The Changing Legacy of the Holocaust in Hebrew Literature." *Salmagundi* 68-69 (Fall-Winter 1985-1986): 245-70.

> Describes significant shifts in the representation of the Holocaust and of Holocaust survivors that have occurred over the course of three decades of Israeli literature.

Fuchs, Esther. *Encounters with Israeli Authors*. Marblehead, Mass.: Micah Publications, 1982, 92 p.

> Candid conversations with nine prominent Israeli writers.

————. *Israeli Mythogynies: Women in Contemporary Hebrew Fiction*. Albany: State University of New York Press, 1987, 147 p.

> Discusses the representation of women in mainstream, contemporary Israeli fiction, focusing on the works of A. B. Yehoshua, Amos Oz, and Amalia Kahana-Carmon.

Halkin, Hillel. "On Translating the Living and the Dead: Some Thoughts of a Hebrew-English Translator." *Prooftexts: A Journal of Jewish Literary History* 3, No. 1 (January 1983): 73-90.

> Comments on the unique challenges of translating works by living Hebrew authors in contemporary Israel.

Patterson, David. *The Shriek of Silence: A Phenomenology of the Holocaust Novel*. Lexington: University Press of Kentucky, 1992, 180 p.

> Probes the artistic struggle to articulate the horrors of the Holocaust through fiction.

Rabin, Chaim, ed. *Books, Articles and Doctoral Theses on Contemporary Hebrew Written in Languages Other Than Hebrew Published in Israel and Abroad (1948-1988)*. Jerusa-lem: Council on the Teaching of Hebrew, 1991, 224 p.
   Bibliography of sources on modern Hebrew linguistics.

Ramras-Rauch, Gila. *The Arab in Israeli Literature.* Bloomington: Indiana University Press, 1989, 227 p.
   Chronological survey of the depiction of Arabs in Israeli fiction.

Shaked, Gershon. *The Shadows Within: Essays on Modern Jewish Writers*. Philadelphia: Jewish Publication Society, 1987, 165 p.
   Collection of cultural and literary essays by the esteemed Israeli critic Gershon Shaked.

Sicher, Efraim, ed. *Breaking Crystal: Writing and Memory after Auschwitz*. Urbana: University of Illinois Press, 1998, 378 p.
   Historical, literary, psychological, and cultural essays on the Holocaust.

Wirth-Nesher, Hana, ed. *What Is Jewish Literature?* Philadelphia: Jewish Publication Society, 1994, 271 p.
   Essays by various contributors on the diverse nature of Jewish literature.

Yudkin, Leon I. *Escape into Siege: A Survey of Israeli Literature Today*. London: Routledge & Kegan Paul, 1974, 197 p.
   Critical introduction to modern Israeli literature.

————, ed. *Hebrew Literature in the Wake of the Holocaust*. Cranbury, N.J.: Associated University Presses, 1993, 130 p.
   Essays on issues and perspectives related to the Holocaust as a subject of Hebrew literature.

————, ed. *Israel Writers Consider the "Outsider"*. Cranbury, N.J.: Associated University Presses, 1993, 143 p.
   Investigates the complexities of Israeli cultural identity as it is represented in contemporary poetry and fiction.

# Politics and Literature

## INTRODUCTION

Politics have been a fertile source for literature since ancient times. Because the success or failure of any one political ideology depends so heavily on the ability of adherents and detractors to promote or defame it, literary pursuits—both fiction and nonfiction—have frequently coincided with political pursuits. The literature of politics has for hundreds of years taken the explicit form of journals, magazines, and newspapers, in which writers openly engage in propaganda or protest. From the early to mid-twentieth century, proponents of socialism and fascism in Europe, the United States, and the newly formed Soviet Union established newspapers in order to spread information about and gain further support for their causes. African Americans in the 1960s and 1970s found that literary journals with a political orientation allowed them an outlet for both protest and creativity, and the number of black political poets quickly grew. Many writers have taken a less direct approach in their political works, often for fear of social or legal repercussions under repressive governments. Political satire first appeared in Greek theater; by the late seventeenth century it had become a sophisticated tool of protest and discontent, employed with much effect by such writers as Jonathan Swift and Alexander Pope. Twentieth-century political satirists like Joseph Heller have often turned to black humor to critique what they consider grossly unjust governmental policies. Writers have also used allegory to voice their dissatisfaction with political regimes and, in Latin American countries in particular, have often added magical realism to their allegorical tales to expose governmental corruption indirectly. The great popularity of novels since the nineteenth century has allowed writers the most versatile medium for promoting their political beliefs. From George Eliot's extended tracts on English law in her novels to the openly racist propaganda of some writers in the American South, novelists have successfully integrated their art and their politics. Nevertheless, writers around the world continue to risk punishment, exile, and even death when they publish their political works, regardless of the literary genre they choose.

---

## REPRESENTATIVE WORKS

Chinua Achebe
*A Man of the People* (novel) 1966
José María Arguedas
*Todas las sangres* (novel) 1964
Samuel Beckett
*Molloy* (novel) 1951
*Malone meurt* [*Malone Dies*] (novel) 1951
*L'innomable* [*The Unnamable*] (novels) 1953

Jorge Luis Borges
*Ficciones* (short stories) 1944
*El Aleph* (short stories) 1949
*El hacedor* [*Dreamtigers*] (poetry and prose) 1960
Robert Coover
*The Public Burning* (novel) 1977
Julio Cortázar
*Hopscotch* (novel) 1966
*Libro de Manuel* (novel) 1973
Thomas Dixon, Jr.
*The Leopard's Spots* (novel) 1902
*The Clansman* (novel) 1905
E. L. Doctorow
*The Book of Daniel* (novel) 1971
John Dos Passos
*U.S.A.* (novel) 1936
Feodor Dostoyevsky
*The Possessed* (novel) 1871
George Eliot
*Middlemarch* (novel) 1871-72
Ralph Ellison
*Invisible Man* (novel) 1952
Nuruddin Farah
*A Naked Needle* (novel) 1976
*Sweet and Sour Milk* (novel) 1979
Hyppolyte-Jean Giraudoux
*La Folle de Chaillot* [*The Madwoman of Chaillot*] (drama) 1946
Ellen Glasgow
*One Man in His Time* (novel) 1922
Nadine Gordimer
"Is There Somewhere Else Where We Can Meet?" (short story) 1953
"The Smell of Death and Flowers" (short story) 1956
"A Soldier's Embrace" (short story) 1980
Peter Handke
*They Are Dying Out* (drama) 1973
Joseph Heller
*Catch-22* (novel) 1961
André Malraux
*L'Espoir* (novel) 1938
*Les Conquérants* (novel) 1949
Gabriel García Márquez
*One Hundred Years of Solitude* (novel) 1967
V. S. Naipaul
*The Mimic Men* (novel) 1967
*In a Free State* (novel) 1978
*A Bend in the River* (novel) 1979
*Guerillas* (novel) 1980
George Orwell
*Animal Farm* (novel) 1945
*1984* (novel) 1949
Boris Pasternak
*Doctor Zhivago* (novel) 1958
Ezra Pound
*Cantos* (poetry) 1925-60

---

# OVERVIEWS

## George Orwell

SOURCE: "The Frontiers of Art and Propaganda," in *My Country Right or Left: 1940-43, The Collected Essays, Journalism, and Letters of George Orwell,* Vol. II, edited by Sonia Orwell and Ian Angus, Harcourt Brace Jovanovich, Inc., 1968, pp. 123-27.

[*Orwell was an English essayist, journalist, and novelist whose works—including the novels* 1984 *and* Animal Farm—*frequently covered political issues. In the following, which was originally broadcast on the BBC Overseas Service in 1941, he argues that English literature beginning in the 1930s sacrificed aesthetics in favor of political didacticism.*]

I am speaking on literary criticism, and in the world in which we are actually living that is almost as unpromising as speaking about peace. This is not a peaceful age, and it is not a critical age. In the Europe of the last ten years literary criticism of the older kind—criticism that is really judicious, scrupulous, fair-minded, treating a work of art as a thing of value in itself—has been next door to impossible.

If we look back at the English literature of the last ten years, not so much at the literature as at the prevailing literary attitude, the thing that strikes us is that it has almost ceased to be aesthetic. Literature has been swamped by propaganda. I do not mean that all the books written during that period have been bad. But the characteristic

writers of the time, people like Auden and Spender and MacNeice, have been didactic, political writers, aesthetically conscious, of course, but more interested in subject-matter than in technique. And the most lively criticism has nearly all of it been the work of Marxist writers, people like Christopher Caudwell and Philip Henderson and Edward Upward, who look on every book virtually as a political pamphlet and are far more interested in digging out its political and social implications than in its literary qualities in the narrow sense.

This is all the more striking because it makes a very sharp and sudden contrast with the period immediately before it. The characteristic writers of the nineteen-twenties—T. S. Eliot, for instance, Ezra Pound, Virginia Woolf—were writers who put the main emphasis on technique. They had their beliefs and prejudices, of course, but they were far more interested in technical innovations than in any moral or meaning or political implication that their work might contain. The best of them all, James Joyce, was a technician and very little else, about as near to being a "pure" artist as a writer can be. Even D. H. Lawrence, though he was more of a "writer with a purpose" than most of the others of his time, had not much of what we should now call social consciousness. And though I have narrowed this down to the nineteen-twenties, it had really been the same from about 1890 onwards. Throughout the whole of that period, the notion that form is more important than subject-matter, the notion of "art for art's sake", had been taken for granted. There were writers who disagreed, of course—Bernard Shaw was one—but that was the prevailing outlook. The most important critic of the period, George Saintsbury, was a very old man in the nineteen-twenties, but he had a powerful influence up to about 1930, and Saintsbury had always firmly upheld the technical attitude to art. He claimed that he himself could and did judge any book solely on its execution, its *manner,* and was very nearly indifferent to the author's opinions.

Now, how is one to account for this very sudden change of outlook? About the end of the nineteen-twenties you get a book like Edith Sitwell's book on Pope, with a completely frivolous emphasis on technique, treating literature as a sort of embroidery, almost as though words did not have meanings: and only a few years later you get a Marxist critic like Edward Upward asserting that books can be "good" only when they are Marxist in tendency. In a sense both Edith Sitwell and Edward Upward were representative of their period. The question is, why should their outlook be so different?

I think one has got to look for the reason in external circumstances. Both the aesthetic and the political attitude to literature were produced, or at any rate conditioned, by the social atmosphere of a certain period. And now that another period has ended—for Hitler's attack on Poland in 1939 ended one epoch as surely as the great slump of 1931 ended another—one can look back and see more clearly than was possible a few years ago the way in which literary attitudes are affected by external events.

A thing that strikes anyone who looks back over the last hundred years is that literary criticism worth bothering about, and the critical attitude towards literature, barely existed in England between roughly 1830 and 1890. It is not that good books were not produced in that period. Several of the writers of that time, Dickens, Thackeray, Trollope and others, will probably be remembered longer than any that have come after them. But there are no literary figures in Victorian England corresponding to Flaubert, Baudelaire, Gautier and a host of others. What now appears to us as aesthetic scrupulousness hardly existed. To a mid-Victorian English writer, a book was partly something that brought him money and partly a vehicle for preaching sermons. England was changing very rapidly, a new moneyed class had come up on the ruins of the old aristocracy, contact with Europe had been severed, and a long artistic tradition had been broken. The mid-nineteenth-century English writers were barbarians, even when they happened to be gifted artists, like Dickens.

But in the later part of the century contact with Europe was reestablished through Matthew Arnold, Pater, Oscar Wilde and various others, and the respect for form and technique in literature came back. It is from then that the notion of "art for art's sake"—a phrase very much out of fashion, but still, I think, the best available—really dates. And the reason why it could flourish so long, and be so much taken for granted, was that the whole period between 1890 and 1930 was one of exceptional comfort and security. It was what we might call the golden afternoon of the capitalist age. Even the Great War did not really disturb it. The Great War killed ten million men, but it did not shake the world as this war will shake it and has shaken it already. Almost every European between 1890 and 1930 lived in the tacit belief that civilisation would last for ever. You might be individually fortunate or unfortunate, but you had inside you the feeling that nothing would ever fundamentally change. And in that kind of atmosphere intellectual detachment, and also dilettantism, are possible. It is that feeling of continuity, of security, that could make it possible for a critic like Saintsbury, a real old crusted Tory and High Churchman, to be scrupulously fair to books written by men whose political and moral outlook he detested.

But since 1930 that sense of security has never existed. Hitler and the slump shattered it as the Great War and even the Russian Revolution had failed to shatter it. The writers who have come up since 1930 have been living in a world in which not only one's life but one's whole scheme of values is constantly menaced. In such circumstances detachment is not possible. You cannot take a purely aesthetic interest in a disease you are dying from; you cannot feel dispassionately about a man who is about to cut your throat. In a world in which Fascism and Socialism were fighting one another, any thinking person had to take sides, and his feelings had to find their way not only into his writing but into his judgments on literature. Literature had to become political, because anything else would have entailed mental dishonesty. One's attachments and hatreds were too near the surface of consciousness to be ignored. What

books were *about* seemed so urgently important that the way they were written seemed almost insignificant.

And this period of ten years or so in which literature, even poetry, was mixed up with pamphleteering, did a great service to literary criticism, because it destroyed the illusion of pure aestheticism. It reminded us that propaganda in some form or other lurks in every book, that every work of art has a meaning and a purpose—a political, social and religious purpose—and that our aesthetic judgments are always coloured by our prejudices and beliefs. It debunked art for art's sake. But it also led for the time being into a blind alley, because it caused countless young writers to try to tie their minds to a political discipline which, if they had stuck to it, would have made mental honesty impossible. The only system of thought open to them at that time was official Marxism, which demanded a nationalistic loyalty towards Russia and forced the writer who called himself a Marxist to be mixed up in the dishonesties of power politics. And even if that was desirable, the assumptions that these writers built upon were suddenly shattered by the Russo-German Pact. Just as many writers about 1930 had discovered that you cannot really be detached from contemporary events, so many writers about 1939 were discovering that you cannot really sacrifice your intellectual integrity for the sake of a political creed—or at least you cannot do so and remain a writer. Aesthetic scrupulousness is not enough, but political rectitude is not enough either. The events of the last ten years have left us rather in the air, they have left England for the time being without any discoverable literary trend, but they have helped us to define, better than was possible before, the frontiers of art and propaganda.

## Irving Howe

SOURCE: "The Idea of the Political Novel," in *Politics and the Novel,* Horizon Press, 1957, pp. 15-24.

[*In the following essay, Howe finds politics to be a "violent intrusion" in literary art and seeks to examine the effect of such political ideas when writers insert them into a text.*]

"Politics in a work of literature," wrote Stendhal, "is like a pistol-shot in the middle of a concert, something loud and vulgar, and yet a thing to which it is not possible to refuse one's attention."

The remark is very shrewd, though one wishes that Stendhal, all of whose concerts are interrupted by bursts of gunfire, had troubled to say a little more. Once the pistol is fired, what happens to the music? Can the noise of the interruption ever become part of the performance? When is the interruption welcome and when is it resented?

To answer such questions one is tempted to turn directly to the concerts, anticipating those rude disharmonies—they will form our subject—which Stendhal hints at but does not describe. And in a moment we shall do that: we shall examine a number of major novels, each of them shaped and colored by a dominant variety of modern thought, to see what the violent intrusion of politics does to, and perhaps for, the literary imagination. But first, a few speculations.

Labels, categories, definitions—particularly with regard to so loose and baggy a monster as the novel—do not here concern me very much. Whether a novel may be called a political or a psychological novel—and it is seldom anything more than a matter of convenience—seems rather trivial beside the question, why does a particular critic, bringing to bear his own accumulation of experience, propose to use one or the other of these labels? What is it that his approach is to make us see more clearly? What mode of analysis does the critic employ, or what body of insights does he command, to persuade us to "grant" him his classification, in the sense perhaps that one "grants" a builder his scaffold?

When I speak in the following pages of the political novel, I have no ambition of setting up still another rigid category. I am concerned with perspectives of observation, not categories of classification. To be sure, distinctions of genre can be very useful in literary analysis: they train us to avoid false or irrelevant expectations and prepare us, within fluid limits, to entertain proper expectations; they teach us, if I may cite a familiar but still useful example, not to expect a lengthy narrative about the deeds of a hero when we read a lyric poem. But we are hardly speaking of genres at all when we employ such loose terms as the political or the psychological novel, since these do not mark any fundamental distinctions of literary form. At most, they point to a dominant emphasis, a significant stress in the writer's subject or in his attitude toward it. They may, that is, be convenient ways of talking about certain rather small groups of novels.

I stress this empirical approach—this commitment to practical criticism  because it has been my experience that a certain kind of mind, called, perhaps a little too easily, the academic mind, insists upon exhaustive rites of classification. I remember being asked once, after a lecture, whether *A Tale of Two Cities* could be considered a political novel. For a moment I was bewildered, since it had never occurred to me that this was a genuine problem: it was, I am now sure, the kind of problem one has to *look for*. I finally replied that one could think of it that way if one cared to, but that little benefit was likely to follow: the story of Sidney Carton was not a fruitful subject for the kind of inquiry I was suggesting. Pressed a little harder, I then said—and this must have struck some of my listeners as outrageous—that I meant by a political novel any novel I wished to treat as if it were a political novel, though clearly one would not wish to treat most novels in that way. There was no reason to.

Perhaps it would be more useful to say that my subject is the relation between politics and literature, and that the term "political novel" is used here as a convenient shorthand to suggest the kind of novel in which this relation is interesting enough to warrant investigation. The relation between politics and literature is not, of course, always the same, and that too is part of my subject: to show the way in which politics increasingly controls a certain kind of novel, and to speculate on the reasons for this change. The chapters on Stendhal and Dostoevsky contain a far heavier stress upon the literary side of things than do the chapters on Koestler and Orwell. And, I think, with good reason. In a book like *1984* politics has achieved an almost total dominion, while such works as *The Possessed* and *The Charterhouse of Parma* cannot be understood without using traditional literary categories.

Having cast more than enough skepticism on the impulse to assign literary labels, I want now, in the hope that it will not seem a merely frivolous sequel, to suggest the way in which I shall here use the term "political novel." By a political novel I mean a novel in which political ideas play a dominant role or in which the political milieu is the dominant setting—though again a qualification is necessary, since the word "dominant" is more than a little questionable. Perhaps it would be better to say: a novel in which *we take to be dominant* political ideas or the political milieu, a novel which permits this assumption without thereby suffering any radical distortion and, it follows, with the possibility of some analytical profit.

Let us for the moment assume a vastly oversimplified schema for the genesis and growth of the novel. Several kinds of prose writing converge to form the novel as we know it, among them the picaresque tale, the pastoral idyll, the romance, the historical chronicle and the early newspaper report. The most important of these is probably the picaresque tale, which flourished during the era in which the bourgeoisie was proving itself to be a vital class but was not yet able to take full political power. Largely good-natured in its moral tone, and often a lively sign of social health and energy, the picaresque novel, through the figure of the rogue-hero, obliquely suggested the new possibilities for social mobility. In acts of sly outrage the rogue-hero broke through the conventional class barriers while refraining from an explicit challenge to their moral propriety; his bravado thus came to seem a mocking anticipation of the regroupment of social strata which would soon take place in the nineteenth century. At the same time, however, the picaresque novel reflected the capacity of society to absorb the shocks of the bourgeois revolution. The atmosphere in which the rogue-hero moved was expansive and tolerant; society had room for his escapades and felt little reason to fear his assaults upon its decorum; in a curious, "underground" way he expressed the new appetite for experiment as a mode of life.

From the picaresque to the social novel of the nineteenth century there is a major shift in emphasis. Where the picaresque tale had reflected a gradual opening of society to individual action, the social novel marked the consolidation of that action into the political triumph of the merchant class; and where the rogue-hero had explored the various levels of society with a whimsical curiosity (for he was not yet committed to the idea of life *within* society), the typical hero of the nineteenth century novel was profoundly involved in testing himself, and thereby his values, against both the remnants of aristocratic resistance and the gross symbols of the new commercial world that offended his sensibility.

Once, however, bourgeois society began to lose some of its élan and cohesion, the social novel either declined into a sediment of conventional mediocrity (as, frequently, in Trollope) or it fractured in several directions. The most extreme and valuable of these directions were the novel of private sensibility, raised in our time to a glory of achievement and a peak of esteem that is without precedent, and the novel of public affairs and politics, which might be warranted in feeling a certain sibling rivalry. . . .

The social novel has always presupposed a substantial amount of social stability. For the novelist to portray nuances of manners or realistically to "cut a slice of life," society must not be too restive under the knife; and only in England was this stability still significantly present during the first half of the nineteenth century.

The ideal social novel had been written by Jane Austen, a great artist who enjoyed the luxury of being able to take society for granted; it was *there,* and it seemed steady beneath her glass, Napoleon or no Napoleon. But soon it would not be steady beneath anyone's glass, and the novelist's attention had necessarily to shift from the gradations within society to the fate of society itself. It is at this point, roughly speaking, that the kind of book I have called the political novel comes to be written—the kind in which the *idea* of society, as distinct from the mere unquestioned workings of society, has penetrated the consciousness of the characters in all of its profoundly problematic aspects, so that there is to be observed in their behavior, and they are themselves often aware of, some coherent political loyalty or ideological identification. They now think in terms of supporting or opposing society as such; they rally to one or another embattled segment of society; and they do so in the name of, and under prompting from, an ideology. [Howe writes in a footnote: I am quite aware that in practice it would often be impossible or not very useful to draw a sharp line of distinction between the political and social novels as I have here described them. Many novels—for example, George Eliot's *Middlemarch*—would seem to straddle the two categories. But I think it is worthwhile making the distinction analytically even if one recognizes that there are few examples of the "pure" type.]

To see this most clearly we must turn to France where Stendhal, though he wrote only a few decades after Miss Austen, was already marking the death of an era. In France, which had known a bourgeois revolution both abrupt and violent, all social contradictions were sharper and the consciousness of them more acute than in England. Through his novels Stendhal repeatedly declared

that the hero, having been deprived of an arena for his talents and energies, must break his way into—and then through—society by sheer force of will. Decades before the world realized it, Stendhal's novels announced that the age of individual heroism was dying, the age of mass ideology beginning to appear.

The political novel—I have in mind its "ideal" form—is peculiarly a work of internal tensions. To be a novel at all, it must contain the usual representation of human behavior and feeling; yet it must also absorb into its stream of movement the hard and perhaps insoluble pellets of modern ideology. The novel deals with moral sentiments, with passions and emotions; it tries, above all, to capture the quality of concrete experience. Ideology, however, is abstract, as it must be, and therefore likely to be recalcitrant whenever an attempt is made to incorporate it into the novel's stream of sensuous impression. The conflict is inescapable: the novel tries to confront experience in its immediacy and closeness, while ideology is by its nature general and inclusive. Yet it is precisely from this conflict that the political novel gains its interest and takes on the aura of high drama. For merely to say that ideology is, in some sense, a burden or an impediment in a novel is not yet to specify its uses—is not yet to tell us whether the impediment may be valuable in forcing upon the novelist a concentration of those resources that are needed to overcome it.

It would be easy to slip into a mistake here, precisely the mistake that many American novelists make: the notion that abstract ideas invariably contaminate a work of art and should be kept at a safe distance from it. No doubt, when the armored columns of ideology troop in *en masse,* they do imperil a novel's life and liveliness, but ideas, be they in free isolation or hooped into formal systems, are indispensable to the serious novel. For in modern society ideas raise enormous charges of emotion, they involve us in our most feverish commitments and lead us to our most fearful betrayals. The political novelist may therefore have to take greater risks than most others, as must any artist who uses large quantities of "impure" matter; but his potential reward is accordingly all the greater. The novel, to be sure, is inconceivable without an effort to present and to penetrate human emotion in its most private, irreducible aspects; but the direction in which the emotion moves, the weight it exerts, the objects to which it attaches itself, are all conditioned, if not indeed controlled, by the pressures of abstract thought.

Like a nimble dialectician, the political novelist must be able to handle several ideas at once, to see them in their hostile yet interdependent relations and to grasp the way in which ideas *in the novel* are transformed into something other than the ideas of a political program. The ideas of actual life, which may have prompted the writer to compose his novel, must be left inviolate; the novelist has no business tampering with them in their own domain, nor does he generally have the qualifications for doing so. But once these ideas are set to work within the novel they cannot long remain mere lumps of abstraction.

At its best, the political novel generates such intense heat that the ideas it appropriates are melted into its movement and fused with the emotions of its characters. George Eliot, in one of her letters, speaks of "the severe effort of trying to make certain ideas incarnate, as if they had revealed themselves to me first in the flesh." This is one of the great problems, but also one of the supreme challenges, for the political novelist: to make ideas or ideologies come to life, to endow them with the capacity for stirring characters into passionate gestures and sacrifices, and even more, to create the illusion that they have a kind of independent motion, so that they themselves—those abstract weights of idea or ideology—seem to become active characters in the political novel.

No matter how much the writer intends to celebrate or discredit a political ideology, no matter how didactic or polemical his purpose may be, his novel cannot finally rest on the idea "in itself." To the degree that he is really a novelist, a man seized by the passion to represent and to give order to experience, he must drive the politics of or behind his novel into a complex relation with the kinds of experience that resist reduction to formula—and this once done, supreme difficulty though it is, transforms his ideas astonishingly. His task is always to show the relation between theory and experience, between the ideology that has been preconceived and the tangle of feelings and relationships he is trying to present. This he does in a number of ways: diseased and intimate emotion twisting ideology into obsessional chimeras, as in Dostoevsky's *The Possessed;* ideology fortifying emotion for an heroic martyrdom, as in Malraux's *Man's Fate;* ideology pure and possessed strangling emotion pure and disinterested, as in Koestler's *Darkness at Noon;* and emotion fatally sapping the powers of ideological commitment, as in James' *The Princess Casamassima.*

The greatest of all political novels, *The Possessed,* was written with the explicit purpose of excommunicating all beliefs that find salvation anywhere but in the Christian God. "I mean to utter certain thoughts," wrote Dostoevsky, "whether all the artistic side of it goes to the dogs or not . . . even if it turns into a mere pamphlet, I shall say all that I have in my heart." Fortunately Dostoevsky could not suppress his "artistic side" and by the time his book reaches its end it has journeyed through places of the head and heart undreamed of in his original plan. But whatever else it does, *The Possessed* proves nothing of the kind that might be accessible to proof in "a mere pamphlet." For while a political novel can enrich our sense of human experience, while it can complicate and humanize our commitments, it is only very rarely that it will alter those commitments themselves. And when it does so, the political novel is engaged in a task of persuasion which is not really its central or distinctive purpose. I find it hard to imagine, say, a serious socialist being dissuaded from his belief by a reading of *The Possessed,* though I should like equally to think that the quality and nuance of that belief can never be quite as they were before he read *The Possessed.*

Because it exposes the impersonal claims of ideology to the pressures of private emotion, the political novel must always be in a state of internal warfare, always on the verge of becoming something other than itself. The political novelist—the degree to which he is aware of this is another problem—establishes a complex system of intellectual movements, in which his own opinion is one of the most active yet not entirely dominating movers. Are we not close here to one of the "secrets" of the novel in general?—I mean the vast respect which the great novelist is ready to offer to the whole idea of *opposition,* the opposition he needs to allow for in his book against his own predispositions and yearnings and fantasies. He knows that his own momentum, his own intentions, can be set loose easily enough; but he senses, as well, that what matters most of all is to allow for those rocks against which his intentions may smash but, if he is lucky, they may merely bruise. Even as the great writer proudly affirms the autonomy of his imagination, even as he makes the most severe claims for his power of imposing his will upon the unformed materials his imagination has brought up to him, he yet acknowledges that he must pit himself against the imperious presence of the necessary. And in the political novel it is politics above all, politics as both temptation and impediment, that represents the necessary.

Abstraction, then, is confronted with the flux of experience, the monolith of program with the richness and diversity of motive, the purity of ideal with the contaminations of action. The political novel turns characteristically to an apolitical temptation: in *The Possessed* to the notion that redemption is possible only to sinners who have greatly suffered; in Conrad's *Nostromo* and *Under Western Eyes* to the resources of private affection and gentleness; in *Man's Fate* to the metaphysical allurements of heroism as they reveal themselves in a martyr's death; in Silone's *Bread and Wine* to the discovery of peasant simplicity as a foil to urban corruption; and in *Darkness at Noon* to the abandoned uses of the personal will, the *I* so long relegated to the category of a "grammatical fiction." This, so to say, is the "pastoral" element that is indispensable to the political novel, indispensable for providing it with polarity and tension; but it matters only if there is already present the public element, a sense of the rigors, necessities and attractions of political life.

The criteria for evaluating a political novel must finally be the same as those for any other novel: how much of our life does it illuminate? how ample a moral vision does it suggest?—but these questions occur to us in a special context, in that atmosphere of political struggle which dominates modern life. For both the writer and the reader, the political novel provides a particularly severe test: politics rakes our passions as nothing else, and whatever we may consent to overlook in reading a novel, we react with an almost demonic rapidity to a detested political opinion. For the writer the great test is, how much truth can he force through the sieve of his opinions? For the reader the great test is, how much of that truth can he accept though it jostle *his* opinions?

In the political novel, then, writer and reader enter an uneasy compact: to expose their opinions to a furious action, and as these melt into the movement of the novel, to find some common recognition, some supervening human bond above and beyond ideas. It is not surprising that the political novelist, even as he remains fascinated by politics, urges his claim for a moral order beyond ideology; nor that the receptive reader, even as he perseveres in his own commitment, assents to the novelist's ultimate order.

## Philip Hanson

SOURCE: "Antibourgeois Anger: Notes on Fiction as a Guide to a Political Sentiment," in *South Atlantic Quarterly,* Vol. 82, No. 3, Summer, 1983, pp. 235-45.

[*In the following essay, Hanson attempts to locate the difference between genuine "social conscience" and "political sentiment" as they are expressed in twentieth-century novels.*]

### FICTION AND POLITICAL SENTIMENT

The political objectivity of fiction compared with that of social science is remarkable. The political economist or social philosopher speaks almost always in a single voice and continues to feign a detached and judicial tone even as he moves from evidence to (contentious) interpretation. He may do the decent thing and signpost his transitions from "is" to "ought." He will probably present, in the course of his argument, points of view opposed to his own. Nonetheless, his own preferences almost invariably become apparent—and usually sooner rather than later. Most social philosophizing is therefore a monologue without drama or conflict; the reader knows that he is being addressed by an advocate who is out to win a case. The novelist, on the other hand, can give persuasive expression to conflicting views. It may not even become clear to the reader which view the writer favors. Sometimes the writer himself does not know; politically, many novelists have been turncoats, floating voters, and "Don't Knows."

So far as politics is concerned, novels that do best are those that depict political sentiments. For political ideas the best sources are the partisan social philosophers. But for the emotions and sensibilities with which individuals embrace some ideas and reject others, fiction—it seems to me—imparts a stronger feeling of understanding than the unnatural sciences[1] of psychohistory or political sociology. Yet in the Anglo-Saxon world, at least, novels written in this century seem seldom to be discussed as political documents. To treat nineteenth-century novels in this way is quite usual, but it is as though novels had to pass through a century or so of processing by literary critics before they were fit for consumption by social critics.

Novelists of any vintage, however, can perform two useful tricks in depicting political sentiment. Both are impressive, though one is more remarkable than the other. The first is to give convincing life to political sentiments that the author himself does not approve of. Even in Russian fiction, with its tradition of strong social commitment, there are striking examples of this in the present century: Maxim Gorky's pitying account of a Tsarist police informer (*The Life of a Useless Man*); Sholokhov's Cossack nationalist, Grigor Melekhov (in the *Don* trilogy), and the recalcitrant villagers in his collectivization novel, *Virgin Soil Upturned;*[2] Solzhenitsyn's labor-camp Leninist, Rubin, in *The First Circle,* not to mention his attempt at (on?) the original Leninist in *Lenin in Zurich.*

The second and more remarkable trick—which must be less consciously performed, as a rule—is that of displaying the seamy side of the author's own political sentiments. Dostoevsky quite often does this, so that a perceptive neo-Marxist commentator can argue that the novels undermine Dostoevsky's own conservative philosophy.[3] And Waugh's famous account of Gilbert Pinfold's misanthropy resembles an *ad hominem* attack on many of his own attitudes: "His strongest tastes were negative. He abhorred plastics, Picasso, sunbathing and jazz—everything in fact that had happened in his own lifetime. The tiny kindling of charity that came to him through his religion sufficed only to temper his disgust and change it to boredom. . . . Shocked by a bad bottle of wine, or a fault in syntax, his mind like a cinema camera trucked (*sic*) furiously forward to confront the offending object close-up with glaring lens. . . . "

### ANTIBOURGEOIS ANGER

Mr. Pinfold's is a Tory style of anger. It is isolationist and defensive. The note is one of slapping down and keeping out. Left, or progressive, or antibourgeois anger is different—and more characteristic of the culture of Western intelligentsias. Indeed, a romantic distaste for the bourgeois world is now so mass-produced, diluted, and tenth-hand that in prosperous societies a large number of otherwise bourgeois people can safely affect it, as a pastime or a manner of speaking.[4] Politically, such part-time alienation may be expressed merely in a propensity to suspicious and indignant hostility toward many of the more conspicuous persons, institutions, and ideas in sight in one's own society: a notion that the establishment or the power structure is generally in the wrong, combined with no great inclination to do anything about it. The same sentiment more passionately entertained shades into anger with and hatred of "the bourgeoisie" and "the system." It is a political sentiment of some importance, and what novelists have told us about it is sometimes unexpected.

Some of them are obviously hostile witnesses. Several Russian writers with direct experience of revolution, for example, concluded that the zeal of revolutionaries was pathological. Pasternak's Yuri Zhivago observes that "those who inspired the revolution aren't at home in anything except change and turmoil: that's their native element; they aren't happy with anything that's less than on a world scale. For them, transitional periods, worlds in the making, are an end in themselves. They aren't trained for anything else, they don't know about anything except that".[5] A similar skepticism about the motives of revolutionaries and builders of new worlds was expressed much earlier by Zamyatin in his novel *We* (1921) and in several of his short stories. This aversion to the whole idea of revolution seems to be shared to this day by all the heterogeneous groupings of Soviet dissidents.

This aversion finds an elaborate—and, to western eyes, exotic—expression in social philosophy in the writings of the Soviet mathematician, Igor Shafarevich. For Shafarevich, socialism is simply an authoritarian, regimented form of social organization such as existed in several past civilizations: his examples include the Third Dynasty of Ur, the Incas, and the Old Kingdom of Egypt. Those who struggle to achieve such a society in modern times are driven, according to Shafarevich, by a pathological propensity to anger, hatred, and destruction—ultimately, a propensity to self-destruction. Dedicated revolutionaries, whatever they may say about their aims for a better world, are actually clear about only what they want to destroy: hierarchy, private property, religion, and the family. That, says Shafarevich, springs from a rage to destroy human individuality. To Shafarevich, socialist revolutionaries really are as Dostoevsky lampooned them in *The Devils,* and socialism is an embodiment of the death-wish.[6]

### LESSING AND SARTRE AS WITNESSES

The opinions of Pasternak, Zamyatin, and Shafarevich are formed by a political experience that is almost the opposite of that of western intellectuals. What is more surprising is that some western novelists of radical or revolutionary sympathies have shown, by implication, a measure of agreement with those opinions. Performing the second kind of novelist's trick in the depiction of political sentiment, they have drawn leading characters whose antibourgeois anger appears pathological.

The best examples I know are two novel-sequences that express attachment (in different degrees) to the revolutionary left. They are Sartre's "Roads to Freedom" trilogy and Doris Lessing's sequence of five *"Martha Quest"* novels grouped under the title "Children of Violence." Each of these cycles was published in a period when left-wing sentiment was strong among the intelligentsias of western Europe: 1945-49 and 1964-69, respectively.

Mathieu Delarue and Martha Quest share one conspicuous trait: a habitual mental state of disgust, irritation, and fretfulness. It is true that there are also large differences between the Delarue and Quest temperaments. There are differences, too, between the two characters' political biographies and between the roles that the two political biographies play in the two novel-sequences. (Quest enters the Communist party near the start of World War II and leaves it after Hungary; she does not find another political home or become enamoured of the bourgeois

world she inhabits. Delarue is attracted to the party but resists joining it. He dies fighting the invading German army and is replaced as a central character—in the last segment of *Iron in the Soul*—by the Communist, Brunet. Brunet's road to freedom is open, while Delarue's is closed.) So far as the depiction of political sentiment is concerned, however, both the similarities and the differences are intriguing.

The habitual state of irritation of both characters is emphasized by their creators. On the first page of the "Children of Violence" novel-sequence Martha Quest is pictured, at the age of fifteen, sitting on the veranda steps of her parents' farm in Rhodesia reading while her mother talks with a neighbor nearby:

> She frowned, and from time to time glanced up irritably at the women, indicating that their gossip made it difficult to concentrate. But then, there was nothing to prevent her moving somewhere else; and her spasms of resentment when she was asked a question, or her name was used in the family chronicling, were therefore unreasonable.

Two pages later:

> She looked down at her book. She did not want to read it; it was a book on popular science, and even the title stiffened her into a faint but unmistakable resentment. . . . Perhaps she was so resentful of her surroundings and her parents that the resentment overflowed into everything near her.

These first few pages of *Martha Quest* describe adolescent anger in a remarkable way. Martha's rages are passionately conveyed, and the reader has to see that they are about real and important things. They are also shown to be a little absurd, but only a little. In the five novels of the "Children of Violence" sequence Martha's anger is traced from adolescence to middle age. It takes many forms and is directed at many targets. The objects of Martha's wrath include her mother (for her narrow views and capacity for self-delusion); the bourgeois white establishment of Rhodesia; her first and second husbands; and her own capacity to play a part she despises (the character she calls "Matty," who charms others by a whimsical exaggeration, and therefore trivialization, of her own nonconformity). The anger becomes more specifically directed and more immediately political during her early period of party membership; later it seems to become a less important part of her temperament and of her responses to what she encounters.

The character of Martha Quest contains a large and changing collection of reactions and perceptions. Many of her antipathies are mingled with other feelings: the element of reluctant (and limited) admiration, for example, in her view of Mr. Maynard, a moderate in the Rhodesian establishment. In other words, her character is so fully represented and so convincingly complicated that it would be absurd to summarize her as some sort of personification of anger. To the reader of "Children of

Violence" she becomes like a close personal friend, impossible to describe briefly in any way at all. But the fretfulness is profound and salient, all the same. Martha Quest spends a very large proportion of her recorded existence in states of annoyance, anger, and disgust—very often with herself. On few pages is she amused, tranquil, enthusiastic, or ecstatic; and she hardly ever falls about, laughing.

Sartrean anger and nausea are, I suppose, more famous. In Mathieu Delarue they are more extreme than in Martha Quest and, as a personal trait, less interesting. Delarue is a small and rather clockwork assembly of attitudes and does not change much over time. (Admittedly, the action in the "Roads to Freedom" trilogy gives him little time in which to change.)

There are only two flashbacks to Delarue's childhood, and they are both exotic in their treatment of frustration and anger. In the first, he is described as savoring the memory of a day when, as a seven-year-old, he (a) tore the wings off a fly; (b) rubbed the fly's head with a kitchen scraper ("the feeble, lackadaisical sport of a bored little boy" in Eric Sutton's translation); (c) picked up and smashed a 3,000-year-old Chinese vase belonging to his uncle (a dentist who, curiously, kept the vase in his waiting room—surely a more imaginative *acte gratuit* than anything Delarue achieves?); and then (d) "felt quite proud" (of (c)), "freed from the world, without ties or kin or origins, a stubborn little excrescence that had burst the terrestrial crust."

The next flashback (immediately following) is to another moment when he felt free or capable of becoming so. He was sixteen "and had just thrashed a lad from Bordeaux, who had thrown stones at him, and he had forced him to eat sand."

The adult Delarue is obsessed with a desire to achieve freedom. When Sartre selects moments in Delarue's experience which have seemed to bring a sense of freedom, these flashbacks are the only two moments he chooses—until the last few minutes of Delarue's life, when he is killing German soldiers. Except for these latter episodes, Mathieu Delarue is shown as constantly angered and revolted by himself and others and, especially, by any behavior characteristic of the bourgeois world he inhabits.

The bourgeois reader can understand this, for Delarue's peacetime world is a nightmare. It is not, however, a world of classes, races, labor, and exploitation—or even a world of political debate. In *The Age of Reason* (the first volume of the trilogy), Delarue's world is composed of a set of venomous pairings, in each of which at least one partner loathes, despises, or at the very least bitterly resents the other: Daniel-Marcelle, Marcel-Mathieu, Mathieu-Ivich, Boris (Ivich's brother)-Lola. On the periphery are a number of other characters who turn out, in the later volumes, to be resented, despised, etc. by their partners (Mathieu's brother Jacques, for example, and Sarah). Then, outside the nightmare of

personal relations, there is the dedicated communist, Brunet, who could slip unnoticed into the better class of Soviet socialist realist novels, and he is unattached.

Mathieu Delarue is attracted to the Communist party and to the idea of fighting in the Spanish Civil War. His obsession with personal freedom, however, prevents him from signing up for either. And the chief attraction of the commitment he is resisting is the scope it would give him for smashing things. He pictures Brunet in Paris " . . . walking through the streets, enjoying the sunshine, light-hearted because he can look ahead, he walks through a city of threaded glass that he will soon destroy, he is walking with rather a mincing, cautious gait because the hour has not yet come to smash it all; he waits, he hopes."

Sartre presents Delarue as a tragic character and a failure. The person he recommends, evidently, is Brunet. But there is no sign that Sartre condemns Delarue's vindictiveness or praises Brunet for acting on some nobler sentiment. The difference between the two men, so far as their political behavior is concerned, is simply that Brunet has decided what to do and gets on with it, whereas Delarue can't make up his mind. (The difference between them as fictional characters is that Delarue has some semblance of life and Brunet none at all.)

Mathieu Delarue is finally presented with a pressing invitation to do something violent. In June 1940 his unit is overtaken by the advancing German army and he has to choose between surrender and a final, doomed resistance. He chooses to shoot—and therefore to be shot—and kills several German soldiers before he dies:

> Mathieu looked at the dead soldier and laughed. For years he had tried, in vain, to act. One after the other his intended actions had been stolen from him: he had been no firmer than a pat of butter. But no one had stolen this. He had pressed a trigger and, for once, something had happened, something definite. The thought made him laugh louder than ever. . . . He looked with satisfaction at his dead man. . . . *His* dead man, *his* handiwork, something to mark *his* passage on the earth. A longing came to him to do some more killing: it was fun and it was easy.[7]

And later: "Each one of his shots revenged some ancient scruple . . . this for everybody in general whom I wanted to hate and tried to understand."

In "Roads to Freedom" Sartre's intellectual stance seems to be that hating is, in the bourgeois world, a truer and more appropriate emotion than the urge to understand. In Part Two of *Iron in the Soul* Brunet, the communist activist, carries the action for the first time in the trilogy. He is a prisoner of war trying to organize a communist cell among his fellow-prisoners. He is shown as brave and determined. If he also exhibits understanding of other people, however, it is a contemptuous and remorseless sort of understanding.

For the great majority of the French prisoners around him he feels the standard Sartrean disgust: ". . . . undersized, nimble, mean . . . with ferrety muzzles." He resents their aptitude for "squalid, poverty-stricken contentment." Communists, he reflects, look different: "tough-looking, with hard eyes." The others are "just animals" or "lily-livered swine." "What they needed was suffering, fear and hatred: what they needed was the spirit of revolt, massacre and an iron discipline."[8]

What are the moods and attitudes of the other prisoners of war which so enrage Brunet? They are familiar from other writings about war: writings by Hašek, Heller, and ex-bombardier Milligan. The men Brunet despises are those who think war is crazy, and shrug, and consider their own comfort. So much for the Good Soldier Schweik.

### THE POLITICAL SENTIMENT OF THE STEPPENWOLF

What is striking about Delarue and Quest is that their antibourgeois anger is presented as a revulsion from their own comfortable lives and not as a revulsion from the squalid and uncomfortable lives of people less fortunate than themselves. The more conventional view, among western intelligentsia, is that all such sentiment against the existing order has an important element of generosity which should command respect. Sartre and Lessing, however, imply something overwhelmingly self-regarding.

There certainly does exist a tradition of radical political sentiment that has something to do with more generous impulses. Describing how socialist ideas began to take hold among the British intelligentsia in the 1880's, Beatrice Webb refers to the growth of a "collective or class consciousness of sin . . . among men of property and men of intellect." This she ascribes to "a growing uneasiness" about an industrial system that kept propertied persons in comfort but "failed to provide a decent livelihood and tolerable conditions for a majority of the inhabitants of Great Britain."[9]

In Mrs. Webb's account, the controversies among socialists, philanthropists, and *laissez-faire* radicals about the problem of poverty influenced her choice of her life's work. Unable to decide who was right, she set out with Victorian energy and seriousness to discover the extent and nature of poverty in the society around her. The aim was to discover what should best be done about it, and she began her work while still disinclined to reach socialist conclusions.

By comparison, the antibourgeois anger described by Sartre and Lessing—considered as a motive for political action—seems childish and petty. It entails, apparently, no concern to investigate what might be going on outside one's own head. The impulse that they depict is an impulse to lash out in order to relieve one's feelings, with little concern for other consequences.

All the same, in these novels by Sartre and Lessing it is constantly indicated that the central character's anger is not a matter simply of personal pathology (allowing, for the moment, that there might be such a thing as "purely personal" pathology). It is something to do with the bourgeois (ordered, prosperous) world in which the character lives, but the exact connection is neither expounded nor implied. The connection is, however, almost formally discussed in an earlier—and more recently fashionable—novel: Herman Hesse's *Steppenwolf.*

Hesse did not depict antibourgeois anger as variously as Doris Lessing or as insistently as Sartre, but he seems to have thought more about its origins and about what it encompassed. Harry Haller (the Steppenwolf) describes his own feelings as follows:

> A wild longing for strong emotions and sensations seethes in me, a rage against this toneless, flat, normal and sterile life. I have a mad impulse to smash something, a warehouse perhaps, or a cathedral, or myself, to commit outrages. . . . For what I always hated and detested and cursed above all things was this contentment, this healthiness and comfort, this carefully preserved optimism of the middle classes, this fat and prosperous brood of mediocrity.

Later a more analytical account of his discontent is transmitted to him, by magic, in the "Treatise on the Steppenwolf."

> Now what we call "bourgeois," when regarded as an element always to be found in human life, is nothing else than the search for a balance. It is the striving after a mean between the countless extremes and opposites that arise in human conduct. [The bourgeois] will never be a martyr nor agree to his own destruction. On the contrary, his ideal is not to give up but to maintain his own identity. . . . His aim is to make a house for himself between two extremes in a temperate zone without violent storms or tempests; and in this he succeeds though it be at the cost of that intensity of life and feeling which an extreme life affords. A man cannot live intensely except at the cost of the self. Now the bourgeois treasures nothing more highly than the self (rudimentary as his may be). And so at the cost of his own intensity he achieves his own preservation and security. . . . The bourgeois is therefore by nature a creature of weak impulses, anxious, fearful of giving himself away and therefore easy to rule.

This is the spectacle of everyday, prosperous life that nauseates Mathieu Delarue, puts Martha Quest in a state of constant fretfulness, and alienates Harry Haller. In literature, sense can no longer compete with sensibility. Where Jane Austen deplored the cultivation of sensibility ("intensity of life") as a highbrow form of dissipation, harmful to others, Hesse deplored its avoidance. It is characteristic of twentieth-century literary culture that his account is aesthetic rather than utilitarian. The result of "living intensely" may be destruction of the self; its consequences for others scarcely enter the picture. In general, the consideration of outcomes—particularly social outcomes—is something to be relegated to the alien, and probably fraudulent, calculus of the politician or businessman.

By the late 1930's even a political economist had noticed this "cultural contradiction." One of Schumpeter's reasons for doubting that capitalism would survive was that the bourgeoisie lacked any sort of romantic allure to help maintain its power; and it zealously built up an intellectual class which was repelled by this lack. One of capitalism's weaknesses in this respect is, paradoxically, its "progressive" replacement of tradition by supposedly rational calculations of costs and benefits. This sort of calculation spreads, in Schumpeter's view, from business into most other human activities, and the element of unseemly, inappropriate calculation is repellent to many. At the same time, one of the distinguishing characteristics of intellectuals, for Schumpeter, was precisely "the absence of direct responsibility for practical affairs"; that is to say, they are defined by him as "people who wield the power of the spoken and written word" without being professionally obliged (unlike, say, diplomats) to concern themselves with the consequences of what they say.[10] As part of an account of the downfall of capitalism, this is a frivolous tale, on the face of it, to follow Marx's surplus value and organic composition of capital, but it is one that is easier to recognize.

Later on, in *Steppenwolf,* Harry Haller passes into one of the shows at the Magic Theatre. It is a war. One side summons the nation "to side with the men against the machines, to make an end at last of the fat and well-dressed and perfumed plutocrats who used machines to squeeze the fat from other men's bodies. . . . " This call for an assault on plutocrats moves immediately into something more general and more frenzied: "Set factories afire at last! Make a little room on the crippled earth! Depopulate it so that the grass may grow again. . . . " The other side proclaims "in a truly impressive way the blessings of order and work and property and education and justice . . ."

To the Steppenwolf both sides appear right: "I stood as deeply convinced in front of one as in front of the other. . . . " But the crucial consideration to any Steppenwolf was that there was a good war going: "a war in which everyone who lacked air to breathe and no longer found life exactly pleasing gave emphatic expression to his displeasure and strove to prepare the way for a general destruction of this iron-cast civilization of ours. In every eye I saw the unconcealed spark of destruction and murder, and in mine too these wild red roses bloomed as rank and high, and sparkled as brightly. I joined the battle joyfully."

#### POLITICAL SENTIMENT AND POLITICS

For reasons both good and bad (or so it seems to me) "this iron-cast civilization of ours" does not please all who inhabit it—though for a great many it does quite well. In particular, it generates among its intellectuals a discontent or irritation or even a settled hostility that is no longer politically insignificant. Shafarevich (disapprovingly), Sartre (approvingly), and Hesse (equivocally) identify this sentiment as destructive. Lessing (in the

*Martha Quest* novels) does not depict the sentiment as destructive in its social implications; in common with Sartre, Hesse, and many other twentieth-century novelists, however, she does convey to the reader a picture of antibourgeois anger as a sentiment stemming above all from a sense that one's own life is being stifled and limited. It is characteristic of Mathieu, Quest, Haller, and whole battalions of like-minded characters in modern fiction that their resentment is to do with an injury which they sense has been done to themselves; it is not to do with the fate of others. By the same token, if the sentiment of antibourgeois anger moves these characters to any strong form of public action, the consequences of that action for others appear only as a secondary consideration.

Antibourgeois anger is often dismissed, smugly, as a childish and irresponsible sentiment. It is not my intention to add to the catalogue of such dismissals. The sentiment, in various forms and degrees, has been too widely shared for too long to be treated merely as an unworthy contrivance of intellectual fashion. What is more to the point is that the sentiment should not be misconstrued. It should not be confused with the workings of social conscience.

As an influence on behavior, therefore, this sentiment occupies a kind of no-man's-land between the world of letters and the world of affairs. All political sentiments, by definition, are forms of feeling rather than calculation and therefore do not include within themselves a consideration of causes and effects. Some political sentiments, however—Beatrice Webb's "collective or class consciousness of sin", for example—would seem to prompt those who entertain them toward a consideration of specific aims and of means to achieve those aims. Antibourgeois anger, on the other hand, is one of the more purely sentimental of political sentiments. The careful weighing of consequences is itself one of the bourgeois habits of mind which arouse this anger in the first place. This sentiment is therefore an impulse toward the politics of upheaval; in more or less normal times it finds strong expression only at the outer fringes of conventional politics, and weak expression only in a general inclination toward the radical Left.

The anomaly is that any set of attitudes should have such a star role in our literature and yet be capable of contributing (I suspect) only harm to our lives as social beings. For all the political activism of (some) literary intellectuals and the literary culture of (some) politicians and "practical men," the gap between literature and politics in the Western world is pathologically large.

#### NOTES

[1] Alexander Zinoviev's phrase (*neestestvennye nauki*), in *The Yawning Heights,* for the social sciences.

[2] Whether the extant Sholokhov, the Grand Old Man of official Soviet literature and the bête noire of the literary

dissidents, really wrote most of the first novel in the *Don* sequence is contested. Computer analysis has been inconclusive. Even if he didn't, *Virgin Soil . . .*, at least, still serves as a striking example.

[3] Leonid Plyushch, *History's Carnival* (London, 1979), p. 118.

[4] An anomaly described, in different styles, by Johannes Gross ("On a German Paradox of "Golden Gloom,'" *Encounter,* April 1981) and by Tom Wolfe ("The Intelligent Coed's Guide to America," in his *Mauve Gloves & Madmen, Clutter & Vine* [New York, 1976]). In his study of the "pilgrimages" of western intellectuals to communist countries, Paul Hollander has explored the consequences of this revulsion from western society for attitudes to the USSR, China, and Cuba (*Political Pilgrims* [London, 1981]).

[5] *Dr. Zhivago* (London, 1958), p. 269. As the Soviet literary establishment correctly observed, *Zhivago* is a profoundly, pervasively, and explicitly antirevolutionary book. It seems strange, now, that Pasternak ever thought it might be published in the Soviet Union. Indeed, the animus is so strong and Pasternak's ability to imagine minds other than his own is so slight that he simply does not depict revolutionary political sentiment "from inside." His revolutionaries are credible only as objects viewed from a distance. Podstrelnikov is a kind of nonfigurative construct apparently intended as a portrait of (it might be better to call it "a meditation upon") the poet Mayakovsky. See Olga Ivinskaya. *A Captive of Time* (London, 1978).

[6] "Socialism in Our Past and Future," in Alexander Solzhenitsyn, ed., *From Under the Rubble* (London, 1975), pp. 26-27. This is an abbreviated version of an extended historical and philosophical work which existed in *samizdat* in the early 1970's.

[7] *Iron in the Soul,* pp. 217-18 of the Penguin edition The original title, *La Mort dans lâme,* fits Shafarevich's diagnosis precisely.

[8] These quotations are taken from Brunet's reflections at several different points, scattered over ninety pages of text.

[9] Beatrice Webb, *My Apprenticeship* (Penguin ed., 1938), pp. 204-06.

[10] Joseph Schumpeter, *Capitalism, Socialism and Democracy,* second ed. (London, 1947), p. 147.

### George Bornstein

SOURCE: "The State of Letters: Can Literary Study be Politically Correct?," in the *Sewanee Review,* Vol. C, No. 2, April-June, 1992, pp. 283-89.

[*In the following essay, Bornstein criticizes the narrowness of political correctness, particularly when applied to literary study, which he argues should not be a limiting exercise.*]

At the height of the terror that established Bolshevism in the Soviet Union, Lenin reportedly sent a famous telegram exclaiming indignantly "We're not shooting enough professors." That was political correctness with a vengeance. The incident reminds us that political correctness is nothing new, that it tends toward the authoritarian, and that it is not likely to contribute much to the welfare, or even the survival, of the professoriate. Although in the last two years one hears the term *political correctness* most loudly from conservative opponents of recent academic trends, the phrase itself has a more complicated history. For example communist intellectuals used it during the 1930s under Stalin. It fit well with a diction that spoke of "the party line," and often appeared in negative usage as "politically incorrect"—for example, it was correct that the world's leading Marxist country had signed a treaty with the world's leading fascist one, but politically incorrect to say so. A half century later, feminists of the 1980s sometimes used the phrase *politically correct,* often with a commendably ironic overtone. So the term appears to span the political spectrum rather than to belong exclusively to any special part of it.

Political correctness, or PC, seems likely to emerge at times of social change, whether of the murderous class displacements of the October revolution in Russia or the more intellectual combat in American universities today. Such changes in constitutive groups, as in canons, seem to me the normal state for universities. To profit from such changes, we need to be fully open in discussing their causes, nature, effects, and even their desirability. Whatever narrows that conversation in advance is limiting. "Damn braces, bless relaxes," wrote William Blake. Particularly in their virulent condemnatory form, doctrines of prior political correctness work against the very openness that they claim to champion.

I welcome as well as defend that increasing openness, being myself the product of it. One of the many instances of the historical amnesia of current political correctness is its erasure of the long discrimination against Jews practiced by elite American universities. In May 1918, for example, Dean Frederick Jones of Yale University spoke for many, when, in a meeting of the Association of New England Deans held at Princeton University, he said that "I think we shall have to change our views in regard to the Jewish element. . . . If we do not educate them, they will overrun us. We have got to change our policies and get them into shape. A few years ago every single scholarship of any value was won by a Jew. I took it up with the Committee and said that we could not allow that to go on. We must put a ban on the Jews. We decided not to give them any scholarships." I don't know if Princeton succeeded in getting me "into shape," but here I am anyway. It took a long time for the vestiges of such discrimination to disappear. Indeed one of my uncles—who with the ethnically indeterminate name of Price became the first member of the family to attend college—had been awarded a scholarship to Columbia, but then it was rescinded when the authorities following the Dean Jones plan discovered that he was Jewish. I myself came East to Harvard as an undergraduate in 1959, two years after its president, Nathan Pusey, forbade the use of the university chapel to a Jewish faculty member wishing to get married in it, and the year after *New York Times* coverage made the anti-Semitism of the Princeton eating clubs known to the nation (those clubs had been praised by an earlier secretary of the university, Varnum Lansing Collins, as "our strongest barrier" to Jewish admissions). In those days, so far as we students knew, Harvard had but one Jewish professor of English (Harry Levin, who seemed more in comparative literature), and Princeton—as I discovered upon arriving there for graduate school—had one. Things were shortly to change so drastically that in a literature class I taught at the University of Michigan this spring, only one of the fifty students knew that Jews had ever suffered discrimination in American academia. As a black friend of mine likes to point out, the predicament of Jewish men of my generation is that we went directly from being discriminated against for being Jewish to being discriminated against for being white males, without ever passing through a period of popularity. Thus to me Harold Shapiro's recent assumption of the presidency of Princeton remains a deeply enigmatic event.

Political correctness is notoriously hard to define, yet I suspect that each of us here has a relatively clear idea of what it means on campus nowadays, and I want to enumerate three components of that idea present in literary study. The first is that PC privileges race, class, and gender in its social and literary analyses. To the extent that those categories recuperate voices previously marginalized or ignored, they seem a clear gain. Who would deny the rightful place of, to pick a few of many writers earlier in our century, Zora Neale Hurston, Langston Hughes, or H.D.? And yet race, class, and gender can generate their own blindness when they become not three of many categories but the dominant—and sometimes the only—ones. Categories that other times and places have thought and still do think fundamental can fall from sight—among them religion, nationalism, or education. To return to Jewish matters for a moment, I like most of my colleagues can rattle off lists of rediscovered female and Afro-American writers prior to 1900, but how many of us can name a single Jewish literary writer in English before 1900? The once marginal have become central, but the still marginal are invisible to the lenses of race, class, and gender. Of course the categories I have suggested loom large in the world today beyond literature: for example, religion in Northern Ireland or in the Middle East, nationalism in central Europe, or education practically everywhere.

We ought not to think that emphasis on race, class, and gender is anything new or that it is automatically progressive. After all, both fascist and Stalinist approaches to

aesthetics highlighted such features, as the art exhibition "'Degenerate Art': The Fate of the Avant-Garde in Nazi Germany" reminds us. A representative book is Paul Schultze-Naumberg's *Kunst und Rasse* [*Art and Race*], published in 1928, which extended Max Nordau's *Entartung* (*Degeneration*), published in 1892, into a full-scale racial analysis of modernism. Race-based approaches to all the arts underlay the Nazis' German Cultural League, which sponsored "art programs" to demonstrate, for example, "why negro culture is contrary to German customs" and to defend "pure German culture." Such positions extended even into the natural sciences. The Nobel prize-winner Philipp Leonard, for instance, argued for pure "German physics" against the pernicious "Jewish science" of Albert Einstein and others. The Nazi press attacked the discoverer of the Uncertainty Principle, Werner Heisenberg, for spreading "Jewish physics" because he used Einstein's relativity theory in his own work. And all such "foreign" influences were seen as threatening aryan womanhood. Meanwhile, in Stalinist Russia, doctrines of "socialist realism" insisted that literature reflect a class-based revolutionary struggle that particularly valorized workers and peasants into cartoon caricatures of virtue. The moral of this, of course, is not that we should abandon race, class, and gender as categories of literary analysis, but only that we should recognize their long and generally shameful history in that enterprise, and should not take their invocation as automatically progressive.

A second characteristic of current PC is its implicit and sometimes explicit casting of the United States as source of the evils identified by analysis according to race, class, and gender—namely racism, classism, and sexism. During its war of national liberation against England earlier in this century, the Irish Republican Army developed a mock catechism around the question "What is the origin of evil?" and its answer, "England." PC often implies a similar catechism, with the answer being America. That is useful insofar as it helps us to struggle against race, class, and gender discrimination. But for all its talk against ethnocentrism, PC seldom includes a comparative perspective on other societies—and for a very good reason. Most other societies, particularly outside the much vilified Europe and Israel, are even less politically correct than the United States. Here some harsh realities need citing: there are not twenty million women walking around America with forced clitorectomies as there are in Africa; slavery was outlawed here nearly a century before it disappeared from the Arab world (and it still hasn't disappeared from some remote corners of that world); and not capitalist America but rather Marxist Russia and China starved to death peasants by the tens of millions as a matter of deliberate state policy. Nations of the so-called Second and Third Worlds are even less politically correct than those of the First World. Indeed it is hardly original to point out that a hallmark of Western tradition is its self-critical attitude on just the points that political correctness holds so dear, including the characteristic one of ethnocentrism.

PC sees the United States not so much as needing reform in order to live up to its own ideals but as so radically flawed as to need to begin all over on a different plan. That plan is usually anticapitalist, and its implicit or explicit socialism constitutes the third characteristic of political correctness. After the spectacular collapse of the Marxist empire in central Europe and the massacres in Tiananmen Square, few PCers willingly identify themselves as Marxists, but instead choose from a range of pathetic evasions: that the Union of Soviet Socialist Republics is not really a Marxist or socialist country, that no Marxist country is really a Marxist country, that they themselves are only cultural but not economic Marxists (whatever that means), or that they have simply renamed themselves materialists. It has become a cliché that the last Marxists in the world are in Western humanities departments, and that virtually none of them have ever studied economics. The general bias leads to a double standard in judging modernist authors of, say, the 1930s: writers who flirted with fascism however long (like Pound) or briefly (like Yeats before he repudiated it) are regularly damned, while those who served Stalinism long after its horrors were known (like Sartre, Simone de Beauvoir, Neruda) suffer no opprobrium at all, but often are admired instead. During my own years in academia, the academic left has regularly glorified one shabby dictatorship after another, and upon its unmasking not questioned the politics that produced the debacle but rather rushed on to a new paradigm—first Cuba, then North Vietnam, then the Khmer Rouge regime in Cambodia, then China, and so on. When I lived in Italy in 1972-73 a favored regime of Italian "democratic leftists" was Albania!

Against such sophistry I would adopt the position of W. B. Yeats when he expressed in 1936 his "horror at the cruelty of governments" and declared that "Communist, Fascist . . . are all responsible according to the number of their victims." By that standard governments we might call Marxist or socialist or communist have a great deal to answer for in our century, where their toll of victims far out does even that of the fascist regimes and, of course, dwarfs the very real sins of the liberal democracies. Current estimates now taught in Russian schools estimate the deaths caused by the Stalinist regime within the Soviet Union to number between 20 and 40 million people, to say nothing of the further millions exterminated outside the nation by Soviet imperialism. And in communist China the internal death toll during the Great Leap Forward (that disaster of the late 50s and early 60s that I and other opponents of the Vietnam war once were taught to admire) is now estimated at between 16 and 27 million people, with 10 million dying in the year 1960 alone. As with genocide, so with ecology. We heard in the 1970s about socialism's respect for the environment and capitalism's cynical exploitation of it, until we learned in the 1980s that the most environmentally polluted regions on earth are in central Europe and Eastern Russia. I do not know whether to be more appalled at the commission of such crimes, or at the silence about them by the academic left today; one has the clear sense that

had such atrocities been committed by liberal democracies, they would be regularly cited by proponents of political correctness. What both Marxist totalitarianism and political correctness have in common on this issue is the idea of group as opposed to individual identity and rights, and the fact that such strategies of identity have been central to the most appalling oppressions of the twentieth century ought at the very least to give us pause about invoking them as somehow automatically on the side of liberation.

In carrying over many of the categories mentioned above (emphasis on race-class-gender; America as the Great Satan; and a loosely leftist orientation) the adherents of PC have already decided what is politically correct and what functions as a moral monitor of past literature. That is, it interrogates the literature of the past according to the standards of the present, rather than using that literature to interrogate the standards of the present. PC thus lacks both humility and the potential for correction: it represents an imperialism of time as obnoxious as an imperialism of space, imposing its own standards on the great world of time with relentless ethnocentrism. Like all imperialisms PC is relentlessly moralistic, in the manner argued against by Shelley in the *Defense of Poetry*. There Shelley defines poetry as the expression of the imagination and maintained against the devotees of Political Correctness in his own time that poetry improved society most by strengthening individual imagination rather than by preaching; hence, he wrote, "a poet would do ill to embody his own conceptions of right and wrong, which are usually those of his place and time, in his poetical creations." The *Defense of Poetry* reminds us that political correctness has recurred throughout history, and that, however admirable some of its goals may be, its means are narrow.

A good example is the controversy over John Synge's *Playboy of the Western World* at the beginning of our century. Synge's rollicking comedy portrayed a mock parricide among the Irish peasantry and the tumultuous love affair between the "hero" Christy Mahon and heroine Pegeen Mike in a language modelled on peasant speech in the West of Ireland. Yet, at its first Irish performances in 1907 and first American tour in 1911, the play provoked riots and denunciations by the then politically correct—the Irish Nationalists in both Ireland and America. Their critique focused on race, class, and gender in political contexts. At that time Ireland was still ruled by England, and Synge was a Protestant Anglo-Irishman writing about Gaelic-speaking Catholic peasants. Politically correct critics like the alderman Michael McInerney, who led the successful fight to ban the *Playboy* in Chicago, labeled it "a studied sarcasm on the Irish race." In Dublin opponents branded it a slander on the peasant class, and argued that it defamed Irish women in particular. In a depressing anticipation of issues that sound familiar today, the Boston police even told Lady Gregory that "they had had the same trouble about a negro play said to misrepresent people of colour." And George Bernard Shaw still sounds highly topical when he defends the *Playboy* by denouncing those whose "notion of patriotism is to listen jealously for the slightest hint that Ireland is not the home of every virtue and the martyr of every oppression, and thereupon to brawl and bully or to whine and protest, according to their popularity with the bystanders." African-American writers were quicker to see the point. "Harlem has the same role to play for the New Negro as Dublin had for the New Ireland," declared Alain Locke in the introduction to his landmark anthology, *The New Negro* (1925), while James Weldon Johnson wrote in *his* important anthology, *The Book of American Negro Poetry* (1922), that "what the colored poet in the United States needs to do is something like what Synge did for the Irish; he needs to find a form that will express the racial spirit by symbols from within rather than by symbols from without." Today, of course, Synge's play is viewed as one of the glories of Irish—and indeed world—literature, even in Ireland. The highly original works that comprise today's canon seldom won the approval of the politically correct of their own day.

The problem with political correctness, then, is not whether it is political or whether it is correct, but that it is narrow. It limits rather than enlarges. To that extent, literary study certainly *can* be politically correct but *ought not* to be. In "Esthetique du Mal" Wallace Stevens quotes Victor Serge's description of a Stalinist prosecutor—"I followed his argument/With the blank uneasiness which one might feel / In the presence of a logical lunatic"—and identifies what we would call a politically correct person as "the lunatic of one idea / In a world of ideas." Political correctness often gives me the same uneasy feeling that it gave Serge and Stevens, and not just because of its narrowness ("one idea") but because it lacks the capacity for self-scrutiny, self-control, and self-criticism. Ezra Pound displayed those qualities when he movingly asked in his last completed canto, "As to where they go wrong, thinking of rightness?" and admitted that "Charity I have had sometimes, / I cannot make it flow through." Similarly T. S. Eliot in the last of his *Four Quartets* lamented "things ill done and done to others' harm / Which once you took for exercise of virtue." Much as I deplore the politics of Pound and Eliot, I admire their capacity for self-criticism, a capacity at odds with all political correctnesses and thus to me central to literary study. For that enterprise I would urge the vision articulated by the great African-American poet Robert Hayden when he wrote:

> We must not be frightened nor cajoled
> into accepting evil as deliverance from evil.
> We must go on struggling to be human,
> though monsters of abstraction
> police and threaten us.
> Reclaim now, now renew the vision of
> a human world where godliness
> is possible and man
> is neither gook, nigger, honkey, wop, nor kike
> but man
>     permitted to be man.

# UNITED STATES

## Joseph Blotner

SOURCE: "The Southern Politician," in *The Modern American Political Novel: 1900-1960,* University of Texas Press, 1966, pp. 191-33.

*[In the following essay, Blotner discusses politics as portrayed in literature of the American South.]*

> Proud, brave, honorable by its lights, courteous, personally generous, loyal, swift to act, often too swift, but signally effective, sometimes terrible, in its action—such was the South at its best. And such at its best it remains today, despite the great falling away in some of its virtues. Violence, intolerance, aversion and suspicion toward new ideas, an incapacity for analysis, an inclination to act from feeling rather than from thought, an exaggerated individualism and a too narrow concept of social responsibility, attachment to fictions and false values, above all too great attachment to racial values and a tendency to justify cruelty and injustice in the name of those values, sentimentality and a lack of realism—these have been its characteristic vices in the past. And despite changes for the better, they remain its characteristic vices today.
>
>                              W. J. Cash
>                      *The Mind of the South*[1]

The Southern Politician naturally takes his character and coloration from his region, this most individualistic of American regions.[2] Students of Southern history and politics object, however, to the stereotypes clustering around such abstractions as "The South," and such figures as "The Southern Demagogue" even while they grant that there is truth in many such stereotypes. It is true that except for North Carolina, Virginia, Tennessee, and Texas, Southern politics has operated until recently under an absolute one-party system. Disfranchisement of most Negroes and many whites has been for nearly a century an accomplished fact. And where disfranchisement leaves off, nonvoting impedes the operation of democratic practices. Experts insist, however, that state politics and leaders are nowhere nearly so homogeneous as is often assumed.

State politics, they declare, presents not one shade or two, but a whole spectrum. Virginia has been dominated most of the years of this century by an organization led by Senator Harry F. Byrd. Stable, powerful, and perspicacious, it can determine which young men will be encouraged in politics and which will be allowed to slip into obscurity. In Tennessee, a working understanding was said to exist in the 1930's and 1940's between the Democratic machine of E. H. "Boss" Crump, based in the city of Memphis and Shelby County, and the Republican faction, based in the mountains of East Tennessee and led by Carroll Reece, for many terms a member of the U.S. House of Representatives and in 1946 Republican National Chairman. The Alabama pattern, however, shows an almost random rise and eclipse of many factions, whereas politics in Florida shows even greater change and variance.[3] North Carolina's government in this century is generally called the most enlightened in the South, but in it the power of the Interests has been stronger and steadier than in perhaps any other Southern state. In the view of one native, "The big interests have known when to give way and when to play ball. They have been willing to be fair but not at the expense of their power."[4] In Mississippi, big delta planters aligned with the Interests have struggled against the hill country people often courted by spectacular demagogues. But here too there are variations and surprises. Mississippi politics sometimes represents an extremity of the Southern dilemma, but it has been observed that in voter turnout, when compared with Virginia "Mississippi is a hot-bed of Democracy."[5] That there are deeply felt attitudes which make for Southern community of ideas—most notably demonstrated on certain issues in Congress—cannot be disputed. But it is also clear that a greater divergence exists from state to state than is commonly assumed even among intelligent laymen.

The figure of the Southern Demagogue has substantially replaced that of the old-style Southern senator. The amply padded figure with flowing locks, pompously declaiming platitudes, has faded. In his place, in books and on film, strides a man burly and unkempt, wily and unscrupulous. His drive to power is aided by an intimate, emphatic knowledge of the plight and aspiration of the mass of the people. He has sprung from this class, but he cynically ignores their interests whenever they conflict with his own. The Southern Demagogue, writes Key, is a national institution: "His numbers are few but his fame is broad. He has become the whipping boy for all his section's errors and ills—and for many of the nation's. His antics have colored the popular view of a region of the United States."[6] A whole series of historical figures stand behind the stereotype. And they appear as early as the turn of the century, appealing to the same feelings that provided a favorable climate for the fervent but short-lived Southern Populism of the 1890's. Pitchfork Ben Tillman of South Carolina, "the first great exponent of the role," was followed by a long list of others who added their own variations.[7] There were Cole Blease and Cotton Ed Smith in South Carolina as well as

> the ineffable Jeff Davis larruping the specter of the black man up and down the hills of Arkansas. Here were Tom Watson and Hoke Smith riding hard upon him in Georgia. Here was W. K. [*sic*] Vardaman roaring to his delighted Mississippians: "The way to control the nigger is to whip him when he does not obey without it . . . and another is never to pay him more wages than is actually necessary to buy food and clothing."[8]

Success bred emulation. In Mississippi, Theodore Bilbo, a self-confessed bribe-taker, followed the path of Vardaman to power. Eugene Talmadge of Georgia, "The Wild Man from Sugar Creek," not only outlasted his downstate rival, Little Ed Rivers (who proclaimed his loyalty to the New Deal while trying to make Georgia strictly his own

political preserve), but left his son Herman a following and a name which helped seat him in the United States Senate. In Texas, W. Lee O'Daniel campaigned with a hillbilly band playing his own compositions. Others displayed markedly individual characteristics: in Memphis, Mister Ed Crump shrewdly built statewide influence on a city and county machine base that would have done credit to a Jersey City or Kansas City politician. The most dramatic of all was a man who belonged "essentially to the traditional pattern of the Southern demagogue," but also managed to be "the first Southern politician to stand really apart from his people and coolly and accurately to measure the political potentialities afforded by the condition of the underdog." He was a man, as he himself readily proclaimed, who was *sui generis*.[9]

> Louisiana [writes Arthur M. Schlesinger, Jr.] was as natural a breeding place for radicalism as its swamps were for fevers. No state in the Union had been so long misgoverned. The old oligarchy, a dreary alliance of New Orleans businessmen and upstate planters controlled by the utilities, the railroads, and Standard Oil of Louisiana, had run things without serious challenge almost since Reconstruction. No state had so high a proportion of illiteracy . . . No state treated its children worse . . . And the submerged people of Louisiana had not only been oppressed, they had been bored: no Cole Blease, no Tom Watson, no Heflin nor Bilbo had arisen to make them laugh and hate and to distract them from the drabness of their days. Half a century of pent-up redneck rancor was awaiting release.[10]

When the instrument for this release came, it came from the north-central Louisiana hill country which had a tradition of revolt as well as deprivation. Refusing to vote for Secession, the parish had been jeered at as the Free State of Winn. In the 1890's Winn had reverberated to the storming Populist oratory of Sockless Jerry Simpson. In 1908 Presidential candidate Eugene V. Debs stumped the parish for the Socialist Party. Mill hands and cotton choppers responded by electing "half of the police jurors and school trustees on the Socialist ticket."[11] These sentiments persisted. "There wants to be a revolution, I tell you," said one man who had seen both Simpson and Debs. "I seen this domination of capital, seen it for seventy years. What do these rich folks care for the poor man? . . . Maybe you're surprised to hear talk like that. Well, it was just such talk that my boy was raised under and that I was raised under."[12] The speaker was Huey Pierce Long, and the boy, the eighth of nine children, was Huey P. Long, Jr. Though theirs was originally a poor white family, college educations were somehow managed for six of the children. But later, on the stump, the boy still claimed that he had worked in the fields from before sunup till after sunset and had known childhood days when he went shoeless as well.

After blooming as an elocutionist at Winnfield High School, Huey P. Long, Jr., had taken to the road at sixteen as a peddler. He sold Gold Dust, a Pinkhamlike compound called "the Wine of Cardui," and ran contests among his customers for the best cake baked with

Cottolene vegetable shortening.[13] He turned briefly from business to education in 1912 when he attended the University of Oklahoma. Then, after another period on the road, he married one of his baking contest winners, young Rose McConnell from Shreveport. Borrowing $400, he began a study of law at Tulane University in New Orleans. The money ran out in seven months, but Long acted with characteristic resourcefulness. He talked the Louisiana bar examination committee into giving him a special examination covering the standard, three-year curriculum of legal studies. He passed it, and on May 15, 1915, he was sworn in as a member of the bar. He was twenty-two years of age.

The pickings were slim at first, and sometimes the pay was humiliation. When he argued against a narrow workmen's compensation law, the chairman of the legislative committee asked whom he represented. His clients, he replied, were several thousand laborers who had paid him no retainer. "They seem to have good sense," commented the chairman. It was a barb Huey never forgot.[14] When the United States entered the war he gained exemption on the grounds that he was married and also a state official. He was a notary public. Working part-time at the law and part-time at the sale of patent medicines, he watched for his opportunity. It came in 1918 when he campaigned for the railroad commissionership of North Louisiana and won the Democratic nomination. And he had his eye on more than railroad matters.

The new commissioner soon began to lay about him. He was, he had let it be known, a friend of the common man. After having Standard Oil's pipelines declared "common carriers," he exerted pressure on Standard's rate-making practices. He compelled the Cumberland Telephone and Telegraph Company to reduce its rates. Meanwhile his Shreveport law practice flourished. In 1920, he helped elect John M. Parker as governor. Three years later, when Parker refused to levy higher taxes on Standard Oil, Long charged betrayal of the people and ran for the gubernatorial nomination. He and his wife and the organization he had built went to work with the old lists of the hill-country customers as well as potential new supporters. Their canvassing extended from the Protestant parishes of northern hill people to the Catholic parishes in the Cajun south. The posters were nailed up, the campaign literature was sent out, and Huey stumped the state. In a rhythmic delivery like the camp-meeting preachers' of his childhood, he roared his invective at the Interests and the "Old Regular" machine of New Orleans. On a rainy January 15th he was defeated, but before 1924 was out, he had been returned to his office as railroad commissioner by a margin of five to one. With the law practice flourishing, he worked to expand his power base.

Four years later Long ran again. His refrain, "Every Man a King but No Man Wears a Crown," was adapted from a Bryan campaign speech of 1900, and it tapped some of the enthusiasm that the Great Commoner himself had aroused. Attacking the wealthy, he called for a financial redistribution. His lament under the Evangeline

Oak became famous. "And it is here under this oak," he declaimed, "Evangeline waited for her lover, Gabriel, who never came . . . but Evangeline is not the only one who has waited here in disappointment." The people, he said, had waited for schools, roads, and institutions. "Evangeline wept bitter tears in her disappointment," he went on, "but it lasted through only one lifetime. Your tears in this country, around this oak, have lasted for generations. Give me the chance to dry the eyes of those who still weep here."[15] This time the skies were fair on Primary Day. Huey P. Long, Jr., carried fifty-six of the sixty-four parishes, and the Pelican State had a new governor.

He got off to a running start. His men went in as speaker of the House and president pro tempore of the Senate. Revenue from new tax bills financed construction of roads and schools and underwrote expanding government bureaus and functions. State patronage was brought firmly under control. When the program needed massive doses of new capital in March of 1929, a special session of the legislature slapped a five-cent-a-barrel levy on the oil refineries. Standard Oil thereupon refused to pay and led the other oil companies in a revolt. Then, on March 25, a senator called for investigation of charges that Long had hired a gunman for a political assassination. Two days later impeachment charges were filed against him. Long prepared for counterattack. With the help of powers such as Robert Maestri of New Orleans and with the encouragement of hill men in overalls come south to stand with him, Long flooded the state with propaganda. But his winning coup came through individual action rather than mass action. Huey threatened and cajoled fifteen state senators into signing a "round robin" letter declaring they would not vote against him. The opposition, now clearly unable to muster the necessary votes for impeachment, collapsed. Standard Oil kept on refining at the old rate per barrel, but Long had repulsed his first major attack. From then on, the temper of his steel began to harden.

By 1930 state government had become an instrument that fitted his hand. His law office prospered in New Orleans, and the Louisiana Democratic Association, which he had organized from the ward and precinct level up, tightened control and funneled unrecorded funds into the organization. A year to the day after the impeachment charges had been drawn up, a newspaper he owned announced that Huey P. Long, Jr., would run for the United States Senate. In the election, one parish, St. Bernard's, went for him 3,979 to 9. He served out his term as governor and then, in January of 1932, boarded the train with his entourage for Washington.

Long had acquired the nickname, "The Kingfish"—taken from the radio serial called "Amos 'n' Andy"—and his behavior in Washington was as colorful as the name. His dress was flamboyant. Strutting on the Senate floor, he slapped backs and ignored protocol.

> In his manners, values, and idiom [writes Schlesinger], Huey Long remained a back-country hillbilly.

But he was a hillbilly raised to the highest level, preternaturally swift and sharp in intelligence, ruthless in action, and grandiose in vision. He was a man of medium height, well built but inclining toward pudginess . . . His face was round, red, and blotched, with more than a hint of pouches and jowls. Its rubbery mobility, along with the curly red-brown hair and the oversize putty nose, gave him the deceptive appearance of a clown. But the darting pop-eyes could easily turn from soft to hard, and the cleft chin was strong and forceful.[16]

He attacked senior senators such as Carter Glass of Virginia and heaped on others his home-style invective. Alben Barkley said he was like a horsefly. "He would light on one part of you," the Kentucky veteran said, "sting you, and then, when you slapped at him, fly away to land elsewhere and sting again."[17] He introduced income-limiting bills and plumped for his "Share-Our-Wealth" program. And he was meditating other things. He had come to Washington convinced that he had played a crucial role in gaining the presidential nomination for Franklin D. Roosevelt. Taking the stump for Roosevelt in territory written off as lost, he had produced results that opened Jim Farley's eyes. What he now wanted in return was the disposal of all federal patronage in Louisiana. Neither Roosevelt nor Farley antagonized him, however, despite provocation. He had decisively helped Senator Hattie Caraway in neighboring Arkansas against six opponents trying to unseat her. Thus when his own man, John H. Overton, took Louisiana's other seat, Long controlled a block of three votes in the nation's upper chamber. He had for some time made references—often humorous or cocky—to himself as a potential occupant of the White House. It was becoming evident that these remarks had more in them than jest.

Long moved forward on two fronts. On election day, 1934, 3,000 battle-dressed Louisiana national guardsmen marched into New Orleans. Long's brother Julius, who had earlier described him as "the greatest political burglar of modern times," saw this move as totalitarian suppression of freedom. "With his well-known record for approving gambling and vice; fraud and ballot-box stuffing," he charged, "supported now by some of the outstanding gamblers and dive owners in and around New Orleans . . . he has the audacity and little respect for the intelligence and liberties of the people to pretend that he sincerely wants to suppress vice and has called out the National Guard and state militia."[18] Less than a month later, the legislature gave his officials practically unlimited control of the Louisiana military and subjected the cities in particular and state in general virtually to authoritarian rule. He turned his weekly paper into a national organ called *American Progress*. In a move traditional with presidential aspirants, he published his autobiography, *Every Man a King*. By February, 1934, the Reverend Gerald L. K. Smith—an antisemite and fascist-to-be—was organizing Share-Our-Wealth clubs on a national basis. In June of 1935 Long gained more national attention with a fifteen-hour filibuster opposing further extension of the New Deal National Recovery Act. By early 1936 he was all but a formally announced candidate. Long did not care if he split the Democratic Party; he was quite prepared to offer an alternative to both major parties. His view of them suggested David Graham Phillips's young radicals and communists in later fiction. Both parties were selling the same nostrums, he said, "And . . . the only difference . . . I can see is that the Republican leaders are skinning the people from the ankle up, and the Democratic leaders are taking off the hide from the ear down. Skin 'em up or skin 'em down, but skin 'em!"[19]

The Administration struck back through a radio broadcast by former NRA administrator, Gen. Hugh S. Johnson, a grizzled and cantankerous veteran who was himself no mean hand at invective. "It was easy," Postmaster General James A. Farley later recalled, "to conceive of a situation whereby Long, by polling more than 3,000,000 votes, might have the balance of power in the 1936 election."[20] After Johnson's blast, Long asked for equal radio time and used it to attack Roosevelt and extol the growing Share-Our-Wealth clubs. The Administration turned to a different kind of weapon. If it could not blast Long directly, it would mine his position. Treasury tax investigators had found out a good deal through an investigation prudently begun in 1930, later suspended, and then resumed. Indictments came through against his organization's smaller fry and plans were made to request a grand jury indictment in October. Long would be charged with evading income taxes on graft he had received through the Win or Lose Corporation deviously operating in the natural gas industry. But the following day a very different causal sequence disposed of the Kingfish forever.

Two opponents who had managed to stand against Long were Judge Benjamin F. Pavy and District Attorney R. Lee Garland. Their judicial district comprised the parishes of St. Landry and, ironically, Evangeline. Evangeline parish had never been able to outvote its yokemate for Long, but the Kingfish had devised a solution. It was the familiar gerrymander: his legislature would make Evangeline a separate district and combine St. Landry with three Long parishes. Like others loyal to Pavy, his son-in-law, Dr. Carl A. Weiss, Jr., was outraged. The mild-mannered eye, ear, nose, and throat specialist was said to be furious, moreover, at Long's insinuations of Negro blood in the Pavy family. Weiss was waiting in a corridor of the capitol building—the skyscraper which Long opponents called "Huey's silo"—on Sunday night, September 8, 1935, when Long emerged from a meeting and strode down the hallway toward the office of his faithful, rubber-stamp governor, O. K. Allen. He never reached it. Weiss stepped from behind a pillar and raised his hand. A gunshot reverberated off the marble walls as Long crumpled to the floor. Weiss fell riddled by the bullets of Long's bodyguards, dying instantly, unrecognizable after the fusillade of lead. Long sustained only one wound, but like Mercutio's it served, and six hours later the Kingfish was dead. The uncertainty about the circumstances of Long's death was increased by the disappearance of the fatal bullet. Weiss had drawn the short straw, said some, in a plot which included some of Long's own men. Weiss had not fired at all, said others, but merely gestured as he tried to intercede for his father-in-law. Long did not, like Eugene O'Neill's Emperor Jones, die by a special, silver bullet. But the bullet was special, and there was something of the element of the macabre, as in the demise of the other, less powerful emperor.

Although the rise and fall of Huey Long was in many ways more dramatic than that of other latter-day demagogues such as Senator Joseph McCarthy, the causes were if anything less complex. It could be argued "that the combination of ruling powers of Louisiana had maintained a tighter grip on the state since Reconstruction than had like groups in other states." Similarly, wrote Key, "the longer the period of unrestrained exploitation, the more violent will be the reaction when it comes."[21] There was no question about the complexity of the man. There were many qualities: "the comic impudence, the gay egotism, the bravado, the mean hatred, the fear."[22] Huey P. Long, Jr., could play the buffoon, but this mask concealed one of the keenest minds in American politics. He was to Alben Barkley "the smartest lunatic I ever saw in my whole life!" to Rebecca West "the most formidable kind of brer fox," and to H. G. Wells "a Winston Churchill who has never been at Harrow."[23] His wit and humor were folksy and bawdy, but they served—and they stung. Neither the enemy in the Standard Oil Company offices in Baton Rouge nor the aristocratic rival in the White House in Washington was immune. Huey could liken the servants of the Interests to devils, his state foes to rats and lice, and the President of the United States to a bird of prey. Herbert Hoover, he said, was like a hoot owl who burst in the hen house, swept the hen from her perch, and then caught her before she touched the floor. Roosevelt, he said, was like a scrooch owl, who "slips into the roost and scrooches up to the hen and talks softly to her. And the hen just falls in love with him, and the first thing you know, *there ain't no hen!*"[24]

The endurance of Long's organization during his lifetime (as he predicted, after him came the deluge) owed much to the fact that he kept faith, by and large, with the people who elected him, the wool hats and red necks, the mill hands and sapsuckers. For their allegiance, writes Schlesinger, "the people of Louisiana got a state government which did more for them than any other government in Louisiana's history . . . Schools, hospitals, roads and public services in general were better than ever before. Poor whites and even Negroes had unprecedented opportunities."[25] Huey had unprecedented opportunities himself, and he made the most of them. When his star was at its zenith, the Kansas City *Star* asserted that "Wall Street has furnished Louisiana about $50,000,000 since the Kingfish took hold . . ."[26] William Allen White saw much more than money involved. "Fascism always comes through a vast pretense of socialism backed by Wall Street money," he wrote. "Huey Long is the type we must fear."[27] Contributions flowed in from the oil, sulphur, railroad, banking, and utility interests.[28] The treasury agent who had led the investigation intended to put Huey

behind bars wrote that he "took plenty and he took it for Huey Pierce Long, which made him a tool of the vested interests he fought so vigorously."[29] Some, however, got little or none at all: "He sprinkled the state with roads and buildings. But he did little or nothing to raise wages for the workers, to stop child labor, to reduce the work day, to support trade unions, to provide pensions for the aged, to furnish relief to the unemployed, even to raise teachers' salaries. He left behind no record of social or labor legislation."[30] In spite of Long's oft-repeated slogan, no one can have been convinced that in the Kingfish's dominions Every Man was a King. But it was clear to see, for all who would, that One Man Wore a Crown.

To many critics, Huey P. Long, Jr., was an American Fascist. Others, while granting like Key that his "control of Louisiana more nearly matched the power of a South American dictator than that of any other American state boss," felt he was innocent of totalitarian ideology.[31] Huey rejected the comparison violently. Mentioned with Hitler, he roared, "don't liken me to that son of a bitch!"[32] He was willing to tolerate a similarity to Abraham Lincoln. Not surprisingly, he came off the better. "Lincoln didn't free the slaves in Louisiana," he boasted, "I did."[33] Another time, he was willing to acknowledge the Great Emancipator as one of his three teachers; the others, he said, were Andrew Jackson and Almighty God.[34] The conjunction of Lincoln and Long was in a strange sort of way apt. In the novels discussed in this chapter the two figures become almost mythic, presenting as through polarized, elements good and evil in American politics and culture.

In the following literary analysis, the Southern Demagogue is subsumed under the figure of the Southern Politician, for there appear in the novels—as there did in the South—leaders of a different stripe. Claude Pepper, a vigorous campaigner and eloquent orator on the stump in Florida, became in Washington one of the strongest advocates of New Deal policies. In Alabama, Big Jim Folsom waxed powerful against the planters and the "big mules" of industry and finance from the commanding position of the governor's chair. The difference between national and local politics for the Southern politician was exemplified by James F. Byrnes. For years a Roosevelt stalwart in Washington, he made White Supremacy his program's keystone in South Carolina. Aspects of conservatism were embodied in fiscal policies of Virginians Harry Byrd and Carter Glass, whereas a conservatism so radical as to give rise to the short-lived Dixiecrat Party of 1948 had as its standard-bearer Governor J. Strom Thurmond of South Carolina. On still another level was Senator J. W. Fulbright, who rose through the faction-ridden politics of Arkansas to a position of power and eminence in the Senate. There he has been not only a liberal Democrat—so far as practical exigencies of Arkansas politics would permit—but a man who has helped shape far-reaching policy under more than one administration. But for all these variants, the stereotype of the demagogue persists. As Cash remarks, it "would not be true to say that . . . the South had no choice save between demagogues of the Right and demagogues of the Left (in their appeal, not their practice, of course). But there would be a good deal of truth in it."[35]

One would not hope to give in a few pages the outlines of the twentieth-century Southern politics which have provided the milieu which produced the novels. But some of the salient features of this political terrain can be seen. After Federal attempts at Reconstruction ceased, the Southern states used the Black Codes to re-establish White Supremacy by substituting peonage for slavery. Then, after Populism foundered upon the rock of cooperation with the Negro, Southern politics emerged as a one-party system. The powerful planters of the Black Belts and new industrialists and financiers of the cities exerted great pressure to maintain the racial and electoral *status quo* (when not in fact extending disfranchisement) and to protect their commercial and financial interests. From the early years of the century they were often opposed by demagogues and popular leaders rising from among the people (or at least giving the appearance of having done so) and making common cause with them against the big planters and the native and absentee industrialists and financiers. Concurrently, industrialization increased and with it the number of industrial workers. But labor's growth into a strong force was militantly opposed by both powerful employers favored under the law and by regional attitudes inimical to such concepts. And though Federal aid was welcomed in the Depression years, the economic structure might prevent it from filtering down as far as it was meant to go—often to the areas where it was most desperately needed—and the incursions of Federal power were resented and repelled.[36]

Whether political or nonpolitical, serious contemporary fiction depicting the South usually emphasizes problems arising out of the racial conflict and dilemma. This is, of course, only one problem, even if the most acute, of a region with a tragic history. It is one aspect of a larger problem: "Obviously the conversion of the South into a democracy in the sense that the mass of people vote and have a hand in their governance poses one of the most staggering tasks for statesmanship in the western world."[37] Surely the extremity of this situation is responsible for much of the power of the best of these novels of Southern politics, the best one of which stands alone.

### LITERARY CHARACTERISTICS

One of the major assertions of twentieth-century American literature has been that the South is not just different from the rest of the country but that it is, as Long liked to call himself, *sui generis*. The work of such artists as William Faulkner, Thomas Wolfe, Eudora Welty, Tennessee Williams, Carson McCullers, and Erskine Caldwell stands as a testimonial to this fact. This same uniqueness is to be seen in the political novel, especially in fourteen novels which appeared in the years between 1922 and 1960. They are novels in which the sense of place is so strong as to set them apart from those of other areas. Often novels of bossism or corruption might as easily

have been set in New York as in Ohio, in New Jersey as in Illinois. The novels in this chapter are set (by statement or inference) in Virginia, West Virginia, Kentucky, Arkansas, North Carolina, Florida, Mississippi, Louisiana, and Oklahoma. None could have been set outside the South, and as the mark of place is upon the novels, so it is upon the men. It has helped create the most dramatic archetypal figure among these novels—the Southern Demagogue—and the best novel—Robert Penn Warren's *All the King's Men.*

The novelists insist on the South's uniqueness. In *The Sound Wagon* a congressman tells T. S. Stribling's Northern protagonist, "In the South we lack system. We have only a few political machines, and they work creakily and uneasily. Our big deciding vote swings with damnable uncertainty on the whim of the voter. You can buy votes in the South, all you want; but you can't get 'em delivered . . . the Southern votes come singly, and the Southern congressman spends his time getting elected."[38] But the regional differences, of course, go deeper than this. They are the products of historical forces which shaped the past and determined the present. In a passage in *The Kingpin* (1953) which shows the often-encountered influence of William Faulkner's rhetoric and cadences, Tom Wicker writes, " . . . out of this past . . . come the people of the country South, the backwoods South . . . timeless, slow-moving, ill-fed, ill-housed, ill-clad, prey to all the dark moods and passions, all the hates and hurts and beliefs of a land and a heritage blighted, diseased, cursed by an old black evil, an evil and a heritage they never saw, never knew, only accepted in some deep and bitter resignation. . . ."[39]

Many of these novelists seem to endorse the view of Southern history which Malcolm Cowley and others see in Faulkner's saga of Yoknapatawpha County. His "Myth of the South," especially in "The Bear" and *Absalom, Absalom!* (1936), portrays a fertile land, developed by powerful aristocrats and aggressive New Men but made vulnerable by the seed of corruption inherent in the moral evil of slavery. The War and its aftermath come as retribution with native and foreign exploiters replacing the armies of occupation to complete the tragedy. The forces leading to the catastrophe were, of course, complex. One contributory force was that form of ancestor worship which Hamilton Basso's protagonist in *The View from Pompey's Head* (1954) calls Southern Shintoism. Robert Rylee's protagonist in *The Ring and the Cross* (1947) contends that General Robert E. Lee should have accepted Lincoln's proffered appointment as commander-in-chief of the Federal forces in order to shorten the war: "And partly due to Lee's loyalty to Virginia, we still sit here in the South, worshipping before the ruined tombs of our corrupt ancestors, blaming others for our ills—and I grant you others have greatly aggravated them—when it was we ourselves who set off the chain of evil circumstance."[40]

In these novels then, the War has left a legacy of poverty, sickness, ignorance, and hatred. Hatred of the Negro is complemented by xenophobia usually directed against the Yankee, the Jew, and latterly, the agents of organized labor. The new order emerging with the dissolution of the old has most of the ante-bellum vices and few of the virtues. Violence and immorality are commonplace. Organizations such as the Ku Klux Klan perpetrate lynchings, mutilations, and beatings. Individuals in public as well as private life commit acts of immorality and sexual pathology which often go beyond simple indices of personal aberration and become symbolic of general social decadence as well. Besides the double standard for men and women, there is the one for white people and Negroes. The heritage of the past is seen not only in the clear and obvious—inadequate schools and roads—but in the devious and covert: leases of state resources to influential entrepreneurs, tax structures which favor the moneyed planters, the utilities, and the corporate interests. Corollary is discrimination against the exploited, underpaid factory hands and hard-pressed share croppers—the "crackers," the "lint-heads," and the "red-necks."

The protagonists produced by these conditions fall clearly into distinct types. Almost all of these Southern politicians are prominent office holders; only a few are Bosses who rule from behind the scenes. These few have a good deal in common with those in Chapter Two. But again, the pervasiveness of the environment, the special conditions in which they attain and exercise power, make them Southern politicians first and Bosses second. Men of lowly birth, usually, they ally themselves with the great mass of the poor. Making their appeal to the "hill-billies" and "wool hats," they pledge roads, schools, and health services, promising to "share the wealth and soak the rich." Others (sometimes these same men once safely ensconced in office) ally themselves with the power companies and large corporations to prey upon the majority of the electorate and the large disfranchised substratum below. A few share the motivation of the Young Knight. Most conform to a pattern, however, which can be called that of the Southern Demagogue—the man who plays upon the emotions of the masses for power, profit, and place. He is usually physically powerful, strong, shrewd, and acute. He has a pragmatic grasp of human psychology in his manipulations of individuals and crowds. He is a dramatic orator whose campaigning combines political issues with the emotions of the revivalist camp meeting and the traveling medicine show. The tones and rhythms of the campaign orations reproduce the antiphonal responses of preacher and congregation. And with them come the twanging of the string bands' hillbilly ballads, the shrilling crescendos of brasses blaring "Dixie."

The Southern Demagogue is usually a complete relativist. He uses what he has to work with, and often the ends are contaminated by the means. He sometimes has an alter ego who may be a villainous henchman or a whipping boy. He is likely to be married to a good woman, whose credentials are sometimes verified by her having been a school-teacher. In almost every instance, however, she has an opposite number too. The Southern Demagogue needs the seductive, loose-moraled sex symbol who becomes his mistress.[41] He is aggressive and ambitious.

Like the Young Knight, he is apt to have Presidential aspirations. But fully half these lives end in violent death.

This violence is in harmony with the violence of the country. In some of these settings, frontier only eighty years before, the democratic processes are often carried out in an atmosphere hostile to them. Politics are almost always conducted under a one-party system. One of David Graham Phillips's protagonists, convinced that both parties were agents paid from the same source, would perhaps have welcomed this simplification. But this system is, if anything, more complicated, with primary elections involving run-offs, strategies for splitting an opponent's strength, and the less subtle devices of innuendo, slander, and fraud. Issues are not uncommonly resolved by gunfire, and in these novels set in the 1930's and 1940's there are fascist overtones. Groups of returning World War II veterans band together, as in the novels of American Fascism, to combat near-totalitarian rule. An analogue of this political violence appears in sexual violence. Seduction, adultery, rape, and deviation do not exhaust it. Sadism is commonplace, and there are ingenious combinations and elaborations which can only be called sexual pathology.

### LITERARY ANCESTORS

The violent passions and events of Reconstruction found violent expression in partisan fiction. Thomas Dixon, Jr., a North Carolina minister who proudly proclaimed himself a nephew of the Grand Titan of the Ku Klux Klan, was fervent and prolific. In novels such as *The Leopard's Spots* (1902), he depicted an outraged South defending itself as best it could against the hateful repression and harassment of a vindictive victor. *The Clansman* (1905) gave even wider currency to Dixon's vehement convictions, especially his anti-Negro feelings, when it was made into one of the first genuine classics of a new medium—the motion pictures. Still perennially showing nearly a half-century after its production, *The Birth of a Nation* caused riots when it was first shown. At the opposite extreme from Dixon was Albion W. Tourgée, an Ohio-born Union officer who resided in the South for fifteen years after the war. Serving as judge of the Superior Court of North Carolina, he had earned the enmity of most of his fellow citizens. In his awkward but intensely-felt novels Tourgée argued that the Federal government had blundered badly in the measures it imposed upon the South. It had failed tragically by thrusting freedom and responsibility upon uneducated masses unable fully to deal with either, then abandoning them and the decent human beings who attempted to ameliorate their lot. The South had predictably responded with repression and atrocity, and Tourgée's novels dilated upon both. In *A Fool's Errand* (1879) and *Bricks Without Straw* (1880) he had diagnosed, prescribed, and preached. "We presumed, that by the suppression of rebellion, the Southern White man had become identical with the Caucasian of the North in thought and sentiment; and that the slave, by emancipation, had become a saint and a Solomon at once," he wrote in the former volume. "So we tried to build up communities there which should be identical in thought, sentiment, growth, and development, with those of the North. It was *A Fool's Errand.*"[42] Later, in a prescription for the future, part of which was to be echoed in the next century by such leaders as Booker T. Washington, Tourgée exhorted: "Make the spelling-book the scepter of national power . . . Poor-whites, Freedmen, Ku-Klux, and Bulldozers are all alike the harvest of ignorance. The Nation can not afford to grow such a crop" (366-367). Although Tourgée's novels dealt more with political processes than did the equally wild farragoes of Dixon, neither author's work was as preponderantly concerned with these processes as the novels which follow. These violent partisans, dealing with the time of dislocation and upheaval, treated at length the larger economic and sociological aspects of the problem as well as its political manifestations. But imperfect as these works were, they enunciated themes which were to recur and sketched in the historical background against which better artists would later set their work.

### EARLY NOVELS: THE RIGHTEOUS

In the three earliest novels of Southern politics in this century, the protagonists were neither Bosses nor demagogues although they briefly achieved both power and notoriety. Two of them emerged from the lower strata of a war-scarred society, making their appeal to an electorate predominantly composed of the impoverished, the uneducated, and the exploited. Unlike most of those to follow, they were unselfishly motivated throughout. The third protagonist was a follower rather than a leader. Although obviously intended to be amusing and even lovable, his effect is the opposite. Insensitive and boorish, he exemplifies aspects of the decadence of his culture. Ironically, in his own limited and insensitive way, he is one of the champions of the right in this culture.

Ellen Glasgow's *One Man in His Time* (1922) is apparently set in Richmond, Virginia, in the years immediately following the first World War. A young aristocrat viewing the present against the dissolution of the past perceives that "the tide of the new ideas was still rising. Democracy, relentless, disorderly, and strewn with the wreckage of finer things, had overwhelmed the world of established customs in which he lived."[43] For Stephen Culpeper the embodiment of this change is Gideon Vetch, white trash born in a circus tent and now governor of the state of Virginia. To another aristocrat he is a demagogue who "deliberately sold his office in exchange for his election—" (148). Vetch does have shady connections. His defense—to be echoed twenty-five years later by the best embodiment of this type—is necessity: "the end for which I work seems to me vastly more important than the methods I use or the instruments that I employ" (173). His goals—new labor laws, social benefits, and eventual nationalization of mines and railroads—are to his aristocratic opponents "mere bombast . . . but the kind of thing that is dangerous in a crowd" (150).

Vetch's figure is immediately familiar, a "tall, rugged figure built of good bone and muscle and sound to the core . . ." (22). This leader of lowly birth smiles down at people "from his great height" (376), impressing even young Culpeper with "the most tremendous dignity a human being could attain—the unconscious dignity of natural forces . . ." (27). Around his story Mrs. Glasgow twists those of Culpeper and Vetch's daughter (another pair of politics-crossed lovers), two older lovers, and the secrets of Vetch's past. In the foreground of the action, he tries to find a solution to an explosive labor dispute while attempting to cleanse his Administration. At this point Mrs. Glasgow does again what she had done twenty years earlier in *The Voice of the People:* she gratuitously kills her protagonist. Again the means is mob violence. Trying to stop a fight, Vetch is shot. Later an opponent eulogizes his "humanity that is as rare as genius itself" (377).

Mrs. Glasgow's intention, as in earlier novels, was to depict another era in Virginia history. Surveying the changes wrought in social and political life by still another war, she contrasted something of the best and worst of the old order and the new. Culpeper was a familiar figure: the enervated aristocrat being thrust aside by the vigorous New Man such as Vetch. Culpeper also demonstrated the process of breakthrough from a stultifying existence to a widening and liberating one. Apart from a few gaucheries in dialogue, the novel is free from obvious awkwardness. But it never wholly succeeds in any of the author's apparent intentions. Each of the explorations is made with a combination of obviousness and insufficiency. And her greatest error, of course, which demonstrates her inability to meet the demands of her theme, is her dispatching of her hero just as he comes to grips with his basic challenges: economic reform in the face of powerful opposition, and the task of escaping contamination by the instruments and methods he has used.

A very different sort of protagonist stands at the center of Glenn Allan's *Old Manoa* (1932). He is a tall, thin man of sixty who wears a mustache and goatee. Old Manoa serves as commissioner of Towhit County, Tennessee, only to oblige his childhood friend Jedge Warmsley, the hideously fat but benevolent Boss of the county.[44] The novel spins out the story of the revolt of Jedge's appointees. In collusion with them is the Phoenix Power Company. Aided by "mountain men" with guns, Jedge and Manoa repulse them in action culminating in arson, assault, and death. Balancing these elements are a romance, the relationship between the two old men, and the character of Manoa himself. Loving the horses he breeds and the blue-grass country where his family has lived for more than a hundred years, he is meant to be a cantankerous but lovable old gentleman. But the humor is thin and Manoa's lovableness is not convincing enough to conceal attitudes also found in some of the worst specimens in these Southern novels. To stop his Negro cook from summoning the doctor, this gallant Southern gentleman throws his whisky glass at her. He flings sticks at his old servant Bunk and refuses to allow Bunk's son Jamie to wear a hat "because Jamie understood a whack or a poke better and quicker than he did an order.[45]

This novel presents a curious kind of authorial innocence. It is meant to be humorous, but the discerning reader is much more likely to feel nausea. Towhit County politics are as much a travesty of the democratic ideal as are those in many novels of corruption, and the "good" men who win in the end (with assistance of the state Boss) are authoritarians with racist mentalities whose characters seem to rest, at least in part, upon substrata of sloth, gluttony, and brutality verging on sadism.

The last of the wholly idealistic protagonists in these novels of the Southern Politician appeared in Charles Morrow Wilson's *Rabble Rouser* (1936). A young red-headed farmhand, he rises to the governorship of Arkansas before he is beaten by the opposition and the Interests (another Power and Light Company). The most interesting aspect of this novel is not Cabe Hargis's career as such but the characteristics which make him an early representative of a common type. His home is Hemmed-in-Holler (threatened by a projected power company dam) in Izard County, and his style, strategy, and values derive ultimately from this fact. His speech is countrified, and the emotion he projects through it is genuine. Hargis turns all his emotional oratory on sympathetic juries when he acts for small litigants against the trusts. On the stump, he loves to see his hearers throw their black hats into the air. He is "for" men with red necks, he tells them, because he is a "redneck" too. (Robert Penn Warren's Willie Stark will later use this pejorative phrase to his own advantage.) He is folksy yet shrewd, campaigning in remote areas other candidates rarely see, sleeping under whatever roof will give him shelter, and wearing down an opponent on a grueling speaking tour. He holds his own in an environment where running a dummy candidate to split an opponent's vote is one of the subtler devices.[46]

*Rabble Rouser* often reads like parody, so broad do its characters and dialects become. Yet it is far from the worst of this group. Amid the overdone accents (sometimes suggesting the raftsmen of Twain's *Life on the Mississippi*) are lyric passages on the seasons, the flow of time, and the fruitfulness of nature. For this study, however, the greatest interest resides in the depiction of this young "rabble rouser" who gains power through a combination of skills. Using intelligence and country-style oratory, he allies his own interests with those of the underprivileged mass of the people from whom he himself comes. And unlike many who rise through the same methods, he does not desert his friends after gaining power.

### THE SOUTHERN POLITICIAN AS BOSS

The few Southern politicians who operate primarily as Bosses work behind the scenes rather than as dynamic leaders openly swaying the masses. They differ from their counterparts elsewhere in their manipulation of regional prejudices and resentments, their reliance upon power and intimidation more than upon favors and agreements, and—in one instance at least—readiness to resort to brutality and violence.

Robert Wilder's *Flamingo Road* (1942) dealt with not just one Boss but two. One of them, like Kevin Costello in Wilder's later *The Wine of Youth* (1955), is a wealthy construction man whose main interest in politics is protecting his investments, although he does what he can to guard Florida "against the predatory instincts of the men who shared some measure of [power] with him."[47] Dan Curtis is a kind of half-hearted Chamber of Commerce Robin Hood, for "What he took came from other men: from the stupidly conniving, the avaricious, the combinations which insisted they were smarter than he, but not from his state. If tax assessments favored his enterprises, franchises and contracts came his way, then he built good roads, operated efficient utilities, and, now and then, cut a small slice of pie for his investors." (201). His enemy is a monstrously obese county sheriff who may owe something to Faulkner's Flem Snopes, possessing as he does "a reptilian treachery and the persistence of a beaver" (237). Titus Semple builds his power carefully, assiduously cultivating both the white farmers and the Negroes. He defeats Curtis's coalition by using evidence of their own corrupt practices, but another familiar Wilder character—the intelligent and ambitious whore with a heart of gold (who also happens to have become Curtis's mistress)—murders him for past insults and injuries. Like *The Wine of Youth*, this novel is technically dextrous. Its fluent prose is almost glossy, and correspondingly, its climaxes have the ring of melodrama, as its assignations have the texture of pulp fiction.

The extremes of Southern politics show up more clearly in a novel by Franklin Coen set in Tennessee or Georgia. *Vinegar Hill* (1950) begins with the retirement of a former congressman and cabinet secretary called typical "of all of the Old Faithfuls," such as Borah, Norris, Hull, Wagner, and McAdoo.[48] He finds a struggle under way between the Boss who made him and returning World War II veterans. Finding that the organization uses intimidation and murder, Secretary Tobias remonstrates with one of Boss Tilden's men: "Red's a puny, inept Huey Long. Or tryin' to be. Long, at least, had some feelin' for people. This'll get you nothin' but trouble" (145). The reply is revealing: "Maybe, Toby. Only understand that Red's playin' for big stakes. The *South*, sir . . . The North ain't sendin' carpetbaggers down here, they're sendin' ideas—damn lousy subversive ideas!" (145). After the Secretary attempts to repudiate his indebtedness to Tilden, the veterans go further. Besieging a hundred deputized out-of-state "gorillas," they breach the courthouse wall with a kind of Bangalore torpedo, killing Tilden in the struggle. The new sheriff solemnly informs the press that "the will of the people had almost been subverted, and that this must not be allowed, even at the cost of so many dead" (308-309).[49]

Tilden's power derives not only from a ruthless machine but also from the skillful use of economic fears and resentment against the North. Every prejudice and attitude likely to be useful is mobilized. Symptomatic of a pervasive immorality and sadism is the deputy sheriff who violates female Negro prisoners and also intimidates a respectable young Negro woman to the same purpose. As a young Congressman, Tobias had been thought a Bull Moose partisan, a trust-buster, and a radical. Although he had later been forced to compromise his principles, his long career had still maintained a fair outward aspect. Supporting it, however, had been the rotten substructure of the machine. Behind the machine's façade had been the decadence of the society which supported it. But in this particular middling novel there were signs of a resurgence of decency and responsibility in the values the veterans defend.

### THE SOUTHERN DEMAGOGUE

The first of the nine novels dealing with the Southern Demagogue appeared in 1941, with five of the rest following within the space of six years. Edward Kimbrough's *From Hell to Breakfast* came eleven years after the death of James K. Vardaman, six years after the demise of Huey Long, and during the lifetime of Theodore S. Bilbo. It displayed a man and a milieu whose characteristics reappeared in the novels that followed and were to be raised to their highest power in Warren's *All the King's Men*. In his foreword Kimbrough declared he was using "the technique of satirical exaggeration," portraying "no specific Mississippi politician . . . but rather . . . satirizing a particular type of man." The object of this satire is Gus Roberts, United States senator and Boss of this state once represented by Vardaman and Bilbo. He is opposed for re-election by the son of an old friend, a pro-labor lawyer glad to argue poor men's cases. (When Roberts's daughter falls in love with the young man, the newspapers naturally enough call it a Romeo-Juliet romance.) Roberts wins easily, and his opponent is lucky to escape from Roberts-organized, white-clad "White Knights" intent on castrating him.

Roberts's perennial success is due to his organization, his conscienceless shrewdness in battle, and his sway over the electorate. Once a Methodist minister and revivalist preacher, he still orates with his old-time fervor. His denunciations of radicalism stem not so much from conviction as from their crowd appeal. Well on in years, he still enjoys his long-time association with a whore-mistress named Fanny. When his long-separated wife sues for divorce on adultery during the campaign, he counters adroitly. He declares he wants no divorce and is saved again at a revival meeting. His rule is characterized by graft and bribery, abuses such as illegal use of prison labor, and hate directed at Negroes, Jews, and outsiders. Most of the characters dilate upon the ills of the South, usually blaming them on someone or something else—Yankee-owned plants or labor organizers within them. There is the usual contempt for idealism and reform. The voters are generally regarded as dolts who can be bought with a paid-up poll tax, corn liquor, a cheap permanent for their wives, or as a last resort, cash money. The constituents most zealously protected are the rich merchants, the mill-owners, and the landowners. Throughout the novel there are references to Hitler, to Naziism, to Fascism. The similarities between their regimes and the local

one, particularly in violence and corruption, are explicitly noted by the defeated candidate at the novel's end. *From Hell to Breakfast* is a tiresome novel presenting a dismal picture of its locale, but it is a picture whose details are corroborated in the novels to come.

A year later Hamilton Basso's *Sun in Capricorn* appeared, its text preceded by the epigraph, "Capricorn is said to be the sign of ambition. It looks like the horns of a goat." The cuckoldry suggested in the second sentence applies neither to Hazzard X, the narrator, nor to Governor Gilgo Slade—whose first name might well set the echoes ringing in the memories of many. Slade is campaigning for the Senate in a northern Louisiana parish, but he has his eye on the Presidency. If anyone is betrayed, it is the voter. Wooed by Slade with old-time, circus-style campaign entertainment—complete with a hillbilly band—he is bombarded from stump and radio by a Big Lie technique suggesting that of contemporary European practitioner, Dr. Joseph Goebbels. The narrator's true and passionate, but unfortunately illegal, love affair is used by Slade against his opponent, the narrator's uncle. Hazzard X's resolve to assassinate Slade is frustrated only by someone else's getting there first. The death of the nobly motivated assassin under the machine guns of Gilgo's bodyguards is another passage likely to set the echoes of memory ringing. At the novel's ironic end, Hazzard X hears two "peckerwoods" regretting Slade's demise and extolling his greatness.

In spite of a convincing narrator, this work is at bottom thin and superficial. There are many untied strands of plot and theme, and Slade, on whom much of the weight of the novel must rest, is only a cardboard ranter and raver. He is, however, another avatar of the type brought to his sinister apotheosis four years later in Warren's Willie Stark.[50]

John Dos Passos's version of the Southern Demagogue archetype, *Number One*, appeared a year after Basso's in 1943. It showed the illness which produced the Demagogue as it flourished in an oil-rich state strongly suggesting Oklahoma. (With *Adventures of a Young Man* [1939] and *The Grand Design* [1948], it formed a partially connected narrative. Following a number of characters through radicalism and corruption in the 1920's and 1930's, the Spanish Civil War, and the early days of the New Deal, the three volumes were finally published together as the trilogy, *District of Columbia*.) Texarcola-born Homer T. "Chuck" Crawford first reaches the District of Columbia as a congressman. The burden of the novel is his rise as he wins a Senate seat and goes on to enrich himself through state oil lands. And when the oil scandal breaks (suggesting a later and smaller Teapot Dome), he is still secure. His secretary, speech-writer, and public-relations man—alcoholic Toby Spotswood, the other major character in the novel—goes to jail.

Crawford is a shrewd tactician running with the hare in public and hunting with the hounds in private. The slogan he offers the people is "Every Man a Millionaire," and he demonstrates the seeming simple-heartedness that makes him one of them by such endearing mannerisms as playing the ocarina. The biography written for his campaign is entitled "Poor Boy to President." His rusticity is no more than skin deep, and like most others of this archetype, he sees the White House as an attainable prize. His relationship with a roadhouse vocalist is as pleasant as that with his Struck Oil Corporation is profitable.[51] And the latter association is disrupted only because of his exercise of his new-found power. A newspaper commentator writes: "his one man filibuster which so neatly upset one of the majority's most cherished applecarts has so angered the Administration stalwarts that they are willing to go the limit. . . ."[52] Crawford differs from most of the other Southern Demagogues in that he meets no serious check. Toby's atonement for his work for Crawford (spurred by the last letter of his younger brother, Glenn, killed fighting in Spain), provides the scapegoat for the income-tax-evasion trial looming as the novel ends.

Though *Number One* is the weakest novel of the trilogy, it is by no means an ordinary novel. Using few of the experimental devices of *U.S.A.,* Dos Passos tells the story often with directness and power. His only special effects are chapter introductions forming a continuous description of "the people"—a farmer, a mechanic, a chainstore clerk, a miner, and a business executive. The concluding italicized passage, in Dos Passos's familiar hortatory manner, adjures the reader:

> weak as the weakest, strong as the strongest,
> the people are the republic,
> the people are you.
>
> (304)

The appeal was a familiar one—heard in the 1930's and earlier, though then warning of a different danger. This appeal sounded much the same as that of Sinclair Lewis in *It Can't Happen Here,* urging the citizen to help preserve political freedom by discharging his duty. But Dos Passos's Demagogue did not, somehow, seem as desperate and threatening as his author's tone suggested.

The sense of *déjà vu* becomes stronger as the reader goes further. And the transparent concealments of several other authors conceal nothing. The title of Adria Locke Langley's novel, *A Lion Is in the Streets* (1945), suggests the "most horrid sights seen by the watch" which Calpurnia describes to Caesar in Act II, Scene ii, of Shakespeare's *Julius Caesar.*[53] But the locale is variously Sherman, Crescent City, or Cypress Bend in Delamore Parish of the Magnolia State. The protagonist is a one-time sharecropper and traveling salesman married to a former schoolteacher. A self-educated lawyer, Hank Martin passes the state bar examination with a phenomenally high score. He rises from commissioner of public works and highways to governor of the state on the strength of his campaign theme of "Divide the Riches." His "kindlin' power" inspires his followers through speeches loaded with Biblical references and rural idiom. It is a camp-meeting technique exercised in revival-style tents. More importantly, however, he organizes a following of country people, paying a stipend to the widows among them out of a $50,000 fee he has frightened out of the Southern Light and Power Co. He insures the franchise of his illiterate followers by "Hank Martin's God-blessed Grandpappy Law," which "says that a man who voted in or before 1867, his sons or his children's children cannot be deprived a' their franchise because of failure t' pass educational or property qualifications."[54] From photostatic copies of lists of these early voters Martin assigns enfranchising ancestors to his followers.

Predictably, corruption follows power as Martin replaces his fanatical immediate followers with a bodyguard of professional "gorillas." He commits adultery, and his disillusioned wife Verity prepares to leave him.[55] She feels he has failed as a governor as well as a husband: "With all her heart she wanted . . . the things Hank planned—freedom from tax for the small cabin and the few acres; for the present taxes on the poor were exorbitant . . . she wanted to see schools, and, yes, free schoolbooks, and fine roads. Did the end justify the means? Hank declared it did. She didn't know. She only knew she hated the method" (329). Though he has built highways and a glistening capital building, an opponent likens him and his tactics to Hitler and his Saar plebiscite. His wife has sadly compared him to Mussolini, and he justifies her estimate as he plans the systematic ruination of the opposition's best men.[56] When the assassin's bullet ends his presidential aspirations, Mrs. Langley's flights of fancy transport her story beyond the bounds of reality. Discovering the assassin in a clothes closet, Verity and her friends promptly aid in his escape as a former member of Martin's staff eulogizes the killer to Martin's dry-eyed relict: "He's all the men of the Boston Tea Party; he's the men at Valley Forge . . . he's all the liberty-loving men who live by Patrick Henry's words" (479). It is here, obviously, that Mrs. Langley has departed from the life of her model in the interests of her fiction. Although Dr. Weiss may well have been concerned for democracy in Louisiana, partisan concerns seem more likely to have been uppermost in his mind.

*A Lion Is in the Streets* was a badly written novel crammed with clichés from the faithful mammy with the syrupy accent to the flashy gangster spectacularly exterminated. The reader is spared neither the melodramatic deathbed message nor the dollops of sex. The novel's principal interest lies in the way it amalgamates the chief characteristics of the Southern Demagogue as they had thus far evolved plus the now nearly ritualized pattern of his rise, rule, and fall. The laws of probability alone would indicate that it was now time for a treatment of this archetype that would do justice to its inherent drama, using its symbolic value to extend its meaning farther beyond the regional. Such a work would comment not only upon man in his political role but also in his engagement in the perennial human dilemma.

When Robert Penn Warren's *All the King's Men* appeared in 1946 it met almost immediate critical and financial success. Seven years later, Warren commented that, "the journalistic relevance of *All the King's Men* had a good deal to do with what interest it evoked. My politician hero, whose name, in the end, was Willie Stark, was quickly equated with the late Senator Huey P. Long, whose fame, even outside of Louisiana, was yet green in pious tears, anathema, and speculation."[57] Warren went on to deny that his novel was a *roman à clef.*

> I do not mean to imply [he wrote] that there was no connection between Governor Stark and Senator Long. Certainly, it was the career of Long and the atmosphere of Louisiana that suggested the play that was to become the novel. But suggestion does not mean identity, and even if I had wanted to make Stark a projection of Long . . . I did not, and do not, know what Long was like, and what were the secret forces that drove him along his violent path to meet the bullet in the Capitol.[58]

As Warren said, the novel was widely construed to be the slightly fictionalized life of Senator Long, in spite of the very different and complex intent and motivation which went into its genesis. This misconception has to a large extent become a part of modern literary folklore. In the average class the student who suggests that the novel is about responsibility or self-knowledge will be outnumbered by those who reply, with the quick assurance of the young, "It's about Huey Long." To do them justice, however, there was much in the novel that *did* suggest the flamboyant personality and spectacular career of the Louisiana senator. The figure who was to become Willie Stark, Warren wrote, was first conceived as

> a man whose personal motivation had been, in one sense, idealistic, who in many ways was to serve the cause of social betterment, but who was corrupted by power, even by power exercised against corruption. That is, his means defile his ends. But more than that, he was to be a man whose power was based on the fact that somehow he could vicariously fulfill some secret needs of the people about him . . . But . . . the politician was to discover, more and more, his own emptiness and his own alienation.[59]

Vastly superior to others like it on the moral, philosophic, and symbolic levels, Warren's novel excels too in its technique and the texture of its often poetic prose. On the narrative levels it has much in common with the others. Willie Stark is, for instance, a farm boy who sells products door-to-door then becomes a self-taught lawyer. County treasurer (in a state resembling Louisiana), he becomes governor and, at least jocularly, a Presidential aspirant.[60] Guided and supported by his wife, another former schoolteacher, Willie is at first a naive idealist. Disillusionment comes after he has been tricked into running for governor by one candidate anxious to split the "cockleburr" vote which will go to another strong in the country districts. With money earned in litigation for independent leaseholders against an oil company, Willie campaigns again, still "symbolically the spokesman for the tongue-tied population of honest men."[61] Even after corruption has set in, Willie's hypnotic oratory still expresses the idealism at first so strong.

And it is your right [he tells them] that every child shall have a complete education. That no person aged and infirm shall want or beg for bread. That the man who produces something shall be able to carry it to market without miring to the hub, without toll. That no poor man's house or land shall be taxed. That the rich men and the great companies that draw wealth from this state shall pay this state a fair share. That you shall not be deprived of hope! (277)

He is a man of extraordinary determination and endurance. Besides his power to fulfill the needs of others, he is a man of other remarkable parts, possessing great shrewdness and an encyclopedic memory. But he is a complete relativist who says that good is made from bad, that "You just make it up as you go along" (273). And his view of the innate sinfulness of human nature lies behind his use of any means to gain his ends: "You got to use what you've got. You got to use fellows like Byram, and Tiny Duffy, and that scum down in the Legislature. You can't make bricks without straw, and most of the time all the straw you got is secondhand . . ." (145). Willie's actions are dictated more and more by expediency, and both he and his methods are contaminated. Turning to blackmail and coercion, he is forced into trafficking with the shadiest elements of his opposition. When death comes from an outraged brother of one of Willie's mistresses, it seems in retribution for all his sins.

Warren had written that "one of the figures that stood in the shadows of imagination behind Willie Stark . . . was the scholarly and benign figure of William James." He added,

> I did have some notions about the phenomenon of which Long was but one example, and I tried to put some of those notions into my book. Something about those notions and something of what I felt to be the difference between the person Huey P. Long and the fiction Willie Stark, may be indicated by the fact that in the verse play [which was the first embodiment of the idea] the name of the politician was at one time Talos—the name of the brutal, blank-eyed "iron groom" of Spenser's *Faerie Queene,* the pitiless servant of the Knight of Justice. My conception grew wider, but that element always remained, and Willie Stark remained, in one way, Willie Talos. In other words, Talos is the kind of doom that democracy may invite upon itself. The book, however, was not intended to be a book about politics. Politics merely provided the framework story in which the deeper concerns, whatever their final significance, might work themselves out.[62]

Warren's words about the character's function regarding democracy's dangers—sounding a good deal like those of Dos Passos and Lewis—are borne out in the pages crammed with political events. There is the depiction of the corrupt machine which invites its own destruction and of the kind of native dictatorship which succeeds it. And besides the study of political psychology, there is a guide, almost, to pragmatic politics: techniques for coercing legislators, quashing impeachment proceedings, and mustering support for candidates while chipping away at the opponents.

But the politics were, after all, a frame for the deeper concerns of the story. These deeper concerns and this functional use of politics were paradoxically responsible for the stature of the novel, so much larger than that of its competitors, a paradoxical situation which will be examined later. The deeper level of *All the King's Men* was indicated by the epigraph chosen from *Purgatorio*, III, of Dante's *Divine Comedy: "Mentre che la speranza ha fior del verde."* Together with the preceding line, it may be translated,

> . . . man is not so lost that eternal love may not
> return
> So long as hope retaineth ought of green.

If the epigraph pointed toward redemption, the title pointed away from it. It was immediately obvious that Warren had drawn on the child's nursery rhyme, "Humpty Dumpty." But he was using it in an anything but childish way, for the key word was "fall." The religious connotation was strongly suggested as well as the secular one. Each of the major characters fell from a state of comparative grace into sin, chiefly through an act of betrayal—of others, of self, or of both, the word "betray" occurring importantly in more than half a dozen contexts throughout the novel. Willie has first been betrayed by the agents of the Harrison machine who gain his trust and induce him to run for governor. He is later betrayed into the hands of his killer by a jealous mistress and a vengeful underling. But as he has betrayed his wife in his liaisons, so he has betrayed the electorate and the best elements in his own nature. Jack Burden, the novel's narrator, has betrayed the faith which his youthful sweetheart, Anne Stanton, had placed in him by refusing to give direction to his life. Later, by revealing her father's misconduct he shatters one of the bases on which she has constructed her scale of values. This in turn leads to her liaison with Willie, destroying one of the last illusions by which Jack has lived. As Jack puts it, "That was the Anne Stanton whom Willie Stark had picked out, who had finally betrayed me, or rather, had betrayed an idea of mine which had had more importance for me than I had ever realized" (327). Burden's real father, Judge Irwin, the friend of Jack's putative father, has betrayed his friend by the adultery with Mrs. Burden in which Jack is begotten. For Willie's political purposes, Jack betrays Judge Irwin. Uncovering evidence of his misdeeds (in which Anne's father was accessory), Jack reveals them to the Judge, precipitating his suicide.

This motif of the fall into sin pervades the novel, appearing even in secondary stories and symbolic incidents. The family story contained in the Cass Mastern papers which are to form the basis of Jack's doctoral dissertation in history—if he can ever come to terms with it and its meaning—has as its most dramatic and meaningful incident the betrayal by one friend of another with the latter's wife.[63] When Jack visits his father he finds that the latest unfortunate whom he has taken in was at one time a circus aerialist. When Jack asks his former specialty, his father informs him, "He was the man who got hanged."[64]

This recipient of Mr. Burden's Christian generosity now specializes in the making of angels out of stale bread masticated into a puttylike consistency. Jack learns that this sculpture is commemorative as well as decorative: his wife, Mr. Burden says, "did the angel act . . . She fell down a long way with white wings which fluttered as though she were flying." Jack completes the story: "And one day the rope broke . . ." (210).

In discussing the transmutation from play to novel, Warren described what he felt as

> the necessity for a character of a higher degree of self-consciousness than my politician, a character to serve as a kind of commentator and raisonneur and chorus . . . I wanted . . . to make him the chief character among those who were to find their vicarious fulfillment in the dynamic and brutal, yet paradoxically idealistic, drive of the politician. There was, too, my desire to avoid writing a straight naturalistic novel, the kind of novel that the material so readily invited. The impingement of that material, I thought, upon a special temperament would allow another perspective than the reportorial one, and would give a basis for some range of style. So Jack Burden entered the scene.[65]

The use of the hard-boiled newspaperman as narrator was not new, but it helped deepen the novel as Warren intended. It is Burden's probing intelligence that explores the multiple problems of identity that arise: *e.g.,* who and what is Willie Stark? And, who and what is Jack Burden? Is Willie the avenger his country partisans think him or the Fascist demagogue his rich enemies call him? Or is he a man compounded of mingled self-interest and idealism, corrupted by power and the means he feels forced to use by the imperfect world in which he lives? Is Jack a wise-cracking cynic, a man concealing the scars of early wounds with braggadocio, or one slowly and painfully coming to terms with himself as he acquires belated maturity? Through Jack's eyes we see both the secular and spiritual rise and fall of Willie Stark. We see the formation of the view of human nature Willie expresses when he tells Jack, "You don't ever have to frame anybody, because the truth is always sufficient" (358). And we also hear the anguished deathbed words, "It might have been all different, Jack . . . You got to believe that . . ." (425).

It is of course through Jack Burden and his life that the motif of redemption is explored, as the reader sees what amounts to the Fall and Rise of Jack Burden. He makes progress along many lines, finally making the right marriage and changing from political hack to student of history. Learning the truth of his own paternity, he takes back the responsibility of conscience he has abrogated in Willie's favor and changes his whole conception of the human dilemma and the human obligation. He rejects the view that life is ultimately meaningless and that actions are not consequential. (This view is expressed in "the Great Twitch," a sardonic philosophical extension of the random and unrelated activity seen in the cheek of a man with a tic, a view explored from another direction in a series of comments upon a prefrontal lobotomy.) Burden makes a transition first to the position objectified in the image of life as a spider web, in which actions are consequential in the extreme. Looking back, he writes,

> I have said that Jack Burden could not put down the facts about Cass Mastern's world because he did not know Cass Mastern [who had betrayed his friend with his wife]. Jack Burden did not say definitely to himself why he did not know Cass Mastern. But I (who am what Jack Burden became) look back now, years later, and try to say why. Cass Mastern lived for a few years and in that time he learned that the world is like an enormous spider web and if you touch it, however lightly, at any point, the vibration ripples to the remotest perimeter and the drowsy spider feels the tingle and is drowsy no more but springs out to fling the gossamer coils about you who have touched the web and then inject the black, numbing poison under your hide. It does not matter whether or not you meant to brush the web of things. (200)

Jack Burden goes beyond this position, however, when he himself gives something of the eternal, redemptive love the epigraph alludes to. He marries Anne Stanton, whom he has wronged. He gives to his mother the mature understanding and love which has previously been beyond him, and he takes into his home his nominal father, now in failing health. And when the old man dictates a heretical tract, Jack finds that he too believes what he has written: "The creation of man whom God in His foreknowledge knew to be doomed to sin was the awful index of God's omnipotence. For it would have been a thing of trifling and contemptible ease for Perfection to create mere perfection . . . The creation of evil is therefore the index of God's glory and His power" (462). And in the last words of the long chronicle, Jack looks forward to the future when, his father dead and the house consumed by mortgages, "we shall go out of the house and go into the convulsion of the world, out of history into history and the awful responsibility of Time" (464)

Warren's design demanded a technique to match it. Ordinary proficiency could not have sustained it. But fortunately Warren is a poet who can combine arresting clusters of image and metaphor with the narrative drive of a novelist possessing a fine ear for accent and nuance. Occasionally these gifts led him into excess. The novel ran to 464 pages, and it could have been at once shorter and better. Warren gained force for his story through a kind of incremental repetition, a reinforcement through repeated phrase, image, and motif. But at times the returns were diminishing ones, just as the sardonic cynicism occasionally turned Jack Burden from the complex and traumatized seeker after his own identity into a plain smart aleck. Working in the tradition of Conrad and Faulkner, Warren manipulated both point of view and time sequence. The novel opens in 1936 and closes in 1939. But Warren expands this time span by extended flashbacks in the years 1850-1864, 1914-1915, and later. Though the reader may grant him his sometimes labyrinthine method, he is not

likely to be so charitable to some of the extended philosophical disquisitions in which fundamental concerns are not so much dramatized as verbalized. But Warren's stylistic resources are still, at their best, dazzling. The dense texture is enriched by subtly used imagery—the death imagery contributes throughout to the force of the dominant themes—and by a kind of epic repetition of characters' attributes, features, and habits. It is a rich prose which can combine the sharpness associated with Hemingway and O'Hara and the rolling rhetoric of that novelist to whom Warren seems much indebted, William Faulkner.

A third of the way through *All the King's Men* Jack Burden declares that "the story of Willie Stark and the story of Jack Burden are, in one sense, one story" (168). As we have seen, it is this cunning strategy that gives the novel its richness. Warren uses these entwined lives to deal with what Dostoevsky called The Eternal Questions—the nature of truth, time, and man, the perception of life as meaningful or meaningless, and the whole problem of cultural and personal values. These are among the considerations Warren designated as "the deeper concerns" which might work themselves out within the political framework of the story. And both these elements were thematically and stylistically related. Talos was "the kind of doom that democracy may invite upon itself" (480) through the refusal to realize that every act is so consequential, that man must assume responsibility and—in an extreme formulation—give love. Correspondingly, Jack shows the kind of doom the individual may invite upon himself through a refusal to recognize consequentiality, assume responsibility, and give love. It is this kind of synthesis, combined with Warren's often brilliant technique, which makes this despite occasional prolixity and obscurity, the best American political novel of this century. It helps, moreover, to make it a work of art with promise of enduring.

Hodding Carter's *Flood Crest* (1947) began with a five-page, poetic description of an oncoming Mississippi flood which suggested the catastrophic dust storm in John Steinbeck's *The Grapes of Wrath*. And like Steinbeck's novel, Carter's used the natural crisis and disaster to parallel one in the social and political realm. U.S. Senator G. Cleve Pikestaff is running for re-election from a state one takes to be Mississippi, the home of newspaper-editor Carter.[66] Pikestaff is a coarse hillman, a nose-picker and bottom-scratcher who has won his way to Congress, the governor's mansion, and the Senate. Combining shrewdness with old-style campaign tactics and oratory, he has an intuitive understanding of the most exploitable of his hearers' prejudices. Running against a young veteran (another hillman campaigning on issues such as Pikestaff's real but unprovable pardon-selling), Pikestaff shows himself as resourceful as ever in the face of changing times and tastes. Pitching his appeal for both the large and small landowners, he hits out at "FEPC. The CIO. Negro suffrage. Social equality. Yankee interference."[67] Like others before him, he makes his guide pragmatism, not principle:

Cleve laughed to himself . . . He ought to write Joe Stalin a thank-you letter, with a carbon to the American Reds. Those fellows had given him something big; something even bigger, if he worked it right, than white supremacy . . . A Red was one who disagreed with you . . . A Red was any nigger who wanted to vote and any white man who thought he ought to. The lowdown, sneaking labor organizers . . . and . . . everybody who belonged to the CIO. Reporters . . . and most college professors, and the Jews and the rest of the foreign element in New York. So were a lot of dissatisfied young no-goods who got ideas overseas, but you had to go slow about them, because they were Veterans. Some of the younger preachers were Reds too, but you mentioned them only as pinks, and sadly, not critically, on account of the Jesus angle. (144)[68]

He combines accusation and innuendo. At his climactic rally, just before the crashing strains of "Dixie," he holds aloft a perjured statement supporting his baseless allegation of Communist influence: "'Here in my hands—' he shouted. 'Here in my hands is the proof of everything Cleve Pikestaff has been warning you about.'"[69] The professor smeared by Pikestaff says of him, "It's his kind who're responsible for the hatred and suspicion. Evil little men, willing to open the floodgates to ensure their elections" (132). But though the literal flood is successfully dealt with (by the lieutenant colonel of Army Engineers who breaks off with Pikestaff's daughter), there is no shoring of the levee against the figurative one. Pikestaff is sick over his intelligent daughter's profligacy, but he has the consolation that his overwhelming re-election is assured.[70] And the lieutenant colonel's words of assurance to his new sweetheart which follow have a somewhat hollow ring. This capably done novel shows the Southern Demagogue at work again—persuasive, cynical, cunning, and adept at combining the effects of old prejudices with new. And he shows no signs whatever of losing any of his power although he undergoes experiences revealing the rottenness around him, and, indeed, very close to him.

A novel published a dozen years later showed the image of the Southern Demagogue just as it had been. Far from changing, it seemed if anything closer to the earlier pattern. In Philip Alston Stone's *No Place to Run* (1959) the setting is again Mississippi. Sixty-one-year-old Eugene C. "Gene" Massie, born into a sharecropper family but a former senator and state power for years, is running in the gubernatorial primary. He relies on personal appearances rather than television, taking off his coat and exposing his red galluses whenever possible.[71] He delivers the only speech he has ever used. It encompasses the themes through which he has played upon his hearers' prejudices successfully for decades: retention of the white primary election and white supremacy in general, a tax policy designed to "soak the rich," and the retention of prohibition. He admits "stealing" $14,000 in a power contract transaction, but he tells his audience he did it "for you."[72] Adultery, bribery, coercion, incarceration, libel, and murder occur before Massie predictably wins the primary. His death by gunshot wounds at the hands of

an outraged husband follows soon after. The nymphomania of the errant wife is a principal aspect of the sexual pathology in the novel. It is complemented by the satyriasis of Massie and the ignorance of drugstore clerk Eurene Hogroth. Unaware of the effects of her seduction, she precipitately gives birth to a child in an alley. The novel's sexual violence is complementary to its other forms of violence. The most spectacular instance is probably displayed by Massie's father. Outraged by a Negro family's arrival on the same land which he farms for shares, he locks the Negro family in the house. Then he burns it before returning to his own dwelling to shoot his family and himself.

This is a competent first novel though a derivative one which shows the influence of Faulkner, Warren, and Tennessee Williams.[73] Stone has a good ear, and he tells a story well, a story here of the basest kind of appeal to abysmal political passions in a nearly mindless electorate. And it is a story in which death is not so much retribution as the result of a destructive drive in the protagonist not so very different from that manifested at various times by his victims.

Two novels published within roughly a half dozen years of each other both dealt with the process by which a new-style Southern Demagogue was created. The protagonists were not successful politicians in mid-career but mature men entering politics. Both stories were set in the early 1950's, and like *Flood Crest,* they showed the adaptation of the techniques and themes of McCarthyism to the milieu of the Southern Demagogue. Tom Wicker's *The Kingpin* (1953) is set in a coastal, tobacco-raising state that suggests North Carolina. Its protagonist is Bill Tucker, campaign manager for Colonel Harvey Pollock, a banker backed by a small group of industrialists and businessmen in the primary election for the United States Senate. Tucker successfully devises a campaign based on anti-Negro and anti-Communist sentiments which discredits Pollock's courageously liberal and ethical opponent. But Tucker's power drive is frustrated when he is ousted by a faithful Pollock adherent who discredits him, using the strategy he devised to ruin Pollock's opponent. Tucker's situation is like Frankenstein's with his monster. He observes Pollock in action:

> the sweat streaming from his fat face, over all of his body, he howled doggedly on, hitting and running and hitting again . . . at the jellied, quivering fear of the people who listened, howling not so cruelly as Talmadge and Bilbo and McDowell, not so piously as his Reconstruction ancestors, not so viciously as the Klan, but somewhere in between, somewhere in that dreamlike state where a Negro is not a nigger but a Nigra, where segregation is neither an evil nor the will of God but a necessity, where an opponent is not a nigger lover nor a Communist but a pink.[74]

Pollock's appeals to the hate and ignorance of a people "slow-moving, ill-fed, ill-housed, ill-clad, prey to all the dark moods and passions" (184) are made even more effective by the tactics of his opponent. He speaks of the Marshall Plan, the Atlantic Pact, Point Four, and asks for "a new evaluation of policy in the Middle East." An aide thinks to himself, "how in the name of God . . . does he expect a peanut farmer to know what even the old policy is?" (115).

The pressing economic problems involve inequitable distribution of land, violent labor-management disputes, poor transportation facilities, and preferential letting of contracts. The tax structure is shaped for the wealthy interests which control the state machine and which find it necessary to unseat Pollock's opponent—who had been appointed rather than elected to the Senate to fill out a term.[75] The political problems and strategies which grow out of this situation include the familiar one of splitting the opponent's rural vote. It is accomplished when Tucker lures an old-style demagogue out of retirement. Rooster Ed McDowell's perennial anti-Jew, anti-Yankee, anti-Negro speeches pull the votes sufficient to require the second primary which Pollock eventually wins.[76] In a newer technique, bogus postcards supporting Pollock's opponent are mailed out from "The National Society for the Advance of Colored People" (116).

The sexual pathology takes familiar forms. Mrs. Pollock's nymphomania in New York, Miami, New Orleans, and Tokyo has been documented by her foresighted husband. Elsewhere, Tucker's bed-partner conveys her contempt for his inferior status through hostile lovemaking, whereas he practices physical violence upon each of the women with whom he is intimate.[77] This combined pathology and violence runs deep in this novel which is thoroughly professional in technique and execution.

Francis Irby Gwaltney prefaced *A Step in the River* (1960) with a conventional disclaimer, remarking, "To those who shall insist that this novel is concerned with the political structure of the author's native state: bad cess." The author's native state was Arkansas, and though the disclaimer was no more convincing than most, it was supported by the fact that the protagonist was not another Huey Long image, although he possessed certain elements in the Southern Demagogue archetype. Like *The Kingpin*, this novel showed the creation and installation of another new-style politician. Wealthy and educated like Colonel Pollock, he is also handsome and magnetic, Thirty-two-year-old John Frank Miller has genius on the platform and shrewdly employs a hillbilly band and a tattooed clown. He also uses of the power of his cousin, who fills many state contracts, and successfully buys off his opposition. The opposition is Preacher Clutts, a backwoods spellbinder who refuses his biennial $50,000 bribe for not running and finally accepts a $100,000 check for his Tabernacle Fund. In return he transfers to Miller a quarter million in cash hotly sought by tax authorities.[78]

This novel's sexual pathology runs riot as Miller and his fiancée engage in a nude orgy including his sister-in-law and the tattooed clown. "I work ten years trying to run a decent establishment," the motel owner complains, "and a candidate for governor organizes a gang bang in my place" (300). This decadence is rejected by the book's narrator, the third of the cousins who serves as their pilot during the campaign. Later to repudiate the old concept of family loyalty, he ironically comments, "I recognize the stench of decay beneath the scent of such a beautiful thing . . ." (79). That the decay is there is clear—in the individuals, the family, the state, and the culture. But it is a decay overlaid with strength which appears capable of perpetuating the rule of this new-style Southern Demagogue on the old power base supporting it. The author has chosen his point of view for reasons, one suspects, which are probably like those of Warren in his creation of Jack Burden. That he does not derive more advantage from this strategy is partly due to the limitations imposed by this particular narrator. Most often tough-talking and taciturn, he is awkward and unconvincing in eloquent passages. Like the others, this book is pervaded by violence. It is competently done, however, and capable at times of bodying forth whole attitudes in a phrase. Preacher Clutts, a man behind "the Confederate Curtain" (107), remarks, "Well I always say . . . if you keep niggers and honest men in their place, they're all right" (287).

## THE SOUTHERN DEMAGOGUE AND THE STATUS QUO

Nineteenth-century political novels set in the South usually fell into three categories. Like Harriet Beecher Stowe's *Uncle Tom's Cabin* (1852)—a novel more political in effect than in content—one showed the evils of the Southern system. Like Tourgée's *A Fool's Errand* (1879), another demonstrated the baleful effects of the mismanaged Reconstruction program frustrated by resurgent Southern nationalism. Like Thomas Nelson Page's *Red Rock* (1898), another embodied the Southern view that federal policies and their results were abominations in both wartime and peacetime.

The reader is struck by the fervor and conviction which run through these novels, whether they are elicited by The Battle Cry of Freedom or The Lost Cause. The novels of the Southern Politician which appeared between 1922 and 1960 were more sophisticated in both form and content and for the most part written from an ethically and politically irreproachable point of view. But they usually depicted fervor and conviction of only the basest kind. The fervor was bred of ignorance and prejudice, and but for the idealism of a few protagonists, the conviction was mostly that of cynical men who had for years successfully made use of ignorance and prejudice. It was a conviction that these conditions were perpetual sources of power which they could continue to tap at will. Symptomatic of this shift from the old to the new is the contest in one of the most recent novels. The victorious Colonel Pollock of *The Kingpin* introduces certain modern restraints and nuances into his demagoguery, but his line of descent is still from Talmadge and Bilbo. The opponent he defeats, able newspaper publisher Ralph Anson, is a man "self-educated in the best Abe Lincoln manner" (112). The character in the tradition of self-seeking demagogue who appeals to the lowest common denominator wins out over the one suggesting the heroic leader.

Although it is patently impossible to return to the antebellum order, the impulse of most of these politicians is a profoundly conservative one aimed at maintaining the *status quo*. A minority works to remedy inequities which favor the wealthy landowner and industrialist while handicapping the impoverished small farmer and tenant farmer. More enter into alliances with the wealthy and powerful, protecting their interests and ranging themselves against organized labor and other forces of change. In one view, the complex of emotions and attitudes which creates a favorable environment for the demagogue has an economic base. His wealthy allies support him in return for preferential treatment which will maintain his state as their economic preserve. The poorer whites support him because his doctrine of White Supremacy offers them support against the economic threat posed by the Negro farmer—who can and must work with less for less. He taps prejudices in them which are both traditional and subrational. And these prejudices show no sign of diminution, at least in these novels. They are still directed with undiminished fervor against the Negro, the Jew, the Yankee, and other outsiders.

Later novels involving the Boss often assert that his very existence has been in jeopardy through the increasing influence of the federal government in local affairs. There is no evidence in any of these novels that a similar force is at work in the area of the Southern politician. When foreign concerns do intrude, they are manipulated to serve the interests of the traditional wielders of power. In these novels, the fascism of the 1930's and 1940's merely provides a new and potent weapon for ruining an opponent with greater dispatch. It is still conceived of merely as a useful political tool, however; the ideology implied by the terms used could not have a remoter significance for those who use them. When Calvin Hall, the narrator of *A Step in the River*, declares he will sue for allegations of communist sympathy made against him, Preacher Clutts, his libeller, is both hurt and aghast. "Now wait a minute!" he exclaims. "Hell! This is a damn political campaign!" (295).

If this amoral adroitness and adaptability of the Southern Politician seems to indicate anything, it is that there has been no material change in the predominant pattern demonstrated through the years of the twentieth century. And equally, there seems in these novels no indication of any fundamental change in sight.

NOTES

[1] W. J. Cash, *The Mind of the South*, pp. 428-429.

[2] In political and cultural studies the South is most often taken to include the eleven Confederate states: Virginia, North Carolina, South Carolina, Georgia, Florida, Alabama, Mississippi, Louisiana, Texas, Arkansas, and Tennessee. In the novels considered in this [essay] the qualities of this region are largely carried over to border states such as West Virginia, Kentucky, and Oklahoma as well.

[3] V. O. Key, Jr., in his exhaustive *Southern Politics*, comments, "Florida's peculiar social structure underlies a political structure of extraordinary complexity. It would be more accurate to say that Florida has no political organization in the conventional sense of the term" (p. 87).

[4] *Ibid.*, pp. 214-215.

[5] *Ibid.*, p. 20.

[6] Key, *Southern Politics*, p. 106.

[7] *Ibid.*, p. 159.

[8] Cash, *South*, p. 248. Goldman notes that Tillman and Vardaman "combined reform and racist attitudes in a formula similar to the one Adolf Hitler was to perfect" (Eric F. Goldman, *Rendezvous with Destiny: A History of Modern American Reform*, p. 65).

[9] Cash, *South*, p. 284.

[10] Arthur M. Schlesinger, Jr., *The Age of Roosevelt: The Politics of Upheaval*, pp. 42-43.

[11] Reinhard H. Luthin, *American Demagogues: Twentieth Century*, p. 239. See also Hartnett T. Kane, *Louisiana Hayride: The American Rehearsal for Dictatorship*, pp. 13-35; Allan A. Michie and Frank Rhylick, *Dixie Demagogues*, p. 110; and Key, *Southern Politics*, pp. 156-159.

[12] Kane, *Hayride*, pp. 36-37.

[13] Michie and Rhylick, *Dixie Demagogues*, p. 109.

[14] Huey P. Long, Jr., *Every Man a King: The Autobiography of Huey P. Long*, p. 27.

[15] Long, *Autobiography*, p. 99.

[16] Schlesinger, *Roosevelt*, p. 48.

[17] As quoted in Schlesinger, *Roosevelt*, p. 53.

[18] As quoted in Luthin, *American Demagogues*, pp. 259 and 260.

[19] As quoted in Schlesinger, *Roosevelt*, p. 65.

[20] As quoted in Luthin, *American Demagogues*, p. 265.

[21] Key, *Southern Politics*, p. 159.

[22] Schlesinger, *Roosevelt*, p. 51.

[23] *Ibid.*, pp. 50 and 66.

[24] *Ibid.*, p. 56.

[25] Schlesinger, *Roosevelt*, p. 58.

[26] As quoted in Michie and Rhylick, *Dixie Demagogues*, pp. 113-114.

[27] As quoted in Schlesinger, *Roosevelt*, p. 89.

[28] Michie and Rhylick, *Dixie Demagogues*, p. 113.

[29] Elmer L. Frey, as quoted in Luthin, *American Demagogues*, p. 250.

[30] Schlesinger, *Roosevelt*, p. 60.

[31] Key, *Southern Politics*, pp. 156 and 164. Rorty and Decter take the opposite view: "He was an ideologue, a theoretician, a planner, an organizer. His library was well stocked with the theoretical literature of both Marxism and Fascism" (James Rorty and Moshe Decter, *McCarthy and the Communists*, p. 113).

[32] As quoted in Michie and Rhylick, *Dixie Demagogues*, p. 112.

[33] As quoted in Schlesinger, *Roosevelt*, p. 60.

[34] Luthin, *American Demagogues*, p. 243.

[35] Cash, *South*, p. 421.

[36] In John Dos Passos's *The Grand Design*, the Reverend Green shows Paul Graves a stricken area. He tells him that in these counties "relief is in the hands of the politicians and the politicians are mostly landlords who save it for their own tenants" (p. 155). For discussion of other inequities, see Goldman, *Rendezvous*, pp. 348-349.

[37] Key, *Southern Politics*, p. 661.

[38] Thomas S. Stribling, *The Sound Wagon*, p. 164.

[39] Tom Wicker, *The Kingpin*, p. 184.

[40] Robert Rylee, *The Ring and the Cross*, p. 285.

[41] This pattern suggests two familiar elements in Southern cultural lore: the idealized image of Southern Womanhood whom the Southern male fanatically praised and venerated, and the seductive woman (often a colored mistress) with whom he found the satisfaction impossible with the idealized Southern Wife and Mother. For an acute analysis of these elements, see Cash, *South*, pp. 82-87 and 128.

[42] Albion W. Tourgée, *A Fool's Errand*, p. 361.

[43] Ellen Glasgow, *One Man in His Time*, p. 2.

[44] The smart fat man becomes a familiar type of Southern politician. Usually he is villainous.

[45] Glen Allan, *Old Manoa*, p. 25.

[46] Describing his campaign for John M. Parker in 1920, Huey Long wrote, "I took the stump for a period of approximately seventy days and went places where no other campaign orator had ever reached, traveling at times by horseback to fill appointments" (Luthin, *American Demagogues*, p. 242).

[47] Robert Wilder, *Flamingo Road*, p. 201.

[48] Franklin Coen, *Vinegar Hill*, p. 4.

[49] The novel's pitched battle strains credibility until one reads of the eviction by a veterans' group of the brutal machine which had for years ruled McMinn County in southeast Tennessee. In the early morning of August 1, 1946, they surrounded the county jail and successfully laid siege to it with bullets and dynamite. The local vassals of the Crump machine and their two hundred hired deputies (many out-of-town and out-of-state plug-uglies) were turned out and the GI slate of candidates installed in office. There were no deaths, but ten of the veterans were wounded and five of the deputies were hospitalized. See Theodore H. White, "The Battle of Athens, Tennessee," *Harper's Magazine*, 194 (January, 1947), 54-60. (It is somehow ironic that the final vote which decided the issue in the state legislature whose ratification made woman suffrage into law should have come from McMinn County. See National American Woman Suffrage Association, *Victory: How Women Won It*, pp. 149 and 152.) In the summer of 1946, former Marine Lieutenant Colonel Sid McMath led a movement in Arkansas which captured the mayoralty of Hot Springs by the following spring, touched off a series of similar actions throughout the state, and placed McMath in the governor's chair in 1948. However, "Not all GI leaders were white knights leading crusades against wicked local machines. The revolts picked up the usual quota of opportunists whose chief sincerity was in their wish to ride the GI band wagon into office. Nevertheless, the movement, if it could be called that, included a number of men of extraordinary idealism coupled with skill and coolness in the hard-boiled tactics of politics" (Key, *Southern Politics*, p. 204). In 1948 McMath, as governor, paid off a debt to a political supporter from a place in the Ozark Mountains called Greasy Creek. He named Orval E. Faubus state highway director. When Faubus went on to the governorship and in his second term drew worldwide attention to Arkansas during the Little Rock integration crises, McMath rued his generosity. "I wish," he lamented, "I had never built the road that led Faubus out of the hills" (*New York Times*, August 5, 1962, Section 4, p. 2E). When Faubus won the nomination for his fifth term, the man who ran third was former governor McMath.

[50] For a discussion of Basso's rejection of the Communist variety of authoritarianism—especially as seen in interchanges with his friend Malcolm Cowley—see Daniel Aaron, *Writers on the Left: Episodes in American Literary Communism*, pp. 339-340.

[51] Schlesinger writes, "if within Long's limits government was benevolent and fairly efficient, it was still intricately and hopelessly corrupt. In 1934, to take an example, Long and several close associates set up the Win or Lose Corporation. The state government considerately made it possible for the new corporation to acquire properties in the natural gas fields; the corporation then persuaded natural gas companies to buy the properties by threatening to increase their taxes if they didn't. Using such persuasive sales methods, Win or Lose cleared about $350,000 in 1935" (*Roosevelt*, pp. 60-61).

[52] John Dos Passos, *Number One*, p. 228. Though bills have been talked to death by a number of legislators, the filibuster is particularly associated with the image of Senator Long. Dos Passos had seen Long and had not been well impressed. He looked, the novelist wrote, "like an overgrown small boy with very bad habits indeed" (as quoted in Schlesinger, *Roosevelt*, p. 49). Other obvious elements in this *roman à clef* include Crawford's start as county road commissioner and subsequent rise to membership on the State Utilities Commission. He manages to get his state delegation accredited over the claims of a rival faction at the national convention, as Long had done in 1932.

[53] What the watch actually reports is that "A lioness hath whelped in the streets." Miss Langley's use of the masculine gender may perhaps suggest simply that a predatory beast is afoot rather than calling up the portents which, to Calpurnia, augur the fall of Rome's dictator.

[54] Adria Locke Langley, *A Lion Is in the Streets*, p. 247. Illiterate whites were able to evade the literacy test for voting through the so-called "grandfather clause" of the state constitution of Louisiana, put into effect without popular vote in 1898. The provisions were identical with those in the novel. Although the stratagem had been rejected in South Carolina because of its doubtful constitutionality, it was adopted by other states before it was declared unconstitutional as a result of litigation begun in Oklahoma. See Key, *Southern Politics*, pp. 538 and 556.

[55] Although one doubts an intentional reference, one may recall the plight of Spenser's Red Cross Knight in Book I of *The Faerie Queene* after Una (Truth, among her other attributes) leaves him.

[56] Though Key does not label the Long machine a case of native Fascism, he notes Long's nearly absolute power: "He dominated the legislature. He ripped out of office mayors, parish officials, and judges who raised a voice against him. Weapons of economic coercion were employed to repress opposition. When they failed the organization did not hesitate to use more direct methods. Huey, at the height of his power, brooked no opposition and those who could not be converted were ruthlessly suppressed" (Key, *Southern Politics*, p. 156).

[57] Robert Penn Warren, "A note to *All the King's Men*," *Sewanee Review*, LXI (Summer, 1953), 479.

[58] Warren, "A note to *All the King's Men*," SR, p. 480. Warren had taught at Louisiana State University in Baton Rouge during the Long era.

[59] *Ibid., SR*, pp. 476-477.

[60] Goldman prints an excerpt from the *New York Times*, November 17, 1935, quoting Long as asserting, "your Kingfish Huey, asittin' in the White House, will know how to handle them moguls." Goldman speaks of Long "clawing his way toward the Presidency," and discusses his potential strength and the threat it was felt to constitute to the Administration in 1935 (*Rendezvous*, pp. 362-363).

[61] Robert Penn Warren, *All the King's Men*, p. 68.

[62] Warren, "A note to *All the King's Men*," SR, p. 480.

[63] An indication of the extent to which the act of betrayal permeates the novel is to be seen in the presumptive betrayal of the guilty wife to the injured husband at the hand of her slave Phebe. The wife's retaliatory act selling her down the river is described by the narrator as "the betrayal of Phebe . . ." (p. 189).

[64] Thinking of the echoes of Dante in Warren, one may wonder here if he has not, like that other echoer of the Florentine, T. S. Eliot, chosen also to echo a different inscriber of myth, Sir James Fraser.

[65] Warren, "A note to *All the King's Men*," SR, p. 478.

[66] Key writes: "Hodding Carter's novel *Flood Crest* . . . builds on the theme of the reconciliation of Bilbo and the delta" (*Southern Politics*, p. 244). Carter knew at first hand political excesses other than those of Mississippi's "Bilbonic Plague." Writing for the *Hammond Courier* as an outspoken critic of the Long regime, Carter had been forced to carry a weapon for his own safety. See Carter, "Huey Long, American Dictator," in Isabel Leighton (ed.), *The Aspirin Age*, p. 341, and Carter's book, *Where Main Street Meets the River*, Chapter Eight.

[67] Hodding Carter, *Flood Crest*, p. 133.

[68] Writing of the strike of textile workers in Gastonia, North Carolina, in the spring of 1929, Cash asserts that it served "to clinch the matter, to fix solidly in the minds of the great mass of Southerners the equation: labor unions+strikers=Communism+atheism+social equality with the Negro—and so to join the formidable list of Southern sentiments already drawn up against the strikers the great central one of racial feeling and purpose; and, in fact, to summon against them much the same great fears and hates we have already seen as giving rise to the Ku Klux Klan" (Cash, *South*, p. 353).

[69] Cash, *South*, p. 124. This same gambit, couched in the familiar phrase, "I have here in my hand," will be seen again in the novels of McCarthyism considered in Chapter Eight.

[70] Discovering the two in a compromising situation, Pikestaff struggles with the convict, who uses his pistol to inflict a scalp laceration on him. Later, speaking at a rally, Pikestaff wears the vote-getting bandage as testimonial to his valor in fighting what he calls the pro-red, anti-American forces which will stop at nothing to silence him. Key writes, "In 1934, Bilbo brought into play his genius for rough-and-tumble campaigning. He wore, from an earlier campaign, a scar won in his oratorical battles for the people. He had been rapped over the head with a pistol butt by an opponent," one he had particularly vehemently calumniated (*Southern Politics*, p. 242).

[71] Describing Eugene Talmadge's first campaign for office in 1926, Key writes that his "lambasting of the corporations was reminiscent of the populists. Then and after his colloquialisms on the hustings and a pair of bright red galluses marked him as a man of the farming people" (*Southern Politics*, p. 116). Key also writes that a candidate "of Talmadge's audacity, occasional uncouthness, iconoclasm, disrespect for established processes always aligned against him a healthy number of Georgians who are usually damned with the designation 'respectable'" (*Southern Politics*, p. 125).

[72] Philip Alston Stone, *No Place to Run*, p. 75.

[73] The author's father, Phil Stone, an Oxford lawyer, had befriended young William Faulkner when he returned to Mississippi from World War I service with the R.A.F., lending him books and providing him with free secretarial services. Like the rest of Oxford, Stone knew many of the exploits of the fabled Faulkner family. In *No Place to Run*, when Massie's career is threatened by accusations of rape, he goes to his sometime mentor, aristocratic old Judge Rogers. When the Judge receives him coldly, Massie is daunted:

> "why, I thought I'd jest come by for a little visit and see you—" "Gene," said Judge Rogers, "our relations are business and political. They are not social. Good afternoon." And he closed the door in his candidate's face and started back up the hall (240-241).

J. W. T. Falkner, the novelist's grandfather, was a supporter of the "redneck" politician, Senator James K. Vardaman. Mr. Falkner allowed a young Mississippian named Lee Russell to read law in his office. After he received his degree from the University, Russell practiced law for a time as an associate of Falkner. He was elected to the state legislature and in 1915 ran successfully for lieutenant governor. The gubernatorial winner that year was Theodore G. Bilbo. One life-long resident of Oxford recalls that one Sunday afternoon following his victory, Russell appeared at the door of the Falkner home. When Falkner asked him what he wanted, Russell replied that he had come to pay a visit. Whereupon Falkner told him that their relations were business and political, not social, and slammed the door.

[74] Tom Wicker, *The Kingpin*, p. 287.

[75] It has been suggested to me that this unsuccessful campaign of liberal Senator Ralph Anson owes something to the defeat of Frank P. Graham, "by all odds the South's most prominent educator and versatile public servant" (Key, *Southern Politics*, p. 206). Graham had left the presidency of the University of North Carolina in 1949 to accept appointment to the U.S. Senate. He was defeated the next year when he ran for election to the post.

[76] Names such as Rooster Ed are plentiful enough in American politics so that one need not necessarily ascribe one to a specific, not to say Southern, source. One thinks of Oklahoma's Alfalfa Bill Murray. But one thinks also of South Carolina's Cotton Ed Smith, a fruitful model for the political novelist, being, in Cash's words, "the archetype of the man who served only the planter and industrial interests in his state, while whipping up and delighting the people with attacks on the Negro, appeals to such vague shibboleths as states' rights, and heroic gasconade of every sort" (*South*, p. 422).

[77] One of these women provides an interesting perspective on the changing role of women. She is observing Pollock's campaign in order to gather material for a Ph.D. dissertation "on the effects of women's suffrage in a specific election" (Wicker, *The Kingpin*, p. 65). Her effect is to provide Tucker with a bed-mate.

[78] The evangelical, revivalist preaching style is often seen in these novels in rallies which have much of the prayer meeting tempo and fervor. Key gives an indication of the continuing efficacy of this technique: "In 1948 in Arkansas 'Uncle Mac' MacKrell was accompanied in his vote-getting tour by his gospel musicians and the hat was passed. 'Uncle Mac's' pastoral experience gave him exceptional skill in the extraction of contributions. Hard-boiled politicians almost wept when they saw the collections" (*Southern Politics*, pp. 479-480). Religion and politics have, of course, been more intimately connected in the South than in most other American regions, particularly during the Reconstruction and after. At the time of Al Smith's candidacy, "the ministers of the evangelical sects finally towered up to their greatest power, until almost literally nobody in the South dared criticize their pronouncements or oppose the political programs they laid out . . ." (Cash, *South*, p. 335). Though the power of the clergy does not extend so far in the more recent novels, it is still formidable.

## Richard Kostelanetz

SOURCE: "The Politics of Ellison's Booker: *Invisible Man* as Symbolic History," in *Chicago Review*, Vol. 19, No. 2, 1967, pp. 5-26.

[*In the following essay, Kostelanetz contends that the narrator of Ralph Ellison's novel* Invisible Man *represents "in symbolic form the overall historical experience of the most politically active element" of African Americans.*]

*Invisible Man* is *par excellence* the literary extension of the blues. It was as if Ellison has taken an everyday twelve-bar blues tune (by a man from down South sitting in a manhole up North in New York singing and signifying about how he got there) and scored it for a full orchestra.

—Albert L. Murray.

I

In his collection of essays, *Shadow and Act* (1964), Ralph Ellison defines the purpose of novelistic writing as "converting experience into symbolic action," and this phrase incidentally captures the particular achievement of his novel, *Invisible Man,* in which he creates a nameless narrator whose adventures, always approximate and unspecific in time and place, represent in symbolic form the overall historical experience of the most politically active element of the American Negro people.

"It is through the process of making artistic forms" Ellison adds elsewhere, "that the writer helps give meaning to the experience of the group," a statement which, especially in its tactile imagery, echoes Stephen Dedalus's ambition, in James Joyce's *Portrait of the Artist as a Young Man,* "to forge in the smithy of my soul the uncreated conscience of my race." In the major sequences of *Invisible Man,* the narrator confronts a succession of possible individual choices which, as they imply changes in group behavior, have a symbolic political dimension for Negro people. When an alternative seems adequate enough to win the narrator's favor, his acceptance becomes, in effect, a pragmatic test of its viability. After he discovers the posited solution is inadequate to his needs, as all of them are, he samples another. Although Ellison does not have his narrator confront every known political possibility, the novel is still the most comprehensive one-volume fictional—symbolic—treatment of the history of the American Negro in the twentieth century.

In the opening quarter of the novel, the narrator eagerly tests opportunities for Negro existence within the Southern system, and just as Voltaire's *Candide* innocently embraces philosophical optimism, so the young Negro assumes the notions prevalent in the early twentieth century of how the colored people can best succeed in the South—those of Booker T. Washington. From a vantage point later in time, the narrator remembers that as a young man about to graduate high school, "I visualized myself as a potential Booker T. Washington," who hoped to follow his idol's advice and perhaps emulate his career.[1] The most successful Negroes, he believed, were those who proved themselves essential to white society, either because they had an employable trade or because they helped to keep order within the Negro communities.

The whole future of the Negro rested largely upon the question of whether or not he should make himself, through his skill, intelligence and character, of such undeniable value to the community in which he lived that the community could not dispense with his presence.

From this proposition stemmed Washington's major corollary: since the South offered the Negro greater social and economic opportunities, the Southern Negro would be wise to remain where he was born. "Whatever other sins the South may be called to bear," he wrote, "when it comes to business, pure and simple, it is in the South that the Negro is given a man's chance in the commercial world." At the base of Washington's politics, then, was a faith that Southern whites would give the respectable Negro a fair opportunity to succeed, and honor whatever success a Negro achieved for himself.

From these positions, Washington, as history and Ellison's narrator saw him, derived the three major lines of conduct implemented at Tuskegee Institute (which distinctly resembles the college in *Invisible Man*). First, Washington believed that to make himself as appealing as possible to white society, the Negro must be industrious in his work, respectful in his dealings with his white superiors, responsible for his family and to his community, and, perhaps most important, scrupulously clean. In *Up from Slavery,* his most influential book, Washington never ceased proclaiming the advantages of an immaculate appearance. For Tuskegee's students, instruction in hygiene was as important as book- and trade-learning:

It has been interesting to note the effect that the use of the toothbrush has had in bringing about a higher degree of civilization among the students. With few exceptions, I have noticed that, if we can get a student to the point where, when the first or second toothbrush disappears, he of his own motion buys another, I have not been disappointed in the future of that individual. Absolute cleanliness of the body has been insisted upon from the first. The students have been taught to bathe as regularly as to take their meals. . . . Most of the students came from plantation districts, and often we had to teach them how to sleep at night; that is, whether between the two sheets . . . or under both of them. The importance of the use of the nightgown received the same attention.

Thus, in the daily schedule at Tuskegee, Washington allocated one-half hour for cleaning one's room, and school officials made periodic inspection tours of the dormitories. A central aim of Tuskegee's education was to take a back-country Negro and, metaphorically, soak him with whitewash.

Secondly, if the Negro were to succeed, he must not challenge the system of white supremacy. In Washington's pet phrase, he must campaign for "responsibility," not "equality." A demand for equal rights, he feared, could only violently disrupt the stability of the South; and not only would revolt have little chance of success, but also the cost in Negro lives would be too exorbitant to make it worthwhile. "The wisest among my race understand that the agitation of questions of social equality is the extremist folly," he wrote, for the Negro must, following

Washington's own example, "deport himself modestly in regard to political claims." Political rights, he argued, "will be accorded to the Negro by the Southern people themselves, and they will protect him in the exercise of those rights," only if the Negro treads the path of humility, impresses white society with his conscientiousness, and contributes to their material prosperity.

Thirdly, the Negro must measure his success in tokens of recognition from white society, rather than in terms of respect of his own people. This is the major lesson Washington drew from his own life, and in the latter half of his autobiography he catalogues the honors he received from white America. He especially enjoyed lecturing before groups of white Southerners, and he saved his most important speeches for the racially mixed audiences of large Southern expositions. Among his deepest desires was to have the President of the United States visit Tuskegee; and when the possibility arose, he twice journeyed to Washington, D.C., to persuade McKinley to come. Furthermore, few things pleased him more than encountering a group of white people who, like some Georgia men mentioned in his book, "came up and introduced [themselves] to me and thanked me earnestly for the work that I was trying to do for the whole South." (Whether they addressed him by his Christian name or "Mr. Washington," he does not disclose.) What a Negro's peers thought of his own work was not as important as what the white folks judged; again, Washington felt that Negroes could best succeed in America by conforming to the prescriptions of entrenched white authority.

Ellison's narrator so thoroughly and innocently subscribes to the Washingtonian ethic that, when he is selected to give the valedictory address at his high school, he echoes both Washington's ideas and his rhetoric. Telling his Negro classmates to cultivate friendly relations with their white neighbors, the narrator quotes the key line of Washington's Atlanta Proclamation Address, "Cast down your bucket where you are," for, it is implied, if the colored southerners look for water elsewhere, they may die of thirst. Likewise, the narrator uses the Washingtonian phrase "social responsibility" to define the role the Negro should play in the South. Upon his graduation the narrator believes that he can rise through the Southern system, perhaps becoming, like his idol, an educational leader or, more modestly, a doctor or lawyer in the Negro South.

The narrator, along with other class leaders, is invited to a gathering of the local white dignitaries; and at the occasion, they ask the narrator to repeat his valedictory address. When he arrives at the meeting, he is first directed to join his classmates in a free-for-all "battle royal" that is a feature of the evening's entertainment. Although he instinctively shies away from bodily contact with boys bigger than himself, the narrator consents to the ordeal to please the white audience. Along with the other Negro youths, he is blindfolded with white cloth; when the bells ring, he is pushed into the ring and throughout the fight, the white citizens on the sidelines

encourage the Negro school boys to "knock" each other's "guts out." This incident, like most of the major scenes in the book, embodies a symbolic dimension that complements the literal action; that is, the scene stands for something larger in the experience of the Southern Negro. Here, Ellison shows how the white powers make the Negroes channel their aggressive impulses inward upon their own race instead of upon their true enemy, who remains on the sidelines, supervising the fray to make sure the violence is directed away from themselves.

To pay for the "entertainment," the hosts put numerous coins and bills upon a rug and encourage the Negroes to pick up "all you grab." Once this new contest starts, they discover the rug is electrified. The shocks lead the boys to jump and shriek, in animal-like movements, to the amusement of the white audience. "Glistening with sweat like a circus seal and . . . landing flush upon the charged rug," one boy "literally dance [d] upon his back, his elbows beating a frenzied tattoo upon the floor, his muscles twitching like the flesh of a horse stung by many flies." In other words, before the Negro receives the pay he earned, he must overcome unnecessary hazards, often arbitrarily imposed, and publicly make a fool of himself. Between the Negro and the money he earns from white society are, symbolically, all the galvanic terrors of an electrified rug; and the price of the white man's pay is the Negro's debasement of his humanity.

After the other boys are paid their pittances and excused, the narrator delivers his speech. Again, he voices the platitudes of Booker T. Washington, feigning the air of sincerity and accents of emphasis. When he mentions the phrase "social responsibility," they ask him to repeat it again and again, until in a moment of mental exhaustion he substitutes the word "equality." Challenged by the audience, he quickly reverts to the traditional, unrevolutionary phrase. Ellison here illustrates that as the speaker's censor relaxes, his true desires are revealed; but as soon as he remembers the power of Southern authority, he immediately represses his wish. At the end of the meeting, the superintendent of the local schools presents the narrator with a briefcase; in it is a scholarship to the state college for Negroes. Again, the political meaning is that the Negro must publicly debase himself and suppress his true desires before he will receive the rewards of Southern society. Washington's guidance would seem to underestimate the price of Negro success in the South.

In the second sequence of the novel, the narrator discovers what kinds of Negroes receive rewards totally disproportionate to their work. As a student, the narrator is assigned to act as a chauffeur for a white trustee, Mr. Norton (whose name at once echoes "Northern" and Charles Eliot Norton, the first professor of art history at Harvard and heir to a certain kind of New England Brahmin liberalism). Responding to Norton's commands, the narrator drives the old man to the Negro slum down below the "white-washed" college on the hill. At his passenger's request, he stops the car before the log cabin of Jim

Trueblood, who, as his name suggests, represents the primitive, uneducated Negro unaffected by the values of white culture. Norton, discovering to his horror that Trueblood has impregnated his daughter, asks the Negro whether he feels "no inner turmoil, no need to cast out the offending eye?" Refusing Oedipus's response to a similar sin, the Negro uncomprehendingly replies, "My eyes is allright," adding, "When I feels po'ly in my gut I takes a little soda and it goes away." Prompted by Norton's queries, Trueblood tells how the officials at the Negro college responded to his misdeed: "[They] offered to send us clean outta the country, pay our way and everything and give me a hundred dollars to git settled with." To the "whitewashed" Negroes, Trueblood represents that elemental humanity that college education must eliminate; and Trueblood's presence near the campus serves as a reminder of the primitive past the college community wants to repudiate.

To escape their strategy of alternate threats and enticements, Trueblood enlists the aid of his white boss who, in turn, refers him to the local sheriff. That official and his cronies so relish Trueblood's tale of sexual indiscretion that they ask him to repeat all the details, giving him food, drink and tobacco in return for their second-hand pleasure.

> They tell me not to worry, that they was going to send word up to the school that I was to stay right where I am. It just goes to show yuh that no matter how biggity a nigguh gits, the white folks always cut him down.

In the days following, Trueblood becomes a celebrity, attracting the interest of white people he had never encountered before.

> The white folks took to coming out here to see us and talk with us. Some of 'em was big white folks, too, from the big school way 'cross the State. Asked me lots 'bout what I thought 'bout things, and 'bout my folks and kids, and wrote it all down in a book.

Presumably, these men were Southern scholars who intended to use Trueblood's confessions as evidence of the inherent immorality of the Negro. Moreover, Trueblood reports, the local white people now give him more work. "I'm better off than I ever been before," he says. "I done the worse thing a man can do in his family and 'stead of things gittin bad, they got better." In short, Trueblood's experience contradicts Washington's belief that white society would reward only those Negroes who live by its expressed morality. Instead, they eagerly appreciate a Negro who conforms to the traditional stereotype of the immoral savage in black skin.

After leaving Trueblood, the narrator follows Norton's command to take him to a roadside bar. Here they encounter a group of hospitalized Negro veterans, mostly psychiatric patients, going to the ironically named "Golden Day" for their weekly round of drinks and whores. Their shepherd is the hospital attendant Supercargo who, as his name suggests, functions as their collective super-ego. Not only does he impose the repressive forces of white society upon them, but he also represents obedience internalized into their own consciences. Therefore, as soon as he disappears to fetch a drink upstairs, the men "had absolutely no inhibitions." A brawl ensues, directed largely against Supercargo and the social forces he represents. As the "veterans" air their complaints, the narrator discovers that they are the dispossessed Negro middle-class. One is an ex-surgeon who was dragged from his home by white men and beaten, it is implied, for saving the life of a white person. Another is a composer on the borderline of lunacy, "striking the [piano] keyboard with fists and elbows and filling in other effects in a bass voice that moaned like a bear in agony." A third "was a former chemist who was never seen without his shining Phi Beta Kappa key." The lesson of their experience is that Southern society destroys Negro talent and genuine accomplishment. Once again, Washington's advice on how the Negro should live in the South proves an inadequate guide.

Back on the campus, the narrator is summoned into the office of the college president to be reprimanded for taking Norton down to the slum, for letting him talk to Trueblood, for leading him to the Golden Day, and for allowing the benefactor to hear complaints of the dispossessed Negroes. He blames the narrator for innocently following Norton's commands and, even worse, for honestly answering his queries. The heart of the young man's error, Bledsoe says, is that "You forgot to lie." "But," the narrator replies, "I was only trying to please him. . . . " To this Bledsoe retorts in anger, "Why, the dumbest black bastard in the cotton patch knows that the only way to please a white man is to tell him a lie! What kind of education are you getting around here?" Bledsoe believes, echoing some cynical implications in Washington's thought, that the Negro college should preach the attainment not of dignity and self-achievement but of surface obsequiousness and underlying cynicism. Had not, the narrator remembers, Bledsoe himself been a model of such behavior. Had not he illustrated how the Negro should play the role of the second-class man.

Since Bledsoe's authority within the college is absolute, the narrator decides to accept punishment for the mistakes his innocence engendered—expulsion; and armed with several of Bledsoe's letters of recommendation, the young man heads for New York. He recognizes that his ethics cannot cope with the reality he finds:

> How had I come to this? I had kept unswervingly to the path placed before me, had tried to be exactly what I was expected to be, had done exactly what I was expected to do—yet, instead of winning the expected reward, here I was stumbling along. . . . For, despite my anguish and anger, I knew of no other way of living, nor other forms of success available to such as me.

Rather than succumb to the new reality he discovers, the young man who scrupulously followed the suggestions of

Booker T. Washington, is forced to disobey his idol's advice and leave the South.

Perhaps the final commentary on Booker T. Washington's ideas is the address given in the college chapel by a Rev. Homer Barbee, a visitor from Chicago. Barbee presents all the optimistic platitudes, predicting the improvement of conditions in the South and greater opportunity for his people to fulfill their worldly ambitions. Instead of bitterness or notions of emigration, revolt and racial conflict, he offers the hope of success within the Southern system—a "bright horizon" through self-improvement. His ideas offer a certain appeal to the narrator and his classmates, until the young man realizes that Barbee wears dark glasses. He is blind, both in the physical sense and in his awareness of political realities. To the Negro in quest of self-fulfillment, the South in fact offers no hope, except to the blind, the immoral, and the cynical. This is the political meaning of the first section of the book.

II

Before he lets his narrator explore much of the North, Ellison introduces a scene which serves as a symbolic portrait of the underlying reality of Negro-white relations in America. Ostensibly, the chapter describes the operation of a paint factory; but the remark that the factory "looks like a small city" indicates symbolic dimensions. The narrator is assigned to mix ten drops of black paint into every can of "Optic White." When he protests that the black would discolor the pure white, his white foreman replies, "Never mind how it looks. You just do what you're told and don't try to think about it." Unaware of the physical principle that mixing small amounts of black paint into white paint actually makes white whiter, the narrator scrupulously follows directions. This process for enriching white paint symbolically parallels the interplay of racial colors in America. The black Negro makes the white world whiter; for since his values and aspirations emulate those of the white world, he reinforces the white American's escatology and, like the black in the can of paint, embellishes the whiteness of American public life. The company's motto is, ironically, "Keep America Pure with Liberty Paints," and, since the paint will be used on a national monument, the passage suggests that all of American history has a similar color composition. Although Negroes have contributed to the American achievement, their effort, like the ten drops, enriches the existing texture. When the narrator inadvertently takes his refill from the wrong tank, the mixture he produces is "not as white and glassy as before; it had a grey tinge." If put on the national monument, it would reveal the heretical truth that American life, underneath the white surface, is, like the color grey, a mixture of black and white. For this mistake, the narrator is removed from his paint-mixing job. If he had likewise revealed the actuality beneath the white-washed surface of America, it is implied, he would have been exiled from the country.

In the second quarter of the novel, the narrator arrives in New York to test the opportunities open to the Negro in the North. He carries seven sealed letters of introduction from President Bledsoe to philanthropic white liberals who are patrons of the college. At six of the offices, the narrator asks to see the man to whom the letter is addressed. The letter is taken from him and delivered; and every time, the secretary returns and informs the narrator that the important man will contact him later. None fulfill his promise; for unbeknownst to the narrator, Bledsoe's letter tells the businessmen that this student has seriously violated some undisclosed rule of the school:

> This case represents one of the rare, delicate instances in which one for whom we held great expectations has gone grievously astray, and who in his fall threatens to upset certain delicate relationships between certain interested individuals and the school.

However, in his concluding sentence, Bledsoe, perhaps disingenuously, asks each recipient to help the young man. The lesson this episode portrays is that the Northern philanthropists will aid "Negroes" in the South, but they will not rescue an individual needy Southern Negro in the North. They suffer from hyperopia: Pain in the distance can be seen clearly, while that close at hand is blurred.

Since one of the businessman is away from New York, the narrator postpones calling at his office. Finally getting an interview, the narrator meets the son of "Mr. Emerson," an heir to the American liberal tradition. He speaks in platitudes, often using a second platitude that doubles back on the first: "Ambition is a wonderful force," he tells the narrator, "but sometimes it can be blinding . . . On the other hand, it can make you successful—like my father . . . The only trouble with ambition is that it sometimes blinds one to realities." He is also extremely self-conscious. "Don't let me upset you," he tells the narrator," I had a difficult session with my analyst last evening and the slightest thing is apt to set me off." When he makes a slip of the tongue, Emerson stops to ponder its significance. He boasts of the number of Negro acquaintances he has—artists and intellectuals all—and of his regular attendance at an important Negro club. Being, as he says, "incapable of cynicism," he reveals to the narrator the deceitful contents of Bledsoe's letter. However, because he is afraid to disobey his father's wishes, young Emerson does not hire the narrator and warns him not to reveal their conversation to anyone. The Northern Emersonian liberal, the novel tells us, is too torn by neurosis, self-doubt and compromise to help the Negro in need.

Recognizing that those who support him in principle offer him few opportunities in practice, the narrator seeks a job as a laborer at Liberty Paints. He is hired, he later discovers, as a "scab," because the company wants to replace its unionized white workers with cheaper non-union Negro labor. The narrator is assigned to the foreman named Kimbro, described as a "slave driver." Assuming this traditional role, Kimbro instructs his Negro workers in their jobs. When a worker makes an error, as does the narrator, Kimbro exercises an overseer's authority and assigns him to another task. After his mistake in mixing the colors, the narrator is assigned to assist Lucius Brockway in the third sub-basement of the plant. Since his job is to control and service the machines that mix the base of the paint, the whole operation of paint-making depends upon his talents. The company has in the past frequently attempted to replace Brockway with white labor—during Brockway's illness an engineer of Italian ancestry was assigned to the job—but it discovered that no one else could do his work. Fearing that someone else will intrude on his domain, Brockway is fanatically anti-union. Entirely subservient to white authority, he takes a childish delight in the company's dependence on him and his special relationship with the boss. When Brockway retired, the Old Man discovered the paint was losing its excellence and personally persuaded Brockway to return to his job. Underpaid and underpraised, Brockway survives in the industrial system by embracing the existing authority and by having indispensable talents.

One day, the narrator inadvertently enters a union meeting in the locker-room. The white workers, assuming that he is applying for membership, at once suspect that he is a company spy. One member proposes that the narrator prove his loyalty to the union before he be permitted "to become acquainted with the work of the union and its aims." Although the novel does not develop the theme of this encounter, the incident suggests that before the labor movement will accept the Negro, he must go to inordinate lengths to justify his right to belong. Once the union people identify him as suspect, they make no effort to ascertain his actual attitude toward unions. "They had made their decision without giving me a chance to speak for myself." As the narrator departs, the meeting chairman tells him, "We want you to know that we are only trying to protect ourselves. Some day we hope to have you as a member in good standing.

What the sequence illustrates is that to both white industry and white unions the Negro is acceptable only if he is either more loyal or more competent than a white; and business would prefer that his labor be less expensive. "The existence of racial prejudice in both employee and employer groups is of course an indisputable fact," wrote Horace R. Cayton and George S. Mitchell in 1939, in *Black Workers and the New Unions*. "If there were no economic advantages in employing Negroes, most employers would prefer a white labor force." This situation creates what the sociologist Robert Merton christens the self-fulfilling prophecy: "In the beginning, a *fake* definition of the situation [evokes] a new behavior which makes the originally false conception come true." If the dominant majority decides that Negroes are unfit to become union members because, it reasons, their lower standard of living allows them to take jobs at less than the prevailing wage, then the Negroes, as a result of exclusion, will become strike-breakers, accepting the lower wage and, it follows, necessarily adjusting their existence to the lower standard of living. Similarly if an employer rules that the Negroes are incapable of

doing important work, then, acting upon their own false belief, they give Negroes only menial jobs. If the Negro, having no other choice, accepts the distasteful labor and handles it competently, then, in the employer's eyes, the Negro has "proved" he is fit only for menial work. Both employers and unions, then, exploit the Negro's second-class position in American society; and neither offers the Negro an acceptable solution. Later in the novel, a misunderstanding, coupled with a difference in attitude, produces a fight between the narrator and Brockway. An explosion occurs, and the narrator finds himself in a hospital. Here he undergoes an unidentified operation somewhat resembling a lobotomy, from which, the doctor promises, he will emerge with a "complete change of personality."

III

In the development of the novel, this chapter and the one following it serve a transitional function; for whereas the narrator once accepted the conventional solutions to the Negro's dilemma, now he is emancipated from this narrow sense of possibility and prepared to sample more radical alternatives. Upon returning to his boarding house, a residence for more ambitious Negroes in New York, he recognizes that his house-mates display the vanities and deceits of those who either failed to climb through the existing system or deluded themselves with artificial tokens of success:

> The moment I entered the bright, buzzing lobby of Men's House I was overcome by a sense of alienation and hostility. My overalls were causing stares and I knew that I could live there no longer, that that phase of my life was past. The lobby was the meeting place for various groups still caught up in the illusions that had just been boomeranged out of my head: college boys working to return to school down south; older advocates of racial progress with utopian schemes for building black business empires; preachers ordained by no authority except their own, without church or congregation, without bread or wine, body or blood; the community "leaders" without followers; old men of sixty or more still caught up in post–Civil War dreams of freedom within segregation; the pathetic ones who possessed nothing beyond their dreams of being gentlemen, who held small jobs or drew small pensions, and all pretending to be engaged in some vast, though obscure, enterprise, who affected the pseudo-courtly manners of certain Southern congressmen and bowed and nodded as they passed like senile old roosters in a barnyard; the younger crowd for whom I now felt a contempt such as only a disillusioned dreamer feels for those still unaware that they dream—the business students from southern colleges, for whom business was a vague, abstract game with rules as obsolete as Noah's Ark but who yet were drunk on finance.

This complements the lobotomy; for just as the narrator assumes a new identity (the operation having caused him to forget his name), so he emerges from his residence hotel with a different set of inclinations.

Soon after, when the narrator discovers some poor old Negroes being evicted from their flat, he makes a speech on their behalf; and as his efforts attract a Harlem crowd, the narrator is accosted by a red-bearded man who introduces himself as "Brother Jack," who says of the narrator's extemporaneous speech: "*History* has been born in your brain." Jack explains that he belongs to a radical action group; and once the conversation becomes more relaxed the narrator accepts Jack's request to see him in the evening. That night, the narrator is introduced to the "Brotherhood," persuaded to become a salaried organizer for the movement, and assigned to a "theoretician" who will educate him in its aims and method. The "Brotherhood" is the American Communist Party in a thin fictional disguise.

This third major section of the novel portrays the narrator's discovery that this radical movement understands neither his existence nor that of his people. From his opening conversation, Brother Jack speaks a language strange to the Negro experience. Addressing the narrator as "Brother," Jack offers him cheese cake, a white delicacy wholly foreign to Negro taste. Furthermore, he muses on how "history has passed by" the old evicted Negroes who are, he adds, "agrarian types, you know. Being ground up by industrial conditions. Thrown on the dump heaps and cast aside. They's like dead limbs that must be pruned away so that the tree may bear young fruit or the storms of history will blow them away." To this the narrator responds, "Look, I don't know what you're talking about. I've never lived on a farm and I didn't study agriculture." Later with an inappropriateness that is typical of him, Jack predicts that the Brotherhood will transform the narrator into "the new Booker T. Washington." A conciliator like Washington is precisely the opposite of the kind of leader a radical group needs; a reference to, say, Frederick Douglass would have been more appropriate. Moreover, the Brotherhood's images of Negro Americans come from the storehouse of bourgeois stereotypes. When one "Brother" asks the narrator to sing a spiritual, the narrator replies that he cannot sing. The Brother's reply is, "Nonsense, *all* colored people sing." Yet, although he senses the Brotherhood's lack of understanding, the narrator is flattered enough to cast his lot with them.

From his earliest contact with the movement, the narrator is aware that he must assume a pre-cast role. When he accepts the job, he is outfitted with a new identity—on a slip of paper is written his new name. At a Brotherhood party, he overhears a female leader say, "But don't you think he should be a little blacker," and the statement prompts him to think, "What was I, a man or a natural resource?" Later, the Brotherhood suggests that he move to a new address and discontinue writing to his relatives for a while. When Jack introduces him to the larger circle under his new identity, the narrator notices, "Everyone smiled and seemed eager to meet me, as though they all knew the role I was to play." Though the narrator senses that the Brotherhood's aims and methods may not coincide with his, he accepts the role they thrust upon him for two reasons—because it offers him a key to understanding his experience and "the possibility of being more than a member of a race."

What the narrator fails to see at this point—and what he discovers later—is that "being more" than a member of his race means being less of a Negro. After he joins the Brotherhood, the narrator symbolically attempts to sever connections between himself and his Southern Negro past. In a boarding house in Harlem, he discovers an object of much ulterior meaning:

> The cast-iron figure of a very black, red-lipped and wide-mouthed Negro, whose white eyes stared up at me from the floor, his face an enormous grin, his single large black hand held palm up before his chest. It was . . . the kind of bank which, if a coin is placed in the hand and a lever pressed upon the back, will raise its arm and flip the coin into the grinning mouth.

The figurine represents an aspect of the historical past that the narrator now wants desperately to forget; it has become "a self-mocking image." When the steam pipe of his room emits a clanking sound, the narrator strikes it with "the kinky iron head," cracking the figurine whose parts scatter across the floor. To escape both the landlady's wrath and his own feelings of guilt, the narrator scrapes the parts into the leather briefcase he received from the Southern businessmen. He drops the package in a garbage can outside an old private house; but its owner demands that he retrieve it (and, all that its contents symbolize). He protests, but when she threatens to call the police, he digs his hand into the muck (that lies between him and his Negro past) and recaptures the load. Two blocks later, he drops it in the heavy snow; but a passerby brings it back to him. The narrator cannot dispose of the package or elements of his character its contents symbolize until near the novel's end. He later acquires from another Negro Brother a link from a work-gang chain which he puts into his pocket; whenever he touches it, he is reminded of his heritage. Through these symbolic devices, Ellison makes the point that not even the Brotherhood can separate the American Negro from his past.

These themes are reinforced by the narrator's introspective monologues. During his affiliation with the Brotherhood, he is haunted by fears of "becoming someone else." For example, just before he is to deliver his first important speech for the Brotherhood, he feels "with a flash of panic that the moment I walked out upon the platform and opened my mouth I'd be someone else. Not just a nobody with a manufactured name which might have belonged to anyone, or to no one. But another personality." The problem is not that the Brotherhood forces him to do things against his will, but that this political life is not an organic outgrowth of his own past. His present experience strikes the narrator as a meaningless series of tacked-on events, chance encounters, and sudden fortunes. He becomes aware of two identities in himself:

> The old self that slept a few hours a night and dreamed sometimes of my grandfather and Bledsoe and Brockway and Mary, the self that flew without wings and plunged from great heights; and the new public self that spoke for the Brotherhood and was

becoming so much more important than the other
that I seemed to run a foot race against myself.

A rigorous schedule prevents the narrator from thinking
too much about this split; only when he is transferred to
a less demanding job does this awareness of his divided
personality oppress him.

If the Brotherhood has little sense of the needs of an
individual Negro, it is even less aware of the actualities
of American Negro life. Once the narrator becomes an
organizer, he quickly rouses a strong, grass-roots movement among the Harlem populace; he makes speeches at
public rallies and regularly visits all the important bars.
His extraordinary success, however, makes his more experienced Negro Brothers jealous; and one, Brother
Wrestum ("rest room"?), accuses him of individual opportunism and dictatorial aspirations. Although one speech
earns applause "like a clap of thunder," the narrator is
condemned by his Brotherhood superiors, because his
talk was "wild, hysterical, politically irresponsible and
dangerous, and worse than that, it was *incorrect!*" The
emphasis upon the last word suggests to the narrator that,
"The term described the most heinous crime imaginable."
They criticize him, he discovers, because he neglected to
include the ideology that would organize the Negro audience behind the Brotherhood. To prepare him more adequately for future speeches, they assign him to an intensive indoctrination program. It is implied, though not
specifically illustrated, that these "correct" ideas and
phrases are incapable of moving the Harlem audience.
After all, if Jack's favorite clichés sound strange to the
semi-educated ear of the narrator, they would be more
wholly foreign to the common Negroes. By not correctly
gauging the attitudes of Harlem, the Brotherhood also
destroys the narrator's usefulness for its cause.

Once he is cleared of suspicions of both disloyalty and
personal opportunism, the narrator returns to Harlem to
discover that in his absence his personal following has
disintegrated. In a symbolic passage, he enters a bar and
addresses two old acquaintances as "Brothers." The tall
one replies inquisitively, "he is relative of yourn?" His
cohort adds, "Shit, he goddam sho ain't no kin of mine!"
The first asks the bartender, "We just wanted to know if
you could tell us just whose brother this here cat's supposed to be?" Since the bartender claims to be the
narrator's "Brother," an argument ensues, the tall one
protesting that since the narrator "got the white fever and
left" for downtown—revealed that his ultimate loyalties
were not to Negroes and Harlem—he was no longer a
"brother" of the Negroes. Later, the narrator discovers
that in his absence the Brotherhood has abandoned its
efforts in Harlem. The work he did, the support he organized, have all disappeared and there seems little likelihood he can retrieve the lost ground. His own labor for
the Brotherhood, he deduces, accomplished nothing. "No
great change had been made."

In one comic interlude, the novel suggests that the
Brotherhood suffered because many of its organizers and
sympathizers had motivations quite distant from politics. After he finishes his speech on the "woman question," the narrator is accosted by an extremely sensual
woman who questions him on "certain aspects of our
ideology." Since the questioning will take a while, she
invites him up to her apartment. Innocently, he accepts
her hospitality. She explains, as he enters her sumptuous
apartment, "You can see, Brother, it is really the spiritual
values of the Brotherhood that interest me." As he answers her questions, she moves closer to him and tells
him how he embodies a "great throbbing vitality." After
he seduces her, he condemns her for "confusing the class
struggle with the ass struggle."

The Brotherhood's failure to gauge the Negro's actual
needs lies not so much in the confusion of motives exemplified by the seductive women as in the blindness intrinsic in the movement's approach to reality. The movement's
ideology contains elements appealing to the impoverished Negroes. It offers colored members equal rights;
yet it is unable to empathize with the people's needs and
spiritual temper. The novel explains this failure in both
symbolic and narrative terms. When the narrator is reprimanded by Brother Jack for not preaching the correct
line at the proper time, the narrator retorts that Jack, a
white man, cannot know "the political consciousness of
Harlem." Jack insists that the committee is the ultimate
judge of reality and that the narrator is disobeying its
"discipline." The narrator rejoins that Jack wants to be
"the great white father" of Harlem, "Marse Jack." A fight
seems imminent; but before it starts, Jack snatches his
glass eye from its socket. The eye, Jack explains, was lost
in the line of duty—by implication, in following the "discipline." The passage suggests not only that Jack is half-
blind to the realities of Harlem—with only one eye his
perception is limited—but also that he is incapable of
seeing Harlem *in depth.* The narrator himself recognizes
the second implication: "The meaning of discipline," he
figures, "is sacrifice . . . yes, and blindness." Once he
discovers this failure of perception, the narrator never
again feels total loyalty to the Brotherhood.

Still, he accepts their command to see Hambro, the chief
theoretician, who reveals more obviously why the Brotherhood is oblivious to the needs of Harlem. It has deserted its drive to recruit Negroes, because, the narrator
is told, its emphasis has switched from national issues to
international ones. When he asks Hambro, "What's to be
done about my district," explaining the decline in membership and the threats from the black nationalists, the
theoretician authoritatively informs him, "Your members
will have to be sacrificed. We are making temporary alliances with other political groups and the interest of one
group of brothers must be sacrificed to that of the
whole." When the narrator argues that exploiting the
Negro people is cynical, Hambro replies, in characteristic
double-talk, "Not cynicism—realism. The trick is to take
advantage of them in their own best interests." The narrator asks what justifies the sacrifice of unwitting people,
and Hambro replies "the laws of reality." Who determines the laws of reality? "The collective wisdom of the

'scientists' of the Brotherhood" is the reply. However, as the narrator perceives, the Brotherhood's science has little contact with hard facts. All they know is ideas about history's movements on the world stage; instead of trying to see Harlem as an individual entity, they see it only as an interdependent cog in a big machine. To the actual lives and hopes of American Negroes, the scientists are completely insensitive.

In talking with Hambro, the narrator concludes, "Everywhere I've turned somebody has wanted to sacrifice me for my good—only *they* were the ones who benefitted." This recognition unlocks the narrator's first general thesis about the relations of white people with the Negro. Both Hambro and Jack, he thinks, are incapable of seeing a human essence either black or white. They believe that only the political part of a man, that segment that could serve the interests of the movement, is worthy of attention; all other problems and aspirations, whether emotional or physical, are ignored. Men could just as well be invisible. "Here I had thought they accepted me," the narrator decides, "because they felt that color made no difference, when in reality it made no difference because they didn't see either color or men." He then recognizes that Jack and Hambro hardly differ from Emerson and Norton. "They were very much the same, each attempting to force his picture of reality upon me and neither giving a hoot in hell for how things looked to me. I was simply a material, a natural resource to be used." As the four white figures blend into one, the narrator discovers the core truth of his relationship with them: "I now recognized my invisibility."

The recognition means that the narrator implicitly accepts the warning Ras the Exhorter, the black nationalist, offered to him earlier in the book:

> Why you with these white folks? Why a good boy like you with them? You *my* brother, mahn. Brothers are the same color; how the hell you call these white men *brother?* Shit mahn Brothers the same color. We sons of Mama Africa, you done forgot? You black, BLACK! You got *bahd* hair! You got thick *lips!* They say you *stink!* They hate you, mahn. You African. AFRICAN! Why you with them? Leave that shit, mahn. They sell you out. That shit is old-fashioned. They enslave us—you forget that? How can they mean a black man any good? How they going to be your *brother?*

Ras's point—that all white men, whether enemy or friend, will use the Negro for their own purposes and finally betray him—is supported by the narrator's own understanding of his experience.

Ras himself proffers a political alternative for the American Negro, as he represents those Negro leaders who have espoused a racism that inverts the Manichean color symbolism traditional to the Christian West. Whereas the Western, which is to say American, mythos makes black synonymous with evil, the Negro racist makes black the color of all that is good. He attracts the support of Negroes by making them proud of their blackness. According to one scholar of black nationalism, C. Eric Lincoln,

> All black nationalist movements have in common three characteristics: a disparagement of the white man and his culture, a repudiation of Negro identity and an appropriation of "asiatic" culture symbols. Within this framework, they take shape in a remarkable variety of creeds and organizations.

The most prominent black nationalist in the period covered by Ellison's novel was Marcus Garvey, as the most famous exemplars in recent years are Elijah Muhammed and Malcolm X. However, there is little reason specifically to identify, as some critics have done, any of these figures with Ras the Exhorter. Although Ras is described as having, like Garvey, a West Indian accent, he favors resettlement in Abyssinia ("Ras" being Abyssinian for prince), whereas Garvey wanted to send American Negroes to West Africa. In this respect, one could say, Ras is closer to the historic Noble Drew Ali, the self-styled leader of the "Moors," who designated Morocco in North Africa as the Negro homeland; moreover, his name evokes a nod to the Ras Tafari movement of colored West Indians. What this multiple reference suggests is that Ras, like other important characters in the novel, is conceived as a fictional prototype embodying a utopian alternative that has been espoused by several historical figures; and sure enough, Ras's group embodies all three of the characteristics Professor Lincoln enumerates as typical of black nationalist movements.

The narrator never allies himself with Ras; for although he knows that Ras is capable of telling the truth about the Negro's relations with whites, the narrator also recognizes that the alternative Ras offers is unrealistic—absurd in everyday practice. Ras advocates a massive return to Africa which—given the costs, the lack of inhabitable space and the difficulties of resettlement—would be too hazardous for an average American Negro. For the United States, Ras preaches counterviolence, which the narrator discovers is ultimately self-destructive.

The Harlem battle Ras eventually wages is most thoroughly characterized by an anonymous Negro who tells his drinking cronies about the riot he has just witnessed. Through this device, Ellison reveals not only the absurdity of the battle itself but also the average Negro's bemused view of the fray:

> You know that stud Ras the Destroyer? Well, man, *he* was spitting blood. Hell, yes, man, he had him a big black hoss and a fur cap and some kind of old lion skin or something over his shoulders and he was raising hell. Goddam if he wasn't a *sight,* riding up and down on this ole hoss, you know one of the kind that pulls vegetable wagons, and he got him a cowboy saddle and some big spurs. . . .

> Hell, yes! Riding up and down the block yelling, "Destroy 'em! Drive 'em out. Burn 'em out! I, Ras, commands you—to destroy them to the last piece of rotten fish!" And 'bout that time some

joker with a big ole Georgia voice sticks his head out the window and yells, "Ride 'em cowboy. Give 'em hell and bananas." And man, that crazy sonofabitch up there on that hoss, looking like death eating a sandwich, he reaches down and comes up with a forty-five and starts blazing up at that window—and man, talk about cutting out! In a second wasn't nobody left but ole Ras up there on that hoss with that lion skin stretched out behind him. Crazy, man.

When he seen them cops riding up he reached back of his saddle and come up with some kind of old shield. One with a spike in the middle of it. And that ain't all; when he sees the cops he calls to one of his goddam henchmens to hand him up a spear, and a little short guy run out into the street and give him one. You know, one of the kind you see them African guys carrying in the moving pictures. . . .

Ras rides hard, "like Earle Sand in the fifth at Jamaica," into the mounted police; and although he manages to knock down two with his spear, a third policeman fells him with a bullet. Meanwhile, the onlookers of Harlem are looting the damaged stores. The political point is quite clear: To the typical Harlemite, Ras's actions are ludicrously ineffectual; for he is neither prepared for a modern battle nor able to win the support of the Negro people. Moreover, the violence he creates causes more deaths among the Negroes than the white enemies. In this respect, the riot echoes the battle royal fought at the beginning of the novel; for in both scenes, the Negroes vent their anger not against their oppressor but against their own people.

Against both Ras and Brother Jack is counterposed Rinehart, who represents the possibilities of Harlem life. As Ras's thugs are closing in upon the narrator, he steps into a drugstore and purchases a disguise of dark glasses and a wide-brimmed hat. Advancing down the street, he notices that several passers-by mistake him for a certain "Rinehart"; within moments, he discovers that Rinehart must be a desirable lover, a gambler, a numbers runner, a police briber, a male whore, a hipster, a zoot-suiter, and a self-ordained Reverend—"Spiritual Technologist." The narrator realizes why Rinehart can fill so many roles, for his own dark glasses reveal that the world of Harlem is "a merging fluidity of forms." In contrast to the Brotherhood, and also to Ras, who try to squeeze the world into rigid categories which limit the dimensions of existence, Rinehart sees that the Negro world in the North offers anonymity and possibility:

> In the South everyone knows you, but coming North was a jump into the unknown. You could actually make yourself anew. The notion was frightening, for now the world seemed to flow before my eyes. All boundaries down, freedom was not only the recognition of necessity, it was the recognition of possibility. And sitting there trembling I caught a brief glimpse of the possibilities posed by Rinehart's multiple personalities. . . .

This recognition echoes the advice an anonymous veteran gave the narrator back in The Golden Day: "Be your own father, young man. And remember, the world is possibility if only you'll discover it." After this revelation, the narrator perceives that "Hambro's lawyer's mind was too narrowly logical" to understand Harlem.

After hastily departing from Hambro's, the narrator decides "to do a Rinehart," to face life with the most ironic of strategies. Remembering his childhood, he repeats to himself his grandfather's deathbed advice: "Live with your head in the lion's mouth. I want you to overcome 'em with yesses, undermine 'em with grins, agree 'em to death and destruction, let 'em swoller you till they vomit or bust wide open." He decides to master the trick of saying yes and no at the same time, yes to please and no to know. "For now I saw that I could agree with Jack without agreeing, and I could tell Harlem to have hope when there was no hope." To please his Brotherhood superiors he fabricates reports of a nonexistent growth in membership, and at the next Brotherhood gathering he entices Sybil, the wife of an organizational functionary, to come to his apartment. Although he knows that she sees him as just another hypersexual Negro, "expected either to sing 'Old Man River' and just keep rolling along, or do fancy tricks with my muscles," he decides this time to exploit his invisibility. However, when she makes "a modest proposal that I join her in a very revolting ritual," the narrator, sometimes a prig, is repelled by what he interprets as an assault on something deeper than mere sexuality. So, he spends the evening torn between the impulse to throw her out of his bed and wondering how Rinehart would have handled the situation. Though he imitates the motions he imagines to be Rinehart's, seducing the girl who calls him "boo'ful," he cannot play the role with the assurance of the master.

This experience with the Brotherhood, along with his recognition of the vanity of Ras's efforts, leads the narrator to a decisive decision: "I knew that it was better to live out one's own absurdity than to die for that of others." Later, he elaborates on the theme:

> I've never been more loved and appreciated than when I tried to "justify" and affirm someone's mistaken beliefs; or when I've tried to give my friends the incorrect, absurd answers they wished to hear. . . . Oh yes, it made them happy and it made me sick. So, I became ill of affirmation, of saying "yes" against the nay-saying of my stomach—not to mention my brain. . . . My problem was that I always tried to go in everyone's way but my own. I have also been called one thing and then another while no one really wished to hear what I called myself. So after years of trying to adopt the opinions of others I finally rebelled.

In the final sequences of the novel, the narrator confronts the problem of how to face what he takes to be the absurdity of society. In escaping from the police, he jumps through a manhole into a bin of coal. Unable to climb out, he experiences a "dark night of the soul," which includes a nightmare in which Norton, Emerson and Jack castrate him of his "illusions." Wading through the tunnels, he finds a large basement cavern which becomes his underground home; in his own way, the man who had Candide's innocence and questing energy eventually accepts Candide's final dictum, "That we must cultivate our [own] garden." Whereas Rinehart exploited absurdity for personal gain, the narrator as underground man accepts, as an expatriate, the condition through his own non-participation.

However, this escape, he discovers, is not satisfactory either. "I couldn't be still even in hibernation," he thinks, "because, damn it, there's the mind, the *mind*. It wouldn't let me rest." The narrator's conscience inspires him to write a book that will explain his experience. "Without the possibility of action," he thinks, existence takes on a meaninglessness, knowledge is forgotten, and the capacities to love and care are suppressed. The narrator achieves what Ellison described in his essay on Wright as the spirit of the blues: "They at once express both the agony of life and the possibility of conquering it through sheer toughness of spirit. They fall short of tragedy only in that they provide no solution, offer no scapegoat but the self." While he agrees with the wisdom of Louis Armstrong's song, "Open the window and let the foul air out," he also believes another song that says, "It was good green corn before the harvest." It is the latter belief that leads him to resolve to "shake off his old skin," to repudiate his form of expatriation, and to seek in the aboveground society an existence that allows him to live primarily for himself. He concludes his story affirming the desire to affirm. "There's a possibility that even an invisible man has a socially responsible role to play." With all his previous experiences and rejections, this becomes the most positive commitment that Ellison's narrator can justifiably make.

### NOTES

[1] What Washington actually believed and said, it should be pointed out, differ slightly from the ideas generally ascribed to him by both followers and enemies. In fact, he spoke out against the grandfather clause, protested lynching, and urged legal action against discrimination. However, since the narrator of Ellison's novel as a high school student subscribes to the prevailing popular image, the following summary deals with the myth, rather than the fact of Washington. History remembers Washington as having primarily urged his fellow Negroes to lead an honest and industrious life within the framework of Southern segregation.

**John Stark**

SOURCE: "Alienation and Analysis in Doctorow's *The Book of Daniel,*" in *Critique: Studies in Modern Fiction,* Vol. XVI, No. 3, 1975, pp. 101-10.

[*In the following essay, Stark explores the relationship between E. L. Doctorow's* Book of Daniel *and the trial of Julius and Ethel Rosenberg.*]

E. L. Doctorow's *The Book of Daniel,* a fine recent novel that has received insufficient attention, perhaps will benefit from renewed interest in Julius and Ethel Rosenberg. Although the novel's tenuous relation to the Rosenberg case creates some of its fascination, the themes that Doctorow develops create most of its substantial intrinsic merit. Doctorow's allusion in his title to the Biblical book of Daniel hints at these themes. The Biblical book describes the Jews enduring as aliens in Babylon and Daniel preserving himself by correctly analyzing bizarre dreams. Similarly, Doctorow makes alienation and analysis the most important themes in *The Book of Daniel.*

Doctorow declines the gambit of writing a fictionalized polemic about the Rosenbergs. Daniel, the narrator, at one point implies that Doctorow does not want to re-adjudicate their case: "I find no clues either to their guilt or innocence."[1] Doctorow rarely includes such clues in *The Book of Daniel.* Occasionally, his determination slackens, and he slips into his novel passing references to the issue. For example, he points out that the prosecution subverted justice by trying the Isaacsons (Doctorow's fictional Rosenbergs) ostensibly for conspiracy but actually for treason (217). At another point Daniel's stepfather, a lawyer, argues that disputing the guilt of Mindish (the novel's David Greenglass) would have been the most effective defense. He thereby implies that a more clever lawyer than Ascher could have proved his clients' innocence. Near the novel's end Daniel speculates that Mindish may have accused the Isaacsons in order to divert attention from real spies. Doctorow could easily have added many more legal arguments because earlier writers have thoroughly discussed the case, but instead he concentrates on the themes of alienation and analysis.

In *The Book of Daniel* the alienation of modern Jews recapitulates their ancestors' alienation during the Biblical Daniel's era. In a discursive passage Doctorow writes of the earlier time: "it is a bad time for Daniel and his co-religionists, for they are second-class citizens, in a distinctly hostile environment" (21). Doctorow uses the furnace into which the Babylonian king thrusts three of Daniel's friends as a symbol of the alien's oppression by the dominant group. The symbol recurs in his novel, particularly in references to the furnace in the basement of the Isaacsons' building and to its attendant, a gruff black named Williams. His fiercely energetic removal of the coal delivered on the sidewalk impresses the young Daniel, and his loud stoking of the furnace at night keeps Daniel awake. The noise of firemaking intensifies during crises, such as the ones immediately after the death of Daniel's grandmother and after the arrest of his parents. During the former crisis, Daniel ventures into the basement to talk with Williams. In one sense, the dominant social class has shunted Williams aside, as it has the Jews, and has made him an alien; in a more important sense, as his psychological domination of Daniel indicates, in their relation and in many other relations between blacks and Jews, the Jew is the alien. Williams, then, tends the furnace, but he does not fear being thrown into it; Daniel, frightened, retreats from the basement and furnace. Doctorow does not state, because he does not need to, the similarity between the furnace images (of the Bible and the novel) and the Nazis' ovens: the ultimate instrument for suppressing aliens.

Doctorow also shows Jewish alienation in other ways besides developing the furnace image. The Isaacsons' trial, like the Rosenbergs', nearly becomes self-enclosed and distinct from WASP society, because judge, accused, major witnesses, and attorneys on both sides are Jewish. At first, the situation may suggest that alienation has nothing to do with the trial, that the verdict does not relate to the defendants' Jewishness. One, however, can also draw the conclusion that persistent alienation makes a group perform the dominant group's work by destroying itself. Doctorow merely hints at such interpretation, but he emphasizes the grandmother's alienation.

> Grandma goes mad when she can no longer consider the torment of her life. My mother's catalogue of the old lady's misfortunes—the abandoned parents whose brown picture she still keeps in her drawer, the death of her first-born in the street, the death of her two sisters in the big fire, the death of her second-born from the flu, the death of her husband, my grandfather who would have loved me if he'd lived. . . . "What killed him and killed them all was poverty and exploitation, and that means being poor and being kept poor by people who grow fat and rich from your labor." (81)

Unlike the Jews, who involuntarily become alienated, the leftist characters in the novel freely choose political alienation. When they accept a leftist theory of history and society and the concomitant political position, they become alienated from people who hold more common positions. Daniel recognizes the effects of accepting his father's political teachings: "that was our relationship—his teaching me how to be a psychic alien" (45). Paul Isaacson, the father, also separates himself and his family from others culturally. Daniel understands the interrelations among culture, politics, and institutions: "what else is to be expected of a Hollywood long since purged of its few humanitarian filmmakers? And what is to be expected of a jury picked however partially from a depraved culture?" (213). In addition to interest in culture that has an obvious political tinge, such as Paul Robeson concerts, the Isaacsons absorb apparently non-political high culture, such as Philharmonic concerts. Moreover, they find their social ideals and heroes in Russia, which alienates them from many of their countrymen. For example, Daniel reveres Bukharin, not because he accepts everything Russian; he admires Bukharin precisely because he opposed Stalin's outrages. Although Doctorow carefully delineates these causes of alienation, he does not show, nor even hint, that the elder Isaacsons' politics impelled them to spy; their criminal conviction, rather, dramatizes their alienation.

The Isaacsons' political alienation admits of degrees; they can assume various political positions at various distances from the common positions. Paul chooses not to separate himself totally from the dominant politics. First, he clings to his belief that one part of the society will correct another part's errors. About the law requiring Communists to register, he says that "only insane men could expect it to survive in the Courts" (98). Shortly, he becomes a victim of the legal system that he expects to nullify Congressional action—and, of course, that legal system kills him. In a cruelly ironic way, then, the hope that signifies refusal to become alienated exacerbates a partially alienated people's anguish; the very things in which they maintain hope become the instruments of further torment and, finally, of death. Looking back at the misplaced hope of people like his father, Daniel dramatizes such irony and indicts those who retain enough hope to be reformers: "it is complicity in the system to be appalled with the moral structure of the system" (243).

In addition to their other difficulties, Paul and his wife, Rochelle, are tormented by the particularly bitter alienation caused by desertion of likely supporters. The Communist Party does not help them until after the sentence, and it helps slightly then only because it anticipates a propaganda advantage, not because it has substantive reasons nor concern for them. Luckily, the parents cannot know about their children's attacks on them after the execution. Daniel attacks mildly, claiming, for example, that Rochelle's "politics was the politics of want. . . . If [she] had been anything but poor, I don't think she would have been a Red" (43). His sister, Susan—Doctorow makes the younger child a girl—attacks much more bitterly. As Daniel deduces later, her suicide attempt occurred as she traveled to New York to give a poster with her parents' picture on it to a radical friend. She wants him to add it to his collage that depicts his enemies. Her act thus repudiates her parents in favor of her radical politics, just as on the same grounds she repudiates her step-parents and Daniel.

By means of time-shifts Doctorow interweaves the Isaacsons' case with the more recent history of the left to show Daniel's increasing political alienation. First, Daniel joins the march on the Pentagon, although only he and his wife know that his presence links the event with his parents; he participates, but not so actively as he would have had he identified his parentage. Then, in the last of the novel's three alternate endings, Doctorow narrates Daniel's eviction by strikers from the Columbia University library, where he has been writing his story. They, too, do not know who he is, and they treat him like any other person impeding their progress. Although their lack of perspective precludes their realizing it, their failure to recognize a survivor from an earlier crucial event in the left's history implies their belief that they are founding the left. Daniel leaves docilely, evicted exactly when he finishes the narration that constitutes the novel, neither opposed to them nor joined with them. Finally, he becomes alienated from the political position for which he much earlier alienated himself from society.

Doctorow also suggests that certain common human traits cause Daniel to become alienated, not only from a group with whose politics he essentially agrees, but also from humanity. In general, Doctorow shows that these traits make alienation difficult for people to avoid, and to clarify such alienation he again uses the image of the furnace. About aggression, one of the general causes of alienation, Daniel says, "the necessary emotional fever for fighting a war cannot be demobilized as quickly as the platoon. On the contrary, like a fiery furnace, at white heat, it takes a considerable time to cool" (33). According to Daniel, his grandmother, too, uses the furnace to represent persecution. He imagines her "calling down cholera and Cossacks and typhoid and wholesale terrors of the burning furnace" (79). At another point, Daniel, seeking to probe more deeply than a conventional Marxist, asserts that "the basis of all class distinctions in society is corporal punishment" (144). To illustrate his point he describes knouting and burning at the stake, the later resembling his image of the persecutorial furnace.

Daniel himself has an aggressive side. Doctorow's description and analysis of it greatly strengthens *The Book of Daniel*. To have portrayed him as the innocent victim of the sadists who killed his parents and who sublimate their sadism so as to corrupt the society in which he lives would have been easier—and much more superficial. More incisively, Doctorow shows in Daniel glimmers of a general problem that underlies the persecution of Jews and leftists: man's inhumanity to man; for example, Daniel enjoys tossing his baby into the air and barely catching him. In addition to endangering the baby and acting out aggression, his action cruelly frightens both the baby and Daniel's wife. Another time he orders his wife to take off her pants; playing masochist to his sadist, she does, and he burns her three times with a cigarette lighter. Thus, Doctorow again connects fire with cruelty.

Doctorow also shows that sexual desires complicate human motivations and alienate one person from another. The Isaacsons' defense includes an effort to show that Mindish accused them at least partly because of his sexual desire for Rochelle and his resulting jealousy of Paul. To develop the sexual theme in this way, Doctorow changes the accuser from the wife's brother, as he was in the Rosenbergs' case, to a friend of the family. The change typifies the modifications that Doctorow makes for literary purposes. In addition to reporting on the factual manifestation of sex—clearly a part of the Isaacsons' defense—Daniel questionably asserts the existence of sexual motivations at other points in his story. For instance, he speculates about Paul's attitude toward Rochelle: "in bad moments alone condemning yourself, cursing yourself for thinking of her centrality, this lady, this soft revolutionary girl and wondering with red ears and hot ears how to get it out of your worthless degenerate mind" (211).

Like aggression and sexual urges, incipient madness alienates some of the characters in *The Book of Daniel*. Daniel claims that madness passes from his grandmother through his mother to his sister. Although his mother has no symptoms, his grandmother, as her response to her tribulations shows, and his sister have serious mental problems. Daniel's own sadism makes him, too, suspect. Rather than showing that the Isaacsons do not meet their society's qualifications for normality or using their mental problems to discredit their politics, Doctorow shows that, like their politics, their mental states differ drastically from those of average people. Daniel is amazed and shocked that the police who find his sister with slashed wrists take her to a mental institution rather than to a hospital. Besides providing the impetus for the plot, their decision shows a quickness to consider anyone mad who is dressed as a political dissenter. The sudden accusation against his parents seems to Daniel like madness. In all of these instances madness and politics intermingle, partly because some people see their political opponents to be mad as well as wrong.

Doctorow shows that only proper analysis can overcome these causes of alienation. The common kinds of rational analysis, however, fail; their advocates either misunderstand completely, comprehend only partially, or fail to act effectively on the basis of their comprehension. The Isaacsons' Marxism does not help them very much to understand their society, especially when that society moves against them, nor would an orthodox Marxist easily understand the more recent developments in leftist politics. Daniel's liberal step-father has a fairly clear understanding of his society but not of his own step-children. The breezy "tough-mindedness" of a journalist who interviews Daniel also fails, even though at first it seems effective when he tells Daniel that his parents were framed. Almost at once, however, he claims that they "*acted* guilty" and that their opponents could not have conspired against them (229-30). Such rational analysis cannot make sense of the world of *The Book of Daniel*.

A poetic sensibility that recognizes the most important images and their meanings has a much better chance of understanding the events of the novel. Artie Sternlicht, the radical who influences Susan, understands the importance of images because he recognizes television's importance. He ends a conversation with Daniel by proclaiming, "we're gonna overthrow the United States with images!" (155). Analyzing images and acting in accordance with this kind of analysis, however, does not guarantee success. Daniel portrays Sternlicht as a colorful, comic leader, not a profound analyst. Similarly, Susan retreats from rational analysis into the most dramatic kind of imagistic thought: by turning herself into a single image, a starfish, she wanders into madness and then into death. Daniel correctly announces that "my sister is dead. She died of a failure of analysis" (317).

The degradation of imagistic thought occurs at Disneyland, Daniel's final stop in his search for the meaning of his parents' execution. He follows Mindish there to question him; although Mindish's senility makes his thoughts about the Isaacsons useless, the physical background of Daniel's meeting with him speaks eloquently yet mutely.

Daniel points out that books, such as *Huckleberry Finn* and *Alice in Wonderland,* and historical reality, such as the development of the Mississippi Valley during the nineteenth century, metamorphose first into Disney's films and then into Disneyland's physical images. The process creates "a separation of two ontological degrees between the Disneyland customer and the cultural artifacts he is presumed upon to treasure in his visit" (304). Daniel points out, like a neo-Marxist, that the interplay between Disneyland and people there usually ends with a purchase and that such interplay has political implications because the culture it portrays influences the customer's understanding of his history and literature.

Although finding and creating images can fail to explain and can even obfuscate, Daniel thinks that he must do these projects because "images are what things mean" (83). Indeed, the meaning of *The Book of Daniel* lies primarily in its images, as Doctorow suggests in one of Daniel's analyses: "technology is the making of metaphors from the natural world. Flight is the metaphor of air, wheels are the metaphor of water, food is the metaphor of earth. The metaphor of fire is electricity" (241). The last point, its significance indicated by Doctorow's placing it in a sentence by itself, reveals how he has composed the novel: from his recurrent image of fire he makes metaphors, including his images of electricity. Specifically, he turns Julius Rosenberg's occupation, owner of a machine shop, into Paul Isaacson's occupation, radio repairman, thereby introducing the motif of electricity. The new image resonates with several important events in the novel: the simultaneous arrival of the first television set in Paul's shop and the arrest of Mindish, Sternlicht's analogy of revolution and television images, and the electrocution of the Isaacsons. Doctorow connects, then, the fire image that derives from the furnace in the Biblical book of Daniel with the electricity image and interweaves these two images in order to develop the theme of alienation. Finally, Doctorow, by finding and creating images, shows the meaning of the Rosenbergs' fate.

The images vary in importance from the fire image to circumstantial details that add little or nothing to the meaning of the novel. A moderately meaningful image of hands communicates by forming an ironic contrast. Early in the novel when Daniel visits Susan in the insane asylum, he looks immediately at her bandaged wrist, the reminder of her suicide attempt. A few pages later a flashback begins with a description of Ascher, the lawyer, taking the two children to a rally for their parents and clutching them too tightly in his strong hands. In neither scene does the bond of human ties that hands can symbolize pertain. Late in the novel Doctorow uses the rejection of heart transplants to represent the self-torment of human emotions. Such analogy relates to the fact that the sensitivity of Daniel's sister and grandmother cause their self-destruction. The earlier passage about the female Isaacsons inheriting madness through their hearts also clarifies the comparison.

The images early in the novel have considerable meaning and show Doctorow's imagistic techniques. Paul's broken arm foreshadows his execution: reactionaries attack a bus returning from a Paul Robeson concert and break Paul's arm when he puts it out the door to summon a policeman. Daniel at first thinks "that was something to be proud of, that he got up to do something. But *what* he did was mysterious and complicated and not anything like what people were saying. . . . I decided he was trying to get the attention of the cop because he really thought the cop would help" (64). In the next paragraph, however, he says that he sees in the action "the quality of calmly experienced planned revolutionary sacrifice." His interpretation changes almost immediately, mainly because he considers the image in isolation. A few pages later in an unobtrusive passage he thinks about an image more effectively: driving in the rain, "he fixed on one drop and followed its career. The idea was that his attention made it different from the other drops. It arrived, head busted, with one water bead as a nucleus and six or seven clusters in a circle around it. . . . Each of the mini-drop clusters combined and became elongated and pulled away in the direction of its own weight" (67). The drop resembles the senior Isaacsons because of its destruction and its interrelations with others. An exemplary image, it seems to change as Daniel observes it, and it relates to other images. The meaning of most of Doctorow's images change as he observes them, and he interrelates them to each other, sometimes as intricately as he relates his furnace image to other images. The novel is to a large extent the sum of these observations and interrelations.

To reinforce the reader's sense that the novel was created primarily by observing and interrelating images, Doctorow uses certain narrative techniques: his narrator is extremely self-conscious, especially in the first few pages, where he even describes his pencil; shifting back and forth between a first-person and a third-person narrator also focuses attention on the author, because the reader recognizes that the author does the shifting and is, ultimately, responsible for the narration. The inclusion of essays breaks the plot's flow and destroys verisimilitude, thereby showing in yet another way that the novel is an author's creation rather than an objective reflection of reality. The time-shifts also create a little bit of chaos and thus focus attention on the author's manipulations. In the most clever shift, the funeral of the elder Isaacsons merges almost imperceptibly with Susan's funeral.

Doctorow's major point, then, is that an analyst should concentrate on images. By so doing Daniel begins to diminish his alienation. He finally faces and describes his parents' execution and his sister's funeral. The book that Daniel has been self-consciously talking about as he narrates it and *The Book of Daniel* end with a passage from the Biblical book of Daniel. It implies that articulating emotions and ideas in a book brings them under control: *"go thy way Daniel: for the words are closed up and sealed till the time of the end."*

### NOTES

[1] E. L. Doctorow, *The Book of Daniel* (New York, 1971; rpt. Signet Books, 1972), p. 145. Subsequent references are to the paperback edition.

## Harry Levin

SOURCE: "Revisiting Dos Passos' *U.S.A.*," in *Massachusetts Review,* Vol. XX, No. 3, Autumn, 1979, pp. 401-15.

[*In the following essay, Levin discusses the political beliefs of John Dos Passos, particularly in* U.S.A.]

John Dos Passos' reputation reached its highest point in 1938, when Jean-Paul Sartre—reviewing the French translation of *Nineteen Nineteen*—proclaimed him without reservation "the greatest writer of our time." Sartre's critical attitudes have always been dictated by the personal or dialectical use he could make of his subjects, and he went on to imitate Dos Passos' method in his own unfinished tetralogy, *Les Chemins de la liberté.* He might not have considered that method so uniquely experimental if he had had any firsthand acquaintance with *Ulysses* (and Joyce was then still alive). But much of *Nineteen Nineteen* had the advantage, from Sartre's point of view, of being set in France. Insofar as he was interested in the larger patterns of interrelated lives, of course he could have found a precedent within that strong tradition of French fiction which had its fountainhead in the *Comédie humaine* and its contemporary manifestation in Jules Romains' *roman-fleuve*. And, as Claude-Edmonde Magny would be pointing out in *L'Age du roman américain* (which in turn would influence the emergent *nouveau roman*), the novel had to register the impact of the cinema. Yet *Nineteen Nineteen,* doubtless because of its sharp confrontations between history and consciousness, fitted in particularly well with Sartre's existentialist position.

Born and nurtured as a romantic individualist, Dos Passos had to work his way toward facing the problems of modern collectivity. His development can be traced from his poems, plays, and travelogues through his two early war novels to his fictional encounters with the city in *Streets of Night* and *Manhattan Transfer,* which Lionel Trilling would hail as perhaps "the most important novel of the decade." When we recall that *An American Tragedy* and *The Great Gatsby* were also published in that same year, or that the decade had already produced *The Age of Innocence* and *Main Street* and would soon be producing *A Farewell to Arms* and *The Sound and the Fury,* we need make no further comment on the vicissitudes of taste. But it was probably *Manhattan Transfer* that went farthest to shock the traditionalists, provoking Paul Elmer More to dismiss it as "an explosion in a cesspool." The more salubrious reaction of Sinclair Lewis may help us to recapture the sense of novelty that it conveyed to sensibilities yet unblurred by nearly a century of metropolitan fiction. Here was, according to Lewis, "the first book to catch Manhattan . . . Here is the city, the smell of it, the sound of it, the harsh and shining sight of it." After all, *The New Yorker* likewise made its first appearance in that *annus mirabilis,* 1925.

Sartre would set his seal of world acclaim on the middle volume of *U.S.A.,* and Dos Passos would win the Feltrinelli if not the Nobel Prize, which has been awarded to many a lesser figure. His decline in standing, during the latter part of his career, was dramatically paralleled by the 180-degree shift in his political orientation. He could scarcely be blamed for sometimes feeling that critics, most of them still more or less liberal, were penalizing him for his congealing conservatism. He rationalized his claims to consistency by restudying Jefferson and the civic fathers in such books as *The Ground We Stand On.* But, as F. O. Matthiessen was able to retort: "They are the ground we stood on a long time ago, before the industrial transformation of our modern world." Moreover, the actual effects of that transformation had been the primary themes of Dos Passos as a novelist. Certain resources of novelistic compassion seem to have withered away, in the process that turned a young man arrested for protesting the Sacco-Vanzetti decision into an old man condoning the Kent State shootings. His second trilogy, *District of Columbia,* is at best a dim sequel to the first; and although *Mid-Century* returns to the documentaries and biographies of *U.S.A.,* significantly it omits the lyrical self-intimations.

Yet there had to be some continuity in which *U.S.A.* was pivotal, if only because it had been poised at a turning point between idealism and disillusionment. The expressionistic play that he wrote in college, *The Moon Is a Gong,* was retitled *The Garbage Man* for its off-Broadway production. Edmund Wilson's novel, *I Thought of Daisy,* sketches out a sympathetic portrait of Dos Passos in his Greenwich Village days: earnest, honest, shy, myopic, dedicated, self-denying, a poetic aesthete by temperament, willing himself by force of conscience to be a radical activist. His period of active radicalism started with the trial of Sacco and Vanzetti and terminated with the defeat of the Loyalists in the Spanish Civil War, which for him was history's wrong turn, exacerbated by the Soviet betrayal of Marxist principles. That was precisely the interval that witnessed the writing of *U.S.A.* As late as 1939 he answered a questionnaire with this credo: "My sympathies lie with the private in the front line against the brass hat; with the hod-carrier against the straw-boss, or the walking delegate for that matter; with the laboratory worker against the stuffed shirt in a mortarboard; with the criminal against the cop." *The 42nd Parallel* contains a vignette from his Harvard days, contrasting the gentlemanly conformities with a millworkers' strike at Lawrence, Massachusetts.

He never strayed very far from such temperamental alignments, though his hatred of the bureaucracy would complicate them by making a bugbear out of the New Deal. Internal conflicts were bound to be reinforced by his mixed ancestry, his illegitimate birth, his upper-class education—not to mention his exposure to war. He had taken his first public stand in 1916 at the age of twenty, with an article for *The New Republic* entitled "Against American Literature." Characteristically it was the establishment that he opposed, in this case the Genteel Tradition, counterposing to it the modernist stance of Walt Whitman. "Our only substitute for dependence on the past is dependence on the future," declared the youthful

Dos Passos. "Here our only poet found his true greatness." Forty years later, after reading *Les Temps Modernes,* he commented to Wilson: "In that connection I read over half of *Democratic Vistas* last night and found it much more based on realities than Sartre." The irony was that when the future toward which Whitman had looked— "Years of the Modern!"—arrived with the twentieth century, Dos Passos found it harder to contemplate than did his admirer, Sartre. To an inquiring student Dos Passos replied that the original slant of his work was "more likely to stem from Whitman (and perhaps Veblen) than from Marx."

Leaving Marx aside as a marginal though by no means irrelevant interest, we proceed through *U.S.A.* from the tutelage of Whitman to that of Thorstein Veblen. The prologue spelling out the title, added after these three novels were conjoined to form a trilogy, moves from the lonely mind of a young man walking "the night streets" to a collective memory of images and echoes: "But mostly *U.S.A.* is the speech of the people." This passage turns out to be nothing less than a poem in Whitman's magnanimous vein; and there are many other such fragments of poetry, notably the composite portrait of the Unknown Soldier that concludes the second volume, "The Body of an American." Dos Passos' democratic conception is rooted in a Whitmanesque unanimism, in the prefatory assumption of *Leaves of Grass* that the United States itself is potentially a great poem, worthy of "gigantic and generous treatment" within the total ambiance of its immediate present. *Manhattan Transfer* had comprised a kind of urban kaleidoscope. Now the panoramic subject matter, to be treated on a scale of 1500 pages, was a cross-section of the entire country during the first three decades of the twentieth century. Modestly conceiving himself as "a second-class historian," the author claimed firsthand access to his age through its language, and asked no more than that his novels be read as "contemporary chronicles."

One of his strengths was his keen reportorial talent for taking in and getting down a locale. Novelists do not have to be circumscribed by a single region, but most of them stick to certain particular backgrounds. Even Balzac hardly covered his lavishly chosen ground in such full detail and over so wide an area as Dos Passos did with his material. At an ever-accelerating pace he zigzags across the continent, with a dip into Mexico and Cuba and a fling at Europe. On the make, his personages gravitate toward a series of capitals, each of them a center for the powers that control American values, all described with atmospheric precision: finance (New York), politics (Washington), industry (Detroit), entertainment (Hollywood), recreation (Miami Beach). As with *Manhattan Transfer,* the titles are large connective symbols. *The 42nd Parallel* roughly runs through Chicago, where, incidentally, Dos Passos was born, eastward to Provincetown, where he did much of his writing, and westward to the Oregon forest, which flashes by in a last reminiscence of his Unknown Soldier. *Nineteen Nineteen* shifts the titular emphasis from a spatial latitude to a temporal axis. And

climactically *The Big Money,* as a central metaphor, universalizes the profit motive and tightens the network of human relations through the cash nexus itself.

*The 42nd Parallel* begins, in a flush of expectation, by celebrating the turn of the century, and ends with the embarkation of troops for the First World War in 1917. *Nineteen Nineteen,* as the date suggests, is less preoccupied with the war itself (previously and more closely rendered in *One Man's Initiation* and *Three Soldiers*) than with its side-effects and disillusioning aftermath, signalized by the Disarmament Conference at Versailles. *The Big Money* deals with the following decade, the razzle-dazzle of the Twenties, the perturbation beneath the debonair surfaces of the so-called Jazz Age, ending with the Wall Street crash of 1929, and portending the strikes and breadlines of the Depression. Hence "this lousy superannuated hypertrophied hell-invented novel," as Dos Passos deprecated it in a letter to Ernest Hemingway, was put together just a few years after the incidents it chronicles. Yet it was conceived and executed as a historical novel, bearing witness to its epoch. Like its greatest prototype in that mode, Tolstoy's *War and Peace, U.S.A.* is concerned with the interweaving and shaping of private existences by public events. Like Tolstoy, Dos Passos shows great respect for history, which is conscientiously presented—unlike E. L. Doctorow in *Ragtime,* who introduces historical figures and then irresponsibly casts them in fictitious roles.

Dos Passos' historicism sets up its social framework through a sequence of biographical sketches. Symmetrically spaced, there are nine of these in each volume, twenty-seven in all, related thematically as well as synchronically to the matter at hand. This assortment of highly typical and widely varied Americans ranges from international bankers (J. P. Morgan) to intransigent radicals (Eugene Debs), from prolific inventors (Thomas Edison) to eccentric artists (Isadora Duncan), from critical thinkers (Randolph Bourne) to film stars (Rudolph Valentino). Technological development has its outstanding proponents: the Wright brothers at Kitty Hawk, the efficiency expert F. W. Taylor, an ambivalent Henry Ford between his "tin lizzie" and his antique collection. Journalism has its playboy in John Reed and its bullyboy in William Randolph Hearst. (Dos Passos' characterization of the latter, "Poor Little Rich Boy," clearly lent inspiration to *Citizen Kane.*) Two presidents are represented: a mock-heroic Theodore Roosevelt and a Woodrow Wilson who comes near to being the arch-villain. "Meester Veelson"—the European accent reflects the hopes for a just peace that he betrayed, after betraying his promise of keeping America out of the war. Dos Passos felt peculiarly embittered, as did Hemingway, because that betrayal debased the language, reducing trusted ideals to rhetorical slogans.

*U.S.A.* is further structured by two formalized devices: the "Newsreel" and "The Camera Eye." Sixty-eight intermittent Newsreels (modeled on a medium then vital but soon obsolescent) frame the time-scheme objectively with reverberating quotations from subtitles, headlines, and popular songs. At the opposite extreme, the fifty-one Camera Eyes are candidly subjective and autobiographical, revealing the mind of the author himself at the moment of his narration. Though the term sounds mechanical, the textures can be rhapsodic; taken together, these passages might constitute Dos Passos' "Song of Myself." James T. Farrell preferred them to all the others, whereas Hemingway's preference was for the portraits from life. The striking—and slightly dampening—implication is that, between the detailed reportage on the one hand and the introspective evocation on the other, the middle territory of sheer fiction seems less arresting or memorable. One wonders how much force it would have carried if the narrative had been straight, without the interventions of collage or montage. Through the trilogy Dos Passos has dispersed a dozen imaginary case histories, five in each volume: six men, six women. The numerical disparity is accounted for by the fact that some drop out, while others enter late. Yet those who cease to be protagonists have walk-on parts in other episodes, so that their life-stories are continued from other viewpoints than their own.

Novels are invariably progressions from innocence to experience, and not less so when—with Proust—they span decades and volumes. Born on the Fourth of July in the century's dewy youth, J. Ward Morehouse is originally viewed through his own eyes as an idealistic high-school debater. Step by step, we watch him from the outside, as he climbs the careerist's ladder: helping to break the Homestead Strike, profiteering as a Dollar-a-Year-Man, pompously and smugly manipulating the wiles of public relations. In a parallel movement, Janey, whom we meet as a lively tomboy, subsequently crushed by the loss of a boyfriend, will reappear as Miss Williams, a colorless old maid and perfect secretary to the important Mr. Morehouse. Mobility goes downward for her brother Joe, who, after wartime adventures with the navy and the merchant marine, is ironically killed in a tavern brawl on Armistice night. Fainy McCreary, the likeable Irish-American printer's devil, is radicalized on his trek to San Francisco, but somehow makes his Mexican peace and disappears from the cycle. Two aspiring girls from different backgrounds in Chicago, Eleanor Stoddard and Eveline Hutchins, pass on from the local Art Institute via an interior decorating studio to intrigues in New York and Paris. Though they get harder and harder to tell apart, one is destined to marry a Russian prince and the other to commit suicide.

The most poignant of these character-sketches, which might stand by itself as a novella, comprises the two sections entitled "Daughter." Anne Elizabeth Trent, a headstrong Texas belle, conscience-stricken after her brother's death as a pilot in training, gets into social work and goes abroad as a postwar Red Cross aide. Made pregnant by an American officer, who temporizes because of other ambitions, she wildly persuades a half-drunk French aviator into looping the loop with her at night, and loses not her baby but her life. A single section is devoted to the radicalization of Ben Compton, a Jewish law student from Brooklyn who goes to jail for his pacifist convictions. Incidental glimpses afterward reveal him as a loyal member of the Communist Party who is ultimately expelled in a doctrinal purge. The comparable case of Mary French, who briefly takes up with Ben Compton at one point, is more fully developed. Ill at ease with the pretentious gentility of her mother, she drops out of Vassar to nurse her beloved doctor-father, who dies of influenza contracted from his patients. After an apprenticeship among the poor at Hull House, she drifts farther leftward: to radical journalism in Pittsburgh, labor organization in Washington, party work as a fellow traveler. Having rejected her family background and been rejected by her Communist lover, she is left to carry on alone.

If the book has any heroine, it is this committed fighter for losing causes, and much of the Sacco-Vanzetti agitation is witnessed from Mary's standpoint. Her opposite number, who also makes her debut in the third volume, is indeed a mock-heroine, a movie queen: the hard-boiled and easygoing Margo Dowling. Sex provides her sordid education; but she learns to use it; and she manages to rise through vaudeville, chorus lines, and nightclubs to the precarious heights of Hollywood stardom. On her way up, she has good-naturedly tried to alleviate the fate of Charley Anderson, which dominates *The Big Money*. That stalwart mechanic from North Dakota was left boarding a troopship at the conclusion of *The 42nd Parallel*. He does not appear in *Nineteen Nineteen* at all; he is too busy fighting and learning all about airplanes. Disembarking at the outset of *The Big Money*, he is now a veteran, a war hero, an ace from the Lafayette Escadrille, trying to realize that the war is over. Demobilization means demoralization for a while. Basically skilled and hard-working, however, he invents a new airplane motor. But an invention must not only be patented; it must be exploited, promoted, and capitalized; stock must be issued, and companies formed. Charley's mechanical know-how would be wasted without the entrepreneurial intercession of shrewd financiers and savvy lobbyists.

His own function, supervising production, inevitably takes him to Detroit, where he is taken up by the country club set. He makes a sort of allegorical choice, when he throws over the engineer's to marry the banker's daughter. He is still most comfortable when tinkering, in his overalls, with his foreman Bill Cermak. But Bill is killed and Charley is badly injured when their plane crashes in taking off for a trial flight. That crash on the runway is emblematic, not merely of Charley's anticlimactic fortunes, but of what will be happening in the stockmarket and throughout the business world. Things fall apart for Charley; his hollow marriage is wrecked; he himself becomes a human wreck, increasingly alcoholic and self-destructive. Drifting down to Florida, where Margo moves in and out of his careening existence, he is fatally injured in a drunken automobile accident, and rival claimants beleaguer his hospital bed as his internal monologue tapers off. In five years, he has promised his assistant, they would be "in the big money"—as everyone has promised everyone else. Unpeeling a roll of fresh hundred-dollar bills, he was tempted to kiss them. "Gosh," he had said to himself at one moment, "money's a great thing." At another he has wished that "he didn't have to worry about money all the time," that instead "he was still tinkerin' with that damn motor."

As Margo Dowling had an opposite number in Mary French, so Charley Anderson has an anti-heroic foil in Richard Ellsworth Savage. He has begun as a well-connected poor relation, a sensitive Harvard poet, who graduates into the war and gets attached to the brass. After a number of safe and easy assignments behind the lines, he goes through the peace negotiations as aide-de-camp to that ever-hustling arch-operator, J. Ward Morehouse, now in charge of opinion-molding for the postwar American public. Through that connection Dick is assured of a future, if not as a man of letters, then as heir apparent to a high-powered advertising agency, as a highly paid apologist for the ensuing materialistic boom. The moral crisis is underlined by his affair with Anne Elizabeth ("Daughter"); when he jilts her, his good faith lies among the casualties. When we take leave of him, in a cynical miasma of worldly success and self-hate, he is suffering the grimmest of hangovers, after a homosexual escapade in Harlem. Dos Passos' classmate, the poet Robert Hillyer, who actually returned to an academic post and took a narrowly traditional line, objected seriously to this character as a caricature of himself. Dos Passos responded, with the usual embarrassment prompted by such identifications *à clef,* that he had simply borrowed certain military associations, along with a few details from their common undergraduate memories.

We might come closer to the significance of Richard Ellsworth Savage if we consider him as an imaginary projection of Dos Passos himself—Dos Passos as he might have become, had he followed the code of snobbery and careerism, had his talent and integrity been compromised by the seductions of the big money, the acquisitive society, and the military-industrial complex. Edmund Wilson remarked that "humanity generally comes off badly" in *Manhattan Transfer,* and it would be hard to gainsay such an impression of *U.S.A.* All too many of its *dramatis personae* wind up as sellouts or losers, just as the war is sold out and the peace is lost. Sartre would interpret this permutation in Marxist terms: "In capitalist society, men do not have lives, they have only destinies." That is why these people seem shallow or two-dimensional, even when contrasted with their historic role-models. And, though we are not given profiles of Sacco or Vanzetti, we hear their voices out of the depths—quoted directly from their correspondence or, most powerfully, from the famous response of Bartolomeo Vanzetti to the death-sentence. Two Camera Eyes record Dos Passos' own emotions before and after the execution. In one he walks through Plymouth, where Vanzetti had worked, and likens those Italian immigrants to the earliest Pilgrim settlers. In the other, he angrily reacts to the defeat of justice: "all right we are two nations."

On a previous page a Camera Eye has recorded his insomniac misgivings, "peeling the speculative onion of doubt," as Peer Gynt did from layer to layer ("topdog? underdog?"). Against the natural grain of skeptical diffidence, "the internal agitator crazy to succeed" had forced Dos Passos to make a soapbox speech in Union Square. Painfully mulling it over, he confesses, "I go home after a drink and a hot meal and read (with some difficulty in the Loeb Library trot) the epigrams of Martial and ponder the course of history and what leverage might pry the owners loose from power and bring back (I too Walt Whitman) our storybook democracy." Here is a pungent contrast: from Whitman to Martial, whom Dos Passos coupled in a letter with Juvenal, read in the same bilingual edition. Both of those Roman poets attest the decline from the virtues of the old Republic to the corruptions of their present Empire. The nostalgia for Whitman's vistas completes the American analogy. His impetus toward panegyric and rhapsody has been transposed into epigram and satire. The keen attraction that this last form held for Dos Passos made itself felt in his introduction to a portfolio of drawings by Georg Grosz, "Satire as a Way of Seeing," where he equated the satirist with the moralist. He identified his own outlook when he accepted the Gold Medal for Fiction from the National Institute of Arts and Letters in 1957, responding to William Faulkner's citation:

> I wonder if any of you have ever noticed that it is sometimes those who find most pleasure and amusement in their fellow man, and have most hope in his goodness, who get the reputation of being his most carping critics. Maybe it is that the satirist is so full of the possibilities of humankind in general, that he tends to draw a dark and garish picture when he tries to depict people as they are at any particular moment. The satirist is usually a pretty unpopular fellow. The only time he attains even fleeting popularity is when his works can be used by some particular faction as a stick to beat the brains out of their opponents. Satirical writing is by definition unpopular writing. Its aim is to prod people into thinking. Thinking hurts.

Dreiser called his most portentous novel *An American Tragedy,* and I suppose that title might subsume many of the destinies—not to say the lives—interwoven through *U.S.A.* Yet it might raise classical questions regarding the stature of the protagonist, since the characters so often seem to be dwarfed by their very multiplicity, if not by the Swiftian perspectives of the author. "We're living in one of the damndest tragic moments in history," he wrote to F. Scott Fitzgerald at about the time he was completing this trilogy. Its tragedy is that of America, and of the world itself. But there are times, he would have read in Juvenal, if he had not felt it in his bones, when it is difficult not to write satire. If the latter-day imperialism could not evoke the verse of a Juvenal or a Martial, then it needed something like the prose of a Petronius or a Tacitus. Given the extraordinary scope of *U.S.A., there* is an additional temptation—which Alfred Kazin has not resisted—to designate it as "a national epic." But critics should be able to discriminate, better than Hollywood press agents, among the fitting literary genres. We might well claim *Moby-Dick* as a national epic, or conceivably the *Leatherstocking* romances.

Other and later American novelists, sometimes rather self-consciously, have touched upon the heroic vein: Frank Norris, Theodore Dreiser, Willa Cather.

Not that *U.S.A.* is lacking in heroes, the underdogs to whom Dos Passos professed his own allegiance, and those who fought and spoke on their behalf: the Unknown Soldier, the legendary Joe Hill, the socialist Debs, the progressive Senator LaFollette, Big Bill Hayward of the I.W.W., Sacco, Vanzetti, and most incisively Veblen, who gradually becomes the presiding spirit. In a letter to Edmund Wilson, written during the composition of *The Big Money,* Dos Passos speaks of gathering ammunition from Veblen's socioeconomic analyses. As the ideologist of the fable, he had been situated to understand—much more comprehensively than Marx—the uses and abuses of technology, its relationship to human factors, and its vulnerability to sabotage at every level. His will included a caveat against any posthumous memoir, which Dos Passos has flouted in a brilliantly satirical psychograph, "The Bitter Drink." That beverage is the hemlock of Socrates, though it has been sipped in small doses and in sporadic classrooms by this twentieth-century gadfly. As a Norwegian-American compatriot of Ibsen, he has not only peeled the onion of doubt; he has slashed out against a shapeless and all-enveloping monster, the Boyg—which Georg Brandes interpreted as the Spirit of Compromise. As a congenital nay sayer, who "suffered from a constitutional inability to say yes," Veblen has his place with Hawthorne and Melville among the iconoclasts of American culture.

Coming closer to the United States than the Marxian class-struggle, the Veblenite antithesis is the tension between producing and consuming. The downfall of Charley Anderson, which Edmund Wilson regarded as "the best part" of the story, is exemplary in that respect. Charley is an inventor; he possesses Veblen's positive "instinct for workmanship." He has a flair for production, but no head for consumption, and consumption is the order of the day. Veblen's negative phrase, "conspicuous consumption," realizes itself in the national spree that Dos Passos satirizes. And, what is economically and politically worse, this is rooted in "conspicuous waste"—waste of energy, of resources, and of lives. "It's the waste," Mary French cries out bitterly in the last scene of the trilogy. "The food they waste and the money they waste while our people starve in tarpaper barracks." These conflicting issues are counterpoised in the epilogue, "Vag." Dos Passos, as a lifelong traveler, had played the vagabond. Here the valedictory young man, who hikes on the transcontinental highway as the young man in the prologue walked the city streets, could obviously be picked up and booked for vagrancy. The contrast, as he seeks to thumb a ride, is with the airline passengers overhead. There is no longer such a contrast today, when the norm of travel is by air, as there was forty years ago, when it was a luxury of the rich to be skyborne.

The decade of this work was the crucial one for commercial aviation, and one of Dos Passos' plays had been *Airways, Inc.* It is not a coincidence that the tragic fall of Charley Anderson or of "Daughter" should be literally enacted as an airplane crash. "Vag" is still vainly thumbing when the long-drawn-out chronicle draws to a close: "A hundred miles down the road." The road is still open nowadays, and the traffic has greatly increased. As a Harvard student, Dick Savage won a prize from *The Reader's Digest* for a sonnet sequence; but the editors wanted it to terminate on "a note of hope"; and he very readily supplied the amelioration, which may have been the first of his many intellectual compromises. Writing back to Malcolm Cowley, who seems to have wanted something more affirmative from *The 42nd Parallel,* Dos Passos promised "a certain amount of statement of position in the later Camera Eyes"—possibly what came out in regard to Sacco and Vanzetti, or what would be made more emphatic by his Veblenite adherence. "But as for the note of hope," he concluded in his sincere and straightforward way, "gosh who knows?" No novelist is under obligation to offer reforms or remedies for the state of affairs he undertakes to expose, and Dos Passos would be far less effective in making such an attempt than was his illustrious and wrong-headed predecessor, Tolstoy.

Veblen could have taught him the futility of his hope "to rebuild the past," to recover the "storybook democracy" of Whitman and Jefferson, and consequently have spared him the embarrassment of campaigning for Barry Goldwater. "The American Dream: What Has Happened to It?" This inquiry was raised in a pair of articles by Faulkner, who lectured and planned a book about it. It has been pursued, in one way or another, by many of the other major novelists of our century. The readiest instance may be the concluding page of *The Great Gatsby,* with its realization that "the last and greatest of all human dreams" has receded from the future into the past. If history has truly become a nightmare, better to reveal it than to keep it veiled in outworn fantasy. Speaking to the students of Choate School, after having received its Alumni Prize, Dos Passos affirmed:

> Writing is and I guess it ought to be one of the hazardous professions.... The first thing a man—striving to come of age in any period of human history—has to do is to choose for himself what is true and what is not true, what is real and what is not real in the picture of society established for him by his elders.... In the search for truth there are no secret formulae that can be handed down from one generation to another. Truth I believe is absolute. Some things are true and some false. You have to find it.

No further explanation was necessary for presenting the panorama as he had found it in *U.S.A.* The achievement was that he had caught so very much of it, thereby enabling Lionel Trilling to say that the whole seemed greater than the sum of its parts. Dos Passos did not need to be—he should not have later become—an ideologue. He was always enough of a moralist to be a genuine satirist. As a reporter, he saw a story in everything, a connecting issue everywhere. As a technician, he developed his own new modes for expressing the complications of modernity.

**Thomas L. Hartshorne**

SOURCE: "From *Catch-22* to *Slaughterhouse V*: The Decline of the Political Mode," in *South Atlantic Quarterly,* Vol. 78, No. 1, Winter, 1979, pp. 17-33.

[*In the following essay, Hartshorne examines the novels* Catch-22 *and* Slaughterhouse V *as fables that may shed light on cultural and political phenomena of the 1960s.*]

Recently several writers have pointed out the risks involved in the use of imaginative literature as a tool for the investigation of American society, culture, and history. Bruce Kuklick, Seymour Katz, R. Gordon Kelly, and Cecil Tate have all questioned the assumptions and practices of what Leo Marx has called the "humanist" approach to American Studies. They have argued that the humanist method usually rests upon unproven assumptions about the meaning and significance of particular works to contemporary audiences, that it does not offer precise evidence concerning the relationship between the writer and his readers, that it ignores the fundamental theoretical problem of distinguishing between a work of literature as a product of an individual mind and as a cultural artifact (or assumes, willy-nilly, that any work of literature may legitimately be treated as a representative cultural expression without investigating precisely what part of the culture is being represented and how).[1]

These criticisms point clearly to the difficulties in using imaginative literature as a "mirror of the past" or as evidence concerning the state of American society at any given time. Yet such uses of literature can be useful by providing for the scholar what it provides for the general reader: perspective, insight, intuitive understanding. One of the critics of the standard approach of American Studies seems to accept such a conclusion when he says that literature can provide "a cognitive model of experience, a hypothetical construction by means of which we may come to know more about experience than experience alone can show. Thus, works of imagistic literature are ways of knowing in themselves. As such, they also enter into the larger cultural process of forming new concepts, or extending, criticizing, or reconstructing already existing concepts."[2] While it is ridiculous to suggest that Henry James's novels prove that there was a tension between American innocence and European corruption in the late nineteenth century, one can argue that a perceptive reading of James may very well help scholars understand the relationship between America and the rest of the world, the ways in which those relationships were perceived at the time, and the intellectual and emotional reactions produced by the perceptions. In other words, imaginative literature may provide clues to fruitful subjects for investigation and approaches to that investigation.

It is in this context that I wish to examine two recent novels, Joseph Heller's *Catch-22* and Kurt Vonnegut, Jr.'s, *Slaughterhouse V,* for the light they may shed on the history of the 1960's. Specifically, I wish to establish some resonances between these novels and left-tending protest movements of the decade by treating the books as fables offering a view of the world and its problems together with a series of rules for coping with them. I will suggest also that a comparison between them can help to illuminate a shift in thought and belief.

We are probably still too close to the sixties to have arrived at a "standard" view of the decade, but I believe that most people would agree with Jim Heath's judgment that it was a Decade of Disillusionment.[3] Something went wrong. The Kennedy Promise turned into the Tragedy of Lyndon Johnson. Americans entered the decade with high hopes, with the conviction that we could engage in a fruitful search for solutions to our most pressing problems and possessing staunch faith in the meliorative potentials of the New Frontier and, later, the Great Society. The decade ended with the nation mired in a seemingly endless war, with assassination, with violence (often perpetrated by those charged with protecting society against violence), with growing frustration and despair. Ken Kesey probably spoke for many when he said, "We blew it."

The various movements of protest and dissent during the decade offer particularly vivid examples of this transition in mood because of the scope of the swing from initial hope to final despair. But the change in mood was not the only thing, nor even the most important thing, that happened to these movements. There was also a change in their assumptions, approaches, tactics, and goals. Speaking very generally, one can see a shift from a commitment to relatively straightforward political protest to what Richard King and others have called cultural radicalism: an attempt to change consciousness rather than society, to alter the way people see and think about their world instead of political and economic relations in it, to transform values instead of social structure.[4] Running parallel with this transition was a gradual expansion of the scope of the demands made by the protesters and a corresponding decline in their specificity. From the sit-ins, freedom rides, and voter registration drives of the civil rights movement of the early sixties to the emphasis on black power; from the community-organizing projects of the early days of the Students for a Democratic Society to the inflexible "revolutionary" rhetoric of the Weatherman Statement; from the demand for the creation of police review boards to indiscriminate attacks on pigs, the same pattern was repeated. Piecemeal reforms became unacceptable because, it was asserted, they had proved inconsequential. It had become necessary to remake the whole system and perhaps even man himself. Reformist politics gave way to revolutionary eschatology.

In this context, a comparison between *Catch-22* and *Slaughterhouse V* offers interesting insights into the shift in attitudes, the change in political culture, and the transition in the general cultural atmosphere. The two books are particularly suited for comparison because there are many points of similarity between them. To mention only the most obvious, both deal with World War II, both assert a strongly antiwar position, both are highly critical of other features of modern life, both present the individual protagonist as a victim, both are written in a narrative style which violates normal time sequence, both are cited as examples of black humor, and both are also cited as examples of the literature of the absurd. With all these similarities, the differences between them become especially revealing and instructive.

Let us first consider *Catch-22*. It deals with an American bomber group stationed on a small island in the Mediterranean and particularly with the efforts of the central character, Captain John Yossarian, to survive in a nightmare world of stupidity, illogic, malignity, and death. Yossarian is painfully aware that the enemy is bent on killing him and equally painfully aware that his commanding officers seem equally bent on seeing to it that they succeed. He manages to survive, barely, and ultimately escapes from the nightmare by following the example of his tentmate, Orr, and leaving for Sweden.

In their treatments of the book, critics have described it as a bitter attack on war, military bureaucracy, and many other features of modern life. The book is certainly an attack, and in many ways it is both bitter and savage. In many ways, however, it is also remarkably innocent, expressing commitment to a set of values and a vision of the world that are not, perhaps, wholly conventional but are quite "straight." For example, one critic, Brian Way, has compared Heller's vision with Kafka's since both authors are concerned with the struggle of the individual against a bureaucratic order.[5] The comparison is imperfect, however, for one of the primary characteristics of Kafka's victim-heroes is that they never know precisely whom or what they are contending against and are never even wholly sure of what the issues are. Yossarian is. He knows who his enemies are and why they are his enemies. He says, "The enemy is anybody who's trying to get you killed, no matter *which* side he's on."[6] It is perfectly true, of course, that for most of the book he is puzzled about what he can do to escape the trap he is in—in fact, Yossarian's search for a strategy for survival is the central dramatic issue in the novel—but ultimately he finds a solution: he "lights out for the territory," thus taking a decisive step in his quest for his own personal salvation.

Now this decision to leave, to desert, has been interpreted as a thoroughly selfish act, as an evasion of profound moral responsibilities.[7] This view, however, misses several essential points concerning the roots and the nature of Yossarian's conflict with the military bureaucracy and his revolt against it. Throughout most of the time span covered by the novel, Yossarian has been a good soldier in the conventional sense. As time goes on, though, he becomes more and more disenchanted and more and more frightened. Worst of all, there seems to be no escape from the system other than death as Colonel Cathcart, his commanding officer, keeps raising the number of missions required for discharge. Finally, Yossarian comes to the conclusion that he has done his share, as much as can reasonably be expected of him. "I've flown seventy goddam combat missions. Don't talk to me about fighting to save my country. I've been fighting all along

to save my country. Now I'm going to fight a little to save myself. The country's not in danger any more, but I am" (p. 455). He has not rejected the ideals for which he was fighting earlier, but he has come to the conclusion that his continued participation in the war would have little practical effect beyond making things easier for the malign and selfish men who command him. They, not he, his country, or his squadron-mates would be the primary beneficiaries of his acquiescence. Thus, his desertion is, among other things, an assertion of the value of the individual life against the claims of a particular group of men who have been clearly revealed as unworthy of respect or obedience. In pursuing his own survival, under the circumstances, he is asserting a profoundly important moral principle.

Furthermore, his act of defiance has important social consequences. It provides his squadron-mates, who are also in danger, with a vivid example of effective resistance. Yossarian's decision is one manifestation of a pattern which is repeated often toward the end of the novel: one example of resistance triggers others. Orr's example nerves Yossarian to attempt his own escape, Yossarian's decision to leave fills the chaplain with a resolve to do what he can to make life miserable for his superiors, and even earlier Yossarian's conduct has created problems for them. His resistance has worried them enough to induce them to make an offer to send him home under certain conditions; they perceive him as a threat to their control because of the possible contagion of his example. As Lieutenant Colonel Korn says: "The men were perfectly content to fly as many missions as we asked as long as they thought they had no alternative. Now you've given them hope, and they're unhappy" (p. 431).

Some critics have taken note of the hopeful, activist, affirmative tone of the ending of the novel and have argued that it is totally inconsistent with the rest of the book and that the ending is, as a result, unconvincing.[8] My own view is that it is possible to discover throughout the book evidences of the attitudes that are clearly and extensively expressed at the end. However, even accepting the idea that the ending is inconsistent, an important question remains: Why did Heller feel impelled to contrive a happy ending and to paste it on to a work which had given no reason for any sort of hope for a way out of the nightmare? Speaking in 1968, Heller said that *Catch-22* was really about Vietnam rather than World War II, "The ridiculous war I felt lurking in the future when I wrote the book."[9] I believe that the book has more to do with World War II than Heller and most of his critics are willing to acknowledge. For all of the savagery of his attack on the military bureaucracy, Heller never attacks the war itself or its goals. In fact, one of his main quarrels with the military bureaucracy is that it is doing a lousy job of achieving what should be its main goal: winning the war. Colonel Cathcart spends hours devising ways of getting a story about himself into the *Saturday Evening Post,* General Peckem insists on tight bomb patterns because they look good in aerial photographs, Milo Minderbinder subordinates everything to his insatiable quest for speculative profits. As the final symbol of the distortion and perversion of goals, Scheisskopf, whose sole military concern is parades, is elevated to command. In deserting, Yossarian can be said to be helping the war effort in the long run by refusing to support those who have demonstrated their incompetence; his act is consistent with the broad goals of the war.

Another important lesson to be drawn from the pattern of Yossarian's resistance concerns its style. The authorities begin to perceive Yossarian as a threat only when he begins to act crazy by doing such things as appearing naked to receive a medal, moaning during the briefing session before the raid on Avignon, and sitting naked in a tree during Snowden's funeral. Before this, his protest had been more conventional. He had asked Doc Daneeka to ground him, he had gone to the squadron commander, Major Major, with the same request, but had had no success. In these instances he found himself impaled on Catch-22, the pseudo-logical form of thinking that the military bureaucracy used to protect and perpetuate itself. Catch-22 enabled the system to absorb, blunt, or deflect ordinary protest: in fact, it seems to be a literary version of what came to be known as co-operation. Yossarian succeeds in escaping Catch-22 by devising modes of protest which those in authority do not expect, which their institutions are unequipped to deal with, which take them unaware.

It is instructive to consider Orr in this context. Orr is a pilot who has great technical skill, but appears vacant, helpless, perhaps slightly mad. He keeps getting himself shot down over the Mediterranean and only giggles inanely when questioned about his peculiar affinity for water. In the end, of course, we discover that he has been practicing his escape. His ineptitude is a masquerade to deceive the authorities; since he does not protest, they do not see him as a threat to the system. It is only overt rebels like Yossarian who are dangerous. Ultimately, Orr is perhaps the most dangerous of all, for he proves that it is possible to buck the system and win. Conventional protest can be handled by Catch-22 (even at the end Cathcart and Korn have plans for dealing with Yossarian if he does not accept their terms), but the system cannot handle the new, unconventional strategy developed by Orr.

From this perspective, *Catch-22* seems almost to be a handbook for the protest movements of the early 1960's. The distinctive feature of these movements was not that they were directed toward new goals, based upon new ideologies, or addressed to the solution of new problems, but rather that they employed new styles of protest: the sit-in (not entirely new but never employed in the widespread fashion of the sixties), freedom rides, direct action, nonviolent resistance, the community organizing of the early years of the SDS, the idea of participatory democracy. At the same time, there was a tendency to avoid explicit ideological commitments and the discussion of long-term blueprints for the wholesale reconstruction of society. The goals of the movements were immediate and concrete: the integration of a particular lunch counter or waiting room, bringing people in a particular neighborhood together in order to achieve specific improvements in the neighborhood.

Here we find another connection with the protest strategy exemplified in *Catch-22*. From the perspective of 1968, Josh Greenfield has argued that the protest of *Catch-22* is relatively mild.[10] Yossarian, after all, is not trying to overthrow the military bureaucracy or subvert Milo Minderbinder's M and M Enterprises; he is simply trying to stay alive, to save himself, to get to Sweden. Similarly, the goals of the protest movements of the early sixties were limited, concrete, and realizable. The strategy was to choose a target which one could hit, to fight a battle one could win, thereby, while the protesters might not be able to remake the system entirely, they would be able to bring about a series of changes which would gradually transform it into something which would begin to resemble what it ought to have been.

In considering *Slaughterhouse V,* we enter a completely different world. The book concerns the adventures of Billy Pilgrim, an infantryman captured during the Battle of the Bulge, taken across Germany as a prisoner of war and imprisoned in Dresden, where he lives through the fire bombing that destroyed the city and killed approximately 130,000 people. Afterwards, he returns home to Illium, New York, where he becomes a successful optometrist, enters into a marriage which is happy by conventional standards, is picked up in a flying saucer and taken to the planet Tralfamadore where he is imprisoned with a female movie star named Montana Wildhack, and somewhere along the line "comes unstuck in time."

It is possible to read *Catch-22* as a political fable, but it is not appropriate to approach *Slaughterhouse V* in this fashion. Vonnegut's concerns and vision are essentially religious rather than political. In *Catch-22* the central problem is how the individual may survive in a hostile system, find methods of beating it or changing it. Vonnegut's central concern, not only in *Slaughterhouse V,* but in most of the rest of his novels, is the relationship between man and his own nature or between man and God. He is trying to come to terms with the dichotomy between man and whatever it is that is responsible for the universe being organized the way it is.

However, if one does read *Slaughterhouse V* as a political fable, the moral is clear: the individual is a pawn of forces he cannot control, and all he can hope to do is to learn to accept, be kind, and to love. Billy Pilgrim is mired in his fate. Even his ability to travel in time does him no good; it does not contribute to his freedom or his happiness; it affords him no way of escaping from or controlling the absurdity, injustice, or brutality of the world; it simply places him in the midst of a system of recurring cyclical patterns which confirm the lesson he learns during his captivity on Tralfamadore: everything that is now, always was, and always will be. In other words, everything is unchangeable. Knowing this, Billy's one major effort to have an effect on his world is to become a crusader for the Tralfamadorian message that it is futile to struggle against one's fate, trying to teach others what he has learned for himself, that the only wise course is to learn to accept things as they are.

Note that the subtitle of the book is "The Children's Crusade." Overtly, this subtitle is intended to reinforce the book's antiwar theme, but it does more than that. It indicates Vonnegut's belief that all crusades are children's crusades. Indeed all crusades are childish, first because they are futile gestures, mere play-acting having no consequences except for the possible release of the aggressive fantasies of those who participate in them, not a wholly desirable occurrence, second because all men are childish, dependent, at the mercy of forces beyond their control. One cannot control one's fate, so one should simply allow things to happen; one will probably be better off in the long run; this is the way to make life reasonably tolerable.

This overt message is reinforced by the tone of the book. Both Heller and Vonnegut have been called black humorists, and *Catch-22,* whatever else it may be, is a very funny book. *Slaughterhouse V,* on the other hand, does not provoke laughter. The dominant mood is, rather, sadness, resigned sadness, and compassion for most of the characters in the book. In addition, while there are more laughs in *Catch-22,* there are also more violence and horror than in *Slaughterhouse V.* The latter certainly does not lack horrifying events—there is nothing in *Catch-22* comparable to the extent of the death and devastation produced by the Dresden raid—but the raid does occur offstage; we do not see it, only its aftermath. It is not so much an event in the novel as its setting, its premise. In *Catch-22* the death of a single individual, Snowden, is presented with more dramatic intensity, in a more shocking fashion, than the death of 130,000 people in Dresden. And this difference in dramatic intensity is characteristic of the books as wholes. There is far more dramatic contrast in *Catch-22* than *Slaughterhouse V.* In fact, it seems that Vonnegut is deliberately writing in a monotone, flattening dramatic rises and falls so as to make one event seem approximately as important as any other event, tending to produce the impression that the sequence of events adds up to nothing more than one damn thing after another. There is climactic action and intensity in *Catch 22* because there are discernible goals for action; things move in a particular direction. In *Slaughterhouse V* they do not; things move in cycles; there is no progress.

*Catch-22* is more invested with feeling, with fear, terror, and at the end, exultation, because Yossarian feels himself to be free in a way that Billy is not and cannot be. Because he is free, he is responsible, and therefore to a degree, guilty. Billy weeps, breaking into tears at odd moments for no apparent reason, but Yossarian fears and agonizes over his inability to help Snowden, over his decision to go in a second time over Ferrara, over his failure to help the victims he sees in his walk through Rome. Billy simply walks through things, feeling compassion for the sufferings of others, but not feeling guilt because he is not guilty; he knows he is not responsible.

He feels no moral pressure beyond the necessity of being nice to other people. Yossarian's goals are wider. "Someone had to do something sometime. Every victim was a culprit, every culprit a victim, and somebody had to stand up sometime to break the lousy chain of inherited habit that was imperiling them all" (p. 414). Thus, while Heller preaches the ethic of action, involvement, and responsibility, Vonnegut preaches the ethic of passivity, tolerance, and love.

A large part of this difference stems from the different angles of vision employed by the two men. Heller's vision is essentially political. As noted before, the central problem of *Catch-22* is the attempts of the individual to survive in a hostile bureaucratic system. Vonnegut's vision, on the other hand, is religious, or perhaps more accurately, cosmic. Yossarian is contending against a human conspiracy; if there is a conspiracy against Billy, it is a cosmic one; if there is a system for him to fight against, it is the whole universe; there are no bad guys for him to defeat, except, perhaps, God. Indeed, Billy is not even engaged in a contest, for there can be no contest where there is no possibility of victory. For Yossarian, to survive constitutes a victory. For Billy, survival is not crucial, for he is fully aware of the inevitability of death; the manner of its coming is a rather trivial issue and makes little difference in the total economy of the universe. All he can hope for is a few good moments in life to cherish. Indeed, from the more general, more cosmic, more universal view that Vonnegut takes, the victories won by Heller's character may very well turn out to be defeats.

Some critics have noted that Yossarian has no guarantee that his future in Sweden will be unrelievedly happy.[11] But the point is that Heller stops short of considering that problem. After saying that Yossarian has achieved a victory, temporary and limited though it may prove to be in the end, he stops. The point he leaves the reader with is that Yossarian has taken a decisive step in his quest for survival and that this is enough. For Vonnegut, however, it would not be enough. He would go on to consider what happens to Yossarian in Sweden and would stress that in the end Yossarian's apparent victory is indeed temporary and limited. Thus, while Heller offers instruction in how we may achieve solutions to our problems, Vonnegut offers perspectives on how we may learn to live tolerably in a world we cannot change.

Let us now see how these conclusions are reflected in the political culture of the 1960's. Advocates of various types of social change began the decade with feelings of openness and optimism, with the firm belief that through proper strategies change was possible, that, in fact, there was a moral imperative to work for improvements, and that to shirk this responsibility was to become a partner in guilt. ("If you are not part of the solution, you are part of the problem.") It was a period of activism, vigor. By the end of the decade, much of this feeling had eroded. The early advances of the civil rights movement, the freedom rides, the sit-ins, the Civil Rights Act of 1964, the Voting Rights Act of 1965 had not, after all, destroyed racism and inequality. The apparent idealism manifested in the Peace Corps and the Alliance for Progress had somehow been swallowed up in the jungles of Southeast Asia. The sense of reawakened commitment, energy, almost euphoria, produced by the New Frontier and the Great Society had not resulted in effective assaults on poverty and urban blight. Instead, defense spending and corporate profits had soared. The nation's idealism and energy seemed to have been diverted into the polluted channels of power politics. The lesson which many drew was this: we have struggled, but we have not overcome; political solutions have failed; the system is not amenable to change by normal methods.

As a consequence, the theoretical orientation of the protest movement changed. In the beginning, it had been based upon the assumption that desirable results could be achieved by concentrating on specific problems, but since this approach had apparently not worked, a new conviction grew steadily in strength: it is not the specific evil to which we must address ourselves, but the evil of the whole system; the specific is simply a reflection of the general and cannot be changed without a change in the system as a whole. It is not racism, poverty, the war, the impersonality of the university which must be destroyed, but the system which has produced and which is responsible for perpetuating all of these. It is necessary, after all, to overthrow M and M Enterprises.[12]

But what, exactly, can we do to make the necessary changes? There were two general answers to this question. One was to reject the reformist approach and to adopt an explicitly revolutionary stance. Part of this transformation involved the decay of the earlier attitude of ideological spontaneity and open-endedness and the corresponding growth of a tendency to become locked into rigid theoretical abstractions. More important than this new dogmatism, however, was a new attitude toward violence. As the sense of a system open to change through political action constricted, it was replaced with bitterness and frustration at the ineffectiveness of previous efforts and at the inertia of that system, and violence began to seem increasingly appropriate, not so much as a rational instrument of change, but as an expression of rage. In fact, the escalation of violence may be seen as a rejection of activism in that its purpose was not so much to transform society in any specific way as to express, as eloquently as possible, one's personal disgust. This is why so much of the violence of the Weathermen seems random and irrational. It is not that it was without purpose—it had a very real purpose—but that purpose was not political but moral, not to produce any specific institutional change, but to "bear witness" in the religious sense to their beliefs and especially the depth of their commitment to them.[13]

The second general response was to alter the field of operations, to take dissent out of the political realm, and to move more and more into the realm of culture and lifestyle, to switch, in short, from political to cultural radicalism. Of course, cultural radicalism had existed earlier in the decade, but the emphasis swung toward it more and

more as time went on. Cultural radicalism is not, of course, a movement. It has no program, no organization, no set of goals. It is rather an orientation, shared by a highly diverse group of people, many of whom have programs and ideologies which are different from and perhaps even contradictory to those held by others in the group. We may distinguish two broad types of cultural radicalism. One is made up of those who believe that their program of cultural radicalism, whatever it is, will produce changes in society. Usually, they feel that the changes produced will be broad and sweeping, revolutionary in fact, transforming the entire society in fundamental ways. Like the revolutionary political groups, they accept the proposition that piecemeal social change and reformist tactics are not adequate to deal with the problems of society, and that more basic alterations are necessary. They differ in that what they want to see changed is not so much institutions as values, and their field of action is culture rather than politics. The Yippies are the best illustration of this tendency. Their life-style was their ideology; craziness was their goal: the medium of their protest, with its outrageous humor, was their message.[14]

The other strand in cultural radicalism we may call escapist. The operating premise here is that society as a whole is probably too corrupt, too massive, too entrenched in injustice or simple inertia, to be effectively changed so as to remove its life-denying characteristics. The goal then became not the transformation of society but the achievement of salvation for oneself in the interstices of or entirely separated from a mad, debased, and dangerous society. If we cannot prevent the building from burning, we can at least flee from the flames.

There are several manifestations of this form of cultural radicalism. The turn toward various forms of mysticism, eastern religions, astrology, the I Ching bespeaks a rejection of the pseudo-rationality upon which contemporary society is based and an attempt to discover and get in tune with the forces that determine what happens in the universe, since it is obvious that we do not and cannot control it. Similarly the commune movement of the late sixties was not usually intended to provide examples of a better life to the rest of the world, but simply to afford refuges from the outside world for commune members. Communes were exclusive rather than inclusive in their tactics, protective rather than exemplary in their goals.[15] Encounter sessions and T-groups multiplied in order to enable the individual to become more aware of himself and thus make it possible for him to manipulate himself into a more suitable relationship with his surroundings. In all these manifestations, the watchword was, "Go with the flow, let it happen." Pretensions to mastery were surrendered, and quasi-Taoism became the preferred strategy for living. Connected with these was a quest for immediacy and authenticity of experience and a tendency to reject goal-oriented behavior and the whole idea of deferred gratification.

To recapitulate, then, *Catch-22,* read as a political fable, offers a moral which is completely consistent with the morally involved, activist, reformist orientation of the early sixties; the system is brutal, unjust, and irrational, but it is also vulnerable. It is run by other human beings, and they are both identifiable and fallible; therefore, effective resistance by the individual may be possible. We must, however, be careful in our choice of methods of resistance; we must devise methods which those in authority do not expect, which their institutions are unequipped to deal with, which will take them unaware. Unconventionality in one's style of resistance is of value in itself. Also of value is the example of resistance. Even minimal success, even the mere fact of having declared oneself in opposition, will encourage others to resist, and there is always the possibility that someone will devise an effective strategy. Even if that strategy results only in one's own salvation as a direct consequence, it may have important indirect consequences in that it may encourage others to undertake their own forms of resistance.

Vonnegut stands in a somewhat different and more complex relationship to the politico-cultural climate which surrounds him. On the one hand, he expresses the more chastened view of the possibilities of political change through individual action that had become widely prevalent at the end of the sixties. Echoing the cultural radicals' idea that society cannot be significantly changed unless men's minds and hearts are changed first, he exemplifies the decay of reformist hopes, just as Heller had earlier exemplified their full flowering. On the other hand, Vonnegut also reacts *against* certain tendencies in the protest movement of the later sixties, especially the tendency toward apocalyptic utopianism. His universe is one in which the basic rule is moral relativism. There are no villains in *Slaughterhouse V,* or indeed in any of his other works. Of course he has moral values, but unlike Heller, he does not feel that the lines between good and evil can be drawn with absolute precision. Further, he feels that those who draw such lines are likely only to cause suffering in the long run. He attacks all pretensions to dominance, mastery, and control based upon convictions of righteous certitude. He is preaching against America's attempt to control the destiny of Southeast Asia, but he is also preaching against those who gave up the hope of achieving limited, immediate, proximate goals in favor of trying to achieve sweeping changes and impose their own vision of the good society, through revolutionary violence if necessary. The Green Berets are not his only targets; so are the Weathermen.

In many ways, Vonnegut's view has much in common with the orientation of the counterculture as described by Theodore Roszak.[16] According to this view, science, technology, and technocratic rationality are tools for the manipulation of things and people in a search for short-run solutions to those problems defined as susceptible of solution by those techniques. This obsessively narrow concern with such problems and techniques ignores the long-term consequences of those acts. For this overemphasis on rationality, we must substitute a reawakened belief in the intuitive, mystical powers of the individual. The vision and the search turn inward. The external world is the province of the technocrats, the bureaucrats, the manipulators, so let us take the internal world for ours. We may not reform society, but at least we will not hurt others; our individual search for peace and tranquility in a regimented, manipulated, absurd world will not destroy the chance of others to do the same. While sympathetic to this view, Vonnegut would find in it a tendency toward oversimplification. He would certainly agree that man's enslavement to science and the machine holds dangers of dehumanization and worse—this, in fact, is the main theme of two of his novels, *Player Piano* and *Cat's Cradle*—but he would also emphasize that the rejection of technology does not guarantee salvation. For Vonnegut, like Hawthorne, the human heart is the fundamental problem, and any change that does not alter man himself will be inconsequential.

In this connection, we may note that Vonnegut is not totally committed to the idea that the individual cannot change his society. Indeed, he writes out of a conviction that artists can have an impact on their world. Art has a purpose to him, and it is an important one, but it is essentially passive. The artist can change the system, but only at the price of not becoming part of it, only by giving up the hope of affecting it directly. Vonnegut has said that his purpose as a writer is to get people before they become generals and presidents and "poison their minds with humanity."[17] But this works only on those who have not yet become generals and presidents, not on those who are generals and presidents already. Another way of saying this is that the artist's function is to provide society with new perspectives, to change people's angle of vision, not to preach direct cures, not to offer prescriptions for social ills, but to point out their existence and to provide new diagnostic techniques. While this is certainly an important, even a vital, function, and while it may over time lead to significant social changes, one must recognize that the artist's influence is likely to be indirect and gradual rather than direct and immediate. The artist's effectiveness as a reformer is limited; substantial improvements, if they can be achieved at all, can be achieved only in the long run, probably a very long run. In the meantime, Vonnegut says, we should be kind, be tolerant, and seize upon and cherish the few moments of simple pleasure that come our way. It is significant that the high point of Billy Pilgrim's life is the nap he takes in the back of a wagon a few days after the destruction of Dresden. So much have the horizons of hope shrunk from *Catch-22* to *Slaughterhouse V.*

NOTES

[1] Bruce Kuklick, "Myth and Symbol in American Studies," *American Quarterly,* 24 (Oct., 1972), 435-50; Seymour Katz, "'Culture' and Literature in American Studies," *American Quarterly,* 20 (Summer, 1968), 318-29; R. Gordon Kelly, "Literature and the Historian," *American Quarterly,* 26 (May, 1974), 141-59; Cecil F. Tate, *The Search for a Method in American Studies* (Minneapolis, 1972); Leo Marx, "American Studies: Defense of an Unscientific Method," *New Literary History,* 1 (Oct., 1969), 75-90.

[2] Katz, *American Quarterly,* 20 (Summer, 1968), 323.

[3] Jim F. Heath, *Decade of Disillusionment: The Kennedy-Johnson Years* (Bloomington, Ind., 1975).

[4] Richard King, *The Party of Eros: Radical Social Thought and the Realm of Freedom* (Chapel Hill, 1972), p. 7.

[5] Brian Way, "Formal Experiment and Social Discontent: Joseph Heller's *Catch-22*," *Journal of American Studies,* 2 (Oct., 1968), 253-70, reprinted in C. K. McFarland, ed., *The Modern American Tradition: Readings in Intellectual History* (New York, 1972), pp. 283-96.

[6] Joseph Heller, *Catch-22* (New York, 1961), p. 127. (Page references are to the Dell paperback edition.)

[7] Douglas Day, "*Catch-22:* A Manifesto for Anarchists," *Carolina Quarterly* (Summer, 1963), 92.

[8] See, for example, Wayne Charles Miller, *An Armed America, Its Face in Fiction: A History of the American Military Novel* (New York, 1970), p. 222; Sanford Pinkser, "Heller's *Catch-22:* The Protest of a *Puer Eternis,*" *Critique,* 7 (Winter, 1964-65), 161-62; Norman Podhoretz, *Doings and Undoings: The Fifties and After in American Writing* (New York, 1962), pp. 232-35.

[9] Quoted in Josh Greenfield, "22 Was Funnier Than 14," *New York Times Book Review,* 3 March 1968.

[10] Ibid.

[11] Tony Tanner, *City of Words: American Fiction, 1950-1970* (New York, 1971), pp. 80-81.

[12] Useful histories of the New Left are Edward J. Bacciocco, Jr., *The New Left in America: Reform to Revolutions, 1956 to 1970* (Stanford, 1970) and Irwin Unger, *The Movement: A History of the American New Left, 1959-1972* (New York, 1974). More sympathetic to the New Left, is Jack Newfield, *A Prophetic Minority* (New York, 1966). The intellectual history of the New Left is treated in Peter Clecak, *Radical Paradoxes: Dilemmas of the American Left, 1945-1970* (New York, 1973) and Richard King, *The Party of Eros: Radical Social Thought and the Realm of Freedom* (Chapel Hill, 1972). Thomas Powers, *The War at Home: Vietnam and the American People* (New York, 1973) is an account of the antiwar movement.

[13] See Thomas Powers, *Diana: The Making of a Terrorist* (Boston, 1971) for an account of the career of one member of SDS. Powers account of life in the SDS communes of the late sixties vividly recalls the accounts in Norman Cohn, *The Pursuit of the Millennium; Revolutionary Millenarians and Mystical Anarchists of the Middle Ages,* 2nd ed. (New York, 1970).

[14] The classic texts of Yippiedom are Free (pseudonym of Abbie Hoffman), *Revolution for the Hell of It* (New York, 1968) and Jerry Rubin, *Do It!: Scenarios of the Revolution* (New York, 1970). The tendency toward cultural radicalism also affected the more purely political wing of the protest movement. See, for example, a letter from, Bernardine Dohrn, quoted in Unger, *The Movement* pp. 189-90. See also Richard Flacks and Milton Mankoff, "Why They Burned the Bank," *Nation* 210 (23 March 1970), 337-40 and "The Changing Base of the American Student Movement," *Annals of the American Academy of Political and Social Science,* 395 (1971), 55-56 and 59-66.

[15] See Laurence Veysey, *The Communal Experience: Anarchist and Mystical Counter-Cultures in America* (New York, 1972).

[16] Theodore Roszak, *The Making of a Counter Culture: Reflections on the Technocratic Society and Its Youthful Opposition* (Garden City, 1969), especially pp. 205-38.

[17] Quoted in Robert Scholes, "A Talk with Kurt Vonnegut, Jr.," in Jerome Klinkowitz and John Somer, *The Vonnegut Statement* (New York, 1973), p. 107.

---

# EUROPE

## Robert Cohen

SOURCE: "Some Political Implications of *The Madwoman of Chaillot*," in *Contemporary Literature,* Vol. 9, No. 2, Spring, 1968, pp. 2210-22.

*[In the following essay, Cohen finds that, despite its "whimsical" surface, Hyppolyte-Jean Giraudoux's* The Madwoman of Chaillot *is an existential drama concerning the political nightmare of World War II.]*

It may seem overly narrow to speak of *The Madwoman of Chaillot* as a political play concerning France in the Second World War. The play is full of fancy, a superbly whimsical collection of farce, fantasy, and flippancy which has achieved as great a popular success as any of Giraudoux's plays. Social seriousness, which continually peeks from the interior of *Siegfried* and *The Trojan War Will Not Take Place,* and is mixed with bothersome intellectual discursions in *Electra,* seems at first totally missing from *The Madwoman.* One American textbook edition even bases its approval of the work on its total removal from the current scene: "For some theatregoers . . . the play seemed too remote from the harsh facts of contemporary history, and many wondered how Giraudoux could write so spirited a comedy during a period of national suffering and despair. Plainly, none of the anguish of the existential drama of the French Occupation is present in Giraudoux's extravaganza. . . . The remoteness of the mood and characters from the dark reality of the day is itself part of the play's charm."[1] Yet I don't think this is "plain" at all, and while the "anguish of existential drama" may not be readily apparent to the theatergoer, it can be found at the very bones of the play.

The play, which was completed in 1942 and first produced after the war, divides society into two races, one of eccentrics and the other of pimps. The former is the carry-over from the army of beggars in *Electra,* and one of their leaders, the Ragpicker, is the more earthly variant of *Electra*'s Beggar, both roles having been first performed by Louis Jouvet. The true leader of this army, however, is the Madwoman Aurélie herself, "A *grande dame.* Silk skirt leading to a train, but gathered up by a metal clothespin. Louis XIII slippers. Marie-Antoinette chapeau. A lorgnette hanging on a chain. A cameo. A basket . . . a dinner bell in the bosom of her dress" (stage direction, p. 102).[2] Supporting the mad fantastical mélange are three more madwomen: Constance, the Madwoman of Passy; Josephine, the Madwoman of la Concorde; and Gabrielle, the Madwoman of Saint-Sulpice; plus a flower girl, a street-singer, a deaf-mute, a lace merchant, a pair of lovers, a sewer king, some historical anti-vivisectionists, and "the friends of vegetables." The enemy army is the one of *mecs* (pimps), a nameless, faceless assortment of presidents, prospectors, barons, brokers, secretaries general, and petroleum lobbyists. Between these two armies, a comic war is waged, but it must not be forgotten that this war, like its contemporary, is a war to the death.

The setting is the Café de l'Alma in the Chaillot district of Paris, and the café represents all which history and culture have deposited in the French capital. "At this same place Molière, Racine and La Fontaine used to come to drink their wine," says the Prospector (p. 101), and it had also been the scene of Giraudoux's meetings with Jouvet. The Madwoman and her friends are long-time residents of the area; the pimps, we see immediately, are newcomers. And they control everything. They corrupt everything. Their goal is to destroy Paris and retrieve the oil which they have found under the city's innards. As the play begins, the Prospector has laid a bomb which he expects will blow up Chaillot. The Ragpicker explains, "There's been an invasion, Countess. The world is no longer beautiful, no longer happy, because of the invasion" (p. 123). The action of the play is simple: it consists of the Madwoman learning of the nature of these "invaders," condemning them *in absentia* in a mock trial, and gloriously ridding the world of them by luring them down into a bottomless pit.

There are three levels of social analogy which are drawn in this colorful adventure, each simultaneously existing as a satiric analysis of the current political scene. On the first, most obvious level, *The Madwoman* parodies capitalism, especially the extreme financial jugglings of those who deal with money as opposed to goods. The *mecs* are the property pimps of Parisian commerce: the "mackerel pimp" and the "white wine pimp," who attach themselves to various objects of man's needs and desires, and work themselves in for a cut on the exchange. The abuses of capitalism had greatly increased during the Occupation,

with the black market substituting for more civil methods of exchange; and the President and his friends sitting around the Café de l'Alma in Giraudoux's play resemble nothing quite as specifically as these black marketeers, described in this 1942 article from the Parisian *France-Europe:*

> M. Nénesse enters a small bar near the Opera. He walks heavily and carelessly on thick, creaking leather soles to his reserved table. The waiters bustle around him. [He adjusts] his gold watch and takes a Chesterfield from his gold cigarette case, weighing at least 300 grams. . . . Out of a bicycle taxi steps either an important colleague or a client of this 1943 tycoon. The new arrival is of indeterminate age. . . . In the abrupt tones that you used to hear in the underworld, the two men converse. The newcomer tears a corner off the paper tablecloth and writes some mysterious figures on it. It all has to do with *"boîtes bleues," "paquets verts,"* and *"douze tonnes de purée."* Finally, the fat man pulls a thick wad of 5,000 franc notes out of his inside pocket, and M. Nénesse stuffs them away without batting an eyelid. The phone rings. It's for M. Nénesse. He doesn't bother to go up to the phone booth; he takes the long-distance call downstairs.
>
> "The trucks from Belgium haven't turned up. And the tobacco. . . . "
>
> Everyone can hear, but what does it matter? N. Nénesse is outside the law. . . .
>
> Before the war, plain Nénesse was in the white slave trade. After the defeat, Monsieur Nénesse traded in meat, poultry and butter. . . . Every day this honest tradesman sells 300,000 francs' worth of goods and collects a cool fifty percent rake-off.[3]

Nénesse, formerly a real pimp and now a vegetable pimp, exactly resembles the Giraudoux *mecs,* who also sport expensive cigarette lighters (with private stock cigarettes), arrogant titles, disrespect for authority, distaste for the human beings about them, and a private code language of financial doubletalk. The president and his friends, like M. Nénesse, exhibit complete freedom from legal prosecution because they control the law; their word is law. "Hundred franc notes belong to the rich, not the poor," the President tells the Ragpicker (p. 89) as he takes the note away. Money belongs to the pimps; it is their language, and the Ragpicker says of them as it was said of M. Nénesse: "When they meet they whisper and pass each other fifty-thousand franc notes" (p. 124).

The attack on capitalism as pimpery was especially meaningful in France, where not only the black market but an outrageously political system of economic policies had hamstrung the country since the First World War. Giraudoux had complained for many years of the system where money had more and more become disassociated with goods, and where the agent of a product became more necessary than its producer. In his last political testament, *Sans Pouvoirs,* he wrote, "Our financial policy has become a money game. . . . It has detached money from its real values; and has allowed our great national resources to go to waste, by detaching money from work, from function, and even from gold itself."[4] It is this aspect of capitalism which, Giraudoux felt, is unnatural and pernicious; the substitution of a seemingly synthetic system of trade for a natural bartering of intrinsic worths. As an economic grievance, however, this may be merely nostalgic, since Giraudoux did not nor could not suggest alternative systems of commerce. The satire against capitalism and economic pimpery is a hollow one. Far from being the principal subject of Giraudoux's interest, it is actually only a sidelight.

More crucial to the play's structure is the analogical relationship of the story to the French-German theme from earlier plays; a theme more deeply buried in the theatrical froth than the other, perhaps, but far more vital. For by this analogy Giraudoux paints his story of the German Occupation of his city: the Madwoman and her cafe friends represent the citizens of Paris (and of France), and the army of pimps represents the German Occupying Forces. Considerable evidence warrants this comparison, admittedly a surprising one considering the play's tone.

The imagery of the script is entirely that of a nation at war. The pimps are "invaders"; their take-over of Paris has been an "invasion"; they are of "another race" and they have arrived in their positions as a result of a series of murders:

> Ten years ago, one day, my heart jumped. Among the passersby I saw a man with nothing in common with anyone else; stocky, stout, his right eye rakish, his left anxious, another race. He swaggered, but in a funny way, somewhat menacing and uneasy, as if he had killed one of my friends to take his place. He *had* killed him. It was just the first. The invasion had begun. Since then not a day has passed without one of my friends disappearing and one of the new ones replacing him. (p. 124)

They take the place of murdered Parisians as the German forces took the places of men killed in the hapless attempt to hold back the Wehrmacht. They are the uniform and uniformed army: faceless, nameless, "locked to one another like alpinists on a chain" (p. 126). When they appear in the final scene, it is in groups of identical robots who follow each other down the bottomless pit, as armies follow each other into war.

They have completely taken over the administration of Paris. "They run everything. They corrupt everything," says the Ragpicker. "The slave era has arrived. We are the last free people" (p. 125). They have appropriated for themselves the grand chateaux in the Loire Valley for their personal residences, and have decorated them with ballet girls from the Opera (p. 160). They are not only above the law, they make it into a rapacious and humiliating weapon. They respect neither tradition, culture, nor personal decency; they "bathe naked, if they choose, in the fountains of the Place de la Concorde. . . . they can turn to you their *derrières*, my dear ladies, and you will smile at them and kiss them as you would their faces.

You *will* kiss . . ." (p. 163). The cruelty of the *mecs* is far more than the cruelty of ordinary capitalists; it is the behavior of a spiteful Nazi empire.

While the German forces were at first kept to fairly rigid standards of conduct during the Occupation, their presence was felt in every corpuscle of the invalided French body. Grey-suited German soldiers mingled almost imperceptibly with Parisians at Auteuil, at the Opera, and in the corner cafés, but the apparent serenity was merely on the surface. One Frenchwoman wrote, "They pass by, two by two, four by four, rarely alone; stiff, grave, hardly talking . . . without the radiant careless smile of youth, without any of the charming abandon that shows real camaraderie. . . . They no longer are human beings; they are creatures galvanized . . .":[5] galvanized by fanaticism, to be sure, also by the incredible power which had fallen into their hands. The Germans, like the Madwoman's *mecs*, had billeted the great chateaux and turned them into military headquarters. They had splashed German highway signs all over Paris, and Parisian nightclubs reverberated to Nazi drinking songs. They were the ones who, in 1942, were buying French girls for their pleasures, swimming nude in the fountains of La Concorde, administering an economy for which they produced nothing, suppressing individual expression and individual belief to the point of committing French citizens to German concentration camps, and in short, running and corrupting Paris without being Parisian. When the pimps disappear at the end of *The Madwoman* and the flower girl cries out, "The armistice must have been signed" (p. 177), it should be obvious what future armistice Giraudoux had then in mind.

Giraudoux does not mention Germany once in the script, and the names of some of the invaders are Duval, Durand, and Boyer; never Schmidt or Ribbentrop or Biedermann. This could possibly be due to an early thought of Giraudoux to produce the play during the Occupation, or it could simply be a measure to maintain the light tone of whimsical fantasy. But there is one precise linkage between the events of the play and of the contemporary situation which is of considerable importance. This is the figure of Adolphe Bertaut.

Adolphe is the former lover of the Madwoman, and their aborted affair haunts the play. They had courted in the 1890's "when the Tsar entered Paris," but had broken apart years afterward, and Adolphe had married a woman named Georgette whom he never loved. "That's the way men are," the Madwoman explains. "They love you because you are good, spiritual, and transparent, and when they get the chance they leave you for some woman who is ugly, colorless, and opaque" (pp. 166-167). Thirty years after that, but still before the play begins, they met again, but that time Adolphe did not recognize his countess Aurélie, and instead he stole a melon from her. Finally, at the end of the play, "all the Adolphe Bertauts of the world" come to return her melon and demand her hand (p. 178). But now she refuses. This is the story of Adolphe Bertaut, and it is a puzzling one since it seems at first to have so little relationship with the rest of the play.

It could be by no accident that this mysterious character has the same name, Adolphe, or Adolf, as the one man whose name virtually personifies the Second World War. In 1942 "Adolphe" could bring thoughts of only one man. Even a hundred years from that date, no parent or author will be able to use the name "Adolf" innocently. Moreover, Adolphe is a very German name in this French play, and he is described as wearing a "cronstadt" (a German stiff hat) and having a suspicion of a harelip (p. 112), which was rumored at the time to be the reason for Hitler's mustache. Through the character of Adolphe Bertaut, Giraudoux shows his own love affair with Germany, his disgust at having been jilted in World War One and having been robbed (the melon) at Alsace-Lorraine, and his final and complete repudiation of the German nation in World War Two. Although Siegfried, speaking for Giraudoux in his 1928 play of that name, refused to dig a "kind of ditch inside myself" between France and Germany; when the Madwoman answers the final, post-armistice appeal of the "Adolphe Bertauts of the world," it is with words of total rejection:

> I say that when they had the 24th of May, 1880, to declare themselves, the most beautiful Pentecost Monday that had ever been seen in the Varrières woods, or the 5th of September 1887 when they took and grilled a pike for our picnic at Villeneuve-Saint-Georges, or even, if necessary, the 21st of August 1897 when the Tsar entered Paris, and when they let all these days pass without saying anything to you, then it is too late! (pp. 178-179)

The cultural bond had never been tied; Germany and France had remained enemies through all opportunities, and had remained unreconciled within the human framework. Speaking from the 1942 vantage, Giraudoux could say nothing else.

Adolphe's story is never told except in sketchy references, and he only appears at the very end of the play. But it is the climactic moment, and the rejection of the Adolphe Bertauts leads directly to the play's concluding statement: "If two beings who love one another let one single minute get between them, it becomes months, years, centuries" (p. 179). Reconciliation in 1942 was beyond hope, the world would have to turn its efforts to the conflicts of the future. The future would learn from the present, and, as in *Electra,* Giraudoux sees beyond the war to the era which will follow. The Madwoman turns to the hesitating young lovers and cries to her friends: "Make them kiss each other, the rest of you, or else in an hour she will be the Madwoman of Alma and he will have a white beard. [They kiss.] Bravo! If only that had happened thirty years ago. I wouldn't be here today" (p. 179). If France had embraced Germany in 1919, if Giraudoux and others had succeeded in making Frenchmen realize the necessity of retaking contact with Germany, as he had attempted in *Siegfried,*[6] the war would not have taken place. Failing that, the time had already come to begin preventing the wars to follow.

The ending of *The Madwoman of Chaillot* is a total capitulation to theatricalism and a violent attempt to escape, even momentarily, from the dialectic. The ending is an act of genocide which only an extreme degree of stylization makes palatable. It is as though the oppression of three years of Nazi Occupation had so burdened Giraudoux that in one enormous, irrational shrug he simply disposed of it through fantasy. A lifetime of concern over Franco-German relations has ended with an act of irredeemable violence and has relinquished all hope of reconciliation short of mass slaughter. In this conclusion Giraudoux adheres to the same basic thought of *Electra,* but with one major difference: *Electra* ends with only the dimmest forecast of what the post-war future would bring, and *The Madwoman of Chaillot* gives us a detailed plan. In 1940 Giraudoux told an audience, "Peace must find us with our programme ready, cut and dried down to the last detail."[7] *The Madwoman,* as much as the political essays in *Sans Pouvoirs* and *Pour Une Politique Urbaine,*[8] became Giraudoux's last will and testament for the future of France, and of European civilization. This is the third, final level of social analogy.

In this light, *The Madwoman* is Giraudoux's warning against the evils of a mechanized, technological society. It is no longer merely Prussianism which concerns him; it is the oppression of technological progress, either American, German, or Russian; the oppression of a technocracy which seeks to devalue individuality, artistry, history, and culture and to insist upon, in their places, efficiency, sterility, neatness, and uniformity. What terrified Giraudoux about this particular war, which was being battled about France's head, was that it led only "to the thought that peace will be no more than a horrible adjustment between a mutilated white race and a triumphant mechanical civilization."[9] It was this thought above all which generated *The Madwoman,* as can be seen in several illustrations.

The pimps are the agents of technological progress; in their faceless anonymity they are the identical pistons in a huge economic machine. Their bent is for progress but their result is destruction. As the Madwoman explains:

> Men everywhere who seem to be building are secretly involved in destruction. The newest of their buildings is only the mannequin of a ruin. . . . They build quays and destroy rivers (look at the Seine), build cities and destroy the countryside (look at Pré-aux-clercs), build the Palace of Chaillot and destroy the Trocadéro. . . . The occupation of humanity is only a universal enterprise of demolition. (p. 141)

Progress, in the technological society, is merely a change from one form to another, and in the wanton sacrifice of the old, Giraudoux feels, vital components of the human character are destroyed.

The technocrats are "cool" people, bespeaking an age where emotion gets in the way of expertise. "They don't run, they don't hurry. You never see them sweat," says the Ragpicker (p. 124). Their motivating source is oil, and their taste for it is sensual, lustful. They find oil under Paris and so will destroy the city to get it. "What do they want to make with it?" asks the Madwoman.

"What one makes with oil—misery, war, ugliness," answers the young lover (p. 122). The interchangeable "presidents of administrative councils, delegate administrators, self-conscious prospectors, contingency stockbrokers, secretaries general of enterprising syndicates, patent expropriators . . . publicity arrangers" (p. 126), who are the ice-blooded arbiters of technological society, have no use for the queer assortment of characters that frequent the Madwoman's café; and the future conflict, we realize, is to be between these technocrats and the less progress-minded. They will either be absorbed or eliminated. The first method is demonstrated at the play's beginning, where the Baron is taken into the fold by the President. The fifty-odd year old Baron exemplifies the degenerated French spirit and his name, Jean-Hippolyte, is the exact reversal of Giraudoux's. He has disposed of his inherited French estates for a series of foreign mistresses. "The more French the name of my estate—the more exotic the name of my mistress," he says pathetically (p. 88), referring to the falling apart of the French Empire, both physically and spiritually.

But many cannot nor will not be absorbed, and these the invaders must liquidate. The Broker summarizes the course of action which must be taken against the Madwoman and her friends, and its reasons, in this peroration from an early draft of the play:

> This madwoman . . . that dealer in shoelaces, that juggler, these are our real enemies, Mr. Prospector. . . . Those who have a sense of humor, a nostalgia for the past (which we abolished!). We others, we pioneers of the modern age, we had thought that by the division of the world into two classes; one of workers and the other a managerial elite; one sweaty and the other perfumed, that by the radical suppression of all connections between money and the poor, between leisure and work, we thought we would have sterilized the epoch once and for all! The diversity of human types has become a major problem for the conscientious managerial executive . . . we have been thinking of reducing them to a single popular type. A thousand exploitees per one exploiter, how convenient that would be, how restful for the conscience. But look! Look about this district which we have filled with the largest number of delegate administrators in Paris, the district which we want to make the citadel of power and money . . . see these flesh and bone ghosts of liberty. . . . These are the phantoms of joyful poverty, of madness. . . . [10]

This statement, somewhat attenuated in the final version in order to preserve the light tone of the play, gives an ironic rationale for all "clean" economic systems, which gain efficiency by reducing man to a uniform figure, easy to program, easy to monitor, easy to keep in line. Such systems were proposed to France during and after the war, first by Hitler through the Vichy government, afterwards by America, via SHAPE, NATO, and European Recovery; and Russia, via the French Communist Party. All of these forces fought for France's destiny in the 'forties and 'fifties, and not until the present Republic under

De Gaulle can France truly be said to have taken her destiny in her own hands. Even this Giraudoux had prophesied. "The only hope rests with De Gaulle,"[11] he had said shortly before his death. While he never was to appreciate the full import of that remark, the relevance of these political concerns became enormous in the post-war period.

The prophesied future for which Giraudoux ultimately hoped was not a sentimentalized fantasy world of mad-women and shoelace peddlers (just as the technocrats were not to be faceless, identical robots—at least in the literal sense), and his rebellion against the mechanized society was considerably more than nostalgic, wistful rumination. He was a political realist, and he had a program. It was not his idea of dramaturgy to use the theater for this sort of exposition—and the play must be seen as a general sounding of alarm rather than a detailed manifesto. Nonetheless, the play offers certain definite guidelines toward the future. It appeals to the Frenchman's love for freedom and to his searching after personal and natural glory. (The President became a pimp only after he sacrificed his dreams of glory and "turned instead to the inexpressive and nameless faces" [p. 89].) It appeals to a respect for tradition, for history, and for a natural state of man and country. It demands a tolerance for all sorts of eccentricities and peculiarities which define the human being. It celebrates the simple qualities of provincial life, and demands that they be protected in an increasingly urban world. To Giraudoux, born in rural Bellac, this was what the war was all about: the preservation of the simple, honest, French way of life. Defending the war, he wrote in 1940:

> What sort of man is a Frenchman? He is a man who likes to spend his time not in the glorification of a race, nor in manifestations of some dark divinity within him, but in simple ways of daily life, the ways of living that his forefathers bequeathed him, in a pleasant, fruitful land, a life based on rational principles and respect for the rights of others. He has his rules of conduct: work, activity, a lively interest in all things. He has his pleasures; the joys of family life and the company of friends; his hobbies, such as fishing, games of bowls. And he has his special passions—a passion for personal freedom . . . with which he tolerates no interference, and a passionate dislike of injustice.[12]

Idyllic? Of course. But Giraudoux was never to shrink from an idea merely because it seemed sentimental. Sentiment, he felt, was one of the distinguishing abilities of the human species, and proper sentimentality was consonant with an honest, natural manner of life. The stability of rural life, which was also that of French life, was in Giraudoux's mind a reflection of French rationality—an essential honesty between body and spirit. "I hate ugliness, I adore beauty," says Irma Lambert, the dishwasher (p. 130). It is the obvious truth which is shocking to hear said, for it is the truth of the body rather than the politic speech of society. By contrast progress is, in Giraudoux's thoughts, an unnecessary demand of the world which continually yanks man from his more natural, honest, and peace-loving destiny; and mere progress, by itself, must be resisted. "France has always had one principle, one programme: to be contented with the existing state of things, and whenever feasible, to turn it to account and to ameliorate it,"[13] said Giraudoux, who craved a society which would slowly evolve by internal movements and august leadership, never by revolution or ideological invasion. Though often thought of as a liberal (as he would probably be called in America), Giraudoux was a staunch conservative. He wished to conserve the trees,[14] conserve the simplicity of rural life, and conserve the importance of love, nostalgia, beauty, and communality. These values are not frequently spoken for in literature, not at least in good literature, for they smack of the super-obvious and the overly sentimental. Yet Giraudoux laced them with such brilliant measures of irony, wit, and savage understatement that they have become palatable.

Peace must bring this freedom to conserve the old while relishing the new, Giraudoux maintained. To the troops fighting for the country, he defined the policy of the war:

> You must look forward to a France equipped for action and well-being on modern lines. While you are defending your country, you must feel assured that, when peace comes, you will find awaiting you not only the heritage of our age-long civilization—which we shall do our best to keep intact for you—but also a larger freedom, a wider field of enterprise, more trustworthy guides and ample safeguards, at last made thoroughly effective against parasites and profiteers.[15]

Giraudoux's activity in establishing the new France "on modern lines" was not strictly limited to polemics. He revived and reorganized the important *Ligue Urbaine et Rurale* and authored its manifestos and policy documents. The league functioned after the liberations and "followed out, on the practical level, the goals which Giraudoux had broadly fixed."[16] He travelled extensively to collect information and spread his gospel—even during the Occupation. He did work in the details as well as the general policies, and worked extensively to preserve certain monuments and parks in the city of Paris in their original forms. It could be argued that this work was trivial, yet that argument is shortsighted. What Giraudoux sought above all for France was a pride in Frenchness, a cultural nationalism, a love, amongst the citizens, of their environment. And no one can now doubt that this pride—or stubbornness as foreigners occasionally consider it—is a major factor in France's international prestige in the post-war world.

For this is the import of *The Madwoman of Chaillot,* and in the 1945 production it came across loud and clear. It was an appeal to Frenchmen not to be swept up in immediate reconstruction and reindustrialization, not to allow any systematized economy to engulf the nation, not to permit France to be left to the mercy of either her enemies or her allies.[17] It is not strictly a matter of Capitalism or Communism, but of "isms" in general. It is an appeal for France to hold on to her eccentricities and irregularities, to protect the individual freedom of her nonconformists, her artists, and her "unproductive" citizens. It is an appeal for the

persistence of history and culture, for the maintenance of national monuments (the Trocadéro, the Café de l'Alma, Paris itself) and rural quiescence. It is an appeal for France to find her destiny in the values of honesty, simplicity, and purity-rather than in mechanical, technological confusion. In France, these issues are entirely real. Giraudoux's appeals, by and large, have been followed.

NOTES

[1] Haskell M. Block and Robert G. Shedd, eds., *Masters of Modern Drama* (New York, 1962), p. 730.

[2] Page references are to the Bernard Grasset 1959 edition of Giraudoux's plays. The translations are my own.

[3] Gerald Walter, *Paris Under the Occupation* (New York, 1960), pp. 101-102.

[4] *Sans Pouvoirs* (Monaco, 1946), p. 64.

[5] Thomas Kernan, *France on Berlin Time* (Philadelphia, 1941), p. 147.

[6] See Frederic Lefevre, *Une Heure Avec . . .* (Paris, 1924). "*Siegfried . . .* is a little pamphlet which I had written to draw to the attention of a certain French public the necessity for reforging our contacts with the Germany of letters and literature" (p. 150).

[7] *The France of To-Morrow* (Paris, 1940), p. 5.

[8] Paris, 1947.

[9] "L'Avenir de France," *Sans Pouvoirs*, p. 134.

[10] *Théâtre Complet* (Paris, 1945-53), XV, 37-38.

[11] Jean Blanzat, "Giraudoux et la Résistance," *Le Figaro,* September 23, 1944, p. 2

[12] *Réponse à Ceux qui nous demandent pourquoi nous faisons La Guerre (Paris,* 1940), p. 4.

[13] *Ibid.*

[14] A common theme. "A nation finds itself in trouble with destiny . . . by its faults . . . such as the citizens wantonly cutting down the trees." *Trojan War,* II, 13.

[15] *The France of To-Morrow,* p. 5.

[16] Raoul Dautry, appendix to Jean Giraudoux, *Pour Une Politique Urbaine* (Paris, 1947), p. 144.

[17] Giraudoux was more afraid of the Allies than Germany. His last days were spent attempting to create an agency which would tabulate French losses in the war as a negotiating weapon for reparations. He was fearful that the Allies would run the entire peacetime show themselves. See Blanzat, p. 2.

**Richard Nickson**

SOURCE: "The Art of Shavian Political Drama," in *Modern Drama,* Vol. XIV, No. 3, December, 1971, pp. 324-30.

[*In the following essay, Nickson attempts to explain and correct readers' common misinterpretations of Bernard Shaw's political beliefs as expressed in his plays.*]

England, arise! the long, long night is over . . .

The unemployed of the Great Depression of the thirties are singing these verses of Edward Carpenter outside number ten Downing Street at the close of Bernard Shaw's *On the Rocks* "to a percussion accompaniment of baton thwacks." Straightway, one critic on the Left observed that "the play ends with the marchers outside the window singing 'England Arise!' which I understand is the theme song of Mosley's Black Shirts."[1] The playwright's conservative biographer, St. John Ervine, propounded an equally ingenious but dissimilar interpretation based on the second line of Carpenter's song, "Faint in the east behold the dawn appear." According to Ervine, "For G. B. S. the east was Russia, and the dawn was a dictator-dominated commune."[2]

At the age of seventy-seven the Good Gray Fabian was still provoking gross misinterpretations of the political content of his drama. For a long time he was even unable to get a theatre in London for his 1933 "Political Comedy," as he subtitled *On the Rocks.* Evidently Ervine was not the only one to believe that this play "marks Shaw's most extreme stand against democracy,"[3] despite what should have been plainly observable—that Shaw was probing, as he had done four years earlier in *The Apple Cart,* for some sort of alternative to the rule of big business as manipulated by venal and inept politicians. He was bent on demonstrating dramatically the warning voiced by Captain Shotover in Act III of *Heartbreak House:* "One of the ways of Providence with drunken skippers is to run them on the rocks." The Captain meant by "skippers" the political pilots of England—and by extension, of Western society. In *The Apple Cart* Shaw portrayed the capitalist quandary of the cabinet skippers getting patched up with a compromise effected by a superior man who happened to be a constitutional monarch. King Magnus just managed to avoid, or postpone, an upsetting of the cart. But in *On the Rocks* the aristocratic man who happens to be the Prime Minister fails to budge the ship of state from its position on the rocks. The change of metaphor in the two titles is ominously significant. Nevertheless, democracy is not the villain of either piece.

Two years after writing *On the Rocks,* Shaw in the preface to *The Millionairess* expressed with directness and scorn his opinions about adult suffrage and about the duly elected Labour and National governments. Although he there declared that he would favor "the most complete Communism and Democracy,"[4] he recognized that no absolute (such as complete democracy) is possible of realization. What has come to pass in the actual world of the "sham-democracies" of the West, Shaw noted, is that "the financier and the soldier are the cocks of the walk; and democracy means that their parasites and worshippers carry all before them."[5] It is, then, not democracy, but sham-democracy (government that always supports profiteering, as Shaw's Prime Minister describes it) which the playwright exposes in *On the Rocks.*

It was said of Shaw early in his career that he was attacking Shakespeare, despite the civilized understanding that only a boor would attack the Bard. Then it began to be more and more widely perceived that the real target of his missiles was "bardolatry." Shaw scored a point. Furthermore he attracted attention, with his levity and exaggeration, to what he was about. Just so, in his later years, he succeeded in attracting attention to his criticism of democracy—as it is perverted, in Shaw's socialistic view, under capitalist management.

Throughout his adult life Bernard Shaw plumped for exchanging the present social order for another, yet most of his lengthy career was dedicated to effecting gradual change in a strictly constitutional manner. He remarked, nevertheless, at the turn of the century, in his (John Tanner's) preface to "The Revolutionist's Handbook," that "all who achieve real distinction in life begin as revolutionists. The most distinguished persons become more revolutionary as they grow older, though they are commonly supposed to become more conservative owing to their loss of faith in conventional methods of reform."[6] For his own faith in such methods had dwindled appreciably by the time of *Man and Superman,* and as he grew older this wisp of faith perished. But the cataclysm of World War I followed by revolutions and *coups* did not damage it so much as did the spectacle of Labour governments of Great Britain, fully staffed with Fabian socialists, putting parliamentary government through what seemed to Shaw to be the same ineffectual paces he had so long derided.

For the most part, the critics and the common readers have continued to misconstrue Shaw's treatment of political matters in his drama. Some of his later plays chiefly come to mind in this regard because in them Shaw dealt directly, for the first time as dramatist, with the problem of British government (in *The Apple Cart* as well as in *On the Rocks*) and with the problem of international government (in *Geneva*). Moreover, the misinterpretations which have ensued are by no means limited to cries of Fascist! from some or Bolshevist! from others (or even the omnifarious Totalitarian!). Indeed, much more frequent are the strictures leveled against The Playwright for not having the good sense to write always as The Polemicist.

Finding in his non-dramatic works an author who can be relied upon to express his opinions sharply, many readers turn away from Shavian dialogue with a feeling of being denied the bounty of a Viewpoint. Not for *them* Doctor Chekhov's prescription to the artist to state a problem correctly, as against solving it. Not for them a Nietzschean *gaya scienza,* let alone a willingness to agree with Wittgenstein that a serious and good philosophical work could be written that would consist entirely of jokes (without being facetious). Still, they might at least keep in mind Shaw's own earnest declaration: "All genuinely intellectual work is humorous."[7]

One person who did keep such matters, or manners, in mind was, as might be expected, a fellow dramatist, and an eminent one—hence another readily maligned one, Bertolt Brecht. Shaw as terrorist is the theme of the gallant Brechtian "Ovation for Shaw,"[8] which certifies the weapon of the senior terrorist to be an unusual one—"that of humor." Shaw's "successful proof that in the face of truly significant ideas a relaxed (even snotty) attitude is the only proper one" apparently formed part of the heritage of the junior, German, terrorist.

But from certain of his non-terrorist friends Shaw the playwright always stands in need of rescue—especially from the friends who would praise the Thinker while apologizing for the Dramatist. A book titled *Bernard Shaw,* with the portentous subtitle *A Reassessment,* was published recently by a self-styled Shaw disciple, Mr. Colin Wilson, in which a kind of querulous tribute is paid the master on every other page. Seldom has praise been uttered with such lavish compunction. For, clearly, the Bernard Shaw of the plays has, time and again, failed to comport himself with that high degree of seriousness required by the no-nonsense disciple. According to the apostolic Word: "it is certainly true that all the plays of his last twenty years seem to go nowhere. And this is not because Shaw's brain was impaired, but because he was unfortunately underworking it."[9]

The simple truth about millions of readers is that they don't quite like drama. Colin Wilson's reservations encompass not just the later plays alone, but the entire repertory. As he condescendingly puts it (and I quote him as a spokesman for Colin Wilsons Limited the world over), "I have tried to show that no matter how successful Shaw's plays may appear to be dramatically, they remain oddly fumbling, journeyman works on their most interesting level—the level of the ideas they set out to dramatise."[10] All such readers doubtless know very well how ideas *should* be dramatized, but meantime we must make do with the example of practicing dramatists. And it is at least possible that practitioner Shaw developed ways of dramatizing ideas—political ideas included—that are better than the descriptions of them by this or that dissatisfied commentator.

It is even altogether likely that the art of political drama, in particular, reached a subtly fine state of development in the hands of Shaw, and never more so than during his final decades, in a few of his most politicized plays. A close examination of them, of what he attempted and did not attempt, uncovers certain assumptions, intentions, and strategies worth remarking, at least for the sake of stressing what is still too lightly overlooked or heavily misinterpreted.

Despite an ever increasing absorption in politics, Shaw as dramatist continued to write, not propaganda, blunt and simple, but plays, elusive and complex: he remained fundamentally, and fortunately, an artist to the end of his days. As an artist he aimed at rendering the social system as he saw it, not as he would like to see it. Yet his plays were never dedicated merely to the recording of facts; they also insinuate a judgment on these facts. For the playwright observed society critically from a definite standpoint—a socialist standpoint, based on convictions which tended to increasing firmness with advancing years. But although a convinced socialist, Shaw never presumed to resolve—much less solve—the social problems explored in his drama. His personal convictions are seldom, if ever, imposed decisively on any of his plays, however much they may happen to be recorded incidentally.

Political solutions or resolutions are provided by society, not by playwrights. The playwright can only, at most, *propose* answers. Playwright Shaw, however, preferred in the main to pose questions and to dramatize situations so as to highlight the basic political matters of which they are a part. As a dramatist he tried to open his readers' eyes to the political facts under which they live—the avowed aim of Shaw the polemical writer.[11] A comparison between the direct expression of his political views in the prefaces and the necessarily indirect expression of them in the plays reveals, besides the marked differences one would expect, how deftly Shaw was able to maneuver within the confines of a rigorous art. Often, of course, the multi-voiced indirect admonition of the dramatist seems but a small echo of the direct advocacy of the polemicist.

All the same, the later plays sweepingly explore and expose contemporary political problems. As has been noted by E. Strauss, a canny observer of Shaw's political drama, they are also devoted to "the psychological effects of the failure to solve them."[12] Interpretations of this failure emphasizing the subjective have been urged more by other critics than by Strauss, who yet sensibly remarked that Shaw's "work is at least as much a document of doubt as of belief. Were it otherwise," he added, "Shaw would not be the great realist that he is; for it would be idle to pretend that the great hopes of his youth have been fulfilled."[13] But while the later plays may be said to objectify, to some degree, a sense of the failure of Shavian ideas, the playwright, by dramatizing the psychological effects *of society* to solve its problems, also objectifies, on the one hand, the need for a solution and, on the other, a criticism of the society which fails to meet this need.

As a member of a capitalist society, writing about and speaking to this society, Shaw is largely concerned with the political problems which he believed to be of moment to such a society. And in the later plays, while posing these problems and criticizing the society under scrutiny for not facing them constructively, he seldom failed to imply—with both his choice of situations and his handling of them—a condemnation of society as it is and a need for its being changed. Without permitting his drama to propound doctrinal matter, and without letting it assume a dogmatic manner, Shaw nevertheless managed often enough to demonstrate the need for social reconstruction.

His detestation of capitalism only mounting with his declining years, Shaw's later plays are in essence a critique, or exposure, of capitalism, especially as it existed in the society he knew best, the British. And he sometimes succeeded brilliantly in pointing up the contradictions within this society. As a communist in theory and a playwright by profession,[14] he received Marxist applause from R. Palme Dutt, who declared that Shaw "exposed capitalist society with a passionate intensity that has never been equalled by any writer of English."[15] E. J. Hobsbawn has gone still further, stating that Shaw has produced "the most remarkable running critique of imperialist civilization from within, that has so far appeared."[16]

Shaw's concentration during his last decades on what he regarded as man's central problem, how to govern himself, led even this master of comedy to somber reflections and eventually to a new genre—apocalyptic comedy, as it might be called. Besides focusing on political predicaments and the failure of society to extricate itself from them, the later plays often proceed to show, or to hint at, the catastrophes to which the failure is leading. By evoking a fantastic, nightmarish atmosphere within the extravaganza medium that he fashioned for this sobering purpose, he was able to record, despite waning powers, the turbulent flux of contemporary life, the social restlessness, the political quandary. What is more, with these final, provocative ventures into new modes on the part of an artist in his seventies, eighties, and beyond, we are treated, paradoxically, to the additional surprise, remarked by James Bridie, of Shaw's artistry dissolving even his most pessimistic plays (*Too True to Be Good* and *Geneva*) in laughter.[17] To characterize them as the fulminations of an old man disillusioned with his earlier convictions is to misrepresent them and their author utterly.

But Shaw did *not* succeed in dramatizing the efficacy of socialist solutions to social problems. He did not attempt to do this. Such an attempt would have but carried him away from his world—at least away from the particular society which he was observing and criticizing. That society failed to solve its problems, and Shavian drama accurately records this failure.

The failure is society's. It is not necessarily the failure of socialist or Shavian ideas, although these ideas must be viewed as at least involved in the failure. It is as sadly plain to his admirers as it was to the aged Shaw that he had failed to be influential in quite the way he had hoped to be. (Such a failure he shares, however, with legions of illustrious figures of history, legend, and myth.) Although many of his proposed reforms were in fact accepted during his lifetime, his socialist proposal for a fundamental change in the structure of society was not accepted. Consequently his plays cannot but reflect the failure of his convictions to prevail. Still, this "sense of failure" dramatically pinpoints as well *the need for change and the failure of society to change itself.* It is in this manner, however deviously, however negatively, that Shaw the dramatist expressed, or suggested, the nature and the strength of his political convictions. Throughout his entire playwriting career, but most especially during his later years, Bernard Shaw staunchly confronted society in the roles that have made him at once both famous and infamous—those of satirist, critic, terrorist!

### NOTES

[1] Robert Forsythe, "The Beauty of Silence," *New Masses,* 5 July 1938, p. 13. "Wolcott Gibbs in his review of *On the Rocks* in the *New Yorker* considers it a Communist play," according to Forsythe, who himself is certain that "without any doubt whatsoever, *On the Rocks* is a fascist play. In addition it stinks."

[2] *Bernard Shaw: His Life, Work and Friends* (New York: William Morrow, 1956), p. 553.

[3] *Ibid.,* p. 355.

[4] *The Simpleton, The Six, and The Millionairess* (London: Constable, 1936), p. 130.

[5] *Ibid.,* p. 123.

[6] *Man and Superman: A Comedy and a Philosophy* (New York: Brentano's, 1909), p. 180.

[7] In *Florence Farr, Bernard Shaw, W. B. Yeats: Letters,* ed. Clifford Bax (New York: Dodd, Mead, 1942), p. 10.

[8] "Ovation for Shaw," trans. Gerhard H. W. Zuther, *Modern Drama,* 2 (1959), 184.

[9] *Bernard Shaw: A Reassessment* (New York: Atheneum, 1969), p. 270. Yet, curiously, on page 264 Wilson states that "Shaw's later works have many virtues; there is not one of them of which we can say . . . that it would have been better for his reputation if he had never written it. One day, someone will write a detailed study of the plays from *Too True to Be Good* to *Why She Would Not,* and it will be an important addition to Shaw criticism."

[10] *Ibid.,* p. 165.

[11] Preface to *Geneva,* in *Geneva, Cymbeline Refinished, and Good King Charles* (London: Constable, 1946), p. 16.

[12] *Bernard Shaw: Art and Socialism* (London: Victor Gollancz, 1942), p. 13.

[13] *Ibid.,* p. 126.

[14] *Everybody's Political What's What?* (New York: Dodd, Mead, 1944), p. 13.

[15] "George Bernard Shaw: A Memoir," *Labour Monthly Pamphlet,* No. 1 (1951), p. 5.

[16] "Bernard Shaw's Socialism," *Science and Society,* 11 (1947), 326.

[17] "Shaw the Dramatist," in *G. B. S. 90: Aspects of Bernard Shaw's Life and Work,* ed. Stephen Winsten (New York: Dodd, Mead, 1946), p. 110.

## Walter G. Langlois

SOURCE: "Anarchism, Action, and Malraux," in *Twentieth Century Literature,* Vol. 24, No. 3, Fall, 1978, pp. 272-89.

[*In the following essay, Langlois discusses the publication of the post–World War I French avant-garde magazine* Action *and its influence on the political writings of André Malraux.*]

In the autumn of 1920, after a long and shattering conflict, French literati were groping in many directions seeking to reformulate an aesthetic for the new, postwar world. It was at that time that the 18-year-old André Malraux published his second literary effort—a prose-poem entitled "Prologue"—together with a negative review of the new André Breton–Philippe Soupault work, *Les Champs magnétiques.* Both items appeared in the October issue of Florent Fels' little avant-garde magazine, *Action.*[1] The text of the review is particularly noteworthy. Although Malraux agreed that Breton's book was "plus susceptible d'être imité que les poèmes de M. Tzara, par exemple, si caracterisés que ses disciples sembleraient des plagiaires," he was nevertheless convinced that "qui voudra écrire une oeuvre en fonction de l'esthétique des *Champs magnétiques* n'en fera qu'un pastiche, donc oeuvre sans valeur." For him, "de nombreux enfants des *Champs magnétiques* vont surgir, mais ils ressembleront trop à leur père" to be really aesthetically valid.

Clearly, the young man felt that the work pointed in a direction which was essentially sterile, and during the next two decades when Surrealism was at its height he maintained a rather aloof attitude toward the movement. As far as he was concerned, there were certain other possibilities being put forth at the time which would ultimately be more fruitful than the one being formulated by Breton and his followers.[2] Although Breton's force of personality and astute leadership enabled his movement rapidly to achieve an almost complete hegemony over the avant-garde in the immediate postwar years, historians who wish to understand the intellectual climate of that period must resurrect and re-examine some of these neglected alternatives which were being proposed around 1920. The one represented by Fels' review *Action* is particularly deserving of such a reappraisal, if for no other reason than that it will help clarify certain elements of the aesthetic context in which young Malraux wrote his three earliest—and most puzzling—works (*Lunes enpapier, Journal d'un pompier du Jeu de massacre*—also known as *Ecrit pour une idole à trompe,* and *Royaume-Farfelu*[3])

and help explain the basis for his rejection of the Dada-Surrealist aesthetic proposed by Breton and his followers.

*Action* appeared for only 12 issues, published between November 1919 and May/June 1922, but it has an unusually interesting history.[4] Essentially it was the brainchild of one man: Florent Fels. Fels was born in Paris in 1893, the child of a bourgeois family named Felsenberg.[5] His father—a middle-level official in the Treasury Department—was highly intelligent and had pronounced Leftist political ideas. A militant member of the Parti Ouvrier Français, he inaugurated a number of programs to benefit workers and their families, and in 1919 he even founded an Ecole Socialiste-Marxiste, supported by Léon Blum, Charles Cachin and Victor Basch.[6] From an early age, Fels was encouraged by his father to read "des auteurs socialisants" and he was taken to rallies where political leaders like Jules Guesde and Jean Juarès spoke out to demand greater social justice for the working masses. In his middle teens, Fels was sent to Denain, near Valenciennes, in the coal and steel producing area of northern France, where he worked as a smith. It was there that he first came into direct contact with Anarchism, a movement which was strong among the local unionists. The French Union-Anarchists were basically not very radical. Primarily what they wanted was for the bourgeois government to cease exploiting the working class and more forcefully to oppose nationalistic wars which always weighed most heavily on that class. The anti-militarism which Fels encountered among his unionist friends was strengthened a few years later when he himself became a soldier during the First World War. His four years in service were more terrible than anything he had ever imagined. As he subsequently recounted in his autobiography, he became particularly opposed to war after the infantry mutinies of the spring of 1917, when he himself—although not directly involved in the rebellions—narrowly missed being shot, "pour l'exemple."[7] Among his comrades in arms, those who were most strongly anti-militarist belonged to a semi-political group called "anarchistes-individualistes," and he soon became good friends with a number of them.

The Individualist Anarchists were one of three branches of a movement which had begun with certain 18th century French philosophers (notably Condorcet, Rousseau, Roux, Varlet and Leclerc), and which had taken general shape in Europe around 1840, with William Godwin in England. Max Stirner in Germany, Kropotkin and Bakunin in Russia, and above all Proudhon in France.[8] Today most people consider the term "Anarchist" to be almost entirely pejorative. It generally suggests wild-eyed radicals who are committed to throwing bombs and other violent acts, but as one of the characters in Malraux's *L'Espoir* points out, Anarchists were fundamentally idealists: "Le Christ? C'est un anarchiste qui aréussi. C'est le seul,"[9] On a political level, they envisaged a society in which the individual would be freed from all governmental coercion and restraint, his conduct being directed by a personal, inner moral commitment.

As the 19th century advanced, this utopian vision won a certain amount of support, but because of the movement's accent on individual freedom it remained rather diffuse in its ideology. However during the latter part of the period—most notably after 1880—three distinct currents became evident. The first of these (the one which Fels had come to know through his father and the men with whom he had worked in northern France) was Union Anarchism. The partisans of that position believed that the fundamental unity of society was the unity of work, and that the best means of abolishing the oppressive capitalist system imposed by the bourgeoisie was the strike, the weapon par excellence of the workers. A second current—less widespread until around 1900 but increasingly important after that date—was what one might call Leftist Anarchism, either Socialist or Communist. Closely linked to Marxism, it differed from Union Anarchism on the questions of the basis of society (the commune and not the work unit), and on the means to be adopted in fighting the bourgeoisie. The Leftist Anarchists believed in strikes, as did the Unionists, but they also advocated more direct or violent action—such as insurrection or revolution—to destroy bourgeois capitalism. Thanks to the success of the Russian Revolution and the increasing diffusion of Communist ideas, after 1919 this current rapidly came to dominate Anarchism. However, paradoxically, in falling under the influence of the Russian Communists—who were predominantly Stalinists, it betrayed its origins and itself became more and more authoritarian, and less and less Anarchist. (This was true to such a point that in 1937 the Russian and Spanish Communists massacred the Anarchists of Catalonia in order to "purify" the movement![10]) In principle the Union Anarchists and the Communist-Socialist Anarchists were both opposed to war, but they nevertheless remained sufficiently nationalist to forget this particular tenet, and in 1914 almost without exception they rallied to the colors.

In late 19th-century Anarchism there was also a third current, which one may call Individualist. In opposition to the ultra-conservative bourgeois mentality so characteristic of the Second Empire, in the years after 1850 many artists and intellectuals began to support this third type of Anarchism. They were attracted to the ideals of personal freedom and social justice which it proposed. By the end of the century, this Individualist current had become quite strong and had won support from some well-known artists and writers. Among the former were Van Rysselberghe, Signac, Vallotton, Van Dongen and—a bit later—Camille and Lucien Pissarro and many of the "Fauves," with Vlaminck in the lead. As for the writers, a majority of the Symbolists were more or less directly linked to Individualist Anarchism, and at *Les Temps nouveaux* Jean Grave counted among his collaborators Tailhade, Richepin, Mirbeau, Bernard Lazare, Paul Adam and Stuart Merrill. Beginning in 1892, under the direction of Francis Viélé-Griffin, the monthly *Entretiens politiques et littéraires* became largely a review of the Individualist Anarchists, numbering among its literary collaborators Valéry, H. de Régnier and Remy de Gourmont, while the strongly anti-militarist *L'Endehors* received the support of men like Mallarmé Verhaeren and Saint-Paul Roux.[11]

It is clear that most of these artists and writers were little concerned with questions of social or political doctrine and even less with programs for revolution. What attracted them above all, as Mallarmé put it in 1895, was the Individualist Anarchist *spirit,* curious about everything that was new in all areas of human endeavor.[12] Moreover the Anarchists' desires for intellectual independence and personal liberty, together with the value which they gave to experience as an end in itself, were also very appealing. After the declaration of war in 1914, this wing of the movement gained additional supporters, particularly among the pacifists; for at a time when almost all the other Anarchists were abandoning their anti-militarism, the Individualists remained faithful to their ideal and continued to proclaim their opposition to *all* wars. It is not surprising that young Fels, deeply interested in literary and artistic questions and more and more horrified by what he was witnessing as a soldier in the trenches, should have been attracted to this group.

In April of 1918, Fels began to collaborate regularly on one of the major Individualist Anarchist publications, the Armand-Chardon bi-monthly newspaper, *La Mêlée*.[13] However after the end of the war he and Marcel Sauvage, one of his co-workers on the paper, became dissatisfied with the increasingly doctrinaire position which the editor was taking on a number of questions. Moreover Fels felt that in many respects *La Mêlée* was too exclusively oriented toward a working-class public and was neglecting the literary and artistic groups in French society. He himself had become involved in several such circles in Paris, most notably the one centered around Max Jacob (through whom he met the writers Paul Morand, Jean Paulhan, Georges Gabory, André Salmon. Pierre Reverdy, Jean Cocteau and—a bit later—André Malraux, Antonin Artaud and the young Raymond Radiguet). A number of these individuals encouraged Fels in his idea that a review would be a better forum than a newspaper for meaningful discussions about literary, political and artistic subjects. In a review, one would be "plus à l'aise pour développer sa pensée, pour y puiser des sujets, pour y contrebalancer les études bourgeoises." As Fels envisaged it, his review would be "hospitalière aux penseurs et aux artistes originaux, un récueil des idées diverses et nouvelles. Son rôle, si le journal doit se disperser parmi les travailleurs et les foules, sera d'attaquer lesmilieux dits intellectuels."[14] In addition it would also support a program of lectures, meetings and art exhibits in various places and would undertake the publication of pamphlets, posters and brochures in order to spread Individualist aesthetic ideas and establish contacts among "tous ceux qui se rapprochent de nous."

It was not until Fels received his demobilization bonus in the spring of 1919 that he had sufficient funds to initiate his project.[15] By early summer he had organized it sufficiently to be able to announce in *La Mêlée* that the first issue of the new *Cahiers individualistes* would appear the following October. He also published a kind of manifesto to indicate the character of this publication (which was soon to become *Action*):

Notre idéal s'identifie bien moins à ce que le monde appelle anarchie, qu'à notre volonté de plus de beauté et d'ordre.

La force des masses est impuissante, si elle n'est pas coordonnée en vue d'atteindre un but plus noble que la satisfaction temporelle de ses appétits immédiats: soif, faim, besoins sexuels, habitation.

L'agitation causée par des meneurs ou leaders est inféconde parce qu'elle atteint la foule en "surface" et non en "profondeur".

Notre action sera peut-être plus lente, mais sachant où nous désirons aller, et pénétrant les milieux les plus vivaces, elle se développera en dépit des persécutions des gouvernements républicains, bolchevistes, ou communistes, malgré les morts que nous laisserons en route; parce qu'elle s'emploie à affirmer une doctrine de vie, la force de l'individu libéré.

Une seule chose mérite d'être sauvée de notre civilisation actuelle, ce sont les monuments d'art passé, et dans le présent l'acquis des lettres et des arts, qui est une chaîne in interrompue de périodes classiques et de recherches esthétiques. . . . [16]

It is difficult to see just where a program founded on something as vague as "la force de l'individu libéré" would lead, even when supported by the theoretical bases of Individualist Anarchism, and this initial manifesto of the *Cahiers individualistes* is a rather surprising mixture of conservatism (order, veneration for the artistic monuments of the past) and of avant-garde political, artistic and literary enthusiasms.

A few weeks later, *La Mêlée* revealed that in order to avoid confusion with *Les Cahiers idéalistes,* the name of the forthcoming *Cahiers individualistes* was to be changed to *Action: Cahiers individualistes de philosophie et d'art.* A quotation from Romain Rolland clarified the choice of the initial word in the new title: "L'action la plus efficace qui soit en notre pouvoir à tous, hommes et femmes, est l'action individuelle d'homme à homme, d'âme à âme, l'action par la parole, l'exemple par tout l'être."[17] As for the word "art," the term was understood to include not only literature and the plastic arts (with which Fels was quite familiar because of his grandmother's long intimate relationship with the great critic and collector, Théodore Duret[18]), but also music and dance—in which the young man was deeply interested as well.

As has been suggested, Fels was in contact with several somewhat different literary cliques in Paris, and it was to friends in these groups that he turned initially for materials for his planned publication. First, there were the intellectuals who were his associates in the Individualist Anarchist movement, notably Han Ryner, Maurice Wullens, Gabriel Brunet, Marcel Martinet, Laurent Tailhade, and Francis Vaud. Then there were the avant-garde writers of Max Jacob's coterie and other Montmartre-Montparnasse literary circles (especially those who collaborated on the reviews *Nord-Sud* and *Sic*)

who could be broadly characterized as "literary Cubists." In addition to Jacob, this included Cendrars, Cocteau, Gabory, Reverdy and Salmon, and to a lesser extent Radiguet, Artaud and Malraux. Finally there were Fels' friends who were artists, art critics, gallery owners, and collectors—both those of the older generation whom he had met through Théodore Duret, and those whom he had come to know during his visits to Montparnasse and to the Bateau Lavoir on Montmartre. Even while gathering materials from these varied literary and artistic sources, Fels wrote several times in *La Mêlée* that he was counting heavily on "les camarades sincères et actifs pour diffuser notre revue qui sera la *première grande manifestation individualiste.*"[19] Indeed, in order to attract the support of the paper's readers—whose interests were primarily doctrinaire, he even took pains to identify the aims of his new publication in terms that would be comprehensible to them: "Que tous comprennent qu'il s'agit d'une v ìtable action philosophique. Entremêlée de poèmes et de nouvelles, afin de toucher le grand public, notre revue sera *individualiste et didactique.* Nous planterons le grain profondément, insensiblement, mais sûrement. Puisse la moisson être belle."[20]

Fels made arrangements with a certain Buschmann, a printer in Antwerp, and sometime around the first week of October of 1919 he sent him the final manuscript of the first number of the new review, scheduled to appear early the following month. How can that ensemble be characterized?[21] It would appear that the young editor counted heavily on the first article, "La Conception stendhalienne du héros: Julien Sorel" by Gabriel Brunet—which took up 26 pages, or almost a third of the publication, to set an "individualist" tone for the issue; in any case it presented Julien as a striking example of a certain "exaltation" of the Individualist personality. Most of the remaining poems and prose works in the issue can be linked to this same Individualist ideology, understood in its broadest sense, particularly the contributions of Marcel Millet, André Salmon, Max Jacob and Georges Gabory. In point of fact, it was young Gabory who made the most extreme (and in the eyes of the authorities most compromising) statement of one aspect of the Individualist Anarchist position in his half satirical, half ironic little essay, "Eloge de Landru." Publication of this first number was delayed considerably by the printer, and when the issues finally arrived at the Franco-Belgian customs in early February 1920 they were immediately confiscated by authorities there. They claimed that Gabory's article in praise of a man—Landru—who had murdered ten women was subversive! It took Fels several months of appeals to various officials before the shipment was released.[22]

During the second half of 1919, while awaiting delivery of the first number of *Action,* Fels had continued his collaboration on *La Mêlée.* An article which he published there in November is particularly interesting and important. The very title of the essay—"Une Littérature d'avant-garde: L'Esprit nouveau"[23]—immediately establishes its links with the seminal lecture of Apollinaire, "L'Esprit nouveau et les poètes," printed a year earlier in the

*Mercure de France.* Since Fels' article suggests the aesthetic principles initially espoused by *Action* and its supporters, it deserves close attention.

Fels began his study by pointing out that—following the example of Rimbaud and Mallarmé—a "certain nombre de poètes ont entrepris de créer une nouvelle forme d'expression du lyrisme, dégagée de toute contrainte prosodique, nourrie de métaphores et d'images rigoureusement neuves, et ne prenant sa force que dans l'esprit." Two contemporary poets in particular: Apollinaire and Salmon; a poet-painter: Max Jacob; and a painter: Picasso had laid the foundations for this new aesthetic in which the *mind* ("l'esprit") was to play an important role. For Fels, this aesthetic had a rather solid philosophical, psychological and emotional basis: "Il est admis communément que derrière le monde des réalités sensibles où nous vivons, existe non moins réel—puisqu'il nous est possible de l'évoquer et même d'y participer—une autre forme de vie. Tout homme a la faculté de se transporter par le jeux de sa sensibilité du monde apparent au monde du rêve; tout homme qui a la faculté de transporter [le] monde apparent au monde du rêve est un poète. Il n'y a point là effect de la volonté, mais bien un phénomène psychologique, dont le sujet est pour ainsi dire irresponsable; c'est le don."

But if it is true that the gifted poet ought to permit his heart to sing freely, he must also "travailler son chant." This second and more intellectual phase of the making of a poet, noted Fels, is "peut-être la plus importante car il ne s'agira pas uniquement d'une aptitude lyrique (ivresse dionysiaque), mais d'un ensemble d'heureuses dispositions dominées par l'harmonie, qui n'est pas une simple qualité naturelle mais le résultat d'un tempérament sain et d'une culture générale sérieuse." Thus, in his view, in order to create poetry there must be not only the lyric exaltation of the Romantics (or the *voyance* of the Surrealists) but also a stable and cultured personality which could formulate or organize that lyricism. Fels also pointed out that modern poetry was directed toward a somewhat different end than had been the case in the past. "Cette sorte d'exaltation, que l'on pourrait appeler l'état lyrique, n'a été mise jusqu'à présent qu'au service de l'évocation directe d'une vision plastique, tendant à évoquer des lignes, des contours, une atmosphère, mais non à créer dans l'esprit du lecteur une émotion précise ressentie par l'artiste, au moment où, animé de cette faculté créatrice, il lui est possible de FAIRE LE POINT." It would appear that the young critic conceived of true modern poetry as "l'expression idéaliste et éternelle" of a world which the individual artist recreates incessantly. In that re-creation, modern poets seek a certain form, but it is "une forme que leur soit personelle et neuve. Ils prétendent être libre de tirer tous les effets possible de la disposition typographique, emploi des 'blancs,' des encres de couleur, [et] absence de ponctuation."

Fels concluded his study by emphasizing that for the previous decade many poets of the young generation had expressed themselves by means of a lyricism which has been designated by the vague—and often pejorative—term of Cubism, but it was clearly evident to him that "le plus pur individualisme règne parmi eux." Yet in spite of their individualism one could distinguish some characteristics that they had in common—in addition to their veneration of certain predecessors like Rimbaud and Mallarmé. In a few sentences, Fels sums up his views of this new poetry which—according to him—was a mixture of Romanticism and of the same intellectualism or idealism that characterized much of the Individualist Anarchist movement:

> La poésie moderne, en réaction contre toute tentative d'explication scientifique du monde, s'affirme anti-didactique, ennemie de la déclamation, de la description, du symbole, des grands impératifs et de ce qui est traditionellement poétique d'expression ou d'esprit . . . , du mot rare, de l'érudition qui pare d'un faux clinquant ce qui ne doit briller que par ses propres charmes composites.

> Elle ne contemple pas la vie, mais la regarde, cherche plus à la rendre aimable qu'à la comprendre. Si l'intelligence peut intervenir à la formation d'un poète, elle reste étrangère à la formation du poème, qu'elle ne pourrait qu'alourdir; il s'agit bien moins de volonté, que d'action spontanée, d'analyse que de synthèse. Ces oeuvres, leurs auteurs n'ont pas la vanité de vouloir les faire revivre dans l'esprit du lecteur, qui [y] apportera sa sensibilité particulière, ses dons imaginatifs, ses goûts . . . Il ne s'agit pas de raconter une petite histoire suivant les troisthèmes généralement adoptés: l'homme, la nature, les forces, mais de créer des oeuvres capables d'exister de leur vie particulière, ayant leur existence propre, individuelle . . .

Of course this conception of literary activity and of the literary work of art (which is closely linked to the ideas of Max Jacob and—subsequently—of Malraux) was going to play an important role in the aesthetic advocated by *Action.*

Sometime in December 1919, when it became clear that Buschmann was not going to deliver the first number of the new review on time, Fels decided to change to a Parisian printer and to proceed with the preparation of the second number, scheduled to appear in late February or early March of 1920. Possibly in the hope of appealing to a larger circle of readers, he dropped the adjective "individualiste" from the title, but the issue still included a number of contributions by writers who were active in that wing of the Anarchist movement, notably Han Ryner and several regular collaborators from Wullens' review, *Les Humbles.* Among the purely literary materials there were essays, poetry and prose pieces from Jacob, Salmon, Suarès, Cocteau, Henri Hertz and Ivan Goll, suggesting a new accent on belles-lettres to the neglect of theory or philosophy. This second number also put a much stronger emphasis on art—particularly painting—indicating that Fels' personal interests had evolved considerably in the nearly six months since he had prepared the initial number of *Action.*[24]

Although Fels did not publish a manifesto, he did prepare a kind of "prière d'insérer" for the press, to clarify the orientation of the review.[25] He noted that after four long years of war "nous avons besoin d'inattendu et surtout de joie" in literature, and he indicated that in *Action* "Nous avons voulu unir des écrivains choisis pour l'originalité de leur esprit et de leur forme . . . individualistes en ce sens qu'ils n'appartiennent à aucune école." This important affirmation emphasizes once again that Fels' individualism was eclectic in the broadest sense of the term, even though it had its origins in certain theories of the Individualist Anarchists with whom he had been closely associated for several years. The second number of *Action* appeared in March of 1920, as planned, followed in a few weeks by the first number, finally pried loose from the censor and put on sale with the fictitious date of "février 1920" printed on its cover. In May, these two issues were reviewed together in the prestigious *Nouvelle Revue française*. After having praised the tone of *Action* ("une revue ingénieuse, charmante, injuste"), the anonymous commentator expressed surprise that two literary figures as different as Han Ryner and Max Jacob were proposed as models, but he alluded favorably to the artistic content of the new periodical ("quelque bois de Derain, un beau dessin au pochoir de Gleizes"). Finally, he spoke of its literary materials, rejoicing that at a time when Dada was dominating much of the Parisian avant-garde there were "pas de dadaistes" in its pages.[26] This is significant, for, as we shall see, Fels—like his friend Malraux—showed himself more and more opposed to the undisciplined, unreasonable, gratuitous and destructive spirit of this movement, which was rapidly coalescing around André Breton.

The intellectual climate in Paris during the immediate postwar period continued to be very unsettled, but during the months of January-February 1920—just as Fels was gathering the materials for his second issue—two events took place which would subsequently become very important. On January 23 the first "manifestation Dada" was held in France, clearly placing André Breton and his clique in opposition to a certain number of the other literary personalities of the avant-garde. The occasion, described in detail by Sanouillet from various sources,[27] was a "matinée poétique" organized by the review *Littérature,* "pour essayer de dire quelque chose" (according to Aragon) in the midst of all the contemporary aesthetic confusion. The manifestation included the reading of literary works, the presentation of some paintings, and the playing of a few musical compositions. At the last moment, Tristan Tzara arrived in Paris from Zurich and it was decided to include him in the program. This was a crucial decision because it changed what had originally been planned as a fairly restrained manifestation of the "Esprit nouveau" under the sponsorship of *Littérature* into a typical "épater-les-bourgeois" manifestation of the Dada—and later, Surrealist—type.

To be sure, the *Littérature* program included a goodly number of avant-garde writers who were not particularly linked to Dada, notably Salmon, Jacob, Reverdy, Cendrars

and Maurice Raynal, but they were grouped in the first part of the matinée. They were followed by Breton who commented upon a number of canvases by Gris, Ribemont-Dessaignes, Chirico, Picabia and Léger, which were presented to the public. Most of these paintings were accepted without problem, although the Double Monde of Picabia, a "parfaite insulte au goût de l'assistance" as one of the eyewitnesses put it, did provoke protests from certain spectators who took modern art seriously. During the second part of the program, there were increased outbursts from the audience, which reached a climax during Tzara's "poetry" recital. When he began to read (to the accompaniment of two bells, energetically rung in the wings by Breton and Aragon) a speech which the arch-conservative Léon Daudet had recently made before the Chambre, a number of those in the audience for whom poetry was not a joke reacted strongly. This protest was led by Florent Fels, who—exasperated—cried out to Tzara: "A Zurich! Au poteau!" in the midst of the uproar. Shortly afterwards, he left the meeting, disgusted and very angry.[28]

Following that *Littérature* matinée, Fels and a few of his friends decided that it was absolutely necessary to organize a countermanifestation to show the other possibilities or directions that were available for the evolution of a new literature and art. This matinée, advertised as "organisée par la revue individualiste *Action,*" took place a month later, on Sunday, February 29, 1920.[29] In order to distinguish it as much as possible from the *Littérature* manifestation (which had been held in a little dance hall in a working-class quarter of Paris), Fels arranged to have his meeting in the Salon des Indépendants at the Grand Palais! Among those present were not only writers, but also critics, artists and members of the *La Mêlée* and *Action* readerships. The matinée began with the recitation of poetry from the works of Rimbaud, Baudelaire, Mallarmé, Jarry and Apollinaire. For the musical part of the program, Jean Cocteau made some brief remarks about the music of Erik Satie which were followed by the performance of several compositions of the master. To give a broader aesthetic dimension to the gathering, Fels called upon Madame Sondaz, the director of a dance school whose talent he greatly admired, to present a ballet.

However the most important part of the program by far—the one which marked without any possibility of misunderstanding the distance that separated the partisans of *Action* from the Breton-Picabia-Tzara group—was the opening lecture, presented by Fels himself.[30] In his discussion of "Les Classiques de l'Esprit nouveau," subsequently published in the pages of the Individualist-Anarchist newspaper, *L'Un,* the young man tried to delineate the basis for a new poetry that would be more valid than the one which was in the process of taking shape around Tzara and Breton. In the course of his commentary, Fels reiterated some of the ideas which he had already presented in his article on the same subject, published in *La Mêlée* three months earlier. However now it was clear that he was directly attacking the Dada movement and—by implication—Breton's nascent Surrealism. He began by pointing out that "ces messieurs du Dada chantent . . . sur un mode mineur, orchestré par M. Picabia," a rather ridiculous and frivolous aesthetic, and he emphasized that "si l'art n'est point sans un certain sérieux, il meurt de l'ennui." Moreover he found it equally unfortunate that among modern writers there were some, "comme ces Messieurs du Dada, plagiant les futuristes italiens," who were (or who pretended to be) mentally unbalanced, in order to "épater les naïfs." At the opposite pole from the writers of Dada, there was an equally sterile conservative group: those who turned their backs on what was happening in the contemporary world in order to busy themselves almost entirely with "acquisitions syntaxiques [et] élégances de style." According to Fels, these "grands couturiers" of literature, these fashionable poets who "travaillant pour la foule, ont tellement le souci du succès immédiat qu'ils mettent leur idéal au niveau de la rue ou du cirque," had no more to do with true or authentic literature than did the posturing Dadaists.

For Fels, true modern poetry was humanist and idealist. As he saw it, "chaque génération éprouve le besoin de briser ses idoles, et chaque recherche l'amène vers des conceptions plus pratiques et plus humaines; la production artistique en est ainsi plus ardente et plus généreuse." But at the same time, "le poète est le témoin à charge du temps . . . A chaque moment solennel de l'histoire, nous retrouvons les poètes comme ces statues antiques, qui, à la croisée des chemins, d'un large geste du bras montraient la route aux égarés." If there are no longer any truly great poets, he said, it is because they will not participate fully in the life of their period; "détachés des contingences et du véritable héroisme du temps, ils dédaignent de venir concourir à la grande oeuvre qui va transmuter le monde." Concerning poetic techniques, Fels conceded that "il n'y a pas de règles définies dans la nouvelle poésie. Il y a des tendances—ne pas plier à l'asservissement de la rime, aux vieux clichés de forme et de métrique. Exposer directement, sans rhétorique, l'objet. De l'image ainsi isolée se dégage l'émotion. Emploi du mot juste, exact, technique." As for the message of modern poetry, "trois thèmes se proposent: l'homme—la nature—les forces." But what was most important was that the poem be born "dans l'enthousiasme," that it be "spontané, vivant de jeunesse ardente." Since a work created in such love and joy would be very fecund, it would be "à son tour génératrice d'idées. Le véritable artiste est toujours audessus de la nature. Il va plus haut, il spiritualise. L'artiste toujours synthétise, car il n'y a pas d'art sans création." Obviously, with such affirmations Fels was placing himself in a current which went counter to the conception of poetry to which the Dada-Surrealist group was increasingly committed.

Toward the end of his lecture, Fels reiterated the general terms of the aesthetic credo which served as the basis for his review, *Action*. This text clearly has definite links with certain of the humanitarian ideals of the Individualist Anarchist movement with which he had long been associated, and it reaffirms the orientation of his new publication (emphasis is his):

*Individualistes nous sommes,* parce que nous écrivons d'abord pour nous, avec le souci d'être d'accord avec notre conscience . . . La littérature [chez d'autres] n'est même plus considérée comme une profession, mais comme une affaire. Pour y atteindre, à défaut d'idées on cultive les mots, et de la littérature à la vie les phrases remplacent l'action. On parle, on rit; on n'agit plus. C'est contre cet esprit que nous avons conçu la revue *Action*—si je n'ai pas fait précéder le premier numéro d'un manifeste, c'est que le seul moyen de nous affirmer était de créer une oeuvre d'union entre les artistes, écrivains, lecteurs,—individualistes en ce sens qu'ils n'appartenaient à aucune tendance, aucun cénacle, aucune école. Choisis simplement pour l'originalité de leur esprit et l'équilibre formel de leur expression. Voici tout notre orgueil: offrir au public des oeuvres recommendables non par le nom de leurs auteurs, mais par leur valeur intrinsique et surtout ne pas sacrifier à l'ambigu, à la pataphysique prétentieuse des néonormaliens de Saint-Sulpice, ou aux excentricités de certains farceurs moroses.

L'art est la fleur d'un cerveau équilibré fécondé par le génie. Je parle de l'art n'ayant à souffrir ni des contingences, ni du temps. La beauté est l'expression de l'infini, dans le temps. L'utilité, je dirai presque, l'utilité matérielle de l'art, c'est de transmettre aux générations successives, les idéaux les plus élevés de l'humanité. Le témoignage le plus haut est du plus grand poète et devient vérité.

It is obvious that such a vision of art—and of poetry in particular—is basically classical, humanist, and idealist. It is at the opposite pole from the one which was gradually taking form among Breton and his disciples, and many of those who were present at the *Action* matinée found it a welcome antidote to the irrationalism and gratuitous pleasantries of Dada.

Following the very successful matinée and the subsequent appearance of the first two issues of *Action,* many young writers rallied to Fels' banner; they came to him "les mains pleines de copie" as he put it.[31] It was at this time that young Malraux—whom Fels had known as a friend of Max Jacob—approached him with his first literary text, a prose poem entitled "Mobilités." Since the piece was entirely in keeping with the general aesthetic orientation of *Action*, Fels was delighted to accept it. He subsequently published some eight other contributions of various kinds by Malraux. When financial pressures forced a reorganization of the administration of the periodical late in 1921, Fels asked Malraux to become a member of his Conseil d'Administration, and the young man actually became a co-editor for the last number of the review, which appeared in the late spring of 1922.[32]

In examining the dozen numbers of this struggling but remarkable little literary magazine (whose demise was largely the result of the increasingly crushing predominance of Breton's Surrealism), what evaluation can be made of it? As we have seen, *Action* had its origins in the Individualist Anarchist movement, but it really took form—if one can use such an expression to characterize a review that was eclectic by principle—primarily in opposition to certain elements in the Dada-Surrealist aesthetic. Unlike many of the other avant-garde publications of the period which were preoccupied above all with maintaining a certain ideological purity, *Action* opened its pages freely—as Fels put it—to "quiconque veut exprimer librement sa pensée," requiring only that contributions be "oeuvres ardentes et novatrices . . . de style viril" which would combat "toutes décadences" and help insure the victory "de tout ce qui a de la valeur."[33]

Obviously the magazine is a mine of information about the intellectual and artistic life of the period, and as we have indicated it is particularly revealing of at least one important alternative which was proposed around 1920-22, immediately before Surrealism became dominant. For those of us who are interested in Malraux, it not only throws a whole new light on his youthful prose poems or tales (which continue to be somewhat of a puzzle, in spite of Professor Vandegans' lengthy exegesis of them), but it also helps to explain the many dark hints during the Phnom Penh trial about the young man's links with certain "subversive" political movements in Paris. Finally, it gives a new depth to the favorable portraits which Malraux makes of certain Anarchists, notably in *Les Conquérants* and in *L'Espoir*. As such, it certainly deserves resurrection, and we can all be grateful that the young Parisian publisher Jean-Michel Place is issuing a facsimile edition of the entire run of *Action,* so that all scholars may study it in greater detail.

## NOTES

[1] A[ndré] M[alraux]. "*Les Champs magnétiques*—André Breton et Philippe Soupault," *Action,* No. 5 (Oct. 1920), p. 69. This unfavorable review was followed by his enthusiastic comments about André Salmon's *La Négresse du Sacré-Coeur* (pp. 69-70). Malraux's prose-poem "Prologue" is on pp. 18-20 of the same issue of *Action.*

[2] Malraux obviously had a certain commitment to the alternative represented by *Action,* for in addition to the two items listed above he also made the following contributions to Fels' magazine:

"La Genèse des *Chants de Maldoror,*" No. 3 (avril 1920), pp. 33-35.

"Mobilités." No. 4 (juillet 1920), pp. 13-14.

"Journal d'un pompier du Jeu de massacre," No. 8 (août 1920), pp. 16-18.

"*L'Entrepreneur d'illuminations,* par André Salmon," No. 9 (oct. 1921), p. 33.

"Aspects d'André Gide," No. 12 (mars/avril 1922), pp. 17-21. The planned second half of this study never appeared because the review ceased publication with this number. Malraux was also listed—along with Paul Dermée and Georges Gabory—as a member of the Comité de Rédaction in the 10th and 11th issues, and for the final number he was a co-editor.

[3] Comparison of texts published (under different titles) in various issues of *Action, Signaux de France et de Belgique, Dés, Accords,* and *'900* indicate that *Journal d'un pompier du Jeu de massacre* and *Ecrit pour une idole à trompe* are actually the same work. For details see various chapters in André Vandegans' exhaustive study, *La Jeunesse littéraire d'André Malraux: Essai sur l'inspiration farfelue* (Paris: Pauvert, 1964).

[4] The dates printed on the numbers are as follows: No. 1—février 1920 (actually originally scheduled to appear in late October or early November, 1919); No. 2—mars 1920; No. 3—avril 1920; No. 4—juillet 1920; No. 5—octobre 1920; No. 6—décembre 1920 (*Almanach 1921*); No. 7—mai 1921; No. 8—août 1921; No. 9—oct. 1921; No. 10—nov. 1921; No. 11—Numéro Hors-serie [Feb. 1922]; No. 12—mars/avril 1922.

[5] For information on Felsenberg, see Florent Fels' autobiography, *Voilà* (Paris: Fayard, 1957), pp. 31-33. The biographical information in the present paragraph was taken from *Voilà,* and from several interviews (in 1961 and 1967) which we had with his friend and associate, Georges Gabory.

[6] See in *Action,* No. 1, p. [86], an advertisement for that school, established to conduct "la recherche de valeurs nouvelles, de doctrines communistes, bolchevistes, maximalistes, etc. par les orateurs et les professeurs les plus compétents du Parti Socialiste international." *Action* shared office space with this school at 18 Rue Feydeau for about six months after its founding.

[7] Fels relates this whole incident in *Voilà,* pp. 57-65.

[8] Our information on the general question of Anarchism has been taken from Jean Maitron, *Histoire du mouvement anarchiste en France: 1894—1914* (1955); Henri Avron, *L'Anarchisme* (1961); George Woodcock: *Anarchism: A History of Libertarian Ideas and Movements* (1962); and Guérin's excellent *Ni Dieu ni maître: Histoire et anthologie de l'anarchisme* (2 vols., 1969). See also the theoretical writings of Proudhon, Benjamin Tucker, Kropotkin, and George B. Shaw.

[9] *L'Espoir* (Paris: Gallimard, 1937), p. 39.

[10] For a summary of this terrible historical incident, see Hugh Thomas, *The Spanish Civil War* (London: Eyre and Spottiswoode, 1961), pp. 424-429.

[11] Woodcock summarizes various aspects of the question of this literary influence of Individualist Anarchism, pp. 305-307.

[12] Cited by Woodcock, p. 306. The foremost theorist of the French Pacifist Individualist Anarchist movement during the first three decades of the 20th century was

Emile Armand. Armand published a number of Anarchist anthologies, translations of English and American Anarchist writers, and a large number of books and pamphlets. Notable among these are: *Refus de service militaire et sa véritable signification: Rapport Présenté au Congrès antimilitariste international d'Amsterdam, juin 1904* (1904); *Qu'est-ce qu'un anarchiste?* (1908); *Les Ouviers, les syndicats et les anarchistes* (1910); *L'Initiation individualiste anarchiste* (1923); *Ce que sont les individualistes anarchistes* (texte de Benjamin Tucker, traduit de l'anglais, 1924); *Les Differents Visages de l'anarchisme* (1927); and *Les Précurseurs de l'anarchisme* (1933). This latter work includes discussions of Prometheus, Gorgias, the Stoics, the Carpo-cratians, various medieval sects, the Abbay of Thélème and the Utopians, La Boétie, Diderot, Sylvain Marechal, Burke, Paine, and William Godwin. Following the mutinies of 1917, Armand was tried for sedition (on the grounds that his pacificist preaching had encouraged dissenters), convicted, and sent to prison for several years.

[13] The complete collection of *La Mêlée*—which is very rare—includes 39 numbers (several of which are double), published roughly bi-mensually between 15 March 1918 and February 1920. In addition several numbers of the newspaper *L'Un*, "anciennement *La Mêlée*" appeared in the spring of 1920, beginning with an issue dated "mars."

[14] For the complete text of these comments made by his co-editor, Marcel Sauvage, see *La Mêlée*, 1-15 mars 1919 (Nos 21/22), p. 5.

[15] *Voilà*, p. 77.

[16] "Les Cahiers individualistes," *La Mêlée*, 15 août 1919 (No. 30), p. 4.

[17] "Les Cahiers individualistes," *La Mêlée*, 1 octobre 1919 (No. 33), pp. 1, 2. The quotation from Romain Rolland is to be found in the same number, p. 2.

[18] On Duret, see *Voilà*, pp. 23-31. Somewhat of a Leftist, his political writings include: *Lettres sur les élections* (1863); *Historie de quatre ans, 1870-1873*, 3 vols. (1876-1880); *Histoire de France de 1870 à 1873* (1893); *Les Napoléons: Réalité et imagination* (1909); and *Vue sur l'histoire de la France moderne* (1913). Fels undoubtedly got some of his political ideas from Duret. The latter's most important book of art criticism is his study of *Les Peintres impressionistes* (1878), expanded and republished in 1906 as *Histoire des peintres impressionistes*. In this text the author discusses Pissarro, Claude Monet, Sisley, Renoir, Morisot, Cézanne and Guillaumin. In addition, during his long career he also published about 15 studies on individual artists such as Cézanne, Courbet, Manet, Whistler, Lautrec and Van Gogh. His *Critique d'avant-garde* (1885) includes essays on the Salon of 1870, several Impressionists, Japanese art, Sir Joshua Reynolds, Gainsborough, Richard Wagner, Arthur Schopenhauer, and Herbert Spenser.

[19] "Essai sur l'individualisme," *La Mêlée*, 1 Oct. 1919 (No. 33), p. 4.

[20] *Ibid.*

[21] In addition to the Brunet and Gabory essays, the first issue of *Action* contained Jacob's "Entrepôt Voltaire," Marcel Millet's "Le Bal du Rector," a poem by Salmon, an essay on fine printing, a short article by Fels on the ballet, and notes on various subjects by Blaise Cendrars, Pierre Bertin and others. It also contained a "dessin au pochoir de A. Gleizes, bois et dessins originaux de Galanis et L. de La Rocha." An article on the ballets of Stravinsky by Leigh Henry was translated from *The Egoist*, a British Individualist publication.

[22] See Gabory's account of the incident, confirmed in our interviews with him, in "Fait divers," *Action*, No. 11, Hors-série [février], 1922, pp. [1-3].

[23] For the full text, see *La Mêlée*, 1-15 novembre 1919 (no. 35), p. 4.

[24] In addition to the "Bois et dessin originaux de: André Derain, A. Domin, Galanis, Max Jacob" the issue featured reproductions of paintings of Alex, Boussingault, Braque, Coubine, Derain, Halicka, Galanis, Gimmi, Gris, Gromaire, Marthe Laurens, Lhote, Simon Lévy, Marchand, Marcoussis, L.-A. Moreau, Picasso, de Segonzac, Severine and Vlaminck. Among some twenty books on art which Fels subsequently published during his long career there are studies on Monet, Matisse, Ensor, Kisling, Utrillo, Van Gogh and Vlaminck.

[25] It was cited in the review of the first two numbers of *Action*, published in *La Nouvelle Revue française*, VII, No. 80 (1er mai 1920), pp. 772-773.

[26] *Ibid.*

[27] See Michel Sanouillet, *Dada à Paris* (Paris: Pauvert, 1965), pp. 142-148, from which the description and quotations here are taken.

[28] Sanouillet, p. 147.

[29] For a description of the *Action* "matinée" (an event which has heretofore escaped the attention of scholars), see *L'Un*, mars 1920, p. 4.

[30] For the text of this lecture, see *L'Un, loc. cit.*

[31] *Voilà*, p. 77.

[32] See above, note 2. Fels also invited Malraux to collaborate on the series *Les Contemporains* which he had inaugurated at Stock, and Malraux complied with a preface for Maurras' *Mlle Monk* (1923).

[33] "A Nos Lecteurs," *Action*, No. 4 (juillet 1920), p. 61. This announcement was repeated in a number of issues of the magazine.

## June Schlueter

SOURCE: "Politics and Poetry: Peter Handke's *They Are Dying Out*," in *Modern Drama,* Vol. XXIII, No. 4, January, 1981, pp. 339-45.

[*In the following essay, Schlueter argues that Peter Handke's play* They Are Dying Out *is more an aesthetic statement than a political one.*]

In 1974, a year after its publication, *They Are Dying Out* was produced at Zürich's Theatre am Neumarkt and Berlin's Schaubühne am Halleschen Ufer. The Schaubühne, like Frankfurt's Theater am Turm, favored politically involved plays with a leftist orientation,[1] and three years earlier it had shown considerable hesitation with respect to *The Ride Across Lake Constance.* There was no such hesitation with *They Are Dying Out,* however, which Horst Zankl (who directed both the Zürich and the Berlin productions) undertook without reservation, apparently feeling its anti-capitalistic message was clear. When the Yale Repertory Theatre produced *They Are Dying Out* in 1979, the play was billed as a "biting, wry comment on the cult of mass marketing and its creators,"[2] with translator Michael Roloff and director Carl Weber "Americanizing" the production to reflect the special embarrassments of our home-grown consumerism.

To be sure, Mr. Quitt (be he the original "Hermann" or the Americanized "Oscar") is by anyone's definition an unconscionable capitalist, who manipulates his colleagues into a position of vulnerability in order to destroy them. And the group of entrepreneurs who gather in his home are unrelenting in their criticism of free enterprise, committing themselves to deception and dissembling while acknowledging that they are cigar-smoking monsters in the public eye.

Nowhere in Handke's work is politics so prominent as in *They Are Dying Out,* yet no critic has satisfactorily accounted for this play's political ideology. Rainer Nägele and Renate Voris, for example, compare the play with Brecht's didactic *St. Joan of the Stockyards* but conclude that Handke's repudiation of capitalistic practices is ambivalent.[3] And Manfred Mixner carefully examines the political framework of the play but denies the existence of any direct political message.[4] The fact is that the play is simply not convincing politically, and one is left with the feeling that Quitt's suicide, effected through successive smashings of his head against a massive stone, is something other than—or more than—his disillusionment with life in a capitalistic society. Politics may indeed offer an entry point for the play, but once one gets beneath the surface texture, he finds himself in a skillfully-wrought playworld which has as much to do with alienation as with capitalism, and more to do with aesthetics than with either. Beneath its political mask, *They Are Dying Out* is a dramatized continuation of the aesthetic dialogue which informs all of Handke's work, and particularly of the growing feeling of loss first suggested in his novel *Short Letter, Long Farewell.*

Like the hero of *Short Letter, Long Farewell,* Quitt is a man in search of self. Quitt has invested much time, effort, and capital in building not only an empire but an image, yet he is not content; though seldom given to displays of emotion, Quitt admits he is a lonely man and, in the play's opening scene, rejects the suggestion of his servant, Hans, to be reasonable. Quitt the businessman suspects there is more to him than his professional pose, and he resolves to prove to Hans—and to himself—that his feelings are "useful."

The entrepreneur becomes preoccupied to the point of obsession with finding the self beneath the camouflage of his businessman's life. In a conversation with Paula Tax, the one female entrepreneur among them, he pleads, "if you look at me now, please become aware of me for once and not my causes,"[5] then begs, "Do I have to bang my head against the floor to make you ask about me?" (p. 202). He tells the story of how the eggman came to the door at the same time each week and how he wanted to scream, "'Can't you be someone else for once?'" (p. 200); and he delights in listening to Kilb relate an event of his (Quitt's) recent past, commenting, "It's beautiful to hear a story about oneself" (p. 174), a remark suggesting that he is looking for verification of his existence. He tells of how some young boys once saw him step out of his house and tauntingly cried out, " . . . I know who you are! I know who you are!", "as though the fact that I could be identified was something bad" (p. 195).

But Quitt's colleagues are disarmed by the unexpected signs of humanization in the entrepreneur. Hearing his long derogatory assessment of the free enterprise system, Koerber-Kent asks, "What were you playing just now? It was just a game, wasn't it? Because in reality you are—", to which Quitt sardonically replies, "Yes, but only in reality" (p. 187). And Kilb, the minority stockholder who faithfully attends all such meetings, asks Quitt, "Can't you distinguish between ritual and reality any more?", warning him, "Know your limits, Quitt" (p. 191).

Quitt does indeed have limitations, and they are not only those of the businessman unable to escape society's labels, but those of a man aware of a self which bears no relationship to the world, to other people, to itself. Quitt longs to be human and speaks to Hans of "Real people whom I can feel and taste, living people. Do you know what I mean? People! Simply . . . people! Do you know what I mean? Not fakes but . . . people. You understand: people. I hope you know what I mean" (pp. 217-218). But despite his hopes, Quitt cannot become any more than a "phantom" of himself, one who suddenly notices that he no longer has anything to do with his face. Quitt's quest ends with the discovery that his reality is defined by his fictions, that his very essence is nothing but role.

Quitt, of course, is no real man but a dramatic character whose search for self must logically end with the cry, "I'm still stuck too deep in my role" (p. 254), for a dramatic character's freedom cannot be had without annihilation. Quitt, in fact, does have an existence beyond his role as businessman, but it is not to be found in the liberation of a necessarily non-existent essential self. It resides, rather, in Quitt's identification of himself as artist. As Joseph A. Federico points out in "The Hero as Playwright in Dramas by Frisch, Dürrenmatt, and Handke," Quitt "sees himself as the hero of a self-authored drama, a 'tragedy'. . . . "[6] In Quitt's words, the tragedy is one of business life, in which " . . . I will be the survivor. And the investment in the business will be me, just me alone" (p. 211). For the artist himself, for Handke, the tragedy expands beyond the world of the play, accounting for Quitt's—and modern man's—loneliness and alienation in terms of no less magnitude than the decline of Western civilization and the consequent loss of a poetic language.

In a 1974 interview for *Die Zeit*, Handke remarked of his characters in this play: "They play as if they were tragic figures. But they remain in the shadow of a parody."[7] The comment is central to the play, not because Handke's "wry humor" (as the Yale Repertory Theatre calls it) precludes a serious treatment of Quitt's fate, but because an advanced capitalistic society, such as the one in which Quitt functions, precludes tragedy. Critic Georg Lukács, tracing the decline of narrative in his *Theory of the Novel* (and elsewhere), speaks of the utopian age of the Greek epic, a form which emanated from a civilization in which there was no disparity between meaning and essence. Tragedy, he contends, developed when the "inner world" and the "outer world" became opposed, but the form permitted their momentary reconciliation, in the tragic crisis. In more recent centuries, there have been only a few writers who have shared this awareness of the schism between man and his environment and who have attempted to restore harmony through narrative.[8] Among the writers whom Lukács regards with especially high esteem is Gottfried Keller,[9] whose masterpiece is the autobiographical *Green Henry*, the novel to which the hero of *Short Letter, Long Farewell* keeps returning.

Indeed, the same sense of loss which the protagonist in *Short Letter, Long Farewell* feels whenever he reads Keller's nineteenth century novel is expressed by Quitt following Hans's reading him a long (slightly edited) passage from Adalbert Stifter:

> How much time has passed since then! In those days, in the nineteenth century, even if you didn't have some feeling for the world, there at least existed a memory of a universal feeling, and a yearning. That is why you could replay the feeling and replay it for the others as in this story ["The Bachelor"]. And because you could replay the feeling as seriously and patiently and conscientiously as a restorer—the German poet Adalbert Stifter after all was a restorer—that feeling was really produced, perhaps. In any event, people believed that what was being played there existed, or at least that it was possible. (pp. 210-11)

Quitt's nostalgia for a lost literature sounds more like Handke the poet than Quitt the capitalist, yet Quitt's status as a promoter of free enterprise has much to do with

aesthetics. For Lukács, the relationship between the decline of Western civilization and the decline of poetry is clear: "The domination of capitalist prose over the inner poetry of human experience, the continuous dehumanization of social life, the general debasement of humanity— all these are objective facts of the development of capitalism . . . The poetic level of life decays—and literature intensifies the decay."[10]

Hegel, of course, also analyzes the effects of capitalism, not in terms of literature but in terms of human relationships, suggesting that mass production prevents the worker from understanding the totality of the events in which he is involved or the product he partially makes. As George Steiner explains Hegel's theory of alienation, capitalism "severs man from the natural rhythms and shapes of creation."[11] The resulting "Verdinglichung," or "reification of life," defines Quitt the capitalist and Quitt the poet as products of the same historical phenomenon. Quitt the capitalist cannot establish contact with the world:

> I would like to snap at the world now and swallow it, that's how inaccessible everything seems to me. And I too am inaccessible, I twist away from everything. Every event I could possibly experience slowly but surely transforms itself back into lifeless nature, where I no longer play a role. I can stand before it as I do before you and I am back in prehistory without human beings. I imagine the ocean, the fire-spewing volcanoes, the primordial mountains on the horizon, but the conception has nothing to do with me. I don't even appear dimly within it as a premonition. When I look at you now, I see you only as you are, and as you are entirely without me, but not as you were or could be with me; that is inhuman. (pp. 202-03)

And Quitt the poet can only complain of failed attempts at poetry:

> All I actually do is quote; everything that is meant to be serious immediately becomes a joke with me, genuine signs of life of my own slip out of me purely by accident, and they exist only at the moment when they slip out. Afterward then they are—well— where you once used to see the whole, I see nothing but particulars now. . . . I would so like to be full of pathos! . . . What slips out of me is only the raw sewage of previous centuries. (p. 211)

Handke's own political inclinations may well be Marxist. But he has repeatedly denied that his writing has political intent, insisting that there is no such thing as an engaged writer, but that there are only engaged men.[12] If Handke's writing, and particularly *They Are Dying Out*, is political, it is so in the sense that Gottfried Keller has referred to all man's activities as "political," not limiting the definition to ideology but referring to man's communal activities, that is, his relationships with other people and with the world at large. *They Are Dying Out* may indeed echo Lukács's aesthetics, but it stops considerably short of becoming a Marxist platform. For Handke's concern in this play is not to attack capitalism but to portray truthfully the condition of modernism, which, whatever the historical reasons (and the rise of capitalism may be one of them), he sees as a nearly unbridgeable schism between the individual and the world.

Speaking of his recently completed *Langsame Heimkehr* in a 1979 Berlin interview, Handke explains that this novel—or, more accurately, he suggests, this epic poem—is an attempt to reach both a world harmony and a universality for himself as a writer. He speaks of history, and particularly the history of the German-speaking world, and of how the past has destroyed the relationship between nature and language, making the poetic creation of men living together a near impossibility. The conflict between the "great nature" of which Hölderlin speaks—for in his time it was still possible to do so—and the modern writer's impotence is what Handke tries to narrate in *Langsame Heimkehr*.[13] Clearly the restoration of a harmonious vision of life is the key for Handke to the restoration of a language which will become the kind of literature Keller and Stifter, as well as Goethe, Schiller, and Hölderlin, were able to create.

So also is the restoration of this vision of life necessary to the creation of epic, or even tragic, figures. Whereas the Greek epic hero felt a continuing sense of union between his inner and outer worlds, and the tragic hero experienced a moment of reconciliation (albeit too late), the modern hero, standing in opposition to his world, can at best be a parody. For Lukács, the prototype of modern literature is the madman, unable to achieve integration. And the characteristic state of the modern artist is impotence. As *New York Times* critic Mel Gussow remarks in his review of the Yale production of *They Are Dying Out,* for Quitt the world ends not with a bang but with a burp,[14] this inarticulate utterance suggesting the final failure of the modern poet.

The extreme pessimism which informs Quitt's fate, however, is not Handke's final comment on modern literature nor the Armageddon of his own writing. For, as Lukács suggests in *The Theory of the Novel,* the grotesque failure of the protagonist in search of himself is inevitable in a world in which no reconciliation is possible, but the work of literature itself can stand as a symbol of the writer's successful integration of matter and spirit. In *They Are Dying Out,* Quitt himself is destroyed, but his servant, Hans, endures. At the end of the play, Hans notices with hope that he is becoming human and, in a parting poem, speaks of learning to dream and of changing the world. If Handke has been using capitalism as a metaphor for the decline of Western civilization, then the survival of Hans, the proletarian, would suggest some hope of a return to an age when the integration of man and his environment was still possible. What suggests the possibility of redemption even more strongly, however, is the fact that Hans has been more than just Quitt's servant throughout the play. He has, in fact, been Quitt's *Doppelgänger.* The strong kinship of the two men is suggested in an early monologue, when Hans, hearing Quitt complain of loneliness and detachment, laments:

> I can't remember anything personal about myself. The last time anyone talked about me was when I had to learn the catechism. "Your humble servant" of "Your Grace." Once I had a thought but I forgot it at once. I am trying to remember it even now. So I never learned to think. But I have no personal needs. Still, I can indulge in a few gestures. (p. 169)

Moments later, Hans explains to Kilb that he is serious only when Quitt is serious, and later, when Quitt invites him to tell him about himself, he replies "You mention me. / Yourself you mean" (p. 207).

In the second part of the play, Hans speaks of his realization of this connection:

> Suddenly I saw that I lacked something. And when I thought about it I realized that I lacked everything. For the first time I didn't just sort of exist for myself, but existed as someone who is comparable, say, with you. (pp. 214-15)

And when Quitt asks Hans, "Would you like to be like me?", the servant replies, "I have to be" (p. 215).

From Hans's point of view, the play has rather a fairy-tale quality to it, the story of the poor servant who perseveres and ultimately becomes king. The analogy is a more substantial one than a first mention would suggest, for, in an interview with Heinz Ludwig Arnold, Handke speaks of his familiarity with the Austrian playwrights Nestroy and Raimund, and particularly the fairy-tale plays of the latter, which he says were the basis for *They Are Dying Out:* "The fairy-tale plays of Raimund have been for me what I still am trying to achieve in my plays. Above all in the last play: *They Are Dying Out* is basically a Raimund-world: the unhappy rich man and the others his comrades."[15] In fact, at one point in the play, a conversation between Quitt and Paula is interrupted by Quitt's wife, who, involved in a crossword puzzle, asks the name of a nineteenth century Austrian dramatist, seven letters. Quitt suggests Nestroy, and she says, "No"; he then suggests Raimund, and she replies, "Of course" (pp. 201-202).

Even without the Raimund clue, however, a lover of fairy tales should recognize the characteristics of the familiar tale of the hero in search of an unspecified kingdom, the attainment of which symbolizes, as Bruno Bettelheim points out, "a state of true *independence,* in which the hero feels . . . secure, satisfied, and happy. . . . In fairy tales, unlike myths, victory is not over others but only over oneself. . . . "[16] If Quitt, the reigning ruler, fails in his quest, then his *Doppelgänger,* his complementary alter ego, does not, and achieves the freedom of self which Quitt sought.

Hans's achievement suggests Handke's idealized vision of the self as the fulfilling union of man and nature, and his hope for a language which can adequately express a relationship he fears is irrecoverable. His survival turns what might otherwise have been a pessimistic, even nihilistic, vision of the future of literature into an earnest hope for new life. It turns *They Are Dying Out* into both a lamentation and a prophecy, conveying the anguish of modern man in search of self and of the writer in search of a language. At one point in the play, Paula accuses Quitt of thinking of himself as "the deputy of universal truth":

> What you experience personally you want to experience for all of us. The blood you sweat in private you bring as a sacrifice to us, the impenitent ones. Your ego wants to be more than itself, . . . (p. 195)

Clearly Quitt's ego has become more than itself, transforming itself not only into the non-capitalistic Hans, who poetically envisions a changed world, but into the poet Handke as well, whose own commitment rests not in any political cause but in a language which offers a renaissance of literature and life.

### NOTES

[1] See Claus Peymann, "Directing Handke," *The Drama Review,* 16 (June 1972), 48, 53.

[2] Promotional advertisement for the Yale Repertory Theatre's fourteenth season, 1979-80.

[3] Rainer Nägele and Renate Voris, *Peter Handke* (München, 1978), p. 92.

[4] Manfred Mixner, *Peter Handke* (Kronberg, 1977), p. 189.

[5] Handke, *They Are Dying Out,* in *The Ride Across Lake Constance and Other Plays,* trans. Michael Roloff (New York, 1976), p. 199. Subsequent citations will appear parenthetically in the text.

[6] Joseph A. Federico, "The Hero as Playwright in Dramas by Frisch, Dürrenmatt, and Handke," *German Life and Letters,* NS 32 (January 1979), 171.

[7] "Gespräch mit Peter Handke über sein Stück," *Die Zeit,* 18 (American edition, 3 May 1974).

[8] Georg Lukács, *The Theory of the Novel,* trans. Anna Bostock (Cambridge, Mass., 1971), pp. 29-39.

[9] See Lukács, *Gottfried Keller* (Berlin, 1946).

[10] Georg Lukács, "Narrate or Describe?", in *Writer and Critic, and Other Essays,* ed. and trans. Arthur Kahn (London, 1978), p. 127.

[11] George Steiner, "Georg Lukács—A Preface," in *Realism in Our Time,* by Georg Lukács (New York, 1964), p. 12.

[12] Handke, "Die Literatur ist romantisch," in *Prosa, Gedichte, Theaterstücke, Horspiel, Aufsätze* (Frankfurt, 1969), pp. 273-87, and *Ich bin ein Bewohner des Elfenbeinturms* (Frankfurt, 1972), pp. 35-50.

[13] See June Schlueter, "An Interview with Peter Handke," *Studies in Twentieth Century Literature,* 4 (1980).

[14] Mel Gussow, "Two Plays That Challenge as They Entertain," *The New York Times,* 11 November 1979, sec. 2, p. 24.

[15] Heinz Ludwig Arnold, "Gespräch mit Peter Handke," *Text + Kritik,* Heft 24/24a (September 1976), 16; my translation.

[16] Bruno Bettelheim, *The Uses of Enchantment: The Meaning and Importance of Fairy Tales* (New York, 1976), p. 127.

## David Morgan Zehr

SOURCE: "Joyce's Bifocal Lens: Politics in Ireland," in the *Midwest Quarterly,* Vol. XXII, No. 2, Winter, 1981, pp. 147-62.

[*In the following essay, Zehr contends that the "Cyclops" chapter of James Joyce's* Ulysses *"dramatizes . . . both forty years of Irish history and the complexity of Joyce's political attitudes and responses to the Irish political situation."*]

One of our most persistent critical images of James Joyce has been that of the politically uninvolved artist—the detached writer sitting above the arena of human affairs paring his fingernails. Although we do associate with Joyce an extensive cultural consciousness of Ireland, we have generally understood that consciousness as free from political partisanship. The "Cyclops" chapter of *Ulysses*—which pits, in a serio-comic style, the humanist Bloom against the bigoted nationalist figure of the Citizen—is usually read as confirming this political detachment; while the chapter clearly reflects Joyce's pervasive knowledge of Ireland's cultural and political affairs, "Cyclops" is commonly seen as a satire on the nationalist movement and as Joyce's own justification of his dissociation from Irish politics. However, Joyce's relationship to Irish politics was considerably more complex. In 1919, when he had just completed "Cyclops," he expressed to Frank Budgen his anxiety over the reception of this chapter in Ireland: "It is a work of a sceptic, but I don't want it to appear the work of a cynic. I don't want to hurt or offend those of my countrymen who are devoting their lives to a cause they feel to be necessary and just" (p. 152). Joyce's response to the Irish struggle was essentially problematic; while he maintained an adversary relationship to the Irish nationalists, he was also deeply and imaginatively concerned with the direction and future of Irish politics.

The fact that throughout *Ulysses* Joyce is never indifferent to political events or to the conflicts between Ireland and England should not be at all surprising, for the years from his birth in 1882 (the year of the Phoenix Park murders) to the publication of *Ulysses* in 1922 (the year of the resolution of Ireland's civil war in the south), were probably the most significant forty years in modern Irish history. Joyce's childhood and adolescence coalesced with the fall of Parnell and the rise of the Gaelic movements in language, sports, and literature, and when he wrote *Ulysses* it was under the shadow of both the First World War and the unsuccessful Easter Rebellion in Dublin in 1916. Not only does a consciousness of these historical-political events permeate the text and tone of *Ulysses,* but the novel also discloses an active and complex response to these, and other, events—a response that demonstrates that Joyce was seldom apolitical when it came to Irish issues.

Although my specific textual attention in this essay will focus on the "Cyclops" chapter, my intention is not that of *explication de texte.* Rather, this chapter is extremely valuable because it dramatizes in such a remarkably coherent manner both forty years of Irish history and the complexity of Joyce's political attitudes and responses to the Irish political situation. First, I think we can best begin to understand the weighty cultural and political "baggage" that Joyce carried with him when he began to write *Ulysses* by looking at the influences that affected his political development in the years preceding his composition of *Ulysses.*

In 1891, Joyce wrote his first published work, "Et tu Healy?", a poem on Timothy Healy's desertion of his political commander, Charles Stewart Parnell. What is interesting about this work is not just that it focuses on a nationalist subject at such an early age, but that it focuses on a conflict between Irish nationalism and what Joyce would later come to identify as an Irish temper—suggesting (as others have done) that there was something about the Irish character that often was at odds with the goals of Irish political action. Joyce elaborates on this attitude in his essay, "Fenianism," in which he ironically approves of the fact that James Stephens had organized the Fenian movement into small cells, indicating that this plan was "eminently fitted to the Irish character because it reduced to a minimum the possibility of betrayal" (Mason and Ellmann, p. 189). I think we will be able to see that Joyce's political satire is aimed not just at Irish nationalism, but at a generalized flaw in the Irish character, which he believed had often subverted the humanist values that he saw as fundamental to the politics of a free and progressive Ireland.

The last decade of the nineteenth century saw the emergency of two Irish nationalist organizations—the Gaelic League and the Gaelic Athletic Association—both of which Joyce was temporarily involved with before he left Dublin in 1904. The concern of Douglas Hyde (the founder of the Gaelic League) with the loss of Irish language, traditions, music, and ideas suggests the kind of nationalist idealism that was compatible with Joyce's own sensibility—a nationalism grounded in a humanist sensibility rather than in rhetoric and ideology. But Joyce came to discover that nationalist ideals could be all too easily transformed into cultural chauvinism and political rhetoric. In a 1906 letter to his brother Stanislaus, Joyce expressed his early problematic relationship to Irish nationalism: "If the Irish programme did not insist on the Irish language I suppose I could call myself a nationalist" (Ellmann, p. 246). While at University College, Joyce was persuaded by his friend Clancy (Davin in *A Portrait*) to take lessons in the Gaelic language—a fact that seems quite inconsistent with the fifth chapter of *A Portrait of the Artist as a Young Man.* However, he gave up the lessons because the instructor, Padraic Pearse (one of the leaders of the Easter 1916 revolt), "found it necessary to exalt Irish by denigrating English" (Ellmann, p. 62). If the Gaelic League, which sponsored Joyce's classes in Gaelic, was intended by Hyde to preserve an Irish cultural heritage, it soon became transformed by an infusion of nationalist ideology. Oliver MacDonagh indicates that Hyde's movement was "infiltrated by extremists" and that as a result it became "a sort of school for rebellion . . . instead of binding Irishmen of all types and opinions together" (p. 64). It was not just the program itself that Joyce rejected, then, but the blinding Irish nationalism that transformed it from a cultural program into a polemical platform.

The Gaelic Athletic Association, which stressed the importance of physical exercise and advocated the revival of native Gaelic sports, also appears to have temporarily attracted the young Joyce, who was made secretary of the new gymnasium while at Belvedere College (the growth of such gymnasiums, and of a renewed interest in sports, was influenced by the GAA). But the Gaelic Athletic Association lacked the humanist impulse that initially informed Douglas Hyde's movement. Oliver MacDonagh says that it "encouraged the idea of a separate people," and that it "sought to insulate native from British sport by a system of exclusion and boycott" (p. 64). Just as with the Gaelic League, the political transformation of this movement into a program for nationalist chauvinism quickly alienated Joyce—and the political subversion of such a cultural organization was not to be lost on Joyce's art. The Citizen, that overblown, myopic nationalist who receives the central satiric focus of "Cyclops," is apparently modelled after Michael Cusack, the founder of the Gaelic Athletic Association; at one point during the chapter, Joe Hynes points at the Citizen and declares him to be the man "that made the Gaelic Sports Revival." Joyce follows this statement with a fantasy meeting of the Slaugh na h-Eireann (the Gaelic name for the Association), the subject of which is the "revival of ancient Gaelic sports and the importance of physical culture, as understood in ancient Greece and ancient Rome and ancient Ireland, for the development of the race" (*Ulysses,* p. 316). Joyce believed that the notion that a sports revival could connect Ireland with a time characterized by such legendary and mythical heroes as Finn MacCool and Cuchulain could only serve to anchor Ireland in the deceiving myth of a golden age, and continue to perpetuate Irish parochialism. At the fantasy meeting it is a lone "L. Bloom," the man who sustains a humanist and modernist sensibility in the novel, who casts the single negative vote.

However, despite Joyce's critical stance toward the nationalists' manipulation of Ireland's internal affairs, when those affairs were interfered with by blatantly discriminatory English practices, Joyce was quick to assume a partisan Irish stance. In "Cyclops" Joyce picks up two nationalist issues that seemed to reflect English prejudice, and interweaves them in order to dramatize his sympathy and support for the Irish cause. In 1904 the British Police Commissioner in Dublin had prohibited the playing of Gaelic games (such as hurling) by the Slaugh na h-Eireann in Phoenix Park, while still permitting the British to play polo there. Joyce gives further force to this issue by interrelating this 1904 incident with a situation that did not take place until 1911, the British embargo on Irish cattle.

As a result of spotted incidents of hoof-and-mouth disease in Irish cattle, the English parliament placed a strict embargo on all Irish cattle, seriously affecting an already weakened Irish economy. The situation was aggravated by the popular belief in England that the Irish were trying to mask the disease and continue to send the diseased cattle to England. Joyce responded strongly enough to the issue to write a short editorial on the conflict in 1912, entitled "Politics and Cattle Disease." He indicates that while concern and careful examination procedures were certainly warranted, the distrust of Irish motives and the doubting of their equal interest in isolating and curing the disease was a continuing insult to the Gaelic nation. Joyce became somewhat involved personally when Henry N. Blackwood Price, an Ulsterman, asked Joyce in 1912 to obtain the address of William Fields, M.P., who was president of the Irish Cattle Trader's Society, in order to inform him of a cure for the hoof-and-mouth disease that he had heard of in Austria. Joyce incorporates this event into the "Nestor" chapter, but does not give the issue political force until the "Cyclops" chapter. Joe Hynes, who has just returned from the Cattle Trader's meeting at the City Arms Hotel, where they are discussing the embargo, comes into Kiernan's Pub in order to give the Citizen the "hard word about it." The Citizen, Joyce's composite portrait of the worst aspects of the nationalist movement, has naturally forsaken the meeting for the more pressing call of drink. Joe Hynes indicates that William Fields and Nannetti are crossing over to London that very night in order to ask about the British embargo on the floor of the House of Commons. At this moment Joyce incorporates into the narrative a short fantasy scene in which a mythical Mr. Cowe Conacre is addressing the House of Commons: "May I ask the right honorable gentleman whether the government has issued orders that these animals shall be slaughtered though no medical evidence is forthcoming as to their pathological condition?" (*Ulysses,* p. 314). However, Joyce does not leave the issue at this merely polemical level.

He raises the cattle issue to a metaphorical level by merging it with the British ban against the playing of Irish games in Phoenix Park. While in London inquiring about the cattle situation, Nannetti is also supposed to inquire for "the league" about the prohibition against the Irish games. Directly following Mr. Cowe Conacre's question, then, an equally imaginative Mr. Orelli stands and inquires, "Have similar orders been issued for the slaughter of human animals who dare to play Irish games in the Phoenix Park?" (*Ulysses,* p. 316). That the answer is in the negative from a learned M.P. does not reduce the irony or the polemical value of relating the two issues—for whether with cattle, or sports, or with politics, Joyce clearly implies that the British exercise a decisive discriminatory policy that stems from a cultural prejudice and that leads to a continued oppression of the Irish people. Thus, although Joyce is clearly satirizing the parochial and polemical nature of the nationalist movement, he also endorses a number of Irish issues, especially those which arise from British interference with Irish affairs.

However, when Joyce left Ireland in 1904, he was less politically conscious and less sympathetic with Irish issues in general than he would be in *Ulysses;* he left Ireland disaffected with his homeland, disenchanted with the Gaelic Revival, and carrying with him an imaginative definition of the Irish character as parochial, idealist, and given to overzealousness. And although he had gone to some socialist meetings in Dublin, his motivation appears to have been less political than personal: he felt convinced that if he was to live as an artist and fly the bonds of a bourgeois life, he would require a government subsidy or a redistribution of wealth. But during his stay in Trieste, Joyce became more polemically involved with socialism, and this renewed interest, combined with the appearance of a new political movement in Ireland, significantly altered Joyce's response to the Irish struggle.

The socialists in Trieste had fomented a general strike in February, 1902, the mood of which was sustained by the Russian Revolution of 1905, and during his early years there Joyce's pronouncements on socialism became more rhetorical and his response to Irish politics more sympathetic. He told his brother, Stanislaus: "You have often shown opposition to my socialistic tendencies. But can you not see plainly that a deferment of the emancipation of the proletariat, a reaction to clericalism or aristocracy or bourgeoism would mean a revulsion to tyrannies of all kinds. Gogarty would jump into the Liffey to save a man's life, but he seems to have little hesitation in condemning generations to servitude. Perhaps it is a case which the piping poets should solemnize" (Ellmann, p. 204). Although Joyce's interest in international politics would soon be on the wane, I do not think that it is accidental that at the same time his sense of alienation from Ireland began to change. He told Stanislaus at this time, "Sometimes thinking of Ireland it seems to me that I have been unnecessarily harsh. I had reproduced (in *Dubliners* at least) none of the attraction of the city for I have never felt at my ease in any city since I left it" (Ellmann, p. 239). Joyce's renewed political interest, and his reassessed relationship with Ireland were intertwined, I think, with his belief that there was a viable political alternative to the dominant nationalist movement in Ireland—Arthur Griffith's Sinn Fein movement, which appeared in the fall of 1904.

Arthur Griffith formulated the program for the Sinn Fein on the basis of Hungary's successful fight for freedom from Austria: the Hungarians had begun their fight by refusing to send representatives to the parliament in Vienna. Griffith put his ideas together in a book, *The Resurrection of Hungary,* which appeared serially in his paper, *The United Irishmen,* between January and June 1904—where it was likely read by the young Joyce. Griffith recognized that the parliamentary actions of Parnell had only led to vetoed Home Rule Bills, and that the violent insurrections of 1803, 1848, and 1867 had proved to be ludicrous failures, and he saw the pervasive nostalgia for a mythical Irish past as merely anchoring the Irish is an unreal, self-deluding world. Griffith, therefore, advocated that "Members of Parliament could begin by withdrawing from Westminster and setting up an Irish Council; after that Irish courts, banks, a civil service, a stock exchange could be established to function alongside their British counterparts until the latter withered away through lack of use" (Caulfield, p. 20). The very name of the movement, Sinn Fein, meaning "Ourselves Alone," suggested that the ideas of self-reliance and pragmatic self-determination (in fact, these were very much the ideas that Swift set forth in *A Modest Proposal*) were more important preliminary steps for independence than the frustrating battle for political recognition. The policy of the Sinn Fein was not bigoted, internally separatist, or polemical; rather, it was a humanist assertion of a modern, non-violent plan to better the social and economic condition of the Irish people, without acquiescing either to the British or to the Irish militants (that it was ultimately subverted by the ideological Irish Revolutionary Brotherhood and taken over by Eamon De Valera in 1917 suggests the power that was recognized in its policy).

Joyce, who was himself convinced of the futility of parliamentary action for Home Rule and was committed to non-violence, declared Griffith to be "the first person in Ireland to revive the separatist idea on modern lines" (Ellmann, p. 245). Joyce expresses his approbation of Sinn Fein in *Ulysses* by suggesting that it is Bloom who gives the idea of the revoluntionary Hungarian methods to Arthur Griffith (Bloom's father was, of course, a transplanted Hungarian, né Virag). By associating the origin of Sinn Fein with Bloom, Joyce not only indicates his endorsement of Sinn Fein, he also manages to give the pacifist, apolitical Bloom an aura of political potential more substantive than that associated with the inflated, violence-declaiming Citizen. While the Citizen's world is narrowly constructed around ideological rhetoric, which Joyce sees as lacking a stable, viable foundation, Bloom embodies a world of moderate humanist values that Joyce sees as a necessary foundation for any progressive, enduring political action. Joyce seems to imply that if Bloom's transmission of the idea for the Hungarian revolution can be so affirmatively transformed, so might his naive ideas of love as the opposite of hatred and of a nation as the same people living in the same place be more tenable as political values than all the fervor and fanaticism of the Citizen.

Joyce's response to a 1907 incident serves to clarify the direction of his political development and the nature of his response to the Irish situation. In February, 1907, J. M. Synge's *The Playboy of the Western World* resulted in riots in Dublin by Irish nationalists; Padraic Colum, arrested during the riots, declared that "nothing would deter him from protesting against such a slander on Ireland" (Ellmann, p. 248). To Slanislaus's amazement, Joyce appeared to side against the literary people and with the nationalists: "I believe that Colum and the Irish Theatre will beat Y. and L.G. and Miss H. [Yeats, Lady Gregory, and Miss Horniman, a supporter of the English and Irish theatres] which will please me greatly . . ." (Ellmann, p. 248). Although this occurrence must have reaffirmed Joyce's sense of Irish parochialism, he believed that Yeats was "quite out of touch with the Irish people," and, therefore, I think we should see his statement less as an anti-intellectual remark than as a partisan Irish reaction against the intellectual Protestants (generally Anglo-Irish) who were controlling the Abbey Theatre. As a result of his interest in the Sinn Fein movement and of his socialist development in Trieste, Joyce took a political stance that was based on his belief that "if the Irish question exists, it exists for the Irish proletariat chiefly" (Ellmann, p. 246).

However, 1907 was a crucial year for Joyce, for in that year he suddenly became acutely aware of the conflict between his art and his socialist interests. He had previously told his brother, "It is a mistake for you to imagine that my political opinions are those of a universal lover; but they are those of a socialistic artist" (Ellmann, p. 240). But in the same month as *The Playboy of the Western World* riots (February 1907), Joyce expressed a fundamental discontent with the direction of his work, and a feeling of need for creative reorganization:

> I have come to the conclusion that it is about time I made up my mind whether I am to become a writer or a patient Cousins. . . . It is months since I have written a line and even reading tires me. I have gradually slid down until I have ceased to take any interest in any subject. . . . I have no wish to codify myself anarchist or socialist or reactionary. . . . Yet I have certain ideas I would like to give form to: not as a doctrine but as the continuation of the expression of myself which I now see I began in *Chamber Music.* (Ellmann, p. 249)

If Joyce did begin to write with renewed consistency and authority at this time (which is clearly demonstrated by his next story, "The Dead"), he nevertheless did not abandon the political ideals and social satire that he had consolidated over the previous decade. He continued to express his distrust and nostalgia for Ireland and his disaffection with British dominance in his 1907 lectures, "Ireland, Island of Saints and Sages," "Fenianism," "Home Rule Comes of Age," and "Ireland at the Bar." If this period demonstrates the complexity and problematic nature of Joyce's commitment to the Irish question, we can now better understand the weighty cultural baggage that Joyce carried with him when he began to write *Ulysses.* In addition, we can now more clearly understand how the events that immediately preceded the composition of "Cyclops"—the First World War and the Easter Rising of 1916—would affect the cultural and political attitudes expressed in that chapter.

Joyce's stay in Zurich from 1915 to 1920 was the major period of the writing of *Ulysses,* during which he was relatively free from immediate financial worries and from the overt disruption of the First World War. Indeed, Ellmann suggests that during the first six months of the war, Joyce was "supremely indifferent to the result and, so long as gunfire could not be heard, to the conflict itself" (p. 394). It is precisely this kind of response that has served to engender our image of a non-political Joyce. But the emotional detachment of his situation in Zurich was suddenly upset in 1916—and, at least temporarily, Joyce became emotionally reinvolved with Ireland and the nationalist struggle.

On Easter Monday, 1916, a revolutionary force led by Padraic Pearse and James Connolly declared Ireland a republic and started the first major insurrection since 1801, but within five days the rebellion was soundly and violently defeated. Joyce followed the events with impatience and pity, slipping for a short time into what Helene Cixous calls a "nostalgic Parnellism" (p. 239), which suggests his latent romantic attachment to his native country. Although he believed that the rising was ultimately futile, he felt emotionally drawn once again to his native country, and declared that one day he and his son would go back to wear the shamrock of an independent Ireland. But when this initial fervor waned, he began to retain his feelings of emotional distance and of ironic personal alienation from Ireland: when asked if he did not look forward to the emergence of an independent Ireland, he replied, "So that I might declare myself its first enemy?" (Ellmann, p. 412).

Nevertheless, the events of 1916 deeply affected Joyce; if he dissociated himself from the violent revolt, he was still moved by those men who had died for a cause in which they believed (cf. Yeats' "Easter 1916"). And in "Cyclops," Joyce implicitly indicts those who voiced a nationalist position but failed to act during the uprising. When Eamon De Valera was being led by the British out of the barricades and through the Dublin onlookers, he is reported to have said, "If only you had come out with knives and forks." The Citizen, sitting in the pub asking for news on the Gaelic League caucus and the Cattle Trader's meeting (neither of which he attends), and having declared himself ready to put "force against force" (*Ulysses,* p. 329), is Joyce's portrait of the vociferous Irish citizen whose ideology is nurtured by heroic rhetoric rather than by action. When the Citizen drinks a toast to the "memory of the dead," his 1904 statement gains clearly ironic overtones in light of the frustrated 1916 revolt. Joyce declared that the "Irish, even though they break the hearts of those who sacrifice their lives for their native land, never fail to show great respect for their dead" (Mason and Ellmann, p. 192). Joyce is thus clearly satirizing the easiness with which the Citizen talks about "the brothers Sheares and Wolfe Tone . . . and Robert

Emmet and die for your country" all in one breath, while he sits drinking in Kiernan's pub. In this instance, Joyce is criticizing not those who have fought and died for the cause, but an Irish character which he sees as anchored in a legendary and nostalgic past rather than in a pragmatic political present.

A concrete manifestation of what Joyce identified as the major problem in the Irish political program, and which helped to define for him the political reality, occurred during the Easter Rebellion when a large number of Dubliners became looters rather than supporters of the struggle. Both Joyce and Sean O'Casey (cf. *The Plough and the Stars*) identified this not as a betrayal of the rebellion, as most nationalists did, but as a reflection of the real interest of the Irish people. The fact that so many of Dublin's citizens had risked being shot not for the proclamation of the Republic but for material goods indicated that their real concern lay with an economic and social revolution, rather than with the specific question of political independence. Although Joyce was not unsympathetic with the Easter Rising, it ultimately reaffirmed for him his belief in the futility of violence and his belief that violent nationalism would only subvert the social revolution and the humanist values necessary for a socially progressive Irish Republic. If the 1916 revolt made a significant impression on Joyce and his art, he saw in the First World War the absurdity and futility of nationalism on an even more magnified scale.

Although Joyce remained detached from the events and issues of the Great War, his attitude in "Cyclops" is clearly the product of a post–World War I consciousness, one that has witnessed the ravaging effects of nationalism throughout Europe. The Citizen dreams of the day "when the first Irish battleship is seen breasting the waves with our own flags," but Bloom, his voice conveying the resonance of a post–World War sensibility, despite the 1904 setting, responds by asking, "Wouldn't it be the same here if you put force against force?" (*Ulysses,* pp. 328-29). Such nationalist aspirations as the Citizen's were not only mocked by the devastating effects of the First World War, they could only result, as Bloom suggests and as Joyce had seen, in "perpetuating national hatred among nations" (*Ulysses,* p. 331). Thus, it is with political and value-laden force that Bloom, who innocently transmitted the idea for Sinn Fein to Griffith, declares: "But it's no use. . . . Force, hatred, history, all that. That's not life for men and women" (*Ulysses,* p. 333). We become increasingly aware that Bloom's humanist sensibility, enunciated in a fictive 1904 world, achieves the impact and meaning that it does because of the events of the First World War (and, for contemporary readers, of the wars that have followed). And Joyce himself demonstrated a Bloomsian sense of the problematic relationship between politics and violence when he told George Borach in October 1918: "Naturally I can't approve of the act of the revolutionary who tosses a bomb in a theatre to destroy the king and his children. On the other hand, have those states behaved any better which have drowned the world in a blood-bath?" (Cixous, p. 239).

Although Joyce is clearly setting up a political dialectic between the humanist Bloom and the ideological Citizen, he still continues to write about specific Irish issues. When John Wyse Nolan raises the subject of England's devastation of Ireland's forests, it is the Citizen who supports an issue with which Joyce appears to be in full sympathy: "Save the trees of Ireland for the future men of Ireland on the fair hills of Eire, O" (*Ulysses*, p. 326). While Joyce is certainly satirizing the Citizen's habit of transforming such issues into heroic rhetoric, there is no satire associated with the subject itself, just as there was not with the cattle issue, or with the banning of Irish games in Phoenix Park. For Joyce, such issues dramatize an unjustifiable British abuse of the Gaelic nation, and permit him to express a partisan commitment, entirely consistent with Sinn Fein policy, to Irish economic, cultural, and social self-determination—while at the same time maintaining the privilege of detached judgment of an Irish temper.

We can now better understand the complex political relationship with Ireland that led to Joyce's anxiety over the reception of "Cyclops" by his countrymen: "It is a work of a sceptic, but I don't want it to appear the work of a cynic. I don't want to hurt or offend those of my countrymen who are devoting their lives to a cause they feel to be necessary and just." Although Joyce dissociated himself from the Irish nationalists, whom he saw as fighting for political independence rather than for a socially progressive Ireland, he did support Griffith's Sinn Fein movement, and he openly attacked English mistreatment of the Irish. Despite the bitterness and distrust that Joyce had learned to associate with the Irish character, Stephen Dedalus is still able to declare toward the end of *Ulysses*, "I suspect that Ireland must be important because it belongs to me." Joyce, then, is never personally or artistically uninvolved with Irish politics. And this dual commitment to Ireland, a commitment to satirize the negative and reactionary aspects, and to assert humanist and cultural values from which his country could establish a modern, unified, progressive state, is, finally, the complex political sensibility that underlies and informs the world of *Ulysses*.

### BIBLIOGRAPHY

Budgen, Frank. *James Joyce and the Making of "Ulysses."* Bloomington, Indiana, 1960.

Caufield, Max. *The Easter Rebellion.* New York, 1963.

Cixous, Helene. *The Exile of James Joyce,* trans. Sally A. J. Purcell. New York, 1972.

Ellmann, Richard. *James Joyce.* New York, 1959.

Joyce, James. *Ulysses.* New York, 1934.

MacDonagh, Oliver. *Ireland.* Englewood Cliffs, N.J., 1968.

Mason, Ellsworth and Richard Ellmann, eds. *James Joyce: The Critical Writings.* New York, 1959.

**Shiraz Dossa**

SOURCE: "*Satanic Verses*: Imagination and Its Political Context," in *Cross Currents*, Dobbs Ferry, Vol. XXXIX, No. 2, Summer, 1989, pp. 204-13.

[*In the following essay, Dossa explains the tension between Western postmodern ideals of freedom—which, he argues, are infused with a rigid and imperialist misunderstanding of other cultures—and traditional "third-world" cultures and argues that Salman Rushdie's* Satanic Verses *relies on both medieval and postmodern European and American stereotypes of Islam, offering no alternatives to the society he criticizes.*]

For many Muslim intellectuals in the West, Salman Rushdie's public biography, since the publication of *Midnight's Children,* has been an exemplary, acclaimed replay of their comparatively anonymous lives. In most cases forced by circumstance to reside in the West, their lives have been less turbulent replicas of Rushdie's, caught between the nativist push to be authentic and the pressure to espouse the ways of their new homeland. No reflective immigrant, especially one educated in the West, can hope to escape this affliction of mind and practice. To live in the metropolitan capitals of the imperial powers, in the cradle of the Eurocentric worldview, is to continually feel in your gut the pull of ethnic allegiance and the dilemmas of divided loyalty.

His huge literary talent aside, Rushdie is a familiar, kindred spirit, a third world Muslim fluent in the language and the culture of the modern West, critical of it yet irresistibly drawn to its sense of undisciplined freedom and possibility. Such intellectuals concede and relish their heritage, play on it endlessly, but are ill at ease with the restrictions that this monotheistic faith foists upon the faithful through its insistence on the truth of its revelation, and with its political ambition to realise this truth in this world.

Like such Muslims, Rushdie has little sympathy for the stringent edicts of the juridical guardians of Islam who wish to harness the secular realm to the law of God. In *Midnight's Children,* and far more sharply in his novel *Shame,* he employed a charming and witty style to lambaste the pretensions of Indian and Pakistani Muslims, particularly political leaders who seemed to get away with self-serving conduct by appealing to selected principles of their comprehensive faith. Though unimpressed by rationalizations employed to justify petty, inhumane and sometimes criminal behavior, he was unwilling to dismiss Muslim politics and ethics *tout court:* his critical touch was temperate and his general tone suggested the solicitousness of an insider who understands the faults of his ethnic compatriots.

In a 1983 opinion piece condemning censorship in Pakistan, particularly the lack of coverage of the involvement of Pakistan's Muslim military rulers in the flourishing heroin trade, Rushdie went on to remark: "How fortunate that the Quran does not mention anything about the ethics of heroin pushing."[1] But whatever offense his novelistic presentation of Muslims may have provoked in the hearts of the faithful was substantially blunted by his scabrous indictment, in his political journalism, of British racism against Asian and black immigrants. In a bitter philippic broadcast on the BBC in 1982, he described Asians and blacks in Britain as members of "the new, imported empire", heavily monitored by "regiments of occupation and control." Unlike the Germans, Rushdie asserted, who had at least attempted to rid themselves of the "pollution" of Nazism in the aftermath of the Third Reich.

> British thought and society has never been cleansed of the Augean filth of imperialism. It is still there, breeding lice and vermin, waiting for unscrupulous people to exploit it for its own ends. The British may be the only people on earth who feel nostalgia for pillage and conquest and war.[2]

Rushdie was applauded, and his criticisms of the third world were taken in stride, not rejected outright, precisely because he had not committed the unforgivable sin of selling out: he had dishonored neither himself nor the third world. No such generosity is apparent in the response to V. S. Naipaul, whose contempt for the third world, for its intransigence in remaining Asian and African—what he calls "bush societies"—is undisguised and unabashed.

For Rushdie, Asia has never ceased to be his homeland, a strand of his soul, a basic facet of his being. Naipaul has poured scorn on Trinidad and other third world nations as unfit for civilized life, a privilege offered only by the West, especially England. Naipaul's spiritual homeland, without apology or qualification, is white Europe and its values. Rushdie's cultural attachments and spiritual milieu, by contrast, will in a central sense always be Asian and Muslim, a fact which he has not sought to downplay or deny.

1

Although *Satanic Verses*[3] is intellectually a bold effort, Rushdie's talent for philosophical thought is inadequate for the sort of mental seminar he has in mind. It is a brilliant literary exercise, sometimes gripping, touching, and intensely humane, but as a venture in imaginative and linguistic virtuosity, a creation of new realms of human feelings and idiosyncracies, it is overall a lesser achievement than *Midnight's Children*.

Rushdie does not write ordinary, straightforward stories with explicit beginnings and endings, tales that make sense to the conventional intelligence. Like Gabriel Garcia Marquez and Milan Kundera, he has carved out an arena of the imagination in which outlandish fantasy lives in comfortable alliance with the everyday and the familiar. As Rushdie tells us again and again: it was and it was not so, it happened and it did not happen.

In Rushdie's pages a veritable panoply of colorful characters, experiences, ideas, dreams, commentaries, questions, clash and merge, assert themselves and vanish, only to reappear to renew their battle. His novels close

without resolutions, only the sense of having been privy to a clutch of insights that seem to enhance our understanding of the messy, lugubrious, frequently shapeless texture of human lives. In *Satanic Verses* Rushdie's focus is once again, as he imagines them, the politics and the culture of South Asia and Britain, and the continuing complex relationship between them that began after the acquisition of formal political independence. This time, however, a key theme is the historical origin and the secular meaning of Islam.

Two Indian Muslims, Gibreel Farishta and Saladin Chamcha, tumble down towards London moments after their plane is blown up by terrorists: both, amazingly, survive the fall. Farishta is a famous and mentally deranged Bombay actor who routinely dreams up a storm of lethal scenarios for other people which invariably end in tragedy for them. Claiming inspiration from the angel Gibreel, he believes himself to be, in his dream life and in his incarnations on earth, variously the angel, Prophet Mohammed, and the Prophetess Ayesha (who leads her "pilgrims" to death in the Arabian Sea, which is parted, as she was reliably informed it would be, by Gibreel Farishta/angel Gibreel).

In England after his fall (Fall), sober, practical Englishmen notice that Farishta sports a holy halo. In India he enjoys the status of a God as a result of having performed countless divine roles in films based on Hindu spiritual epics—the Bombay "theologicals". Farishta's fevered mind is, consequently, incapable of separating fantasy from reality.

Farishta's fellow survivor, Saladin Chamcha, is a British citizen with a "first-class British passport"; he has lived in England for many years and more or less despises his native India and things Indian. Chamcha is in love with the aristocratic England of culture, etiquette and class, and to realize his dream of becoming an Englishman has acquired an English wife, Pamela. Paradoxically, she has no passion for *his* England but espouses radical feminism and third world causes.

His second life on British soil proves to be tiresome and depressing: Chamcha is subjected to a tirade of racist insults and physical abuse by an English policeman and is rejected by his wife. That he smells badly and has sprouted satanic horns and a tail in his new incarnation, makes his life especially intolerable: he has literally been transformed into the dirty, devilish immigrant the British mind supposes him to be. Chamcha's tribulations serve as a parable of the real condition of Asian and black immigrants in Thatcher's England—an England in the throes of ethnocentric bravado, rediscovering its imperial pride in the great power that once ruled much of the world, including India. Saladin Chamcha, despite his cloying allegiance to Proper England, to "Proper London", is Britain's internal other, the despised native colonial, and he suffers accordingly.

*Satanic Verses* is forthright, detailed and candid in its depiction of British racism, institutionalised and retail, but not uncompromising in its condemnation. Rushdie also notices the unrecognized immorality in the conduct and business dealings of British Asians and blacks, the tendency a number of them have to elide or scant ethical questions. British racism is a terrible, sickening reality but Britain is not all evil: it has frequently offered refuge to radical dissidents of various ideological stripes:

> Would the United States, with its are-you-now-have-you-ever-beens, have permitted Ho Chi Minh to cook in its hotel kitchens? What would its McCarran-Walter Act have to say about a latter-day Karl Marx, standing bushy-bearded at its gates, waiting to cross its yellow lines?[4]

## 2

Unfortunately, Rushdie's capacity for nuance and ambiguity is far less conspicuous in his reconstruction of the origins of Islam, in his secular rendition of the life and the motives of the Prophet Mohammed. By now it is notorious that the "satanic" facet of the *Satanic Verses* lies in his resorting to the medieval Christian polemical tag Mahound for the Prophet, his implying that God's messenger was willing to compromise with the money-gods of Mecca, and his bad taste in fabricating a sequence in which Arabian prostitutes in Mecca assume the names of the Prophet's wives and service their clients in their new identities.

To protest, as Rushdie and his mainly Western admirers have done, that *Satanic Verses* is a species of fiction, that the entire episode of the Prophet and the Muslims is an uncontrollable dream that takes shape in the unstable mind of the mentally deranged Farishta, is understandable and legitimate. Fiction has no obligations to anything or anybody apart from the imaginative muse that compels a writer, irrespective of how farfetched and preposterous it may seem to many.

In this century, memorable fiction has routinely sought to do exactly that, to challenge and disturb the pieties of our political managers. Fiction's function as an adversarial play in the continuing conflict over values and truth in the modern world, is no longer controversial among intellectuals. Rushdie is painfully and rightly aware of his mandate to contest and disable the conventional self-understandings that rule our minds and our lives.

It seems to me that *Satanic Verses'* relatively few pages on Islam have outraged innumerable Muslims, including the well educated, not because they are superbly fictional, but because they are insufficiently imaginative. Rushdie's protagonists and lesser figures, his treatment of the rise of Islam, his choice of names, his description of the progress of the faith, are too close to the facts of Muslim history. But his version of that history was bound to offend because it is recast in a way that scorns the ethical and spiritual claims of the faith, and of the messenger of Allah together with his wives and his companions. In other words Rushdie's writing, in this instance, *comes across as history, not as fiction, as though it were the real history of Islam that Muslim leaders and believers had repressed.*

Failure of imagination, not the reverse, is the actual problem as far as his Islam is concerned: Rushdie manages to present the faith as an Arab businessman's scam (abscam?), as too lax and flexible in its ethics. In the novel, Salman Farsi, the Persian scribe who wrote down the revelation (Quran), asserts that the Prophet did not recognise and acceded to the fabrications he introduced in the holy book. Farsi, replying to a query regarding the Prophet's character, says, "The closer you are to the conjurer . . . the easier to spot the trick."[5]

Such sentiments articulate an image of Islam and the Prophet that is surely insulting. To say that these feelings are the malign products of Farishta's hardly balanced mind is true but unconvincing to sincere believers. In their common-sense judgement, Rushdie is the final author of these lines and thoughts. When he leaves the traditional interpretation of Islam and explicitly invents, Rushdie invariably has his characters say things that can and do cause offense.

No writer worth his salt is ever innocent, and Rushdie is one of the least innocent of the new group of third world authors presently pushing the boundaries of the English language to the limit. Innocence, which means a lack of experience and reflection, is a liability of the first order—in a serious writer. Rushdie may have underestimated the impact of his history of Islam on his Muslim readers, but in the light of his two previous novels, which show him to be a fastidious and deliberate writer, he cannot plead the kind of innocence he now seems to be claiming.

No matter how self-conscious a particular writer's craft, his literary imagination assumes concrete form in a specific cultural and public space. Writers write in identifiable political and spiritual contexts, and their writing is necessarily appropriated in terms of the discourses that constitute these contexts. In Rushdie's case, the Islamic standpoint on literary liberty and the commanding Western disposition towards the Muslim Orient impinge centrally on the way we read *Satanic Verses*. What Rushdie writes are not merely complex, dense works of fiction but fictional political tracts suffused with investigations of the politics of exile, identity, religion, ethics, racism, and so forth.

*Satanic Verses* was plunged into bitter controversy precisely because, written in a Western language for a Western or Westernised audience, it asserted a skeptical, cynical thesis about Islam that played into and reinforced the rampant, contemptuous, crusading anti-Islamism that has seized the leaders and populace of the Western world in the wake of the Iranian revolution. That it was written by a Muslim author celebrated by the literati in the West, that it invoked standard Orientalist cliches in its descriptions of the Prophet ("Mahound") and of the Muslim faithful and the Imam biding his time in London, as medieval figures hostile to modernity, history and reason, lent further authority to the Western calumnies against Islam.

In Islam generally, and in Iran particularly, politics and religion are conceptually intertwined. Ayatollah Khomeini's furious reaction to *Satanic Verses* was a traditional Muslim response simultaneously political and religious, though separable for analytical purposes. Politically, Khomeini was incensed by what he saw as a political assault on Islam and the Prophet in a book published and supported by the West in a climate in which Westerners universally denigrate Muslims. The novel legitimated Western antipathy to Islam.

From the strictly Islamic standpoint, Rushdie's secular, irreverent dissection of the beginnings of the faith and of the Prophet's motives is, in the words of a leading scholar of Islam, Bernard Lewis, "tantamount to apostasy. Apostasy for all schools of classical Islamic jurisprudence is a capital offense."[6] In principle Khomeini's high-handed death sentence on Rushdie was within the bounds of classical Muslim law, but he was only half-right: Muslim law explicitly specifies that the accused person should be brought to trial, allowed to defend himself and should then be sentenced if he is found guilty.[7]

In the Muslim tradition, literature is not only highly prized, it is ranked at the zenith of Islamic arts. Muslim writers have a fair amount of leeway in the use of imagination, but fairly clear limits circumscribe literary liberty. Since Islam is the foundation of Muslim religion as well as Muslim culture and the Muslim way of life, its literary writers are compelled to head the transcendental leitmotif that suffuses Muslim thought and practice. Nor can they pretend that literature has no impact on Muslim self-understanding and on the cultural life of the Muslim community. Muslims, like Jews, tend to see life whole and consistently, not as a clump of disconnected, self-enclosed compartments.[8]

Khomeini's fury was in part the authentic rage of a Muslim against a fellow-Muslim who had poisoned, in his merciless judgment, the wells of the communal faith worldwide. Rushdie had failed to understand his position as a Muslim, as a member of the faith. As Wilfred Cantwell Smith points out, "Membership in the community is not something distinct from, or added to, is not simply consequent upon, but is an aspect of personal Islam."[9] In Khomeini's eyes, Rushdie had deliberately violated the sanctity of the Muslim community; he had insultingly renounced his citizenship in the Muslim cosmopolis. Rushdie, though a Muslim by birth, had tried to say in the *Satanic Verses* what is inconceivable and makes no sense to Muslims generally: that he was no longer a Muslim, that he was abandoning his origins. Rushdie has not understood this elementary fact about the Islamic view of Muslims.

To many Muslims, Khomeini's death sentence was uncalled for and unnecessary, even bizarre, but one suspects they all understood the reasons that led him to vent his fury.

3

For the vast majority in the West, the overriding issue in the Rushdie affair was his freedom to write as he pleased,

his liberty to unleash his imagination, on any subject of his own choosing. John Stuart Mill and Voltaire, among other luminaries, were pressed into service. Nothing else was remotely relevant: Rushdie's freedom as an author was (ironically) sacred and absolute, and it was defended with unflinching zeal. The argument was postulated, predictably, in terms of liberal democracy and the protracted ordeal of the enlightened West in securing this and other freedoms for itself and mankind.[10] Nothing was said, naturally, of how severely restricted this liberty was for so many on the fringes of liberal-capitalist democracies, or for radical writers such as Noam Chomsky and Israel Shahak who tackled such taboo subjects as U.S. imperialism, Israeli oppression of the Palestinians, and so on.

A few hardy intellectuals with the gumption to dissent from the collective outpourings of freedom's frontline soldiers, managed to surface. For instance, J. P. Stern defended liberty but was compelled to say that he was "reluctant and deeply troubled" because of what the novel implied about Islam. Edward Mortimer observed that Rushdie "must have known when he wrote *The Satanic Verses,* that many Muslims would be unable to take the novel in the playful, sardonic spirit in which it was apparently meant. . . . By naming the book and the characters as he did, Mr. Rushdie courted such a reaction."[11]

Khomeini's lethal pronouncement *was* infuriating, but it occurred to hardly any of Rushdie's defenders that Muslims just might have a rational case: the stalwarts of secular modernity seemed incapable of even imagining the depth of the outrage felt by Muslims, let alone understanding it. In liberty's name hoary, medieval insults against Islam, Iran and Muslims flooded liberal journals, their language and tone vigorously Orientalist: Muslims were at bottom uncivilized, barbarian, irrational, violent, crazed, and of course fundamentalist.

It was not really so surprising that these Western liberals were so illiberal, so imperious in their attitude to Islam and Muslims. Liberal hostility to religion, a legacy of the post-Enlightenment ethic, is legendary. Muslim attachment to the transcendent and the spiritual is beyond their modernist sensibility and intrinsically incomprehensible.

In Islam's case, Western liberal contempt is specially acute because it is buttressed by a Western tradition of suspicion and political fear of Islam that has been part of the Western *weltanschauung* since the Crusades. As the classical scholar Peter Brown succinctly noted, "no other non-European civilization has been so persistently gagged and bridled by European stereotypes as has Islam."[12] In *Satanic Verses,* Rushdie seems to have espoused these very damaging stereotypes.

For a writer who identifies with the third world, and with the predicament of third world citizens of the west, Rushdie's Orientalist musings seem unintelligible. To raise critical questions about evil proclivities in Islam, to query the moral texture of the Prophet's mission, to imply that the evil that occurs in South Asia is equivalent to the evil of British racism, to insinuate that Muslim believers are naturally reactionary—to raise and then slide over such controversial issues within an international political context saturated with contempt for the faith and the people of Islam, is to commit an act of literary injustice against Muslims.

Rushdie's questions are philosophical and scholarly, unanswerable in a novel, and not the kind he is intellectually equipped to answer. A writer of great fiction who has penetrating insights is not necessarily a practiced scholar. Rushdie, thoroughly secular and post-modern, has the leftist's ideological antipathy to religion, but his mental style is Nietzschean. He is an anti-foundationalist who thinks that there are no absolute or stable truths: everything is fluid and shifting, everything in principle is questionable, and presumably permissible, as Nietzsche discovered.

Leftist Nietzscheanism has its radical uses in dismantling and displacing the Western discourses of mastery and oppression of the third world, and in unmasking native discourses of domination within the third world. Rushdie is entirely justified in lambasting corruption and inhumanity in Muslim nations, and he is right in excoriating the abuses of power by Muslims under the cover of their religion.

But Islam, the faith of nearly one billion human beings, is not a doctrine of injustice. In Wilfred Cantwell Smith's words:

> Surely the Islamic enterprise has been the most serious and sustained endeavour ever put forward to implement Justice among men; and until the rise of Marxism was also the largest and the most ambitious.[13]

Nor was the Prophet, venerated by millions of Muslims, a mountebank—the Mahound of the medieval Christian imagination. For Rushdie to speculate, in his fictional *Satanic Verses,* that the Prophet may be the real author of the Quran, or that he was possibly immoral in his personal and public conduct, is a colossal *faux pas,* aesthetically and intellectually.

Post-modernism, the fashionable leading edge of contemporary scholarship, has been a positive development insofar as it has led to a revaluation of the entrenched epistemologies, and to a radical understanding of the politics of knowledge and theorizing in the social sciences and the humanities. Third world studies and third world scholars in particular have benefitted considerably from post-modernism's scrutiny of the West's privileging of its own values, and the consequent claim that it was the responsibility of the West to instruct and police the non-European world.

Yet post-modernism's limitations are obvious, philosophically and ethically. The absence of permanent ground on which to structure national or international values, the lack of some notion of the transcendent on which to base a theory of human rights, as distinct from a tenuous and malleable humanism, has made it very difficult, if not impossible, to fashion a universally common and credible ethics which all nationalities can accept as minimally rational and humane.

If ambiguity was the typical impulse of late modernism, radical uncertainty and radical unclarity is the typical stance of post-modernism. Salman Rushdie's *Satanic Verses,* both in its literary accomplishments and its moral mistakes, is an authentic product of this post-modernist sensibility. Rushdie offers no vision of the good society, no sketch of truths from which such a global polity might emerge.

NOTES

[1] Salman Rushdie, "Last Chance?", *Index on Censorship* (December 1983), p. 2.

[2] Salman Rushdie, "The New Empire within Britain", in *New Society,* (December 9, 1982), pp. 417-420; see also the response to Rushdie by Lincoln Allison in the same journal, January 13, 1983; pp. 53-54. For another English reaction to Rushdie's general view on Britain and India, see Richard West, "Rushdie and the Raj", in the *Spectator* (April 7, 1984), pp. 18-19.

[3] Salman Rushdie, *The Satanic Verses* (New York: Viking, 1988).

[4] *Ibid.,* p. 399.

[5] *Ibid.,* p. 363.

[6] Bernard Lewis, "Rushdie and the Law of Islam," in the *Manchester Guardian Weekly,* March 5, 1989, p. 18.

[7] *Ibid.*

[8] For a discussion of these points, see James Kritzeck (ed.), *Anthology of Islamic Literature* (New York: Mentor, 1964), introduction pp. 15-26; Seyyed Hossein Nasr, "Reflections on Islam and Modern Thought," *Studies in Comparative Religion* (Summer-Autumn, 1983), pp. 164-176; Wilfred Cantwell Smith, *Islam in Modern History* (New York: Mentor, 1957), Chs. 1 and 2.

[9] Cantwell Smith, *Islam in Modern History,* p. 27, *passim.*

[10] For representative examples of this defense, see the editorial, "Two Cheers for Blasphemy" *New Republic* (March 13, 1989), pp. 7-9, and Carlos Fuentes' reflections on this affair, *Manchester Guardian Weekly* (March 5, 1989), pp. 8-9.

[11] J. P. Stern, "By any Other Name," *Manchester Guardian Weekly* (February 26, 1989), p. 25, and excerpts from the piece by Edward Mortimer, London *Financial Times* reproduced in the editorial in *New Republic,* cited in note 10.

[12] Peter Brown, "Understanding Islam," *New York Review of Books* (February 22, 1979), pp. 31-33. For excellent

analyses of the Muslim–Western Christian relationship since the Crusades, see Norman Daniel, *Islam and the West: The Making of an Image* (Edinburgh: Edinburgh University Press, 1960) and R. W. Southern, *Western Views of Islam in the Middle Ages* (Cambridge: Harvard University Press, 1962). For a polemical, humanist critique of Western discourse on Islam, see Edward Said, *Orientalism* (New York: Vintage, 1979).

[13] Cantwell Smith, *Islam in Modern History,* p. 32.

# LATIN AMERICA

### Gene H. Bell

SOURCE: "Borges—Literature and Politics North and South," in *The Nation,* New York, Vol. 222, No. 7, February 21, 1976, pp. 213-17.

[*In the following essay, Bell discusses Jorge Luis Borges's literary output during a fifteen-year period of personal and political crisis, and assesses his subsequent influence on North American literary and cultural theory.*]

I

Surveying the sum total of Borges's works, one is struck by a kind of "bulge" at approximately the middle of his career. This bulge constitutes the relatively brief spell—1939 to the middle 1950s—during which the Argentine writer produced the stories gathered in *Ficciones* and *El Aleph,* as well as the prose parables in *Dreamtigers.* Until then, Borges had published many of his strangely provocative essays and some lovely books of verse—but little as yet of universal import. Years later, during the 1960s and 1970s, well after his writing career had reached its peak, he reaped the benefits of his sudden and deserved fame, living the life of a much-esteemed public figure, journeying from podium to podium, prize to prize—and meanwhile issuing the anti-climactic narratives of *Doctor Brodie's Report* or playful trifles like *The Book of Imaginary Beings.* What is noteworthy about those luminous fifteen years—the *Ficciones* and *El Aleph* years—is that they closely coincide with a biographical and historical moment, a specific period of acute, seemingly endless crises in Borges's life as well as in the larger world itself.

In 1937, at the age of 38, Borges started work as a cataloguer in a dreary suburban library. Borges somehow spent nine years in that shabby place, earning very little, doing pointless tasks amid what seems to have been an unpleasant crew of Philistines. It was Borges's first regular job, and his only extended encounter with the coarse world of non-literature. But his troubles had only begun.

In February 1938, Borges's father died. In December, Borges himself was injured in a fall from a stairway and nearly died of blood poisoning. Upon recovering, Borges began writing his greatest works—though, ironically, these went largely unrecognized for more than a decade, the annual prizes regularly going to authors far below his level. Borges has never forgiven or forgotten this last fact.

Beyond these personal troubles there was the growing socio-political nightmare. From 1930 onward, the Fascist wave abroad—in itself distressing for a Borges sympathetic to liberal Europe—had set in motion a number of local equivalents. In contrast to the rest of Spanish America, which was passively in favor of the Allies, an idiosyncratic political militarism was to arise in Argentina. Perhaps less pro-German than it was anti-English, it was in some degree swept to power by widespread anti-imperialist (i.e., anti-British) sentiment, culminating finally in the right-wing military populism of Perón. For though the political outlook of the *peronista* and other officers' sects of the time was more or less corporative-nationalist rather than left-wing socialist, they drew a significant amount of support by their opposition to British capitalism—a key issue in a country long dominated by English finance.

As was inevitable under a right-wing nationalist regime, those mildly liberal, pro-English (the labels roughly overlap) sectors of Argentine society were subjected to cultural isolation and political harassment. The Borges family had ties with precisely this grouping. (Borges's grandmother was English; his grandfather had fought on the liberal side in the 19th-century civil wars; and his father had taught in a British school.) At the outset of Perón's Presidency, Borges was dismissed from his library post. A clerk at City Hall explained to him, "Well, you were on the Allies' side, what do you expect?" The government later had Borges shadowed by the police; on various occasions, Borges's mother, sister, and nephew were actually put in prison.

Borges understandably looks back on these fifteen years as his worst. The events must have seemed shocking to a 38-year-old man of letters, one whose pleasantly *aisé* existence hitherto had seldom been ruffled by cares other than literary. Then came boring work and unpleasant company, bereavement and near-death, forced cultural isolation, political persecution. The piling up of disagreeable experiences no doubt appeared to him irrational, beyond comprehension.

Such were the circumstances under which Borges brought out his greatest stories. From his vantage point of chaos—his altered family situation, a miserable job, and an anti-Liberal dictatorship—creating the stories served him as his concrete means of organized defense. The act of writing the *Ficciones* and *El Aleph* is thus a classic instance of literature thriving in an adversary role, nourished by a struggle against untoward personal and political conditions. The subjective attitude of Borges the man is of course a complex matter, but in its literary version there are two noteworthy components: a nostalgia for combat in the past, and a learned and urbane liberalism vis-à-vis the present. It is highly significant that Borges's best knife stories, with 19th-century heroism as their subjects, were written at the height of the military-populist dictatorship in Argentina. In such a context the stories assume a character of subtle protest, of opposition through counter-example: the true courage of the days of Republican Argentina (a time when the Borges family, and its values, were at their peak of class dominance) stands in implicit contrast to the shabby, dictatorial 1940s (when the economically ruined Borges family, together with their social allies, were politically deprived).

Far better known is the opposition stance exemplified by Borges in his richest, most celebrated tales of fantasy. In "Tlön, Uqbar, Orbis Tertius" the narrator looks back on the lure, during the 1930s, of such false and facile "symmetries"—as in his words—"dialectical materialism, anti-Semitism, Nazism," all of which have culminated in the reigning hysteria over the planet Tlön. Impervious to, but alone amid these omnipresent Idealisms, the narrator finds silent refuge in Sir Thomas Browne's *Urn Burial,* an evocatively nostalgic work on classical archaeology. (The easy juxtaposition of Nazism with Marxism may suggest the extent of Borges's acquaintance with the latter.)

This essentially is the apology of the civilized man of letters, the cultivated gentleman who, in a time of social upheaval, can side neither with the rebels nor with the reactionaries; experientially removed from the arena of social battles, lacking even the political information available in books, he dismisses Left and Right as equally false, unaware of how untenable his position is, though perfectly well aware of his irrelevance, in a crumbling social panorama. Ironically, Borges's fanciful view of the Hitler decade is itself an Idealist intellectual's interpretation. It sees the political turmoil as being brought about not by economic dislocations but by the mass appeal of a few seductive ideas—recalling those old-fashioned historians who felt that the French Revolution was "caused" by the writings of Rousseau and Voltaire. For all of Borges's artfulness and sophistication, the dizzying final paragraphs of "Tlön, Uqbar, Orbis Tertius" ultimately reflect the bewildered middle-way position of 1930s moderates, who, while fearful of the Axis, for ideological reasons were unwilling to make common cause with the anti-Fascist Left, tending instead to brush off both sides and label them fanatics.

Much the same spirit informs the last few pages of "The Library at Babel." There the narrator-librarian surveys a universe beset by ignorance, violence and plague, by ideological splintering and a tired sense that all has been said—much as Europe and Argentina must have appeared to Borges in 1941. The narrator, in need of reassurance, finds consolation in the fact of the Library itself, its untapped riches, its order, its grandeur. The story, unlike "Tlön, Uqbar, Orbis Tertius," avoids any explicit social or political judgments, focusing instead on an epistemological question. Rather than attack the Right and the

Left as equally and hopelessly Utopian, it depicts the scientific search for knowledge as futile and pointless. Though certain fundamental truths about the Library-Universe are occasionally hit upon—such as the decisive discovery that twenty-five letters form the basic components of all the books—these only whet people's appetite, giving rise to feverish quests for more knowledge, about one's self and about the cosmos, finally generating social division and personal despair. The truth seekers, unfortunately, cannot grasp what the narrator knows: that the Universe is "infinite," "useless" and "secret." The note on which the story ends is thus intellectual quietism rather than explicit social conservatism. But then, since in this story the Library is the world, to cease seeking to uncover its laws does correspond to social withdrawal.

This is the muted agony of an essentially traditionalist intellectual, a nostalgic man of letters whose world has become opaque, incomprehensible, and whose readings in the cultural heritage of a happier, more stable past furnish him no concrete hold on the present, when things crumble; he then projects his own historical bewilderment onto others. Borges's philosophical nihilism by no means enjoys universal acceptance, however. Views such as these can scarcely characterize a practicing politician or a research scientist. And the fact is that Borges, his celebrated erudition notwithstanding, is scarcely informed about natural science—its mode of knowing, its praxis—while his sense of 20th-century social thought is particularly limited. Even Freud's discoveries Borges has shrugged off as the ravings of "a kind of madman," and in a 1945 essay Borges actually puts Freud in the same camp with the Nazis and assorted modern barbarians. In his nonliterary readings, Borges amuses himself with mystics, rather likes Jung and dabbles in Schopenhauer—speculative thinkers who spun highly provocative fancies and conceits, but whose contributions in the way of significant knowledge are in the end minimal.

These and other darkly brooding tales, written during a time of personal torment for Borges, of political struggles in Europe and Argentina, demonstrably exist due to the prompting of these larger crises. The proof of this is that when Borges finally emerged from his woes in 1955, his work began losing its textural and philosophic richness. By the same token, little of Borges's output before 1938 suggests the future writer of fiction of worldwide and revolutionary impact. It is probable that, had Borges not been compelled to undergo these unsettling experiences, he would have remained what he had been until his middle 30s: a good and fairly interesting poet, erudite and skilled, a talented literary gentleman much like others of his kind, those numerous upper-class Latin American men of letters who write a certain amount of excellent verse and seldom attain major stature. (Although there are critics who try to make a case for Borges as the poetic equal of Neruda or Paz, that is wishful thinking. Borges's poetry is nostalgically neat but narrow, intellectually fanciful but slightly prosy, touchingly warm but lacking in larger passions.) Similarly, the earlier essays, though filled with fresh insights and conceits, are still the work of an eccentric genius who has not yet hit upon his most fitting medium and subject matter.

Borges's sudden leap into literary greatness around 1940, then, appears to have been catalyzed by a freak situation, the unique congruence of his personal crisis with an unusual historical moment—that of the period of the 1930s and 1940s, when the liberal, Anglophile upper class in Argentina was under siege by a mass movement of the Right—much as were the liberal anti-Fascist forces in Europe. When, with the anti-Perón coup of 1955, the struggle against the populist Right came to an end, the notorious spiritual sterility of the old upper-class milieu reasserted itself. Since then, it has reverted, in its sociopolitical preoccupations, to orthodox anti-communism, an ideology well-known for the vacuity of its intellectual products. Borges himself has shared in the political crudities of that social nucleus, even to the point of signing petitions favoring the Bay of Pigs invaders, pleading for the execution of Régis Debray in Bolivia, dedicating a book to Richard Nixon and quietly supporting the Onganía dictatorship in the 1960s.

Whatever the limitations of his early and late phases, Borges's innovations in the Spanish language and in prose fiction give rise to a Latin American literary movement that is still in force. He is the prime mover in that impressive series of novels which includes Cortázar's *Hopscotch,* García Márquez's *One Hundred Years of Solitude* and Cabrera Infante's *Three Trapped Tigers.* As Carlos Fuentes remarked, without Borges the modern Latin American novel simply would not exist. Nonetheless, at the same time that Borges's work initiates a new literary period, it also signals a culmination, perhaps an ending to an earlier, lengthier social and cultural era, that of the domination of Latin America by its Europhile, moderately liberal upper classes. It is one of those ironies of history that this social milieu—so often legitimately criticized, so remote from basic human concerns, from those larger struggles which can nourish great art—accidentally found itself during the 1930s and 1940s in a position of active opposition to the national and international Right, and holding the view that the latter is the greatest threat to civilization. It was the first time since the days of the Rosas dictatorship that Argentina's pro-English liberals had been politically victimized and thereby drawn into the broad arena of their nation's conflicts. And, as in the Rosas days, the so-called "Second Dictatorship" gave rise to a formidable, impressive literature on the part of the opposition. Borges's best stories, which exalt the old Europe of humane letters, and evoke a lost, courageous 19th-century Argentina in which knives figure in place of guns, are the greatest literary works to emerge from the historical myths and longings of Argentina's old upper class.

Significantly, the novelists that have followed in Borges's wake have for the most part no personal links with his preferred social arrangements, their values and practices. Products of the urban middle class rather than the rural old-rich, they have depended not on family money or aristocratic patronage but on full-time work in such fields as teaching, translating, clerking, journalism and diplomacy. Their literary sources and subjects also differ substantially from those familiar Borgesian themes—on the one hand gaucho wistfulness, on the other Western culture under siege by the barbarians, by raiders of libraries, by vandals under the spell of Nazism, Marxism, Freudism, Peronism, Tlönism. . . . Julio Cortázar, for example, draws freely on French thought and surrealism, on anthropology and jazz. In another vein, Manuel Puig, Cabrera Infante and the younger Mexicans have found a locus of their own in films and Pop culture, while García Márquez, Fuentes and Vargas Llosa are varyingly influenced by Faulkner, Spanish American regionalism and Marx. Borges's urbane, erudite concern for minor Edwardians and the glories of Western civilization must appear quaint and irrelevant to these novelists—however much they admire his literary achievement.

II

The impact of Borges on American writing may be almost as great as was his earlier influence in Latin America. The American 1950s were a desert, a bleak stretch relieved only by one or two entertainments by Nabokov; for barrenness few literary epochs can match the cold-war years. The quiet arrival of Borges's Englished fictions was to make a difference for the 1960s; his dreamlike artifices helped to stimulate a writing culture steeped in WASP-suburban metaphysics and Jewish neo-realism. The Argentine master reawakened for us the possibilities of far-fetched fancy, of formal exploration, of parody, intellectuality and wit. There are fantasies by Coover and Barthelme scarcely conceivable without the originating presence of Borges; allusions to the latter appear in Pynchon; and the longer novels of Barth are shaped in great degree by a theory of parody derived from Borges.

Still, Borges's fame in the United States shows nuances of difference from his reputation in Latin America. For one thing, his standing in our country is much higher, both in relative and absolute terms. Curiously enough, no other Latin American author of fiction has caught on with comparable force, even though the Spanish-speaking continent now boasts numerous novelists as eminent in their respective fields as Borges once was in his. Most North American literary types at least know of Borges, while relatively few have heard of Cortázar, García Márquez, Carpentier, Fuentes, Vargas Llosa. It is an added irony, moreover, that the peak of the Borges cult on the American campus came at a time—the late 1960s and early 1970s—when the younger authors of the Hispanic world had for more than a decade simply assumed the existence of Borges and gone beyond him—indeed, when Borges's work had become less of a revolution, an innovation, a surprise, and had assumed its rightful place in the Latin American literary landscape.

There are identifiable reasons for the somewhat lopsided quality of Borges's American fame, some purely circumstantial, others profoundly historical, "political." Among the former reasons one must note Borges's simple physical presence in those 1960s, crowded years when he delivered literally hundreds of lectures across the land, and in fine English, with a fluency equaled by few Latin American authors, whose second language is more often French. It is a reasonable guess that most of Borges's serious United States readers have actually heard him speak on some occasion—a wish not to be realized by, say, Cortázar or Beckett devotees. Similarly, Borges's willingness to talk with all manner of interviewers has given him further visibility, planting his name in national weeklies and newspapers as well as in drugstore paperbacks and "little" magazines. All this could not help but stimulate interest; it gave Borges enthusiasts some sense of having real ties with him, of knowing him more than as an authorial abstraction, while people who had not read Borges found their curiosity aroused by these reminders of his existence. Probably no other non-English-language author of recent times has been so much in the American limelight. Finally, Borges's childlike pro-Americanism—surpassed only of late by Solzhenitsyn's—inevitably flattered his audiences, enhanced his acceptability with Americans who would be easily discomfited by the anti-imperialism of a García Márquez or a Carpentier.

But there are social facts and institutional forces which contribute just as significantly to Borges's influence in America. Among these is the vastness of the North American academic subculture—more colleges and universities than there are in all of Europe, let alone in Latin America. Many of these schools were quite rich during the 1960s, and could pay Borges well for the myriad seminars and lectures (so many talks, in fact, that he inevitably repeated himself). Even more important, here was a bookish author with a great deal of obscure erudition, an Argentinian Eliot-Pound-Joyce whom several hundred Spanish professors could carefully explicate in their classes and weave about him a network of articles in two or three dozen special-interest journals—articles which were read by thousands of graduate students, who then wrote papers derived from those articles and set their sights on being future authors of articles on Borges. The nature of this Argentine author's *oeuvre* is such that it generated a new professional specialty and came to play a well-established part in the American publishing machine, like Chaucer anthologies or Chinese cookbooks. And although general interest in Borges has subsided somewhat, the managers of the Borges market continue to produce reviews and *Festschriften,* holding seminars and symposia in which Borges's work is dealt with as a self-contained entity, to be considered in a vacuum, ahistorically, as if the two books he wrote thirty years ago were still a prime issue in Latin American writing.

Aside from the decisive boost given Borges by academia, however, there is the deeper role of the stories themselves, the uses to which their meanings lend themselves. For, while the stylistic and formal manner of Borges gave the literary professionals a task to perform, on the other hand the content of *Ficciones* supplied his readers with a precise political optics, a cluster of historical attitudes, a

mode of social feeling that helped strengthen and define their ideological posture. During the 1960s the United States was torn by social conflict: riots in the ghetto, a hopeless war in Asia and the campus revolts ultimately created by that war. In this disorderly picture (comparable to that of Europe in the 1930s or Argentina in the 1940s) Borges's artifices provided a defense for those American academics who were as confused by the whole spectacle as our informant on Tlön or the librarian at Babel are bewildered by the sinister forces they evoke. Departmental chairmen, professors pushing the New Criticism, apolitical novelists like John Updike all shared a vague, inarticulate opposition to the war in Indochina, combined with an inability to sympathize with the highly vocal anti-war Left. They found in Borges's nightmares a sophisticated, inspired, vividly argued affirmation of their own position—i.e., an urbane aloofness, a middle-way quietism, a studied, even-handed, occasionally snobbish indifference to Right and Left, and in this case to the physical slaughter of the war and to the moral anger of the opposition activists. The literary people, in their alienation from, and ignorance of, the political situation, carved out for themselves—as do Borges's raconteurs—a refuge in seminars and old books, in the monumental libraries of the American university system. For, just as at the end of "Tlön, Uqbar, Orbis Tertius" the narrator shuts his eyes to politics and hides in his Quevedian translation of Sir Thomas Browne, in like manner some professors of the 1960s took their stand in the past, in the great traditions of the West, that accumulated store of rich and complex culture which, during those years, irate radicals and blacks on the one hand, and weekly body counts and B-52 strikes on the other, seemed to have rendered marginal, useless, "irrelevant."

That our literary milieus found in Borges's fiction not only a peculiar artistic greatness but a useful social content as well, becomes clearer when one considers the comparatively small following thus gained in the United States by other Latin Americans. The fact is that, though García Márquez, Cortázar or Carpentier are comparable major artists—whose novels are read throughout the Spanish-speaking world, well received by North American reviewers, and intensely examined by professional Hispanists (who often as not miss the social meaning of their books)—they have not generated the cult, let alone the academic market, enjoyed here by Borges.

Part of the explanation for this must lie in the unsettling tone and content of these authors' works. The atmosphere of threat in Borges's tales comes off as bookish and abstract when contrasted, say, with the more concretely physical horrors in the stories of Julio Cortázar. The latter's *Hopscotch* puts into question the very value of European thought and learning; and his Dadaistic *Cronopios*—a commercial failure here—tweaks the nose of bourgeois respectability by disrupting routine. Alejo Carpentier's close affiliation with the Castro government could hardly promote his standing in the United States. His best-known novel, *The Lost Steps,* is built on a suggestion that "Europe," with all her rich culture, may be far more barbaric than the Indians of Venezuela—a notion contemplated by but a fringe of educated Americans; and *Explosion in a Cathedral* pins down the various ideological nuances and posturings brought into being by revolution—an experience too remote for most American liberals who, with their relatively conflict-free history, tend toward political consensus and compromise.

Similarly, García Márquez's *One Hundred Years of Solitude,* one of the great novels of our time, has failed to arouse any literary excitement comparable to that inspired by the works of Borges. Again, however, the politics—anti-Americanism, pro-revolutionism—embedded within the texture of that book probably puts off and excludes a fair number of American readers. Moreover, García Márquez's humane, understanding portraits of his characters, so unlike the "literary" aura surrounding Borges's gauchos and hoods, probably meets with a certain amount of cultural incomprehension, even condescension, on the part of readers whose attitudes of superiority have everything to do with the generally low status of Latin American immigrants in this country. Finally, the novels of Fuentes and Vargas Llosa, steeped as they are in Marxist concepts, must inevitably fall on deaf ears with an American public largely hostile or indifferent to or ignorant of the cluster of issues raised by that strand of thought.

None of this diminishes Borges's stature as a literary artist. There were aspects both modish and ideological to his American fame in the 1960s but the intrinsic worth of his contribution is now accepted. His stories, moreover, have a special significance in that they clear the way for numerous literary trends on both American continents, determining the shape of much fiction to come. In his part of the world, Borges's meticulous use of language—his careful construction of each sentence, his strict avoidance of Hispanic bombast, his cool understatement—has revolutionized Spanish prose; he thus stands in the same relation to current Latin novelists as Flaubert once did to numerous authors in Europe. At the same time, by rejecting realism and naturalism, he has opened up to our Northern writers a virgin field, led them to a wealth of new subjects and procedures—in a word, provided an alternative to Updike and Bellow. In successfully transcending the old modes of representation and discourse, Borges has accidentally done for us a job previously performed elsewhere by Poe, the fantast from a "barbarous," backward land who, by way of Baudelaire, freed French verse from its classic and romantic dead weights.

The art of every author has also its social origins and functions, however, and Borges's stories, as we have seen, emerged in their time from the anti-fascism *cum* anti-communism of Argentina's liberal Anglophile upper class. Later, this outlook, masterfully given shape in Borges's best books, furnished artistic fuel for the supine anti-war and hostile anti-Left politics of our 1960s literati. Hence, besides being a catalyst, a Poe to our new writers, Borges took on a conserving function, one allotted earlier to Camus, who deemed life absurd, history a nightmare, and action meaningless, preaching as man's sole path to salvation an indulgent metaphysics of subjectivity. The 1960s were too angry, too rough to be soothed by so callow a pessimism; Borges furnished a more concrete and objective stance, one built on more than personal feeling. To what he and others perceived as a mindless Left, and knowledge and history without hope or meaning, Borges gallantly counterpoised a consolation through books, through the verbal treasures of the past.

The 1970s are a rather different matter, what with universities in the doldrums, enthusiasm for "pure" learning on the wane, students shying away from literature, and a widespread skepticism about personal salvation through art. There is no war, no strife, but the *status quo,* less persuasive than it was some years ago, needs a more fitting advocate to prop up its image. After being badly bruised in Asia, the non-Left American reader wants a less sophisticated, less urbane, less witty anti-communism, one that doesn't cloud things up with mental fancies or old books, wastes no time on right-wing threats as well; the system now needs a sterner, more openly "political" conservatism that will drown out the din of American violence abroad and proffer arguments against the political disillusionment back home. That function seems, for now, to have been assigned to Solzhenitsyn.

## Mario Vargas Llosa

SOURCE: "Social Commitment and the Latin American Writer," in *World Literature Today,* Vol. 52, No. 1, Winter, 1978, pp. 6-14.

[*In the following essay, Llosa explains the obligation Latin American writers feel to be not only artists but political activists as well.*]

The Peruvian novelist José María Arguedas killed himself on the second day of December 1969 in a classroom of La Molina Agricultural University in Lima. He was a very discreet man, and so as not to disturb his colleagues and the students with his suicide, he waited until everybody had left the place. Near his body was found a letter with very detailed instructions about his burial—where he should be mourned, who should pronounce the eulogies in the cemetery—and he asked too that an Indian musician friend of his play the *huaynos* and *mulizas* he was fond of. His will was respected, and Arguedas, who had been, when he was alive, a very modest and shy man, had a very spectacular burial.

But some days later other letters written by him appeared, little by little. They too were different aspects of his last will, and they were addressed to very different people: his publisher, friends, journalists, academics, politicians. The main subject of these letters was his death, of course, or better, the reasons for which he decided to kill himself. These reasons changed from letter to letter. In one of them he said that he had decided to commit suicide because he felt that he was finished as writer, that he no longer had the impulse and the will to create. In another he gave moral, social and political reasons: he could no longer stand the misery and neglect of the Peruvian peasants, those people of the Indian communities among whom he had been raised; he lived oppressed and anguished by the crises of the cultural and educational life in the country; the low level and abject nature of the press and the caricature of liberty in Peru were too much for him, et cetera.

In these dramatic letters we follow, naturally, the personal crises that Arguedas had been going through, and they are the desperate call of a suffering man who, at the edge of the abyss, asks mankind for help and compassion. But they are not only that: a clinical testimony. At the same time, they are graphic evidence of the situation of the writer in Latin America, of the difficulties and pressures of all sorts that have surrounded and oriented and many times destroyed the literary vocation in our countries.

In the USA, in Western Europe, to be a writer means, generally, first (and usually only) to assume a personal responsibility. That is, the responsibility to achieve in the most rigorous and authentic way a work which, for its artistic values and originality, enriches the language and culture of one's country. In Peru, in Bolivia, in Nicaragua et cetera, on the contrary, to be a writer means, at the same time, to assume a social responsibility: at the same time that you develop a personal literary work, you should serve, through your writing but also through your actions, as an active participant in the solution of the economic, political and cultural problems of your society. There is no way to escape this obligation. If you tried to do so, if you were to isolate yourself and concentrate exclusively on your own work, you would be severely censured and considered, in the best of cases, irresponsible and selfish, or at worst, even by omission, an accomplice to all the evils—illiteracy, misery, exploitation, injustice, prejudice—of your country and against which you have refused to fight. In the letters which he wrote once he had prepared the gun with which he was to kill himself, Arguedas was trying, in the last moments of his life, to fulfill this moral imposition that impels all Latin American writers to social and political commitment.

Why is it like this? Why cannot writers in Latin America, like their American and European colleagues, be artists, and only artists? Why must they also be reformers, politicians, revolutionaries, moralists? The answer lies in the social conditions of Latin America, the problems which face our countries. All countries have problems, of course, but in many parts of Latin America, both in the past and in the present, the problems which constitute the closest daily reality for people are not freely discussed and analyzed in public, but are usually denied and silenced. There are no means through which those problems can be presented and denounced, because the social and political establishment exercises a strict censorship of the media and over all the communications systems. For example, if today you hear Chilean broadcasts or see Argentine television, you won't hear a word about the political prisoners, about the exiles, about the torture,

about the violations of human rights in those two countries that have outraged the conscience of the world. You will, however, be carefully informed, of course, about the iniquities of the communist countries. If you read the daily newspapers of my country, for instance—which have been confiscated by the government, which now controls them—you will not find a word about the continuous arrests of labor leaders or about the murderous inflation that affects everyone. You will read only about what a happy and prosperous country Peru is and how much we Peruvians love our military rulers.

What happens with the press, TV and radio happens too, most of the time, with the universities. The government persistently interferes with them; teachers and students considered subversive or hostile to the official system are expelled and the whole curriculum reorganized according to political considerations. As an indication of what extremes of absurdity this "cultural policy" can reach, you must remember, for instance, that in Argentina, in Chile and in Uruguay the Departments of Sociology have been closed indefinitely, because the social sciences are considered subversive. Well, if academic institutions submit to this manipulation and censorship, it is improbable that contemporary political, social and economic problems of the country can be described and discussed freely. Academic knowledge in many Latin American countries is, like the press and the media, a victim of the deliberate turning away from what is actually happening in society. This vacuum has been filled by literature.

This is not a recent phenomenon. Even during the Colonial Period, though more especially since Independence (in which intellectuals and writers played an important role), all over Latin America novels, poems and plays were—as Stendhal once said he wanted the novel to be—the mirrors in which Latin Americans could truly see their faces and examine their sufferings. What was, for political reasons, repressed or distorted in the press and in the schools and universities, all the evils that were buried by the military and economic elite which ruled the countries, the evils which were never mentioned in the speeches of the politicians nor taught in the lecture halls nor criticized in the congresses nor discussed in magazines found a vehicle of expression in literature.

So, something curious and paradoxical occurred. The realm of imagination became in Latin America the kingdom of objective reality; fiction became a substitute for social science; our best teachers about reality were the dreamers, the literary artists. And this is true not only for our great essayists—such as Sarmiento, Martí, Gonzáles Prada, Rodó, Vasconcelos, José Carlos Mariátegui—whose books are indispensable for a thorough comprehension of the historical and social reality of their respective countries, but it is also valid for the writers who only practiced the creative literary genres: fiction, poetry and drama. We can say without exaggeration that the most representative and genuine description of the real problems of Latin America during the nineteenth century is to be found in literature, and that it was in the verses of the poets or the plots of the novelists that, for the first time, the social evils of Latin America were denounced.

We have a very illustrative case with what is called *indigenismo,* the literary current which, from the middle of the nineteenth century until the first decades of our century focused on the Indian peasant of the Andes and his problems as its main subject. The indigenist writers were the first people in Latin America to describe the terrible conditions in which the Indians were still living three centuries after the Spanish conquest, the impunity with which they were abused and exploited by the landed proprietors—the *latifundistas,* the *gamonales*—men who sometimes owned land areas as big as a European country, where they were absolute kings who treated their Indians worse and sold them cheaper than their cattle. The first indigenist writer was a woman, an energetic and enthusiastic reader of the French novelist Emile Zola and the positivist philosophers: Clorinda Matto de Turner (1854-1909). Her novel *Aves sin nido* opened a road of social commitment to the problems and aspects of Indian life that Latin American writers would follow, examining in detail and from all angles, denouncing injustices and praising and rediscovering the values and traditions of an Indian culture which until then, at once incredibly and ominously, had been systematically ignored by the official culture. There is no way to research and analyze the rural history of the continent and to understand the tragic destiny of the inhabitants of the Andes since the region ceased to be a colony without going through their books. These constitute the best—and sometimes the only—testimony to this aspect of our reality.

Am I saying, then, that because of the authors' moral and social commitment this literature is good literature? That because of their generous and courageous goals of breaking the silence about the real problems of society and of contributing to the solution of these problems, this literature was an artistic accomplishment? Not at all. What actually happened in many cases was the contrary. The pessimistic dictum of André Gide, who once said that with good sentiments one has bad literature, can be, alas, true. Indigenist literature is very important from a historical and social point of view, but only in exceptional cases is it of literary importance. These novels or poems written, in general, very quickly, impelled by the present situation, with militant passion, obsessed with the idea of denouncing a social evil, of correcting a wrong, lack most of what is essential in a work of art: richness of expression, technical originality. Because of their didactic intentions they become simplistic and superficial; because of their political partisanship they are sometimes demagogic and melodramatic; and because of their nationalist or regionalist scope they can be very provincial and quaint. We can say that many of these writers, in order to serve better moral and social needs, sacrificed their vocation on the altar of politics. Instead of artists, they chose to be moralists, reformers, politicians, revolutionaries.

You can judge from your own particular system of values whether this sacrifice is right or wrong, whether the immolation of art for social and political aims is worthwhile or not. I am not dealing at the moment with this problem. What I am trying to show is how the particular circumstances of Latin American life have traditionally oriented literature in this direction and how this has created for writers a very special situation. In one sense people—the real or potential readers of the writer—are accustomed to considering literature as something intimately associated with living and social problems, the activity through which all that is repressed or disfigured in society will be named, described and condemned. They expect novels, poems and plays to counterbalance the policy of disguising and deforming reality which is current in the official culture and to keep alive the hope and spirit of change and revolt among the victims of that policy. In another sense this confers on the writer, as a citizen, a kind of moral and spiritual leadership, and he must try, during his life as a writer, to act according to this image of the role he is expected to play. Of course he can reject it and refuse this task that society wants to impose on him; and declaring that he does not want to be either a politician or a moralist or a sociologist, but only an artist, he can seclude himself in his personal dreams. However, this will be considered (and in a way, it is) a political, a moral and a social choice. He will be considered by his real and potential readers as a deserter and a traitor, and his poems, novels and plays will be endangered. To be an artist, only an artist, can become, in our countries, a kind of moral crime, a political sin. All our literature is marked by this fact, and if this is not taken into consideration, one cannot fully understand all the differences that exist between it and other literatures of the world.

No writer in Latin America is unaware of the pressure that is put on him, pushing him to a social commitment. Some accept this because the external impulse coincides with their innermost feelings and personal convictions. These cases are, surely, the happy ones. The coincidence between the individual choice of the writer and the idea that society has of his vocation permits the novelist, poet or playwright to create freely, without any pangs of conscience, knowing that he is supported and approved by his contemporaries. It is interesting to note that many Latin American men and women whose writing started out as totally uncommitted, indifferent or even hostile to social problems and politics, later—sometimes gradually, sometimes abruptly—oriented their writings in this direction. The reason for this change could be, of course, that they adopted new attitudes, acknowledging the terrible social problems of our countries, an intellectual discovery of the evils of society and the moral decision to fight them. But we cannot dismiss the possibility that in this change (conscious or unconscious) the psychological and practical trouble it means for a writer to resist the social pressure for political commitment also played a role, as did the psychological and practical advantages which led him to act and to write as society expects him to.

All this has given Latin American literature peculiar features. Social and political problems constitute a central subject for it, and they are present everywhere, even in works where, because of the theme and form, one would never expect to find them. Take the case, for example, of the "literature of fantasy" as opposed to "realist literature." This kind of literature, whose raw material is subjective fantasy, does not reflect, usually, the mechanisms of economic injustice in society nor the problems faced by urban and rural workers which make up the objective facts of reality; instead—as in Edgar Allan Poe or Villiers de L'Isle-Adam—this literature builds a new reality, essentially different from "objective reality," out of the most intimate obsessions of writers. But in Latin America (mostly in modern times, but also in the past) fantastic literature also has its roots in objective reality and is a vehicle for exposing social and political evils. So, fantastic literature becomes, in this way, symbolical literature in which, disguised with the prestigious clothes of dreams and unreal beings and facts, we recognize the characters and problems of contemporary life.

We have many examples among contemporary Latin American writers of this "realistic" utilization of unreality. The Venezuelan Salvador Garmendia has described, in short stories and novels of nightmarish obsessions and impossible deeds, the cruelty and violence of the streets of Caracas and the frustrations and sordid myths of the lower middle classes of that city. In the only novel of the Mexican Juan Rulfo, *Pedro Páramo* (1955)—all of whose characters, the reader discovers in the middle of the book, are dead people—fantasy and magic are not procedures to escape social reality; on the contrary, they are simple alternative means to represent the poverty and sadness of life for the peasants of a small Jalisco village.

Another interesting case is Julio Cortázar. In his first novels and short stories we enter a *fantastic* world, which is very mischievous because it is ontologically different from the world that we know by reason and experience yet has, at first approach, all the appearances—features— of real life. Anyway, in this world social problems and political statements do not exist; they are aspects of human experience that are omitted. But in his more recent books—and principally in the latest novel, *Libro de Manuel* (1973)—politics and social problems occupy a place as important as that of pure fantasy. The "fantastic" element is merged, in this novel, with statements and motifs which deal with underground militancy, terrorism, revolution and dictatorship.

What happens with prose also happens with poetry, and as among novelists, one finds this necessity for social commitment in all kinds of poets, even in those whom, because of the nature of their themes, one would expect not to be excessively concerned with militancy. This is what occurred, for instance, with religious poetry, which is, in general, very politicized in Latin America. And it is symptomatic that, since the death of Pablo Neruda, the most widely-known poet—because of his political radicalism, his revolutionary lyricism, his colorful and schematic ideology—is a Nicaraguan priest, a former member of the American Trappist monastery of Gethsemane: Ernesto Cardenal.

It is worth noting too that the political commitment of writers and literature in Latin America is a result not only of the social abuse and economic exploitation of large sectors of the population by small minorities and brutal military dictatorships. There are also cultural reasons for this commitment, exigencies that the writer himself sees grow and take root in his conscience during and because of his artistic development. To be a writer, to discover this vocation and to choose to practice it pushes one inevitably, in our countries, to discover all the handicaps and miseries of underdevelopment. Inequities, injustice, exploitation, discrimination, abuse are not only the burden of peasants, workers, employees, minorities. They are also social obstacles for the development of a cultural life. How can literature exist in a society where the rates of illiteracy reach fifty or sixty percent of the population? How can literature exist in countries where there are no publishing houses, where there are no literary publications, where if you want to publish a book you must finance it yourself? How can a cultural and literary life develop in a society where the material conditions of life—lack of education, subsistence wages et cetera— establish a kind of cultural apartheid, that is, prevent the majority of the inhabitants from buying and reading books? And if, besides all that, the political authorities have established a rigid censorship in the press, in the media and in the universities, that is, in those places through which literature would normally find encouragement and an audience, how could the Latin American writer remain indifferent to social and political problems? In the practice itself of his art—in the obstacles that he finds for this practice—the Latin American writer finds reasons to become politically conscious and to submit to the pressures of social commitment.

We can say that there are some positive aspects in this kind of situation for literature. Because of that commitment, literature is forced to keep in touch with living reality, with the experiences of people, and it is prevented from becoming—as unfortunately has happened in some developed societies—an esoteric and ritualistic experimentation in new forms of expression almost entirely dissociated from real experience. And because of social commitment, writers are obliged to be socially responsible for what they write and for what they do, because social pressure provides a firm barrier against the temptation of using words and imagination in order to play the game of moral irresponsibility, the game of the enfant terrible who (only at the level of words, of course) cheats, lies, exaggerates and proposes the worst options.

But this situation has many dangers, too. The function and the practice of literature can be entirely distorted if the creative writings are seen only (or even mainly) as the materialization of social and political aims. What is to be, then, the borderline, the frontier between history, sociology and literature? Are we going to say that literature is only a degraded form (since its data are always dubious because of the place that fantasy occupies in it) of the social sciences? In fact, this is what literature becomes if its most praised value is considered to be the testimony it offers of objective reality, if it is judged principally as a true record of what happens in society.

On the other hand, this opens the door of literature to all kinds of opportunistic attitudes and intellectual blackmail. How can I condemn as an artistic failure a novel that explicitly protests against the oppressors of the masses without being considered an accomplice of the oppressor? How can I say that this poem which fulminates in assonant verses against the great corporations is a calamity without being considered an obsequious servant of imperialism? And we know how this kind of simplistic approach to literature can be utilized by dishonest intellectuals and imposed easily on uneducated audiences.

The exigency of social commitment can signify also the destruction of artistic vocations in that, because of the particular sensibility, experiences and temperament of a writer, he is unable to accomplish in his writings and actions what society expects of him. The realm of sensibility, of human experience and of imagination is wider than the realm of politics and social problems. A writer like Borges has built a great literary work of art in which this kind of problem is entirely ignored: metaphysics, philosophy, fantasy and literature are more important for him. (But he has been unable to keep himself from answering the social call for commitment, and one is tempted to see in his incredible statements on right-wing conservatism—statements that scare even the conservatives—just a strategy of political sacrilege in order not to be disturbed once and for all in his writings.) And many writers are not really prepared to deal with political and social problems. These are the unhappy cases. If they prefer their intimate call and produce uncommitted work, they will have to face all kinds of misunderstanding and rejection. Incomprehension and hostility will be their constant reward. If they submit to social pressure and try to write about social and political themes, it is quite probable that they will fail as writers, that they will frustrate themselves as artists for not having acted as their feelings prompted them to do.

I think that José María Arguedas experienced this terrible dilemma and that all his life and work bears the trace of it. He was born in the Andes, was raised among the Indian peasants (in spite of being the son of a lawyer) and, until his adolescence, was—in the language he spoke and in his vision of the world—an Indian. Later he was recaptured by his family and became a middle-class Spanish-speaking Peruvian white. He lived torn always between these two different cultures and societies. And literature meant for him, in his first short stories and novels (*Agua* [1935], *Yawar Fiesta* [1949], *Los ríos profundos* [1958]), a melancholic escape to the days and places of his childhood, the world of the little Indian villages—San Juan de Lucanas, Puquio—or towns of the Andes such as Abancay, whose landscapes and customs he described in a tender and poetic prose. But later he felt obliged to renounce this kind of lyric image to fill the social responsibilities that everybody expected of him. And he wrote a very ambitious book, *Todas las sangres* (1964), in which he

tried, escaping from himself, to describe the social and political problems of his country. The novel is a total failure: the vision is simplistic and even a caricature. We find none of the great literary virtues that made of his previous books genuine works of art. The book is the classic failure of an artistic talent due to the self-imposition of social commitment. The other books of Arguedas oscillate between those two sides of his personality, and it is probable that all this played a part in his suicide.

When he pressed the trigger of the gun, at the University of La Molina, on the second day of December in 1969, José María Arguedas was too, in a way, showing how difficult and daring it can be to be a writer in Latin America.

**Enrico Mario Santí**

SOURCE: "Politics, Literature and the Intellectual in Latin America," in *Salmagundi,* Vol. 82-83, Spring/Summer, 1989, pp. 92-110.

[*In the following essay, Santí explores the "paradox" engendered when Latin American writers are expected to represent their geographical region's entire intellectual community while literature is generally excluded from intellectual discussion.*]

Our subject is vast and to attempt to cover it in an essay this size is perhaps mad. The reader may also wonder how a professor of literature can presume to address the complex and tumultuous world of politics and the intellectual in Latin America. I would wonder myself, were it not for the fact that literature and the writer—the poet, the novelist, the playwright, the essayist—continue to play a crucial role in the shaping of that world. In fact, so closely has the institution of literature been identified with the political debates among Latin American intellectuals, that often general discussions on the subject take the terms writer and intellectual to be synonymous, despite their obvious differences. Not too long ago, for example, *The New York Times Magazine* carried a long and interesting piece by Alan Riding on "Revolution and the Intellectual in Latin America" which featured a number of literary celebrities—notably, García Márquez and Octavio Paz, but also Borges, Cardenal, Cortázar, Fuentes, Rulfo and Vargas Llosa, among others.[1] Despite the comprehensive title, Riding's piece focused exclusively on these writers and their ideological differences without ever mentioning the existence of other Latin American intellectuals who are not literati—artists, economists, historians, journalists, academics—and who presumably participate as well in the same debate. More significant, I think, is that despite this glaring absorption of the intellectual by the writer, Riding's piece contains hardly any discussion of literature per se. The works of these writers indeed provide the background and identity that make their political differences significant, but these works are never discussed. It is only in the final paragraph of the piece, when Riding's need to justify his approach becomes evident, that he mentions how this political debate "has contributed to the region's literature," and concludes, hurriedly and cryptically, that "Latin America's social models may so far have failed, but its writers have made the failures memorable."

I realize of course, that I may be asking of Riding's journalism a scholarly precision which it never intended. Be that as it may, what interests me about his article, and which I would like to make the theme or at least the goal of my essay, is the significance of Riding's omission of literature from his discussion of the role of the writer in the current political debate in Latin America. I wish to explore, in part, the paradox that this omission dramatizes—the virtual exclusion of literature from the concept of the intellectual while at the same time calling upon the writer to represent that intellectual. The paradox is not, to be sure, a cultural phenomenon which is peculiar to Latin America. It constitutes, rather, one more version of the general problematic that binds literature and the intellectual; and even more generally, of the contradictory relationship between the intellectual and his own discipline. About this general relationship I shall have more to say later. My immediate purpose, in citing this telling example from *The New York Times,* was to demonstrate that literature does play an important role in that debate—indeed, to judge from its systematic exclusion from articles like Riding's—a much more crucial role than would appear at first sight. Consequently, any serious discussion of the relationship between the writer and the intellectual cannot simply chronicle from the outside, as it were, the broad political opinions that writers may or may not share. It must also broach those specific problems, complex and slippery as they are, that are peculiar to the writer and to literature as both human experience and as an institution.

Before attempting to take up the specific literary question that I have just raised, let me begin as broadly as possible and review with you some of the themes that constitute the current political debate among Latin American writers and intellectuals. My comments must be necessarily general, more in an attempt to outline a conceptual framework that would help us understand the various positions than to give a comprehensive or exhaustive survey. It is true that, as Riding points out, at the heart of this debate, "is the search for new political models for a continent . . . viewed as desperately in need of change". Within the growing strategic importance that the Third or underdeveloped world assumes in the East-West conflict, the question of a reliable political and economic model for Latin America has become, to say the least, urgent. The United States and Soviet Union continue to provide, of course, the alternative models of development. But in a continent where democratic political institutions are constantly on the verge of collapse and the local economies suffer from a chronic instability, despite the proximity to and influence of the United States, the prestige of a Western democratic model has waned. At the same time, however, the continuing economic failure, repressive policies and militarization of the Soviet Union have cast doubts on its own viability as a model for Latin America, particularly as that model has already been proven a failure in the areas of economic and ideological dependence, as the case of Cuba demonstrates.

It would of course be too simple to say that all of the positions assumed by Latin American writers and intellectuals derive from this debate regarding political models. At the same time, however, one must admit that the implicit choice of models determines not only the various ideological positions but, more importantly, different concepts of the intellectual. Should the writer and intellectual be a dissident and adopt, for example, a constantly negative position toward the State; become a permanent critic of government, as it were, in defense of a universal ethic or morality? Or should he be a public defender instead; attempt to identify, that is, the social and political problems that require immediate redress and thereby take the side of so-called revolutionary governments and national liberation movements which make these problems their object of reform? I put this question in an either/or formula, reductive though I find it, because this is the way that most Latin American intellectuals themselves often pose it. García Márquez will ask, for example, "how can the intellectual enjoy the luxury of debating the destiny of the soul when the problems are of physical survival, health, education, ignorance, and so on?" Octavio Paz, on the other hand, will assert that "as a writer, my duty is to preserve my own marginality before the State, before political parties, before all ideologies and before society itself."[2] Thus while intellectuals of the left, such as García Márquez or Mario Benedetti, will accuse their liberal counterparts of selling out to American imperialism because of the liberals' occasional criticism of the Cuban and Sandinista Revolutions, liberal intellectuals, such as Octavio Paz or Mario Vargas Llosa, will charge their counterparts on the left with support of so-called revolutionary causes and governments for the sake of opposing United States influence in the area, even while allowing that kind of support to curtail their freedom to criticize those same cases and governments.

I am deliberately overstating the rift between the two sides for the sake of clarity. In reality, the distinctions between the two groups are not as clear-cut, although the issues remain as real. Neither Octavio Paz nor Mario Vargas Llosa spend their days, as García Márquez apparently hints, debating the destiny of the soul. In the current intellectual scene I can think of no more outspoken critic of concrete political and social issues ranging from Mexico's one-party system to birth control—than Octavio Paz. Likewise, Vargas Llosa's actions on behalf of certain causes—like freedom of the press in his native Peru and the fate of Argentina's "disappeared"—is also well-known. At the same time, both García Márquez and Benedetti, like the late Julio Cortázar, have been able to speak out against Washington's complicity with repressive military dictatorships and in support of the Cuban and Sandinista revolutions precisely because they assume a marginal position both as exiles and as critics. I suspect, therefore, that what divides these groups is more strategy than substance, although there are clear substantial differences, of course. All of these writers oppose dictatorial regimes; all of them criticize, albeit in various degrees, the pervasive influence of the United States; and all of them defend intellectual freedom. What does divide them, I think, is two things: one, localized issues which both determine and reflect their implicit choice of political models; and two, each group's skeptical views of the other's intellectual status. I want to pursue the second of these divisive reasons.

A moment ago, I described the reciprocal opinions of liberal and left intellectuals. We can now refine that description by adding these two statements. First, in suppressing any criticism of the socialist countries that actively support national liberation movements in Latin America, intellectuals of the left are accused by their liberal counterparts of ideological dogma, thus betraying in effect their role as critics and reformers. As Vargas Llosa stated recently, in a spirited debate with Benedetti, "I criticize equally all of those regimes that throw their adversaries into exile (or into jail, or kill them off) while he (Benedetti) seems to think all this is somehow less serious if it's done in the name of Socialism."[3] Second, in withholding blanket support of national liberation movements and criticizing all dictatorial regimes equally and without distinction of their ideological sign, the liberal intellectual is accused by his counterpart on the left of diluting any specific criticism of the United States, thus betraying their social conscience. "How can we be content," writes Benedetti in the same debate with Vargas Llosa, "if every minute a Latin American child dies of hunger and disease; if every five minutes there's a political murder in Guatemala; if 30,000 people have disappeared in Argentina?"[4] As we can see, then, what is at stake in each of these positions is nothing less than the very identity of the intellectual. One ceases being an intellectual as soon as the other side believes you to have betrayed the essence of intellectual identity: unceasing criticism and reform, in the case of the liberal; conscience and solidarity, in the case of the left.

It would perhaps seem obvious to us, standing safely outside of the debate, that the figure of the intellectual includes or should include *both* of these functions. The intellectual should be, at once, the unceasing critic of society and of the state, ever alert to point out deceit, irresponsibility or mismanagement in the public domain; but the intellectual should also be the conscience of society and the state, the keeper of cultural and social values, the mirror in which society reflects itself in order to legitimize the status quo. The first, critical or reformist function determines a negative, marginal position before society at large. The intellectual points out problems and wrongdoings and suggests ways of resolving them. The second, moral function determines a positive, central position in society. The intellectual defends policies and actions and justifies their implementation. I would venture, however, that it would be difficult to get Latin American intellectuals to agree on the distribution of functions which I am offering here. Whereas the liberal (certainly Paz and Vargas Llosa) would be the first to

describe him/herself as the true conscience, the first to appropriate a moral function to his or her criticism, though not necessarily a central position in society, the intellectual of the left (García Márquez or Benedetti), on the other hand, would argue instead that in denouncing the hidden complicity between Washington and military regimes, for example, it is s/he who fulfills a truly critical, negative position. The problem, of course, is that both positions are correct because descriptions of the type that I have made rest ultimately on the point of view chosen to evaluate the debate.

One can gather, then, that much of the problem of discussing the subject of the intellectual in Latin America revolves around our lack of an adequate vocabulary to describe such a figure. It would certainly be tempting, in this regard, to apply concepts about the intellectual developed in Europe to a description of the Latin American version. I am thinking in particular of the categories formulated by Antonio Gramsci, the first (and in my opinion the most acute) modern Marxist to make the intellectual the central part of his sociopolitical analyses. As we know, Gramsci says that intellectuals are usually of two kinds: *organic* intellectuals, who appear in connection with an emergent social class and who prepare the way for that class's conquest of civil society by preparing it ideologically; and *traditional* intellectuals, those who seem to be unconnected with social change and who occupy positions in society designed to conserve the traditional processes by which ideas are produced—teachers, writers, artists, priests and so forth.[5] But if we were seriously to apply these Gramscian categories we would immediately run into problems. The organic intellectual's ideological work on behalf of the emergent class would certainly fit certain aspects of the intellectual of the left. But the defensive, almost reactionary dogma with which the left guards its political advances would seem to draw them closer to Gramsci's definition of the traditional intellectual. Conversely, the traditional intellectual's established position in society would seem to describe the liberal intellectual's privileged status; and yet, the pluralism which the liberal intellectual advocates would seem to counter the traditional conservative process by which ideas are produced in the underdeveloped societies of Latin America.

Compounding the difficulty attendant to the lack of a general theory of intellectual production in the Latin American tradition are the intrinsic difficulties stemming from the concept of the intellectual itself, what I earlier referred to as the general paradoxical relationship between the intellectual and his discipline. "The intellectual," wrote Jean-Paul Sartre in one of his many *meddling* essays, "is someone who *meddles* in what is not his business."[6] Indeed, in order to qualify as an intellectual, what Sartre calls "a specialist in practical knowledge," one must stand apart from one's particular specialization, take cognizance of its universal implications, and discuss these implications publicly. Charles Oppenheimer and Carl Sagan, for example, were a physicist and is an astronomer, respectively; but it was only when both scientists began to discuss publicly the implications of their research for the threat of nuclear war that they actually joined the ranks of the intellectual. (Noam Chomsky and Andrei Sakharov are two other names that come to mind.) How does this paradox work in the case of the writer? Must the writer, along with the physicist, the astronomer and the linguist, stand apart from his particular work and take cognizance of its universal implications before s/he can become an intellectual? For Sartre, whose views on the subject are revealing, the answer is no. "The writer," he says, "is not an intellectual *accidentally,* like others, but *essentially.*"[7] That is, unlike the physicist, the astronomer or the linguist, the writer, by the very nature of his work, is always engaged in the contradiction between the particular exigencies of his craft and the universal implications of his message. Moreover, the writer makes of that contradiction the theme and substance of his work.

"Not all intellectuals are writers," writes Octavio Paz, "but all (or almost all) writers are intellectuals."[8] To Paz's succinct formula, with which I agree, of course, I would simply add the following: Indeed, all writers are intellectuals *but* their intellectual status will be recognized insofar as they address something other than their writing, insofar as they meddle, that is, in what is not their business, namely literature. This is not, incidentally, my own personal opinion; I am merely describing an institutional reality. Nobody would deny, for example, that Jorge Luis Borges was an intellectual; and yet, the fact that in his last few years Borges devoted himself almost exclusively to literary concerns and no longer wrote about politics—and when he did speak about politics it was to thank an honoring regime like Pinochet's Chile or to praise democratic elections, like the recent ones that ousted the Argentine junta and put Alfonsin in power—cast Borges, in the public eye at least, as a curious non-intellectual of sorts. Is it by chance, I wonder, that in his piece Riding refers to Borges as a poet ("the continent's greatest living poet") or that he should barely mention Borges, or Juan Rulfo, another famous non-meddler, in the course of his discussion of other literary celebrities whom he does not hesitate to call "intellectuals"? Thus, while the writer would seem to be the essential, rather than the accidental, intellectual, still he appears to fall prey to the same paradox that riddles the figure of the intellectual in general. Indeed, in the case of the writer that paradox seems to loom even larger. For when the physicist and the astronomer discuss publicly the universal implications of their work, they punctuate their discussion with precise details of their research for the simple reason that everyone expects them to share those details. And yet, when the writer discusses publicly the universal implications of his writing, or of literature in general, how can he possibly do this without risking a loss of his status as an intellectual? The question, in other words, is how can a writer be an intellectual and still remain a writer?

Facing this particular quandary of the writer as intellectual, liberals like Octavio Paz and Vargas Llosa have given an answer with which I happen to sympathize. The

essence of the writer as intellectual, they say, is determined by his creative use of language, which thereby presupposes his undertaking a critique of language—precisely the medium that intellectuals must use in order to exchange ideas. Such a critique does not necessarily produce, as opponents from both left and right have charged, an irresponsibly aestheticist or solipsistic form of literature—texts that comment on their own aesthetics while excluding all historical and existential issues. Rather, in making language the object of his criticism, the writer opens himself and his work to the realm of systematic inquiry, to an analytical reason and doubt that necessarily binds his writing to his historical and political context. In this sense, writing, like politics, becomes as Octavio Paz points out, "the space where political freedom is displayed—circus, arena, theatre, tribunal, philosophical academy, scientific laboratory and open-air church, all rolled into one."[9] Vargas Llosa, less lyrically perhaps, has put it this way: "The literary vocation is born out of one man's disagreement with the world, out of his detection of the deficiency, the emptiness and the rubbish that surround him."[10] If statements such as Paz's and Vargas Llosa's sound primitive and perhaps even naive to an American or European ear, it may be because they advocate the kind of minimal level of intellectual freedom which already forms part of a modern Western consciousness but which in Latin America, languishing on the margins of the West, has been the exception. On the other hand, by posing such a primitive position, in restating the minimal conditions of intellectual activity, one achieves a distinct advantage over Western discussions of the intellectual which, in the case of the writer at least, as we have seen, lead to a quandary. Such a restatement restores, that is, the intellectual essence of the writer by pointing to the centrality of language—the medium that embodies the writer, identifies the intellectual and allows for the critical exchange of ideas.

In order to exchange ideas critically we must have, as a minimum, a willingness to establish a dialogue with others—those whose ideas are opposite, or at least different from, ours. Dialogue means sharpening our language in order to communicate our ideas, sharpening our reason in order to question those ideas with which we happen to disagree, and sharpening our conscience in order to have the courage to modify ideas whenever we are persuaded by the dialogue. These truisms are the staple of any liberal intellectual establishment, such as that of the American university, but unfortunately not those that prevail in Latin America. The predicament of the intellectual in Latin America, I fear, is that while differences of opinion do abound, very little face to face exchange of these differences actually takes place. Disagreements either with the State or among intellectuals themselves are taken as betrayals, breaches of conduct and personal affronts, rather than as the necessary and healthy differences stemming from one's intellectual and moral conscience. Simply to understand, as he does, the important issues of his history, society and culture is not enough for the intellectual. Such understanding often stagnates for the lack of a meaningful circuit of exchange. And yet, as C. Wright

Mills wrote once about the predicament faced by the post-War American intellectual:

> Knowledge that is not communicated has a way of turning the mind sour, and finally of being forgotten. For the sake of the integrity, discovery must be effectively communicated. Such communication is also a necessary element in the search for clear understanding, including the understanding of one's self. For only through the social confirmation of others whom we believe adequately equipped do we earn the right of feeling secure in our knowledge.[11]

The historical roots of this tragic absence of intellectual dialogue in Latin America are well known. A heritage of violent conquest and colonization; a climate of authoritarianism stemming from the anti-modern spirit of the Counter-Reformation; the fracture of a single culture into twenty-one artificial republics; the endemic weakness, since Independence, of democratic institutions; the wholesale absence of liberal values. With this desolate background, it is no surprise that since Independence the Latin American intellectual has pursued the question of his or her cultural identity, and that he should have pursued it, by and large, in exile. What exactly is Latin America, who exactly is the Latin American and what do these things mean, are the questions that underlie much of the literature written in Latin America, from Simón Bolívar to Carlos Fuentes, during the 19th and 20th centuries. The questioning itself, however, has often suffered under the very fragmentation that elicits it. For usually the question is not who exactly is the Latin American, but rather who exactly is the Argentine, the Brazilian, or the Cuban? What is the national psychology of the Peruvian? Or, how do we arrive at an ontology of the Mexican? Such questions may seem silly to us jaded Americans, but they have been felt to be and are of course necessary to Latin Americans; and they are interesting and useful insofar as they stem from and refer back to the broader cultural context which they attempt to interrogate. Such questions about cultural identity reflect, in turn, other more fundamental, less rarefied questions. Why are we so bad off, how did we get this way, and how do we get out of this mess? The question about identity—the ontological question, if you will—thus becomes indistinguishable from the question about process—the historical question; and these two questions, in turn, merge into one broad social question: what is the history of relations not only among the Latin American nations themselves, but between Latin America and the rest of the world?

Such a monumental history, essential though it is, still awaits its Arnold Toynbee—and I am certainly not it. But whereas Latin America has lacked encyclopaedic historians of the breadth and talent of Toynbee it does have a tradition of equally encyclopaedic writers whose work makes up in visionary depth what it has lacked in scholarly breadth. In other words, it has been in the language of literature, rather than in that of strict scholarship, that the Latin American intellectual has always asked the fundamental questions about his or her cultural identity. Which thus means that the answers that literature has provided have themselves posed other (or perhaps the same) questions in a perhaps endless chain of historical interpretation. The late visionary style of a writer like José Martí—Cuba's foremost 19th century poet and one of the principal figures of Latin American intellectual history—stems, for example, from a desperate attempt, toward the end of his short life, to synthesize historical wisdom, moral judgment, political action and poetic insight. The argument of an essay like "Nuestra América" (Our America) (1891), in which Martí pleas for the self-knowledge and self-government of Latin America through original ideas and original institutions, cannot be divorced from its rhetorically-charged language and visionary sweep. It would not be excessive to say that in this particular essay Martí's critique of the dual faults of provincialism and servile imitation, so rampant in the politics and culture of 19th century Latin America, is couched in an intricate poetic logic where ideology becomes indistinguishable from metaphor. In my own literal and surely crude translation of two of the essay's memorable sentences: "We were but a mask: underwear made in Britain, vest made in Paris, coat from the United States, and a little beret made in Spain. . . . Let our wine be made of bananas; it may turn out bitter but it is still our wine." Of course, banana wine exists only in language, in Martí's metaphor for cultural independence; but the metaphor itself embodies a will to invent, or invent anew, a synthesis which Martí found lacking in the fractured colonial mask of 19th century Latin American society. Intellectuals of the left today claim Martí, with all good reason, as a precursor of their own anti-imperialism; but they somehow always manage to overlook that Martí's revolution, carried out throughout a lifetime of exile, actually takes place in language, and therefore that his contributions to ideology presuppose a linguistic critique of certain received ideas of his time.

The poetic logic and visionary sweep of a writer like Martí therefore deceive us into dismissing his work as unscientific and perhaps even politically useless. Indeed, Martí was a critic of Positivism, so we can expect his style to reflect an abiding distrust of scientific method and a sympathy for intuitive understanding. And yet his work, like that of any writer and thinker, has limits and problems—particularly insofar as that work both unveils and conceals the broader question of cultural identity. In this sense Martí is no different from most 19th century Latin American intellectuals, whose anti-analytical prejudice left an equivocal legacy. They urge us, on the one hand, to assume our cultural identity, but they never inform us, on the other, about how exactly that identity came about, let alone what that identity means in relation to other cultures. They urge, in other words, the pursuit of ontology, without pursuing the more significant details of history, and ultimately ignore, for the sake of self-definition, the social context that necessarily determines that identity.

One can find a useful corrective to such a legacy, I believe, in the historical meditations of a writer like Octavio Paz. In a series of essays on the subject of history and society—starting with the classic *Labyrinth of Solitude,* which dates from 1950, and on with the *Critique of the Pyramid* (1969), *El ogro filantrópico* (1978), *Sor Juana Inés de la Cruz* (1982), and *Tiempo nublado* (1983)— Paz has sought to uncover the hidden traumas, so to speak, of Latin American history. I use the word trauma advisedly, for Paz's intention in these and other essays has been nothing less than to psychoanalyze Latin American history; to do psychohistorical interpretations of certain moments and institutions in the hope that such interpretations might effect an eventual therapy. Paz himself would prefer calling his essays "moral criticism," "the description of a harmful, hidden reality," as he has stated, rather than a straight psychohistory, and there is good cause to follow him on this.[12] *The Labyrinth of Solitude,* for example, describes certain traits of the Mexican character—hermeticism, hypocrisy, formality, the death wish, violence, etc.—which are explained as symptoms of psychic conflicts caused by historical traumas—the violence of the Spanish Conquest, the humiliation of the Indian during the Colonial period, the ensuing bad faith of Mexican intellectual and political movements like the Porfirato and even the Mexican revolution. In this sense, the history of Mexico, from the Aztecs to the present, becomes a kind of text which the poet, as a privileged reader, can decipher in terms of the traumas found in the day-to-day behavior of today's Mexican.

One may or may not agree with Paz's original and at times inventive links between symptoms and traumas in the course of his argument. But one cannot deny that unlike earlier attempts to describe the Mexican character, such as Samuel Ramos's *Profile of Man and Culture in Mexico* (1934), Paz's solid grounding in history represents a breakthrough. Such a breakthrough is possible, moreover, because unlike previous attempts to deal with the subject, undertaken mostly by academics (philosophers or social scientists), *The Labyrinth of Solitude* was the work of a writer, and specifically of a poet. In fact, Paz has stated on occasion that his original plan was to write a novel about Mexican history, but that once he wrote it he decided to change it into an essay because the only good thing about the novel turned out to be the characters' dialogue, which of course discussed ideas about Mexico. Even the title—*El laberinto de la soledad*—is poetic, let alone the goal of the book: one poet's reading of history for the sole purpose of feeling himself (and making others feel) less lonely. Although the influence of Marx, Freud and Nietzsche is evident throughout the book, what is ultimately interesting about it is the personal, almost intimate attitude that Paz assumes toward his subject. Neither Marx, nor Freud, nor Nietzsche, not even the Sartre of *Being and Nothingness*—had ever granted loneliness the status of a separate philosophical category. But Paz had, if not as a philosophical category at least as an existential reality, scrutinized it in his early introspective poetry as well as in a brilliant earlier essay entitled "Poetry of Solitude and Poetry of Communion", partly devoted to Saint John of the Cross. As the central formula of that early essay had been that "the poet starts out from loneliness, and guided

by desire, goes toward communion," so Paz's reading of Mexican history follows such an itinerary to end, finally, in the discovery of loneliness as a universal human problem rather than a specifically Mexican trauma. To quote from the haunting lines of the last chapter: "There in open loneliness, transcendence awaits us too: the hands of other lonely people. For the first time in our history, we are the contemporaries of all men."[13]

In citing the examples from Martí and Paz I have attempted to show how the cultural and political meditations of the Latin American intellectual necessarily involve a literary consciousness. This consciousness flares up, as Martí's daring metaphors dramatize for us, even at those moments when the notion of literature seems to be furthest removed from the writer's mind, involved as he is in the unmediated moral reading of his society. There is something of this in Paz's statement that historical knowledge, being neither quantitative nor subject to constant laws, falls halfway between science and poetry. "The historian," says Paz, "makes descriptions like a scientist and has the visions of the poet. History allows us to understand the past, and also, at times, the present. More than a form of knowledge, history is a form of wisdom."[14] Thus poetry or literature would seem to constitute not just the formal or rhetorical framework of the historical text—its "mode of encodement", to use Hayden White's handy term—but the very essence and justification of the historian's task, the very source of its meaning, as it were. The historian, just like the writer as intellectual, would therefore appear to be constituted by a literary or poetic consciousness which he does not and indeed cannot acknowledge, but without which—without "visions" and "wisdom" in Paz's view—his identity would not be possible.

We readily accept the opposite view, of course—literature can be historical, philosophical, or political without any loss of its specificity. In fact, the more historical, philosophical or political, the more modern and indeed the more literary we believe that literature to be. The appeal to modernity is in fact that—an appeal to immediacy, to action, to the anti-historical moment that can be experienced through the senses, through sentiment, through any medium that is *not* language. Literature feeds upon its own self-denying gestures, and the abandonment of literature (as in Cervantes and Flaubert) is itself one of the greatest literary themes. It is significant that some of the most representative texts of modern Latin American literature also dramatize this paradox. Pablo Neruda's *Heights of Macchu Picchu,* for example (a poem I always like to come back to), narrates a flight out of the alienation of the modern world and into the pre-Columbian past that the ruins of the famous Incan city represent. The speaker, whom I now take to be a figure of the Latin American intellectual, ascends to the ruins searching for an unmediated contact with a past untouched by the distortions wrought by five centuries of Western domination. And yet, the poem shows us not only that the speaker's flight cannot be a flight out of time, for he remains locked into the present, but that the very meaning of the ruins he so anxiously sought is constituted by the very history he attempted to avoid. That history includes, of course, the speaker's own literary consciousness, held to be an accomplice of Western cultural domination; and the poem goes on to implement that consciousness as a subversion of the Western library.[15] The poem's flight out of literature and into the mode of historical action ends up affirming the role that literature plays in the realization of that action. A similar pattern emerges from Alejo Carpentier's *The Lost Steps,* the novel of an alienated Latin American musicologist's voyage from New York City to the South American jungle in search of primitive musical instruments. After locating the instruments in a remote jungle village where he feels at home at last with himself and his context—he decides to return to civilization one last time in order to bring back the paper that will allow him to write down his musical *magnum opus.* When the musicologist returns to the jungle, however, he discovers that the signs that marked the way to the village have been covered over by the torrential rains, and therefore that this flight into the jungle, and the implicit rejection of the historical world, is impossible. The only world given to the intellectual is the present, however corrupt and disenchanting he may find it. I want to quote you from the last lines of the novel: "The gloomy mansions of romanticism, with its doomed loves, are still open. But none of this was for me, because the only human race to which it is forbidden to sever the bonds of time is the race of those who create art. They not only must move ahead of the immediate yesterday, represented by tangible witness, but must anticipate the song and the form of others who will follow them, creating new tangible witness with full awareness of what has been done up to that moment."[16]

Both *Heights of Macchu Picchu* and *The Lost Steps* are allegories of the plight of the Latin American intellectual called upon to explore his cultural identity, tempted to abandon literature for the world of committed action, and forced always to return to literature as the ground of his personal identity and the field of that action. Both texts narrate a process of conversion to the cause of that historical action, only their common argument further describes that conversion as an open, infinite process, ever subject to eventual scrutiny and revision, as if anticipating, as the end of *The Lost Steps* tells us, "the song and form of others that will follow." Both *Heights of Macchu Picchu* and *The Lost Steps* are classics, to be sure, of modern Latin American literature. And yet the knowledge—and the *wisdom,* as Paz would have it—including political knowledge and wisdom, that these two classics, among other texts, have to offer, have been little heeded by most Latin American intellectuals, including, alas, Neruda and Carpentier themselves. Throughout the twenty odd years following the publication of his poem, Neruda remained an obedient Stalinist, a virtual accomplice of the Soviet mass murders, persecutions and the Gulag. Carpentier, in turn, went on to become a solemn, respectful bureaucrat in Paris, where he lived for the better part of his last twenty years, enjoying all the comforts and luxuries that he so piously denounced as an echo of the regime that he served.

Fortunately, however, the wisdom of literature is distinct from the human foibles of its authors, and literature tells us things that authors themselves are incapable of articulating, except of course in the very literary language which they seem condemned to ignore, or at least to misunderstand. If literature constitutes, as I have tried to argue, a separate valid mode of knowledge or wisdom, then it will be necessary to develop a reading method that would respect that mode and not simply reduce it to another master discourse. Philosophers, historians, politicians, social scientists, journalists like Alan Riding, and even some literary critics, are fond of invoking and using literary texts for the purpose of illustrating ideas and theories. Literature, in this restricted sense, becomes an object to be interpreted and decided upon by the master discourse of *other* disciplines—which thereby become the subject that decides where meaning lies and what to make of it. A reversal of such a scheme whereby philosophy, history, politics, *The New York Times* and even literary criticism itself would become the object of interpretation of literature would not only allow literature to be heard, but also would probably uncover the arbitrary and ultimately fictional strategies that are at work in preserving the power structures of those disciplines. Literature, in this other, unrestricted sense, would become that "minor horror" which Jorge Luis Borges, our intellectual nonintellectual *par excellence,* once invoked as his idea of Paradise: "a vast, contradictory library, whose vertical deserts of books run the incessant risk of metamorphosis, which affirm everything, deny everything, and confuse everything—like a raving God."[17]

NOTES

[1] *The New York Times Magazine* (March 13, 1983), pp. 29-40.

[2] *El ogro filantrópico* (Barcelona: Seix Barral, 1979), p. 306. All translations, here and elsewhere, are mine.

[3] *Vuelta,* 92 (July, 1984), p. 51.

[4] Ibid., p. 48.

[5] See "The Function of the Intellectuals" and "The Different Position of Urban and Rural-Type Intellectuals", in *Selections from the Prison Notebooks,* ed. Quintin Horare and G. M. Smith (New York: International Publishers, 1971), pp. 3-23.

[6] *Between Existentialism and Marxism* (New York: Random House, 1974), p. 230.

[7] Ibid., p. 284.

[8] *El ogro filantrópico,* p. 20.

[9] Ibid., p. 302.

[10] *Contra viento y marea* (1962-1982) (Barcelona: Seix Barral, 1983), p. 135.

[11] *Power, Politics and People,* ed. Irving Louis Horowitz (New York: Oxford University Press, 1963), p. 300.

[12] *El ogro filantrópico,* p. 20.

[13] My translation from *El laberinto de la soledad* (1950; Mexico: Fondo de Cultura Económica, 1973), p. 174. Incidentally, I would prefer to translate Paz's *soledad* as "loneliness" instead of "solitude", as it is usually rendered. Loneliness refers more precisely to Paz's theme of the lack of intimate association with, rather than a wilful separation from, others.

[14] *El ogro filantrópico,* p. 21.

[15] For such a reading of the poem, see my *Pablo Neruda: The Poetics of Prophecy* (Ithaca and London: Cornell University Press, 1982), especially pp. 104-75.

[16] *The Lost Steps,* 2nd ed. Trans. Harriet de Onís (New York: Alfred Knopf, 1971).

[17] "The Total Library", in *Borges: A Reader,* ed. E. Rodríguez Monegal and Alastair Reid (New York: E. P. Dutton, 1981), p. 96.

## Neil Larson

SOURCE: "The Boom Novel and the Cold War in Latin America," in *Modern Fiction Studies,* Vol. 38, No. 3, Autumn, 1992, pp. 771-84.

*[In the following essay, Larson questions whether or not there is a correlation between global cultural, intellectual, and political anti-communism and the "canonization of Latin American modernism."]*

I

One of the collateral if perhaps somewhat fortuitous benefits of the current preoccupation with postmodernism in the humanities is that it has now become much more difficult to sustain what for decades was the dominant mode of apology for modernism itself, and the underlying ideology of its "canonicity": the idea that modern*ism* and modern*ity* were consubstantial categories, that modern*ism* was somehow already precontained in the raw and immediate experience of contemporary life. To defend, say, the Joycean interior monologue or the surrealist principles of *montage,* it was once necessary only to declare the fidelity of the aesthetic device to "modern" life itself. Modernism had succeeded, for a time at least, in laying ideological claim to being the *realism* of our (or its) time. Given this fundamental premise, one might or might not concede the existence of a modernist "politics." But even supposing one did, such a "politics" tended to be viewed as likewise consubstantial with "modernity" rather than, say, as the expression of some particular group or even class interest. Above all, one thinks

here of the Adornian and generally left-formalist theory of aesthetic negation as constituting a new sphere for emancipatory activity after the decline of "politics" in its traditional modes.

Although one can still find serious efforts to attribute to modernism both a lived immediacy and a kind of teleological necessity (see, for example, Marshall Berman's *All That Is Solid Melts into Air*), this sort of thinking must now confront the sense among intellectuals and cultural consumers generally that modernism has failed to keep its utopian promises—and that contemporary experience may not after all be of a piece with modernist aesthetics. For some, no doubt, the same premise of consubstantiality now restates itself, *mutatis mutandis,* as the relationship of *post*modern*ism* to *post*modern*ity.* But modernist burn-out has also made it easier to begin to think about the politics of modernism without in turn feeling obliged to erect modernism into a metapolitics with its own unique pertinence to contemporary experience. Perhaps, after all, modernism did serve the interests of some while effectively thwarting those of others. And perhaps there were, or are, other modernities, unexpressed and unsuspected in canonically modernist aesthetic categories and practices. In any event, the relation of modernism to both modern experience and to other aesthetic and cultural practices has come increasingly to be seen as hegemonic and exclusionary rather than transparent and totalizing.

One of the many areas opened up for critical investigation by this line of thinking is the historical connection between modernism and the anti-Communist politics of the Cold War. (In precise fact, this connection was already being drawn by, among other Old Left intellectuals, the Lukács of the early 1950s [see, *inter alia, The Meaning of Contemporary Realism* and the epilogue to *The Destruction of Reason*]). But the—as one might put it—one-two punch of Cold War thinking itself, together with the generally promodernist stance of the New Left, had until recently kept this question outside the limits of acceptable discourse.) Serge Guilbaut, in his 1983 *How New York Stole the Idea of Modern Art,* argues, for example, that the rise of Abstract Expression in the U.S. after World War II was less the result of some spontaneous shift of aesthetic sensibility on the part of artists and critics than the product of a self-consciously political drive to decanonize the old Popular Front realism of the 1930s and replace it with a depoliticized art compatible with the U.S. imperial elite's new image of itself as the guardian of aesthetic culture. A similarly political connection is uncovered in Lawrence H. Schwartz's *Creating Faulkner's Reputation.* Here Schwartz analyzes the shift in Faulkner's literary fortunes from relative obscurity in the 1930s and early 1940s to the super stardom of the 1950s and after as a function of the same Cold War cultural campaign to delegitimize the Left-leaning social and proletarian realism that thrived in the pre–Cold War United States through the creation of a new, distinctly "apolitical" and purportedly authentic "American" novelist. Guilbaut and Schwartz emphasize the key role played in both instances by the New York Intellectuals gathered around the *Partisan Review,* as well as, in the case of Faulkner, by New Critics such as Allen Tate and Cleanth Brooks. James Murphy, in his recent and valuable study *The Proletarian Moment,* argues similarly that the current neglect of the proletarian fiction of the 1930s stems directly from an institutionalization of the politically aggressive promodernism of the New York intellectuals. And one should note here as well Barbara Foley's important new reading of the North American proletarian novel itself, in which she has shown that the initial reception of works by authors such as Erskine Caldwell, Josephine Herbst, Mike Gold, Richard Wright, and others, not only by Left-wing but by more "mainstream" critics as well, was generally enthusiastic. If this major body of literature, stigmatized for its supposed aesthetic crudity and propagandism, later languished in the shadow of modernists such as Faulkner, this, she shows, was at least as much a result of the Cold War cooptation of formerly friendly critics and publishers as it was of any properties intrinsic to the novels themselves.

What these and other studies point to is certainly not, let it be said, a conspiracy theory of modernism as an anti-Communist plot, but rather the tendency of cultural and literary institutions on the "Western" side of the Cold War divide to promote the *canonization* of modernist works—many of which long predated and/or had no direct relationship to the aggressively anti-Communist policies of the post–World War II years. These works suited the cultural dictates of the Cold War not so much for what they said or represented, but for what they *did not say or represent,* for their scrupulously maintained neutrality as purely self-referential languages of form, or what Guilbaut calls their "political apoliticism" (2). The politics of the Cold War do not create modernism. To suppose so would be to fall into an obvious historical fallacy. But it bears considering whether or not it is the politics of the Cold War that create the institutional and cultural forces that in turn have inculcated into several generations, including my own, the creed of a modernist consubstantiality with contemporary life—of modernism, even, as historico-aesthetic *telos.*

The question I wish to pose in the present essay is whether or not something analogous to the aesthetic-political change traced by Guilbaut, Schwartz, Foley, and others in the United States takes place in Latin America. More particularly: can a correlation be drawn between the global ideological demands of the Cold War, above all the elevation of anti-Communism into a virtual touchstone not only for political but for virtually all cultural practice as well, and the canonization of Latin American modernism, especially modernist narrative?

Initially, however, some clarification is required. "Modernism" is in some ways an unaccustomed term in the sphere of Latin American literary discourse. Its Spanish cognate—*modernismo*—refers to a literary movement appearing in Spanish America at roughly the turn of the century, mainly in poetry, and with affinities for French symbolism and Parnassianism. By any account, however, *modernismo* would have to be deemed a pre- or at best proto-modernist phenomenon, if the more Eurocentric or metropolitan designation is maintained. *Vanguardismo* probably comes closest to translating the English term. But the lexical difficulty aside, there remains the question of whether there *is* a Latin American modernism directly assimilable to some metropolitan, or would-be global modernist canon. Much of Latin American critical debate over the last three to four decades has dwelled on this general issue, often claiming that such an assimilation does considerable violence to a modern Latin American body of literature that, while not quite outside the orbit of canonical modernism, nevertheless turns on its own unique substrate of contemporary, lived experience. For a time the preferred term became "magical realism," in reference to a mode of literary narrative that, while resembling modernism in its penchant for formal experiments, also differed from it by virtue of its purportedly mimetic relationship to a Latin American reality that was said to exceed traditionally realist modes of representation.[1]

But with the proviso that its Latin American variant typically lodges the claim to an autonomy of form within a prior claim to an autonomy of content, I think it can be agreed that, at least in the narrative sphere, a Latin American modernism has its origins in the works of authors such as Borges, Mario de Andrade, Asturias, Carpentier, Rulfo, and Guimarães Rosa. There can also be little dispute that the so-called "boom" phase of Latin American fiction that, beginning in the 1960s, follows on the work of the latter—comprising works by, *inter alia,* Fuentes, Cortázar, Vargas Llosa, and García Márquez—fully merits the modernist designation. Indeed, as Gerald Martin has recently written, the "boom" should be regarded not only as the "product of the fiction that had gone before" but even more so as the "climax and consummation of Latin American Modernism . . ." (239).

But I would, in fact, go even further and maintain that it is only after the onset of the "boom," and the vastly enhanced visibility of its representative authors and works both within the Latin American ambit itself and internationally, that the pre-"boom" modernists themselves come to be tacitly regarded as belonging to a uniform literary current. It is now a standard article of Latin American literary historiography that without a Borges, no Cortázar, without a Rulfo or Asturias, no García Márquez, and so on. From a certain narrowly philological standpoint, this is certainly a fact. But the effect of the genealogy here is not only to register the inheritance per se, but also to make it appear to be the fulfillment of a kind of literary destiny: we needed Rulfo so that we could get a García Márquez, thus realizing the true latent possibilities of the Latin American literary genius.

That is: the "boom," if I am right about its effective success in rewriting Latin American literary history with itself as *telos,* might be seen as achieving, vis-à-vis its literary prehistory, what the rise of Faulkner, or of Abstract Expressionism achieve in their respective

North American spheres: the decisive and *a priori* exclusion from (or marginalization within) the canon of nonmodernist works and movements.

But does this elevation of modernism to a hegemonic position likewise obey, even if only indirectly, a Cold War political logic? Here the analogy to North American developments appears much more problematic. Certainly, the standard theories of the "boom" would not appear to support such a view. These theories can, very schematically, be classified as belonging to three different types. The first, and probably still the most commonly alleged theory may be termed the *aestheticist.* Typically advanced by the "boom" authors themselves, the aestheticist account of the "boom" explains it as simply the discovery of a new literary language in which to express Latin American reality with, for the first time, complete authenticity. Cortázar, Fuentes, and Vargas Llosa all made notorious pronouncements to this effect, and there has been no lack of critics to echo them back. But we would scarcely expect to find any emergent historical or political critique of modernism in this version of the "boom," since, in keeping with what is obviously its own modernist self-understanding, the aestheticist theory takes as its point of departure the idea of an immanent formal rupture that must, finally, be accepted on faith. Any attempt at a historical or political explanation of this aesthetic rupture would only rob it of the claim to formal immanence. Moreover, even if one were inclined to give credence to it, it would have to be observed that the formal "revolution" had already in large measure been carried out by pre-"boom" modernists such as Borges, Asturias, Guimarães Rosa, and others.[2]

A second theory of the "boom" that has gained some currency holds that, as the term "boom" itself implies, the "aesthetic" revolution was really nothing more than a major expansion of Latin American literary commodities into domestic and international markets. Its best known advocate has been Angel Rama, whose essay "El 'boom' en perspectiva" ("The 'Boom' in Perspective") remains one of the most informative pieces of criticism ever to be written on the subject. Here Rama equates the "boom" with the emergence in Latin America of a larger reading public, together with the production and the marketing tools required to service it. The "boom" marks the "absorption of literature within the mechanisms of consumer society" (53, my translation), and along with it the appearance of the author not only as professional but as media-star.

This is certainly a useful corrective to the aestheticist myth, but it will likewise not take us very far in the exploration of the links between the "boom" novel and the global politics of the Cold War. Rama regards the political orientations of the "boom" authors, ranging, at different times, from socialist to liberal to conservative, to be, by reason of this very plurality, of secondary importance. What mattered was exclusively the new reading public; the "boom" novel was such by virtue of its ability to command this new market, to supply it with

a set of self-images that, for whatever reason, met a pre-existing demand. That is, Rama adopts what might be called the *vulgar sociological* standpoint, according to which phenomena such as market trends, demographic shifts and changing consumption and work patterns are separated from questions of both politics and aesthetics.

Finally, there is the theory, which might be designated the *revolutionary-historicist,* that sees the "boom" novel as the literary manifestation of the new political consciousness generated in Latin America by the Cuban Revolution. The Colombian critic Jaime Mejía-Duque, for example, concedes the significance of both the purely formal and commercial aspects of the "boom," but regards these as "over-determined" by the new political reality supposedly inaugurated in 1959 (86). The fact that, particularly after the Padilla affair of 1971,[3] many of the "boom" authors withdrew their initial support of the revolution demonstrates the "constitutive ambiguity" of the politics of the "boom" but does not negate the objective historical connection. The "boom" is, in Mejía-Duque's words, "something exterior to [the] revolution, but not foreign to it" (86, my translation). More recently Gerald Martin has taken a similar position, seeing the "boom" as:

> a confused and contradictory moment, marked deeply by the Cuban revolution. . . . The sense of diverse ideological alternatives offered by Cuba and the various social democratic experiments of the day, combined with the new cosmopolitanism bred by a consumption-oriented capitalist boom and an expansion of the Latin American middle classes (nouveau read?)—buyers and consumers of novels—created a period of intense artistic activity throughout the subcontinent. (204-05)

Within this theoretical trend there might also be included those more negative assessments of the "boom"—see for example Fernández Retamar's *Calibán*—that indict the "boom" novelists with being *too* "exterior" to the revolution . . . but without ceasing to insist on the Cuban experience as the historical precondition for the aesthetic developments as such, however they are to be evaluated.

From the standpoint of basic methodology, it is this latter, *revolutionary-historicist* approach to the "boom" that I think is most adequate. Here, at least, in contrast to the aestheticist approach, an effort is made to historicize and politicize modernist aesthetic categories, but without thereby succumbing to the vulgar sociological tendency to treat the aesthetic aspect as intrinsically arbitrary. But the insistence on the Cuban revolution as the principal historical determinant of the "boom" novel has always seemed somewhat dubious to me. The profound subjective impact of the revolution and the events it unleashed on Latin American intellectuals and artists certainly cannot be denied. And in a sense it is through Cuba, especially post-1961, that the Cold War exerts its most direct influence on Latin America. But how does one proceed from the anti-imperialist, and later would-be socialist revolution to the modernist "revolution" in literary form (or, if one prefers, the uncontroversially capitalist revolution in book publishing and marketing) without converting the analogous term here into the thinnest of abstractions? Such a notion does not answer but merely begs the questions: what was there particularly "modernist" in the Cuban Revolution? and/or what particular anti-imperialist or socialist objectives were furthered through the consecration of modernist narrative as the authentic mode of contemporary Latin American literary expression?

In this regard it will be useful to give an account of still another critical-theoretical approach to the "boom," in this case belonging to the Latin American historian Tulio Halperín Donghi. In his wonderfully incisive and lucid essay "Nueva narrativa y ciencias sociales hispano-americanas en la década del sesenta" ("The New Narrative and Spanish American Social Sciences in the 1960s"), Halperín notes the curious contradiction between the initially pro-Cuban, and generally radical anti-imperialist stance of the "boom" authors and the fact that the same authors "elaborate a literature that scarcely alludes to the dramatic conjuncture from which it stems . . ." (149, my translation). The "boom" novel, according to Halperín, "rests on a renunciation of a certain image of the reality of Spanish America as historical, that is, as a reality collectively created through a temporal process whose results are cumulative" (150, my translation). He attributes this renunciation in part to the fact that attempts to create a historical novel in Latin America had been predominantly the work of the pathological-determininist view of history embodied in naturalism—a view which, given the political effervescence of the 1960s, could only seem perversely out of date. But the "boom," in Halperín's account, answers naturalism not with a deeper historical realism but rather with an adoption of "new techniques," that is, with modernism. This, in the politically charged atmosphere of the 1960s, leads to the "paradox" that "this literature, neither militant nor escapist, and seeming to evoke what was once viewed as Spanish America's historical calvary as if its governing fatalities had entirely lost their potency—this literature is nevertheless recognized as being the most akin to a mass readership increasingly militant in spirit" (154, my translation). And he continues:

> The readers of García Márquez were those who found it easy to believe that a landowner from Rio Grande, educated in the political school of gaucho factional disputes and in the no less ambiguous one of populism [the reference is to Juan Perón], was in fact the unexpected Lenin required by his country to lead the revolution to victory, or that the Chilean propertied classes were prepared to swallow, and even savour as delectably traditional in flavor the revolutionary medicine wisely prescribed for them by Dr. Allende (155, my translation).

But, continues, Halperín, alluding to the violent military repression of the 1970s, "there is no need to be reminded of what bloody horrors were effectively required in order to destroy a set of illusions too pleasing to be easily renounced; 'magical realism' now appears as an echo of a time in Spanish America whose magic those horrors have dispelled for ever" (155).

With some extrapolation, the emergent picture here is that of a modernism that, while remaining, as the Old Left might have put it, "right" in substance, nevertheless finds itself for a time in the peculiar historical conjuncture of being "Left" in appearance. Unlike its North American analog of roughly a decade earlier, *this* modernism refuses the mantle of "political apoliticism" and, at least at first, openly encourages an image of itself as somehow *engagé*. Why? Perhaps because, putting it bluntly, the Latin American "boom" modernist is an anti-*yanqui* nationalist before s/he is an anti-Communist. When the populist illusions of the 1960s are dispelled by the brutal reaction of the 1970s in Latin America (in fact the death of Che in 1967 can be taken as the symbolic inauguration of a period of counter-insurgency and repression that begins as early as 1964 in Brazil), the seeming Right/Left aphasia of the "boom" vanishes with it. (It is at this point, some have argued, that the moment of the "boom" passes, giving way to that of the more politically motivated "testimonio," or "testimonial novel"). But Halperín adduces another factor here as well. This is that, again in contrast to the North American situation, the modernism of the "boom" does not appear to answer the elite need to counter-hegemonize a tradition of increasingly Left-tending realism but rather the outwardly progressive impulse to overcome a much older tradition of naturalistic portrayal in Latin America. It was in and through this tradition—stretching, conservatively, from Domingo Faustino Sarmiento's *Facundo* to the novels of the Mexican revolution and even, perhaps, into Spanish America's scattered experiments with "socialist realism" itself—that the neocolonial intelligentsia had articulated its deep-seated pessimism regarding the capacity of the masses to overcome their purportedly pathological "backwardness" and usher Latin America onto the threshold of modern civilization. In novels as otherwise diverse as Cambaceres' *En la sangre*, for instance, and Revueltas' *El luto humano*—the former a frankly reactionary screed, the latter a supposedly progressive, even revolutionary one—there operates much the same reduction of human agencies in Latin America to the irresistible working out of a naturally, even racially or biologically predetermined tragedy. It is against this background, Halperín argues, that the flight from historical portrayal into the modernist "boom" novel's utopias of form and language can appear liberating. The key factor in Halperín's own rather tragic view of Latin America's *literary* destiny, however, is that the moment of authentic, historical *realism* is missing. While in Halperín's view, the Latin American social sciences do effect a rupture with naturalist historicism—for which he above all thanks the path-breaking work of the Peruvian Marxist José Carlos Mariátegui—no such breakthrough occurs in literature. If the "boom" enacts a "revolution," it remains, for Halperín, a "revolución Boba"—a "fool's revolution," that "solves" the basic difficulty by resolutely turning its back on it (164).

II

But is the literary breakthrough into a modern historical realism in fact an unrealized moment in Latin America? Here I think that Halperín, although substantively correct insofar as the "boom" authors he has in mind do not work either out of or against such a tradition of realism, nevertheless risks error by omitting what may be the grand exception to the rule here—the literature of Brazil. To be sure, the naturalist tradition finds as firm an anchor here as elsewhere in Latin America. One thinks, above all, of Euclides da Cunha's vastly influential work, *Os sertões.* So, indeed, does modernism, as witness the examples of a Mario de Andrade, or what is perhaps the Joycean Ur-text of Latin American modernism, Guimarães Rosa's *Grande sertão: veredas.* But then what does one do with a Machado de Assis? One might argue the case for a nineteenth-century anomaly here, perhaps, were it not for the strong claims to realism attributable in turn to a whole series of twentieth-century authors as well, among them Lima Barreto, Rachel de Quierós, Graciliano Ramos, and Jorge Amado.

Without at this point exploring any further the case to be made for a Brazilian exceptionalism, I do nevertheless wish to devote additional consideration, in light of my original query regarding modernism and the Cold War, to one of the above authors in particular—namely, to Jorge Amado. My reasons for this are several. First of all, I would maintain that Amado's narrative fictions of the 1940s and 50s, specifically from *Terras do sem fim* in 1943 until the publication of *Gabriela, cravo e canela* in 1958, represent the highest attainment of modern historical realism in Brazil . . . if not in Latin America as a whole. To say this is not to discount the serious flaws that distort some of these works, perhaps especially his more orthodox socialist realist novels (*Seara vermelha,* and the urban trilogy *Os subterrâneos da liberdade*). These flaws notwithstanding, however, I think that Amado's work of this period effectively refutes the postulate of Latin America as condemned to choose between a naturalist, pathological realism and a modernist antirealism.

This is not the place to engage in a lengthy analytical presentation of the sources and specific configuration of Amadian historical realism. Suffice it, here, to suggest that Amado's intense personal involvement in the class struggles that lead up to the "revolution" of 1930 and subsequently ushered in the period of the fascist-inspired "New State" of Getulio Vargas, together with his strong literary debts to Brazil's "Northeastern," and distinctly antimodernist school of rural proletarian realism, are what ultimately make possible the great achievement of a work such as *Terras do sem fim,* together with its sequel in the "cacao cycle," *São Jorge de Ilhéus:* the fully epical portrayal of Brazil's evolution, out of a state of semifeudal land tenure and rural clientelism (the Brazilian term is *coronelismo*) into one of modern, dependent capitalism. What, in the naturalist tradition, presents itself as the iron subjugation of human agency to the prehistorical factors of environment and "race"—and, in the later "boom" novel appears as the "magical" incongruity of life in the

traditional, "backward" sector with the other, increasingly urbanized and hypermodern Latin America—emerges in Amado's fiction as the *economically* determined distortions suffered by human beings who *do* live in thrall, not to "nature" but to commodities . . . and, in this case, to a single, export commodity: cacao. Amado is obviously not the first or the last Latin American novelist to grasp the reality of neocolonial, dependent capitalism. But he is, I would argue, one of, if not *the* first to discover the most effective artistic means for portraying this reality as something fully historical and dynamic—as, in the final analysis, the cumulative product of human agencies.

This fact alone makes Amado an interesting foil to the various versions of the "boom." But there is still another reason for bringing Amado into the picture here. And that is that Amado himself undergoes a suspiciously "boom"-like transformation at a very discrete moment not only in his own literary and political career, but in Cold War historiography as well.

The story merits telling in some detail.[4] Amado had spent the latter half of the 1930s in militant opposition to the Vargas dictatorship, an opposition which resulted in several jailings, exile, and even the public burning of his works in the capital of his native Bahía province, Salvador. In the 1940s he formally joins the Brazilian Communist Party and is elected, in 1945, to the Chamber of Deputies on the Party slate. Renewed repression sends him into a European exile in 1948, from which he is not to return until 1952. In 1954 he publishes the militantly socialist realist trilogy of underground life under Vargas, *Os subterrâneos da liberdade.*

In February of 1956 there occurs an event, however, that was to shake not only Amado's political convictions but the ideological foundations of the international Communist movement of the time: Khrushchev's "secret" speech denouncing Stalin, delivered at the XXth Party Congress of the Soviet Communist Party. The speech itself turns out to be a vague, obviously self-serving harangue in which Krushchev advances the absurd thesis that all the ills of Soviet society up to present moment are to be blamed on the individual Stalin and the mystical "cult of personality" that he had somehow been able to instigate. But few, if any, party loyalists around the world seem to have been in a position to perceive this at the time, awed, as most were, by the supreme political and ideological authority of Krushchev himself. In fact, I would propose, this becomes a turning point not only for international Communism but for the conduct of the Cold War itself, insofar as the "East," still represented by the USSR (the Sino/Soviet split, although brewing, is still some seven years away), now adopts an increasingly defensive, conciliatory position in the face of the "West's" unrelentingly aggressive anti-Communism. (A few years later Khrushchev promulgates the doctrine of "peaceful coexistence" between socialist and capitalist states.)

Amado is, by all accounts, devastated by the sudden political turn. His personal friend and fellow Communist

Pablo Neruda records in his memoirs that the "revelations [in Kruschchev's speech] had broken Amado's spirit. [ . . . ] From then on he became quieter, much more sober in his attitudes and his public statements. I don't believe he had lost his revolutionary faith, but he concentrated much more on his literary work, and eliminated from it the directly political aspect that had previously characterized it" (cited in Wagner 240, my translation). For several months after the speech, Amado maintains a political silence. Then, in October of 1956 he publishes a letter in a Brazilian Party newspaper calling for open discussion of the Krushchev report and condemning the "cult of personality." Although he remains a Party member, from this point on Amado begins to withdraw from political life and, as Neruda notes above, to devote all his energies to his literary career.

The result, published in 1958, is the novel for which he is still probably best known: *Gabriela, cravo e canela.* Set, like the earlier "cacao cycle" in the southern Bahian port of Ilhéus, *Gabriela* is the ludic, mock-epical and, as some have termed it, "picaresque" love story of Nacib, a local Syrian merchant, and the novel's heroine, a beautiful "cinnamon"-skinned refugee from the draught-stricken Northeast whom Nacib first hires to be his cook. Through the vagaries of this cross-class and "inter-racial" liaison—from premarital to marital and finally to postmarital—Amado weaves the narration of the changing sexual and gender mores of Ilhéus as it gradually undergoes the transition (previously portrayed in *Terras do sem fim* and *São Jorge de Ilhéus*) from *coronelismo* to modern commercial capitalism. The novel ends with the landmark legal conviction of one of the local cacao "colonels" for the murder of his adulterous wife—the first time in local memory that such a conviction has been obtained. But the story Amado had previously told through epic means, in which a series of personal destinies is presented in such a way that their determination by historical and economic factors is made tangible and concrete, becomes, in *Gabriela,* a kind of domestic idyll, or, to adopt Doris Sommer's term in *Foundational Fictions,* a "romance." No longer depicted as necessary if likewise tragic and contradictory in its outcome, the transition to modern capitalist dependency, symbolized by the fall of the colonels and the rise of the port-based trading houses, becomes, in *Gabriela,* a subject for farce. Politics recede into the background, to be replaced in the foreground by the theme that is to characterize Amado's fiction from 1958 on: the exotic, eroticized piquancy of Bahía's Afro-Brazilian culture, most often as epitomized in women, music, and food.

With *Gabriela,* Amado achieves almost instantaneous acceptance by the Brazilian bourgeois literary establishment. His past sins, above all his orthodox socialist realist or "Zhdanovite" phase, are forgiven, and he is welcomed into the literary circles and *salons* that had for years excluded him. The record here is dramatic indeed. Up until 1959 Amado, despite becoming both nationally and internationally famous, had received only two literary prizes: the Premio Graça Aranha in 1936 and the Stalin Prize in 1951. In 1959 alone he receives, for *Gabriela,* four major awards, with more to follow in 1961. And, most dramatic of all, in April of 1961 he is unanimously elected to a seat in the Brazilian Academy of Letters—a seat for which, in a historical first, he is the sole and uncontested candidate. Sales of *Gabriela* are unprecedented for a Brazilian work of fiction. Critics, from the Catholic conservative Tristão de Athayde to the existentialist Jean-Paul Sartre hail the Party "dissident" Amado as a literary genius. And, as Wagner observes, those that rush to valorize Amado's new departure invariably discover in *Gabriela* a wealth of "advances" in literary form and technique (246). Only a few old Communist stalwarts object to the political apology clearly being enacted in Amado's new novel.[5] Even high-level Brazilian politicians, including presidents Kubitschek and Quadros, eager to plug into Amado's mass readership, declare themselves fans of *Gabriela.*

Do we not thus have, in *Gabriela,* what may virtually be the first "boom" novel? The required characteristics seem to be there: the self-consciously "literary" concern for new formal techniques, the mass sales, the conversion of the author into a national celebrity, and so on. In all honesty it must be admitted that *Gabriela,* despite its retreat from Amado's earlier epic and politically empassioned mode of narration, is still a work concerned with the historical portrayal of Brazilian society at a decisive phase. Amado the realist remains very much present in this work, despite the new tone of preciosity and farcical remove from history as "grand récit." The obsession with purely formal experiments and "language" has not reached (nor will it in Amado's subsequent work) anything like the extreme of, say, García Márquez's *Autumn of the Patriarch.* There is no Joycean or Faulknerian imprint here. It would perhaps even require some imagination to characterize *Gabriela* as a work of "modernism" in the full sense of the term. But there can be, to my mind, no doubt about the novel's distinctively Cold War modernist subtext: above all, the careful retreat from the objectives of social or socialist realism and the avoidance of any open signs of political engagement.

Needless to say, *Gabriela* will not satisfy the revolutionary-historicist theory of the "boom" novel by sheer virtue of chronology. Amado was certainly to become a supporter of the Cuban revolution, but in the years 1956-1958 the crucial historical experience for Amado is clearly the Cold War itself, and its political impact on the very considerable Left-led mass movement in Brazil. But perhaps this suggests a closer link between the canonical "boom" novel and the Cold War than is typically thought to exist. Certainly none of the standard "boom" authors duplicate Amado's history of intense political activity. Nor do they, like Amado, emerge into modernism out of a prior history of historical and social realism. The new political and ideological reality that, in 1956, rushes upon an author such as Amado with catastrophic effect becomes, for the somewhat younger and more politically disengaged figure of a Fuentes or Cortázar something more in the nature of a horizon of ideologically unquestioned assumptions. The budding "boom" novelist is more likely an Existentialist—via readings of Sartre and Camus—than a militant Leninist. But if the Cuban revolution results in a sudden, seemingly Leftwing inflection within the overall rightward evolution, then its effect, it seems to me, is largely superficial and temporary. As Halperín justly notes, it never induces the new phase of historical realism that might have been expected if the ideological impact of Cuba were really as profound as is sometimes claimed. What Cuba elicits from the "boom" is, I would argue, a somewhat more militant version of a Latin American nationalism that just as easily supports a Perón or an Omar Torrijos as it does a Fidel.

The value of rereading the "boom" through a technically extracanonical novelist such as Amado is, at the very least, that it gives us a clearer picture of what was politically at stake in the generation of a literary moment about which there has grown the myth that it was both inevitable and the expression of a Latin American *essence.* By looking at *Gabriela* as a virtual "boom" text—but also within the context of the Amadian historical realism with which it breaks—the myth of essence, or what we have also termed the myth of modernism itself as consubstantial with a raw, prepolitical level of contemporary experience, is more easily shattered. And shattering this myth remains, in my view, a vital task. For, if, as we are told, the Cold War is over, its ideological and cultural legacy is still very much with us.

### NOTES

[1] The classic argument for "magical realism" is to be found in Alejo Carpentier's original, 1949 prologue to his novel, *El reino de este mundo.*

[2] Martin points this out in *Journeys through the Labyrinth* (241).

[3] A bitter controversy surrounding the jailing of poet Heberto Padilla by the Cuban government for purportedly subversive activities.

[4] For much of the information in what follows I rely on Wagner's immensely useful study, *Jorge Amado: Politica e Literatura.*

[5] Wagner cites the criticism of Paulo Dantas, who sees in *Gabriela* not a process of "maturation" but rather one of "accommodation," implying a "substantial loss in the most primitive and authentic qualities of [Amado as] novelist" (248, my translation). Jacob Gorender, in Wagner's citation, writes that "in *Gabriela* there disappears the revolutionary sense of the whole that characterizes Amado's earlier works: the social conflicts are superficial, and the workers come to occupy a very remote and secondary plane" (249, my translation). Gorender agrees that in *Gabriela* Amado transcends some of the schematism of *Os subterrâneos da liberdade,* but not without paying the price of a political shift to the right.

### WORKS CITED

Amado, Jorge. *Gabriela, cravo e canela.* Lisbon: Publicações Europa-America, 1970.

———. *São Jorge de Ilhéus.* Lisbon: Publicações Europa-America, 1970.

———. *Os subterrâneos da liberdade.* Lisbon: Publicações Europa-America, 1976.

———. *Terras do sem fim.* São Paulo: Livraria Martins, 1942.

Berman, Marshall. *All That Is Solid Melts into Air: The Experience of Modernity.* New York: Simon, 1982.

Carpentier, Alejo. *El reino de este mundo.* 1949. Barcelona: Editorial Seix Barral, 1967.

Foley, Barbara. *Radical Representations: Politics and Form in U.S. Proletarian Fiction, 1929-1941.* Unpublished manuscript, 1991.

Guilbaut, Serge. *How New York Stole the Idea of Modern Art.* Trans. Arthur Goldhammer. Chicago: U of Chicago P, 1983.

Halperín Donghi, Tulio. "Nueva narrativa y ciencias sociales hispanoamericanas en la década del sesenta." Viñas 147-164.

Lukács, Georg. *The Destruction of Reason.* Trans. Peter Palmer. London: Merlin, 1980.

Martin, Gerald. *Journeys through the Labyrinth: Latin American Fiction in the Twentieth Century.* London: Verso, 1989.

Mejía-Duque, Jaime. *Narrativa y neocoloniaje en América Latina.* Bogotá: Ediciones Tercer Mundo, 1977.

Murphy, James. *The Proletarian Moment.* Urbana: U of Illinois P, 1991.

Rama, Angel. "El 'boom' en perspectiva." Viñas 51-84.

Retamar, Fernández. *Calibán.* Montevideo: Aqui Testimonio, 1973.

Schwartz, Lawrence H. *Creating Faulkner's Reputation: The Politics of Modern Literary Criticism.* Knoxville: U of Tennessee P, 1988.

Sommer, Doris. *Foundational Fictions: The National Romances of Latin America.* Berkeley: U of California P, 1991.

Viñas, David, et al., eds. *Másallá del boom: Literatura y mercado.* Mexico City: Marcha Editores, 1981.

Wagner Berno de Almeida, Alfredo. *Jorge Amado: Politica e Literatura.* Rio de Janeiro: Editora Campus, 1979.

## AFRICA AND THE CARIBBEAN

**Helen Pyne Timothy**

SOURCE: "V. S. Naipaul and Politics: His View of Third World Societies in Africa and the Caribbean," in *CLA Journal,* Vol. XXVIII, No. 3, March, 1985, pp. 247-62.

[*In the following essay, Timothy examines V. S. Naipaul's view, as expressed in his fiction, of Third World political attitudes and issues.*]

There is a certain sense in which V. S. Naipaul is an anachronism in Third World writing: He is the writer-in-exile trained in the metropole and still resident there after thirty years. He is the writer who left the West Indies at a time when the colonial system was well entrenched and who has never returned to his homeland except in fleeting visits. He has never participated in any political movement dedicated to the notion of political independence; rather he has eschewed nationalistic pronouncements. Now a citizen of Britain, he has revealed how sincerely he depends on what he calls the "literate" persuasion of that society. According to him, the Third World environment does not provide this atmosphere.

The Third World writer who has maintained this "observer status" is more usually associated with a pre-1950 era. Yet Naipaul is now regarded internationally as the foremost expositor of Third World political philosophy, attitudes, and movements. This paper attempts to set out what, according to Naipaul, these attitudes might be, what their motivations are, and how they might be evaluated. Finally, an attempt is made to assess the kinds of contributions which Naipaul makes to a larger understanding of the Third World political person.

The works which are here examined deal primarily with independent post-colonial societies in the Caribbean and in Africa. They are fictional writings. It is perhaps best, therefore, to justify the claim that the political stances which follow are in fact those of the author himself and not merely those of the characters who exist only within the counterfeit world of *The Mimic Men* or *A Bend in the River.* As this paper will show, Naipaul's perspectives on Third World development are repeated explications of a personal paradigm, an intensely private way of viewing Third World societies. Whether it be African or the Caribbean coincidence of the assessment leaves little doubt that the author's convictions are being ventilated.

Within the Naipaulian cosmos the characters are the distinct product of their environment. They can never become anything or *do* anything other than what the environment makes it possible for them to produce. And the Caribbean environment as depicted in *The Mimic Men* and in *Guerrillas* is appreciably unstable and insecure. Kripalsingh, the hero in *The Mimic Men,* is the West Indian of Hindu ancestry, a personality who is emotionally and psychologically crippled (the name is iconic) by the society in which he has been born. Kripalsingh's social environment is unstable: his father, although of middle-class origin and a teacher, is socially insecure and unhappy because his wife, through her marriage to him, becomes a poor relation of a suddenly wealthy family. The invidious comparisons which the boy and his sisters make of their own status vis-a-vis that of their in-laws is at the base of his uncertain childhood.

But a more important factor seems to be present within the structure of the society. Naipaul seems to think that it is only within a Third World country, where the society is in a state of flux, that people like Kripalsingh's grandfather can become a millionaire through the lucky purchase of the correct franchise. Similarly, in such societies, which are without tradition, the only thing respected is money. Thus, Kripalsingh's father, for all his admirable qualities, becomes acutely frustrated by his inability to obtain a position of respect or prominence within his family. Moreover, Kripalsingh's awareness of his own blemished personality is shown by Naipaul as merely a reflection of the "distress" of the whole society. It is part of Naipaul's metatheory that human beings can only be secure when they are born and nurtured within the shadow of their ancestors.

Societies in the Caribbean, then, can only breed individuals whose problems are incapable of resolution and whose impotence flows from this root cause. Naipaul carefully reinforces the message. Kripalsingh is the descendant of the uprooted Indian in the Caribbean; but the descendants of the other races fare just as badly. Hok, the representative of the Chinese races, and Browne, the African descended boy, and, by extension, all the boys of Kripalsingh's era are locked in a blemished world where they only survive by excluding the reality of their environment and their existence. They are all of high intellectual calibre, sensitivity, and astuteness. They are physically well balanced and graceful. Yet their survival depends on a denial of existence. They are refugees in the world of the intellect, in Latin books, in temperate climates. To put it tritely, only apples exist where oranges abound. Their affliction resides in the overwhelming shoddiness of their environment. Born to disgrace within a disgraceful backwater, only imaginative and emotional escape makes life bearable.

What kind of action can be expected from people like these? Where their action is political it cannot be ideological. It cannot derive out of consensus or plurality of views. It becomes rather of the nature of a howl in the dark, a desperate individual response to distress, an emotional reaching out to fellow sufferers. Thus Kripalsingh's father becomes the focus of a political movement. His own anxiety and dejection happen to coincide with that of exploited dock workers, and he becomes their leader. But a political act which surfaces from these blighted roots has no solid basis, no real direction. Singh has to fall back on the relics of his ancestral Hindu religion. He becomes a source of solace to people who have no other hope. The assessment here is clear: The Indian in these societies, although likewise uprooted, does have the possibility of drawing on his rich underlying cultural and religious heritage for philosophical direction, succor, and support. Although his understanding of its wholeness is imperfect, he nevertheless can offer the Negro (the dock workers) a glimpse of the meaningfulness of existence which they are wholly incapable of producing for themselves. But even this unsubstantial cultural link is being lost between the generations of these uprooted peoples. It is interesting to note that Singh's larger humanity can only be perceived by his son when it has been revealed to him by an English aristocrat in England. As Naipaul so clearly believes, it is the European who must reveal every aspect of his existence to the Third World persona since there is no system of value in that environment against which the individual can judge either the quality of his beliefs and existence or his environment.

The assessment of Third World political action and interaction given in *The Mimic Men* is a devastating one. But its outlines are very clear, and its ramifications are further explored in *Guerillas*. Jimmy Ahmed's irremediably blemished self is the result of the squalor of his birth: a half-caste "born in the back room of a Chinese grocery."[1] This ramshackle beginning cannot be transcended. The society which spawns births like these cannot produce men of substance. The Caribbean is therefore "a place that had exhausted its possibilities. . . . Nothing that happened here could be important."[2]

Like all Third World personalities, Ahmed has no real understanding of himself or his society. His image of himself is a reflection of that created by those people in England who perceived him according to their own wrong-headed predilections. Yet this deficient personality is to be expected to act, to create vital social change within the society. Like Singh he becomes the eye of an evanescent emotional expression of the frustration and impotence of the more severely disadvantaged elements of society, and for a time he is able to channel and express it. But again, like Singh, his actions end in lonely and random violence, a violence which it is suggested has some darkly ritualistic and primitive meaning, a faulty and debased attempt to recapture the ancestral past.

These dramatic politically motivated events are brief and transient, again precisely because the society is incapable of producing the intellectual depth which could encourage an ideological or philosophical response to these scintillae of pain. Browne and Kripalsingh in *The Mimic Men* are university trained as is Meredith in *Guerillas*. But their attempts at political action are equally ineffectual, equally doomed to failure. They despise themselves and their societies. Browne is the Black Power advocate: but his newspaper "The Socialist" is "petty and absurd," and he satirizes his people, the smell of the mob, their ignorance, the narrowness of their aims and desires. Even worse is his total lack of respect for the people whom he purports to serve: on the subject of their exclusion from jobs in the bank he says: "If I thought black people were handling my few cents I wouldn't sleep too well."[3] Browne and Kripalsingh represent the new politicians of the post-colonial Caribbean world: in such hands independence can only be a farcical exercise.

Naipaul's further explorations of the genesis and effects of political action in the Third World are set in Africa. Within *In a Free State* the projections are tentatively developed: *A Bend in the River* examines them in greater detail. The "free state" is a newly independent African country. But independence has meant the outbreak of civil war. The act of war is political: it is an attempt by the president to assert his jurisdiction over the king's people. It may be noted here that whereas in relation to the Caribbean the politicians were presented as being incapable of any real action, in the African setting real action is war. But like the violence in *Guerrillas* it is a negative, destructive act. Moreover, its motivation is perfectly irrational. It is based on a precolonial, preideological motive. Mysterious and primordial, it is further strengthened by the African desire to enslave. It is Naipaul's suggestion both in *In a Free State* and in *A Bend in The River* that slavery and the desire to enslave are peculiarly African conditions.[4]

The president in the African state controls the army, the helicopters, the impressive outputs of modern technology created in another civilization, that of, as Naipaul says: "the makers and doers." Their "legitimate" uses are being perverted in Africa. The president himself is a pure pragmatist. He is the accommodator who wears his hair "in the English style" and affects Western-type suits. Without the dignity of an ideological system, ennobling nationalism, or even racial pride, he imports white mercenaries to hunt down his own people. In other words, with independence in Africa the systems of modern Europe are being used to serve wholly irrational and ignoble ends.

But what of the citizen of this "free state"? Free peoples are certainly those who must enjoy the rights and privileges of citizens within the boundaries of their particular state. The important corollaries, commonplace but nevertheless true, are the commitment and the intelligence to operate the reticulated network of rights and privileges and responsibilities. It is difficult to imagine the African citizens of *In a Free State* as having the capability of functioning within a modern political system.

Firstly, the educated middle classes who belong to the president's people share the fruits of the president's power, as Naipaul describes them:

> The Africans were young . . . could read and write,
> and were high civil servants, politicians or the
> relations of politicians, non-executive directors and
> managing directors of recently opened branches of
> big international corporations. They were the new
> men of the country and they saw themselves as
> men of power.[5]

But if the middle classes are contemptible, the masses are "pathetic." In crowds they are "blank-faced," "featureless," docilely being herded into trucks.[6] Their clothes are cast-off European clothes, shabby, and patched. In other words, it appears that they have made some external adaptations towards European culture, but it is an imperfect accommodation, unsightly, and at variance with the indigenous sense (as symbolized by the colorful patches on their clothes). Single representatives of the common people are no more admirable. For example, the African at the Hotel, although invested with more individuality and personality (his clothes "fitted"), is equally dirty and sweaty. His face shows "age alone rather than a quality of experience. . . . His smile was fixed."[7] The picture is a negative one: the Africans seem to understand only hate and rage. This sense of smouldering rage causes Naipaul to invest their personalities with a kind of menace which seems to emanate from the secrecy of their primitive ceremonies and the total irrationality and unpredictability of their behavior.

The king's people add further dimensions to this picture of the citizens of the modern African state. The king himself, the African version of an aristocrat, is shallow, unthinking. A "forest-person," his authority had been fraught with the same insubstantiality and impermanence which is intrinsic to a forest culture. During the period of colonialism there had been an attempt to invest him with permanence and presence in the shape of a concrete palace. But in the post-colonial era he has reverted to insubstantiality. He becomes victim to the primal disorder of his society, falls prey to the savagery of his ancient enemy. But there is no real sympathy for the "poor little king": having assumed the norms and attitudes of his colonial masters, he has lost even his native forest cunning: he attempts to escape not by disappearing into the bush, but by taking a taxi. The rest of the king's people are semi-literate forest dwellers, totally unsuited for the modern world and incapable of even the simplest manual labour which is associated with civilization: that of cleaning the windows of a car or pumping gas. They cannot even collect money or understand a monetary system.[8]

Many other motifs apparent in *In a Free State* are further developed in *A Bend in the River*. The postcolonial era has meant violence and destruction of all the permanent structures created by colonialism. The destruction has been caused by African rage at European domination:

> The steamer monument had been knocked down
> with all the other colonial statutes and monuments.
> Pedestals had been defaced, protective railings
> flattened, floodlights smashed and left to rust.
> Ruins had been left as ruins; no attempt had been

> made to tidy up. . . . The wish had only been to
> get rid of the intruder. It was unnerving. The depth
> of the African rage, the wish to destroy, regardless
> of the consequences. (p. 33)

Again, then, African action is imperfect; it is destructive, unthinking violence, almost a perverse and inevitable desire to revert to the bush.

Naipaul's pervasive sense of the return of Africa to a primeval state is recorded in his treatment of the environment in this novel. He compares the order, the beauty, the care given to a European city with the chaos of the African city:

> I was walking on the Embankment, beside the
> river. . . . On the Embankment wall there are
> green lamp standards. I had been examining the
> dolphins on the standards, dolphin by dolphin,
> standard by standard. I was far from where I had
> started, and I had momentarily left the dolphins to
> examine the metal supports of the pavement
> benches. These supports . . . were in the shape of
> camels. . . . I stopped, stepped back mentally . . .
> and all at once saw the beauty in which I had been
> walking—the beauty of the light, the river and the
> sky, the soft colours of the clouds, the beauty of
> light on water, the beauty of the buildings, the
> care with which it had all been arranged. (p. 163)

> This was the President's city. . . . This was where,
> in colonial days he had got his idea of Europe.
> The colonial city . . . with many residential areas
> rich with decorative, sheltering trees . . . was still
> to be seen. It was with this Europe that, in his own
> buildings, the President wished to compete. The
> city while decaying in the center, with dirt roads
> and rubbish mounds just at the back of the great
> colonial boulevards, was yet full of new public
> works. (p. 267)

All facilities are third class, and there is the strong sensation that the timelessness of the river and the jungle will eventually reassert itself and that the feeble efforts of the African at civilized endeavour will simply and inexorably disappear.

With this brooding sense of impending destruction, political action must be essentially meaningless. Like leaders in the Caribbean, the Big Man, a city boy and therefore a rootless person in the African context, is driven only by the psychological imperative of exorcising the frenzy caused by the humiliating circumstances of his birth; his mother had been a hotel maid during the colonial era. The Big Man is a wily politician, a soldier who at first seems to irradiate intelligence and guidance for the masses from the capital. But he soon begins to demonstrate the usual Naipaulian flaws of the Third World politician: He trusts his white advisors and mercenaries rather than his own people; he apes the mannerisms of the aristocratic European ruler. But his posturings soon become more dangerous: he becomes *malin,* bullying, murderous. He rules by the invocation of symbols, fetishes, dreams. He adopts some of these symbols from

European civilizations but only in order to parody them. How can there be a *citoyen* in a state where rights, freedoms, law and order are unknown? His use of the African Madonna, his *maximes* and portraits are simply frauds. As he moves more and more into the shadow of his ancestral persona, even his "Window to the World," "The Domain," is revealed as a shoddy hoax which cannot be saved from destruction, even with the greatest amount of idealism and intensity.

The unhealthiness of the Big Man's psyche and system must affect the whole society and, with the deficiencies of that society, together create an irredeemable state. It is nonsense to speak of law, justice, citizenship where the people understand only exploitation:

> Asians, Greeks and other Europeans remained prey, to be stalked in different ways. Some men were to be feared, and stalked cautiously: it was necessary to be servile with some. . . . It was in the history of the land: here men had always been prey. (p. 62)

Africans are *malins*—"not wicked," "mischievous," "bad-minded," but

> *malins* the way a dog chasing a lizard was *malin* or a cat chasing a bird. The people were *malins* because they lived with the knowledge of men as prey. (p. 62)

The animal imagery is intentional here: it conveys the mindless, inhuman cruelty inherent in African personality, the lack of appreciation or understanding of other people as human beings.

This assessment of African personality is not surprising since in the picture of Ferdinand we are presented with the modern African who has his roots in the forest village in the "real" ancestral life (his mother is a sorceress). Ferdinand is the prototype of the African civil servant who interprets and administers the desires of "the Big Man." But his limitations are severe, although his future at first seems secure: "how easy it had been made for him." But he begins as a bush African, and for Naipaul, Africans have truly dwelt for centuries in darkness where no societal organization, no cultural continuity has been etched on their minds. They know of magic, dreams, superstitions; but that is all. Ferdinand's mind is truly a *tabula rasa*:

> You took a boy out of the bush and you taught him to read and write: you levelled the bush and built a polytechnic and you sent him there. It seemed as easy as that, if you came late to the world and found ready-made those things that other countries and peoples had taken so long to arrive at—writing, printing, universities, books, knowledge. The rest of us had to take things in stages. . . . [W]e were so clogged by what the centuries had deposited in our minds and hearts. Ferdinand, *starting from nothing* had with one step made himself free and was ready to race ahead of us. (p. 112; emphasis mine)

African culture and knowledge are simply of no value.

Of course, Ferdinand cannot "race ahead" of anyone: the society does not permit it. He must fall prey eventually to the madness which leads the president to victimize and annihilate everyone, even those he has created.

Politics in Africa, then, is the world of the exploiter and the exploited, the shabby and the corrupt. Blood and iron is the substitute for law and order. Viciousness, dishonesty, and trickery have replaced political philosophy. But those things are to be expected because all Third World endeavors are useless. Modern Africa, after all, is almost an unsubstantial creation, "flimsy," on the verge of returning to the bush. The root cause of the "frenzy" is the awareness of their insignificance among the creators, "the makers and the doers of the world." As Salim says; "I had just come from Europe; I had seen the real competition" (p. 266).

The sentiments which are encapsulated in the above quotation may be interpreted as the overt expression of an underlying presumption in this work, and indeed in all the novels which are being considered here. There is always the feeling that Naipaul is using Europe as the standard against which the Third World is measured. This unabashedly Euro-centered view of the world is remarkable in a writer of Third World origins and one who in fact continues to write about India, Africa, Latin America, and the Caribbean. At the root of the comparison between Europe and the Third World is the perception that Europe represents civilization, law, order. It is seen as the repository of history, the cradle of ideas, of creative endeavour, of intellectual depth. Towards the end of *A Bend in the River,* where narrative voice fractures and focus moves from Salim, the major character to spotlight the long monologue of the other two Indian characters who are also born in Africa, the reader is struck by the fact that their life experiences are concerned with their relationships to Europe and European peoples and societies, their fears of the consequences of the massive intrusions of Third World peoples with their inadequate perceptions of order, and their diverse social values into these carefully developed civilizations. At this stage the authorial voice becomes extremely self-evident, and the style takes on the more realistic mode of the journalist. This stress on opinions lessens the feeling of verisimilitude and confirms that the author is in fact attempting to disseminate his opinions.

But is Europe really "the competition"? If this view is accepted, then it would entail corollaries that there is only one model for human development, that only one area of the world is worthy of emulation. This would imply a presupposition that one's historical sense must confine itself to the post-industrial sector of human history and must ignore the facts of continuous human development and the diversity of human attitudes which a wider ranging look at history and societies must surely reveal. Is the common man in any of the world's major societies which are outside the scope of European thought and endeavour really engaged in attempting to "catch-up" with European education, mores, norms, political and social organization which Naipaul seems to suggest as the only path for Africa and the Caribbean? Is there no possible awareness of self save by comparison with the European awareness of that identity as unique, and therefore the source of definition for the entire world?

Acceptance of this viewpoint must be regarded as part of the intellectual milieu of the writer who sees the act of literary creation as confined to "literate societies," and as presenting an avenue for self-awareness and self definition. The quotation:

> The World is what it is; men who are nothing, who allow themselves to become nothing have no place in it.[9]

is relevant here. It expresses the strong conviction that the individual can, by his own efforts, escape the limitations of his origins. But this escape is only for those who are sensitive, talented and aware: not for the group as a whole. There exists the possibility of linking even this viewpoint to the traditionally elitist viewpoint of European societies and education, where the privileged few are accorded a higher social and intellectual value.

It could also be argued that the presentation of the Third World environment as barren not only serves to reinforce the ironic mode of these works and to transfer the modern intellectual theme of the wasteland into the Third World environment, but it also recalls the well-known, almost axiomatic European view which maintained that "nothing" existed south of the Sahara until one arrived at South Africa. This perception has been somewhat moderated through the additional knowledge of the meanings of culture and civilization, of the variety of endeavors which might be named "creative." But in a strange way, Naipaul appears to remain impervious to these more sensitive and inclusive assessments of human endeavour.

These remarks should not be taken to mean that Naipaul is always totally wedded to the European viewpoint. Indeed there are places where he condemns European hypocrisy and lies, the self-interested use of Third World situations to further individual careers or to further individual ambitions. He also marvels at the arrogance which led them to create civilized settlements in places "whose future had come and gone." Again, in *A Bend in the River* the European god has not approved of the mixing of peoples as the motto "Miscerique que probat populos et foedera jungi" seemed to suggest. [He approves of the mingling of peoples and their bands of union.] European arrogance has assumed that peoples could be united: but to Naipaul this is anathema. The mingling of peoples in the Third World has led to disastrously insecure individuals. In Africa it has meant loss of power, identity, and individuality for the Arabs. In modern Europe, "where hundreds of people like myself from parts of the world like mine had forced themselves in to work and live," (p. 247), the mixing of peoples is causing Europe

to be "shrunken and mean and forbidding." The disorganization, the squalor of the Third World, the dishonesty in trading, and the slavery are catching up with Europe and subverting its culture.

Of course, it is difficult to speak of modern Third World societies and avoid the subject of the relationships of the races. And for Naipaul, the Third World writer, this subject is interestingly handled. In both *The Mimic Men* and *A Bend in the River* the major characters are Indians born in the Caribbean and in Africa. They are the most sensitively perceived and the most fully developed characters in these works. But they are on the fringes of their societies, not relating in any profound way to members of the other races. In *The Mimic Men,* as we have seen, Kripalsingh does become for a moment part of a political movement. But his involvement in the society is short-lived, and he is a withdrawn, isolated personality. The Indians here also have unsatisfactory relationships with Europeans of both sexes. With Africans they are uneasy, anxious, fearful of exploitation. The Indians, though born in Africa, have no interest in, or understanding of, African culture, societal relationships, aims, or aspirations.

In *The Mimic Men* and again in *Guerrillas* Naipaul suggests that the French Creoles, representatives of the white colonial power structure, retain prestigious positions in the Caribbean, although like the Arabs in Africa they have lost real power since "the tarbrush passed there." Their relationship with the black peoples is analyzed as being one of tolerance and understanding, best expressed by the phrase that those locked in a slave-owner–slave relationship for centuries understand each other. But the tolerance on both sides is mixed with an ironic view of the posturings of the newly powerful blacks and a desire to continually remind them of their past. Within this linked relationship of former slave-owner and slave, the Indian has no place.

The European in Africa and in the Caribbean is either a sloppily sentimental liberal without clearly defined aims and with a flawed personality such as Bobby in *In a Free State* or Peter in *Guerrillas* or a failed intellectual attempting to regain a power position in the Third World like Raymond. In any event the "mingling of races," an event brought about by European political expansion, is, in Naipaul's view, a disaster.

These stances lead to a perception which is explicitly antisocialist. The mingling of peoples from the various races is after all a physical manifestation of the kind of inherent equality which socialism attempts to express in ideological terms. But this political philosophy stands in direct contrast to Naipaul's abiding faith in the elitism of the talented. Accordingly, Naipaul discusses socialism in the Third World as "a Third World socialistic pose." He makes it clear that all the new politicians mouth socialism—but necessarily meaninglessly, because where are the community, the honesty, the intellect, the belief in human endeavour which must support this political philosophy? It is interesting that in spite of his knowledge of the history within a society, he does not use his knowledge of the history of the Third World to arrive at any dialectical position which postulates the necessity for change, growth, or development. For the masses there is no hope.

It is a negative and pessimistic view, unrelieved by any positive features which may truly show an awareness of the possibility of the evolution of states in political terms, of the value of political ideology, be it socialist or nationalistic within these societies, or of the immeasurable increase in pride, self-awareness, emotional health, and material benefit which political independence brings to Third World peoples.

### NOTES

[1] V. S. Naipaul, *Guerrillas* (New York: Random House, 1980), p. 18.

[2] Ibid., pp. 50-51.

[3] V. S. Naipaul, *The Mimic Men* (London: Deutsch, 1967), p. 118.

[4] V. S. Naipaul, *A Bend in the River* (London: Deutsch, 1979), pp. 19, 62, 83. Hereafter cited in the text by page reference only.

[5] V. S. Naipaul, *In a Free State* (New York: Penguin, 1978), p. 104.

[6] Ibid., p. 121.

[7] Ibid., p. 130.

[8] Ibid., pp. 146-48.

[9] Naipaul, *A Bend in the River*, p. 91.

### Barbara Eckstein

SOURCE: "Pleasure and Joy: Political Activism in Nadine Gordimer's Short Stories," in *World Literature Today,* Vol. 59, No. 3, Summer, 1985, pp. 343-46.

[*In the following essay, Eckstein considers Nadine Gordimer's short stories as an attempt to break down dichotomies in South African political culture.*]

I know a recent college graduate, a young white man from an ordinary, comfortable suburb of an American Midwestern city. At Kenyon College he studied Central American history and culture, and now he is a political activist, living sometimes in Central America but mostly in the city where he grew up. Not too long ago I asked him if he sees much of his parents, who still live in the suburb across town. "No, not much," he explained. "They're into pleasure and I'm into joy." When I began

thinking about all the characters in Nadine Gordimer's short stories who try to be activists or try not to be, I was reminded of my friend and his parents. Because true political activism does aspire to a secularized transcendence and political passivity does seek pleasure to numb reality, his dichotomy is useful in pinpointing what distinguishes political activists from others. One would think, moreover, that in a society as compartmentalized as South Africa's, this distinction between activists and others—in fact, any self and other—would be clearcut. However, most particularly in a nation whose official governmental policy since 1948 has been to mystify the black other as enemy and so promote dichotomist, we-they thinking, no dichotomy of humanity can withstand careful scrutiny. Careful, skeptical, but compassionate scrutiny is exactly the method of Nadine Gordimer's short stories.

John Cooke, Stephen Clingman, and others who have studied Gordimer's novels see in them a general movement from personal to political interaction and, in many of the novels, a direct response to the political context of a particular phase in South African history.[1] I am persuaded that this perception of a progression in the novels is well founded. The short stories, however, are different. Because short stories, at their best, have the resonance of a lyric, they can often be prescient in a way a novel cannot. A writer may well have an inkling of a complex vision beyond social dichotomies, find an image to embody that inkling, and thus create a very provocative short story. Still, a writer needs more than an inkling and an image to sustain a fictional society for the course of a novel. Even though Gordimer's novels show a development away from compartmentalized personal lives toward a holistic social vision, from the 1950s onward her short stories have suggested the kind of ambiguities that confound one's efforts to separate self from other, hero from enemy, even pleasure from joy.

"Is There Somewhere Else Where We Can Meet?" published in 1953, is just such a story. Simply put, it seems to be the story of a young white woman who, finding herself alone in a deserted lot, encounters a ragged black man who robs her. This is the apparent action of the story, but there is no unequivocal evidence to confirm the truth of this appearance. Cooke, who does himself read the story as a robbery, nevertheless provides the terms to describe the story in another way. He suggests the terms *camera-eye* and *painterly* for two techniques Gordimer uses: the first is a detached perspective; the second, engaged.[2] "Somewhere Else" is a painterly story. The writer is very engaged in the fearful perception of the white woman as her eye flies past the landscape to the one use of red paint, the cap on the black man's head. Plunged into blind fear and unable to focus on anything else, the woman is thrown totally off balance as she and the red cap approach one another. The characters' movement has such a dizzying effect that after they are face to face, it is impossible to tell exactly what their ensuing actions are. Writer and reader are enveloped in the fear felt by the woman, who is the central consciousness: "Every vestige of control, of sense, of thought, went out of her as a room plunges into dark at the failure of power."[3]

In this dark room of fear without sense or thought, she sees what she has anticipated all her life: assault by a black man. However, in this dark room the reader cannot be certain that the character's "awful dreams came true," because the black man's movements are always a response to the white woman's; he may be steadying her, after all, and not robbing her. In her fear she is not able to consider this possibility. So when she "fumbled crazily" with her packages, and then "his hand clutched her shoulder," she is forced to interpret this as "grabbing out at her." She fights him; he responds by "jerking her back." She drops her packages; he responds—as she puts it—by "falling upon them." He may, in fact, be picking them up. In the dark room of fear one sees only the images of one's own nightmares; they may or may not truly be embodied in some external reality.

The beautifully created tension and ambiguity in this story allow for a vision beyond personal fear. Because the woman has confronted her fear of the other, she may have taken the first step toward political commitment to change herself and her society. When she first enters the barren dreamscape at the beginning of the story, her eye is riveted on the red cap. Knowing that it is what she fears, she is propelled toward it, not in a death wish, as Freud might have it, but rather in an instinctual desire for survival. The desire to know that which one fears, to imagine what is real—no matter its horror—is the raw material for the thought and action that makes personal and social survival possible.[4] Thus the young South African woman is compelled to leave her white female isolation and confront the two-personed other she has been conditioned to fear and distrust: the black "peril" the South African Nationalist Party has created to unify white voters, and the black male with whom sexual interaction is illegal and immoral. When she does face the mythical other, she discovers that, though she cannot see clearly, she can survive.

Only after literally grappling with the black man does she realize, first, that she is relieved when she stops fighting and, second, that whether or not he was robbing her, it was silly to fight for her money, which she needs so much less than he. She uncovers at least this much reality by jeopardizing her security. At the end of the story she is described as an "invalid" picking burrs from her stockings. No longer protected and imprisoned by the pleasures and forces of isolation, she is vulnerable. Transcendent joy is hardly at hand, but it is now a possibility for this survivor. Her meeting with the black man has not been pleasant, but for a moment she and the African did stand on the common ground of Africa, which runs from under one prison to under another.[5]

In "The Smell of Death and Flowers," a more discursive story published in 1956, a young white woman takes her first overt political action. Having just returned to Africa after five years in England, she is very correct and bored with her prettiness. At a party given by white liberals she "feels nothing," she thinks, and so it is only whimsy that makes her decide to join the white activists on a protest march into the black quarter. Her participation at the march is like her attendance at the party: unfeeling politeness. Only her sense of etiquette prevents her from leaving. Even after the marchers are arrested, she again thinks, "I feel nothing"; but in the police station her "psychic numbing"[6] constitutes an even more emphatic defense against seeing what is real than it did at the party. Not until she is being booked and thereby becoming the victim whom others, including blacks, observe does she recognize the observer she has been and so see the arbitrary will of white supremacy which they have felt. Gordimer writes, "And she felt suddenly, not *nothing*."[7]

Not nothing" is something, but it is not much. Unlike the young woman in the earlier story who enters the dark room alone, this woman moves disinterestedly into an established society of activists. Her transformation is sudden and guarded. Unable to feel pleasure at the party, she also stands at a great distance from any joyful release that follows political engagement. She does not grapple with her fear in pursuit of knowledge that will free her from an isolated, inherited point of view. Her vision of herself as a victim of the white god, as the blacks have been victims, and the feeling that attends this vision may be a genuine epiphany, but the vision may also be a sentimental one which cannot break down the barriers of dichotomies. This pretty protagonist may be like some of the American activists in the sixties whom Christopher Lasch describes: young people from the suburbs who demonstrated not out of commitment or even fear, but because demonstrations suddenly produced a feeling that broke through numbness like a hallucinogen or amphetamine.[8] Because "The Smell of Death and Flowers" is a camera-eye account and not a painterly story, and because its protagonist is more thoroughly numbed, it is less successful in complicating dichotomies than is "Somewhere Else." It does clearly show, however, that all the folks on one side of the police barriers are not of the same self. It also suggests that the distance between liberalism and political activism is no shorter than that between conservatism and political change.[9]

Even armed with awareness and feeling, those who take action to alleviate injustice so as to break out of the isolation into which they were born cannot suffer the exact fate of those without choice. In South Africa this means no white activist, no matter how often she is jailed, will ever be black. After the heyday of interracial political action in the fifties, then the Sharpeville massacre in 1960 and the subsequent banning of the African National Congress, this fact came home to South Africa's black activists. Forced to go underground, they chose to work alone. The white activists were left to wonder if they would ever be able to struggle with or know the Africans.

Never sanguine about the possibilities of interracialism, Gordimer most explicitly shows this skepticism in several stories from the sixties and seventies, particularly "Not for Publication," "Open House," and "A Soldier's Embrace." Of these, "A Soldier's Embrace" is the most confounding, for it shows that even when black and white activists work together and succeed, their success inexplicably segregates them. In this story a white woman is caught up in a street party celebrating the liberation of an African state from a white-minority government. The woman and her husband, a lawyer who has defended black activists, have worked with the blacks for just such a liberation. So when, simultaneously, she is hugged in the street by both a white soldier (a European mercenary) and a black soldier, the visceral experience seems the perfect image of the new state. After the liberation, however, their black friends are, in fact, cool; they are engrossed in the task of setting up a government independent of any whites' advice. Sadly, with or without whites' advice, the likelihood is that independence will not be freedom for the new state, because all southern Africa is economically dependent upon South African white-supremacist capitalism.[10] So this new state is destined to flounder and suffer, and even the most well-meaning whites are destined to move elsewhere to a stable economy, where they can practice their professions and run their businesses. Still, when the white couple in the story finally do decide to move, their African friend, earlier businesslike and cool, now cries. There is some genuine feeling embedded in their history of struggle together, however separate that togetherness has been, yet their success confounds everyone's identity. As they drive away, the woman thinks, "The right words would not come again."[11] The woman's pleasure in the soldiers' embraces might have been joy, since they have all worked for such liberation; but it is not.

Gordimer has stated several times that in South Africa no division is more absolute than that between the races.[12] In her short stories, however, she does not always accept the inevitability of this division. In a number of stories about activism and marriage, she explores all the permutations and combinations of connection and disjunction: is the most pronounced difference between activists and nonactivists (regardless of race and sex), between men and women (regardless of political commitment and race), or between blacks and whites (regardless of sex and political commitment)? Gordimer's stories of marriage, like Chaucer's "Marriage Group," come up with every possible answer to the questions they raise. Though others might well be added, the stories to which I am referring are "Six Feet of the Country" (1956), "Something for the Time Being" (1960), "A Chip of Glass Ruby" (1965), "Some Monday for Sure" (1965), and "A Soldier's Embrace" (1975). The complexities of the connections in these stories make them some of Gordimer's best.

"A Chip of Glass Ruby" must be singled out because it contains an Indian heroine with a true Gandhian heart. She succeeds if not in all her political goals, at least in being thoroughly alive by remembering and attending to the myriad details of political commitment and family. When her surly husband is both annoyed and awed by his wife's ability to remember his birthday even when she is

in prison, his daughter explains her mother to him: "'It's because she doesn't want anybody to be left out [that] she always remembers.'"[13] Even the husband comes to realize he desires his wife because she not only survives, she lives. She has the very rare ability to sustain joy.

Due to the limits of space, I will have to leave the intricacies of the "Marriage Group" for another essay. Instead I would like to look at Gordimer's most recent work, the novella *Something Out There,* in which the dichotomies of activists and others, men and women, and blacks and whites all have an opportunity to complicate one another. At the beginning of the story, what is "out there" is some sort of wild primate which is terrorizing the white suburb, an obvious invasion of Africa into the isolated white enclave. Fear prohibits even those who see the primate from describing it with any accuracy, and fear feeds on itself until all the self-involved insecurities of the white suburbanites are externalized in the body of the primate "out there." The great irony of the novella is that while the newspapers and neighbors are obsessed with the ape, four human terrorists establish themselves on the edge of the suburb and, after careful planning, blow up the power station. This irony works nicely, but it is not what most interests me about the novella.

What interests me is that the terrorists enter the area and rent a house without fuss because the white man and woman terrorist pose as a young married couple soon to have a baby. Of course, the suburbanites are taken in by the disguise, but it is the meaning of the sham marriage and sham pregnancy for the terrorists that is intriguing. Once lovers, the young couple, Charles and Joy, continue to pursue their radical political action despite the dissolution of their personal relationship. This is admirable enough in light of several of the marriage stories in which characters refuse to see their compromised ideals in order to maintain a marriage. The novella certainly too gives ample evidence of joyless married suburbanites assuaged by pleasure. Nevertheless, Charles and Joy's ability to feign marriage and pregnancy without any notable second thoughts is a numbness of its own. Joy, in particular, can play the game of the young pregnant wife at the suburban grocery store with aplomb but is never shown making any connections with this life from which she originated.[14] For her, the white suburbanites are as other and "out there" as the ape is to the suburbanites. They are simplified, externalized evil. Because she does not feel the loss of what she has left or the viability of others' lives—however narrowly lived—her political commitment is its own ideological, walled garden. Joy does not live up to her name. That she would be only feigning pregnancy seems appropriate.

Still, I am not sure that this failure is entirely to be blamed on the character. Gordimer's portraits of the Afrikaners who rent Charles and Joy the house and of the other nouveau-riche whites terrorized by the ape are stinging portrayals of the pettiness of the bourgeoisie. So when we are told that Joy has come from such a home, it is not surprising that she thoroughly rejects it; but neither is her decision as human or as interesting as it could be. Despite the novella's being a satire, it is in other regards realistic enough to incorporate less exaggerated, more complex portraits of the rising white middle class.

I am not defending the values of the white middle class—let alone white supremacy—or even any intrinsic worth of marriage and pregnancy. However, when individuals born into this system of being leave it without any apparent struggle, I am skeptical of their ability to become truly engaged in any other struggle. Nonetheless, I should also say that Gordimer's novels demonstrate that she has been very aware of the struggle to leave home, however distasteful its values.[15]

The novella does present one character who ventures out to connect with the society that the radicals seek to change. Eddie, a young black activist, risks going into Johannesburg, the core of apartheid. Like the white woman in "Somewhere Else," he seems compelled to do the thing which most jeopardizes him. In the daytime the city is teeming with the lives of all races, and Eddie becomes a part of that life. He wanders the grocery-store aisles as though at a "vast exhibition," window-shops along busy streets, buys himself some curried chicken, and is propositioned by a prostitute. South African society has treated him far worse than it has Joy, but he feels the necessity to remind himself of concrete lives and a bustling economy. Contrasting alienated, white, Western antiheroes to African heroes, Gordimer has explained that African heroes, like Eddie, say yes, yes, yes by saying no; they suffer but are not sick at heart.[16] Eddie derives pleasure from what he must destroy, and so he knows the price not only of his failure—death or imprisonment or exile—but of his success. Knowledge does not change his commitment; it keeps that commitment human.

When Eddie returns to the hideout, he and Joy dance while Vusi plays his homemade saxophone and Charles looks on.[17] Eddie again connects. In their isolated activist community, the white woman can approach the black man without fear and the black man can approach the white woman without rags. They all know, however, that the connection they make will soon be lost. After the power station is blown, one may be killed, all will be scattered, most will be in exile. It will be a long time before the filaments Eddie noiselessly and patiently sends out can stick and permanently hold. Perhaps that time will never come. In the meantime there is the possibility of joy for those who will risk it.

At their engaged and engaging best, Gordimer's short stories offer the reader not just "the pleasure of the text," but the joy of the text as well. We do not just luxuriate in the language; we rejoice in the commitment that confounds all dichotomies.

NOTES

[1] See Stephen Clingman, "Multi-Racialism, or *A World of Strangers*," *Salmagundi*, 62 (Winter 1984), pp. 32-61;

John Cooke, *Only Pursue: The Novels of Nadine Gordimer*, Baton Rouge, Louisiana State University Press, 1985 (forthcoming); and John Cooke, "African Landscapes: The World of Nadine Gordimer," *WLT* 52:4 (Autumn 1978), pp. 533-38.

[2] Cooke, *Only Pursue*, p. 154.

[3] Nadine Gordimer, "Is There Somewhere Else Where We Can Meet?" in her *Selected Stories*, New York, Penguin, 1976 (rpt. 1983), pp. 17-20.

[4] Robert Jay Lifton, *The Life of the Self: Toward a New Psychology*, New York, Basic Books, 1976 (rpt. 1983), pp. 129-30.

[5] In "The Novel and the Nation in South Africa" (*TLS*, 11 August 1961, pp. 520-23), Gordimer writes: "It is unlikely that while you are within the stockade thrown up around your mind by the situation about which you are reading, you will be aware that a common ground runs beneath your feet to beneath the stockade of another particular situation, and another."

[6] Lifton replaces the Freudian term *denial* with *psychic numbing*, because denial focuses on individual, infantile repression, and Lifton wants to emphasize the individual affecting and affected by society.

[7] Nadine Gordimer, "The Smell of Death and Flowers," in her *Selected Stories*, pp. 122-44.

[8] Christopher Lasch, *The Culture of Narcissism*, New York, Warner, 1979, pp. 57-70.

[9] For more on the limitations of liberalism, see Kenneth Parker on *A World of Strangers* in "Nadine Gordimer and the Pitfalls of Liberalism," in *The South African Novel in English: Essays in Criticism and Society*, Kenneth Parker, ed., New York, Africana, 1978, pp. 114-30.

[10] Donald Denoon, with Balam Nyeko and J. B. Webster, *"Nationalisms" in Southern Africa since 1800*, Washington, D.C., Praeger, 1973, pp. 214-29. More recently, Claude Robinson has demonstrated this same fact in his discussion of a Mozambique—South African pact in "Delicate Peace with Apartheid," *The Nation*, 22 September 1984, pp. 235-36.

[11] Nadine Gordimer, "A Soldier's Embrace," in her collection *A Soldier's Embrace*, New York, Viking, 1980, pp. 7-22.

[12] Nadine Gordimer, in "A Conversation with Nadine Gordimer" [interviews with Robert Boyers, Clark Blaise, Terence Diggory, and Jordan Elgrably], *Salmagundi*, 62 (Winter 1984), pp. 3-31.

[13] Nadine Gordimer, "A Chip of Glass Ruby," in her *Selected Stories*, pp. 264-74.

[14] Elizabeth Gerver notes the importance of Lukács's emphasis on connections ("Everything is linked to everything else") in her consideration of some of the women in Gordimer's novels, "Women Revolutionaries in the Novels of Nadine Gordimer and Doris Lessing," *World Literature Written in English,* 17 (1978), pp. 38-50.

[15] Cooke, "Leaving the Mother's House," in his *Only Pursue,* pp. 59-117, provides a great deal of evidence to support Gordimer on this point.

[16] Nadine Gordimer, *The Black Interpreters: Notes on African Writing,* Johannesburg, Ravan, 1973, p. 9.

[17] Nadine Gordimer, *Something Out There, Salmagundi,* 62 (Winter 1984), pp. 118-92. See particularly pp. 165-72.

## Charles R. Larson

SOURCE: "The Precarious State of the African Writer," in *World Literature Today,* Vol. 60, No. 3, Summer, 1986, pp. 409-13.

*[In the following essay, Larson examines the effects of governmental corruption on African writers.]*

These are not good times for African writers—or Third World writers almost anywhere, for that matter. Political and economic factors (determinants even in the best of times) have become so unstable in recent years that the African literary scene has begun to resemble a barren wasteland, unprecedented at any time since the early 1960s, the era of independence. What can be more ironic than to glance back to the final days of colonialism and regard them nostalgically as the golden days of African literature—stifled by the increasing political instability across the continent once Africans shook off their colonial shackles? African writers, it appears, have paid for their independence with their creativity.

Before I begin my tale of woe, however, let me illustrate with one lengthy example the economic obstacles operating against African writers even in the best of times (those infrequent periods when publishers are receptive to creativity and the books they publish are widely read, if not sold). For this hypothetical example, I shall use Chinua Achebe's *Things Fall Apart,* since this work has probably been the most popular African novel of all time. (My students are convinced that Achebe is getting rich.)

To follow the course of Achebe's riches, we have to begin with the original edition of the work, since that is where much of the problem begins for any writer, William Heinemann published the English hardback edition in 1958. Assuming a standard contract between publisher and author, Achebe would have received a 10 percent royalty on all copies of his novel sold *within* England. Copies sold overseas—and that would include Nigeria, Achebe's homeland—would have earned him half-royalties

or 5 percent. African writers have often been shocked to discover that copies of their books sold within their own country earn them reduced royalties, yet this is only one of the prices Third World writers pay for publishing "overseas."

When paperback rights are sold to another publisher, the royalty is traditionally split fifty-fifty between the author and the hardback publisher of the work. No doubt such an arrangement existed between Achebe and the African Writers Series, in 1962, when *Things Fall Apart* first appeared in a paperback edition. It is possible that those terms were subsequently renegotiated when Achebe became the editor of the series, but if they were not, all those copies of his first novel (said to be in the hundreds of thousands) have earned him half-royalties. (This, one hopes, was not a case of a double jeopardy: half-royalties for "overseas" sales and then half-royalties again for the paperback edition.)

Reprint rights in other countries are more complicated. The royalties paid on the American hardback edition of *Things Fall Apart* were probably split in the traditional manner: half to the author and half to William Heinemann. The American publisher was McDowell, Obolensky (1959), which had its own trade paperback in print for a number of years; but then in 1969 the mass-market paperback rights were sold to Fawcett Books, and the novel suddenly became much more widely available.

The explosion in black studies in the United States in the early 1970s undoubtedly helped increase the sales of Achebe's book. It is possible that *Things Fall Apart* sold twenty-five or thirty thousand copies yearly for a while, until black-studies courses experienced declining enrollments. The original Fawcett edition of the novel sold for seventy-five cents, though several years later the price had escalated to $1.95—the figure we can use to demonstrate why Chinua Achebe (or any African writer) will never get rich from American readers.

By rounding off the price to two dollars, increasing the yearly sales to fifty thousand copies, and assuming a 10 percent royalty base (unlikely for a paperback contract negotiated in 1969), the figures look like this: 50,000 copies at $2 = $100,000 gross X 10% royalties = $10,000. That $10,000 in royalties looks quite respectable until one remembers that half of it has to go to Obolensky (the American hardback publisher). That immediately cuts Achebe's potential share to $5,000, a figure that has its own set of restrictions.

Once we earmark $5,000 for Achebe at this stage, we have to figure out the portion that will go to the Internal Revenue Service. I mention this fact because it is inescapable. Just as the United States designates certain countries as most-favored nations and exempts businesses from paying dual income taxes, the United States—and many European countries—offers similar reciprocity to writers within those countries. Thus, when Graham Greene publishes a novel in the United States, he pays income taxes on his American royalties only in England and not in both countries. Norman Mailer pays income taxes to the American government on his English royalties and not both. That reciprocity does not exist with African nations, however, so the IRS takes a 30 percent cut (or $1,500) out of Achebe's American royalties. That reduces the figure to $3,500, which must be split equally between Heinemann and the author, further decreasing Achebe's royalties to $1,750. Since Nigeria and England do have a tax agreement, Achebe gets to keep the full $1,750—except, of course, for that portion he has to pay in tax to his own government.

African writers who publish outside the continent have the economic cards stacked against them. They'll never get wealthy under these conditions, which give no indication of changing. Pity the poor writer who experiences only modest sales in the United States or any other Western country. For the most part, however, the options for publishing in Africa are still greatly limited. Worse, several African writers have said that when they have chosen to publish on the continent, the publishers have paid them no royalties at all.

Economically, the African writer is hardly better off today than he was during colonial times. Though literacy has improved greatly across the continent in the last twenty-five years, the situation for most writers has barely altered. African governments are so economically strapped that very little money can be spent on the arts. Even funds for education (the most logical area for a trickle-down effect to reach the writer) have been cut because of the servicing of national debts, the financing of defense, and so on. Can one imagine, for example, Samuel Doe or Idi Amin showing much interest in the state of their respective countries' literatures?

There are probably only two writers in all of tropical Africa who can live by their royalties: Chinua Achebe and Wole Soyinka.[1] That in itself belies the pathetic situation for most African writers. They are forced to support themselves by other means—an affinity they share with many writers throughout the world. Few writers anywhere take up the pen expecting to become rich by their efforts. But let's consider what many writers in the West do to supplement their serious writing. They free-lance; they write articles and reviews for newspapers and magazines to help earn their bread and butter. Those outlets do not really exist for the writer in tropical Africa. Economically, almost everything is against him.

Let's be optimistic about this and assume that good writing will always survive and that the writer who struggles hard enough will find a publisher for his work. Thus, the African writer—like his counterpart anywhere else—will find his readers. He may not become wealthy or famous, but he will see his work in print and derive comfort from that. Naïvely, I used to believe that the African writer could overcome all these factors and find his niche in world literature. Lately, however, I've begun to feel differently, as I've looked at what can only be called a decline in African literature—both in quality and quantity. (The former is more upsetting than the latter.)

What's happened to Chinua Achebe, who must be Africa's most famous novelist yet hasn't published a novel since *A Man of the People* (1966)—twenty years ago? What about Ayi Kwei Armah, who looked for a while as if he might become Africa's most prolific novelist? His last novel, *The Healers*, was published in 1978. What about Kofi Awoonor? Bessie Head? Cyprian Ekwensi? Amos Tutuola? Mongo Beti? Cheikh Hamidou Kane? J. P. Clark? Richard Rive? Gabriel Okara? Yambo Ouologuem? Ferdinand Oyono? Lenrie Peters? Taban lo Liyong? Charles Mangua?

The list could go on, but I've tried to name only those writers who demonstrated major talent and then—for the most part—fell silent. Out of fairness, this roster should be balanced with the names of those writers who have continued to be visible; yet that list is much, much shorter: Wole Soyinka, Ngugi wa Thiong'o, Nuruddin Farah. There are also a number of popular writers (such as Buchi Emecheta) whose visibility has increased, but it is difficult to treat their work seriously. More significant, it seems, is the situation in which so many of these writers have found themselves caught during the last few years.

Chinua Achebe is again the best example. After *A Man of the People,* he published other works: a volume of short stories and a collection of poems. Achebe's poems are minor works, however, and even his collection of short stories contains substantial material written prior to his last published novel. Turning instead to his last published book, *The Trouble with Nigeria* (1983),[2] the dilemma becomes immediately apparent. If the continent's major novelist has been reduced to publishing a treatise such as this, the intellectual climate for the African writer has become appalling. One quotation from this work will suffice.

> Nigeria is *not* a great country. It is one of the most disorderly nations in the world. It is one of the most corrupt, insensitive, inefficient places under the sun. It is one of the most expensive countries and one of those that give least value for money. It is dirty, callous, noisy, ostentatious, dishonest and vulgar. In short, it is among the most unpleasant places on earth!

Great writers have always been social critics. *The Trouble with Nigeria* belongs to a distinguished list of polemics written by major writers through the years. Still, shouldn't the Nigerian government be embarrassed by this latest publication by its major writer? And shouldn't those of us who admire Achebe for his creative brilliance be enraged that he's felt compelled to publish a work such as this instead of his long-promised fifth novel? To what extremes will African governments drive their artists?

That is the rub, of course: the African governments, the powers that be, the politicians in charge. Achebe had fun with this years ago in *A Man of the People.* In that novel he satirically described Chief Nanga (the Minister of

Culture of an unnamed African country, though clearly Nigeria) as a man who "announced in public that he had never heard of his country's most famous novel," presumably *Things Fall Apart,* though "he prophesied that before long our great country would produce great writers like Shakespeare, Dickens, Jane Austen, Bernard Shaw, and—raising his eyes off the script—Michael West and Dudley Stamp."

Has Achebe lost his sense of humor? Probably not. Rather, it looks as though he has concluded that satire is meaningless if the objects of that satire no longer realize that they are being attacked. Only a frontal approach will be noticed; hence *The Trouble with Nigeria.* Yet the trouble with Nigeria is the trouble with African governments in general. They will apparently do anything to silence their writers. African governments have a) imprisoned their writers (Soyinka, Ngugi, Awoonor, René Philombe, and too many South African writers to list here); b) censored their writers' works (Ngugi, Philombe, Legson Kayira, Camara Laye, Nuruddin Farah, plus dozens of South African writers); c) forced their writers into exile (Laye, Kayira, Farah, S. Henry Cordor, Solomon Deressa, Achebe [after the civil war], Oswald Mtshali, Dennis Brutus, Bessie Head, Ezekiel Mphahlele, Peter Abrahams, and numerous other South African writers); and d) pushed their writers to the brink of insanity (Head, Laye, Yambo Ouologuem). When all these tactics have failed, African governments have silenced their writers with one of the most effective muzzles: assimilating them into the government bureaucracy or, worse, the diplomatic corps (Laye, Awoonor, Cyprian Ekwensi, Amos Tutuola, Wilton Sankawulo, Abioseh Nicol, Syl Cheyney-Coker).

What impresses one most about African writers' responses to these intrusions on their corporeal and intellectual existence is that so few of them have compromised their positions. Rather, they have met the enemy (the state) with silence, which of course is the reason why so many of the writers mentioned here have apparently stopped publishing. They have seen what has happened to a writer like Ngugi, who has continued publishing. They have fully understood why a novel that satirized the colonial government is acceptable (even de rigueur), whereas one criticizing the postindependent political situation can only get them into trouble.

It is fear of reprisals, then, that has led to the steady decline of African writing during the last twenty-five years. The older generation of writers (those who began publishing in the 1950s and the early 1960s) have been silenced, and the younger ones have quickly followed suit, though some of the latter have chosen another route and written fluff, devoid of any artistic merit or meaningful social context. Still, these are difficult times, no matter what road taken.

Several years ago I was asked to write an article about younger African writers—those who had begun publishing during the 1970s. The intent of the essay (which was to be published in a United States government publication

widely distributed in Africa) was to describe as many writers as possible and thereby increase their exposure among African readers. It was only after I agreed to write the piece that I began to reflect upon the sorry state of African writing and realize that there were only a few writers who had demonstrated great promise (comparable to those who had begun writing earlier).

I picked three writers: Nuruddin Farah of Somalia, S. Henry Cordor of Liberia, and T. Obinkaram Eschewa of Nigeria. The article I subsequently wrote was never published but was censored instead, because authorities in the State Department—I was told—decided that the praise I had lavished on Farah would offend officials in Somalia, where he had been declared persona non grata. I was appalled that the censorship of African writers had reached American soil, though I have never had any illusions about Ronald Reagan's political myopia. Examining the careers of these three writers, we can observe a kind of pattern typical of the situation in general.

Of the three, Nuruddin Farah has been the most visible, though he has had to remain in exile for most of his career. His first novel, *From a Crooked Rib,* published in 1970, was written while he was a student in India. It identified Farah immediately as one of his continent's most sensitive and understanding writers about African women. Elba, the young woman in the story, runs away from her village in order to avoid an arranged marriage with an older man. She tells a friend, "That is what we women are—just like cattle, properties of someone or other, either your parents or your husband." What she ponders is why a man can have four wives but a woman only one husband.

Farah's championing of women's rights has been unacceptable to some of his African readers, though it has not been the reason for his exile. That problem has been political, the subject of all his recent novels: *A Naked Needle* (1976), *Sweet and Sour Milk* (1979), *Sardines* (1981), and *Close Sesame* (1983). The last three (powerful and disturbing works) constitute a trilogy with the overall theme of African dictatorship. The pathway of his fiction, then, has been overtly political, with only one possible escape route: exile. His books are not available in Somalia, where they have been banned, and Farah himself—determined to continue writing—has become a kind of cosmopolite, picking up teaching and journalistic assignments wherever possible to supplement the meager income from his novels.

S. Henry Cordor's situation parallels Farah's. He too has been trapped by politics, though ironically by the regime he initially chose to embrace. The body of his creative work is still quite small because so much of it has never been published. As Liberians often say, they never enjoyed the benefits of being a colony. That has posed special problems for the country's writers, who find it almost impossible to publish overseas. Self-publication tends to be the norm.

Cordor's stories demonstrate a rare sensibility. In a few brief paragraphs he is able to size up character and situation, often with a subtle wit and a polished manner far beyond that of his most daring contemporaries. "In the Hospital," for instance, is an almost perfect example of what can be done with the short-story form. Sadly, however, Cordor has found himself in recent years becoming a spokesman for Liberian intellectuals and compelled to abandon fiction for political commentary. When Doe became president of Liberia, Cordor was enthusiastic, but he quickly soured when he witnessed the president's intolerance of free speech (especially among students). Today Cordor lives in exile in the United States, waiting for the day when politics back home will change.

In contrast to the works by Farah and Cordor, T. Obinkaram Echewa's novel *The Land's Lord* is much more traditional and free of contemporary commentary. The three principal characters (Father Higler, a Catholic priest; his African acolyte, Philip; and a juju priest called Ahamba) are engaged in a kind of philosophic dialogue about good and evil and, by extension, about Christianity and animism, Africa and the West. When *The Land's Lord* was published by Heinemann in 1976, comparisons were made between Echewa and Achebe and Ngugi, largely because of the novel's traditional setting, though Echewa has also said of his writing: "I expect to go over the social and historical terrain that has been traversed by Achebe and others and till it more deeply. I am interested right now in the problem of 'evil' in African societies without reference to colonialism or the white man."

Although Echewa's novel has been widely praised, it has been followed by a ten-year silence. A second novel, called *The Crippled Dancer* and announced for publication in 1982, has never appeared. It is probable that Echewa's writing career has been stifled by Heinemann's decision to curtail drastically the scope of its African Writers Series, the major publishing outlet for the continent's writers during the last twenty years. At the moment many publishers in the West are interested in publishing only those African writers whose work is already widely known and deemed profitable.

The fact is that Africa cannot afford its writers today— and neither can the West, though their reasons are somewhat different. As long as African governments regard their writers as threats to their longevity, most of the continent's serious writers will be forced to remain silent and the decline of African writing will continue. One has only to think of the career of Ngugi wa Thiong'o and the continual harassment he has experienced both in and out of prison at the hands of the Kenyan government. A lesser man would have caved in long ago.

The West, of course, could help the situation, particularly in the area of publishing, but the indications are that that will not happen. Why is it, for example, that South Africa's white writers are embraced by American publishers (and readers) while the country's black writers still remain virtually unknown? Years ago there was a rumor going around that an African writer who tried to get published in the United States was told that his book wasn't African enough. A similar myopia about Africa on the part of Western publishers still exists, in spite of the commercial success of books about Africa by writers who are not African (Isak Dinesen and Alice Walker, to mention two current favorites).

For years the literary image of Africa in the West was largely controlled by writers who were not African. In the late 1950s and early 1960s it looked as if that were about to change. A dozen or so writers achieved international recognition, though only one of them (Wole Soyinka, the continent's major writer) has enhanced his visibility in the West. Politics and economics have pushed most of the others to the side. If the situation does improve, it will not be the result of worldwide political and economic fluctuations but rather because of the resilience of the writers themselves.

## NOTES

[1] On the various authors discussed or referred to in this essay, see the following articles in *BA/WLT*: Chinua Achebe, 48:1 (Winter 1974), p. 74; Wole Soyinka, 60:1 (Winter 1986), pp. 31-32; Ngugi wa Thiong'o, 59:1 (Winter 1985), pp. 26-30; Nuruddin Farah, 58:2, (Spring 1984), pp. 215-21; Ayi Kwei Armah, 59:3 (Summer 1985), pp. 337-42; Ferdinand Oyono, 59:3 (Summer 1985), pp. 333-37; Buchi Emecheta, 59:1 (Winter 1985), pp. 9-13; J. P. Clark, 52:2 (Spring 1978), pp. 216-23; Dennis Brutus, 55:1 (Winter 1981), pp. 32-40; Bessie Head, 57:3 (Summer 1983), pp. 414-16; Camara Laye, 54:3 (Summer 1980), pp. 392-95.

[2] For a review of Achebe's book *The Trouble with Nigeria*, see *WLT* 59:3 (Summer 1985), p. 478.

---

# FURTHER READING

## Secondary Sources

Bettman, Elizabeth R. "Joyce Cary and the Problem of Political Morality." *Antioch Review* XVII, No. 2 (June 1957): 266-72.
  Discusses the ways in which Joyce Cary wove political symbolism into his final three novels.

Britt, Theron. "Literature and Politics: Same Difference?" *College Literature* 23, No. 2 (June 1996): 171-76.
  Reviews three works on politics and literature.

Brown, Clarence. "Into the Heart of Darkness: Mandelstam's 'Ode to Stalin'." *Slavic Review* XXVI, No. 4 (December 1967): 584-604.
  Examines the events that led up to Osip Mandelstam's composition of his "Ode to Stalin".

Bryant, Jerry H. "John A. Williams: The Political Use of the Novel." *Critique* XVI, No. 3 (1975): 81-100.
 Surveys political elements in the novels of John A. Williams.

Crick, Bernard. *Essays on Politics and Literature.* Edinburgh: Edinburgh University Press, 1989, 259 p.
 Collection of essays on politics and literature.

Edwards, Jorge. "Chilean Writing after the Coup." *Partisan Review* 57, No. 3 (Summer 1990): 378-84.
 Explores writing in Chile after the military coup of September 1973.

Eliot, T. S. "The Literature of Politics." In *To Criticize the Critic and Other Writings*, pp. 136-44. London: Faber and Faber, 1965.
 Lecture originally delivered at a literary luncheon arranged by the London Conservative Union in 1955; Eliot discusses the literature of conservatism.

Felstiner, John. "Poetry and Political Experience: Denise Levertov." In *Coming to Light: American Women Poets in the Twentieth Century*, edited by Diane Wood Middlebrook and Marilyn Yalom, pp. 138-44. Ann Arbor: University of Michigan Press, 1985.
 Explains the poetic and political philosophy of poet Denise Levertov.

Gass, William H., and Lorin Cuoco, eds. *The Writer in Politics.* Carbondale and Edwardsville: Southern Illinois University Press, 1996, 191 p.
 Collection of essays and panel discussions by noted writers presented at a conference at Washington University in 1992.

Groman, George L. "W. A. White's Political Fiction: A Study in Emerging Progressivism." *Midwest Quarterly* VIII, No. 1 (October 1966): 79-93.
 Examines the larger impact of William Allen White's progressive political stance.

Gross, Seymour L., and Eileen Bender. "History, Politics, and Literature: The Myth of Nat Turner." *American Quarterly* XXIII, No 4 (October 1971): 487-518.
 Confronts critics of William Styron's *The Confessions of Nat Turner*, arguing that Turner is a mythic figure of symbolic meaning rather than a historical reality.

Kucich, John. "Postmodern Politics: Don DeLillo and the Plight of the White Male Writer." *Michigan Quarterly Review* XXVII, No. 2 (Spring 1988): 328-41.
 Contends that DeLillo has consistently infused his works with political issues despite their lack of overt ideology.

Lee, L. L. "*Bend Sinister*: Nabokov's Political Dream." *Wisconsin Studies in Contemporary Literature* 8, No. 2 (Spring 1987): 193-203.
 Discusses Nabokov's *Bend Sinister* as an exploration of political and personal devolution into madness.

Nelson, Harland S. "Steinbeck's Politics Then and Now." *Antioch Review* XXVII, No. 1 (Spring 1967): 118-33.
 Contrasts Steinbeck's political stance in his early novel *The Grapes of Wrath* with that of his later novel *The Winter of Our Discontent*, concluding that both novels contain elements of radicalism and conservatism.

Nyce, Benjamin. "Joyce Cary's Political Trilogy: The Atmosphere of Power." *Modern Language Quarterly* 32, No. 1 (March 1971): 89-106.
 Describes "the atmosphere of political power" as portrayed in Cary's novel trilogy, notably, the "confusion, mistrust, violence, and enthusiasm which permeates the world of a man who uses political power like an artist."

Ogunghesan, Kolawole. "The Political Novels of Peter Abrahams." *Phylon* 34, No. 4 (December 1973): 419-32.
 Examines Abrahams' theme of spiritual freedom as a means of achieving social integration and political equality.

Rowse, A. L. "The Contradictions of George Orwell." *Contemporary Review* 241, No. 1402 (October 1982): 186-94.
 Finds in Orwell's political ideology a "restrictive Puritanism."

Siddiq, Muhammad. "The Contemporary Arabic Novel in Perspective." *World Literature Today* 60, No. 2 (Spring 1986): 206-11.
 Notes that contemporary Arabic literature is never "entirely divorced from politics."

Wilding, Michael. "The Politics of *Nostromo*." *Essays in Criticism* XVI, No. 4 (October 1966): 441-56.
 Argues that Conrad's novel *Nostromo* is not explicitly political, but that instead Conrad posited politics as one of many means to human corruption.

Williams, C. E. "Writers and Politics: Some Reflections on a German Tradition." *Journal of European Studies* 6, No. 21 (March 1976): 75-99.
 Presents an overview of political theory as represented in the German literary and intellectual tradition.

Winter, Helmut. "A Note on History and Politics in Recent German Drama." *Modern Drama* XIII, No. 3 (December 1970): 247-53.
 Explores political theory and historical events in post–World War II German drama.

# Women in Modern Literature

## INTRODUCTION

Gender issues have been a topic in written literature since ancient times, when Greek poets such as Sappho and Homer wrote of female sexuality, marriage, and emotional bonds between women and their families, and philosophers questioned, and usually denigrated, the role of women in society. Christianity brought to literature the dichotomous virgin-whore—or "good girl-bad girl"—archetype, modeled after the seemingly contradictory figures of the Virgin Mary and the Biblical prostitute Mary Magdalene, which has survived to the present day in literature and popular culture. In the Victorian period female literary paradigms began to shift as more women openly published their writings and women's emancipation became a major societal issue. At one end of the spectrum was the Victorian "Angel of the House," which placed women in the position of helpmate, homemaker, and superior social conscience, but which ultimately limited women's options to the realm of home and occasional volunteer work. At the other end was the newly emerging liberated woman who candidly demanded her right to education, suffrage, and the single life but who was generally treated as an outcast by respectable society and still could not vote, inherit property, or easily cultivate a career. Both figures appeared in and were scrutinized by the literature of the time. In the early twentieth century, as the psychoanalytic theories of Sigmund Freud became widely read, literature by and about women took on an interiorized dimension. Many later feminist thinkers considered Freud's ideas about women misogynistic and claimed that they said more about Freud's own insecurities and neuroses than about the actual state of women's psyches, but it cannot be denied that concepts such as castration anxiety, penis envy, and Oedipal and Electra complexes strongly influenced Western notions about women, particularly in literature, throughout the twentieth century. Literature by and about women in Latin American, Caribbean, Asian, and African countries has tended to focus on many of the same issues, in addition to more fundamental questions of human rights and the effects of colonization and slavery on women. In the modern feminist era—particularly after women earned the right to vote in many Western countries and gained greater access to education and the workplace—literature has concentrated increasingly on women's changing roles and continued obstacles to equality.

## REPRESENTATIVE WORKS

Zoe Akins
*The Old Maid* (novel) 1935

Ciro Alegría
*La serpiente de oro* (novel) 1935
Margaret Atwood
*The Edible Woman* (novel) 1969
Claire Booth
*The Women* (drama) 1936
Charlotte Brontë
*Jane Eyre* (novel) 1847
Hortense Calisher
"The Rabbi's Daughter" (short story) 1975
Willa Cather
*My Ántonia* (novel) 1918
Alice Childress
*Wine in the Wilderness* (drama) 1969
*Wedding Band* (drama) 1972
Kate Chopin
*The Awakening* (novella) 1899
Rachel Crothers
*A Man's World* (drama) 1909
*Mary the Third* (drama) 1925
*When Ladies Meet* (drama) 1932
George Eliot
*Middlemarch* (novel) 1871-72
Gustave Flaubert
*Madame Bovary* (novel) 1857
J. E. Franklin
*Black Girl* (drama) 1971
Zona Gale
*Miss Lulu Bett* (drama) 1920
Elizabeth Gaskell
*Ruth* (novel) 1853
*Wives and Daughters* (novel) 1864-66
Susan Glaspell
*Trifles* (drama) 1916
*The Verge* (drama) 1921
*Alison's House* (drama) 1930
Lillian Hellman
*The Children's Hour* (drama) 1934
Merle Hodge
*Crick Crack Monkey* (novel) 1970
Henrik Ibsen
*A Doll's House* (drama) 1879
C. L. R. James
*Minty Alley* (novel) 1936
Henry James
*The Portrait of a Lady* (novel) 1881
*The Wings of the Dove* (novel) 1909
Sarah Orne Jewett
*Country of the Pointed Firs* (novel) 1896
James Joyce
*Ulysses* (novel) 1922
Margaret Laurence
*The Stone Angel* (novel) 1964
Mary Lavin
*The Becker Wives* (novella) 1946

D. H. Lawrence
  *The Rainbow*  (novel)  1915
  *Women in Love*  (novel)  1920
L. M. Montgomery
  *Anne of Green Gables*  (novel)  1908
Brian Moore
  *I Am Mary Dunne*  (novel)  1968
Toni Morrison
  *The Bluest Eye*  (novel)  1970
  *Sula*  (novel)  1973
  *Song of Solomon*  (novel)  1977
Yigal Mossensohn
  *The Way of Men with Women*  (novel)  1953
Flora Nwapa
  *Efuru*  (novel)  1966
Tillie Olsen
  "Tell Me a Riddle"  (short story)  1961
Cynthia Ozick
  "Envy; Or, Yiddish in America"  (short story)  1977
Grace Paley
  "Faith in the Afternoon"  (short story)  1983
  "The Immigrant Story"  (short story)  1983
Sylvia Plath
  *Ariel*  (poetry)  1965
  *Crossing the Water*  (poetry)  1971
Katia Saks
  *La Rifa*  (novel)  1968
Mario Vargas Llosa
  *La casa verde*  (novel)  1965
Edith Wharton
  *The House of Mirth*  (novel)  1905
Virginia Woolf
  *Mrs. Dalloway*  (novel)  1925
  *Orlando: A Biography*  (novel)  1928
  *A Room of One's Own*  (essay)  1929
William Butler Yeats
  *The Wind among the Reeds*  (poetry)  1899
  *In the Seven Woods*  (poetry)  1903
  *The Wild Swans at Coole*  (poetry)  1917

---

# OVERVIEWS

## Ashley H. Thorndike

SOURCE: "Woman," in *Literature in a Changing Age*, The Macmillan Company, 1920, pp. 192-22.

[*In the following essay, Thorndike examines the portrayal of women in works by both male and female writers from the Victorian period into the modern age.*]

During the last century women shared in the profits that arose from the vast progress in education, democracy, industry, and invention. Indeed, they appear to have acquired some excess of profits and to have gained ground relatively to men. The wife in relation to the husband, the sister in comparison with her brother, the spinster in comparison with the bachelor, may still have inferior opportunities and privileges, but their inferiority is far less marked than a century ago. The advance has been by no means uncontested or unheralded. Woman has been the subject of discussion and legislation as never before. Women's education, women's rights, woman suffrage have become current terms representing great social movements. The rights of free association and free speech, which have been used by Englishmen with such important results in social and political change, have been employed even more effectively by Englishwomen. The feminist movement, by which term we may include all efforts for increasing the opportunities and activities of women, has availed itself of every weapon of organization and association, of public debate and propaganda. The woman question has taken its place alongside of the problems of poverty, labor, government, and religion as one of the permanent occupations for our minds and consciences. The tendency to treat of all the millions of individuals as compressed into the abstraction Woman, set off over-sharply against that other abstraction Man, doubtless often darkens and confuses counsel; but it is a symptom of the progress of women which has marked the century and still continues, conscious, militant, and expectant. We can scarcely discuss changing literature without asking what did changing woman have to do with it?

I

Woman and sex have always received a large amount of attention in literature, and notably in periods and places where culture has developed most highly. The influence of women both as readers and writers has often been considerable, although of course exercised only by a small class. Just as literature for and by men was usually a matter for the courtly or priestly classes, so literature for and by women was restricted to the lady. Possibly the most remarkable development of a feminist literature is to be found in Japan of the tenth and eleventh centuries, when the court was dominated by the queen mother and the court ladies. But the rise of courtly poetry in the Middle Ages and in the Paris Salons of the Bourbon era furnish striking examples of feminine influence. With the growth of the middle classes in England through the seventeenth and eighteenth centuries, the influence of women rapidly widened. The leisure class came to include not only the great ladies but a large number of the wives and daughters of merchants. The "city madam" receives a good deal of notice in the Jacobean drama, and by Addison's time the *Spectator* and the *Tatler* rely for their support upon the fair sex. Indeed, a case might be made for the assertion that the growing preponderance of sentiment in the eighteenth century and finally the romantic movement itself were due in no small measure to the influence of women of leisure on manners, morals, and literature. If Rousseau was the father of romanticism, woman was its mother, or at least its nurse.

To whatever degree women were responsible for romanticism, they certainly did much to impose a decency, at least outward, upon English letters. The protest against the licentiousness of the Restoration drama came from the middle classes where women were becoming readers and theater-goers. From that time, the masculine pen has been more and more restrained by the consciousness that its products were to be sold to women, and to women looking to books for refinement and education as well as for entertainment. Since Fielding and Smollett there have been few robustious and masculine pens. In Victorian literature woman was the censor.

In addition to the host of women who wept over the sentiments of Richardson or Rousseau, or who wrote in imitation, there was also a growing class of professional women writers. These women were usually forced by some domestic disaster to earn their own living by the pen, and turned to the theater, the periodical, or the novel. At first these venturesome females were somewhat lacking in respectability, as Mrs. Afra Behn or Mrs. Manley, and Grub Street offered no road to reinstatement in polite society. But the growing popularity of the novel supplied a market in which women could readily compete. By the beginning of the nineteenth century there was a considerable number of women writers.

The novel provided a popular form with a technic much less exacting than the poem or the drama, and such as might be acquired by the novice or the amateur. Further, it required no extensive or specialized learning as did the more serious forms of prose, and no acquaintance with affairs such as was demanded by the pamphlet or periodical. Novels had for their themes love and marriage, which were supposed to be the main interests of women, and they soon had many women among their readers. Manifestly, a young girl might scribble away at home, despatch her manuscript to a publisher, and await the success or failure of her story without unduly infringing on any of the conventions by which her sex was bound and without going outside of the limits set by a narrow conception of women's sphere either in her reading or her experience. Young girls were, in fact, soon scribbling away behind their parents' backs with surprising results. Fanny Burney amazed her father and his friends, Dr. Johnson and Burke, by her *Evelina,* and opened the way for future novelists to deal with domestic and feminine affairs. Maria Edgeworth similarly astonished her father and his philosophical friends by the stories drawn from her experience in Ireland and in fashionable London. In Steventon rectory a girl of twenty-one wrote *Pride and Prejudice* and thereby gained a sure title to immortality. The acclaim of the great, large money payments, immortality—such were the rewards opened to women by the novel. Its significance for them, and theirs for it, have indeed gone on broadening and are now enormous; but they cannot be regarded as changes operating for the first time in our period. As we have seen, during the fifty years before Victoria came to the throne, woman had made the novel very much her own.

II

What then are the changes most manifest in the relations between women and literature in the Victorian era? Woman's increased opportunities and occupations have had abundant reflection, but it would be difficult to state precisely how the reflection of their interests has differed from that of preceding epochs. Moreover, they have shared in the great changes in education, religion, industry, politics, and morals which we have been considering as affecting the literature of the mid-century. It would again be difficult to state precisely in what way the resulting changes in literature have been due to women rather than to men. If such exact balancing is impossible, we may still be guided in our search for a reflection of changing woman by two important considerations. First, in the nineteenth century, women, in comparison with men, did more writing and more reading than ever before. Literature is one of the fields in which their increased activity is most apparent. Second, the literature of the century records in some measure the aims and effects of that increasing advance which we have called the feminist movement. The progress of woman like the advance of democracy, empire, religion, labor, and science, has left its effect on literature.

Who were these Victorian authoresses? The books, or at least the names, of a few are known to everyone—Mrs. Browning, Christina Rossetti, the Brontë sisters, Mrs. Gaskell, and George Eliot. But there were many others whose names were once on every tongue, though the fame of some has passed with the snows of yesteryear. There was Harriet Martineau, sturdy disciple of the utilitarians, who wrote a whole library of useful literature; and the Honorable Mrs. Norton, the brilliant and beautiful granddaughter of Sheridan and the original of *Diana of the Crossways;* and the much admired Letitia E. Landon who wrote countless novels and met a wretched fate, and Mrs. Mary Sewell, the most popular ballad writer of the century, of whose pathetic *Mother's Last Words* over one million copies were sold. And there were Felicia Hemans and Jean Ingelow among the poets; and Mary Mitford, Charlotte Yonge, Dinah Mulock Craik, Ouida, Mrs. Trollope, and Mrs. Oliphant among the novelists; and the Strickland sisters and Mrs. Jameson among the writers of miscellaneous prose. Much of the writing of these ladies is very feminine, if you will; but it is also very Victorian. In comparison with the work of men, it is easier to find general likenesses than general differences. Most of the women were moralists, but so were most of their brother writers. Most of their writing seems sentimental, but so does much of the poetry and fiction produced by male Victorians. The women were ardent in reforms, but so were Dickens and Ruskin. The most individual and sensitive and perhaps most feminine of the women, Christina Rossetti, displays in her verse no virtues or defects strikingly different from those to be found in other poets of the century from Coleridge to Francis Thompson. The most important woman writer in her influence upon subsequent literature has been George Eliot, but this influence can be defined in terms of the use of scientific knowledge and an analytical method in fiction, changes that might have been initiated by a man as well as by a woman. Charlotte Brontë in giving a woman's view of passion, made what was probably the most distinctly feminine contribution to fiction, but such a disclosure was inevitable, once women took to writing novels. It is rather in the variety and quantity of the literature produced than in any markedly feminine qualities that the Victorian women will be remembered. They were not so very unlike the Victorian men, but in letters they won a place as equals, competitors, and coöperators beside their brothers and husbands. In no other field did they accomplish such a public service or gain such public recognition.

Some of these women writers held established and comfortable positions in society and had normal experiences in life, but others were involved in domestic entanglements. The ancient gossip may be revived, not to intimate any discredit to the ladies of the past, where indeed very little discredit can be charged, but to suggest that these personal experiences had a certain effect on literature. George Eliot estranged herself from Victorian womankind by living as his wife with George Lewes, Mrs. Norton freed herself from an impossible dolt of a husband, but not without gossip that long pursued her. Letitia Landon suffered from an absurd scandal, a broken engagement, an unhappy marriage, and died from an overdose of prussic acid. There were disappointments and estrangements in the lives of Christina Rossetti and Charlotte Brontë. Even Mrs. Browning eloped with her husband and was never forgiven by her father. Personal discontent and sufferings have often enough found expression in literature, but with these women the expression is not so much that of personal unhappiness as of the unhappiness which is the peculiar lot of their sex. Their imagination, to be sure, was sensitive to any suffering, to that of the poor, the toilers, the oppressed, and especially to the wrong and pain inflicted upon children. But sympathy, protest, and revolt all quicken in behalf of woman tyrannized over by lover, husband, family, or society. Woman's work in letters may perhaps be sufficiently illustrated if we glance at the careers of two women, not of the first importance as writers, but who both exemplify special feminine service in letters and who both were active in the early stage of the feminist movement.

### III

Caroline Norton was one of three sisters, granddaughters of Sheridan, who astonished early Victorian society by their beauty and talent. Married at nineteen to a stupid and niggardly husband, she sought the publishers not less from the need of money than from the desire for fame. Of her first volume of verse, published when she was twenty-one, she tells us that it defrayed "the first expenses of my son's life." The success of the young mother in both society and letters was immediate, and she was soon making a considerable income as editor and chief contributor to those Annuals which were one of the most curious literary products of the Victorian era. They appeared as Christmas gift books, handsomely adorned by steel engravings and containing prose and verse contributions, largely from persons of title or fashion, who presumably wrote for love rather than for money. Critics who consider the present state of literature to be degenerate

might recover their optimism by consulting the insipidities of the Annuals, Keepsakes, and Garlands of the mid-century. They represent the popularization of belles lettres as an entertainment for the leisure class; but with all their sentimental banality they offered a certain field for women of real talent. The Countess of Blessington was the chief promoter of this sort of publication, and it was well supported by Mrs. Norton's abundant cleverness. After her separation from her husband, when she was in still greater need of money, she sometimes made £1500 a year through her pen. A few poems, such as "Bingen" and "Juanita" still survive, but her verses and stories are much less readable to-day than her letters, which still retain the gaiety and wit that everyone admired in her conversation. Beneath the imitative rhetoric, however, one may discern in her published work some of the generous emotions that were arousing the women of that day, pity for the children of the working classes and a growing sympathy for women subject to tyranny.

Mrs. Norton's quarrel with her husband received full publicity at the time and has been frequently retold, but without ever eliciting any sympathy for Mr. Norton. She left her petty tyrant in 1836. His ridiculous suit against Lord Melbourne failed utterly in court, and was supposed to have been instigated by political enemies of the prime minister. The wife had no chance to appear in the trial, and under the English laws of that time the husband kept possession of the three young children and even had a right to his wife's earnings. After long negotiations over the custody of the children and pecuniary matters, a legal separation was arranged; but the husband's malice increased with his wife's fame and fortune, the quarrel was again resumed and got into court in 1853 on the issue of the validity of a contract between them. Both husband and wife, he then fifty-two and she forty-five, stated their cases with much temper in long letters to the *Times*. The letters as human documents have not lost their force after these seventy years, and they constitute an important record of the tyranny of husbands and the rebellion of wives. From our point of view, however, their most significant feature is the wife's eloquent apology for her outburst on the ground that she is a writer, a woman responsible to the public and posterity.

> I will, as far as I am able, defend a name which might have been only favourably known, but which my husband has rendered notorious. The little world of my chance readers may say of me, after I am dead and gone and my struggles over and forgotten, "The woman who wrote this book had an unhappy history," but they shall not say, "The woman who wrote this book was a profligate and a mercenary hypocrite." Since my own gift of writing gives me friends among strangers, I appeal to the opinion of strangers as well as that of friends. Since, in however bounded and narrow a degree, there is a chance that I may be remembered after death, I will not have my whole life misrepresented.
>
> Let those women who have the true woman's lot of being unknown out of the circle of their homes thank God for that blessing—it is a blessing; but

for me publicity is no longer a matter of choice.
Defence is possible to me, not silence.

The wife had not only rebelled, she had carried her rebellion before the public; and she fought not merely for herself and her children but for wives and mothers in general. She put much of her own story into her novels and also into pamphlets and letters in support first of the infant custody bill, and later in the controversy over the marriage act of 1857. It was in no small measure due to her efforts that this law gave a wife the right to inherit and bequeath property, and, if separated from her husband, to contract and sue and to be protected in her earnings. Her friends usually attempted to dissuade her from the publicity that was thought unfeminine, but a reader of today must admire unreservedly the high temper and gallant courage with which she fought her cause. The writer for the fashionable keepsakes and scrap-books proved herself a real public servant. Apart from specific legislation, the whole case of the wife against the husband gained a general hearing because this particular wife happened to be a woman of letters. It must not be thought that she wrote as a thorough-going champion of her sex. It is in a conformist and not an ironical mood that she earnestly declares her belief that women are inferior to men and were so created by God, and disavows any intention to plead for equality. She was attacking particular tyrannies upheld by law. Though she might have been capable of the epigram that Meredith attributes to his Diana, "Menmay have rounded Seraglio Point; they have not yet doubled Cape Turk"; yet the main point of her attack on marital tyranny was financial and not sexual. But this is another sign of the times, for our commercial system manifestly has developed new difficulties between husband and wife as well as between capitalist and laborer.

Mrs. Norton's rebellion was more typical of the time and more significant of the advance of women than she herself could have realized. Through literature she was able to present to a large public the spectacle of a wife obviously superior to her husband in every intellectual and moral quality, and also excelling him as a money earner. In what did man's superiority consist? The legal status which permitted the indignities and persecutions that she suffered was doomed to destruction as soon as it was exposed to the reading public. Through literature she could win her own independence, and she could present a convincing plea for the greater independence of all wives.

IV

Very different from Mrs. Norton's career was that of Harriet Martineau. She never possessed the senses of smell and taste, by the age of sixteen she had become very deaf, and during a large portion of her seventy-four years of life she suffered from serious illness. Yet it would be difficult to find a lifetime marked by more varied interests and occupations or by more copious industry.

Her girlhood, with its indigestion, nerves, broken schooling, and Unitarian pietism, does not seem to have directed her fancy to romance, for her first published work at the age of nineteen was an essay on "Female Writers on Practical Divinity." Her father's death left the family in poverty, and her virtual engagement to marry a fellow-student of her brother was opposed by his family and finally ended with insanity and death for him and long and prostrating illness for her. At twenty-seven she was penniless and struggling to earn a living by needle-work and writing. Success came through an offer by the Unitarian Association of prizes for three essays designed to convert the Catholics, the Jews, and the Mohammedans. Miss Martineau wrote for them all, won them all, and had forty-five guineas to the good. The money gave her leisure and encouragement to devise a scheme of a series of stories illustrating the principles of political economy.

The suggestion came partly from reading Mrs. Marcet's *Conversations on Political Economy,* and that lady must be regarded as Miss Martineau's predecessor in the art of popularizing knowledge. Among her books, some of which went through many editions, were, *Conversations on Chemistry, intended more especially for the Female Sex, Conversations on Natural Philosophy* designed for very young children, *Game of Grammar,* and *Willy's Travels on the Railroad. Miss* Martineau's *Illustrations of Political Economy* filled nine volumes and made a great success. They were followed by other series of similar tales, *Poor Laws and Paupers Illustrated* and *Illustrations of Taxation.* At thirty-two she was a literary celebrity, the friend of all the radical and whig writers and politicians, and the chief glory of the Society for the Diffusion of Useful Knowledge. Her health demanded a vacation, and after a voyage of forty-two days from Liverpool to New York, she spent two years in travel in the United States.

Such was her entrance into the field of letters, but space is lacking to describe the variety and extent of her continued activities. She refused several offers of pensions and persisted in relying on an independent pen. Her travels in America, where she consorted with the abolitionists and thereby aroused much antipathy, resulted in two books. She wrote various novels and a series of children's stories that are among her best remembered works. After an illness pronounced incurable had been relieved by mesmerism, she wrote *Letters on Mesmerism,* which aroused more antipathies. She travelled in Europe and in Egypt and Palestine, and under the influence of Henry G. Atkinson became more addicted to mesmerism and philosophical atheism, and became estranged from her brother James. In one twelve-month she wrote a two-volume history of contemporary England that is still a most readable and interesting narrative. She became a disciple of Comte and translated and condensed his philosophy. She wrote constantly for the reviews and newspapers, contributing in the course of fifteen years over sixteen hundred articles to the *Daily News* alone. She continued to fictionize and popularize useful information in various forms, such as *Forest and Game Law Tales* (information supplied by John Bright), *Household Education and Guides to Service,* including a handbook on *The Maid of*

*All Work.* When expecting to die from heart disease she wrote her *Autobiography,* but she lived for twenty years more. These she occupied with running a farm, lecturing to workingmen, taking an active interest in all current events and reforms, including the American War and a building society, and with writing on *The Factory Controversy, British Rule in India,* and, in order to help Miss Nightingale, *England and her Soldiers.*

Much of Miss Martineau's writing interprets or applies the utilitarian principles and much of it was in response to that movement for diffusing useful knowledge, in which Brougham was a leader. But the range of her interests and knowledge is no less amazing. Almost every theory or ism which perplexed the mid-century received her study. Unitarianism, abolition, utilitarianism, political economy, mesmerism, and positivism at one time or another received her devoted support. This loyal devotion to causes was united with a faculty for idolizing leaders or teachers, which she sometimes carried to the verge of fanaticism. Last Carpenter, a Unitarian minister, Priestly, her brother James, and Comte, successively, and Henry G. Atkinson finally and permanently, were the gods of her idolatry. Devotion and idolization are often deemed essentially feminine qualities, but so too perhaps is the shrewd practicality which Miss Martineau displayed in the conduct of her affairs and in the production of books. She wrote modestly of herself, "With small imaginative and suggestive powers, and therefore nothing approaching to genius. . . . she could popularize while she could neither discover nor invent." One new and important function of literature in the nineteenth century was this popularizing of knowledge, this extension of education to an enlarged reading public. To this service she brought notable gifts of expression and a mind at once progressive and practical. In a century of schoolmarms, she was their chief.

Her good sense was displayed in all her activities in the feminist movement. She was not much troubled by theories about woman's rights but very much concerned with every movement or means for bettering the position of women. From the day she wrote of *Female Writers on Practical Divinity,* she maintained a special interest in women, and felt herself responsible before the public as their representative. She was actively interested in their education and notably in their new part in industry and in various legislation to remove legal disabilities; and in later years in the agitation of the early seventies for suffrage. But her great influence upon the changing ideas as to woman's ability to take an enlarged part in the work of the world, was exercised not so much through her advocacy of various reforms as by the example of her own active and industrious life. Here was a woman with pronounced physical disabilities, and with no opportunity for the usual feminine domesticity, who made a name for herself and spent fifty years in constant public service. This atheist with her ear trumpet became a literary lion, a figure in society, capable even of managing the ursine Carlyle upon the lecture platform; also this teacher of children and workingmen and factory girls was influencing and directing public opinion and the general progress of ideas. She traveled about the world and she studied economics, politics, theology, philosophy, and nearly everything else that men studied. She taught men as well as women, and had statesmen and philanthropists as well as the youthful and ignorant among her pupils. In her own experience she enlarged woman's sphere, and she did this through literature. For Harriet Martineau, literature proved an opportunity not to display her own personality and sensibility but to show how efficiently women could help in that share of the work of the world which modern literature must perform.

V

The careers of Miss Martineau and Mrs. Norton, so different in many respects, illustrate ways in which women were making an advance in freedom and usefulness through literature. The career of almost any woman writer would similarly illustrate both a literary service in some measure peculiarly feminine and a particular contribution to the general emancipation of the sex. The steps in that emancipation were too numerous and often too imperceptible at the time to secure full record in the careers of women writers; but in the writing of men as well as of women, and indeed in the whole course of literature, there is a continuous response to the gradual though rapid changes which the century was bringing to woman. It must suffice here to glance at some of the more striking connections which mark this extended relationship between literature and the feminist movement.

I have already noted in the writing of Mrs. Norton and Miss Martineau an interest in improving the conditions of employment of women and children, in the better education of women, and in freeing wife and mother from some of the ancient tyrannies sustained by law. At the middle of the century the most important ideas at work to affect woman's position undoubtedly focussed on higher education. The enormous advances that have since been made in England and America had a starting point in the establishment of Queen's College in 1848 through the initiative of Frederick Denison Maurice. In the preceding year appeared "The Princess" by his intimate friend Tennyson. Though no one now views the poem as a revolutionary or radical document on the woman question, still it was a response to the most advanced ideas of its own day. If we remember that even Mrs. Norton was then proclaiming the God-created inferiority of women, there is a forward-moving sweep in Tennyson's oft-quoted generalizations—

> In true marriage lies
> Nor equal nor unequal.
>
> For woman is not undevelopt man
> But diverse.

Within a dozen years the agitation for woman suffrage had advanced to the foreground. The election of John Stuart Mill to the House of Commons in 1865 gained a parliamentary discussion for the proposal, and his essay four years later "On the Subjection of Women" placed the question in the forum of literature. The active effort that continued through the seventies and eighties to make woman suffrage a part of the Liberal program of electoral reform, was, however, only an advance guard engagement. The progress of the army of women was being made in other ways and was slowly but surely moving up to the support of the advanced detachment.

In literature this general progress was naturally best represented in the novel. The freedom offered by the novel for the depiction of changing woman was, however, seriously fettered by two of its established conventions. In the first place, it was expected to tell a story of youthful love culminating in marriage for better or worse until death do us part. In the second place, the heroine was expected to be very good as well as very beautiful, faultless in heart and face—requirements not easy to jibe with reality. The effort to present the new woman was compelled to attack these two conventions, and was first manifested in the presentation of married woman and her difficulties and in the greater reality applied to the analysis of women, whether good or bad. Two novels by masters of fiction that were appearing simultaneously in the late forties illustrate both of these tendencies. In Edith of *Dombey and Son,* Dickens attempts without success to portray the unhappy wife in modern circumstances. In Becky Sharp, Thackeray draws a full portrait triumphant in its reality and satire. A few years later in America, Hawthorne's *Blithedale Romance* more explicitly recognizes the struggle of a woman against the confines of sex. In England the application of reality to the presentation both of the passion of love and of the aspirations and social sympathies of women was accomplished with fine art in the novels of Charlotte Brontë and Mrs. Gaskell, and with a still more profound and searching knowledge by George Eliot.

In her great series of women, Maggie, Romola, Dorothea, and Gwendolen, we have the tragedies of high-souled women, moved by great aspirations which end in resignation or reconciliation, related with the profoundest knowledge not of woman's heart alone but of all the possibilities of her nature for intellectual and moral progress. It was given to the most highly educated and intellectual woman of the century to lead in intellectualizing the novel and its presentation of women.

Within a few years of *Middlemarch* Meredith and Hardy were publishing novels appreciative of the wide potentialities of women in modern society. In 1879, the year after *Daniel Deronda,* appeared Ibsen's *Doll's House* and Meredith's *Egoist.* In the English novel the attack is made on the masters of the dolls' houses, who in the person of Sir Willoughby Patterne are covered with ridicule for their masculine egoism. If *The Egoist* did not make the immediate commotion produced by Ibsen's play, it was no less a revolutionary document for rebellious women, and five years later Meredith won his first popular success with a brilliant imaginative re-creation of the career of Mrs. Norton. Unfortunately the crucial incident of

*Diana of the Crossways* was taken from a false bit of gossip that attributed to Mrs. Norton the betrayal of the secret of Peel's intended *volte face* on the repeal of the corn laws, an errancy even less conceivable in Meredith's heroine than in the more violent-tempered original, and perhaps as falsely aimed at the sex as at Mrs. Norton. But the novel elevated to romance that modern battle of a woman for independence from the restrictions of sex which her career had typified. By this time Meredith's poems, Hardy's novels, and many other books were representing the struggle of women with the bonds of flesh and circumstance and sex toward a participation and leadership in the advance of civilization. Though there were still many tenants of dolls' houses in fiction, there were also many women refusing tenancy or revolting against their landlords. The movement was worldwide, and the literatures of various countries were debating the good and evil in women with a growing recognition that her further participation in affairs of all kinds was inevitable.

It is not contended that this late-Victorian reading of women discloses a superiority in manners or brains over Shakespeare's heroines or a truth to fact greater than in those of Miss Austen. Undoubtedly imaginative art had placed women at least on an equality with man long before the Victorian era. Jane Eyre is not superior to Juliet, or Diana to Beatrice. Miss Austen's Emma with a little practice could doubtless run a modern department store. The change is not so much in proving woman's abilities as in establishing her freedom and greater opportunity. Juliet and Beatrice exist only as they are being wooed, visions of convincing reality but glimpsed only through the radiances of romance. Emma has no goal except to marry the best man of her limited acquaintance. In Dorothea, Gwendolen, Clara Middleton, and Diana, the complexities of woman's opportunities in modern society receive full exposition; and if she is still a creature to be wooed, she is not to be won without a full appreciation of her purposes and efficiencies. In George Eliot and Meredith, women appear not merely as wonderful individuals but as participants in social progress and in the march of ideas.

VI

In spite of Meredith's insistence on "more brain" as essential for women's work in civilization, and in spite of his denunciation of sentimentalism as "fiddling harmonics on the strings of sensualism," fiction has not been wholly converted. With all her greater accomplishments and interests in comparison with her older sisters, the heroine of the modern novel is often studied mainly as a creature of sex. The two most persistent attitudes in such presentation are, first, that of conventional sentimental fiction which passes hero and heroine through familiar vicissitudes to complete happiness, and, second, that of the ancient legend of the fall of man which views woman as his temptress and hence chiefly to blame for all the ills that arise from the sexual instinct. Even in these venerable attitudes of art, I think we may discern considerable change of late.

The sentimentality that still characterizes popular fiction scarcely seems as dangerous as it did to Meredith. The Keepsakes and Annuals of Mrs. Norton's day have their successors in hundreds of novels and thousands of short stories that amuse and entertain us in about the same way as a game of backgammon or cribbage. There is no real uncertainty, no real tension on the emotions, only a little superficial perplexity and a faint curiosity as to just how the hero will be rescued or what substitute for Desdemona's handkerchief will cause the misunderstanding. Such novels have just as little to do with sex as our popular detective stories have to do with crime, or our game of backgammon with intellectual progress. If they fill our leisure with a meaningless entertainment, they are no worse in this respect than the Galaxies and Keepsakes. Indeed, if some tireless student would make a tabulation, our magazines and best sellers would probably be found to present an improved class of heroines, less insipid and timorous, more self-reliant and intelligent than those of the mid-century. They would be found more likely to rescue the hero and less likely to be rescued by him, more readily triumphant over misunderstandings caused by handkerchiefs or otherwise, and exhibiting prowess in many fields outside of the art of fascination. Though popular fiction continues to multiply the permutations and combinations in its game of youthful love, it appears to have lost most of that certain condescension toward females which distinguished Victorian sentimentality.

The second persisting view of woman, that of Adam toward Eve, has received a peculiar reënforcement through modern realists. In the protest against sentimentalism and idealism, the realists have been always prone to search out the more physical and less spiritual aspects of sex as well as its more morbid or baser connections. In part, this has resulted in a wholesome enough frankness and honesty, in striking contrast with the earlier Victorian prudishness. In part, however, it results in the persistence of a very masculine explanation of the ills of the universe in terms of woman. If one marked outcome of the sexual instinct is the idealization of one sex by the other, there is also a manifest tendency for each to blame the other for the evils and disasters accompanying sex. This recurs in many forms, in the adventuress or temptress of conventional fiction, in the sensual woman of the modern realist, in the satirical extravagance of Mr. Shaw or in the pessimism of Mr. Hardy. It has been remarked that his women however charming and lovable, are likely to be regarded as the most irrational elements in a confused universe, as somehow especially blamable for the complications of sex which make the destiny of man the more hopeless. English literature, however, has never gone to the length of continentals such as Zola or Strindberg, either in the exploitation of the physical and pathological accompaniments of sex or in piling the blame for these upon woman.

The change to be noted in this persistent Adamite conception lies in the greater truth and honesty brought to the study of sex. Not only is there more frankness and more science, there is manifest both in such a philosopher as Hardy and such a wit as Shaw an effort to view the facts. Though masculine prejudice will doubtless continue to survive, it is less likely to be unsupported by at least a partial study of reality. We may expect in the future a still greater frankness in respect to the facts of sex, and we may expect—what was spared to the Victorian era—woman's imaginative reaction to these facts. The Victorian era did not itself contribute but it prepared the way for what the world has long waited—Eve's account of the Fall of Man, and of Woman. This will unquestionably shock a good many men but in the end it may contribute to that mutual understanding of the sexes which Meredith held forth as a worthy goal for imaginative art. His "Essay on Comedy" thus sums up the new attitude of art toward women.

> Comedy is an exhibition of their battle with men, and that of men with them; and as the two, however divergent, both look on one object—namely, Life—the gradual similarity of their impressions must bring them to some resemblance. The comic poet dares to show us men and women coming to this mutual likeness: he is for saying that when they draw together in social life, their minds grow liker.

VII

In *The Education of Henry Adams* there is a rather metaphysical discussion under the caption, "The Dynamo and the Virgin." The phrase suggests the contrast between old gods and new, between medieval and modern faiths, and also the possibility of a profound change in women themselves if they desert the ancient ideal of the Madonna for the modern ideal of an increased production of commodities. With these perplexities the literature of the mid-century has had small concern, yet it may afford a clue to their answer.

Certainly it is full of the worship of motherhood. That excites the tenderest tributes even from its satirists like Carlyle and Thackeray, and is the crown of womanhood for its idealized Pompilias or its realized Dianas. The mother, to be sure, is no longer worshipped only as a saint, but as the indispensable life-giver, eternally sacrificing herself for us. For men swayed by the ideas of democracy and biology her function is no less august and her sacrifice no less beautiful than for those worshippers who built the cathedrals of Notre Dame at Paris and Chartres. If art in the nineteenth century has offered no such monuments, literature has at least been loyal in its devotion, offering as it never has before, even in its Shakespeare or Chaucer, the tribute of its imagination to the mothers of the race.

With the mother is joined the child. In no earlier epoch is literature so devoted to children. The beginning of this tide of imaginative interest, as we have noted, goes back to the end of the eighteenth century, to the followers of Rousseau, to the infant schools, to the paintings of Reynolds, and to the poems of Wordsworth and Blake. But it has continued and grows apace. With our changing ideas, it is no longer the child as the type of the natural man or the child as the innocent breath of the divine, uncorrupted by the contagion of men, that we worship, but the child as the heir of the ages and the next step in a progressive humanity. He is our creation and our hope; and, as never before, the emotions of mankind have been engrossed in watching his early years.

Children crowd the novels of the century. On this host of children in Dickens, Thackeray, Eliot and elsewhere, the humor, tenderness, and sympathy of both their authors and millions of readers have been lavished. The imagination of many an author has worked with most enthusiasm when it has turned back to recollections of his own childhood. From infancy through boyhood and girlhood and adolescence, the novel of the last century has journeyed over and over again, garnering a harvest that the preceding centuries left unreaped. There has grown too a vast literature for boys and girls. The greatest of our novelists and poets have written for them, and in recent years the foremost of our men of letters, Stevenson, Kipling, and Barrie, have been at their very best when writing for children. The child's world has been brought into literature, and a large amount of literature has been created for childhood and youth. The education of the child has become one of the functions of literature, a function carried on not only by some of the masters of the art but by an army of translators, adapters, and teachers who have made books for his guidance. I have noted some of the humblest educational booklets which prepared the way for Harriet Martineau's tales; and, after all, a book which tries to adapt natural philosophy to children is not so very distant in aim from the wonderful *Jungle Books* or the *Child's Garden of Verse*. They are all seeking an imaginative kinship with the child in his awakening sense of the wonderful world he has inherited.

Women have shared with men in making these books for and about boys and girls. And who have read them? Who have read them to the children if not the mothers and older sisters and teachers? It is rather a hopeless task to speculate on the choice of reading between men and women. But, if woman's influence as a reader has been exercised decidedly anywhere, it is in this field of juvenile books. Not that the fathers may not also enjoy with the children "Peter Pan" and the "Jungle Books," and "Alice in Wonderland," but it is surely the mothers who have encouraged the vast creation of entertainment, instruction, sympathy, and fancy for their children. And the teachers too, who have the duty of guiding children into the world of imagination, they have had a quick welcome for those books which really reached the child's mind and won from it a voluntary response. We may be sure that among the many changes that literature has undergone, this is likely to be one of the most permanent—its more intimate appeal to childhood and youth; and we are safe enough in attributing this acquired function in no small part to the increased numbers and intelligence of women readers.

The mother and the child, so far as literature can reassure us, seem in no danger of diminishing influence. The imagination will doubtless continue to be excited by variabilities of the eternal feminine, but it seems likely to continue its devotion to the responsibilities and nobilities of motherhood and to the romance and education of childhood. As to the dynamo, it may be the most appropriate symbol for the age in which we are about to live, and perhaps both women and men are modelling themselves and their lives on its example rather than on the precedents of the saints or the sages. In current fiction women are sometimes described as live wires, and I have noted signs in literature of an increasingly dynamic character in the heroines. Literature of the future must view woman in many new occupations, increasingly concerned with industry, business, and politics, and it may have to relate her struggle with the dynamo. Some hints of that conflict are to be found in the writers who preached a selected production whether by dynamo or madonna, restricted by considerations of quality and welfare; and possibly the literature of the future may support this philosophy. All we can conclude from our survey is that the literature of the Victorian era records no trepidation at the conflict and no fears for the result. Perhaps it has too little knowledge of the dynamo, but it exhibits great confidence in the madonna.

Our survey has revealed a larger number of women engaged in creating literature than ever before. They have been active not only as poets and novelists but in the many miscellaneous kinds of writing that have so increased, especially in those that may be called educational. Heretofore literature has been made by men; henceforth, probably in an increasing degree, this work will be shared by women. But this does not indicate any great change in the character or functions of literature. It has already recognized the equality of women, pled for their independence, and idealized their attributes. The greater participation of women as writers and readers has already maintained a decency and refinement of expression, it seems likely to encourage an increase of good sense and a diminution of masculine prejudice in the treatment of sex. Woman as the worker, as the companion of machines, as the toiler and thinker, should demand increasing attention; and the problems of sex should become less enigmatical to a literature designed for and by both sexes. Then, the devotion of the imagination of the last century to motherhood and children will prove itself one of the most efficient preparations for the battle which the coming epoch must wage to subdue the dynamo to the service of a humane civilization.

## Naomi Lewis

SOURCE: "In Spite of Lit," in *The Twentieth Century*, Vol. 164, No. 978, August, 1958, pp. 114-25.

[*In the following essay, Lewis discusses various stereotypes of women in nineteenth- and twentieth-century literature.*]

Anyone would think from reading Literature that it is by no means an agreeable thing to be a woman. (By Literature I mean, at this moment, practically any invented narrative, good or bad.) It is a curious error, and it may be one of the reasons why, for many years, I have given up reading the stuff at all. To be sure, in the course of professional duty one's eye travels in a month over many more thousands of pages of Lit—current fiction and all—than one would like to believe. It is surprising what the system will tolerate (as doctors, lawyers and plumbers must think sometimes) in the way of Work. Left to myself, however, I find it harder and harder to read the fictional page; *Lucky Jim,* for instance, and *Bonjour Tristesse* go so heavily that after two years or so I have not reached the end of either. I sometimes wonder what those conclusions may hold.

Life may have come before letters, but life (that is, behaviour) is a follower, often years or centuries behind the thoughts that speed it along. And so it happens that Literature (fiction) starts as our reflection and ends too often as our model, imposing ideas and emotions that would never otherwise have troubled us. Love, tastes, manners, desires, beliefs—practically all the conventions in these important affairs come out of books. The relation between parents and young, assumptions about forgiveness, fidelity, duty, kinship, monogamousness, virginity—how many people in the past few hundred years have been untouched by the current fictional rulings on these matters? Florence Nightingale herself, when past the age of thirty, still felt a sense of sin in crossing the will of her appalling parents, and in leaving the subservience of her home. Genius does not always go with intelligence. Here, the comment by Mrs Browning on Miss Nightingale's later activities is of peculiar interest. Look through the personal irritation and you see a really shrewd attack on one of the most popular aspects of the myth.

> Every man is on his knees before ladies carrying lint, calling them 'angelic she's', whereas if they stir an inch as thinkers and artists from the beaten line (involving more good to general humanity than is involved in lint), the very same men would curse the impudence of the very same women. . . . I do not consider the best use to which we can put a gifted and accomplished woman is to *make her a hospital nurse.*

There is a comical note about this, of course, but we can see what she means. Why should woman be merely an 'angelic she'? Why—to carry the question further—should we assume that every woman desires to be a wife or a mother, or to have a 'career' (whatever that may be) as a rigid alternative? What if she wants to live happily alone, without even a budgerigar? Perhaps it is hard to make a novel about a delicious solitude, but, if a poem is possible, why not a tale? Only do not make the fictional mistake of placing the lady inside convent walls. Nothing could be less solitary than this communal world, with its ordered dependence even in private thoughts.

The conventions do not remain constant, it may be observed. I cannot, for instance, feel that the unmarried girls in Jane Austen's novels—the Bennets and others—suffered from sexual frustration or other such textbook neuroses of our time. Chagrin, failure, boredom with home life—but nothing more than that: the other things had not been invented. I can remember myself, at the age of eighteen, being puzzled for a moment by a lecturing don (eighteenth century Lit) who spoke of 'the battle of the sexes'. The phrase was meaningless. Battles between siblings, of every kind, I well understood; but there it was prestige of age or youth that turned the jealous scale. This, as I see it now, was a clear—perhaps unique—case of ignorance of or uncontamination by Lit.

The laws of fiction have rarely been on the side of women, but is it not largely the fault of women when such injustices persist? As readers they believe: as writers, with very few exceptions, they betray. Novelists do not all go as far as Charlotte Yonge, who stated, on grounds that she would have thought were theological: 'I have no hesitation in declaring my full belief in the inferiority of women, nor that she brought it upon herself'—and used her female characters accordingly. 'Self-denial is always best, and in a doubtful case the most disagreeable is always the safest' was one of her rules. It seemed to her quite in order that Dr Moberly, father of fifteen children, should make her promise that she would never let Ethel May of *The Daisy Chain* marry, nor the philoprogenitive Dr May of her story ever die. Theology has always been one of the most dangerous forms of Lit, particularly to female victims. Few have recovered: not one has come out unscarred.

Foreground women (as opposed to servants, needy relatives and other furniture) may have had a slightly better time in other novels of that day, but certain rules were almost invariably observed. Women who sinned, whether professionally (poor Nancy in *Oliver Twist*) or by a single lapse (poor Em'ly in *David Copperfield,* or Ruth in Mrs Gaskell's *Ruth*) had to die, and that was that. Becky Sharp, remember, was a lawfully married woman before many chapters were gone. But in our own liberal age, there is a dreadful impulse still to *torment* one's female characters. Plays like *Nine till Six* or *The Women,* or *Autumn Crocus*—O that theme about the sad teacher—Miss Hepburn or another—having her one and only fling ('the last chance') on her Continental hols!—where do you or I fit in with all this crowd? And ought it all to go on and on and on as it does? Literature, as I have said before, is a model for life; it is a wonderful weapon, a means of creation or revenge, a sort of magic, the unanswerable word, in fact, if you happen to have the gift. See what Jane Austen did with it—an achievement on the side of women (no yearning stuff, no squalor and yet no cheating either)—that could still serve as a model.

Horrifying as its power may be in its time, nothing is more absurd than a convention that has decayed. This should be a warning to women, if they will (or would) but take it. The position of the governess in nineteenth century England is a fair example; any member of this melancholy profession had to be poor but of good family, a compulsorily depressed gentlewoman, in order to be able to mix with the children of the house but also to be treated as an inferior by her employers. God has ordained that this is, was and ever will be the way of Life, the theory ran. We know to-day, of course, that it was one of the teachings of Lit. Mrs Pryor, in *Shirley,* has some enlightening things to say about the matter.

> You told me before you wished to be a governess; but, my dear, if you remember, I did not encourage the idea. I have been a governess myself a great part of my life . . . when I was young, before I married; my trials were severe, poignant. I should not like you to endure similar ones. It was my lot to enter a family of considerable pretensions to good birth and mental superiority. . . . I was early given to understand that 'as I was not their equal', so I could not expect 'to have their sympathy'. It was in no sort concealed from me that I was held 'a burden and a restraint in society'. The gentlemen, I found, regarded me as a 'tabooed woman,' to whom 'they were interdicted from granting the usual privileges of the sex', and yet who 'annoyed them by frequently crossing their path'. The ladies too, made it plain that they thought me 'a bore'. The servants, it was signified, 'detested me'; *why,* I could never clearly comprehend. . . . It was intimated that 'I must live alone, and never transgress the invisible but rigid line which established the difference between me and my employers'. My life in this house, sedentary, solitary, constrained, joyless, toilsome . . . began ere long to produce mortal effects on my constitution—I sickened. The lady of the house told me coolly I was the victim of 'wounded vanity'. She hinted that if I did not make an effort to quell my 'ungodly discontent', to cease 'murmuring against God's appointment,' and to cultivate the profound humility befitting my station, my mind would very likely 'go to pieces' on the rock that wrecked most of my sisterhood—morbid self-esteem—and that I should die an inmate of a lunatic asylum.

All the 'quoted' phrases in this speech are taken from that famous essay which appeared as a perfectly serious contribution to *The Quarterly* after the publication of *Jane Eyre.* Some of the prize assertions, however, are to follow, from the lips of the eldest daughter of the house.

> There were hardships (allowed this young lady) in the position of a governess, but . . . it must be so. *She* had neither view, hope, nor *wish* to see these things remedied; for in the inherent constitution of English habits, feelings, and prejudices, there was no possibility that they should be. Governesses, she observed, must ever be kept in a sort of isolation: it is the only means of maintaining that distance which the reserve of English manners and the decorum of English families exact. . . . We need the imprudences, extravagances, mistakes, and crimes of a certain number of fathers to sow the seed from which WE reap the harvest of governesses. The daughters of tradespeople, however well-educated, must necessarily be underbred, and as such unfit to be inmates of our dwellings. . . . We shall ever prefer to place those about our offspring who have been born and bred with somewhat of the same refinement as ourselves.

This is really a peerless example (note the hammering use of the word 'ever') of the effect of Lit at its most fantastic, on manners and beliefs. And also, for once, of the riposte through the same medium. Remember, though, that there were a hundred meek, voiceless, nameless governesses in the fictional background of the earlier nineteenth century for one Jane Eyre.

For *Jane Eyre,* the all-level best seller, is one of the few novels on the high level of genius which are aware of the power of Lit over life, and *use it in the heroine's cause.* (In her later governess-book, *Villette,* the author quailed and fell into the old guilty heroine-punishment pattern.) But Jane herself is superb, succeeding entirely on her own (that is her author's) terms. She is prim and neat, small and plain (well, sort of), sharp in speech, prickly in temper, and alone, an orphan. She is Miss Charlotte Brontë with the foil of a Rochester. Her wardrobe is Quakerish and slight—a black stuff gown for day, a dove-colour for occasions: 'my best dress (the silver-gray one, purchased for Miss Temple's wedding and never worn since) . . . my sole ornament the pearl brooch'. *The* pearl brooch—we know it as if it were our own. How cunningly she describes the 'beauty' of her rival, Miss Ingram, with her 'noble bust' and 'rich raven ringlets', her 'arched and haughty lip'. 'Queen Boadicea, leaning back against those purple cushions,' is Mr Rochester's contribution. Jane gets all the benefit of the contrast.

> 'Don't address me as if I were a beauty; I am your plain, Quakerish governess.'
>
> 'You are a beauty' (Mr Rochester returns) 'in my eyes, and a beauty just after the desire of my heart—delicate and aërial.'

A fairy from elf-land, he calls her. 'You shall sojourn,' he promises, 'at Florence, Venice and Vienna . . . wherever I have stamped my hoof, your sylph's foot shall step also.' He describes their first conversation.

> Impatiently I waited for evening, when I might summon you to my presence. An unusual—to me— a perfectly new character I suspected was yours: I desired to search it deeper and know it better. You entered the room with a look and air at once shy and independent: you were quaintly dressed—much as you are now. I made you talk: ere long I found you full of strange contrasts. Your garb and manner were restricted by rule; your air was often diffident, and altogether that of one refined by nature, but absolutely unused to society . . . yet when addressed you lifted a keen, a daring, and a glowing eye to your interlocutor's face; there was penetration and power in each glance you gave; when plied by close questions you found ready and round answers . . .

Ready and round answers! How we long to be able to give them on the spot, like the ladies in *The Importance of Being Earnest,* or *The Way of the World,* or *The School for Scandal,* or the novels of Miss Compton Burnett. This is what Charlotte Brontë achieves on her own behalf, and on behalf of all the downtrodden governesses whose state was fixed 'for ever' in *The Quarterly.*

Still, the virgins and matrons continued to hold the centre of the stage for some time yet. Sometimes an audacious variation—the Amazonian maiden—might appear. To find one such in Tennyson, who soon in life developed settled views on women, is a surprise—but the poem belongs to his early days.

> I know her by her angry air,
> Her bright black eyes, her bright black hair,
>     Her rapid laughters wild and shrill,
> As laughter of the woodpecker
>     From the bosom of a hill.
>     'Tis Kate—she sayeth what she will;
> For Kate hath an unbridled tongue,
>     Clear as the twanging of a harp.
>     Her heart is like a throbbing star.
> Kate hath a spirit ever strung
>     Like a new bow, and bright and sharp
>     As edges of the scymetar.
> Whence shall she take a fitting mate!
>     For Kate no common love will feel;
> My woman-soldier, gallant Kate,
>     As pure and true as blades of steel.
>
> Kate saith, 'the world is void of might.'
> Kate saith, 'the men are gilded flies.'
>     Kate snaps her fingers at my vows;
> Kate will not hear of lover's sighs.
> I would I were an armed knight . . .

Compare Stevenson's rather frightening

> Steel-true and blade straight
> The great artificer
> Made my mate.

These are instances—there are other variations in male writing—of defence-by-Lit. This is not to be confused with attack-by-Lit, most formidably employed in recent times, I suppose, by Shaw. Women have never made sufficient use of either of these weapons on their own behalf.

But even at the turn of the present century the fictional uneasiness about the 'earning' woman persisted. Gissing did his best for the sad respectable shop girl or clerk, but he imposes so dejected an air on his characters that they seem forcibly taken out of the silent background; they are not natural heroines like Jane. Wells, who was on the side of women, had a try with Ann Veronica though, if he succeeded, it was because Ann was really the virgin-into-matron heroine of fifty years earlier. Still, he did bring the trouble to the surface.

> 'It's no good flying out at that, Vee; *I* didn't arrange it. It's Providence. That's how things are; that's the order of the world. Like appendicitis. It isn't pretty, but we're made so. Rot, no doubt; but we can't alter it. You go home and live on the G.V., and get some other man to live on as soon as possible. It isn't sentiment, but it's horse sense. All this Woman-who-Diddery—no damn good. After all, old P.—Providence I mean—*has* arranged it so that man will keep you, more or less. He made the universe on those lines. You've got to take what you can get.'

That was the quintessence of her brother Roddy.

He played variations on this theme for the better part of an hour.

'You go home,' he said at parting; 'you go home. It's all very fine and all that, Vee, this freedom, but it isn't going to work. The world isn't ready for girls to start out on their own yet; that's the plain fact of the case. . . . You go home and wait a century, Vee, and then try again. Then you *may* have a bit of a chance. Now you haven't the ghost of one—not if you play the game fair.'

It was remarkable to Ann Veronica how completely Mr Manning, in his entirely different dialect, indorsed her brother Roddy's view of things. He came along, he said, just to call, with large, loud apologies, radiantly kind and good. Miss Stanley, it was manifest, had given him Ann Veronica's address. The kindly-faced landlady had failed to catch his name, and said he was a tall handsome gentleman with a great black moustache. Ann Veronica, with a sigh at the cost of hospitality, made hasty negotiations for an extra tea and for a fire in the ground-floor apartment, and preened herself carefully for the interview. In the little apartment, under the gas chandelier, his inches and his stoop were certainly very effective. In the bad light he looked at once military and sentimental and studious, like one of Ouida's guardsmen revised by Mr Haldane and the London School of Economics and finished in the Keltic school.

'It's unforgiveable of me to call, Miss Stanley,' he said, shaking hands in a peculiarly high, fashionable manner, 'but you know you said we might be friends. It's dreadful for you to be here . . . but your aunt told me something of what had happened. It's just like your Splendid Pride to do it. Quite!'

He sat in the arm-chair and took tea, and consumed several of the extra cakes which she had sent out for, and talked to her . . . looking very earnestly at her with his deep-set eyes, and carefully avoiding any crumbs on his moustache the while. Ann Veronica sat firelit by her tea-tray with, quite unconsciously, the air of an expert hostess.

'Your father, of course,' he said, 'must come to realize just how Splendid you are! He doesn't understand. I've seen him, and he doesn't a bit understand. *I* didn't understand before that letter. It makes me want to be just everything I *can* be to you. You're like some splendid Princess in Exile in these dreadful dingy apartments!'

'I'm afraid I'm anything but a Princess when it comes to earning a salary,' said Ann Veronica. 'But frankly, I mean to fight this through if I possibly can.'

'My God!' said Manning in a stage-aside. 'Earning a salary!'

What the last half-century has done, by way of Lit, has been to bring practically all of the background figures to the front—the very old, the very young, the servant, the spinster, the prostitute, the 'other' woman. Some have taken the leading rôle better than others. *All Passion Spent* is one of the best pieces of Lit on the side of old age that exists. Servants have been 'done' by Henry Green and Ivy Compton Burnett as well as, rather self-consciously, by George Moore. 'Earning a salary' is a commonplace—indeed, a necessity. Your heroine must have an occupation of sorts to take the place of conversation. And yet, I begin to wonder, what are novels really about even now? Nothing is more generally uninteresting than an average young woman on the way to getting married—yet this is the theme of almost every fictional volume on the public library shelves. Sex, which can be a nice sort of subject, runs to extremes: nymphomania or nothing. Well, if we must have our nymphs, let them do their stuff with style, like Iris March—perhaps the only nymph of genius that our century has produced.

> The light that plunged through my half-open sitting room door fought a great fight with the shadow of her green hat and lit her face, mysteriously. She was fair. As would they say it in the England of long ago—she was fair. And she was grave, so grave. That is a sad lady, I thought. To be fair, to be sad . . . why, was she intelligent, too? And white she was, very white, and her painted mouth was purple in the dim light, and her eyes, which seemed set very wide apart, were cool, impersonal, sensible, and they were blazing blue. Even in that light they were blazing, like two spoonfuls of the Mediterranean in the early morning of a brilliant day. The sirens had eyes like that, without a doubt, when they sang of better dreams. But no siren, she! That was a sad lady, most grave. And always her hair would be dancing a tawny, formal dance about the small white cheeks.

> 'I know what you are thinking,' she said.

> 'I wonder!'

> 'Yes. You like Gerald, don't you?' She thought about that. 'Well, what you are thinking is, whether it is fair to him to take me up there in case he is drunk . . .'

> 'If only it was "in case",' I said. 'You see?'

> She closed her eyes.

> 'Poor Gerald,' she whispered. 'Isn't it a shame!'

> I could not see her face, her back was to me. The leather jacket, the brave green hat, the thoughtful poise. But I heard her whisper the name of the inert thing sprawling half on a broken Windsor chair and half across the littered table . . . and I thought to myself that these twins must have been great playmates once upon a time. . . . Suddenly I found her looking at me over her shoulder, so thoughtfully. I can see her now, the way she suddenly looked at me, half over her leather shoulder, thinking I knew not what, and her right hand spread out on her brother's arm. There was a striking emerald on the third finger of her right hand, livid against the dark thing that was Gerald March.

Rather fine, really, that last sentence. Soon, however, Iris moves to go.

> She painted her mouth, staring moon-struck into the daylight. 'Yes, I would die for purity. I wouldn't mind dying anyhow, but it would be nice to die for purity . . .'

> I said thus and thus.

> 'Yes,' she said, not having heard a word of mine, 'it is not good to have a pagan body and a Chislehurst mind, as I have. It is hell for the body and terror for the mind. There are dreams, and there are beasts. The dreams walk glittering up and down the soiled loneliness of desire, the beasts prowl about the soiled loneliness of regret. Goodbye.'

> 'Then it must be "good-bye"?'

> 'Because of shame,' she said. 'But if I were different, I would like you for my friend——'

> She said she was in London now only on business that would last a few weeks, and lived always abroad.

> 'But this is the telephone number,' she said . . . and her leather arm darted to the floor and came up with a book, and on the fly-leaf of the book she scrawled the number with her lip-stick.

> High above the sharp noises of the young day I heard the scream of an electric horn.

The electric horn still sounds for those who read Mr Arlens' book—though perhaps one should be about the age of ten or twelve, and simple at that, when you find it first in a corner of the shelves. For purity, though—it takes a lot of charm or piquancy to carry *this* thing off. Lucrece of the Tarquin episode is by contrast an anti-woman invention. But Daisy Miller, dying for much the same reason on her Continental tour, is not. The Jamesian bachelor Winterbourne hears that 'the little American flirt' is dangerously ill. He calls to ask news, and Daisy's mother tells him:

> 'She spoke of you the other day. . . . She gave me a message; she told me to tell you. She told me to tell you that she was never engaged to that handsome Italian. I am sure I am very glad; Mr Giovanelli hasn't been near us since she was taken ill. I thought he was so much of a gentleman; but I don't call that very polite! . . .'

> But . . . it mattered very little. A week after this the poor girl died; it had been a terrible case of the fever. Daisy's grave was in the little Protestant cemetery, in an angle of the wall of imperial Rome, beneath the cypresses and the thick spring flowers. Winterbourne stood there beside it, with a number of other mourners; a number larger than the scandal excited by the young lady's career would have led you to expect. Near him stood Giovanelli, who

came nearer still before Winterbourne turned away. Giovanelli was very pale; on this occasion he had no flower in his buttonhole; he seemed to wish to say something. At last he said, 'She was the most beautiful young lady I ever saw, and the most amiable.' And then he added in a moment, 'And she was the most innocent.'

Winterbourne looked at him, and presently repeated his words, 'And the most innocent?'

'The most innocent!'

Winterbourne felt sore and angry. 'Why the devil did you take her to that fatal place?'

Mr Giovanelli's urbanity was apparently imperturbable. He looked on the ground for a moment, and then he said, 'For myself, I had no fear; and she wanted to go.'

Winterbourne leaves Rome, but a year later he meets his aunt, Mrs Costello, at Vevey.

In the interval Winterbourne had often thought of Daisy Miller and her mystifying manners. One day he spoke of her to his aunt—said it was on his conscience that he had done her injustice.

'I am sure I don't know how,' said Mrs Costello. 'How did your injustice affect her?'

'She sent me a message before her death which I didn't understand at the time. But I have understood it since. She would have appreciated one's esteem.'

. . . He presently said, 'You were right in that remark that you made last summer. I was booked to make a mistake. I have lived too long in foreign parts.'

For Henry James was never, I think, unfair to women in the way in which women are to themselves. What he chose to describe was the difficulty of contact between differing patterns of Lit.

It may be objected that a good many women who run (about a house or thereabouts) are not also those who read. Do not forget the women's magazines, with their ready appeal for us all. Their fiction would appear to be aimed at the coarsest of readers; the taste for it seems to me strange and perverted, like a taste for blancmange or tripe. But it is more false and more dangerous than either of these dishes. Vigorous young women such as those who feature in the tales are either coldly getting engaged to dull young men, or are involved, perhaps, in relationships which never by any chance get a partisan hearing in these pages. Lit is displayed here at its most insidious. Ah, but turn to the section at the end—the letters from those who have taken this diet of Lit as a basis for life. All those marriages, all those lovely kiddies—nothing turns out like it does in books. Is this the best plan of behaviour after all?

And even if you do not read, the myths come through. The fairy tale teaches the laws of luck; if you are the youngest, with butter-coloured hair and not over bright in mind, you will get not only the king's son or daughter, but a second chance or even a third when you go wrong. Is Cinderella an edifying tale? Certainly not in the gross modern versions. In the French original the sisters were haughty, elegant, proud; not creatures of vulgar low comedy. Cinderella's *type* makes the story wrong. Would she not have been sitting at home reading the film magazines by the fire while her sisters went, say, to the Festival Hall? It is time some genius rewrote the Cinderella tale—a woman preferably—and many another legend too. Most human unhappiness comes from wrong ideas; but it is not too late to create a new sort of heroine, an anti-De Montherlant woman. It has come to a pretty pass when women as well as men are not on the side of themselves.

> O but he was as fair as a garden in flower,
> As slender and tall as the great Eiffel Tower,
> When the waltz throbbed out on the long
>       promenade
> O his eyes and his smile they went straight to my
>       heart;
> 'O marry me, Johnny, I'll love and obey':
> But he frowned like thunder, and he went away.

That—and there is a lot more of it—was by young Mr Auden. You see what I mean? On the other hand *The Green Hat* and *Zuleika Dobson*, were both the work of men. A sad thought, I was going to say, but best, after all, to take it as a compliment: a talisman.

## Carolyn Heilbrun

SOURCE: "The Woman as Hero," in *The Texas Quarterly*, Vol. 8, No. 4, Winter, 1965, pp. 132-41.

[*In the following essay, Heilbrun finds female fictional heroes largely unique to modern literature because these female heroes represent the struggles of both women and men in the modern age.*]

It appears that having chosen such a title as "the woman as hero," I ought to begin with some definitions. What do I mean by a woman, and what do I mean by a hero? I hope you will be immeasurably relieved to learn that I have no intention of defining a woman. For one thing, it would involve defining a man, and I'm not hero enough for that. Let us say that if there are two doors, one marked "women" and one marked "men," we shall be talking about those people who will go through the door marked "women."

What I *shall* try to define is a particular literary phenomenon involving women. This literary phenomenon, which can be given an opening and closing date, like any other proper historical occurrence, does involve our knowing what a hero is. Clearly it will not do to put up a door marked "heroes" and wait to see who walks through it. Almost as clearly, it will not help to track the concept of "hero" through the forests of literary criticism and literary history: that is the sort of undertaking for which a scholar must be prepared to devote a large portion of his life. Therefore, I asked my seven-year-old son, who happened to be reading about Wyatt Earp at the time, what a hero was, and he said: "the main character in a book, of course." Which I think is a pretty good definition.

Still, let me, womanlike, enlarge on it a little. The hero of a work is the protagonist, the central character who undergoes the major action. If we can borrow Kenneth Burke's phrases, the hero begins with a purpose he believes himself sufficiently in control of circumstances to carry out; but—to be human is to act on partial knowledge; and so events he could not foresee, the past which he has forgotten, rise up to thwart him. He undergoes a passion, he is acted upon, he suffers. He emerges from this suffering with a new perception of what the forces are which govern his world. We all know, or soon learn, what it is to think that we can plan the future, what it is to suffer as these plans go awry, what it is to learn at last what past acts—our own or other people's—were at work to render impossible our illusion of being in control of destiny. This action—purpose through passion to perception—which the hero undergoes is a universal, perhaps an archetypal action. It is at least of sufficient universality to allow us, as we say, to "identify" with the hero, regardless of our age or sex.

Now it is quite clear that if we put up a literary door for literary characters marked "heroes," most of the characters who walk through it will be men. I'm aware that we have a word for central women characters—heroines—but what we mean by this word, almost always, is that female character who plays the largest, or most important role in the life of the hero, who is the chief sexual event in his life; or we mean the central character in a work, like soap opera, written for women, with which no man could possibly identify, his usual reaction to such heroines being that they richly deserve the slow torture they are so lugubriously undergoing. Perhaps you will see then why I speak of a woman as "hero." I am speaking not of a woman who occupies the traditional place of women in literature, but of a woman who is the protagonist of a work, the character who undergoes the central action, the character whom men, as well as women, may view as an actor in a destiny possible for them.

The traditional place for women in literature can be seen clearly, if distantly, in the *Aeneid.* Which of us can forget the picture of Aeneas as he leaves the burning city of Troy? On his shoulders he carries his aging father, Anchises; by the hand he leads his son, Ascanius. Of his wife Creusa we seem to have lost account; so has Aeneas, so almost has Virgil. She has produced Aeneas's son, and can now only be an encumbrance to everyone. Aeneas's other hand is not offered to her; she is left to follow, and is lost in the shadows.

As a contemporary novelist has said to me, "What do you *do* with women characters, except have the men characters make love to them? Then either they marry them or they don't." Virgil would not, one assumes, have put it so

inelegantly, but one senses the emotion, nonetheless, in the *Aeneid.* Dido is a queen, the builder of a great city, the ruler of a great people. But all of it is lost for love of Aeneas. Unlike Aeneas, she has no sense of destiny to sustain her. Seized with unrequited love for a man who must follow *his* destiny undeterred by casual affairs in caves, she forgets everything but passion as she throws herself upon her sword.

In discussing the phenomenon I have called "the woman as hero" I am going to speak only of women heroes created by male authors. Though some of the greatest women heroes are the creation of women authors, I am limiting my discussion to the work of male authors for several reasons. First, when a man has been forced, possibly against his inclination and by the deepest demands of his artistic vision, to use a woman as hero, the choice he has made reveals far more powerfully than could the work of a woman writer the particular qualities of a woman which make her a hero. To put this frivolously, if D. H. Lawrence chooses a woman as hero, that is news; if Virginia Woolf does, that is just what everyone expected.

Second, by choosing male writers, one avoids, neatly if unfairly, those women writers against whom can be leveled a "masculine protest." Though most men do not respond to women writers in this way, there are others who loathe Jane Austen, and, at the moment at least, many men seem to recoil from Virginia Woolf's work as from the screech of chalk on blackboard. Norman Mailer's dismissal of women writers, while extreme, is perhaps not totally unrepresentative: "I doubt if there will be a really exciting woman writer until the first whore becomes a call girl and tells her tale."

Finally, by choosing male writers, it is possible to avoid "feminism" as an issue. We may feel certain that men chose women heroes not out of any urge to fight the feminist battle but because woman's place in the universe provided the proper metaphor for the place of the heroic in a work of literary art. A male writer with a woman hero may be antifeminist or antiwoman in his personal life or in his discursive writings; this is not to the point. Ibsen, a man unusually sympathetic to the dilemma of women, still denied that he was writing about women's rights: "I am writing about humanity," he said.

Ibsen and James, then, almost at the same moment, discovered the woman as hero. Certainly within a year of each other, each had conceived his first major, tragic work, and each had determined that in this new work a woman would bear the burden of the tragic action. Thus, in 1880, was born the woman as hero, a creature quite distinct from the "heroine." Greatly significant, she has been little noticed, and now, indeed, the wench is dead. But for a period of nearly fifty years such major writers as Ibsen, James, Shaw, Lawrence, and Forster were to find that, at the height of their powers, it was a woman hero who best met the requirements of their imaginations. The woman hero became the embodiment of the masculine artistic vision.

Ibsen made the first notations for *A Doll's House* in 1878. We are told (by Halvdahn Koht) that he called it at first simply "a modern tragedy, so great and inclusive did it seem in his mind." What he wished to show was the contrast and conflict between "the natural feelings on one side and belief in authority on the other." For Ibsen, the woman was the proper spokesman for the "natural."

The following year, in 1879, Henry James wrote to his brother: "I have determined that the novel I write this next year shall be 'big.'" What James had determined to do (in the words of Oscar Cargill) was to make the heroine of *The Portrait of a Lady* "focal rather than contributory, which neither Shakespeare nor George Eliot, however deeply interested in their heroines, had done, and to center everything in her consciousness, particularly emphasizing her view of herself." One recalls James's phrase about his cousin, Minny Temple, who died young: "She would have given anything to live." It is the phrase which, with all the force James intended behind the verb "to live," describes the modern hero, man or woman.

The woman hero of modern literature is sustained by some sense of her own autonomy as she contemplates and searches for a destiny; she does not wait to be swept up by life as a girl is swept up in a waltz. Ralph Touchett, in *The Portrait of a Lady,* thinks of Isabelle: "but what was she going to do with herself? This question was irregular, for with most women one had no occasion to ask it. Most women did with themselves nothing at all; they waited, in attitudes more or less gracefully passive, for a man to come that way and furnish them with a destiny." Before the 1880s it was shocking—to many it still is—to think of a woman as a person before she is thought of as mistress, wife, or mother. Even Frau Raabae, the German actress who played Nora in one of the first productions of *A Doll's House,* flatly refused to perform the conclusion of the play as Ibsen had written it; "I would never leave my children," she said. Almost no one bothered to notice—many still haven't—that Ibsen, using his woman hero, was writing of the need of every human being to be himself freely and strongly.

"The main thing," Ibsen once wrote in a letter, "is to remain sincere and true in relation to one's self. It is not a matter of willing this or that, but of willing what one absolutely must do because of one's self, and because one cannot do otherwise. Everything else leads only to falsehood." Ibsen's plays with a woman hero are not, as they have so often been called, "social dramas"; they are tragedies.

Tragedy, like psychoanalysis, offers no superhuman salvation, only the perceptions of the limits of human power, and the freedom which such perception brings. Nora faces the world at the end far more stripped of everything than Oedipus. Though blind, symbolically dead, his "occupation gone," he is still a great man. It has been prophesied that the land where he is buried will flourish. Nora, on the other hand, has come to realize that in the sense in which Forster will later use the phrase, she does not "exist." She is called mother, wife, housekeeper, but in fact she is none of these things, and without these she ceases to be. The hero of our modern tragedies is no king whose death brings about the salvation of society. Our modern hero is a man searching for himself. Both *Oedipus Rex* and *A Doll's House* are Aristotelian tragedies because they possess plot, which we know to be of the first importance; there is present the imitation of an action. *Ghosts,* for example, is not a social drama about syphilis, or even about the narrow mores of a provincial society. It is a tragedy of a hero who looks now to the future when all joy may be possessed, when the past has been "paid off," a hero who then discovers, as Oedipus discovered, that the past has only just begun to reveal itself, and that the future holds only a revelation of the power of the past. Mrs. Alving has, like Oedipus, apparent autonomy; her husband is dead, she has a son, she has the chance to tell off the man who betrayed her passion many years ago. Triumphant and arrogant, she follows the inevitable path of human tragedy. She is a hero.

Have there not been women heroes before the age of "modern" literature? Yes: we may mention Shakespeare's plays, and *The Scarlet Letter.* But the woman as hero is more frequent in great modern literature precisely because the peculiar tension that exists between her apparent freedom and her actual relegation to a constrained destiny is a tension experienced also by men in the modern world. "She would have given anything to live." Woman, serving as a metaphor for modern man striving to express himself, to *be* himself within a mechanical society, discovers her greatest wish is to *live,* a wish for which she will give anything or everything, even that which we have decided is innate in women: the love of children and the passionate desire for a man. Not even these two "innate" qualities are allowed, in modern literature, to stand between a woman and herself. Nora will leave even her children; Isabelle Archer will leave even the man she has come passionately to desire. It is, incidentally, noteworthy how many commentators insist that Isabelle "fears" passion in *The Portrait of a Lady:* in fact, she does not flee from the passion of Casper Goodwood's kiss. She flees from the temptation that kiss offers away from the moral act to which, by marrying Osmond and promising Pansy to return, she has committed herself.

"We do not see women," Consol Bernick says at the end of one of the drafts of Ibsen's *Pillars of Society,* and indeed she has been harder to *see* than any other human being, harder to visualize as a person. Conrad was, together with Joyce, one of the only two major modern writers in English who could not so visualize a woman, who did not use a woman as a hero. Yet Conrad and Joyce avoided the woman as hero in startlingly different ways and for different reasons. Conrad could no more have conceived of a woman hero than could Dickens. Though we should not, after the common fashion, call him a writer of sea stories, this label does at least emphasize his creation of artistic worlds in which women have no part, or no continually essential part. In his most characteristic, perhaps his most profound work, *Heart of*

*Darkness,* women are explicitly characterized as outside the range of reality, the experience of truth. "It's queer how out of touch with truth women are," Marlow says; "they live in a world of their own, and there has never been anything like it, and never can be." Kurtz's fiancée could no more be told the truth of her lover's death than a foreigner could, on a sudden, be initiated into sacred rites. For Conrad, women are outside the range of action. This is not, of course, a criticism of Conrad; such a criticism would be absurd.

Joyce is quite another matter. Suffice it to say that the woman as hero, like the man as hero, exists in one character in *Ulysses, Leopold* Bloom. No one surely can deny Bloom's feminine (I do not mean effeminate) characteristics; he is both man and woman, he is everyman. In the "Circe" episode he becomes a woman, but I speak of something closer to his conscious nature than this. His empathy with women is extraordinary: he alone in the book is sympathetically present during childbirth; he is sympathetically aware, though not in awe of, the problems of menstruation; he is sexually passive at times, even masochistic. Molly says of him, "I saw he understood or felt what a woman is." Apart from Leopold Bloom, all men and all women, we have in *Ulysses* only woman in childbirth, woman as sexually exciting girl (though crippled) and woman as the sexual object of man's quest. And Molly is perhaps, as some women critics have testified, closer to a man's sexual fantasies of a woman, than to a woman. It is Leopold who performs the rites of homecoming, Leopold who makes the cocoa he drinks, in a kind of communion, with Stephen. Hero and anti-hero, Bloom who is Jew and Gentile, Moses and Christ, is man and woman too.

In creating Isabelle Archer in *The Portrait of a Lady,* James was able (as Fred B. Millett has written) to bestow on her "a considerable number of traits of his younger self." Essential to the creation of the woman as hero is the ability of the male author to transpose his own experience to a woman character. Thus Lawrence bestows on Ursula his own early experiences, the traits of his younger self. In the figure of the "hero" (as Maud Bodkin has pointed out) we have the human spirit which has found expression where differences of male and female cease to be of first importance. As it happened, it was modern woman, with her strange destiny of slavery and freedom inextricably combined, who best symbolized the modern, existential, "absurd" lot. Bodkin knows that in the experience of any gifted woman her "imaginative life has been largely shaped by the thought and adventure of men." For modern authors, the imaginative life can be largely shaped by the thought and adventure of women, particularly the gifted woman "affronting her destiny" and refusing to be trapped by the usual expectations which society has for her. As Isabelle Archer puts it: "I don't know whether I succeed in expressing myself, but I know that nothing else expresses me. Nothing that belongs to me is the measure of me; on the contrary, it's a limit, a barrier, and a perfectly arbitrary one." The artist is, as Coleridge and others have said, androgynous; and

here it is the woman who, through the vision of the androgynous artist, speaks for modern man: "I know that nothing else expresses me."

It is possible to find, in Leon Edel's brilliant biography, statement after statement of James's in which he tells us that woman is not to be contrasted with man, as something "other" to be criticized by him, but is simply a vision of man's own "inner economy." It is interesting to know that a man who saw much of James in London was sufficiently fascinated by James's great attractiveness to women to attempt to determine the essential reason for it. James, he discovered, "seemed to look at women rather as women looked at them. . . . Women look at women as persons; men look at them as women." In many cases the young women who are the focal points of his great novels made present, so to speak, the possibility of a woman hero to many men, particularly many authors, who followed James.

It is doubtful if Henry James's first perception of the woman as hero came from his cousin Minny Temple. What seems far more likely is that after the concept of the woman as hero had formed itself in his mind he, with his artist's imagination which works always in the concrete, never in the abstract, allowed these ideas temporarily to crystalize around the figure of his dead cousin. However that may be, in describing Minny Temple, he described the woman as hero: "Life claimed her and used her and beset her—made her range in her groping, her naturally immature and unlighted way from end to end of the scale. . . . She was absolutely afraid of nothing she might come to by living with enough sincerity and enough wonder. . . . " As James reached maturity as an artist, the female protagonist preëmpted the scene. True, there would be heroes also; but the woman had become a "hero" for James.

E. M. Forster began by writing fantasies, short stories of youths who turned into trees and omnibuses which left with regularity for the celestial regions where Shelley dwelt. When he came to exchange fantasy for plot, he wrote novels whose essentially revolutionary quality was not immediately recognized, largely because he seemed to deal with the nature of reality rather than the problems of social revolution. In his first three novels, the moral burden is borne almost entirely by men. By the time of *Howards End,* however, Forster has found his woman hero and given her, moreover, a female moral progenitor from whom she inherits, not only England, but the sense of reality which will enable her properly to pass the inheritance on. Margaret Schlegel is a hero, but so new and outrageous a one that even today we squirm uncomfortably in contemplation of her.

In *Howards End,* Forster is writing of appearance and reality; by appearance he seems to mean that which has only the sanction of social and cultural approval; by reality that which a person discovers to be true expression of himself. Margaret and Helen Schlegel, who refuses to be bound by what culture or society considers "right" or "normal," still have the power to shock us; at best we feel that Forster has somehow failed in his presentation of them. It is, for example, shocking and inexplicable to us that Margaret should marry so stuffy a businessman as Mr. Wilcox: it is so clearly not, on her part, a marriage of love. I might note here that in teaching modern fiction in several institutions, I have found that the fictional events most unacceptable to students are Margaret Schlegel's marriage to Mr. Wilcox and Leopold Bloom's acceptance of his wife's infidelity. On the other hand, Molly Bloom's uncorseted memoirs, and Lady Chatterley's abandoned moments of passion, while provocative, are in no way shocking. Students do not call "shocking" in novels that which really shocks them: this they call improbable. That a marriage between unlike people should be undertaken for reasons emphatically not romantic disturbs our sense of fitness.

Still more shocking, however, is the fact that Forster permits his women heroes to eschew the most widely acceptable of female attitudes. Lionel Trilling, in one of the first and still the best book on Forster, reproves him sharply: "Helen confesses that she cannot love a man, Margaret that she cannot love a child." Here, in Mr. Trilling's eyes, Forster has failed. Yet the precise demand made by Forster in this novel is for a new concept of identity, especially for women, the most restricted of modern creatures. Margaret, the hero, speaks: "It is only that people are far more different than is pretended. All over the world men and women are worrying because they cannot develop as they are supposed to develop. Here and there they have the matter out, and it comforts them. . . . Don't you see that all this leads to comfort in the end? It is part of the battle against sameness. Differences—eternal differences, planted by God in a single family, so that there may always be colour; sorrow perhaps, but colour in the daily gray. . . . "

"Can't it strike you—even for a moment—" Helen asks Margaret, "that your life has been heroic?" The question is addressed to us.

Many critics have discussed James's "limited heroines," yet none surely is as truly limited as Adele Quested in Forster's *A Passage to India.* Hysterical, unsatisfied, uncharming, unpretty—she seems, she is, a negation of femininity, or heroine-ism; no man from Tom Jones to Mellors would look at her twice. But she performs the one act most difficult to all of us: she makes a fool of herself in the cause of justice. She does this, moreover, as a public act. Neither Aziz nor Fielding, both greater than she, is capable of this. Even Mrs. Moore, who sees the truth, is too repelled by human perfidity to remain for the trial; she escapes into death. In speaking the truth Adele Quested, the hero of the modern "quest," alienates everyone, those who will never forgive her for accusing Aziz, and those who will never forgive her for withdrawing the accusation. As a woman, Adele owes nothing to Aziz; he has been affronted that so ugly a woman, with no breasts, could have imagined he would make love to her. But she will not sacrifice him, even to that fury which hell hath

nothing like. She finds her function beyond the range of her womanhood in an act of public heroism. This is not to say that the woman hero must be unfeminine: it is to say that she cannot be confined within her femininity. The woman who is hero does not fulfill herself by being wife or mother or mistress; she makes decisions, she affects events which shake the world.

Yet the question of sexuality has been considered central to our time—let us say, from *Hard Times* onward. The great modern failure of sexuality, and the prophet of this new doom and this new vision is, of course, D. H. Lawrence. It is therefore all the more fascinating that when Lawrence began writing not books which others might have written, but (in the words of Graham Hough) books which no one but Lawrence could write, his imagination should have chosen a female protagonist. It is clear from *The Rainbow* and *Women in Love* that only a woman could properly embody for Lawrence the new artistic vision. Modern woman (Marvin Mudrick writes) "in her unforeseen and disastrously unprepared-for homelessness, true representative of modern mankind—has nothing at all of what, outside themselves, sustained the two generations before her." With her consciousness only of herself, of her sexuality, with her awareness of her lack of inheritance, of place in the community, of satisfactory role in the world, she became precisely *the* searcher after the new prophetic vision. It is probably also likely that Lawrence, who had written out his "sickness' in *Sons and Lovers,* was enabled, as other artists have been, to find the proper objectivity of true art by making the hero a different sex from his own.

After *Women in Love,* Lawrence's greatest novel, he divided the masculine from the feminine more sharply, leaving as feminine that which only *receives* passion, and finally, in *The Plumed Serpent,* that which is properly denied consummation by her lover. Norman Mailer's "The Time of her Time" with its gymnastics, its dubbing of the male organ "avenger," carries the late Laurentian, Miltonic view of the sexes to its extreme, if logical, conclusion. But in Ursula, Lawrence created a hero. As artist he understood that the mortal risk was not, or was no longer, death; it had become the possibility that life, the lived life, might be evaded.

In modern times, men and women have moved nearer to each other in their experience of the fear that life might be unlived. So much of our modern fiction—one need instance only Hemingway, Joyce's *The Dead,* Tolstoy's *The Death of Ivan Illych,* James's *The Beast in the Jungle*—concerns itself with the sudden, tortured awareness of the unlived life, the knowledge that too often in modern times it is only at the moment of death that the experience of life is actually undergone. The life which dared nothing that society had not prescribed for it, hitherto mainly the lot of women, became also in our modern world the lot of many men.

But there was still another reason for the choice of the woman hero. Women, never the possessors of the military and business virtues, need not, as heroes, assume or pretend commitment to these outworn ideals. If Henry James, for example, sent an American young man to Europe, he had still to account for him professionally, for his commitment to the business of life. The alternative was to render his hero a dilettante, or dying like Ralph Touchett in *The Portrait of a Lady.* A young woman nicely avoided all these problems as life made no demands upon her of bravado and money-making and choice of profession. Hers was to be the heroism of those from whom a lived life is not demanded. The only demand the woman hero made on life was Minny Temple's demand to *live.*

The so-called "new woman" is not the woman as hero; to be more exact, few women heroes are "new women." Shaw, for example, is one of those writers whom we think of immediately, almost instinctively, in connection with the "new woman." His *Quintessence of Ibsenism* discusses modern woman at length and is, incidentally, largely responsible for the general impression that this was what Ibsen was "discussing" also. Shaw is important to the history of the modern woman hero, not because he portrayed "new women," but because he portrayed St. Joan.

Shaw's St. Joan is an extraordinary creation largely because Shaw knows that Joan is not only a woman hero, she is the prototype of the woman hero. We have had other great revolutionaries, and other great soldiers from the ranks. We have had other saints, others who talked with God and acted at His bidding. But in Shaw's play we have a hero so preposterous that had the historical Joan not existed, not even Shaw would have had the nerve to invent her. Shaw knows she is not a hero because she saved France, or because her heart would not burn in the fire, or because she was destroyed by just-thinking men acting wrongly, and resurrected by unjust-thinking men acting rightly. She is a hero only because, coming from nowhere, with few or no predecessors, looking forward only to the most circumscribed of lives, she lived in such a way as to change the world, to give her life for a purpose. The cause, moreover, for which she chose death, was simply freedom—not France, not God, not the Catholic Church, but freedom to live as a functioning moral being in the world. She was mocked, and revered, and destroyed and annointed because she was a hero, and because she was a special kind of hero: the person of no apparent importance from whom heroism, or even complete humanity, cannot logically be expected.

Shaw's *St. Joan* was first presented in 1923. One year later, in 1924, came Adele Quested, mocked and unloved, yet fighting for right and bearing scorn in public. They are a strange group of heroes reaching back to 1880: Nora, and Isabelle Archer; Mrs. Alving and Margaret Schlegel; Ursula Brangwen, and St. Joan. By the end of the nineteen thirties this kind of hero has vanished, and the door has slammed behind her. In the contemporary literature which followed World War II, she is an unknown creature; the female protagonist, at least in novels by men, has again donned her traditional dress, or undress. She has become only an event in the life of a man.

Like all heroes, she had a strange birth and came to a sudden end. Can we postulate some reasons for her disappearance from literature? Perhaps it was the triumph of equality over disability, of sophistication over innocence. Perhaps it was the discovery of new outsiders, Jews, Negroes, Angry Young Men. Perhaps the dread of lost masculinity prevents contemporary men from envisioning heroes as women.

A woman hero speaks: "I have no father nor mother nor lover, I have no allocated place in the world of things, I do not belong to Beldover nor to Nottingham nor to England nor to this world, they none of them exist. I am trammelled and entangled in them, but they are all unreal." Perhaps there are no more women heroes because there are no longer women who could say these words, nor men who could imagine a woman saying them.

## Cynthia Griffin Wolff

SOURCE: "A Mirror for Men: Stereotypes of Women in Literature," in *The Massachusetts Review,* Vol. XIII, Nos. 1 & 2, Winter-Spring, 1972, pp. 205-18.

[*In the following essay, Wolff analyzes various conventional portrayals of women in literature throughout history.*]

Insofar as it mirrors the world, literature reflects the prevalent social attitude toward women; and since this attitude so often values men and masculine pursuits over women and feminine hobbies, women's concerns seem devalued. In *A Room of One's Own,* Virginia Woolf describes the situation with characteristic acuity:

> It is obvious that the values of women differ very often from the values which have been made by the other sex; naturally, this is so. Yet it is the masculine values that prevail. Speaking crudely, football and sport are "Important"; the worship of fashion, the buying of clothes "trivial." And these values are inevitably transferred from life to fiction. This is an important book, the critic assumes, because it deals with war. This is an insignificant book because it deals with the feelings of women in a drawing-room. A scene in a battlefield is more important than a scene in a shop—everywhere and much more subtly the difference of value persists.

Those of us who have studied "women in literature" are not wanting for men to explain this "realistic fallacy." As the husband of a friend pointed out with exasperated patience: "Maybe it's not fair, but that's how it is. Men *are* more important in society because they do, in fact, hold the principal roles which govern it. Wars are more important than female thoughts in a drawing-room."

This is a tidy explanation. The trouble is that it doesn't really fit the problem. If the treatment of women merely reflected their relative lack of influence in the public world, then one might expect to find that literature dealt mainly with men. Yet such is strikingly not the case. Since the Renaissance in English literature (and in many major literary epochs before that time), women have figured prominently; and at some periods, literature flows so enticingly around the feminine character that it is men who seem to be excluded. If this is so, why do we complain, why do we women still feel slighted? This further question can be answered only by examining *how* women are portrayed in literature.

In society as we know it, there are a number of specifically masculine problems that shape every man's life: "Oedipal" problems (accepting the fact of the mother's relationship to the father and turning sexual energy towards other, appropriate objects); establishing masculine identity (this frequently involves testing one's courage, independence, or physical competence); resolving conflicts with authority, either by accepting the authority's right to govern or by freeing oneself from a guilty obligation to it; entering into an appropriate marriage; performing a series of public roles in an acceptable way (or, perhaps, choosing not to); acting as a good father (another variation on the problem of authority); and accepting the inevitable loss of power and potency that accompanies old age. A very large proportion of the works which people generally term literature are focused on one or another of these problems: one thinks of *Hamlet, King Lear, Paradise Lost, David Copperfield, Lord Jim,* all of Dostoyevsky, *Huck Finn*—one could go on almost *ad infinitum.* There are, of course, a corresponding set of essentially feminine problems: resolving the "Electra" problem; establishing feminine identity (among other things, coming to understand and accept the fluctuations of the menstrual cycle and resolving conflicts of power with the mother); entering into an appropriate marriage; acting as a mother (this entails resolving one's own desire for oral gratification, resolving fears concerning childbirth, accepting the responsibilities of rearing a child—or redefining the role so that the task of rearing will be shared by others—or even choosing *not* to undertake the task of mothering); accepting the private sphere as the appropriate one (or redefining woman's role so that an accommodation can be made between public and private); and dealing with loss of beauty and with menopause. Unlike the masculine problems, these feminine problems are very seldom the principal subject of literary interest; and when women's problems *are* discussed, the discussion is virtually always limited to problems of courtship and of accepting the private sphere as the proper one. Of course there are exceptions, especially in the twentieth century; the important thing is not, however, that there are exceptions. Rather it is that there are so few, and that this "feminine" literature balances so insignificantly against that massive body of literature which is dominated by masculine dilemmas.

How seldom a major work of literature deals primarily with a power conflict between two women (though such exist in real life for every woman); in literature when women compete, it is always for the attentions of a man. Childbirth (its rewards, its terrors) exists in literature primarily as a convenient plot device for eliminating extraneous young women. Mothering, when it is portrayed at all, is shown from the viewpoint of the child (male) who either resents it or idealizes it; the genuine happiness and difficulty of mothering don't exist in traditional literature. Menopause is portrayed as a snide joke—a rouged woman with a young lover, or a grasping harpy of a wife and mother—a figure to be scorned or pitied, but one not worthy of sustained analysis. All of these are genuine, serious problems that real women deal with daily (even within the context of their subordinate social position). Yet literature seldom if ever shows them doing so. Instead, the relationship between women and men is treated as if it were the only meaningful relationship that a woman has; thus her relationships with other women, with children, and with society in general are significantly diminished. What is more, while women are seen as subsidiary parts of essentially masculine problems, men are seldom seen as subsidiary parts of feminine problems (ironically, when men do figure in what might be termed a feminine problem, they often end up playing a dominant role—as Knightley does in *Emma*).

In general there is a whole range of feminine characterization which is delimited at the one extreme by a very narrow consideration of the "problem of women" ("problem of women" here is usually taken to mean problems of courtship and marriage) and which concludes at its other extreme in gross misrepresentation. What is more significant, all of these characterizations of women are dominated by what one might call the male voice. The definitions of women's most serious problems and the proposed solutions to these problems are really, though often covertly, tailored to meet the needs of fundamentally *masculine* problems. To a greater or lesser extent, then, this kind of feminine characterization must be termed prejudiced or stereotyped because it tends always to emphasize one aspect of character while leaving out others of equal or greater importance. To be more explicit, the bias is carefully chosen so that certain types of masculine behavior (toward women and toward the world in general) might be justified. The stereotypes of women vary, but they vary in response to different masculine needs. The flattering frequency with which women appear in literature is ultimately deluding: they appear not as they are, certainly not as they would define themselves, but as conveniences to the resolution of masculine dilemmas.

The final irony is, of course, that Nature often imitates art. When a society gives its sanction, even its praise, to stereotyped images of womanhood, the women who live in that society form their own self-images accordingly. A stereotype may become, by a sort of perversity, an image of reality that even women seek to perpetuate.

### THE VIRTUOUS WOMAN AND THE SENSUOUS WOMAN

The psychological origins of these first two stereotypes—treated together here because they so often appear together in the same literary work—are reasonably clear; they have been spelled out in Freud's three essays entitled *Contributions to the Psychology of Love.* A little boy first forms ties of affectionate dependence with his mother; as he matures, he adds to these a more explicitly sexual attachment (and the accompanying realization that his beloved, "pure" mother has a sexual relationship with his father). Freud would claim that the problem of uniting these two forms of love is never completely solved in modern society. In pathological cases, they become completely separate in the adult man: he projects his own broken emotions on to the women around him, dividing them into two distinct classes. There are "good" women—for whom he feels fondness and respect; and there are "bad" women who arouse him sexually; in literature these projections of the man's feelings become the stereotypes of the virtuous woman (who reflects his inhibitory tendencies—his "super-ego") and the sensuous woman (who reflects his libidinal or "id" tendencies). The value to the man of creating these stereotypes is clear; it relieves him from the difficult task of trying to unite the two forms of love which have become distinct in his experience. These stereotypes are much reinforced by two literary traditions: the Christian tradition, with its twin figures of Mary Magdalen and Mary the Mother of Christ, and the Courtly Love tradition, which refined some of the distinctions already implicit in certain Christian attitudes.

Once we understand the origins and function of these stereotypes, some of their distinctive characteristics become clear. First, although literature dealing with them frequently appears to focus on a woman, the real focus is usually the man who is affected by the woman he describes. For example, there are a number of early Saints' lives which treat the conversion of whores who later become venerated for their purity and piety; although the ostensible subject of these lives is the female Saint, the real focus is usually the male narrator, who describes with elaborate detail the various effects (bad and good, before and after) that the subject has had on him. Similarly, Dante's *La Vita Nuova* is supposedly about Beatrice; it is really about Beatrice's effect on Dante. In Elizabethan sonnet cycles the declared subject is the lady; often our principal interest is the poet who has been inspired by her. This stereotype imputes enormous power to the woman, a power which is demonstrated by the *man's* reaction to her.

Usually the chaste woman is identified with the positive elements in a man's life; typically she inspires literary productivity or other virtuous acts such as patriotism (as in Scott's novels). The sensuous woman, on the other hand, is identified not only with sex but with other forms of non-virtuous behavior (Shakespeare's Dark lady keeps him from writing; Milton's Delilah tries to divert Samson from fulfilling his heavenly destiny). And the language which is used to depict these women reflects the moral evaluation of them. Assuredly certain physical characteristics are assigned to each: blond hair, blue eyes, fair skin to the chaste; dark hair, etc. to the sensuous. More interesting, however, is the frequency with which the modalities of praise and blame are employed to describe the "love" relationship. In the Courtly Love tradition, especially, the lover repeatedly seeks his lady's approval—she sometimes becomes an external conscience according to which he may judge himself and his life (the evolution of Petrarch's Laura throughout the course of his songs and sonnets illustrates this tendency clearly—as does Petrarch's repeated concern with problems of praise and blame). When the lady is virtuous, the lover is in a humbled position; but when the woman is sensuous, the situation is reversed. Now she (and all those unacceptable emotions she is made to represent) becomes the object of contempt and derision. Ovid, in the *Amores,* has contempt for the lady whose sexual favors he seeks; and when English poets (such as Donne) write in the Ovidian tradition, they adopt much the same air of contempt for "loose" women. The lady's social status also seems to reflect the built-in moral bias: chaste women tend to be well-born; sensuous women are low-born—or they are gypsies or foreigners.

The sensuous woman is defined as sensuous because she affects men in a certain way (she arouses them, she makes them tend toward "sinful" behavior, she intrudes into their domestic arrangements—in short, she is disruptive); and there is no place for such a character in any work of literature that is meant to conclude with social order. So sensuous women are killed off, or they move on, or they enter a convent. Now this hasty removal often has nothing intrinsically to do with the woman as an individual; it is behavior which does not grow easily and convincingly out of the demands of her character; it is merely a literary convenience too often offered as realism.

We might observe that the usual identification of the chaste woman with all that is good and the sensuous woman with all that is bad is sometimes reversed. The chaste woman (as embodiment of conscience) sometimes becomes so destructively critical that her disapproval renders the man unable to act (because he can never meet her exacting standards). In such situations—Joyce's *Portrait,* Lawrence's *Sons and Lovers*—the young man must flee his "good" but devouring "ideal woman." By the same token, the sensuous woman sometimes receives gentler treatment—most often when she appears in subliterature, the official aesthetic status of which makes her moral position clear. (I am *not* talking about the prostitute with a heart of gold; that is in the Sentimental tradition.) Hence Cleland feels no need to condemn Fanny Hill; the genre of her *Adventures* is condemnation enough.

### THE SENTIMENTAL STEREOTYPE

There is a long tradition which maintains that woman is essentially emotional; the literary form of the heroic epistle accommodates this view to some extent. Nevertheless, portraits of women in English literature are remarkably free from the taint of hysteria until the eighteenth-century cult of Sentimentalism. Since the specific aesthetic and moral origins of this stereotype are of major importance, we will begin by outlining them.

The Sentimental definition of woman was largely supported by the Moral Sentiment school of philosophy. Such men as Shaftesbury, Hutcheson, and Adam Smith claimed that every man had a natural inclination toward good; and this "natural affection," as it was called, expressed itself as an inclination toward justice and fair behavior and as a spontaneous and deep response to human suffering (Adam Smith especially emphasizes the empathic component of man's moral sentiment). In practical terms, this view of morality holds that a man engages in moral behavior *not* on the basis of a set of rationally apprehended principles, but as a sympathetic (emotional) response. One could either share the happiness of others or respond with pity to their suffering; in aesthetic practice the tendency toward shared happiness usually took the form of poetic expression, while pity was aroused by suffering depicted in the drama and the novel. Such a moral system *seems* humane enough; however, one fact emerges upon reflection. If an important aspect of man's moral behavior is a response to suffering, then someone must be victimized if a man is to engage in this form of moral behavior. The "moral" man cannot feel sympathy in a vacuum.

Under the influence of this moral system, the status of victim—and all those qualities which might lead someone to be victimized—gained public recognition and even approval. The Moral Sentiment view did not make sex distinctions (though Burke's *Essay on the Sublime and the Beautiful* gives some indication of the kind of quasi-sexual terminology that could be used to describe aesthetic relationships). In theory the sufferer could be either a man or a woman; however, in literary practice it was usually—indeed, almost always—a woman or a child. Those who are physically smaller and legally dependent were prized for their vulnerability. In characterizing women, authors employed a whole series of devices to reinforce our view of them as helpless: the epithet "little" first came into vogue at this period as a sign meant to coerce affection—little Emily; little Dora; Amelia (in Fielding's novel), described repeatedly as a "little helpless lamb"—and of course, diminutive size became a sign of beauty. Weak health, the tendency to unnamed and often fatal illnesses, became an appropriate fate for fictional heroines: Richardson's Clarissa dies for absolutely no discernible physical reason, and in *Grandison,* Clementina's grief slides rapidly and inevitably into failing health. Most important, the woman was by definition incompetent; she must look to the men in her environment to resolve her dilemmas (after all, her competence would remove from them the possibility of engaging in "moral" behavior). *Vanity Fair* demonstrates this belief lucidly, though not without irony: the narrator perceives Becky with distaste not merely because she is immoral but also (perhaps principally) because she is so determinedly self-sufficient; and the passivity of Amelia, though disappointing in the end, is more emotionally satisfying to him.

Partly because of the greater value placed on women's incompetence, but even more because of the increased attention which came to be paid to their emotional life

(the moral sentiment being an "affection"), the display of emotions became a supposedly reliable index to character: good women cried easily; bad women were self-contained. One could make a long list of weeping heroines in this stereotype. With this obsessive focus on emotionality, women came increasingly to be defined as *purely* emotional, without rational competence worth mentioning (Rousseau is very explicit in *Emile*).

Yet the "proper" emotional sphere for women was rigidly limited. Her proper realm was the private one, her proper emotions domestic. A woman could suffer; she could feel love (especially unrequited or betrayed love), but seldom sexual passion; she could feel sympathy for others (typically responding with kindness on a personal level), but she was portrayed as incapable of moral outrage. Most strikingly, she was never permitted to feel anger; the absence of rage in these otherwise highly emotional women is truly striking. And of course, she was never moved by public ambitions (no one who believed in the Sentimental ethic could have written *Macbeth*). As the denial of her public self and her rational capacities is completed, woman is relegated entirely to the domestic scene. Her role as wife is of passing but subsidiary importance (there is little hint of married sexuality), and her emotional energies are channeled into her relationship with her children. Thus the role of mother became idealized; and in some works, as in Dickens', one feels that a woman married only to have children.

Whereas the sensuous woman and the virtuous woman were described in modalities of praise and blame, the Sentimental woman is described in terms of submission and suffering; and this view of woman as essentially submissive or masochistic is accompanied by an interesting shift of aesthetic intention. Aristotle declared that tragedy should inspire pity and terror. Traditionally, the central figure is a person of great parts and renown who suffers calamity; and the tragedy takes its force from the impressiveness of his struggle and the disaster of his defeat. During the Sentimental era this formula shifts very much in the direction of pity, and the central character becomes correspondingly weaker. We are meant to sympathize with his pain, not admire his struggles; and there emerges a literature not of great men and women, but of helpless victims (usually women). To give one example, in the traditional rendering of the Heloise/Abelard story, Abelard is castrated; in Rousseau's adaptation, Julie (the heroine) suffers and dies.

What male problems are projected into this stereotype? Most obviously problems having to do with the expression of sadistic impulses. The "Byronic" hero is the complement to the Sentimental heroine (and incidentally, he appears much before Byron). Frequently the heroine finds him attractive precisely *because* he is cruel (his rough treatment being a kind of perverse gesture of attention and/or affection). In other cases his cruelty is seen as regrettable, but understandable: men of strong passions *do* act sadistically and (so the implicit argument runs) women are intended by Nature to be victimized.

### THE LIBERATED WOMAN

The picture of "the liberated woman" which appears in 19th and 20th century literature is less stereotypical than any of the others that we shall deal with; perhaps, indeed, it is less of a distortion than it is an exaggeration of certain real problems. Yet its plausibility makes it, ultimately, all the more seductive; and perhaps more than any other stereotype, it has been accepted not only by men but by women as well.

In many ways, the picture of the liberated woman is the exact obverse of the Sentimental stereotype; this relationship is not accidental, for liberation entailed rejecting the clichés of Sentimentalism. The first great spokesman for liberation was Mary Wollstonecraft, who set out explicitly to rebut what she felt to be the outrageous claims of Rousseau. Wollstonecraft's image of woman— an image which was to become fundamental to the stereotype of the liberated woman—was drawn from the liberal political writings of the day. Thomas Paine saw man(kind) as essentially rational and based his theory of government upon that assumption; Wollstonecraft saw women as part of mankind, and therefore claimed (against the emotionalism advanced by Rousseau) that they, too, are essentially rational. Women are, she asserted, not fundamentally different from men; and the "feminine" character is merely the product of socialization. Wollstonecraft's treatise does not offer a stereotype; however, the insistence upon women's intellectual capacities and the complete disregard for their emotional and domestic lives which serves Wollstonecraft's argument is used by later authors to turn the liberated woman into a freak.

Thus the first element which we may discern in the stereotype of the liberated woman is an insistence upon her intelligence and/or talent. Prior to Wollstonecraft, it is difficult to find a description of a heroine that gives any information about her intelligence; afterwards, there is a veritable flood of bluestockings. Emma is "handsome, clever, and rich," Dorothea Brooke was "usually spoken of as being remarkably clever," Jane Eyre is formidably, destructively bright—and the list extends right to the present. When the author is sympathetic to women, their intelligence is problematical but not bizarre; when he is not, her abilities (however real) are seen as aberrations (as in *Princess Ida,* "Mighty maiden with a mission, / Paragon of common sense, / Running fount of erudition, / Miracle of eloquence"). It is amusing, or even "unnatural" that women should develop such capacities.

If the liberated woman has potential, then her problem, a problem which is repeated with endless variations, is that she desires to find meaningful (usually public) employment of that talent. In this endeavor, the liberated woman is almost always doomed to failure: Emma, if she was ever truly liberated, submits to Knightley's wisdom; Dorothea and Dinah recognize the far-reaching significance of private acts; Mary Barton, one of the few working women in 19th century fiction, longs for a husband to support her; Sue Bridehead and Eustacia Vie are destroyed in their attempts to move beyond the domestic world.

Sometimes woman's failure to find public fulfillment is depicted as an adjustment (however violent) of personal aims; in other cases, the woman's "wrong-headed" attempts at self-fulfillment are represented as political rebellions against the system of male-dominated marriages. Sue feels she must submit herself to Phillotson as obedient wife; in Tennyson's *Princess,* the heroine ultimately renounces all talk of equality between the sexes; and in pulp literature (see *A Woman in Spite of Herself*), the woman's "proper" submission to her husband is postulated in more dramatic and degrading forms. During this period there grew a large body of self-proclaimed "responsible" medical opinion to the effect that women are mysteriously unreliable. They must submit (for their own good) to the restraints of male-dominated marriage; for their intelligence, however great, cannot compensate for biological inadequacy.

In addition to their sex-linked inadequacy, ambitious women were often portrayed as sexually perverse. Sue Bridehead is not a lesbian, but she is certainly frigid. Hermione and Gudrun (in Lawrence's *Women in Love*) are sexual grotesques. Even George Eliot's heroines tend to channel their sexual forces into unhealthy directions until they have recognized and accepted the essentially domestic quality of their talents. The notion that a liberated woman must be sexually aberrant is, of course, still with us; and female intellectuals are labeled promiscuous or lesbian according to the fantasies of the accuser.

Accompanying this sexual distortion is a more general distortion of the woman's domestic life. For example, so long as she is liberated, a woman is presumed to have no interest in—no feeling for—children and mothering. This stereotype seems to presume (in an ironic acceptance of the Sentimental ethic) that intellect and mothering are incompatible. One thinks of the haste with which Nora divests herself of family in *The Doll's House.* Perhaps Ibsen's psychology is correct; perhaps the ties are too binding and too close—so that freedom can only come with renunciation. Still, what is unreal is Nora's lack of conflict, regret, remorse. Once she has found her mind, all domestic affections seem to have been supplanted. Shaw's heroines have children, but there is no affection since these children become mere expressions of ambition. Even Mill, who spoke so eloquently for women, assumed that a mother, though she might wish time to develop her intellect, would have no public ambitions. The Suffragists (many of them women with children— daughters who followed in their mothers' way) were pictured in the press as sexual and emotional freaks.

It is not difficult to see the male end served by this stereotype; simply put, it is the maintaining of power. If by implication, insinuation, bullying, bravado, women can be convinced that there can be no working accommodation among their varying needs and desires, if they can be convinced of the necessity to submit, then men need not fear their competition.

THE AMERICAN GIRL

The stereotype of the liberated woman ultimately served a political end—the conservative maintenance of a male-dominated marriage, which in turn reflected the power structure of a male-dominated society. The stereotype of the American Girl grows out of economic and moral issues: woman's function, according to this stereotype, is to magnify the men who support her; she is the visible manifestation of their success and the repository of that traditional morality which they so often suspended during the process of amassing wealth.

This stereotype is a post-Civil-War phenomenon. Very little literature focused on the American woman before 1860, although the early nineteenth century saw much feminist activity (Mt. Holyoke, the first women's college, was established in 1837), and women more than proved their usefulness at supposedly masculine tasks during the war. In 1860, then, there were a large number of women who were educated and conscious of their special role as women (often not satisfied with the prejudice against them); women became a large potential reading public and (now) an apparently appropriate subject for study in literature. A great deal of literature after 1860 is directed at woman, written about women; and in this literature we find the emerging stereotype.

The most important characteristic of the American Girl is her accomplishment: she is an "educated" woman, and her thoughts about herself take this consciously into account. A striking example can be seen in Alcott's descriptions of the March girls (all under eighteen); they speak several foreign languages, read Shakespeare, refer casually to the works of Dickens, do some Latin, play the piano, draw—all of this with ease and grace. They make Emma or even Dorothea Brooke seem clumsy by comparison. Yet, this education is deliberately designed to be unconnected with any real-life adult role (save perhaps that of teaching school). Veblen defines leisure as the "non-productive consumption of time. . . . an evidence of pecuniary ability to afford a life of idleness." No facet of American life better illustrates Veblen's theory than the girl whose father can afford to send her to school (rather than have her engage in household industry) and whose father and husband can *both* afford not to have that education put to financial use. A woman becomes, then, the ornament of prosperous society.

The irony, pathos, even tragedy of this situation did not escape perceptive writers. Alcott shows us Jo's troubles; Howells develops the theme repeatedly—most strikingly in a less-known work entitled *A Woman's Reason;* and Edith Wharton draws an impoverished Lily of the field in *House of Mirth.* Yet none of these portraits went so far as to suggest that woman should train her intelligence (as man does) for active social roles. No productive intellectual life is seen for her, and perhaps that is why she is always most captivating as a girl. If intellectual growth is denied, then the process of aging seems unnatural.

Although genuine public activity is prohibited, the American girl is given one rather nebulous task—that of bearing the torch of culture (while the menfolk are out working). The one genuine profession open to her is that of school teacher; in the East she may direct only young minds, but in the rough, masculine world of the frontier she tries to tame the anti-social spirits of grown men as well (in this connection Owen Wister's *The Virginian* is the archetypal work). Yet as teacher, she becomes someone to run from or to reform by wooing her away from her books. When she does not actually hold a position teaching, she nevertheless continues her "civilizing" work (as Twain termed it). Small boys understandably avoid her and her husband may learn to fear her bossy ways (Silas Lapham's wife was a teacher before her marriage, and when she gave up that job, she turned all her energies into making Silas socially respectable). Henry Adams makes the case even more clearly and tragically in *Esther* and *Democracy.* In both novels the heroines take the task of reformation seriously—the one in religion and the other in government. Both of his heroines refuse to capitulate to what their lovers might have termed practical realities. Because they are women, they cannot enter the drama of public life directly; and their persistent high-mindedness serves only to destroy their chances for personal happiness. Both society and the women themselves lose.

In James we find, perhaps, the most articulate statement of woman's dilemma. Many of James' heroines are women with a truly American capacity for generosity; they develop their intellects, their fortunes, their spirits to no end (save, perhaps, a Christ-like transcendence of the cares of this world). Varena Tarrant in *The Bostonians* comments most clearly on this stereotype; her gift is permitted no final public outlet, and she becomes—as the wife of Basil Ransom—the final flower of an impoverished tradition.

The woman of this stereotype is placed in an inherently contradictory position. She must develop her talents, but she must not do so with practical ends in mind; she is instilled with a sense of purpose and moral destiny, and permitted no more serious occupations than women's clubs; she is not permitted to age gracefully, yet she is scorned for clinging to youth; she is expected to bear responsibility for the transmission of culture (and morality), and avoided as a captious wife and possessive mother. Ultimately, what this stereotype offers is not so much the denial of certain female roles as a hopelessly contradictory definition of them.

CONCLUSION

We scarcely have space here to discuss the implications of these stereotypes; however, we can make a few tentative comments. One very common response to the observation that women are characterized stereotypically is an indignant assertion that after all, men, too, are confronted with literary stereotypes. Of course. To claim that for the most part feminine characterization is distorted is to make no claim at all about the characterization of men; and surely anyone who has studied literature would have to be a dunce not to notice that there are masculine stereotypes. We have mentioned one, the Byronic hero; another is the Warrior or the Soldier, and there are others.

The really interesting question is whether these masculine stereotypes are analogous to the stereotypes of women. In several significant ways they are not. Whereas the characterization of women is distorted to meet masculine needs and the feminine stereotype becomes a useful justification for male behavior of one sort or another, the stereotypes of men do not always serve this function for women. The Byronic stereotype is problematical; probably it fuels both masculine and feminine fantasies. However, the image of the Warrior has very little at all to do with women; and except in classical epics, the poem, play, or novel which includes this stereotype very often has no significant female figures at all. Thus men may appear stereotypically in literature, but when they do, the stereotype is usually a fantasied solution to an essentially masculine problem. The supremacy of the male voice remains unchallenged. Moreover, there is a genuinely significant body of literature which recognizes the limitations of some of these masculine stereotypes and which attempts to reveal their inadequacy as standards for defining character or guiding behavior: one finds Tennyson's "Ulysses," *Lord Jim,* or *The Red Badge of Courage.* There is no comparable body of antistereotype literature about women, unless one wishes to view the image of the liberated woman as an answer to Sentimentalism (and as we have seen, that course has its pitfalls).

Indeed, the persistent acceptance of the stereotypes of women is remarkable. Even women writers (to our embarrassment) seem to adopt them. Austen, who never married, condemns Emma for her resolution to remain single; and having chastised her heroine, promptly corrects Emma's "masculine" need to manage things by having her submit to the wisdom of Knightley. George Eliot, who lived openly with a married man, does not permit Dorothea Brooke the same independence. How often in literature, especially before 1900, is a woman's view of herself, of her own rights, of her needs, described entirely by the convenience of the male-authored stereotypes of women.

One might take an amused, almost archeological view of the literary remains of these stereotypes if they were only remains. The trouble is, they are still taken seriously. A modern novel (enormously popular) in the Sentimental tradition begins: "What can you say about a twenty-five-year-old girl who died?" The motion picture captures the image of the liberated woman (played by Barbara Stanwyck, Rosalind Russell, or more recently, Doris Day), successful women executives who wear mannish suits, who are tough, and who, if they are lucky, are saved by the intervention of a strong man who puts things to right. Television is the appropriate medium for the display of the American Girl, that beauty-contest winner who must have not only the proper measurements but also demonstrable (though unusable) schooling and a

"talent" for amusing. A girl whose loftiest function is, apparently, that of endorsing products.

How many girls have made their lives miserable by trying to mold themselves to one or another of these caricatures of human nature? How many have thought that they might be virtuous or sexual but not both? How many have been counselled into emotionalism (and scorned for their lack of intellect)? How many have feigned stupidity lest they frighten suitors by their unfeminine intelligence? How many have been forced to obtain an education which they were absolutely prohibited from using?

Confronted with these mutilated and demeaning images of feminine character, it is all too easy for women to dismiss them as totally lacking in truth. Such an attitude is not profitable. Insufficient as they are for describing a woman's experience, these images do grow out of genuine male experience. Thus for example, if a man is psychologically incapable of uniting his affectionate and libidinal impulses, he will inevitably perceive his relationships with women in terms of the first two stereotypes we have considered. Now his view of women as either virtuous or sensuous may tell us very little about women; but it reveals a great deal about *him.* And the same may be said of all these stereotypes. The ultimate truth of these images of women does not rest in their ability to capture feminine experience or women's life-problems; it inheres, ironically, in their capacity for revealing masculine dilemmas and postulating fantasied solutions to them. These are women—not as they are, but as *men wished they were.* Better than rejecting these stereotypes, women might say to men: "Look, and learn about yourselves."

---

## AMERICAN LITERATURE

### Kimberley Snow

SOURCE: "Women in the American Novel," in *Women: A Feminist Perspective,* edited by Jo Freeman, Mayfield Publishing Company, 1975, pp. 279-92.

[*In the following essay, Snow examines the evolution of female characterization in American literature from the embodiment of goodness and purity to that of conniving temptress.*]

In 1852 Melville described Lucy Tartan in *Pierre:*

> . . . her cheeks were tinted with the most delicate white and red, the white predominating. Her eyes some god brought down from heaven; her hair was Danae's, spangled with Jove's shower; her teeth were dived for in the Persian Sea.

In 1930 Faulkner described Temple Drake in *Sanctuary:*

> Her face was quite pale, the two spots of rouge like paper discs pasted on her cheek bones, her

mouth painted into a savage and perfect bow, also like something both symbolical and cryptic cut carefully from purple paper and pasted there. . . . her eyes blank right and left looking, cool, predatory and discreet.

This change from flower to Venus's flytrap took place neither suddenly nor completely. The earlier image of woman as the hand-wrought creation of the gods permeated our culture to such an extent that remnants and distortions of it may still be found. Despite its persistence on the periphery, however, it was gradually obscured and replaced by a more dominant image. In turn, that image was eclipsed by a newer one, until an evolving pattern emerged in which a series of images grew out of, or in opposition to, one another. The contemporary image of woman as a mechanical yet threatening creature is but the current one in this succession. It is not difficult to trace the broad outlines of the evolutionary process that turned the darling of the gods into the witch of the Industrial Revolution.

There are, of course, individual characterizations of women that transcend the usual pattern and works that do not correspond to the dominant trend. [Such individual portraits as Isabel Archer and Hester Prynne immediately spring to mind.] In spite of these exceptions, if one reviews a cross section of American literature for a certain time span, one finds that in general a common attitude toward women prevails and a particular image dominates. In works of literary merit, this portrait is presented in depth, while in popular literature, it tends to be more one-dimensional or stereotyped. But whether the characterization is deep or shallow, within a given time period the underlying attitude toward woman is often depressingly consistent.

In early American literature a number of different types of female characters are found. Several are transplants from European soil, although one, at least, reflects a more specifically American treatment. By the nineteenth century, these types of women and the attitudes behind them had jelled into an idealized portrait of woman. A change occurred around the end of the nineteenth century, and by the middle of the twentieth, the earlier image of woman was almost reversed. In order to trace the change in our literature from the idealized heroine of the nineteenth century to the current demonic one, it is necessary first to review a few of the conventional female types that were carried over into our literature from the European tradition.

The earliest American novels feature the sentimental heroine inherited from Samuel Richardson's *Clarissa Harlow,* published in 1748. The formula for these novels is simple: a heroine is (reluctantly or through chicanery) seduced, impregnated, and abandoned. In the end the parent/guardian/friend who initially drove her into the arms of the seducer arrives (miraculously) in time for a deathbed scene. Amid copious tears, recriminations, and forgiveness all around, the heroine presents them with her spotless baby (usually a girl) to bring up before she

"raised her eyes to Heaven—and then closed them forever."[1] William Hill Brown's *The Power of Sympathy* (1789), Susanna Rowson's *Charlotte Temple* (1794), and Hannah Foster's *The Coquette* (1797) are all popular examples of this type.

Another popular heroine in the early literature is the one-dimensional female who flits through the historical romances of James Fenimore Cooper and William Gilmore Simms and their imitators. This woman exists essentially as a prop to be brought on stage to swoon, scream, or sigh at the appropriate moment. Her chief function, apparently, is to be rescued by the hero.

Of all the early American novelists, Charles Brockden Brown was the most innovative in his treatment of women. Many of his contemporaries dealt with the idea of the "American Adam"—a second Adam who is given another chance in the second Eden of the New World. Brown, however, was the only one to deal with the New Woman [The New Woman is a term applied to the independent, self-motivated heroine of the Restoration drama. Her immediate origins lie in the Renaissance, although the liberated heroine appears throughout epic literature and mythology.] in the New World. In 1798 Brown, who had been influenced by Mary Wollstonecraft and the French feminists, wrote a dialogue called *Alcuin* that deals with the education and emancipation of women. In his novels he explored these ideas further by creating rational, self-directed heroines who embody many feminist ideals. Although Brown was not always successful in developing his heroines, his treatment of women, especially in *Wieland* (1798) and *Ormond* (1799), is extremely interesting.[2] His efforts in this area were truly pioneering, for it was not until nearly the end of the nineteenth century that the New Woman emerged as a dominant type in American letters.

In American literature of the late eighteenth and early nineteenth centuries, the sentimental and historical heroines are dominant. These two did not remain pure types, but became inextricably mixed. Leslie Fiedler, however, has pointed out that there is a curious lack of women of any type in many of the American classics throughout the nineteenth century. He points to *Moby Dick, Huckleberry Finn, The Last of the Mohicans,* and *The Red Badge of Courage* as examples. It is his thesis that excessive sentimentality has prevented American authors from portraying either woman or sex in a natural manner. The American novel, he writes, "is different from its European prototypes, and one of its essential differences arises from its chary treatment of woman and of sex."[3]

But Fiedler has oversimplified and exaggerated his case. The English novelists of the same period were no more realistic about sex than the Americans. Dickens, who had a tremendous influence on American novelists, was excessively sentimental about women and never failed to idealize them. Still, Fiedler is right in observing that sex and women do not play a dominant part in our nineteenth-century literature. The reason for this is simple:

American novelists—in their novels—were simply concerned with other things. Since early American writers were strongly influenced by the Puritan meditative tradition, in which the soul is constantly being examined, American literature tends to deal more with the state of the soul than with the individual in society. Theoretically, souls have no sex, but in a sexist society, they are perceived as male and represented as such. [One is reminded of the husband's comment: "My wife and I are one and I am he."] Since women are thus seen in social, not metaphysical terms, it is not surprising that they play a large part in English novels, which deal with society and social relationships, but have a paler role in American literature, which deals with the isolated soul of man, his relationship with himself, or his relationship to God. Up to the novels of Henry James, social relationships, especially between men and women, are not as important in American literature as they are in English or Continental literature.

The Romantic movement in the United States, for example, has a peculiarly desexed quality about it when compared to the Romantic movement in Britain. None of the major American writers of this period show the combined interest in women and sex displayed by Blake and Shelley. Whitman was interested in sex, but except for "Children of Adam," not necessarily in connection with women. The high-minded Mr. Emerson and Mr. Thoreau were concerned neither with women nor with sex, but with philosophy. Poe has many women characters, but they all seem to be dead—or dying.

In spite of Fiedler's claims, the great American fiction writers of this period—Poe, Melville, and Hawthorne—created many women characters. Frequently, however, as would be expected in the type of novel involved, women are treated not as individuals but as symbols of some aspect of man's soul. Of course, to see women in symbolic terms was nothing new. In the Western tradition, with its persistent ideas of a Manichean universe, the dual aspects of man's nature have frequently found symbolic form. In Plato's parable of a chariot pulled by a black horse and a white horse, the dual aspects of man's nature are symbolized by the black horse, which pulls the chariot downward, and the white horse, which pulls it upward, while the charioteer struggles to keep a steady course. [Freud, using the same paradigm, calls them the id, ego, and superego.] Women are substituted for the horses in much of Western literature, but the basic struggle and the underlying symbolism remain the same. In this traditional, even archetypal pattern, the Dark Woman as Fiedler calls her, who symbolizes the evil side of man's nature, is placed in opposition to what he calls the Fair Maiden, who represents the good side. The hero is symbolically caught between the two. This symbolic representation, of course, prevents a realistic portrayal of the woman herself, as an individual in her own right. [Also, the fact that women are always connected with sex and are seen only in their relationships to men gives them a lopsided appearance in literature and prevents realistic characterization. The nonsexual aspects of a woman's life are almost never explored by male authors, and

women characters do not think about anything except men. No doubt the fact that women exist in fiction as symbols of man's inner conflicts or as necessary props to his fantasy life indicates their true position in society.]

In the earlier versions of this symbolism, such as the one set forth in the sixteenth century by Spenser in *The Faerie Queene,* The Fair Maiden is closely identified with God and with the powers of the Establishment. Conversely, the Dark Woman is a temptress who is the agent of the underworld and the darker powers. By the Romantic era, however, the Dark Woman is no longer truly evil but has become increasingly idealized. At the same time she has also become more autonomous and self-motivated, for she is no longer the agent of the devil. In Scott's *Ivanhoe,* for example, Rebecca's Jewish ancestry connects her with the archetypal Dark Woman, although she is not evil herself. In the novels of Scott and his American followers, the Dark Woman becomes depressingly vapid and virtuous, only a pale carbon of the dangerous creature she once was. Even in Oliver Wendell Holmes's *Elsie Venner,* where the heroine has deep affinities with the dark powers, her viciousness is sympathetically attributed to a snake bite received by her mother. In the end Elsie repents in a tearful deathbed scene and dies like a good sentimental heroine.

This symbolic representation of the Dark Woman and the Fair Maiden is seen in Poe's "Ligeia," Melville's *Pierre,* and Hawthorne's *The Marble Faun,* as well as in numerous other American works. Usually the Dark Woman is pictured as being in love with the hero, and it is only some unfortunate circumstance (she is his sister, she is married, etc.) that prevents her from marrying him. Unlike her progenitors, she exists only for the hero; certainly she has no outside interests such as witchcraft or pacts with the devil. Frequently she has a past, but it remains shrouded in mystery and she gives up all connections with it for the hero. In fact, the Dark Woman's darkness lies mainly in the color of her hair and the obscurity of her origins. Likely as not, she loves the hero as purely and virtuously as the Fair Maiden. Usually, the hero is fascinated or even obsessed with the Dark Woman, but because she is outside the accepted structures of society, he marries the Fair Maiden. [In Melville's *Pierre* the hero chooses the Dark Woman and all three members of the triangle are destroyed.]

By the end of the century, when the image of woman was generally undergoing a change, novelists shifted their emphasis from the hero's struggle between the Dark Woman and the Fair Maiden to the point of view of one of the women. As the psychology of the Dark Woman was explored, she was portrayed in increasingly sympathetic terms. Ellen Olenska in Edith Wharton's *The Age of Innocence,* for example, is much more appealing than the fair, cold May Welland. In William Dean Howells's *The Rise of Silas Lapham,* a major portion of the plot hinges on the fact that the hero is in love with the Dark Woman, while everyone (including the women themselves) assumes that he is in love with the Fair Maiden.

To today's reader the Dark Woman of the earlier novels is infinitely more interesting than her pale, pious sister, but this was not always the case. [Even as late as 1957, when the girls in a high school class were asked if they identified with Scarlett O'Hara or Melanie Wilkes, only one chose Scarlett. In 1970, however, three-fourths of the girls in a similar class said they identified with Scarlett.] Contemporary reviews of these novels reveal that the nineteenth-century sympathies were with the Fair Maiden, who stayed well inside the traditional woman's role.

The early women novelists, too, tended to keep women within the usual boundaries, but a study of the domestic novel reveals an unsuspected twist. These novels—written by, about, and for women—have long been dismissed with a sniff by academicians as being unworthy of study. It is true that their literary quality is usually very poor, and their portrayal of the ordinary woman's daily trials and sacrifices in the home, ludicrously heroic. But it was not because of literary quality that the work of such women as Mrs. E. D. E. N. Southworth and Augusta Jane Evans Wilson outsold that of better writers each year by a wide margin.

In one domestic novel after another, the heroine, who embodies all of the idealized traits of womanhood, glories in her role as wife and mother. She is worshipped because she is that mystical thing known as Woman, and she rules her father, husband, and children through "love." She is the mawkish product of the fireside poets, the epitome of the Victorian ideal of motherhood. The men in the novel, alas for their brute natures, do not always have the higher sensibilities necessary to appreciate these paragons. Thus in the domestic novel the roles of long-suffering martyr, forgiving wife, and indispensable helpmeet reach their apotheosis. No doubt these novels, with their glorification of women, served to keep women satisfied with their roles as wives and mothers, but they also helped to work out unconscious feelings of aggression and hostility by means of fantasy.

On the surface the domestic novel is merely a sentimentalization of woman, but this is only on the surface. When Helen Waite Papashvily analyzed a number of the books, she found that by the end, the husband's or father's great powers had been diminished or destroyed. Frequently the hero died and the novel ended in an orgy of tears at his bedside. (Did someone say wish-fulfillment?) Other times the hero was somehow mutilated, emasculated, bedridden, blinded, or otherwise incapacitated in the course of the novel, and was put under the complete control of the heroine by the end. Sometimes the hero reformed his evil ways (frequently he gave up drinking), but his burden of guilt rendered him as manageable to the heroine as the physical injuries sustained by the heroes of other novels did.

Papashvily writes that although their women characters retained the traditional women's roles, the domestic novels were "a witches' broth, a lethal draught brewed by women and used by women to destroy their common enemy, man": "No man, fortunately for his peace of mind, ever discovered that the domestic novels were handbooks of another kind of feminine revolt—that these pretty tales reflected and encouraged a pattern of feminine behavior so quietly ruthless, so subtly vicious that by comparison the ladies at Seneca appear angels of innocence."[4] Perhaps the true viciousness of these novels lies in their absolute lack of self-knowledge and honesty. While the self-righteous heroines exploit the roles that are sanctioned by society, their hate and hostility are completely unconscious and completely buried under sentimentality. Thus these women are able to devour their families by "love" and crush them with guilt—while God and society look on approvingly.

In the nineteenth-century popular literature written by men, the heroine shows many of the same characteristics found in the domestic novel, without her proclivities toward castration. A combination of the sentimental and Fair Maiden heroines, she emerges as an idealized, desexed creature, brimming over with piety, purity, and innocence. She has an innate moral sense vastly superior to that of the men around her. She is ethereally beautiful, sensitive, loving, kind, and generous, and if she is occasionally willful, she is just headstrong enough to add spice. She is all heart, and she acts on feminine instinct rather than on the basis of rationality. She is spoken of in diminutives and is invariably described with flower imagery. In fact, she could be called the Dew Drop heroine. Naturally, Dew Drop has no goal in life except marriage and few concerns outside of the domestic.

Dew Drop enjoyed a widespread revival in the popular culture of the 1950's. She was modernized to the extent that she was no longer pious and became inordinately fond of baseball, but she remained incorrigibly virginal and kittenish. Dew Drop reached her apotheosis in Doris Day, and while today the type may still easily be found in popular literature, girls' books, women's magazines and innumerable television series and commercials, her popularity is somewhat diminished.

Even in the nineteenth century, there was a reaction against the saccharine Dew Drop, and by the late 1900's, two different reactions were easily discernible. One reaction sprang from the intellectual currents set in motion by realism and naturalism, and eventually led to a more realistic treatment of women. The other stemmed from the feminist movement and led to the reintroduction of the New Woman into American literature. In the case of the former, it is obvious that at first American novelists could be realistic and naturalistic about almost everything except their heroines. Generally, their women characters continue in the tradition of Dew Drop or they are lightly varnished over with a thin coating of realism or naturalism.

Such a novelist as Frank Norris, for example, who is hailed as a pioneer in naturalism, has given us the following description of a young woman: "She sat thus, as on a throne, raised about the rest, the radiance of the unseen crown of motherhood glowing from her forehead, the beauty of the perfect woman surrounding her like a glory."[5] Even in the most frequently cited example of American naturalism, *Maggie: A Girl of the Streets*, Stephen Crane is able to evoke sympathy for Maggie because she initially embodies so many of Dew Drop's characteristics: blushing shyness, innate delicacy and daintiness, love of beauty and flowers, and so on. Similarly, Theodore Dreiser's *Sister Carrie* is said to be naturalistic because it shows a woman controlled by external circumstances and animal instincts. However, much of the novel's naturalism is undercut by the sentimental overtones in Dreiser's description of Carrie. In time, of course, the heroine was treated with brutal realism, but the early attempts at realism and naturalism reveal how deeply the stereotype of the ideal heroine was imbedded at the turn of the century.

That the tide against Dew Drop was turning, however slowly, becomes clear when we consider the emergence of a new type of heroine—the New Woman. She has been described by Beatrice K. Hofstadter:

> At the turn of the century a new heroine appeared, epitomized in the drawings of Charles Dana Gibson and hailed everywhere as the "New Woman." She was tall and active, she held her body straight and her head high. Her free and easy manners shocked her genteel mother, and her determination to live her own life appalled her father and his world of domineering men.[6]

The New Woman, however, was not as universally admired as Hofstadter would lead one to believe. In many of the popular novels written by men around the turn of the century, the New Woman is shown declaring her independence, making a mess of things, and then confessing that her way of thinking was mistaken and gratefully reverting to her role of Dew Drop. In other novels she is simply satirized and her principles are deliberately misrepresented for a humorous effect. But despite these distortions and jibes, the New Woman had entered our literature for good. She was a product of the feminist movement and frequently, like Mary Johnston's Hagar, a fervent advocate of women's rights. At other times, as in the novels of Hamlin Garland, she simply embodied the feminist ideals—independence and control over her destiny—without actually advocating the franchise for women.

The New Woman is guided by her rational mind rather than intuitive emotion. This heroine is interested in specific reform instead of being invested with a vague spirituality and goodness. She is portrayed as having a sharp mind and an indomitable will, a combination that makes her successful in her attempts to control her destiny. The New Woman is more physical than spiritual; thus for the first time sex begins to enter into the portrait of the American heroine.

The New Woman is still with us today, but unfortunately she is no longer the dominant stereotype. She is most clearly seen in the figure of the popular girl detective, Nancy Drew. In the Nancy Drew stories Nancy is flanked by the dark and fair standbys of American literature. The blond is overly feminine, formless, and afraid of things, while the brunette lacks true feminity and womanly grace. With archetypal simplicity, Nancy is titian-haired, and she combines the best qualities of the blond and the brunette. In addition, she is a marvel of efficiency, independence, and self-reliance, rivaled only perhaps by Batman. When a homing pigeon falls at her feet, she immediately exclaims, "I'll wire the International Federation of American Homing Pigeon Fanciers and give them the number stamped on the bird's leg ring. All homing pigeons are registered by number so the owners can be traced."

Nancy would never be guilty of fluttering over the pigeon wondering what was to be done or looking to her football-hero friend, Ned Nikerson, for advice. In fact, when examined closely, Ned exists solely as a prop to Nancy—much as the Ken doll is a useful accessory for Barbie. Nancy's father, too, is only a shadowy figure in the background who supplies her with legal advice and new cars from time to time. Judging from the Nancy Drew cult that exists among young girls today, one can conclude that these books serve much the same function as the domestic novels did in the nineteenth century. [In a recent conversation about various heroines, a nine-year-old girl dismissed Beth of *Little Women* as one of those things in literature that are "not real—like houses that fly and animals that talk." She considered Nancy Drew to be quite real because "after all, girls do get kidnapped and things and they area lot smarter than their boyfriends and fathers and policemen and everybody."]

In addition to supplying little girls with a model of feminism, the emergence of the New Woman in American letters had an adverse effect. Male authors, as Virginia Woolf pointed out, were so unsettled by this display of feminism that they came to write with what she called "the male side of their minds." The excessive maleness of Hemingway's novels are classic examples of this preoccupation with the masculine. [It is difficult, however, to really hate Hemingway now that we have Norman Mailer.]

From out of all this maleness, a new female stereotype emerged in American literature—the American Bitch. Prime examples are Temple Drake in Faulkner's *Sanctuary*, Daisy Buchanan in Fitzgerald's *The Great Gatsby*, and the heroines in Hemingway's "The Snows of Kilimanjaro" and "The Short Happy Life of Francis Macomber." No longer the innocent, suffering woman or the pliable Dew Drop, the American Bitch is utterly shallow and inhumane. She is the spoiled product of luxury and freedom, the self-centered child whose favorite pastime is destruction—especially the destruction of men. In many cases she is not only a bitch but a hypocrite, retreating behind the code that traditionally protects the ladies when she is challenged. Far from being pure, she is portrayed as being sexually insatiable, devouring the hapless men who attempt to satisfy her lust. Just as Dew Drop grew out of the Fair Maiden stereotype, the American Bitch is an updated version of the Dark Woman.

Even while the novelists of the 1920's and 1930's were creating these destructive monsters, many were also presenting an alternative image of woman: that of the mother-savior. This character is a strong, primitive matriarch, usually nonwhite, who symbolizes the traditional enduring qualities of love, sacrifice, maternal strength, and devotion. If the rest of the characters in the novel survive at all, it is because of her. Dilsey in Faulkner's *The Sound and the Fury,* Pilar in Hemingway's *For Whom the Bell Tolls* and Ma Joad in Steinbeck's *The Grapes of Wrath* are typical examples of the mother-savior figure.

Various critics have pointed out that the heroine created by a male author is frequently a projection of his own hopes, fears, and frustrations.[7] William Wasserstrom feels that in American literature the heroine reflects the national spirit as frequently as she does the personal aspirations of her creator. It is his thesis that Dew Drop embodies the optimism of nineteenth-century America and that Henry James's fledgling heroines in Europe reflect the emergence of our young country into the world arena. In these terms it could be argued that the novelists of the 1920's and 1930's used the American Bitch and mother-savior stereotypes to symbolize the conflicting value systems in American society—specifically the modern versus the traditional.

Certainly, the American Bitch is sometimes so closely identified with industrialization as to be indistinguishable from it. She is described in mechanical imagery, and her emasculating, threatening qualities seem to reflect the depersonalizing influences of an industrial society. In contrast, the mother-savior is a primitive or peasant woman closely connected with the simple agrarian life and the traditional values associated with it.

By the 1960's, however, the two characters, savior and destroyer, had merged, and only the negative side remained. The strong matriarch was replaced by Ken Kesey's Big Nurse in *One Flew Over the Cuckoo's Nest.* Thus the destroyer absorbed the savior, and symbolically, all hope that the agrarian ethic would save modern man was lost. Big Nurse became the objective correlative for the Super State, a monster with complete legal control over man, but inhuman and rotten to the core.

Also by the 1960's, the American Bitch had reached hysterical proportions in the novels of such writers as Norman Mailer, Bernard Malamud, Gore Vidal, and John Updike. Not since the days of Saint Augustine has woman been so reviled as she is by these novelists. As one would expect when woman is viewed as an evil force, man-woman relationships in these novels are reduced to a vicious battle. The struggles range from the relatively mild ones in Updike's *Couples,* where the relationships are based on a tedious expediency, to the more violent ones in Mailer's *An American Dream,* which are filled with pain and hate. Kate Millett points out that much of Mailer's degradation of women lies in his specifically lower-class attitude toward them.[8] No doubt it is

machismo—an excessive concern with maleness—that makes his novels read like extended castration fantasies.

In addition to serving as a sort of inkblot into which the author projects his personal fears, the Ultramodern American Bitch is identified with her society, as was the traditional American Bitch before her:

> Woman becomes something far more insidious than a mere scold; she becomes that force in life which not only has its own unconquerable and even indefinable power but also operates to rob man of his last shred of purpose and dignity. Sexually, she is all hunger and depredation. In terms other than those of sexual desire she is an empty shell, as empty and meaningless as the society in which we find her and with which she has come to be so disastrously identified.[9]

Thus, as our society has disintegrated, so has our heroine—both to the point that one wonders whether either can be redeemed.

In order to rebalance and humanize the image of woman in American literature—to show that she, too, is the victim and not just the product of our society—women novelists must present the female point of view. Moreover, they must write as well as men novelists and receive equal consideration from readers and reviewers. Within our culture, however, the difficulties involved in doing this are almost overwhelming. In order to write well, as Virginia Woolf points out, a woman must have a substantial income and a room of her own with a lock on the door.[10] Even then, just writing well is not enough, as the fate of Kate Chopin and of her novel, *The Awakening,* painfully shows.

This novel, published in 1899, is the story of the awakening of Edna Pontellier, the wife of a wealthy but stuffy New Orleans businessman. Through a lover she awakens first to physical passion and then to herself as a human being. In her quest for self-discovery and personal growth, she gradually awakens to the true nature of the position of woman in society and to the restrictions imposed on her because she is a woman. Edna begins to realize that her lover, like her husband, is insensible to her need for autonomy. As she awakens from her illusions about romantic love, she realizes that a series of lovers will probably follow her present one and that such socially unacceptable behavior on her part will destroy her children. In the end she decides not to sacrifice her essential being by resuming her empty role as wife and mother, and chooses death instead.

Naturally, Kate Chopin had trouble getting her novel published. Not only is its theme outrageous for 1899, but the novel is written with a detached simplicity that never argues for or against the heroine's actions. When it was finally published, it created a scandal. Even in her home town, Saint Louis, the citizens—including T. S. Eliot's mother—demanded that it be removed from the library shelves. A newspaper proclaimed that it was "too strong drink for moral babes and should be labeled poison." Chopin, stunned by these vicious attacks, withdrew from society, never to write again. She died a few years later.

Although *The Awakening* is beautifully written and contains many themes that were later to become major ones in American fiction, it has been forgotten. Since it not only contains a deeply unsettling image of woman that totally contradicted the prevailing stereotype at the time of its publication but also projects a most unflattering portrait of a successful businessman, one suspects that it was too disconcerting to win the attention it deserved. Even today, when Kate Chopin is mentioned at all, her name is usually mispronounced [It should be pronounced like the composer's name.] and she is relegated to that innocuous pigeonhole of "local colorists." She is noted for her Creole stories, but *The Awakening* is rarely mentioned. The novel itself remained virtually unknown until it was reprinted in 1964. Even the cover of the 1964 edition hails it as "an American *Madame Bovary*." This comparison not only somehow gives Flaubert the credit for the book's excellence but also undercuts its meaning, for if anything, *The Awakening* is a woman's answer to *Madame Bovary*.

The fate of Kate Chopin's *The Awakening* is but one example of how the feminine world view is banished from literature. Women are just beginning to be aware of—and to rebel against—the process that keeps the male mythology intact.[11] In the field of criticism, the male critic is able to destroy a book that threatens to present a dissenting view by ignoring it, by damning it with faint, paternalistic praise, or by distorting its meaning, whether as a result of simple blindness to feminine nuance or of a more conscious attempt to denigrate the feminine viewpoint. A subtle form of distortion is to relegate all feminine works to either the mediocrity of "popular" literature or the quaintness of "local color."

Another perennial tactic in criticism is to see women characters and authors only in biological terms. [This is known among critics as "innovative criticism" and among feminists as "the biological put-down."] One critic, for example, divides Faulkner's women into cows and bitches, while another relates the poems of Emily Dickinson to her menstrual cycles. Male characters and authors, however, are not reduced to their biological functions. No one divides Faulkner's men into studs and geldings or relates Carlyle's work to his indigestion, although the evidence is certainly there in both cases.

Women authors and characters are also frequently distorted in classroom discussions. It is not uncommon for a literature teacher to agonize over the trials that beset modern man as they are reflected in Quentin Compson's character, but to dismiss Caddy as a slut. Often women authors are completely ignored. It is perfectly possible today to received a bachelor's degree in literature without studying any female author other than Emily Dickinson; a master's degree by adding only Edith Wharton, Ellen Glasgow, and Willa Cather; and a doctorate by adding only another handful, usually the "local colorists."

While it is true that writers such as Sylvia Plath, Doris Lessing, and Joan Didion have begun to create new images of women, their work is usually not dealt with except in the few courses that deal specifically with women in literature. These specialized courses are a valuable first step, but until their insights and perspectives are incorporated into the larger literary framework, the image of women in literature, as in life, will continue to be created and perpetuated by the patriarchy. Since what is known as literature is almost entirely dictated by the taste of the male critic/publisher/professor, the image of woman is defined in *his* terms. Naturally this image tends to reinforce the traditional ideas of women with which the male is most comfortable. Thus, a woman striving to create a mature, well-integrated image for herself certainly cannot find a model for it in our well-known literature. Nor will she find her special problems honestly confronted, explored, or transcended there. Instead she will find stereotyped heroines—monstrous extremes of virtue and bitchery—acting out stereotyped responses.

In order to rebalance this image of woman in literature, it is not enough merely to increase the number of honest women authors or to rediscover perceptive female writers of the past. Only when women can make their influence felt in the fields of criticism, publishing, and education will literature serve to liberate rather than enslave the woman. Only then will the image of woman in American literature change and begin to reflect woman as a human being rather than a stereotype, symbol, or scapegoat.

### NOTES

[1] This line from Susanna Rowson's *Charlotte Temple* is typical of the rhetorical tone of most sentimental novels.

[2] For a complete discussion of Brown's treatment of women, see my article "The Continuity of Charles Brockden Brown: Feminism in *Alcuin, Weiland,* and *Ormond,*" *Women's Studies,* Fall 1973.

[3] Leslie Fiedler, *Love and Death in the American Novel* (New York, 1960), p. 11.

[4] Helen Waite Papashvily, *All the Happy Endings* (New York, 1956), p. xvii.

[5] Frank Norris, *The Octopus* (New York, 1956), p. 504.

[6] Beatrice K. Hofstadter, "Popular Culture and the Romantic Heroine," *American Scholar,* XXX (Winter, 1960-61), 98-116.

[7] See Simone de Beauvoir, *The Second Sex* (New York, 1968); William Wasserstrom, *The Heiress of All the Ages* (Minneapolis, 1959); and H. R. Hays, *The Dangerous Sex: The Myth of Feminine Evil* (New York, 1964).

[8] Kate Millett, *Sexual Politics* (New York, 1970).

[9] Diana Trilling, "The Image of Women in Contemporary Literature," in *The Woman in America,* ed. R. J. Lifton (Boston, 1965), p. 63.

[10] Virginia Woolf, *A Room of One's Own* (New York, 1957).

[11] See Mary Ellman, *Thinking About Women* (New York, 1968).


**Barbara Meldrum**

SOURCE: "Images of Women in Western American Literature," in *The Midwest Quarterly,* Vol. XVII, No. 3, 1976, pp. 252-67.

[*In the following essay, Meldrum surveys women characters in Western American literature, finding them largely confident and independent compared with portrayals of women in other regional literatures.*]

Women played a major role in the settlement of the American West, and they have often had prominent roles in the literature of the westward movement. In spite of these facts, scarcely any attention has been given to western American literature in the numerous anthologies of women in literature that have appeared in recent years. Since the westward movement was so integral to the formation of an American national character (at least as claimed by Frederick Jackson Turner and his successors), a study of women in western American literature should provide some insights into the character of American woman, as envisaged by various authors. Such a study is, of course, beyond the scope of a single essay. I would, however, like to suggest three possible approaches to the subject and exemplify the kinds of insights which these approaches can yield. First (thematic approach), woman has frequently been portrayed in western fiction as a civilizing force (usually identified with the East) in a western, uncivilized environment. Second (archetypal approach), the masculine vs. feminine ideals provide dramatic tension and thematic importance in some western fiction. Third (historical role approach), the pioneer woman—probably the most typical role of western women—provides a wide range of images of women on the western frontier as portrayed in the fiction.

The first area of consideration—woman as civilizing force—is very clearly represented in one of Bret Harte's short stories, "The Idyl of Red Gulch." Mary, the schoolmarm, is a newcomer from the East and is literally idolized by the rough Westerners. In contrast, the women in the story who are most closely identified with the West are "bad" women. When the unwed mother of Tommy (one of Mary's pupils) comes to Mary and asks her to take Tommy and get him into a good school, she says, "'Do with him what you like. The worst you can do will be kindness to what he will learn with me. Only take him out of this wicked life, this cruel place, this home of

shame and sorrow. . . . You will make him as pure, as gentle as yourself.'" The contrast between East and West and the important role of woman as a force for civilization and virtue are clearly portrayed in this tale of an eastern schoolmarm.

Owen Wister's Molly in *The Virginian* (1902) is also an eastern schoolmarm, though much better developed than Bret Harte's Mary. Wister's schoolmarm is one who has spunk, is somewhat appalled by western roughness, is beautiful and cultured, and therefore is attractive to the hero who proves his worth in part by becoming more cultured (or at least able to "pass" in eastern society). One can of course argue as to whether the West capitulates to the East, or whether the easterner Molly becomes a westerner, or whether the marriage of Molly and the Virginian represents an ideal amalgam of the best traits of both worlds. The latter was, I believe, the intention of Wister and is analogous to the view expressed by Cooper in his Preface to *The Leather-stocking Tales:* Cooper asserted that Leatherstocking represented the best traits of the white man and the red man, of civilization and savagery. In a parallel way, Wister sought to suggest in the marriage of East and West an ideal union which would point the way for productive development of the West. This thesis is undercut by several aspects of the story: the Virginian is from Virginia originally and contrasts with the more identifiably western men such as Trampas. Moreover, although the Virginian reads books recommended to him by Molly, he doesn't broaden his literary tastes significantly. Molly's role as civilizing force is limited largely to prompting the Virginian to settle down to marriage and a family; the Virginian is not appreciably more civilized at the end of the tale than he was at the beginning. Indeed, in the first chapter, the narrator, newly arrived from the East, concludes that the tall hero is more of a gentleman than himself.

Thus, whether in fact or fancy, the woman in western fiction is often portrayed as a civilizing force opposing the irresponsible freedom of the West. Though typically this role is filled by an eastern schoolmarm, the role can be played in other capacities. Mary Hallock Foote, for example, in her early novel *Led-Horse Claim* (1892) uses as her eastern woman the sister of a mining superintendent in a Colorado mining town. In this tale the West, as seen through the eyes of the eastern newcomer, is rough, violent, greedy and destructive. Significantly, the hero with whom she falls in love is really an easterner who has managed to adapt to the West, and their love is consummated in the East, not the West.

We find, then, a dichotomy in the typical western tale: the woman represents that which is eastern, cultured, and feminine; she is the worthy prize for the most virtuous and masculine hero. The man is western (or at least identified significantly with the West), is rough but appreciates culture, and is of course very masculine. In some tales this simple dichotomy becomes far more complex, and in a novel such as Walter Van Tilburg Clark's *The Ox-Bow Incident* (1940), the masculine ideal is shown to be destructive. Max Weatherbrook has dealt with this notion very skillfully and convincingly:

> The American Dream . . . has emphasized individuality, which is both the price and privilege of democracy. As it releases man from cultural and political tyranny, individualism also begins to imprison man within the confines of his own temporal powers of creation. Too often, the emphasis on free will leads to an emphasis on ego and degenerates into greed and into an exaggerated evaluation of the male ego. Clark . . . holds that the male ego tends to separate man from the permanent, to distort projection. The intellect, also severed from the permanent, is associated with a degrading version of the feminine. Thus the lynch mob in *The Ox-Bow Incident* misappropriates for itself a monopoly on virtuous masculinity, and thus the protestations of Davies and Gerald Tetley are repeatedly associated—both in language and action— with a degrading femininity (*Western American Literature,* Summer 1966).

What we see in the novel are fragments of human beings; what is needed, is unity.

Westbrook focuses his discussion on the men in the novel; I would like to suggest a few points about some of the women. None of them are major characters in this male-dominated novel, but they are important for the light they shed on the masculine vs. feminine concepts which are so crucial to an understanding of how the men regard each other and how they become involved in executing three innocent men.

Frena is a woman who champions Kincaid, the cowboy who has supposedly been murdered; when the lynch mob is slow to form and get on its way to avenge the death of Kincaid, Frena tries to shame the men into action with sarcasm. Later, young Gerald Tetley says of her that she wants power; men are the biggest part of a woman's power; Frena can't get a man, so she'd like to see them all dead and gone—then she would have power over the other women. What is significant about Gerald's view of Frena is that he suggests a similar goal for both men and women: power. They are different only in their manner of pursuit—the men are bullies, the women are sneaks.

Ma Grier is physically a very big, buxom woman, strong as any man in town, reputed to have a bad past. She dresses like a man, and hates women. She too is a fragment of a person, as represented by her perverted femininity. She tries to be a man, and thus she too is caught up in the masculine ideal which motivates the men in the lynch mob. The others are afraid of her. However, she fears one person, and that is Tetley (the father of Gerald), who eventually leads the mob. It is his notion of he-man masculinity which prompts him to force his son's participation in the lynching—a participation which eventuates in Gerald's suicide. Tetley says at one point, "I'll have no female boys bearing my name." Ma Grier, then, exemplifies the power of what might be called the "masculine mystique," whereas Frena, who fails with men, thereby fails to prove her femininity.

Rose Mapen is the most feminine woman in the novel. She is feared by the women of Bridgers Wells, who succeed in driving her out of town because they are afraid she will do something; because she is attractive to most of the men, she is feared by the other women. Rose is a somewhat ambiguous woman, her image depending on one's point of view: the narrator Art sees her as a tart, but his pal Gil wants to marry her. She is capable of sustaining contrasting images of women projected on her by men with varying perspectives. After being driven out of town, she goes to San Francisco and marries Mr. Swanson, then returns to show off her husband to Bridgers Wells. On this return trip the stage runs into the lynch mob while they search for the rustlers. Her husband, we find, represents a different kind of masculinity which contrasts with the western masculine ideals of the mob. Although Art's first impression is that Swanson is a "weak sister," he begins to revise his opinion. Swanson has a kind of strength the cowboy Gil can't cope with. "I don't know how to start a decent fight with that kind of a guy," Gil concludes. The character of Swanson is not sufficiently developed for us to make any sweeping conclusions, but it is significant that Clark here gives us a man who achieves recognizable masculinity without the destructive distortions typical of the men in the lynch mob. Rose gains an advantage by her marriage, for she gains the power of a man, and in this instance a man set apart from those of Bridgers Wells. Yet she is not, I believe, presented as an ideal woman, for she flaunts her conquest in marriage before the townspeople. Also, more important, at the end of the novel, after the mob has returned to Bridgers Wells in shame and guilt for having hanged three innocent men, Rose and her husband are in the tavern, and Rose's vivacity and attractiveness lead to laughter—at a time that is hardly appropriate for frivolity. Her role here reminds one of the complaint in "My Fair Lady"—you take a woman to a play or ballet and she sits there searching for her gloves. Woman is here represented as empty-headed, not concerned with values apart from her own vanity.

The image of woman in this novel is quite grim. The women may not be any worse than the men, but Clark does seem to use the image of woman to suggest generally negative qualities. The men who seek to be masculine are undone by their efforts—their egos lead them into the actions of a murdering lynch mob. The men who are weak and ineffectual are characterized as feminine. The masculine woman (MaGrier) is at best humorous, at worst disgusting. The most feminine woman (Rose Mapen) is basically frivolous. What is needed, then, is unity of self, rather than the fragmented projections of parts of the self. In sexual terms, what is needed is a unity of masculine and feminine (the androgynous ideal), but this is not achieved in the novel. In fact, the thrust of the story tends to confirm Westbrook's notion that the emphasis on individualism in the western experience is ultimately destructive. Ironically, the individualism which focuses on ego eventually results in conformity to the group, in the story of the lynch mob in the novel.

When we turn to the role of the pioneer woman, we are confronted by a large body of material, for the pioneer woman's experience has attracted western writers (both men and women) for many years. The pioneer woman usually was the follower of her husband in their western venture; as exemplified in A. B. Guthrie's *The Way West* (1949), the man typically took the lead in wanting to go West, and the woman followed, with varying degrees of willingness and adaptability. Although certainly not all men were constitutionally and temperamentally suited for such an adventure, those who were not seldom made the effort; whereas the women, in their role as followers of their husbands, might find themselves forced to make adaptations for which they were not well suited. In this process, some were crushed; others survived and, in doing so, often achieved dimensions of character that had been dormant during their earlier pre-pioneer experience. Guthrie, in *The Way West,* shows us how the women learn to cope with their new experiences. It is not easy. Rebecca, the wife of Lije Evans, concludes that men are "queer. . . . The more miles they made the better-spirited [her husband] was, as if there wasn't any aim in life but to leave tracks, no time in it but for go." When they sight Fort Laramie, Lije is jubilant to see this landmark of his progress toward the Pacific; Rebecca, however, is jubilant because the Fort means buildings and probably chairs. "I just want to set in a chair," she says. In spite of the difficulties, most of the women not only manage to survive but become contributing members of the party. Guthrie tells us, "the women did their part and more. They traveled head to head with men, showing no more fear and asking no favor. . . . They had a kind of toughness in them that you might not think, seeing them in a parlor. So, on a trail, women came to speak and men to listen almost as if to other men. It was lucky for the pride of men that few traveled with their wives to Oregon. They'd never quite believe again a woman was to look at but not to listen to."

The demands placed on the pioneer women were great. Not only did they have to learn to make do without the conveniences of the homes they had known before, but they often had to do men's work, and pregnancy might come when things were most difficult, during their journey or during the early back-bending days of breaking the sod and building a new home. Some simply were not able to bear the strain. One of the most poignant pictures of a woman crushed by the pioneering experience is the picture of Kari, in Rolvaag's *Giants in the Earth* (1927). Kari, the pioneer woman who has lost her child on the prairie, is crazy with grief and must be tied inside the wagon lest she leave it in search of her dead son. The anguish of grief, the frightening immensity of the prairie spaces— these are too much for Kari. And her husband, though trying to help, is a bungling novice; he lacks the ingenuity, common sense, and stamina of a Per Hansa, and as the wandering family fades away into the distance, we feel that they are wandering closer to despair and death.

Mari Sandoz portrays many failures (both men and women) in her biography of her father, *Old Jules* (1935).

One example is a woman who takes the lives of her children, then commits suicide. The context is significant. The winter is bleak and difficult; the men can break away from the isolation when the storms let up, but the women cannot: "They had only the wind and the cold and the problems of clothing, shelter, food, and fuel." One neighbor woman says as the bodies are prepared for burial, "If she could a had even a geranium—but in that cold shell of a shack." The brutalities of nature, and the economic difficulties, prove to be more than this woman can bear.

But many of the pioneer women did achieve a measure of success in their experience. I would like to consider here a few of the more successful ones, in an ascending scale of achievement. Near the bottom would be the women in Vardis Fisher's *The Mothers* (1943), a historical novel based on the Donner Party. The title suggests the focus Fisher achieved in this work; the wives and mothers proved to have greater stamina, ingenuity, and general survival capacity than the strongest men. The reason for their advantage seems to lie in their roles in the family— their drive to protect and care for their offspring and/or their husbands (and usually the ties to children proved to be stronger than ties to husbands). These mothers could be self-sacrificing for their own loved ones, but some could also be ruthless towards others, even the children of others. In this grim study of starvation and desperation, Fisher portrays both the noble and the horrifying lengths to which these women will go for the sake of those whom they value. Here, the strenuousness of totally new experiences engendered by conditions peculiar to the western environment as experienced by novices produces a crucible for human character.

Beret, wife of Per Hansa in Rolvaag's *Giants in the Earth,* is nearly defeated in her western experience. In this novel Rovaag explores with great sensitivity the psychological trauma of a woman who is not able to adjust easily to the open spaces of the prairie or the rigors of pioneer life and who must also endure the shock of these adjustments while pregnant. She becomes increasingly neurotic during her pregnancy, but regains a degree of mental health when she gives birth to a child graced by the good omen of being born with a caul, and when she surprises herself by living through the birth. For a time, the demands of caring for her new child restore her will to live. But she has not yet adjusted to the open prairie where there is nothing to hide behind; during harvest, when the locusts swarm over the little farms and eat many of the crops, Beret suffers a nervous collapse. Her condition continues for several years, with periods of relative sanity and insanity. She regains control of herself when she realizes that God has not deserted them there on the prairie (the visiting minister plays an important role here) and when she learns that Per Hansa has confidence in her. She has had to come to terms with herself in relation to the natural environment, which in its seeming hostility was pagan to her, and in relation to her husband, who has brought her to this forbidding land. The fact that she has indeed become reconciled to her situation is evident in the next novel, *Peder Victorious*

(1929), when she decides to remain after Per Hansa's death, for she now realizes that this is her children's home as well as Per Hansa's dream and that it must, therefore, be her home too. As the settlement grows and some of the traditional elements of civilization (particularly the church and the school) become well-established, she finds it easier to manage, and she is even successful in fulfilling a supposedly male role when she engineers the construction of the barn which had been her husband's dream.

Mari Sandoz portrays a variety of pioneer women in the gallery of Old Jules' four wives. In addition, there is Rosalie—the girl back home who refuses Jules' many invitations to join him. She is Jules' childhood sweetheart in the old country who remains his goddess, the vision of perfect love which he will never know, and which consequently is never tarnished by the realities of pioneer life. Estelle, Jules' first wife, is abandoned by him because he believes she is lazy and won't work. Jules demands much of a wife and little from himself in return toward his wife, so we are inclined to believe Jules has treated his first wife harshly—until we meet her later in the book. Though she is no villain, she is hardly admirable and fails to win much sympathy. Jules' second wife, Henriette, comes to him from Switzerland on the recommendation of her good friend, Jules' sister. She finds life hard on the Nebraska prairie, but stays with Jules until a financial settlement leaves her independent, whereupon she promptly kicks Jules out and files for divorce. The two later become good friends, and on one occasion Henriette mortgages her farm to help Old Jules, but the years of drought are too much for her, and she, like so many others, goes insane. Although she has periods of recurrent sanity, Henriette is a victim of the land. She succeeds in gaining an adjustment of self with her husband, but never achieves reconciliation with the land.

Emelia, Jules' third wife, also comes from the old country, encouraged by Jules' glowing descriptions of the land. But what he has written has been his dream, not reality. And so she comes, expecting to be mistress of the fine house of a well-to-do husband. What she finds, is grizzled Old Jules and his two-room shack, no dishes to eat from, no cloth for the table, a stove propped up by bricks. And Jules invites her to his bed with its greasy blankets, no sheets. Emelia stays for two weeks, then disappears and makes a new life for herself, though remaining in Nebraska. Here is one who makes a working adjustment to the demands of life in the pioneer West, and who does not allow herself to be smothered by a mistake.

Mary, the fourth wife, is the most able one of all. She nearly leaves Jules during their early marriage but waits too long and becomes pregnant. Thereafter she remains primarily to care for her children. Mary labors very hard—she is up early and works late, whereas Jules sleeps until nearly noon and exerts himself only to care for his orchard and to go hunting (which is his masculine escape, not available to Mary, when things get tense around home). One example will demonstrate the role of husband and wife in this family and the desperate plight of Mary. She tries to get Jules to castrate the calves before they get too big for her to handle. But Jules procrastinates, and when he finally attempts the job, Mary is unable to hold the large calf when he kicks. Jules, furious, says, "I learn the goddam balky woman to obey me when I say 'hold him.'" He chases Mary and beats her with a handful of wire stays; she rushes into the house, grabs poison from the poison drawer, and tries to take it, but is intercepted by the grandmother and then by Jules. The grandmother shields Mary, and Jules leaves on a hunting expedition. The children cower under the bed like frightened rabbits.

Life is very difficult for Mary, and she is nearly defeated. But she manages to endure, even to gain some of her own wishes by skillful diplomacy, which always leaves Jules with the impression that he is the boss and the provider. But it is an extremely hard life, and Mary ages prematurely. It is no wonder that the daughter Mari never marries.

Another author of midwestern pioneer life, Sophus Keith Winther, has given us, in the character of Meta Grimsen, a pioneer woman who succeeds admirably on the frontier. In a series of three novels, *Take All to Nebraska* (1936), *Mortgage Your Heart* (1937), and *This Passion Never Dies* (1938), Winther traces the history of a family of Danish immigrants from about 1898 to the early 1920s. This is not the more rugged pioneer period of Rolvaag or even Sandoz and Cather; the forces to be contended with here are in part nature, but more especially the social and economic forces facing immigrants attempting to adjust to a rural community. Again we see the husband as the driving leader, the one who wanted to go West; Meta would just as soon return to Denmark, but her destiny is with her husband. Again we see the hardships faced by the pioneer woman; she loses her only daughter through illness, which might have been cured had adequate medical care been available on the prairie. Meta's working hours are long, and she seldom gets a day off. More often than not, when a trip to town must be made, she must remain behind, and her husband has the pleasure of a change of routine. Although she often does little things to please her children and husband, they seldom think to do something special for her. The bleakness of her life is typified by her efforts to make their home a little brighter: she talks Peter into buying some wallpaper and they work hard to put it up. That evening, she goes to bed tired but happy with the new look in her home. But the next morning, she awakens to find the paper in shreds on the floor; the walls are simply too old and musty to hold the paper. In spite of the disppointments, hard work and economic set-backs, Meta endures and inspires her children with a quiet courage. She is a symbol of the triumphant pioneer woman whose fulfillment is in the lives of her children.

No discussion of the pioneer woman would be complete without mention of Willa Cather's *My Antonia* (1918). In this beautiful nostalgic evocation of the past, Cather has given us several successful women. There is Tiny Soderball, who goes West to try her fortune. She does very well in the Klondike and eventually settles in San Francisco. Here is one who succeeds in a career of her own. She leads a life of adventure, but eventually her only interest is making money. I quote here the narrator's comment: "She was satisfied with her success, but not elated. She was like someone in whom the faculty of becoming interested is worn out." Another woman who, in psychological terms, might be regarded as even more successful than Tiny is Lena Lingard. She becomes a seamstress and thus enjoys an independent career, first in Lincoln, then in San Francisco. She avoids marriage and a family, for she has seen enough of the rigors of family life as an immigrant child on the prairie, and as for married life she says, "It's all being under somebody's thumb." Her independent life seems to bring with it a great deal of satisfaction and fulfillment, and she faithfully contributes financially to the family she has left behind.

But Willa Cather's focus is of course on Antonia. This immigrant girl endures many hardships as a child and young woman. She works in the fields until she becomes hard and coarse, but friends and relatives of the narrator help to rescue her from this situation before it is too late. While working as a hired girl in town, she learns much from the Harlings that helps her to adjust to her American environment. Although seduced and enticed away from her friends by a young man who soon abandons her, she returns, has her baby, and rises above this trauma to marry a man who can help her achieve fulfillment as a mother. The narrator describes her, when he visits her surrounded by her children: "she still had that something which fires the imagination, could still stop one's breath for a moment by a look or gesture that somehow revealed the meaning in common things. . . . It is no wonder that her sons stood tall and straight. She was a rich mine of life, like founders of early races."

One could of course object to Cather's portrayal by pointing out that she, like so many others, follows the old stereotype that woman can achieve fulfillment of self only through the biological function of sex and the sociological role of mother. The image of Antonia at the end of the book tends to confirm this notion. However, it is worth noting that Lena Lingard and Tiny Soderball do achieve a large measure of self-realization. More important, perhaps, is the significance of comparisons between these characters and the narrator, Jim Burden. He marries, but his marriage is childless, and we get the impression that his marriage is not happy or rewarding. Jim Burden loves the land of his childhood and the memories of his past more than his present situation. Thus, although Antonia as the earth-mother founder of races may demonstrate the greatest degree of self-fulfillment, I would rank Lena Lingard second, ahead of Jim Burden. In Willa Cather's approach, self-fulfillment is not markedly different for men or for women.

In reviewing the images of women presented in western fiction, I find one stereotype generally missing, and that is the image of the submissive wife. Hamlin Garland portrays some pretty beaten down women, but they often reveal real gumption. For example, in "A Branch Road," Agnes responds to her childhood sweetheart and deserts her husband and escapes the dismal life she has had with him. In "Mrs. Ripley's Trip," the wife saves money, a dime at a time, for a trip back to New York State; she declares her intention to her husband, who soon realizes there is no use contradicting; she carries through with her trip, and then returns home and resumes her role as hardworking, faithful wife. Willa Cather's Antonia is clearly head of the household, and Mary firmly and effectively bans Old Jules from her bedroom when she has had enough of child-bearing. In H. L. Davis' *Honey in the Horn,* more often than not it is the woman who leaves her husband in the pursuit of some other man, and not vice versa. And even Beret—in response to her urging Per Hansa goes out into the snowstorm that claims his life. One can find examples of the submissive wife in western fiction, but they are more typically the Indian squaws than the white American wives: Teal Eye, who is Boone's squaw in Guthrie's *The Big Sky* (1947), or Hugh Glass' squaw in Frederick Manfred's *Lord Grizzly* (1954). The white pioneer wife may have started out as the submissive wife when her husband told her they were going out West, but the ones who succeeded in their roles as pioneer wives also attained a degree of independence and resourcefulness that made them no longer totally submissive. If we can say that the westward movement exemplified the capitalistic drive to a growth economy wherein the white pioneer assumed an aggressive role toward natural resources and typically sought to conquer his environment, then perhaps we may conjecture that the pioneering experience placed the women in a similar role: they stood beside their husbands, and they too became aggressors. Also, the western experience often contributed to a breakdown of traditional roles; in some cases the individuals felt less bound by marriage vows than did their counterparts in the East. Because of circumstances, then, the women often did men's work and often attained independence of thought and action. All this is not to say that the women of western fiction are truly "liberated." But then, neither are the western men.

## Victoria Aarons

SOURCE: "The Outsider Within: Women in Contemporary Jewish-American Fiction," in *Contemporary Literature,* Vol. 28, No. 3, Fall, 1987, pp. 378-93.

[*In the following essay, Aarons examines the writing of several contemporary Jewish American women writers, finding in their works a consistent awareness of being outside both American culture and Judaism.*]

For quite some time now the issue of ethnic identity in Jewish-American fiction has posed a central concern for critics and writers alike, a concern bred from the necessity to identify the place of Jewish fiction within the broader scope of American literary culture. Not unlike other literatures that we have come to call "ethnic," black or chicano fiction, for instance, or even those which comprise the "immigrant experience" in fiction (such as Maxine Hong Kingston's novels of Chinese-Americans), Jewish-American writing emerges as yet another example—if not the primary paradigm—of both an "ethnic" and an "immigrant" fiction. Certainly the Jewish-American literature that directly grew out of the early immigrant experience in America, Abraham Cahan's *The Rise of David Levinsky* (1917), and Anzia Yezierska's *Hungry Hearts* (1920), for example, yielded to such literary concerns as dialect and a preoccupation with themes of assimilation and ethnic identity. Perhaps the best-known novel of the Jewish immigrant's journey from steerage to New York tenement life, Henry Roth's *Call It Sleep* (1934), self-consciously calls attention to the problematic mingling of languages and customs that characterized the "greenhorn's" struggle to integrate into American culture. This novel in many ways stands as a beacon to the immigrant's epic survival, much as Roth's metaphorical description in the prologue of the towering statue in New York's harbor ironically illuminates the immigrant's precarious passage into mainstream America: "the rays of her halo were spikes of darkness roweling the air; shadow flattened the torch she bore to a black cross against flawless light—the blackened hilt of a broken sword. Liberty." By its very nature, then, early Jewish-American fiction was relegated to a certain *outsider* status. Both the writers and their fictions were situated on the outskirts of our perceived notions of the American literary heritage.

For post World War II Jewish writers, however, this outsider posture seemed no longer a requirement. Bellow, Malamud, and Philip Roth merge into the mainstream of American literature to stand alongside Faulkner, Hemingway, and Steinbeck. More and more, Jewish writers speak about and within American culture, transcending an earlier "immigrant" identity imposed by an alien culture. In *Jewish Writing and Identity in the Twentieth Century*,[1] Leon Yudkin suggests such a shift in the place of American Jewish writers from the outskirts to the mainstream of literary culture when he argues that:

> By the 1940's, a substantial native-born generation considered itself as much a part of the national fabric as any other element, religious or ethnic. To be an American Jew became increasingly one of the ways of being an American. . . . This did not mean that there was no longer a characteristically Jewish literature but its form of expression changed. The Jew could not easily see himself as an immigrant if he was of local provenance and an English-speaking American national. He was already, on the whole, commercially successful, socially established if not totally integrated, and did not have another mother country to look back to nostalgically or to summon as a measure. (112)

Yudkin's point here seems particularly significant in light of our attention to defining literature in terms of its ethnic origins. He argues even further that in American literature since the 1940s,

> the Jewish voice is not only heard but increasingly accepted as the norm. Jewish terminology, except

in certain instances of specialist exposition, is no longer explained to the reader. Yiddish has entered the American language, and the Jewish type with the implication of his cultural, social and historical background is understood as part of the scene. Bellow does not have to translate to the extent that Cahan did. And the Jew is not seen on the fringes of society, trying to edge his way in. In many ways, he exemplifies that society. And Jewish literature is peculiarly American literature. (112-13)

Yet Jewish women writers, at least in our formal recognition of them, remain beyond the pale of established critical acclaim. Less recognized than their male counterparts, yet nonetheless emerging in the American literary scene, contemporary Jewish women writers continue to be faced with issues of ethnic identity and self-definition, reinforcing the "immigrant" status that defined earlier Jewish fiction in America. For, if Jewish fiction in America has been marked by a certain outsider status, it may be all the more so for Jewish women writers, who are outsiders to the traditional, male-dominated literary culture, as well as to the more traditional Jewish laws, which limit women's roles in public worship and in institutional power.

What we find in the writing of many contemporary Jewish women, such as Grace Paley, Tillie Olsen, Cynthia Ozick, and Hortense Calisher, is a self-conscious recognition of an outsider position in both American culture and Judaism. When coupled as oft-perceived products of a literary subculture, Jewish ethnic identity and an emerging "women's fiction" become finally questions of voice, a voice that is at once a source of richness and tension in the fiction of contemporary Jewish-American women. In defining that voice, we come somewhat closer, I believe, to securing a coherent vision, a common world view, shared by many Jewish women writers in America.

I do not mean to suggest that literary concerns of ethnicity no longer remain central to the more established male Jewish writers. Indeed, the ethnicity of writers such as Malamud and their categorization as Jewish writers result in critical debate still. Robert Alter, in *After the Tradition*, suggests this tension:

> It is by no means clear what sense is to be made of the Jewishness of a writer who neither uses a uniquely Jewish language, nor describes a distinctively Jewish milieu, nor draws upon literary traditions that are recognizably Jewish.[2]

Here the complexity of the issues surrounding Jewish identity in the fiction of American writers crystallizes. Unlike other literary subgenres that call attention to questions of ethnicity and identity (such as black, hispanic, native American, or lesbian literatures), Jewish-American fiction seems to raise issues of a distinctively different nature. Because the Jews assimilated so quickly (unlike other minority groups still pursuing their rights and fashioning their American identities), Jewish identity has been complex enough to force itself upon the design of

American fiction. While group affiliation would be the apparent linking concept of minority literatures, such *public* matters of identity give way to more *private* concerns with personal identity for the Jew in America. Jewish-American literature is still an "immigrant fiction" because of the complexities of the question of what it means to *be* a Jew in America. Can one *remain* a Jew in a secular "melting pot" and still feel at home there, still maintain a posture of economic and social success? This is the essential focus for contemporary Jewish-American writers. The question of whether one can remain a Jew in America, that is, can remain connected to the faith, underlies the thematic tensions in works as diverse as I. B. Singer's "The Son from America," Grace Paley's "The Loudest Voice," and Philip Roth's "Defender of the Faith." As one might expect, however, the issue of whether one can remain a Jew in America is not only a matter of faith, but involves an even deeper connection to the heritage, to the past, to the disappearing world of the "fathers."

Because of these complexities, a singular "Jewish" voice is untenable. Before one could identify *a* Jewish voice, one would have to answer some very vexing questions: How does one define the ethnicity of a writer: by his or her direct political statements? By his or her depiction in fiction of Jewish characters, environment, and issues? By his or her birth alone? Must a writer address particular Jewish issues or situations to be considered a Jewish writer? These questions are difficult because of the uncertainty in the definition of a uniquely Jewish character or context in America, where the character is as much American as Jewish and the context grounded in an American ethos. Questions of Jewish identity in writing are not unlike those currently faced by contemporary women writers, who have often felt compelled to address the issue of a "women's fiction," whether or not they consider themselves advocates of the genre. The current controversy among feminist critics and writers highlights this concern.[3] As Adrienne Rich and others have argued, how we define ourselves involves complex personal and political issues. This process of self-definition—especially for women who have been alienated historically from the Western literary heritage—presents itself in the literature by women as more than a search for identity, for a fixed personal identity. (I make the distinction here, knowing that it is a controversial one, between feminist writers, unified by a political ideology, and writers who are women.) Rather it seems to me that the attempts at self-definition through literature become a process of self-fashioning, of forging an identity. For contemporary Jewish-American women writers, faced with dual issues of sexual and ethnic identity, the process of self-definition is further complicated.

Can we make certain assumptions about Jewish women writers that will not simply reinforce well-worn stereotypes about both Jews and women? Does a self-perceived "ghettoization," the formative influence in the development of the Jew as "outsider," keep Jewish women writers on the margin of American literary culture? Such self-conscious distinctions go no little way in reinforcing an outsider status, despite, for example, Leon Yudkin's contention that the Jew in literature has secured a firm place by moving "from the periphery to the centre" (113) of American literary tradition.

The motif of the outsider as fictional stereotype has been overly simplified in much of the writing about Jewish literature. To call the Jewish writer simply an outsider, distanced from both the American experience and from his or her Jewish heritage, ignores the dichotomy that lies at the heart of the problems of ethnic identification in fiction. As outsider, the Jew—as fictional character and as writer—becomes much more than a stereotype. The very tension in the fiction of Jewish-American writers is the insider-outsider *paradox,* the ability of the Jew to be at once insider and outsider, in terms of both America and Judaism.

Nonetheless, Jewish-American writers, I would maintain, remain in many ways on the periphery of the literary culture still, in no little part as a result of their own self-consciousness of their position in the literary community. Cynthia Ozick defines this troublesome position well when she depicts herself as "a third-generation American Jew (though the first to have been native-born) perfectly at home and yet perfectly insecure, perfectly acculturated and yet perfectly marginal."[4] Ozick's description of the Jewish writer as defined by a precarious balance between acculturation and estrangement reflects a self-consciousness on the part of the Jewish writer, a self-conscious Judaism that extends to the characters' visions of themselves and to their perceived place in America.

Tillie Olsen's famous story, "Tell Me a Riddle,"[5] depicts a woman, an immigrant, who has spent her adult years struggling for equilibrium and comfort in America, who finally when her children are grown, when her death is imminent, renounces Judaism, renounces a connection to any specific faith. In the hospital, when told she is on the Jewish list for visiting rabbis, she proclaims: "Not for rabbis. At once go and make them change. Tell them to write: Race, human; Religion, none" (89). For this old woman, Judaism—the religion and inherent traditions—represents backwardness, persecution, and restriction. Her daughter, American-born, tries to recreate tradition, ritual. She looks to her mother for a key to the past, for a link to Judaism, hoping to enrich the present. However, instead of being drawn to the tradition of her youth, the dying woman regards such rituals as the lighting of candles as "Superstition! From our ancestors, savages, afraid of the dark, or of themselves: mumbo words and magic lights to scare away ghosts" (90). Her vision of Judaism militates against her principles of humanity, principles for which she fought in Olshana, in the old country, principles that flew in the face of a centuries-long stronghold of oppression. In a bitter recollection of what it meant to be Jewish, Olsen's protagonist decries the faith of her "fathers":

> Candles bought instead of bread and stuck into a
> potato for a candlestick? Religion that stifled and

said: in Paradise, woman, you will be the footstool
of your husband, and in life—poor chosen Jew—
ground under, despised, trembling in cellars. And
cremated. And cremated. . . .

Heritage. How have we come from our savage past,
how no longer to be savages—this to teach. To
look back and learn what humanizes—this to teach.
To smash all ghettos that divide us—not to go back,
not to go back—this to teach. (90; ellipses added)

Olsen's protagonist rebels against a determined adherence to a faith that persecutes and against long-ingrained
gender expectations that reinforce her alienation from a
religion that persecutes even more because of her status
as a woman. To the amazement of her family, she cannot
respond to her grandchildren. Her husband scolds her:
"Unnatural grandmother, not able to make herself embrace a baby" (92). The kind of isolation felt by the protagonist in "Tell Me a Riddle" is derived from the pressure to be what she is not, to live up to an externally
defined posture of doting Jewish grandmother, solicitous
wife, acquiescent old woman, content with the passage of
age. She views these predetermined roles as denials of
the progressive secular humanist she sees herself to be.
She tells her granddaughter, "'it is more than oceans
between Olshana and you'" (113), and yet her hopes for
equality and freedom, values symbolized by America,
plummet in the face of continued oppression. Those socialist ideologies of her youth in the old country—ideologies that gave her life-blood—failed to materialize in the
"land of the free," and so she remains an immigrant still,
ghettoized, as she was in the *shtetl,* by her refusal to
"move to the rhythms of others," to accept the diminished
circumstances willed to her. The old woman's husband
finally comes to understand his wife's longing and loss,
and remembering the ideals of the past, sees them now in
the light of betrayal and failure of the twentieth century:
"' "in the twentieth century ignorance will be dead,
dogma will be dead, war will be dead, and for all human-
kind one country—of fulfillment?" Hah!'" (120).

The immigrant's distance from his or her homeland, the
"outsider" status, provides us with a vision of loss, disappointment, and disillusion. In Cynthia Ozick's brilliant
short story, "Envy: Or, Yiddish in America,"[6] the main
character, Edelshtein, must forever remain un-noticed
because he writes his poetry in Yiddish and has no English translator. He derides America as "the empty
bride" (171), without dowry, without history, without
identity. The wry humor with which he is portrayed by
Ozick is constantly checked by our sympathies for him.
Edelshtein's despair over the fate of Yiddish in America
is momentarily arrested by his delight in finding a young
woman, American-born, who reads Yiddish. Edelshtein's
delusion that he has finally found a translator who will
make him famous, will make his works known in America,
founders when he discovers that Hannah, the would-be
translator of his work, will not translate poems of the
"ghetto." She is interested only in poetry that reflects
universal concerns, poetry in the mainstream, "'In the
world. . . . Not in your little puddles'" (173). Edelshtein's

response to Hannah's attack demonstrates the enormous
gap between the immigrant and the American-born Jew,
the latter a Jew by descent only:

"Again the ghetto. Your uncle stinks from the
ghetto? Graduated, 1924, the University of Berlin,
Vorovsky stinks from the ghetto? Myself, four God-
given books not one living human being knows, I
stink from the ghetto? God, four thousand years
since Abraham hanging out with Jews, God also
stinks from the ghetto?"

"Rhetoric," Hannah said. "Yiddish literary rhetoric."
(173)

Hannah, unlike the American-born daughters in Tillie
Olsen's "Tell Me a Riddle," perceives her "heritage" not
as a source of richness and continuity, but rather as a
preoccupation with suffering, as a curse: "'Suffer suffer,'
she said. 'I like devils best. They don't think only about
themselves and they don't suffer'" (174). Hannah seeks a
universal—not a peculiarly Jewish—history, much in fact
like Olsen's protagonist, a history without the emotional
vestiges of the "old country," free from suffering, from
defeat, from self-delusion. Edelshtein's outrage at
Hannah's neglect of the past emphasizes the chasm between generations, between cultures. He, in turn, denies
her a past, curses her: "'Forget Yiddish!' he screamed at
her. 'Wipe it out of your brain! Extirpate it! Go get a
memory operation! You have no right to it, you have no
right to an uncle, a grandfather! No one ever came before
you, you were never born! A vacuum!'" (175).

As Edelshtein cries out, it ultimately may be a matter of
"rights," that the birthright, the right of identity, a connection to the past, to Judaism, carries with it the emotional baggage of the outsider. However, being a Jew in
twentieth-century America takes on a decidedly different
meaning from what it meant to be a Jew in the Eastern
European shtetls. This difference in definition finally
prevents Hannah and Edelshtein, Tillie Olsen's dying
mother and her American-born children, and the host of
Jewish characters separated by generations, from residing
comfortably under the same "roof."

Problems with generational differences and with "place"
are deeply connected to issues of identity and ethnicity.
Grace Paley's protagonists, especially the women,
struggle with identity, with their physical place in the
world, and in relationships with other people—parents,
husbands, children, peers. For Paley, Judaism often appears in her short stories as a nagging reminder of the
past, a loss, a constant source of disquiet for many of her
characters. The main character, Faith, in Paley's short
story, "Faith in the Afternoon,"[7] for example, is caught
between differing visions of the world. On the one hand,
she remains connected to the world of the "fathers," as
characterized by her parents, and on the other, she lives
in a more modern America, a world seemingly free from
the bonds of historical and religious dictates. Having left
Judaism in a formal sense, reinforced by her marriage to
a gentile, a union that finally—acrimoniously—leaves

her to raise her children on her own ("'I love their little goyish faces'" [48], her father says of his grandchildren), Faith attempts to bridge the two worlds. Although she has abandoned the old neighborhood of her childhood, she nostalgically turns to her mother in search of information of people from her past, and feels connected to them; their *tsouris,* their suffering, is akin to her own. Yet she remains inevitably outside of both worlds, her predicament ironically similar to the very immigrant parentage against which she shields herself:

> Her grandmother pretended she was German in just the same way that Faith pretends she is an American. Faith's mother flew in the fat face of all that and, once safely among her own kind in Coney Island, learned real Yiddish, helped Faith's father, who was not so good at foreign languages, and as soon as all the verbs and necessary nouns had been collected under the roof of her mouth, she took an oath to expostulate in Yiddish and grieve only in Yiddish, and she has kept that oath to this day.

> Faith has only visited her parents once since she began to understand that because of Ricardo she would have to be unhappy for a while. Faith really is an American and she was raised up like everyone else to the true assumption of happiness. (33)

Yet in her failure to achieve the American image of happiness—the immigrant's dream—Faith can neither reconcile herself to her family, which is her past, nor adjust to the present. So her relationship with both parents, but especially with her father, is wrought with emotional turbulence; her "Judaism" becomes self-conscious, very much on the surface of her actions and responses.

While the father figure in Jewish literature is a powerful force with whom to be reckoned, the figure of the mother provides a deep connection to the past. Unlike Olsen's protagonist in "Tell Me a Riddle," it is often the mother who, because of her garrulity and penchant for participating actively in the lives of her neighbors and friends (frequently depicted humorously), is a rich source of information and continuity. It is not surprisingly the mothers who strongly adhere to the "world of the fathers," the mothers to whom the American-born children return time and time again. The tradition of the mother in Jewish literature—a tradition that unfortunately often lends itself to the worst kind of stereotyping—has a long history for both male and female Jewish writers. Shenandoah Fish, for instance, in Delmore Schwartz's short story, "America! America!,"[8] suffers from a loss of identity while traveling abroad and returns home to his mother's kitchen where, almost despite himself, he listens and is drawn to his mother's stories of old family ties. In them he recognizes his connection to the people in his past, not without a good deal of self-recognition and guilt, born from his conscious attempt to distance himself from his mother's immigrant history and to intellectualize his family's past. He comes to recognize his condescension toward his family and their friends with no little self-disgust:

> Shenandoah was exhausted by his mother's story. He was sick of the mood in which he had listened, the irony and the contempt which had taken hold of each new event. He had listened from such a distance that what he saw was an outline, a caricature, and an abstraction. How different it might seem, if he had been able to see these lives from the inside, looking out.

> And now he felt for the first time how closely bound he was to these people. His separation was actual enough, but there existed also an unbreakable unity. (32)

Despite Shenandoah's recognition of his unbreakable connection to his heritage, an insight he has not come upon without considerable turmoil, he remains an outsider still: "'I do not see myself. I do not know myself. I cannot look at myself truly'" (33). Shenandoah, like many of the fictive American-born children of immigrant parentage, suffers from a self-imposed but equally uncomfortable "immigrant" condition. He *is* and is *not* a part of his parents' world. Thus in characters like Shenandoah and Faith, we see, not a transcendence of traditional values, but a fragmentation of identity resulting from, on the one hand, a guilt-ridden attraction to the old ways and, on the other, the realization that the attraction, both curiosity and instinct, is felt inevitably from the "outside."

The outsider's sense of difference often results in a perceived failure to live up to the expectations of one's parents—a theme itself consistently found in the literature. We find it, for example, in such works as Chaim Potok's *The Chosen,* Bernard Malamud's *The Assistant,* Susan Fromberg Schaeffer's *Falling,* and Herbert Gold's "The Heart of the Artichoke," in which the conflict of values and choices between children and their parents—mothers who know intimate details of the lives of their neighbors, fathers who ascribe to postwar American notions of success, parents who believe in fixed absolutes, such as family loyalty, hard work, and the like—creates considerable ambivalence for the protagonists. This tension manifests itself, I believe, most strikingly in the depiction of the "modern" Jewish woman, who is, in many ways, expected to carry on the tradition. In Hortense Calisher's short stories this ambivalence manifests itself in a quiet recognition, but by no means an unqualified acceptance, of change. In "The Rabbi's Daughter,"[9] for example, Calisher's protagonist leaves the refined "world of the fathers," for her the relatively genteel world of the Jewish middle class, surrenders her career as a pianist for marriage to a man who works with his hands, yields finally to a style of dress and decorum unlike those to which she is accustomed, and takes up a life of transience. The difference in the rabbi's daughter's two hands, one more roughened than the other, reflects with understated power the dual nature of her existence. Gazing at her hand, she proclaims: "This one is still 'the rabbi's daughter'" (288), the hand unmarred by work, unblemished by worries about finances and domestic concerns.

Characteristic of many of the protagonists uncovered in the fiction of Jewish-American women, the rabbi's daughter breaks from the tradition, the life, but can never entirely leave the world of her "father," that world so ingrained, so very much at the heart of her identity and her struggle. This kind of ambivalence prevents the female protagonists from living comfortably in either world. For the rabbi's daughter, it breeds resentment, dissatisfaction, a sense of self as "visitor." The rabbi's daughter, upon leaving her family and moving into new temporary lodgings found by her husband, "heard her own voice, sugared viciously with wistfulness. 'Once I change [my attire] I'll be settled. As long as I keep it on . . . I'm still a visitor'" (288; ellipsis in original). Shedding her "travel" clothes—an adornment of past luxury—becomes a metaphor for relinquishing a past life for a much less certain future, a future without the fixed values and traditions of the "fathers."

Similarly, Paley's character Faith is equally infused with an ambivalence that causes both shame and anxiety, manifested by an uneasy love for her father, whom she can no longer look in the eye:

> He leaned over the rail and tried to hold her eyes. But that is hard to do, for eyes are born dodgers and know a whole circumference of ways out of a bad spot. . . .
>
> Mr. Darwin reached for her fingers through the rail. He held them tightly and touched them to her wet cheeks. Then he said, "Aaah . . ." an explosion of nausea, absolute digestive disgust. And before she could turn away from the old age of his insulted face and run home down the subway stairs, he had dropped her sweating hand out of his own and turned away from her. (48-49)

The image presented here is strikingly visual; Faith's father virtually pulls on her, drawing his daughter to him, begging her to return to the fold. A tug of war ensues, from which neither emerges as victor.

Paley's characteristically ironic—often tentatively humorous—voice balances the pathos of her characters and situations. This voice might best be characterized as a kind of self-irony, born perhaps from the inherent problems of self-definition and from the recognition of the precarious posture of the American Jew. Jewish writers thus are ironically detached from, yet identify with, their characters.

As distanced from traditional Jewish values and culture as many of the characters are—Hannah, the rabbi's daughter, the dying old woman who denounces a faith that denies humanity, the young mother in Paley's story who recognizes the disparate needs of her father and herself—they have nonetheless a bond, a haunting connection to Judaism, an obsession with the past, an often unspoken alliance with "the fathers." Susan Fromberg Schaeffer metaphorically suggests this link to a collective sense of identity:

> they remembered with wonder, how their lives, and their characters, and their morals and their fates had always hung there like long clothes in the closet, waiting for them to grow into them.[10]

This compelling link to the past, a past experienced often elusively as a sort of collective memory for the American-born children, is nowhere more apparent than in the fiction that draws heavily upon the tension between the immigrant parent and his or her American-born child. This reliance on collective memory is what allows Grace Paley's narrator in "Mom" to relate the images of her childhood memory of her mother, like all mothers, who calls to the child from the window to come in off the street: "I am not the child. She isn't my mother. Still, in my head where remembering is organized for significance (not usefulness), she leans far out."[11] For the American-born children of Jewish immigrants, life in America is both a blessing and a curse, ironically for the same reason: because one is not in Europe. Paley, in "The Immigrant Story,"[12] establishes this paradox, when a young couple attempt to grapple with their parents' lives, and with their own childhoods (a common theme in Paley's works):

> Jack asked me, Isn't it a terrible thing to grow up in the shadow of another person's sorrow?
>
> I suppose so, I answered. As you know, I grew up in the summer sunlight of upward mobility. This leached out a lot of that dark ancestral grief. . . .
>
> What if this sorrow is all due to history? I asked.
>
> The cruel history of Europe, he said. In this way he showed ironic respect to one of my known themes. (171)

The narrator of the story remembers her childhood perception of America, reflected by an incantation: "I made an announcement to the sixth-grade assembly thirty years ago. I said: I thank God every day that I'm not in Europe. I thank God I'm American-born and live on East 172nd Street where there is a grocery store, a candy store, and a drugstore on one corner and on the same block a shul and two doctors' offices" (173). Yet as the narrator itemizes the gains, her luck in being an American, Jack recounts the losses of the immigrant experience, of his parents' past. For him, America symbolizes the ultimate sacrifice, that of parents for children who constantly deny the promise. The misery, the guilt, and the confusion Jack feels stem primarily from his own sense of failure. Jack remembers the comparative ease of his life in juxtaposition with his pieced-together fictional picture of his parents' struggle, a picture that comes together in his "memory" of likely events:

> My mother and father came from a small town in Poland. They had three sons. My father decided to go to America, to 1. stay out of the army, 2. stay out of jail, 3. save his children from everyday wars and ordinary pogroms. He was helped by the savings of parents, uncles, grandmothers and

set off like hundreds of thousands of others in that year. . . . Mostly he put his money away for the day he could bring his wife and sons to this place. Meanwhile, in Poland famine struck. Not hunger which all Americans suffer six, seven times a day but Famine, which tells the body to consume itself. . . . My father met my mother at the boat. He looked at her face, her hands. There was no baby in her arms, no children dragging at her skirt. . . . She had shaved her head, like a backward Orthodox bride, though they had been serious advanced socialists like most of the youth of their town. He took her by the hand and brought her home. They never went anywhere alone, except to work or the grocer's. They held each other's hand when they sat down at the table, even at breakfast. Sometimes he patted her hand, sometimes she patted his. He read the paper to her every night. (174-75)

Their story is the immigrant's story, and their sorrow, their loss, becomes that of their children, American-born, both finally outsiders. Jack's efforts to explain his parents' lives in America, like the obsessive queries made of Olsen's resistant protagonist—"Day after day, the spilling memories. Worse now, questions, too. Even the grandchildren: Grandma, in the olden days, when you were little" (98)—speak to, I think, an attempt at alleviating the fragmentation that has become the by-product of contemporary Jewish-American life. Such attempts often fail, however, because of the tensions inherent in the outsider's relation to his or her culture, expressed again by Shenandoah Fish:

Shenandoah tried to imagine their arrival in the new world and their first impression of the city of New York. But he knew that his imagination failed him, for nothing in his own experience was comparable to the great displacement of body and mind which their coming to America must have been. (27)

It is not so simple to argue that what we finally uncover in Jewish-American writing is a conflict of generations, a struggle between the immigrants and their American-born children. A struggle, certainly. However, it is a struggle that connects as well as divides. For such children in fiction, even those long since grown, the oral history embedded in their memories remains paradoxically a source of both connection and estrangement. Despite the host of characters caught in an ambivalent, often warring posture with their heritage, the guiding voice of the writer, almost without exception, tempers the conflict, makes sense of the tension through empathy. It is no wonder, then, that this conflict has as its center the family, for, as Robert Alter has recently argued, "the family, after all, is the matrix of our psychological lives, of our political, moral, and theological imaginings."[13]

While this ambivalence is articulated most pronouncedly in the language of the vanishing immigrant in Jewish-American literature, the insidiousness of separateness, of identity by ethnicity, appears also in that literature remote from the immigrant experience. Hortense Calisher's short story, "Old Stock,"[14] for example, suggests a different vision of the outsider. The assimilated and refined Mrs. Elkin, who considers herself and her daughter removed from those "Jews whose grosser features, voices, manners offended her sense of gentility all the more out of her resentful fear that she might be identified with them" (263), finds herself the very brunt of anti-Semitism, all the more disturbing because of her own anti-Semitic inclinations. While vacationing in the Catskills, where she considers herself beyond reproach, Mrs. Elkin tries her best to shun the other Jews staying at her lodgings; she considers any such association intrusive and presumptuous. Much to her embarrassment, however, Mrs. Elkin's "disguise" is exposed by an elderly local woman, and her unease, finally out in the open, reflects the denial of her own and her daughter's Jewish lineage and ironically causes her daughter to seek such a connection:

"I told Elizabeth Smith," Miss Onderdonk said. "I told her she'd rue the day she ever started taking in Jews." . . .

Mrs. Elkin, raising her brows, made a helpless face at Hester [her daughter], as if to say, "After all, the vagaries of the deaf . . ." She permitted herself a minimal shrug, even a slight spreading of palms. Under Hester's stare, she lowered her eyes and turned toward Miss Onderdonk again.

"I thought you knew, Miss Onderdonk," said her mother. "I thought you knew that we were— Hebrews." The word, the ultimate refinement, slid out of her mother's soft voice as if it were on runners.

"Eh?" said Miss Onderdonk.

Say it, Hester prayed. She had never before felt the sensation of prayer. Please say it, Mother. Say *"Jew."* (272-73; first ellipsis added)

Her mother's obvious distress paradoxically causes Hester to define herself once and for all as Jewish, and so to put an end to her mother's attempts to be what she is not.

We finally return to the question: can one remain a Jew in America? This question, born of the Jewish immigrant experience, depends for its answer on the definition of Judaism, which in many ways "looks different" in America, and on the acceptance of change, the tolerance of an evolving Jewish character in the literature of Jewish-American writers, the denial of old stereotypes and archetypal patterns.

How does one reconcile the Jewish-American experience with its past, with its immigrant origins? The steerage across the waters left behind more than miles. And the sense of loss is increasingly perceptible as the generations turn for American Jews, creating a need for a new identity, a new sense of what it means to be Jewish, a need intensified for women by the inevitably transformed feminine postures available in the "new" culture of America. In the fiction I've examined, a new vision of what it means to be Jewish in America emerges. No longer do we find, as we did with the earlier immigrant fiction and even with that which came after World War II, characters who feel excluded from and at odds with American socioeconomic ideals. Malamud, Bellow, and Philip Roth, it might be argued, worked through the evolution of the Jewish male character who, always a step out of line with the rest of America, struggled unsuccessfully to merge with the American main-stream, to shed the weighty baggage of his heritage. Contemporary Jewish-American women writers present a different sense of the "outsider." No longer on the outskirts of American culture, nor even of the literary tradition, the characters find themselves paradoxically alienated from and drawn to a heritage from which they are excluded, and yet in which they play an important function—the silent foil of a male-dominated tradition. This paradox of simultaneous exclusion and inclusion results in the fragmentation of identity we've seen in these stories, a fragmentation that causes the characters to seek to resolve their ambivalent feelings toward their pasts by trying to recreate them. Often, such characters are torn between a longing for the past, for a sense of absolutes (rituals, traditions, beliefs), and a determination to forge ahead, to fashion an identity that "fits" for this time and this place. Though their defiance of the "world of the fathers" results in new possibilities for the Jewish-American woman, it remains a vision fraught with ambivalence, with mistrust of one's "place," yet with an "insider's" instinct for continuity and the potential reaffirmation of identity. It is in this way that the Jewish-American woman, and perhaps, even more so, the Jewish-American woman writer, is the "outsider within."

### NOTES

[1] Leon Yudkin, *Jewish Writing and Identity in the Twentieth Century* (New York: St. Martin's Press, 1982). All quotations are from this edition.

[2] Robert Alter, *After the Tradition: Essays on Modern Jewish Writing* (New York: E. P. Dutton, 1969) 18.

[3] While my intentions in this essay do not allow for a comprehensive analysis of the identity politics of women's literature, I would call attention to the following texts which I have found useful: Rosalind Coward, "Are Women's Novels Feminist Novels?" in *The New Feminist Criticism: Essays on Women, Literature and Theory,* ed. Elaine Showalter (New York: Pantheon, 1985) 225-39; Nelly Furman, "The Politics of Language: Beyond the Gender Principle?" in *Making a Difference: Feminist Literary Criticism,* eds. Gayle Greene and Coppélia Kahn (London: Methuen, 1985) 59-79; Gayle Greene and Coppélia Kahn, "Feminist Scholarship and the Social Construction of Woman," in *Making a Difference* 1-36; and Elaine Showalter, "Women's Time, Women's Space: Writing the History of Feminist Criticism," *Tulsa Studies in Women's Literature* 3 (Spring/Fall 1984): 29-43.

[4] Cynthia Ozick, "Toward a New Yiddish: Note," in *Art & Ardor: Essays by Cynthia Ozick* (New York: Knopf, 1985) 152.

[5] Tillie Olsen, *Tell Me a Riddle* (New York: Dell, 1961) 72-125. All quotations are from this edition.

[6] Cynthia Ozick, "Envy; Or, Yiddish in America," in *Jewish-American Stories,* ed. Irving Howe (New York: New American Library, 1977) 129-77. All quotations are from this edition.

[7] Grace Paley, "Faith in the Afternoon," in *Enormous Changes at the Last Minute* (New York: Farrar, 1983) 29-49. All quotations are from this edition.

[8] Delmore Schwartz, "America! America!," in *In Dreams Begin Responsibilities and Other Stories,* ed. James Atlas (New York: New Directions, 1978) 10-33. All quotations are from this edition.

[9] Hortense Calisher, "The Rabbi's Daughter," in *The Collected Stories of Hortense Calisher* (New York: Arbor House, 1975) 276-88. All quotations are from this edition.

[10] Susan Fromberg Schaeffer, *Falling* (New York: Avon Bard Books, 1973) 9.

[11] Grace Paley, "Mom," in *Esquire* 85 (Dec. 1975): 84.

[12] Paley, "The Immigrant Story," in *Enormous Changes at the Last Minute* 169-75. All quotations are from this edition.

[13] "Kafka's Father, Agnon's Mother, Bellow's Cousins," *Commentary* 81 (Feb. 1986): 48.

[14] Calisher, "Old Stock," in *The Collected Stories* 263-75. All quotations are from this edition.

---

## OTHER NATIONAL LITERATURES

### Jane S. Jaquette

SOURCE: "Literary Archetypes and Female Role Alternatives: The Woman and the Novel in Latin America," in *Female and Male in Latin America: Essays,* edited by Ann Pescatello, University of Pittsburgh Press, 1973, pp. 3-27.

[*In the following essay, Jaquette analyzes images of women in Peruvian literature in an attempt to discover the changing roles of women in Latin American culture.*]

It is the intent of this paper to examine literary images of women in Peru (a "prerevolutionary" society in the sense that, in contrast to Castro, the new military elite has not focused on changing female roles as an aspect of its "revolutionary" program) in order to cast new light on sociological perspectives of women in Latin American society. It is assumed, as female studies have assumed in the North American and British context, that there is a vital link between literature and social behavior, that literature both represents existing social relationships and at the same time socializes women into their roles. Thus literature can be a legitimate source of data and a useful generator of hypotheses for empirical research.

In examining Peruvian literature I found that there was a tendency among Peruvian writers to avoid creating "real" female characters. In the case of Ciro Algería and the social protest novelist in general, this was due to the use of females as *symbols*. In the case of José Maria Arguedas, however, the absence of female characters seemed to result from the author's preference for male characters and his tendency to equate human existence with male existence in the modern urban context. In this way women become part of the existential problem for men, an additional cross to bear. Mario Vargas Llosa treats female and male characters as interacting *stereotypes;* character development is simply not a part of his style. The absence of female characters in novels by male authors is contrasted with the centrality of the female psyche in *La Rifa* by female novelist Katia Saks: the plot of her very short but polished novel is the unsuccessful attempt of an upper-class *Limeña* to free herself from the traditional female roles.

While the Peruvian novel gives ample opportunity to deal with male attitudes toward women, it is weak in behavioral imagery. For this reason I have gone to a book which has been described as a "mythic representation of a third-world culture," Gabriel García Márquez's *Cien años de soledad.* In Macondo, women play at least as significant a part as the men; in fact, women seem to dominate in many respects. As in Vargas Llosa's writing, women appear as stereotypes rather than as individuals, but the stereotypes are developed in detail; they become true *archetypes.* The goal of the novel is the presentation of exterior relations, not interior conflict, and the use of stereotypes is suited to the "mythical" atmosphere that García Márquez generates. From *Cien años de soledad* I have drawn three archetypes which I think represent female role alternatives in Latin American society: woman as Mother, as Witch, and as Wife/Concubine. Further illustrations are provided from the writings of Carlos Fuentes, Julio Cortázar, and Octavio Paz.

Of importance throughout the section on archetypes and roles is an implied comparison between female options in Latin America and those available in the United States. This is significant not only as an abstract exercise in sociology but from the standpoint of strategy for the feminist movement in Latin America. I conclude that the availability of strong female roles in Latin American culture is a sign of the vitality of the "traditional" forms of role differentiation and that *machismo,* often thought by North

Americans as the clearest evidence of the oppression and powerlessness of women in Latin America, is really a social convention in which women have an important stake, for male "immorality" is basic to female legitimacy and influence. Thus the prospects for winning converts to North American-style "liberation" seem dim indeed.

### WOMEN IN THE PERUVIAN NOVEL

The direction of modern Peruvian literature has been most strongly influenced by the figures of Ciro Alegría and José María Arguedas, writers who combined the traditions of the local-color novel and the novel of social protest to bring about a new perspective on Indian culture and to raise the question of the future role of the Indian in the national society. As Earl M. Aldrich[1] has written: "Rural Peru, Indians and mestizos, local color and social protest are primary elements in their works; but these elements are consciously and masterfully blended with stylistic and linguistic techniques calculated to express as never before the complexities of character and environment." Given the "complexity" of character development and the success of both writers in evoking the "essence" of Peru, their books seem a logical starting place in the search for images of women.

Alegría, who had his first major literary success with the publication of *La serpiente de oro* in 1935, concentrates on the conflict between the exploited Indian population and the dominant criollo culture. In offering a sympathetic view of Indian culture, however, Alegría idealizes the life of the Indians, not by underplaying the hardships they suffer as a result of exploitation, but by portraying utopian social relations. As a result, female characters become a set of props, useful in the task of symbolizing the essential harmony between man and nature, in showing the positive personal qualities of male characters, or in providing appropriate romantic interludes.

Thus in the opening lines of *La serpiente de oro* he begins with a lyrical description of a valley near the Marañón in which the woman is little more than an extension of nature:

> We *cholos* whose story this is live in Calemar. We know many other valleys which have been formed where the hills have retreated or been eaten away by the river, but we do not know how many there are downstream. We do know that they are all beautiful and that they speak to us with their haunting ancestral voice which is strong like the voice of the river. . . .
>
> It was Lucinda who was rattling the cooking gourds about inside. Lucinda was from the town. In her green eyes there was rain with sunshine and she was all grace as she walked, her pliant body swaying like a papaya tree. From her womb she had borne a son named Adán.[2]

We learn that Lucinda is at one with nature and fertile, but we are also told that fertility is her only reason for being: "[Adán] was really the link between [Lucinda and Arturo], for what good is a sterile woman? She is complete only if she has children. Then she is water for thirst, bread for life, and besides a furrow—a furrow for life."[3]

Lucinda's qualities of "womanliness" serve to emphasize Arturo's "manliness." Lucinda first meets Arturo, her husband and father of her child, while serving food in her mother's inn in "the town." Arturo was immediately attracted to her ("In the two years they had missed coming to the festival she had ripened like a fruit") and takes her to the dance. They engage in a courtship in which Lucinda holds her own fairly well ("What a pretty girl you've become" / "And what a liar you've become") and they dance and drink a great deal. In the end Lucinda decides to return to Calemar with Arturo and runs away with him without telling her mother. During the festival itself, Lucinda provides Arturo with the opportunity to defend her against the advances of two state troopers (who represent the repressive coastal culture); after the general melee that results Arturo decides it is time to go. Lucinda is hesitant, but she bends to Arturo's will and to the call of nature: "She wanted to go into the house and throw her arms about her mother and never let go of her. But at the same time she felt an inescapable command within her, a powerful voice that came from some far off world of dreams . . . and she walked swiftly toward it."[4] Later she has doubts and begins to cry, and Arturo asserts himself in the expected male way:

"Are you crying?"

"My mamma. My little brother."

He answered almost brutally: "There's nothing to do about it. . . . It's too late now."

It is the voice of the river, imperious and relentless. . . . Lucinda now heard only that voice and she yielded, without further resistance, to the current.[5]

In another novel, *El mundo es ancho y ajeno,* Alegría again returns to the theme

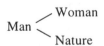

Here the symbolism is emphasized by being posed as an unanswerable question in the mind of the Indian Rosendo Maqui, hero of the novel. Rosendo is contemplating his home, the town of Rumi:

Rumi was both forbidding and gentle, stern and friendly, solemn and benign. The Indian Rosendo believed that he understood its physical and spiritual secrets as though they were his own. Or, rather, those of his wife, for love is a stimulus to knowledge and possession. Except that his wife had grown old and sick, while Rumi was always the same, haloed by the prestige of immortality.

"Which is better," Rosendo tried to decide, "the earth or woman?"

He had never thought it through clearly, but he knew that he loved the earth very much.[6]

But within Alegría's philosophical system, the question is pointless (as earth and woman are the same) and serves only to illustrate the "good" quality of males, that they concern themselves with these difficult questions. (Should the male superiority contention made here seem farfetched, try imagining a female character pondering the relative worth of males and the earth.) When Alegría returns to the question, it is to emphasize the oneness of female and earth, although Rosendo, strangely enough, gains rather than loses stature after all this pointless pondering:

Marguicha had grown like a flourishing plant. . . . When the time came her lips and cheeks became flowers and her young breasts fruit. Her solid hips promised the fecundity of the deep furrow. . . . In a word, she was life which fructifies and is eternal, for the destiny of woman is the same as the earth. Once more Maqui asked himself, "Which is better, woman or the earth?"

A sudden rush of wind shook the ears of wheat and carried away his thoughts.[7]

Woman is a "pliant tree," a "furrow," "fruit." Like the earth she has but one purpose, to reproduce. And like the earth she is merely one part of the universe man contemplates, he thinking, she one of the possible objects of his thought. It should perhaps be remembered that the audience that will respond to this imagery is in Lima and not in Rumi.

Alegría uses descriptions of sexual relations between men and women in Indian culture and between men and women from the "coast" to symbolize contrasts between the two cultures themselves. In *El mundo es ancho y ajeno,* lovemaking takes place between a boy and girl with the harvest as a backdrop: "The afternoon came with shimmering heat and the penetrating exhalation of the earth mingled with that of ripe plants. Juan was a branch and Simona a fruit, and neither was more than twenty." As the afternoon wore on the two separate themselves from the group; Juan chases Simona and they wrestle in the alfalfa. The scene is both spontaneous and morally acceptable, for this is the "real thing": "Simona's body discovered the joy of a man, and Juan, who had laid many a girl under the hedges and in the fields, felt that call of the blood which makes a man select one woman among all others."[8] One wonders what the effect would have been if Simona had been "just another girl" with whom Juan was making it. Would her healthy spontaneity then have been a little misplaced? And as for all the "others" treated so lightly by Juan—are their futures ruined because they cannot any longer offer men the gift of their virginity? But these comments are inappropriate, of course. The point Alegría is making is that Indian relations between men and women are spontaneous, healthy, and moral in comparison with the unhealthy, artificial, and decadent sexual behavior characteristic of coastal criollo culture.

The coastal lovers are Bismark Ruiz and Melba Cortez. We first come upon Bismark Ruiz fleeing from his home and family into the arms of Melba, madam of the "house of La Costeña."[9] He is being sought by Rosendo Maqui and others from Rumi to serve as lawyer for the townspeople in a case involving the status of their legal claims to the land on which they have been living. The bordello atmosphere as contrasted with the innocence and purpose of the Indians who enter it is a perfect device for contrasting the purity of the Indians with the decadence of the lawyer and, by extension, coastal culture. It is interesting that the bordello is a recurring theme in the Peruvian novels discussed in this paper. It appears to function as a sort of "men's house": relationships in the bordello are among men, not between men and women. In fact, the house of prostitution often seems to be the only place in town with any life in it, the place where men fight, exchange information, and conduct business.

In the particular scene Alegria paints, the Indians first go to the house of Bismark Ruiz and find that he is not at home. We are given the picture of the "deserted" wife and the neighbor women who support her in condemning her husband's licentiousness:

> The calvalcade stopped before the house of Bismark Ruiz. . . . A woman came out carrying a baby over her shoulder. Her deep circled eyes and drawn face showed traces of tears.
>
> "What?" she asked. "You are asking for Bismark? You come to his house to look for him? What an ideal"[10]

When the Indians look properly confused, a neighbor explains: "That man stays at La Costeña's. He's there all the time and I know the wicked creature has bewitched him. Oh, the faithless one. He almost never comes home. To leave his children like this, poor helpless babies."[11]

But the conflict of the novel does not lie here and we are not encouraged to linger over this woman whose problems are, after all, simply a normal part of the corrupt (i.e., non-Indian) culture. "They weren't all babies," Alegría informs us, as if to show us how our sympathies have been misplaced. "A tall son appeared who acted as his father's secretary . . . and offered to conduct them to his father."[12] If children can act as accomplices, it is clear that the system is to be condemned, not the individuals within it.

Melba has arrived at her position as a "fallen woman" partly out of a natural skill at it (she "enjoyed coquetting") and partly out of economic need. When the Indians led by Rosendo enter the house, Melba, "tall and fair, rather stout, with eyes shaded by long lashes and a full, red mouth" looks at the Indians "with condescending aloofness."[13]

At this moment Bismark Ruiz appears, the epitome of duplicity, criollo-style:

> "Here are my best clients," said the lawyer. "They are the villagers of Rumi, hard-working honorable men against whom an iniquitous robbery is being plotted. . . . "
>
> "Bring out beer for my clients," shouted the lawyer, and his friends smiled and even Melba Cortez smiled a little. They brought out the beer in big glasses crowned with foam. Abram and his son declined. Rosendo and Goyo Auca politely drank theirs. . . .
>
> The lawyer wore a greenish suit, heavy rings on his fingers, and across his stomach, from one vest pocket to the other, stretched a chain of gold. His eyes were bleary with drink and he reeked of brandy as though he had been soaked in it. He half closed the door as they went into the room.
>
> "It's a pity that just now . . . with this party going on. . . . Not the best moment to deal with weighty matters."[14]

In Alegría novels the good women are fecund, strong but dominated by their husbands, in touch with nature and indistinguishable from it. The good woman represents the best qualities of the Indian culture. The bad woman, representing criollo culture, is artificial, weak (Melba is always presented as dependent and clinging), and decadent. Given this use of female characters it is very difficult to see women as individuals in Alegía's novels. The most that can be extracted are generalizations about "healthy" sexual behavior that will appeal to the morality of a coastal audience. The woman should be premaritally chaste, yet capable of "knowing a man"; there is a value placed on monogamy and on the family unit in contrast to the bordello which, while "normal," is not ideal. The conflict between the good and the bad woman is a choice made by males in the plot of many novels. In Alegría, however, the choice is not an internal, psychological conflict between man's carnal nature and his moral self, rather the conflict is presented on a totally different plane as the choice between cultures. Yet in Peru the real choice is between cholification—Indian acceptance of coastal values—and *preservation* of Indian culture against the encroachments of criollo values. The third possibility, coastal acceptance of Indian culture, has never been a serious choice, and thus the analogy is not fully satisfactory.

With José Maria Arguedas the problem of female imagery is more difficult. On the one hand, Arguedas has had tremendous success in creating a form of dialogue which transmits directly an Indian world view. Like Alegría, he is deeply concerned with the implications of cultural conflict in Peru, but in contrast to Alegría his insights and writing technique dispel the feeling of being on the outside looking in. As Aldrich has said, in the past "the Indian has seemed largely 'inscrutable' because our vision has been largely external."[15] But, as in Alegría's work, his images of women are positive in the Indian context only. Arguedas does not perceive the problem of women as in any way analogous to the problem of the Indian, and female characters are again used as symbols, although in a more subtle way and with ultimately more damaging effect.

Arguedas's final novel, written in 1969 when he was contemplating suicide, alternates between chapters of fiction and notes from a personal diary of his thoughts while he is writing. The theme is the conflict between two cultures (as indicated by the title, *El zorro de arriba y el zorro de abajo*), but significantly the setting is not the sierra but a city on the coast, Chimbote, where the Indian is out of his own environment and under tremendous pressure. Arguedas successfully evokes the depressing atmosphere of Chimbote, a town that has expanded very rapidly due to the development of the fish-meal industry. It is a collection of cinder-block shacks hastily thrown up on the sand and strung along the desolate Pan-American Highway, reeking with the smell of fish meal and constantly illuminated by the red glow of the ovens, a city on the brink of hell.

We first come to know Chimbote through the "red-light district," a series of ill-built rooms very near the highway. Again, the function of the *prostibulo* is that of a men's house, the scene of fights and discussions. Rumors circulate, men are drawn together by their need to escape, and women have very little to do with what is going on. In the cheapest house, women lie on their backs with their legs spread, waiting for customers. Thus female is reduced to cunt, which gives Arguedas the opportunity to point out a play on words: the word for cunt is *zorra, zorro*—the *zorro* of the title, Chimbote, is the *zorra* of Peru, the stinking, garbage-hole *zorra* of capitalist penetration. It is interesting that the most shocking, repulsive description Arguedas can apply to Chimbote is to compare it to female genitalia and that the effect of such a description is to equate the vagina with a putrid wound. A comparable and well-known imagery is suggested by Octavio Paz's analysis of the verb *chingar:* "to injure, to lacerate, to violate. . . . The verb is masculine, active, cruel; it stings, wounds, gashes. . . . The person who suffers this action is passive, inert, and open."[16]

Within the novel the only woman who receives any attention is Jesusa, wife of an ex-miner, don Esteban, who is dying of lung disease. Jesusa, like don Esteban, is a migrant; she supports her husband and child by selling vegetables in the market. She cares for don Esteban when he is sick, and cooks for him and his black *compadre, el loco* Moncada. Moncada is the crazy man who is sane, and it is from Moncada's lips that we hear the truths about imperialism and exploitation in Chimbote.

In a scene that is repeated more than once, Arguedas writes of the relationship between Jesusa and don Esteban. Jesusa is trying to convince him to see a priest to save himself from death. However, don Esteban has his own solution: to cough up five ounces of carbon from

his lungs and thus rid himself of the disease. Jesusa has just told him that he will surely die anyway, and don Esteban tries to kick her but fails:

> His wife murmured to herself, she did not speak aloud, she moved her lips. Don Esteban knew, he understood, that when his wife spoke that way, for herself, she was speaking to him as though he were a corpse. "All the others from my town who went to the Cocalón Mine have died; you'll die that way too," she said. "Your kick is weaker than a chicken's. You are dead but you are alive, curse of God. The devil is in your body 'in all his power', and your mouth speaks, it spits carbon."

Don Esteban lies down; his chest rattles. Jesusa continues:

> "Your eyelashes are like the feet of San Jorge Volador, witch-animal, your chest is the bellows of the Devil. You don't confess! You don't want to talk to the Brother," she thought.

> "I will not speak of my filthiness with the Brother— ever!" said don Esteban with a weak and cavernous voice as though he had heard the woman's thoughts. "I'll speak with God directly."

> The woman realized that the baby was crying. It had been crying monotonously for quite a while. The few buyers who still looked for things in that corner of the market saw a small man, extremely thin, with raised shoulder blades, they saw him try to kick the woman, then lie down. . . . They observed him with particular curiosity. Those who saw the quarrel through to the end were left calm, although surprised when they saw that the body of the man stretched out on the ground did not seem so small as it had when he was standing. "There are men like that one," said one, "made up of all there is that is human. Small, but with the outline of a man."[17]

On one level don Esteban is becoming "more human" by rejecting Jesusa—he is rejecting both religion and fatalism by rejecting her. But here too the woman is symbolic, one side of a philosophical conflict that occurs within *male* consciousness. By trying to kick his wife, then withdrawing to his own world, don Esteban is credited with becoming more *human* (!)—"Small, *pero con traza de hombre.*"

The most interesting insights into Arguedas's views of women come not from the novel itself but from the accompanying diaries. Women are mentioned only briefly, but significantly, among discussions of Arguedas's attempt to climb out of his emotional abyss through writing, his disgust at the literary artifices of writers like Carlos Fuentes and Julio Cortázar, his admiration for the Brazilian, Guimarães Rosa, and his search for life: *"Muchas veces he conseguido jugar con los pueblos de los perros como perro con perro. Y asi la vida es más vida para uno"* ("Many times I have played with the dogs in the towns, dog to dog. And thus is life made richer for one").[18] Yet there is always the thought of suicide, the dream of the revolver. He begins the book by telling us that the desire to kill himself

has occurred to him many times, and that once he was brought back to the zest of life by contact with a woman:

> In April of 1966, a little more than two years ago, I tried to kill myself. In May of 1944 a psychological illness I contracted in childhood came to a head and I was unable to write for almost five years. A meeting with a plump *zamba,* young, a prostitute, returned me to what the doctors call *"tono de vida."* The meeting with that happy woman was the subtle touch, very complex, that my body and soul needed to restore the broken link with the world. When this link became intense I was able to transmit to words the feeling of things. From that moment I have lived, with interruptions, somewhat mutilated.[19]

It is significant that a prostitute, with no claims on him, could restore Arguedas to health. His relationship to his wife appears much more complicated and more ambivalent, which may affect the way in which women are represented in his urban novel.

Arguedas refers to his wife (his second) twice in the diaries, once to say that he feels fortunate to be loved by good people, among them his wife, and that for her he has the greatest respect. The second time he is in Arequipa, trying to write:

> I spent twelve days in Arequipa. There I wrote fifteen pages, the last ones of chapter three. For the first time I lived in a state of happy integration with my wife. For the first time I did not feel afraid of a loved woman, rather I felt a happiness that was only frightening at times.[20]

Six months later, Arguedas shot himself. He left the following note:

> I am choosing this day because it won't interfere with the university schedule. I believe that the term has closed. It is possible that my friends and the authorities will lose Saturday and Sunday, but it is their time and not that of the U. J.M.A.

Mario Vargas Llosa is representative of a new departure in Peruvian literature, the emergence of the urban novelist. In the work of Vargas Llosa, as in the short stories of Enrique Congrains Martin or Sebastián Salazar Bondy, the city becomes the focal point and in a sense the protagonist, as the jungle or nature has been the protagonist of so many Latin American novels. The "urban" novel goes beyond the limitations of the "local color" or "social protest" novel to touch more universal concerns, to treat, as Aldrich describes it, "moral and spiritual problems common to modern man." He continues:

> The rejection or loss of tradition and the frantic quest for new values on the Peruvian scene are understood to be a reflection of modern civilization. Likewise, the confusion, misery and desperation which dominate contemporary Peruvian society are seen as but one example of a complex moral and spiritual bankruptcy that is universal.[21]

In addition, as Jean Franco has noted, the function of the modern Latin American novel has changed. In the social protest novel, the solution to the oppression of the Indians lies in the possibility of a mass uprising which will initiate an era of revolution and eventually bring social justice. "In the modern novel, revolution is no longer seen as a panacea; at best it is only an essential first step. The real battle, it is suggested, is in the human mind and particularly within the minds of the upper and middle classes, whose failure to construct a reasonable society is one of the tragedies of Latin America."[22]

In *La casa verde* (1965) Vargas Llosa uses a technique of constantly changed time sequences to suggest the complexity and interdependence of human lives and human actions. The Green House is a brothel, but also suggests the jungle, an escape and a prison. Within these constraints, Vargas Llosa's characters, men and women, become less important than the action itself, less real than the situations they are caught in. In a sense they are victims of their expectations of one another, sets of interacting stereotypes. The complexity of time sequences and interdependencies avoids resolution and blurs moral judgment about individuals; it leaves the reader feeling that society itself must be condemned. One of the main characters, a Sergeant from Piura, decides to marry an Indian girl recently let out of a convent school for unlocking a gate and letting the other children escape. Bonifacia, the Indian girl, has been introduced to us in the convent as the "innocent" who reveals the hypocrisy of the nuns in her eager effort to be "good" in their terms. Outside the convent she is subject to a different set of conventions into which she is more readily drawn. When the Sergeant decides to propose, it sets off a series of reactions over which no one has control:

> And when he got back they would be married, sweety, and his voice broke and he began to laugh like an idiot, while Lalita shouted and burst out onto the terrace, resplendent, her arms open, and Bonifacia went to meet her and they embraced. Nieves the pilot shook hands with the Sergeant whose voice was breaking with emotion. Don Adrián, he had gotten all shaken up: he wanted them to stand up with them, of course. She could see, Señorita Lalita, he'd fallen into her trap, and that was that, and Lalita had known from the beginning that the Sergeant was a proper Christian, he should let her embrace him. . . . Bonifacia, confused, was hugging the Sergeant, Lalita, she kissed the pilot's hand, she picked up the children and held them in the air, and they would be very glad to stand up with them, Sergeant, he should stay for dinner tonight. Her green eyes were sparkling, and Lalita they would build their house right here next door, they became sad, they would help them, they became happy, and the Sergeant she would have to take very good care of her, Ma'am, he didn't want her to see anybody while he was away on the trip, and Lalita of course, she wouldn't even let her out of the door, they'd tie her up.[23]

What emerges in Vargas Llosa's writing is a set of stereotypes or expected behavior patterns, not characters. We never see what is happening inside people's heads; we never know what Bonifacia *thinks* about the nuns or about the Sergeant. Instead we see Bonifacia in certain roles for which we can fill in any missing details from our own experience. Bonifacia is the "innocent," Lalita the "mother," and the Sergeant is a *"macho"* type. But there is a twist: in *La casa verde* the stereotypes which apply to each character are often made to alternate with their opposites, leaving the reader in doubt as to which qualities to attribute to a single individual. What is more confusing is that opposing stereotypes of necessity evoke opposing judgments by the reader which further contribute to the tension the novel creates.

Ironically, the stereotypes are reinforced in this process as it is not the evaluation of the stereotyped behavior itself that is called into question, but the absence of consistency in behavior. Thus the reader can never quite decide about Lalita, the good mother type who has many children by serial husbands, each of whom finds her attractive and satisfying. The exception is her first husband, a leper escaping from the law, who is fleeing on a raft through most of the novel; he always describes Lalita as a "dirty whore"—split images that cannot be made to converge.

In the case of Bonifacia we have the child/woman of the convent who becomes a prostitute in the Green House in Piura, after her Sergeant-husband is sent off to jail for his involvement in a bar killing. The day comes, of course, when the Sergeant (Lituma) returns home and finds his wife (Wildflower) in the brothel:

> "Lituma got in this afternoon," Josefino said, as if he were giving an order, "He's downstairs, with the Leon's."
>
> A quick shudder passed through Wildflower's body, her hands were motionless, stuck between the bottonholes. But she did not turn or speak.[24]

She dresses, forces her wide feet into the high heels that don't fit, and follows Josefino downstairs. Lituma is at the bar: "Good to see you, sweety, and a grimace came over his whole face, his small eyes showed unbearable uneasiness now, good to see you, Lituma, Wildflower said. . . . 'This is meeting night, old man,' Lituma said. 'Now you can see how I've behaved myself'." Later Lituma and his cousins beat the shit out of Josefino and return to the Green House. Wildflower is being asked to dance by a fat man as the madam (Chunga) looks on:

> "What's wrong with this one, Chunga?" the fat man asked, panting.
>
> "What's wrong with you?" Chunga said. "They're inviting you to dance, don't be rude. Why don't you accept the gentleman's invitation?"
>
> But Wildflower was still struggling.

> "Lituma, tell him to let go of me."
>
> "Don't let go of her, friend," Lituma said. "And you do your duty, whore."[25]

Child-prophet in the jungle, whore in the city, and for Lituma a similar shift from nice guy-victim in the jungle to oppressor-victim in Piura on the coast. The city is unhealthy, and the jungle is better if only by comparison. A faint return to a familiar theme. But the Sergeant could never have stayed in the jungle. He missed the lights, the people, the action.

Traditions break down and conventional behavior patterns no longer hold people and no longer protect them. They seem part of a stabler, simpler past. Bonifacia/Wildflower, child/whore: when the dichotomies collapse and individuals must live out conflicting roles, it is very costly in human terms. In *La casa verde* the old stereotypes are rotting but the new forms of social relationships are inhuman and disgusting. Yet it seems that to debate the advantages of the past is pointless, for there is no going back.

By beginning with Alegria and the social protest novel I have ignored earlier trends in Peruvian literature. Before the social protest novel became central there was a "decadent" phase in Peruvian writing exemplified by Clemente Palma's *Cuentos malévolos*.[26] In the decadent novel, "boredom is the bane of the hero's existence, his constant companion, goading him into perversion and sadism; but since perversion and sadism, once experienced, lose their savor, he falls prey again to ennui."[27] *La Rifa*, a novella by Katia Saks, is in part a return to the style of the decadents and in part a modern commentary on the existential alternatives open to women. The heroine is an upper-class *Limeña;* the scene is a peculiarly truncated Lima—the Lima of the Karamanduke restaurant, a villa at Ancón, the old suburb of Chorrillos. It is a Lima that seems unchanging and unchangeable, almost frozen in modern time, shimmering under the relentless brightness of the summer sun.

The theme is a triangle trying fairly ineffectually to become a quadrangle. Liliana, her husband Julyan, and her cousin Maya are the triangle, maintained by a love between Julyan and Maya that is compelling, often cruel, and pointless. Pablo is Liliana's lover, peripheral. The stifling ennui is broken by sex, violence, and eventually death. Its decadence lies in Liliana's masochism from which she is unable to break free and her role as accomplice to Julyan and Maya: she is the permanent spectator to the pain they inflict on one another. Maya, witch/child, sensuous, a spirit, dances before another man. Julyan decides to punish her for her boldness, for arousing another man in his presence. Liliana is witness:

> She shrank away, suddenly on guard, and eyed him with mistrust. But the sense of defiance prevailed; she shrugged and continued to look at him with cold, impertinent eyes. He leaned over her, still smiling. He grasped her long shocks of hair and twisted them into a thick luxurious rope

that he wound around her throat. She gasped. Her hands caught his wrists as she strained to free herself.

"Wicked little creature," Julyan said sweetly. "Wicked little bitch, isn't she, Liliana?"

"Please," I said.

"A bitch," he said, "among bitches."

Maya was struggling to push him away and free herself. She jerked her head from side to side in a violent effort to escape. I thought, the old instinct. She fought him with eyes wide open and teeth clenched. . . . He tightened the knot around her neck so brutally that she gasped for breath, and her hands flew to her sides, clutching the air.

She felt his urgency. His will. Hers was no longer existent. . . .

"Julyan," I cried, "she's suffering."

"Nonsense," he said placidly. "She needs someone to initiate her into the art of suffering."

"Her head!" I cried.

"Yes," he mused, "a rare, inscrutable head, isn't it?"

"Enough!"

I turned my head and saw his eyes. They were fixed upon her, bold, transparent, untroubled. I saw his face, a face that could be as rigidly ascetic as it could be charming, voluptuous. A naked face. Deeply stirring. I dropped my eyes.

There was silence and the glare of dawn. I lay back on the bed, quite still, my arms and legs stretched out on the white sheet. I thought, a stone effigy, alone, forgotten, eternal.[28]

Yet the "decadence" of Katia Saks is a modern decadence, arising out of the rigor mortis of the old traditions, the absurdity of the old social controls. Tradition is represented by Liliana's mother; Liliana's response is not to fight it but to withdraw:

"I don't understand why you should insist upon exposing me to her society."

"Peruvian etiquette," I said. "She is our cousin, is she not?"

"It would not be the first time we excluded from our society a member of our own family. Her mother, as you will remember, was denied permission to visit the family."

I burst out laughing.

"Mother," I said, "you are an exemplary woman."

"I have a certain line of conduct," Mother said dryly, "and I adhere to it.

I simply cannot justify your tolerance. You behave toward her as though you were her—her accomplice."

A chill, A silence. A false peace. A false freedom. The loop of a rope. . . .

"What have I done to make this happen to me? That I should live to witness the moral disintegration of my own child, my own flesh and blood. What have I done to be punished so mercilessly? Again and again. First your father. Now you. Both of you. It's wicked. There's no pride left in this house. No dignity. God knows I have always conducted myself with honor and humility. Your father betrayed the high regard he enjoyed in this house. I endured. You were left to me. I bestowed upon you the dignity of our name. You have violated it."

"That makes me very wanton, doesn't it?" I said, and I smiled at Mother. . . .

"I pray that the good Lord will have mercy on your soul."

"Mother," I said, "the good Lord and I make no demands upon each other."

"It will not be long before I go," Mother said. "When I go your sins will be your own."

I looked at her eyes, her mouth. Her mouth was a thin, rigid line. I rested my forehead against the edge of the bathtub. The water was gray. Like ashes.[29]

It is interesting that Katia Saks's novel, in contrast to those of the male novelists, is devoted exclusively to a concern about the nature and quality of the relations between men and women. The conflict in *La Rifa* is provided by Liliana's attempt to break through the traditional role alternatives; ironically, Pablo, her lover, offers her the least freedom from conventional expectations. Liliana has our sympathy for she has all the valued "modern" qualities: an analytical bent, detachment, tolerance. But in the end her sense of self is too weak, based as it is on the unlikely combination of confidence derived from her class position and a willingness to admit her sexual needs. It is hardly a strong enough foundation for the development of a new identity. She is trapped, and in the end she succumbs:

[Julyan] rose with a listless air. He walked away from the bed and began to undress with a dull look in his eyes and a distraught expression on his face, as though he were unable to shake off the fresh anxieties, the seed-bearing thoughts. I saw his dim, hesitant silhouette, the purity of his nakedness, his face, his wide-staring eyes.

I drew a deep breath and closed my eyes. Julyan crossed the room with his slow silent stride. He leaned over me and pressed me to him and kissed me lightly on the lips. A sudden thrill ran up my body, and I leaned against the narrow brass bed, breathless, dazzled, lost. . . .

We lay outstretched on the narrow brass bed, inert, oppressed, our bodies barely touching.[30]

### LITERARY ARCHETYPES AS ROLES: *Cien años de soledad*

The relative absence of female characters in Peruvian literature is itself an interesting commentary on the position of women in Peruvian society. However, it makes it very difficult to pursue the goal of this paper which is to compare literary images with some psychological and sociological generalizations about Latin American women, with the clichés we all recognize. In comparing Alegria and Arguedas to Vargas Llosa, it is possible to make the distinction between woman as symbol (e.g., of nature or of Indian culture) and woman as stereotype or archetype (woman behaving according to a recurring, predictable pattern of rules). In what follows I use the novel of Gabriel Garcia Márquez to develop three archetypes which I believe represent three alternative roles available to women within the "transitional" society of Latin America. *Cien años de soledad* is particularly suited to this purpose, first because it is an attempt to portray the uniqueness and variety of Latin American social experience as a distinct totality, as a culture, and second because, in contrast to Vargas Llosa, Garcia Márquez develops his male and female characters as positive "ideal types," rather than as the carriers of advanced social deterioration. In the literary sense, the use of archetypes is quite consistent with the epic form of the novel: as in the *Chanson de Roland,* characters represent values or qualities in conflict among themselves. Real characters could only result from having conflict occur *within* individuals, a distinction which separates most modern Western writing from the tradition of the epic. On the level of sociological interpretation, the use of archetypes and the relevance of the epic form in the modern Latin American novel may be due to the persistence of traditional patterns of social relations in conditions of political and economic "modernization."[31]

The three archetypes I develop here are the roles of Mother, Witch, and Wife/Concubine. In dealing with the first two, I would like to stress the contrast between these roles and literary role images in North American writing and to discuss the implications of the availability of these roles for women in Latin America in terms of the prospects for a feminist movement there. The mutual dependence of the roles of wife and concubine (the opposite of the common view that they are mutually hostile) is relevant to our interpretation of the "double standard" and our concept of *machismo.*

*Woman as Mother.* It is perhaps not surprising that sociologists and political scientists raised in a culture with a Judeo-Protestant heritage, one which emphasizes patriarchal authority, bars women from certain religious roles, and has a male image of God, should fail to grasp the breadth of female influence and power in a society in which the Virgin is an important religious figure and where male resentment (e.g., Arguedas) of the link between women and religion is still an important literary theme. From the imagery in *Cien años de soledad* it is possible to describe certain patterns of female dominance which are not commonly available in North American culture. On the whole, women in *Cien años de soledad* represent the forces of stability as against the male characters who are always disrupting society by their futile military exploits, their misguided scientific adventures, and their total lack of common sense. The male principle of technology, which Lionel Trilling has characterized as "hard, resistant, unformed and unpleasant,"[32] has not yet taken over in Latin America, as it has in so many other parts of the West, and Úrsula, the archetypical Mother of the novel, can still scoff at the scientific experiments of her husband as "impractical." Úrsula is the strongest, the only positive force in the novel. It is she who tries to keep the family together, who concerns herself about the daily needs such as a roof over their heads and food to eat, who fights off the encroachments of the ants and the cobwebs, and who tries to regulate social/sexual relations to avoid the event that will signify the end of the family line: the birth of a child with the tail of a pig.

Úrsula's strength is the force of her will: shortly after he establishes the town of Macondo, her husband, José Arcadio Buendía, decides that it is time to leave again.

> "We will not leave," [Úrsula] said. "We will stay here, because we have had a son here."
>
> "We have still not had a death," he said. "A person does not belong to a place until there is someone dead under the ground."
>
> Úrsula replied with a soft firmness:
>
> "If I have to die for the rest of you to stay here, I will die."
>
> José Arcadio Buendia had not thought that his wife's will was so firm. He tried to seduce her with the charm of his fantasy, with the promise of a prodigious world where all one had to do was sprinkle some magic liquid on the ground and the plants would bear fruit whenever a man wished, and where all manner of instruments against pain were sold at bargain prices. But Úrsula was insensitive to his clairvoyance.
>
> "Instead of going around thinking about your crazy inventions, you should be worrying about your sons," she replied. "Look at the state they're in, running wild just like donkeys."
>
> José Arcadio Buendia took his wife's words literally. He looked out the window and saw his barefoot children in the sunny garden and he had the impression that only at that instant had they begun to exist, conceived by Úrsula's spell. Something occurred inside of him then, something mysterious and definitive that uprooted him from his own time and carried him adrift through an unexplored region of his memory. While Úrsula continued sweeping the house, which was safe now from being abandoned, he stood there with an absorbed look, contemplating the children until his

eyes became moist and he dried them with the back of his hand, exhaling a deep sigh of resignation.

"All right," he said. "Tell them to come help me take the things out of the boxes."[33]

It would be possible to analyze the conversation between Úrsula and her husband at some length, to point out some of the interesting implications of the children coming to exist "by Úrsula's spell" and José Arcadio's "deep sigh of resignation." But for the sake of brevity let us concentrate on the importance of the family as an institution in Latin American society and the meaning of the phrase heard so often there, "woman rules in the home."

The prevalence of the extended family and of *compadrazgo*, the relative lack of geographical mobility, and the survival of the family as an important instrument of social regulation over a fairly broad range of activities give women who dominate their families a considerable degree of power and influence. The figure of the "matriarch" is a common one in Latin America. One sociologist has explained the prevalence of strong mother-figures as a carry-over from the old Spanish concept of "saint-mother" who is the "focal personality around whom all members of the family group themselves, tied by spiritual and sentimental bonds."[34] The "saint-mother" preserves the family as a strong, united institution; "she keeps alive traditions, preserves memories dear to the heart, encourages everything that strengthens family unity, rejects everything that might threaten to weaken it. She is, as it were, the family priestess, who watches over the life of its members from cradle to grave."[35] Not the least of the personal relations a mother can rely upon is that between herself and her sons. Thus Úrsula is the only person who can intervene against the arbitrary will of her son, Colonel Aureliano Buendía; she is the only one, he realizes, who "penetrates his misery." In *La Rifa*, Liliana no longer respects her mother's value system, but she still respects her mother's right to demand a degree of external conformity.

A significant factor in judging female influence is the scope and legitimacy of social sanctions emanating from the family itself, affecting prestige, marriage partners, inheritance, "acceptable" behavior, even political influence. Don Apolinar Moscote, the "magistrate sent by the government" to rule in Macondo, remains utterly powerless until his family is socially accepted by the Buendías.

Contrast the Latin American family with the institution which carries the same name in North America. There the woman who "rules the home" rules four walls, some household appliances, and two or three small children. She lacks access to the "male sphere" which the extended family and the matriarchal role make available to the Latin American woman. She cannot rely on the effectiveness of social sanctions to control behavior outside of the immediate nuclear family. In fact, I would argue that it is the severe decline in the prestige, size, and function of the family in the United States which has brought about the deep frustration with the female role which is the basis of modern feminism. I do not mean the decline of the family as an institution of "fulfillment" in the individual, psychological sense in which the term is used. I refer to the decline of the family as a source of power and influence for women. In the name of a false egalitarianism (false because it has never been achieved), the North American woman has been deprived of self-respect and the respect of others through the severe limitation of her role. Under the banner of the feminine mystique she has taken over the duties of a full-time maid, and it has been assumed that, in spite of her education, she has the intellectual capacities of a maid as well. She cannot rely on the role differentiation which is so obvious in Latin American society, which allows the woman (particularly the upper-class woman who can presumably afford household help) to maintain her image as a person of culture and of valid experience, to acquire wisdom and dignity with age (instead of obsolescence), and even to combine a career with marriage, an opportunity which is ironically much less available to her North American counterpart.

Insofar as the North American feminist movement is based on frustration with female powerlessness on the personal as well as the political level, and I think the obvious desire of women to break into the "male" world is clear evidence of this kind of frustration, then the feminist movement will not have the same appeal in Latin America nor can it expect "consciousness" on the part of Latin American women. This is not to say that accusations of "male chauvinism" are irrelevant to the dynamics of male-female relations in the Latin context: like the tradition of *machismo* it serves to increase the opportunities for "emotional blackmail" of males by females (see Wife/Concubine below). It is to say, however, that feminism will not be a healthy transplant. A whole generation of North American women have become convinced of their powerlessness relative to males and have moved to destroy the role differentiation they perceive as its cause. The Latin American woman correctly perceives role differentiation as the key to her power and influence. Even the notions of the "separateness" and "mystery" of women, which are viewed in the North American context as male propaganda chiefly used to discriminate against women, are seen in the Latin American context as images to be enhanced, not destroyed.

*Woman as Witch.* The image of the female as mysterious, unfathomable, somehow beyond men's rules, is the second significant archetype in Latin American literature. Because of man's mysterious and often frightening relationship with elements in his environment (e.g., the "jungle" or death), it is a pattern that often degenerates into a symbol: woman is the unknown personified. Yet it can be a true character type and is a recurring one, even in the Peruvian novel. Bonifacia and Maya are both "mysterious" in this sense; in Alegría's *El mundo es ancho y ajeno* there is the female figure of the *curandera*, literally a witch who possesses certain kinds of magic powers. While the role of *curandera* has survived in the urban areas,[36] it appears to be a lower-class phenomenon. The intellectual particularly is too immersed in the Western view of "objective" reality[37] to take witchcraft seriously. What remains is the emphasis on female as "other" and/or the female who is living outside the ordinary social role expectations.

In *Cien años de soledad* a number of women have witchlike characteristics, among them Rebeca who eats earth and whitewash and has tremendous silent energy; she carries her parents' bones with her in a bag. The peculiar timelessness of the novel, and much of its wonder, comes from the powerful female images that García Márquez creates. His most extreme creation in this archetype is Remedios the Beauty, a ravishing simpleton. Like Bonifacia, she exposes the absurdity of human conventions:

> She was becalmed in a magnificent adolescence, more and more impenetrable to formality, more and more indifferent to malice and suspicion, happy in her own world of simple realities. She did not understand why women complicated their lives with corsets and petticoats, so she sewed herself a coarse cassock that she simply put over her and without further difficulties solved the problem of dress, without taking away the feeling of being naked, which according to her lights was the only decent way to be when at home. They bothered her so much to cut the rain of hair that already reached to her thighs and to make rolls with combs and braids with red ribbons that she simply shaved her head and used the hair to make wigs for the saints. The startling thing about her simplifying instinct was that the more she did away with fashion . . . the more disturbing her incredible beauty became and the more provocative she became to men.[38]

A man once fell through the roof tiles watching Remedios the Beauty take a bath; she had a subtle, lingering odor that followed him to the grave. The end García Márquez provides for her is suitably incredible:

> Remedios the Beauty stayed [in the family], wandering through the desert of solitude, bearing no cross on her back, maturing in her dreams without nightmares, her interminable baths, her unscheduled meals, her deep and prolonged silences that had no memory until one afternoon in March, when Fernanda wanted to fold her brabant sheets in the garden and asked the women in the house for help. She had just begun when she noticed that Remedios the Beauty was covered all over with an intense paleness.
>
> "Don't you feel well?" she asked her.
>
> Remedios the Beauty, who was clutching the sheet by the other end, gave a pitying smile.
>
> "Quite the opposite," she said. "I never felt better."
>
> She had just finished saying it when Fernanda felt a delicate wind of light pull the sheets out of her hands . . . and she tried to grasp the sheet so that she would not fall down at the instant in which

> Remedios the Beauty began to rise. Úrsula, almost blind at the time, was the only person who was sufficiently calm to identify the nature of that wind and she left the sheets to the mercy of the light as she watched Remedios the Beauty waving goodbye in the midst of the flapping sheets that rose up with her, abandoning her environment of beetles and dahlias and passing through the air with her as four o'clock in the afternoon came to an end, and they were lost forever with her in the upper atmosphere where not even the highest flying birds of memory could reach her.[39]

There is another more sinister dimension to the stereotype of the "mysterious" woman, of the type who is unable to so fully leave the world of things, of social conventions, of the envy of men who may try to destroy her. A fascinating portrayal of this kind of woman is La Maga,[40] a female character in Julio Cortázar's *Rayuela*. *Rayuela*, if read from chapter 1, introduces the relationship of La Maga and Oliveira, meeting each other "by chance" in Paris: "We did not go around looking for one another, but we knew that we would meet just the same. . . . La Maga was fascinated with the strange mix-ups she had become involved in because of the breakdown of the laws governing her life. She was one of those people who could make a bridge collapse by simply walking on it, or who could sobbingly remember having seen in a shop window the lottery ticket which had just won five million."[41]

Oliveira describes himself as a "searcher": "It was about this time that I realized that searching was my symbol, the emblem of those who go out at night with nothing in mind, the motives of a destroyer of compasses."[42] La Maga is the very opposite of a compass, but she will be destroyed just the same. She is out of logic, out of time: "It didn't take me long to understand that you didn't discuss reality with La Maga. Praise of disorder would have terrified her as much as criticism of it." And, with La Maga talking, "What do you call the past? As far as I'm concerned, everything happened yesterday, last night, no earlier."[43] Their relationship is a "play," one with frightening implications for male-female relationships.

> Oliveira felt that La Maga wanted death from him, something in her which was not her awakened self, a dark form demanding annihilation, the slow wound which on its back breaks the stars at night and gives space back to questions and terrors. Only at that time, off center like a mythical matador for whom killing is returning the bull to the sea and the sea to the heavens, he bothered La Maga in a long night which they did not speak about much later. He turned her into a Pasiphaë, he bent her over and used her as if she were a young boy, he knew her and demanded the slavishness of the most abject whore, he magnified her into a constellation, he held her in his arms smelling of blood, he made her drink the semen which ran into her mouth like a challenge to the Logos, he sucked out the shadow from her womb and her rump and raised himself to her face to anoint her with herself in that ultimate work of knowledge which only a man can give to a woman. . . .

Later on Oliveira began to worry that she would think herself jaded, that their play would move on to sacrifice. Above all he feared that most subtle form of gratitude which turns itself into doglike love. He did not want freedom, the only suit that fit La Maga, to be lost in any strong femininity. He didn't have to worry. . . .

Since he did not love her, since desire would stop (because he did not love, desire would stop), he would have to avoid like the devil any kind of sacred ritualizing of their play. For days, for weeks, for some months, every hotel room, every square, every position of love and every dawn in a marketplace café; a savage circus, a subtle operation, and a rational balance. That's how it came to be known that La Maga was really waiting for Horacio to kill her and that hers would be a phoenix death, entry into the council of philosophers, that is to say, the discussions of the Serpent Club. La Maga wanted to learn, she wanted to be ed-you-kay-ted. Horacio was the exalted, the chosen one, the one to fulfill the role of purifying priest.[44]

La Maga wishes to be destroyed and Oliveira, it would seem, is only doing his duty. Only "for days, for weeks, for some months" it is a slow death, an eternal put-down.

As with Oliveira, so with Julyan. The mysterious, the nonrational in women is both desirable and deserving of punishment. As Octavio Paz has written:

> Woman is a living symbol of the strangeness of the universe and its radical heterogeneity. As such, does she hide life within herself, or death? What does she think? Or does she think? Does she truly have feelings? Is she the same as we are? *Sadism begins as a revenge against female hermeticism or as a desperate attempt to obtain a response from a body we fear is insensible.*[45]

It is possible for women to escape the conventional role expectations in Latin American society as the prevalence and variety of the female as "witch" reveals. But unless relationships with males are avoided altogether, the price is punishment and even death.

*Woman as Wife/Concubine.* Georgie Anne Geyer has written of *machismo* that it implies a fairly rigid set of behavioral rules in which males and females both have a stake: "It is probably true that many women preferred and today prefer the ordered, stable life of Latin society in which the family is sacrosanct and in dissolvable and where they know they will always be the respected, virginal wives and mothers, no matter what other women their husbands enjoy."[46] The truth of this statement lies less in the assumption of stability in family life and more in the insight it gives into the self-image of the woman in the family: women retain respect as wives and mothers in part from their ability to maintain their *virginal* image, and *machismo* is the mechanism by which this is accomplished. Without *machismo* the wife could not employ the emotional leverage on her husband and sons which is a result of her "moral superiority." Without the image

(and reality) of the concubine, there would be no measure of sin against which the wife could contrast her purity and retain her traditional influence.

*Cien años de soledad* provides one of the clearest descriptions of the archetype in the character of Fernanda, the very beautiful, quite socially proper wife of Aureliano Segundo; a woman who uses a gilded chamberpot. Fernanda came to Macondo from "the highlands" to marry Aureliano; she views herself as the martyred carrier of the traditions of her family and class in this town in the sticks. To maintain her resolve and self-righteousness she attacks her husband's infidelity:

> She had the right to expect a little more consideration from her husband because, for better or for worse, he was her consecrated spouse, her helpmate, her *legal despoiler,* who took it upon himself of his own free and sovereign will the grave responsibility of taking her away from her paternal home, where she never wanted or suffered from anything, and where she wove funeral wreaths as a pasttime, since her godfather had sent a letter with his signature and the stamp of his ring on the sealing wax simply to say that the hands of his goddaughter were not meant for tasks of this world except to play the clavichord, and nevertheless her insane husband had taken her from her home with all manner of admonitions and warnings and had brought her to that frying pan of hell where a person could not breathe because of the heat, and before she had completed her Pentecostal fast he had gone off with his wandering trunks and his wastrel's accordion to loaf in adultery with a wretch of whom it was only enough to see her behind, well, that's been said, to see her wiggle her mare's behind in order to guess that she was a, that she was a, just the opposite of her, who was a lady in a palace or a pigsty, at the table or in bed, a lady of breeding, God-fearing, obeying His laws and submissive to His wishes, and *with whom he could not perform,* naturally, the acrobatics and trampish antics that he did with the other one.[47]

Lest this seem an exaggerated image of the "Wife," let us go back to the Western bourgeois novel and the so-called "Victorian" view of women in our own culture. Leslie Fiedler, in his *Love and Death in the American Novel*, describes the female heroines of the bourgeois novel as "feminist," a term he uses in a very special sense to describe female characters that are, for the first time since the Greek plays perhaps, as strong as their male competitors. The novel he uses as an illustration is Samuel Richardson's *Clarissa*, written in the mid-eighteenth century. The standard theme of novels is seduction, and Lovelace, Clarissa's aristocratic, articulate suitor, is compared to Don Juan:

> Don Juan . . . is essentially the impenitent; he can be damned but not persuaded, punished but not defeated. . . . Don Juan is unequivocally condemned, at least in the conscious judgments of the playwrights who evoke him; but he is the sole

hero of the dramas through which he moves, and becomes easily . . . the sympathetic rebel loved by the Romantics. Lovelace, on the other hand, though equally courageous, equally irresistible in love, meets an opponent who is stronger than God— stronger, that is, than any religious scruple the seventeenth century had been able to set in the way of the principle of sexual conquest. The women who surround Don Juan . . . do not add up to one single Clarissa, a *female force equal and opposite to the male force.*[48]

Against a force like Clarissa, the universal lover is transformed into the "monogamous Seducer" which "leads finally to submission to the lady and repentance before her, if not before God in whose name she speaks." Yet, this "feminist" principle rests on female chastity, a quality that has been dealt a strong blow in the West by the Freudian revolution: now orgasm is every woman's sacred duty. In Latin America, however, the persistence of *machismo* allows the bourgeois "feminist" principle to survive; it is significant that the severing of the tie between femininity and chastity has elsewhere coincided with a real decline in female prestige and power, a decline concealed by the myth of female equality.

Of course, as Katia Saks's novel indicates, Latin American women have not been immune to the Freudian "disease." Another Latin American writer, Carlos Fuentes, has treated the conflict between the social power of chastity and the post-Freudian awareness of human sexual drives as a literary theme. In two of his novels there are major female characters who are caught between their sexual desires and their desire to control men. Catalina, "bought" wife of Artemio Cruz (in *La muerte de Artemio Cruz,* 1964) struggles to achieve complete self-control, to deny her husband by denying herself:

> I won't tell you: at night you conquer me, but I defeat you during the day. . . .
>
> Why can't I accept it without feeling wrong, without reserve? I want it to be proof that he can't resist my body, but I take it as only proof that I have overcome him, that I can evoke love from him every night and freely deprecate it the next day with my coldness and distance. Why can't I decide? Why do I have to decide?[49]

And there is doña Asunción, lying beside her dull and pompous husband, touching her own body, secretly attracted to her young nephew, in *Las buenas consciencias* (1961): "[N]othing must hint at her secret desires; they must remain so secret that she does not know them herself, covered, in the silence of dreams, by vague imagination and over that a black hood of suppression."[50]

In spite of the conflict, however, both doña Asunción and Catalina achieve something tangible for their self-denial: legitimate control over certain aspects of their social milieu, the reinforcement of social traditions which they accept. Contrast with this gain the lot of the concubine who is exploited by the wife and by the husband, as well, who has no security, not even the security of raising legitimate children. The treatment of prostitution in the novels we have discussed seems simplistic: in Vargas Llosa's novel, for example, Bonifacia is considered to be an economic and spiritual victim, an inevitable casualty, lacking in will. In *Cien años de soledad* there are two concubine figures, both of which are secure in their external sexual power over men, a power that in the real world, however, declines drastically with age.

Thus it is significant to find in Fuentes's *Artemio Cruz* a description of the frustrations of a kept woman that sounds almost like something out of a women's liberation journal. The woman is Lilia, Artemio's long-term companion, a woman who has superseded his own wife as his hostess, a woman who at one time was a stylish consumer good for Artemio. Lilia is childless, functionless, and climbing the walls:

> Was it necessary for her to interrupt his meditation? Lilia's heels clicking indolently. Her unpainted fingernails scratching the salon door. Her grease-plastered face. She had come to inquire whether her rose dress would be appropriate for tonight? She didn't want to wear the wrong thing, like last year, and provoke his irritation and anger. Ah, he was already drinking! Why not invite her to join him? She was getting damn tired of the way he mistrusted her, keeping the bar locked. . . . Was she bored then? As if he didn't know! She almost wished she were old and ugly so he would throw her out once and for all and let her live as she wanted to. He wasn't stopping her? And then where would she have such luxury, this big house, his money? Plenty of money. almost too much luxury, and no happiness at all, no fun, not even free to have a little drink, if you please, damn it. Well: of course she loved him very much. Hadn't she said it a thousand times?[51]

And later, at the party, after a few drinks:

> He went toward her with his difficult, faltering pace. With every step he took her voice fluted higher. "I'm sick of watching TV all day, little old manny-man! I already know all those cowboy stories. Bang-bang-bang! The marshal of Arizona, camp of redskins. Bang-bang! I dream about their damn voices, old man! Have a Pepsi . . . and that's all, old man. Security with comfort. Policies . . ."
>
> His arthritic hand struck her and the dyed curls fell over her eyes.[52]

Economic dependence, boredom, paternalism backed with the threat of physical force. Dyed curls and greased face. It sounds quite familiar, and yet there is little prospect for an alliance even here. The concubine owes her existence to one principle which the North American woman rejects: the bourgeois principle of power through chastity where the "wife" could not exist without the "concubine" and the concubine has influence in part due to the wife's self-control. Within the Latin American context, the availability of some strong female images and viable alternative roles is a sign of the continued health of the system. On the other hand, it is equally clear that the Latin American model of male-female relations offers no solutions to the North American feminist who rejects not only the principle of chastity as a means to power, but also the unchallenged principle of role differentiation between males and females on which the Latin American system rests.[53]

NOTES

[1] Earl M. Aldrich, Jr., *The Modern Short Story in Peru* (Madison: University of Wisconsin Press, 1966), pp. 114-15.

[2] Ciro Alegría, *The Golden Serpent* (New York: Signet, 1963), p. 8 and p. 22. English translations were used for quotations where available.

[3] Ibid., p. 23.

[4] Ibid., p. 40.

[5] Ibid., p. 41.

[6] Ciro Alegría, *Broad and Alien Is the World* (New York: Farrar & Rinehart, 1941), p. 5.

[7] Ibid., pp. 39-40.

[8] Ibid., p. 130.

[9] Note symbolism in name: la Costeña not only comes from the coast, her role is coastal.

[10] Ibid., p. 69.

[11] Ibid.

[12] Ibid.

[13] Ibid., p. 70.

[14] Ibid., p. 73.

[15] Aldrich, *Modern Short Story in Peru*, p. 130.

[16] Octavio Paz, *The Labyrinth of Solitude; Life and Thought in Mexico*, trans., Lysander Kemp (New York: Grove Press, 1961), pp. 77 ff.

[17] José Maria Arguedas, *El zorro de arriba y el zorro de abajo* (Buenos Aires: Editorial Losada, 1971), pp. 158-59.

[18] Ibid., p. 13.

[19] Ibid., p. 11.

[20] Ibid., pp. 205-06.

[21] Aldrich, *Modern Short Story in Peru*, p. 142.

[22] Jean Franco, *The Modern Culture of Latin America,* rev. ed. (Harmondsworth, Eng.: Penguin, 1970), p. 255.

[23] Mario Vargas Llosa, *The Green House,* trans., Gregory Rabassa (New York: Harper and Row, 1968), p. 195.

[24] Ibid., p. 149.

[25] Ibid., p. 173.

[26] Son of Ricardo Palma, author of the famous *Tradiciones Peruanos.*

[27] Aldrich, *Modern Short Story in Peru,* p. 17.

[28] Katia Saks, *La Rifa* (New York: William Morrow, 1968), pp. 49-50. Katia Saks lives currently in New York; the novel was not, to my knowledge, published in Peru.

[29] Ibid., pp. 28-31.

[30] Ibid., p. 156.

[31] The absence of real characters in the Latin American novel has been commented upon by others; it is hardly the transitional style throughout the Third World, however. Contrast modern African novels, for example.

[32] Quoted in an essay by Peter Nettl.

[33] Gabriel Garcia Márquez, *One Hundred Years of Solitude* (New York: Avon, 1971), pp. 22-23.

[34] Rosa Signorelli de Marti, "Spanish America," in *Women in the Modern World,* ed. Raphael Patai (New York: Free Press, 1967), p. 202.

[35] Ibid., p. 202.

[36] See, for example, the work of Oscar Lewis.

[37] As the most recent work by Carlos Castañeda attempts to challenge, an outstanding example of an alternative to the "myth of the objective consciousness."

[38] Garcia Márquez, *One Hundred Years,* p. 217.

[39] Ibid., pp. 22-23.

[40] Note symbolism of names La Maga, Maya—they suggest magic; *maya* has a number of antirational possibilities.

[41] Julio Cortázar, *Hopscotch* (New York: Signet, 1967), p. 15.

[42] Ibid., p. 15.

[43] Ibid., p. 56.

[44] Ibid., pp. 32-33.

[45] Paz, *Labyrinth of Solitude,* p. 44. Italics mine.

[46] Georgie Anne Geyer, *The New Latins* (Garden City, N.Y.: Doubleday, 1970), p. 92.

[47] Garcia Márquez, *One Hundred Years,* p. 301. Italics mine.

[48] Leslie A. Fiedler, *Love and Death in the American Novel,* rev. ed. (New York: Delta, 1966), p. 66. Italics mine.

[49] Carlos Fuentes, *The Death of Artemio Cruz* (New York: Farrar, Straus and Giroux, 1964), p. 100.

[50] Carlos Fuentes, *The Good Conscience* (New York: Farrar, Straus and Giroux, 1961), p. 83.

[51] Fuentes, *Death of Artemio Cruz,* p. 245.

[52] Ibid., p. 248.

[53] Some interesting corroboration of the gap between Latin American women and North American women is provided by Anne Steinmann and David J. Fox, "Specific Areas of Agreement and Conflict in Women's Self Perception and Their Perception of Men's Ideal Woman in Two South American Urban Communities and an Urban Community in the United States," *Journal of Marriage and the Family,* 31, no. 2 (May 1969), pp. 281-89.

## Isobel McKenna

SOURCE: "Women in Canadian Literature," in *Canadian Literature,* No. 62, Autumn, 1974, pp. 69-78.

[*In the following essay, McKenna provides an overview of women in Canadian literature from 1769 to the 1970s.*]

> Most women don't even live lives of quiet desperation. (Quiet desperation is far too dramatic.) Most women live lives like doing the dishes, finishing one day's dishes and facing the next, until one day the rectal polyp is found or the heart stops and it's over. And all that's left of them is a name on a gravestone.

Brian Moore's heroine comments thus in *I Am Mary Dunne* (1968), his study of the confused Canadian woman of today. Moore may have been only transiently a Canadian writer, but he has caught exactly the mood of the Canadian girl who seeks a way out of the faceless secondary role the world offers her.

How did the situation arise? For Canadians the best record is found in Canadian fiction. Literature, much more than sociological or psychological studies, provides the rounded picture, the most complete expression of the social and psychological nature of a society, and does so not necessarily in the best writing.

Since the essence of literary art is to show us what a human being is within a particular culture, in a particular time and place, a glance at some fairly representative Canadian novels in English can be expected to demonstrate what has been the position of women in English Canadian society. Fashionable plots and popular attitudes, varying over the years, provide the clues to understanding the society contemporary to both author and audience.

The earliest novel in English which had a Canadian setting and was to some extent written here is Frances Brooke's *The History of Emily Montague* (1769). In popular epistolary style it gives a rather charming but limited view of garrison life in old Quebec at the end of the eighteenth century. Romantic love triumphs amid sleigh rides, balls, and afternoon teas. The position of women is simply that of transplanted Englishwomen. To understand Emily's place in society one cannot seek for Canadian roots, but must look back to England and its current *mores.* That, in fact, is just what Emily does.

Emily's story is concerned with only English men and women in a then new and rather exotic setting. Garrison officers and government appointees have social importance; they are pleasantly surprised to discover elegance and charm in seignorial society. But the French Canadian girls are more coquettish—hence less "ladylike"—than the English girls, and this not only causes the English women to accept this as proof of their own superiority; it also seems to be the first example of what Ronald Sutherland terms "the myth of *la femme fatale canadienne*" (*Second Image*). All the women have importance only as wives or daughters of important men, and this attitude was to prevail not only in Canadian colonial society but long after the creation of the nation.

Such was the basis of Canadian novels until reading books became more of an activity of the lower and middle classes, since people like to read about themselves, or what might be their own situations. The English ideal dominated in Canadian society generally and therefore in its literature. Both actively and passively the influence was reinforced to produce a watered-down imitation of English social values. The Church of England was fashionably inclined to poetic expression; Methodists and Presbyterians believed in education but for practical, "useful" purposes; English-speaking Roman Catholics were often poor, and like their French Canadian contemporaries, were usually encouraged to make the most of the situation in life to which they had been born. The priesthood was a high vocation that attracted bright young men since it offered education along with its dedication, but cultivation of a deep interest in literature was rarely part of their training. Every congregation's admiring dependence upon its clergy increased the latter's influence and encouraged the *status quo,* which in turn meant that the secondary role of women in society was praised as the true one. The romantic place of nature in nineteenth century fiction encouraged the popularity of "nature" novels, where the absence of women is a negative indication of woman's place in contemporary society.

Managing a well-run household was the proof of the Canadian woman's worth. In pioneer circumstances, this was a necessity. Physically, it was a natural division of the vital work to leave outside work to the men and inside work to the women. The Strickland sisters, Susanna Moodie and Catherine Parr Traill, were unusual in the cultivation they brought to the backwoods. They exemplified the educated Englishwoman of genteel birth whose leisure might well be occupied in writing. To express herself, or to earn some much-needed money, there was little else that a woman could do, apart from the manual labour to which some hard-pressed women were reduced, though if she were sufficiently well-born, she might open a school for young ladies, where a doubtful education would be dispensed, along with some training in managing a household.

There was still something of the feudal lady of the manor in the style in which women administered the many facets of running a home. Even Mrs. Moodie was conscientious about such duties, since to her, as to her contemporaries, this was only doing her share in the partnership of marriage. Every mother of young women became the administrative manager, assigning actual duties to daughters and to servants. Mrs. Moodie might despair of the servants available in Canada, but she had them; the work involved in running a house then was accomplished by a great deal of manual labour done by those who usually had no education at all. In a supposedly democratic country, varied social levels were an accepted fact of life.

During the 1850's and 1860's, Rosanna Leprohon wrote with some success when she turned her emphasis towards Canadian society as she knew it in and near Montreal. She quite accepted the established social hierarchy, and her stories seem to vary from the currently popular style chiefly in their novel setting, involving French Canadian society, with women who did belong to their environment.

In large part, Canadian writers sought the more lucrative and prestigious American markets, which determined the kind of writing they could undertake. Most of the fiction appeared serially in magazines, in stories that were usually highly moral and infinitely dull. About the time of Confederation, the American market had become even larger, and more Canadian writers were attracted. Most simply catered to popular tastes, but some, like Sara Jeannette Duncan, had genuine talent and some originality.

Besides literary ability, Duncan demonstrates shrewd objectivity and an accurate eye for her society. *The Imperialists* (1904) remains the best portrayal of life in a small Ontario town during the latter part of the nineteenth century. Duncan's characters are closer to actuality than those of her rivals, and the gossipy atmosphere of little towns is clearly mirrored. The central character, Lorne Murchison, is romantically in love with Dora Millburn. Dora is not very bright, the product of the superficial standards of her society, and she turns from Lorne to a young man, shallow as she is, whose greatest recommendation is that he is English. This lends him a cachet which home-grown heroes cannot equal—except in the author's eyes. Here we see the tide turning against the former tendency to worship anyone and anything imported from Britain. Here, at least, England no longer sets the pace, though the ties are not yet cut.

Dora and her young Englishman illustrate the false social standards condemned by Miss Duncan, and they deserve one another. Lorne's sister, Advena, is much more the ideal young Canadian woman of the period. She is high-minded, kindhearted, pure and constant in her love. She has also something of the martyr complex, then considered attractive since it implied faithful endurance of great trials and misunderstandings. The hard work and self-sacrifice so vital in the pioneer are now metamorphosed into a kind of subservience to society. The original importance of the group over the individual has been replaced by the Victorian male domination of the family and especially of the women in it. Negation of personal desires is no longer a requirement for survival but a quality sanctified by society as the mark of the true "lady".

The only gratification of such martyrdom is a self-deluding smugness entailing a clouded, hypocritical view of social roles. But Advena is Canadian, with an honesty and independence which the author feels are typical. Advena endures so much and no more; the role of martyr is not to be accepted without a struggle. She does something about her frustrated love for the new young minister in town, and in the end, through Advena's initiative, she and her young minister are free to fall into one another's arms. The solution is rather pat, but the point is made that custom and manners are superficial and often false: the true values of kindness, faithfulness, and sincerity count in both men and women. Both sexes can be dominated by false values only to their own misfortune. Despite the moral tone, Duncan also makes the point that to achieve any kind of fulfilment in life, sincerity requires an independent spirit to accompany it. Although Duncan's theme here is political, the women she portrays are realistically part of the story. In Advena especially, we see one who is all that her society expected and admired, but who also has some of that freedom of thought balanced by native intelligence which the author herself displayed. Like Duncan, Advena manages to get what she truly wants and at the same time to get along within her society. It was the kind of compromise that had then to be made, but at least it involved much more than simple mindless compliance.

Materialistic values and illogical snobbery are also attacked in Duncan's other, and lesser, novels, which are not set in Canada. In *A Canadian Girl in London* (1908),

Mary Trent's father, a Senator, has sent her with her brother Graham to become acquainted with London society, but they are glad to escape its hypocrisies to return to the more direct simplicity of Canada. But Mary's admiration for her wealthy self-made father and her handsome brother betrays, in its acquiescence to them, her own sense of inferiority: she sees clearly but can act only directly.

This is the kind of situation which gave rise to the popularity of the Victorian belief that "the hand that rocks the cradle rules the world." For all her independent intelligence and tactful firmness, Mary's role is still that of an adjunct to the males in the family. The pioneer concept of the family working together to gain achievement still dominates the role of the woman. It is father who makes the decisions regarding the aims of the family—which are his own. Duncan's women are always conformist to a degree that allows them to fit within their society, but at the same time they are individuals with no time for false pretenses, conforming only within the limits of their sense of justice.

Not long after Duncan's books appeared, L. M. Montgomery published the first of her stories about Anne of Avonlea, *Anne of·Green Gables,* 1908). An attractive, imaginative little girl, Anne learns to blend her independence with the conventionality of her time and place, and through necessity as much as through following her own wishes, she gains a career, she becomes a teacher, then a rather new and honourable profession open to women. Teachers in the public schools had formerly most often been men; women who taught had either been nuns or faded gentlewomen who provided a meagre education to those whose parents could afford to pay.

Much of the long popularity of Anne of Green Gables is due to her independent spirit, her confidence that she can accomplish something for herself. She is intelligent and better educated than previous generations of Canadian-born women had been. Her children, who appear in later stories, receive her encouragement in expanding their horizons. Women in Montgomery's books still belong to the rural society that dominates then, but they feel fortunate in comparison to preceding generations. Life is less difficult, and it offers many new chances; careers in nursing and secretarial work as well as teaching were then just opening up as fields of exciting opportunity for women.

In the early days of the present century, the west was just beginning to develop while the east had already gone through its pioneering stages. Ralph Connor recalled in his novels the Glengarry area and the Scottish pioneers among whom he grew up. He portrayed women as he had known them—vital to their society, though confined by their settlers' lives. The chief reason for the existence of women was the necessity for good wives and mothers, according to pioneer standards. In *Glengarry Schooldays* (1902) Connor described Mrs. Finch, his most admired example of such womanliness, as "last to bed and first to stir", with a "steadfast mind and unyielding purpose":

> Her husband regarded her with a curious mingling of reverence and defiance . . . but while he talked much about his authority, and made a great show of absolutism with his family, he was secretly conscious that another will than his had really kept things moving . . . withal her soft words and gentle ways, hers was a will like steel . . . Besides the law of order, there was . . . the law of work . . . To the mother fell all the rest. At the cooking and cleaning, and the making and the mending, all fine arts with her, she diligently toiled from long before dawn till after all the rest were abed. But besides these and other daily household chores there were, in their various seasons, the jam and jelly, the pumpkin and squash preserves, the butter-making and cheese-making, and more than all, the long, long work with the wool.

The laws of order and work that Connor mentions meant that each could accomplish what his or her talents suggested, in terms of their society. Where girls were concerned, creative and administrative talents were not only encouraged but were vital to the farm life most people followed, and to contemporary urban life.

Despite the unadmitted fact that both knew that she indeed ran the farm, Mrs. Finch was a good wife who, in her awareness of his need to appear absolute master, never argued with her husband. In quiet, devious ways, she arranged that injustices should not last long, and the family accepted this oblique kind of authority. When this ideal wife and mother became ill, no one related this to the physical exhaustion she must have felt, and no one was more surprised than her husband, lost without her. Mrs. Finch demonstrated the strength of character for which she was noted, and suffered in silence. This martyrdom illustrates the endurance which pioneer life demanded; when it turned out that she had "malignant cancer" for which nothing could be done, her early training served her well. Mrs. Finch was granted after her death the supreme accolade: "all her life . . . she lived for others."

The other woman prominent in this story is Mrs. Murray, the minister's wife, described as "fine and fair and saintly", the inspiration of all. The influence of a good woman was acknowledged and appreciated in pre-Freudian novels, and women were well aware of this power which society granted them. They regarded it a duty to use it well, and this in turn encouraged a more selfless attitude.

There is indeed something almost frighteningly simple in the standards Connor portrays. Women were not expected to work outside the home in any capacity that interfered with their first duty, the household—but most lived the life of Mrs. Finch, with plenty to occupy them. Certainly Connor grants to women ability, intelligence, charm, along with a kind of superiority to men. In his later novels, he attempts to fathom character more deeply, but society has changed, and although he recognizes this, he cannot cope with it.

Later, beginning with *Jalna* in 1927, came the stories of Mazo de la Roche, widely read outside this country but never considered great literature here, largely owing to the unrealistic settings and their author's soap-opera imagination. But her characters sometimes display the faults and virtues of real people. Meg is sweet but unyielding, in the manner of her contemporaries who still felt the need to be martyred by their convictions without ever examining them honestly. Old Adeline may be a dominating, rather irritating old woman, but she is true to her times. Such tyranny within the family was a woman's sole outlet if she had the qualities of leadership, and Gran had no special talents outside them: she merely liked to run things. Her own generation had considered her ambitions not only acceptable but necessary: the family must be united in the common cause. By virtue of her position as matriarch, she had a duty to perform which society felt was absolutely incumbent upon her. She was an exaggerated representation of the kind of woman considered "good" in the author's youth, and her portrait seems drawn partly in admiration and partly in irritation

As the years pass in the Jalna stories, women make greater efforts to attain independence. Often as not, they suffer for it, or are shown to be ridiculous and not very bright. In the author's own society a woman was always faced with a choice: either a life of her own, or life with a husband as mother-homemaker, based on the pioneer concept updated to the disadvantage of women.

As society develops beyond the pioneer stage, women are considered as restricted by their own natures, although in practice the restriction is imposed by society itself. But the pioneer evaluation of women as individuals still lingers. Frederick Philip Grove shows sympathy for the overworked and downtrodden immigrant wives on the prairies, who work there much as they would have done in their homes in Europe. *Our Daily Bread* (1928) and *Fruits of the Earth* (1933), like his other prairie novels, reflect the west of the first decades of this century, still the time of the pioneers. In *Settlers of the Marsh* (1925), Mrs. Amundsen is a victim of the cruelty of her husband's harsh peasant attitude, and this in turn deeply wounds, psychologically, her daughter Ellen. This kind of loveless slavery disgusts Clara Vogel so much that she turns completely against everything that might have been good in farm life. Uneducated and untrained, Clara turns to her only alternative in the city, where easy virtue brings an easy life. Ellen and Clara are both victims of their society: the only future offered to them is marriage and homemaking and child-rearing, and when they refuse this, little remains. Ellen earns her reward through patient suffering, while Clara did as she chose until caught by the nemesis of violent death.

Despite Grove's empathy with these women characters, the moral views of his time dictate what they may do, or be. In *The Master of the Mill* (1944), different times and circumstances are involved, and the women have differing roles. The three Mauds of the story are the three faces of Eve, granted characteristics which belong to individuals nevertheless. As R. E. Watters suggests in his "Introduction" to the 1961 edition, the three Mauds encompass "the trinity of mind, heart, and spirit", but it is notable that each can only symbolize one of these qualities. It is also notable that in Maud Dolittle we see a woman who is brilliant, with keen business ability along with a warm heart. Grove knew well that many women were indeed capable of more than housework, and in this novel he has a situation where such a woman fits in. But the society portrayed seems to share the views of Mazo de la Roche: these women either marry *or* have a career, and the only career is Maud Dolittle's as secretary.

Grove accurately reflects the times of which he wrote. In *Two Generations* (1946) he not only portrays the "generation gap" long before the phrase became trite, but he demonstrates his belief in the "new" woman, who wanted her own life as well as a husband and a home. Like the other Patterson children, Alice feels frustrated by her father's narrow attitude. She, too, is determined to leave the family farm, although her own ambition is subordinated to that of her brother Phil. Their almost incestuous love for one another is meant to show the shared ideas and beliefs of the younger generation who feel that there is more to life than physical labour. They are surprised at the support their mother provides, and come to realize that she, too, was once young and dream-filled. The most modern woman of them all is Nancy, their brother George's wife: she has struggled to become a dancer, and has no intention of giving up her hardwon opportunities. Grove allows Nancy to make everyone eventually happy: she bears George's son, the first grandchild, but continues to plan for her career. The opposite pole to Nancy and Alice is Cathleen, brother Henry's wife. Grove loses no opportunity to point out the stupidity and conformity which make her uninteresting to all, even to Henry.

No matter how dated the story's details, Grove positively supports the notion of women as individuals with talents and abilities to be encouraged. He is one of very few writers of his time to do so. Despite women having the vote and being recognized as persons before the law, few novels, then or later, reflect any great change in their attitude to women, whose characters are usually portrayed as more restricted and less free than in real life they need be. Society in general was slow to adopt new ideas or to face realities, and fiction reflected the lag.

For instance, in Callaghan's *Such is My Beloved* (1934), the two prostitutes are convincing in terms of the novel's theme, but add nothing to the portrayal of women as they exist in this century; they are Eve in modern dress, man's downfall, leading him out of Paradise.

Callaghan sees the Christian virtue of self-negation as the woman's role. In *They Shall Inherit the Earth* (1935), Anna's lack of self-centredness may be the giving of spirit which man must learn in order to live in this world, but it also seems to be the old martyr-complex of women in different terms. Certainly it projects an ideal of which Ralph Connor would have approved.

*More Joy in Heaven* (1937) is deliberately a martyr story, with Kip Caley condemned by society because it cannot understand his Biblical sense of charity. But his mother and Julie are martyrs too, whose suffering is only intensified through association with Kip. Only the "bad" characters gladly suffer nothing.

In *The Loved and The Lost* (1951) Peggy Sanderson embodies another version of the martyr role. In her common sense, Sara Jeanette Duncan would be impatient with Peggy's lack of understanding of reality, although she would recognize the traces of Victorian gentility in Peggy's difficulties. No matter how high her intentions, Peggy suffers for flouting society's rules, since she does not recognize that society is still insistently conformist to outworn ideas. One can imagine a Mrs. Finch, for instance, finding a way to cope, even though it would be through an attitude which Peggy could not abide.

Generally, Callaghan's themes are seen through male characters who have a strength which raises them against the background of his flat style. The women tend to be paler, blending into this background. His more recent novels change somewhat in technique, but though the settings are contemporary, there is little difference in the characters of the women, despite the author's sympathy.

One of Hugh MacLennan's best portrayals of women is rather oddly, in his early novel, *Barometer Rising* (1941). Penny Wainwright is almost a complete metaphor of twentieth century womanhood: she is caught between the conflicting rules of the older generation of her father and his friends, and the newer freedom with its stress on individuality. She refuses to be a martyr, but acts to solve her difficulties. Penny's circumstances are not far removed from the present as far as her position in society is concerned. In MacLennan's later books, however, women tend to be merely types, with even less individuality and sense of purpose than Sara Jeannette Duncan's characters.

Not surprisingly, the most penetrating studies of women tend to be in novels written by women. Ethel Wilson portrays women sometimes tied by marriage, or by love alone, but still as individuals with some freedom of choice, often preoccupied with the search for a meaning to their lives. Margaret Laurence has much the same attitude. In *The Stone Angel* (1964), for example, she shows how one woman born out of her time remains strongly individualistic, reacting to the restrictions of her world. In the end, Hagar has been defeated by her turn-of-the-century small-town society as much as by the simple fact of age. For such as Hagar there was no place.

The push-and-pull of contemporary society and its effects on a sensitive, intelligent Canadian woman are perhaps best expressed in Margaret Atwood's *The Edible Woman* (1969). Marion McAlpin, the central character, leads the conventional life of the recent university graduate. Atwood herself is quoted on the book's jacket as stating that the novel is "about ordinary people who make the mistake of thinking they are ordinary", which sums up Marion's situation. She does all the expected things, even to being almost engaged to a young-man-on-the-make. But suddenly Marion cannot eat: unknowingly, but literally, she is fed up with conformity, and understands this only when she realizes that she herself is being eaten up by society. Symbolically, she frosts a cake as the image of a woman and serves it to her friends. They are appalled, so Marion happily finishes by eating it herself. The old martyr-complex had subtly pushed her into contemporary "nonconformist" conformity, but rather like Duncan's Advena, Marion is saved by a sturdy independence she had never suspected in herself. With none of Advena's social and moral commandments to guide her, Marion must find her own way, and it is difficult. She is involved in a war, not between the sexes at all, but of one kind of society against another. The "edible" woman is the loser, the contemporary martyr—unless, like Marion, she turns against the society that is nibbling away her individuality.

Like Susanna Moodie, Mrs. Finch, or Nancy or Alice Patterson, Marion realizes that femininity is only a part of her own unique person, and is not to be worn as a hair-shirt.

**Edna N. Sims**

SOURCE: "Notes on the Negative Image of Woman in Spanish Literature," in *CLA Journal*, Vol. XIX, No. 4, June, 1976, pp. 468-83.

[*In the following essay, Sims studies negative images of women in Spanish literature, finding it to be "the country in which the most universal negative feminine prototype was created."*]

In view of the attention which is given today to the theme of women's rights, it seems fitting that we examine the literature of the country in which the most universal negative feminine prototype was created. With Fernando de Rojas' Celestine as the motivating personality in our quest for greater understanding of the dilemma of man's distinguished helpmate, we shall investigate in this treatise the literary origins of many of the pejorative characteristics commonly ascribed to woman.

A careful study of the literature of Spain from its genesis through the first half of the year 1560 (the year of publication of Fray Luis de Leon's *Perfecta casada*) convinces us that, in subsequent centuries, there is probably very little material to be added in the portrayal of the negative feminine archetype. The descriptions of woman's behavior and the multiple interpretations of the various authors who scrutinize customs from the early medieval period through the first half of the Spanish Renaissance can be envisioned as an imaginary literary trajectory which reveals five particular aspects of our theme.

The popular fables, often referred to as "enxiemplos," represent the first literary genre where we discover a predominance of feminine types depicted from a negative point of view. The second grouping includes protagonists from the works of Juan Ruiz, the famous Archpriest of Hita; Alfonso Martínez, more commonly referred to as the Archpriest of Talavera and the notorious Celestine of Fernando de Rojas' *Tragicomedia de Calixto y Melibea* to which we have already alluded. The works of the second group are distinguishable from those of the first due to the intent of the authors to substitute the generalized portraiture of the protagonists of the fables with a more detailed characterization of the feminine personality.

The third division leads us to a series of sentimental novels where, in a unilateral projection of abstract elements, Juan Rodríguez del Padrón, Diego de San Pedro and Juan de Flores, together with certain personal observations which they manage to express through the characters of their creation, offer their singular interpretations of the misdeeds of several enamoured females. The conduct of woman continues to undergo a similar censorship in the early picaresque novels where, due to political, social or religious influence, the male subconscious persuades him to accept and even, in some cases, to imitate the notorious strategems of the female life style.

The trajectoral cycle completes itself with the humanists Juan Luis Vives, Cristóbal de Villalón and Fray Luis de León presenting a series of didactic treatises describing the vices of both pagan and Christian women. These zealous writers, who see themselves as counselors singularly commissioned to rectify the social ills of their society, direct their advice to the female with the intention of improving her destiny and, simultaneously, that of future generations.

As we have indicated above, the genesis of the misogynist element in Spanish literature is seen in the fables, the greater part of which were introduced to Spain with the migration of various segments of the North African populace. Without taking women very seriously, the members of clergy utilized the antifeminist propaganda from the literature of the "enxiemplos" as didactic anecdotes for their sermons. As they spoke of man's unfortunate counterpart from the pulpit, their sincere efforts to "enseñar deleitando" converted the amusing comportment of the "nice but sometimes wicked little woman" into a predilect theme not only for sermons but for several other literary genres. Consequently, after their long journey of translation from the Arabic to the Romance languages, the Spanish adaptations of these entertaining fables were to become known throughout Europe.

It is apparent, if one thoughtfully considers the image of woman in the literature of the "enxiemplos," that she is rarely depicted in a positive manner. This is not to discount the one or two fables where she is presented as the victim of some thoughtless spouse or as a "poor little creature" unjustly pursued by the less liberal minded forces of her society; however, leaving aside these infrequent exceptions, it is immediately apparent that her scandalous reputation evokes abundant negative narrative for her enthusiastic biographers. In accordance with the findings of John Esten Keller,[1] who has completed a scholarly investigation of the subject matter of more than one thousand exempla, we again emphasize the fact that not all the motifs of the popular fables can be designated as originating with Spanish authors.

In a summary of the various roles which are commonly ascribed to women, the most frequently portrayed archetypes are the adulteress, the procuress, the unscrupulous maternal figure, the temptress and the habitual talebearer. Less frequent but relatively abundant stereotyped figures in the exempla include portrayals of cruel daughters, disobedient wives, avaricious peasants, murderesses and widows who fail to respect the memory of their departed husbands. Feminine types depicted even less frequently in the exempla are women who have allowed themselves to be deceived by fast-talking gentlemen callers, women portrayed as unethical salespersons, participants in incestuous liaisons, servants whose presence in the household precipitate havoc and nuns whose mundane behavior reveals little or no religious commitment. The works which narrate these exempla include the *Disciplina clericalis,* the *Libro de los castigos, Calila e Dymna,* the *Libro de las consolaciones, Barlaam e Iosaphat,* and the *Libro de los engaños,* which contains the *Historia del Príncipe Erasto, Scala celi* and the *Historia de los siete sabios.*

Among the various sketches of wicked females appears an old woman whose conduct sometimes coincides with that of the procuress. The mother-in-law figure, although she is not considered to be as destructive as the "alcahueta," demonstrates a similar aptitude for instigating illicit love affairs. The comportment of the maternal figure is underscored in the fables when the mother, during the absence of her son-in-law, collaborates in her daughter's extramarital escapades. The daughter's husband has no scruples about leaving the vigilance of his youthful wife to the "little old lady of saintly carriage," but the reputation of the ancient silver-haired relative is destroyed in the "Ejemplo de la espada" (No. XI) which appears in Pedro Alfonso's *Disciplina clericalis.*

Alfonso presents a doting mother-in-law who was held in such high esteem by her daughter's husband that he, on departing for a business venture in a distant city, considered his home and his marriage secure due to the presence of the older woman. Immediately after his departure, the young wife with her mother's consent, called her lover and while the three of them were enjoying the repast of the day, the husband returned unexpectedly. The experienced elderly woman, who calmly assured the nervous couple she could handle the situation, gave the young suitor a naked sword and instructed him to stand behind the door and to remain perfectly silent. When the suspicious husband saw that the trembling young man would answer none of his accusations he turned to his "amada señora madre" and trustingly accepted her convincing reply:

> Fijo honrado, el caso es este. Aquí vinieron tres ombres tras este ombre que está a la puerta queriéndolo matar, e nosotras lo dexamos entrar con la mano en la espada assí, porque entonces estaua la puerta abierta, e él piensa ahora que tu eres alguno dellos, e por miedo que ha non te responde.[2]

The deceived husband saw only "las buenas acciones" of the two women and, believing they had saved the life of a poor young man, offered the latter his hand of friendship.

Before the fourteenth century the literary portrait of the female in the fables and in most other genres depicted an abstract archtype who often remained nameless and who was repeatedly lacking in individualizing qualities. The authors of the exempla underscored her defects but, in their generalized portraiture, failed to perceive a well delineated feminine figure. During the period following the popular exempla Juan Ruiz initiates the first attempt towards a more concrete literary characterization of women and, followed by Alfonso Martínez, who authored the *Corbacho* and Fernando de Rojas, who created the *Tragicomedy of Calixto y Melibea,* the fondness for creating more realistic types increased. With the antithesis of the holy Virgin as his model of the perfect woman, Juan Ruiz managed to express his ingenious comprehension of the human condition in his realistic projection of the vices of women whose eyes were so full of sand ("llenos de arista")[3] that they, innocently accepting the friendship of astute procuresses and other individuals of similar ambition, were unable to perceive the traps of the cunning parasites who set about to deceive them ("andan por escarnecerla[s]").[4] At the same time, the humorous attitude of the author permitted him to bestow his protagonists with exaggerated sobriquets with which "mocetas," "vejezuelas," "arrepintajas," "magrillas y gordillas" or sensual "tornavacas" and "chatas malditas retozoñas cual cabras monteses"[5] exchanging their last vestiges of femininity for masculine qualities which almost coincide with the author himself, Juan Ruiz

> da todavía un paso más en el proceso de descomposición de un cuerpo femenino presentado como repelente hasta desintegrarse en una odiosa masa de miembros animales . . . [6]

In a clear transition between the Trotaconventos of the Archpriest of Hita and the culmination of the procuress archetype in Fernando de Rojas, Alfonso Martínez, the Archpriest of Talavera, defines several feminine failings that have been earlier cited in the exempla. Not entirely unlike Juan Ruiz, a limitless zest for the observation of the most minute details leads Alfonso Martínez to the intimate confines of the chambers of women from several social classes but, while the first Archpriest infuses life into his characters with his rude mockery of their physical appearance, the Archpriest of Talavera concentrates on their coarse speech patterns. Two similar works in the Catalonian language offering more concrete portraits of female prototypes are the *Llibre de les Dones* where the less pessimistic Fray Fransech Eiximenis describes the misdemeanors of women of his day from a moralist's point of view. *Spill,* known also as the *Libre de Consells* and written by Jaume Roig, is, in spite of its resemblance to the prose of Fernando de Rojas or the Archpriest of Talavera, a direct forerunner of the picaresque novel. Its author, who was a prominent physician of the pre-Renaissance period, describes in a naturalistic fashion the misconduct of women of society's lower strata, especially in terms of the infirmities related to the state of motherhood.

On passing to the "novela sentimental," the traditional prototype of the wicked woman is counterbalanced, somewhat, by a series of dialogued debates or discourses in her favor. In spite of the absence of the well delineated negative female figure depicted in the awkward "serranas" of the Archpriest of Hita, and even without discounting what has been recognized as the justifiable victory of the male in the famous debate, a well defined antifeminist projection can be traced in the works of Juan Rodriguez del Padrón, Diego de San Pedro and Juan de Flores, three principal authors of the sentimental novel. Among the various themes and subthemes of these novels, the most important emphasis is the authors' underscoring of the various dimensions of tragedy which their male protagonists suffer as they become enamoured of several designing young women. The focus of the misogynist element falls, therefore, not on the innovative debates nor on the multiple and shocking misdeeds of women but, rather, on the one hand, in the manner in which the authors themselves and the various characters of their creation interpret the actions of the female and, secondly, in the unilateral projection of certain abstract elements—Fortune, Honor, and Irony—in the lives of these characters.

The classification of the sentimental novel as antifeminist may be questioned when one considers that the authors of this genre substitute the scatterbrained types of the exempla with discreetly intelligent women who display ability to reason with a profundity heretofore unattributed to the members of their sex. (Bear in mind that the alleged intellectual ability is not the point of view of the authors). The defense of our thesis approaches affirmation with the following observations: Although the women display positive intellectual capacity, there consistently exists a unilateral tendency to ignore their good judgement. A primary example of this biased favoritism comes to the fore when, in spite of the excellent manner in which Braçayda champions the cause of women in her encounter with Torrellas in the famous story of *Grisel y Mirabella,* Juan de Flores declares the male to be the winner of the debate.

The exemplary virtue of the protagonist of the *Cárcel de amor* is interpreted from a negative point of view when Laureola, in determining her true feelings for a would-be suitor, refuses to mistake "piedad" for "amor." Although his protagonist feels compassion for the suffering of the rejected pretender, the author, ignoring woman's God given right to select her own mate and, depicting the rejected Leriano as a martyr to love, prefers to underscore the suffering of the male:

. . . dolor le atormenta, pasión le persigue,
desesperança le destruye, muerte le amenaza, pena
le secuta, pensamiento lo desuela, deseo le atribula,
tristeza le condena, fe no le salua, que de todo
esto tu eres causa.[7]

Directing our attention now to the ill fame of the woman
of the early picaresque novel, it can be stated that an
accelerated projection of the vices heretofore cited continues but, this time, the impulse which marks woman's
merciless comportment is attributed to the unhappy economic situation to which she finds herself almost permanently condemned. In anti-feminist literature prior to *La
Loçana Andaluza,* the idea of misogyny is communicated
in the criticism which society, with the assistance of several favorably disposed authors, inflicts traditional stereotypes on its female inhabitants. Unlike their literary
precursors, Francisco Delicado and the anonymous author of *Lazarillo de Tormes* underscore the negative aspects of the female with indications of (1) woman's own
interpretation of her role in society (2) the unscrupulous
schemes she employs in order to earn a living in that
society and (3) the singular impact of her influence over
the persons with whom she comes into contact. Ranpín,
as the constant companion of the protagonist of *La
Loçana Andaluza,* is the character whose lifestyle is most
significantly altered by his "maestra." In the second
novel (*Lazarillo de Tormes*) the youthful rogue follows in
the footsteps of a woman who, at first glance, appears to
play only a minor role in the life of her impressionable
victim.[8] With the advent of the Humanist era, the close
scrutiny of female customs continues. An unlimited presentation of her vices of past centuries is rendered to
meet the Hispanic literary synthesis of pagan and Christian concepts with each writer concentrating on his favorite philosophies of the two currents as he attempts to
devise the formula for his ideal woman.

This synthesis of Christian and pagan concepts depicts,
first, a woman who, emphasizing the philosophy of Clas-
sicism, struggles interminably for the harmonious development of her intellectual facilities. There is also the
woman who, ignoring the medieval plea of preparation
for the spiritual life after death, seeks complete equality
with her male counterpart by concentrating on the pleasures of the flesh. In sharp contrast to this dual ideology
of pagan origin is depicted an exemplary maiden whose
chief concern is for the unadulterated teachings of Christianity. With the writings of Erasmus as their primary
source of inspiration, these authors depict the female as
a weak minded creature whose only hope of salvation lies
in their leader's admonition of "la religiosidad interior."

Inasmuch as the above cited philosophies tend to reveal
not only the vices of women of earlier times but also
some of her more positive qualities, it must be concluded
that the humanist writers are neither "for" nor "against"
women. They have, however, consistently demonstrated a
vital interest in her comportment. We do not negate the
well intentioned efforts of these authors in their attempt
to present an objective commentary on the unparalleled

problems of the women of the era. They view themselves
as counselors commissioned to rectify the ills of their
society but, in spite of their lack of malice towards the
female, their treatment of her misfortune clearly reflects
several stereotyped ideas concerning the women of whom
they write.

Juan Luis Vives, reiterating the Erasmian philosophy of
moderation and inner spirituality, expresses his ideas
for the betterment of the female of the species in *De
institutione Christianae Foeminae.* This treatise, which
was published in the latter part of 1523, is a relatively
vivid commentary on the role of the women of the period
and is dedicated to Maria Tudor, the daughter of Henry
VIII and Catherine of Aragon, his academic advisee.
Underscoring the wicked nature of Earth's first female
inhabitant, Vives looks upon the women of his day as the
unfortunate recipients to which Eve transmitted a great
repertory of debilitating evils. Doubtful of the intellectual
capacity of women, he discourages their scholarly pursuits suggesting that man's sinful counterpart limit her
reading to spiritual literature. In the same manner as Juan
Ruiz, Vives criticizes the "flirtatious" women who attend
public gatherings solely to be admired by prospective
suitors and recommends the young woman's activities be
home-centered. If she abstains from associations with
other females, her own chaste habits will remain uncorrupted. Vives demonstrates little confidence in the ability
of young maidens to wisely select their own husbands
and in the same manner in which he counsels young
maidens to respectfully submit themselves to their parents he admonishes the female spouse to obey her husband: "¡Estarás debajo del poder de tu marido, y él te
dominará!"[9] Juan Luis Vives shows no mercy for the
adulterous woman and condemns the acute tendency towards jealous behavior which he finds prevalent among
innumerable housewives. Although he portrays the
woman as inferior to her husband, he expects her to be
superior in her capacity to forgive the iniquities of the
male: "Santifíquese el marido infiel por la esposa fiel."[10]

Cristóbal de Villalón, who also writes with the didactic
intention of rectifying the ills of the society in which he
lives, reconciles his adventuresome spirit and vivid capacity for fictitious production with a singular evaluation
of the customs of women he has either known or created
from epochs and cultures other than his own. In Turkey
he turns his attention to the habits of women who have
earned the favor of numerous sultans. *El Crotalón* takes
him to the confines of splendid harems where he observes
the intimate life of the country's courtesans in the manner
of a twentieth century detective. Villalón is so appalled at
his findings that he, in *El Scholástico,* vehemently ad-
vises the young men under his imaginary tutelage to
make a concerted effort to avoid associations with members of the opposite sex. The female prototypes of his
major works are not as well delineated as those of Juan
Ruiz or Fernando de Rojas, but the animated dialogue of
*El viaje de Turquía* and *El Crotalón,* and the descriptive
narration of *El Scholástico* offer a wealth of information
concerning the character commonly ascribed to women.

Villalón's earliest treatise, *El viaje de Turquía,* takes us to the Muslim household where the men of the nation are depicted as the most cruel misogynists of all time. The indifferent attitude of the male sovereigns towards women is casually revealed in the skilfully directed conversations between Pedro de Urdemalas and Mátalas Callando, whom the author utilizes to summarize his own observations:

> . . . que no estiman las mujeres ni hacen más caso dellas que de los asadores, cuchares y cazos que tienen colgados de la espetera; en ninguna cosa tienen voto, ni admiten consejo suyo.[11]

Despite his recognition of the ill will of the male in matters concerning the female, Villalón does not excuse the conduct of the members of the weaker sex. Women of the general Turkish society are offered very little freedom. Those fortunate enough to reside in palatial harems must resign themselves to the troublesome vigilance of the sultan's loyal eunuchs. Their less fortunate sisters are ordered to cover themselves in public and do so in spite of the physical discomfort occasioned by the unsympathetic climate. Indeed, their modest attire has been so severely designed that frequently members of their own families have failed to recognize them in the market place.

The author explains that the excessive controls with which the male has attempted to regulate the activities of the female have met with little success. The rigid surveillance has resulted in a greater feminine insight for resolving the annoying restrictions to such a degree that they have been widely acclaimed for their ability to convert almost all such obstacles into inconceivable victories. One such example is seen in the traditional group visits of the young maiden to the public bath houses, a weekly ritual which almost becomes a burlesque outing:

> . . . y de camino hace cada una lo que quiere, pues no es conocida, buscando su aventura.[12]

Some of the women, instead of utilizing the public bath, invent pretexts for bathing "en privado" and, frequenting the mansions of wealthy gentlemen in order to enjoy the exquisite toiletries imported from the far corners of the globe, willingly engage in prostitution on a regular basis. The women of Turkey are as insistent in their efforts to acquire material goods as the other women we have discussed, but, due to the excessive number of female residents in the most exclusive harems, perhaps their greatest problem is finding a landowner who is willing to support them:

> Cuando van por la calle, si les decís amores, os responden, y a dos por tres os preguntarán si tenéis casa, y si decís que no, os dirán mill palabras injuriosas; si decís que sí, dirán se que se la mostréis disimuladamente, y métense allí, y veces hay que serán mujeres de arraeces; otras tomaréis lo que viniere, y si os paresce tomeréis de allí amistad para adelante, y si no, no querrá deciros quien es.[13]

The authors mentioned above have restricted their observations to the negative aspects of female behavior, but Luis de León is the man whose works bear the distinct signature of one seeking an honest solution to the dilemma of his nation's most ridiculed figures. The good friar sets forth his ideas in a treatise entitled *La perfecta casada* where, in a painstaking analysis of the behavior pattern of the women of his century, he offers the formula by which the members of the weaker sex may restore not only their own good fortune, but that of the entire Hispanic kingdom.

Yielding to the implicit limitations of his vocation, he refused to comment on the misdeeds for which many of his predecessors had censored the conduct of the female members of the cloister and, dedicating his didactic efforts to María Varela Osorio, a young aristocrat on the threshold of matrimony, he prescribed a formula for successful conjugal relationships. The perfect wife must take special care to uphold the good name of her husband. As sole administrator of her household she must untiringly master the skills required to serve its members. The model housewife rises at daybreak. Aware of the hazards of physical fatigue, she nourishes herself substantially but, stressing the benefits of a well ordered kitchen rather than a well rested body, she is frequently the lastto retire:

> . . . más debe a su oficio que a su cuerpo, y mayor dolor y enfermedad es traer de contino su familia desordenada y perdida, que padecer un poco . . .[14]

Functioning in the role of family comforter, her sympathetic concern for the problems of her spouse and her honest efforts to encourage him in his moments of depression will be rewarded. According to Fray Luis, there are many foolish women who must be held accountable for failing to be responsive to the most important task their Creator has demanded of them. In his exacting reproof of their casual attitude towards the sacred mission which can be effectively executed only by themselves, he attempts their reform reminding them that the well disciplined woman, even in her moments of leisure, devotes her activities to the welfare of her household. Reiterating the value of self-sacrifice, the perceptive friar describes the perils of commissioning another to fulfill one's own responsibilities:

> Mucho se engañan las que piensan que mientras ellas, cuya es la casa, y a quien propiamente toca el bien y el mal della, duerman y se descuidan, cuidará y velará la criada, que no le toca y que al fin lo mira como todo ajeno.[15]

Fray Luis also reminds his readers of certain calamitous entanglements which can result from unnecessarily provoking the enmity of faithful servants and, with equal fervor, writes of the honor and serenity which can be permanently enjoyed by the woman whose well treated servant contentedly sings her praises at home and abroad. His most severe criticism concerning the delicate bond between housemaids and their mistresses censors the consuming excesses of arrogance of which numerous employers are guilty:

> . . . y hay tan vanas algunas, que casi desconocen su carne, y piensan que la suya es carne de ángeles, y la de sus sirvientas de perros, y quieren ser adoradas dellas, y no acordarse dellas si son nacidas; y si se quebrantan en su servicio, y si pasan sin sueño las noches, y si están ante ellas de rodillas los días, todo les parece que es poco y nada para lo que se les debe, o ellas presumen que se les ha de deber.[16]

Luis de León criticizes, as did Juan Ruiz, the women who unceasingly admire their own beauty seated before the mirrors of their boudoirs hour after hour. Elaborating on many of the vain displays which echo the statements of Martínez de Toledo when, in his *El Corbacho,* he identified himself as a spy in the private chambers of several of his country's most illustrious females, Luis de León, with less deliberate self incrimination, reiterates his predecessor's disapproval of the female's unlimited fondness for fine clothing and expensive jewelry. This extended description also illustrates the thoroughness with which he observes the toilet articles of the woman's dressing rooms as he describes the time consuming process with which she, "rodeada de botellas y arquillas,"[17] endangers her vision in an attempt to alter the appearance of her eyes. Alluding to a lack of moderation in her application of powder and rouge, he sees the conversion of what was once a pretty face to a clown-like mask:

> . . . en caso que fuesen hermosas, se tornan feas con sus mismas manos.[18]

He cites uncleanliness, greed and avarice as vices common to the members of the weaker sex and, like Villalón, suggests men avoid associations with beautiful women. Reiterating the suspicions of earlier members of his profession, he depicts them as unchaste seductresses possessing dangerous powers over the will of even the most temperate men:

> . . . la belleza es peligrosa porque atrae a sí y enciende en su cobdicia los corazones de los que la miran.[19]

Convinced of woman's inferiority, he discourages her scholarly pursuits and her ambitions in the business world as endeavors unsuited to the feminine temperament:

> . . . la naturaleza no la hizo para el estudio de las ciencias ni para los negocios de dificultades. . así les limitó el entender, y por consiguiente, les tasó las palabras y las razones.[20]

Contrasting somewhat with the educated female protagonist of *El Scholástico,* Fray Luis suggests the model woman must also learn to sew. This valuable craft will free her from reading

> . . . libros de caballerías, y del traer el soneto y la canción en el seno, y del terrero [lugar donde se tiraba al blanco con la ballesta] y del sarao, y de otras cien cosas de este jaez . . . [21]

He condemns the idle women who spend too much time away from home. Loitering about the streets to engage in malicious gossip or in other unbecoming mischief corrupts their minds. He excuses the male members of the species who, as the bread-winners of the family, are obliged to get about in the world in search of their fortunes and suggests only three acceptable missions for which women should be seen in public:

> . . . o es visita de algún enfermo, o es ver la misa, o el oir la palabra de Dios.[22]

He alludes with approbation to the ingenious manner in which the ancient Chinese managed to restrict the tale-bearing vagabonds of their society:

> . . . les tuercen a las niñas los pies, por que cuando sean mujeres no los tengan para salir fuera, y porque, para andar en su casa, aquellos les bastan.[23]

One of the vices which for Fray Luis is least tolerable is committed by women whose warped conception of motherhood inflicts irreparable damage upon their offspring. Proud of themselves for adhering to the teachings of the Catholic church, they boast of their large numbers of offspring, but almost immediately after giving birth to their children, leave their complete care to doting nurse-maids. These self-centered women, in an effort to preserve their own beauty, direct the substitute mothers to breastfeed their newborn, but their profound ignorance of human relationships causes them to react with bitter astonishment when the children demonstrate more loyalty for the ones who truly rear them than for their biological parent. The stepmother was the most frequently ridiculed maternal figure of early medieval literature, but the wicked strategy of the female parents described by Fray Luis easily surpasses the similarly conceived portrayals of the exempla.

Although he has followed the path of former antifeminist proponents in his condemnation of female comportment, it must be concluded that Fray Luis de León does not completely despair. Mindful of the redeeming qualities of spiritual concentration, he prayerfully awaits the transformation of man's "troublesome helpmate" in whose delicate hand lies the key which will open or close for good or for ill the door of his country's future:

> S'l souligne fortement la constitutive debilité feminine et ses deficiences nombreuses, ce n'est, semble-t-il, qu'afin de mieux faire ressortir le mérite de la femme vertueuse, qui sait triompher d'une condition defavorable et fragile pour réaliser en elle la perfection morale la plus achevée.[24]

The general tendency of the above mentioned authors to underscore the negative aspect of almost all facets of the life of women might very well have tempted us to accept this antifeminist current as a biased exploitation with a deliberate attempt to condemn the members of the opposite sex. If, at the same time, one accepts the Biblical rendering of earth's first two human beings and the well known explanation it offers for man's loss of paradise, one will probably ask whether it is reasonable to convict the male of such a grave accusation. In view of Mother Eve's weaknesses in her confrontation with the serpent, the ill fate of womankind has been accepted not as the result of a preconceived campaign on the part of the male but, rather, as the fulfilling of a divine law[25] which proposed to punish any earthling who attempted to make himself equal to his Creator. In accordance with this interpretation, the first representative of the members of the feminine gender of the human race was chastized for her desire to become a sage goddess and, thusly, condemned to become the slave of the male.

These ideas, needless to say, are accepted by some and refuted by others but, in accordance with the information we have gathered from our study, we would tend to question the suggestion of a deliberately designed campaign to exploit women. It is true we have discovered a strong misogynist tendency and, if we consider the material herein treated in its entirety, we note in the beginning, a strong element of negativism in the general characterization of the female prototype. What we must remember, however, is that this literary trajectory of negativism is interrupted. The female protagonists of the sentimental novel are permitted to speak in their own defense. Also, after Rojas and the picaresque novel our authors, while continuing to present the vices of the female, make an honest effort to be objective. We submit that total objectivity on our part cannot permit the complete rejection of the authors' professions of sincerity as they explain their purpose: The didactic writers claim to be interested, first and foremost, in the betterment of society and their understanding of the important role of woman in this mission inspires them to instruct her.

There is nothing abnormal in their preoccupation with the fate of woman. Even a cursory glance at Spanish literature reveals that, at least until the latter part of the sixteenth century, the female protagonist has been presented not only to entertain but also to spiritually fortify her reading public. Man's interest in her destiny continues in the present century, but it is difficult to believe that antifeminist portraits could really depict more vices than those we have already encountered.

NOTES

[1] John Esten Keller, *Motif-Index of Medieval Spanish Exempla* (Knoxville, 1949), pp. ix-x.

[2] Pedro Alfonso, *Disciplina clericalis,* ed. Angel González Palencia (Madrid, 1948), p. 125.

[3] Juan Ruiz, *Libro de Buen Amor,* ed. Manuel Criado de Val (Madrid, 1965), p. 248.

[4] Ruiz, p. 248.

[5] Ruiz, pp. 350-351.

[6] Ruiz, p. 351.

[7] Diego de San Pedro, *Cárcel de amor* (Madrid, 1904), p. 16.

[8] See my book on this subject: Edna N. Sims, *El antifeminismo en la literatura española hasta 1560* (Bogota, 1972), pp. 88-94.

[9] Juan Luis Vives, *Obras completas,* ed. Lorenzo Riber (Madrid, 1947), p. 1086.

[10] Vives, p. 1089.

[11] Cristóbal de Villalón, *Viaje de Turquía,* ed. Antonio G. Solalinde (Buenos Aires, 1942), p. 241.

[12] Villalón, p. 243.

[13] Villalón, p. 246.

[14] Luis de León, *La perfecta casada,* ed. Espasa-Calpe (Madrid, 1963), p. 62.

[15] León, p. 60.

[16] León, p. 85.

[17] Ruiz, p. 221.

[18] León, p. 89.

[19] León, p. 146.

[20] León, p. 124.

[21] León, p. 54.

[22] León, p. 113.

[23] León, p. 130.

[24] Alain Guy, *La Pensée de Fray Luis de León* (Paris, 1943), p. 648.

[25] Pierre Thomas Dehau, *Eve et Marie,* ed. las monjas dominicanas del rosario perpétuo (La Crosse, 1958), p. 59.

**Ruth Beizer-Bohrer**

SOURCE: "Images of Women in Israeli Literature— Myth and Reality," in *Judaism: A Quarterly Journal,* Vol. 33, No. 1, Winter, 1984, pp. 91-100.

*[In the following essay, Beizer-Bohrer discusses the contrast between starkly realistic plots and elaborate rhetorical styles in the works of female Israeli writers.]*

Like their pioneering parents who rebelled against old traditions and left their homes to build a new society in Israel, the second generation and native born Israelis (the 1948, or War-of-Independence-generation) share with their parents an ideology based on the highest values of humanism and egalitarianism. Like those parents, these young Israeli men and women had to face a harsh and hostile landscape, and defend their homes and lives against enemies in order to fulfill a national dream. Both generations were inspired by myths of equality, among them the equality of men and women, which was nourished by the Narodniki and socialist movements in Russia, and the humanitarian vision of writers like Tolstoi and Turgeniev, especially the latter's image of a forthright and accomplished new woman.

One of the striking features of the literature of these native speakers of Hebrew is that, on the one hand, it clings very closely to reality, depicting mundane aspects of working and fighting in an egalitarian society, but, on the other hand, it resorts, contrary to our expectations, to a very high flown style, using language which is very rhetorical and literary, excessively decorative and rich in neologisms and archaisms. It is language that aims at an exalted stylistic level, that attempts to elevate daily life rather than stooping down to it. Characters who are young Sabras, whose qualities and actions are quite typical and ordinary, may be presented with a pathos and with rhetorical stylistic devices that aim to create around them an aura of utter importance as in the following description from Moshe Shamir's novel *He Walked In The Fields:*[1]

> He was a lad whose education could have been somewhat better, and with somewhat less flaws, but he was, in fact, one hundred lads put together, if not more . . . He was a vintner, and someday perhaps he would return to being one again; then he would tend the vines, carefully handling the bunches so as not to cause them any harm . . . He was a young talent, good at field training and at skirmishes in particular . . . He was a beloved child of one of the kibbuzim . . . He was one Jew, young and tanned of skin, marching on the road of Migdal-Karem . . . He was a finger, that knew to press, firmly and knowingly, on a trigger of a Brenn machine-gun . . . He was the mystery of the sudden awakening presence . . . He was the commander of a platoon marching back from a voyage of field training.[2]

The works of all of these young writers, especially during the Forties and early Fifties, display this common stylistic tendency of elevating and stylizing mundane daily occurrences, which Prof. Gershon Shaked calls *pathetic realism.*[3] Writers like Shamir and Yizhar, Megged, Shaham and Mossensohn, despite the vast differences between them, share an attitude that sees in the simple daily actions of work and defense, of a young

growing society, manifestations of heroism and uniqueness. Consequently, the characters and the collective group that appear in the fiction of that period are portrayed in heroic terms, and are surrounded by a certain mythical aura. This heroic treatment and myth-making tendency becomes further evident when one observes the presentation of the male characters in the stories as compared with the females, a sample of the former being obvious in the paragraph quoted above. It is further amazing that in this literature we see only a society of men; no women participate in the central plots of the stories or, rather, the women stay in the background, while the action is reserved only for the men. The roles of the men, furthermore, are made heroic and their images and actions are magnified by means of the high style and the rhetorical intensification, as demonstrated above. In this whole literature we see these young men going to battle, building, defending, and facing trying conditions. We meet them in the Underground against the British and in prison (Yigal Mossensohn), mobilizing the Hagganah and the Palmah (Moshe Shamir, Nathan Shaham), and participating in battles and defense (S. Yizhar, Shaham and others).

This fact, of presenting the history of the formation of the State of Israel, as carried out by men only, is rather surprising, since it is well known that the women participated with the men in all of the actions; they worked, fought and died side by side with them. It seems to me, also, that there is a significant relationship between the magnification of the roles of men and the minimizing of the roles of women that is manifested in the works of these writers. I will try to illustrate this point by a closer examination of the images of women in the works of five authors.

Nathan Shaham's novella, *Always We,*[4] deals with the transition period in Israel from an informal and ideological Underground army (the Hagganah)—to a formal army structure. The story presents several analogical tales of some young lads who are appointed to official higher commanding ranks, but prefer, instead, to volunteer for more dangerous tasks. Each one of them confronts tests of moral and ideological commitments to the values of the Hagganah, and each one of them has to leave behind him an unhappy girl-friend. Thus, Ram, who volunteers as commander of a dangerous mission, has his ability to exercise authority severely hampered and doomed to failure because of a neglectful upper-level commander, a lazy bureaucrat. This is, for him, a test of his manhood and of his moral character. Young Avi, another fellow, and an only son; also volunteers for action in the front line, despite the objections of his mother. The test for his call to action is high-lighted by a scene with his girlfriend Batya, who turns off the alarm clock so as to keep him longer in bed with her. Thus, he wakes up too late to join his troop in their early morning departure. Consequently, he leaves alone and, as said, too late, an action which results in his eventual death. Avi feels cheated by the girl but does not communicate to her the seriousness of his obligation. He feels contempt for her in her inability to understand, as well as for his mother, who tries to keep him behind by pretending sickness. The girl-friend, on her part, cannot understand why he cannot sacrifice a few hours for the sake of their love.

There is a deep gulf between the world of the man and that of the woman. The man faces his duty and destiny alone. He has to leave the comfortable world of the woman, to tear himself away from her seductive sexual attraction, in order to *get out* and fulfill himself.

The following descriptions of women (pp. 95, 98) are typical to Shaham's stories:

> *Ilana:* She was short and her features were small, except for her bosom, which rose in front of her with a maternal tranquility and glorious ripeness.

> *Semadar:* He saw that her lips were thin and well formed and her breast beautiful . . . He leaned towards her under the jacket above their heads, and her breast rubbed against him. The fresh smell that came from her body, mixed with the smell of the rain and the aroma of the atmosphere intoxicated him . . .

The repeated words and phrases describing women are: gentle, pleasant, motherly with soft breasts, warm eyes, moist lips, etc. . . . These images evoke a sense of comfort and associations with bedrooms. Military offices are decorated by the girls with curtains and flowers that are reminiscent of home, and the characterizations of the girls are made in indiscriminate sexy clichés.

The world of men, in contrast, is tough, full of action and of moral and ideological tests. The man controls his emotions and is non-talkative. The woman tries to lure him to stay "in her arms," she wants to spoil him with domestic and sexual comforts. The world of battle and conflict seems to be completely outside of her realm. The exception to the rule is Gipka, the *tomboy,* who tries to imitate the boys and accompany them on their skirmishes. But even she has to use manipulation in order to be allowed to join them.

Similar to Shaham in this aspect of a complete separation between the worlds of men and women is Moshe Shamir in his previously mentioned novel, *He Walked in the Fields.* Shamir, however, characterizes his women with greater individuality, endowing them with emotional articulation and expressiveness, while the men, by contrast, cannot express their emotions. Mikka, who has recently come to Palestine with the Youth Aliyah, also wants Uri, the hero of the story, to remain with her. They have just fallen in love, and have spent only a few weeks together in an affair that has come to a climax by their having sexual relations on their trip in the open fields. This scene, which is the high point of the book and of their intimacy, is also imbued with innocence and youthful trust. Uri, however, is immediately afterwards called to duty in the Hagganah, in spite of his father's and Mikka's pleas. He claims:

> I must go . . . I will not agree that someone else will defend me and you and give his life instead of me. . . . One must go because it was so decided, and those who will return, if they do, will return to the wife, the children, the work and triviality.

The man must go out, away from "triviality," and selfishly free himself from the challenges of personal complications such as Mikka's pregnancy, about which he prefers not to find out. Uri feels himself masculine, free and strong, away on the mountains, leading his soldiers:

> He hops over masses of rock fast, agile and smart; a knapsack tight on his hip. Just rely on Uri, he does need to look where he is going on those heights. His legs, his eyes, his nostrils move as if on their own . . . In only two months he was elevated to the rank of platoon commander . . . his own privates now at his command, adapting themselves to his steps.[5]

The love affair between Uri and Mikka is interrupted by Uri's enlistment in the Hagganah and ends with his untimely death in action two months later. He leaves behind him a pregnant Mikka, who will not abort the child so that she will keep his legacy alive. She is a biological enabler, the progenitor for the mythic father; carrying his seed she will bear the fruit of this young god.

Yigal Mossensohn's book, *The Way of Man with Women,*[6] as the title of the book implies, openly deals with the battle of the sexes. It takes place some time in 1946, during the resistance against the British and the imprisonment of Jewish leaders, and focuses on the man-woman relationships of three married couples on one of the kibbuzim. Two of the men, Joseph Alon and Raphael Huber, whose story is narrated from their point of view, alternating between an omniscient narrator and their own interior monologues, have adulterous wives. Both of the wives are attracted to the same man—Ruben Bloch, the grand seducer of the kibbuz, who is also married, who is attractive and tanned, handsome and smiling, and "who seems to wipe the women off their feet without any effort" (p. 20). The two cheated husbands, whose stories are strictly analogical, are ugly, tormented by jealousy, self-doubt and misgivings. One of them ends up committing suicide, while the other is driven to a crime of passion, killing Ruben as if by accident, an act which, in itself, solves the problem of the seducer's presence on the kibbuz.

The third couple serves as antithesis to the triangles of passion. Nahum Genkin and his wife, Ruth, have an ideal marriage. He, the kibbuz intellectual, sits in his workroom writing "of things that deal with struggle, things that delve into depth" (p. 16), worrying about the many chores to be done the next day. His wife, in the meanwhile, after their happy love making, sleeps in the bedroom, "her yellow hair adorning her narrow face, her fist resting next to her on the pillow, in a peaceful dreamless sleep. She, he thinks to himself, lives her uncomplicated life, a creature being rejuvenated every new day" (p. 19).

The women in this book are presented in stereotyped sexual roles with no individual characterization. They are either sexual nourishers or sexual destroyers. The men, on the other hand, struggle and suffer, think and fight, both among themselves and against the British, each one of them engaged on two fronts—the political, ideological one and the sexual battleground. This dual aspect of the men's lives is epitomized in a scene in which the men of the kibbuz, locked up in Latrun by the British after the "Black Saturday," are anxiously watching Ruben, the seducer, being released before their eyes, and returning alone to the women, free from the competition of the husbands. According to Mossensohn—*"Cherchez la femme"*—behind every man there is a woman who determines his sexual fate, is the secret agent for his life and for his death.

The most sophisticated and accomplished artist among this group of writers is S. Yizhar. In his stories, which concentrate almost entirely on the War of Independence, we also meet primarily groups of men, with no women participating in the plots or in the action. Like the other writers, Yizhar emphasizes the theme of *going out* as indicated by the title of one of his stories. "Before the Departure."[7] His men are tested in action, in confrontations with death and in their loyalty to each other and to the values of the group. In spite of the focus on the men at war, the testing and the call for action, Yizhar does not share the heroic point of view of his contemporaries, but, rather, ironically views the ultimate meaning of man's existence, in war as well in peace. He exercises the critical judgment of a moralist, mixed at times with pathetic enthusiasm when referring to the enterprise of the group as a whole.[8]

Yizhar's images of women, however, are also quite similar to those of the other writers. The women are neither individualized nor characterized, but are a composite. They exist only in fantasies of the main characters and are the objects of their yearnings. Each is an idealized female, whose features are suggested more as a silhouette:

> That special way of pushing back the falling mass of hair, of turning her neck as she bobby-pinned the unruly lock, her curved hand and fingers moving in the silent dexterity of the casual and the calm.[9]

The main character usually notices with fascination the sight of "a quarter of her profile . . . the hair descending over her shoulders with mocking and divine coquetishness."[10] She is also a fantasized mystery of a romantic lady with whom he would escape to "a distant place, with a magnificent citadel built on top of a hill . . . and bring her there like a princess."[11] In fact, she is an adolescent ideal of pure beauty, an unreachable cruel lady who frightens him, and whose presence he really avoids, preferring to be left alone on guard in the quarry, rather than spending the time there with her, so that he can adore her from afar; "she is so distant from being grasped, so fascinating in her absence, so regal in her glory."[12]

This woman appears in Yizhar's stories as a love ideal of a dream girl, to whom he devotes some of the most beautiful lyrical expressions, and who inspires longing and imagination. She is a *love* ideal and not a *sex* ideal; a personification of beauty and of poetry, and there is no mature love relationship in any of the stories. In addition, besides being a love ideal, the woman is also a symbol of the *home* and its *stability*. She provides the place to which the soldiers can return after the battle, so that, despite the threat of war, its destructiveness and meaninglessness, Yizhar's soldiers have the assurance that—

> There is a Ruthie, or a Rena, or a Nira, or a Dali, who waits at home . . . to whom you can return from the fields and the cold . . . for this girl is sure to welcome you when you return, and be kind and loving, gracious and domestic.[13]

Similarly, the young soldiers at Ziklag,[14] amidst frightful enemy attacks, hug the memories of their girl-friends back home. The girls' reality provides them with a sense of security about their own existence. Throughout the lengthy interior monologues of each of the soldiers, the girls are described in a dispassionate and controlled fashion, discussing their sensuality without really communicating it (p. 571-572), not even in the descriptions of Amihai's red-headed girl-friend. The young men's associations with the girls disclose feelings of *trust* and *security,* rather than sexual lust; the girls are symbols of *home* rather than embodiments of *Eros.* In addition to the idealized girl-friends, there also appear in Yizhar's stories incidental women figures, who are shown as loyal home makers and trusting wives preparing food, or welcoming their husbands back from work.[15]

The images of women common to this whole group of young writers, who also represent a unified cultural phenomenon in Israeli literature, are stereotyped sexual and domestic models, relegated to secondary roles, while the male figures are elevated to almost mythic proportions. This is a literature written by men about men, who make a separation between a superior world of men and an inferior world of women. This gulf is bridged by the power of the sex drive and by the men's need for domestic comfort and stability as provided by the women. In many ways this is a *sexist literature* which reveals the minds of men, who are very young, which reflects cultural attitudes of condescension towards women, while it reveals very little about the qualities or the inner world of the women themselves. Shaham and Mossensohn share a sharp sexist approach, consistent throughout; even in their later works, expressed by a sense of male superiority that either claims women's ineptness, or takes on a patronizing attitude of protectiveness. The women in their stories are portrayed as incapable of comprehending the complexities and difficulties of the men's world; they are motivated by the need for love expressed via sex or the wish to possess a man and keep him home. This simplistic and man-centered viewpoint results in total stereotyping of the women along sexual models, and the complete separation of the realms of men and women. The women are located in the home, the bedroom, the kitchen, while the men go out to war, to prison, to hardships. The war seems not to touch the women at all; they remain on its periphery, except when their lovers or husbands get killed.

Shamir and Yizhar reveal greater complexities in the treatment of the man-woman relationship, and in the characterizations of both men and women. Shamir's hero is aware of the challenges of involvement with the woman and opts to avoid them by escaping into the heroic and glamorized world of the man and of the war. Yizhar's heroes also reveal a complex psychological attitude to women, expressed by avoidance and youthful adoration of an idealized woman. The young heroes in both Shamir and Yizhar's worlds display the complexities and complexes of immature young men.

The central metaphor employed by all of these writers and which expresses their common cultural attitudes is, as mentioned before, the *going out,* accompanied by a physical separation of territories. The men must go out to a different realm than that of the women in order to meet challenges and prove themselves. They must be able to tear themselves away from that world which is characterized by comfort, pleasure, reassurance and sexuality. The separate worlds are portrayed in opposing images—hardness versus softness, toughness versus pleasure, action versus talk, challenges versus emotions, sacrifice and death versus security and stability. The world of this young *macho* male society measures itself in terms of heroism and confrontations, wishing to create through the fiction and the language a new mythic male model, reminiscent of Hemingway's world of men.

The picture that emerges from this literature stands in sharp contrast to the ideals of equality between the sexes which Socialism and Zionism included in its ideology. What, then, happened to the ideals? Leslie Hazelton, in her book, *Israeli Women, The Reality Behind the Myth* (1977),[16] claims that the myth of equality of women exists only as a rationalization, not as a reality, because "myths compel respect, not necessarily by their truth, but because they are needed by those who believe in them" (p. 21). The myth presents an admirable Israeli woman, strong and independent, sharing and contributing equally with her male pioneer countryman in the army, on the land and in politics. Indeed, the myth exists, but it is mostly conveyed in parades and in photographs that show "a gun toting woman fighter, ready to sacrifice her life for her country, looking tough, dressed in fatigues, hair severely pulled back under caps, training with full concentration and deadly seriousness." In reality, women did learn how to use guns but it was generally the men who did the guard duty and the women who welcomed them and, if necessary, nursed them. In the first stages of the War of Independence women soldiers were essential for convoy duty since they could conceal guns and grenades under their clothes and evade detection by the British troops manning the road blocks. Some women served in the Palmah as well as in the underground organizations of Ezel and Lehi, but few were actually involved in combat, once the war was under way. Later, in spite of the women's protest against the discrimination, they were

trained for defense warfare only, which meant that they served as wireless operators, nurses and quartermasters. There were some women who actually fought and died in battle, but it was solely on these exception that the rule of the myth was to be based.

Deeply revealing and most important documentary material on how the women themselves felt and acted is offered by Netiva Ben-Yehuda's biographical novel—*Bein Hasfirot* (Between Calendars),[17] 1981, which deals with her experiences as a 19 year old commander in the Palmah during 1947-48. She says:

> The girl in the Palmah had a very hard time. We were only three women commanders in the whole third battalion. We did not seek to become commanders, we were not suffragettes, the Palmah was. It inscribed on its flags the principle of equality of the sexes, but it did not uphold it. We continuously had to prove that we deserved that right, that we were able and capable, a thing no male had to do. Our success did not count, our previous achievements did not add up, each time we had to prove ourselves anew. In 1947 we were only 3,000 Palmah members ready for combat in a country of 60,000 Jews, and half of us were women. On November 29, 1947 came the order—to remove all the females from the front to the rear. This left only 1500 men ready to defend the country . . . my heart was ready to explode, we were waiting all these months, dying to go out to the real fighting . . .[18]

Netivah's book gives expression to her outrage and continuous struggle against male chauvinistic attitudes summed up in the familiar slogan, "no female will be in charge of us." Two central incidents vividly illustrate the nature of the dual struggle that these young women (and men) had to face. On the one hand, they were teenagers, who unpreparedly but enthusiastically were caught in a situation of "making history" with their own bodies. On the other hand, they were women and, as such, encountered additional difficulties from their male comrades. Two incidents which occurred in the Galilee before the formal outbreak of the war illustrate this situation. In the one, Netivah participated in an ambush of an Arab bus carrying important Arab agitators. She suddenly found herself alone facing the head Arab terrorist who had jumped out of the disabled bus. Unflinchingly, and for the first time in her life, she pulled the trigger and killed him. This story gave rise to an immediate legend about a demonic Jewish woman fighter. The other incident took place in Ramot Naftali while taking her thirteen newly arrived trainees to the fields to teach them the use of the rifle, when, suddenly and unexpectedly, they were surrounded by thousands of attacking Arab enemies. Under a hellish barrage of fire she taught those trainees to use the rifle and carry out field retreat, and succeeded, after a tense and breathtaking five hour period (and a remove of one kilometer), to bring them back to safety. One man got killed immediately and she had to leave him behind. Afterwards, she had to fight off the rumors and the slander by the very same commander who himself selected those training grounds where they were ambushed, and who blamed her for leaving the dead man behind on account of her being "a woman."[19]

*Conclusion:* The documentary material from the period about male attitudes towards women in Israeli society confirms, in many ways, the picture that comes forth from the literary evidence. The literary and the historical material reveal the same gap between the ideological declarations of equality between the sexes and the real psychological attitudes of male chauvinism and discrimination against women that are deeply imbedded in the existing cultural patterns. It is a phenomenon, common to revolutionary and battling societies, quickly to create new myths that project a new self image, which do not always strike root in the actual cultural-social patterns of life. Both myths, the one of women's equality, the other of a new male hero, ironically contradictory to one another, grew simultaneously from the same ideological roots of an emerging new society in Palestine. Both were projections of ideals; neither was true to reality.

Even later developments in Israeli society have not much altered these patterns. The many wars and the continuous state of siege have directed the concerns of society towards national priorities, rather than to the status of its individuals. Issues like equal rights for women in social, economic and religious matters, and the attempts at creating a feminist political platform in the Knesset have met with little success or popularity, even among the women in Israel. With the continuous need for a large, stable male military structure (the women's divisions being relegated to service roles only), the tendencies towards the preservation and cultivation of a strong male self image have continued to prevail. At the same time, the insecurities on the outside have continued to emphasize the need for security and stability in the home and the traditional roles of women. Few dare to rock the boat and challenge the foundations of society's structure, and much is rationalized by excuses of national unity and existing myths of equality. The needs, however, for an improved quality of life for both women and men, and the need to share equally the responsibilities for the nation are more and more felt, as well as the yearnings for a state of peace, in which these just and fair goals might be implemented.

### NOTES

[1] Moshe Shamir, *Hu Halakh Bassadot* (*Sifriyat Poalim*, 1947), pp. 269-270. Translations my own (RBB).

[2] Note the recurring anaphora "he was." It is repeated twenty times in a passage extending over one and a half pages and devoted to the descriptions of the qualities of Uri, the hero of the novel.

[3] Gershon Shaked, *Gal Hadash Bassiporet Haivrit* (Tel-Aviv: *Sifriyat Poalim*, 1971), p. 41.

[4] Nathan Shaham, *Tamid Anakhnu* (*Sifriyat Poalim*, 1952). Translations from Shaham my own.

[5] *Hu Halakh Bassadot*, p. 240.

[6] Yigal Mossensohn, *Derekh Gever* (Tel-Aviv: Tversky, 1953). Translations from Mossensohn my own.

[7] S. Yizhar, *"B'terem Yeziah,"* (1949) in *Arba'ah Sippurim* (Tel-Aviv: Hakibbuz *Hameuhad*, 1967), sixth printing, p. 46. Translations my own.

[8] See the concluding parts of S. Yizhar, *Midnight Convoy*, trans. Reuven Ben-Yosef, (Jerusalem: Israel Universities Press, 1969) and *"B'terem Yeziah."*

[9] *Midnight Convoy*, p. 199.

[10] *"B'terem Yeziah,"* p. 29.

[11] Ibid, p. 20.

[12] S. Yizhar, *"Laila B'li Yeriyot,"* 1939, in *Hahorshah Bagivah,* (*Sifriyat Poalim*, 1947), p. 329. Translations my own.

[13] *"B'terem Yeziah,"* p. 29.

[14] S. Yizhar, *Yemei Ziklag*, 2 vols. (Tel-Aviv: Am-Oved, 1958).

[15] S. Yizhar, *B'fa'atei Negev* (*Hakibbuz Hameuhad*, first edition 1945, revised edition 1978); and *"Massa' El Gedot Ha'erev,"* 1941, in *Hahorshah Bagivah*.

[16] Leslie Hazelton, *Israeli Women* (New York: Simon and Schuster, 1977).

[17] Netivah Ben-Yehuda, *Bein Hasfirot* (Jerusalem: Keter, 1981).

[18] Ibid., paraphrased and translated by me from pages: 86, 107, 121, 160, 278, 280.

[19] This exciting and realistic account, written in reportage style, can be found on pp. 218-235.

---

# FICTION

## Ford Madox Ford

SOURCE: "The Woman of the Novelists," in *The Critical Attitude*, Duckworth & Co., 1911, 190 p.

[*In the following essay, Ford presents, in the form of a letter, an analysis of the "Woman of the Novelists," which he defines as the amalgam of women as portrayed in literature, finding that presentations of female characters are generally harmful to women in society and personal life.*]

My dear mesdames, X, Y, and Z.

We should like you to observe that we are writing to you not on the women, but on the Woman of the novelists. The distinction is very deep, very serious. If we were writing on female characters—on the women of the novelists—we should expect to provide a series of notes on the female characters of our predecessors or our rivals. We should say that Amelia (Fielding's Amelia) was too yielding, and we should look up Amelia and read passages going to prove our contention. Or we should say we envied Tom Jones—and again give our reasons for that envy. We should say that Amelia Osborne (Thackeray's Amelia) was a bore. And we should bore you with passages about Amelia. We should flash upon you Clarissa and Pamela; Portia and the patient Grisel; Di Vernon and Lady Humphrey's Daughter (perhaps that is not the right title); Rose (from *Evan Harrington*)—we adore Rose and very nearly believe in her—and Mr Haggard's "She." We should in fact try to present you with a series of *Plutarch's Lives* in tabloid form, contrasting Amelia Osborne with Fielding's Amelia; Rose Harrington with Lady Rose's Daughter (we have got the title right this time) or Portia with the heroine of *What Maisie Knew*. It would be fun and it would be quite easy: we should just have to write out a string of quotations, and there would be an end of it.

But the "Woman of the Novelists" is quite other guess work. It is analysis that is called for—analysis that is hard to write and harder to read. To put it as clearly as we can, all the women of the novelists that you have read make up for you the Woman of the Novelists. She is, in fact, the creature that you average out as woman.

For you who are women, this creature is not of vast importance as an object lesson. For us men she is of the utmost. We fancy that, for most of us she is the only woman that we really know. This may seem to some of you an extravagant statement. Let us examine it a little more closely.

Has it occurred to you to consider how few people you really know?—How few people, that is to say, there are whose biographies, whose hearts, whose hopes, whose desires and whose fears you have really known and sounded! As you are women and a good many of you are probably domestic women, this will not appear to you as clear as it will to most men. Yet it will be clear enough. Let us put a case—the case we know best—our own, in fact.

We have a way of putting ourselves to sleep at night by indulging in rather abstruse mental calculations. Lately we figured out for ourselves how many people we know, however slightly. The limits we set were that we should know their names, be able to sit next them at table. We could reckon up rather over a thousand—to be exact, one thousand and forty.

But of all of these how many do we really *know?* The figure that we have arrived at may seem a little preposterous, but we have considered them rather carefully. We know intimately the circumstances and the aspirations of eight men and two women and we are bound to say that both women say we do not understand them. Still for the purposes of our argument we will say that we do.

In the present-day conditions of life, as we have said, men are more prone to these acquaintanceships that are not knowledge. They go to business and negotiate with great numbers of simulacra in the shape of men. Some have eyes, beards, voices, humours and tempers; some are merely neckties, waistcoats or penholders. But as to how these simulacra live, what they really desire—apart from their functional desires to outwit us in the immediate business in hand—as to what they are as members of society, we have, as a rule, no knowledge at all.

We meet at our club every day from twenty to thirty men of whose circumstances we have not the least idea. One of them is, for instance, quite good company, distinguished and eminently conversational. We know what his public function is: we know his politics: we know his vices. But as for knowing *him:* why, we have never even looked him up in *Who's Who* to see if he is married!

And, if we are so walled off from men, how much more are we walled off from women? I should say that, out of that odd thousand acquaintances, about six hundred are women. Yet the conventions of modern life prevent us from really knowing more than two—and those two, we are told, we do not understand.

We daresay we don't. But who is to blame? Why, the Woman of the Novelists.

We trust that, by now, you know what we are driving at.

For the conditions of modern life are such that for experience of our fellow men we have to go almost entirely to books. And the books that we go to for this knowledge are those of the imaginative writers.

(Thus among novelists—or the greatest of English novelists—we should include Shakespeare. We should also include Chaucer and perhaps the English dramatists up to Sheridan—the dramatists like Congreve, that is, who are read and not performed. We have reasons for making these inclusions that we will not dwell upon.)

We may take ourself to be the average man: the man in the street. And you will find that the man in the street—or rather the men on your hearthstones—your husbands and brothers—are in much the same case as ourself. You will find that they know up to a score or so of men. You will—if you are the average wife—take care that they don't know more than a couple of women, one of them being yourself. And you will all agree with us when we say that your husbands and your brothers do not understand you. They think they do; but they do not. Poor simple, gross creatures, for them two and two will be four. For you—I wonder how much two and two are?

Yet your man of the hearthstone will talk about woman. He will talk about her with a simple dogmatism, with a childish arrogance. He will tread on all your corns. He will say that women are incapable of humour. (Of course, in his mind he will exclude you and his sister and mother—but he will never make you believe that.) He will say that women are changeable. (He will probably include you in that.) He will say that every woman is at heart a rake. (We do not know where you come in there.) He will say that a certain lane is called Dumb Woman's Lane because it is so steep that no woman's feet ever carried her up it. Well, you know all about what he will say as well as we do.

But you observe: he is talking about Woman; he talks with the confidence of an intimate. But what woman is it that he talks of? Why is it that you are not torn with pangs of jealousy when he thus speaks? Who is this creature; incapable of humour, steadfastness, virtue or reticence? You are not alarmed: you do not suddenly say to yourself: "Are these the women he spends his time with when he pretends to be at his office, his club, his golf-links or his tailor's?" You are quite tranquil on that account; you hate him for his conceit, but you know you have him safe. This is no woman of prey that he is analysing. Women of prey are more attractive: they bewilder, they ensnare, they do not leave room for dogmatism. No, This is the Woman of the Novelist!

We do not mean to say that there have never been men whose views of women were founded upon actual experience, who took lines of their own and adhered to them. There have even been imaginative writers who have done this: there have been, that is to say, misogynists, as there have been women worshippers, and there have been a few men to whom the eternal feminine presents eternal problems for curiosity.

We do not recall, at this moment, any great novelist who has actually been a misogynist: it would indeed be a little difficult to write a novel from a misogynistic point of view—though there are several novelists who come as nearly as is possible to a pitch of altogether ignoring the Fair Sex.

The Fair Sex! Do not these two words bring to mind the greatest of all misogynists—Arthur Schopenhauer? For, says he, that we should call the narrow-chested, broad hipped, short-legged, small waisted, low-browed, light-brained tribe, the Fair Sex, is that not a proof of the Christo-Germanic stupidity from which all we Teutons suffer?

We wonder how many of you have read Schopenhauer's *Über die Weiber?* If you have not you should certainly do so. It is an indictment of what—owing to various causes—women may sink to. It is, of course, exaggerated; but it is savagely witty in the extreme. (And, if it enrage you, go on to read the other monograph in *Parerga and Paralipomena* in which Schopenhauer attacks carters who crack whips. *Über Lärm und Geräusch* it is called. There you will see that what Schopenhauer attacks—along with one type of woman—is the middling sorts of men.)

The one type of woman that he attacks—the garrulous, light-headed, feather-brained type that he says includes all woman-kind—this one type was drawn from the one woman from whom Schopenhauer really suffered. Schopenhauer was—his pasquinades apart—a mystic and dogged thinker, and the thinker is apt to consider that his existence is the all important thing in this world—and that the disturber of his existence is the greatest of criminals.

The one woman from whom he suffered was his mother. All other women he stalled off; his mother he could not. And Johanna Schopenhauer was what you might call a terror.

To begin with, for a considerable portion of Schopenhauer's life, she held the purse strings. She was an indomitable, garrulous creature. (Need we say that she was one of the most successful women novelists of her day?) She had the power to approach Schopenhauer at all times: to talk to him incessantly: to reproach this needy and lofty thinker with his want of success as a writer: to recommend him to follow her example and become a successful novelist.

So that, actually, it was his mother's type that he was attacking when he thought—or pretended to think—that he was attacking all womenkind. And that, upon the whole, is what has happened to most of the few writers who have systematically attacked women. We do not think, as we have said, that there are many of these, but some writers have had rather narrow escapes. There was, for instance, Gustave Flaubert.

Flaubert was several times pressed to marry, but he always refused and he gave his reason that: "Elle pourrait entrer dans mon cabinet"—"She might come into my study." From this you will observe that he found just such another woman as was Johanna Schopenhauer. And indeed it *was* just such another—the lady he called La Muse—that he found. The Muse was the only woman with whom he came really into contact—and she was a popular novelist, a writer of feuilletons and of fashion pages, an incessant chatterer. She was no doubt a sufficiently attractive woman to tempt Flaubert towards a close union. But his own wisdom and the fact that she plagued him incessantly to read her manuscripts let him save himself with a whole skin. He was not minded to give her the right—or at any rate the power—to come into his study.

If he had done so—who knows?—under the incessant stimulus of her presence he might have joined the small band of writers who have been women haters.

As it is he was—not so much a misanthropist—a hater of his kind as a lover of what is shipshape. He had in fact The Critical Attitude. And seeing how badly—how stupidly—the affairs of this world are governed—this loving the Shipshape rendered him perpetually on the look-out for the imbecilities of poor humanity.

If he was hard upon women, he was harder, without doubt, upon men. Madame Bovary is idle, silly, hyper-romantic, unprincipled, mendacious—but she is upon the whole more true to her poor little lights than most of the male characters of the book—than Homais the quack, than her two lovers—and she is less imbecile than her husband. And indeed, the most attractive and upon the whole the wisest in the conduct of life and in human contacts—the most attractive and wisest character that Flaubert ever drew is Madame Arnoux in *L'Education Sentimentale*. She is nearly a perfect being, recognising her limitations and fulfilling her functions. I do not think that Flaubert drew more than one other such—the inimitable Félicité, the patient household drudge, in the *Cœur Simple*. Bouvard and Pécuchet are lovable buffoons or optimists, brave and impracticable adventurers into the realms of all knowledge: these two dear men are one or the other as you look at them. Flaubert drew them lovingly but we are not certain that he loved them; it is impossible to doubt that he loved Madame Arnoux, the lady, and Félicité of the Simple Soul. He drew each of them as being efficient—and since he drew two efficient women, and no efficient man at all—we may consider him to have given us the moral that, in an imbecile world, as he saw it, woman had a better chance than man.

We are not quite certain whether we regard Flaubert or Turgenev as having been the greatest novelist the world ever produced. If we introduce a third name—that of Shakespeare—we grow a little more certain. For we should hesitate to say that Flaubert was greater than Shakespeare—in fact we are sure we should not say it—but we are pretty certain that Turgenev was.

His personality was more attractive than Flaubert's—and his characters are more human than Shakespeare's were. So we should give the palm of the supreme writer to Turgenev—and so, we fancy, would every woman if she were wise. For Turgenev was a great lover—a great champion—of women. He was a great lover—a great champion, too, we may say—of humanity. Where Flaubert saw only that humanity was imbecile, Turgenev, kindlier and more sympathetic, saw generally that men were gullible and ineffectual angels. And it is significant that all the active characters—all the persons of action—in Turgenev's novels are women, There is just one man of action—of mental and political action—in all Turgenev's works—and that man, Solomin, the workman agitator, is the one great failure of all Turgenev's projections. He is wooden and unconvincing, an abstractly invented and conventional figure.

And this preponderance of the Fair Sex in Turgenev's action does not come about because Turgenev was a champion of women: it arises simply because of the facts of Russian life as Turgenev saw them. (And let us offer you as an argument, when you are most confounded with the dogma that women never *did* anything political, the cases of Russia and Poland. For, when the history of the Russian Revolution comes to be written it will be seen that an enormous proportion of the practical organising work of the revolution was done by women, the comparatively ineffectual theorising has been in the main the

work of men. As for Poland—the Polish national spirit has been kept alive almost solely by the women.)

So with Turgenev: if you take such a novel as *The House of Gentlefolk* you will find that it is Lisa who is the active character, taking a certain course which she considers as the course of duty and persevering in it. Her lover, Lavretsky, on the other hand, is an ineffectual being, resigned if you will, but resigned to the action of destiny. And, roughly speaking, this is the case with all Turgenev's characters. It is Bazaroff the Nihilist who is in the hands of the woman he loves: it is only in the physical activities of the peasants that the man takes the upper hand.

But Turgenev, if he was a great lover of women, did not idealise them. We love Lisa with a great affection: she might be our patient but inflexible sister: we love her and believe in her because she is the creation of a patient and scrupulous hand.

Let us now consider the woman of the English novelist—because, alas, we are a nation of readers so insular that only a few thousands of us have heard of Madame Bovary and a very few hundreds of Lisa. Consequently, these figures hardly bulk at all as colouring the figure of the Woman of the Novelist as she affects us English.

Let us consider the best known woman of action in English imaginative writing; let us consider Portia. Here we have a woman witty a little beyond woman's wit: graceful a little beyond woman's grace: gracious a little beyond the graciousness of women: with a knowledge of the male heart a little beyond the knowledge that woman ever had. She is, in fact, the super-woman.

If we love Liza, we adore Portia: but if we believe in Turgenev's heroine do we ever quite believe in Shakespeare's? Do we ever quite—to the very back of our minds—believe in Cordelia? Or in Beatrice? Or in Desdemona? Or in Juliet? Do we believe that we shall ever meet with a woman like these? And—what is more important still—do we ever believe that these woman will "wear," that their qualities will not pall, their brilliances create in us no impatience, or cause in them no reactions that in their effects would try us beyond bearing? Portia might get us out of a scrape: Juliet might answer passion with passion: Desdemona might bear with our ill-humours: Beatrice would pique us delightfully whilst we were courting. We might, in fact—we *do* certainly—believe in these super-women during certain stages of our lives. But . . . what a very big "But" that is!

And yet, with the women of Shakespeare the tradition of the Woman of the Novelist is already in full swing. This particular good woman—the heroine of an episode—is a peculiarly English product—a product of what Schopenhauer called, as we have said, Christo Germanisch Dummheit (Christo Germanic stupidity.) It is hardly, in fact, stupidity: it is rather idealism. (But then in the practical affairs of the world idealism is very nearly the same thing as stupidity.) The man, in fact, who would marry Beatrice would be a stupid man, or one obsessed by erotic idealism. (For certainly—quite certainly—she would "entrer dans son cabinet.")

Do not please imagine that these are mere cheapnesses. Or, if they are, consider how life itself is a matter of infinite cheapnesses. And then consider again how this tradition of the super-woman heroine, the woman who is the central figure of an episode—has come right down to our own time on the wings of the English novel. She is always, this super-woman, gliding along some few inches above the earth, as we glide when we dream we are flying. She is a sort of Diana with triumphant mien before whose touch all knotted problems dissolve themselves. So she has traversed, this woman of the novelist, down and across the ages until we find her, triumphant and buoyant still, in the novels of Mr Meredith. Do not we all adore Rose and Diana and Letty—and all these other wonderful creatures? And do not we all, at the back of our minds, disbelieve in them?

You will say that Mr Meredith is the great painter of your sex. But you will not believe that: the statement is a product of emotion. You mean that he is the great pleader for your sex.

Ah! the Woman of the Novelist—the Woman of the Novelist: what great harm she has done to the cause of women in these days and for centuries back!

For consider what she has done: when Elizabethan England put Portia on the stage the Elizabethan Englishman considered that he had in public treated Woman so handsomely that she had got as much as she could reasonably expect. He proceeded in private, to cheat her out of nine-tenths of what she deserved.

You have only to read any of the innumerable *Advices to a Son,* written by various Tudor gentlemen to realise to what an extent this was really the case. The son was advised to regard his wife as a very possibly—a very probably—dangerous adjunct to a house. She was esteemed likely to waste a man's substance, to cheat his heirs in the interests of an almost inevitable second marriage. She was not to be chosen for her talkativeness as that would distract a man: (elle pourrait, in fact, entrer dans son cabinet) She was not to be of a silent disposition because she could not entertain him when he needed entertainment.

And so—hardly and coldly—with that peculiar hardness and coldness that distinguished all the real manifestations of Tudor prudence—were the lines of women's life laid down in these Tudor testaments. Woman was a necessary animal, a breeder of children; but she was a very dangerous one, or at least a very uncertain beast—a chestnut horse exhibited most of her characteristics. Desdemona and the patient Grisel were acknowledged to be dreams: Beatrice of the ready tongue was to be eschewed, and as for Portia—the Elizabethan was pretty sure, even *his* lawyers with their settlements could not bind her!

So that, in Elizabethan days, as to-day, you had a Woman of the Novelists, a Super-Woman—set on high and worshipped. But you had a very different woman whom you contemplated—if you were a man—from behind the locked doors of your *cabinet.*

To-day we have still the Woman of the Novelists—the woman of Mr Meredith. Like Portia she is inimitable in episodes: she will get a man out of a scrape: she will be inimitable too during a season of courtship. We do not, being English, go in for the novel of life: we do not want to: we do not want to face life. When we marry, it is a woman something like Portia, or Di Vernon, or Sophia Western, or Rose Harrington that we marry. We have given up as impracticable the Elizabethan habit of attempting, by selection or settlements, to choose and to tie down a partner for life. We have given it up; we say: "The Woman of the Novelists is one thing; but as for the woman we shall marry, she is an incomprehensible creature, bewildering and unknowable. We must take our chance."

But we should like to point out to you that we might say almost the same thing if we were going to make an indissoluble life-partnership with any man. We have, as it were, a romantic—a novelist's—idea that men, as distinguished from women, are upright, logical, hardworking, courageous, businesslike. We do not really believe this. But, if we go into partnership with a man, we do it because we like him or believe in him; because, in fact, he appeals to us. We cannot tell how he will wear, any more than we can tell how the woman we marry, or want to marry, will wear. He may go off with the till: it may prove intolerable to sit day after day in the same office with such a bounder; the fact that he comes in at night full of energy and loquacity may be intolerable, too, if he is sharing our rooms.

This will not much surprise us in a man. It is apt to disconcert us very much in our Portia—and we say: "What a strange beast woman is! She was so clever with Shylock. Has not she got the tact to see that we need our studies to ourselves?"

Of course, the woman that we know, the woman, that is to say, that eventually each of us gets to know, is fused at last into the Woman of the Novelists. This invariably happens, for we woo a Portia who has neither a past nor a future, and life welds for us this Portia into an ordinary woman. This combination of the Woman of the Novelists who is always in one note with a creature of much the same patiences, impatiences, buoyant moments, reactions, morning headaches and amiabilities, as our own— this hybrid of a conventional deity and a quite real human being is a very queer beast indeed. We wonder if you ever quite realise what you are to the man on your hearthstone? We do not know if any woman ever really thinks—really—truly—and to the depths of her whole being—thinks that she has a bad husband. We do not know about this, but we are perfectly certain that no husband ever thinks that he has a bad wife. You see—

poor, honest, muddled man with the glamour of the novelist's woman on him—he is always looking about somewhere in the odd and bewildering fragments of this woman who has the power to bedevil, to irritate, to plague and to madden him. He looks about in this mist of personal contacts for the Cordelia that he still believes must be there. He believes that his Sophia Western is still the wise, tolerant, unjealous Sophia, who once made him with the blessing of some Parson Adams, the happiest of men. God forbid that we should say she is not there. We are certain that the man believes she is, only he cannot find her. He is so close to her, and you know that if you hold your nose very close to a carpet, it is useless to hope to see its pattern. But no—believe us when we say that no man in the silence of his study believes that he has a bad wife. She may drink, but he will think that some action, some attribute, or the circumstances of the life that she has led with him, gives excuse. She may nag, but he will believe that it is because he has never really taken the trouble to explain the excellencies of his motives and his actions. She may be unfaithful, but in his heart he will believe that it is because he has been unable to maintain the strain of playing Benedick to her Beatrice. And this poor, honest, simple man may declaim against his wife to his friends, may seek in new Amelias new disillusionments, may seek amid the glamour of *causes celèbres* his liberty—but he will listen to the words of his K.C.—of his special pleading conscience—with a certain contrition, for before his eyes, dimly radiant, there will stand the figure of the Woman of the Novelists.

Now, if this man never believes that his wife is a bad wife he will yet pick up certain little salient peculiarities. He will not believe that any given manifestation of unreasonableness is a part of the real character of his Di Vernon; he will regard it as an accidental, as what Myers called a supra-liminal, exhibition, just as when he himself, having travelled first class with a third-class ticket, neglects to pay the excess fare. It is not the sort of thing he would do, it is only what by accident he has done. He remains honest and upright in spite of it. So when his wife calls him a beast he does not believe that the word "beast" is really a part of the vocabulary of, let us say, Dolly of the "Dolly Dialogues." It is all one with his excess fare that he carelessly—and it was so unlike him!—neglected to pay.

At the same time a constant aggregation of these little nothings becomes impressed upon his mind. They are the reaction from the Woman of the Novelists. He does not believe that they are part of his individual woman's nature, he cannot quite make them out—so he attributes them to her sex. (If he lived with a man he would not attribute them to this man's sex but he would say it was because poor so-and-so went to Eton instead of Winchester, or because he smokes too much, or because he takes after his parents.)

The woman of the music-hall, in fact—"My wife who won't let me" and "My wife's mother who has come to stay"—this creature is the direct product of *à rebours* of

the Woman of the Novelists. For, if no man really believes that his wife is a woman of the music-hall, he is not so loyal to the wife of his friend Hunter. His own wife was *Diana of the Crossways*. She still, if she would only be serious for a minute—is Diana of the Crossways. Mrs Hunter, however, is only Mrs Hunter. To Hunter she was once St Catherine of Siena and still is saintly. But our friend catches certain phases of the intercourse of the Hunters; he hears an eloquent discourse of Hunter about the action of the tariff on the iron industry in Canada, he hears this eloquent and learned discourse interrupted by Mrs Hunter's description, let us say of the baby linen of the Prince of the Asturias. He does not know that Mrs Hunter was once St Catherine—is still St Catherine—and, as such, has a right to be more interested in infants than in iron trades. And, just as in the newspapers, crimes are recorded and the normal happenings of life let alone, so a number of irrational, unreasonable, illogical actions of real women become stored in our poor friend's mind. Thus he arrives at his grand question with which he will attempt to stump you, when you ask for a certain little something:

"Why can't you," he asks, "learn to be logical, patient, businesslike, self-restrained?"

"You cannot because of your sex? Then give up talking and try to be the womanly woman."

And by the womanly woman he means the Woman of the Novelists. And if you achieved this impossibility, if you became this quite impossible she, he would still squash you with the unanswerable question:

"What does St Catherine, what on earth does St Catherine of Siena, want with a vote?"

You see this terrible creation, this Woman of the Novelists has you both ways. Man has set her up to do her honour, and you, how foolishly and how easily you have fallen in the trap!—you, women, too, have aided and applauded this setting up of an empty convention. Women are not more illogical than men, but you are quite content as a rule to allow yourselves to be called illogical if only you may be called more subtle. Women are not less honourable than men, but you are quite content to be called less honourable than men if only you may be called long-suffering. In the interests of inflated virtues you have sacrificed the practical efficiencies of life, you are content to be called hysterical, emotional and utterly unworthy of a place in any decently ordered society, in order that you may let men bamboozle themselves into thinking that in other ways you are semi-divine. Well, this has recoiled upon your own heads and now the average man, whilst believing that in certain attributes you are semi-divine, believes that in the practical things of this life you are more incapable—the highest and most nearly divine of you is more incapable of exercising the simplest functions of citizenship than the lazy and incompetent brute who carries home your laundryman's washing. I do not know which of you, woman or novelist, is the more culpable. The novelist, being a lazy brute, has evolved this convenient labour-saving contrivance. You, thinking it would aid you in maintaining an ascendancy over a gross and stupid creature called man, have aided and abetted this crime against the Arts, and the Arts have avenged themselves, the gross and stupid creature has found his account and you are left as the Americans say "in the cart."

Whether there will ever come a reaction, the God Who watches over all to-morrows alone can tell. But you have the matter a great deal in your own hands, for to such an extent is the writer of imaginative literature dependent on your suffrages, that if women only refused to read the works of any writer who unreasonably idealises their sex, such writers must starve to death. For it should be a self-evident proposition that it would be much better for you to be, as a sex, reviled in books. Then men coming to you in real life would find how delightful you actually are, how logical, how sensible, how unemotional, how capable of conducting the affairs of the world. For we are quite sure that you are, at least we are quite sure that you are as capable of conducting them as are men in the bulk. That is all we can conscientiously say and all, we feel confident, that you will demand of us.

## Gordon W. Thompson

SOURCE: "Conrad's Women," in *Nineteenth-Century Fiction*, Vol. 32, March, 1978, pp. 442-63.

[*In the following essay, Thompson argues that Joseph Conrad's turn to stories focusing largely on his protagonists' relationships with women in his later career was a conscious decision, not an unconscious shift in the author's thoughts on women.*]

We have learned to think of Joseph Conrad's writing career as falling into two distinct periods. The first, from 1895 until 1910, is the period of great achievement during which a skeptical Conrad portrayed isolated, deluded individuals stumbling into a moral abyss and either being destroyed or emerging with a stoical dedication to human solidarity. The second period begins in 1910 when Conrad, after completing *Under Western Eyes,* suffered some kind of breakdown. With the exception of *The Shadow-Line* (1917), his late fiction is weakened by the absence of the earlier skepticism and austerity; in these works, Conrad's writing is sentimental and romantic, full of unconvincing tales of timid heroes who are inspired by powerful women.

This change in Conrad's fiction is called a "decline" by Douglas Hewitt, Thomas Moser, and Albert J. Guerard,[1] all of whose books appeared in the 1950's. The key to the decline is what Moser calls "the uncongenial subject"—women, especially women in love. Moser demonstrates that Conrad had difficulty finishing books about love (*The Sisters* and *The Rescue,* for example), that he was unable to dramatize emotions, that sexual subject

matter was inhibiting for him. Moser suggests that Conrad could not write about love because he didn't really "believe in" it: "We must guard against being surprised, shocked or horrified at Conrad's negative attitude toward love. How could it be otherwise? Conrad sees man as lonely and morally isolated, harried by egoistic longings for power and peace, stumbling along a perilous path, his only hope benumbing labor or, in rare cases, a little self-knowledge. Conrad could not possibly reconcile so dark a view with a belief in the panacea of love, wife, home, and family."[2] By persistently writing about women and love, as he does in six out of seven of his last works, Conrad could not avoid failure, for he invariably fell into "creative bewilderment in the presence of a sexual situation."[3]

Critical consensus supports Hewitt, Moser, and Guerard,[4] and I share the view that Conrad's later works lack the power and moral complexity of the earlier ones. It is troubling, however, that we have not reflected adequately on the *artistic* reasons for Conrad's returning to a love theme over and over again—and not only in his last works. (As Bernard C. Meyer, M.D., points out, the protagonist is emotionally involved with a woman in twenty-five out of Conrad's thirty-one stories.)[5] Instead of assuming that Conrad had legitimate artistic purposes in mind when he placed his uncertain heroes under the spells of strong women, commentators have sought extrinsic explanations for the recurrence of this stereotypic situation in his books. Some suggest that Conrad had grown weary of being a difficult and unpopular writer, so that the female love interest of *Chance* and *Victory* is a concession to the expectations of the reading public.[6] (The fact that Conrad's later works sold fairly well lends some credibility to this view.) Most scholars offer psychological explanations for Conrad's "obsession" with female-dominated men. Moser says, for example, that Conrad had a fear of women; in his mind they were somehow related to death and destruction, which explains his excessive concern with a hero's loss of masculinity to a powerful woman.[7] C. B. Cox finds Conrad a subconscious misogynist who lapses into vague, dreamlike, sentimental writing about women because he "could only find expression for his hidden fear of sex in these terms."[8] The fullest explanation is offered by Bernard C. Meyer, whose psychoanalytic biography contains an analysis of Conrad's subconscious attitudes toward women. According to Meyer, Conrad was indeed a misogynist, whose female characters destroy men either by symbolically devouring them or by consuming them in flames. Meyer argues that Conrad's artistic decline was brought about by his nervous breakdown in 1910, which caused him to lose all control over his misogyny and write a series of books depicting "phallic woman" destroying "castrated man."[9]

These theories are interesting, but they do not deal with Conrad's *conscious* motives for writing about the impact of strong women on imaginative and potentially heroic men. If art is to some extent the product of careful thought and planning, as well as the expression of inner compulsions, then we must supplement the psychological explanations with literary analysis. Since Conrad insisted that "my work . . . has the solid basis of a definite intention" and that writing is "intelligent action guided by a deliberate view of the effect to be attained,"[10] it is important that we provide an explanation of the Conradian love theme, not in terms of the author's psychological condition, but in terms of his apparent intended meaning as revealed by the text. Conrad wanted his readers to take seriously "the claims of the ideal"—the possibility of transcendent truth—and he usually embodied this possibility in stereotyped female characters; Conrad wanted his readers to take equally seriously the possibility that this world is without higher meaning and all claims of the ideal are illusions—and this possibility is played out in the fates of his male characters; the novels of Conrad thus remain ambiguous, not revealing whether ideals are illusions or higher truths; and, finally, this is as true for Conrad's early works as it is for his late ones.

Let us begin with *Victory* (1915), a novel with more admirers than any other late work of Conrad. Because F. R. Leavis and others have maintained that *Victory* is one of Conrad's masterpieces, it is the book most severely attacked by those who find it representative of Conrad's female-related decline after 1910.[11] The descriptions of Lena as she gives her life for the unarmed hero, Axel Heyst, are considered typical of Conrad's loss of control. "We can only justify this language if we see it as heavily ironic, but words such as 'flush,' 'divine radiance,' and 'shades of death' suggest that Conrad has lost himself in sentimentality."[12] I submit that Conrad has not "lost himself," but is carefully trying to articulate his conception of man's fate in the world.

Lena embodies a vital alternative to Heyst's detachment. Heyst cannot effectively combat the worldly evil manifested in Jones, Ricardo, and Pedro because he has followed his father's instructions to endure life as a spectator rather than as a participant; he has never killed a man or loved a woman. Heyst is paralyzed because action requires commitment, hope, and belief, and he is too knowledgeable to succumb to such illusions. "He had been used to think clearly and sometimes even profoundly, seeing life outside the flattering optical delusion of everlasting hope, of conventional self-deceptions, of an ever-expected happiness."[13] Lena, however, is not a thinker. Instinctively, passionately, she offers fierce resistance to the evil invaders and demonstrates that "it is not the clear-sighted who lead the world. Great achievements are accomplished in a blessed, warm mental fog" (92). Heyst's detachment has been useless, no more than a "fine attitude before the universally irremediable" (Author's Note, p. x).

Lena's ability to act is generally explained in terms of her love for Heyst, her passionate nature, and her womanhood. She is seen as trying "to prove her love to Heyst,"[14] and thereby help him recognize "the active role he should have played in the human scene."[15] She is a representative of life whose passion and intuitive wisdom achieve a victory—perhaps an illusory victory—over

Heyst's detachment. This is by no means a false reading. Lena is a creature of the world, and her simple earthiness and years of suffering enable her to recognize danger instinctively and move boldly to face it.

The text, however, also attaches a more sublime meaning to the character of Lena. Her function in the novel is highly symbolic, which helps to explain why so many readers have found her a stereotype, as if Conrad is more concerned with making her "mean" than with making her "be." Lena is the embodiment of a spiritual state which (if it exists) transcends the earthly realm of pettiness, suffering, and evil. She brings into Conrad's harsh world the mystical suggestiveness of beauty, divine love, and life eternal. This spiritual—one might almost say Platonic[16]—dimension seems to be lacking, or even ridiculed, in Conrad's earlier fiction and, with a few exceptions,[17] critics have been inclined to pass over it in *Victory;* that is, while Lena is sometimes recognized as "transcendent," this quality is not regarded as particularly important, nor is the extent and purpose of such characterization carefully judged. It is, nevertheless, an important aspect of Lena's character, and it contributes mightily to the novel's meaning.

Conrad uses a number of conventional devices to emphasize the otherworldly side of Lena's character. She is, for example, repeatedly described as a ghost, a spirit, a "white, phantom-like apparition" (83); when Heyst meets her outside Schomberg's hotel, she is "white and spectral . . . putting out her arms to him out of the black shadows like an appealing ghost" (86). She is dressed in white throughout the novel until Heyst makes her wear black for the final encounter with evil at the book's end. (Since she is entering the earthly battlefield, the change of color is perhaps appropriate.) In spite of Conrad's suggestions that she is a fallen woman (she is twice called Magdalen), the whiteness is also used to convey her innocence. She is often pictured as childlike (306, 309, 355, 405), or, as Conrad describes her in his Author's Note, "the very image of dreamy innocence" (p. xvii). Lena's spiritual nature is also implied by the magical quality of her voice. Hers is a voice "suggesting infinite depths of wisdom and feeling" (209), which strikes Heyst with special force, for he is a man who has lived in silence. The voice, of course, is a nonphysical manifestation of Lena, and, like the whiteness, the childlike innocence, and the ghostliness, it is a conventional attribute which confirms our impression of her as a spiritual being.

Conrad suggests, at times, that Lena is as much a dream or an idea as she is a living woman. Lena says, "It seems to me, somehow, that if you were to stop thinking of me I shouldn't be in the world at all" (187), and the narrator says that, for Heyst, her caresses "might have been the unsubstantial sensations of a dream invading the reality of waking life; a sort of charming mirage in the barren aridity of his thoughts" (319).

Lena makes it clear that her vision of life is one in which God has "got to do with everything—every little thing"

(359). She is able to repel Ricardo's attack "because of the faith that had been born in her—the faith in the man of her destiny, and perhaps in the Heaven which had sent him so wonderfully to cross her path" (292). Heyst, whose view of life is precisely the opposite—God has nothing to do with anything—blames Lena's Sunday school lessons for such silly optimism. Lena understands the difference between their visions and condemns Heyst's earthbound realism when she says to him, "It seems to me that you can never love me for myself, only for myself, as people do love each other when it is to be for ever" (221). It is this sense of the infinite that enables Lena to love selflessly and act heroically. Heyst comes to see that she embodies a simple and timeless faith, for he wonders "whether you are just a little child, or whether you represent something as old as the world"; he sees himself, correctly, as the modern man, locked by his own skepticism into a particular moment in time: "I date later—much later. I can't call myself a child, but I am so recent that I may call myself a man of the last hour" (359). Lena, however, is never shaken by Heyst's lack of faith and, even as she dies, believes that her heroic sacrifice has made her love eternal: "Exulting, she saw herself extended on the bed, in a black dress, and profoundly at peace; while, stooping over her with a kindly, playful smile, he was ready to lift her up in his firm arms and take her into the sanctuary of his innermost heart—for ever! The flush of rapture flooding her whole being broke out in a smile of innocent, girlish happiness; and with that divine radiance on her lips she breathed her last, triumphant, seeking for his glance in the shades of death" (407).

While this final vision may be merely Lena's private delusion, the narrator insists it is Lena's spirituality that has enabled her to act: "She had been prompted, not by her will, but by a force that was outside of her and more worthy" (394). Lena is even granted a kind of divinity in two scenes in which men sit at her feet, looking up at her in adoration; Heyst assumes this posture on the hill in Samburan, and Ricardo kneels at Lena's feet in Heyst's bungalow and cries, "You marvel, you miracle, you man's luck and joy" (398). These heavy-handed scenes present the stereotypic paralyzed male, gazing worshipfully at the equally stereotypic female, whose exalted vision has guided her to resolute action. They are tableaux which formalize what Conrad's characterization, imagery, and narrative point of view have made clear throughout *Victory:* that Lena is a representative of the spiritual sphere who enters Heyst's godless, loveless, meaningless world, and offers the possibility of transcendent love and joy.

It may be that this dimension of her character detracts from Lena as a "real" woman with sexual and psychological needs, but Conrad has worked hard to keep us from such a one-sided view. Sometimes he suggests that Lena's spirituality is a sentimental delusion of Heyst's; at other times, it seems to be a self-conception of her own arising from her childish religiosity; at still other times, the narrator hints that Lena's spiritual nature exists outside the mind of either character. What is inescapable is

Conrad's determination that Lena be seen as both a woman in the flesh and the embodiment of a transcendent ideal.

Once one recognizes Lena's symbolic significance in *Victory,* the most perplexing problem becomes determining whether or not Conrad is serious about this spiritual dimension of the novel. He is, after all, the writer of numerous tales in which dreams of noble deeds—such as Kurtz's notion of taking light into the heart of darkness or Lord Jim's desire to act heroically or Charles Gould's determination to save Costaguana through material interests—are either ridiculed or shown to be dangerously deficient. The world is too tough a place to sustain such illusions, and Conrad treats man's desire to transcend it with relentless irony. When it is a woman who possesses the lofty view of things, she can only retain her silly faith by being shielded from the awful truths of life.

Surely *Victory* can be read as another story in this anti-Platonic collection. Heyst suspects that he is jeopardizing his safety by rescuing Lena, and he is right, for it is Lena, indirectly, who brings destruction to his island. The world beguiles men into thinking action will matter in their lives, and Lena acts as the world's temptress, luring Heyst out of his safe isolation. There are Adam and Eve associations in *Victory,* which suggest that Lena can be seen as man's temptress, leading him on to the knowledge and action that will destroy him. Heyst knows that the great struggles of life are metaphysical—"the real dangers of life, for him, were not those which could be repelled by swords or bullets" (255)—and Lena's inspirational sacrifice is not much help in combating those dangers. From this perspective, Lena's higher vision seems a fatal delusion, and her "victory" is ironic indeed; she has not borne her love to another sphere, she has not defeated the forces of evil, she has not even sacrificed very effectively, for the man she means to save soon destroys himself in despair. This is the inevitable result of taking one's spiritual longings seriously.

Thus, *Victory* is a novel in which the author seems to take away the very thing he offers. In the "spiritual" scenes, Conrad suggests—through a "heavenly" female character—that the world can be transcended through love, sacrifice, and commitment to life; at the same time, the fate of the male character suggests that the world cannot be escaped, that "feminine" visions are illusions, and that stoic detachment might be the wisest response to life. Is Lena's nature truly spiritual? Yes and no. Has there been a real victory in the novel? Yes and no. Is "Victory" an ironic title? Yes and no. Conrad wants to leave the reader torn between belief and negation, between commitment and detachment, between vision and open-eyed realism. The world of *Victory* is thoroughly ambiguous and any response to it is likely to be insufficient and uncertain. In addition to wondering what unconscious motivation would drive a gifted ironist like Conrad to writing sentimental prose, we need to concede that *Victory* achieves an ambiguity, a precarious equipoise between irreconcilable extremes, that has been consciously sought by the novelist.

The stories that Conrad tells in his other late novels are, of course, various, but he always manages to include a female who seems to open the spiritual realm to an adoring male. Love inspires both men and women to dream of self-sacrifice; the protagonists become hesitant "knights," gingerly rescuing their inspirational "damsels." Love and the commitment to the ideal that it inspires, however, frequently lead to betrayal and destruction. As in *Victory,* Conrad's women are destroyers of their men; they bring not only the vision that makes life worth living but the fatal commitment as well—the commitment to a dream that renders man vulnerable and makes his worldly failure certain.

This is not to say that Conrad tells the same story over and over again, or that his characters are all the same. Lena and Flora de Barral and Edith Travers, for example, are quite different women: Lena is inspired through suffering and love; Flora is inexperienced and torn by conflicting loyalties; Mrs. Travers is rather sullen and pampered. Their needs, their sufferings, and their minds are hardly the same, but symbolically, they are quite similar—they all bring the spiritual realm (or the illusion of the spiritual realm) into the lives of highly idealistic men.

In *Chance* (1913), the story of Captain Anthony's chivalrous rescue of Flora de Barral is told by Marlow, a cynical antifeminist who tends to sneer at the sentimental strength of women and the "hackneyed, illusions, without which the average male creature cannot get on" (94). Flora de Barral, a "phantom-like girl" (50), innocent, white, childlike, has sought a way "to escape from the world" (189) because she is "a woman for whom there is no clear place in the world" (281). She is of this world too, of course; her sense of family responsibility, her suffering at the hands of the governess, her sexuality (and confusion over her husband's honorable absence from the marriage bed) all contribute to the social and psychological dimensions of the work. She is rescued by Roderick Anthony, who idealizes her as "that wisp of mist, that white shadow homeless in an ugly dirty world" (332). Like Lena, Flora shows remarkable physical courage when she helps young Powell light a flare during a storm; and Anthony, like Heyst, makes himself vulnerable to the forces of evil (in this case, Flora's father) by deciding to follow an idealistic and sentimental course of action.

Marlow regards all these romantic doings with considerable scorn. He believes that most men's difficulties are brought about by "transcendental good intentions, which, though ethically valuable, I have no doubt cause often more unhappiness than the plots of the most evil tendency" (376). Even as he takes this realistic view, however, Marlow finds in women a spiritual quality that is beautiful and ennobling:

> "Man, we know, cannot live by bread alone, but hang me if I don't believe that some women could live by love alone. If there be a flame in human beings fed by varied ingredients earthly and spiritual which tinge it in different hues, then I seem to see the colour of theirs. It is azure. . . .

> You say I don't know women. Maybe. It's just as well not to come too close to the shrine. But I have a clear notion of *woman.* In all of them, termagant, flirt, crank, washer woman, bluestocking, outcast and even in the ordinary fool of the ordinary commerce there is something left, if only a spark. And when there is a spark there can always be a flame . . ." (353)

Thus, through Marlow's observations on Flora and Captain Anthony, Conrad has once again presented the conflict of world and spirit as ambiguous and irreconcilable. The dilemma of *Victory* is present in *Chance:* on the one hand, the transcendental realm that men perceive through women may be a sentimental illusion that leaves one defenseless in a cruel world; on the other hand, those spiritual visions may be the only force that inspires man to action that is not brutish—to deeds of heroic self-sacrifice.

The fact that *Chance,* unlike *Victory,* ends with a happy marriage and bright promise for the future may lessen the ambiguity somewhat. Powell is a solid, down-to-earth sort of man who will not spiritualize Flora in the way that Captain Anthony does, and perhaps we should conclude that her ideal significance is only one of Anthony's illusions. *Chance* offers us that possibility, of course, but it also teases us with the possibility that the ideal embodied by Flora has an existence outside the troubled mind of Captain Anthony.

The conflict of world and spirit reappears in *The Rescue* (1920). Tom Lingard is a strong and capable man who leaves himself as "defenceless as a child before the shadowy impulses of his own heart" (11) by chivalrously rescuing people in trouble. Like Heyst's, his chivalry fatally involves him in life, and again like Heyst, he faces the final struggle "unarmed" (70, 226, 287). He is, simply, "a man of infinite illusions" (466).

Lingard's first dangerous commitment is to Hassim and Immada, the exiled prince and princess of Wajo. His final romantic commitment is to Edith Travers, whose husband's yacht has run aground off Lingard's secret Shore of Refuge. This woman has the customary feminine effect on a man's worldly projects: she makes Lingard forget his commitment to Hassim and Immada, she fails to deliver the ring that signals their capture, and she keeps him from negotiating quickly with Belarab. In short, her participation in Lingard's affairs contributes to the destruction of his "kingdom" and the loss of several lives.

Edith Travers is not only a destructive force, however; she is a bored society woman who, at the same time, represents the spiritual potential in a man's life. Conrad uses the now-familiar technique of describing her as a victim of the world (122), as white, radiant, luminous (139), and as possessing a magical voice (141). Typically, she resists the banality of the world and longs to devote herself to the ideal: "As a young girl, often reproved for her romantic ideas, she had dreams where the sincerity of a great passion appeared like the ideal fulfillment and the only truth of life. Entering the world, she discovered that ideal to be unattainable because the world is too prudent to be sincere. Then she hoped that she could find the truth of life an ambition which she understood as a lifelong devotion to some unselfish ideal" (151).

Edith's encounter with Lingard fills her with a sense of purpose, a determination to assert life even at the risk of death. She sees her task as saving Lingard from himself, which is precisely what Lena must do for Heyst. To Lingard she is "Indestructible—and, perhaps, immortal!" (432); "he was in the state of a man who, having cast his eyes through the open gates of Paradise, is rendered insensible by that moment's vision to all the forms and matters of the earth" (415). Thus, it is Edith Travers who provides Lingard with his "glimpse of Paradise" (433, 436, 449), and it is also Edith who helps him bungle all his earthly projects. This dual function of the main female character makes *The Rescue* another book which, in a quite different context from that of *Victory* or *Chance,* insists on the impossibility of reconciling the claims of the transcendent and the terrestrial.

Rita de Lastaola, in *The Arrow of Gold* (1919), is one of Conrad's least subtle creations. She is a former shepherdess who has used her beauty to achieve power and influence among the artists, adventurers, and exiled Spanish nobility living in Marseilles in the 1870's. She is clever and worldly, and yet she is another female stereotype who embodies grace, perfection, and absolute harmony. We are told that she stands for "all the women in the world" (67, 101, 300). She too has a mysterious, magical voice, and she seems to be a heavenly emissary: she possesses a "form wherein there seemed to beat the pulse of divinity rather than blood" (88), and her beauty is "loveliness with a divine breath" (121). Although she has been the mistress of the artist Allègre, Conrad stresses the fact that she has been kept from the world like a nun and still has "childlike innocence" (93).

When the hero, Monsieur George, falls in love with Rita, he feels himself in touch with eternity: "I imagined her to be lost in thought, removed, by an incredible meditation while I clung to her, to an immense distance from the earth. The distance must have been immense because the silence was so perfect, the feeling as if of eternal stillness. I had a distinct impression of being in contact with infinity" (219). At another point he says, "I had never tasted such perfect quietness before. It was not of this earth. I had gone far beyond. It was as if I had reached the ultimate wisdom beyond all dreams and all passions. She was that which is to be contemplated to all Infinity" (288). As before, in the case of Captain Anthony, the reader will not be able to decide whether this is the sentimental illusion of a dreamer or the exalted inspiration of a visionary.

Like other Conrad heroines, Rita inspires her adorers to perform heroic deeds. But this heroism is wasted in a hopeless, unrealistic cause—the attempt to restore Don Carlos to the throne of Spain. This woman (who is all the women in the world) may bring to men a glimpse of Infinity, but she also directs them to worldly projects that are quixotic.

Conrad's last complete work, *The Rover* (1923), is less a love story than the other late novels. Nevertheless, in the character of Arlette, Conrad portrays a woman who instinctively turns to God when she falls in love with Lieutenant Réal and conceives of him as "free from all earthly connections" (175). She brings to him "the sense of triumphant life" (260) which is, for Conrad, the customary impact of the feminine vision upon men. And it is Arlette who inspires old Peyrol to destroy himself in heroic self-sacrifice.

These explications show that all of Conrad's last novels except *The Shadow-Line* contain sexually stereotyped protagonists who serve a thematic function. The novels are not felicitously done, it is true; the writing about women as carriers of the Ideal, the Eternal, and the True is clumsy and unoriginal. It is important to recognize, however, that this use of sexually stereotyped characters is a feature of Conrad's masterpieces as well as his lesser works; indeed, the exaggeration of the late novels helps us to understand the earlier, subtler writings. As we have seen, the idea that fascinates Conrad is this: the perception (or presumed perception) of transcendent truths is what gives life meaning and makes men long to sacrifice themselves to an exalted ideal. This spiritual perception is thoroughly feminine, so that women inevitably bear the vision to men, who are the primary actors in earthly dramas. The bitter ambiguity of life is such that the vision is at once sustaining and destructive, truthful and illusory, beautiful and ridiculous.

This ambiguity differs from the Romantic-Realism that readers have been discovering in Conrad since the 1920's. These readers maintain that Conrad achieves his unique effects by striving for a balance between Romance and Realism—that is, by treating the subject matter of Romance in the method of a Realist to produce Actuality itself.[18] Ernst Bendz sees in Conrad's Romanticism a "subtle tinge of transcendentalism,"[19] but he is almost alone in this view. Others associate Romance with adventure, melodrama, youth, mystery, sentimentality, Nature, exoticism, glamour, and suspense—but not "transcendentalism." As David Thorburn wisely observes, Romanticism leads, in fact, to a concentration on the ordinary world, "a place in which elemental necessities join men to one another, a place in which men are not entirely cut off from their kind, because they share similar feelings, fear death and want to keep living, ally themselves together when they must, and carry on long continuities of labor and struggle."[20] In other words, it would be a mistake to equate Conrad's insistence on the possibility of transcendent truth with the Romanticism that leads him to write adventure stories about sea voyages and faraway places. Conrad himself says, "the feeling of the romantic in life lies principally in the glamour memory throws over the past and arises from the contact with a different race and a different temperament."[21] There is no "tinge of transcendentalism" in that statement.

Conrad's ambiguity is missed when one studies only the perspective evoked by the experience of the "masculine" stereotypes—nihilism, skepticism, pessimism, etc. This perspective is, of course, crucial to any understanding of Conrad. But it is an error to overlook the opposing perspective, the "feminine" fascination with the Ideal. As Conrad remarked to Sidney Colvin in 1917: "I have been called a writer of the sea, of the tropics, a descriptive writer, a romantic writer—and also a realist. But as a matter of fact all my concern has been with the 'ideal' value of things, events and people."[22] Edward W. Said maintains that it was World War I that convinced Conrad that the world is more ideal and less mechanistic than he had suggested in his early works: "But, as Whitehead has put it, the only way to mitigate mechanism is by discovering that it is not mechanism. And this is what Conrad had just discovered. Because the war proposed itself to his *heart* with explosive, cataclysmic force, with a recognizable individuality of its own, with a beginning and a foreseeable end to it, Conrad now felt that universal existence was lively and dramatic."[23]

Said's argument is attractive and certainly correct for the later Conrad, but I am not persuaded that Conrad's interest in higher truth developed only at the end of his life. Apparently, something happened after 1910 that led Conrad to represent the ideal as potentially, or momentarily, attainable in the love between a man and a woman. But even Conrad's masterpieces, those ironic and toughminded stories he wrote early in his career, continually focus on man's longing for a transcendent reality (either embodied in a woman or described in female imagery) and the apparent hostility of the world to this longing. The tension between idealism and skepticism is a feature of all Conrad's work.

Natalia Haldin, the unhappy Russian emigrée in *Under Western Eyes* (1911) is symbolically not unlike the women in Conrad's later fiction. She is naïvely ignorant of the affairs of men, and persists in a blind—and probably foolish—belief that the world is approaching a bright future of peace and loving concord. Yet, in spite of (or because of) her "ignorance of the baser instincts of mankind" (142), she is the inspiration for Razumov's sacrificial act of truthfulness—his confession that he betrayed Victor Haldin to the Russian authorities. He says that he has been moved by her "pure heart which had not been touched by evil things" (359); he tells her that "it was as if your pure brow bore a light which fell on me, searched my heart and saved me from ignominy, from ultimate undoing" (361). As we would expect, Razumov is destroyed for succumbing to a woman's inspiration, for heeding the call of the ideal.

In *Nostromo* (1904), Emilia Gould is represented as childlike, fairylike, and almost divine, as her association with the blue-robed Madonna overlooking the steps of Casa Gould implies. Her spiritual nature is expressed in the way she endows facts with ideal significance, whether the "facts" are silver ingots from the San Tomé mine or the important events of Costaguana's past. Though her husband abandons her in order to pursue his belief in justice through material interests, Emilia Gould is an object of reverence for Dr. Monygham, to whom she "suggested ideas of adoration, of kissing the hem of her robe" (513), and for Nostromo, who sees her as "Shining! Incorruptible!" (560). Nostromo even tries to make confession to her on his deathbed. Her effect on men, even on the cynical Dr. Monygham, is to inspire them to heroic action.

Antonia Avellanos, also in *Nostromo,* has a similar effect on Martin Decoud. Because of her, "his only aspiration was to a felicity so high that it seemed almost unrealizable on this earth" (192). Decoud knows that this is "a sentimental basis for his action" (216), but it is the only power that can inspire him to put aside his clear-eyed skepticism and join the fight against the Monterists.

In *Lord Jim* (1900), the hero is influenced by an ideal of heroic action that is often described in feminine terms, such as his opportunity for redemption which comes to him "veiled . . . like an Eastern bride" (243-44). In addition, a real woman—Jewel—protects Jim and rescues him from the four assassins of Sherif Ali. With her heroism and love, she is able to keep Jim on Patusan, cut off from the harsh world of men, leaving "his earthly failings behind him" (218)—like going to a star. Jewel's relationship to Jim causes Marlow to reflect: "Our common fate fastens upon the women with a peculiar cruelty. . . . One would think that, appointed to rule on earth, it seeks to revenge itself upon the beings that come nearest to rising above the trammels of earthly caution; for it is only women who manage to put at times into their love an element just palpable enough to give one a fright—an extra-terrestrial touch" (277). As in *Victory,* the cruel ironies of the world are opposed by the actions of a stereotyped female character who is loving, faithful, and spiritual.

The point of *Lord Jim* is not that Jewel's love and Jim's idealism are character deficiencies in a world that requires stern stoicism; the primary concern of the novel is the ambiguous nonresolution of the encounter between a transcendent ideal and a brutalizing environment. The underlying "Platonism" of *Lord Jim,* which goes well beyond the male-female relationship, has been identified by Tony Tanner in his brilliant analysis of the butterfly and beetle imagery. The butterfly is "a creature of beauty, a creature with wings which can carry it above the mere dead level of an earth which beetles crudely hug." The beetles, of course, are "ugly earth-bound creatures, devoid of dignity and aspiration, intent merely on self-preservation at all costs." Humanity contains both butterflies and beetles, the images suggest, and beetlelike humans survive far better than those special individuals who spurn the earth and pursue the transcendent beauty of the butterflies. What Tanner calls "Marlow's tentative Platonic musings" leave us with a choice between butterflies and beetles, a choice between survival without beauty and short-lived exaltation.[24] The impossible choice of *Lord Jim* is a feature of most of Conrad's other stories, in which the promise of the Ideal is offered to the male protagonists by female characters. (Or, one might say, the protagonists *believe* the Ideal is offered to them by women.) This is important for us to recognize, for it means that we must readjust our received notions of Conrad. Criticism has so concentrated upon Conrad as the poet of darkness, as the spokesman for Schopenhauerian despair, as the ironical observer of gullible men discovering their own capacities for betrayal, that we have slighted the other half of the picture in which Conrad tries to capture the overwhelming attraction of the Ideal.

It is possible in reading "Heart of Darkness" to mistake the insufficiency of Kurtz for the insufficiency of his ideal. The "moving appeal to every altruistic sentiment" (118), which we associate with Kurtz's Intended in the sepulchral city, is in fact noble and inspiring. It is currently fashionable to find the idea of taking "light" into the dark places of the world contemptible because it destroys the beauty and integrity of native societies, but that is not Conrad's objection to the "fantastic invasion." He was no lover of primitive cultures. The point is that Kurtz is too inherently savage to carry his conception of goodness beyond empty eloquence, that the avaricious agents of civilization are hypocritically invoking ideals as they grab the loot, and that the Intended is too far removed from the realities of existence to recognize that this is so. But the vision of "light"—the idea that redeems—may be the only alternative to the "triumphant darkness," unless we settle for Marlow's beetlelike survival technique of frantically working on the steamer in order to avoid the call of the wild. It is man, not the dream, that is insufficient.

If I have established that Conrad both affirms and denies the transcendent aspirations of men, there remains the task of explaining why he does so. This "having it both ways" is a feature not only of his novels but of his nonfictional writing as well. We find the pessimistic Conrad rejecting higher truths in a letter to R. B. Cunninghame Graham in 1898: "Faith is a myth and beliefs shift like mists on the shore; thoughts vanish; words, once pronounced, die; and the memory of yesterday is as shadowy as the hope of tomorrow—only the string of my platitudes seems to have no end. As our peasants say: 'Pray, brother, forgive me for the love of God.' And we don't know what forgiveness is, nor what is love, nor where God is. Assez."[25] We find the affirming Conrad in his 1905 essay "Books": "It must not be supposed that I claim for the artist in fiction the freedom of moral Nihilism. I would require from him many acts of faith of which the first would be the cherishing of an undying hope; and hope, it will not be contested, implies all the piety of effort and renunciation."[26] Some of the most perceptive readers of Conrad have recognized that he expresses irreconcilable views and have criticized him for failing to resolve them. Surely that is what lies behind E. M. Forster's famous observation that Conrad's obscurity comes from his refusal to resolve "the discrepancies between his nearer and further vision"[27] and Ian Watt's judgment that "Conrad seems to accept an impasse to which his great contemporaries, more ambitious, and

perhaps less deeply alienated from the possibilities of belief, tried to find solutions."[28] I would argue that this "impasse" is, in fact, a vision of life that requires considerable integrity and courage to sustain. In the life of a sensitive man, cursed (and blessed) with both imagination and intellect, these points of view will be in constant and dynamic conflict, so that any action must be taken in a state of thorough confusion; but a man who does not feel the burden of life's ambiguousness, who can maintain and act upon a single affirmative or nihilistic view of the world, is less a man for all his clarity.

It will not do to insist that the pessimistic Conrad was "early" and the affirmative Conrad was "late." Conrad's late books are not the work of a man who has become "simple and serene,"[29] nor do they represent a "retreat from a complex awareness of the mingling of evil and good in human nature and of the untrustworthiness of the ideals which we set up for ourselves."[30] If Conrad's late novels are inferior works of art, it is not because of a significant change in his view of men or women or the universe they inhabit. In spite of the falling off of his artistic powers, Conrad preserved an unchanging vision throughout his career; but Conrad criticism has not adequately defined that vision or shown how Conrad expressed it in his works of art. What is needed is a study of fiction which "admits to the validity of irreconcilable points of view."[31] One can begin such a study by analyzing the way Conrad embodies irreconcilable points of view in sexually stereotyped characters.

For Conrad, existential problems are masculine problems. It is men who must find meaningful actions in a world that is unsympathetic—perhaps even hostile—to humanity. Some of Conrad's characters (Gentleman Brown in *Lord Jim,* and Jones, Ricardo, and Pedro in *Victory*) become agents of the world and participate in the harsh destructive process themselves. Others adopt a defensive attitude and simply struggle to survive—without principles, without aspirations, without plans. There are a few male characters in Conrad who survive impressively by remaining faithful to a code that has evolved as a way to behave in this tough world. Old Singleton, who bravely steers the *Narcissus,* and Captain MacWhirr, who rides out a typhoon, are examples of such steadfast men. There are some men, like the grotesque revolutionaries in *The Secret Agent* and *Under Western Eyes,* who manage to exist only by ignoring the "darkness" of the world and pursuing fantastic utopian visions. There are "civilized" men who live in societies designed to keep unpleasant realities at bay as long as possible; these are the people who so infuriate Marlow when he returns from the horror of Africa and sees them as "people hurrying through the streets to filch a little money from each other, to devour their infamous cookery, to gulp their unwholesome beer, to dream their insignificant dreams. . . . Their bearing, which was simply the bearing of commonplace individuals going about their business in the assurance of perfect safety, was offensive to me like the outrageous flauntings of folly in the face of a danger it is unable to comprehend" (152).

Women, on the other hand, are "out of it." They are the custodians of the dream—the dream of love, of beauty, of faith, of hope. One can only believe in these things by remaining innocent of the world, for the darkness is a destroyer of visions. Those men who think they have seen the world's darker side feel obligated to lie to women in order to keep their dreams alive. Gould lies to his wife, Razumov lies (for a time) to Natalia Haldin, Nostromo tells Giselle he comes to the Great Isabel to visit her when in fact he comes to tap his supply of stolen silver, Marlow and Kurtz both lie to Kurtz's Intended, and Decoud wants Antonia to be told that his mission has been "accomplished gloriously and successfully" (300). Because of her exalted vision, a woman can act heroically, as Lenadoes, or she can inspire a man to noble actions, as Antonia Avellanos does. Hence, Conrad's women are associated with the "sustaining illusion," the affirmative faith which, regardless of its truthfulness, makes action possible. This faith constitutes a rejection of the ironical skepticism of some of Conrad's male characters; as Sophia Antonovna says in *Under Western Eyes,* "women, children and revolutionists hate irony, which is the negation of all saving instincts, of all faith, of all devotion, of all action" (279). Conrad is less interested in the truth or illusion of the feminine vision than he is in the impact of that vision on a man seeking meaningful action.

While Conrad's books contain many of the stereotypic male and female characters just described, these characters, however, are not his great interest. Again and again, he returns to a different character that fascinates him: the man who has enough integrity to recognize the terrible truths of the world and enough imagination to respond passionately to the transcendent vision. Lord Jim, Martin Decoud, Razumov, Axel Heyst, Captain Anthony, Monsieur George, and Tom Lingard are all versions of this character. Each one of these men is drawn to an idealized concept of the world that is, to some degree, feminine; each one of them also discovers that this is a perverse world in which hopes are crushed and dreams come to naught. It is not Conrad's "exhaustion," therefore, that leads him to portray his protagonists as men who are paralyzed, unarmed, and impotent. Action must be almost impossible for someone utterly torn between two conflicting views of the universe. No doubt Conrad admired the single-minded devotion to duty of a Captain MacWhirr; but, for the most part, he did not find such men artistically very interesting. When one has no dreams of his own and is convinced that idealistic hopes are illusions, then the proper course of action is clear: one must faithfully steer the ship. But when one is not sure that dreams are illusions, when the earthly and celestial claims are both powerful and cancel each other out, then one does not steer well, and the likelihood of failure and even betrayal is great.

The presentation of men being pulled apart by conflicting visions requires narrative technique of extreme sophistication; Moser is quite right when he insists that "the essence of Conrad is his complexity."[32] In order to write stories in which the desired effect is ambiguity, inconclusiveness, and uncertainty, Conrad must both affirm the Ideal and ironically undercut it at the same time. The multiple narrators and the abolition of chronological sequence are devices Conrad employs for simultaneously affirming and negating. Royal Roussel shows that it is through the complexity of Marlow's narrative that Jim becomes the kind of enigma Conrad wanted him to be: "Marlow's approach suggests that he is attempting to blend both sides of Jim, the light and the dark, by drawing the shadowy line between his success and failure so thin that the two are confused. If Jim's case could be made totally ambiguous, if Jim could be wrapped completely in the enigma, then perhaps a no man's land could in fact be established in which the darkness and the light could coexist."[33] As readers of *Lord Jim,* we must remain unsure of our estimation of him. A reader who is confident that Jim's dreams are either contemptible illusions or divine ideals has missed the point.

Throughout his life, Conrad admired those writers who shared his fascination with the ambiguity of the human situation. He wrote of Anatole France: "He knows that our best hopes are irrealisable; that it is the almost incredible misfortune of mankind, but also its highest privilege, to aspire towards the impossible; that men have never failed to defeat their highest aims by the very strength of their humanity which can conceive the most gigantic tasks but leaves them disarmed before their irremediable littleness."[34] In his late works as well as his early ones, Conrad, like France, sought to show that a man's greatest misfortune—that he is a dreamer—is also his highest privilege. If, after 1910, he more explicitly equated man's aspirations with the vision of love brought to him by a woman, his insistence upon the ambiguity of the human situation did not diminish; we should be no more certain of Heyst's "victory" than we are of Jim's. There are many possible explanations for the artistic decline in Conrad's career, but a change in his perception of men and women and their predicament on earth is not one of them.

## NOTES

[1] Hewitt, *Conrad: A Reassessment* (Cambridge: Bowes and Bowes, 1952; rpt. Folcroft, Pa.: Folcroft, 1969); Moser, *Joseph Conrad: Achievement and Decline* (Cambridge, Mass.: Harvard Univ. Press, 1957; rpt. Hamden, Conn.: Archon, 1966); and Guerard, *Conrad the Novelist* (Cambridge, Mass.: Harvard Univ. Press, 1958).

[2] Moser, p. 127.

[3] Guerard, p. 96.

[4] Some critics have not accepted the theory of artistic decline. See, for example, Adam Gillon, *The Eternal Solitary: A Study of Joseph Conrad* (New York: Bookman, 1960), who insists that love is by no means an uncongenial subject to Conrad but the key to his vision of mankind (p. 87); Sharon Kaehele and Howard German, "Conrad's *Victory:* A Reassessment," *Modern Fiction*

*Studies,* 10 (1964), 55-72, who maintain that the later Conrad is still concerned with the old preoccupations of illusions and loyalty; George Thomson, "Conrad's Later Fiction," *English Literature in Transition,* 12 (1969), 165-74, who sees in the last books a resolution—through women—of the tension that characterizes the early works; and John A. Palmer, *Joseph Conrad's Fiction: A Study in Literary Growth* (Ithaca, N.Y.: Cornell Univ. Press, 1968), who insists that Conrad's artistic development was continuous throughout his career.

[5] *Joseph Conrad: A Psychoanalytic Biography* (Princeton: Princeton Univ. Press, 1967), pp. 273-74.

[6] Paul L. Wiley, *Conrad's Measure of Man* (Madison: Univ. of Wisconsin Press, 1954), p. 3.

[7] Moser, p. 126.

[8] *Joseph Conrad: The Modern Imagination* (London: Dent; Totowa, N.J.: Rowman and Littlefield, 1974), p. 163.

[9] Meyer, pp. 174, 232.

[10] Conrad to Blackwood, 31 May 1902, cited in Jocelyn Baines, *Joseph Conrad: A Critical Biography* (New York: McGraw-Hill, 1960), p. 284.

[11] In addition to Leavis, *The Great Tradition* (London: Chatto and Windus, 1948), p. 209, *Victory's* defenders include: M. C. Bradbook, *Joseph Conrad: Poland's English Genius* (Cambridge: Cambridge Univ. Press, 1941); Morton Dauwen Zabel, *Craft and Character: Texts, Method, and Vocation in Modern Fiction* (New York: Viking Press, 1957); Robert F. Haugh, *Joseph Conrad: Discovery in Design* (Norman: Univ. of Oklahoma Press, 1957); Frederick R. Karl, *A Reader's Guide to Joseph Conrad* (New York: Noonday Press, 1960); J. I. M. Stewart, "Conrad," *Eight Modern Writers,* Oxford History of English Literature, 12 (Oxford: Clarendon Press, 1963), pp. 184-222; R. W. B. Lewis, "The Current of Conrad's *Victory,*" *Trials of the Word: Essays in American Literature and the Humanistic Tradition* (New Haven: Yale Univ. Press, 1965), pp. 148-69; and Kaehele and German, Wiley, Baines, and Palmer, all cited above.

Among those who join Hewitt, Moser, and Guerard in attacking *Victory* are Marvin Mudrick, "Conrad and the Terms of Modern Criticism," *Hudson Review,* 7 (1954), 419-26, and "Introduction," *Conrad: A Collection of Critical Essays,* ed. Marvin Mudrick (Englewood Cliffs, N.J.: Prentice-Hall, 1966); G. S. Fraser, *The Modern Writer and His World* (1953; rpt., 3rd ed., Penguin, 1964); and René Kerf, "Ethics *versus* Aesthetics: A Clue to the Deterioration of Conrad's Art," *Revue des Langues Vivantes* (Brussels), 31 (1965), 240-49.

[12] Cox, p. 136.

[13] Joseph Conrad, *Victory,* Vol. 15 of *Joseph Conrad: Complete Works,* Canterbury Edition, 26 vols. (New York: Doubleday, 1924-26), p. 82. Further page references in my text are to this edition, and subsequent references to other Conrad novels are also to the Canterbury Edition and appear parenthetically in the text.

[14] Baines, p. 396.

[15] Karl, p. 248.

[16] Conrad once wrote to Garnett (28 August 1908), "There is even one abandoned creature who says I am a neoplatonist? What on earth is that?" *Letters from Joseph Conrad, 1895-1924,* ed. Edward Garnett (Indianapolis: Bobbs-Merrill, 1928), p. 214. At least two critics regard this protest as disingenuous and have persevered in finding a kind of Platonism in Conrad's work. See Robert Penn Warren's introduction to *Nostromo,* Modern Library Edition (New York: Random House, 1951), p. xxxiii; and Tony Tanner, "Butterflies and Beetles—Conrad's Two Truths," *Chicago Review,* 16, No. 1 (1963), 123-40, rpt. in *Lord Jim,* ed. Thomas C. Moser (New York: Norton, 1968), pp. 447-62.

[17] See Walter F. Wright, *Romance and Tragedy in Joseph Conrad* (Lincoln: Univ. of Nebraska Press, 1949); and Seymour L. Gross, "The Devil in Samburan: Jones and Ricardo in *Victory,*" *NCF,* 16 (1961), 81-85.

[18] Ruth M. Stauffer, *Joseph Conrad: His Romantic-Realism* (Boston: Four Seas, 1922; rpt. New York: Haskell House, 1969), p. 20.

[19] *Joseph Conrad: An Appreciation* (Gothenburg, Sweden: N. J. Gumpert, 1923), p. 30.

[20] *Conrad's Romanticism* (New Haven: Yale Univ. Press, 1974), pp. 146-47.

[21] *Joseph Conrad: Letters to William Blackwood and David S. Meldrum,* ed. William Blackburn (Durham, N.C.: Duke Univ. Press, 1958), p. 130.

[22] Joseph Conrad, *Joseph Conrad on Fiction,* ed. Walter F. Wright (Lincoln: Univ. of Nebraska Press, 1964), p. 35.

[23] *Joseph Conrad and the Fiction of Autobiography* (Cambridge, Mass.: Harvard Univ. Press, 1966), p. 72.

[24] Tanner, *Chicago Review,* 16, No. 1 (1963), 124, 127, 134; *Lord Jim,* Norton Critical Edition, ed. Thomas C. Moser, pp. 448, 450, 456.

[25] *Joseph Conrad's Letters to R. B. Cunninghame Graham,* ed. C. T. Watts (Cambridge: Cambridge Univ. Press, 1969), p. 65.

[26] Joseph Conrad, *Notes on Life and Letters* (New York: Doubleday, Page, 1923), p. 8.

[27] *Abinger Harvest* (New York: Harcourt, Brace, 1936), p. 139.

[28] "Joseph Conrad: Alienation and Commitment," in *The English Mind,* ed. Hugh Sykes Davies and George Watson (Cambridge: Cambridge Univ. Press, 1964), p. 275.

[29] Guerard, p. 292.

[30] Hewitt, p. 103.

[31] Cox, p. 172.

[32] Moser, p. 8.

[33] *The Metaphysics of Darkness: A Study in the Unity and Development of Conrad's Fiction* (Baltimore: Johns Hopkins Press, 1971), p. 104.

[34] *Notes on Life and Letters,* p. 33.

## Elizabeth Ammons

SOURCE: "Going in Circles: The Female Geography of Jewett's *Country of the Pointed Firs*," in *Studies in the Literary Imagination,* Vol. 16, Fall, 1983, pp. 83-92.

[*In the following essay, Ammons discusses the narrative structure of Sarah Orne Jewett's* Country of the Pointed Firs *as unconventional because of its circular, nonlinear, and peculiarly feminine style.*]

Sarah Orne Jewett realized very early that plot was not her strong suit. She wrote to Horace E. Scudder, an editor at the *Atlantic Monthly,* in 1873 (Jewett was born in 1849): "But I don't believe I could write a long story as . . . you advise me in this last letter. In the first place, I have no dramatic talent. The story would have no plot. I should have to fill it out with descriptions of character and meditations. It seems to me I can furnish the theatre, and show you the actors, and the scenery, and the audience, but there never is any play!" At this early point in her career, Jewett worried about her inability to produce conventional dramatic structure. "I could write you entertaining letters perhaps, from some desirable house where I was in most charming company, but I couldn't make a story about it. I seem to get very much bewildered when I try to make these come in for secondary parts. And what shall be done with such a girl? For I wish to keep on writing, and to do the very best I can."[1]

Jewett never did become skillful at conventional plotting. Her attempt to create an interesting historical novel in *The Tory Lover* (1901) is notably unsuccessful; her three novels for girls, while pleasant, are very ordinary. Probably because conventional, long, dramatic structures requiring exposition, complication, climax, and resolution—the standard protagonist/antagonist model—did not work well for her, she wrote few long works. The problem of how to sustain a long narrative without relying on stock dramatic architecture was not easy to solve. She could do a respectable job with conventional form if her subject matter was fairly predictable, as *A Country Doctor* demonstrates in 1884; but even this novel, interesting thematically, is not particularly exciting aesthetically. It remained for *The Country of the Pointed Firs* a dozen years later to reveal a solution to Jewett's problem of putting together a long piece of fiction that would not attempt to imitate conventional dramatic structure yet would be unified and exciting. To accomplish that end, Jewett structures the novel around two essentially female psychic patterns: one of web, the other of descent.

In *In a Different Voice: Psychological Theory and Women's Development* the developmental theorist Carol Gilligan argues that men and women value different areas of life. She says that "the vision of maturity can be seen to shift when adulthood is portrayed by women rather than men. When women construct the adult domain, the world of relationships emerges and becomes the focus of attention and concern." Basing her findings on research undertaken by others as well as herself, she comes to the conclusion that "while men represent powerful activity as assertion and aggression, women in contrast portray acts of nurturance as acts of strength."[2] She continues in a statement that might well be used to explicate the fictive world of Sarah Orne Jewett: "Women's development delineates the path not only to a less violent life but also to a maturity realized through interdependence and taking care" (Gilligan, p. 172). This less violent female orientation comes, in Gilligan's view, from the fact that female development promotes a relational over a competitive approach to life, something which has often been construed as aberrant or maladjusted by modern psychological theory because such theory is based on a male rather than a female model. For example, in the existing literature, Gilligan points out that "women appear as the exception to the rule of relationships, by demonstrating a love not admixed with anger, a love arising neither from separation nor from a feeling of being at one with the external world as a whole, but rather from a feeling of connection, a primary bond between other and self." Speaking directly to the major modern theoretical model, she explains: "Throughout Freud's work women remain the exception to his portrayal of relationships, and they sound a continuing theme, of an experience of love which, however described—as narcissistic or as hostile to civilization—does not appear to have separation and aggression at its base" (Gilligan, pp. 46-47). This specifically female experience of love described by Gilligan, an experience not grounded in separation and aggression but in connection, in feelings of intimate relatedness to others, animates *The Country of the Pointed Firs.* The book turns its back on the competitive world of men, literally leaving cantankerous Boston miles behind, and explores the quiet, affectional realm of women.

Jewett's structure reflects her subject matter. Rendering one woman's easy, undramatic, fundamentally *un*conflicted accumulation of relationships over the course of one summer—her nurturance and development of bonds with a number of other people—represents the artistic challenge of Jewett's book. The task is to keep the narrative free of conflict ("action") trumped up for its own sake, yet make it cohesive, even compelling. Jewett does that in part, I think, by structuring the book like a web.

To help us visualize male and female modes of perception, Gilligan extrapolates from her material two dominant images. "The images of hierarchy and web," she says, "drawn from the texts of men's and women's fantasies and thoughts, convey different ways of structuring relationships and are associated with different views of morality and self." They "inform different modes of assertion and response: the wish [of men] to be alone at the top and the consequent fear that others will get too close; the wish [of women] to be at the center of connection and the consequent fear of being too far out on the edge" (Gilligan, p. 62). Conventional Western written narrative such as Jewett inherited corresponds in important ways to the hierarchical mode described here by Gilligan. Created by men, standard dramatic structure is linear (starts at one point and moves forward to another point), pinnacle-oriented (moves by stages or steps, often clearly identifiable, to a climactic top point); asymmetric (the high point usually occurs between the middle and the end); and relationally exclusive rather than accumulative (relationships compete with and replace each other to keep the action moving forward, as opposed to side-ways, up-and-down, backwards, or three-dimensionally). The result is narrative structure that works on a ladder principle: action and tension mount as we progress through the fiction to its climax, its high point, situated close to the end.

Jewett's structure in *The Country of the Pointed Firs* is, in contrast, webbed, net-worked. Instead of being linear, it is nuclear: the narrative moves out from one base to a given point and back again, out to another point, and back again, out again, back again, and so forth, like arteries on a spider's web. Instead of building to an asymmetric height, it collects weight at the middle: the most highly charged experience of the book, the visit to Green Island, comes at the center of the book (in the eighth through eleventh of twenty-one chapters), not toward the end. And instead of being relationally exclusive, it is inclusive and accumulative: relationships do not vie with but complement each other. The narrator does not go through a series of people; she adds new friendships onto her life multidirectionally.

Like a web, which consists of strands radiating from a common nucleus, *The Country of the Pointed Firs* begins with, constantly returns to, and ends in the relationship between the narrator and her landlady Mrs. Todd. Symbolic of that nuclear bond, which deepens and broadens but does not undergo fundamental or unexpected change—it is steady, solid, unshakable—is Mrs. Todd's house at Dunnet Landing, place of shared habitation and point of repeated return and embarkation. The events of the narrator's summer ray out from this central edifice/relationship in disparate and seemingly random directions, but they always return (until the end when the narrator heads out alone to Boston). Jewett makes the image "circle of friends" a literal, geographical reality in this book. She calls the first chapter "The Return," and the picture she gives of the narrator's coming back to Dunnet Landing after her winter's work in the city, indeed the whole concept of re-turn, of turning (a circular movement of course) back to where one has been—this circularity comprises the first "action" in the book—is structurally paradigmatic. The narrative continually turns back to where it has been, enriched by its journey out, but not needing to alter or improve upon the nucleus: the relationship between the narrator and Mrs. Todd. All that "happens" in this book is that the circle expands.

One might map *Huckleberry Finn* as an upside-down L: the action moves down the Ohio and then the Mississippi. A map of *The Sun Also Rises* might look like a pendulum, with a line starting in Paris, running down into Spain, and then back up to Paris. A map of "plot" in *The Country of the Pointed Firs* might look, in contrast, scattered and indecisive. Instead of one line, even an extremely complicated one (as would have to be the case for most novels, of course), it would need many lines raying out, some straight, some crooked, some looped, from the Dunnet Landing heart of the book. (This seeming disorder may explain how Willa Cather was led to ruin the book structurally when she edited its reissue in 1925 and stuck in Dunnet Landing stories not contained in Jewett's original 1896 version.[3]) The central principle of Jewett's narrative, very much like the web Gilligan identifies as basic to female relational experience, is aggregation. Experiences accumulate in many directions.

First the narrator renews her bond with the land and meets Mrs. Todd. (Chapter 1 is "The Return," Chapter 2, "Mrs. Todd.") Then the narrator heads inland from their shared home to a vacant schoolhouse where she strikes up a friendship with Captain Littlepage, a retired mariner with whom she journeys out on yet another voyage, this one in imagination rather than fact, as he tells her about a kingdom of the dead—of eerie "fog-people"—encountered by sailors in the frozen north years ago. This relationship with Captain Littlepage and his strange tale of a ghastly arctic purgatory she then carries back with her to Mrs. Todd. The next unit of narrative (four chapters long in contrast to two for the Littlepage yarn) follows Almira Todd and the narrator out to Green Island, the home of Mrs. Todd's mother, Mrs. Blackett. Within this bigger trip out from land is a smaller one out from Mrs. Blackett's earthy home to a sacred grove, virtually a shrine, where the intimacy between the narrator and Mrs. Todd deepens. The experience is carried back by both women, first to Mrs. Blackett's home, then to their own on the mainland. For the fourth cluster of chapters (twelve through fifteen) Susan Fosdick arrives as a houseguest at Dunnet Landing: the circle of two women expands to three and then in spirit to four as the country women recreate narratively the bleak world of Joanna Todd, who years ago turned Shell-Heap Island into a hermitage when disappointed in love. The penultimate narrative unit, which like the Green Island trip is four chapters long (and of symmetrical weight thematically as well), shows Mrs. Todd and the narrator journeying out once again from

Dunnet Landing, this time inland and with Mrs. Blackett enlarging the circle, to attend the Bowden family reunion, a ritualistic pulling together of a large but scattered family circle. The last person added to the narrator's summer is Elijah Tilley, a forlorn widower whose grief for his lost mate does not diminish with time. Following that chapter (the 20th) is the narrator's leavetaking, appropriately titled in this book of journeying forth and carrying back "The Backward View."

Jewett's separate narrative units do not lead inexorably one to the next. They could be scrambled—the Green Island chapters could be switched with the Bowden reunion section, for example, or the Elijah Tilley meeting with the Captain Littlepage one, and so forth—and the book would not disintegrate. The composition of Jewett's narrative, like the composition of the women's days she chronicles, does not follow an inviolable order.[4] Our understanding of each event is not built on our knowledge of what preceded it; the narrative does not stairstep. Yet there is a pattern. Although the book's pieces could be rearranged without plunging the whole into chaos (something one could never do to a well-constructed linearly plotted fiction), one would not want to rearrange them. *The Country of the Pointed Firs* is not aimless. The pattern Jewett creates has its own coherence, its own rhythm, its own emotional and intellectual logic.

Most obvious, for example, is the book's alternation of joyful and sorrowful episodes: we first meet robust Mrs. Todd, then sad Captain Littlepage, then lively Mrs. Blackett, then tragic Joanna, then delighted Bowden reunioners, then tearful Elijah Tilley. Certainly this pattern of affirmation and depression, of happiness and sadness constantly exchanging places, mirrors the reality of many people's, but especially women's, lives. If relationships are the focus rather than the background of one's world, as has traditionally been the situation of women,[5] one inevitable rhythm (since we are mortal and sentient) is constant oscillation between vitality and morbidity, happiness and sadness, life and death, addition and loss. The rocking structure of Jewett's narrative echoes, beautifully, many women's domestic, affectional experience.

A second large pattern noticeable in *The Country of the Pointed Firs* is the way the male figures (Captain Littlepage, William Blackett, Elijah Tilley) move in and out of the narrative singularly. Whereas women function in groups—the narrator, Mrs. Todd, and Mrs. Blackett visit on Green Island and later travel together to the reunion; the narrator, Mrs. Todd, and Susan Fosdick visit for days and talk at length about Joanna—the men in the book show up solitarily. Captain Littlepage wanders alone into the schoolhouse where the narrator sits trying to write; William is so shy that at first he hides from the narrator when she visits Green Island (and he does not come along to the reunion even though his mother and sister wish he had); Elijah Tilley is not at all outgoing—he normally communicates only with three other people and "appeared to regard a stranger with scornful indifference."[6] The widely spaced introduction of these men,

each separate from the other and each surrounded by narrative in which women relate warmly and easily with one another, calls attention to the gap between the world of women and the world of men in this book. In part, as critics have pointed out, the small number and isolation of men in *The Country of the Pointed Firs* are realistic; the great seafaring days are gone and with them the men who made their living from ships. But Jewett's presentation of men individually and as outsiders is not merely economic in *The Country of the Pointed Firs*. From the perspective of female community, which is the perspective of this book, men are minor characters. They are not *as a group* of major importance in women's psychological reality. They appear and disappear as individuals, passing through women's emotional life intermittently and singly. Only occasionally is one essential in certain women's relational life, as William is in his mother's and sister's (but not, it should be noticed, in the narrator's, although she is very close to both women in his family). The affectional world of women, this book shows structurally as well as thematically, resides mainly in bonds with other women.[7] Men are quite literally isolated, relatively unimportant presences.

Undergirding these large designs, much as the radial lines of a spider's structure support various surface networks, is Jewett's fundamental pattern of web, which enables her to create an ordered and emotionally satisfying long narrative without relying on conventional "plot" to give the book shape. Web holds the book together both mechanically and psychically. Mechanically, the repeated trips back to Dunnet Landing create cohesion by tying the separate strands of narrative to one unifying point, home. Psychically, the aggregative structure of Jewett's narrative reproduces female relational reality. Neither linear nor exclusive, that reality consists in a process of valuing relationships above other goals in life (notice how the narrator's work—she is a writer—degenerates almost into oblivion over the summer) and of developing friendships in an interconnected pattern that has at its core the powerful mythic energy of primal female love. That myth, I now wish to suggest, generates Jewett's other major structuring device, allowing her to move the book beyond coherence to drama, still without drawing on the aggression-based protagonist/antagonist model of conventional male plot structure.

If Willa Cather mangled the general structure of Jewett's book, adding chapters where none were wanted, she certainly did not mistake the book's controlling energy. Introducing the 1925 edition, she begins her concluding paragraph: "If I were asked to name three American books which have the possibility of a long, long life, I would say at once, 'The Scarlet Letter,' 'Huckleberry Finn,' and 'The Country of the Pointed Firs.'"[8] The grouping is not as eccentric as it may look. Although these three books differ in many ways, they share an essential similarity. At the emotional center of each stands not an individual but a relationship, a couple: Hester and Dimmesdale, Huck and Jim, the narrator and Mrs. Todd. Moreover, each is a love story, though none conventional. The standard man/woman/marriage love-plot is replaced with a narrative about a passionate bond between two people whose relationship falls outside that narrow frame.

Jewett makes the dramatic center of *The Country of the Pointed Firs* unmistakable. In the tenth of her twenty-one chapters, titled "Where Pennyroyal Grew," the narrator and Mrs. Todd descend together into a silent, sacred, lush, female space in nature where past and present, self and other, myth and reality merge. In journeying "down to the pennyroyal plot," a place Mrs. Todd explicitly calls "sainted," the two women leave behind "the plain every-day world" (78, 77) to come together in the presence of the sacred earth, the healing Mother, herself. As Marjorie Pryse says in an excellent Introduction to a recent edition of the book, "it is clear that Mrs. Todd, in her role as guide, herbalist, and priestess, is here helping her summer visitor to go directly to the source of all vision and inspiration."[9] That source is primal, archetypal female love.

Christine Downing in *The Goddess: Mythological Images of the Feminine* speaks poetically of the Great Mother, Gaia, grandmother and great-grandmother to Demeter, Hera, Hestia, Athene, and Artemis, as "the mother of the beginning. . . . She is the mother who is there before time . . . a mother from whom we are not separated, as in time, in consciousness, we find ourselves to be separated from the mother of the present. She is a fantasy creature behind the personal mother, construed of memory and longing, who exists only in the imagination, in myth, archetypally—who is never identical with the personal mother." Although this figure "is there from the beginning," Downing points out that "our discovery of her is always a return, a re-cognition."[10] Most often this re-turn, or re-cognition, occurs in nature. It comes about by journeying into the earth: giver of life and death, progenitor of us all, symbol of the Great Mother. For Downing the descent occurred at Delphi in the company of a beloved woman friend. As the two women sat together in a pine grove, she "never had such a sense of a deep communion with another human being. It seemed to me as though my soul entered her body as hers had entered mine." Years later, Downing learned that before the grove at Delphi had been dedicated to Apollo it had been Gaia's. The communion she and her friend experienced was not apollonian but primal and female; it was the mysterious energy of the Great Mother.[11]

This descent into a sacred female space in nature, a grove, a cave,[12] is of course retold not invented by Downing. Jewett's own feelings for Greece, with its "blinding light" over a sea "dazzling and rimmed by far-off islands and mountains to the south," and her intense attraction to myth and to ritual—for example, "the Bacchic Dance"—she described in a letter to a woman friend in 1900 as "too much for a plain heart to bear."[13] It is the journey Thea Kronborg takes in Cather's *The Song of the Lark* (1915) when she descends into the canyon of her spiritual forebears, Native American mothers and artists, and finds

her creative strength reborn. Likewise, it is the journey the narrator and Mrs. Todd take to the sacred plot of pennyroyal on Green Island at the center of Jewett's *Country of the Pointed Firs*. Mrs. Todd shows the narrator a treasured picture of her mother and then bares her feelings, taking the narrator into her most intimate confidence. In so doing Almira Todd evokes the ancient, perhaps timeless, grief and courage of all women: "She might have been Antigone alone on the Theban plain. . . . An absolute, archaic grief possessed this countrywoman; she seemed like a renewal of some historic soul, with her sorrows and the remoteness of a daily life busied with rustic simplicities and the scents of primeval herbs" (78). Her "favorite," not surprisingly, is pennyroyal (211).

Pennyroyal is the special herb of women, specifically of womb. It is used in childbirth to promote the expulsion of the placenta; it is also an emmenagogue, an agent used to induce or increase menstrual flow.[14] Thus associated with both the beginning and the end of new life, pennyroyal suggests maternal power itself: the central awesome power of women, like the Earth, to give or not to give life.

Home of "such pennyroyal as the rest of the world could not provide" (76), the place to which Jewett's two women descend marks the sacred female center of *The Country of the Pointed Firs*. The narrator says "I felt that we were friends now since she had brought me to this place" (77). Here the two women know each other fully. They enter into a communion with each other and with the earth that can only be expressed ritualistically: "There was a fine fragrance in the air as we gathered it [the pennyroyal] sprig by sprig and stepped along carefully, and Mrs. Todd pressed her aromatic nosegay between her hands and offered it to me again and again" (76).

Lush, secret, and earthily female, the space to which Jewett's women descend at the middle of *The Country of the Pointed Firs* represents the dramatic core of Jewett's narrative, which instead of being climactic might be described as concentric, even vortical. The emotional energy of the book collects most intensely in Chapter 10, "Where Pennyroyal Grew," from which, in every direction, like rings spreading out when a stone is dropped in a pool, emanates Jewett's drama of female love, which is noncombative and nonlinear. Just as Dunnet Landing, point of constant egress and return, holds the book together mechanically, and the similarly weblike pattern of building relationships out from that base gives the book psychic coherence, so "Where Pennyroyal Grew," in its reproduction of basic female mythic material, holds the book together dramatically and emotionally. At the center, rather than near the end, Jewett's love-story grows most concentrated, and nothing on either side of this midpoint significantly diminishes, conflicts with, or changes that basic female drama.

The artistic geography of *The Country of the Pointed Firs,* a book, as its title signals, about geography, is complex. Instead of relying on conventional inherited forms, at which she was not very good anyway, Jewett made a book that locates itself formally outside the masculine mainstream. Patterns of concentricity, net-work, web, and oscillation mold a narrative that does not know how to march and scale. Rather, it rocks, circles, ebbs, and swells. That Jewett never mastered conventional form was no loss at all.

NOTES

[1] Richard Cary, ed., *Sarah Orne Jewett Letters* (Waterville, Maine: Colby College Press, 1967), p. 29.

[2] Carol Gilligan, *In a Different Voice: Psychological Theory and Women's Development* (Cambridge, Mass.: Harvard Univ. Press, 1982), pp. 167-68.

[3] See Willa Cather, ed., *The Best Stories of Sarah Orne Jewett* (Boston and New York: Houghton Mifflin Co., 1925). For the thought that Cather was probably just following the lead of Jewett's publishers, who added stories to posthumous editions of the book (1910, 1919), see Francis Fike, "An Interpretation of *Pointed Firs,*" *Appreciation of Sarah Orne Jewett: Twenty-nine Interpretive Essays,* ed. Richard Cary (Waterville, Maine: Colby College Press, 1973), p. 179, n. 2; rpt. from *New England Quarterly,* 34 (December 1961), 478-9. Happily, Jewett's original version of *The Country of the Pointed Firs* is now available in a 1981 Norton paperback edited by Mary Ellen Chase.

[4] As sociologist Nancy Chodorow observes of the domestic activities of women, they "have a nonbounded quality. They consist, as countless housewives can attest and as women poets, novelists, and feminist theorists have described, of diffuse obligations." Therefore, in contrast to "work in the labor force—'men's work'—[which] is likely to be contractual, to be more specifically delimited, and to contain a notion of defined progression and product," "the work of maintenance and reproduction [in the home] is characterized by its repetitive and routine continuity, and does not involve specified sequence or progression." See Chodorow, *The Reproduction of Mothering: Psychoanalysis and the Sociology of Gender* (Berkeley: Univ. of California Press, 1978), p. 179.

[5] As Chodorow states succinctly: "women's work is 'emotion work'" (*Reproduction of Mothering,* p. 178).

[6] Sarah Orne Jewett, *The Country of the Pointed Firs* (Boston and New York: Houghton Mifflin, 1896), p. 186. References in the text are to this edition.

[7] For discussion of female friendship in the nineteenth century from an historical perspective, see Carroll Smith-Rosenberg's groundbreaking essay, "The Female World of Love and Ritual: Relations between Women in Nineteenth-Century America," *Signs* 1 (Autumn, 1975), 1-30.

[8] Cather, "Preface," *Best Stories,* p. xviii.

[9] Marjorie Pryse, "Introduction to the Norton Edition," *The Country of the Pointed Firs and Other Stories* by Sarah Orne Jewett, ed. Mary Ellen Chase (New York: W. W. Norton, 1981), p. xv.

[10] Christine Downing, *The Goddess: Mythological Images of the Feminine* (New York: Crossroad Publishing Co., 1981), p. 135.

[11] *Ibid.,* p. 143.

[12] For description of a modern and very personal experience, see Downing, pp. 144-45.

[13] Annie Fields, ed., *Letters of Sarah Orne Jewett* (Boston and New York: Houghton Mifflin, 1911), pp. 172-73.

[14] Emrika Padus, *Woman's Encyclopedia of Health and Natural Healing* (Emmaus, Pa.: Rodale Press, 1981), pp. 292, 299, 302.

## Paul Schwaber

SOURCE: "Molly Bloom and Literary Character," in *The Massachusetts Review,* Vol. XXIV, No. 4, Winter, 1983, pp. 767-89.

[*In the following essay, Schwaber suggests reasons for Joyce's decision to end his novel* Ulysses, *which otherwise focuses on the experiences of men, with the soliloquy of Molly Bloom, a conspicuously feminine persona.*]

James Joyce took big chances, to great effect. He left Ireland to write about it and except for brief visits stayed away, in time returning magnificently in his books. An antic testimony of his achievement occurred on Bloomsday 1982 (the centenary year of Joyce's birth) when citizens of Dublin with their Mayor enacted a chapter of *Ulysses* in the streets, and for an hour Irish life actually followed his art. Joyce, in life, expected disapprobation or worse from the Irish. Nevertheless, for years he risked the publication of *Dubliners,* although he dearly wanted it, preserving some offending words. In *Ulysses* he transformed Homeric precedence, democratizing the epic with a very funny tale of a middle-aged Dublin advertising canvasser, a tormented young man he befriends, and the canvasser's intriguing wife. *Finnegans Wake* transformed everything, including known languages into something unique, unheard elsewhere before or since, yet quite ordinary. It is by now commonly acknowledged that Joyce's work pressed ever innovative narrative forms and variations of language with the persistent play of genius, rendering worlds—all of them Dublin—and earning extraordinary respect and influence. *Ulysses* and *Finnegans Wake,* of course, but *Dubliners* and *Portrait* too delight, puzzle, invite more interpretation and, still, befuddle. A vast commentary has accumulated, some of it, not surprisingly, addressing the locus I wish to consider again: Molly Bloom's soliloquy.

What fascinates me is how risky her soliloquy remains—in itself and as the end of *Ulysses*—though not as at first because of sexual explicitness, lack of punctuation or utter, unspoken interiority. Six glacial decades later, readers who do not blanche when called "post-modern" seem to take these matters in stride. My students, for example, question Molly's characterization with a current feminist urgency. Older critics have been questioning characterization itself, among other things. For 19/20ths of *Ulysses* Molly figures all but entirely in the awareness of others, most of them men, and preoccupyingly in the broodings, interests, memories and fantasies of her husband, whom with Stephen Dedalus we get to know well during the depicted course of June 16, 1904 and the first two hours of June 17. Joyce chortled that her soliloquy would be "the indispensable countersign to Bloom's passport to eternity"; and whatever he may have meant by that, it doubtless included validation for our troubled caring for Leopold Bloom while reading the book and his continuing play in our minds.

It seems important, then, and only fair that we know her thoughts. But given the elaborately nuanced development of *Ulysses,* the duration and drama of our involvement with Stephen and Leopold, why end solely with her? Why, from Joyce's cornucopia of craftable fictions, a radically interior monologue that gives her silent and ambiguous, to be sure, but no less final say? No analogue to Penelope requires that. Nor does Joyce's previous work, focused like most of *Ulysses* on the experiences of men, anticipate it. "I am going to leave the last word with Molly Bloom," he wrote to Frank Budgen—and later, cunningly, to Harriet Shaw Weaver: "I sent the *Penelope* episode to the printer. . . . The *Ithaca* episode which precedes it I am now putting in order. It is in reality the end as *Penelope* has no beginning, middle or end." The soliloquy has often been anthologized—hence, has been perceived as detachable. Admiring critics of it have been known to think it a poor conclusion to the book. In sum, even for the enigmatic genius who made risk integral to his creativity, suspension of our close knowledge of Molly to the very end has had perils. I take encouragement from a remark of Richard Ellmann's: "we must listen to what, in spite of his cardplayer's face and the ostentatious shuffling of the deck, Joyce is saying to us." More is at work in the final section of *Ulysses* than a gambler stretching his luck—although he certainly is doing that.

II

Let us contemplate her as she lies awake in the old brass bed at #7 Eccles Street. Poldy, as she sometimes calls her husband, sleeps soundly beside her. He kissed her on the buttocks getting into bed and woke her; but that, like his wily account of the day and surprising request for eggs and tea for breakfast—and like all the ordinary yet special events we have followed—is over for him. Having wandered, the exhausted Jewish Odysseus of Dublin sleeps, his "cold feet" as usual where his head should be.

That afternoon Molly has been to bed with a man other than him for the first time. At nearly 2:45 A.M., she is

well on in her thoughts, taking note at the moment of her daughter's recent behavior, the inadequacies of her cleaning lady, and an assignable cause: Leopold's deficiencies as a provider. She begins to pity herself, when suddenly she realizes she is menstrual: "every day I get up theres some new thing on sweet God sweet God well when Im stretched out dead in my grave I suppose Ill have some peace I want to get up a minute if Im let wait O Jesus wait yes that thing has come on me now wouldnt that afflict you of course all the poking and rooting and ploughing he had up in me." Boylan's forcefulness brought it on, she supposes, discomfited by their intention to do it again four days hence: "wouldnt that pester the soul out of a body," she sighs, "unless he likes it some men do." Sorely disappointed, she airs a general complaint: "God knows theres always something wrong with us 5 days every 3 or 4 weeks usual monthly auction isnt it simply sickening." Soon we learn of her relief not to be pregnant by him. But the period surprises her. Hers may not be predictable—"5 days every 3 or 4 weeks," she says and before long calculates 3 weeks since her last. Perhaps she's inattentive. Later, wondering whether something might be wrong with her "insides," she thinks fleetingly of seeing a doctor.

At once she recalls a similarly unexpected onset one night at the theater. It was their "one and only time" in a box. A fashionable fellow stared through glasses at her, Bloom talked on impercipiently about "Spinoza and his soul thats dead I suppose millions of years ago," while she smiled, leaned forward, and trying to look interested felt "all in a swamp." They had gone expecting "a fast play about adultery," but some "idiot" in the gallery hissed and shouted at the adulteress all the same. Molly fancies the fellow finding a woman in the next lane after the show "to make up for it," adds "I wish he had what I had then hed boo," and whisks back to the present:

> I bet the cat itself is better off than us have we too much blood in us or what O patience above its pouring out of me like the sea anyhow he didnt make me pregnant as big as he is I dont want to ruin the clean sheets the clean linen I wore brought it on too damn it damn it and they always want to know youre a virgin for them theyre such fools too you could be a widow or divorced 40 times over a daub of red ink would do or blackberry juice no thats too purply O Jamesy let me up out of this pooh.

This glimpse in the midst of things may help us to fathom Joyce's gamble on her, as well as her husband's abidingly detailed fascination with her. Through the windings of the book Molly has been a source of entertainment and pride to Leopold, the powerful magnet too of his regrets, guilts, pleasurable self-punishments and attempts at recovery, such as they are. Not with total consistency, it is true, she has seemed from afar a scold and layabout, a disloyal if much-tried wife, a singer possessed of a strong but untrained voice and heaving embonpoint, a goad for masculine jokes, timidities and stories, an earth mother, and once, Gea-Tellus herself. She did not leave the house and much of the time was in bed. We saw her toss a coin from her window to a crippled beggar—an uncommon act of charity in the book; and we know of the singing tour to be managed by Boylan and their appointment that afternoon. But for the most part, except as we might gauge her more complexly through Bloom's thoughts, Molly has been the stuff of gossip and wish. Indeed, she attracts attention—while remaining subject to Dublin's expectations, like the other women we ponder: the milk-woman and midwives, Josie Breen, Stephen's sister Dilly, the barmaids Misses Kennedy and Douce, Gerty MacDowell, Mrs. Purefoy at last delivered of her 9th child, and the whoremistress Bella Cohen. Molly's very ruminations, moreover, proceed from stereotype: a woman in bed and on her back, emotional and garrulous, with little to do but conjure sex, endure biological vulnerability and *be.* These are long odds.

Yet as in the passage quoted, when we are as if present while she thinks, Molly proves alert, witty and playful though in pain, complaining and engaging in distress. Her perceptions tumble into one another, suggesting acuity and mental richness if also muddle. Her spontaneity allies with sharply etched images to produce exaggerations that resonate: "its pouring out of me like the sea"; "a widow or divorced 40 times over." Divorce or Bloom's death—the thought has occurred formulaically but more than once. She has an eye for fakery, whether her own or others': "a daub of red ink would do." She lacks education but has a knowing, cunning intelligence and ready opinions. Dismayed here, she shows willingness to find fault and distribute it, for unlike Bloom, she does not assume the weight of the world's blame. Her mind moves swiftly, liltingly. "Flow" or "stream" are the usual metaphors for it, as in "stream of consciousness." Molly's reflects convention, stereotype and her variety: her zest, fun and shrewdness, her acerbity, outrage, wonder and pain—and more, as we shall see.

Because although earthy and direct, she is evasive too. Her surprise about her period jibes with her diction: "that thing" has come upon her; something in her "insides" has produced "pooh." There are specificities she ducks, even with herself. "I was coming for about 5 minutes with my legs round him," she has exulted; "I had to hug him after O Lord I wanted to shout out all sorts of things fuck or shit or anything at all." But she didn't. She said nothing: "who knows the way hed take it . . . I gave my eyes that look with my hair a bit loose from the tumbling and my tongue between my lips up to him the savage brute"—only to go on: "Thursday Friday one Saturday two Sunday three O Lord I cant wait til Monday." Molly functions within constraints, her inner ones flexible enough to allow her to displace her aggression ("fuck," "shit") to Boylan (who has enough of his own, "the savage brute") through time, and retrospectively to increase her pleasure. She wanted to shout but didn't; as she remembers it, she came for 5 minutes; and through the length of her soliloquy, the number of times they had intercourse increases from at least 2 to "5 or 6." It may be by way of compromise with her contradictory impulses, therefore,

that she slips into comical but contained metaphors like "all in a swamp" and the "usual monthly auction."

She seems comfortable with half-knowledge ("he didnt make me pregnant as big as he is") and with superstitious explanations ("the clean linen I wore brought it on too damn it"). Perhaps she is straining here for distancing humor, but typically Molly fuzzes or distorts a bodily focus of knowledge. She also imposes precipitous finality on what she knows ("unless he likes it some men do"), with the dependable effect of switching her objects of attention rather than pursuing any one. Of course, she's tired, still excited and thinking associatively. She does run her diverting idiom to absurdity, however. That Boylan hoped to find her—Bloom's wife and Milly's mother—a virgin is much to be doubted, though the drift may alert us to a wish. Neither Gea-Tellus nor Penelope, Molly Bloom evokes both and more, because she is realized, contradictory, idiosyncratic—a specific woman who combines lively curiosity with puzzling limitations on it. From that bind she indulges in philistinism, like her dismissal of Spinoza, as elsewhere she notices only to disdain politics, religious disputes, nationalism and wars—matters of import to others in *Ulysses.* She continues untroubled about countering frankness with avoidance, furthermore, because apparently unaware of it.

Given her many mentions of God, her chiselled memory of the hissed stage adulteress suggests guilt; and earlier she remembered awakening terrified to the thunderstorm: "as if the world was coming to an end God be merciful to us I thought the heavens were coming down about us to punish." Overridingly in this passage, however, Molly is angry: bitter about her marriage and the demandingness of men ("theyre such fools"), distressed by the monthly exigencies of her body, thus encompassingly disgusted when she calls out for help—"O Jamesy let me up out of this pooh"—to Joyce! A vaudevillian flash relaxes the tension. O Jamesy might help; O Jesus didn't. But this flash illuminates a pattern it breaks: our willing suspension of disbelief, that is, that we have been following an actual woman's thoughts. Molly's cry recalls us to the text it undermines. Deconstruction at the wish of an anguished character who wants her rights and comforts as a design of words: we may call it a *mise-en-abîme,* but what are we to make of it?

III

We could take it as a joke and no more. Whose, then? We could think it cute or too cute, welcome or tasteless, brush it aside while we turn again to Molly, just as the text does. Bestirred that much, though, we might wonder at a character out of bounds (how does she know Jamesy?) or at an author competing with a character of his own making. We could resent the intrusion, grumble that he set a trap for us, preen ourselves for spotting it, or wish to transcend such pettiness. Our own self-awareness, in short, no less than Joyce's would have entered the picture, even while we were resolving to forget the whole thing. The man Joyce (1882-1941), knowable from letters, memoirs, Ellmann's magnificent biography and other sources, would not bear directly on the sustained and now compromised illusion of Molly's reality. Our experience as readers, however, our awarenesses and decisions, surely would.

The reader's recognition that literature is structured of language, conventions, presuppositions of thought, feeling, and strategies has provided what unity there has been to critical theories of literature in this century. For several decades in this country, for instance, an informing way of judging aesthetic, psychoanalytic, Marxist, historical, sociological, biographical or mythic contributions to literary criticism has been to attend to their adequacy of address to the detailed properties of the text. At our insistence no less than her own, Molly Bloom remains at least and always a structure of words. Her cry to Jamesy goes to a crux of critical concern, laying bare the truth that books are made, while exemplifying the active use of that truth in *Ulysses.* For beginning within daring but available conventions of psychological interiority and spatial form, *Ulysses* pulsates through the past-ridden consciousnesses of Stephen and of Leopold as they interact with present persons and circumstances and eventually revels in narrative innovation. This latter pronounced turn, adumbrated in the overview of Dublin, "Wandering Rocks," gets decisively inaugurated in the next episode, where male and female Siren songs sound and words play like musical notes. From "Sirens" through "Penelope," the end—that is, in "Cyclops," in which Bloom confronts the Citizen in Barney Kiernan's bar; "Nausicaa," in which he masturbates to Gertie's teasing from the beach; "Oxen of the Sun," set in the Holles Lying-In Hospital, "Circe" in the red-light district, "Eumaeus" in the Cabman's shelter; and "Ithaca," in which Stephen and Leopold, at 7 Eccles Street, converse, drink cocoa, urinate under the stars, and separate—each section has a distinct idiom, a unique pattern of presentation. For the greater bulk of *Ulysses,* therefore, we read page by page a story we perceive is being told by James Joyce, whose transformable presence is integral to it. *Ulysses* offers no mirroring of an objective reality, no approach to such through a consistent point of view, no omniscient narrator on whose dependable voice or manner we can rely. We learn to get our bearings instead in each new section and cumulatively, haltingly, to recognize aspects of a protean narrator—entertainer, verbal conjurer and show-off, historical scribe, journalist, folklorist and observer of mores and persons, puzzler, heir of all the literary ages, creator, and at the instant of Molly's cry savior: "O Jamesy." That hovering presence makes possible as it mediates our complex and slow, often comical, uncertain, unprecedented but nonetheless comprehensible experience—which includes discernible characters, their city, society and time: 1904. The year *Ulysses* was published, Joyce remarked of the work-in-progress that would become *Finnegans Wake:* "I would like it to be possible to pick up any page of my book and know at once what book it is." In much of *Ulysses,* it seems to me, he had already accomplished that.

This direction of commentary toward complex rendering, open yet persuasive reference, and alertness required of readers to the text and to themselves, ought not, I believe, prove objectionable *in principle* to current European or American practitioners of formalist criticism, whether in the Structural-Linguistic, Russian or Anglo-American traditions. Emphases as well as terminologies would differ drastically, but all could find some legitimacy in my procedure. Formalists do not condemn mimetic illusion, nor necessarily suspect communicable meanings or assumptions of literature as shareable social discourse. They oppose reifications, blunt equations of work and world. They refute both disengaged content and disengaged form. Their focus is verbal, the patterned convention and invention by which representations and meanings are enabled, complicated, qualified. Far more systematic fomalists then L. C. Knights, therefore, have approved his spirited 1933 essay aptly entitled "How Many Children had Lady Macbeth?" Knights attacked 19th-century notions of literary characters as actual persons, exemplary figures or accompanying friends separable from the works in which they appear. Such simplicity, he argued, not only could not be tested in the works but distorted the fulness of experience otherwise available through language, imagery, tone and form. I risk that error, as, traditionally, psychoanalytic critics of literature have, from Freud on.

So if I intend to return to the illusion of Molly Bloom's reality—and by extension to representations of society, history, places and persons in literature—I had better be textually focused. I had better account for the unfolding of her vivid, apparently random thoughts, the absence of punctuation but presence of paragraphs in her interior monologue, its multiplicities of momentary meanings and discontinuities, its diction and the intrusion of Jamesy. Some of that I've begun. But if, clinging quaintly to Aristotelian experience at this late date, I go on to ask why *now* Molly has started an affair, why it seems appropriate that she married Leopold in the first place and why she has stayed with him—I had better not be reductive, or even worse in the critical rankings, naive. Fair enough. After all, I hope not to align myself with the fellow who proved capable of shouting at a stage character, both for my own well-being and because I have noted Molly's scorn for him. She called him an idiot. I do, however, wish to respect my sustained perception, based on my experience reading the final structure of words in *Ulysses,* that her scorn would matter.

Post-formalist criticism plays for other stakes. It has perhaps as many modes as practitioners, but all would swoop through the broken boundary where Molly cries out to Jamesy and call both radically into doubt—each now being a signifier within the text—along with all other privileged assumptions of comprehensibility, such as separate persons, texts separable from other texts, and sustainable illusions of reality however indeterminately structured and mediated. Decentered perception disrupts traditional arrangements of meaning, allowing others to accumulate apparently without end. The daring pursuit of post-formalism seems to be language itself, the uncertain reality it makes, how it encodes us and how we know (or think we do) what we know. "The really difficult task," Geoffrey Hartman writes, "is, as always, the hermeneutic one: to understand understanding through the detour of the writing/reading experience. *Detour* is meant ironically, for there is no other way. The new theory, whether we approach it through Heidegger or Derrida, puts the straight line in doubt. Writing is a labyrinth, a topological puzzle and textual crossword; the reader, for his part, must lose himself for a while in hermeneutic 'infinitizing' that makes all rules of closure appear arbitrary." In practice, though, hermeneutic infinitizing about literature has meant *not* attending to traditional and apparent privileged meanings, which may well turn out to be qualified or negated—for example, a refusal even to credit the illusion of a believable character within a literary work. Neither Hartman nor Derrida (as I read them) requires it, but the practice of post-formalism has meant no shareable stories or meanings, no discernible common ground of imagination. It is as if all conscious discourse can aspire only to the condition of dreams: there is no way of saying what one means, not even manifestly. I don't claim to understand why—except that political and erotic faiths are involved, which seems an altogether different matter—but I wish to confront the issue, for I think both sides need one another. Colin MacCabe poses it succinctly as a choice. "*Ulysses* and *Finnegans Wake*," he writes, "are concerned not with representing experience through language but with experiencing language through a destruction of representation. Instead of constructing a meaning, Joyce's texts concern themselves with the position of the subject in language." Ironically enough, formalism with no hermeneutical ambitiousness can lead to the same thing. Hugh Kenner has averred recently: "There is no Bloom. There is language"; and "On nothing is *Ulysses* more insistent than that there is no Stephen . . . simply language." Ostensible differences meet, both in effect denying that we communicate in comprehensible ways through working fictions, however indeterminately, playfully and randomly; both denying in practice the apparent experience of centuries that notions of reality are shareable—and thereby understandable, challengeable, and often at a cost in human suffering, changeable.

IV

Molly is wide awake, tired but in no hurry to sleep. Her thoughts current associatively, through switch words (images, the floating pronoun "he") and moods. The liveliness and disparate movement of her mind impress quickly; and before long one adjusts for its persistence, because Molly's thoughts pulsate on and on. Her silent soliloquy, its logic and focus elusive, its contiguities insistent, admits little inner silence. Can she bear no rest, no time to absorb? For 45 crowded pages the only cessations occur when she cries to Jamesy—a moment instantly closed round by more thoughts—and at 8 paragraph endings, the last of which ends the book. We can know her closely only this way: keyed up, mulling

present and future and remembering her past, hours after frolicking with Boylan and soon after her husband requested breakfast in bed.

Not since the City Arms Hotel has he asked that—and then he did it under guise of being ill. They lived at the City Arms more than a decade ago when he worked for Mr. Cuffe at the Cattle Market, at the time their son, Rudy, was born and after 11 days died. Leopold now gets breakfast for her—did so, in fact, that very morning. "I love to hear him falling up the stairs of a morning with the cups rattling on the tray," she muses. In big and little as *Ulysses* ends, Molly ponders change. Too fed up to continue as she has—witness the first adultery, the cry to be let up out of pooh—she explores other of her feelings as well: guilt, to be sure, but far more recurrently indulgence and appreciation, nostalgia, sadness, anger, competitiveness, joy and desire. Several of these converge to anxiety when she comes close to fantasizing murder contemplating a Mrs. Maybrick, who poisoned her husband—Molly imagines for love of another man. She remarks disliking being alone in the big "barracks of a place" at night. But usually anxiety is not something Molly feels. It is what she avoids—what translates into the constant press of her thoughts. Her mind here has a runaway tone, suggests an implicit panic attributable only in part to the specialness of the day. Molly's thoughts push on, I believe, to fill the unknown *and* to suppress or otherwise contain what frightens her, because given who she is—who she reveals herself to be—the changes already begun endanger her.

This dynamic of her characterization—anxiety diverted to pulsating consciousness—may explain why the critics, who have been perceptive about her, have oddly delimited her. It is as if one would drown in that stream of consciousness if immersed too long. Neither the earlier mythologizers nor more recently the feminists have offered an informing understanding of her as a character. Nonetheless, Molly is, as they have said, a yea-sayer, often evokes delight in physical being and may well embody comic hopefulness. Surely she has mythic resonance—her fame alone establishes that; and she too worries that she has been whorish, though she bitterly blames Bloom for it. She can be viewed as a proto-feminist without benefit of theory and, less sympathetically yet appropriately, as the projected image of a brilliant male author's quite traditional wishfulness about women. But these are aspects that separately do not open to her and together do not add up to her—assuming, of course, that she is a realized character. Marilyn French does not. She argues that Molly represents the life force and is splendid that way but impossibly contradictory, a disaster as a character. I find the revisionism of Stanley Sultan, David Hayman and Father Robert Boyle, among others, more genuinely useful. They distinguish carefully between Bloom's notions about Molly's admirers and lovers, her own thoughts about specific men, and her actual adultery that day, eliminating the possibility of presuming her either a loose woman or a heroine of free love. By establishing such consensual facts, they clarify a good deal about her and appreciate the difficulty with which she decides, finally, to give Leopold one more chance. They too, however, do not provide an inclusive and psychologically plausible reading of her. Abstracted and empiricized, Molly Bloom's living image has not been apprehended sufficiently, with all its confusingly attractive, manifest chaos. Valuable as the commentaries have been, a poignant irony emerges: that readers of *Ulysses* have matched Molly's depicted contemporaries in their readiness to foreclose her.

About some things we can be clear. She was born on Gibraltar 33 years earlier. She never knew her mother, for reasons that remain mysterious. Her father, Brian Tweedy, an Irish Sergeant-Major in the British Army, raised her with the aid of several elderly women, most notably pious and stern Mrs. Rubio, whom Molly remembers with annoyance—an attitude she transfers easily to her cleaning lady and to Mrs. Riordan, Stephen's aunt, whom the Blooms knew in the City Arms Hotel. Old women do not please her. Contrastingly, her father figures kindly in her thoughts. As a soldier's daughter she has glowing memories of parades, ceremonies and colors, of officers' talk and band night strolls on an officer's arm. She remembers Gibraltar's hot sun, the flowers and the sea, the multiplicity of peoples on the island and her discoveries of early adolescence there. Although she mentions no presently close women friends, she longingly invokes Hester Stanhope, a Gibraltar friend nearly her own age and married to a much older man. Molly and Hester's husband had begun to be somewhat aware of one another when the Stanhopes left. That was awful: "it got as dull as the devil after they went I was almost planning to run away mad out of it . . . so bored sometimes I could fight with my nails." She remarks sadly: "people were always going away and we never." Eventually she and her father settled in Dublin, she met Bloom and at 18 married him, already pregnant with their first child, Milly. By now they have been married for 16 years. Milly, herself an adolescent, lately has left home to work as a photographer's assistant in Mullingar. Her mother supposes Bloom behind the move, suspecting his prescience and possible permission about herself and Boylan, but she recognizes that she and Milly no longer could abide under the same roof. Milly leaves an empty nest: only Molly and Leopold at 7 Eccles Street; Molly has to remind herself not to shop for three. And since their little son died, sexual contact between them has been exceedingly strange, involving attentiveness and often tenderness, varieties of fore- and alternative play, his selecting pornographic books for her to read, and as the parodically objective previous section reports it, "a period of 10 years, 5 months and 18 days during which carnal intercourse had been incomplete, without ejaculation of semen within the natural female organ."

So Molly turned to Boylan after an epic wait—one as long as the Trojan War. The aftermath we can observe in her unremitting stream of consciousness early the next morning, which channels her anxiety, thereby energizing her process of thoughts without her being conscious of it.

Maybe, you might say, but what other evidence can I point to? And what could Molly be so deeply anxious about—other than change, that is, which may be crucial for her but as formulated is too abstract, too conceptual, for such sounding? My answer will be roundabout, essayed by way of the specific contents that bring her thoughts to a halt, however briefly. The paragraph endings thus prove revealing.

The first, for example, occurs when she reflects about Mrs. Maybrick, who put arsenic in her husband's tea. "Theyre not brutes enough to go and hang a woman surely are they," Molly wonders—and halts, presumably not liking the retort she could adumbrate. Then she darts in a different direction, albeit a related one, toward men who have desired her with some success: Bloom, while courting; and Boylan; Bartell d'Arcy, the tenor who kissed her on the stairs after a choir concert; and the mysterious Gardner 5 years back, the one Leopold knows nothing about, who embraced well, whom she did not sleep with, and who died of enteric fever in the Boer War. This drift ends when she recalls trying to persuade Mr. Cuffe, whom Bloom had insulted, not to fire him. Cuffe refused—Molly notes with pride—regretfully: "I just half smiled I know my chest was out that way at the door when he said Im extremely sorry and Im sure you were." Puffed with her attractiveness, triumphant in that way, she holds for a moment, delighted. The third paragraph finishes passionately: Thursday Friday one Saturday two Sunday three O Lord I cant wait til Monday"; and the fourth desperately: "my goodness theres nothing else its all very fine for them but as for being a woman as soon as youre old they might as well throw you out into the bottom of the ash pit."

Equally charged thoughts mark the ends of the other paragraphs. She passes wind with accompanying mental rebuke of her husband while a distant train whistle provides cover: "I wish hed sleep in some bed by himself with his cold feet on me give us room to let a fart or do the least thing . . . quietly sweeeee theres that train far away pianissimo eeeeeeee one more song . . . that was a relief." She urinates gleefully attending to her period on the chamberpot. After articulating a prolonged imaginative scenario about Stephen, who would be her young, clean, intelligent poet lover, curiously linked to Rudy, who would now have been the age Stephen was when first she saw him—she startlingly remembers Boylan: "O but then what am I going to do about him though." So many men to keep track of! It brings her up short. At the last, her lyrical "yes" ends the book as she merges Bloom with her first beau, Mulvey, who kissed her under the Moorish wall, and Gibraltar and father with Howth Hill, where she got Bloom to propose, affirming felt continuities between her happiest memories, her present and her future—again, at least for the moment.

Murder and adulterous love, pride of beauty, aroused sexual desire, fear of ageing and of desertion, bodily discharges and an anal shove, a confusion of admirers, ecstatic fulfillment: these intensities arrest her inner flow of language. For moments they cannot be contained. Our focusing example, which has its own breakthrough—Molly's association of menses and pooh—provides more clues about the range of what has stirred in her, and the urgency. After calling out to Jamesy, she follows with grumbles about women's lot, a revery about sex being better in the afternoon, and this fantasy, combining retaliatory hostility and exhibitionism with a wishful flight to pre-puberty: "I think Ill cut all this hair off me there scalding me I might look like a young girl wouldnt he get the great suckin the next time he turned up my clothes on me Id give anything to see his face." In turn this issues to concern that the chamberpot might break from her weight, self-conscious snippets of herself and Boylan ("he was so busy where he oughtnt to be") and a tendentious thought about urinating: "God I remember one time I could scout it out straight whistling like a man almost," before ending a paragraph with overt fantasizing about being a man:

> I bet he [Boylan] never saw a better pair of thighs than that look how white they are the smoothest place is right there between this bit here how soft like a peach easy God I wouldnt mind being a man and get up on a lovely woman O Lord what a row youre making like the Jersey lily easy O how the waters come down at Lahore.

In the aspect of lover to Lily Langtree, Molly here becomes the King of England.

This material bespeaks wayward desires awash, a psychic fluidity that approaches boundarylessness and diffusion, that sweeps forward to renewed genitality and back to the earliest stages of development. It includes bisexuality, murderousness, dire vulnerability and a resurgent, flamboyant assertiveness so pleasurable, so intense, that she backs off. Furthermore, it dovetails with aggressive and libidinous preoccupations dealt with throughout the soliloquy by being presented, diverged from and continually recurred to, and in that way (if I may be permitted a pun) mollified—though never fully. Her thoughts press on: "Goodbye to my sleep for this night." Molly's act of adultery and these early morning ruminations show oedipal configurations. She has made a triangle by adding Boylan, perhaps to replace the one with Milly. She considers one in which Stephen would replace Boylan, connects Stephen and Rudy, remembers her father and Mrs. Rubio, and her incipient awareness of Captain Stanhope. She is fascinated with male arousal ("can you ever be up to men the way it takes them"; "you never know what freak theyd take alone with you theyre so savage for it": "arent they fearful trying to hurt you"). For example: quiet, mild Mr. Mastiansky taking his wife from behind; Bloom's fondness for stockings and drawers, smutty pictures and rumps; his "mad crazy letters" during their courtship ("Precious one everything connected with your glorious body everything underlined that comes from it is a thing of beauty and a joy for ever") that had her masturbating 4 or 5 times a day; Boylan attracted by her foot; Boylan sucking at her breasts, making them firm and her thirsty; sailors flashing; all men "mad to get in there

where they came out of youd think they could never get far enough up." Her own arousal is palpable and polymorphous, stretching to all areas of the body and to preoedipal rebelliousness, rage and orality. She would like to suck a young boy's penis; she'd like to give Boylan a "great suckin"; and she can feel her soul in a kiss: "theres nothing like a kiss long and hot down to your soul almost paralyzes you."

So as Molly Bloom, a somewhat exotic but discreet Dublin housewife, who until that day even by strict Victorian standards was a respectable one—who committing adultery wanted to shout obscenities but didn't—thinks through what to do now about Boylan and what about Bloom, including the possibility of having another child with him ("yes thatd be awfully jolly," she remarks early and rushes on), she simultaneously gives expression to a flood of id impulses and struggles to control it. She isn't always like this. She is in crisis—when potentials always present clamor to the fore. Two examples will suffice. She remembers herself at ten years of age: "standing at the fire with the little bit of a short shift I had up to heat myself I loved dancing about in it then make a race back into bed Im sure that fellow opposite used to be there the whole time watching." And she remembers herself courted by Leopold, who perversely beseeched her for a pair of her drawers. Pleased and wonder-struck, she gave him not hers but her doll's. She still had one.

Molly's ego, one might say, both in its conscious and unconscious aspects, works overtime. She is not without controls, though they are tested. I have emphasized that the persistent process of her thoughts counts for much, and psychoanalysts will recognize in it defensive maneuvers of displacement, projection, splitting, isolation, denial, repression ("that thing" has come again), reaction-formation and regression. She is also markedly ambivalent, which provides a kind of ballast. Molly gives and takes back, asserts and lightens, expresses distaste only to find something admirable. She intends to take her ring off before going to Belfast with Boylan, "or they might bell it round the town in their papers or tell the police on me but theyd think were married O let them all go and smother themselves for the fat lot I care he has plenty of money and hes not a marrying man so somebody better get it out of him." In a more pliant mood, but critical of her cleaning lady, she notes: "arent they a nuisance that old Mrs Fleming you have to be walking round after her putting things into her hands sneezing and farting into the pots well of course shes old she cant help it." When concerned about her "insides," she brings Dr. Collins to mind, whom before her marriages she consulted about emissions she now thinks were caused by her masturbating—though she would not use that term: "asking me had I frequent omissions where do those old fellows get all the words they have omissions with his short-sighted eyes on me cocked sideways I wouldnt trust him too far to give me chloroform or God knows what else still I liked him when he sat down to write the thing out frowning so severe his nose intelligent like that." Later, feeling possessive and ruefully proud of

Poldy, she thinks of his coming in late, of Paddy Dignam's funeral and the men who attended it:

> this is the fruits of Mr Paddy Dignam . . . well theyre not going to get my husband into their clutches if I can help it making fun of him when behind his back I know well when he goes on with his idiotics because he has sense enough not to squander every penny piece he earns down their gullets and looks after his wife and family good-for-nothings poor Paddy Dignam all the same Im sorry in a way for him what are his wife and 5 children going to do unless he was insured comical little teetotum always stuck up on some pub corner and her or her son waiting Bill Bailey wont you please come home.

Or consider her asseverations on women: "either he wants what he wont get or its some woman ready to stick her knife in you I hate that in women no wonder they treat us the way they do we area dreadful lot of bitches I suppose its all the troubles we have makes us so snappy." Molly can't be nasty without making amends, or flatly changing the subject.

Writ large, her pattern of doing and undoing becomes her path for deciding about Boylan and Bloom—although given the style, reversals are always possible. Clearly, Boylan thrilled her: "O thanks be to the great God I got somebody to give me what I badly wanted to put some heart up into me." But early on she resents him slapping her behind, just as if she were one of his father's horses. She plays with running off with him and provoking a scandal. In time, however, Boylan's crassness and stupidity compare terribly with her hopes for Stephen: "the ignoramus [Boylan] that doesnt know poetry from a cabbage . . . of course hes right enough in his way to pass the time as a joke sure you might as well be in bed with what with a lion God Im sure hed have something better to say for himself an old Lion would." By the end, via the fantasy about Stephen, linked to Rudy and leading to Bloom, Blazes Boylan seems dismissed from her thoughts. A similar route, going the opposite way, affects Leopold. Stanley Sultan has shown persuasively that through the course of her soliloquy Molly arrives at her decisive attitude toward her husband, answering in kind his odyssean return to her. From initial mild favor in her thoughts, Poldy plummets; but by the end she crystallizes her acceptance of him. Molly's inner oscillations contain and ventilate, can serve stasis or adaptation.

All commentators have remarked how enmeshed Molly is with Bloom. No matter how far she travels mentally, she always returns to him, and whether puzzled, annoyed, dismayed, fascinated, amused or pleased, her attention plays on him. Thus too she complements him, answers his consistent preoccupation with her during the day. She reveals qualities akin to his: "because the day before yesterday he was scribbling something a letter when I came into the front room for the matches to show him Dignams death in the paper as if something told me and he covered it up with blotting paper pretending to be thinking about business." The parallel to his noticing that morning that she'd hidden Boylan's note under her pillow is obvious. Molly watches him as closely and as surreptitiously as he does her. She thinks he has been having sex elsewhere: "so very probably that was it to somebody who thinks she has a softy in him . . . and then the usual kissing my bottom was to hide it." She has other traits like his. She gave charity, as did he, more than he could afford, to Dignam's family; and he acted charitably toward Stephen. When Molly hears the train whistle's "weeping tone," she pities the "poor trainmen" far from their families; and remembering bullfights on Gibraltar she registers dislike for the violence done to the horses. So there is kindness to her. She fits the lonesome man who threw Banbury cake to the gulls.

Several times she affirms his preferability to other women's husbands. She likes his manners and cleanliness, his caring and his learning, such as it is—though she mocks it. "[S]till he knows a lot of mixed up things especially about the body and the insides": that she respects. And he is polite to old women. Her anger and complaints are manifest: "any man thatd kiss a womans bottom Id throw my hat at him after that hed kiss anything unnatural where we havent 1 atom of any kind of expression in us the same 2 lumps of lard before ever I do that to a man pfooh the dirty brutes . . . of course a woman wants to be embraced 20 times a day almost to make her look young no matter by who so long as to be in love or loved by somebody if the fellow you want isnt there sometimes by the Lord God. . . . " Still, "something always happens" with Leopold. A willful fellow, officious about his knowledge of music and women's clothes, not sufficiently successful and at times embarrassing, he is always interesting. She enjoys the oddity in him. Fondly and laughably she remembers her swollen breasts hurting her after weaning Milly, "till he got doctor Brady to give me the Belladona prescription I had to get him to suck them they were so hard he said it was sweet and thicker than cows then he wanted to milk me into the tea well hes beyond everything I declare somebody ought to put him in the budget if only I could remember the one half of the things and write a book out of it the works of Master Poldy yes." Poldy is her problem; but psychologically, in her crisis-ruminations, she may be said to organize around him.

There is one more pattern of containment cooperating with the ongoing process of her thoughts, her balancing ambivalence and her recurrence to Bloom: Molly's narcissism. She refers everything to herself—assesses herself validated by it or not, triumphant or failed. That is why she is so competitive. How better to secure a diffusable self than to bang up against what one is not? That accounts for the edge of battle in her pride of beauty, as with Mr. Cuffe; her temper about men who distract Poldy from attending to her; her shortness with causes and learning. Her self-reference bears on her generalized dislike of men or women at different moments, her fascination with who has what and with who gets more: "nice invention they made for women for him to get all the pleasure"; "they have friends they can talk to weve none." She thinks of Boylan at her breasts: "he couldnt resist they excite myself sometimes its well for men all the amount of pleasure they get off a womans body were so round and white for them always I wished I was one myself for a change just to try with that thing they have swelling upon you so hard and at the same time so soft when you touch it." Gardner, she remembers, "said no man could look at my mouth and teeth and not think of it." Compliments gratify her deeply. And ordinariness appalls. She has tart things to say of other Irish women singers: "Kathleen Kearney and her lot of sparrow-farts skitting around talking about politics they know as much about as my backside anything in the world to make themselves someway interesting Irish homemade beauties soldiers daughter am Iay and whose are you bootmakers and publicans I beg your pardon coach I thought you were a wheelbarrow." It's a nice touch on Joyce's part that Molly remembers whistling "there is a charming girl I love" when tossing the coin to the crippled sailor. For self-regard preserves her, just as crucially as what she knows about Bloom does: "I saw he understood or felt what a women is and I knew I could always get round him." Without both, but especially that sense of her power over him, she could be nothing.

v

Why, then, did Molly commit adultery, and why this tremulous aftermath? After long holding to a pattern of complicitly non-genital interaction with Leopold—one they both trace to the death of their infant son Rudy and obviously different from their preceding pattern, which produced two children, the first conceived prior to marriage—Molly has pushed forward again to genitality. Her adultery with Boylan broke a regressed tie to Bloom, and that inner change contributes to her tremulousness. What apparently provided the impetus, however, was Milly's puberty—her attendant acerbity to Molly and flirtatiousness with Leopold, and the path she has now taken toward a separate life. Molly reflects on the family name she acquired in marriage, prefers it to Breen, Briggs, Mulvey, Boylan "or those awful names with bottom in them Mrs Ramsbottom or some other kind of bottom," and suddenly links three generations of women: "my mother whoever she was might have given me a nicer name the Lord knows after the lovely one she had Lunita Laredo the fun we [Mulvey and she] had running along Willis road to Europa point twisting in and out all round the other side of Jersey they were shaking and dancing in my blouse like Millys little ones now when she runs up the stairs I loved looking down at them." Milly's development has revived Molly's wishfulness about her mother and vibrant memories of her own young sexuality. Annoyed with but proud of Milly, Molly registers delight in herself and her fears of getting old: "[Leopold] helping her into her coat but if there was anything wrong with her its me shed tells not him . . . I suppose he thinks Im finished out and laid on the shelf well Im not no nor anything like it"; "her tongue is a bit too long for my taste your blouse is open too low she says the pan calling

the kettle blackbottom and I had to tell her not to cock her legs up like that on show on the windowsill before all the people passing they all look at her like me when I was her age." Before confronting the empty nest, Molly knew the enlivening challenge of an all-too full one and began to reclaim her desire.

Her thrust forward includes her thought, briefly aired early in the soliloquy, of trying for another child with Leopold; and near the end, during the prolonged revery about Stephen through which she arrives at her decisive acceptance of her husband, she has a poignant series of associations:

> when do you ever see women rolling around drunk like they do or gambling every penny they have and losing it on horses yes because a woman whatever she does she knows where to stop sure they wouldnt be in the world at all only for us they dont know what it is to be a woman and a mother how could they where would they all of them be if they hadnt all a mother to look after them what I never had thats why I suppose hes running wild now.

It is Stephen she means, whose mother died and whose father Molly has called "a criticizer": "well its a poor case that those that have a fine son like that theyre not satisfied and I none." The imagined lover to replace Boylan thus leads to her dead infant: "that disheartened me altogether I suppose I oughtnt to have buried him in that little woolly jacket I knitted crying as I was but give it to some poor child but I knew well Id never have another our 1st death too it was we were never the same since O Im not going to think myself in the glooms about that any more."

This sequence unlocks a good deal, I think. Their little son's death long ago touched Molly's ache of absence; and she retreated from genitality—Poldy did too, but that is for another day—to avoid another such loss. Nothing ventured, nothing gained to potentially and so painfully lose again. Rudy's was *their* first death but not Molly's. It evoked hers: the core inner one of the mother "to look after her" she never had, though everyone else did. Hence the halt to intercourse, though she knew she could bring Poldy round if she wanted to. Hence the importance to her of Hester, who taught her and held her: "Hester we used to compare our hair mine was thicker than hers she showed me how to settle it at the back when I put it up and whats this else how to make a knot on a thread with the one hand we were like cousins what age was I then the night of the storm I slept in her bed she had her arms round me then we were fighting in the morning with the pillow what fun." Hence the idealization of Gibraltar—an inclusive, warm, colorful, nurturing place, a maternal substitute or screen—compared with which her life in Dublin inevitably seems grey. Other strands connect with her missing mother too: Molly's aggrandizing narcissism—a compensation; her vulnerability, which she counters with competitive thoughts; her store of anger and ambivalence; her fear of ageing; her nostalgia. Her imprecision about bodily knowledge also may derive from this. Freud taught that the ego is first and foremost a body ego. But Molly had no mother whose dependable touching, washing, hugging and overseeing could help her to define her boundaries. So she thinks about Milly, for example, "of course she cant feel anything deep yet I never came properly til I was 22 or so," as if the two statements relate simply and logically. Even her belief in God has maternal echoes: "for them saying theres no God I wouldnt give a snap of my two fingers for all their learning why dont they go and create something I often asked him atheists or whatever they call themselves." Create something—the way mothers, she knows, even when not there, can.

"[P]eople were always going away and we never"; "I suppose theyre dead long ago . . . its like all through a mist makes you feel so old"; "were never easy where we are." Loss is what she is heir to, what she guards against most, in living memorial to her old injury of soul. However much she accepts or wants the present changes in her life, therefore, they reverberate deeply and frighteningly. She has lost Milly now, and Poldy too—not actually or completely, of course, but as she has depended on them being for quite a while. Of the mother for whom she still longs, she knows only a name and that her eyes and figure were like her own. Careful and perhaps ashamed about the mystery of her mother, she did not tell Leopold about it until they were engaged. That fact alone invites speculation. But one thing Molly has believed: that Lunita Laredo either was Jewish or looked Jewish. And thus Lunita's daughter was ready for Leopold Bloom. She remembers their first meeting vividly: "he excited me I dont know how the first night ever we met when I was living in Rehoboth terrace we stood staring at one another for about 10 minutes as if we met somewhere I suppose on account of my being jewess looking after my mother." Their mutual recognition was mutual transference: "we stood staring . . . as if we met somewhere." From that instant Poldy fulfilled her abiding wish for a *maternal* person, whatever else she saw and liked in him. And since the blow to them both of Rudy's death, he has "looked after" her: caring, making breakfast, being the butt of her assertiveness and making no genital demands. For more than a decade they maintained a holding environment involving mother and child. Consequently, Molly's desire to leave it now and her new experience of adultery bestir her from core to periphery.

A few comments instead of a summary: Joyce ended *Ulysses* with Molly to mark her move back to Poldy in a manifestly happy ending. Thereby he extended the democracy of his epic interest from Stephen and Leopold to her, and potentially to everyone. Presenting a woman, he made her specific, real and free—capable of talking to him. [She entered his dreams that way, escaping his control and this interpretation: "I saw Molly Bloom on the hillock under a sky full of moonlit clouds rushing overhead," he wrote down for Herbert Gorman. "She had just picked up from the grass a child's black coffin and flung it after the figure of a man passing down a side road by the field she was in. It struck his shoulders, and she said, 'I've done with you.' The man was Bloom seen from behind. There was a shout of laughter from some American journalists in the road opposite, led by Ezra Pound. I was very indignant and vaulted over a gate into the field and strode up to her and delivered the one speech of my life. It was very long, eloquent and full of passion, explaining all the last episode of *Ulysses* to her. She wore a black opera cloak, or *sortie de bal,* had become slightly grey and looked like *la Duse.* She smiled when I ended on anastronomical climax, and then, bending, picked up a tiny snuffbox, in the form of a little black coffin, and tossed it towards me, saying, 'And I have done with you, too, Mr. Joyce.'"] So thoroughly did he render her that one can perceive and ponder her and offer a psychoanalytically informed interpretation of her. Molly has an actual situation, inner dynamics and an internalized past. She exists, an illusion of verbal art that counters a generation of critics who deny her very possibility. I like to imagine Joyce in 1922, his weather eye to the future, making it harder for them.

If I have made more difficult their bias toward non-referentiality, I think that only fair. They have made mine—toward the representation of reality and credible literary characters—more difficult. If I have given the lie to pieties that a psychoanalytic reading of a literary character cannot be done or if done must be reductive or bad, so much the better. About Molly's silence I trust we all agree. She is no more silent than Stephen, Leopold, or anyone in *Ulysses,* because like them she is a creature printed in words in a book. A creature of words: I have been trying to restore the weight of *creature* in that phrase.

**Carolyn L. Karcher**

SOURCE: "Male Vision and Female Revision in James's *The Wings of the Dove* and Wharton's *The House of Mirth,*" in *Women's Studies,* Vol. 10, No. 3, 1984, pp. 227-44.

[*In the following essay, Karcher asserts that* The House of Mirth *was Edith Wharton's attempt to reclaim female authorship and authority—her own and that of her women characters—-from Henry James's "angel-monster" dichotomy in* The Wings of the Dove.]

In their groundbreaking study of female authorship, *The Madwoman in the Attic,* Sandra Gilbert and Susan Gubar have theorized that authorship has traditionally aroused deep anxiety in women of our culture, because our "fundamental definitions of literary authority are . . . overtly and covertly patriarchal."[1] Chief among the cultural paradigms that have hampered female creativity, according to Gilbert and Gubar, are the "extreme images of 'angel' and 'monster' which male authors have generated" of women. The image of the angel has inculcated an ideal of self-renunciation incompatible with authorship—an ideal most perfectly realized in death, whether as martyred saint or as static objet d'art. Equally pernicious, the image of the monster has served to frighten women away from authorship by representing its very essence—plotting, scheming, manipulating—as loathsome and deadly in women. Thus in order to define themselves as authors, women have had to engage in a "revisionary struggle" against these cultural paradigms—a process which has often entailed rewriting the texts of their male precursors and retelling, from a female point of view, the cautionary stories that men have told about women.

Though not discussed by Gilbert and Gubar, the literary relationship between Edith Wharton and Henry James provides a fascinating illustration of their thesis. James was more than a precursor for Wharton; he was a mentor, and one who took a notoriously authoritative stand on matters of narrative technique and proper choice of subject.[2] Early in her career, Wharton had begun sending him samples of her fiction. When the master had responded by patronizingly indicating his desire to "pump the pure essence of my wisdom and experience" into this "almost too susceptible *élève*", Wharton had been both gratified and nettled.[3] James's criticism of one story had devastated her. Significantly, she had assuaged her wounded pride by "composing a little parody of James's current style of writing"—significantly because parody, as Gilbert and Gubar point out, is "one of the key strategies" to which women writers have resorted in their "quest for self-definition."[4] Even more revealing is Wharton's reaction to James's comments on her first novel, *The Valley of Decision* (1902). While she was sufficiently flattered by his praise to send copies of his letter to three close friends, and while she took the advice he proceeded "earnestly, tenderly, intelligently" to give her—"Profit, be warned, by my awful example of exile and ignorance. . . . *Do New York!* The 1st-hand account is precious"—she privately disparaged the master's own latest creation. "Don't ask me what I think of *The Wings of the Dove!*" she grumbled to one of the very correspondents with whom she shared James's accolade.[5]

It is no accident that Wharton picked *The Wings of the Dove* as the terrain of her "revisionary struggle" against the master; for it contains nearly all the elements of the patriarchal mythology that Gilbert and Gubar have found so destructive to literary women. To begin with, the novel projects a dualistic image of womanhood, with Kate Croy representing the scheming, plotting "monster-woman . . . [who] embodies intransigent female autonomy" and Milly Theale representing the "angelic sister" whom the monster-woman "threaten[s] to replace."[6] Kate literally seeks to achieve her autonomy by stepping into the dying Milly's place as heiress to a vast fortune. In this way, she hopes to author her own script—one that would permit her to marry her lover, Merton Densher, a man of modest means, and still have the wherewithal to live in comfort and succor her needy father and sister. Otherwise, she would have to choose between the equally undesirable scripts her lover and family have authored for her, which oblige her either to marry for love and abandon her family, or to marry for money and abandon

her lover. Far from endorsing Kate's script, however, the novel condemns it as monstrous, because it calls for Densher's marrying Milly on her deathbed, so that he and Kate can inherit her money.

By implication, *The Wings of the Dove* thus suggests that authorship itself is monstrous in women. Bearing out such a reading is the novel's denigration of its other female plotters. The chief author of the family script dictating a marriage of convenience, for example, is Kate's wealthy aunt and principal source of economic support, Maud Lowder, who vies with her niece in sinister manipulativeness. Mrs. Lowder frankly regards her niece as a marketable commodity which she has been "letting . . . , as you say of investments, appreciate," and which she intends to exchange only for entrée into the English aristocracy, by marrying Kate off to a Lord.[7] Kate's widowed sister, Marian Condrip, who, along with their bankrupt father, supports Mrs. Lowder's plan, has herself proved inept at plotting. Having married a portionless clergyman and been left with four small children to provide for, she stands as a "grave example" of what an impractical match "might make of a woman," even while she pitilessly urges on Kate the "duty" of marrying well for her family's sake (WD, I, 37, 42).

The strongest evidence for discerning in *The Wings of the Dove* a patriarchal attack on female authorship is its satiric portrayal of a literal female author, the New England local colorist Susan Shepherd Stringham. At the outset, Mrs. Stringham appears merely parasitical and silly. In quest of grist for a romantic novel, she attaches herself to Milly Theale, whom she recognizes with an excitement that "positively [makes] her hand a while tremble too much for the pen," as "the real thing, the romantic life itself" (WD, I, 107). Later, however, she, too, discloses the lineaments of patriarchal mythology's predatory monster-woman: when she confesses an inclination to "put Kate Croy in a book and see what she could so do with her," Kate wonders apprehensively whether the redoubtable "Susie" intends to "Chop me up fine or serve me whole" (WD, II, 46). Whether as a comic or as a sinister figure, in sum, Mrs. Stringham personifies the freakishness of female authorship.

Not only does *The Wings of the Dove* perpetuate the traditional stereotypes so inimical to female authorship; it also vindicates the male right to pronounce judgment on women, and hence, by extension, to assume sole authorship of their stories. Except in the opening chapters of the book, we see Kate Croy almost entirely through the eyes of Merton Densher. As a journalist, Densher obviously incarnates the profession of authorship. He also incarnates the life of the mind, to which, as Kate perceives to her "lasting honour," she can have access only with "some such aid as his" (WD, I, 50-51). It follows that whatever weaknesses of character Densher displays in passively lending himself to Kate's designs against Milly, his judgment is never at issue. And where Kate is concerned, that judgment is increasingly negative. At first Densher judges Kate primarily in relation to himself.

Because he, unlike her, has never actively lied to Milly—if he had, he emphasizes, he would have "chucked" Kate to make his lie a truth—he feels morally superior to her (WD, II, 199, 326). Ultimately, however, Densher judges Kate in relation to Milly, whose angelic image interposes itself between the lovers after she has forgiven Densher on the eve of her death. In two climactic scenes at the end of the novel, Densher invokes Milly's ghost against Kate, first by giving her Milly's unopened Christmas letter, then by sending her the sealed announcement of Milly's bequest to him. When Kate casts the unopened letter into the fire, but breaks the seal of the bequest announcement, thus failing the moral tests Densher has devised for her, he confronts her with a final choice: either to renounce him, in exchange for the legacy, or to forego the legacy as the price of marrying him. With this ultimatum, delivered at the very moment Kate's plot comes to fruition, Densher wrests from her the power of authorship and reduces her once more to a character in a male author's script. In accordance with patriarchal tradition, Densher's—and James's—script now completes the moral repudiation of the monster-woman who chooses autonomy over love, by enshrining the dead angel-woman in her place.

Such, then, are the features marking *The Wings of the Dove* as what Gilbert and Gubar would call patriarchal myth. Since, as they contend, women writers attempting to struggle free from myths so deadly to their creativity inevitably had to reexamine the society that had produced them, it is not surprising that the main flaw Edith Wharton cited in *The Wings of the Dove* was its abstract moral treatment of a quintessentially social problem, its failure to illuminate the economic and cultural conditions limiting a woman's freedom and influencing or dictating her choices. "The characters in 'The Wings of the Dove' . . . seem isolated in a Crookes tube for our inspection," she complained in her autobiography, *A Backward Glance,* written after James's death.[8] Privately she went much further. Greeting with enthusiasm the harsh critique of James's recent fiction published by her friend William Brownell in 1905, Wharton confided that it expressed her views "so exactly" that she felt as if it had been "celestially written" for her.[9] Among the passages she singled out for special praise was one reproaching James for showing so little "knowledge of and interest in the sociology of the human species" that the world of his late novels was "a little like Lilliput without Gulliver."[10]

Wharton would have had very personal reasons for feeling that the stricture applied especially well to *The Wings of the Dove;* for the social situation James had presented so abstractly in that novel was one with which she was intimately acquainted. Not that Wharton had ever faced the necessity of marrying for money—her family, unlike Kate Croy's, was extremely wealthy. She had, however, experienced the social pressures defining marriage as the primary goal of a woman's existence and setting personal happiness, fulfillment, and intellectual compatibility below considerations of status, economic security, and family convenience in determining what was a suitable match. Even more to the point, she had had much exposure

to the masculine type Merton Densher epitomized—a type whose pursuit of a feminine ideal too rarefied for any earthly woman to live up to actually masked a deep-seated fear of marriage, as Wharton would show in *The House of Mirth.*[11]

Several factors thus combined to spur Wharton into undertaking a female revision of her mentor's patriarchal fable: the sympathetic insight her own life had given her into the plight of a woman caught, like Kate Croy, between the economic dependency patriarchal society imposed on women and the unattainable ideal of transcendency it held up to them; the need she felt, as James's disciple, to declare her independence of him and to prove herself more than the master's "echo";[12] and finally, the special burden she shared with other women writers, of overturning a literary model that denied women the power of authorship.

In order to reclaim Kate Croy's story for female authorship, Wharton had to translate what was essentially a cautionary tale—how the wicked witch earns her discomfiture at the hands of the prince when she attempts to step into the shoes of the fairytale princess—into an inside view of woman's entrapment in patriarchal society. This entailed a number of fundamental changes: (1) replacing the "Crookes tube" in which Kate Croy, Milly Theale, and Merton Densher "seem isolated" with a fully delineated social world, governed by behavioral codes and value systems that rigidly circumscribe its inhabitants' freedom; (2) fusing the split images of woman as monster and angel, fallen temptress and innocent martyr, into a single figure whose aspirations and limitations derive from social causes; (3) presenting this woman's experiences of entrapment and asphyxiation primarily through her own consciousness, rather than through that of a male observer-author; (4) exposing the male observer-author's judgments as obtuse and self-serving; (5) providing glimpses of alternative roles and relationships for women that point the way toward an eventual solution of their predicament in patriarchal society.

Let us begin with Wharton's first major departure from patriarchal script in *The House of Mirth*—her sociological reformulation of the moral choice its heroine confronts. Lily Bart, like Kate Croy, has been thrown by her father's bankruptcy and her mother's death on the mercy of a rich aunt who has engaged to support her until she can make a "good marriage," and who, in the meantime, fosters in her niece "a salutary sense of dependence."[13] Like Kate, Lily is also torn between a marriage that would offer her wealth and social prestige and one that would offer her love, intellectual communion, and spiritual growth. Wharton's focus, however, is not on which Lily will choose or how she will attempt to reconcile the two—the problems that preoccupy James in *The Wings of the Dove*—but on what has made wealth and social prestige so vital to Lily and so impossible to obtain except through marriage—questions about Kate that James does not address. In raising this issue, Wharton's aim is to explore the factors that restrict women like Lily to dependent roles and condition them to regard themselves as "beautiful object[s]" destined for male consumption.[14]

From the start, Wharton characterizes Lily as "so evidently the victim of the civilization which had produced her, that the links of her bracelet seemed like manacles chaining her to her fate" (HM, p. 7). The arresting simile betrays Wharton's rootedness in a female literary tradition that Gilbert and Gubar have found pervaded by images of imprisonment. Wharton uses many such images to suggest Lily's imprisonment in *The House of Mirth:* the succession of houses from which she flees, the various "ladylike . . . costumes" for which she mortgages her reputation, the mirrors in which she constantly peers, and the paintings on which she models her appearance in one of the novel's most memorable scenes.[15]

The task Wharton sets herself is to explain how the civilization that produced Lily fashioned her into the exquisitely specialized, yet fragile and non-functional object she is. The first explanation Wharton advances is biographical: Lily's mother has brought her up to be "ornamental," to crave luxury and despise "dinginess," and to prize her beauty, especially after her father's bankruptcy, as "the last asset in their fortunes, the nucleus around which their life was to be rebuilt," the means of purchasing the luxury that enhances and is enhanced by her beauty (HM, pp. 34, 297). In other words, as a female custodian of patriarchal values, Lily's mother has instilled in her two potentially conflicting lessons: that she must seek to embody the aesthetic equivalent of that deadly moral ideal, the angel, by turning herself into an object d'art; and that she must cultivate the skills needed to market herself to the right male buyer. Ironically, however, those skills—plotting, scheming, manipulating—are precisely the ones patriarchal society discourages in women. Unable to resolve the contradiction, Lily never succeeds in authoring her own life, even along the lines of patriarchal script.

The biographical explanation Wharton offers of Lily's fate becomes a sociological explanation when applied to the other women of her set, all of whom have been taught to trade in their charms and to rely for their support on wealthy husbands. The most obvious examples are Bertha Dorset, who acts as Lily's nemesis, and the divorcée Carry Fisher, whose tutelage Lily half-heartedly follows. Bertha feeds her self-esteem by engaging in extramarital affairs, while taking care not to furnish her disgruntled husband with the evidence of infidelity that he needs to divorce her. Carry maintains herself between marriages by sponging off her friends' husbands and grooming rich parvenus to enter Old New York's inner circle, at the same time keeping an eagle eye out for eligible men. The fate of those women who have no charms to trade in merely reinforces the lesson. Lily's dour spinster cousin Grace Stepney, for instance, is relegated to the obscurity of a drab boarding house, excluded from dinner parties, and dependent on their Aunt Peniston's charity until she inherits Aunt Peniston's fortune in Lily's stead. And Lily's childhood friend Gerty Farish, likewise a spinster,

"has a horrid little place, and no maid, and such queer things to eat" (HM, p. 7). True, Gerty's commitment to social work infuses more meaning into her "dingy" life than Lily can appreciate; nonetheless, Gerty remains pathetically conscious of her inability to compete with Lily for the love of Lawrence Selden: "What right had she to dream the dreams of loveliness? A dull face invited a dull fate" (HM, p. 162). Throughout the novel, Wharton uses these other women as doubles mirroring Lily's predicament. Once again, it is a strategy linking Wharton with her nineteenth-century female precursors, who often projected their own self-divisions onto characters functioning as doubles for the heroine.[16]

When Wharton explains Lily's dilemma in sociological terms, she does not confine herself to dramatizing the impact of patriarchal values on upper-class women. By taking Lily out of her narrow upperclass milieu and sending her on a downward spiral through New York society, Wharton shows us that the same pernicious cultural assumptions trammel women of every class. Nowhere in *The House of Mirth* do we meet women who do not depend on men for their self-esteem, their economic security, or both. This is true even of the working women among whom Lily ends her career after her disinheritance. Netty Struthers is fairly representative. She ascribes her will to begin life over again, following her abandonment by a lover, to her husband George, who "cared for me enough to have me as I was," and she explicitly discounts the thought of an independent life: "I'd never have had the heart to go on working just for myself" (HM, pp. 314-15).

Wharton's attempt to depict the working-class world, which she did not know at first hand the way she did New York high society, has been criticized as an artistic lapse.[17] But the glimpse Wharton gives us of working women's lives is indispensable for putting Lily's tragedy into perspective and for generalizing it into a statement about woman's fate in patriarchal society. Indeed one might argue that the absence of such a perspective in *The Wings of the Dove,* where the aesthetic shudder aroused by Marian Condrip's "lumpishly" furnished suburban flat provides our only sense of what Kate's life would be like without wealth, is a far more serious flaw of artistry (WD, I, 36-37; II, 364-65).

Lily's fall into the working class allows Wharton both to expose her heroine's limitations in the strongest possible light and to gauge the extent to which they are shared by women of other classes. The main limitations Lily displays as she comes into contact with working women are her complete insensitivity to their plight and her inability to adapt to their condition. Hitherto, comments Wharton acerbically, Lily has "accepted with philosophic calm the fact that such existences as hers were pedestalled on foundations of obscure humanity"; the wintry "mud and sleet" lying outside her "hot-house" world have no more disturbed her than they would an "orchid basking in its artificially created atmosphere" (HM, p. 150). Only when herself subjected to the "sedentary toil" in unwholesome air that has given her sister milliners in Mme. Regina's hat shop their "fagged profiles," "sallow" complexions, and uniform look of "dull and colourless" middle age does Lily acknowledge her kinship with them (HM, p. 282). Even then, she fondly hopes at first to establish her superiority "by a special deftness of touch." Instead, she finds herself "an object of criticism and amusement to the other work-women" because after two months of apprenticeship, "her untutored fingers [are] still blundering over the rudiments of the trade" (HM, pp. 284-85). Lily is forced in the end to recognize that she has "neither the aptitude nor the moral constancy to remake her life on new lines; to become a worker among workers"—that unlike these women she has always dismissed, she cannot earn her own living (HM, p. 301).

While contrasting Lily unfavorably with working-class women in this respect, Wharton exhibits their world as but a "fragmentary and distorted image" of Lily's. They, too, she charges, are "awed only by success—by the gross tangible image of material achievement" that determines a woman's rank in society (HM, pp. 285-86). They, too, as Netty Struthers indicates, consider marriage the ultimate criterion of "success" for a woman. Thus from the highest to the lowest levels of patriarchal society, Wharton shows women unquestioningly accepting the system that locks them into economic and psychological dependency. Hardly able to conceive of developing a sense of worth outside marriage, much less of seeking autonomy, such women patently belie the patriarchal stereotype of female plotting run amok.

In sum, the sociological dimension Wharton has added to her version of Kate Croy's story has fundamentally altered its meaning. By presenting Lily Bart as the victim of social constraints that operate against all women, whatever their class, Wharton makes it impossible for readers to see in her the conniving monster James would have them see in Kate.

Wharton's Lily is more than a humanized avatar of James's Kate, however. After all, Kate describes herself as "a person, thank goodness, who can do what I don't like" (WD, II, 226), whereas Lily repeatedly recoils at the crucial moment from the subterfuge and self-prostitution necessary to land a wealthy husband. Lily's moral fastidiousness and the vulnerability that results from it, manifested most nakedly in her death from an overdose of sleeping potion, identify her not with the monster-woman, but with her martyred "angelic sister." Lily is thus Kate Croy and Milly Theale rolled into one flawed, suffering being, who enacts within herself the Manichaean struggle that patriarchal mythology projects outward onto the icons of monster and angel. By fusing these sundered icons, Wharton has symbolically indicated the means of restoring woman to wholeness. That process, she implies, must begin with woman's rejection of the double bind in which patriarchy traps her when it forces her to choose between submitting to the angel's lingering death and courting the monster's punishment.

Restoring woman to wholeness also entails granting her experiences of entrapment and asphyxiation in patriarchal society a significance independent of the one a male observer would discern. That is, it entails restoring to woman the right of authorship which the male observer has usurped from her. We have already seen how Merton Densher usurps Kate's right of authorship. Less obviously, he also usurps Milly's by translating her death into a moral and aesthetic drama staged for his benefit. In contrast, as Cynthia Griffin Wolff has brilliantly demonstrated, Wharton's treatment of Lily's slow decline and death compels us to "revaluate" the tradition of rendering the "death of a beautiful woman . . . through the eyes of . . . a highly sensitized, loverlike man."[18] Except in the opening and closing scenes of *The House of Mirth*, Wharton turns this patriarchal tradition on its head: entering the consciousness of the woman "thus exalted and objectified" (to quote Wolff again), she "reveal[s] the psychological distortions, the self-alienation, that a woman suffers when she accepts the status of idealized object." In those opening and closing scenes, however, Wharton limits the reader to the traditional male viewpoint, presenting Lily as her would-be lover Lawrence Selden sees her. The gap between his perceptions and those Wharton allows us through a direct view of Lily makes for a devastating indictment of the male observer-author's myopia and sanctimoniousness.

Nowhere does the opposition between James's male vision and Wharton's female revision emerge more starkly than in her recreation of Merton Densher as Lawrence Selden. Wharton mercilessly accentuates in Selden the traits James obfuscates in Densher: his fear of marriage, which the moral perfection he exacts of women and the unacceptable conditions he poses for marriage serve to cover up; his dishonesty with regard to "material things," which he looks down on women for accounting so vital, while himself clinging to the skirts of the wealthy; and his self-righteous cruelty, which he passes off as love.

Selden himself hints at his fear of marriage in the very first chapter. When Lily reproaches him for not coming to see her more often though they "get on so well," he answers "promptly": "Perhaps that's the reason" (HM, p. 8). His frankness here is unusual. More typically, he tries to blame his own irresolution on Lily. That way he enjoys the luxury of denigrating her values, without the risk of inviting her to share his "republic of the spirit" (HM, 68, 72-73). True, Lily continues to angle after wealthy suitors, despite her attraction to Selden. Yet Selden seizes all too eagerly on every pretext she offers him for disengaging himself.

The most striking instance occurs, significantly, on the heels of a scene reverberating with echoes from *The Wings of the Dove*.[19] In the Brys' evening of tableaux vivants, Wharton boldly restages the famous dinner party in Venice, evocative of a Veronese painting, at which Milly makes her valedictory appearance. The Brys' "Venetian ceiling" is reportedly by Veronese, and among the tableaux they recreate is a "Veronese supper" (HM, pp. 132, 134). Although Lily's model is a Reynolds portrait, rather than a Veronese banquet scene, her graceful white robe recalls the "wonderful white dress" donned by Milly for her gala occasion (HM, p. 137; WD, II, 213). Lily's ethereal beauty inspires in Selden a combination of the sexual passion that draws Densher to Kate and the worship of a feminine ideal that draws him to Milly. This time, Selden determines to marry Lily and take her "beyond the ugliness, the pettiness, the attrition and corrosion of the soul" which characterize her life in New York high society (HM, p. 154). He even recognizes that if he is to rescue Lily, he must not expect to free her from her old life overnight ("Perseus's task," he reminds himself, "is not done when he has loosed Andromeda's chains, for her limbs are numb with bondage"); nor must he allow "his own view of her . . . to be coloured" by the vulgar minds in which he sees her reflected (HM, pp. 158-59). Still, these insights do not prevent him from once again abandoning Lily and casting the blame on her, when he sees her emerging from Gus Trenor's house around midnight. Selden's haste in crediting "appearances" and rumors that impugn Lily's purity stands in signal contrast to the unwavering faith that a less refined suitor, the Jewish parvenu Simon Rosedale, maintains in her.

Belying the moral fastidiousness Selden displays toward Lily, moreover, is his own previous indulgence in an extramarital affair with Bertha Dorset, the loosest and most cynical woman in Lily's circle. Clearly, the double standard Selden applies to Lily serves as a defense against commitment to her—a defense he does not need against a married woman, which is precisely what constitutes Bertha's appeal.

Wharton shrewdly analyzes Selden's fear of marriage. "It had been Selden's fate," she explains, "to have a charming mother. . . . Unfortunately . . . his views of womankind in especial were tinged by the remembrance of the one woman who had given him his sense of 'values'" (HM, p. 152). Selden, in other words, has an oedipal fixation on his mother, and this fixation lies at the root of his deep ambivalence toward women, expressed in the very ideal he pursues: "a pretty woman" blending in character "the stoic's carelessness of material things" and "the Epicurean's pleasure in them" (HM, p. 152).

Ambivalence is the keynote, not only of Selden's relations with women, but of his relations with the social world he professes to despise—quite properly, since the two are intertwined in the "values" he has imbibed from his mother. "You spend a good deal of your time in the element you disapprove of," Lily observes in response to his assertion that his ideal, unlike hers, is "personal freedom"—freedom "from money, from poverty, from ease and anxiety, from all the material accidents" (HM, pp. 68, 70). Lily herself embodies the attraction which "material things" hold for him, notwithstanding his desire to transcend them; for Wharton makes amply clear that Selden views Lily primarily as an exquisite objet d'art which "must have cost a great deal to make" (HM, p. 5).[20] She also emphasizes how much it costs to maintain the kind of beauty Selden so admires in Lily—a beauty dependent, like that of an objet d'art, on being displayed in a tasteful setting and enhanced by objects of equal value (in Lily's case expensive clothes and jewels). Just as a museum piece would lose its effect in a cheap storefront, so Lily would lose her charm in dingy surroundings and "dowdy clothes," and under the load of cares that go with them; she would look indistinguishable from the "shallow-faced girls in preposterous hats, and [the] flat-chested women struggling with paper bundles and palm-leaf fans," who strike Selden, when he contrasts them to her, as belonging to a different race (HM, pp. 5, 73). Thus even were Selden psychologically capable of marriage, he would soon tire of the Lily his modest means would support. As Cynthia Griffin Wolff puts it, "Lily unadorned would, after all, fail to sustain his interest."[21] But of course he can no more admit this to himself than he can acknowledge his fear of marriage.

It is in the final scenes of *The House of Mirth* that Wharton most completely discredits her version of James's hero. James, though making Densher partially responsible for Milly's death, had allowed him the absolution denied Kate. Wharton, on the contrary, exposes Selden as sanctimonious and self-serving to the last. The moment of truth she seems to grant Selden when he confronts Lily's death is ironically short-lived. Hardly does he come to "a realization of the cowardice which had driven him from [Lily] at the very moment of attainment" than he proceeds to justify himself at Lily's expense: "He saw that all the conditions of life had conspired to keep them apart; since his very detachment from the external influences which swayed her had increased his spiritual fastidiousness, and made it more difficult for him to live and love uncritically. But at least he *had* loved her—had been willing to stake his future on his faith in her" (HM, pp. 328-29).

Unlike James, Wharton does not let her "negative hero"[22] get away with this self-righteous reaffirmation of moral superiority to the woman he claims to have loved. Instead, she once again shows how little faith Selden has in Lily and how easily it is shaken. Once again, Lily's mysterious entanglement with Gus Trenor affords the pretext for annulling the "personal stake" Selden feels in her affairs as a result of "their last hour together" (HM, p. 327). Among Lily's papers, Selden finds an unsealed envelope addressed to Trenor. Too chivalrous to open it, he "put[s] it from him with sudden loathing," only to discover in the course of examining Lily's checkbook that all the envelope contains is a check discharging Lily's debt to Trenor with nearly the full amount of her aunt's $10,000 legacy. The reference to Selden's and Lily's "last hour together" conceals another barbed irony; for it reminds us that Selden has "hardly noticed" the most significant occurrence of that hour—Lily's heroic gesture of casting into the fire the incriminating letters between him and Bertha Dorset which she could have used to purchase her social reinstatement (HM, p. 310).

The reversal Wharton has effected here of the twin scenes climaxing *The Wings of the Dove* is unmistakable:

Kate's brutal act of tossing Milly's letter into the fire has become both Lily's generous act of self-sacrifice and Selden's obtuse disregard of it; Densher's noble renunciation of Milly's legacy has become Lily's far nobler renunciation of her aunt's legacy; Densher's veneration of Milly's sacred tribute has become Selden's base suspicion of Lily. In rewriting the ending of *The Wings of the Dove* to exonerate Kate-Lily and condemn Densher-Selden, Wharton is repudiating once and for all the right of moral judgment claimed by the male observer-author, insisting once and for all on the female author's right to tell woman's own story from her own point of view.

Although that story, as Wharton tells it, centers on the victimization of women in patriarchal society, it also offers hints of how women may escape their crippling psychological and economic dependency. One such hint is embodied in Gerty Farish's career as a social worker and in Lily's dream of using her aunt's legacy to set herself up as a milliner like Mme. Regina. Granted, neither of these options proves feasible for Lily. Nevertheless, Wharton seems to be suggesting that the availability of satisfying and remunerative careers is a prerequisite for ending women's dependency. The other prerequisite she indicates seems more nearly attainable in *The House of Mirth:* sisterhood. Counterbalancing the women who betray or exploit Lily, like Judy Trenor, Bertha Dorset, Mrs. Peniston, and Grace Stepney, are women who try to help her, either by finding her alternative means of livelihood, as do Carry Fisher and Gerty Farish, or by commiserating with her, as do the working women Miss Kilroy and Netty Struthers. These gestures of sisterhood, while they do not succeed in saving Lily, point toward the creation of a feminine support network that promises to facilitate women's achievement of independence. The significance of such implied resolutions to the feminine predicament Lily exemplifies becomes all the more apparent when we realize that Wharton offers them in lieu of the resolution to which James brings *The Wings of the Dove:* the redemption of the male observer, effected when the angel-woman's sacrificial death arms him against the monster-woman's blandishments.

As a case study of the female author's problematic relationship with her male mentor, Wharton's prolonged dialogue with James presents an especially intriguing confirmation of Gilbert's and Gubar's hypothesis, because the two authors' comments on each other's work permit critics to spy not only on the female chafing under her yoke, but on the male squirming over his bed of coals. That James sensed the revisionary spirit of *The House of Mirth* is obvious from his discomfort with the novel. Whereas critics have unanimously ranked it among Wharton's finest works, James ranked it below a far inferior novel, which he himself criticized for its "strangely infirm composition and construction." Even more telling is the main fault he found with *The House of Mirth:* that Lawrence Selden, who ought to have been the novel's center of consciousness, was "too *absent.*"[23] Wharton's shaft had hit home.

For her part, Wharton continued the process of revision. As Cynthia Griffin Wolff has shown, Wharton's *The Age of Innocence* revises James's *The Portrait of a Lady* in much the same way that *The House of Mirth* does *The Wings of the Dove.*[24] And in her autobiography, Wharton similarly characterizes her novel *The Custom of the Country* as an attempt to incorporate James's favorite theme, the encounter of American and European, into a broader social chronicle.[25]

Wharton saved her boldest challenge to male literary authority for posthumous publication, however. The Beatrice Palmato manuscript, which she left in embryo among her private papers, may be the first explicit account of female sexual arousal written by a woman. As R.W.B. Lewis has pointed out, it startlingly revises both the strait-laced, ladylike image of Wharton that male critics like Percy Lubbock helped transmit to posterity and the phallocentric descriptions of female sexual response that male authors like Lawrence and Joyce were introducing to Wharton's contemporaries.[26] Yet Wharton must have realized that the time was not ripe for a woman to flout taboos which men were only beginning to violate. The Beatrice Palmato fragment remained a private record, and Wharton bequeathed to a new generation of female revisionists the task of reclaiming woman's right to author—and publish—the text of her own erotic experience.

### NOTES

[1] Sandra M. Gilbert and Susan Gubar, *The Madwoman in the Attic: The Woman Writer and the Nineteenth-Century Literary Imagination* (New Haven: Yale University Press, 1979), pp. 17, 25, 28-30, 34, 45-49.

[2] On James's "rigid" literary views, see Edith Wharton, *A Backward Glance* (1933; rpt. New York: Scribner's, 1964), pp. 180-83, 234. Also James himself, cited in Millicent Bell, *Edith Wharton and Henry James: The Story of Their Friendship* (New York: George Braziller, 1965), p. 247: "if a work of . . . fiction, interests me at all (and very few, alas, do!) I always want to write it over in my own way. . . . "

[3] Bell, 246-47; R.W.B. Lewis, *Edith Wharton: A Biography* (New York: Harper & Row, 1975), pp. 126, 131: Leon Edel, *The Master: 1901-1916,* Vol. V of *Henry James* (Philadelphia: Lippincott, 1972), 202.

[4] Lewis, *Edith Wharton,* p. 125; Gilbert and Gubar, pp. 76, 80.

[5] Lewis, *Edith Wharton,* p. 127; Bell, pp. 76-77. 222. Wharton had in fact anticipated James's advice to "Do New York" in a novel she subsequently abandoned to write *The House of Mirth.*

[6] Gilbert and Gubar, p. 28.

[7] Henry James, *The Wings of the Dove* (New York: Scribner's, 1909), I, 82. All further page references will be

to this edition of *The Wings of the Dove* and will be given parenthetically in the text, keyed to the abbreviation WD.

[8] Wharton, *Backward Glance,* p. 190.

[9] Bell, p. 222.

[10] William C. Brownell, *American Prose Masters,* ed. Howard Mumford Jones (1909; rpt. Cambridge, Mass.: Belknap Press of Harvard Univ. Press, 1963), p. 263. The essay was originally published in *Atlantic Monthly,* 95 (April, 1905), 496-519. The quotation refers specifically to *The Awkward Age,* but it is clear from the context that Brownell considers that novel typical of James's late fiction.

[11] Bell, p. 241, points out that "Wharton was herself a victim of the compulsion to 'make a good marriage.'" For biographical details on the men in Wharton's life, see Lewis, *Edith Wharton,* pp. 37-51; also Wharton, *A Backward Glance,* p. 95.

[12] "The continued cry that I am an echo of Mr. James (whose books of the last ten years I can't read, much as I delight in the man) . . . makes me feel rather hopeless." Cited in Bell, p. 221.

[13] Edith Wharton, *The House of Mirth* (1905; rpt. New York: Scribner's, 1969), p. 38. All further page references will be to this easily accessible edition and will be given parenthetically in the text, keyed to the abbreviation HM.

[14] See Cynthia Griffin Wolff, *A Feast of Words: The Triumph of Edith Wharton* (New York: Oxford Univ. Press, 1977), pp. 110-33, for an extremely illuminating discussion of Lily as an objet d'art.

[15] Gilbert and Gubar, p. 85, discuss the use of these symbols in nineteenth-century literature by women.

[16] Gilbert and Gubar, p. 78.

[17] See Diana Trilling, "*The House of Mirth* Revisited," in Irving Howe, ed., *Edith Wharton: A Collection of Critical Essays* (Englewood Cliffs, N.J.: Prentice-Hall, 1962), p. 107. Also in Howe, ed., see Alfred Kazin, "Edith Wharton," pp. 92-93 for a sweeping assertion of Wharton's alleged ignorance of "how the poor lived."

[18] Wolff, p. 132.

[19] R.W.B. Lewis, *Trials of the Word: Essays in American Literature and the Humanistic Tradition* (New Haven: Yale Univ. Press, 1965), p. 136, has also noted these echoes.

[20] I am indebted here to Wolff, pp. 120-24.

[21] Wolff, p. 121.

[22] The epithet Wharton applied to Selden in a letter to a friend, cited in Lewis, *Edith Wharton,* p. 155.

[23] James's comments are cited in Bell, p. 259, and Lewis, *Edith Wharton,* pp. 153, 180-181.

[24] Wolff, pp. 310-13.

[25] Wharton, *A Backward Glance,* pp. 182-83.

[26] Lewis, *Edith Wharton,* p. 525; see also his Appendix C, pp. 545-48, for the outline and text of the Beatrice Palmato fragment.


## Barbara Weiss

SOURCE: "Elizabeth Gaskell: The Telling of Feminine Tales," in *Studies in the Novel,* Vol. 16, No. 3, Fall, 1984, pp. 274-87

[*In the following essay, Weiss contends that, rather than disrupting or devaluing her works, Elizabeth Gaskell's use of stories inserted into her texts allowed the author to explore feminine thought and experience across a broad spectrum of ages and social status.*]

In considering the works of Elizabeth Gaskell, the critic is immediately confronted with those twin damning adjectives, "charming" and "minor," which have clung to the reputation of Gaskell in the present century and prevented a balanced and serious consideration of her works.[1] Discussions of her talent usually suggest her marginal status, portraying her as a homemaker and an amateur, rather than as a serious professional writer.[2] And no quality has been held against the author more than her natural gift of storytelling. Her love of plot-making, her appreciation of the good anecdote, story, or melodrama has been cited against her, as if her very charm and natural ability as a spinner of tales were evidence of an absence of art and purpose in her works.[3] In particular, the interpolated tales which frequently crop up in all but her most mature works are likely to strike the modern critic as disruptive and unnecessary. In recent years, however, feminist criticism has shed a new light on the act of storytelling and its psychological implications for the female artist. Sandra Gilbert and Susan Gubar, for example, in *The Madwoman in the Attic* have explored the difficulties inherent in the position of the woman writer in an age in which ideal women were supposed to have no stories and in which the act of making stories of one's own life or the lives of other women could be considered a subversive activity.[4] In a tradition of patriarchal literature, great anxiety and self-doubt seem to have been the portion of those women who attempted to give a feminine shape to reality by telling their own tales. Viewed in such a context, then, the interpolated tales in Gaskell's works may have been the means through which the author was able to work out the anxieties and ambiguities inherent in the role of female artist. Indeed, in the seemingly artless and random tales which her characters tell to one another, Gaskell may well have explored her own attitude toward fiction and the act of making fiction, and her perceptions about the difference between the fiction of men and the fiction of women.

Gaskell's life-long love of a good story is well documented; her letters attest to an early interest in local customs, legends, and superstitions.[5] Her dramatic skill as a raconteuse was valued by the Howitts, who praised her ability to tell ghost stories around the fire, while her friend Charles Eliot Norton wrote, "She is a wonderful story-teller . . . always dramatic."[6] Several of her published stories suggest her delight in a rattling good ghost story ("The Old Nurse's Tale" and "The Poor Clare") and many reflect her interest in local folklore, embroidering or reworking local tales with an introduction tracing something of their origins.[7] But it is her fondness for interpolating a seemingly unrelated tale into the midst of an ongoing narrative that has marked Gaskell in the eyes of her critics as a naturally gifted but essentially artless amateur. Even Edgar Wright, who in *Mrs. Gaskell: The Basis for Reassessment* makes the most persuasive case for her "unity" and "development" as an important writer, is forced to take her to task for her interpolated tales: "Mrs. Gaskell was one of those who find it difficult to resist a digression; to this extent her fondness for reminiscence and local tales affects the mechanics of her art as well as the tautness of her style."[8] And indeed it cannot be denied that Gaskell was sometimes guilty of interrupting the continuity of her work with an unrelated tale or anecdote. The gentle, pastoral tone of *My Lady Ludlow,* for example, is seriously disrupted by the gory tale of Clément, a melodrama which occupies about one-third of the book with only the lamest excuse of connection to the main plot. More often it was the comic anecdote which tempted Gaskell from the flow of her narrative. In *Mary Barton,* for example, Margaret tells an involved story of a seemingly dead scorpion her grandfather brought home, only to have it thaw out by the fire.[9] Often such stories are put in the mouth of a local character to serve the function of local color as well as comedy. One of the delights of *Ruth* is to be found in the comic stories of the servant Sally, which cannot fail to entertain the reader, even if they do nothing to speed the progress of the narrative. In one memorable and long-winded tale, Sally tells of the clerk who got down on his knees while she kneeled at her cleaning tasks and proposed marriage instead of the "Methodee" prayer she had expected. The story meanders on for eleven pages; its avowed purpose, which it accomplishes, is to "talk" Ruth to sleep.[10] Other equally verbose tales include Sally's recovery of Christian cheerfulness after causing Mr. Benson's accident and the making of her will, in which she pays an extra sixpence for each fancy "law-word" included (*R,* pp. 191-94). Such comic tales serve as the very staple of *Cranford,* which consists largely of remembered anecdotes of such local and domestic events as the old woman dressing her cow in flannel, or the cat swallowing the old lace. The verve of such anecdotes cannot fail to amuse the reader, but it is their seemingly random quality which has earned their author the epithets "charming," "minor," and "artless."

To defend Elizabeth Gaskell fully from such pejorative terms, it would perhaps be necessary to prove that she did indeed possess a conscious aesthetic in the creation of literary fiction, a task made difficult by the author's own self-effacement as a writer. Seldom in her letters did Gaskell discuss the artistic principles of her work; she was, of all Victorian authors, perhaps the least likely to make grand pronouncements upon her own art. For this reason it will be necessary to turn to the work itself to discover what Gaskell considered to be the function of fiction, and an interesting starting point is a seldom remarked episode in *Sylvia's Lovers,* in which the hero Phillip finds consolation for his troubles in the reading of old tales. Estranged from Sylvia by his own failure of truth and her lack of charity, Phillip goes off to war, returning home poverty-stricken and disfigured, to take refuge as a bedesman. Seeking diversion, he immerses himself in a "tattered old volume" of the *Seven Champions of Christendom* and reads of how Sir Guy, Earl of Warwick, came home from war disguised as a beggar and was unrecognized by his own wife until he sent for her to come to his deathbed. There "they had many sweet and holy words together, before he gave up the ghost, his head lying on her bosom."[11] Obsessed with this literary image, Phillip dwells upon it as comfort and inspiration: "All night long, Guy and Phillis, Sylvia and his child, passed in and out of his vision" (*SL,* p. 492). The story of Sir Guy and his wife, of course, neatly forecasts and encapsulates the destiny of Phillip and Sylvia, who will be reunited in compassion and forgiveness on Phillip's deathbed. Gaskell had this ending firmly in mind from the very beginning of the composition of *Sylvia's Lovers:* she seems to have felt that the emotional truth of her tale was embodied in this ending, for she wrote to her reader, W. S. Williams at Smith and Elder, asking him not to judge the book until he could see how it would be justified by the ending (*L,* 499, pp. 674-75). The function of the story from the *Seven Champions of Christendom,* then, is to foreshadow the reconciliation and Christian harmony in which *Sylvia's Lovers* is destined to conclude. This connection is significant, for it seems to suggest that literary fictions, such as the story of Sir Guy, can convey the hard-won emotional lessons which characters are often too blind to recognize clearly. The telling of a tale can often encapsulate emotional truths which function as either warning or inspiration, functions which Gaskell, like her Victorian contemporaries, would have considered to be the first obligations of literature. Seen in this light, then, the tales and anecdotes which interrupt the flow of a narrative are hardly likely to be random or artless, and an examination of the other interpolated tales of *Sylvia's Lovers* should bear out this theory.

Unlike the tale of Sir Guy, which comes from a "tattered old volume," the other tales of the novel come from an oral tradition of legends and local history; one of them is clearly an indulgence by the author in her weakness for ghost stories—a sailor's tale of how his uncle was saved from robbers by his brother's ghost. Other stories, however, are more closely related to the theme and unifying images of the novel. Kinraid, for example, first impresses

Sylvia with his tales of the sights he has seen on his whaling voyages. As she listens in "fascinated wonder," he tells her what seems to be a typical sailor's tall tale about his glimpse of the "mouth o' hell"—a wall of ice seventy miles long with burning flames inside it, and black demons darting about it. The story is significant, for it marks the first impression which Kinraid makes upon Sylvia; but it also is significant for the way in which its fiery images seem to jar with the pastoral milieu of Sylvia's life. Kinraid's suggestion that it was the daring of the sailors which led them to "peep at terrors forbidden to any on us afore our time" (*SL*, p. 108) hints of a wild and reckless nature in the young sailor; while he is not developed as an evil or demonic character, the nature of his tale certainly suggests that he is neither destined nor suited to be the hero of the pastoral romance in which Sylvia is casting him. Similar in nature is the tale which Daniel Robson uses to cap the young sailor's story, also a sailor's yarn and one with which the young Robson first fascinated and courted Sylvia's mother years before. Like Kinraid's tale, Robson's nautical story about a wild ride upon the back of a whale suggests a nature unsuited for domestic harmony and responsibility, and perhaps forecasts Robson's reckless end, riding on and at the same time imprisoned by a wave of mob violence.[12]

Opposed to these stories of terror, wonder, and adventure told by male characters, there is the simple anecdote of local history told by Sylvia's mother. The story of poor "crazy Nancy" has an obvious reference to the romance of Sylvia and Kinraid. A young man, "as nobody knowed" but who had "summat to do wi' the sea" turns the head of a young serving girl "just to beguile the time, like," and then he abandons her. Poor Nancy can no longer perform her tasks and ends her days chained to the kitchen dresser of the workhouse, unable to utter anything but one phrase: "He once was here" (*SL*, pp. 198-99). Mrs. Robson's story is a warning which Sylvia chooses not to hear, but its message is clear to the reader. A woman who abandons herself to an unwise love risks abandoning her duty, her serenity, and even her sanity. Madness is another "doorway to hell," as fearsome as that glimpsed by Kinraid or Robson in their travels, and closer to the truth of Sylvia's own life than any image of masculine adventure, for with Kinraid's abandonment Sylvia will come precariously close to madness and to abandoning her Christian path. Her mother's story clearly embodies the same emotional truth which the novel embodies for the reader; the function of the telling of tales, then, can clearly be the same as that of writing novels—to reach the heart of the listener with a symbolic truth made powerful by imagination and art. In addition, there seems to be a special truth concerning the nature of women's lives which can only be conveyed by the fiction-making powers of a woman who tells tales for other women.

If such a large claim may be made for most of the interpolated tales of *Sylvia Lovers*, then it would seem worth the reader's while to consider the function of the tales which the characters tell to one another in other works of Gaskell, and it would seem valid also to consider what role the sex of the storyteller plays. For it is apparent from even a cursory look at the interpolated stories in *Sylvia's Lovers* that there is a great difference between the tales that men tell and the tales that women tell, a difference which is surely significant in an age when the function of the female writer was much in doubt.

The attitude of Gaskell concerning her role as a woman writer was at best problematical. Her letters reflect a recurring conflict between what she called "home duties" and "the development of the individual," (i.e., her work as a writer) and her anxieties, which she referred to as "my puzzle," apparently were never resolved (*L*, 68, p. 106). Modern attempts to portray her as a feminist seem equivocal or exaggerated. In spite of her acknowledgment of the special disadvantages under which a talented woman labored, Gaskell was far from a doctrinaire supporter of feminism; it was only with reservations that she signed a petition for the Married Women's Property Act, and her advice to an aspiring woman writer was to concentrate on household duties (*L*, 151, p. 693). Nevertheless, she was vocal on the need for meaningful work for women and was anxious that her writing be taken seriously. Like Mary Ann Evans and the Brontë sisters, who published under masculine or neutral names, she wished to avoid the connotation of frivolity and sentimentality which plagued works by "lady" novelists. Gaskell consulted her publisher about the possibility of using a masculine pseudonym (*L*, 28, p. 59) and eventually published her first novel anonymously. But in spite of her desire to have her writing judged apart from considerations of her sex, Gaskell was far from disclaiming sexual differences in literary perspective. No critical praise for *Mary Barton* pleased her more than that of Thomas Carlyle, who began his letter with an intuition of the novel's female authorship,[13] and Gaskell was extremely chagrined to discover that she had guessed wrongly at the sex of the author of *Adam Bede*.[14] Though assuredly not a feminist writer, no Victorian woman writer of major stature was more aggressively *feminine* than Gaskell. Active and even strenuous as her life as a writer and minister's wife was, it seems to have convinced her that the feminine sphere of interest was not only different from that of men—it required a different literary perspective, an act of feminine fiction-making, to give reality and shape to it. Such an attitude may be discerned in the voice of the feminine narrator of *Cranford*, who dismisses a letter from her father, noting disdainfully that it was "just a man's letter; I mean it was very dull and gave no information beyond that he was well, that they had had a good deal of rain, that trade was very stagnant, and there were many disagreeable rumors afloat."[15] The letter from Mary Smith's father is not unimportant, for the "disagreeable rumours" pertain to the imminent failure of Miss Matty's bank, a key thread in the plot of *Cranford*. But the narrator's disdain for this "man's letter" is significant in an author who was herself a prolific and accomplished letter-writer. What a "woman's letter" might have contained is suggested by the collected letters of Gaskell herself and by the closely observed feminine perspective of the narrator of *Cranford:* domestic details, gossip, the trivia of human connectedness, and hints of the rich inner emotional life. Mary Smith's father warns of the failure of a bank, but only Mary herself can report on the effect of this event on Miss Matty's character, on her relationships with the community, and on her view of herself and of her world. To say that *Cranford* could have been written and observed only by a woman writer is not to trivialize the book, but to suggest that there existed in the nineteenth century a world of domestic concerns, human relationships, and inner needs which could scarcely have been attained from a masculine literary perspective.

It is little wonder, then, that in the works of Gaskell, the stories that women tell differ greatly from those of men. As the stories in *Sylvia's Lovers* have already suggested, the tales of men are likely to be filled with adventures, journeys, and marvels—like the sailor's ghost story or the nautical tall tales of Kinraid and Daniel Robson. Edgar Wright has detected in the scene in *North and South* in which Mr. Thornton first impresses Margaret with the chronicle of his early struggles, a suggestion of Othello's seducing Desdemona with his marvelous tales.[16] The Othello courting motif is observable in the interpolated tales of other Gaskell heroes; as has already been noted, Kinraid in *Sylvia's Lovers* first impresses Sylvia with his nautical tales, just as Daniel Robson had once courted Sylvia's mother. Similarly, in *Mary Barton* Will Wilson comes home from the sea to make an impression on the heart of Margaret Legh with his fireside tales of flying fish and mermaids with bright green hair. Again, in *Cranford,* the old bachelor Peter comes home from his travels to enchant the ladies of Cranford with "more wonderful stories than Sinbad the Sailor" (*C,* p. 185). Other tales that men tell are likely to revolve around some great journey or adventure. In *Mary Barton,* John Barton tells how the workmen took their petition to London, only to have Parliament refuse to hear it, and Job Legh tells a comic epic of two old men bringing back an infant granddaughter from London. The tales of these men are not at all random or unrelated to the progress of the narrative. Barton's adventure is a key motivation for the eventual murder of the mill owner's son, and the whole episode of the workmen's petition is crucial to the theme of the misunderstanding between the working men and the managerial class. Job Legh's comic tale embodies another of the novel's themes, the compassion and humanity of the poor for one another. The comic journey of the two grandfathers to rescue an infant echoes other acts of charity which the poor perform for one another in *Mary Barton.* The old men's ignorance and incompetence at child care are the stuff of high humor, but the readiness with which their own class, and particularly the women of their class come to their aid, is a recurring motif in the works of Gaskell. These masculine stories of adventure are thus hardly random or without purpose. Exciting yarns in their own right, they are also a part of the cumulative method by which Gaskell piles up her novels' impressions. The stories are chosen deliberately to display something of the teller's character; moreover, they generally reflect the broader themes and images of the novel.

Unlike the adventure stories of the masculine characters, on the other hand, the tales that women tell, like Mrs. Robson's story of Crazy Nancy, usually convey an emotional truth about the lives of women. Their messages in themselves are not likely to be overtly subversive; often in fact they reinforce prevailing stereotypes of the ideal Victorian "angel in the house." The mere act of female storytelling, however, becomes a means, not unlike the writing of novels, by which the female characters may name and give shape to the reality of their lives in a patriarchal society. Often the stories are told by one woman to another, to inspire her, to warn her, or to serve as some sort of clue by which she may find her path in the midst of the perplexities and trials with which feminine lives are fraught. In Gaskell's earliest novel, for example, almost every story told by a woman is told to Mary Barton herself, or is intended for her benefit, and each of them contains some feminine guidance about the duties and needs of a womanly life which the heroine desperately needs to hear. Left motherless at an early age, Mary is in danger of abandoning domestic duties and family ties for the empty flattery and false temptations offered to her by Harry Carson. (The luxury and idleness of the life of a "lady," which Mary hopes to attain through Carson, are embodied in the ironic portrait of Carson's sisters; in *North and South,* Mr. Thornton's sister and Margaret's cousin are similar portraits which suggest that the vain and idle life of a lady is not the ideal of the true woman.) With her mother dead and her father increasingly absorbed by his obsession with the workers' struggle, Mary has only the guidance of the other women in her life, and in their tales and conversation, these characters often act as surrogate mothers by suggesting to Mary the advice which her own mother might have provided had she lived. Old Alice Wilson, for example, relates the story of her youth to Mary and Margaret Legh, both young and motherless girls. Alice tells of leaving her home in the country to go into "service" in Manchester and of how it hurt her own mother that she was so willing to go. In subsequent years she often plans to go home again, but is unable to do so before her mother's death. The motif of Alice's futile desire to see her old home once more is repeated again and again throughout the novel; it serves as a warning to Mary about the value of the "home ties" she is tempted to abandon. Even the ballad which Alice sings about "the golden hills o' heaven" which remind her of the hills of her country home serves as a veiled warning to Mary and Margaret. The old folk ballad is about "a lover that should hae been na lover" (*MB,* p. 35) and about the girl who succumbed to him and was therefore barred forever from the golden hills, a tale which forecasts presciently the danger that Mary herself will skirt. Another tale is offered to Mary by Mrs. Wilson, who is destined to become Mary's mother-in-law. She tells Mary of the time early in her marriage when, in her domestic ignorance, she boiled potatoes all day until she had produced "a nasty brown mess, as smelt through all the house" (*MB,* p. 137). Mrs. Wilson is a weak and foolish character, and her recital of small domestic tribulations is comic, but the implications of her tale are serious and are intended for

Mary's instruction. Mary has already neglected her social duties and domestic ties by failing to visit this old family friend more often, and her failure is symptomatic of the fact that she is neglecting the honest love of Jem Wilson for the false blandishments of Harry Carson. Mrs. Wilson's story, then, is a reminder of the importance of women's true duties. The subsequent discussion about the tendency of factory women toward "putting their little ones out at nurse, and letting their house go all dirty, and their fires all out" (*MB*, p. 137) serves as another reminder of where Mary's true duty and true fulfillment lie. But the novel's most important tale is clearly the one told by Mary's Aunt Esther. The story of Esther's life cannot, of course, be told directly to Mary, for Esther is a prostitute, and Mary must be protected from such contact and from the direct knowledge of such a sordid tale. But Esther tells her chronicle of seduction and betrayal with the express intention of preventing Mary from following such a course, and thus she seeks out first Mary's father and then Mary's suitor, Jem Wilson, to force them to listen to her story in the hopes that they can prevent a similar fate from befalling Mary. Like the Ancient Mariner accosting wedding guests, Esther forces her listener to hear the truth about her ruin in the hopes that it will serve as guidance for Mary's path in life. (Indeed, it is not unlikely that Esther's tale forecasts Gaskell's purpose in her own tale of a seduced woman, her novel *Ruth*.) As in other stories that women tell in *Mary Barton*, Esther's tale is intended to convey the same symbolic truth about women's lives as the novel itself, indeed the same truth that Victorian society heartily endorsed—that true fulfillment comes from the emotional and spiritual ties that bind a woman to hearth and family. The very telling of such tales, however, seems to suggest the existence of a feminine community of interests which differ radically from those of men, a community which supports and gives validity to the act of feminine fictionmaking.

The stories that women tell each other in *Ruth* seem to perform a similar function. Once again a motherless young heroine is embarked upon a life fraught with moral peril, and once again she finds solace and guidance in the tales of the women she meets. Ruth's first storyteller is a fat old lady who comforts the weeping girl on a coach journey by telling of her own lost sons, "soldiers and sailors, all of them," all very far from home, "and yet, you see, I can laugh and eat and enjoy myself" (*R*, p. 131). The sympathy of this traveller suggests a community of women sharing the values of nurturing, love, and compassion and linked by the common bond of motherhood which Ruth is about to share. The existence of such a bond is demonstrated again toward the end of the novel when Ruth's son hovers on the verge of death and an old crippled woman comes to inquire and pray for him, "stirred with a sharp pang of sympathy, and a very present remembrance of the time when she too was young, and saw the life-breath quiver out of her child" (*R*, p. 309). Later, after Leonard's recovery, Ruth listens, weeping at the old woman's story of how her own child had sickened and died, "and the two were henceforward

a pair of friends" (*R*, p. 310). Significantly, the old woman herself no longer sheds tears, but sits "patient and quiet, waiting for death" (*R*, p. 310). The jolly woman traveller and the crippled old woman are both linked to Ruth through their common motherhood, and the stories they tell of the loss of their sons imply a Christian resignation in the face of life's adversity, which is surely the novel's most prevalent theme. Their resignation, however, is at least partially belied by the relish with which they make stories and dramas out of their lives and use those stories to create a bond with other women. But the supreme storyteller of the novel is, of course, the servant Sally, and it remains for Sally to tell the tale which drives the moral of the novel home to Ruth. Watching Ruth perform household tasks with a languid and depressed spirit, Sally tells of her own experience as a young servant girl. Despondent over the accident which had crippled Master Thurstan, Sally "took to praying and sighing, and was careless about dinner and the rooms" (*R*, p. 173). She is reprimanded by her mistress, who points out that Sally's beloved Master Thurstan cannot eat the sodden pudding, and asks her if she thinks we are put into the world to "do nothing but see after our own souls? or to help one another with heart and hand, as Christ did to all who wanted help?" (*R*, p. 174). Sally's tale, and her accompanying admonition that "making a bed may be done after a Christian fashion," (*R*, p. 173) remind Ruth that she must find her proper work in the world through Christian love and resignation, the tale thus encapsulating in comic form the central theme of the novel. Indeed, the character of Sally is pivotal to this theme, and all of her tales suggest the same motif, even when they are intensely comic. The story of Sally's refusal of a proposal of marriage from the kneeling clerk is really the proof of her devotion to her master, whom she will not leave even for a life and home of her own, and the story of the drawing up of her will, with its fancy "law-words," is the tale of another act of Christian love and charity, for she is leaving her savings to her master. Thus Sally endorses the typically Victorian role of the selfless heroine; her triumph lies in her ability to give purpose and dimension to her life by her own considerable verbal powers.

The tales that women tell to the heroines of *Ruth, Mary Barton,* and *Sylvia's Lovers* are all aimed at conveying the central truths about the lives of women that the novels themselves embody; in each case the interpolated tale reflects upon the shared experience of women in a way that mirrors the novels' larger themes and, by implication, the very function of the female novelist. In other Gaskell works, the tales of women are not central to the development of a heroine, but nonetheless are in keeping with the concern of the novels with the emotional drama of women's lives and their attempts to gain some control over this drama by makng it the stuff of their tales. *Cranford*, as has previously been observed, is a collage of stories told by the ladies of the town and by the female narrator, comic and slight in their effect, but slowly creating a portrait of a stable, traditional, nurturing, and *feminine* community, as opposed to the masculine world

of the neighboring city. Nina Auerbach has pointed out the role of "fancy" (i.e., tale-telling) in uniting the feminine community of Cranford in such a way that a private, feminine, fictional vision is created out of magic burglars, ghosts, spies, Frenchmen, witches, and the "white lies" told to Miss Matty to preserve her dignity, all acts of feminine fiction-making which in the end subvert "public, masculine truth."[17] The only story which jars in this stable, communal experience is the wild adventure related by the conjuror's wife, but the "Signora," as she is called, is another woman bonded by the common experience of motherhood, for she has lost six children and possesses, as the narrator observes, "those strange eyes that I've never noticed but in mothers of dead children" (*C*, p. 130). The feminine community of Cranford rallies itself to her aid, with even the formidable Miss Pole drawn into this sisterhood of compassion and humanity. The tale of the conjuror's wife concerns her journey through India to save the life of her last surviving child, and the kindness that she receives along the way, particularly from an officer's wife whose own children have died. The story is remarkably similar to the story in *Mary Barton* in which Job Legh takes his infant granddaughter home from London, helped along the way by women who have lost their own children. (Job, of course, is a masculine taleteller, but he is more of a nurturing figure than the other male storytellers, being older and having raised his granddaughter alone.) In any case, the story of the conjuror's wife is decidedly a contrast to that of the other traveller returned from India to Cranford, Miss Matty's brother. Peter returns home to tell such traditionally masculine tall tales as the one about shooting a cherub off a mountain top, whereas the story of the "signora" revolves around the feminine themes of sacrifices made for a child and the bond between women who have suffered loss. Like the other ladies of Cranford, the conjuror's wife uses storytelling to impose verbal control on a life in which she otherwise has little power.

There are fewer interpolated tales in *North and South.* Mr. Thornton's recital of his early struggles, which fits into the Othello-Desdemona pattern of courting noted in Gaskell's works, is an integral part of the developing of the hero's personality and the theme of the harsh, sturdy Northern character. But there is one clearly anecdotal story of great interest in the novel, and it is told by Margaret Hale herself. A sturdier heroine than those of Gaskell's previous novels, Margaret Hale does not seek much guidance from other women and specifically rejects the advice of such surrogate mothers as Mrs. Thornton and her own Aunt Shaw. Margaret relies, sometimes to her regret, largely upon her own judgment, and the story she tells is interesting in that it contains her own vision of the inner reality of women's lives. The story emerges in the midst of a heated discussion between Margaret and Mr. Thornton about the conduct of the masters toward their workers. Mr. Thornton compares the workers to children and declares himself in favor of governing such children by autocratic laws. Margaret responds with a strange story of a wealthy man in Nuremberg, who lived for many years with a child he kept shut up in his

immense mansion. Upon the death of the father, the son is discovered to be "an over-grown man, with the unexercised intellect of a child," who is unable to take care of himself in the world and falls prey to every bad counsellor and evil influence. Eventually this "great old child" must be cared for by the city authorities, for "he could not even use words effectively enough to be a successful beggar."[18] Margaret's story is clearly related to the political and economic discussion at hand, for it suggests that the workers, deprived of education and independence, will grow to be both ignorant and dangerous. Margaret implies that in order to be capable of governing themselves rationally, the workingmen must be educated to understand the economic conditions which govern their lives and must be given some control over their own destiny. Such an argument is clearly central to the major economic theme of the novel, but it is related as well to an equally central theme: the dilemma of women's lives. As John Pikoulis has noted, in *North and South* "the theme of women searching for an expansion of the possibilities for living that are open to them is combined with the theme of the dispute between masters and men."[19] In the discussions between Margaret and Mr. Thornton, Gaskell depicts an intricate blending of economic and sexual tensions; as a woman suffering the limitations forced upon her by male society, Margaret identifies strongly with the equally powerless industrial workers. Her anecdote serves a double function, then; it establishes her political position in opposition to Mr. Thornton and it also suggests Margaret's clear-sighted vision of the central problem in the lives of nineteenth-century women—the lack of experience and education which might teach them to function independently. With Margaret Hale, Gaskell seems finally to have created a heroine strong enough to articulate her own visions in fictions of her own making.

In view of Gaskell's increasingly subtle use of the feminine anecdote or tale to convey the central concerns of her novels, it is interesting to note that there are fewer and fewer interpolated tales in her later works. *Cousin Phillis* contains almost no tales, although, of course, it is, like *Cranford,* a narrated reminiscence. Peter Keating has pointed to a significant difference between the female narrator of *Cranford* and the masculine narrator of *Cousin Phillis* which is consistent with the way that Gaskell used male and female storytellers in other works: "whereas Mary Smith had embodied Mrs. Gaskell's own perceptions of Cranford, [the narrator of *Cousin Phillis*] lacks any truly sympathetic understanding of the lives and events he describes."[20] (The measure of the gulf between Mary Smith and Paul Manning as narrators may be gauged by the effect of their respective interventions in the events of their stories. Mary Smith arranges for the return of Peter from India, and intuitively suggests the perfect genteel employment for Miss Matty in her reduced circumstances; Paul's well-intentioned itervention in his cousin's love affair, on the other hand, brings about the bleak ending of *Cousin Phillis*.) But aside from the blundering ignorance of the masculine persona of her narrator, Gaskell shows

little interest in the act of tale-telling in *Cousin Phillis* and none at all in her last novel, *Wives and Daughters.*

It is apparent that the dwindling role of the interpolated tale in Gaskell's later work is related to some development in her ideas about her role as a woman writer; just what this development might have been is difficult to document. Aina Rubenius has postulated a change in Gaskell's writing from the publication of *The Life of Charlotte Brontë,* which "marks the transition in Mrs. Gaskell's authorship from the writing of novels with a purpose, such as *Mary Barton, Ruth,* and *North and South,* to the writing for art's sake."[21] According to Rubenius, Gaskell later came into contact with ideas about women's rights and Goethean ideas of self-development, and thus came to regard the demands of her art as paramount.[22] Although evidence for such an intellectual change is hard to pinpoint, it is at least certain that her literary success in later years brought her economic confidence and independence. Her letters show that by the end of her life she had taken control of her own income generated from writing and had no qualms about using it at her own discretion.[23] It is possible that in later years her admiration for Charlotte Brontë may have inspired her with greater self-assurance about the role of the woman writer, or that the very act of writing the biography (the story of a woman who outwardly had no story) may finally have laid to rest her doubts about the validity of women creating stories out of the reality of feminine lives.

Whatever the cause, at the end of her career, Gaskell seems to have had less need to work out a justification for feminine fiction-making through the interpolated tale. *Wives and Daughters,* in particular, is imbued with such a forceful vision of the painful inner drama of seemingly prosaic feminine lives, that the author seems not to have needed the help of her characters to tell stories which hammer home her themes. And yet, to say that there are no tales and stories in Gaskell's most mature work is not to suggest that the tales are necessarily random or intrusive in the earlier works. Rather, they seem to be the mark of a growing artist, striving to control her material and her artistic vision within the bounds of an exuberant and bountiful talent, and striving also to justify the very act of feminine creation. Taken as a whole, the stories and tales of these novels show an astonishing range of fiction-making, from the comic and the marvelous to the pathetic. Each is appropriate in some way to the character of its narrator, and each in some way reflects upon the major concerns of the novels. The act of storytelling in Gaskell's works, particularly when the teller is a woman, is an artistic and literary act of faith—the passing on of tradition, the sharing of experience or vision, the strengthening of communal bonds—in the same way that writing a novel is, for a woman, an act of faith. Each of the storytellers of these novels is a literary artist in his or her own right; and in particular, the female tellers of tales seem to convey the inner truths of feminine experience which Gaskell would have considered to be the particular province of the woman novelist. Far from being artless or intrusive, then, the interpolated tales of Gaskell's novels are a measure of the author's early power to absorb the broadest possible range of life's experience, to make it serve the purposes of her art, and to work out the implications of a uniquely feminine making of fiction.

### NOTES

[1] F. R. Leavis, for example, cites her as one of those "minor novelists" like Charlotte Yonge and Wilkie Collins whose work has blurred the recognition due to the truly "classical" novelists (*The Great Tradition* [New York: New York Univ. Press, 1973], pp. 1-2). John Gross begins his evaluation of her work by conceding that her "charm" has "led to her being treated as a lightweight, automatically consigned to the ranks of the miniaturists and minor talents" ("Mrs. Gaskell," in Ian Watt, *The Victorian Novel: Modern Essays in Criticism* [London: Oxford Univ. Press, 1971], p. 217). And Laurence Lerner, in his introduction to the Penguin edition of *Wives and Daughters* tempers his praise of *Cranford* with the same disparaging phrases: "charming" and "minor" (Harmondsworth: 1969, p. 20).

[2] See Edgar Wright in his excellent study, *Mrs. Gaskell: The Basis for Reassessment* (London: Oxford Univ. Press, 1965), pp. 4-5.

[3] Wright discusses the stereotype of the "moderately cultured amateur with . . . a talent for story-telling" (p. 4).

[4] Sandra M. Gilbert and Susan Gubar, *The Madwoman in the Attic: The Woman Writer and the Nineteenth Century Imagination* (New Haven: Yale Univ. Press, 1979), p. 39 et passim.

[5] *The Letters of Mrs. Gaskell,* ed. J. A. V. Chapple and Arthur Pollard (Manchester: Manchester Univ. Press, 1966), 12, pp. 28-33; 15, p. 42; and 29, p. 61. Hereafter cited in the text as *L,* followed by letter and page references.

[6] Winifred Gérin, *Elizabeth Gaskell* (Oxford: The Clarendon Press, 1976), pp. 123, 184.

[7] Wright, pp. 79-82. According to Wright, "there is an obvious link between her love of tradition and legend, and her delight in ghost stories and morbidly tinged tales, which are a staple of any mythology" (p. 165).

[8] Wright, p. 82.

[9] *Mary Barton,* Knutsford Edition (London: Smith and Elder, 1906; rpt. New York: A. M. S. Press, 1972), pp. 43-44. All references to the works of Gaskell will be to the Knutsford Edition.

[10] *Ruth,* pp. 164-69.

[11] *Sylvia's Lovers,* p. 492.

[12] Angus Easson in *Elizabeth Gaskell* (London: Routledge and Kegan Paul, 1979) has noted how "the sense of exaggeration in Robson's tale" demonstrates the way in which "Gaskell modifies or finds a story appropriate to her characters" (p. 167).

[13] Carlyle began his letter, "Dear Madam, (For I catch the treble of that fine melodious voice very well)" and went on to praise the "beautiful, cheerfully pious, social, clear and observant character [which] is everywhere recognisable in the writer. . . . " In Gérin, p. 89. For Gaskell's reaction, see *Letters,* 33, p. 64; 37, p. 68; 38, pp. 68-69; and 39, pp. 69-71.

[14] Gaskell's discomfort with the feminine authorship of *Adam Bede* had mainly to do with the irregularities of "Mrs. Lewes'" life. See *Letters,* 431, p. 559; 438, pp. 566-67; 449, p. 592; and 451, p. 594.

[15] *Cranford,* p. 143.

[16] Wright, p. 140.

[17] *Communities of Women: An Idea in Fiction* (Cambridge: Harvard Univ. Press, 1978), pp. 87, 117.

[18] *North and South,* pp. 141-42.

[19] "*North and South:* Varieties of Love and Power," *Yearbook of English Studies,* 6 (1976), 176.

[20] Introduction to *Cranford/Cousin Phillis* (Harmondsworth: Penguin, 1976).

[21] *The Woman Question in Mrs. Gaskell's Life and Works* (Essays and Studies on English Language and Literature, The English Institute in the University of Upsala, ed. S. B. Liljegren, Cambridge: Harvard Univ. Press, 1950), pp. 60-61.

[22] Rubenius, pp. 61-62.

[23] Early letters report her husband coolly pocketing her check for "Lizzie Leigh" (*Letters,* 70, p. 113). In her later years she used her income without her husband's knowledge to purchase a house for his retirement and the future of her unmarried daughters.

## Jane S. Bakerman

SOURCE: "Failures of Love: Female Initiation in the Novels of Toni Morrison," in *American Literature,* Vol. 52, No. 4, January, 1981, pp. 541-63.

*[In the following essay, Bakerman explores the attempts and failures of women to initiate themselves into both personal and social maturity in a culture in which they are automatically considered outsiders in the novels of Toni Morrison.]*

I

Toni Morrison, contemporary writer and senior editor at Random House, has achieved major stature through the publication of only three novels. *The Bluest Eye* (1970)[1] and *Sula* (1973)[2] are brief, poetic works which explore the initiation experiences of their black, female, adolescent protagonists. *Song of Solomon* (1977)[3] is a much longer but still lyrical story relating Macon (Milkman) Dead's search for familial roots and personal identity. Milkman's development is framed and illuminated by the maturation stories of three women important in his life, and the presence of these subplots in the tale of a male protagonist is a good indication of the importance of female initiation in Morrison's thought.

For Toni Morrison, the central theme of all her work is

> Beauty, love. . . . Actually, I think, all the time that I write, I'm writing about love or its absence. Although I don't start out that way. . . . But I think that I still write about the same thing, which is how people relate to one another and miss it or hang on to it . . . or are tenacious about love.[4]

Certainly, this theme is evident in *The Bluest Eye, Sula,* and *Song of Solomon,* their female characters searching for love, for valid sexual encounters, and, above all, for a sense that they are worthy.

Traditionally, the initiation rite is painful but enlightening, and the chief theme of novels of novels of adolescence has been identified as "the individual's search for genuine values."[5] Morrison's early works explore the results for black women when the values are real and powerful but are designed primarily for middle-class whites. This concept certainly appears importantly in *Song of Solomon,* but that book also explores what happens to women whose values (and value) are determined by the men who control their lives. From the outset, these values are known by some of Morrison's female characters to be useless, even damaging, to them. Claudia, the narrator of *The Bluest Eye,* for instance, recognizes her position.

> Being a minority in both caste and class [being poor, black, female], we moved about anyway on the hem of life, struggling to consolidate our weaknesses and hang on, or to creep singly up into the major folds of the garment. (p. 11)

For Pecola Breedlove, Sula Peace, Nel Wright Greene, Pilate Dead, Hagar Dead, and First Corinthians Dead, as for many other female characters,

> Female aspiration is a joke. Female rebellion may be perfectly justified, but there is no good universe next door, no way out, young potential revolutionaries can't find their revolution. So they marry in defeat or go mad in a complicated form of triumph, their meaning the inevitability of failure.[6]

In Toni Morrison's novels, she joins her basic theme with the initiation motif, and the initiation experiences, trying and painful as they are, fail.[7] Pilate invents her own standards and lives almost outside society, a choice which eventually brings tragedy upon her family. Sula rebels and is rejected. Nel marries; Corinthians takes a lover, and both are diminished. Hagar and Pecola attempt to transform themselves; Hagar dies, and Pecola goes mad. All live lives of profound isolation in a society which does not want them.

II

*The Bluest Eye* employs two frames; the outer frame demonstrates the elementary school reader standards for family behavior and beauty. The inner frame is the family life of the MacTeers; the younger MacTeer daughter, Claudia, tells us the story of her friend, Pecola Breedlove, and in doing so describes her own stable family as a point of comparison and contrast.

Pecola seems to have been born knowing that the Breedloves were damaged people, undervalued by both whites and blacks. She wishes to emerge not only from the isolation of childhood, but also from the isolation of this family stigma: They are poor, and they are ugly.

> You looked at them and wondered why they were so ugly; you looked closely and could not find the source. Then you realized that it came from conviction, their conviction. It was as though some mysterious all-knowing master had given each one a cloak of ugliness to wear, and they had accepted it without question. (p. 28)

Because white children appear to be beloved by both white and black adults, Pecola determines to achieve beauty and acceptance by acquiring blue eyes.

> Each night, without fail, she prayed for blue eyes. Fervently, for a year she had prayed. Although somewhat discouraged, she was not without hope. To have something as wonderful as that happen would take a long, long time. (p. 35)

Morrison's point is clear:

> When the strength of a race depends on its beauty, when the focus is turned to how one looks as opposed to what one is, we are in trouble. . . . The concept of physical beauty as a *virtue* is one of the dumbest, most pernicious and destructive ideas of the Western world, and we should have nothing to do with it. Physical beauty has nothing to do with our past, present or future. Its absence or presence was only important to *them,* the white people who used it for anything they wanted—[8]

But there is no one to explain this point to Pecola. Her parents, Cholly and Pauline, have accepted the idea that they are ugly and in doing so have come to hate one another. Equally importantly, they do not know how to love; and they cannot give their children a sense of self, for they have none of their own. Cholly, parentless, set adrift by the death of his guardian, taunted and humiliated by white men during his first sexual encounter, does not know about nurturing love, and feeling love, he is incapable of expressing it healthfully:

> Cholly was free. Dangerously free. Free to feel whatever he felt. . . . He was free to live his fantasies, and free even to die, the how and the when of which held no interest for him. . . . Abandoned in a junk heap by his mother, rejected for a crap game by his father, there was nothing more to lose. He was alone with his own perceptions and appetites, and they alone interested him. (pp. 125-26)

Indulging those perceptions and appetites, Cholly courts and marries Pauline, but she cannot teach him, for she, too, has been isolated and unloved.

> Slight as it was, this deformity [a maimed foot] explained for her many things that would have been otherwise incomprehensible: why she alone of all the children had no nickname; why there were no funny jokes and anecdotes about funny things she had done; why no one ever remarked her food preferences—no saving of the wing or neck for her—no cooking of the peas in a separate pot without rice because she did not like rice; why nobody teased her; why she never felt at home anywhere, or that she belonged anyplace. Her general feeling of separateness and unworthiness she blamed on her foot. (p. 86)

Pauline's isolation is exacerbated by the couple's removal to the North, where she is unlike other blacks and unaccepted by them. Eventually, her loneliness and Cholly's futile struggle to support them decently destroy every possibility of love, and they learn to use their children as weapons against one another.[9] The impending failure of Pecola's initiation, then, is first foreshadowed by the failure of love within her family.

There are a series of these lesser, foreshadowing encounters, all centering on failure of love, equated with the failure to be accepted or even to be considered worthy of acceptance. Frequently, these encounters have sexual overtones, for positive initiation is symbolized here by healthy sexuality, and we meet Pecola at the onset of menstruation. She and her friends, Claudia and Frieda MacTeer, like other girls, are curious, puzzled, and enticed by their sexuality. For Claudia and Frieda, questioning is colored with romance:

> My sister comes in. Her eyes are full of sorrow. She sings to me: 'When the deep purple falls over sleepy garden walls, someone thinks of me . . . ' I doze, thinking of plums, walls, and 'someone.' (p. 7)

For Pecola, it is tinged with terror:

> What did love feel like? she wondered. How do grown-ups act when they love each other? Eat fish together? Into her eyes came the picture of Cholly and Mrs. Breedlove in bed. He making sounds as though he were in pain, as though something had him by the throat and wouldn't let go. Terrible as

his noises were, they were not nearly as bad as the no noise at all from her mother. It was as though she was not even there. Maybe that was love. Choking sounds and silence. (p. 44)

The foreshadowing encounters also incorporate the motifs of race and ugliness, so that at every turn the reader is made to understand that Pecola's state is hopeless. Even the most casual exchanges teach her that she is unworthy. At school, the boys taunt her; she is the scapegoat for their own humiliation and pain,

> 'Black e mo. Black e mo. Yadaddsleepsnekked. Black e mo black e mo ya dadd sleeps nekked. Black e mo . . . '

> They had extemporized a verse made up of two insults about matters over which the victim had no control: the color of her skin and speculations on the sleeping habits of an adult, wildly fitting in its incoherence. That they themselves were black, or that their own father had similarly relaxed habits was irrelevant. It was their contempt for their own blackness that gave the first insult its teeth. They seemed to have taken all of their smoothly cultivated ignorance, their exquisitely learned self-hatred, their elaborately designed hopelessness and sucked it all up into a fiery cone of scorn that had burned for ages in the hollows of their minds—cooled—and spilled over lips of outrage, consuming whatever was in its path. (p. 50)

Buying the Mary Jane candies that she likes to eat because of the blond, blue-eyed child on the wrapper, Pecola is made aware that for many people, she doesn't really exist:

> He does not see her, because for him there is nothing to see. How can a fifty-two-year-old white immigrant storekeeper with the taste of potatoes and beer in his mouth, his mind honed on the doe-eyed Virgin Mary, his sensibilities blunted by a permanent awareness of loss, *see* a little black girl? . . .

> She looks up at him and sees the vacuum where curiosity ought to lodge. And something more. The total absence of human recognition—the glazed separateness. She does not know what keeps his glance suspended. Perhaps because he is grown, or a man, and she a little girl. But she has seen interest, disgust, even anger in grown male eyes. . . . it is the blackness that accounts for, that creates, the vacuum edged with distaste in white eyes. (pp. 36-37)

And she assuages her resulting, unearned shame with "nine lovely orgasms with Mary Jane. Lovely Mary Jane, for whom a candy is named" (p. 38).

As they multiply, the foreshadowing encounters grow more painful and frightening. Seemingly befriended by a pretty little girl, the darling of the teachers and the demon of the other children, Pecola begins to relax, only to discover that she's being tricked into revealing "humiliating" facts about her family in exchange for Maureen's specious information about sex.

> 'Did you ever see a naked man?'

> Pecola blinked, then looked away. 'No. Where would I see a naked man?'

> 'I don't know. I just asked.'

> 'I wouldn't even look at him, even if I did see him. That's dirty. Who wants to see a naked man?' Pecola was agitated. 'Nobody's father would be naked in front of his own daughter. Not unless he was dirty too. . . . '

> 'How come you said 'father'?' Maureen wanted to know. (p. 55)

The most terrible of the rejections occurs when a young boy makes her the scapegoat for his own pain, which stems directly from the fact that his mother, embracing white, middle-class standards, forces him to reject his own blackness and invests her affection in her cat.

> How beautiful, she thought. What a beautiful house. There was a big red-and-gold Bible on the dining-room table. Little lace doilies were everywhere. . . . Potted plants were on all the windowsills. A color picture of Jesus Christ hung on a wall with the prettiest paper flowers fastened on the frame. She wanted to see everything slowly, slowly. . . . She was deep in admiration of the flowers when Junior said, 'Here!' Pecola turned. 'Here is your kitten!' he screeched. And he threw a big black cat right in her face. She sucked in her breath in fear and surprise and felt fur in her mouth. The cat clawed her face and chest in an effort to right itself, then leaped nimbly to the floor. (pp. 69-70)

Pecola is unable to save the cat from further torture and she is unable to save herself, for Junior's mother, interrupting, cannot allow herself to see the moment for what it really is; to do so would be to acknowledge kinship with Pecola, poor, ugly, and black, "'You nasty little black bitch. Get out of my house'" (p. 72).

Thus, Pecola is carefully taught that there is no one to love her, that whites do not see her, that blacks scorn her. For Pecola, the healthy sexual encounter symbolizing initiation into the adult world is forbidden, for when someone does *see* her as lovable, it is her father, and he rapes her.

> The sequence of his emotions was revulsion, guilt, pity, then love. His revulsion was a reaction to her young, helpless, hopeless presence. . . . Guilt and impotence rose in a bilious duet. What could he do for her—ever? . . . What could a burned-out black man say to the hunched back of his eleven-year-old daughter? If he looked into her face, he would see those haunted, loving eyes. . . . How dare she love him? Hadn't she any sense at all? What was he supposed to do about that? Return it? How? . . . a bolt of desire ran down his genitals,

giving it length. . . . His soul seemed to slip down to his guts and fly out into her, and the gigantic thrust he made into her then provoked the only sound she made—a hollow suck of air in the back of her throat. Like the rapid loss of air from a circus balloon. (pp. 127-28)

The resulting baby dies, but Pecola lives, the victim of failed initiation, though she makes one more attempt to come to terms with the world. Because her prayers have come to no account, she seeks the aid of a magician. If he can give her blue eyes, all will be reversed. The result is bitter and ironic; she finds the only refuge available to her—madness. Through her false belief that she has, indeed, acquired blue eyes, beauty, Pecola escapes to the deepest isolation of all.

> The damage done was total. She spent her days, her tendril, sap-green days, walking up and down, up and down, her head jerking to the beat of a drummer so distant only she could hear. (p. 162)

For the community, Pecola's madness, coupled with her family history, excites scorn rather than sympathy. She becomes the scapegoat not merely for frustrated children, but for all of society. She assumes

> All of our waste which we dumped on her and which she absorbed. And all of our beauty, which was hers first and which she gave to us. All of us—all who knew her—felt so wholesome after we cleaned ourselves on her. We were so beautiful when we stood astride her ugliness. Her simplicity decorated us, her guilt sanctified us, her pain made us glow with health. . . . Even her waking dreams we used—to silence our own nightmares. And she let us, and thereby deserved our contempt. We honed our egos on her, padded our characters with her frailty, and yawned in the fantasy of our strength. (pp. 162-63)

The novel is effective because of the importance of its theme and the skill with which the inevitability of the failed initiation is developed through the compelling foreshadowing encounters. This device keeps the story convincing even while distancing Pecola from the reader, perhaps the final dramatization of her hopelessness and her eventual ostracism from a society which would rather destroy than accept her.

### III

Though the initiations of Sula Peace and Nel Wright also fail, *Sula* differs from *The Bluest Eye* in both complexity and the assignment of responsibility. Here, while it is still made clear that Sula and Nel are undervalued and that their families legislate toward the initiation failure, both girls make specific decisions and choices which also contribute. Pecola struggles with the fate assigned to her; Sula and Nel help to choose their fates.

Like *The Bluest Eye, Sula* is highly episodic, and flashbacks dramatize the damage done to adult family members who influence and shape Sula and Nel.[10] In *Sula*, as in *The Bluest Eye*, the protagonists undergo a series of experiences, each incorporating racial and sexual overtones, but here the encounters fall into two categories: those undergone individually and those suffered together. The division is important, for the experiences within the families have made the girls what they are as individuals; the experiences outside the families, all shared, indicate one of Morrison's most important points in the novel—the personalities of Sula and of Nel, could they have been merged, would have amounted to one whole person.

Just as their friendship is essential to their well-being as children, so would their learning from one another's faults have made them adult women capable of well-being. The real tragedy in *Sula* is that Nel and Sula are unable to learn that lesson; their friendship ruptures and they live isolated, frustrated lives. The interrelationship of the girls' personalities, symbolized by their friendship, and the recurring sexual and racial themes provide unity; the results are powerful and effective.

Both the Peace and Wright families are essentially fatherless; thus, the girls learn their most important lessons from their mothers, and in each case, the mother fails her daughter. Helene, Nel's mother, is absolutely conventional, being "constantly on guard for any sign of her [own] mother's wild blood" (p. 17), and she passes her rigid attitude about sex along to Nel. She seems strong and capable, but on a journey south, Nel watches her mother cringe before a white railway conductor under the disgusted, scorn-filled, impotent eyes of a group of black soldiers. The effect is lifelong:

> If this tall, proud woman, this woman who was very particular about her friends, who slipped into church with unequaled elegance, who could quell a roustabout with a look, if *she* were really custard, then there was a chance that Nel was too.
>
> It was on that train . . . that she resolved to be on guard—always. She wanted to make certain that no man ever looked at her that way. That no midnight eyes or marbled flesh would ever accost her and turn her into jelly. (p. 22)

Nel's individual initiation hardens her so that when the final, terrible test of her friendship with Sula comes, she turns her back on love and affirmation and finds refuge in that hardness—and in isolation.

Sula's home is governed by her grandmother, Eva, and run by her mother, Hannah. Both women are popular with men—Eva has a troop of male friends, Hannah a succession of lovers, but though they feel genuine love for them, "it was manlove that Eva bequeathed to her daughters" (p. 41), neither is able to express her affection for her children in a way that is acceptable or apprehendable to them. Sula's perceptions about sex are not formed by one of the initiation experiences, but rather are accumulated over the years by her mother's promiscuousness.

Seeing her step so easily into the pantry and emerge looking precisely as she did when she entered, only happier, taught Sula that sex was pleasant and frequent, but otherwise unremarkable. Outside the house, where children giggled about underwear, the message was different. So she watched her mother's face and the face of the men when they opened the pantry door and made up her own mind. (p. 44)

These perceptions are, however, also colored by her individual initiation experience which occurs when she overhears Hannah talking to a friend about their daughters:

'You love her, like I love Sula. I just don't like her. That's the difference. . . . '

She only heard Hannah's words, and the pronouncement sent her flying up the stairs. In bewilderment, she stood at the window fingering the curtain edge, aware of a sting in her eye. Nel's call floated up and into the window, pulling her away from dark thoughts back into the bright, hot daylight. (p. 57)

It is significant that Nel's call draws Sula into their most crucial shared initiation. Both girls have been prepared for it by their families, but they have been prepared to fail.

This preparation for failure has, however, been social as well as familial. Their friendship has sustained them under some societal and familial pressures, and they know it.

Because each had discovered years before that they were neither white nor male, and all that freedom and triumph was forbidden to them, they had set about creating something else to be. Their meeting was fortunate, for it let them use each other to grow on. Daughters of distant mothers and incomprehensible fathers . . . they found in each other's eyes the intimacy they were looking for. (p. 52)

One preparatory initiation episode occurs when the girls are threatened by four white boys, newcomers in the community who assert themselves by tormenting black children on the way home from school. Sula, generally the leader in their comradeship, determines to end the problem, and she does so by slashing off the tip of her left forefinger before their eyes, "'If I can do that to myself, what you suppose I'll do to you?'" (pp. 54-55). While, in a sense, she has solved the immediate problem, and while the girls have become "blood sisters," she has reacted with the violence which is her family pattern, and she has clearly indicated that while she can *act,* she does so irresponsibly. Nel reacts by refusing to consider herself really a part of the moment. The pattern of failure is set; just as they will never be free of family influence, they will be unable to cope with the pressures of society except by damaging themselves.

Their ultimate joint initiation occurs on the river bank, immediately after Sula's rejection by her mother and very shortly after the blood rite. The initiation confirms their unity, their sexuality, and their joint responsibility for what is about to happen; Morrison sets up the moment by a heavily symbolic description of play.

Sula lifted her head and joined Nel in the grass play. In concert, without ever meeting each other's eyes, they stroked the blades up and down, up and down. Nel found a thick twig and, with her thumbnail, pulled away its bark until it was stripped to a smooth, creamy innocence. Sula looked about and found one too. When both twigs were undressed Nel moved easily to the next stage and began tearing up rooted grass to make a bare spot of earth. When a generous clearing was made, Sula traced intricate patterns in it with her twig. At first Nel was content to do the same. But soon she grew impatient and poked her twig rhythmically and intensely into the earth, making a small neat hole that grew deeper and wider with the least manipulation of her twig. Sula copied her, and soon each had a hole the size of a cup. Nel began a more strenuous digging and rising to her knee, was careful to scoop out the dirt as she made her hole deeper. Together they worked until the two holes were one and the same. When the depression was the size of a small dishpan, Nel's twig broke. With a gesture of disgust she threw the pieces into the hole they had made. Sula threw hers in too. Nel saw a bottle cap and tossed it in as well. Each then looked around for more debris to throw into the hole: paper, bits of glass, butts of cigarettes, until all of the small defiling things they could find were collected there. Carefully they replaced the soil and covered the entire grave with uprooted grass.

Neither had spoken a word. (pp. 58-59)

They are interrupted by a little boy, Chicken Little, and, still playing, still seemingly happy, Sula grasps his hands, swinging him about in a great circle—until their hands slip apart, and he is thrown into the river.

The water darkened and closed quickly over the place where Chicken Little sank. The pressure of his hard and tight little fingers was still in Sula's palms as she stood looking at the closed place in the water. They expected him to come back up, laughing. Both girls stared at the water. . . .

The water was so peaceful now. There was nothing but the baking sun and something newly missing. (p. 61)

The initiation is complete; their friendship has been promising, but they have been shaped to failure. Their maturity is flawed because they successfully conceal their part in the death, and they will never have really successful unions with men because those unions are doomed to be marked with blood and pain.

The complete failure of the initiation is not apparent at first; Nel marries, and on the wedding day, Sula leaves town to be gone for years, exploring the outside world.

Nel's marriage, however, is limiting rather than defining. Morrison makes clear that Nel's life-long search for conformity is the result of her mother's training and Nel's refusal to admit to herself that she has any responsibility for Chicken Little's death. The marriage provides her with respectability, a house to keep, children to rear, but it is doomed both through her own and her husband's lack of self-worth. The union is made because Nel is a tool for Jude's ego, his sense of maturity having been denied him by society.

> So it was rage, rage and a determination to take on a man's role . . . that made him press Nel about settling down. He needed some of his appetites filled, some posture of adulthood recognized, but mostly he wanted someone to care about his hurt, to care very deeply. Deep enough to hold him, deep enough to rock him, deep enough to ask, 'How you feel? You all right? Want some coffee?' And if he were to be a man, that someone could no longer be his mother. (p. 82)

When Sula returns, years later, the initiation failure is dramatized, for she engages in an affair with Jude. The discovery of the affair ends their friendship; both women are to remain incomplete—and isolated—for life.

Sula undertakes the affairs because she is a damaged personality:

> hers was an experimental life—ever since her mother's remarks sent her flying up those stairs, ever since her one major feeling of responsibility had been exorcised on the bank of a river with a closed place in the middle. The first experience taught her that there was no other that you could count on; the second that there was no self to count on either. She had no center, no speck around which to grow. . . . For that reason she felt no compulsion to verify herself—to be consistent with herself. (pp. 118-19)

Nel cannot cope with the affair because of her resolution, formed on that train south, to be hard; never to be "soft" before the eyes of any man. Further, to admit that Sula's frailty is human would be to face her own part in the accidental murder of Chicken Little. She does not do so for years, not until after Sula's death, when Eva, Sula's grandmother, forces the question:

> What did Eva mean by *you watched?* How could she help seeing it? She was right there. But Eva didn't say *see,* she said *watched.* 'I did not watch it. I just saw it.' But it was there anyway, as it had always been, the old feeling and the old question. The good feeling she had had when Chicken's hands slipped. She hadn't wondered about that in years. 'Why didn't I feel bad when it happened? How come it felt so good to see him fall?'

All these years she had been secretly proud of her calm, controlled behavior when Sula was uncontrollable, her compassion for Sula's frightened and shamed eyes. Now it seemed that what she had thought was maturity, serenity, and compassion was only the tranquility that follows a joyful stimulation. Just as the water closed peacefully over the turbulence of Chicken Little's body, so had contentment washed over her enjoyment. (p. 170)

Separated by Nel's resolution to settle for respectable calm, both women live lives of desperate isolation; Sula becomes the scapegoat for the town's ills; Nel lives a cold, severely respectable life as a put-upon woman. Symbolically, neither ever achieves a truly sustaining sexual union. When, finally, they do meet again, for Nel, meeting with the dying Sula is merely a part of her "respectable" role; they converse, but they do not come together, and it takes still longer for Nel to realize that the *great* loss she has suffered is really the destruction of their friendship, the one chance they had to learn to be full, complete women.

*Sula,* a more multifaceted book than *The Bluest Eye,* uses the maturation story of Sula and Nel as the core of a host of other stories, but it is the chief unification device for the novel and achieves its own unity, again, through the clever manipulation of the themes of sex, race, and love. Morrison has undertaken a more difficult task in *Sula.* Unquestionably, she has succeeded.

IV

*Song of Solomon* is a somewhat more hopeful book than *The Bluest Eye* or *Sula;* Milkman's quest is ironically successful, and this note of modified hope is echoed in the female initiation patterns in that one of them leads to happiness—at least temporary happiness—for the initiated, First Corinthians Dead. Morrison reveals her admirable tendency to adapt rather than to adopt traditional patterns in these initiation stories by delaying the initiations of both Corinthians and her cousin, Hagar Dead, until the women are well beyond their teens; Corinthians is in her forties; Hagar is in her thirties. The device is successful, indicating the extreme difficulty of the black woman's search for self-determination, and certainly the results of these initiations underscore that point.

The initiation of Pilate Dead, however, takes place during her adolescence, as is traditional. During the main action of *Song of Solomon,* Pilate, aunt of the protagonist, Milkman, has no real identity at all, and in a long flashback, Morrison reveals the reasons for this lack as she recounts Pilate's initiation experiences. Pilate has never known her mother's name, and her father's, that of the first Macon Dead (Milkman's grandfather), was invented by a careless, belittling white official. Even the circumstances of Pilate's birth dramatize her rootlessness; immediately

> after their mother died, she had come struggling out of the womb without help from throbbing muscles or the pressure of swift womb water. As a result . . . her stomach was as smooth and sturdy as her back, at no place interrupted by a navel. (p. 27)

The first years of Pilate's life are, nevertheless, promising, almost Edenic; she and her father and brother live and thrive on their Pennsylvania farm until a powerful white family covets their land and murders the first Macon Dead. The murder is the first step in Pilate's initiation; "I saw Papa shot. Blown off a fence five feet into the air. I saw him wigglin on the ground'" (p. 140).

On her own—she and Macon soon separate after a quarrel over a man he has murdered and over gold buried at the murder site—her initiation continues, for she painfully learns that she is not welcome in any community; "'I was cut off from people early. You can't know what that was like'" (p. 141). Twice, she joins bands of pickers and gets on well with them until she takes lovers who report that she has no navel. Taking the lack to be a sign that she is unnatural, the groups expel her. When she finds a haven on an isolated island off the coast of Virginia, she contrives to conceal her belly from her lover, and after their baby is born, refuses to marry him, reasoning that she cannot hide her lack of a navel from a husband forever. She is cut off from permanent sexual commitment, a symbol in Morrison's work for fruitful maturity. Pilate's uniqueness marks her:

> It isolated her. Already without family she was further isolated from her people, for . . . every other resource was denied her: partnership in marriage, confessional friendship, and communal religion. Men frowned, women whispered and shoved their children behind them. (p. 148)

Pilate's initiation is complete; she has learned the lessons of the world. She knows the danger of the white world because it blew her father off the fence; she has learned that the black world cannot or will not truly accept her. Being strong, she undertakes, then to build a world of her own.

> Finally Pilate began to take offense . . . when she realized what her situation in the world was and would probably always be she threw away every assumption she had learned and began at zero. . . . Her mind traveled crooked streets and aimless goat paths, arriving sometimes at profundity, other times at the revelations of a three-year-old. Throughout this fresh, if common, pursuit of knowledge, one conviction crowned her efforts: since death held no terrors for her (she spoke often to the dead), she knew there was nothing to fear. That plus her alien's compassion for troubled people ripened her and . . . kept her just barely within the boundaries of the elaborately socialized world of black people. (p. 149)

But Pilate's place within those boundaries is marginal; she is the black district's bootlegger, and people come to her house for goods, not for companionship. Her world is both huge and small. Her vision is broad as a consequence of giving up "all interest in table manners or hygiene" and acquiring in its place "a deep concern for and about human relationships" (p. 149). It is small in that it includes almost no people except her daughter,

Reba; her granddaughter, Hagar—and her father's ghost; "'I seen him since he was shot. . . . It's a good feelin to know he's around. I tell you he's a person I can rely on. I tell you something else. He's the *only* one'" (p. 141). Her father's spirit becomes the source of the wisdom around which she constructs her life.

> It was right after Reba was born that her father came to her again. Pilate had been extremely depressed and lonely after the birth . . . and she spent some dark lonely hours along with the joyous ones with the baby. Clear as day, her father said, 'Sing, Sing,' and later he leaned in at the window and said, 'You just can't fly on off and leave a body'. . . . And she knew he was telling her to go back to Pennsylvania and collect what was left of the man she and Macon had murdered. (p. 147)

Pilate does sing; she sings often (and her song is a major clue in Milkman's search for the family origins, one of Morrison's cleverest, most effective foreshadowing devices). Furthermore, she returns to the scene of the murder and reclaims the dead man's bones which she carries about with her throughout her life, but these gestures of obedience, the center of her world structure, are informed by an overwhelming irony.

Pilate does not really understand her father's messages at all; she cannot because she does not know her family history. The self-definition she builds, the world view she constructs based upon his advice keeps her sane and active, but it further isolates her, cuts her off from her community. Pilate's initiation has failed because her family have not been able to equip her for success, and the resulting singularity also colors and controls the lives of her daughter and granddaughter. The failure of Pilate's way of life foreshadows Hagar's tragedy.

Hagar is the center of her mother and grandmother's attention; "they did their best to satisfy every whim Hagar had" (p. 92), but the youngster is not like her family.

> Hagar was prissy. She hated, even as a two-year-old, dirt and disorganization. At three she was already vain and beginning to be proud. She liked pretty clothes. Astonished as Pilate and Reba were by her wishes, they enjoyed trying to fulfill them. They spoiled her, and she, as a favor to their indulgence, hid as best she could the fact that they embarrassed her. (pp. 150-51)

Most of the time, Hagar is successful at hiding her feelings about her mother and grandmother. Only once, when she is seventeen, does she speak out, and then she speaks elliptically and takes care to heal the brief breach. She says,

> 'Some of my days were hungry ones'. . . .
>
> 'Baby?' Reba's voice was soft. 'You been hungry, baby? Why didn't you say so?' Reba looked hurt. 'We get you anything you want, baby. Anything. You *been* knowing that'". . . . [Pilate's] face was like a mask. It seemed . . . that somebody had just

clicked off a light. . . . Reba's had crumpled. Tears were streaming down her cheeks. Pilate's face was still as death, but alert as though waiting for some signal. Hagar's profile was hidden by her hair. She leaned forward, her elbows on her thighs. . . . The quiet held. . . .

Then Pilate spoke. 'Reba, She don't mean food.' . . . Pilate began to hum. . . . After a moment, Reba joined her, and they hummed together in perfect harmony. . . .

When the two women got to the chorus, Hagar raised her head and sang too. (pp. 48-49)

As always, Pilate turns to her father's misunderstood command as a way of solving problems, a way of making sense of perplexing life. Conditioned to this response, loving her mother and grandmother, and ignorant of any other option, Hagar joins in. The moment passes; the chance for understanding or change is gone, and Hagar moves forward to her initiation unprepared. The overwhelming love of her immediate family will not be enough.

It is significant that Hagar's single act of rebellion takes place during Milkman's first visit to her home, for he is responsible for her long delayed initiation. The cousins become lovers and remain lovers for years. For Hagar, the commitment is absolute; "Totally taken over by her anaconda love, she had no self left, no fears, no wants, no intelligence that was her own" (p. 137); Milkman represents something of her own, and he also represents a regulated life quite different, potentially, from the careless, disorganized life of her family. But Milkman never considers Hagar seriously as a mate, and he finally breaks off the affair.

With nothing on earth to cling to but her concept of herself as Milkman's lover, Hagar fails her initiation test. She sees herself only as she imagines he sees her and comes to doubt her own very great beauty. In her view, that is the one means she has to hold Milkman, and holding Milkman is the only thing worth doing. When she comes to believe that he prefers another kind of beauty, she has nothing, and she determines to kill him.

> Hagar. Killing, ice-pick-wielding Hagar, who, shortly after a Christmas thank-you note, found herself each month searching the barrels and cupboards and basement shelves for some comfortably portable weapon with which to murder her true love.

> The 'thank-you' cut her to the quick, but it was not the reason she ran scurrying into cupboards looking for weapons. That had been accomplished by the sight of Milkman's arms around the shoulders of a girl whose silky copper-colored hair cascaded over the sleeve of his coat. . . . As regularly as the new moon searched for the tide, Hagar looked for a weapon and then slipped out of her house and went to find the man for whom she believed she had been born into the world. (pp. 126-27)

Her mother and grandmother take the only steps they know; they respond with violence—Pilate beats her—and love, "All they knew to do was love her and since she would not speak, they brought things to please her" (p. 308). But that is not enough; it never has been, and Milkman's friend, Guitar, thinking of Hagar and reasoning through her problem, correctly identifies it as isolation. Hagar has never learned to cope with the world, has never learned who she is because her mentors—Pilate and Reba—also do not know. There has been no community to love and teach her, no place for her to belong except the home of which she disapproves.

> Pretty little black-skinned girl. What had Pilate done to her? Hadn't anybody told her the things she ought to know? He thought of his two sisters, grown women now, who could deal, and the litany of their growing up. Where's your daddy? Your mama know you out here in the street? Put something on your head. You gonna catch your death a cold. Ain't you hot? Ain't you cold? Ain't you scared you gonna get wet? Uncross your legs. Pull up your socks. I thought you was goin to the Junior Choir. Your slip is showin. Your hem is out. Come back in here and iron that collar. Hush your mouth. Comb your head. Get up from there and make that bed. Put on the meat. Take out the trash. Vaseline get rid of that ash.

> Neither Pilate nor Reba knew that Hagar was not like them. Not strong enough, like Pilate, nor simple enough, like Reba, to make up her life as they had. She needed what most colored girls needed: a chorus of mamas, grandmamas, aunts, cousins, sisters, neighbors, Sunday school teachers, best girl friends, and what all to give her the strength life demanded of her—and the humor with which to live it. (p. 307)

But Hagar has neither inner strength nor humor; Morrison sees her clearly as the symbol of the "wild," outside-the-community faction of the poor black district of their Midwestern town, the faction that has neither roots nor structure, that can rely upon its own untutored intensity:

> there was something truly askew in this girl. . . . here was the wilderness of Southside. Not the poverty or dirt or noise, not just extreme unregulated passion where even love found its way with an ice pick, but the absence of control. Here one lived knowing that at any time, anybody might do anything. Not wilderness where there was system, or the logic of lions, trees, toads, and birds, but wild wilderness where there was none. (p. 138)

All her life Hagar has known (as all of Southside knows) that the white community has no use for her; all her life she has known that she is only marginally tolerated by the black community. For a time, she has believed that her beauty, passion, and desirability were the keys to a life structured around Milkman. When he rejects her, when it is time for her to initiate herself into a life of her own, she cannot, and when even violence fails her (her attempts to murder Milkman abort), she decides to transform herself. She intends to sacrifice her one great asset, her beauty, to change herself into the kind of woman Milkman will love and value forever. Even this attempt, impassioned, chaotic, and pitiful as it is, fails, and in the process, Hagar becomes fatally ill. She cannot possibly succeed because nothing in her life has prepared her to define herself; she cannot succeed even in imitating Milkman's "real" girl friends because nothing in her background arouses in him a sense of her true value. There remains nothing else for her to do but to die.

At first glance, the story of Milkman's sister, First Corinthians Dead, seems to be a sharp contrast to the tragic story of Hagar, her cousin, though like Hagar's initiation, Corinthians' is delayed until late in her life, and also like Hagar's, it centers around her willingness to meet the needs of a man. But unlike Hagar, Corinthians manages the accommodation.

Until well into adulthood, Corinthians, like Pilate, has absolutely no identity of her own:

> She was First Corinthians Dead, daughter of a wealthy property owner and the elegant Ruth Foster, granddaughter of the magnificent and worshipped Dr. Foster; who had been the second man in the city to have a two-horse carriage. (p. 197)

but even that identity is fragile, for Corinthians' father is bitter toward her and her sister, Magdalene.

> The disappointment he felt in his daughters sifted down on them like ash, dulling their buttery complexions and choking the lilt out of what should have been girlish voices. Under the frozen heat of his glance they tripped over doorsills and dropped the salt cellar into the yolks of their poached eggs. The way he mangled their grace, wit, and self-esteem was the single excitement of their days. (pp. 10-11)

Corinthians cannot turn to her mother for support or enlightenment because Ruth Foster Dead is herself helpless, abandoned, and immobilized by the death of her father and the scorn of her husband.

In their own eyes, Macon and Ruth Dead have done their best by their daughters, for they have been sent to the finest colleges and have traveled abroad. The result is, however, that the two are over-qualified for roles as wives of rising black professional men, and the white world will offer them no jobs except as domestics. For years, they spend their time making artificial roses to sell to a local department store, pitying their mother, and being browbeaten by their father. Finally, Corinthians rebels and secretly becomes the maid of the town's "lady author"; to do so, she must deny herself and assume a mask.

> Corinthians was naïve, but she was not a complete fool. She never let her mistress know she had ever been to college or Europe or could recognize one word of French Miss Graham had not taught her.

> . . . Actually, the work Corinthians did was good for her. In that house she had what she never had in her own: responsibility. She flourished, in a way, and exchanged arrogance occasionally for confidence. The humiliation of wearing a uniform . . . and deceiving people was tempered by the genuine lift which came of having her own money rather than receiving an allowance like a child. (p. 190)

The first step in Corinthians' initiation is partially successful; she has asserted herself and stepped away from her father's shadow. The value of the effort, however, is dimmed by the lies and repression she must practice to sustain her new life.

Her most important test comes when she meets and falls in love with Henry Porter, who does yard work for a living. The pair date like teenagers, but Porter never meets the Deads; Corinthians dreads her father's reaction:

> Corinthians knew she was ashamed of him, that she would have to add him to the other secret, the nature of her work, that he could never set foot in her house. And she hated him a lot for the shame she felt. Hated him sometimes right in the middle of his obvious adoration of her, his frequent compliments about her looks, her manners, her voice. But those swift feelings of contempt never lasted long enough for her to refuse those . . . sessions where she was the sole object of someone's hunger and satisfaction. (p. 194)

Eventually, Porter forces the issue, telling Corinthians that she must defy her father or give up her lover. When Corinthians makes her choice, she does so by subjugating and humiliating herself completely:

> He did not move. In a panic, lest he shift gears and drive away, leaving her alone in the street, Corinthians climbed up on the fender and lay full out across the hood of the car. She didn't look through the windshield at him. She just lay there, stretched across the car, her fingers struggling for a grip on steel. She thought of nothing. Nothing except what her body needed to do to hang on, to never let go. Even if he drove off at one hundred miles an hour, she would hang on. Her eyes were shut tight with the effort of clinging to the hood, and she didn't hear the door open and shut, nor Porter's footsteps as he moved around to the front of the car. She screamed at first when he put his hand on her shoulders and began pulling her gently into his arms. He carried her to the passenger's side of the car, stood her on her feet while he opened the door and helped her ease into the seat. In the car, he pressed her head onto his shoulder and waited for her soft crying to wane before he left the driver's seat to pick up the purse she had let fall on the sidewalk. He drove away then to number 3 Fifteenth Street, a house owned by Macon Dead, where sixteen tenants lived, and where there was an attic window, from which this same Henry Porter had screamed, wept, waved a shotgun, and urinated over the heads of the women in the yard. (p. 199)

Once her choice is made, Corinthians is happy with it; she suppresses the hatred born of shame:

> Standing there, barefoot, her hair damp with sweat and sticking to her cheeks like paint, she felt easy. In place of vanity she now felt a self-esteem that was quite new. She was grateful to him, this man who rented a tiny room from her father, who ate with a knife and did not even own a pair of dress shoes. A perfect example of the men her parents had kept her from (and whom she had also kept herself from) all her life because such a man was known to beat his woman, betray her, shame her, and leave her. Corinthians moved close to him, tilted his chin up with her fingers, and planted a feathery kiss on his throat. (p. 201)

She even summons the courage to move away from the Deads' home and into a place she and Porter share. The sexual phase of her initiation, like the economic phase, seems to be acceptable to her, given the fact that she can make the necessary accommodations. And there is one further factor here. In a very real way, Corinthians has rejected her father's false values, values assumed and copied from whites, by embracing Porter, for Porter also has a secret life. He is one of the Seven Days, a band of black men who avenge their race every time the white community murders a black. However, the fact remains that to live with Porter, she must subjugate herself utterly.

For the careful reader, this compromise calls into serious question the ultimate worth of Corinthians' choice. Guitar, Milkman's friend who has been so right in his assessment of Hagar's problem, has, at one point, tried to dissuade Hagar from her headlong passion for Milkman, and his comment to Hagar also holds true for Corinthians:

> 'Could you really love somebody who was absolutely nobody without you? You really want somebody like that? Somebody who falls apart when you walk out the door? You don't, do you? And neither does he. You're turning over your whole life to him. Your whole life, girl. And if it means so little to you that you can just give it away, hand it over to him, then why should it mean any more to him? He can't value you more than you value yourself.' (p. 306)

The answer is that to both Hagar and Corinthians, life *has* no worth without the men they love; they have no identity save the reflection of themselves in the eyes of those men. Hagar has never learned to value herself; Corinthians' pride is arid and useless in the society in which she finds herself. Perhaps she is luckier than Hagar—but quite possibly, Morrison suggests, she is not—and the reader is left to wonder how long Porter will value a life found valueless in the eyes of its owner.

*Song of Solomon,* then, offers three portraits of women whose initiation experiences fail because their families have not prepared them for the transition into fruitful maturity. Each of the three defines herself only according to the standards and desires of a beloved man: Pilate lives her entire life under her misapprehension of her father's messages; Hagar dies because she cannot be the kind of woman Milkman desires; and Corinthians abandons the self-image she has cherished for a lifetime to find menial work in a white-controlled world and to find sexual release with a man who demands that she submit completely. Of the three, only Corinthians has any chance for even modified happiness. Corinthians' slim chance makes *Song of Solomon* Morrison's least despairing portrait of the black woman's condition. At best, this note of hope is muted.

V

In her fiction, then, Morrison has united her theme, the explorations of love, and a traditional device, the initiation motif, along with a series of brilliantly dramatized foreshadowing events, skillfully made frames, and splendid characterizations. The resulting novels are compelling statements of the failure of human values. The inversion of a traditional motif—that is, the treatment of failed initiations—is successful, its effect devastating. The achievement is remarkable, making it clear that Toni Morrison is, indeed, a major American novelist.

NOTES

[1] Toni Morrison, *The Bluest Eye* (New York: Holt, Rinehart and Winston, 1970). All further references are indicated in the text.

[2] Toni Morrison, *Sula* (New York: Alfred A. Knopf, 1973). All further references are indicated in the text.

[3] Toni Morrison, *Song of Solomon* (New York: Alfred A. Knopf, 1977). All further references are indicated in the text.

[4] Jane S. Bakerman, "The Seams Can't Show: An Interview with Toni Morrison," *Black American Literature Forum,* 12 (1979), 60.

[5] Frederic I. Carpenter, "The Adolescent in American Fiction," *English Journal,* 46 (1957), 315.

[6] Patricia Meyer Spacks, *The Female Imagination* (New York: Alfred A. Knopf, 1975), p. 158.

[7] Other commentaries about the initiation experience and/or the *Bildungsroman* include Suzanne Howe, *Wilhelm Meister and His English Kinsmen* (New York: Columbia Univ. Press, 1930), pp. 1-10 especially; Lionel Trilling, "The Princess Casamassima," *The Liberal Imagination* (New York: Doubleday & Company, 1953), pp. 55-88; and Jane A. Bakerman, "The Long Journey from Somersetshire: A Commentary on the Apprenticeship Novel," *Indiana English Journal,* 6 (1971), 14-20. These sources show that for the traditional adolescent hero, the acceptance of society's tarnished values symbolizes the ability to be "mature," to be accepted and to

live successfully within the society. For Morrison's female characters, that option is not viable.

[8] Toni Morrison, "Behind the Making of *The Black Book*," *Black World*, Feb. 1974, p. 89.

[9] *Eye* incorporates the failed initiations of Cholly and Pauline Breedlove in flashbacks, a device common in Morrison's work. Further, Pauline's comments about her responses to the North give compelling evidence of the problems of transplanted southern black women.

[10] One of the most fascinating motifs in *Sula* is the exploration of mother-daughter relationships, and in the flashbacks, Morrison provides insight into the relationship between Sula's mother, Hannah, and her grandmother, Eva, as well as that of Nel's mother, Helene, to her grandmother, Rochelle. In both cases, the difficulties stem not simply from the women's personalities, but also from the poverty and racial pressures which have shaped them.

## Evelyn Torton Beck

SOURCE: "Kafka's Traffic in Women: Gender, Power, and Sexuality," in *The Literary Review*, Vol. 26, No. 4, Summer, 1983, pp. 565-76.

[*In the following essay, Beck discusses the male-centeredness of Kafka's works, maintaining that the absence of women in the texts represents Kafka's attempt to control and marginalize them.*]

When, in 1952, the Austrian writer Ilse Aichinger received the prestigious Group 47 prize, her work was so often compared to Franz Kafka's that one of the group members allowed himself a little joke and referred to her as "Fräulein Kafka," only to correct himself at once, "That isn't really the lady's name; she only writes as if it were."[1]

In spite of the high praise intended by this somewhat backhanded compliment, Aichinger was not pleased. She did not wish to be viewed as an epigone, not even a Kafka epigone. She may also have understood that what these critics thought was so good about her work was that she was able to write *like a man*. Moreover, she may have recognized that something in this renaming process was off balance, that the very process by which she had been elevated to a "Fräulein Kafka" could only work in one direction, since, as every schoolchild learns quite early, in Western culture it is *never* a compliment for a man to be dubbed a female *anything*. Such a reversal is so far from our imagination, that a witty reference to a Herr Lasker-Schüler in Germany or a Mr. Stein, or Mr. O'Keefe or Mr. Dickinson in the United States would probably be mistaken as a reference to these artists' *fathers*. Moreover, no woman's writing has, like Kafka's and the work of other male writers, ever been viewed as representative of that supposedly unmarked category, "the universal."

It is by questioning the conception of Kafka's universality that a feminist reading of Kafka must begin. We might start by asking, "What does it mean when critics, one after the other, using different formulations, all come to the same conclusion—that Kafka is the spokes*man* for modern *man?* I have no intention of challenging the sexist language of this assertion; it is, in fact, quite correct—so long as we can agree that when Kafka and Kafka critics claim to be speaking for *man,* they do not at the same time claim to be speaking for *woman.* A poem by the late Muriel Rukeyser on this theme might prove to be instructive:

> "Myth"
>
> Long afterwards, Oedipus, old and blinded, walked the roads.     He smelled a familiar smell.     It was the Sphinx.     Oedipus said, "I want to ask one question.
>
> Why didn't I recognize my mother?"     "You gave the wrong answer," said the Sphinx.     "But that was what made everything possible," said Oedipus.     "No," she said.
>
> "When I asked, what walks on four legs in the morning, two at noon, and three in the evening, you answered, Man.     You didn't say anything about woman."
>
> "When you say Man," said Oedipus, "you include women too. Everyone knows that."     She said, "That's what you think."[2]

Sobered perhaps by this feminist retelling of one of our most revered myths, let us stand back for a moment from our received truths about Kafka and look again "with fresh eyes" (to quote both Bertold Brecht and Adrienne Rich) and approach his texts from a new critical direction.

It is not difficult to show that the question of gender is the single most ignored aspect of Kafka's work, while at the same time it is one of his most outstanding characteristics. Let us begin with a few simple observations on which I think we can all agree:

1. *Kafka's fictional world is male—homosocial and at moments subtly and not so subtly homoerotic.* Think, for example, of the Stoker chapter in *Amerika,* the Titorelli chapter in *The Trial,* the Bürgel episode in *The Castle.* In at least a dozen short pieces *woman is literally absent* from the text (for example, "An Old Manuscript," "Jackals and Arabs," "A Visit to a Mine," "Eleven Sons"). There is not even an Eve in Kafka's Paradise parables; in Kafka's world there is only Adam and God. When woman is not absent, *her presence is obliterated, obscured or trivialized;* for example, in "The Penal Colony," "A Hunger Artist," "A Fratricide." Where she is not obscured, *she is seen as purely instrumental;* she becomes the vehicle or conduit for male activity, specifically for the male quest which is at the center of Kafka's works.

2. *The essential power struggles in Kafka's texts are between the males:* Joseph K. and the representatives of the Law in *The Trial;* K., Klamm, and the castle officials (and messengers) in *The Castle,* Georg Bendemann and his father in "The Judgment," Gregor and his father in "The Metamorphosis," the Officer and the Explorer in "The Penal Colony." In the monologue pieces *a male voice always speaks into a male ear*—"The Investigations of a Dog," or the Ape speaking to the "Honored Gentlemen of the Academy." In the one or two instances where a female figure seems to be the center, as in "Josephine the Mouse" or "A Little Woman," the male narrator speaks for her. *Nowhere in Kafka does woman speak for herself.*

3. Because it is his male heroes who organize the text's way of seeing, *the angle of vision in Kafka's texts is necessarily androcentric*—i.e., male-centered. The full import of this becomes particularly clear when that male eye looks out at woman. What it never sees is the "person" of a woman, but always the body or part of a body. In *The Trial,* Fräulein Bürstner, exhausted though she is at the end of the day, having been surprised by K. in her room, and obviously uneager to speak to him, is nonetheless seen by K. as "slowly caressing her hip," as if to attract his sexual attentions (which he eventually forces on her). Another example is provided by the washerwoman's "warm voluptuous body under the coarse dress," as if it existed simply in order to invite/incite the male eye. Woman is seen as an intrusion to the male equilibrium; she disrupts by her very presence.

It is therefore no accident that Kafka's heroes have been spoken of in strictly male terms, as modern day Fausts, or *shlemiels,* or even as little boys. Woman in Kafka's world can help or hinder the hero, but never can she herself be an active participant in the quest. Moreover, as Kafka represents her, she is quite incapable of understanding the impulse to act or of comprehending its spiritual dimension. *Woman does not struggle toward writing; she is what is written.*

If this were a longer study it would be useful to provide a contextual history of Kafka's highly problematic relationship to women in his life—beginning with his 1913 question in a letter to Max Brod: "Could it be that one can bind a girl by writing?" We would continue with the recognition that Kafka used the hundreds of letters he elicited (indeed coerced) from Felice (to whom he was twice engaged) *as a nourishment for his own writing.* Kafka was well aware of the fact that she, in turn, had no idea of whom she was thus nourishing. I would also explore more fully his desire to keep "nocturnal writing" to himself, specifically asking Felice *not* to write to him at night because "nocturnal writing belongs to men everywhere, even in China." We would thus see more clearly the degree to which his understanding and representation of the world were androcentric. I would also explore the impact of Jewish family life on his imagination, the fact that his own Jewish father was an arch-patriarch of whom

he was afraid, and that women are structured into Orthodox Judaism in ways that place them at the center of the culture, but outside some religious obligations and ritual participation. (For example, women do not count as part of the ten men needed for a *minyan,* the minimum number to start a prayer service. Women are considered "unclean" during menstruation and in the synagogue, they sit either upstairs or at the back behind a curtain, so they do not distract the praying men. While Kafka's family was reformed, Kafka was fascinated with the Orthodox Law and these attitudes, in any case, permeate the Orthodox Jewish view of women.)

The most serious implications of the texts' male-centered angle of vision is that it makes impossible the existence of real women, and substitutes in their place false constructs, projections of male fears and fantasies, idealizations and demonizations of woman, and asks us to accept these as real representations of ourselves. Virginia Woolf, who understood much about gender/power relationships, was distressed by the sharp discrepancy she noted between the actual lives of historical women and the representations of woman in male writings. In *A Room of One's Own* she writes: "[Woman] pervades poetry from cover to cover; she is all but absent from history."[3] As astute as Woolf was, she was only half-right. Women are indeed absent from recorded history, but in spite of the variety of female creations, she is also absent from literature. Feminist film criticism has developed this analysis: "Man imposes meaning on the silent image of woman who is tied to her place as the bearer of meaning, not a maker of meaning."[4]

The German theorist Sylvie Bovenschen articulates the analysis in these words:

> The wealth of representations of woman is supposed to compensate for the silence of women. But even this silence has been mythologized. . . . Mostly, however, the silence of women remains unnoticed. It has been drowned out by the substitutionary dialogue about the feminine.[5]

However subversive some aspects of Kafka's vision may be, his work carries the dominant ideology about woman. By creating figures like those of Fräulein Bürstner and Leni in *The Trial,* Frieda and Olga in *The Castle,* Clara and Brunelda in *Amerika,* Frieda Brandenfeld in "The Judgment," he participates in the mythologizing process and also contributes to the substitutionary dialogue. Most fascinating in a feminist reading of Kafka is the recognition that even as he perpetuates the mythology about woman, he also unmasks it, and in so doing, lays bare the structures that bind woman. We need to be "resisting readers" of Kafka only to the extent that we continue to believe in the universality of his vision. Once we accept its partiality, we are freer to understand in what ways woman is structured into his texts, what functions she serves, and in what ways she is necessary to his discourse.

Kafka's works demonstrate the ways in which women's services are essential for male survival. It is not necessary to document elaborately that throughout Kafka's texts women are expected to, and do perform domestic and sexual services for men. In *The Trial* Leni is cook, nurse, maid, and mistress to the Lawyer, much as Frieda ministers to K.'s needs in *The Castle* (and to Jeremiah after she abandons K.). Virginia Woolf calls this woman's "civilizing" function for men. In *The Trial* Josef K. articulates it well: "'Women's hands are quietly effective,' . . . He himself might have smashed the dishes on the spot, but he certainly could never have quietly carried them away."[6] Woman provides the nurturance that keeps men going.

Kafka also understands that access to women is essential to the maintenance of male power. In a patriarchal world, men develop a sense of entitlement to women; they have rights to women that women do not have to themselves. With the exception of Amalia in *The Castle,* Kafka's women are domesticated and seen as objects of exchange between male partners. Where the phallus carries power and the meaning of difference, the phallus passes from one male to another through the medium of woman. Thus men are linked to one another through woman. She is both central and utterly peripheral. Woman, on the other hand, is not ever in a position to realize the benefits of her own circulation.[7]

Virginia Woolf also understood this pattern: What these illustrious men got from their alliance with women, aside from "comfort, flattery and the pleasures of the body" was "something that their own sex was unable to supply."[8] In Kafka's works men are the rightful owners of women's nurturing. This becomes clear when, for example, Gregor's wound (in "The Metamorphosis") begins *to throb* as he sees that his mother and sister, having left their work lying, "drew close to each other and sat cheek to cheek."[9] Similarly, after Gregor's death, Mr. Samsa is upset when he sees the mother and daughter clasping each other tightly. He interrupts their embrace, "And you might have some consideration for me!"[10] thus refocusing attention onto himself. At the end, he places himself between the two women, having successfully disrupted their alliance.

Throughout, Kafka's male characters think of women in the language of ownership. "I'm not thinking of handing the girl over to you," says the country doctor to his groom. "The body belonged to Wese . . ." in "A Fratricide." Even the weakest, most powerless male feels entitled to exercise some power over women. When Josef K. loses access to the washerwoman because the student carries her off to the Examining Magistrate, K. sees this loss of the woman as his "first unequivocal defeat." To have won the woman would have been to win power over the other men. Woman has no place in this struggle; she is the booty to be won. She does not exist for herself and she cannot speak in her own name. "There could be no more fitting revenge on the Examining Magistrate and his henchmen than to wrest this woman from her and take her himself."[11] Clearly if Josef K. had won her, he would have won power over his opponent. The woman becomes

the means of his revenge. Josef K. even fantasizes that someday the woman might "belong to K. and K. alone." He also pictures using his prostitute whom he visits weekly, as a means of putting down the student. She would refuse the student her favors, the student would beg for them on his knees, and K. would then be the victor. That the body of the woman becomes the battleground for the male partners should be self-evident.

But Kafka goes one step further in annihilating woman: he allows Josef K. to speak for her, to name her experience. Angry at losing the washerwoman, and angry at what he perceives as her lack of resistance (against obviously heavy odds), K. shouts at her, "And you don't want to be set free."[12] One might well ask, what would "freedom" for her mean here? Whether she is carried off by the student or by Josef K., her position of powerlessness remains the same. Feminist theorist Andrea Dworkin suggests that in a patriarchy, woman is at the mercy of male power even if that power seems to be in warring male factions—men rape; men protect women from rape. The system operates to make women dependent on male power.[13] But the crowning blow in the washerwoman episode is K.'s reinterpretation of her behaviour: he insists that her abduction (read rape, coercion, seduction) is "her own fault" a judgment in which her husband all too readily concurs: "She's actually the most to blame of all."[14] Could there be a clearer statement of the patriarchal myth that women not only enjoy rape, but that they ask for it?

Woman is also powerless to express her own sexuality. She is called a whore if she initiates or appears to initiate sexual activity (Josef K.—"So this is all that it amounts to, she's offering herself to me. She's corrupt."[15]), but it is her refusal of the male that brings down the full force of patriarchal wrath. The Amalia episode in *The Castle,* whatever its spiritual or symbolic meanings, must also (perhaps first) be read on the literal level. "Access is one of the faces of Power. . . . Total power is unconditional access, total powerlessness is being unconditionally accessible."[16] The slave who denies access thereby declares herself not a slave. Amalia's is the story of the slave who said no.

Amalia's story is at once very simple and extremely complex. It both supports and exposes the patriarchal power system that enslaves woman. Part of its complexity arises from the narrative perspective: It is not as simple as one woman (Olga) telling another woman's story (Amalia's) to a man (K.). Kafka creates two very different female figures whom he sets off one against the other. Amalia, the pariah, whose act of refusal sets her outside the community, remains virtually silent; it is Olga, the "gentler of the sisters," the adapter, the woman who identifies with and accepts male power, who sees herself and other women through male eyes, who speaks for the rebel Amalia. Thus, though the voice that speaks is a woman's, the male value system permeates her story. It is no accident that it is Olga who introduces K. to the Herrenhof, an inn whose very name establishes it as a precinct of patriarchal power, and it is in the Herrenhof that Olga reveals her relationship to that power system. For this reason, the scene is worth quoting in some detail. K. is feeling powerful, so he orders Olga to take him home. But Olga gets caught up in her circle of friends.

> The peasants would not let her go; they had made up a dance in which she was the central figure, they circled round her yelling all together and every now and then one of them left the ring, seized Olga firmly round the waist and whirled her round and round; the pace grew faster and faster, their yells more hungry, more raucous, until they were insensibly blended into one continuous howl. Olga, who had begun laughingly by trying to break out of the ring, was now merely reeling with flying hair from one man to another.[17]

The contradictions in this picture are as glaring as they are revealing. The peasants (the men) have created a dance (a set of conventions, a pattern, a structure) in which Olga (woman) is trapped. Though she is the central figure and is absolutely necessary to the structure, she is clearly out of her own control and at the mercy of the shouting, leering men. This image not only represents the position of woman in patriarchy, but also follows closely the dialogue in which K. admits his urge to take Frieda from Klamm. It may well provide a correlative for Frieda's passage from Klamm, to K. to Jeremiah, to who knows what man next?

It is this whirling female figure that we need to juxtapose to Amalia, the woman who stands alone, who, we are told, has a "direct and serious gaze, which is unflinching." Amalia's unabashed open gaze should warn us. If man is the owner of the gaze and woman its object, who should appropriately look down in modesty, then any woman who herself gazes, will be considered insurrectionary. Like the Medusa's, her eye will be seen as cold and hard, and monstrous. Amalia's fortune (or misfortune) is that she becomes the object of a castle official's gaze. On that day, Amalia is the only one who does not participate in the celebration of the new fire-engine (a symbol of male power?); she stands apart from the others and is thus noticed by the official who, having seen her, desired her; desiring her, he demands access to her and expects to be obeyed. (Olga tells K. "There is no such thing as an official's unhappy love affair."[18] He always gets the girl if he wants her.) If the woman in question "knows her place," she complies, as Frieda did when she herself had been called by Klamm. Sortini's request in the form of a vulgar letter which Amalia tears up and throws out the window, reveals the degree to which the official felt disrupted by his attraction to Amalia.

Olga believes that Amalia, by being chosen, is somewhat at fault. She explains to K., "Sortini was obviously enraged because the sight of Amalia had disturbed and distracted him in his work . . . even overnight he had not succeeded in forgetting her."[19] Sortini's letter has the force of rape: it commands, threatens, and brings shame on its victim, not on the perpetrator, in spite of the fact

that it is widely acknowledged in the community that it represents "an abuse of power." Olga also explains that it is not simply refusing that was Amalia's crime. A woman can refuse, so long as she pretends to comply. "It wasn't that she didn't go that the curse was laid upon our family. . . . for there are many ways of getting around it, another girl might have decked herself up and wasted some time in doing it and then gone to the Herrenhof only to find that Sortini had left . . . but Amalia neither did that nor anything else. If only she had made some pretense of complying."[20] The family too could have re-established itself in the community if it had avoided ever mentioning the matter.

In order for the patriarchal power system to continue to operate, women must comply in keeping silent the violations of power. Amalia's "shamelessness," as Olga puts it, is that she refused to pretend that nothing had happened. By tearing up the letter, she fought back. "She stood face to face with the truth and went on living."[21] The woman who speaks the truth, the woman who tries to control her own destiny, if only by refusing, becomes a pariah and calls down the wrath of the power structure. "What would happen if one woman told the truth about her life? The world would split open,"[22] is Muriel Rukeyser's articulation of this understanding. K. has a hard time accepting or understanding this truth. His own understanding is limited by his desire to find a place in the power structure. If he had to choose between Amalia and Olga, he wouldn't give it much reflection (and would choose Olga).[23] K. also refuses to see that his liaison with Frieda is no different from Frieda's with Klamm, or from what Amalia's would have been. K. wants to idealize male-female transactions. Here Kafka's analytic vision comes surprisingly close to that of Emma Goldman who first recognized that the traffic in women was a result of women being treated as a sex commodity.

> Nowhere is woman treated according to the merit of her work, but rather as a sex. It is therefore almost inevitable that she should pay for her right to exist, to keep a position in whatever line, with sex favors. Thus it is merely a question of degree whether she sells herself to one man, in or out of marriage, or to many men.[24]

There is considerable irony in Kafka's sharing such a radical critique of the uses of women's sexuality in a patriarchy, and I am not certain how much of what he represents he himself takes in as critique.

What is even more ironic, is that despite Kafka's personal sense of alienation from the sources of patriarchal power, he nonetheless embeds masculist values in his world, a world, to quote Virginia Woolf, in which "men harbor in their breasts an eagle, a vulture, forever tearing the liver out and plucking at the lungs—the instinct for possession, the rage for acquisition which drives them to desire other people's fields and goods perpetually [and, one might add, other men's women], to make frontiers and flags, battleships and poison gas."[25] Kafka may not approve of such a world, but he is undoubtedly of it: he supports and perpetuates as he unmasks. Looking at Kafka's *oeuvre* with even only slightly more open vision, we cannot fail to see that his fiction (and letters, diaries, and fragments) are filled with images and acts of mutilation, gratuitous violence, murder, rape, death, abduction, wounds, carrion, blood.

Setting aside *The Penal Colony* since that can too easily be seen as an exception, let us look at a few less well known pieces that illustrate the point amply. Consider "A Fratricide" in which one man, without any apparent motivation, murders another while the narrator watches: "Right into the throat and left into the throat and a third time deep into the belly stabbed Schmar's knife. . . . 'Done' said Schmar, and pitched the knife, now superfluous blood-stained ballast, against the nearest house front. 'The bliss of murder! The relief, the soaring ecstasy from the shedding of another's blood.' . . . Wese, old nightbird, friend, alehouse crony, you are oozing away into the dark earth below the street. Why aren't you simply a bladder of blood so I could stamp on you and make you vanish into nothingness? Not all we want comes true, not all the dreams that blossomed have borne fruit. . . . "[26] Another example is "The Vulture" which is hacking at the narrator's feet, who overhears the narrator ask a gentleman for help, and "It took wing, leaned far back to gain impetus, and then like a javelin thrower thrust its beak through my mouth, deep into me. Falling back, I was relieved to feel him drowning irretrievably in my blood, which was filling every depth, flooding every shore."[27] A celebratory blending of violence, sexuality and death is fairly obvious here.

The same perspective holds in "The Bridge," in which the narrator is stiff and cold, stretched over a ravine. The human step he hears tells him to prepare. But when the man was on the bridge, he "jumped with both feet on the middle of my body. I shuddered with wild pain . . ." and finally, turning around to see him, "I. . . . began to fall, I fell and in a moment I was torn and transpierced by the sharp rocks."[28] A somewhat different version occurs in "An Old Manuscript" in which the butcher throws a live ox to the nomads while the narrator covers his ears with his bed clothes "to keep from hearing the bellowing of that ox, which the nomads were leaping on from all sides, tearing morsels out of its living flesh with their teeth."[29] The self-hating quality of these passages will not surprise us, especially when we also recognize their strong homoerotic component, an aspect of his sexuality which Kafka had great difficulty accepting. (We might add that he also had difficulty with heterosexuality, but he did not create such violent images in his descriptions of male-female sexuality, though Frieda and K. do "claw at each" other in a desperate attempt to find fulfillment. In these all-male pieces, the violence is always tinged with pleasure-pain. Kafka bears out the observation that the legend of male violence is the most celebrated legend of *man*kind.[30]

Most Kafka critics (except psychoanalytically oriented ones) look past the surface of these violent images to consider their "deeper meanings." My question: what could lead us to want to look past the surface, to not see what is so clearly there? Only some degree of participation in a system that naturalizes and celebrates violence, that accepts a brutalized version of sexuality. In this sense, Kafka's world is not exceptional, it is the rule.

In the heterosexual realm, there is a degree of cannibalism in Kafka's descriptions. One critic refers to "pornological" elements in Kafka which relate to male pornography. Robinson's description of Brunelda in *Amerika* is a good example: "How lovely she looked. . . . You felt you could eat her. [The German is *ablecken*— "lick her"] You felt you could drink her up."[31] In similarly imbibing and objectifying terms, Kafka describes Josef K.'s advances to Fräulein Bürstner, "He rushed out, seized her, and kissed her first on the lips, then all over the face, like some thirsty animal lapping greedily at a spring of long-sought-for fresh water."[32] If woman is the water to be imbibed, the food to be eaten, how is she to nourish herself?

This is not a question that the androcentric writer poses (nor the androcentric critic either), since his focus is on the well-being of the male psyche. For this reason, the feminist critic must focus on the small ruptures in the text that come more clearly into our vision once the male ceases to be the central and only reference point in our readings. For instance, in "A Report to an Academy," we may wish to account for the ape's wife, who turns up only at the very end of the ape's report. She is a "half-trained little chimpanzee" who waits every evening for her performing husband to return home late at night, "and I take comfort from her, as apes do. By day I cannot bear to see her, for she has the insane look of the bewildered, half-broken animal in her eye."[33]

What are we to make of this insertion? Why does Kafka bother to give his ape a wife at all? Why a half-crazed one, only half-domesticated at that? Or are all women, like Leni, "freaks of nature"? Is Kafka trying to tell us something about the situation of woman, particularly academic wives with performing husbands? Are we to take this representation as a critique—or is he simply making a report? When are the two the same? When and how do they differ?

Kafka's manipulation of the narrative perspective makes it difficult to answer these questions definitely. They are in fact, the central questions asked by feminist critics. What is the relationship between fictional representation and a writer's world view? What responsibility does the writer have? If the writer merely *represents*, is he or she responsible for perpetuating a power structure and a way of thinking that needs to be changed? Kafka's extraordinary skill as a writer whose words have the power to seduce, to make us see with him, to accept his vision, makes him a dangerous writer. The central male figures in Kafka's texts seek and struggle, but never find. For him, there is no way out *but* the struggle itself. The female is placed in a far more powerless position, for she is at the mercy of even the smallest, most inconsequential male. For her, there can be no quest; at best, she can be a conduit; her power is temporary and derivative, bestowed upon her by the male. She is never in a position to learn anything, since she herself cannot act. A male can read Kafka against the grain. He can refuse to answer the Law when it beckons, he can refuse a false trail or trial. Woman exists only on the margins, entrapped in a power system in which she is never an actor, only acted upon.

For this reason, as Rich suggests, "a radical critique of literature, feminist in its impulse, would take the work first of all as a clue to how we live, how we have been living, how we have been led to imagine ourselves. . . . how we can begin to see—and therefore live—afresh."[34]

A first step in seeing anew is our willingness to recognize that even our most canonized texts, those we have imagined to be most universal, are in fact, not gender neutral. Faust after all, is and can only be male; Gretchen "the eternal feminine that leads 'us' on high" is irrevocably female. We must be willing to recognize that gender has been a determining factor in our myth-making, in the way power and sexuality are structured into literary texts. If we recognize this, then what follows is the awareness that even our most "objective" readings of these texts are also not gender neutral. In this arena we could speak of Fräulein Hartmanns or Fräulein deMans or Fräulein Derridas and Lacans.

For women have been taught to see through an androcentric lens; it is a way of seeing we all have to un-learn. Such a paradigm shift is both exhilarating and disorienting, since it forces us to rethink our received truths about literary study and about the world. It challenges our codified values, especially about "old masters" and "eternal truths." It forces us to rethink and reconceptualize the value systems by which we live. Such disruptions are never comfortable, but to paraphrase a Kafka aphorism, a book should act on us like a sharp blow—it should serve as an ax for "the frozen sea within us." Though I would prefer less violent language, this perception well describes the kind of awakening a feminist analysis of literature can catalyze. We ought to welcome it.

### NOTES

[1] See Elisabeth Endres, "Ilse Aichinger," *Neue Literatur der Frauen,* ed. Heinz Fuknus (Munich: Verlag C. H. Beck, 1980), p. 44.

[2] Muriel Rukeyser, "Myth," in *I Hear My Sisters Saying: Poems by Twentieth Century Women,* ed. Carol Konek and Dorothy Walters (New York: Thomas Y. Crowell, 1976), p. 243.

[3] Virginia Woolf, *A Room Of One's Own* (New York: Harcourt, Brace and World, 1957), p. 45.

[4] This concept is analyzed in some detail in an unpublished dissertation-in-process, on feminist criticism by Lucie Arbuthnot; probable date of completion, May 1982, New York University.

[5] Silvia Bovenschen, *Die imaginierte Weiblichkeit: Exemplarische Untersuchungen zu kulturgeschichtlichen und literarischen Präsentationsformen des Weiblichen* (Frankfurt am Main: Suhrkamp Verlag, 1979), p. 41. Translation mine.

[6] Franz Kafka, *The Trial,* definitive edition (New York: Schocken Books, 1968), p. 18.

[7] This analysis is based in part on the excellent theoretical work of Gayle Rubin, "The Traffic in Women," in *Toward an Anthropology of Women,* ed. Rayna R. Reiter (New York and London: Monthly Review Press, 1975), pp. 157-210. Rubin's work is based on a feminist reinterpretation of the works of Levi-Strauss, Freud, and Lacan.

[8] Woolf, *Room,* p. 90.

[9] Franz Kafka, "The Metamorphosis," in *The Complete Stories,* ed. Nahum N. Glatzer (New York: Schocken Books, 1976), p. 125.

[10] Kafka, *Stories,* p. 139.

[11] Kafka, *Trial,* p. 56.

[12] Kafka, *Trial,* p. 58.

[13] Andrea Dworkin, *On Pornography: Men Possessing Women* (New York, 1981). Dworkin's analysis comes close to Josef K.'s recognition that the apparent parties of the Right and the Left were all colleagues, all wearing the same badge as even the Examining Magistrate (*Trial,* p. 47). What Josef K. does not comprehend is that no matter how outside the system he may perceive himself to be, as a male, he too is a colleague, wearing a male badge of power, power which he believes he ought to be able to exert on women.

[14] Kafka, *Trial,* p. 61.

[15] Kafka, *Trial,* p. 52.

[16] Marilyn Frye, "Some Reflections on Separatism and Power," *Sinister Wisdom* 6 (Summer 1978), pp. 35-36.

[17] Franz Kafka, *The Castle* (New York: Alfred A. Knopf, 1947), p. 52.

[18] Kafka, *Castle,* p. 254.

[19] Kafka, *Castle,* p. 248.

[20] Kafka, *Castle,* p. 250.

[21] Kafka, *Castle,* p. 270.

[22] Muriel Rukeyser, "Käthe Kollwitz," in *No More Masks,* ed. Florence Howe and Ellen Bass (Garden City, New York: Anchor Press, 1973), p. 103.

[23] Kafka, *Castle,* p. 298.

[24] Emma Goldman, *"The Traffic in Women" and Other Essays in Feminism* (Washington, N.J.: Times Change Press, 1970 reprinting of 1917 edition), p. 20.

[25] Woolf, *Room,* pp. 38-39.

[26] Kafka, *Stories,* p. 403. Earlier in the piece the narrator had commented, "Unriddle the mysteries of human nature" (p. 402). This seems an excellent example of a generalization about the *human* condition which is, in fact, accurate only in a description of *male* behavior in western culture. This kind of violence is simply not condoned or encouraged in women as it is in men. It is men who have been the perpetrators of gratuitous violence; most often, women are its victims.

[27] Kafka, *Stories,* p. 443.

[28] Kafka, *Stories,* p. 412.

[29] Kafka, *Stories,* p. 417.

[30] See Dworkin, *On Pornography,* which develops this idea in some detail.

[31] Franz Kafka, *Amerika* (New York: Schocken Books, 1962), p. 234.

[32] Kafka, *Trial,* p. 29.

[33] Kafka, *Stories,* p. 259.

[34] Adrienne Rich, "When We Dead Awaken: Writing as Re-Vision," in On *Lies, Secrets, and Silence* (New York: Norton, 1971) p. 35.

**Alfred Habegger**

SOURCE: "Macho Businessmen Take Control of America," in *Texas Quarterly,* Vol. 21, No. 4, Winter, 1989, pp. 149-56.

[*In the following essay, Habegger examines social forces during America's "gilded age," after the Civil War, that may have contributed to the image of the American Girl in the literature of William Dean Howells and Henry James.*]

### MACHO BUSINESSMEN TAKE CONTROL OF AMERICA

#### Howells says Social Queen Wears Leather Not Lace

#### AMERICAN GIRL STILL UNCORNERED

To corner someone is to master him by driving him into a corner where he can't get away. In the last century, *cornering* acquired an extended meaning on the stock exchange, where you *cornered* a stock by getting control of it or *cornered* another speculator by manipulating the market and ruining him. The quarter century following the Civil War was that period in our country's history when the violent American male cornered vast sectors of the United States. One man, Jay Gould, tried to corner gold, but fortunately didn't succeed. Another, helped by the rapid building of railroads, cornered the meatpacking industry. Carnegie cornered steel. Edison cornered electric power. Rockefeller cornered oil and put together such an unimaginable concentration of wealth and power that a century later his grandson was able to corner the vice-presidency. At the fountain-head of our corporations, monopolies, and family dynasties there was a powerful male ego with great skill in the martial art of cornering.

That period after the Civil War has always had the reputation of being a very ugly time. The reputation is well deserved, but it deludes us into looking at that time as exceptional. The so-called Gilded Age was exceptional only in the openness with which the American male lived his fantasies of war and conquest, and in the success with which he realized them. The Gilded Age was our formative time, when the lords of darkness made the rings and consolidated the power that we still live under. A few ruthless go-getters did it all because they wanted to be king. When the Vanderbilts put their French chateaux on Fifth Avenue, they seemed out of place to people of refinement. A castle, after all, belongs on an estate, not on the dirty, crowded streets of New York. But the dirty, crowded streets of New York *were* the Vanderbilt's estate.

It's hardly surprising that our best novelists of the time wrote about powerless folks somewhere off on the edges. The local color movement, which arose after the Civil War, celebrated the old traditional people and ways of life, far from the urban centers where the cornering was in full force. The best book of the period, *Huckleberry Finn,* took place in a pre-industrial era, and its hero was a boy just the reverse of the pushy, barn-storming masculine ideal (embodied in Tom Sawyer). Henry James and William Dean Howells hit their stride as novelists only when they began writing about a character as remote as Huck from the fury of commerce and industry, the "American girl."

The American girl was conceived as a new kind of person, peculiar to America and its social conditions. She was brave, independent, adventurous, and full of the inflated American dream of grand self-fulfillment that up to then had been reserved for men only. One of James's American girls, the aptly named Miranda Hope, does the unthinkable and explores Europe all by herself, always alert to the "condition of women." Most of the others— Daisy Miller, Isabel Archer, and, in Howells, Kitty Ellison, Lydia Blood, and Florida Vervain—are also seen in transit only, and never in the context of the community from which they derive. That is because the American girl can never fulfill herself at home. Her travels are the expression of an inner restlessness that cannot be satisfied within her culture. Once she stops moving and settles down to marriage, the American girl passes out of the stage of hopeful promise and turns into a lady.

The best-known American girl is Daisy Miller, innocent and vulgar, plain as her first name, common as her last, and with a gritty integrity that says, *Don't tread on me.* She looms all the larger for being seen through the tiny aperture of Winterbourne's sensibility, with his virginal obsession over the issue of her sexual purity. Daisy pays no attention at all to the arbitrary code of propriety imposed on women by European society, and by American ladies living in Europe; and she pays for her cheeky freedom with her life. *The Portrait of a Lady,* written a few years after *Daisy Miller,* is about an American girl who submits to ladyhood. James originally conceived of Isabel Archer, the heroine, as a "presumptuous" girl "affronting her destiny." In the novel, Isabel proves to be a young woman challenging the definition and limits of womanhood. But at the end, the wide world she sets out to explore has shrunk to "a very straight path," with the potent, commanding presence of Caspar Goodwood at one end and the evil, tyrannical shadow of her husband at the other. For Isabel, adulthood means the suffocation of her heart's desire, a final submission to an absurd set of constraints, an endless checkmate with a husband who hates her. These, for James, are the conditions of adulthood. In accepting them, the American girl grows up into a lady.

Without Henry James we might not know about the American girl, but it was Howells who discovered her and, in my opinion, wrote about her with the greater insight. She made her first appearance in Howells's novel of 1873, *A Chance Acquaintance.* Kitty Ellison, the heroine, comes from an abolitionist family in the West and has strong liberal ideals. She venerates Boston as the cradle of liberty. She becomes acquainted with a proper Bostonian by accidentally placing her arm in his—thus taking the initiative and reversing the usual gender roles. She and Arbuton fall in love and become engaged even though he seems far more prim and censorious than her ideal abolitionist Boston. In the end, Arbuton refuses to introduce her to his fashionable friends and she decides to break the engagement. Her hopes are disappointed by Eastern snobbishness, or the brutality inherent in any developed society, and she's disappointed by a man because the man, whether in *Daisy Miller* or *A Chance Acquaintance,* has a much bigger stake in society than does the American girl.

But there's another character in Howells and James with an even bigger stake in society, and especially in good society, than masculine snobs like Winterbourne and Arbuton, and that is the lady. In her successive avatars in James's fiction—Madame de Bellegarde, Madame Merle, Mrs. Brookenham (in *The Awkward Age*), and Mrs.

Lowder—she is rigid yet amoral, a devious, powerful, freedom-hating tyrant who generally has a younger woman under her thumb. James hated her, but Howells hated her even more, having married her. His wife Elinor was the model for Isabel March, a brittle, unreasonable, and childish person who confines her life and that of her husband to maddeningly narrow circuits. Then there is Mrs. Pasmer, in *April Hopes,* who lies by instinct, has no dignity, flatters everyone, and enjoys a complete "sovereignty" over her husband, who sits in perfect idleness in the reading rooms of hotels. Mrs. Pasmer has the integrity of a slave whose sly wits have taken her all the way to the top. Even worse is a leader of society like Mrs. Munger, in *Annie Kilburn,* who plans to establish a social union for the poor workers of Hatboro' in order to win a higher grade of status for herself. Mrs. Munger dresses in leather; in fact, as Howells says, she wears leather where other women would wear lace. And that is the secret of Howells's ladies—discipline. Strict, irrational, life-denying discipline.

Howells's manly men are a different species. Hatch (in *The Undiscovered Country*), Bartley Hubbard, Silas Lapham, Fulkerson, and Jeff Durgin (in *The Landlord of Lion's Head*) are casual, easygoing, and hard working. Interested in power, they feel great contempt for status. They are in the workaday world, journalism or business, and they don't live under the same strain as Howells's ladies. In Howells's best-known couple, Basil and Isabel March, the man is a humorous Westerner and the woman a strict, dutiful New Englander who holds her man on a very tight leash. Reverend and Mrs. Sewell have the same kind of marriage: "She was the custodian of their potential virtue, and he was the instrument, often faltering and imperfect, of its application to circumstances." The man seems to come from a free, uncensored place, and the woman regards him as a kind of barbarian and never gives up trying to civilize him.

In Howells the two sexes are two nations: the barbarians hold the power and keep the wheels turning, while the mandarins have the manners, the culture, the ideals, the gentility. The culture was split along the line of gender. There was a masculine domain full of cigar smoke, loud laughter, profanity, and a readiness to ignore the law or anything else that got in the way. And there was a feminine domain, a rigid, artificial, and expensive place where common sense could not be tolerated. This cultural situation had a thousand different consequences, some trivial, some very serious. A man could corner a sizable piece of the new world, yet not have the freedom to adjust his balls if ladies were present (an elementary comfort still denied us). Writers like Mark Twain had to censor themselves at every point because the language actually used by men could not be printed, books being in the female domain. And the American girl was encouraged to develop a vague, lofty conception of herself, and then had to lace herself into the fearful bondage of being a lady.

Howells wrote novel after novel about people living in the no person's land between the masculine and feminine domains. He was absorbed by the predicament of the decent, unaggressive man who was scorned by the "hard, practical men" as a sissy and a lightweight. He was no less absorbed by the struggle of independent women to carve out a dignified way of life for themselves, and he traced this struggle in its most important phase—working for a living. In *A Woman's Reason* a well-bred, high-strung Brahmin has to enter the workaday world after her father dies insolvent. She tries to support herself by decorating pottery with pictures from Flaxman's Homer. When that fails to bring in any money, she turns to hat making, selling her tasteful creations made of lace and dead birds to working-class women. That fails too, and she finally evades the problem of earning a living in a ladylike way by marrying. *A Woman's Reason* isn't a good novel, but it's honest in showing exactly how useless the rich young lady really was.

There are several self-supporting women in Howells's books. In Amanda Grier and Statira Dudley, two factory workers in *The Minister's Charge,* Howells tried to imagine what it would be like to be both female and proletarian. But most of his self-supporting women are artists. One of these, Cornelia Root in *A Woman's Reason,* is a stern, no-nonsense chip of New Hampshire granite. She resembles Dr. Prance in Henry James's *Bostonians,* who has not only renounced being a lady, but has renounced womanhood itself for the sake of her profession.

In *Doctor Breen's Practice* Howells wrote about an American girl who tries to be a lady, a doctor, and a free woman all at the same time. She is fearfully knotted up by the strain of reconciling these incompatible roles, and at the end, after losing her nerve on her first case, she gives up medicine for marriage. Or maybe she chooses marriage in order to give up medicine. In either case, the story of Grace Breen's brief practice is Howells's most realistic, down-to-earth treatment of the American girl. Also, it amounts to a surprisingly full picture of the torments of a pioneering professional woman.

Doctor Breen has gone into medicine not because she finds it an attractive field but because of her New England sense of duty and her hope of being useful among the Fall River mill workers. Instead of studying real medicine, she went to a homeopathic school in New York, where she saw herself more as a lady than as a professional:

> There had been a time when, in planning her career, she had imagined herself studying a masculine simplicity and directness of address; but the oversuccess of some young women, her fellows at the school, in this direction had disgusted her with it, and she had perceived that after all there is nothing better for a girl, even a girl who is a doctor of medicine, than a ladylike manner.

But as she sets out on her medical practice, she finds it almost impossible to reconcile the lady with the doctor. With men, she is self-conscious and constrained. She puts on a severe, professional act for them, and yet, as a lady,

she must be handed up the stairs. Even the men who feel well disposed to her, and most of them do, can't help blushing as they try to deal with her both as helpless lady and commanding physician. She is in an extremely jumpy and suspicious state as the novel opens.

Dr. Breen has almost more trouble with women than with men. The scene of the novel is laid at a small New England coastal hotel, where virtually all the guests are respectable ladies whose husbands remain at work in the city. Most of these ladies have "complaints" of one sort or another. They pass their days in ennui and idle talk, and inevitably exclude Breen from their vacuous pastimes. They force her to play the role of authority and then revert to little giggling girls.

> "I presume," said young Mrs. Scott, with a deferential glance at Grace, "that the sun is good for a person with lung difficulty."
>
> Grace silently refused to consider herself appealed to, and Mrs. Merrit said, "Better than the moon, I should think."
>
> Some of the others tittered, but Grace looked up at Mrs. Merritt and said, "I don't think Mrs. Maynard's case is so bad that she need be afraid of either."

Although the empty-headed ladies defer to Breen, secretly they think she's "more scandalous than if [she] were the greatest flirt alive."

It's easy to see why the young woman should be so tense and anxious as she enters on her professional career. And there are other irritations. Her first patient is a petulant, irresponsible woman who has left her husband and thrown herself on Breen. The difficulties of being both friend and doctor to the childish Mrs. Maynard are insurmountable: when Mrs. Maynard wants to evade her responsibilities, she treats Breen as her doctor; but when the prescriptions don't suit her, she ignores them as if they were the recommendations of a friend. The careless woman catches pneumonia and coughs up blood.

> "Now," she said, "I *am* sick, and I want a *doctor!*"
>
> "A doctor," Grace meekly echoed.
>
> "Yes. I can't be trifled with any longer. I want a *man* doctor!"

Breen regards this quite sensibly as a patient's foolish whim. But in the end, as Mrs. Maynard gets worse, Breen loses her nerve and relinquishes the case to a male rival, Dr. Mulbridge.

Mulbridge has achieved the professional manner that Breen so badly needs. He masters his patients with a "rude moral force," and appears to regard the woman doctor with the same "contemptuous amusement" he feels for his women patients, who love to flatter and submit to him. Mulbridge is "a tall, powerfully framed man" with a "shaggy head" and a dark "grizzled" beard. The emancipation of women strikes him as "droll." His grandfather was captain of a slave ship, and his father was a Copperhead in the Civil War. He is compared to Rochester in *Jane Eyre* by one of the hotel women, the giddy Miss Gleason. He is the oppressive male world incarnate, but he's still vulnerable. If he seems to be the strong, silent type, it's because he has found this an effective pose with his voluble and hysterical patients. And there's a blot on his record from the Civil War, a suggestion that he may have deserted or been given an irregular discharge: "'I never rightly understood,' said Hackett, 'just what it was about him, there in the army—coming out a year beforehand, that way.'" The pig may be secretly a coward.

Mulbridge not only refuses to take Breen seriously as a physician, but decides to marry her. When his mother suggests that Breen might not have him, the pig reveals himself: "his jaw closed heavily" and his face momentarily assumed "a certain brutal look." In proposing, he fights with everything he has. He makes Breen sit on a tree stump while he remains erect. He leans "forward over her, and seem[s] to seize a physical advantage in the posture." Like a remorseless Puritan minister, he begins by catechizing her on her failure and makes her admit she is utterly insufficient in herself. He beats her down and then offers himself as her salvation. Astonished, Breen turns him down, but he argues and insists even when she tells him off:

> "I think you are a tyrant, and that you want a slave, not a wife. You wish to be obeyed. You despise women. I don't mean their minds—they're despicable enough in most cases, as men's are—but their nature."

> He only laughs, and Grace has to use the ultimate weapon: "I'm engaged—engaged to Mr. Libby!" Mulbridge is stupified and broken.

And who is this Mr. Libby that Breen is going to give up her career for? He is a mild, well-mannered son of a mill owner who does nothing but dangle around Mrs. Maynard and go sailing. He leads the elegant life of leisure that a lady like Grace Breen was expected to lead. He is a faceless, characterless blank, and a milksop too, for when it's time to propose, he simply doesn't have the courage to tell Breen he loves her. In desperation Grace Breen (like a number of Howells's women) has to take the risk herself and make the decisive sexual advance.

> She suddenly put up her arms across her eyes, with the beautiful, artless action of a shame-smitten child, and left her young figure in bewildering relief. "Oh, don't you see that I love *you?*"

So Grace Breen escapes the doubts and torments of freedom by offering her "young figure" to a man and reverting to a young girl's gesture of shamed surrender. Yet her escape remains as equivocal as her brief professional life. If she acts like a girl in covering her eyes, she nonetheless acts like a man by openly declaring her love. If she

commits herself to the role of wifehood, it's only after taking the husband's initiative. Does she choose marriage in order to avoid the problems of adulthood and independence? Or does she want to retain the sovereign independence of the American girl by marrying a drone she can dominate as easily as Mulbridge thought he could dominate her?

Like the other American girls in Howells and James who skim over land and sea in quest of a social role that doesn't exist, Grace Breen refuses to commit herself to either the masculine or the feminine domain. In what little we see of her married life at the end of the novel, she seems bored, restless, and unhappy. She goes to museums, as good ladies must, but she doesn't like doing it. She resumes her medical practice among the factory children at her husband's mills, but only at his urging. (The adult workers are apparently taken care of by a man doctor.) Howells blames her dissatisfaction on her Puritan conscience, but it might also be attributed to her failure to find something to do and someone to be. She has succeeded in frustrating Mulbridge in his attempt to corner her, but married to Libby she remains at loose ends, without a piece of the action that is hers alone. She hasn't cornered anything at all.

---

# POETRY

## Samuel Hynes

SOURCE: "All the Wild Witches: The Women in Yeats's Poems," in *The Sewanee Review,* Vol. LXXXV, No. 4, Fall, 1977, pp. 565-82.

[*In the following essay, Hynes discusses the women in William Butler Yeats's poetry in light of Yeats's idea of the poetic muse as a sexual, maternally creative, and pantheistic force.*]

"We poets would die of loneliness but for women, and we choose our men friends that we may have somebody to talk about women with." This is Yeats in a letter written near the end of his life, playing a characteristic life-long role—the poet writing to a woman about men, women, and love. The generalization that he makes is not, of course, as universal as it sounds; but certainly it is true of Yeats himself: he belongs in the category of lovers of women, those men for whom the company of women is more important than the company of men. Everything that we know about his life, all the copious biographical records that he left, gives the same impression of a life defined and supported by relationships with women, from Madame Blavatsky and Maud Gonne at the beginning to Dorothy Wellesley and Margot Ruddock at the end. The published letters make this point very clearly: more than half were written to seven women. And of all his correspondence the most moving letters are those addressed during his last years to an old woman who had been his mistress forty years before—an intimacy sustained for all that time on remembered feeling alone.

For Yeats the interaction of the sexes was a source of energy, and a paradigm of that energetic conflict of opposites that he saw at the core of existence. "The polarity which we call sex," as he put it, was one of an infinity of polarities in existence, but for Yeats it was the most dynamic and creative one. His philosophic system begins with the copulation of God and woman, and moves by the interpenetration of opposites, and even after death there is the intercourse of angels. And as with the Creation, so with creation: sexual energy is a source of poetic energy, the muse is a sexual being.

I am concerned here not either with biography or with Yeats's philosophical system, but with poems only, and specifically with the women in the poems, though the roles that they play will obviously be related to Yeats's experience of and ideas about women. A reasonable place to begin is a poem about three particular women—the poem in *Responsibilities* entitled "Friends." "Now," Yeats begins, "must I these three praise." But he doesn't praise them, exactly: what he does is to *justify* his will-to-praise, taking each woman in turn as a separate case of praiseworthiness:

> One because no thought,
> Nor those unpassing cares,
> No, not in these fifteen
> Many-times-troubled years,
> Could ever come between
> Mind and delighted mind;
> And one because her hand
> Had strength that could unbind
> What none can understand,
> What none can have and thrive,
> Youth's dreamy load, till she
> So changed me that I live
> Labouring in ecstasy.
> And what of her that took
> All till my youth was gone
> With scarce a pitying look?
> How could I praise that one?
> When day begins to break
> I count my good and bad,
> Being wakeful for her sake,
> Remembering what she had,
> What eagle look still shows,
> While up from my heart's root
> So great a sweetness flows
> I shake from head to foot.

The three women here are all clearly actual people who were important in Yeats's life—Lady Gregory, Olivia Shakespeare, and Maud Gonne—but their specific identification is not crucial to the poem. What *is* crucial is the women's roles that they represent—and Yeats's attitude toward those roles. Yeats begins with the least complicated relationship—his long connection with Lady Gregory. Like other men of his time (or perhaps I should

simply say like other men) Yeats was inclined to separate the intellectual from the sexual powers in woman, and to see the two together as a sure source of conflict. He describes his friendship with Lady Gregory as entirely a communion of mind with mind; it is therefore a comfortable relationship, and easy to praise: there are no conflicts and no impediments here, because there are no bodies.

The second woman enters the poem in a more complicated way, in the role of sexual priestess, the woman who initiates the poet into the rites of maturity and so frees him from the prison of his youth and releases his creative energies. As with the first woman her role in his life is positive but partial: the instrument of the first was *mind;* this woman is a strong *hand*—an instrument of physical contact. That contact was important, but it belongs to the past: initiation is a *stage,* not a condition; and when it is over what remains is only vestigial intimacy, based on sex recollected in tranquillity. Yeats seems to have had such an intimate friendship with Olivia Shakespeare, and of course he found it praiseworthy, since it too contained no present source of conflict and no emotional expense.

But the third woman is another matter, and it is her presence in the poem that gives it its strength. Biographically she is Maud Gonne, but she is Maud Gonne transformed and mythologized into a figure of female sexual energy. Note how she enters: first as memories of suffering and loss, and of her indifference, and then as the cause of present feeling—present wakefulness, present sweetness. Unlike the other two she is given no positive role in the poet's past; she is simply there, like a natural force, an erotic emotional center to be acknowledged. This sexual figure appears many times in Yeats's poems, in various forms: she is imaged as a lion, an eagle, a burning cloud, a tightened bow—all nonhuman, violent, kinetic things. When she appears as a woman it is often as Helen of Troy, a woman who in Yeats's mind was not an ideal of beauty, but a symbol of beauty's unconscious *power:* perfectly beautiful, but perfectly unthinking, and so potentially destructive, but unaware of her destructiveness—Helen, the burner of cities, a symbolic female figure of which Maud Gonne is also a type.

Another way to describe this powerful threatening figure is to say that she is a witch. Yeats said of Maud Gonne that "she had to choose (perhaps all women must) between broomstick and distaff and she has chosen the broomstick—I mean the witches' hats." Yeats's witches are not the grotesque creatures of popular mythology, but sexually powerful women: "All the wild witches, those most noble ladies," he calls them in a poem. Their wildness is potentially destructive (it is an attribute of Maud Gonne in several poems), but it is compatible with nobility and with great beauty, and it is a source of creative energy.

It is not so easy to praise this sexual witch as it was to praise the other women: "How *could* I praise that one?" Yeats asks. The answer is simply that he *does:* the ending of the poem is not a justification of his praise, but simply a rendering of the intense emotions that thoughts of this woman stir in his heart. Such feelings are a form of praise, and so is the poem that contains them. So, you might say, the witch who stirs these feelings creates the poem.

All three women in the poem are treated as active shapers of the poet's life: they have *wrought* what joy is in his days, and he exists as a poet because they have existed. (No man played so significant a role in Yeats's creative life.) But it is the *third* woman, the cause of suffering, who is Yeats's real muse, because she alone is a present source of feeling, and so of essential creativity. Because of her this poem about women and sex is also a poem about poetry.

Yeats usually worked from actual persons to general ideas, as he does in "Friends," but there is one poem about women that starts from generalizations: "On Woman" in *The Wild Swans at Coole.* The poem begins:

> May God be praised for woman
> That gives up all her mind,
> A man may find in no man
> A friendship of her kind
> That covers all he has brought
> As with her flesh and bone,
> Nor quarrels with a thought
> Because it is not her own.

Not, one must admit, a very enlightened view; "the polarity which we call sex" is here set in mind/body terms, with man supplying the thought, and woman clothing it in her flesh: Man brings, Woman gives. This is a conception of the relation between the sexes that Yeats expresses elsewhere, and we must take it to be a part of his whole attitude toward women—not so much an ideal perhaps as a commonplace male daydream of what an agreeable life would be, a fantasy of cheerful female subordination.

But as the poem proceeds, this daydream dissolves into a different image of man-woman relations, the love of Solomon and Sheba.

> . . . Solomon grew wise
> While talking with his queens,
> Yet never could, although
> They say he counted grass,
> Count all the praises due
> When Sheba was his lass,
> When she the iron wrought, or
> When from the smithy fire
> It shuddered in the water:
> Harshness of their desire
> That made them stretch and yawn,
> Pleasure that comes with sleep,
> Shudder that made them one.

Sheba here manifests the qualities that Yeats praised in "Friends": she is wise, she is a maker, and she is a lover. With her, Solomon experiences that condition of perfect union that Yeats called Unity of Being. It is Sheba, then, rather than Helen of Troy, who is Yeats's ideal woman; being sexually powerful, she is a witch, but

she is a positive one; and her union with Solomon, which is both intellectual and sexual, is an ideal relationship.

Yeats said that he had dramatized himself as a man in this poem, and he must have seen himself in the role of Solomon, grown wise while talking with his queens. But Yeats also enters the poem at the end in his own voice, to utter a prayer for love:

> God grant me—no, not here,
>
> . . . . .
>
> But when, if the tale's true,
> The Pestle of the moon
> That pounds up all anew
> Brings me to birth again—
> To find what once I had
> And know what once I have known,
> Until I am driven mad,
> Sleep driven from my bed,
> By tenderness and care,
> Pity, an aching head,
> Gnashing of teeth, despair;
> And all because of some one
> Perverse creature of chance,
> And live like Solomon
> That Sheba led a dance.

These lines serve as a gloss on the preceding Solomon and Sheba passage. Yeats ended that account of perfect love with the shudder of consummation. But what happens then? The lovers reenter time, desire begins again, and the suffering that deep feeling brings returns. Sexual love is not a mode of being, but a dance: Unity of Being *is* achievable in the act of love, but it is momentary. Yeats expands on this point in another poem about these perfect lovers ("Solomon and the Witch"), which ends with Sheba crying "O! Solomon! let us try again." That is Yeats's point about sexual love: it is a continual trying again. The same is true of the creative act of the poet. So you might say that sexual love is the poem you write with your body; and that poems are the intercourse of the imagination with its muse. And indeed Yeats did say essentially that: "A man's work thinks through him," he wrote in his journal (1909). "Man is a woman to his work, and it begets his thought."

By the end of "On Woman" the tone has changed radically. By introducing the sufferings of sexual love in his own voice, Yeats has transformed his poem from a male daydream of easy dominance to a tense expression of sexual need. The sexes remain complementary—Solomon needs Sheba, and Yeats at fifty needs his rightful woman—but the woman's role is no longer a subordinate one; in the sexual dance, it is Sheba who calls the tune.

These two poems are useful because they develop in similar ways, beginning with relatively simple views of men and women, and moving to the assimilation of more complicated and contradictory feelings. The same could be said of the development of Yeats's whole career: it begins with conventional stereotyped expressions of sexual attitudes and grows in complexity of understanding right up to the great sexual poems of his old age. If this account seems to make Yeats's career one long study of women and sex, one need only point out that his muse was a sexual woman and that he was therefore doing only what a poet should, in devoting his life to the contemplation of her nature.

If we look at Yeats's early love poems—at poems such as "He Bids His Beloved Be at Peace," "He Gives His Beloved Certain Rhymes," and "A Poet to His Beloved" (all from *The Wind among the Reeds,* 1899)—we can see how simple and conventional his initial attitudes were. Though these poems were addressed to an actual woman, Olivia Shakespeare, during an actual love affair, there are no woman, no man, and no sexuality in them: the beloved is reduced to an inventory of poetical parts—long hair, pearl-pale hands, passion-dimmed eyes—and the lover is only a weary voice. In the first published versions of these poems Yeats gave his speaker various pseudonyms—Aedh, Mongan, Robartes, O'Sullivan Rua—as though to say, "Please don't think that this is *me* uttering these Pre-Raphaelite clichés." And indeed it isn't: it is a conventional poetical figure who is speaking *to* a conventional poetical figure, about a man/woman relationship that is also conventional. It is all made out of poetry.

Actual women, and actual feelings about them, begin to enter the poems in Yeats's next volume, *In the Seven Woods,* written when Yeats was in his late thirties. It was a time for him of sexual deprivation: "Since my mistress had left me," he later wrote of this period, "no other woman had come into my life, and for nearly seven years none did. I was tortured by sexual desire and disappointed love." So the first real poems of love came not out of fulfillment, but out of loss and desire. And out of an increasing sense of Time. The relation between love and time is one that Yeats returned to throughout his career, and was still brooding over at the end of his life, in poems like the Crazy Jane cycle and "The Wild Old Wicked Man." It is no doubt an inevitable aspect of the theme of love—to love is to be aware of mortality—but for Yeats it was an especially insistent subject. For Yeats saw both woman's beauty and love itself as poignantly vulnerable to that mutability which was at the base of his tragic sense of life. Two poems in particular from *In the Seven Woods* introduce this theme: "Adam's Curse," in which love and romantic ways of loving wane like the hollow moon, and "The Folly of Being Comforted," a poem about the mutability of beauty.

> One that is ever kind said yesterday:
> "Your well-belovèd's hair has threads of grey,
> And little shadows come about her eyes;
> Time can but make it easier to be wise
> Though now it seems impossible, and so
> All that you need is patience."
>          Heart cries, "No,
> I have not a crumb of comfort, not a grain.
> Time can but make her beauty over again. . . . "

> O heart! O heart! if she'd but turn her head,
> You'd know the folly of being comforted.

This seems at first a conventional lover's protestation: don't try to comfort me with the effects of time; to me she is still beautiful—and still unattainable. But there are actually *two* comforts offered in the poem—the friend's attempt to comfort and the heart's response—and *both* are foolish. The lover will go on loving, and the well-beloved will go on aging, and there is no comfort in either process. If she'd but turn her head the lover would see that he still loved her but he would also see that she was aging. Man and woman must live in time; neither love nor mortality can be altered by thinking about it.

The woman in this poem is sharply, even cruelly rendered: gray hairs and shadows are scarcely the traditional materials of love poetry. No doubt this is Maud Gonne as she actually looked in her late thirties. The identification is not important, but the *actuality* of the woman is; from this point on, the women in Yeats's poems begin to be real distinguishable people existing in the real world: Lady Gregory, Ann Gregory, Florence Farr, Mabel Beardsley, Maud Gonne's daughter Iseult, Eva Gore-Booth, and Con Markiewicz, and later George Yeats, Margot Ruddock, and Dorothy Wellesley. As they appear they begin to form a collective myth of female energy in its various forms—the child, the virgin, the witch, the wild woman, the crone: a configuration of female roles not unlike the myth of Robert Graves's white goddess. It is inevitably a *man's* myth, not simply because a man is the maker of it, but because in Yeats's mind the sexual interaction of male and female was a paradigm of the creative process; in these poems a cast of energetic women engage the imagination of the poet, and out of that engagement come the poems.

In the most powerful of these mythologized women energy is a kind of madness, and it sometimes seems that Yeats regarded madness as simply the superlative form of femaleness.

> It's certain that fine women eat
> A crazy salad with their meat
> Whereby the Horn of Plenty is undone.

These lines are from "A Prayer for My Daughter," but there are many other poems that make the same point: that in some "fine women" an excess of sexual energy deflects them from their true female functions into the alien world of history and action and into a kind of mad activity. Yeats's argument is that sexual energy (being natural and *female*) should ideally exist outside history (which is *male*). This is the essential male sexist assumption—that nature and history have gender—and Yeats was certainly sexist in his theorizing about women; but the actual women in his poems of this middle period do not conform to his theory: they are all in history, and passionately so. In poems like "No Second Troy," "Easter 1916," "On a Political Prisoner," and "To a Friend Whose Work Has Come to Nothing" Yeats wrote about women who had turned their energies to public political ends; it was not the ideal role for women that he imagined, but it was a reality that he acknowledged, and to which he was attracted. Clearly he *liked* fine women, even crazy ones.

It seems at first surprising that though Yeats was a lover of women, he did not write many love poems to them (that is, if we take a love poem to be a private I-Thou communication, the subject of which is present feelings about the relationship). Even his poems concerning Maud Gonne are almost never love poems in this sense: instead they are poems *about* love, which is a very different thing. There are two sets of poems that Yeats grouped together that we might call his Maud Gonne cycles: one group, in *The Green Helmet,* begins with "A Woman Homer Sung" and runs through "Against Unworthy Praise"—seven short poems in all. The other, in *The Wild Swans at Coole,* begins with "Memory" and ends with "Presences"—eight poems. Neither is, strictly speaking, a cycle of love poems; rather both are concerned in different ways with loss, and so belong with Yeats's other meditations on the larger theme of the relation between love and time. In the first cycle the subject is the loss of the beloved, and the consequences of that loss for Yeats's poetry; the poems were written in the years following Maud Gonne's marriage, and together they constitute a sort of Yeatsian Dejection Ode, in which the muse withdraws her sexual energy and leaves the poet with only the lifeless matter of language. The point is made most clearly in "Reconciliation":

> Some may have blamed you that you took away
> The verses that could move them on the day
> When, the ears being deafened, the sight of the
>     eyes blind
> With lightning, you went from me, and I could find
> Nothing to make a song about but kings,
> Helmets, and swords, and half-forgotten things
> That were like memories of you. . . .
> But, dear, cling close to me; since you were gone,
> My barren thoughts have chilled me to the bone.

Here the woman is clearly the muse whose presence lends the poet's verses their power to move. What is left when she goes is only the stage properties of poetry, which take such life as they have from memories of her. There is a paradox here, which Yeats repeated in his later poem on the same theme, "The Circus Animals' Desertion": poems are only dream versions of the reality of love. If one were truly loved, it seems, one would not need to write poems. Yet it is the *loss* of love that turns the poet to his poor words and barren thoughts, and so creates the poem of love out of its absence.

The second cycle, written some ten years later, focuses on the losses that time inflicts on the beloved: the loss of youth and beauty, the loss of reputation, the loss of authority in the world. Like the earlier poems they treat Maud Gonne as the muse, but a muse grown old, whose power to inspire is retrospective: "I knew a phoenix in my youth" is the refrain of one poem, but another repeats "vague memories, nothing but memories." It is appropriate and inevitable that Yeats's muse should age, for everything in his created world is subject to the same destructive power of time. "Everything that man esteems/ Endures a moment or a day"—including love and beautiful women, poems and poets, civilization itself. From this point in Yeats's career (we are at 1917, his fifty-second year, the year of his marriage) the powerful historical women begin to grow old and fade from the poems, and when they do appear, they do so in the role of powerless age: Maud Gonne in "Among School Children," Lady Gregory in "Coole Park and Ballylee," the Gore-Booth sisters in the elegy to them.

Love passes, the sexual energy of actual loved women fades—and what is one to make poems of then? Who will be an old man's muse? We can find a hint of a solution in a letter from Yeats to Olivia Shakespeare written in July 1926: "Some time ago you asked me for some love poems I had written. I did not send them because they want revision. They are part of a series. I have written the wild regrets, for youth and love, of an old man, and the poems you asked for are part of a series in which a woman speaks, first in youth and then in age." The two series to which Yeats refers are "A Man Young and Old," published in *The Tower* in 1928, and "A Woman Young and Old," published in *The Winding Stair* (1933). Yeats calls them love poems, but one must radically redefine the term to make it fit. For in these poems there is no identifiable *I* or *you,* only generic Man or Woman, old or young. Being stripped of specific human identity, the poems are also stripped of the trappings and consolations of romantic love: there are no pearl-pale hands and passion-dimmed eyes here, *body* appears as an unmodified noun, sex is violent, and old age is ugly. In these bare poems love is—not *reduced,* exactly, but rendered in its essential naked sexuality, whether felt or remembered. They are the love poems of the genders, not of individuals.

Like the earlier Maud Gonne poems, these are poems *about* love—the sufferings of young love, and the wild regrets of age. The poems of youth are passionate and harshly honest—the lover is a "lout," struck dumb by his heart's agony; the poems of old age have a Becketty savagery—intimate and sexual, but never tender. What they all have in common is a great fierce energy: even to the old man, love is a shriek, a blow, a harsh laugh, a thumping heart. They are energetic poems, and the source of the energy is sexuality.

Take for example one of the Old Man's songs, "His Memories."

> We should be hidden from their eyes,
> Being but holy shows
> And bodies broken like a thorn
> Whereon the bleak north blows,
>
>    . . . . .
>
> The women take so little stock
> In what I do or say

They'd sooner leave their cosseting
To hear a jackass bray;
My arms are like the twisted thorn
And yet there beauty lay;
The first of all the tribe lay there
And did such pleasure take—
She who had brought great Hector down
And put all Troy to wreck—
That she cried into this ear,
"Strike me if I shriek."

The poem begins with a familiar theme of Yeats's later poems—his hatred of age and physical decay. The old body is an object of loathing—a broken thorn, a "sort of battered kettle at the heel," "a tattered coat upon a stick." But though age brings loss of sexual attractiveness (women, as he says here, take no stock in what he does), it does not diminish sexuality itself. There are great energy and great physicality in this poem, as there are in other poems of this time—"The Tower," for example, and "Sailing to Byzantium"—and though it begins in hatred and loathing, it ends in love. The poem turns on the words "And yet," and what follows provides a kind of balance: remembered beauty balancing present ugliness, sexual love balancing hatred. The beauty is once more Helen, the wrecker of Troy, woman understood as sexual power; but she is remembered not mythically but intimately, in a blunt physical way, as a passionate woman making passionate love.

The poem is called "His Memories," though there is really only one memory in it; but that one memory is rendered more vividly and immediately than the old man's present agedness is. The point made about old age is not very comforting: memory doesn't fade, nor desire diminish, and there will be no philosophic calm. Nevertheless in its frank celebration of sexual love the poem is curiously heartening, because it sounds honest: old age probably *will* be like that. It is a courageous statement for an old ailing poet to make.

But the most surprising thing about these late love poems is that in the second group Yeats speaks as a woman—in a woman's voice and with a woman's sensibility. His woman is passionately physical, takes pleasure in "lively lads," and enjoys her own body in a very unladylike, unrestrained way. She is also, like the Man, frankly and directly carnal. The seventh poem, for example, is a Yeatsian variation on the aubade from *Romeo and Juliet:*

"Parting"

*He.* Dear, I must be gone
    While night shuts the eyes
    Of the household spies;
    That song announces dawn.

*She.* No, night's bird and love's
    Bids all true lovers rest,

. . . . .

*He.* Daylight already flies
    From mountain crest to crest.

*She.* That light is from the moon.

*He.* That bird . . .

*She.*            Let him sing on,
    I offer to love's play
    My dark declivities.

Here darkness and the sexual woman have the last word, as they did in "Solomon and the Witch" (and don't in *Romeo and Juliet*). Love is *play* here, but it is serious play, and it is physical play: *declivities* is a topographical word, which makes the woman's body a little earth—and not in the lover's eyes but in her own.

In "A Woman Young and Old" Yeats had, you might say, become his own muse, by the extraordinary act of assuming a woman's private sexual identity as a poetic persona. Three years later he did it again, even more brilliantly, in "Words for Music Perhaps," a sequence of twenty-five poems of which fifteen are uttered by that same persona, the sexual woman. Of these, seven are Crazy Jane poems. Jane is a wonderfully rich character, but what she essentially represents in these poems is the changeless female principle, as Yeats understood it. Living as she does out of history, and subject only to natural cyclical change, she can express sexual energy even in old age (as Maud Gonne and Lady Gregory couldn't—at least not in Yeats's poems). To call her *crazy* is simply to recognize that, being the essential woman, she contains the generic madness of femaleness: she is the wild old wicked muse, the last of Yeats's witches.

The Crazy Jane poems, taken together, make an important point about the sexuality of Yeats's later poems. In the dramatis personae of the cycle there are three characters: two men, the bishop and Jack the journeyman, and one woman, Jane. Between Jane and the bishop a lively dialogue goes on; they are the antinomies of the poems—Sex and Anti-Sex. But Jack gets only one line to speak in the whole sequence—if indeed it is he who says wearily "That's certainly the case" during one of Jane's speeches. As the Lover he has virtually no existence independent of Jane—he is simply the sexual partner, the "solid man," who lives in Jane's memory rather as Helen lives in the Old Man's. But the energy of the poems comes from Jane alone.

One sees a similar assignment of energy in the "Three Bushes" cycle in *Last Poems,* where the Lady and the Chambermaid plan and comment on the sexual action, leaving the lover with nothing to do but perform his necessary act, utter a six-line song, and then go out and fall on his head and die. In both cycles it is the women who are the sexual dynamos, the initiators and the articulators of love's play; the men are there because the polarities of sex require them, but they are passive and mute.

The other poems of "Words for Music Perhaps" are in the mood of "A Woman Young and Old," though with perhaps a greater sexual tenderness in some (I am thinking especially of the beautiful little lyrics "Three Things" and "After Long Silence"). Once more Yeats insisted that these were "love poems." Writing about *The Winding Stair* to Olivia Shakespeare, he said: "'Crazy Jane' poems (the origin of some of these you know) and the little group of love poems that follow are, I think, exciting and strange. Sexual abstinence fed their fire—I was ill and yet full of desire." One recalls that time thirty years earlier, when Yeats was, as he said, "tortured by sexual desire" and writing the poems of *In the Seven Woods*. Like the others these are "love poems" only in the sense of being about the experience of love, especially of love remembered. It is appropriate that he should have written about them to Olivia Shakespeare, for to him she *was* the "woman young and old"—a woman then in her sixties as Yeats was, but also a woman remembered as young, the woman he had loved more than thirty years before.

Should we say then that Yeats achieved in the end an androgynous mind? Coleridge said that a great mind *must* be androgynous, and Virginia Woolf agreed. Certainly Yeats *had* a great mind, and in his last years he *said* that it was an androgynous one. In a letter to Ethel Mannin in 1935 he wrote: "You are doubly a woman, first because of yourself and secondly because of the muses, whereas I am but once a woman"; and in the following year he wrote to Dorothy Wellesley: "My dear, my dear—when you crossed the room with that boyish movement, it was no man who looked at you, it was the woman in me. It seems that I can make a woman express herself as never before. I have looked out of her eyes. I have shared her desire." And that is true—in his last poems he *could* do that. Yet for all that, he was scarcely what Virginia Woolf meant by androgynous. "It is one of the tokens of the fully developed mind," she wrote in *A Room of One's Own,* "that it does not think specially or separately of sex"; and "it is fatal," she thought, "for any one who wrote to think of their sex." Yeats did think specially and separately of sex, and thought about it a great deal. He believed in essential, antinomial sexual differences, and he thought in Man/Woman dichotomies (though he also believed in the equivalence of sexual pleasure, and in the power of Sheba to direct the sexual dance). In his own sexual orientation he was entirely masculine. But though a man, he was a man who loved women, and because he loved women, he could imagine their feelings—for isn't love just that, a living into another person's being?

Yeats's world moved by the interaction of opposites, and of these the most fundamental and fertile was the interaction of man and woman in sexual love, the dance of Solomon and Sheba. That dance is the essential act of creation, in which Self engages its own opposite, and becomes unified with it. "The marriage bed is the symbol of the solved antinomy," Michael Robartes says in *A Vision. In* this sense the dance is a marriage, a poem is a marriage, sex is a marriage. Even marriage is a marriage. They are all acts of the imagination, by which a self transcends its separateness by creating something more. In this process sex is a metaphor, and the sexual woman—old or young, historical or mythical, crazy or sane—is the muse of all creation. If that is true, then in

his last years Yeats's imagination had become like a marriage bed—a coupling of male and female, a solved antinomy. Perhaps that is why those last poems are the greatest lyric poems of our time.

## Sherry Zivley

SOURCE: "Plath's Will-less Women," in *Literature and Psychology*, Vol. XXXI, No. 3, 1981, pp. 4-14.

[*In the following essay, Zivley examines works in which Sylvia Plath exhibited passivity and possible schizophrenia.*]

When most people think of the poetry of Sylvia Plath, they think of "Daddy," of "Lady Lazarus," of "Lesbos," the *Ariel* poems of strong will and incredible energy. Such Plath poetry is often remembered as charged with dangerously high voltage. Nevertheless, much of Plath's poetry is extremely passive in tone and theme. Much of her poetry presents personae who are passive and helpless and who often yearn to achieve a state of even greater passivity and numbness.

Such helplessness and will-lessness have been discussed by most major psychoanalytic writers who agree that such passivity is a symptom of a human being in the throes of serious depression or schizophrenia.

In his early and major clinical studies of schizophrenia, Harry Stack Sullivan pointed out that a primary indicator of the illness is regression. Sullivan explains that the patient's "mental structure [is] . . . disassociated" and that "the disintegrated portions [of the patient's mental structure] may regress to various earlier levels of mental ontology." He explains, "This disparity of depths seems the essence of that which is schizophrenia, as distinguished from other mental disorders."[1] Recovery from schizophrenia, Sullivan points out, depends on the degree of hope the patient sees for the future. He says,

> . . . the social milieu to which the patient has to return, has a great deal to do with his future. If . . . the patient . . . belie[ves] that he can circumvent ·or rise above environmental handicaps . . . his recovery proceeds.[2]

If a person is unable "to secure the requisite balance between desire and satisfaction, then he recoils from the world—either physically, by flight into the hinterland or suicide, or by the route of symbols, schizophrenia."[3] Sullivan distinguishes between depression and schizophrenia:

> While the true depressive is preoccupied with thoughts of the enormity of the disaster, of punishment, hopelessness, and the like the incipient schizophrenic is not the host of any simple content, but is burdened with pressing distresses, and becomes more and more wrapped up in fantastic explanation

and efforts at remedy. The distinction is one fundamentally dynamic: Pure depression is practically a standstill of adjustment; the schizophrenic depression is a most unhappy struggle. Instead of literally or figuratively sitting still, these people are striving to cut themselves off from painful stimuli, escape the situation by mystic and more or less extraordinary efforts, and justify themselves by heroic measures.[4]

Sullivan explains that "in every case of schizophrenic illness there is found in the history of the individual a point at which there had occurred what might well be called a disaster to self-esteem," which in turn led them to experience panic.[5] Having lost his self-esteem, the schizophrenic begins to experience feelings of helplessness and consequently will-lessness, which Silvano Arieti points out is a predominant symptom of schizophrenia. Many schizophrenics refuse to believe in the "influence of will on one's life." Arieti says,

> . . . many schizophrenics believe that they do not live or will. They are lived, they are caught in a network of situations where other people, other facts, other events determine their life. They have no part whatsoever in determining the world but are reduced to the state of inanimate objects. If that is all their life is about, they either give up entirely or become even more passive.
>
> . . . . .
>
> They believe that other people . . . do have a will and determine the world. Such function is denied only to them, and therefore they cannot accept this deprivation. Inherent in their mental condition is this lifelong protest.[6]

If a person experiences a "complete loss of the capacity to will," he becomes catatonic; he not only loses his belief in his own ability to will, he loses the ability to even move his own body.[7] Arieti explains,

> During the catatonic illness the patient attaches a tremendous sense of responsibility to any manifestation of his will, even in reference to actions which are generally considered of little importance. Every willed movement comes to be seen not as a function but as a moral issue; every motion is considered not merely as a fact but as a value. Such an abnormal sense of responsibility reaches the acme of intensity when it becomes associated with delusions of negative cosmic power or negative omnipotence. The patient comes to believe that a little movement that he can make, by producing a change in the state of the universe, may be capable of harming his whole community or even of destroying the whole world.
>
> . . . . .
>
> Although he is not pyschologically paralyzed, he is, for practical purposes, petrified. Like a statue he cannot respond to people who touch him, bump into him, smile at him, or caress him. But unlike

a statue he hurts in the most atrocious way, having lost something more precious than his eyesight, the most human of his possessions—his will.[8]

It is obvious from these analyses that a regression into will-lessness has extremely serious consequences for anyone. Yet this is precisely the kind of regression demonstrated in many of Plath's poems, in which the personae either yearn for or have achieved extreme conditions of will-lessness.

Nearly all of these will-less personae are women, which is not surprising. Many of them suffer from what David McClelland and Norman Watt call "sex-role alienation,"[9] or an unwillingness to act out the roles or do the work ordinarily expected of women in our culture.[10] Since these women are unable to balance their desires with the demands of their culture, they are much more likely to suffer from schizophrenia.

Many of Sylvia Plath's will-less women do manifest serious schizophrenic symptoms of will-lessness. These personae see absolutely no hope, no possibilities for their lives.

Many powerful and recurring images in Plath's poetry reveal the personae's frustration, helplessness, and fury. Some of these are images of a Jew in Nazi Germany, a prisoner in jail, a patient in a hospital, a queen bee in her hive, and other incarcerated characters.

In the imagery in which Plath identifies the persona's predicament with that of a Jew in Nazi Germany, the main implications of Plath's imagery of oppression appear. The speaker is trapped and hates her oppressor; she sees nothing but further suffering and death as her future. In "Daddy"[11] the speaker associates her father/oppressor with "the snows of the Tyrol, the clear beer of Vienna," "a swastika," describes him with the words "your Luftwaffe," "your Aryan eye," and "Meinkampf look," and calls him "Panzer-man, panzer-man." He is himself like a Panzer in his obliteration of all vulnerable creatures who stand in his way. The speaker characterizes her father's egocentricity by his recurrent "Ich, ich, ich," and because of him she thinks the German "lanuage obscene." She is so fearful of him that she cannot speak; her tongue is "stuck in a barb [sic] wire snare." She epitomizes him as

> An engine, an engine
> Chuffing me off like a Jew
> A Jew to Dachau, Auschwitz, Belsen
> I begin to talk like a Jew
> I think I may well be a jew.

She considers both her father and her husband (who resembles her father) to be her jailors, persecutors, and potential murderers. She appears to realize that *her* problem is that she seeks out dictatorial men and assumes a passive, scapegoat role in her relationships with them. Yet this intellectual recognition has not prevented her from becoming emotionally involved with such men. She says,

> Every woman adores a Fascist,
> The boot in the face, the brute
> Brute heart of a brute like you.

Plath's writing from the time she wrote *The Bell Jar* has portrayed women complaining bitterly of their submission to such male tyrants. Again and again she uses the image of the Jew in Nazi Germany to dramatize a woman's oppression by such men. In "Lady Lazarus" (A5-9) the speaker describes her skin as "Bright as a Nazi lampshade" and her face as "a featureless, fine Jew linen." No longer seeing herself as a complete human being, the speaker feels reduced by persecution to her physical elements: "a cake of soap/A wedding ring/ A gold filling." She calls the men in her life "Herr Doktor," "Herr Enemy," "Herr God," and "Herr Lucifer" and warns them to "Beware/Beware." Yet the speaker is never seen turning her furious energy to freeing herself from these men. Instead, she merely explodes and vents her anger in what is probably merely one or more explosions in repetitive cycles of passively accepting abuse or domination, of getting angry, and of making threats. In "Getting There" (A36-39), the speaker imagines herself in Germany, surrounded by "Krupp [the munitions manufacturer], black muzzles" and says that to reach freedom, "It is Russia I have to get across . . . / I am dragging my body/ Quietly through the straw of the boxcars." It would be such a long and demanding journey that she feels helpless to succeed. In "Mary's Song," the speaker's concern expands to include her child. She fears that either she or her child will become sacrificial lambs in "The same fire" that melts "the tallow heretics" and ousts Jews from their native lands. Such images may be excessively dramatic but they reveal how Plath apparently viewed marriage in the 1950's and early 1960's.

Plath portrays other helpless women as hospital patients. These women feel that they have lost their identities and that they are not completely human and alive any more. Many of these women even feel only partially animate. They feel helpless against the doctors who would purge them of their faults to turn them into ordinary women and submissive wives. In "Tulips" (A10-11), the speaker says,

> I am nobody . . .
> I have given my name and my day-
> clothes up to the nurses
> And my history to the anaesthetist
> and my body to the surgeons.

These surgeons "have swabbed me clean of my loving associations," and the speaker feels, consequently, "I am a nun now, I have never been so pure." In "Tulips," she feels reduced to only a part of herself, only "an eye between two white lids." In "Death & Co." (A28-30) the speaker is reduced still further and feels that "I am red meat," no more important than meat in a butcher's counter. Likewise the patient in "Paralytic" (A77-80) thinks of herself as merely a "Dead egg." And in "The Stones" (C82-84): the speaker feels that she is treated as if she were a piece of machinery being repaired or a jewel being chiseled by a gem cutter. In none of these poems does the speaker think of herself as having value to her family, to her doctor, or to the attendants in the hospital in which she finds herself.

One of Plath's most powerful images of a woman trapped in a role from which she cannot extricate herself and in which she feels controlled by society, family, and husband appears in her bee-keeping poems. In these poems, Plath shows the queen bee as doubly imprisoned by beekeeper and worker bees. In "The Beekeeper's Daughter" the queen is owned and controlled by the "hieratical" beekeeper, "the Maiestro of the bees" (C73). In "The Bee Meeting" Plath shows the queen bee as surrounded, trapped, and enslaved by thousands of worker bees. This queen is threatened yearly by the young virgin queens who "Dream of a duel [with the older queen] they will win inevitably" because she is becoming "old, old, old" and "exhausted" (A57). Likewise she is threatened in the poem "The Bee Meeting" by the bee-keeper who may search out and kill the old queen in order to replace her with a younger, stronger queen to guarantee the health of the hive. Like the queen, the female novice beekeeper becomes a scapegoat in "The Bee Meeting" (A55-57) in a village ritual she does not understand. In this poem the newcomer is outnumbered by other villagers and, unlike them, wears a "sleeveless summery dress' with "no protection" while "they are all gloved and covered." By the end of this poem, queen bee and novice beekeeper become fused into a scapegoat who is sacrificed in order that the hive and society may continue their traditional functions.

Still another image Plath uses to show the domination of a woman is that of the vampire and his victim in "Daddy" and other poems. In this image the woman feels that she is the victim of a parasite who drinks and depletes her lifeblood.

Plath occasionally shows persecution through images which portray the persona as a persecuted Christ. The speaker in "Apprehensions" identifies herself with Christ during his crucifixion. The protagonist of "Gigolo" (WT6) says "My mouth sags" like "the mouth of Christ." And another persona expresses "a terror/Of being off under crosses and a rain of pieties" (WT 3). These images portray a person who feels as helpless as someone being crucified would be.

A different image utilizes Christian tradition to portray woman's helplessness. The woman in "Getting There" (A36-38) thinks of herself as Adam's rib and says,

> It is Adam's side
> This earth I rise from, and I in agony.
> I cannot undo myself.

Plath uses the image of a prisoner in jail to indicate some of her protagonists' feelings of helplessness. One speaker feels she is a captive of the devil, to the "Man in Black" in "the dim barbed wire headland of Deer Island prison" (C52). The speaker in "Daddy" believes she has been controlled and tormented for so long that she has developed "a love of the rack and screw." And in "The Jailer"[12] the wife complains (as a mere component of another person's body, she obviously feels helpless to will any actions of her own) of a variety of abuses from her husband, saying she has been "locked in," "drugged," "raped," "tortured," "hung, starved, burned, and hooked." In the process, her will has atrophied.

In many of these images that describe Plath's female protagonists' loss of freedom, the protagonist can anticipate nothing but death. The Jew in Nazi Germany, the queen bee, the vampire's victim, the crucified Christ, and others are reduced to corpses in the only peace that Plath offers these protagonists.

All of these personae appear to be unable to "circumvent or rise above [their] environmental handicaps," as Sullivan has said is common of schizophrenics. They are, consequently, unable to make any decisions that could make their lives more tolerable. Instead, like the patients Sullivan describes, they "become more and more wrapped in fantastic explanation and efforts at remedy." The very nature of the images with which they describe themselves are fantastic and extreme, and those personae who suggest efforts at remedy, like the speakers in "Lady Lazarus" and "Daddy", vent their anger in wild threats but do little to change their predicaments.

According to R. D. Laing, a person who feels he lacks identity and autonomy "may feel more unreal than real; in a literal sense, more dead than alive .... He may feel more insubstantial than substantial."[13] Such a person may experience what Laing calls "petrification and depersonalization." Specifically, he may fear "being turned from a live person into a dead thing, into a stone, into a robot."[14] And in order to avoid being turned into an inanimate being by other people or external forces, he chooses to turn himself into an inanimate being. For such a person, Laing says,

> Utter detachment and isolation are regarded as the only alternative to a clam- or vampire-like attachment in which the other person's life-blood is necessary for one's own survival, and yet is a threat to one's survival. Therefore, the polarity is between complete isolation or complete merging of identity rather than between separateness and relatedness.[15]

Plath not only uses a variety of situations in which one human being has totalitarian rule over another to portray the role of contemporary women; she also utilizes other images which portray her personae as helpless bodies or inanimate objects. These persons are completely devoid of will. They are like the schizophrenic patients Arieti describes who "believe that they do not live or will." In "Paralytic" (A77-78), the speaker says,

> My God the iron lung
> That loves me, pumps
> My two
> Dust bags in and out.

In such a predicament, as Plath says in "Edge," "The woman is perfected" only when she is dead and

> Her dead
> Body wears the smile of accomplishment,
> The illusions of a Greek necessity
> Flows in the scrolls of her toga,
> Her bare
> Feet seem to be saying:
> We have come so far, it is over.

Even worse off than the women Plath portrays as victims are these who are so helpless that they think of themselves as corpses. Although charged with less immediate emotional impact than the many images in which a female protagonist is compared to a sensate, suffering victim with whom the reader can empathize, much more chilling in their cumulative impact are the images in which Plath shows sensitive women reduced to inanimate objects. These women have numbed their sensations in order to endure their suffering or have had their wills broken by suffering. In either case they are completely defenseless and helpless. Plath describes these women with imagery that suggests that they are less than human. There is a skeleton which mimics the dead body of a once-living being, a mannequin that imitates human form, a mechanical watch, which has movement, and Plath's most frequently used inanimate image—that which is furthest removed from a human being—the rock or stone.

In "All the Dead Dears" the speaker describes her reaction to "a stone coffin of the fourth century A.D. containing the skeletons of a woman, a mouse, and a shrew" (C29-30), which she saw in the archaeological museum in Cambridge. Referring to "This antique museum-cased lady," Plath asserts

> This lady here's no kin
> Of mine, yet kin she is: she'll suck
> Blood and whistle my marrow clean
> To prove it. As I think now of her
> head,
> From the mercury-backed glass
> Mother, grandmother, greatgrandmother
> Reach hag hands to haul me in;

Here Plath sees the dead woman as representative of all women and identifies with the corpse, feeling as dead and trapped as the mummy. In "The Rival" the speaker wakes in a "mausoleum" (A p. 48). And in "Tulips" she feels like a weighted body ready to be submerged, with "A dozen red lead sinkers round my neck" (A p. 11). The women presented as inanimate objects believe that they have no will power at all. Some are presented as dolls or mannequins. They still have the appearance of human beings but are treated as objects and lack both will power and feelings. In both "The Applicant" and (A p .4-5) the woman is kept in a closet and sold as one would sell a suit of clothes. She is called a "living doll," an automation that "can sew," "can cook," and "can talk, talk, talk," and that will serve as an inanimate "Poultice" or "image" to the man who purchases her. In "The Munich Mannequins" (A pp. 73-74) the prostitutes are described as mannequins, store dummies, old-fashioned dummies with heads and arms, but with steel rods instead of bodies, they are described as "Orange lollies on silver sticks." These mannequins seem immobile as they "lean tonight/ In Munich" waiting to be moved about, dressed, undressed, and used by the men who purchase them. In "Amnesiac" the woman is called "The little toy wife" (WT p. 19). And in "Witch Burning" the woman becomes both doll and scapegoat because she is shown as a voodoo doll (CW p. 53).

No human qualities remain in the imagery of stones or paper that Plath uses to describe women. Such images suggest that these women have not only lost all will power, but also have become numb, dumb, and totally insensate objects. They are completely passive. They have given up. In "Tulips," the speaker says "My body is a pebble to them [the hospital staff], they tend it as water/ Tends to the pebbles it must run over" (A p. 10). In "The Beekeeper's Daughter," the speaker complains to the beekeeper that her heart is "under your foot" and that she is a "sister of stone" (C73). In "The Rival" the speaker says her rival's first "gift is making a stone out of everything" (A p. 48) thus implying that she feels she herself has been turned to stone by her rival. In "The Stones" the speaker feels she is lying "on a great anvil" where a pestle is gradually diminishing her. She says "I become a still pebble . . . /In a quarry of silences" (C82). The speaker finds the peacefulness that comes with this stone-like numbness desirable and preferable to the suffering she has experienced when she still perceived her feelings. In "Lorelei" the speaker seeks both numbness and total oblivion, saying, "Stone, stone, ferry me down there" (C23). Again and again Plath uses the image of woman as stone. In "Leaving Early" the speaker says "We slept like stones" (CW p. 19). In "Love Letter" the speaker claims "then I was dead/ . . . like a stone" (CW p. 27). In "Who" the pregnant woman insists, "I am a root, a stone, an owl pellet" (CW p. 48).

Plath often uses paper as an image to describe the experience of being insensate and disembodied. In "Cut" the speaker says she has a "thin/Papery feeling" (A p. 13). And in "Tulips" she calls herself a "cut-paper shadow" (A p. 11). The miscarrying secretary in "Three Women" believes she has become like men who are "like cardboard."

Other images of people as paper appear in "Crossing the Water" in which the people are described as paper dolls—"cut-paper people" (CW p. 56).

A particularly painful variant on the paper image is that of paper burning, an image in which the woman described is as helpless as paper, but who suffers from burning pain. The speaker in "Eavesdropper" (WT pp. 25-27) feels she is being held and destroyed by the eavesdropper, whom she describes as

> one
> Long nicotine finger
> On which I,
> White cigarette,
> Burn.

And in another image, the paper is reduced even further, to ashes: a widow is described as "a sheet of newsprint in a fire" (CW p. 22).

In other images that connote helplessness, numbness, and often death or inanimateness, Plath describes women as "Jade" in "Purdah" (WT p. 40), and as ivory in "Childless Woman" (WT p. 34). In "In Plaster" the speaker is imprisoned in an alter ego who is like a plaster cast containing her. She feels she "shall never get out of this!" (CW p. 16). In "Love Letter" the speaker claims that she slept like "a snake" (CW p. 27). And in "Two Campers in Cloud Country" the speaker complains, "I lean to you, numb as a fossil. Tell me I'm here." In "Face Lift" as the speaker is anesthetized. She describes her experience: "At the count of two/Darkness wipes me out like chalk on a blackboard . . ." (CW p. 5). In "Gigolo" the speaker claims to be merely a "Pocket watch" and says, "I tick well" (WT p. 6). Also in "An Appearance" the woman's body "opens and shuts—/A Swiss watch" (WT 10). These women retain no human qualities at all. They have become objects.

All of Plath's will-less and helpless women are potential candidates for or already suffer from, severe mental illness. They are likewise potential suicides, since they can see no possibilities for themselves other than lying down and playing dead. Perhaps they suffer because they feel entrapped or enslaved in their role as housewives. Perhaps they represent all twentieth century people—men and women. But, if Plath herself felt as her female protagonists do, if she felt as oppressed and dependent as they, if she thought there were as few possibilities for a woman living independently, one can see that such beliefs would have contributed to her own self-destruction. For all their fury and ugliness, Plath's images of oppression are primarily very sad: They show human beings for whom life is a living hell, and for whom the only alleviation of their suffering will come in death, which many, like the speaker in "I am Vertical," long for. She says, I am Vertical but I would rather be horizontal (CW p. 12). She yearns to be like the flowers and trees, wishing, first, for their respective "daring" and "longevity," and, then, for death. She says,

> It is more natural to me, lying down.

>      . . . . .

> And I shall be useful when I lie down finally:

Then the trees may touch me for
once,
and the flowers have time for me.
(CW p. 12)

Here is the source of the fury and anger and helplessness: these women feel they have no worth, that they would be more useful as fertilizer for flowers and trees.

Plath's personae long for total passivity or death. They wish to become like the catatonic schizophrenic whom Arieti has described. According to Arieti, such a patient

> . . . has a special type of schizophrenia which fortunately has become much less common in recent years in most parts of the world. At times after a certain period of excitement and agitation, at other times without warning, the patient slows down, reaching sooner or later a state of partial or complete immobility. He may become so stiff, rigid, and incapable of movement that he resembles a statue. He then becomes unable to move around and take care of his physical needs. He cannot dress or undress, does not have the initiative to feed himself in the presence of food or to talk in the presence of other people, nor does he answer questions. At other times, the patient is not so severely affected, but his activities are reduced to a minimum. He gives the impression of being paralyzed, but there is nothing wrong with his motor equipment, musculature, nerves, articulation, etc. What is disturbed is his faculty to will. He cannot will and therefore cannot will to move.

. . . . .

> Before becoming acutely ill, the patient generally is confronted with a very important decision to make, or with a challenge for which he was not prepared. Such a task seems gigantic, impossible to cope with, and finally overwhelming to the patient.[16]

> These patients usually had a parent who made all of their decisions for them. When the patients later had to make their own choices, they found themselves unable to act; if they acted, they were criticized and made to feel guilty. Catatonia is an avoidance of action in order to remove the panic connected with willed action. The panic, at first connected with one or a few actions becomes generalized. When it is extended to every action, the patient lapses into a state of complete inability to will and consequent immobility. At other times it is an obsessive-compulsive anxiety rather than a definite fear which does not permit the patient to move. Is it better to move or not to move, to talk or not to talk, to choose this word or another one? In the midst of this terrifying uncertainty the patient decides not to will at all.[17]

Many of Plath's personae are women who long for just such passivity. Yet they can be juxtaposed against other more famous Plath personae, like those in "Daddy" and "Lady Lazarus," who are screaming that they want more independence and that they are autonomous. It is not surprising that of Plath's many kinds of images of torment, oppression, and imprisonment, the most vivid and horrible are those which are neither symbolic nor metaphoric. These are the poems in which she attempts to realistically portray a wife or mother in a kitchen. These images are often hellish and nightmarish. In these examples, the woman seems more trapped, more frustrated, more in pain than in any of the images that reduce woman to a lower form of existence. These images are painful because, although helpless, the woman still is sensitive to her suffering; yet the suffering is compounded both by her inability to do anything about it and, often, by the fact that she is trapped in her suffering with children who are likewise suffering and whom she can do little for. As classic wives of the 1950's, they are dependent creatures who have abdicated all major responsibilities to their husbands. They have thus robbed themselves of independence, autonomy, and self-esteem. Thus, they have submitted to oppression and robbed themselves of their wills and their humanity.

In "A Birthday Present" the protagonist, while cooking, complains against having to adhere "to rules, to rules, to rules" (A p. 42) both in cooking and in life. In "Cut" the violence with which the protagonist describes her thumb which she cut while chopping onions indicates the hatred and violence she feels as she stands there working in her kitchen. She calls the thumb "Saboteur, / Ka kase man," recognizing that in cutting herself so often do, her anger against herself, attacking her thumb as "Trepanned veteran, / Dirty girl, / Thumb stump" (A p. 14).

The poem which may show the speaker's greatest anger and frustration at the imprisonment as a housewife, is "Lesbos." "Lesbos" (A pp. 30-31) begins with lines that reverberate with horror and describe a hideous scene:

> Viciousness in the kitchen!
> The potatoes hiss.
> It is all Hollywood, windowless,
> The fluorescent lights wincing on and
> off like a terrible migraine,
> Coy paper strips for doors————
> Stage curtains, a widow's frizz.

. . . . .

> Meanwhile there's a stink of fat and
> baby crap
> (A p. 30).

The speaker goes on to describe the walls as "windowless" and providing no means for escaping or even viewing the outside world. Hers is a solitary confinement of the most intense sort. Consequently, she feels "silent" and in "hate"./hate/Up to my neck,/Thick, "thick" (A 32), in a statement that perhaps explains why Plath shows many women as imprisoned and frustrated. They cannot find alternatives to the dilemmas in which they find themselves; therefore they hate their husband, their predicaments, their children, and, most importantly, themselves. They find no alternative to their roles as housewives because they lack the courage to live independently. As the speaker in "The Bee Meeting" says, "I could not run without having to run forever" (A p. 57).

The speaker in "the Jailor" epitomizes the helplessness and fury of Plath's women personae. She claims to be jailed, "drugged and raped." She claims to have been tortured: "He has been burning me with cigarettes." She claims to have been starved: "My ribs show." She claims to being killed: "Hung, starved, burned, hooked!" She feels that her only chance of being freed is if her husband is "dead and away." But "That, it seems is the impossibility/ That being free." And although the speaker insists that it is her husband that is responsible for her imprisonment, she reveals an even more important cause of her entrapment when she admits, "I am myself. That is not enough." The most important cause of her suffering is apparent here: She has no self-esteem and therefore she chooses to live in a situation in which she is abused. Similarly in most of the other images of oppression that Plath uses, the woman thinks of herself as helpless and passive. Plath recognizes that "Every woman adores a Fascist" but she fails to perceive that to "adore a Fascist" one must first loathe oneself. Consequently she blames the oppressor for her misery, but her only freedom must come from stopping being passive (and complaining about her helplessness and oppression) and taking some control over her life. She needs to choose to become a woman, a complete human being who can make decisions, act, and accept the responsibilities of her actions. Unfortunately most of Plath's personae choose to seek oblivion and insensateness and to think of themselves as prisoners, stones, paper, or other subhuman or inanimate objects.

### NOTES

[1] Harry Stack Sullivan, *Schizophrenia as a Human Process,* 2nd ed. 1962; rpt. (New York: Norton, 1974).

[2] Ibid., p. 15.

[3] Ibid., p. 96.

[4] Ibid., pp. 114-115.

[5] Ibid., p. 158.

[6] *The Will to Be Human* (New York: Dell, 1972), p. 48.

[7] Silvano Arieti, *Interpretation of Schizophrenia,* 2nd ed. (1955; rpt. New York: Basic Books, 1974), pp. 211-212.

[8] Ibid., p. 213-214. Arieti explains,

> The fear of the willed action accounts for other characteristics of catatonia. The patient may not be able to will to act independently, but may still be able to accept commands for others. He may passively follow orders given by someone else because the responsibility will not be his: when he

obeys, he substitutes another person's will for his own. When the patient is put into a given position, the will or responsibility of someone else is involved. If he wants to change his position, he has to will the change, and this causes anxiety or guilt. Thus the passivity to the suggestion of others is not an acceptance of power from others, as in hypnosis, but a relief from responsibility.

[9] Phyllis Chessler, *Women and Madness* (Garden City, New York: Doubleday, 1972), quoting David C. McClelland and Norman Watt, "Sex Role Alienation in Schizophrenia," *Journal of Abnormal Psychiatry,* Vol. 73, No. 3, 1968.

[10] Phyllis Chessler reports, p. 50, that in Dr. Shirley Angrist's 1961 study of female ex-mental patients she

> . . . found that the rehospitalized women had refused to function "domestically" in terms of cleaning, cooking, child care, and shopping. The rehospitalized women were no different from the ex-mental patients in terms of their willingness to participate in "leisure" activities, such as traveling, socializing, or enjoying themselves. The rehospitalized women were, in Angrist's terms, slightly more "middle class and more frequently married than their non-returned counterparts." Further, the husbands who readmitted their wives expressed significantly lower expectations for their total human functioning. They seemed more willing to tolerate extremely childlike and dependent behavior in their wives—such as incessant complaining and incoherence—as long as the dishes were washed. These husbands also expressed great alarm and disapproval about their wives' "swearing," "cursing," and potentially violent "temper tantrums." Angirst, et al, "Rehospitalization of Female Mental Patients," *Archives of American Psychiatry,* Vol. 4, 1961.

[11] References to collections of Plath's poetry will be indicated by abbreviations of the titles within parentheses within the text:

*Colossus* (New York: Random House, 1962).

*Ariel* (New York: Harper & Row, 1965).

*Crossing the Water* (New York: Harper & Row, 1971).

*Winter Trees* (New York: Harper & Row, 1972).

[12] Encounter XXI (1963), p. 51.

[13] R. D. Laing. *The Divided Self* (New York: Pantheon Books, 1960), p. 43.

[14] Ibid., p. 48.

[15] Ibid., p. 54.

[16] Arieti, *Will*, pp. 211-212.

[17] Ibid., p. 213.

# DRAMA

## Jeanne-Marie A. Miller

SOURCE: "Images of Black Women in Plays By Black Playwrights," in *CLA Journal,* Vol. XX, No. 4, June, 1977, pp. 494-507.

[*In the following essay, Miller examines the attempts of African American playwrights after the 1950s to bring black female characters to the forefront in American drama.*]

In 1933, in an essay entitled "Negro Character as Seen by White Authors," the brilliant scholar-critic Sterling A. Brown wrote that Blacks had met with as great injustice in the literature of America as they had in the life of their country. In American literature, then, including the drama, Blacks had been depicted most often as negative stereotypes: the contented slave, the wretched freeman, the comic Negro, the brute Negro, the tragic mulatto, the local color Negro, and the exotic primitive.[1] Black female characters have been scarce in only one of these categories—the brute Negro. They have been most plentiful as the faithful servant. In American drama, where, seemingly, many more roles have been written for men than women, Black or white, it is the Black female character who has faced double discrimination—that of sex and race.

As early as the nineteenth century Black women have been written about by playwrights of their own race. Melinda, in William Wells Brown's *The Escape,* for example, is a mulatto who is not tragic,[2] and Rachel, in Angelina Grimke's early twentieth-century play of the same name, is a young, educated, middle-class Black woman who protests against the indignities suffered by her race.[3] Though there were many plays written by Blacks after the dawn of the twentieth century, the Civil Rights Movement of the 1950's and the Black Consciousness Movement of the 1960's produced many new Black playwrights who brought to the stage their intimate inside visions of Black life and the role that Black women play in it.

Alice Childress, a veteran actress, director, and playwright, in several published plays, has placed a Black woman at the center. Childress noted early that the Black woman had been absent as an important subject in popular American drama except as an "empty and decharacterized faithful servant."[4]

Childress' *Florence,* a short one-act play, is set in a railroad station waiting room in a very small town in the South.[5] The time of the play is the recent past. Emphasized is the misunderstanding by whites of Blacks, brought on by prejudice and laws that keep the two races apart. The rail separating the two races in the station is symbolic.

In the station a Black woman of little means, with a cardboard suitcase and her lunch in a shoebox, has a chance meeting with a white woman also bound for New York. In the conversation that takes place between them, the prejudices of the whites and their myths about Blacks are exposed, such as that of the tragic mulatto. Revealed also is the determination to keep Blacks in the places set aside for them by whites. Marge, the Black woman's daughter living at home, has accepted her place; Florence, the daughter seeking an acting career in New York, has not. Because of the revelations of the white woman, Florence's mother, enroute originally to bring her daughter home and end her fumbling New York career, changes her mind and instead mails the travel money to Florence so that she can remain where she is. Thus, a docile-appearing Black woman, who stays in her place in the South, acts to help her child transcend the barriers placed there by those trying to circumscribe her existence.

Childress' two-act comedy *Trouble in Mind,* while concentrating on discrimination in the American theatre, also brings into focus the troublesome racial conditions in the United States of the 1950's.[6] The framework of *Trouble in Mind* is the rehearsal of the play "Chaos in Bellesville," a melodrama with an anti-lynching theme, in reality a white writer's distorted view of Blacks. The principal character, Wiletta Mayer, a middle-aged Black actress, a veteran of "colored" musicals, appears at first to have found a way to survive in the prejudiced world of the theatre. Coerced by the white director, however, she explodes and reveals her long pent-up frustrations. Specifically, Wiletta disagrees with the action of the character she is playing—a Black mother who sends her son out to be lynched by a mob seething with hatred because the Black man had tried to vote. Wiletta, alone among the play's interracial cast, demands script changes that will portray Black life realistically. Though she loses her job in the attempt, she in no way seems to regret the stand she has taken after a lifetime of acceptance.

In *Wine in the Wilderness,* Tommy Marie, a young Black woman from the ghetto, teaches real pride to her newly acquired middle-class acquaintances.[7] This play is set during the Black revolutionary period of the 1960's. It is one of those Harlem summers popularly described as long and hot. A riot is taking place outside the apartment of Bill, a Black artist currently engaged in painting a triptych entitled "Wine in the Wilderness"—three images of Black womanhood. Two canvases have been completed: one depicting innocent Black girlhood and the other, perfect Black womanhood, an African queen, this artist's statement on what a Black woman should be. The third canvas is empty because Bill has not found a suitable model for the lost Black woman, the leavings of society. Unknown to Tommy, she has been picked out by two of Bill's friends to serve as the model for that hopeless creature. At first sight Tommy is unpolished and untutored but is essentially a warm, likeable human being. Once a live-in domestic and now a factory worker, at the present time she has been burned out and then locked out of her apartment as a result of the riot.

Later, dressed in an African throw cloth and with her cheap wig removed, Tommy undergoes a transformation as she overhears Bill, to whom she is attracted, describe his painting of the African queen. Believing that he is referring to her, she assumes the qualities he praises: "Regal . . . grand . . . magnificent, fantastic. . . . " For the first time she feels loved and admired. While Bill is trying to get into the mood to paint her, she recites the history of the Black Elks and the A. M. E. Zion Church, all part of her background. With her new look and the new knowledge he has gained about her, Bill cannot now paint Tommy as he had intended, for she no longer fits the image he sought.

The next day Oldtimer, a hanger-on, unthinkingly tells Tommy about the three-part painting and the unflattering role she was to play in it. She, in anger, teaches Bill and his middle-class friends about themselves—the hatred they have for "flesh and blood Blacks"—the masses, as if they, the others, have no problems. To the white racist, they are all "niggers" she tells them. But she has learned—she is "Wine in the Wilderness," "a woman that's a real one and a good one," not one on canvas that cannot talk back. The real thing is *inside,* she states.

Bill changes the thrust of his painting. Oldtimer—"the guy who was here before there were scholarships and grants and stuff like that, the guy they kept outta the schools, the man the factories wouldn't hire, the union wouldn't let him join . . ."—becomes one part of the painting; Bill's two friends—"Young Man and Woman workin' together to do our thing"—become another. Tommy, the model for the center canvas, is "Wine in the Wilderness," who has come "through the biggest riot of all, . . . 'Slavery'" and is still moving on against obstacles placed there by both whites and her own people. Bill's painting takes on flesh. Tommy has been the catalyst for change.

Unlike Childress' other plays, *Wedding Band* is set in an earlier period—South Carolina in 1918.[8] The central character, Julia Augustine, the Black woman around whom the story revolves, is an attractive woman in her thirties. A talented seamstress, she has only an eighth-grade education. The play opens on the tenth anniversary of her ill-fated love affair with Herman, a white baker who has a small shop. This illegal love affair is the theme of the play. In direct violation of South Carolina's laws against miscegenation, the pair has been meeting and loving clandestinely for years. On this day, in celebration of their anniversary, Herman gives Julia a wedding band on a thin chain to be worn around her neck. This day, too, is the first that Julia has spent in this impoverished neighborhood. She has moved often because her forbidden love affair has caused her to be ostracized by both Blacks and whites.

A series of encounters clearly delineates the kind of woman Julia really is. Though she is lonely between Herman's visits and sometimes allows wine to fill in the void, she is a woman of strength. She endures the criticism of her affair. She is unselfish, warm, and forgiving. With compassion she reads a letter to a new neighbor who cannot read. Unknown to her lover's mother, Julia sews and shops for her. When confronted by this woman who hates her and whose rigid racism drives her to exclaim that she would rather be dead than disgraced, Julia rises to her full strength and spews out the hatred that momentarily engulfs her. And even in her sorrow she is able to give a Black soldier a fitting sendoff to the war and the promise that the world will be better for all Blacks after the war's termination. In the end, Julia forgives her weak, timid lover who is dying from influenza. He could never leave South Carolina for a region more suitable for their love and marriage, he explains, because he had to repay his mother the money she gave him for the bakery. In reality, history stands between Julia and Herman. South Carolina belongs to both of them, but together they could never openly share the state. The promised escape to the North and marriage never materialize. Julia stands at the end of a long line of Childress' strong Black women characters. In this backyard community setting of *Wedding Band* are other images of Black womanhood—the self-appointed representative of her race, the mother protecting her son from the dangers awaiting him in the white South, and the woman, abused by a previous husband, waiting loyally for the return of her thoughtful and kind merchant marine lover.

The promising talent of the late Lorraine Hansberry was perhaps best displayed in the well-known *A Raisin in the Sun,* which portrays an interesting variety of female characters, none more so than Lena Younger, who has grandeur, strength, patience, courage, and heroic faith.[9] She is strong in the belief of her God who has sustained her throughout life. She mightily loves her family to whom she teaches self-respect, pride, and human dignity, protects them, sometimes meddles in their affairs, and does not always understand their needs and desires. Above all else, she wants a home for her family, a physical structure large enough to house them all comfortably. Acquiring this home would mean the realization of a long deferred dream. She wants, too, to help Beneatha, her daughter, fulfill her dream of being a medical doctor. But the attitudes of the younger generation Lena sometimes does not fathom—Beneatha's toward religion and Walter's toward money which to him symbolizes success. The wise, sensitive woman that she is, Lena Younger realizes before it is too late that her son, in desperation, is reaching out to manhood at the age of thirty-five, and she helps him by making him the head of the household over which she has presided since the death of her husband. Theirs is a household of working-class people struggling to survive with dignity.

Beneatha, young, spoiled, spirited, and sensitive, has social pride. Her ideas about women's liberation and her interest in her African heritage were to burst in full force in the decade that followed the production of *A Raisin in the Sun.*

Ruth, Lena's daughter-in-law, a gentle woman, weary with life, loves her husband, who at first falsely blames her for his lack of materialistic success. She wants him to have that chance to be a man. In this household Ruth acts as a peacemaker between the generations.

*A Raisin in the Sun* is a drama of affirmation. Man's possibilities are manifold, and in this work this family, with the help of the women, changes its world, if only a little.

Like Childress, Hansberry turned to the past for materials for one of her plays. In *The Drinking Gourd,* a drama about slavery, written for television, one of the principal characters is Rissa, a cook who is also one of the more privileged slaves on Hiram Sweet's plantation.10 On the surface, she is like the cherished, fictionalized image of the Black mammy who philosophically accepts her status, showers love and devotion on her white master and his family, forgives her white family of all wrong-doing, and hums or sings away all personal pain and sorrow. But unlike that unrealistic mammy, Rissa is concerned about her own family. To make life easier for her son Hannibal, she obtains a place for him in the Big House, only to have him refuse the favor. Slavery to him in any form is repulsive. After Hannibal is brutally blinded at the order of the plantation owner's son—for daring to learn to read—Rissa seeks vengeance for the crime. Though the fate is unknown of one son, Isaiah, who ran away from slavery, she assists the blind Hannibal, his sweetheart Sarah, and Isaiah's son, Joshuah, in escaping from slavery to freedom. Moreover, for protection, she gives them a gun that she has stolen from Hiram Sweet's cabinet. Thus Rissa reverses the myth of the faithful, contented slave—faithful to her master and contented in her servitude. Unlike Carson McCuller's Berenice, who continues to care for her white charge while a mob seeks to murder one of her own family, Rissa rivets her attention on her son, while her white master, calling to her for help, dies outside her cabin.

J. E. Franklin's *Black Girl,* which takes place in the present in a small town in Texas, has several generations of Black female characters, all representing different types.[11] Two sisters, who have succumbed to the limiting factors of their ghetto environment and are locked into dreary marriages, work, sometimes with extreme measures, to prevent their half-sister, Billie Jean, from realizing her dream to become a dancer. Having failed themselves, they want her to fail. Billie Jean's aspirations are met with hostility.

Billie Jean wants to break out of her suffocating environment and seek her own identity. Her ambition far exceeds any that her family might have, a family of women, who, for the most part, have given up dreaming.

Mama Rosie, a strong, rough woman, the mother of the three young women, is undemonstrative in her love for them. Because of past bitterness, stemming perhaps from her relationships with her two former husbands, she finds it easier to believe in strangers—girls of no kin, whom she has taken into her home from time to time—than it is to believe in her own. In reality she is disappointed in her older daughters and does not understand her youngest. She is fearful that all of her children will end up like her. Her love for her children is buried so deep that she cannot express it. She holds up to them as an example to follow, Netta, one of the girls she has helped. She feels that Netta, who is now in college, will return after graduation and buy her a house. Mama Rosie's children, in turn, unify in their hatred for this young woman.

Mu' Dear, Mama Rosie's mother, who also lives in the home, acts with moral authority and helps Billie Jean break out of the stultifying environment. "God knows I ain't crazy about her wanting to be no dancer, either," she states, "but that's her life, Rosie. If she don't make nothing out-a it, it'll be her nothing. . . . She can't do no worse with her'n than you have done with your'n. None of you . . . Now, take your hands off-a that child and be quick about it." She also causes Mama Rosie finally to confess her love for her family.

Whereas the grandmother makes it possible for Billie Jean to break the home barriers around her, it is Netta, who inspires her to finish high school, enter college, and join the dance company that is going on a national tour. Like Beneatha Younger, Billie Jean has enthusiasm for a dream that will improve and enrich her life as well as that of others.

Ron Milner, in *Who's Got His Own,* one of the significant plays of the Black theatre in the 1960's, is concerned with a young, angry Black man who finds a positive channel for his agitation only after he reaches an understanding of his father whom he has hated most of his life.[12] It is the father's funeral that has brought the son home. The son, in gaining the knowledge he needs to help himself, forces revelations from his sister and mother.

The sister is a sympathetic character, a young woman who has rejected Black men because she associated with them the ugly brutality that she saw in her father. After a shattering experience with a young white man, she became a recluse. The confession, which her brother forces from her, gives her the desire to try life once again.

The son learns that his God-fearing mother protected her husband when he was alive. She placed herself between his rage and the white world and thus absorbed the violence he would have reeked on that world. In his childhood he had had the terrifying experience of seeing his own father lynched and burned for trying to protect his wife. It is the mother who explains the father to her children, and it is her daughter who endeavors to have them all look to the future. Yesterday is past, she tells them; yesterday is the place where they have been.

In a one-act play, *The Warning—A Theme for Linda,* the emphasis is on Black women, especially on Linda, who, while approaching womanhood, is trying to understand it.[13] In a manless home, she is exposed to other women who have varying attitudes toward love: her younger sister and cousin who equate love with sex; her grandmother, whose experiences with her weak husband have left her bitter; and her own mother, whose affairs with several men have left her void of feeling. Linda concludes, especially after learning of her grandmother's relationship with her husband, that she will be a woman of strength and will demand strength from the man of her choice.

In both plays Milner's aim was to make his Black women characters complete human beings. Like the son in *Who's Got His Own,* Linda is made to define herself and thus live a fuller, more meaningful life. Milner's concern about the Black woman was continued in *What the Wine-Sellers Buy,* a contemporary morality play, in which a flashy hoodlum attempts to ensnare the soul of a Black youth, whom he tries to turn into a pimp and the youth's pretty, young girl friend into his first commodity.[14]

In his plays Ed Bullins, one of Black America's most prolific playwrights, focuses mainly on Black folk in an urban setting. His female characters include a lesbian who protects her love affair in a South Philadelphia ghetto.[15] A woman massive in size and strong in personality, she has accepted the rough life around her and has learned to cope with it. In comparison, the weak girl, whom she loves, wandered into this affair because she was not prepared for life by her family and was disappointed in an affair with a man. In another play, a woman tired of life's hardships turns to religion as an opiate, forsaking the ways of the world as well as her own son.[16]

In several of Bullins' full-length works—*Goin' a Buffalo, In the Wine Time, In New England Winter, The Duplex,* and *The Fabulous Miss Marie*—strong dramas couched in tough ghetto terms, the characters, though hemmed in by their environment, fight to survive. They often hold on to the dream that the future will be better. In *Goin' a Buffalo,* whose major characters are petty underworld figures, Pandora turns over her earnings as a prostitute and a dancer to her husband to help them toward their move from Los Angeles to Buffalo, where their lives will improve.[17] Pandora explains: "I'm just makin' this money so Curt and me can get on our feet. One day we gonna own property and maybe some businesses when we get straight . . . and out of this town." She believes in her husband—believes that they both can move up in the underworld or out of this world altogether whenever they choose. She does not see herself as a prostitute—just helping out until she and her husband can get something better. She works to help them realize a dream that proves in the end to be elusive. Lou, in *In the Wine Time,* wants to protect her nephew whom she took into her home when his mother died.[18] Her husband Cliff, who sometimes abuses her, will not accept the menial labor reserved for Black men. She stays with him, and, at times, speaks her mind. In *In New England Winter,* Steve, Cliff's half brother, commits a robbery in order to get money to return to New England where Liz, the

half-mad girl he loves, still lives.[19] When he last saw her, because of suspicions about him planted in her mind by his rival, her mind had snapped. In *The Duplex: A Black Love Fable,* Steve now in California has a protective love for his landlady Velma, who, brutalized by her husband, reaches out to her tenant for the fulfillment denied to her in marriage.[20] Velma always wanted her own home—away from the farm where she lived with her parents. She and her husband came to the city, where he went to school and then obtained a good job. Velma got her home, but lost her husband. Bullins, in *The Fabulous Miss Marie,* focuses on a group of superficial middle-class types, who, symbolized by the fortyish Marie, live a life filled with parties replete with drinking, sex, and vulgar conversations.[21] Pretense is the order of the day, and realities, often painful, are buried, temporarily, in the endless round of social gatherings.

In addition to his realistic plays about some aspects of Black urban life, Bullins wrote plays with a polemical thrust, many of them influenced by the Black Revolutionary Theatre of the 1960's. In one of these plays, *The Gentleman Caller,* a one-act play whose framework is symbolic, a seemingly stereotypical Black maid, dependable and faithful, murders her white employers and then calls for the unity of Black people and the destruction of the oppressor.[22]

From the middle to the late 1960's, perhaps the best known Black American playwright was Imamu Amiri Baraka (LeRoi Jones), who wrote plays calling for a revolutionary change among Black people. He was the prime mover of the Black Revolutionary Theatre, which, he wrote, should force change as well as be change. Black audiences must be cleansed of their ugliness. They must be forced to see their beauty—the strength in their minds and in their bodies. It must take dreams and give them a reality. It was to show what the world is and what it should be.[23]

Black women played only minor roles in many of the published plays of Baraka, for the 1960's was a time when the Black man, oppressed by many years of slavery and Post Civil War prejudice, was asserting himself and reclaiming his manhood. The Black woman was to be his helpmate, so to speak. Thus Black female characters in the plays growing out of the Black Revolutionary Theatre were sometimes negative types to be shunned or virtuous paragons to be emulated.

In *A Black Mass,* set early in history, at a time when life was pure, a Black woman, virtuous in nature, becomes the innocent victim of a white monster, an evil thing, a product of the only one of the original Black magicians who creates for creation's sake.[24] At the end of the play, she is white in color and imitates the repulsive actions of her defiler. In *Experimental Death Unit #1,* which takes place in modern times, during a war between whites and Blacks, a Black revolutionary army murders a vulgar Black woman of the streets and the two white men who have had sex with her.[25] Types repugnant to

Black revolutionary aims are to be annihilated.[26] In a fourth one-act play, *Madheart: A Morality Play,* two Black women, a mother and her daughter, who have spent their lives worshipping the foul white Devil Woman, are held up as types to be scorned or changed.[27] Because of their adoration of this creature, they have become materialistic and have turned to prostitution and alcoholism. Continuing to instruct Black women in what they should *not* be, the playwright, through another character, teaches a lesson in feminine submission. In an article entitled "Black Woman," Baraka once wrote that in contributing to the development of the Black nation, the Black woman must inspire, submit to, compliment, and praise her Black man. Once separated by physical and then by mental slavery, the Black man and the Black woman must now reach out for each other—not as equals but she as "the single element in the universe that perfectly completes [his] essence."[28]

Unlike the majority of Black American playwrights, who use realism in dramatizing their ideas, Adrienne Kennedy, an *avant gardist,* experiments with expressionism and surrealism. A poet of the theatre, she uses impressions and images rather than treat plot and character in a traditional manner. Despite the mode of treatment Kennedy draws her material from the Black experience. Her female character Sarah, in *Funnyhouse of a Negro,* is a young, tortured Black woman who has nightmarish agonies about being Black.[29] The action takes place on the last day in her life—before she commits suicide. The fantasy characters, all well known historical figures—Queen Victoria, the Duchess of Hapsburg, Patrice Lumumba, and Jesus—represent the various selves of Sarah. In a monologue she reveals pertinent information about herself. The daughter of a light-skinned mother and a dark-skinned father, she spends some of her time writing poetry. She also spends time with a Jewish poet interested in Blacks. Because of guilt feelings about her treatment of her father, whose black skin she abhors, she imagines that she has killed him with an ebony mask and believes, at other times, that he committed suicide when Lumumba was murdered. After her own suicide, it is revealed by her Jewish lover that, in reality, Sarah's father is married to a white whore. The material possessions he has are those which Sarah herself craved—European antiques, photographs of Roman ruins, walls of books, oriental carpets, and a white glass table on which he eats his meals. The pressures of being Black in America are the subject of this work. These pressures, in turn, have produced madness in this sensitive Black woman who has an identity problem as well as a problem with love, God, and parents.

In a second play by Kennedy, *The Owl Answers,* the racial identity problem is repeated.[30] The scenes, a New York subway, the Tower of London, a Harlem hotel room, and St. Peter's, are fantasies in the mind of the principal character, a Black woman named She Who Is. Her mother, a cook, was impregnated by a white man of English ancestry, who declared the child a bastard. But the child, now a woman, dreams about her white father's world. The English ancestors, whom she claims—Shakespeare, William the Conqueror, Chaucer, and Anne Boleyn—in rejecting her, jeer her. She cannot find her place in either the Black or white world.

Thus Black women in the plays of many Black playwrights receive varied treatment, and their images, for the most part, are positive. The women often have great moral strength. In contrast to many of the white-authored dramas in which Black women have appeared, usually as servants dedicated to the families for whom they work, in the plays of Black writers, these women's concerns are for what interests them, mainly their own families. In many of these plays it is their lives that are on stage. In Black-authored dramas depicting ghetto lifestyles, Black women hold on to life, however harsh it may be, and sometimes work for a better future. In the dramas written by women, except in the plays of Kennedy, Black women often look to the future with optimism. Even Childress' Julia Augustine's plans for a move to the North with her lover terminate only with his death. In the plays written by Black males, Black women's happiness or "completeness" in life depends upon strong Black men. Thus Black playwrights bring to their works their vision, however different, of what Black women are or what they should be. Missing, however, is a wealth of dramas with positive images of Black middle-class women, Black middle-class women who work to improve the quality of life for themselves, their families, their race—the Mary McLeod Bethunes, the Mary Church Terrells, and the unsung Black women who help to improve the world, if only a little.

NOTES

[1] *The Journal of Negro Education,* 2 (April 1933), 179-203.

[2] *The Escape; or, A Leap for Freedom* (Boston: R. F. Wallcut, 1858).

[3] *Rachel* (Boston: The Cornhill Company, 1920).

[4] "A Woman Playwright Speaks Her Mind," *Anthology of the American Negro in the Theatre: A Critical Approach,* ed. Lindsay Patterson (New York: Publishers Company, Inc., 1969), pp. pp. 75-79.

[5] *Masses and Mainstream,* 3 (October 1950), 34-47.

[6] *Black Theater,* ed. Lindsay Patterson (New York: Dodd, Mead and Company, 1971), pp. 135-174.

[7] *Wine in the Wilderness* (New York: Dramatists Play Service, Inc., 1969).

[8] *Wedding Band* (New York: Samuel French, Inc., 1972).

[9] *Black Theater,* ed. Lindsay Patterson, pp. 221-276.

[10] *Les Blancs: The Collected Last Plays of Lorraine Hansberry* (New York: Vintage Books, 1973), pp. 217-313.

[11] *Black Girl* (New York: Dramatists Play Service, Inc., 1971).

[12] *Black Drama Anthology*, ed. Woodie King and Ron Milner (New York: New American Library, 1971), pp. 89-145.

[13] *A Black Quartet* (New York: New American Library, 1970), pp. 37-114.

[14] *What the Wine-Sellers Buy* (New York: Samuel French, Inc., 1974).

[15] "Clara's Ole Man," *Five Plays by Ed Bullins* (Indianapolis: Bobbs-Merrill Co., 1968), pp. 249-282.

[16] "A Son, Come Home," *Five Plays by Ed Bullins*, pp. 185-213.

[17] *New Black Playwrights*, ed. William Couch, Jr. (Baton Rouge: Louisiana State University Press, 1968), pp. 155-216.

[18] *Black Theater*, ed. Lindsay Patterson, pp. 379-406.

[19] *New Plays from the Black Theatre*, ed. Ed Bullins (New York: Bantam Books, 1969), pp. 129-174.

[20] *The Duplex: A Black Love Fable* (New York: William Morrow and Company, Inc., 1971).

[21] *Scripts*, 1 (February 1972), 56-80.

[22] *Contemporary Black Drama*, ed. Clinton F. Oliver and Stephanie Sills (New York: Charles Scribner's Sons, 1971), pp. 365-380.

[23] "The Revolutionary Theatre," *Home* (New York: William Morrow and Company, 1966), pp. 211-213.

[24] *Four Black Revolutionary Plays* (Indianapolis: Bobbs-Merrill Company, 1969), pp. 17-39.

[25] *Four Black Revolutionary Plays*, pp. 1-15.

[26] See Sonia Sanchez' "The Bronx Is Next," *The Drama Review*, 12 (Summer 1968), 77-83 and Jimmy Garrett's "We Own the Night: A Play of Blackness," *Black Fire: An Anthology of Afro-American Writing*, ed. LeRoi Jones and Larry Neal (New York: William Morrow and Co., Inc., 1968), pp. 527-540.

[27] *Four Black Revolutionary Plays*, pp. 65-87.

[28] *Black World*, 19 (July 1970), 8-9.

[29] *Contemporary Black Drama*, ed. Clinton F. Oliver and Stephanie Sills, pp. 187-205.

[30] *Cities in Bezique* (New York: Samuel French, Inc., 1969), pp. 3-29.

## Cynthia Sutherland

SOURCE: "American Women Playwrights as Mediators and the Woman Problem," in *Modern Drama*, Vol. XXI, No. 3, September, 1978, pp. 319-36.

[*In the following essay, Sutherland argues that early twentieth-century American women playwrights openly addressed women's issues such as divorce, careers, and sexual expression, while women in the suffrage movement became notably more conservative about such concerns.*]

Ibsen's Nora shut the door of her "doll's house" in 1879. Among the generation of American women born in the 1870's and 1880's, Zona Gale, Zoe Akins, and Susan Glaspell all won Pulitzer Prizes. Rachel Crothers, the successful dramatist who wrote more than three dozen plays, characterized her own work as "a sort of Comédie Humaine de la Femme." In an interview in 1931 she said: "With few exceptions, every one of my plays has been a social attitude toward women at the moment I wrote it. . . . I [do not] go out stalking the footsteps of women's progress. It is something that comes to me subconsciously. I may say that I sense the trend even before I have hearsay or direct knowledge of it."[1] During a period in which most American playwrights confined their work to representations of the middle class, these women were distinctive because they created principal roles for female characters whose rhetoric thinly veiled a sense of uneasiness with what Eva Figes and others more recently have called "patriarchal attitudes."

By the turn of the century, the mostly "abolitionist" women who had originated the battle for suffrage in the 1840's and 1850's were either dead or retired, and a new generation of leaders was attempting to expand popular support through the use of muted political rhetoric which intentionally avoided controversy.[2] The majority of women resisted arguments advocating changes in sex roles on the grounds that their inherent femininity would be diminished and their homes threatened. In the *Ladies' Home Journal*, Jane Addams argued benignly that a woman who wanted to "keep on with her old business of caring for her house and rearing her children" ought to "have some conscience in regard to public affairs lying outside her immediate household."[3] The conciliatory strategy of feminist leaders like Addams and Carrie Chapman Catt exalted the family, motherhood, and domestic values, minimized conflicts between self-realization and inhibiting social conditions, and often disregarded the arguments of radical feminists who insisted that only basic alterations in the organization of the family and sexual relationships could effect substantive changes in women's lives.

For many members of audiences, political issues continued to be dissociated from personal lives in which an equator divided the world of human activity marking "homemaking" and "breadwinning" as hemispheres. In 1924, a study of a fairly large group of young girls indicated that a substantial number planned to choose marriage over a "career" and that few had developed alternative goals. Asked to "name the four heroines in history or fiction whom [they] would most like to resemble," only two of 347 chose women identified chiefly or even at all with feminist causes.[4] They elected, rather, to live vicariously through husbands and children, accepting the traditional sex-role differentiation in which "instrumental/task functions are assigned to males, and expressive/social functions to females."[5]

Glaspell, Akins, Gale, and Crothers chronicled the increasingly noticeable effects of free love, trial marriage, the "double standard," career, divorce, and war on women's lives. Public rhetoric generally subsumed private sexual rhetoric in the theatre during this period, and dramatic discourse tended to mediate conflicting views of women's "legitimate" place in society more often than it intensified dispute. Although the sector of life subtended by domesticity was being steadily decreased by technological and economic developments in the early years of the century, feminist leaders, artists, and housewives shared the common inability to suggest an alternative social structure through which discontent might be alleviated.[6] To the extent that female characters on the stage accepted the traditional sex role, a diminished state of consciousness manifested itself in language that avoided strong or forceful statements, evinced conformity, consisted of euphemism and question-begging,[7] and celebrated the processes which safely domesticated erotic pleasure.[8] As contemporary critics, we tend to be disappointed by portrayals of women who cannot express, much less resolve, their problems. Yet, here, precisely, I believe, is the reason for the popular success and the "critical" failure of many of these plays. The spectacle of dramatic characters conducting themselves in the ironic guise of people only half aware of conflicts between individuation and primary sex role has usually been interpreted as trivial, the result of mediocre artistry, rather than what it is—the theatrical encoding of a "genderlect," or to put it another way, a language that reflects the internalizing by members of society of a particular system of sex differentiation and values.

However, during the period before the thirty-sixth state ratified the Nineteenth Amendment in 1920, a significant number of plays did present exceptionally articulate female artists as figures incarnating the dilemma of people torn by the conflicting demands of sex role and career.[9] In *A Man's World* (National Theatre, Washington, D.C., October 18, 1909), Rachel Crothers's protagonist Frank Ware is a novelist who oversees a club for girls who "need another chance."[10] She has published anonymously a defense of women's rights which even her friends—themselves painters, writers, and musicians—agree is much too good to have been written by a woman. After accidentally discovering that her fiancé, Malcolm Gaskell, has fathered her adopted seven-year-old son (the deserted mother had been her friend and died in childbirth), she renounces him. Avoiding a facile reconciliation, Crothers chose rather to stress Frank's abhorrence of her lover's complacent refusal to acknowledge

responsibility for the deplorable consequences of his own sexual license. In the final curtain scene, their relationship is abruptly severed:

> FRANK. Oh, I want to forgive you. . . . tell me you know it was wrong—that you'd give your life to make it right. Say that you know this thing is a crime.
>
> GASKELL. No! Don't try to hold me to account by a standard that doesn't exist. Don't measure me by your theories. If you love me you'll stand on that and forget everything else.
>
> FRANK. I can't. I can't.[11]

In *He and She* (Poughkeepsie, 1911), Crothers again explored the dilemma of a woman who must decide between sex role and career, in this instance, motherhood or sculpting. Ann Herford surrenders the commission she has won in a national competition to her husband, Tom, who has been openly skeptical that his wife could do "anything for a scheme as big" as the project required for the contest. When he wins only the second prize, his ego is badly shaken, and he retrenches to the familiar rhetorical stance of chief breadwinner. Reconciliation comes only after Ann abandons her prize in response to the needs of her teenage daughter. Crothers, although she shows a woman conceding final "victory" to her primary sex role, allows her character to voice bitterness and disappointment:

> TOM. . . . you've not only beaten me—you've won over the biggest men in the field—with your own brain and your own hands; in a fair, fine hard fight. . . . there'll be times when you['ll] eat your heart out to be at work on it—when the artist in you will *yell* to be let out.
>
> ANN. I know. . . . And I'll hate you because you're doing it—and I'll hate myself because I gave it up—and I'll almost—hate—her . . . my heart has almost burst with pride—not so much that *I* had done it—but for all women. . . . then the door opened—and Millicent [their daughter] came in. There isn't any choice Tom—she's part of my body—part of my soul.[12]

Ann's uneasy capitulation to the obligations of motherhood is carefully orchestrated by the simplistic attitudes of two women who are in love with her husband's close friend, a partially caricatured "male chauvinist" hardliner; one woman accepts a promotion in her job rather than tolerate what she views as his suffocating demands, the other chases him because she believes that "all the brains a woman's got [are]—to make a home—to bring up children—and to keep a man's love."[13] That Tom and Ann might exchange roles, he taking over as parent temporarily while she carves her frieze, is outside the realm of dramatic choice, because, in Crothers's dialectical structure, the men and women are shown to be incapable of conceiving this as an alternative.[14] General expectations that a shift towards a more egalitarian society would lead to personal and social enfranchisement in the progressive era as middle-class women moved in the direction of greater self-consciousness are clearly undercut in the endings of Crothers's plays.[15]

A vastly more imaginative if less independent playwright, Susan Glaspell both directed and acted in her own plays. From 1913 until 1922, she worked with the Provincetown Players.[16] A sounding board for new ideas, the Provincetown group produced plays that sometimes spoofed feminist excesses, yet usually respected the seriousness of the "movement's" political aims.[17] In *Suppressed Desires* (Wharf Theatre, Provincetown, Summer, 1915),[18] Glaspell ridiculed a woman who nearly wrecks her marriage by testing psychoanalytic theories on her sister and husband, and in *Close the Book* (Playwright's Theatre, 1917), she poked fun at a liberated girl who naively insists, *"Hand on heart,"* that she is "not respectable."[19] In *Woman's Honor* (Playwright's Theatre, 1918), she presents a satiric sketch of the effects of the "double standard." A young man accused of murder refuses to provide himself with an alibi by identifying his married mistress. He is beleaguered by a bevy of volunteers, each of whom wants to sacrifice her own "honor" to save him by claiming that *she* has been the anonymous lover. The women are comic types with predictable opinions about female honor: "The Shielded One," "The Motherly One," "The Silly One," "The Mercenary One," and "The Scornful One."[20] The last of these expresses her resentment of society's definition of "woman's honor": "Did it ever strike you as funny that woman's honor is only about one thing, and that man's honor is about everything but that thing?" With amusing logic, she tells the prisoner that since "woman's honor means woman's virtue," the lady for whom he "propose[s] to die has no virtue" (p. 134). Caught in the midst of chatter, he resigns himself: "Oh, *hell, I'll plead guilty"* (p. 156), rather than be faced by another speechifying female.

But in her most famous play, *Trifles* (Wharf Theatre, Provincetown, Summer, 1916), Glaspell began to explore seriously the more violent psychological aspects of women trapped in loveless marriages. Minnie Wright has strangled her husband. The wives of the sheriff and a neighbor have come to her home to collect a few things to make her more comfortable in jail.[21] As their husbands search for evidence that would provide a motive, the women discover among Minnie's "trifles" a canary's carcass and decide to defy the law by concealing it, guessing that her husband "wrung—its neck. . . . Wright wouldn't like the bird—a thing that sang—She used to sing. He killed that, too" (p. 25). The neighbor expresses her regret: "I might have known [Minnie] needed help! I know how things can be—for women. . . . We live close together and we live far apart. We all go through the same things—it's all just a different kind of the same thing" (p. 27). As they leave, the women explain to the men who have ridiculed Minnie's "trifles" that she was going to "knot" her quilt, a subdued, ironic, and grisly reminder of the manner in which a stifled wife has enacted her desperate retaliation. In the theatre of the next decade, the

motifs of the caged bird and the lost singing voice were to become the hallmarks of numerous "domesticated" women who abandoned careers.

In *Trifles*, Glaspell had negotiated that portrayal of a woman's violent repudiation of her husband's narrow notion of sex role by removing her from the sight of the audience (a technique she later was to repeat in *Bernice* and *Allison's House*).[22] But the play in which she confronted most vehemently the sex-role imprisonment of women is *The Verge,* first performed by the Playwright's Theatre in its last season (November 14, 1921). Claire Archer rejects her daughter and murders her lover. Her insane passion to breed a fresh botanical species which she calls "Breath of Life," one which may be "less beautiful—less sound—than the plants from which [it] diverged,"[23] expresses her radical rejection of biological and cultural inheritance—she is identified as the "flower of New England . . . what came of men who made the laws that made . . . [the] culture" (pp. 18-19). She has divorced a "stick-in-the-mud artist and married—[a] man of flight" (p. 32), who she has hoped will "smash something," but who also has turned out to be baldly conventional. The son who had shared her vision of transcendence is dead. Driven by frustration and disappointment, in a terrifying scene, she strikes her daughter across the face with the roots of an "Edge Vine," believing that both the girl and the plant are incurable conformists. Her words echo horribly those of familiar mythic murderesses: "To think that object ever moved in my belly and sucked my breast" (p. 56). When the lover who has rejected her frenetic sexual advances returns because he wants to keep her "safe" from harm, she strangles him as a "gift" to the plant, choosing to break "life to pieces in the struggle" to cast free from traditional sex role. A demented Demeter, Claire has been mesmerized by an apocalyptic vision: "Plants . . . explode their species—because something in them knows they've gone as far as they can go. Something in them knows they're shut in. So [they] go mad—that life may not be imprisoned. Break themselves up—into crazy things—into lesser things, and from the pieces—may come one sliver of life with vitality to find the future. How beautiful. How brave. (p. 34) Glaspell's representation of a failed Goddess-Mother was treated respectfully by reviewers in England, but in this country it was largely misunderstood or ignored.[24]

Written a year earlier, another study of a woman's plight, Zona Gale's *Miss Lulu Bett,* opened at the Belmont Theatre on December 27, 1920 and subsequently won the Pulitzer Prize.[25] Like Rachel Crothers and Susan Glaspell, Zona Gale had come to New York from the Midwest and was sympathetic to feminist causes despite her mother's caveat to shun radical politics and women's groups—"I would let that mess of women alone!" she had advised her daughter.[26] The novel on which Gale had based her play had been immediately successful, and in eight days, she had hastily, though with considerable dramatic skill, adapted it for production.[27] Even though *Miss Lulu Bett* did not present a threatening subject (for "old maids" were commonly seen not as electing spinsterhood but as having had it thrust upon them by faithless lovers or deprivation),[28] strong critical pressure influenced Gale to alter the last act, in which, like Ibsen's Nora, Lulu walks out of the house in which she has been a virtual servant to become an independent woman.[29] Gale rewrote the last act so that it conformed more closely to her popular novel, which concluded with Lulu comfortably established as a respectable wife.[30] This story of a drab but resourceful and dry-witted woman—whom Fannie Hurst called a "shining star" reflected in "greasy reality"[31]—ran for 186 performances. Such capitulation to public opinion evident in the modification of the ending by a writer who had supported the Woman's Peace Union, the Woman's Peace Party (Wisconsin), Jane Addams and the Hull-House workers, and who later helped to write the Wisconsin Equal Rights Law,[32] has considerable significance. It anticipated the new style of mediation used by playwrights who continued to dramatize aspects of the "woman problem" in the 1920's.

After World War I and the extension of the franchise, the momentum towards fully equal status for women slowed considerably. One of Rachel Crothers's characters sees herself as an exception to what was to become an increasingly regressive trend: "I haven't slipped back one inch since the war. Most women who sort of rose to something then have slumped into themselves again, but I've gone *on*. My life gets much fuller and wider all the time. There's no room for men. Why, *why* should I give up my own personal life—or let it be changed in the slightest degree for a man?"[33] But the woman who speaks these somewhat fatuous lines will, during the course of the dramatic action, reveal her disingenuousness by seducing a member of the British upper class so that her "personal life" and career are, in fact, exchanged for marriage.

Statistics on employment indicate that the percentage of females in the total labor force had decreased from 20.9 in 1910 to 20.4 in 1920.[34] Among women, the proportion of the total college enrollment dropped-three of every four new professionals chose traditionally female-dominated fields, and the number of doctors decreased by nearly one-third. Female architects and lawyers continued at less than three percent, and attendance at professional schools increased only slightly.[35] When members of Pruette's test group were questioned, only thirty-two percent indicated that they would like to be successful *themselves* in "some chosen work"; the remainder opted for success "through" husband and family.[36] The choice between marriage and career continued to be polarized;[37] and the divorce rate rose steadily.[38] By 1929, Suzanne la Follette was to comment that "the traditional relations of the sexes is far from being reversed in this country, [but] . . . has shifted away enough to cause alarm among those to whom it seems the right and inevitable relation *because* it is conventional."[39] Many of the changes affecting women's lives were seen as detrimental to their femininity. George Jean Nathan opined that " . . . women more and more have ceased to be the figures of man's illusion and more and more have become superficially indistinguishable from man himself in

his less illusory moments. In sport, in business, in drinking, in politics, in sexual freedom, in conversation, in sophistication and even in dress, women have come closer and closer to men's level and, with the coming, the purple allure of distance has vamoosed."[40] The plays of this period characterize masculine responses that range from reactionary to adjustive but are rarely innovative. Crothers spoofs (or does she?) a gentleman's overreaction to a woman who aggressively courts him: " . . . it seems to be awfully important . . . nowadays to be a woman . . . I'm not criticizing. Men *are* totally unnecessary, I s'pose, except for breeding purposes. And we go on taking ourselves for granted in the same old relationships with women. Stupid of us, isn't it?"[41]

Early in the 1920's, the struggle against social oppression had shifted towards a rebellion against convention in which the manipulation of style was both means and end. The flapper was sometimes a flamboyant flouter, as Zelda Fitzgerald's life apparently proved, but she generally strayed only temporarily from acceptable patterns of conduct, because her values were essentially the same as those of her parents.[42] Cocktail in one hand and cigarette in the other, she made an avocational pretense of "rebellion" that was quite compatible with middle-class wisdom, as she mimicked the demands of earlier feminists for sexual equality.

The plays that Crothers wrote in the 1920's signal her own ambivalence toward the contrived stance of young women whose gold-plated philosophy was an amalgam of "free-thinking" writers like Ellen Key, Mona Cairn, Havelock and Edith Ellis. Like Congreve's Millamant, they were choosing to "dwindle into a wife" rather than persevere in a search for practical alternatives. Crothers's formulaic plot for flappers continued to have the staple elements described by Clara Claibourne Park in her study of the young women in Shakespeare's comedies: "Invent a girl of charm and intellect; allow her ego a brief premarital flourishing; make clear that it is soon to subside into voluntarily assumed subordination; make sure that it is mediated by love."[43] But Crothers's perspective is ironic, because she juxtaposes romantic courtship and the harsh antagonisms that often grow between marriage partners. The plays she wrote during these years strongly emphasized deteriorating sexual relationships over a period of time, thus undermining the power of the traditional plot to sustain communal custom through ritual reenactment. In *Mary the Third* (Thirty-ninth Street Theatre, February 5, 1925), the playwright presented three generations of women in the throes of choosing mates. The grandmother, Mary the First, traps a mate with flirtation in 1870; the mother, Mary the Second, yields to the proposal of her most vigorous but most unsuitable lover in 1897. These two women are seen as mere anachronisms by Mary the Third, in 1923, who fecklessly flaunts convention by insisting that she will choose her mate only after going off to the country on an experimental trip with two men and another woman to "live naturally and freely for two weeks—doing a thing we know in the bottom of our souls is *right,* and knowing perfectly well the whole town is going to explode with horror."[44] However, after only a few hours, Mary rationalizes her own lack of persistence, deciding to be "magnanimous" to the "deep prejudices" of her parents. She returns home. Fearful of being scolded, she and her brother hide and are horrified when they accidentally overhear their parents in a fight (reminiscent of Strindberg and foreshadowing Albee) that shaves off the thin skin concealing the bleeding tissue of their marriage. They hear their father tell their mother: "I'm flabbergasted at you. You seem to have lost what sense you did have. . . . I can't count on you. You aren't *there.* Sometimes I think you aren't the woman I married at all," and their mother's even more devastating reply: "And sometimes I think you're a man I *couldn't* have married. Sometimes I loathe everything you think and say and do. When you grind out that old stuff I could *shriek.* I can't breathe in the same room with you. The very sound of your voice drives me insane. When you tell me how right you are—I could strike you."[45] The fate of the marriage of Mary the Second is left unresolved at the conclusion. Even though Mary the Third has seen her mother's agonized entrapment and recognized its partial basis in her inability to earn an independent income, the daughter herself yields to the pressures of convention and enters marriage knowing just as little about her future husband as her grandmother and mother had known of theirs. Self-deceived, she has only partly digested the teachings of those writers who had argued for new kinds of marriages:[46] " . . . you *ought* to be able to [make your own living]. . . . I shall have my own money. I'll *make* it. I shall live with a man because I love him and only as long as I love him. I shall be able to take care of myself *and* my children if necessary. Anything else gives the man a horrible advantage, of course. It makes the woman a kept woman." (p. 92) Significantly, Mary has rejected an intelligent suitor who has warned her that "unless we change the entire attitude of men and women towards each other—there won't be any marriage in the future" (p. 96), and disregarded the fact that she is as ill-trained to support herself as her mother had been.

Crothers's plays signal changes in the treatment of the "woman problem" in the theatre during the twenties. The dialectic between the "new woman" and her "old-fashioned" relatives increasingly undercut conventional comic endings as reconciliation with older patterns became a hollow act. In a series of skillfully constructed one-act plays, Crothers continued her mordant comment by creating the character of a successful but shallow politician, Nancy Marshall, whose words expose a growing "tokenism" in the feminist views of many of her contemporaries:

> We women must be considerate of each other. If I am nominated I'm going to be awfully strong for that. . . . Men have made a mess of it—that's all. The idea that there aren't enough houses in New York to go 'round. What nonsense! . . . All those awful people with money who never had any before in their lives ought not to be allowed to crowd other people out. It's Bolshevism—just

> Bolshevism. . . . And not enough school teachers to go 'round. . . . People ought simply to be made to teach school, whether they want to or not. . . . I can't teach school. God knows I'd be glad to— and just show them if my hands weren't so full now of—I'm going to have awful circles under my eyes from standing so long.[47]

She contrasts her own knowledge of the nuances of political style with her female opponent's corpulent presence on the hustings: "She is so unpopular I should think she'd withdraw from sheer embarrassment . . . she is so unattractive. That's why the men have put her up . . . they're not afraid of her because they *know* she'll never get anywhere." (pp. 19-20) The sheer vacuousness of Nancy Marshall's political views elicits the response from her best friend that "Between you and her I'd vote for the best man going," and comes into sharp relief when compared to the comment of Mary Dewson, director of women's work for the Democratic party, after the election of 1932: " . . . we did not make the old-fashioned plea that our candidate was charming, . . . we appealed to the intelligence of the country's women."[48]

In a one-act sequel, after the same friend calls her an "old maid," Nancy Marshall suddenly comprehends the real "importance of being a woman" and hastily puts on a proper gown for the purpose of attracting a proposal of marriage. The customary import of the courtship scene is compromised, because the gentleman of her choice has been rejected, in an earlier scene, by Patti Pitt, a young woman who sees herself as public property (she is an entertainer!), but who actually has meant it when she said "It's power, . . . I've got it and I mustn't throw it away. . . . Any woman can get married, but I have something more important to do" (*The Importance of Being a Woman,* p. 77). The satiric treatment of both women by Crothers indicates that she was sensitive to the processes of rationalization used by women confronted by the choice between career and marriage, and had identified in those who opted for the latter an erosion of energy that was to continue to perpetuate, for a number of years in the theatre, the prominence of the "feminine mystique."

In the 1930's, Clare Boothe's satire, *The Women* (Ethel Barrymore Theatre, December 26, 1936), slashed at materialistic Park Avenue matrons, but also reflected an underside of the cultural milieu as female characters turned increasingly to divorces, affairs, and sometimes to temporary careers. In a late play by Crothers, *When Ladies Meet* (Royale Theatre, October 6, 1932), the scenario of the struggle of female characters for economic and moral independence receives less emphasis than the failing and futile relationships all the women have with the men. Mary, a writer, and Claire, a wife, are both in love with the latter's philandering husband. Mary has continued to reject the persistent courtship of good-natured Jimmie, a friend who puts women "in pigeon holes and tab[s] them—[according to] a *man's* idea of women."[49] Jimmie shrewdly arranges a meeting of mistress and wife at a mutual friend's country house. The play's title is drawn from a remarkable scene that occurs "when ladies meet" to discuss the fictional case in Mary's novel in which a mistress tells her lover's wife that she wants to live for a year with him on a trial basis. Claire's comments on the verisimilitude of Mary's novel barely conceal her response to her own situation:

> I suppose *any* married woman thinks the other woman ought to know enough not to believe a married man—if he's making love to her. . . . I happen to be married to a man who can no more help attracting women than he can help breathing. And of course each one thinks she is the love of his life and that he is going to divorce me. But he doesn't seem to . . . I can always tell when an affair is waning. He turns back to the old comfortable institution of marriage as naturally as a baby turns to the warm bottle . . . I'd say [to the mistress] *of course* something *new* is interesting. *Of course* I look the same old way—and sound the same old way—and eat the same old way and walk the same old way—*and so will you*—after awhile. I'd say *of course* I can understand his loving you—but are *you prepared to stand up to the job of loving him?* Most of the things you find so irresistible in him are terribly hard to live with. You must love him so abjectly that you're glad to play second fiddle just to keep the music going for *him*. (pp. 109-13)

When her husband unexpectedly blunders into the room, fiction becomes reality—true to Claire's prediction—he begs to return, but she rejects him with a newly discovered decisiveness: "You can't conceive that I *could* stop loving you. It happened in just one second—I think—when I saw what you'd done to [Mary]. . . . I'm not going *home—now—or ever*." (p. 135) Mary will continue to write and to live alone. The theme of the emotional consequences of both disintegrating marriages and the pursuit of careers had been introduced earlier in the play by their hostess, who diagnoses women's restlessness as due to a far-reaching lack of fulfillment in either institution: "Men mean a great deal more to women than women do to men. . . . I don't care *what* strong women—like Mary tell you about loving their work and their *freedom*—it's all *slush*. Women *have got to be loved*. That's why they're breaking out so. . . . They're daring to have lovers—good women—because they just *can't stand being alone*." (p. 64)

Crothers had managed to write, on the average, a play a year since 1904. The incipient thirty-year-long quietism in feminist activities produced by apathy, factionalism, and personal loneliness is evident in the uneasy resignation of her later female characters. The playwright's response to a reporter, in 1941, revealed her final alienation from feminist causes and repeated her earlier assertion that her plays had mirrored, *mutatis mutandis,* the social evolution of sex roles: "What a picayune, self-conscious side all this woman business has to it. . . . I've been told that my plays are a long procession reflecting the changing attitudes of the world toward women. If they are, that was completely unconscious on my part.

Any change like that, that gets on to the stage, has already happened in life. Even the most vulgar things, that people object to with so much excitement, wouldn't be in the theatre at all if they hadn't already become a part of life."[50]

In 1931, the Pulitzer Prize was given to Susan Glaspell, the first woman to win it in a decade.[51] In *Alison's House* (Civic Repertory Theatre, December 1, 1930), her last play, she again returned to the dramatic techniques she had used during her years with the Provincetown a decade earlier. Zoe Akins won the Prize, in 1935, for *The Old Maid* (Empire Theatre, January 7, 1935),[52] but her skillful dramatic adaptation (like Edith Wharton's novelette published eleven years earlier) is set back in time. Both prize-winning plays safely distanced controversial feminist issues by presenting women tethered by Edwardian proprieties rather than more immediately recognizable topical restraints. It is possibly worth pointing out that the plays for which American women have won Pulitzer Prizes deal essentially with the "old maid" figure in whom the threat of sex-role conflict is "neutralized," as did the near-winner, Lillian Hellman's *The Children's Hour* (Maxine Elliott Theatre, November 20, 1934), which dealt with the cruel ostracism of suspected lesbians.[53]

The efforts of women to understand and determine their own lives, their failure to develop effective strategies for the realization of personal gratification, their continuing attachment to the perimeters of capitalism were portrayed by Glaspell, Gale, Crothers, and Akins less as a passionate subjugation than as the restless sojourn of half-articulate captives in a land that seemed alien to them. Marriage continued to be the first choice and a career the second of most women, as their enrollment percentage in colleges continued to drop steadily from 40.3 in 1930 to 30.2 in 1950.[54] In the theatre, divorcees and professional women continued to be perceived as "threats" to the institution of marriage, because they personified women's fulfillment through chosen alternative social roles.[55] Not until the late 1950's would public attention again focus on the issues probed so searchingly by this generation of playwrights. Certainly, isolated expressions of "feminist" theatre, like Sophie Treadwell's *Machinal* (Plymouth Theatre, September 7, 1928), had continued, but they were generally short-lived, and for a quarter of a century, there was no reappearance of the serious concern with the "woman problem" that had characterized the work of America's women playwrights from the Midwest.

My comments have been limited to plays written by middle-class women who bring to issue kinship rules and incest taboos in which primary sex role determines generic restrictions for dramatic action. A thoroughgoing analysis would have included, among others, the ordinary females and heteroclites created by Clare Kummer, Rose Pastor Stokes, Alice Gerstenberg, Alice Brown, Sophie Treadwell, Rita Wellman, Neith Boyce, Lula Vollmer, Maurine Watkins, Charlotte Perkins Gillman, and Julie Herne. Nor have I mentioned Edward Sheldon, George

Middleton, Bayard Veiller, Sidney Howard, George Kelly, Eugene O'Neill, and S. N. Behrman, who were remarkably sensitive to the predicaments of female characters and deserve to be reevaluated in this light.

As theatre historians and critics, we must now attempt to refine our working lexicon. Beyond female roles dictated by kinship structures (e.g., wife, mother, daughter, sister, bride, mother-in-law, widow, grandmother), there exist other roles which are more or less independent (e.g., coquette, ingénue, soubrette, career woman, servant, shaman, witch, bawd, whore) as well as interdependent roles (e.g., the other woman, mulatto). Only by developing descriptive categories with some historical precision can we hope to account for both formulaic successes and changes in dramatic modes. A more accurate vocabulary for female "dramatis personae" could help us to understand the inter-relationships between the theatre and evolving social milieus in this and other periods.

### NOTES

[1] Interview with Henry Albert Phillips, March 15, 1931; Scrapbook III, p. 59. Quoted by Irving Abramson, "The Career of Rachel Crothers in the American Drama" (Ph.D. diss., University of Chicago, 1956), p. 193. Also see, Lois C. Gottlieb, "Obstacles to Feminism in the Early Plays of Rachel Crothers," *University of Michigan Papers in Women's Studies* I (June 1975), 71-84.

[2] *Cf.* Deborah S. Kolb, "The Rise and Fall of the New Woman in American Drama," *ETJ* 27 (1975), 149-60. Also see, William H. Chafe, *The American Woman: Her Changing Social, Economic, and Political Role, 1920-1970* (London and New York, 1972), pp. 3-22; Aileen S. Kraditor, *The Ideas of the Woman Suffrage Movement 1890-1920* (New York, 1965); William L. O'Neill, *Everyone Was Brave: A History of Feminism in America* (Chicago, 1969); June Sochen, *Movers and Shakers: American Women Thinkers and Activists, 1900-1970* ([Chicago], 1973).

[3] Jane Addams, "Why Women Should Vote," *Ladies' Home Journal* 27 (1910). Also see, *Democracy and Social Ethics* (New York, 1902), *passim*.

[4] Lorine Pruette, *Women and Leisure: A Study of Social Waste* (New York, 1924), pp. 123, 138, *passim*. Jane Addams was chosen once, Frances Willard twice. Pruette's figures actually do not indicate clearly if the same person chose both women, so that it is possible that three girls were involved.

[5] See David Tresemer and Joseph Pleck, "Sex-Role Boundaries and Resistance to Sex-Role Change," *Women Studies* 2 (1974), 72. Tresemer and Pleck acknowledge their indebtedness to T. Parsons and R. F. Bales's *Family, Socialization, and Interaction Process* (Glencoe, Ill., 1955). See also, Harriet Holter, *Sex Roles and Social Structure* (Oslo, 1970).

[6] A notable exception, Charlotte Perkins Gillman, had written original and pithy sociology in works like *Women and Economics* (1898), *The Home, Its Work and Influence* (1903), and *His Religion and Hers* (1923). However, in her plays, she relied heavily on "romance" to mitigate feminist political content. See, for example, *Three Women* (1911) and *Something to Vote For* (1911), published in *The Forerunner*.

[7] The "reduced state of consciousness" that is "favorable to political conformity" and its manifestation in the "decline of language" is elegantly described by George Orwell in "Politics and the English Language," in *A Collection of Essays by George Orwell* (Garden City, N.Y., 1957), pp. 162-77.

[8] My generalization here is based, of course, on Claude Lévi-Strauss's *The Elementary Structures of Kinship*, rev. ed., trans. Bell, Sturnes, and Needham (Boston, 1969) and Georges Betaille's *Death and Sensuality: A Study of Eroticism and Taboo* (New York, 1969).

[9] In Crother's earliest full-length play, *The Three of Us* (Madison Square Theatre, October 17, 1906), the heroine is an independent woman who breaks horses, runs a gold mine, and raises two orphaned younger brothers in California. Rhy McChesney goes alone at night to her would-be seducer's lodgings to ask that he release her from a promise of silence concerning a business deal. Discovered in a "compromising situation" by her future fiancé, she defends her honor, and her freedom to come and go as she wishes. The play's formulaic ending resolves problems on the basis of mutual faith.

[10] Arthur Hobson Quinn judges *A Man's World* to be "one of the most significant dramas of the decade." *A History of the American Drama from the Civil War to the Present Day*, rev. ed. (New York, 1936), 2: 52. Unless otherwise noted, dates of first performances are those listed in Quinn's "Bibliography and Play List." Also see, Phyllis Marschall Fergusson, "Women Dramatists in the American Theatre, 1901-1940" (Ph.D. diss., University of Pittsburgh, 1957).

[11] *A Man's World* (Boston, 1915), p. 112. A contemporary reviewer praised Crothers for facing the "consequences of the premises without hesitation or faltering." *The Nation* 90 (February 10, 1910), 146. Cf., Eleanor Flexner, *American Playwrights 1918-1938* (New York, 1938), p. 240.

[12] *He and She*, in *Representative American Playwrights*, ed. Arthur Hobson Quinn, 7th rev. ed. (New York, 1953), p. 928. The play was also produced as *The Herfords* (Plymouth Theatre, January 12, 1912). It was revived in New York (The Little Theatre, February 12, 1920). Significant revisions, in Crothers's handwriting, appear in the typescript in the New York Public Library.

[13] *Ibid.*, p. 916. In his review of a performance in New York, Alexander Wollcott aptly observed that "*He and*

*She* seems peopled less with folks than with embodied points of view, and the play seems less a dramatic story than a symposium." *New York Times* (February 13, 1920), 16: 3.

[14] Sixteen years later, Crothers's play *Venus* (Masquerade Theatre, December 26, 1927) presented people on an interplanetary flight reversing their masculine and feminine characteristics under the influence of a compound. The play folded (not surprisingly) after only eight performances. See Abramson, p. 378. Brooks Atkinsons's review (*New York Times* [December 26, 1927], 23: 26) suggests a number of reasons why the play failed. No one has located the play text.

[15] Heywood Broun denounced the ending when the play was finally acted in New York: "The play espouses a side of the feminist question with which we are in the most complete disagreement. We have always found that the soup tastes just the same whether it is opened with loving care or by the hired help. Nor are we convinced that young daughters tend to become entangled in unfortunate love affairs the instant a mother begins to paint a picture or deliver a series of lectures or write short stories for the magazines." *New York Tribune* (February 13, 1920), 11. Although Broun's point is one with which today's feminists might well agree, a glance at the headline on the front page reveals a political context for his stance: "Arizona Ratifies Suffrage Amendment, Is the 31st State, Only 5 More Needed."

[16] Henrietta Rodman's Little Theatre and the Washington Square Players had been performing in Greenwich Village since 1912. For an account of feminist activity in the Village, see June Sochen, *The New Woman: Feminism in Greenwich Village, 1910-1920* ([Chicago], 1972).

[17] Henrietta Rodman, however, was ruffled by Floyd Dell's comic treatment of women's suffrage in *What Eight Million Women Want,* and called a meeting of the Liberal Club to protest it. See Dell's *Homecoming* (New York, 1933), pp. 260-66; and Sochen, *The New Woman,* p. 85. Crothers shared Glaspell's more relaxed view of what was fair game for the comic artist: "Why on earth shouldn't the same person write a comedy satire on advanced feminism and a serious play which is based on the plea for a double standard. . . . Surely the most militant feminist can't fail to see that if some of her radical ideas were at once adopted and acted upon they'd be very funny and would produce chaotic results." *New York City Sun* (January, 1914), quoted by Abramson, p. 216.

[18] Glaspell had read some of Freud's works after his visit to the United States in 1909 had "literally caused an earthquake in public opinion." Oscar Cargill, *Intellectual America: Ideas on the March* (New York, 1941), p. 601. Another "Village" manifestation of contemporary awareness of Freudian theory was Alice Gerstenberg's expressionistic play *Overtones* (Washington Square Players, 1915), in which two women are portrayed simultaneously as primitive selves and socialized personae.

[19] Susan Glaspell, *Plays* (Boston, 1920), p. 84. All subsequent quotations from her work will be identified in the text in parentheses.

[20] The part was acted by Ida Rauh, who was arrested for distributing birth control pamphlets with Rose Pastor Stokes. See Sochen, *The New Woman,* pp. 65-66; also the *Boston American* (May 6, 1916). In 1916, the first birth control clinic had opened in New York. See David Kennedy, *Birth Control in America: The Career of Margaret Sanger* (New Haven, 1970).

[21] The theme of imprisonment appears again in Glaspell's first full-length play, *Bernice* (Playwright's Theatre, March 21, 1919), in *The Inheritors* (Playwright's Theatre, March 21, 1921), and in *Alison's House* ( (Civic Repertory Theatre, December 1, 1930).

[22] *Enemies,* written by Glaspell's friends Neith Boyce and Hutchins Hapgood for the Provincetown Players in the same year, presents a clash between husband and wife which ends in an uneasy truce rather than murder, but which confronts an audience with the unmediated raw threat of the wife's version of a Shavian "life force": "You, on account of your love for me, have tyrannized over me, bothered me, badgered me, nagged me, for fifteen years, . . . Men and women are natural enemies, like cat and dog—only more so. They are forced to live together for a time, or this wonderful race couldn't go on. . . . The shock and flame of two hostile temperaments meeting is what produces fine children." Neith Boyce and Hutchins Hapgood, *Enemies,* in *The Provincetown Plays,* edd. George Cram Cook and Frank Shay (Cincinnati [1921]), p. 130. The play, in addition to its obvious debt to *Man and Superman* (1903), dramatizes a marital argument less vicious than but remarkably similar to the one shown by Strindberg in *The Dance of Death* (1901) and its dramatic "progeny."

[23] *The Verge: A Play in Three Acts* (Boston, 1922), p. 52.

[24] The Berg Collection in the New York Public Library is the repository of reviews which the playwright had received through a clipping service.

[25] The premiere had been presented by David Belasco at Sing Sing, December 26th, on a portable stage. See Jane F. Bonin, *Prizewinning American Drama* (Metuchen, N. J., 1973), p. 8.

[26] August Derleth, *Still Small Voice: The Biography of Zona Gale* (New York, 1940), p. 100. "Zona was already at that time heart and soul with the feminist movements of her time, and was particularly interested in suffrage for women, going so far as to speak on the subject on several occasions to gatherings." (p. 101)

[27] The other play under consideration was a domestic comedy by Frank Craven, *The First Year.* The jury, consisting of Hamlin Garland, William Lyon Phelps, and Richard Burton elected to waive the requirement that the

play be an "original" American drama. Garland wrote to Frank Fackenthal: "Feeling that it would be a handsome thing to give the prize to a woman, Burton will join Phelps and me in giving the award to *Lulu Bett*." John Hohenberg, *The Pulitzer Prizes: A History of the Awards in Books, Drama, Music, and Journalism Based on the Private Files Over Six Decades* (New York, 1974), pp. 50-1. Also see, Harold P. Simonson, *Zona Gale* (New York, 1962), p. 79.

[28] See Dorothy Deegan, *The Stereotype of the Single Woman in American Novels* (New York, 1951; rpt. 1969).

[29] Ludwig Lewisohn, "Native Plays," *The Nation* 112 (February 2, 1921), 189. Lewisohn preferred the original ending, which, he argued, had "turned [Gale's] original fable into a play and had given it a weightier and severer ending. . . . the most inevitable that we recall in the work of any American Playwright."

[30] In the revised third act, Lulu's "husband's" missing first wife is discovered to have died, a circumstance making his second marriage legal. In the novel, Lulu had married another less attractive but more stable suitor. See Simonson, pp. 85-6.

[31] *Ibid.*, p. 82; letter from Fannie Hurst to Zona Gale, n. d.

[32] *Ibid.*, pp. 64-5; Derleth, pp. 45-6, 211, 261. Also see, Zona Gale, "What Women Won in Wisconsin," *The Nation* 115 (August 23, 1922), 184-85.

[33] *The Importance of Being a Woman,* in *Six One-Act Plays* (Boston, 1925), p. 71.

[34] Chafe, p. 53.

[35] *Ibid.*, p. 58. Also see Elizabeth K. Nottingham, "Toward an Analysis of the Effects of Two World Wars on the Role and Status of Middle-Class Women in the English Speaking World," *American Sociological Review* 12 (1947), 666-75; Mabel Newcomer, *A Century of Higher Education* (New York, 1959).

[36] Pruett, pp. 132-33. Also see, O'Neill, pp. 251-52.

[37] See Margaret Mead, "Sex and Achievement," *Forum* 94 (1935), 301-3.

[38] See Sochen, pp. 27-8, 102.

[39] Quoted in Anne Firor Scott, ed., *Women in American Life: Selected Readings* (Boston and New York, 1970), p. 130.

[40] "Clinical Notes," *American Mercury* 19 (1930), 242. *Cf.* H. L. Mencken's *In Defense of Women* (Garden City, N.Y., [1922]), a clever plea for old-fashioned "femininity": " . . . all of the ladies to [*sic*] take to this political immolation seem to me to be frightfully plain. . . . there were not five women at either national convention who

could have embraced me in camera without first giving me chloral." (p. 132)

[41] *The Importance of Being a Woman,* p. 87.

[42] Nancy Milford, *Zelda* (New York, 1970); Sochen, pp. 98-9; Chafe, pp. 94-8.

[43] "As We Like It: How a Girl Can Be Smart and Still Popular," *American Scholar* 42 (1973), 275.

[44] *Mary the Third* (Boston, 1925), pp. 35-6. Crothers puts a damper on her daring when Mary specifies that their relationships will be platonic.

[45] The quarrel between the father and mother had been published earlier as a one-act play with the title *What They Think.* Ludwig Lewisohn saw *Mary the Third* as "a blanket attack on marriage and nearly everything connected with it." *The Nation* 116 (March 7, 1923), 278.

[46] See William L. O'Neill, *Divorce in the Progressive Era* (New Haven, 1967); Sidney Ditzion, *Marriage, Morals and Sex in America* (New York, 1953; rept. 1969).

[47] *The Importance of Being Clothed,* in *Six One-Act Plays,* pp. 18-19.

[48] *Buffalo Evening News* (January 12, 1933) clipping, Dewson Papers, SL, Box 1; quoted by Chafe, p. 40.

[49] *When Ladies Meet* (New York, 1932), p. 13.

[50] Interview with Catherine Hughes, "Women Playmakers," *New York Times Magazine* (May 4, 1941), 10, 27. Zoe Akins, Rose Franken, and Lillian Hellman are quoted as sharing these opinions.

[51] "There was more disagreement than usual over the award . . . [for] *Alison's House* is what drama critics most frequently describe as a literary play." Burns Mantle, ed., *The Best Plays of 1930-31 and the Year Book of the Drama in America* (New York, 1931), pp. 222-23. Also see, Hohenberg, pp. 105-6.

[52] Like the other playwrights, Akins had Midwest origins. Born in the "heart of the Ozarks," Humansville, Missouri, in 1886, she had travelled widely. Between 1916 and 1947, she produced well over two dozen plays and filmscripts.

[53] See Richard Moody's *Lillian Hellman* (New York, 1972), Chapter IV, pp. 36-61, for a full account of the dramatist's imaginative adaptation of William Roughead's story "Closed Doors; or, The Great Drumsheugh Case" from his collection of crime stories in *Bad Companions.*

[54] Newcomer, p. 46.

[55] *Cf.* Donald Nelson Koster, "The Theme of Divorce in American Drama, 1871-1939," (Ph.D. diss., University of Pennsylvania, 1942).

**Susan L. Carlson**

SOURCE: "Two Genres and Their Women: The Problem Play and the Comedy of Manners in the Edwardian Theatre," in *The Midwest Quarterly,* Vol. XXVI, No. 4, Summer, 1985, pp. 413-24.

[*In the following essay, Carlson considers whether the Edwardian problem play and comedy of manners contain relevant truths despite their sexual stereotypes.*]

Mrs. Lucy Dane, the "problem" in Henry Arthur Jones's *Mrs. Dane's Defense,* is a typical Edwardian problem-play woman. She is intelligent, graceful, sensitive, and sensual. She has a dangerous, though exciting ebullience and an admirable tenacity. And she is just enough unacceptably déclassé so that audiences can pity her while accepting her final banishment as a necessary relief. The conflicting response of other characters to her type is also typical. On the one hand, and most prominently, Sir Daniel Carteret righteously and religiously condemns her for her affront to moral categories. Lady Eastney, on the other hand, sympathizes with Mrs. Dane and seethes at the injustice of a double standard that condemns "problem" women like Mrs. Dane. These antithetical responses understandably have opened the door to similarly irreconcilable critical responses. Critics who decry problem plays like *Mrs. Dane* complain of the outdated, almost laughable rigidity of a Sir Daniel; critics who defend problem plays praise the enduring human flexibility the plays offer in a Lady Eastney.

Who is right? Do problem plays endorse the preachings of Sir Daniel or the tolerance of Lady Eastney? Are they lifeless, laughable period pieces or can they still be viable social commentary?

To answer these questions and explain the paradoxical responses, I want to dissect the Edwardian problem play along side its contemporary comedies of manners. It is easy to overlook how much the two types of play share—their attention to sexual stereotypes and double standards and their heady atmospheres of social art and artifice—because the two conclude so differently. That is, in comedies of manners, society is a school in which women learn about themselves and gain power; and in problem plays, this same society not only denies women power, but also destroys them. Yet these nearly opposite endings emphasize differences that are not as significant as the similarities between the two dramatic worlds. In both, social portraits are distorted by conflicting responses to social problems. Problems are studied in both and solved in neither.

Consider first how in *Mrs. Dane* Jones attempts to balance the two very different responses his problem "Mrs. Dane" elicits. As I began by suggesting, Lucy Dane is the stereotypical "problem" woman. With her conniving she has lured away young Lionel's heart, attracted the attention of every man in the play (excepting only butlers), gained the sympathy of good women, and almost fooled the great Sir Daniel. But her trickery marks her moral weakness, not any social cleverness. She has broken Sir Daniel's hard rules by having an affair and an illegitimate baby with a married man and cannot be tolerated at Sunningwater. As society's sanctioned judge and jury, the formidable Sir Daniel uses absolutes to brand her "wrong," and others "right."

Nevertheless, as Jones intends, we retain a measure of sympathy for Mrs. Dane, a result of the double standard she suffers from. The similarities between her past and Sir Daniel's are striking; he was once in love with a married woman and made plans to run off with her, plans she broke, not he. Striking too are the nearly opposite social attitudes to the two cases of indiscretion. Sir Daniel has no qualms about telling his story; he tells it, in fact, to the woman he wants to marry, *to convince her that he's a good, loving man.* Mrs. Dane, on the other hand, maintains a false identity out of a well-founded fear of revealing her past. Through Lionel and Lady Eastney especially, Jones registers his abhorence of the double standard that condemns Mrs. Dane while letting Sir Daniel prosper. But Jones also accepts the double standard. The "problem" in this play is clear; a transgressing woman is caught in the bind of a harsh double standard. One response (ultimately the one Jones favors) to the problem is equally clear; the double standard is unfair, but it is the best society has, the accepted social convention people have agreed to live by. Mrs. Dane is not a solution to the "woman problem" and offers none. As she cowers under the rules, she accepts Sir Daniel's moralistic, rigid world. She remains a problem.

A possible solution to the "woman problem" *is,* however, outlined in Lady Eastney. She is everything Mrs. Dane is supposed to be, but is not: a graceful, charming, intelligent, sensitive, and wise widow. Like Mrs. Dane's, her life is a calculated response to a society where the ideal is upheld that appearances and manners are true indicators of individual worth. And for Lady Eastney, the mannered world does work as a flexible yet moral one where witty conversation and occasional masks are gracious and successful ways to deal with others while protecting one's vulnerabilities. Lady Eastney is very much like the comedy of manners heroine who glides successfully and thoughtfully through her dangerous world. Both Lady Eastney and Mrs. Dane have gained a social power by learning to convert an awareness of double standards to indirect control. But the fact that Lady Eastney has not transgressed makes all the difference in her exercise of power and our attitude to it. What has deteriorated to lying and conniving for Mrs. Dane remains studied, controlled, and graceful interaction for Lady Eastney. Not only has Lady Eastney accepted the existence of the double standard, but she has also learned to use it to her advantage. And at the end of the play, for example, she brilliantly displays her power over people and events. By remaining in the system and playing by the rules, she gains the chance to triumph, she gains the opportunity to condemn the double standard and its disastrous effect on Mrs. Dane, and she retains about her an aura—what amounts to a social armour—that promises she *could* change things. In this problem play about women and a double standard, she represents much more of a solution to the "woman problem" than Mrs. Dane can. We are not to accept her answers, however. She is to act as a palliative to lure those of us who agree with her into accepting Sir Daniel's very different conclusions.

While *Mrs. Dane,* vintage 1900, houses these two contradictory responses to the "woman problem" at the beginning of the Edwardian decade, Maugham's *Penelope,* Pinero's *Mid-Channel,* and Granville-Barker's *The Madras House* illustrate similar dramatic tensions at the end of the decade. *Penelope* and *Mid-Channel* are evidence of the continuing dissonance of *Mrs. Dane's* antithetical responses to the woman problem. *The Madras House* towers above them all as a breakthrough revision of the problem play, its women, and its world.

W. S. Maugham's *Penelope* is a light, bright, frollicksome comedy of manners. It is not divorced from the social relevance of a play like *Mrs. Dane,* however, nor from its problem women; its social commentary is simply more oblique. This comedy, like most, forces a crisis on its characters, in effect taunting them to use their time-tested system of rules and manners to cope with rule-breakers and role reversals. Its issues are those of the problem play: how does society deal with transgressors? how do people deal with problematic social codes? how does one cope with a double standard? how are matters of right and wrong determined? Its answers are those of Lady Eastney: some ingenuity and a generous dose of accommodation can almost always set things right.

Maugham's titular character, Penelope, faces the dilemma of dealing with a philandering husband. While she rushes to the conclusion that divorce is her salvation, her father, Professor Golightly, shows her the comic way back to happiness in saving her marriage, using social rules and codes that one need not break since they can so conveniently be bent. If Penelope had divorced Dickie, her action would be an acknowledgment that the system does fail, and the play would conceivably enter the realm of the problem play. But her father's social wisdom saves Pen from that fate and preserves a comic realm.

Like *Mrs. Dane's Defense,* this play studies social rights and wrongs. When Professor Golightly suggests to Pen that she play along with Dickie's affair, both Pen and Mrs. Golightly charge him with immorality, presumably because his advice counsels the breaking of rules. However, the rest of the play proves that their charges are irrational and that Professor Golightly has not only pragmatic but also very moral solutions to social dilemmas. He shows his family that accommodating supposed immoralities is a very moral art, a key to comedy's resilience.

As Maugham's spokesperson in this study of Edwardian value systems, Professor Golightly teaches Pen, Mrs. Golightly, and eventually Dickie that, for all their protestations, they do *not* believe in a system of well-defined rules. Rather, they believe in somewhat elastic social codes which can let them welcome back Dickie when he sees he has been wrong, and which can allow them to accept and live with the human frailty that could next time be their own.

Maugham intensifies his message about the need for social flexibility by making Pen—a woman—its main receptor. In this comic world as in the world of the problem play, women are most likely to need an understanding of social mores, because in a system full of sexual double standards they are most likely to suffer. As Lady Eastney shows and Pen learns, an added knowledge often gives women a way to by-pass double standards and offers them a makeshift equality. Yet although Pen gains the upper hand in her marriage, there is a paradox in her reconciliation with Dickie. To assert her new power over Dickie she must leave him at the end of the play. And to keep him, Pen must cease to be only herself and wear the masks of "half a dozen different women." Even with her new understanding, Pen, like Mrs. Dane and Lady Eastney, will continue to live in a world where she is at an automatic disadvantage as a woman.

In the end, for all its promise as a purveyor of solutions to women's problems, this comedy—like *Mrs. Dane*—stops short of endorsing its pragmatic, flexible solutions. Pen controls her life and warms us with laughter as Mrs. Dane and Lady Eastney could not. But the seemingly joyous end of Maugham's play is compromised by Pen's step back to the unresolved double standards of marriage, in her acceptance of a social system she suffers in. Although *Penelope* is not about the "woman problem" in the obvious way *Mrs. Dane* is, it shows how useless even the compromise of comedy is to solve "woman" problems. We do not suspect Professor Golightly's good-natured pronouncements in the same way we suspect Sir Daniel's, but our lack of suspicion should not blind us to the way this play, like *Mrs. Dane,* undermines its own criticism. For all of its talk about social change and moral flexibility, this play counsels acceptance of the status quo. It is simply less ashamed than a problem play to admit it. Maugham shows that simple comedy is not the way out of the self-defeating paradox of the problem play.

In A. W. Pinero's *Mid-Channel,* these paradoxical attitudes reappear in their problem-play form. Centering on the Blundell marriage, this is a mechanical play full of dated melodrama, hideous images, and predictable characters. When Theo and Zoe Blundell separate and each conducts a love affair, the double standard becomes the issue of their failing marriage, and the play. Zoe may take her friend Leonard Ferris as her lover out of desperation and loneliness, but in doing so she still breaks the rules. When she returns from her European tour in Act II, her body shows signs of her transgression. She is "wan and there are dark circles around her eyes."

Theo has suffered too with his "bad color." However, his suffering is comparable to Zoe's only until their friend

Peter Mottram brings the two sinners together. Theo confesses his affair and painlessly clears his conscience; much like Sir Daniel, he uses his confession *to prove his love.* In turn, he perfunctorily asks Zoe to confess, assuming that she'll have nothing to admit. He is unable to accept it when she does. *From* her he expects accommodation; *for* her he has only hard, unbending rules: "it's impossible for us ever to live under the same roof again under *any* conditions. . . . I couldn't stoop to that." Like Mrs. Dane and Pen, Zoe is the victim of a double standard.

The end result of the rules Theo pronounces is Zoe's suicide. Realizing that she is not a fit wife for Theo and certainly too tarnished for young Leonard, Zoe disposes of herself. Pinero has presented the "problem" of a young woman caught in the double standard, but he has not solved it any more than Jones did. Even his echo of the comic voice in Peter Mottram is more destructive than comforting. Like *Mrs. Dane, Mid-Channel* paradoxically exposes, indicts, and then accepts a society which bases its sexual relationships on a double standard.

Despite their better intentions, Jones and Pinero signal us in their problem plays that no alternative to the sad end for women like Mrs. Dane and Zoe exists. Lady Eastney and Peter Mottram remain as spectres of comic solutions neither the authors nor their characters can fully accept, but *Penelope* suggests how finally fruitless even their solutions are. Only in *The Madras House* does Harley Granville-Barker show that the alternatives his fellow authors flirt with but always reject could work, but perhaps only in a changed world and a changed drama. Recognizing the paradox that stymies the others, he begins to move beyond it.

While *The Madras House* is ostensibly about Philip Madras's move from industrial mogul to civil servant, Philip's most important role is to act as tour-guide for our journey through an Edwardian world obsessed with defining its changing sexual roles. There is no "problem woman," but through its groupings of women on stage, the play makes several clear, condemning statements about the way Edwardian society treats its women. In Act I the six grown, unmarried Huxtable sisters are a haunting reminder of the pitiable uselessness of unmarried upper-middle-class women. The tenacious wives and lonesome lovers of Act II and the ghostly living mannequins of Act III further documents the range of problematic roles Edwardian women fill. Curiously, the men in the play, not such sympathetic women, do the talking about the "problem" all of these women represent.

Constantine Madras defines the problems of Edwardian womanhood, castigating his fellow men throughout Act III for allowing women to be no more than sex objects. His solution to the problem is a hard-to-swallow sexist escape to his Mohammedan lifestyle where women admittedly are domestic objects. Yet his observations remain as undeniable as they are lucid. Unlike Sir Daniel, who ended up living a paradox, Constantine acknowledges

the double standard for what it is and brazenly but honestly takes advantage of it. Constantine pinpoints Edwardian hypocrisy about women. His son Philip does something about it.

Sensitive to the nuances of the woman question, Philip realizes how the objectification of women his father decries is the result of men's social dominance, and in the course of the play he offers his support to the various women suffering from their dependence on men—his Huxtable cousins, his mother, Miss Yates, and his wife Jessica. Yet during the long, discursive third act he is largely silent, seemingly unresponsive to his father's perorations. His silence is not acquiescence, however, but contemplation, the results of which he expresses in Granville-Barker's experimental fourth act.

Acts I through III are Granville-Barker's complex statement of the "woman problem." His statement *includes* the range of failed Edwardian dramatic answers we've seen bounded by Pen's compromise and Zoe's suicide. In Act IV, Philip searches for a solution to the problem beyond the ineffective accommodation of his comic predecessors, Lady Eastney, Professor Golightly, Pen and Peter, as he considers social change, a solution to a problem.

In his final conversation with Jessica in Act IV, Philip extends his play-long trail-blazing search for a world free of double standards to his own marriage. Unlike his predecessors in the drama, he looks for a solution which changes the existence of both women *and* men. First, Philip realizes that to clear the way for such change he must give up the mannered, cultured world so dear to him. He must deny a world premised on the rules of *Mrs. Dane's Defense* or *Mid-Channel* or *Penelope.* Second, he realizes that women will have to pay a price for the change they need, as he warns his wife: "There's a price to be paid for free womanhood, I think . . . and how many of you ladies are willing to pay it?" The play ends with Jessica agreeing to meet him "halfway" to build a new society with the egalitarian rules Philip describes: "And I want an art and a culture that shan't be just a veneer on savagery . . . but it must spring in good time from the happiness of a whole people." This utopia is no *fait accompli,* of course, as Granville-Barker's intentionally tentative ending reminds us with Jessica's witness to a tenacious double standard and the author's concluding words that "there is no end to the subject." Yet for the first time, social change is a viable alternative. Theatrically, Granville-Barker's final act may be weak, but its theoretical conversation confronts and dissects the paradox of social attitudes that rendered other similar plays gutless.

Granville-Barker labels his innovative play a "comedy." But it rarely resembles the form of comedy in *Penelope* or the comic tone of Lady Eastney. Neither is it a problem play in the Jones-Pinero tradition. Granville-Barker has realized that to find a dramatic world free from the double standard strangling men and women in problem plays and comedies, he must find a form—as well as a content—that questions the status quo. In three acts of self-conscious study of the antithetical responses to "problem" women in both problem plays and comedies, he clears the way for the refreshing open-endedness of his final act. In *Mrs. Dane's Defense* and *Mid-Channel* personal tragedy was the result of unbendable rules, yet the rules remained intact. In *Penelope,* the comic atmosphere was right for social questioning, but the results of that questioning were circumscribed by the very accommodation that is comedy's strength. In problem plays as in comedies a play's ending returns us to established social order and belief. Only Granville-Barker pens the social commentary that his fellow Edwardian playwrights set out to write, because he consciously rejects the inherent limits both the problem play and the comedy of manners impose on women characters.

Problem plays by both Jones and Pinero and comedies by Maugham have not often been revived in the last 70 years. Ironically, Granville-Barker's plays, which never enjoyed the initial popular success of the others, have much more potential for our contemporary stage. *The Madras House* was, in fact, done in London in 1977-78. Because they defy not only Edwardian standards but also Edwardian dramatic forms, Granville-Barker's plays have the potential of explaining to us our own social problems and revolutions, not just Edwardian ones. "Problem women" do not exist for us as they did for the Edwardians, but their problems of combatting a stolid social order do. For the "problem women" of the problem play and their sisters in comedy we can extend our sympathy from a comfortable distance. We are asked to do no more; solutions are implied in the statements of the problems. But faced with the "problem women" of Granville-Barker, we are challenged to join in the fray. We want to do so because there is hope of change.

---

# FURTHER READING

## Anthologies

Showalter, Elaine, ed. *Women's Liberation and Literature.* New York: Harcourt Brace Jovanovich, Inc., 1971, 338 p.
    Contains selections of fiction, poetry, drama, and nonfiction that have dealt with the issue of women's rights and suggests topics for classroom discussion and research writing.

## Secondary Sources

Ackley, Katherine Anne, ed. *Misogyny in Literature: An Essay Collection.* New York: Garland Publishing, Inc., 1992, 393 p.
    Examines misogyny in literature through history and across various genres, including poetry, science fiction, and horror.

Bell, Roseann P., Bettye J. Parker, and Beverly Guy-Sheftall, eds. *Sturdy Black Bridges: Visions of Black Women in Literature.* Garden City, N.Y.: Anchor Books, 1979, 422 p.
    Essay collection focusing on writings by and about black women; includes selections from poetry and fiction.

Boos, Florence, and Lynn Miller, eds. *Bibliography of Women and Literature.* 2 vols. New York: Holmes and Meier, 1989, 439 p. and 342 p.
    Bibliography of works by and about women from 600 A.D. to 1975.

Bradham, Margaret C. "Barbara Pym's Women." *World Literature Today* 61, No. 1 (Winter 1987): 31-37.
    Argues that Pym's writing deserves greater exposure and that critics who have focused on Pym as a feminist author or a modern Jane Austen have misinterpreted Pym's female characters.

Chessman, Harriet S. "Women and Language in the Fiction of Elizabeth Bowen." *Twentieth Century Literature* 29, No. 1 (Spring 1983): 60-85.
    Locates the identities of Bowen's female characters within their use of language and their place in the narrative.

Cornillon, Susan Koppelman, ed. *Images of Women in Fiction: Feminist Perspectives.* Ohio: Bowling Green University Popular Press, 1972, 399 p.
    Collection of essays covering various feminist issues in literature.

Deegan, Dorothy Yost. *The Stereotype of the Single Woman in American Novels: A Social Study with Implications for the Education of Women.* New York: King's Crown Press, 1951, 252 p.
    Examines American novels for their "sociopsychological content" regarding single women and women's education.

Féral, Josette. "Writing and Displacement: Women in Theatre," translated by Barbara Kerslake. *Modern Drama* XXVII, No. 4 (December 1984): 549-63.
    Attempts to analyze feminine discourse in plays written by women.

Fernando, Lloyd. *"New Women" in the Late Victorian Novel.* University Park: Pennsylvania State University Press, 1977, 168 p.
    Uses Victorian social history and the history of the emancipation movement to analyze liberated female characters in Victorian fiction.

Foster, Jeannette. *Sex Variant Women in Literature.* Baltimore: Diana Press, 1956, 420 p.
    Examines depictions of lesbians in literature through history.

Gasiorowska, Xenia. *Women in Soviet Fiction, 1917-1964.* Madison: University of Wisconsin Press, 1968, 288 p.

Surveys portrayals of women in Soviet fiction; includes a glossary and bibliography.

Gottlieb, Lois C., and Wendy Keitner. "Images of Canadian Women in Literature and Society in the 1970's." *International Journal of Women's Studies* 2, No. 6 (November-December 1979): 513-27.
> Contends that Canadian literary and media images of women in the 1970s were essentially adversarial and "hostile."

Guggenheim, Michel, ed. *Women in French Literature.* Saratoga, Calif.: Anma Libri, 1988, 242 p.
> Collection of essays that examine depictions of women in the works of major French writers. Some essays are in French.

Hoffman, C. G., and A. C. Hoffman. "Re-Echoes of the Jazz Age: Archetypal Women in the Novels of 1922." *Journal of Modern Literature* 7, No. 1 (February 1979): 62-86.
> Argues that despite changes in women's social conditions after World War I, images of women in literature written in 1922 continued to depict women as either love goddesses or mother figures.

Holbrook, David. *Images of Woman in Literature.* New York: New York University Press, 1989, 295 p.
> Psychoanalytic examination of women in literature, focusing particularly on the female characters in Shakespeare.

Miller, Beth, ed. *Women in Hispanic Literature: Icons and Fallen Idols.* Berkeley: University of California Press, 1983, 373 p.
> Collection of essays covering major gender issues in the literatures of Spain, Mexico, Latin America, and American Chicano communities.

Pannill, Linda. "Willa Cather's Artist-Heroines." *Women's Studies* 11, No. 3 (1984): 223-32.
> Discusses Cather's conception of what it means to be a woman artist in light of the conflicting demands of career and conventional gender roles.

Rule, Jane. *Lesbian Images.* Garden City, N.Y.: Doubleday and Company, Inc., 1975, 246 p.
> Discussion of lesbian writers and characters intended as a "common reader" rather than a comprehensive survey.

Schipper, Mineke, ed. *Unheard Words: Women and Literature in Africa, the Arab World, Asia, the Caribbean, and Latin America.* Translated by Barbara Potter Fasting. London: Allison and Busby, 1984, 288 p.
> Covers the history, development, and major contemporary trends in writings by and about women in Africa, the Middle East, Asia, the Caribbean, and Latin America; includes several interviews with representative women writers and a recommended reading section.

Trilling, Diana. "The Image of Women in Contemporary Literature." In *The Woman in America,* edited by Robert Jay Lifton, pp. 52-71. Boston: Houghton Mifflin Company, 1965.
> Speech originally presented at a conference on the "superior woman student"; discusses the conflict between women's education and the depiction of women in contemporary literature.

Yellin, Jean Fagan, and Cynthia D. Bond, eds. *The Pen Is Ours: A Listing of Writings by and about African-American Women before 1910 with Secondary Bibliography to the Present.* New York and Oxford: Oxford University Press, 1991, 349 p.
> Includes listings of works by and about women published in both periodicals and books, as well as works by and about female slaves.

# How to Use This Index

The main references

---

**Calvino, Italo**
1923–1985 ....... **CLC 5, 8, 11, 22, 33, 39,**
**73; SSC 3**

---

list all author entries in the following Gale Literary Criticism series:

*BLC* = *Black Literature Criticism*
*CLC* = *Contemporary Literary Criticism*
*CLR* = *Children's Literature Review*
*CMLC* = *Classical and Medieval Literature Criticism*
*DA* = *DISCovering Authors*
*DAB* = *DISCovering Authors: British*
*DAC* = *DISCovering Authors: Canadian*
*DAM* = *DISCovering Authors: Modules*
    *DRAM*: *Dramatists Module*; *MST*: *Most-Studied Authors Module*;
    *MULT*: *Multicultural Authors Module*; *NOV*: *Novelists Module*;
    *POET*: *Poets Module*; *POP*: *Popular Fiction and Genre Authors Module*
*DC* = *Drama Criticism*
*HLC* = *Hispanic Literature Criticism*
*LC* = *Literature Criticism from 1400 to 1800*
*NCLC* = *Nineteenth-Century Literature Criticism*
*PC* = *Poetry Criticism*
*SSC* = *Short Story Criticism*
*TCLC* = *Twentieth-Century Literary Criticism*
*WLC* = *World Literature Criticism, 1500 to the Present*

The cross-references

---

See also CANR 23; CA 85-88;
  obituary CA116

---

list all author entries in the following Gale biographical and literary sources:

*AAYA* = *Authors & Artists for Young Adults*
*AITN* = *Authors in the News*
*BEST* = *Bestsellers*
*BW* = *Black Writers*
*CA* = *Contemporary Authors*
*CAAS* = *Contemporary Authors Autobiography Series*
*CABS* = *Contemporary Authors Bibliographical Series*
*CANR* = *Contemporary Authors New Revision Series*
*CAP* = *Contemporary Authors Permanent Series*
*CDALB* = *Concise Dictionary of American Literary Biography*
*CDBLB* = *Concise Dictionary of British Literary Biography*
*DLB* = *Dictionary of Literary Biography*
*DLBD* = *Dictionary of Literary Biography Documentary Series*
*DLBY* = *Dictionary of Literary Biography Yearbook*
*HW* = *Hispanic Writers*
*JRDA* = *Junior DISCovering Authors*
*MAICYA* = *Major Authors and Illustrators for Children and Young Adults*
*MTCW* = *Major 20th-Century Writers*
*NNAL* = *Native North American Literature*
*SAAS* = *Something about the Author Autobiography Series*
*SATA* = *Something about the Author*
*YABC* = *Yesterday's Authors of Books for Children*

# Twentieth-Century
# Literary Criticism

Cumulative Indexes
Volumes 1-94

# Literary Criticism Series
# Cumulative Author Index

**20/1631**
See Upward, Allen
**A/C Cross**
See Lawrence, T(homas) E(dward)
**Abasiyanik, Sait Faik** 1906-1954
See Sait Faik
See also CA 123
**Abbey, Edward** 1927-1989 ................ **CLC 36, 59**
See also CA 45-48; 128; CANR 2, 41; MTCW 2
**Abbott, Lee K(ittredge)** 1947- ............... **CLC 48**
See also CA 124; CANR 51; DLB 130
**Abe, Kobo** 1924-1993 **CLC 8, 22, 53, 81; DAM NOV**
See also CA 65-68; 140; CANR 24, 60; DLB 182;
MTCW 1, 2
**Abelard, Peter** c. 1079-c. 1142 .......... **CMLC 11**
See also DLB 115, 208
**Abell, Kjeld** 1901-1961 ......................... **CLC 15**
See also CA 111
**Abish, Walter** 1931- .............................. **CLC 22**
See also CA 101; CANR 37; DLB 130
**Abrahams, Peter (Henry)** 1919- ............. **CLC 4**
See also BW 1; CA 57-60; CANR 26; DLB 117;
MTCW 1, 2
**Abrams, M(eyer) H(oward)** 1912- ......... **CLC 24**
See also CA 57-60; CANR 13, 33; DLB 67
**Abse, Dannie** 1923- **CLC 7, 29; DAB; DAM POET**
See also CA 53-56; CAAS 1; CANR 4, 46, 74;
DLB 27; MTCW 1
**Achebe, (Albert) Chinua(lumogu)** 1930- **CLC 1, 3, 5, 7, 11, 26, 51, 75; BLC 1; DA; DAB; DAC; DAM MST, MULT, NOV; WLC**
See also AAYA 15; BW 2, 3; CA 1-4R; CANR 6, 26, 47; CLR 20; DLB 117; MAICYA; MTCW 1, 2; SATA 38, 40; SATA-Brief 38
**Acker, Kathy** 1948-1997 ................ **CLC 45, 111**
See also CA 117; 122; 162; CANR 55
**Ackroyd, Peter** 1949- ...................... **CLC 34, 52**
See also CA 123; 127; CANR 51, 74; DLB 155;
INT 127; MTCW 1
**Acorn, Milton** 1923- .................... **CLC 15; DAC**
See also CA 103; DLB 53; INT 103
**Adamov, Arthur** 1908-1970 ..... **CLC 4, 25; DAM DRAM**
See also CA 17-18; 25-28R; CAP 2; MTCW 1
**Adams, Alice (Boyd)** 1926- **CLC 6, 13, 46; SSC 24**
See also CA 81-84; CANR 26, 53, 75; DLBY 86;
INT CANR-26; MTCW 1, 2
**Adams, Andy** 1859-1935 ....................... **TCLC 56**
See also YABC 1
**Adams, Brooks** 1848-1927 .................. **TCLC 80**
See also CA 123; DLB 47
**Adams, Douglas (Noel)** 1952- **CLC 27, 60; DAM POP**
See also AAYA 4; BEST 89:3; CA 106; CANR 34, 64; DLBY 83; JRDA; MTCW 1
**Adams, Francis** 1862-1893 .................. **NCLC 33**
**Adams, Henry (Brooks)** 1838-1918 **TCLC 4, 52; DA; DAB; DAC; DAM MST**
See also CA 104; 133; CANR 77; DLB 12, 47, 189;
MTCW 1
**Adams, Richard (George)** 1920- .. **CLC 4, 5, 18; DAM NOV**
See also AAYA 16; AITN 1, 2; CA 49-52; CANR 3, 35; CLR 20; JRDA; MAICYA; MTCW 1, 2;
SATA 7, 69
**Adamson, Joy(-Friederike Victoria)** 1910-1980
**CLC 17**

See also CA 69-72; 93-96; CANR 22; MTCW 1;
SATA 11; SATA-Obit 22
**Adcock, Fleur** 1934- ............................. **CLC 41**
See also CA 25-28R; CAAS 23; CANR 11, 34, 69; DLB 40
**Addams, Charles (Samuel)** 1912-1988 .. **CLC 30**
See also CA 61-64; 126; CANR 12, 79
**Addams, Jane** 1860-1945 ..................... **TCLC 76**
**Addison, Joseph** 1672-1719 .................... **LC 18**
See also CDBLB 1660-1789; DLB 101
**Adler, Alfred (F.)** 1870-1937 ................ **TCLC 61**
See also CA 119; 159
**Adler, C(arole) S(chwerdtfeger)** 1932-. **CLC 35**
See also AAYA 4; CA 89-92; CANR 19, 40;
JRDA; MAICYA; SAAS 15; SATA 26, 63, 102
**Adler, Renata** 1938- ......................... **CLC 8, 31**
See also CA 49-52; CANR 5, 22, 52; MTCW 1
**Ady, Endre** 1877-1919 .......................... **TCLC 11**
See also CA 107
**A.E.** 1867-1935 ................................. **TCLC 3, 10**
See also Russell, George William
**Aeschylus** 525B.C.-456B.C. **CMLC 11; DA; DAB; DAC; DAM DRAM, MST; DC 8; WLCS**
See also DLB 176
**Aesop** 620(?)B.C.-564(?)B.C. .............. **CMLC 24**
See also CLR 14; MAICYA; SATA 64
**Affable Hawk**
See MacCarthy, Sir(Charles Otto) Desmond
**Africa, Ben**
See Bosman, Herman Charles
**Afton, Effie**
See Harper, Frances Ellen Watkins
**Agapida, Fray Antonio**
See Irving, Washington
**Agee, James (Rufus)** 1909-1955 ..... **TCLC 1, 19; DAM NOV**
See also AITN 1; CA 108; 148; CDALB 1941-1968; DLB 2, 26, 152; MTCW 1
**Aghill, Gordon**
See Silverberg, Robert
**Agnon, S(hmuel) Y(osef Halevi)** 1888-1970 **CLC 4, 8, 14; SSC 30**
See also CA 17-18; 25-28R; CANR 60; CAP 2;
MTCW 1, 2
**Agrippa von Nettesheim, Henry Cornelius** 1486-1535 .................................................. **LC 27**
**Aherne, Owen**
See Cassill, R(onald) V(erlin)
**Ai** 1947- ....................................... **CLC 4, 14, 69**
See also CA 85-88; CAAS 13; CANR 70; DLB 120
**Aickman, Robert (Fordyce)** 1914-1981 . **CLC 57**
See also CA 5-8R; CANR 3, 72
**Aiken, Conrad (Potter)** 1889-1973 .. **CLC 1, 3, 5, 10, 52; DAM NOV, POET; PC 26; SSC 9**
See also CA 5-8R; 45-48; CANR 4, 60; CDALB 1929-1941; DLB 9, 45, 102; MTCW 1, 2; SATA 3, 30
**Aiken, Joan (Delano)** 1924- .................. **CLC 35**
See also AAYA 1, 25; CA 9-12R; CANR 4, 23, 34, 64; CLR 1, 19; DLB 161; JRDA; MAICYA;
MTCW 1; SAAS 1; SATA 2, 30, 73
**Ainsworth, William Harrison** 1805-1882 **NCLC 13**
See also DLB 21; SATA 24
**Aitmatov, Chingiz (Torekulovich)** 1928- **CLC 71**
See also CA 103; CANR 38; MTCW 1; SATA 56

**Akers, Floyd**
See Baum, L(yman) Frank
**Akhmadulina, Bella Akhatovna** 1937- **CLC 53; DAM POET**
See also CA 65-68
**Akhmatova, Anna** 1888-1966 **CLC 11, 25, 64; DAM POET; PC 2**
See also CA 19-20; 25-28R; CANR 35; CAP 1;
MTCW 1, 2
**Aksakov, Sergei Timofeyvich** 1791-1859 **NCLC 2**
See also DLB 198
**Aksenov, Vassily**
See Aksyonov, Vassily (Pavlovich)
**Akst, Daniel** 1956- ............................. **CLC 109**
See also CA 161
**Aksyonov, Vassily (Pavlovich)** 1932- **CLC 22, 37, 101**
See also CA 53-56; CANR 12, 48, 77
**Akutagawa, Ryunosuke** 1892-1927 ..... **TCLC 16**
See also CA 117; 154
**Alain** 1868-1951 ................................. **TCLC 41**
See also CA 163
**Alain-Fournier** ...................................... **TCLC 6**
See also Fournier, Henri Alban
See also DLB 65
**Alarcon, Pedro Antonio de** 1833-1891 .. **NCLC 1**
**Alas (y Urena), Leopoldo (Enrique Garcia)** 1852-1901 ............................................... **TCLC 29**
See also CA 113; 131; HW 1
**Albee, Edward (Franklin III)** 1928- **CLC 1, 2, 3, 5, 9, 11, 13, 25, 53, 86, 113; DA; DAB; DAC; DAM DRAM, MST; DC 11; WLC**
See also AITN 1; CA 5-8R; CABS 3; CANR 8, 54, 74; CDALB 1941-1968; DLB 7; INT CANR-8;
MTCW 1, 2
**Alberti, Rafael** 1902- ............................. **CLC 7**
See also CA 85-88; CANR 81; DLB 108; HW 2
**Albert the Great** 1200(?)-1280 ........... **CMLC 16**
See also DLB 115
**Alcala-Galiano, Juan Valera y**
See Valera y Alcala-Galiano, Juan
**Alcott, Amos Bronson** 1799-1888 ......... **NCLC 1**
See also DLB 1
**Alcott, Louisa May** 1832-1888 **NCLC 6, 58; DA; DAB; DAC; DAM MST, NOV; SSC 27; WLC**
See also AAYA 20; CDALB 1865-1917; CLR 1, 38; DLB 1, 42, 79; DLBD 14; JRDA; MAICYA;
SATA 100; YABC 1
**Aldanov, M. A.**
See Aldanov, Mark (Alexandrovich)
**Aldanov, Mark (Alexandrovich)** 1886(?)-1957
**TCLC 23**
See also CA 118
**Aldington, Richard** 1892-1962 .............. **CLC 49**
See also CA 85-88; CANR 45; DLB 20, 36, 100, 149
**Aldiss, Brian W(ilson)** 1925- **CLC 5, 14, 40; DAM NOV**
See also CA 5-8R; CAAS 2; CANR 5, 28, 64; DLB 14; MTCW 1, 2; SATA 34
**Alegria, Claribel** 1924- **CLC 75; DAM MULT; PC 26**
See also CA 131; CAAS 15; CANR 66; DLB 145;
HW 1; MTCW 1
**Alegria, Fernando** 1918- ....................... **CLC 57**
See also CA 9-12R; CANR 5, 32, 72; HW 1, 2
**Aleichem, Sholom** ............. **TCLC 1, 35; SSC 33**

See also Rabinovitch, Sholem
**Alepoudelis, Odysseus**
See Elytis, Odysseus
**Aleshkovsky, Joseph** 1929-
See Aleshkovsky, Yuz
See also CA 121; 128
**Aleshkovsky, Yuz** ............................. **CLC 44**
See also Aleshkovsky, Joseph
**Alexander, Lloyd (Chudley)** 1924- ........ **CLC 35**
See also AAYA 1, 27; CA 1-4R; CANR 1, 24, 38, 55; CLR 1, 5, 48; DLB 52; JRDA; MAICYA; MTCW 1; SAAS 19; SATA 3, 49, 81
**Alexander, Meena** 1951- ..................... **CLC 121**
See also CA 115; CANR 38, 70
**Alexander, Samuel** 1859-1938 ............. **TCLC 77**
**Alexie, Sherman (Joseph, Jr.)** 1966- ... **CLC 96; DAM MULT**
See also AAYA 28; CA 138; CANR 65; DLB 175, 206; MTCW 1; NNAL
**Alfau, Felipe** 1902- ............................... **CLC 66**
See also CA 137
**Alger, Horatio, Jr.** 1832-1899 ................ **NCLC 8**
See also DLB 42; SATA 16
**Algren, Nelson** 1909-1981**CLC 4, 10, 33; SSC 33**
See also CA 13-16R; 103; CANR 20, 61; CDALB 1941-1968; DLB 9; DLBY 81, 82; MTCW 1, 2
**Ali, Ahmed** 1910- ................................. **CLC 69**
See also CA 25-28R; CANR 15, 34
**Alighieri, Dante**
See Dante
**Allan, John B.**
See Westlake, Donald E(dwin)
**Allan, Sidney**
See Hartmann, Sadakichi
**Allan, Sydney**
See Hartmann, Sadakichi
**Allen, Edward** 1948- ............................. **CLC 59**
**Allen, Fred** 1894-1956 .......................... **TCLC 87**
**Allen, Paula Gunn** 1939- . **CLC 84; DAM MULT**
See also CA 112; 143; CANR 63; DLB 175; MTCW 1; NNAL
**Allen, Roland**
See Ayckbourn, Alan
**Allen, Sarah A.**
See Hopkins, Pauline Elizabeth
**Allen, Sidney H.**
See Hartmann, Sadakichi
**Allen, Woody** 1935- ...... **CLC 16, 52; DAM POP**
See also AAYA 10; CA 33-36R; CANR 27, 38, 63; DLB 44; MTCW 1
**Allende, Isabel** 1942-**CLC 39, 57, 97; DAM MULT, NOV; HLC; WLCS**
See also AAYA 18; CA 125; 130; CANR 51, 74; DLB 145; HW 1, 2; INT 130; MTCW 1, 2
**Alleyn, Ellen**
See Rossetti, Christina (Georgina)
**Allingham, Margery (Louise)** 1904-1966**CLC 19**
See also CA 5-8R; 25-28R; CANR 4, 58; DLB 77; MTCW 1, 2
**Allingham, William** 1824-1889 ........... **NCLC 25**
See also DLB 35
**Allison, Dorothy E.** 1949- ..................... **CLC 78**
See also CA 140; CANR 66; MTCW 1
**Allston, Washington** 1779-1843 ............. **NCLC 2**
See also DLB 1
**Almedingen, E. M.** ................................. **CLC 12**
See also Almedingen, Martha Edith von
See also SATA 3
**Almedingen, Martha Edith von** 1898-1971
See Almedingen, E. M.
See also CA 1-4R; CANR 1
**Almodovar, Pedro** 1949(?)- ... **CLC 114; HLCS 1**
See also CA 133; CANR 72; HW 2
**Almqvist, Carl Jonas Love** 1793-1866 . **NCLC 42**
**Alonso, Damaso** 1898-1990 .................... **CLC 14**
See also CA 110; 131; 130; CANR 72; DLB 108; HW 1, 2

**Alov**
See Gogol, Nikolai (Vasilyevich)
**Alta** 1942- .............................................. **CLC 19**
See also CA 57-60
**Alter, Robert B(ernard)** 1935- .............. **CLC 34**
See also CA 49-52; CANR 1, 47
**Alther, Lisa** 1944- ............................ **CLC 7, 41**
See also CA 65-68; CAAS 30; CANR 12, 30, 51; MTCW 1
**Althusser, L.**
See Althusser, Louis
**Althusser, Louis** 1918-1990 ................ **CLC 106**
See also CA 131; 132
**Altman, Robert** 1925- ..................... **CLC 16, 116**
See also CA 73-76; CANR 43
**Alvarez, A(lfred)** 1929- ..................... **CLC 5, 13**
See also CA 1-4R; CANR 3, 33, 63; DLB 14, 40
**Alvarez, Alejandro Rodriguez** 1903-1965
See Casona, Alejandro
See also CA 131; 93-96; HW 1
**Alvarez, Julia** 1950- ............... **CLC 93; HLCS 1**
See also AAYA 25; CA 147; CANR 69; MTCW 1
**Alvaro, Corrado** 1896-1956 ................. **TCLC 60**
See also CA 163
**Amado, Jorge** 1912- ..... **CLC 13, 40, 106; DAM MULT, NOV; HLC**
See also CA 77-80; CANR 35, 74; DLB 113; HW 2; MTCW 1, 2
**Ambler, Eric** 1909-1998 .................... **CLC 4, 6, 9**
See also CA 9-12R; 171; CANR 7, 38, 74; DLB 77; MTCW 1, 2
**Amichai, Yehuda** 1924- ........ **CLC 9, 22, 57, 116**
See also CA 85-88; CANR 46, 60; MTCW 1
**Amichai, Yehudah**
See Amichai, Yehuda
**Amiel, Henri Frederic** 1821-1881 ......... **NCLC 4**
**Amis, Kingsley (William)** 1922-1995**CLC 1, 2, 3, 5, 8, 13, 40, 44; DA; DAB; DAC; DAM MST, NOV**
See also AITN 2; CA 9-12R; 150; CANR 8, 28, 54; CDBLB 1945-1960; DLB 15, 27, 100, 139; DLBY 96; INT CANR-8; MTCW 1, 2
**Amis, Martin (Louis)** 1949-**CLC 4, 9, 38, 62, 101**
See also BEST 90:3; CA 65-68; CANR 8, 27, 54, 73; DLB 14, 194; INT CANR-27; MTCW 1
**Ammons, A(rchie) R(andolph)** 1926-**CLC 2, 3, 5, 8, 9, 25, 57, 108; DAM POET; PC 16**
See also AITN 1; CA 9-12R; CANR 6, 36, 51, 73; DLB 5, 165; MTCW 1, 2
**Amo, Tauraatua i**
See Adams, Henry (Brooks)
**Amory, Thomas** 1691(?)-1788 ................... **LC 48**
**Anand, Mulk Raj** 1905- **CLC 23, 93; DAM NOV**
See also CA 65-68; CANR 32, 64; MTCW 1, 2
**Anatol**
See Schnitzler, Arthur
**Anaximander** c. 610B.C.-c. 546B.C. .... **CMLC 22**
**Anaya, Rudolfo A(lfonso)** 1937- .. **CLC 23; DAM MULT, NOV; HLC**
See also AAYA 20; CA 45-48; CAAS 4; CANR 1, 32, 51; DLB 82, 206; HW 1; MTCW 1, 2
**Andersen, Hans Christian** 1805-1875**NCLC 7, 79; DA; DAB; DAC; DAM MST, POP; SSC 6; WLC**
See also CLR 6; MAICYA; SATA 100; YABC 1
**Anderson, C. Farley**
See Mencken, H(enry) L(ouis); Nathan, George Jean
**Anderson, Jessica (Margaret) Queale** 1916-**CLC 37**
See also CA 9-12R; CANR 4, 62
**Anderson, Jon (Victor)** 1940-**CLC 9; DAM POET**
See also CA 25-28R; CANR 20
**Anderson, Lindsay (Gordon)** 1923-1994 **CLC 20**
See also CA 125; 128; 146; CANR 77
**Anderson, Maxwell** 1888-1959 ... **TCLC 2; DAM DRAM**

See also CA 105; 152; DLB 7; MTCW 2
**Anderson, Poul (William)** 1926- ........... **CLC 15**
See also AAYA 5; CA 1-4R; CAAS 2; CANR 2, 15, 34, 64; CLR 58; DLB 8; INT CANR-15; MTCW 1, 2; SATA 90; SATA-Brief 39; SATA-Essay 106
**Anderson, Robert (Woodruff)** 1917- .... **CLC 23; DAM DRAM**
See also AITN 1; CA 21-24R; CANR 32; DLB 7
**Anderson, Sherwood** 1876-1941 **TCLC 1, 10, 24; DA; DAB; DAC; DAM MST, NOV; SSC 1; WLC**
See also AAYA 30; CA 104; 121; CANR 61; CDALB 1917-1929; DLB 4, 9, 86; DLBD 1; MTCW 1, 2
**Andier, Pierre**
See Desnos, Robert
**Andouard**
See Giraudoux, (Hippolyte) Jean
**Andrade, Carlos Drummond de** ............. **CLC 18**
See also Drummond de Andrade, Carlos
**Andrade, Mario de** 1893-1945 ............. **TCLC 43**
**Andreae, Johann V(alentin)** 1586-1654 ... **LC 32**
See also DLB 164
**Andreas-Salome, Lou** 1861-1937 ......... **TCLC 56**
See also DLB 66
**Andress, Lesley**
See Sanders, Lawrence
**Andrewes, Lancelot** 1555-1626 ................... **LC 5**
See also DLB 151, 172
**Andrews, Cicily Fairfield**
See West, Rebecca
**Andrews, Elton V.**
See Pohl, Frederik
**Andreyev, Leonid (Nikolaevich)** 1871-1919**TCLC 3**
See also CA 104
**Andric, Ivo** 1892-1975 ............................. **CLC 8**
See also CA 81-84; 57-60; CANR 43, 60; DLB 147; MTCW 1
**Androvar**
See Prado (Calvo), Pedro
**Angelique, Pierre**
See Bataille, Georges
**Angell, Roger** 1920- ............................. **CLC 26**
See also CA 57-60; CANR 13, 44, 70; DLB 171, 185
**Angelou, Maya** 1928-**CLC 12, 35, 64, 77; BLC 1; DA; DAB; DAC; DAM MST, MULT, POET, POP; WLCS**
See also AAYA 7, 20; BW 2, 3; CA 65-68; CANR 19, 42, 65; CDALBS; CLR 53; DLB 38; MTCW 1, 2; SATA 49
**Anna Comnena** 1083-1153 .................. **CMLC 25**
**Annensky, Innokenty (Fyodorovich)** 1856-1909 **TCLC 14**
See also CA 110; 155
**Annunzio, Gabriele d'**
See D'Annunzio, Gabriele
**Anodos**
See Coleridge, Mary E(lizabeth)
**Anon, Charles Robert**
See Pessoa, Fernando (Antonio Nogueira)
**Anouilh, Jean (Marie Lucien Pierre)** 1910-1987 **CLC 1, 3, 8, 13, 40, 50; DAM DRAM; DC 8**
See also CA 17-20R; 123; CANR 32; MTCW 1, 2
**Anthony, Florence**
See Ai
**Anthony, John**
See Ciardi, John (Anthony)
**Anthony, Peter**
See Shaffer, Anthony (Joshua); Shaffer, Peter (Levin)
**Anthony, Piers** 1934- .......... **CLC 35; DAM POP**
See also AAYA 11; CA 21-24R; CANR 28, 56, 73; DLB 8; MTCW 1, 2; SAAS 22; SATA 84
**Anthony, Susan B(rownell)** 1916-1991 **TCLC 84**

See also CA 89-92; 134
**Antoine, Marc**
 See Proust, (Valentin-Louis-George-Eugene-) Marcel
**Antoninus, Brother**
 See Everson, William (Oliver)
**Antonioni, Michelangelo** 1912- ............ **CLC 20**
 See also CA 73-76; CANR 45, 77
**Antschel, Paul** 1920-1970
 See Celan, Paul
 See also CA 85-88; CANR 33, 61; MTCW 1
**Anwar, Chairil** 1922-1949 ................... **TCLC 22**
 See also CA 121
**Apess, William** 1798-1839(?) ... **NCLC 73; DAM MULT**
 See also DLB 175; NNAL
**Apollinaire, Guillaume** 1880-1918**TCLC 3, 8, 51; DAM POET; PC 7**
 See also Kostrowitzki, Wilhelm Apollinaris de
 See also CA 152; MTCW 1
**Appelfeld, Aharon** 1932- ................. **CLC 23, 47**
 See also CA 112; 133
**Apple, Max (Isaac)** 1941- ................... **CLC 9, 33**
 See also CA 81-84; CANR 19, 54; DLB 130
**Appleman, Philip (Dean)** 1926- ............. **CLC 51**
 See also CA 13-16R; CAAS 18; CANR 6, 29, 56
**Appleton, Lawrence**
 See Lovecraft, H(oward) P(hillips)
**Apteryx**
 See Eliot, T(homas) S(tearns)
**Apuleius, (Lucius Madaurensis)** 125(?)-175(?) **CMLC 1**
 See also DLB 211
**Aquin, Hubert** 1929-1977 ...................... **CLC 15**
 See also CA 105; DLB 53
**Aquinas, Thomas** 1224(?)-1274 .......... **CMLC 33**
 See also DLB 115
**Aragon, Louis** 1897-1982**CLC 3, 22; DAM NOV, POET**
 See also CA 69-72; 108; CANR 28, 71; DLB 72; MTCW 1, 2
**Arany, Janos** 1817-1882 ...................... **NCLC 34**
**Aranyos, Kakay**
 See Mikszath, Kalman
**Arbuthnot, John** 1667-1735 ........................ **LC 1**
 See also DLB 101
**Archer, Herbert Winslow**
 See Mencken, H(enry) L(ouis)
**Archer, Jeffrey (Howard)** 1940- .. **CLC 28; DAM POP**
 See also AAYA 16; BEST 89:3; CA 77-80; CANR 22, 52; INT CANR-22
**Archer, Jules** 1915- ............................ **CLC 12**
 See also CA 9-12R; CANR 6, 69; SAAS 5; SATA 4, 85
**Archer, Lee**
 See Ellison, Harlan (Jay)
**Arden, John** 1930- **CLC 6, 13, 15; DAM DRAM**
 See also CA 13-16R; CAAS 4; CANR 31, 65, 67; DLB 13; MTCW 1
**Arenas, Reinaldo** 1943-1990**CLC 41; DAM MULT; HLC**
 See also CA 124; 128; 133; CANR 73; DLB 145; HW 1; MTCW 1
**Arendt, Hannah** 1906-1975 ............. **CLC 66, 98**
 See also CA 17-20R; 61-64; CANR 26, 60; MTCW 1, 2
**Aretino, Pietro** 1492-1556 ....................... **LC 12**
**Arghezi, Tudor** 1880-1967 .................... **CLC 80**
 See also Theodorescu, Ion N.
 See also CA 167
**Arguedas, Jose Maria** 1911-1969 .. **CLC 10, 18; HLCS 1**
 See also CA 89-92; CANR 73; DLB 113; HW 1
**Argueta, Manlio** 1936- .......................... **CLC 31**
 See also CA 131; CANR 73; DLB 145; HW 1
**Ariosto, Ludovico** 1474-1533 ..................... **LC 6**

**Aristides**
 See Epstein, Joseph
**Aristophanes** 450B.C.-385B.C. .... **CMLC 4; DA; DAB; DAC; DAM DRAM, MST; DC 2; WLCS**
 See also DLB 176
**Aristotle** 384B.C.-322B.C. **CMLC 31; DA; DAB; DAC; DAM MST; WLCS**
 See also DLB 176
**Arlt, Roberto (Godofredo Christophersen)** 1900-1942 .............. **TCLC 29; DAM MULT; HLC**
 See also CA 123; 131; CANR 67; HW 1, 2
**Armah, Ayi Kwei** 1939-**CLC 5, 33; BLC 1; DAM MULT, POET**
 See also BW 1; CA 61-64; CANR 21, 64; DLB 117; MTCW 1
**Armatrading, Joan** 1950- ...................... **CLC 17**
 See also CA 114
**Arnette, Robert**
 See Silverberg, Robert
**Arnim, Achim von (Ludwig Joachim von Arnim)** 1781-1831 ........................ **NCLC 5; SSC 29**
 See also DLB 90
**Arnim, Bettina von** 1785-1859 ............. **NCLC 38**
 See also DLB 90
**Arnold, Matthew** 1822-1888 .... **NCLC 6, 29; DA; DAB; DAC; DAM MST, POET; PC 5; WLC**
 See also CDBLB 1832-1890; DLB 32, 57
**Arnold, Thomas** 1795-1842 .................. **NCLC 18**
 See also DLB 55
**Arnow, Harriette (Louisa) Simpson** 1908-1986 **CLC 2, 7, 18**
 See also CA 9-12R; 118; CANR 14; DLB 6; MTCW 1, 2; SATA 42; SATA-Obit 47
**Arouet, Francois-Marie**
 See Voltaire
**Arp, Hans**
 See Arp, Jean
**Arp, Jean** 1887-1966 .............................. **CLC 5**
 See also CA 81-84; 25-28R; CANR 42, 77
**Arrabal**
 See Arrabal, Fernando
**Arrabal, Fernando** 1932- ........ **CLC 2, 9, 18, 58**
 See also CA 9-12R; CANR 15
**Arrick, Fran** ......................................... **CLC 30**
 See also Gaberman, Judie Angell
**Artaud, Antonin (Marie Joseph)** 1896-1948**TCLC 3, 36; DAM DRAM**
 See also CA 104; 149; MTCW 1
**Arthur, Ruth M(abel)** 1905-1979 .......... **CLC 12**
 See also CA 9-12R; 85-88; CANR 4; SATA 7, 26
**Artsybashev, Mikhail (Petrovich)** 1878-1927 **TCLC 31**
 See also CA 170
**Arundel, Honor (Morfydd)** 1919-1973 ... **CLC 17**
 See also CA 21-22; 41-44R; CAP 2; CLR 35; SATA 4; SATA-Obit 24
**Arzner, Dorothy** 1897-1979 ................... **CLC 98**
**Asch, Sholem** 1880-1957 ...................... **TCLC 3**
 See also CA 105
**Ash, Shalom**
 See Asch, Sholem
**Ashbery, John (Lawrence)** 1927-**CLC 2, 3, 4, 6, 9, 13, 15, 25, 41, 77; DAM POET; PC 26**
 See also CA 5-8R; CANR 9, 37, 66; DLB 5, 165; DLBY 81; INT CANR-9; MTCW 1, 2
**Ashdown, Clifford**
 See Freeman, R(ichard) Austin
**Ashe, Gordon**
 See Creasey, John
**Ashton-Warner, Sylvia (Constance)** 1908-1984 **CLC 19**
 See also CA 69-72; 112; CANR 29; MTCW 1, 2
**Asimov, Isaac** 1920-1992 **CLC 1, 3, 9, 19, 26, 76, 92; DAM POP**
 See also AAYA 13; BEST 90:2; CA 1-4R; 137; CANR 2, 19, 36, 60; CLR 12; DLB 8; DLBY 92; INT CANR-19; JRDA; MAICYA; MTCW 1,

2; SATA 1, 26, 74
**Assis, Joaquim Maria Machado de**
 See Machado de Assis, Joaquim Maria
**Astley, Thea (Beatrice May)** 1925- ....... **CLC 41**
 See also CA 65-68; CANR 11, 43, 78
**Aston, James**
 See White, T(erence) H(anbury)
**Asturias, Miguel Angel** 1899-1974**CLC 3, 8, 13; DAM MULT, NOV; HLC**
 See also CA 25-28; 49-52; CANR 32; CAP 2; DLB 113; HW 1; MTCW 1, 2
**Atares, Carlos Saura**
 See Saura (Atares), Carlos
**Atheling, William**
 See Pound, Ezra (Weston Loomis)
**Atheling, William, Jr.**
 See Blish, James (Benjamin)
**Atherton, Gertrude (Franklin Horn)** 1857-1948 **TCLC 2**
 See also CA 104; 155; DLB 9, 78, 186
**Atherton, Lucius**
 See Masters, Edgar Lee
**Atkins, Jack**
 See Harris, Mark
**Atkinson, Kate** ....................................... **CLC 99**
 See also CA 166
**Attaway, William (Alexander)** 1911-1986**CLC 92; BLC 1; DAM MULT**
 See also BW 2, 3; CA 143; DLB 76
**Atticus**
 See Fleming, Ian (Lancaster); Wilson, (Thomas) Woodrow
**Atwood, Margaret (Eleanor)** 1939-**CLC 2, 3, 4, 8, 13, 15, 25, 44, 84; DA; DAB; DAC; DAM MST, NOV, POET; PC 8; SSC 2; WLC**
 See also AAYA 12; BEST 89:2; CA 49-52; CANR 3, 24, 33, 59; DLB 53; INT CANR-24; MTCW 1, 2; SATA 50
**Aubigny, Pierre d'**
 See Mencken, H(enry) L(ouis)
**Aubin, Penelope** 1685-1731(?) ................... **LC 9**
 See also DLB 39
**Auchincloss, Louis (Stanton)** 1917- **CLC 4, 6, 9, 18, 45; DAM NOV; SSC 22**
 See also CA 1-4R; CANR 6, 29, 55; DLB 2; DLBY 80; INT CANR-29; MTCW 1
**Auden, W(ystan) H(ugh)** 1907-1973**CLC 1, 2, 3, 4, 6, 9, 11, 14, 43; DA; DAB; DAC; DAM DRAM, MST, POET; PC 1; WLC**
 See also AAYA 18; CA 9-12R; 45-48; CANR 5, 61; CDBLB 1914-1945; DLB 10, 20; MTCW 1, 2
**Audiberti, Jacques** 1900-1965 ..... **CLC 38; DAM DRAM**
 See also CA 25-28R
**Audubon, John James** 1785-1851 ........ **NCLC 47**
**Auel, Jean M(arie)** 1936-**CLC 31, 107; DAM POP**
 See also AAYA 7; BEST 90:4; CA 103; CANR 21, 64; INT CANR-21; SATA 91
**Auerbach, Erich** 1892-1957 ................. **TCLC 43**
 See also CA 118; 155
**Augier, Emile** 1820-1889 ..................... **NCLC 31**
 See also DLB 192
**August, John**
 See De Voto, Bernard (Augustine)
**Augustine** 354-430 . **CMLC 6; DA; DAB; DAC; DAM MST; WLCS**
 See also DLB 115
**Aurelius**
 See Bourne, Randolph S(illiman)
**Aurobindo, Sri**
 See Ghose, Aurabinda
**Austen, Jane** 1775-1817**NCLC 1, 13, 19, 33, 51; DA; DAB; DAC; DAM MST, NOV; WLC**
 See also AAYA 19; CDBLB 1789-1832; DLB 116
**Auster, Paul** 1947- ............................... **CLC 47**
 See also CA 69-72; CANR 23, 52, 75; MTCW 1

See Rolfe, Frederick (William Serafino Austin
    Lewis Mary)
**Barondess, Sue K(aufman)** 1926-1977 .... **CLC 8**
    See also Kaufman, Sue
    See also CA 1-4R; 69-72; CANR 1
**Baron de Teive**
    See Pessoa, Fernando (Antonio Nogueira)
**Baroness Von S.**
    See Zangwill, Israel
**Barres, (Auguste-) Maurice** 1862-1923**TCLC 47**
    See also CA 164; DLB 123
**Barreto, Afonso Henrique de Lima**
    See Lima Barreto, Afonso Henrique de
**Barrett, (Roger) Syd** 1946- .................. **CLC 35**
**Barrett, William (Christopher)** 1913-1992 **C L C
    27**
    See also CA 13-16R; 139; CANR 11, 67; INT
    CANR-11
**Barrie, J(ames) M(atthew)** 1860-1937 . **TCLC 2;
    DAB; DAM DRAM**
    See also CA 104; 136; CANR 77; CDBLB 1890-
    1914; CLR 16; DLB 10, 141, 156; MAICYA;
    MTCW 1; SATA 100; YABC 1
**Barrington, Michael**
    See Moorcock, Michael (John)
**Barrol, Grady**
    See Bograd, Larry
**Barry, Mike**
    See Malzberg, Barry N(athaniel)
**Barry, Philip** 1896-1949 ...................... **TCLC 11**
    See also CA 109; DLB 7
**Bart, Andre Schwarz**
    See Schwarz-Bart, Andre
**Barth, John (Simmons)** 1930-**CLC 1, 2, 3, 5, 7, 9,
    10, 14, 27, 51, 89; DAM NOV; SSC 10**
    See also AITN 1, 2; CA 1-4R; CABS 1; CANR 5,
    23, 49, 64; DLB 2; MTCW 1
**Barthelme, Donald** 1931-1989**CLC 1, 2, 3, 5, 6, 8,
    13, 23, 46, 59, 115; DAM NOV; SSC 2**
    See also CA 21-24R; 129; CANR 20, 58; DLB 2;
    DLBY 80, 89; MTCW 1, 2; SATA 7; SATA-
    Obit 62
**Barthelme, Frederick** 1943- .......... **CLC 36, 117**
    See also CA 114; 122; CANR 77; DLBY 85; INT
    122
**Barthes, Roland (Gerard)** 1915-1980**CLC 24, 83**
    See also CA 130; 97-100; CANR 66; MTCW 1, 2
**Barzun, Jacques (Martin)** 1907- .......... **CLC 51**
    See also CA 61-64; CANR 22
**Bashevis, Isaac**
    See Singer, Isaac Bashevis
**Bashkirtseff, Marie** 1859-1884 .......... **NCLC 27**
**Basho**
    See Matsuo Basho
**Bass, Kingsley B., Jr.**
    See Bullins, Ed
**Bass, Rick** 1958- .................................. **CLC 79**
    See also CA 126; CANR 53; DLB 212
**Bassani, Giorgio** 1916- ........................... **CLC 9**
    See also CA 65-68; CANR 33; DLB 128, 177;
    MTCW 1
**Bastos, Augusto (Antonio) Roa**
    See Roa Bastos, Augusto (Antonio)
**Bataille, Georges** 1897-1962 ................. **CLC 29**
    See also CA 101; 89-92
**Bates, H(erbert) E(rnest)** 1905-1974 .... **CLC 46;
    DAB; DAM POP; SSC 10**
    See also CA 93-96; 45-48; CANR 34; DLB 162,
    191; MTCW 1, 2
**Bauchart**
    See Camus, Albert
**Baudelaire, Charles** 1821-1867 **NCLC 6, 29, 55;
    DA; DAB; DAC; DAM MST, POET; PC 1;
    SSC 18; WLC**
**Baudrillard, Jean** 1929- ........................ **CLC 60**
**Baum, L(yman) Frank** 1856-1919 .......... **TCLC 7**
    See also CA 108; 133; CLR 15; DLB 22; JRDA;

MAICYA; MTCW 1, 2; SATA 18, 100
**Baum, Louis F.**
    See Baum, L(yman) Frank
**Baumbach, Jonathan** 1933- ............... **CLC 6, 23**
    See also CA 13-16R; CAAS 5; CANR 12, 66;
    DLBY 80; INT CANR-12; MTCW 1
**Bausch, Richard (Carl)** 1945- ............. **CLC 51**
    See also CA 101; CAAS 14; CANR 43, 61; DLB
    130
**Baxter, Charles (Morley)** 1947-**CLC 45, 78; DAM
    POP**
    See also CA 57-60; CANR 40, 64; DLB 130;
    MTCW 2
**Baxter, George Owen**
    See Faust, Frederick (Schiller)
**Baxter, James K(eir)** 1926-1972 .......... **CLC 14**
    See also CA 77-80
**Baxter, John**
    See Hunt, E(verette) Howard, (Jr.)
**Bayer, Sylvia**
    See Glassco, John
**Baynton, Barbara** 1857-1929 ............... **TCLC 57**
**Beagle, Peter S(oyer)** 1939- .......... **CLC 7, 104**
    See also CA 9-12R; CANR 4, 51, 73; DLBY 80;
    INT CANR-4; MTCW 1; SATA 60
**Bean, Normal**
    See Burroughs, Edgar Rice
**Beard, Charles A(ustin)** 1874-1948 .... **TCLC 15**
    See also CA 115; DLB 17; SATA 18
**Beardsley, Aubrey** 1872-1898 ............... **NCLC 6**
**Beattie, Ann** 1947- **CLC 8, 13, 18, 40, 63; DAM
    NOV, POP; SSC 11**
    See also BEST 90:2; CA 81-84; CANR 53, 73;
    DLBY 82; MTCW 1, 2
**Beattie, James** 1735-1803 .................... **NCLC 25**
    See also DLB 109
**Beauchamp, Kathleen Mansfield** 1888-1923
    See Mansfield, Katherine
    See also CA 104; 134; DA; DAC; DAM MST;
    MTCW 2
**Beaumarchais, Pierre-Augustin Caron de** 1732-
    1799 ................................................... **DC 4**
    See also DAM DRAM
**Beaumont, Francis** 1584(?)-1616 .. **LC 33; DC 6**
    See also CDBLB Before 1660; DLB 58, 121
**Beauvoir, Simone (Lucie Ernestine Marie
    Bertrand) de** 1908-1986 **CLC 1, 2, 4, 8, 14,
    31, 44, 50, 71; DA; DAB; DAC; DAM MST,
    NOV; SSC 35; WLC**
    See also CA 9-12R; 118; CANR 28, 61; DLB 72;
    DLBY 86; MTCW 1, 2
**Becker, Carl (Lotus)** 1873-1945 ......... **TCLC 63**
    See also CA 157; DLB 17
**Becker, Jurek** 1937-1997 .................. **CLC 7, 19**
    See also CA 85-88; 157; CANR 60; DLB 75
**Becker, Walter** 1950- ........................... **CLC 26**
**Beckett, Samuel (Barclay)** 1906-1989**CLC 1, 2, 3,
    4, 6, 9, 10, 11, 14, 18, 29, 57, 59, 83; DA;
    DAB; DAC; DAM DRAM, MST, NOV; SSC
    16; WLC**
    See also CA 5-8R; 130; CANR 33, 61; CDBLB
    1945-1960; DLB 13, 15; DLBY 90; MTCW 1, 2
**Beckford, William** 1760-1844 ............. **NCLC 16**
    See also DLB 39
**Beckman, Gunnel** 1910- ........................ **CLC 26**
    See also CA 33-36R; CANR 15; CLR 25;
    MAICYA; SAAS 9; SATA 6
**Becque, Henri** 1837-1899 ....................... **NCLC 3**
    See also DLB 192
**Beddoes, Thomas Lovell** 1803-1849 ...... **NCLC 3**
    See also DLB 96
**Bede** c. 673-735 .................................. **CMLC 20**
    See also DLB 146
**Bedford, Donald F.**
    See Fearing, Kenneth (Flexner)
**Beecher, Catharine Esther** 1800-1878 **NCLC 30**
    See also DLB 1

**Beecher, John** 1904-1980 .................... **CLC 6**
    See also AITN 1; CA 5-8R; 105; CANR 8
**Beer, Johann** 1655-1700 ........................... **LC 5**
    See also DLB 168
**Beer, Patricia** 1924- ............................... **CLC 58**
    See also CA 61-64; CANR 13, 46; DLB 40
**Beerbohm, Max**
    See Beerbohm, (Henry) Max(imilian)
**Beerbohm, (Henry) Max(imilian)** 1872-1956
    **TCLC 1, 24**
    See also CA 104; 154; CANR 79; DLB 34, 100
**Beer-Hofmann, Richard** 1866-1945 .... **TCLC 60**
    See also CA 160; DLB 81
**Begiebing, Robert J(ohn)** 1946- .......... **CLC 70**
    See also CA 122; CANR 40
**Behan, Brendan** 1923-1964**CLC 1, 8, 11, 15, 79;
    DAM DRAM**
    See also CA 73-76; CANR 33; CDBLB 1945-1960;
    DLB 13; MTCW 1, 2
**Behn, Aphra** 1640(?)-1689**LC 1, 30, 42; DA; DAB;
    DAC; DAM DRAM, MST, NOV, POET; DC
    4; PC 13; WLC**
    See also DLB 39, 80, 131
**Behrman, S(amuel) N(athaniel)** 1893-1973 **C L C
    40**
    See also CA 13-16; 45-48; CAP 1; DLB 7, 44
**Belasco, David** 1853-1931 ...................... **TCLC 3**
    See also CA 104; 168; DLB 7
**Belcheva, Elisaveta** 1893- ...................... **CLC 10**
    See also Bagryana, Elisaveta
**Beldone, Phil "Cheech"**
    See Ellison, Harlan (Jay)
**Beleno**
    See Azuela, Mariano
**Belinski, Vissarion Grigoryevich** 1811-1848
    **NCLC 5**
    See also DLB 198
**Belitt, Ben** 1911- .................................. **CLC 22**
    See also CA 13-16R; CAAS 4; CANR 7, 77; DLB
    5
**Bell, Gertrude (Margaret Lowthian)** 1868-1926
    **TCLC 67**
    See also CA 167; DLB 174
**Bell, J. Freeman**
    See Zangwill, Israel
**Bell, James Madison** 1826-1902**TCLC 43; BLC 1;
    DAM MULT**
    See also BW 1; CA 122; 124; DLB 50
**Bell, Madison Smartt** 1957- .......... **CLC 41, 102**
    See also CA 111; CANR 28, 54, 73; MTCW 1
**Bell, Marvin (Hartley)** 1937- .. **CLC 8, 31; DAM
    POET**
    See also CA 21-24R; CAAS 14; CANR 59; DLB
    5; MTCW 1
**Bell, W. L. D.**
    See Mencken, H(enry) L(ouis)
**Bellamy, Atwood C.**
    See Mencken, H(enry) L(ouis)
**Bellamy, Edward** 1850-1898 .................. **NCLC 4**
    See also DLB 12
**Bellin, Edward J.**
    See Kuttner, Henry
**Belloc, (Joseph) Hilaire (Pierre Sebastien Rene
    Swanton)** 1870-1953 ..... **TCLC 7, 18; DAM
    POET; PC 24**
    See also CA 106; 152; DLB 19, 100, 141, 174;
    MTCW 1; YABC 1
**Belloc, Joseph Peter Rene Hilaire**
    See Belloc, (Joseph) Hilaire (Pierre Sebastien
    Rene Swanton)
**Belloc, Joseph Pierre Hilaire**
    See Belloc, (Joseph) Hilaire (Pierre Sebastien
    Rene Swanton)
**Belloc, M. A.**
    See Lowndes, Marie Adelaide (Belloc)
**Bellow, Saul** 1915-**CLC 1, 2, 3, 6, 8, 10, 13, 15, 25,
    33, 34, 63, 79; DA; DAB; DAC; DAM MST,

1945; DLB 19; MTCW 1, 2

**Brooke-Haven, P.**
See Wodehouse, P(elham) G(renville)

**Brooke-Rose, Christine** 1926(?)- ......... **CLC 40**
See also CA 13-16R; CANR 58; DLB 14

**Brookner, Anita** 1928- ... **CLC 32, 34, 51; DAB; DAM POP**
See also CA 114; 120; CANR 37, 56; DLB 194; DLBY 87; MTCW 1, 2

**Brooks, Cleanth** 1906-1994 ..... **CLC 24, 86, 110**
See also CA 17-20R; 145; CANR 33, 35; DLB 63; DLBY 94; INT CANR-35; MTCW 1, 2

**Brooks, George**
See Baum, L(yman) Frank

**Brooks, Gwendolyn** 1917-**CLC 1, 2, 4, 5, 15, 49; BLC 1; DA; DAC; DAM MST, MULT, POET; PC 7; WLC**
See also AAYA 20; AITN 1; BW 2, 3; CA 1-4R; CANR 1, 27, 52, 75; CDALB 1941-1968; CLR 27; DLB 5, 76, 165; MTCW 1, 2; SATA 6

**Brooks, Mel** .......................... **CLC 12**
See also Kaminsky, Melvin
See also AAYA 13; DLB 26

**Brooks, Peter** 1938- ....................... **CLC 34**
See also CA 45-48, CANR 1

**Brooks, Van Wyck** 1886-1963 .............. **CLC 29**
See also CA 1-4R; CANR 6; DLB 45, 63, 103

**Brophy, Brigid (Antonia)** 1929-1995 . **CLC 6, 11, 29, 105**
See also CA 5-8R; 149; CAAS 4; CANR 25, 53; DLB 14; MTCW 1, 2

**Brosman, Catharine Savage** 1934- ......... **CLC 9**
See also CA 61-64; CANR 21, 46

**Brossard, Nicole** 1943- ........................**CLC 115**
See also CA 122; CAAS 16; DLB 53

**Brother Antoninus**
See Everson, William (Oliver)

**The Brothers Quay**
See Quay, Stephen; Quay, Timothy

**Broughton, T(homas) Alan** 1936- ....... **CLC 19**
See also CA 45-48; CANR 2, 23, 48

**Broumas, Olga** 1949- ....................... **CLC 10, 73**
See also CA 85-88; CANR 20, 69

**Brown, Alan** 1950- ................................. **CLC 99**
See also CA 156

**Brown, Charles Brockden** 1771-1810 NCLC **22, 74**
See also CDALB 1640-1865; DLB 37, 59, 73

**Brown, Christy** 1932-1981 ..................... **CLC 63**
See also CA 105; 104; CANR 72; DLB 14

**Brown, Claude** 1937- ..... **CLC 30; BLC 1; DAM MULT**
See also AAYA 7; BW 1, 3; CA 73-76; CANR 81

**Brown, Dee (Alexander)** 1908-**CLC 18, 47; DAM POP**
See also AAYA 30; CA 13-16R; CAAS 6; CANR 11, 45, 60; DLBY 80; MTCW 1, 2; SATA 5

**Brown, George**
See Wertmueller, Lina

**Brown, George Douglas** 1869-1902 .... **TCLC 28**
See also CA 162

**Brown, George Mackay** 1921-1996**CLC 5, 48, 100**
See also CA 21-24R; 151; CAAS 6; CANR 12, 37, 67; DLB 14, 27, 139; MTCW 1; SATA 35

**Brown, (William) Larry** 1951- .............. **CLC 73**
See also CA 130; 134; INT 133

**Brown, Moses**
See Barrett, William (Christopher)

**Brown, Rita Mae** 1944- ... **CLC 18, 43, 79; DAM NOV, POP**
See also CA 45-48; CANR 2, 11, 35, 62; INT CANR-11; MTCW 1, 2

**Brown, Roderick (Langmere) Haig-**
See Haig-Brown, Roderick (Langmere)

**Brown, Rosellen** 1939- ......................... **CLC 32**
See also CA 77-80; CAAS 10; CANR 14, 44

**Brown, Sterling Allen** 1901-1989**CLC 1, 23, 59;** BLC 1; DAM MULT, POET
See also BW 1, 3; CA 85-88; 127; CANR 26; DLB 48, 51, 63; MTCW 1, 2

**Brown, Will**
See Ainsworth, William Harrison

**Brown, William Wells** 1813-1884**NCLC 2; BLC 1; DAM MULT; DC 1**
See also DLB 3, 50

**Browne, (Clyde) Jackson** 1948(?)- ........ **CLC 21**
See also CA 120

**Browning, Elizabeth Barrett** 1806-1861**NCLC 1, 16, 61, 66; DA; DAB; DAC; DAM MST, POET; PC 6; WLC**
See also CDBLB 1832-1890; DLB 32, 199

**Browning, Robert** 1812-1889 NCLC **19, 79; DA; DAB; DAC; DAM MST, POET; PC 2; WLCS**
See also CDBLB 1832-1890; DLB 32, 163; YABC 1

**Browning, Tod** 1882-1962 ..................... **CLC 16**
See also CA 141; 117

**Brownson, Orestes Augustus** 1803-1876 **NCLC 50**
See also DLB 1, 59, 73

**Bruccoli, Matthew J(oseph)** 1931- ........ **CLC 34**
See also CA 9-12R; CANR 7; DLB 103

**Bruce, Lenny** ......................................... **CLC 21**
See also Schneider, Leonard Alfred

**Bruin, John**
See Brutus, Dennis

**Brulard, Henri**
See Stendhal

**Brulls, Christian**
See Simenon, Georges (Jacques Christian)

**Brunner, John (Kilian Houston)** 1934-1995 C L C **8, 10; DAM POP**
See also CA 1-4R; 149; CAAS 8; CANR 2, 37; MTCW 1, 2

**Bruno, Giordano** 1548-1600 ..................... **LC 27**

**Brutus, Dennis** 1924- .... **CLC 43; BLC 1; DAM MULT, POET; PC 24**
See also BW 2, 3; CA 49-52; CAAS 14; CANR 2, 27, 42, 81; DLB 117

**Bryan, C(ourtlandt) D(ixon) B(arnes)** 1936-C L C **29**
See also CA 73-76; CANR 13, 68; DLB 185; INT CANR-13

**Bryan, Michael**
See Moore, Brian

**Bryant, William Cullen** 1794-1878 NCLC **6, 46; DA; DAB; DAC; DAM MST, POET; PC 20**
See also CDALB 1640-1865; DLB 3, 43, 59, 189

**Bryusov, Valery Yakovlevich** 1873-1924**TCLC 10**
See also CA 107; 155

**Buchan, John** 1875-1940 **TCLC 41; DAB; DAM POP**
See also CA 108; 145; DLB 34, 70, 156; MTCW 1; YABC 2

**Buchanan, George** 1506-1582 ..................... **LC 4**
See also DLB 152

**Buchheim, Lothar-Guenther** 1918- ........ **CLC 6**
See also CA 85-88

**Buchner, (Karl) Georg** 1813-1837 ...... **NCLC 26**

**Buchwald, Art(hur)** 1925- ..................... **CLC 33**
See also AITN 1; CA 5-8R; CANR 21, 67; MTCW 1, 2; SATA 10

**Buck, Pearl S(ydenstricker)** 1892-1973 **CLC 7, 11, 18; DA; DAB; DAC; DAM MST, NOV**
See also AITN 1; CA 1-4R; 41-44R; CANR 1, 34; CDALBS; DLB 9, 102; MTCW 1, 2; SATA 1, 25

**Buckler, Ernest** 1908-1984 **CLC 13; DAC; DAM MST**
See also CA 11-12; 114; CAP 1; DLB 68; SATA 47

**Buckley, Vincent (Thomas)** 1925-1988 . **CLC 57**
See also CA 101

**Buckley, William F(rank), Jr.** 1925- **CLC 7, 18, 37; DAM POP**
See also AITN 1; CA 1-4R; CANR 1, 24, 53; DLB 137; DLBY 80; INT CANR-24; MTCW 1, 2

**Buechner, (Carl) Frederick** 1926-**CLC 2, 4, 6, 9; DAM NOV**
See also CA 13-16R; CANR 11, 39, 64; DLBY 80; INT CANR-11; MTCW 1, 2

**Buell, John (Edward)** 1927- ..................... **CLC 10**
See also CA 1-4R; CANR 71; DLB 53

**Buero Vallejo, Antonio** 1916- ......... **CLC 15, 46**
See also CA 106; CANR 24, 49, 75; HW 1; MTCW 1, 2

**Bufalino, Gesualdo** 1920(?)- .................. **CLC 74**
See also DLB 196

**Bugayev, Boris Nikolayevich** 1880-1934**TCLC 7; PC 11**
See also Bely, Andrey
See also CA 104; 165; MTCW 1

**Bukowski, Charles** 1920-1994**CLC 2, 5, 9, 41, 82, 108; DAM NOV, POET; PC 18**
See also CA 17-20R; 144; CANR 40, 62; DLB 5, 130, 169; MTCW 1, 2

**Bulgakov, Mikhail (Afanas'evich)** 1891-1940 **TCLC 2, 16; DAM DRAM, NOV; SSC 18**
See also CA 105; 152

**Bulgya, Alexander Alexandrovich** 1901-1956 **TCLC 53**
See also Fadeyev, Alexander
See also CA 117

**Bullins, Ed** 1935- ..... **CLC 1, 5, 7; BLC 1; DAM DRAM, MULT; DC 6**
See also BW 2, 3; CA 49-52; CAAS 16; CANR 24, 46, 73; DLB 7, 38; MTCW 1, 2

**Bulwer-Lytton, Edward (George Earle Lytton)** 1803-1873 ............................... **NCLC 1, 45**
See also DLB 21

**Bunin, Ivan Alexeyevich** 1870-1953**TCLC 6; SSC 5**
See also CA 104

**Bunting, Basil** 1900-1985 **CLC 10, 39, 47; DAM POET**
See also CA 53-56; 115; CANR 7; DLB 20

**Bunuel, Luis** 1900-1983**CLC 16, 80; DAM MULT; HLC**
See also CA 101; 110; CANR 32, 77; HW 1

**Bunyan, John** 1628-1688 LC **4; DA; DAB; DAC; DAM MST; WLC**
See also CDBLB 1660-1789; DLB 39

**Burckhardt, Jacob (Christoph)** 1818-1897**NCLC 49**

**Burford, Eleanor**
See Hibbert, Eleanor Alice Burford

**Burgess, Anthony****CLC 1, 2, 4, 5, 8, 10, 13, 15, 22, 40, 62, 81, 94; DAB**
See also Wilson, John (Anthony) Burgess
See also AAYA 25; AITN 1; CDBLB 1960 to Present; DLB 14, 194; DLBY 98; MTCW 1

**Burke, Edmund** 1729(?)-1797**LC 7, 36; DA; DAB; DAC; DAM MST; WLC**
See also DLB 104

**Burke, Kenneth (Duva)** 1897-1993 .... **CLC 2, 24**
See also CA 5-8R; 143; CANR 39, 74; DLB 45, 63; MTCW 1, 2

**Burke, Leda**
See Garnett, David

**Burke, Ralph**
See Silverberg, Robert

**Burke, Thomas** 1886-1945 .................. **TCLC 63**
See also CA 113; 155; DLB 197

**Burney, Fanny** 1752-1840 .............. **NCLC 12, 54**
See also DLB 39

**Burns, Robert** 1759-1796**LC 3, 29, 40; DA; DAB; DAC; DAM MST, POET; PC 6; WLC**
See also CDBLB 1789-1832; DLB 109

**Burns, Tex**
See L'Amour, Louis (Dearborn)

**Burnshaw, Stanley** 1906- ............ **CLC 3, 13, 44**

See also CA 9-12R; DLB 48; DLBY 97

**Burr, Anne** 1937- .................................... CLC 6
See also CA 25-28R

**Burroughs, Edgar Rice** 1875-1950 **TCLC 2, 32; DAM NOV**
See also AAYA 11; CA 104; 132; DLB 8; MTCW 1, 2; SATA 41

**Burroughs, William S(eward)** 1914-1997CLC **1, 2, 5, 15, 22, 42, 75, 109; DA; DAB; DAC; DAM MST, NOV, POP; WLC**
See also AITN 2; CA 9-12R; 160; CANR 20, 52; DLB 2, 8, 16, 152; DLBY 81, 97; MTCW 1, 2

**Burton, SirRichard F(rancis)** 1821-1890 **NCLC 42**
See also DLB 55, 166, 184

**Busch, Frederick** 1941- ........ CLC **7, 10, 18, 47**
See also CA 33-36R; CAAS 1; CANR 45, 73; DLB 6

**Bush, Ronald** 1946- ................................ CLC **34**
See also CA 136

**Bustos, F(rancisco)**
See Borges, Jorge Luis

**Bustos Domecq, H(onorio)**
See Bioy Casares, Adolfo; Borges, Jorge Luis

**Butler, Octavia E(stelle)** 1947- ..... CLC **38, 121; BLCS; DAM MULT, POP**
See also AAYA 18; BW 2, 3; CA 73-76; CANR 12, 24, 38, 73; DLB 33; MTCW 1, 2; SATA 84

**Butler, Robert Olen (Jr.)** 1945- .. CLC **81; DAM POP**
See also CA 112; CANR 66; DLB 173; INT 112; MTCW 1

**Butler, Samuel** 1612-1680 .................. LC **16, 43**
See also DLB 101, 126

**Butler, Samuel** 1835-1902TCLC **1, 33; DA; DAB; DAC; DAM MST, NOV; WLC**
See also CA 143; CDBLB 1890-1914; DLB 18, 57, 174

**Butler, Walter C.**
See Faust, Frederick (Schiller)

**Butor, Michel (Marie Francois)** 1926- CLC **1, 3, 8, 11, 15**
See also CA 9-12R; CANR 33, 66; DLB 83; MTCW 1, 2

**Butts, Mary** 1892(?)-1937 .................... TCLC **77**
See also CA 148

**Buzo, Alexander (John)** 1944- .............. CLC **61**
See also CA 97-100; CANR 17, 39, 69

**Buzzati, Dino** 1906-1972 ....................... CLC **36**
See also CA 160; 33-36R; DLB 177

**Byars, Betsy (Cromer)** 1928- .............. CLC **35**
See also AAYA 19; CA 33-36R; CANR 18, 36, 57; CLR 1, 16; DLB 52; INT CANR-18; JRDA; MAICYA; MTCW 1; SAAS 1; SATA 4, 46, 80; SATA-Essay 108

**Byatt, A(ntonia) S(usan Drabble)** 1936- CLC **19, 65; DAM NOV, POP**
See also CA 13-16R; CANR 13, 33, 50, 75; DLB 14, 194; MTCW 1, 2

**Byrne, David** 1952- ................................ CLC **26**
See also CA 127

**Byrne, John Keyes** 1926-
See Leonard, Hugh
See also CA 102; CANR 78; INT 102

**Byron, George Gordon (Noel)** 1788-1824NCLC **2, 12; DA; DAB; DAC; DAM MST, POET; PC 16; WLC**
See also CDBLB 1789-1832; DLB 96, 110

**Byron, Robert** 1905-1941 ....................... TCLC **67**
See also CA 160; DLB 195

**C. 3. 3.**
See Wilde, Oscar

**Caballero, Fernan** 1796-1877 .............. NCLC **10**

**Cabell, Branch**
See Cabell, James Branch

**Cabell, James Branch** 1879-1958 ......... TCLC **6**
See also CA 105; 152; DLB 9, 78; MTCW 1

**Cable, George Washington** 1844-1925 **T C L C 4; SSC 4**
See also CA 104; 155; DLB 12, 74; DLBD 13

**Cabral de Melo Neto, Joao** 1920- CLC **76; DAM MULT**
See also CA 151

**Cabrera Infante, G(uillermo)** 1929-CLC **5, 25, 45, 120; DAM MULT; HLC**
See also CA 85-88; CANR 29, 65; DLB 113; HW 1, 2; MTCW 1, 2

**Cade, Toni**
See Bambara, Toni Cade

**Cadmus and Harmonia**
See Buchan, John

**Caedmon** fl. 658-680 ............................ CMLC **7**
See also DLB 146

**Caeiro, Alberto**
See Pessoa, Fernando (Antonio Nogueira)

**Cage, John (Milton, Jr.)** 1912-1992 ....... CLC **41**
See also CA 13-16R; 169; CANR 9, 78; DLB 193; INT CANR-9

**Cahan, Abraham** 1860-1951 ................. TCLC **71**
See also CA 108; 154; DLB 9, 25, 28

**Cain, G.**
See Cabrera Infante, G(uillermo)

**Cain, Guillermo**
See Cabrera Infante, G(uillermo)

**Cain, James M(allahan)** 1892-1977CLC **3, 11, 28**
See also AITN 1; CA 17-20R; 73-76; CANR 8, 34, 61; MTCW 1

**Caine, Mark**
See Raphael, Frederic (Michael)

**Calasso, Roberto** 1941- .......................... CLC **81**
See also CA 143

**Calderon de la Barca, Pedro** 1600-1681 . LC **23; DC 3; HLCS 1**

**Caldwell, Erskine (Preston)** 1903-1987CLC **1, 8, 14, 50, 60; DAM NOV; SSC 19**
See also AITN 1; CA 1-4R; 121; CAAS 1; CANR 2, 33; DLB 9, 86; MTCW 1, 2

**Caldwell, (Janet Miriam) Taylor (Holland)** 1900-1985 ......... CLC **2, 28, 39; DAM NOV, POP**
See also CA 5-8R; 116; CANR 5; DLBD 17

**Calhoun, John Caldwell** 1782-1850 ..... NCLC **15**
See also DLB 3

**Calisher, Hortense** 1911- CLC **2, 4, 8, 38; DAM NOV; SSC 15**
See also CA 1-4R; CANR 1, 22, 67; DLB 2; INT CANR-22; MTCW 1, 2

**Callaghan, Morley Edward** 1903-1990CLC **3, 14, 41, 65; DAC; DAM MST**
See also CA 9-12R; 132; CANR 33, 73; DLB 68; MTCW 1, 2

**Callimachus** c. 305B.C.-c. 240B.C. ..... CMLC **18**
See also DLB 176

**Calvin, John** 1509-1564 .......................... LC **37**

**Calvino, Italo** 1923-1985CLC **5, 8, 11, 22, 33, 39, 73; DAM NOV; SSC 3**
See also CA 85-88; 116; CANR 23, 61; DLB 196; MTCW 1, 2

**Cameron, Carey** 1952- .......................... CLC **59**
See also CA 135

**Cameron, Peter** 1959- ............................ CLC **44**
See also CA 125; CANR 50

**Campana, Dino** 1885-1932 .................... TCLC **20**
See also CA 117; DLB 114

**Campanella, Tommaso** 1568-1639 ............ LC **32**

**Campbell, John W(ood, Jr.)** 1910-1971 . CLC **32**
See also CA 21-22; 29-32R; CANR 34; CAP 2; DLB 8; MTCW 1

**Campbell, Joseph** 1904-1987 ................. CLC **69**
See also AAYA 3; BEST 89:2; CA 1-4R; 124; CANR 3, 28, 61; MTCW 1, 2

**Campbell, Maria** 1940- ................ CLC **85; DAC**
See also CA 102; CANR 54; NNAL

**Campbell, (John) Ramsey** 1946-CLC **42; SSC 19**
See also CA 57-60; CANR 7; INT CANR-7

**Campbell, (Ignatius) Roy (Dunnachie)** 1901-1957 .............................................. TCLC **5**
See also CA 104; 155; DLB 20; MTCW 2

**Campbell, Thomas** 1777-1844 .............. NCLC **19**
See also DLB 93; 144

**Campbell, Wilfred** .................................. TCLC **9**
See also Campbell, William

**Campbell, William** 1858(?)-1918
See Campbell, Wilfred
See also CA 106; DLB 92

**Campion, Jane** ........................................ CLC **95**
See also CA 138

**Campos, Alvaro de**
See Pessoa, Fernando (Antonio Nogueira)

**Camus, Albert** 1913-1960 CLC **1, 2, 4, 9, 11, 14, 32, 63, 69; DA; DAB; DAC; DAM DRAM, MST, NOV; DC 2; SSC 9; WLC**
See also CA 89-92; DLB 72; MTCW 1, 2

**Canby, Vincent** 1924- .......................... CLC **13**
See also CA 81-84

**Cancale**
See Desnos, Robert

**Canetti, Elias** 1905-1994 .. CLC **3, 14, 25, 75, 86**
See also CA 21-24R; 146; CANR 23, 61, 79; DLB 85, 124; MTCW 1, 2

**Canfield, Dorothea F.**
See Fisher, Dorothy (Frances) Canfield

**Canfield, Dorothea Frances**
See Fisher, Dorothy (Frances) Canfield

**Canfield, Dorothy**
See Fisher, Dorothy (Frances) Canfield

**Canin, Ethan** 1960- ................................ CLC **55**
See also CA 131; 135

**Cannon, Curt**
See Hunter, Evan

**Cao, Lan** 1961- ...................................... CLC **109**
See also CA 165

**Cape, Judith**
See Page, P(atricia) K(athleen)

**Capek, Karel** 1890-1938 TCLC **6, 37; DA; DAB; DAC; DAM DRAM, MST, NOV; DC 1; WLC**
See also CA 104; 140; MTCW 1

**Capote, Truman** 1924-1984CLC **1, 3, 8, 13, 19, 34, 38, 58; DA; DAB; DAC; DAM MST, NOV, POP; SSC 2; WLC**
See also CA 5-8R; 113; CANR 18, 62; CDALB 1941-1968; DLB 2, 185; DLBY 80, 84; MTCW 1, 2; SATA 91

**Capra, Frank** 1897-1991 ....................... CLC **16**
See also CA 61-64; 135

**Caputo, Philip** 1941- .............................. CLC **32**
See also CA 73-76; CANR 40

**Caragiale, Ion Luca** 1852-1912 ........... TCLC **76**
See also CA 157

**Card, Orson Scott** 1951- CLC **44, 47, 50; DAM POP**
See also AAYA 11; CA 102; CANR 27, 47, 73; INT CANR-27; MTCW 1, 2; SATA 83

**Cardenal, Ernesto** 1925- . CLC **31; DAM MULT, POET; HLC; PC 22**
See also CA 49-52; CANR 2, 32, 66; HW 1, 2; MTCW 1, 2

**Cardozo, Benjamin N(athan)** 1870-1938TCLC **65**
See also CA 117; 164

**Carducci, Giosue (Alessandro Giuseppe)** 1835-1907 .............................................. TCLC **32**
See also CA 163

**Carew, Thomas** 1595(?)-1640 .................. LC **13**
See also DLB 126

**Carey, Ernestine Gilbreth** 1908- ........... CLC **17**
See also CA 5-8R; CANR 71; SATA 2

**Carey, Peter** 1943- ...................... CLC **40, 55, 96**
See also CA 123; 127; CANR 53, 76; INT 127; MTCW 1, 2; SATA 94

**Carleton, William** 1794-1869 ................ NCLC **3**
See also DLB 159

**Carlisle, Henry (Coffin)** 1926- .............. CLC **33**

**Clash, The**
See Headon, (Nicky) Topper; Jones, Mick; Simonon, Paul; Strummer, Joe
**Claudel, Paul (Louis Charles Marie)** 1868-1955 **TCLC 2, 10**
See also CA 104; 165; DLB 192
**Claudius, Matthias** 1740-1815 ............ **NCLC 75**
See also DLB 97
**Clavell, James (duMaresq)** 1925-1994 **CLC 6, 25, 87; DAM NOV, POP**
See also CA 25-28R; 146; CANR 26, 48; MTCW 1, 2
**Cleaver, (Leroy) Eldridge** 1935-1998 **CLC 30, 119; BLC 1; DAM MULT**
See also BW 1, 3; CA 21-24R; 167; CANR 16, 75; MTCW 2
**Cleese, John (Marwood)** 1939- ............. **CLC 21**
See also Monty Python
See also CA 112; 116; CANR 35; MTCW 1
**Cleishbotham, Jebediah**
See Scott, Walter
**Cleland, John** 1710-1789 ..................... **LC 2, 48**
See also DLB 39
**Clemens, Samuel Langhorne** 1835-1910
See Twain, Mark
See also CA 104; 135; CDALB 1865-1917; DA; DAB; DAC; DAM MST, NOV; DLB 11, 12, 23, 64, 74, 186, 189; JRDA; MAICYA; SATA 100; YABC 2
**Cleophil**
See Congreve, William
**Clerihew, E.**
See Bentley, E(dmund) C(lerihew)
**Clerk, N. W.**
See Lewis, C(live) S(taples)
**Cliff, Jimmy** ........................................... **CLC 21**
See also Chambers, James
**Cliff, Michelle** 1946- ............... **CLC 120; BLCS**
See also BW 2; CA 116; CANR 39, 72; DLB 157
**Clifton, (Thelma) Lucille** 1936- **CLC 19, 66; BLC 1; DAM MULT, POET; PC 17**
See also BW 2, 3; CA 49-52; CANR 2, 24, 42, 76; CLR 5; DLB 5, 41; MAICYA; MTCW 1, 2; SATA 20, 69
**Clinton, Dirk**
See Silverberg, Robert
**Clough, Arthur Hugh** 1819-1861 ........ **NCLC 27**
See also DLB 32
**Clutha, Janet Paterson Frame** 1924-
See Frame, Janet
See also CA 1-4R; CANR 2, 36, 76; MTCW 1, 2
**Clyne, Terence**
See Blatty, William Peter
**Cobalt, Martin**
See Mayne, William (James Carter)
**Cobb, Irvin S(hrewsbury)** 1876-1944 ... **TCLC 77**
See also CA 175; DLB 11, 25, 86
**Cobbett, William** 1763-1835 ................ **NCLC 49**
See also DLB 43, 107, 158
**Coburn, D(onald) L(ee)** 1938- ............... **CLC 10**
See also CA 89-92
**Cocteau, Jean (Maurice Eugene Clement)** 1889-1963 **CLC 1, 8, 15, 16, 43; DA; DAB; DAC; DAM DRAM, MST, NOV; WLC**
See also CA 25-28; CANR 40; CAP 2; DLB 65; MTCW 1, 2
**Codrescu, Andrei** 1946- ..... **CLC 46, 121; DAM POET**
See also CA 33-36R; CAAS 19; CANR 13, 34, 53, 76; MTCW 2
**Coe, Max**
See Bourne, Randolph S(illiman)
**Coe, Tucker**
See Westlake, Donald E(dwin)
**Coen, Ethan** 1958- ................................. **CLC 108**
See also CA 126
**Coen, Joel** 1955- ................................... **CLC 108**

See also CA 126
**The Coen Brothers**
See Coen, Ethan; Coen, Joel
**Coetzee, J(ohn) M(ichael)** 1940- **CLC 23, 33, 66, 117; DAM NOV**
See also CA 77-80; CANR 41, 54, 74; MTCW 1, 2
**Coffey, Brian**
See Koontz, Dean R(ay)
**Coffin, Robert P(eter) Tristram** 1892-1955 **TCLC 95**
See also CA 123; 169; DLB 45
**Cohan, George M(ichael)** 1878-1942 ... **TCLC 60**
See also CA 157
**Cohen, Arthur A(llen)** 1928-1986 ..... **CLC 7, 31**
See also CA 1-4R; 120; CANR 1, 17, 42; DLB 28
**Cohen, Leonard (Norman)** 1934- **CLC 3, 38; DAC; DAM MST**
See also CA 21-24R; CANR 14, 69; DLB 53; MTCW 1
**Cohen, Matt** 1942- ...................... **CLC 19; DAC**
See also CA 61-64; CAAS 18; CANR 40; DLB 53
**Cohen-Solal, Annie** 19(?)- ................... **CLC 50**
**Colegate, Isabel** 1931- ......................... **CLC 36**
See also CA 17-20R; CANR 8, 22, 74; DLB 14; INT CANR-22; MTCW 1
**Coleman, Emmett**
See Reed, Ishmael
**Coleridge, M. E.**
See Coleridge, Mary E(lizabeth)
**Coleridge, Mary E(lizabeth)** 1861-1907 **TCLC 73**
See also CA 116; 166; DLB 19, 98
**Coleridge, Samuel Taylor** 1772-1834 **NCLC 9, 54; DA; DAB; DAC; DAM MST, POET; PC 11; WLC**
See also CDBLB 1789-1832; DLB 93, 107
**Coleridge, Sara** 1802-1852 ................. **NCLC 31**
See also DLB 199
**Coles, Don** 1928- ................................. **CLC 46**
See also CA 115; CANR 38
**Coles, Robert (Martin)** 1929- ............. **CLC 108**
See also CA 45-48; CANR 3, 32, 66, 70; INT CANR-32; SATA 23
**Colette, (Sidonie-Gabrielle)** 1873-1954 **TCLC 1, 5, 16; DAM NOV; SSC 10**
See also CA 104; 131; DLB 65; MTCW 1, 2
**Collett, (Jacobine) Camilla (Wergeland)** 1813-1895 **NCLC 22**
**Collier, Christopher** 1930- ................... **CLC 30**
See also AAYA 13; CA 33-36R; CANR 13, 33; JRDA; MAICYA; SATA 16, 70
**Collier, James L(incoln)** 1928- ... **CLC 30; DAM POP**
See also AAYA 13; CA 9-12R; CANR 4, 33, 60; CLR 3; JRDA; MAICYA; SAAS 21; SATA 8, 70
**Collier, Jeremy** 1650-1726 ..................... **LC 6**
**Collier, John** 1901-1980 ..................... **SSC 19**
See also CA 65-68; 97-100; CANR 10; DLB 77
**Collingwood, R(obin) G(eorge)** 1889(?)-1943 **TCLC 67**
See also CA 117; 155
**Collins, Hunt**
See Hunter, Evan
**Collins, Linda** 1931- ............................. **CLC 44**
See also CA 125
**Collins, (William) Wilkie** 1824-1889 **NCLC 1, 18**
See also CDBLB 1832-1890; DLB 18, 70, 159
**Collins, William** 1721-1759 **LC 4, 40; DAM POET**
See also DLB 109
**Collodi, Carlo** 1826-1890 ................... **NCLC 54**
See also Lorenzini, Carlo
See also CLR 5
**Colman, George** 1732-1794
See Glassco, John
**Colt, Winchester Remington**
See Hubbard, L(afayette) Ron(ald)
**Colter, Cyrus** 1910- ............................. **CLC 58**

See also BW 1; CA 65-68; CANR 10, 66; DLB 33
**Colton, James**
See Hansen, Joseph
**Colum, Padraic** 1881-1972 ................... **CLC 28**
See also CA 73-76; 33-36R; CANR 35; CLR 36; MAICYA; MTCW 1; SATA 15
**Colvin, James**
See Moorcock, Michael (John)
**Colwin, Laurie (E.)** 1944-1992 **CLC 5, 13, 23, 84**
See also CA 89-92; 139; CANR 20, 46; DLBY 80; MTCW 1
**Comfort, Alex(ander)** 1920- . **CLC 7; DAM POP**
See also CA 1-4R; CANR 1, 45; MTCW 1
**Comfort, Montgomery**
See Campbell, (John) Ramsey
**Compton-Burnett, I(vy)** 1884(?)-1969 .. **CLC 1, 3, 10, 15, 34; DAM NOV**
See also CA 1-4R; 25-28R; CANR 4; DLB 36; MTCW 1
**Comstock, Anthony** 1844-1915 ........... **TCLC 13**
See also CA 110; 169
**Comte, Auguste** 1798-1857 ................. **NCLC 54**
**Conan Doyle, Arthur**
See Doyle, Arthur Conan
**Conde, Maryse** 1937 **CLC 52, 92; BLCS; DAM MULT**
See also Boucolon, Maryse
See also BW 2; MTCW 1
**Condillac, Etienne Bonnot de** 1714-1780 . **LC 26**
**Condon, Richard (Thomas)** 1915-1996 **CLC 4, 6, 8, 10, 45, 100; DAM NOV**
See also BEST 90:3; CA 1-4R; 151; CAAS 1; CANR 2, 23; INT CANR-23; MTCW 1, 2
**Confucius** 551B.C.-479B.C. **CMLC 19; DA; DAB; DAC; DAM MST; WLCS**
**Congreve, William** 1670-1729 **LC 5, 21; DA; DAB; DAC; DAM DRAM, MST, POET; DC 2; WLC**
See also CDBLB 1660-1789; DLB 39, 84
**Connell, Evan S(helby), Jr.** 1924- **CLC 4, 6, 45; DAM NOV**
See also AAYA 7; CA 1-4R; CAAS 2; CANR 2, 39, 76; DLB 2; DLBY 81; MTCW 1, 2
**Connelly, Marc(us Cook)** 1890-1980 ....... **CLC 7**
See also CA 85-88; 102; CANR 30; DLB 7; DLBY 80; SATA-Obit 25
**Connor, Ralph** ..................................... **TCLC 31**
See also Gordon, Charles William
See also DLB 92
**Conrad, Joseph** 1857-1924 **TCLC 1, 6, 13, 25, 43, 57; DA; DAB; DAC; DAM MST, NOV; SSC 9; WLC**
See also AAYA 26; CA 104; 131; CANR 60; CDBLB 1890-1914; DLB 10, 34, 98, 156; MTCW 1, 2; SATA 27
**Conrad, Robert Arnold**
See Hart, Moss
**Conroy, Pat**
See Conroy, (Donald) Pat(rick)
See also MTCW 2
**Conroy, (Donald) Pat(rick)** 1945- .. **CLC 30, 74; DAM NOV, POP**
See also Conroy, Pat
See also AAYA 8; AITN 1; CA 85-88; CANR 24, 53; DLB 6; MTCW 1
**Constant (de Rebecque), (Henri) Benjamin** 1767-1830 ..................................... **NCLC 6**
See also DLB 119
**Conybeare, Charles Augustus**
See Eliot, T(homas) S(tearns)
**Cook, Michael** 1933- ........................... **CLC 58**
See also CA 93-96; CANR 68; DLB 53
**Cook, Robin** 1940- .............. **CLC 14; DAM POP**
See also BEST 90:2; CA 108; 111; CANR 41; INT 111
**Cook, Roy**
See Silverberg, Robert

See also CA 9-12R

**Ehrenbourg, Ilya (Grigoryevich)**
See Ehrenburg, Ilya (Grigoryevich)

**Ehrenburg, Ilya (Grigoryevich)** 1891-1967 **CLC 18, 34, 62**
See also CA 102; 25-28R

**Ehrenburg, Ilyo (Grigoryevich)**
See Ehrenburg, Ilya (Grigoryevich)

**Ehrenreich, Barbara** 1941- ............... **CLC 110**
See also BEST 90:4; CA 73-76; CANR 16, 37, 62; MTCW 1, 2

**Eich, Guenter** 1907-1972 ...................... **CLC 15**
See also CA 111; 93-96; DLB 69, 124

**Eichendorff, Joseph Freiherr von** 1788-1857 **NCLC 8**
See also DLB 90

**Eigner, Larry** ......................................... **CLC 9**
See also Eigner, Laurence (Joel)
See also CAAS 23; DLB 5

**Eigner, Laurence (Joel)** 1927-1996
See Eigner, Larry
See also CA 9-12R; 151; CANR 6; DLB 193

**Einstein, Albert** 1879-1955 ................ **TCLC 65**
See also CA 121; 133; MTCW 1, 2

**Eiseley, Loren Corey** 1907-1977 ............ **CLC 7**
See also AAYA 5; CA 1-4R; 73-76; CANR 6; DLBD 17

**Eisenstadt, Jill** 1963- ........................... **CLC 50**
See also CA 140

**Eisenstein, Sergei (Mikhailovich)** 1898-1948 **TCLC 57**
See also CA 114; 149

**Eisner, Simon**
See Kornbluth, C(yril) M.

**Ekeloef, (Bengt) Gunnar** 1907-1968 .... **CLC 27; DAM POET; PC 23**
See also CA 123; 25-28R

**Ekelof, (Bengt) Gunnar**
See Ekeloef, (Bengt) Gunnar

**Ekelund, Vilhelm** 1880-1949 ............... **TCLC 75**

**Ekwensi, C. O. D.**
See Ekwensi, Cyprian (Odiatu Duaka)

**Ekwensi, Cyprian (Odiatu Duaka)** 1921- **CLC 4; BLC 1; DAM MULT**
See also BW 2, 3; CA 29-32R; CANR 18, 42, 74; DLB 117; MTCW 1, 2; SATA 66

**Elaine** ................................................... **TCLC 18**
See also Leverson, Ada

**El Crummo**
See Crumb, R(obert)

**Elder, Lonne III** 1931-1996 .......................... **DC 8**
See also BLC 1; BW 1, 3; CA 81-84; 152; CANR 25; DAM MULT; DLB 7, 38, 44

**Elia**
See Lamb, Charles

**Eliade, Mircea** 1907-1986 ...................... **CLC 19**
See also CA 65-68; 119; CANR 30, 62; MTCW 1

**Eliot, A. D.**
See Jewett, (Theodora) Sarah Orne

**Eliot, Alice**
See Jewett, (Theodora) Sarah Orne

**Eliot, Dan**
See Silverberg, Robert

**Eliot, George** 1819-1880 **NCLC 4, 13, 23, 41, 49; DA; DAB; DAC; DAM MST, NOV; PC 20; WLC**
See also CDBLB 1832-1890; DLB 21, 35, 55

**Eliot, John** 1604-1690 .................................. **LC 5**
See also DLB 24

**Eliot, T(homas) S(tearns)** 1888-1965 **CLC 1, 2, 3, 6, 9, 10, 13, 15, 24, 34, 41, 55, 57, 113; DA; DAB; DAC; DAM DRAM, MST, POET; PC 5; WLC**
See also AAYA 28; CA 5-8R; 25-28R; CANR 41; CDALB 1929-1941; DLB 7, 10, 45, 63; DLBY 88; MTCW 1, 2

**Elizabeth** 1866-1941 ............................. **TCLC 41**

**Elkin, Stanley L(awrence)** 1930-1995 **CLC 4, 6, 9, 14, 27, 51, 91; DAM NOV, POP; SSC 12**
See also CA 9-12R; 148; CANR 8, 46; DLB 2, 28; DLBY 80; INT CANR-8; MTCW 1, 2

**Elledge, Scott** ........................................ **CLC 34**

**Elliot, Don**
See Silverberg, Robert

**Elliott, Don**
See Silverberg, Robert

**Elliott, George P(aul)** 1918-1980 ............. **CLC 2**
See also CA 1-4R; 97-100; CANR 2

**Elliott, Janice** 1931- .............................. **CLC 47**
See also CA 13-16R; CANR 8, 29; DLB 14

**Elliott, Sumner Locke** 1917-1991 ......... **CLC 38**
See also CA 5-8R; 134; CANR 2, 21

**Elliott, William**
See Bradbury, Ray (Douglas)

**Ellis, A. E.** ............................................. **CLC 7**

**Ellis, Alice Thomas** ............................... **CLC 40**
See also Haycraft, Anna
See also DLB 194; MTCW 1

**Ellis, Bret Easton** 1964- **CLC 39, 71, 117; DAM POP**
See also AAYA 2; CA 118; 123; CANR 51, 74; INT 123; MTCW 1

**Ellis, (Henry) Havelock** 1859-1939 ...... **TCLC 14**
See also CA 109; 169; DLB 190

**Ellis, Landon**
See Ellison, Harlan (Jay)

**Ellis, Trey** 1962- ................................... **CLC 55**
See also CA 146

**Ellison, Harlan (Jay)** 1934- **CLC 1, 13, 42; DAM POP; SSC 14**
See also AAYA 29; CA 5-8R; CANR 5, 46; DLB 8; INT CANR-5; MTCW 1, 2

**Ellison, Ralph (Waldo)** 1914-1994 **CLC 1, 3, 11, 54, 86, 114; BLC 1; DA; DAB; DAC; DAM MST, MULT, NOV; SSC 26; WLC**
See also AAYA 19; BW 1, 3; CA 9-12R; 145; CANR 24, 53; CDALB 1941-1968; DLB 2, 76; DLBY 94; MTCW 1, 2

**Ellmann, Lucy (Elizabeth)** 1956- ........... **CLC 61**
See also CA 128

**Ellmann, Richard (David)** 1918-1987 ..... **CLC 50**
See also BEST 89:2; CA 1-4R; 122; CANR 2, 28, 61; DLB 103; DLBY 87; MTCW 1, 2

**Elman, Richard (Martin)** 1934-1997 ..... **CLC 19**
See also CA 17-20R; 163; CAAS 3; CANR 47

**Elron**
See Hubbard, L(afayette) Ron(ald)

**Eluard, Paul** ....................................... **TCLC 7, 41**
See also Grindel, Eugene

**Elyot, Sir Thomas** 1490(?)-1546 ............... **LC 11**

**Elytis, Odysseus** 1911-1996 .... **CLC 15, 49, 100; DAM POET; PC 21**
See also CA 102; 151; MTCW 1, 2

**Emecheta, (Florence Onye) Buchi** 1944- **CLC 14, 48; BLC 2; DAM MULT**
See also BW 2, 3; CA 81-84; CANR 27, 81; DLB 117; MTCW 1, 2; SATA 66

**Emerson, Mary Moody** 1774-1863 ....... **NCLC 66**

**Emerson, Ralph Waldo** 1803-1882 . **NCLC 1, 38; DA; DAB; DAC; DAM MST, POET; PC 18; WLC**
See also CDALB 1640-1865; DLB 1, 59, 73

**Eminescu, Mihail** 1850-1889 ............... **NCLC 33**

**Empson, William** 1906-1984 **CLC 3, 8, 19, 33, 34**
See also CA 17-20R; 112; CANR 31, 61; DLB 20; MTCW 1, 2

**Enchi, Fumiko (Ueda)** 1905-1986 .......... **CLC 31**
See also CA 129; 121; DLB 182

**Ende, Michael (Andreas Helmuth)** 1929-1995 **CLC 31**
See also CA 118; 124; 149; CANR 36; CLR 14; DLB 75; MAICYA; SATA 61; SATA-Brief 42; SATA-Obit 86

**Endo, Shusaku** 1923-1996 **CLC 7, 14, 19, 54, 99; DAM NOV**
See also CA 29-32R; 153; CANR 21, 54; DLB 182; MTCW 1, 2

**Engel, Marian** 1933-1985 ................. **CLC 36**
See also CA 25-28R; CANR 12; DLB 53; INT CANR-12

**Engelhardt, Frederick**
See Hubbard, L(afayette) Ron(ald)

**Enright, D(ennis) J(oseph)** 1920- .. **CLC 4, 8, 31**
See also CA 1-4R; CANR 1, 42; DLB 27; SATA 25

**Enzensberger, Hans Magnus** 1929- ...... **CLC 43**
See also CA 116; 119

**Ephron, Nora** 1941- ......................... **CLC 17, 31**
See also AITN 2; CA 65-68; CANR 12, 39

**Epicurus** 341B.C.-270B.C. ................. **CMLC 21**
See also DLB 176

**Epsilon**
See Betjeman, John

**Epstein, Daniel Mark** 1948- ................... **CLC 7**
See also CA 49-52; CANR 2, 53

**Epstein, Jacob** 1956- ............................. **CLC 19**
See also CA 114

**Epstein, Jean** 1897-1953 ...................... **TCLC 92**

**Epstein, Joseph** 1937- ........................... **CLC 39**
See also CA 112; 119; CANR 50, 65

**Epstein, Leslie** 1938- ............................. **CLC 27**
See also CA 73-76; CAAS 12; CANR 23, 69

**Equiano, Olaudah** 1745(?)-1797 .. **LC 16; BLC 2; DAM MULT**
See also DLB 37, 50

**ER** ...................................................... **TCLC 33**
See also CA 160; DLB 85

**Erasmus, Desiderius** 1469(?)-1536 .......... **LC 16**

**Erdman, Paul E(mil)** 1932- ................... **CLC 25**
See also AITN 1; CA 61-64; CANR 13, 43

**Erdrich, Louise** 1954- .. **CLC 39, 54, 120; DAM MULT, NOV, POP**
See also AAYA 10; BEST 89:1; CA 114; CANR 41, 62; CDALBS; DLB 152, 175, 206; MTCW 1; NNAL; SATA 94

**Erenburg, Ilya (Grigoryevich)**
See Ehrenburg, Ilya (Grigoryevich)

**Erickson, Stephen Michael** 1950-
See Erickson, Steve
See also CA 129

**Erickson, Steve** 1950- ......................... **CLC 64**
See also Erickson, Stephen Michael
See also CANR 60, 68

**Ericson, Walter**
See Fast, Howard (Melvin)

**Eriksson, Buntel**
See Bergman, (Ernst) Ingmar

**Ernaux, Annie** 1940- ........................... **CLC 88**
See also CA 147

**Erskine, John** 1879-1951 .................... **TCLC 84**
See also CA 112; 159; DLB 9, 102

**Eschenbach, Wolfram von**
See Wolfram von Eschenbach

**Eseki, Bruno**
See Mphahlele, Ezekiel

**Esenin, Sergei (Alexandrovich)** 1895-1925 **TCLC 4**
See also CA 104

**Eshleman, Clayton** 1935- ....................... **CLC 7**
See also CA 33-36R; CAAS 6; DLB 5

**Espriella, Don Manuel Alvarez**
See Southey, Robert

**Espriu, Salvador** 1913-1985 .................... **CLC 9**
See also CA 154; 115; DLB 134

**Espronceda, Jose de** 1808-1842 .......... **NCLC 39**

**Esse, James**
See Stephens, James

**Esterbrook, Tom**
See Hubbard, L(afayette) Ron(ald)

**Estleman, Loren D.** 1952- .. **CLC 48; DAM NOV,**

**POP**
See also AAYA 27; CA 85-88; CANR 27, 74; INT
CANR-27; MTCW 1, 2
Euclid 306B.C.-283B.C. ...................... **CMLC 25**
Eugenides, Jeffrey 1960(?)- .............. **CLC 81**
See also CA 144
Euripides c. 485B.C.-406B.C.**CMLC 23; DA; DAB;
DAC; DAM DRAM, MST; DC 4; WLCS**
See also DLB 176
Evan, Evin
See Faust, Frederick (Schiller)
Evans, Caradoc 1878-1945 .................. **TCLC 85**
Evans, Evan
See Faust, Frederick (Schiller)
Evans, Marian
See Eliot, George
Evans, Mary Ann
See Eliot, George
Evarts, Esther
See Benson, Sally
Everett, Percival L. 1956- ..................... **CLC 57**
See also BW 2; CA 129
Everson, R(onald) G(ilmour) 1903- ....... **CLC 27**
See also CA 17-20R; DLB 88
Everson, William (Oliver) 1912-1994**CLC 1, 5, 14**
See also CA 9-12R; 145; CANR 20; DLB 212;
MTCW 1
Evtushenko, Evgenii Aleksandrovich
See Yevtushenko, Yevgeny (Alexandrovich)
Ewart, Gavin (Buchanan) 1916-1995 **CLC 13, 46**
See also CA 89-92; 150; CANR 17, 46; DLB 40;
MTCW 1
Ewers, Hanns Heinz 1871-1943 ........... **TCLC 12**
See also CA 109; 149
Ewing, Frederick R.
See Sturgeon, Theodore (Hamilton)
Exley, Frederick (Earl) 1929-1992 ..... **CLC 6, 11**
See also AITN 2; CA 81-84; 138; DLB 143; DLBY
81
Eynhardt, Guillermo
See Quiroga, Horacio (Sylvestre)
Ezekiel, Nissim 1924- ........................... **CLC 61**
See also CA 61-64
Ezekiel, Tish O'Dowd 1943- ................. **CLC 34**
See also CA 129
Fadeyev, A.
See Bulgya, Alexander Alexandrovich
Fadeyev, Alexander ........................ **TCLC 53**
See also Bulgya, Alexander Alexandrovich
Fagen, Donald 1948- .............................. **CLC 26**
Fainzilberg, Ilya Arnoldovich 1897-1937
See Ilf, Ilya
See also CA 120; 165
Fair, Ronald L. 1932- ............................... **CLC 18**
See also BW 1; CA 69-72; CANR 25; DLB 33
Fairbairn, Roger
See Carr, John Dickson
Fairbairns, Zoe (Ann) 1948- ................. **CLC 32**
See also CA 103; CANR 21
Falco, Gian
See Papini, Giovanni
Falconer, James
See Kirkup, James
Falconer, Kenneth
See Kornbluth, C(yril) M.
Falkland, Samuel
See Heijermans, Herman
Fallaci, Oriana 1930- ...................... **CLC 11, 110**
See also CA 77-80; CANR 15, 58; MTCW 1
Faludy, George 1913- ............................. **CLC 42**
See also CA 21-24R
Faludy, Gyoergy
See Faludy, George
Fanon, Frantz 1925-1961 **CLC 74; BLC 2; DAM
MULT**
See also BW 1; CA 116; 89-92
Fanshawe, Ann 1625-1680 ...................... **LC 11**

Fante, John (Thomas) 1911-1983 ..... **CLC 60**
See also CA 69-72; 109; CANR 23; DLB 130;
DLBY 83
Farah, Nuruddin 1945- .. **CLC 53; BLC 2; DAM
MULT**
See also BW 2, 3; CA 106; CANR 81; DLB
125
Fargue, Leon-Paul 1876(?)-1947 ... **TCLC 11**
See also CA 109
Farigoule, Louis
See Romains, Jules
Farina, Richard 1936(?)-1966 ............ **CLC 9**
See also CA 81-84; 25-28R
Farley, Walter (Lorimer) 1915-1989 ..... **CLC 17**
See also CA 17-20R; CANR 8, 29; DLB 22; JRDA;
MAICYA; SATA 2, 43
Farmer, Philip Jose 1918- .................. **CLC 1, 19**
See also AAYA 28; CA 1-4R; CANR 4, 35; DLB
8; MTCW 1; SATA 93
Farquhar, George 1677-1707**LC 21; DAM DRAM**
See also DLB 84
Farrell, J(ames) G(ordon) 1935-1979 ...... **CLC 6**
See also CA 73-76; 89-92; CANR 36; DLB 14;
MTCW 1
Farrell, James T(homas) 1904-1979 **CLC 1, 4, 8,
11, 66; SSC 28**
See also CA 5-8R; 89-92; CANR 9, 61; DLB 4, 9,
86; DLBD 2; MTCW 1, 2
Farren, Richard J.
See Betjeman, John
Farren, Richard M.
<indSee Betjeman, John
Fassbinder, Rainer Werner 1946-1982 . **CLC 20**
See also CA 93-96; 106; CANR 31
Fast, Howard (Melvin) 1914-**CLC 23; DAM NOV**
See also AAYA 16; CA 1-4R; CAAS 18; CANR
1, 33, 54, 75; DLB 9; INT CANR-33; MTCW 1;
SATA 7; SATA-Essay 107
Faulcon, Robert
See Holdstock, Robert P.
Faulkner, William (Cuthbert) 1897-1962**CLC 1,
3, 6, 8, 9, 11, 14, 18, 28, 52, 68; DA; DAB;
DAC; DAM MST, NOV; SSC 1, 35; WLC**
See also AAYA 7; CA 81-84; CANR 33; CDALB
1929-1941; DLB 9, 11, 44, 102; DLBD 2; DLBY
86, 97; MTCW 1, 2
Fauset, Jessie Redmon 1884(?)-1961**CLC 19, 54;
BLC 2; DAM MULT**
See also BW 1; CA 109; DLB 51
Faust, Frederick (Schiller) 1892-1944(?) **T C L C
49; DAM POP**
See also CA 108; 152
Faust, Irvin 1924- .................................. **CLC 8**
See also CA 33-36R; CANR 28, 67; DLB 2, 28;
DLBY 80
Fawkes, Guy
See Benchley, Robert (Charles)
Fearing, Kenneth (Flexner) 1902-1961 . **CLC 51**
See also CA 93-96; CANR 59; DLB 9
Fecamps, Elise
See Creasey, John
Federman, Raymond 1928- ................ **CLC 6, 47**
See also CA 17-20R; CAAS 8; CANR 10, 43;
DLBY 80
Federspiel, J(uerg) F. 1931- ................. **CLC 42**
See also CA 146
Feiffer, Jules (Ralph) 1929- **CLC 2, 8, 64; DAM
DRAM**
See also AAYA 3; CA 17-20R; CANR 30, 59; DLB
7, 44; INT CANR-30; MTCW 1; SATA 8, 61
Feige, Hermann Albert Otto Maximilian
See Traven, B.
Feinberg, David B. 1956-1994 ................ **CLC 59**
See also CA 135; 147
Feinstein, Elaine 1930- ......................... **CLC 36**
See also CA 69-72; CAAS 1; CANR 31, 68; DLB
14, 40; MTCW 1

Feldman, Irving (Mordecai) 1928- ..... **CLC 7**
See also CA 1-4R; CANR 1; DLB 169
Felix-Tchicaya, Gerald
See Tchicaya, Gerald Felix
Fellini, Federico 1920-1993 ............. **CLC 16, 85**
See also CA 65-68; 143; CANR 33
Felsen, Henry Gregor 1916- .............. **CLC 17**
See also CA 1-4R; CANR 1; SAAS 2; SATA 1
Fenno, Jack
See Calisher, Hortense
Fenollosa, Ernest (Francisco) 1853-1908**TCLC 91**
Fenton, James Martin 1949- ................. **CLC 32**
See also CA 102; DLB 40
Ferber, Edna 1887-1968 .................. **CLC 18, 93**
See also AITN 1; CA 5-8R; 25-28R; CANR 68;
DLB 9, 28, 86; MTCW 1, 2; SATA 7
Ferguson, Helen
See Kavan, Anna
Ferguson, Samuel 1810-1886 ............. **NCLC 33**
See also DLB 32
Fergusson, Robert 1750-1774 ................. **LC 29**
See also DLB 109
Ferling, Lawrence
See Ferlinghetti, Lawrence (Monsanto)
Ferlinghetti, Lawrence (Monsanto) 1919(?)-**CLC
2, 6, 10, 27, 111; DAM POET; PC 1**
See also CA 5-8R; CANR 3, 41, 73; CDALB 1941-
1968; DLB 5, 16; MTCW 1, 2
Fernandez, Vicente Garcia Huidobro
See Huidobro Fernandez, Vicente Garcia
Ferrer, Gabriel (Francisco Victor) Miro
See Miro (Ferrer), Gabriel (Francisco Victor)
Ferrier, Susan (Edmonstone) 1782-1854**NCLC 8**
See also DLB 116
Ferrigno, Robert 1948(?)- ..................... **CLC 65**
See also CA 140
Ferron, Jacques 1921-1985 ......... **CLC 94; DAC**
See also CA 117; 129; DLB 60
Feuchtwanger, Lion 1884-1958 ............. **TCLC 3**
See also CA 104; DLB 66
Feuillet, Octave 1821-1890 ................. **NCLC 45**
See also DLB 192
Feydeau, Georges (Leon Jules Marie) 1862-1921
**TCLC 22; DAM DRAM**
See also CA 113; 152; DLB 192
Fichte, Johann Gottlieb 1762-1814 ...... **NCLC 62**
See also DLB 90
Ficino, Marsilio 1433-1499 ....................... **LC 12**
Fiedeler, Hans
See Doeblin, Alfred
Fiedler, Leslie A(aron) 1917- ...... **CLC 4, 13, 24**
See also CA 9-12R; CANR 7, 63; DLB 28, 67;
MTCW 1, 2
Field, Andrew 1938- ............................. **CLC 44**
See also CA 97-100; CANR 25
Field, Eugene 1850-1895 ....................... **NCLC 3**
See also DLB 23, 42, 140; DLBD 13; MAICYA;
SATA 16
Field, Gans T.
See Wellman, Manly Wade
Field, Michael 1915-1971 .................. **TCLC 43**
See also CA 29-32R
Field, Peter
See Hobson, Laura Z(ametkin)
Fielding, Henry 1707-1754 **LC 1, 46; DA; DAB;
DAC; DAM DRAM, MST, NOV; WLC**
See also CDBLB 1660-1789; DLB 39, 84, 101
Fielding, Sarah 1710-1768 .................. **LC 1, 44**
See also DLB 39
Fields, W. C. 1880-1946 ....................... **TCLC 80**
See also DLB 44
Fierstein, Harvey (Forbes) 1954- **CLC 33; DAM
DRAM, POP**
See also CA 123; 129
Figes, Eva 1932- ...................................... **CLC 31**
See also CA 53-56; CANR 4, 44; DLB 14
Finch, Anne 1661-1720 .................. **LC 3; PC 21**

See also CA 45-48; CANR 2, 48, 74; MTCW 1

**Fraser, Sylvia** 1935- .............................. **CLC 64**
See also CA 45-48; CANR 1, 16, 60

**Frayn, Michael** 1933- ... **CLC 3, 7, 31, 47; DAM DRAM, NOV**
See also CA 5-8R; CANR 30, 69; DLB 13, 14, 194; MTCW 1, 2

**Fraze, Candida (Merrill)** 1945- ........ **CLC 50**
See also CA 126

**Frazer, J(ames) G(eorge)** 1854-1941 ... **TCLC 32**
See also CA 118

**Frazer, Robert Caine**
See Creasey, John

**Frazer, Sir James George**
See Frazer, J(ames) G(eorge)

**Frazier, Charles** 1950- ........................ **CLC 109**
See also CA 161

**Frazier, Ian** 1951- ................................ **CLC 46**
See also CA 130; CANR 54

**Frederic, Harold** 1856-1898 ................ **NCLC 10**
See also DLB 12, 23; DLBD 13

**Frederick, John**
See Faust, Frederick (Schiller)

**Frederick the Great** 1712-1786 ................ **LC 14**

**Fredro, Aleksander** 1793-1876 .............. **NCLC 8**

**Freeling, Nicolas** 1927- ........................ **CLC 38**
See also CA 49-52; CAAS 12; CANR 1, 17, 50; DLB 87

**Freeman, Douglas Southall** 1886-1953 **TCLC 11**
See also CA 109; DLB 17; DLBD 17

**Freeman, Judith** 1946- .......................... **CLC 55**
See also CA 148

**Freeman, Mary Eleanor Wilkins** 1852-1930 **TCLC 9; SSC 1**
See also CA 106; 177; DLB 12, 78

**Freeman, R(ichard) Austin** 1862-1943 **TCLC 21**
See also CA 113; DLB 70

**French, Albert** 1943- ............................ **CLC 86**
See also BW 3; CA 167

**French, Marilyn** 1929- ... **CLC 10, 18, 60; DAM DRAM, NOV, POP**
See also CA 69-72; CANR 3, 31; INT CANR-31; MTCW 1, 2

**French, Paul**
See Asimov, Isaac

**Freneau, Philip Morin** 1752-1832 ......... **NCLC 1**
See also DLB 37, 43

**Freud, Sigmund** 1856-1939 .................. **TCLC 52**
See also CA 115; 133; CANR 69; MTCW 1, 2

**Friedan, Betty (Naomi)** 1921- ............... **CLC 74**
See also CA 65-68; CANR 18, 45, 74; MTCW 1, 2

**Friedlander, Saul** 1932- .......................... **CLC 90**
See also CA 117; 130; CANR 72

**Friedman, B(ernard) H(arper)** 1926- ...... **CLC 7**
See also CA 1-4R; CANR 3, 48

**Friedman, Bruce Jay** 1930- ............ **CLC 3, 5, 56**
See also CA 9-12R; CANR 25, 52; DLB 2, 28; INT CANR-25

**Friel, Brian** 1929- ..... **CLC 5, 42, 59, 115; DC 8**
See also CA 21-24R; CANR 33, 69; DLB 13; MTCW 1

**Friis-Baastad, Babbis Ellinor** 1921-1970**CLC 12**
See also CA 17-20R; 134; SATA 7

**Frisch, Max (Rudolf)** 1911-1991**CLC 3, 9, 14, 18, 32, 44; DAM DRAM, NOV**
See also CA 85-88; 134; CANR 32, 74; DLB 69, 124; MTCW 1, 2

**Fromentin, Eugene (Samuel Auguste)** 1820-1876 **NCLC 10**
See also DLB 123

**Frost, Frederick**
See Faust, Frederick (Schiller)

**Frost, Robert (Lee)** 1874-1963**CLC 1, 3, 4, 9, 10, 13, 15, 26, 34, 44; DA; DAB; DAC; DAM MST, POET; PC 1; WLC**
See also AAYA 21; CA 89-92; CANR 33; CDALB 1917-1929; DLB 54; DLBD 7; MTCW 1, 2;

SATA 14

**Froude, James Anthony** 1818-1894 ..... **NCLC 43**
See also DLB 18, 57, 144

**Froy, Herald**
See Waterhouse, Keith (Spencer)

**Fry, Christopher** 1907- ..... **CLC 2, 10, 14; DAM DRAM**
See also CA 17-20R; CAAS 23; CANR 9, 30, 74; DLB 13; MTCW 1, 2; SATA 66

**Frye, (Herman) Northrop** 1912-1991 **CLC 24, 70**
See also CA 5-8R; 133; CANR 8, 37; DLB 67, 68; MTCW 1, 2

**Fuchs, Daniel** 1909-1993 ................... **CLC 8, 22**
See also CA 81-84; 142; CAAS 5; CANR 40; DLB 9, 26, 28; DLBY 93

**Fuchs, Daniel** 1934- ............................. **CLC 34**
See also CA 37-40R; CANR 14, 48

**Fuentes, Carlos** 1928-**CLC 3, 8, 10, 13, 22, 41, 60, 113; DA; DAB; DAC; DAM MST, MULT, NOV; HLC; SSC 24; WLC**
See also AAYA 4; AITN 2; CA 69-72; CANR 10, 32, 68; DLB 113; HW 1, 2; MTCW 1, 2

**Fuentes, Gregorio Lopez y**
See Lopez y Fuentes, Gregorio

**Fugard, (Harold) Athol** 1932-**CLC 5, 9, 14, 25, 40, 80; DAM DRAM; DC 3**
See also AAYA 17; CA 85-88; CANR 32, 54; MTCW 1

**Fugard, Sheila** 1932- ............................. **CLC 48**
See also CA 125

**Fuller, Charles (H., Jr.)** 1939- **CLC 25; BLC 2; DAM DRAM, MULT; DC 1**
See also BW 2; CA 108; 112; DLB 38; INT 112; MTCW 1

**Fuller, John (Leopold)** 1937- ................. **CLC 62**
See also CA 21-24R; CANR 9, 44; DLB 40

**Fuller, Margaret** ............................ **NCLC 5, 50**
See also Ossoli, Sarah Margaret (Fuller marchesa d')

**Fuller, Roy (Broadbent)** 1912-1991 ... **CLC 4, 28**
See also CA 5-8R; 135; CAAS 10; CANR 53; DLB 15, 20; SATA 87

**Fulton, Alice** 1952- ............................... **CLC 52**
See also CA 116; CANR 57; DLB 193

**Furphy, Joseph** 1843-1912 ................... **TCLC 25**
See also CA 163

**Fussell, Paul** 1924- ............................... **CLC 74**
See also BEST 90:1; CA 17-20R; CANR 8, 21, 35, 69; INT CANR-21; MTCW 1, 2

**Futabatei, Shimei** 1864-1909 ................ **TCLC 44**
See also CA 162; DLB 180

**Futrelle, Jacques** 1875-1912 ............... **TCLC 19**
See also CA 113; 155

**Gaboriau, Emile** 1835-1873 .................. **NCLC 14**

**Gadda, Carlo Emilio** 1893-1973 .............. **CLC 11**
See also CA 89-92; DLB 177

**Gaddis, William** 1922-1998**CLC 1, 3, 6, 8, 10, 19, 43, 86**
See also CA 17-20R; 172; CANR 21, 48; DLB 2; MTCW 1, 2

**Gage, Walter**
See Inge, William (Motter)

**Gaines, Ernest J(ames)** 1933-**CLC 3, 11, 18, 86; BLC 2; DAM MULT**
See also AAYA 18; AITN 1; BW 2, 3; CA 9-12R; CANR 6, 24, 42, 75; CDALB 1968-1988; DLB 2, 33, 152; DLBY 80; MTCW 1, 2; SATA 86

**Gaitskill, Mary** 1954- ............................. **CLC 69**
See also CA 128; CANR 61

**Galdos, Benito Perez**
See Perez Galdos, Benito

**Gale, Zona** 1874-1938 ...... **TCLC 7; DAM DRAM**
See also CA 105; 153; DLB 9, 78

**Galeano, Eduardo (Hughes)** 1940-**CLC 72; HLCS 1**
See also CA 29-32R; CANR 13, 32; HW 1

**Galiano, Juan Valera y Alcala**

See Valera y Alcala-Galiano, Juan

**Galilei, Galileo** 1546-1642 ...................... **LC 45**

**Gallagher, Tess** 1943-**CLC 18, 63; DAM POET; PC 9**
See also CA 106; DLB 212

**Gallant, Mavis** 1922-**CLC 7, 18, 38; DAC; DAM MST; SSC 5**
See also CA 69-72; CANR 29, 69; DLB 53; MTCW 1, 2

**Gallant, Roy A(rthur)** 1924- ................. **CLC 17**
See also CA 5-8R; CANR 4, 29, 54; CLR 30; MAICYA; SATA 4, 68

**Gallico, Paul (William)** 1897-1976 .......... **CLC 2**
See also AITN 1; CA 5-8R; 69-72; CANR 23; DLB 9, 171; MAICYA; SATA 13

**Gallo, Max Louis** 1932- .......................... **CLC 95**
See also CA 85-88

**Gallois, Lucien**
See Desnos, Robert

**Gallup, Ralph**
See Whitemore, Hugh (John)

**Galsworthy, John** 1867-1933 .. **TCLC 1, 45; DA; DAB; DAC; DAM DRAM, MST, NOV; SSC 22; WLC**
See also CA 104; 141; CANR 75; CDBLB 1890-1914; DLB 10, 34, 98, 162; DLBD 16; MTCW 1

**Galt, John** 1779-1839 ............................... **NCLC 1**
See also DLB 99, 116, 159

**Galvin, James** 1951- ............................... **CLC 38**
See also CA 108; CANR 26

**Gamboa, Federico** 1864-1939 .............. **TCLC 36**
See also CA 167; HW 2

**Gandhi, M. K.**
See Gandhi, Mohandas Karamchand

**Gandhi, Mahatma**
See Gandhi, Mohandas Karamchand

**Gandhi, Mohandas Karamchand** 1869-1948**TCLC 59; DAM MULT**
See also CA 121; 132; MTCW 1, 2

**Gann, Ernest Kellogg** 1910-1991 .......... **CLC 23**
See also AITN 1; CA 1-4R; 136; CANR 1

**Garcia, Cristina** 1958- .......................... **CLC 76**
See also CA 141; CANR 73; HW 2

**Garcia Lorca, Federico** 1898-1936**TCLC 1, 7, 49; DA; DAB; DAC; DAM DRAM, MST, MULT, POET; DC 2; HLC; PC 3; WLC**
See also CA 104; 131; CANR 81; DLB 108; HW 1, 2; MTCW 1, 2

**Garcia Marquez, Gabriel (Jose)** 1928-**CLC 2, 3, 8, 10, 15, 27, 47, 55, 68; DA; DAB; DAC; DAM MST, MULT, NOV, POP; HLC; SSC 8; WLC**
See also AAYA 3; BEST 89:1, 90:4; CA 33-36R; CANR 10, 28, 50, 75; DLB 113; HW 1, 2; MTCW 1, 2

**Gard, Janice**
See Latham, Jean Lee

**Gard, Roger Martin du**
See Martin du Gard, Roger

**Gardam, Jane** 1928- ............................... **CLC 43**
See also CA 49-52; CANR 2, 18, 33, 54; CLR 12; DLB 14, 161; MAICYA; MTCW 1; SAAS 9; SATA 39, 76; SATA-Brief 28

**Gardner, Herb(ert)** 1934- ...................... **CLC 44**
See also CA 149

**Gardner, John (Champlin), Jr.** 1933-1982**CLC 2, 3, 5, 7, 8, 10, 18, 28, 34; DAM NOV, POP; SSC 7**
See also AITN 1; CA 65-68; 107; CANR 33, 73; CDALBS; DLB 2; DLBY 82; MTCW 1; SATA 40; SATA-Obit 31

**Gardner, John (Edmund)** 1926- ... **CLC 30; DAM POP**
See also CA 103; CANR 15, 69; MTCW 1

**Gardner, Miriam**
See Bradley, Marion Zimmer

**Gardner, Noel**

Gunn, William Harrison 1934(?)-1989
See Gunn, Bill
See also AITN 1; BW 1, 3; CA 13-16R; 128;
CANR 12, 25, 76
Gunnars, Kristjana 1948- ..................... CLC 69
See also CA 113; DLB 60
Gurdjieff, G(eorgei) I(vanovich) 1877(?)-1949
TCLC 71
See also CA 157
Gurganus, Allan 1947- ....... CLC 70; DAM POP
See also BEST 90:1; CA 135
Gurney, A(lbert) R(amsdell), Jr. 1930- CLC 32,
50, 54; DAM DRAM
See also CA 77-80; CANR 32, 64
Gurney, Ivor (Bertie) 1890-1937 ......... TCLC 33
See also CA 167
Gurney, Peter
See Gurney, A(lbert) R(amsdell), Jr.
Guro, Elena 1877-1913 ....................... TCLC 56
Gustafson, James M(oody) 1925- ........ CLC 100
See also CA 25-28R; CANR 37
Gustafson, Ralph (Barker) 1909- ......... CLC 36
See also CA 21-24R; CANR 8, 45; DLB 88
Gut, Gom
See Simenon, Georges (Jacques Christian)
Guterson, David 1956- ........................... CLC 91
See also CA 132; CANR 73; MTCW 2
Guthrie, A(lfred) B(ertram), Jr. 1901-1991 C L C
23
See also CA 57-60; 134; CANR 24; DLB 212;
SATA 62; SATA-Obit 67
Guthrie, Isobel
See Grieve, C(hristopher) M(urray)
Guthrie, Woodrow Wilson 1912-1967
See Guthrie, Woody
See also CA 113; 93-96
Guthrie, Woody ...................................... CLC 35
See also Guthrie, Woodrow Wilson
Guy, Rosa (Cuthbert) 1928- .............. CLC 26
See also AAYA 4; BW 2; CA 17-20R; CANR
14, 34; CLR 13; DLB 33; JRDA; MAICYA;
SATA 14, 62
Gwendolyn
See Bennett, (Enoch) Arnold
H. D. ................. CLC 3, 8, 14, 31, 34, 73; PC 5
See also Doolittle, Hilda
H. de V.
See Buchan, John
Haavikko, Paavo Juhani 1931- ........ CLC 18, 34
See also CA 106
Habbema, Koos
See Heijermans, Herman
Habermas, Juergen 1929- ................... CLC 104
See also CA 109
Habermas, Jurgen
See Habermas, Juergen
Hacker, Marilyn 1942-CLC 5, 9, 23, 72, 91; DAM
POET
See also CA 77-80; CANR 68; DLB 120
Haeckel, Ernst Heinrich (Philipp August) 1834-
1919 ...................................... TCLC 83
See also CA 157
Hafiz c. 1326-1389(?) .......................... CMLC 34
Haggard, H(enry) Rider 1856-1925 ..... TCLC 11
See also CA 108; 148; DLB 70, 156, 174, 178;
MTCW 2; SATA 16
Hagiosy, L.
See Larbaud, Valery (Nicolas)
Hagiwara Sakutaro 1886-1942 TCLC 60; PC 18
Haig, Fenil
See Ford, Ford Madox
Haig-Brown, Roderick (Langmere) 1908-1976
CLC 21
See also CA 5-8R; 69-72; CANR 4, 38; CLR 31;
DLB 88; MAICYA; SATA 12
Hailey, Arthur 1920- .. CLC 5; DAM NOV, POP
See also AITN 2; BEST 90:3; CA 1-4R; CANR 2,

36, 75; DLB 88; DLBY 82; MTCW 1, 2
Hailey, Elizabeth Forsythe 1938- .......... CLC 40
See also CA 93-96; CAAS 1; CANR 15, 48; INT
CANR-15
Haines, John (Meade) 1924- ................ CLC 58
See also CA 17-20R; CANR 13, 34; DLB 212
Hakluyt, Richard 1552-1616 ...................... LC 31
Haldeman, Joe (William) 1943- ........ CLC 61
See also CA 53-56; CAAS 25; CANR 6, 70,
72; DLB 8; INT CANR-6
Hale, Sarah Josepha (Buell) 1788-1879NCLC 75
See also DLB 1, 42, 73
Haley, Alex(ander Murray Palmer) 1921-1992
CLC 8, 12, 76; BLC 2; DA; DAB; DAC; DAM
MST, MULT, POP
See also AAYA 26; BW 2, 3; CA 77-80; 136;
CANR 61; CDALBS; DLB 38; MTCW 1, 2
Haliburton, Thomas Chandler 1796-1865 N C L C
15
See also DLB 11, 99
Hall, Donald (Andrew, Jr.) 1928- CLC 1, 13, 37,
59; DAM POET
See also CA 5-8R; CAAS 7; CANR 2, 44, 64;
DLB 5; MTCW 1; SATA 23, 97
Hall, Frederic Sauser
See Sauser-Hall, Frederic
Hall, James
See Kuttner, Henry
Hall, James Norman 1887-1951 .......... TCLC 23
See also CA 123; 173; SATA 21
Hall, Radclyffe
See Hall, (Marguerite) Radclyffe
See also MTCW 2
Hall, (Marguerite) Radclyffe 1886-1943TCLC 12
See also CA 110; 150; DLB 191
Hall, Rodney 1935- ................................. CLC 51
See also CA 109; CANR 69
Halleck, Fitz-Greene 1790-1867 ......... NCLC 47
See also DLB 3
Halliday, Michael
See Creasey, John
Halpern, Daniel 1945- ........................... CLC 14
See also CA 33-36R
Hamburger, Michael (Peter Leopold) 1924- C L C
5, 14
See also CA 5-8R; CAAS 4; CANR 2, 47; DLB 27
Hamill, Pete 1935- ................................ CLC 10
See also CA 25-28R; CANR 18, 71
Hamilton, Alexander 1755(?)-1804 ...... NCLC 49
See also DLB 37
Hamilton, Clive
See Lewis, C(live) S(taples)
Hamilton, Edmond 1904-1977 ................ CLC 1
See also CA 1-4R; CANR 3; DLB 8
Hamilton, Eugene (Jacob) Lee
See Lee-Hamilton, Eugene (Jacob)
Hamilton, Franklin
See Silverberg, Robert
Hamilton, Gail
See Corcoran, Barbara
Hamilton, Mollie
See Kaye, M(ary) M(argaret)
Hamilton, (Anthony Walter) Patrick 1904-1962
CLC 51
See also CA 176; 113; DLB 191
Hamilton, Virginia 1936- CLC 26; DAM MULT
See also AAYA 2, 21; BW 2, 3; CA 25-28R;
CANR 20, 37, 73; CLR 1, 11, 40; DLB 33, 52;
INT CANR-20; JRDA; MAICYA; MTCW 1,
2; SATA 4, 56, 79
Hammett, (Samuel) Dashiell 1894-1961CLC 3, 5,
10, 19, 47; SSC 17
See also AITN 1; CA 81-84; CANR 42; CDALB
1929-1941; DLBD 6; DLBY 96; MTCW 1, 2
Hammon, Jupiter 1711(?)-1800(?)NCLC 5; BLC
2; DAM MULT, POET; PC 16
See also DLB 31, 50

Hammond, Keith
See Kuttner, Henry
Hamner, Earl (Henry), Jr. 1923- ........... CLC 12
See also AITN 2; CA 73-76; DLB 6
Hampton, Christopher (James) 1946- .... CLC 4
See also CA 25-28R; DLB 13; MTCW 1
Hamsun, Knut ...............................TCLC 2, 14, 49
See also Pedersen, Knut
Handke, Peter 1942-CLC 5, 8, 10, 15, 38; DAM
DRAM, NOV
See also CA 77-80; CANR 33, 75; DLB 85, 124;
MTCW 1, 2
Hanley, James 1901-1985 .......... CLC 3, 5, 8, 13
See also CA 73-76; 117; CANR 36; DLB 191;
MTCW 1
Hannah, Barry 1942- ................. CLC 23, 38, 90
See also CA 108; 110; CANR 43, 68; DLB 6; INT
110; MTCW 1
Hannon, Ezra
See Hunter, Evan
Hansberry, Lorraine (Vivian) 1930-1965CLC 17,
62; BLC 2; DA; DAB; DAC; DAM DRAM,
MST, MULT; DC 2
See also AAYA 25; BW 1, 3; CA 109; 25-28R;
CABS 3; CANR 58; CDALB 1941-1968; DLB
7, 38; MTCW 1, 2
Hansen, Joseph 1923- ........................... CLC 38
See also CA 29-32R; CAAS 17; CANR 16, 44, 66;
INT CANR-16
Hansen, Martin A(lfred) 1909-1955 .... TCLC 32
See also CA 167
Hanson, Kenneth O(stlin) 1922- ........... CLC 13
See also CA 53-56; CANR 7
Hardwick, Elizabeth (Bruce) 1916-CLC 13; DAM
NOV
See also CA 5-8R; CANR 3, 32, 70; DLB 6; MTCW
1, 2
Hardy, Thomas 1840-1928TCLC 4, 10, 18, 32, 48,
53, 72; DA; DAB; DAC; DAM MST, NOV,
POET; PC 8; SSC 2; WLC
See also CA 104; 123; CDBLB 1890-1914; DLB
18, 19, 135; MTCW 1, 2
Hare, David 1947- ........................... CLC 29, 58
See also CA 97-100; CANR 39; DLB 13; MTCW
1
Harewood, John
See Van Druten, John (William)
Harford, Henry
See Hudson, W(illiam) H(enry)
Hargrave, Leonie
See Disch, Thomas M(ichael)
Harjo, Joy 1951- .............. CLC 83; DAM MULT
See also CA 114; CANR 35, 67; DLB 120, 175;
MTCW 2; NNAL
Harlan, Louis R(udolph) 1922- ............. CLC 34
See also CA 21-24R; CANR 25, 55, 80
Harling, Robert 1951(?)- ....................... CLC 53
See also CA 147
Harmon, William (Ruth) 1938- ............. CLC 38
See also CA 33-36R; CANR 14, 32, 35; SATA 65
Harper, F. E. W.
See Harper, Frances Ellen Watkins
Harper, Frances E. W.
See Harper, Frances Ellen Watkins
Harper, Frances E. Watkins
See Harper, Frances Ellen Watkins
Harper, Frances Ellen
See Harper, Frances Ellen Watkins
Harper, Frances Ellen Watkins 1825-1911TCLC
14; BLC 2; DAM MULT, POET; PC 21
See also BW 1, 3; CA 111; 125; CANR 79; DLB
50
Harper, Michael S(teven) 1938- ........ CLC 7, 22
See also BW 1; CA 33-36R; CANR 24; DLB 41
Harper, Mrs. F. E. W.
See Harper, Frances Ellen Watkins
Harris, Christie (Lucy) Irwin 1907- ..... CLC 12

See also CA 5-8R; CANR 6; CLR 47; DLB 88; JRDA; MAICYA; SAAS 10; SATA 6, 74
**Harris, Frank** 1856-1931 ..................... **TCLC 24**
See also CA 109; 150; CANR 80; DLB 156, 197
**Harris, George Washington** 1814-1869**NCLC 23**
See also DLB 3, 11
**Harris, Joel Chandler** 1848-1908**TCLC 2; SSC 19**
See also CA 104; 137; CANR 80; CLR 49; DLB 11, 23, 42, 78, 91; MAICYA; SATA 100; YABC 1
**Harris, John (Wyndham Parkes Lucas) Beynon** 1903-1969
See Wyndham, John
See also CA 102; 89-92
**Harris, MacDonald** ................................ **CLC 9**
See also Heiney, Donald (William)
**Harris, Mark** 1922- ................................ **CLC 19**
See also CA 5-8R; CAAS 3; CANR 2, 55; DLB 2; DLBY 80
**Harris, (Theodore) Wilson** 1921- ......... **CLC 25**
See also BW 2, 3; CA 65-68; CAAS 16; CANR 11, 27, 69; DLB 117; MTCW 1
**Harrison, Elizabeth Cavanna** 1909-
See Cavanna, Betty
See also CA 9-12R; CANR 6, 27
**Harrison, Harry (Max)** 1925- ................ **CLC 42**
See also CA 1-4R; CANR 5, 21; DLB 8; SATA 4
**Harrison, James (Thomas)** 1937-**CLC 6, 14, 33, 66; SSC 19**
See also CA 13-16R; CANR 8, 51, 79; DLBY 82; INT CANR-8
**Harrison, Jim**
See Harrison, James (Thomas)
**Harrison, Kathryn** 1961- ....................... **CLC 70**
See also CA 144; CANR 68
**Harrison, Tony** 1937- ........................... **CLC 43**
See also CA 65-68; CANR 44; DLB 40; MTCW 1
**Harriss, Will(ard Irvin)** 1922- .............. **CLC 34**
See also CA 111
**Harson, Sley**
See Ellison, Harlan (Jay)
**Hart, Ellis**
See Ellison, Harlan (Jay)
**Hart, Josephine** 1942(?)- .... **CLC 70; DAM POP**
See also CA 138; CANR 70
**Hart, Moss** 1904-1961 ..... **CLC 66; DAM DRAM**
See also CA 109; 89-92; DLB 7
**Harte, (Francis) Bret(t)** 1836(?)-1902**TCLC 1, 25; DA; DAC; DAM MST; SSC 8; WLC**
See also CA 104; 140; CANR 80; CDALB 1865-1917; DLB 12, 64, 74, 79, 186; SATA 26
**Hartley, L(eslie) P(oles)** 1895-1972 ... **CLC 2, 22**
See also CA 45-48; 37-40R; CANR 33; DLB 15, 139; MTCW 1, 2
**Hartmann, Geoffrey H.** 1929- ................. **CLC 27**
See also CA 117; 125; CANR 79; DLB 67
**Hartmann, Sadakichi** 1867-1944 ......... **TCLC 73**
See also CA 157; DLB 54
**Hartmann von Aue** c. 1160-c. 1205 ..... **CMLC 15**
See also DLB 138
**Hartmann von Aue** 1170-1210 ........... **CMLC 15**
**Haruf, Kent** 1943- ................................. **CLC 34**
See also CA 149
**Harwood, Ronald** 1934- .. **CLC 32; DAM DRAM, MST**
See also CA 1-4R; CANR 4, 55; DLB 13
**Hasegawa Tatsunosuke**
See Futabatei, Shimei
**Hasek, Jaroslav (Matej Frantisek)** 1883-1923 **TCLC 4**
See also CA 104; 129; MTCW 1, 2
**Hass, Robert** 1941- ....... **CLC 18, 39, 99; PC 16**
See also CA 111; CANR 30, 50, 71; DLB 105, 206; SATA 94
**Hastings, Hudson**
See Kuttner, Henry
**Hastings, Selina** ................................... **CLC 44**

**Hathorne, John** 1641-1717 ................... **LC 38**
**Hatteras, Amelia**
See Mencken, H(enry) L(ouis)
**Hatteras, Owen** .................................. **TCLC 18**
See also Mencken, H(enry) L(ouis); Nathan, George Jean
**Hauptmann, Gerhart (Johann Robert)** 1862-1946 **TCLC 4; DAM DRAM**
See also CA 104; 153; DLB 66, 118
**Havel, Vaclav** 1936-**CLC 25, 58, 65; DAM DRAM; DC 6**
See also CA 104; CANR 36, 63; MTCW 1, 2
**Haviaras, Stratis** ................................... **CLC 33**
See also Chaviaras, Strates
**Hawes, Stephen** 1475(?)-1523(?) .............. **LC 17**
See also DLB 132
**Hawkes, John (Clendennin Burne, Jr.)** 1925-1998 **CLC 1, 2, 3, 4, 7, 9, 14, 15, 27, 49**
See also CA 1-4R; 167; CANR 2, 47, 64; DLB 2, 7; DLBY 80, 98; MTCW 1, 2
**Hawking, S. W.**
See Hawking, Stephen W(illiam)
**Hawking, Stephen W(illiam)** 1942-**CLC 63, 105**
See also AAYA 13; BEST 89:1; CA 126; 129; CANR 48; MTCW 2
**Hawkins, Anthony Hope**
See Hope, Anthony
**Hawthorne, Julian** 1846-1934 .............. **TCLC 25**
See also CA 165
**Hawthorne, Nathaniel** 1804-1864 **NCLC 39; DA; DAB; DAC; DAM MST, NOV; SSC 3, 29; WLC**
See also AAYA 18; CDALB 1640-1865; DLB 1, 74; YABC 2
**Haxton, Josephine Ayres** 1921-
See Douglas, Ellen
See also CA 115; CANR 41
**Hayaseca y Eizaguirre, Jorge**
See Echegaray (y Eizaguirre), Jose (Maria Waldo)
**Hayashi, Fumiko** 1904-1951 ................ **TCLC 27**
See also CA 161; DLB 180
**Haycraft, Anna**
See Ellis, Alice Thomas
See also CA 122; MTCW 2
**Hayden, Robert E(arl)** 1913-1980**CLC 5, 9, 14, 37; BLC 2; DA; DAC; DAM MST, MULT, POET; PC 6**
See also BW 1, 3; CA 69-72; 97-100; CABS 2; CANR 24, 75; CDALB 1941-1968; DLB 5, 76; MTCW 1, 2; SATA 19; SATA-Obit 26
**Hayford, J(oseph) E(phraim) Casely**
See Casely-Hayford, J(oseph) E(phraim)
**Hayman, Ronald** 1932- ........................... **CLC 44**
See also CA 25-28R; CANR 18, 50; DLB 155
**Haywood, Eliza (Fowler)** 1693(?)-1756 . **LC 1, 44**
See also DLB 39
**Hazlitt, William** 1778-1830 ................. **NCLC 29**
See also DLB 110, 158
**Hazzard, Shirley** 1931- ........................ **CLC 18**
See also CA 9-12R; CANR 4, 70; DLBY 82; MTCW 1
**Head, Bessie** 1937-1986**CLC 25, 67; BLC 2; DAM MULT**
See also BW 2, 3; CA 29-32R; 119; CANR 25; DLB 117; MTCW 1, 2
**Headon, (Nicky) Topper** 1956(?)- .......... **CLC 30**
**Heaney, Seamus (Justin)** 1939-**CLC 5, 7, 14, 25, 37, 74, 91; DAB; DAM POET; PC 18; WLCS**
See also CA 85-88; CANR 25, 48, 75; CDBLB 1960 to Present; DLB 40; DLBY 95; MTCW 1, 2
**Hearn, (Patricio) Lafcadio (Tessima Carlos)** 1850-1904 ................................................ **TCLC 9**
See also CA 105; 166; DLB 12, 78, 189
**Hearne, Vicki** 1946- .............................. **CLC 56**
See also CA 139

**Hearon, Shelby** 1931- ......................... **CLC 63**
See also AITN 2; CA 25-28R; CANR 18, 48
**Heat-Moon, William Least** .................... **CLC 29**
See also Trogdon, William (Lewis)
See also AAYA 9
**Hebbel, Friedrich** 1813-1863 .... **NCLC 43; DAM DRAM**
See also DLB 129
**Hebert, Anne** 1916-**CLC 4, 13, 29; DAC; DAM MST, POET**
See also CA 85-88; CANR 69; DLB 68; MTCW 1, 2
**Hecht, Anthony (Evan)** 1923-**CLC 8, 13, 19; DAM POET**
See also CA 9-12R; CANR 6; DLB 5, 169
**Hecht, Ben** 1894-1964 ........................... **CLC 8**
See also CA 85-88; DLB 7, 9, 25, 26, 28, 86
**Hedayat, Sadeq** 1903-1951 .................... **TCLC 21**
See also CA 120
**Hegel, Georg Wilhelm Friedrich** 1770-1831 **NCLC 46**
See also DLB 90
**Heidegger, Martin** 1889-1976 ................ **CLC 24**
See also CA 81-84; 65-68; CANR 34; MTCW 1, 2
**Heidenstam, (Carl Gustaf) Verner von** 1859-1940 **TCLC 5**
See also CA 104
**Heifner, Jack** 1946- ...............................**CLC 11**
See also CA 105; CANR 47
**Heijermans, Herman** 1864-1924 ......... **TCLC 24**
See also CA 123
**Heilbrun, Carolyn G(old)** 1926- ............ **CLC 25**
See also CA 45-48; CANR 1, 28, 58
**Heine, Heinrich** 1797-1856 . **NCLC 4, 54; PC 25**
See also DLB 90
**Heinemann, Larry (Curtiss)** 1944- ....... **CLC 50**
See also CA 110; CAAS 21; CANR 31, 81; DLBD 9; INT CANR-31
**Heiney, Donald (William)** 1921-1993
See Harris, MacDonald
See also CA 1-4R; 142; CANR 3, 58
**Heinlein, Robert A(nson)** 1907-1988**CLC 1, 3, 8, 14, 26, 55; DAM POP**
See also AAYA 17; CA 1-4R; 125; CANR 1, 20, 53; DLB 8; JRDA; MAICYA; MTCW 1, 2; SATA 9, 69; SATA-Obit 56
**Helforth, John**
See Doolittle, Hilda
**Hellenhofferu, Vojtech Kapristian z**
See Hasek, Jaroslav (Matej Frantisek)
**Heller, Joseph** 1923- **CLC 1, 3, 5, 8, 11, 36, 63; DA; DAB; DAC; DAM MST, NOV, POP; WLC**
See also AAYA 24; AITN 1; CA 5-8R; CABS 1; CANR 8, 42, 66; DLB 2, 28; DLBY 80; INT CANR-8; MTCW 1, 2
**Hellman, Lillian (Florence)** 1906-1984**CLC 2, 4, 8, 14, 18, 34, 44, 52; DAM DRAM; DC 1**
See also AITN 1, 2; CA 13-16R; 112; CANR 33; DLB 7; DLBY 84; MTCW 1, 2
**Helprin, Mark** 1947- .. **CLC 7, 10, 22, 32; DAM NOV, POP**
See also CA 81-84; CANR 47, 64; CDALBS; DLBY 85; MTCW 1, 2
**Helvetius, Claude-Adrien** 1715-1771 ....... **LC 26**
**Helyar, Jane Penelope Josephine** 1933-
See Poole, Josephine
See also CA 21-24R; CANR 10, 26; SATA 82
**Hemans, Felicia** 1793-1835 .................. **NCLC 71**
See also DLB 96
**Hemingway, Ernest (Miller)** 1899-1961**CLC 1, 3, 6, 8, 10, 13, 19, 30, 34, 39, 41, 44, 50, 61, 80; DA; DAB; DAC; DAM MST, NOV; SSC 1, 25; WLC**
See also AAYA 19; CA 77-80; CANR 34; CDALB 1917-1929; DLB 4, 9, 102, 210; DLBD 1, 15, 16; DLBY 81, 87, 96, 98; MTCW 1, 2

10, 15, 35, 44, 108; BLC 2; DA; DAB; DAC; DAM DRAM, MST, MULT, POET; DC 3; PC 1; SSC 6; WLC
See also AAYA 12; BW 1, 3; CA 1-4R; 25-28R; CANR 1, 34; CDALB 1929-1941; CLR 17; DLB 4, 7, 48, 51, 86; JRDA; MAICYA; MTCW 1, 2; SATA 4, 33

Hughes, Richard (Arthur Warren) 1900-1976 CLC 1, 11; DAM NOV
See also CA 5-8R; 65-68; CANR 4; DLB 15, 161; MTCW 1; SATA 8; SATA-Obit 25

Hughes, Ted 1930-1998 CLC 2, 4, 9, 14, 37, 119; DAB; DAC; PC 7
See also Hughes, Edward James
See also CA 1-4R; 171; CANR 1, 33, 66; CLR 3; DLB 40, 161; MAICYA; MTCW 1, 2; SATA 49; SATA-Brief 27; SATA-Obit 107

Hugo, Richard F(ranklin) 1923-1982 CLC 6, 18, 32; DAM POET
See also CA 49-52; 108; CANR 3; DLB 5, 206

Hugo, Victor (Marie) 1802-1885 NCLC 3, 10, 21; DA; DAB; DAC; DAM DRAM, MST, NOV, POET; PC 17; WLC
See also AAYA 28; DLB 119, 192; SATA 47

Huidobro, Vicente
See Huidobro Fernandez, Vicente Garcia

Huidobro Fernandez, Vicente Garcia 1893-1948 TCLC 31
See also CA 131; HW 1

Hulme, Keri 1947- .................................. CLC 39
See also CA 125; CANR 69; INT 125

Hulme, T(homas) E(rnest) 1883-1917 . TCLC 21
See also CA 117; DLB 19

Hume, David 1711-1776 .............................. LC 7
See also DLB 104

Humphrey, William 1924-1997 ............. CLC 45
See also CA 77-80; 160; CANR 68; DLB 212

Humphreys, Emyr Owen 1919- ............. CLC 47
See also CA 5-8R; CANR 3, 24; DLB 15

Humphreys, Josephine 1945- ........ CLC 34, 57
See also CA 121; 127; INT 127

Huneker, James Gibbons 1857-1921 ... TCLC 65
See also DLB 71

Hungerford, Pixie
See Brinsmead, H(esba) F(ay)

Hunt, E(verette) Howard, (Jr.) 1918- ....... CLC 3
See also AITN 1; CA 45-48; CANR 2, 47

Hunt, Kyle
See Creasey, John

Hunt, (James Henry) Leigh 1784-1859 NCLC 1, 70; DAM POET
See also DLB 96, 110, 144

Hunt, Marsha 1946- .............................. CLC 70
See also BW 2, 3; CA 143; CANR 79

Hunt, Violet 1866(?)-1942 .................... TCLC 53
See also DLB 162, 197

Hunter, E. Waldo
See Sturgeon, Theodore (Hamilton)

Hunter, Evan 1926- ....... CLC 11, 31; DAM POP
See also CA 5-8R; CANR 5, 38, 62; DLBY 82; INT CANR-5; MTCW 1; SATA 25

Hunter, Kristin (Eggleston) 1931- ........ CLC 35
See also AITN 1; BW 1; CA 13-16R; CANR 13; CLR 3; DLB 33; INT CANR-13; MAICYA; SAAS 10; SATA 12

Hunter, Mollie 1922- ............................. CLC 21
See also McIlwraith, Maureen Mollie Hunter
See also AAYA 13; CANR 37, 78; CLR 25; DLB 161; JRDA; MAICYA; SAAS 7; SATA 54, 106

Hunter, Robert (?)-1734 ............................ LC 7

Hurston, Zora Neale 1903-1960 . CLC 7, 30, 61; BLC 2; DA; DAC; DAM MST, MULT, NOV; SSC 4; WLCS
See also AAYA 15; BW 1, 3; CA 85-88; CANR 61; CDALBS; DLB 51, 86; MTCW 1, 2

Huston, John (Marcellus) 1906-1987 .... CLC 20
See also CA 73-76; 123; CANR 34; DLB 26

Hustvedt, Siri 1955- ............................. CLC 76
See also CA 137

Hutten, Ulrich von 1488-1523 .................. LC 16
See also DLB 179

Huxley, Aldous (Leonard) 1894-1963 CLC 1, 3, 4, 5, 8, 11, 18, 35, 79; DA; DAB; DAC; DAM MST, NOV; WLC
See also AAYA 11; CA 85-88; CANR 44; CDBLB 1914-1945; DLB 36, 100, 162, 195; MTCW 1, 2; SATA 63

Huxley, T(homas) H(enry) 1825-1895 NCLC 67
See also DLB 57

Huysmans, Joris-Karl 1848-1907 ... TCLC 7, 69
See also CA 104; 165; DLB 123

Hwang, David Henry 1957-CLC 55; DAM DRAM; DC 4
See also CA 127; 132; CANR 76; DLB 212; INT 132; MTCW 2

Hyde, Anthony 1946- ............................. CLC 42
See also CA 136

Hyde, Margaret O(ldroyd) 1917- ........... CLC 21
See also CA 1-4R; CANR 1, 36; CLR 23; JRDA; MAICYA; SAAS 8; SATA 1, 42, 76

Hynes, James 1956(?)- ........................... CLC 65
See also CA 164

Ian, Janis 1951- .................................... CLC 21
See also CA 105

Ibanez, Vicente Blasco
See Blasco Ibanez, Vicente

Ibarguengoitia, Jorge 1928-1983 .......... CLC 37
See also CA 124; 113; HW 1

Ibsen, Henrik (Johan) 1828-1906 TCLC 2, 8, 16, 37, 52; DA; DAB; DAC; DAM DRAM, MST; DC 2; WLC
See also CA 104; 141

Ibuse, Masuji 1898-1993 ........................ CLC 22
See also CA 127; 141; DLB 180

Ichikawa, Kon 1915- .............................. CLC 20
See also CA 121

Idle, Eric 1943- .................................... CLC 21
See also Monty Python
See also CA 116; CANR 35

Ignatow, David 1914-1997 ......... CLC 4, 7, 14, 40
See also CA 9-12R; 162; CAAS 3; CANR 31, 57; DLB 5

Ihimaera, Witi 1944- ............................. CLC 46
See also CA 77-80

Ilf, Ilya ................................................ TCLC 21
See also Fainzilberg, Ilya Arnoldovich

Illyes, Gyula 1902-1983 ........................... PC 16
See also CA 114; 109

Immermann, Karl (Lebrecht) 1796-1840 NCLC 4, 49
See also DLB 133

Ince, Thomas H. 1882-1924 .................. TCLC 89

Inchbald, Elizabeth 1753-1821 ............. NCLC 62
See also DLB 39, 89

Inclan, Ramon (Maria) del Valle
See Valle-Inclan, Ramon (Maria) del

Infante, G(uillermo) Cabrera
See Cabrera Infante, G(uillermo)

Ingalls, Rachel (Holmes) 1940- ........... CLC 42
See also CA 123; 127

Ingamells, Reginald Charles
See Ingamells, Rex

Ingamells, Rex 1913-1955 ................... TCLC 35
See also CA 167

Inge, William (Motter) 1913-1973 CLC 1, 8, 19; DAM DRAM
See also CA 9-12R; CDALB 1941-1968; DLB 7; MTCW 1, 2

Ingelow, Jean 1820-1897 ...................... NCLC 39
See also DLB 35, 163; SATA 33

Ingram, Willis J.
See Harris, Mark

Innaurato, Albert (F.) 1948(?)- ........ CLC 21, 60

See also CA 115; 122; CANR 78; INT 122

Innes, Michael
See Stewart, J(ohn) I(nnes) M(ackintosh)

Innis, Harold Adams 1894-1952 .......... TCLC 77
See also DLB 88

Ionesco, Eugene 1909-1994CLC 1, 4, 6, 9, 11, 15, 41, 86; DA; DAB; DAC; DAM DRAM, MST; WLC
See also CA 9-12R; 144; CANR 55; MTCW 1, 2; SATA 7; SATA-Obit 79

Iqbal, Muhammad 1873-1938 ........ TCLC 28

Ireland, Patrick
See O'Doherty, Brian

Iron, Ralph
See Schreiner, Olive (Emilie Albertina)

Irving, John (Winslow) 1942- .. CLC 13, 23, 38, 112; DAM NOV, POP
See also AAYA 8; BEST 89:3; CA 25-28R; CANR 28, 73; DLB 6; DLBY 82; MTCW 1, 2

Irving, Washington 1783-1859 NCLC 2, 19; DA; DAB; DAC; DAM MST; SSC 2; WLC
See also CDALB 1640-1865; DLB 3, 11, 30, 59, 73, 74, 186; YABC 2

Irwin, P. K.
See Page, P(atricia) K(athleen)

Isaacs, Jorge Ricardo 1837-1895 ........ NCLC 70

Isaacs, Susan 1943- ............CLC 32; DAM POP
See also BEST 89:1; CA 89-92; CANR 20, 41, 65; INT CANR-20; MTCW 1, 2

Isherwood, Christopher (William Bradshaw) 1904-1986CLC 1, 9, 11, 14, 44; DAM DRAM, NOV
See also CA 13-16R; 117; CANR 35; DLB 15, 195; DLBY 86; MTCW 1, 2

Ishiguro, Kazuo 1954-CLC 27, 56, 59, 110; DAM NOV
See also BEST 90:2; CA 120; CANR 49; DLB 194; MTCW 1, 2

Ishikawa, Hakuhin
See Ishikawa, Takuboku

Ishikawa, Takuboku 1886(?)-1912TCLC 15; DAM POET; PC 10
See also CA 113; 153

Iskander, Fazil 1929- ............................ CLC 47
See also CA 102

Isler, Alan (David) 1934- ....................... CLC 91
See also CA 156

Ivan IV 1530-1584 ................................. LC 17

Ivanov, Vyacheslav Ivanovich 1866-1949TCLC 33
See also CA 122

Ivask, Ivar Vidrik 1927-1992 ................. CLC 14
See also CA 37-40R; 139; CANR 24

Ives, Morgan
See Bradley, Marion Zimmer

Izumi Shikibu c. 973-c. 1034 ............. CMLC 33

J. R. S.
See Gogarty, Oliver St. John

Jabran, Kahlil
See Gibran, Kahlil

Jabran, Khalil
See Gibran, Kahlil

Jackson, Daniel
See Wingrove, David (John)

Jackson, Jesse 1908-1983 ..................... CLC 12
See also BW 1; CA 25-28R; 109; CANR 27; CLR 28; MAICYA; SATA 2, 29; SATA-Obit 48

Jackson, Laura (Riding) 1901-1991
See Riding, Laura
See also CA 65-68; 135; CANR 28; DLB 48

Jackson, Sam
See Trumbo, Dalton

Jackson, Sara
See Wingrove, David (John)

Jackson, Shirley 1919-1965CLC 11, 60, 87; DA; DAC; DAM MST; SSC 9; WLC
See also AAYA 9; CA 1-4R; 25-28R; CANR 4, 52; CDALB 1941-1968; DLB 6; MTCW 2; SATA 2

**Jacob, (Cyprien-)Max** 1876-1944 .... **TCLC 6**
See also CA 104
**Jacobs, Harriet A(nn)** 1813(?)-1897 ... **NCLC 67**
**Jacobs, Jim** 1942- ................................ **CLC 12**
See also CA 97-100; INT 97-100
**Jacobs, W(illiam) W(ymark)** 1863-1943 **TCLC 22**
See also CA 121; 167; DLB 135
**Jacobsen, Jens Peter** 1847-1885 ........ **NCLC 34**
**Jacobsen, Josephine** 1908- ........... **CLC 48, 102**
See also CA 33-36R; CAAS 18; CANR 23, 48
**Jacobson, Dan** 1929- ..................... **CLC 4, 14**
See also CA 1-4R; CANR 2, 25, 66; DLB 14,
207; MTCW 1
**Jacqueline**
See Carpentier (y Valmont), Alejo
**Jagger, Mick** 1944- .............................. **CLC 17**
**Jahiz, al-** c. 780-c. 869 ...................... **CMLC 25**
**Jakes, John (William)** 1932- **CLC 29; DAM NOV,
POP**
See also BEST 89:4; CA 57-60; CANR 10, 43, 66;
DLBY 83; INT CANR-10; MTCW 1, 2; SATA
62
**James, Andrew**
See Kirkup, James
**James, C(yril) L(ionel) R(obert)** 1901-1989 **C L C
33; BLCS**
See also BW 2; CA 117; 125; 128; CANR 62;
DLB 125; MTCW 1
**James, Daniel (Lewis)** 1911-1988
See Santiago, Danny
See also CA 174; 125
**James, Dynely**
See Mayne, William (James Carter)
**James, Henry Sr.** 1811-1882 ............... **NCLC 53**
**James, Henry** 1843-1916 **TCLC 2, 11, 24, 40, 47,
64; DA; DAB; DAC; DAM MST, NOV; SSC
8, 32; WLC**
See also CA 104; 132; CDALB 1865-1917; DLB
12, 71, 74, 189; DLBD 13; MTCW 1, 2
**James, M. R.**
See James, Montague (Rhodes)
See also DLB 156
**James, Montague (Rhodes)** 1862-1936 . **TCLC 6;
SSC 16**
See also CA 104; DLB 201
**James, P. D.** 1920- .......................... **CLC 18, 46**
See also White, Phyllis Dorothy James
See also BEST 90:2; CDBLB 1960 to Present; DLB
87; DLBD 17
**James, Philip**
See Moorcock, Michael (John)
**James, William** 1842-1910 ............ **TCLC 15, 32**
See also CA 109
**James I** 1394-1437 ................................ **LC 20**
**Jameson, Anna** 1794-1860 ................... **NCLC 43**
See also DLB 99, 166
**Jami, Nur al-Din 'Abd al-Rahman** 1414-1492 **LC 9**
**Jammes, Francis** 1868-1938 ................ **TCLC 75**
**Jandl, Ernst** 1925- .............................. **CLC 34**
**Janowitz, Tama** 1957- ........ **CLC 43; DAM POP**
See also CA 106; CANR 52
**Japrisot, Sebastien** 1931- ..................... **CLC 90**
**Jarrell, Randall** 1914-1965 **CLC 1, 2, 6, 9, 13, 49;
DAM POET**
See also CA 5-8R; 25-28R; CABS 2; CANR 6, 34;
CDALB 1941-1968; CLR 6; DLB 48, 52;
MAICYA; MTCW 1, 2; SATA 7
**Jarry, Alfred** 1873-1907 ....... **TCLC 2, 14; DAM
DRAM; SSC 20**
See also CA 104; 153; DLB 192
**Jarvis, E. K.**
See Bloch, Robert (Albert); Ellison, Harlan (Jay);
Silverberg, Robert
**Jeake, Samuel, Jr.**
See Aiken, Conrad (Potter)
**Jean Paul** 1763-1825 ............................. **NCLC 7**
**Jefferies, (John) Richard** 1848-1887 .. **NCLC 47**

See also DLB 98, 141; SATA 16
**Jeffers, (John) Robinson** 1887-1962 **CLC 2, 3, 11,
15, 54; DA; DAC; DAM MST, POET; PC 17;
WLC**
See also CA 85-88; CANR 35; CDALB 1917-1929;
DLB 45, 212; MTCW 1, 2
**Jefferson, Janet**
See Mencken, H(enry) L(ouis)
**Jefferson, Thomas** 1743-1826 ............. **NCLC 11**
See also CDALB 1640-1865; DLB 31
**Jeffrey, Francis** 1773-1850 ............. **NCLC 33**
See also DLB 107
**Jelakowitch, Ivan**
See Heijermans, Herman
**Jellicoe, (Patricia) Ann** 1927- ............. **CLC 27**
See also CA 85-88; DLB 13
**Jen, Gish** .......................................... **CLC 70**
See also Jen, Lillian
**Jen, Lillian** 1956(?)-
See Jen, Gish
See also CA 135
**Jenkins, (John) Robin** 1912- ............... **CLC 52**
See also CA 1-4R; CANR 1; DLB 14
**Jennings, Elizabeth (Joan)** 1926- ..... **CLC 5, 14**
See also CA 61-64; CAAS 5; CANR 8, 39, 66;
DLB 27; MTCW 1; SATA 66
**Jennings, Waylon** 1937- ....................... **CLC 21**
**Jensen, Johannes V.** 1873-1950 ........... **TCLC 41**
See also CA 170
**Jensen, Laura (Linnea)** 1948- ............. **CLC 37**
See also CA 103
**Jerome, Jerome K(lapka)** 1859-1927 .. **TCLC 23**
See also CA 119; 177; DLB 10, 34, 135
**Jerrold, Douglas William** 1803-1857 ... **NCLC 2**
See also DLB 158, 159
**Jewett, (Theodora) Sarah Orne** 1849-1909 **T C L C
1, 22; SSC 6**
See also CA 108; 127; CANR 71; DLB 12, 74;
SATA 15
**Jewsbury, Geraldine (Endsor)** 1812-1880 **N C L C
22**
See also DLB 21
**Jhabvala, Ruth Prawer** 1927- . **CLC 4, 8, 29, 94;
DAB; DAM NOV**
See also CA 1-4R; CANR 2, 29, 51, 74; DLB 139,
194; INT CANR-29; MTCW 1, 2
**Jibran, Kahlil**
See Gibran, Kahlil
**Jibran, Khalil**
See Gibran, Kahlil
**Jiles, Paulette** 1943- ....................... **CLC 13, 58**
See also CA 101; CANR 70
**Jimenez (Mantecon), Juan Ramon** 1881-1958
**TCLC 4; DAM MULT, POET; HLC; PC 7**
See also CA 104; 131; CANR 74; DLB 134; HW
1; MTCW 1, 2
**Jimenez, Ramon**
See Jimenez (Mantecon), Juan Ramon
**Jimenez Mantecon, Juan**
See Jimenez (Mantecon), Juan Ramon
**Jin, Ha** 1956- ...................................... **CLC 109**
See also CA 152
**Joel, Billy** ............................................. **CLC 26**
See also Joel, William Martin
**Joel, William Martin** 1949-
See Joel, Billy
See also CA 108
**John, Saint** 7th cent. - ........................ **CMLC 27**
**John of the Cross, St.** 1542-1591 ............. **LC 18**
**Johnson, B(ryan) S(tanley William)** 1933-1973
**CLC 6, 9**
See also CA 9-12R; 53-56; CANR 9; DLB 14, 40
**Johnson, Benj. F. of Boo**
See Riley, James Whitcomb
**Johnson, Benjamin F. of Boo**
See Riley, James Whitcomb
**Johnson, Charles (Richard)** 1948- **CLC 7, 51, 65;**

**BLC 2; DAM MULT**
See also BW 2, 3; CA 116; CAAS 18; CANR 42,
66; DLB 33; MTCW 2
**Johnson, Denis** 1949- ........................... **CLC 52**
See also CA 117; 121; CANR 71; DLB 120
**Johnson, Diane** 1934- ..................... **CLC 5, 13, 48**
See also CA 41-44R; CANR 17, 40, 62; DLBY 80;
INT CANR-17; MTCW 1
**Johnson, Eyvind (Olof Verner)** 1900-1976 **CLC 14**
See also CA 73-76; 69-72; CANR 34
**Johnson, J. R.**
See James, C(yril) L(ionel) R(obert)
**Johnson, James Weldon** 1871-1938 **TCLC 3, 19;
BLC 2; DAM MULT, POET; PC 24**
See also BW 1, 3; CA 104; 125; CDALB 1917-
1929; CLR 32; DLB 51; MTCW 1, 2; SATA 31
**Johnson, Joyce** 1935- .......................... **CLC 58**
See also CA 125; 129
**Johnson, Judith (Emlyn)** 1936- ......... **CLC 7, 15**
See also CA 25-28R, 153; CANR 34
**Johnson, Lionel (Pigot)** 1867-1902 ..... **TCLC 19**
See also CA 117; DLB 19
**Johnson, Marguerite (Annie)**
See Angelou, Maya
**Johnson, Mel**
See Malzberg, Barry N(athaniel)
**Johnson, Pamela Hansford** 1912-1981 **CLC 1, 7,
27**
See also CA 1-4R; 104; CANR 2, 28; DLB 15;
MTCW 1, 2
**Johnson, Robert** 1911(?)-1938 ............ **TCLC 69**
See also BW 3; CA 174
**Johnson, Samuel** 1709-1784 .. **LC 15; DA; DAB;
DAC; DAM MST; WLC**
See also CDBLB 1660-1789; DLB 39, 95, 104, 142
**Johnson, Uwe** 1934-1984 ....... **CLC 5, 10, 15, 40**
See also CA 1-4R; 112; CANR 1, 39; DLB 75;
MTCW 1
**Johnston, George (Benson)** 1913- ........ **CLC 51**
See also CA 1-4R; CANR 5, 20; DLB 88
**Johnston, Jennifer** 1930- ....................... **CLC 7**
See also CA 85-88; DLB 14
**Jolley, (Monica) Elizabeth** 1923- **CLC 46; SSC 19**
See also CA 127; CAAS 13; CANR 59
**Jones, Arthur Llewellyn** 1863-1947
See Machen, Arthur
See also CA 104
**Jones, D(ouglas) G(ordon)** 1929- .......... **CLC 10**
See also CA 29-32R; CANR 13; DLB 53
**Jones, David (Michael)** 1895-1974 **CLC 2, 4, 7, 13,
42**
See also CA 9-12R; 53-56; CANR 28; CDBLB
1945-1960; DLB 20, 100; MTCW 1
**Jones, David Robert** 1947-
See Bowie, David
See also CA 103
**Jones, Diana Wynne** 1934- ................... **CLC 26**
See also AAYA 12; CA 49-52; CANR 4, 26, 56;
CLR 23; DLB 161; JRDA; MAICYA; SAAS 7;
SATA 9, 70, 108
**Jones, Edward P.** 1950- ......................... **CLC 76**
See also BW 2, 3; CA 142; CANR 79
**Jones, Gayl** 1949- **CLC 6, 9; BLC 2; DAM MULT**
See also BW 2, 3; CA 77-80; CANR 27, 66; DLB
33; MTCW 1, 2
**Jones, James** 1921-1977 ......... **CLC 1, 3, 10, 39**
See also AITN 1, 2; CA 1-4R; 69-72; CANR 6;
DLB 2, 143; DLBD 17; DLBY 98; MTCW 1
**Jones, John J.**
See Lovecraft, H(oward) P(hillips)
**Jones, LeRoi** .................... **CLC 1, 2, 3, 5, 10, 14**
See also Baraka, Amiri
See also MTCW 2
**Jones, Louis B.** 1953- ........................... **CLC 65**
See also CA 141; CANR 73
**Jones, Madison (Percy, Jr.)** 1925- ......... **CLC 4**
See also CA 13-16R; CAAS 11; CANR 7, 54; DLB

152

**Jones, Mervyn** 1922- .......................... **CLC 10, 52**
See also CA 45-48; CAAS 5; CANR 1; MTCW 1

**Jones, Mick** 1956(?)- ................................. **CLC 30**

**Jones, Nettie (Pearl)** 1941- ..................... **CLC 34**
See also BW 2; CA 137; CAAS 20

**Jones, Preston** 1936-1979 ......................... **CLC 10**
See also CA 73-76; 89-92; DLB 7

**Jones, Robert F(rancis)** 1934- .................. **CLC 7**
See also CA 49-52; CANR 2, 61

**Jones, Rod** 1953- ...................................... **CLC 50**
See also CA 128

**Jones, Terence Graham Parry** 1942- ... **CLC 21**
See also Jones, Terry; Monty Python
See also CA 112; 116; CANR 35; INT 116

**Jones, Terry**
See Jones, Terence Graham Parry
See also SATA 67; SATA-Brief 51

**Jones, Thom** 1945(?)- ............................... **CLC 81**
See also CA 157

**Jong, Erica** 1942-CLC **4, 6, 8, 18, 83; DAM NOV, POP**
See also AITN 1; BEST 90:2; CA 73-76; CANR 26, 52, 75; DLB 2, 5, 28, 152; INT CANR-26; MTCW 1, 2

**Jonson, Ben(jamin)** 1572(?)-1637 **LC 6, 33; DA; DAB; DAC; DAM DRAM, MST, POET; DC 4; PC 17; WLC**
See also CDBLB Before 1660; DLB 62, 121

**Jordan, June** 1936- . **CLC 5, 11, 23, 114; BLCS; DAM MULT, POET**
See also AAYA 2; BW 2, 3; CA 33-36R; CANR 25, 70; CLR 10; DLB 38; MAICYA; MTCW 1; SATA 4

**Jordan, Neil (Patrick)** 1950- ................ **CLC 110**
See also CA 124; 130; CANR 54; INT 130

**Jordan, Pat(rick M.)** 1941- .................... **CLC 37**
See also CA 33-36R

**Jorgensen, Ivar**
See Ellison, Harlan (Jay)

**Jorgenson, Ivar**
See Silverberg, Robert

**Josephus, Flavius** c. 37-100 ................ **CMLC 13**

**Josipovici, Gabriel** 1940- .................... **CLC 6, 43**
See also CA 37-40R; CAAS 8; CANR 47; DLB 14

**Joubert, Joseph** 1754-1824 .................... **NCLC 9**

**Jouve, Pierre Jean** 1887-1976 .............. **CLC 47**
See also CA 65-68

**Jovine, Francesco** 1902-1950 .............. **TCLC 79**

**Joyce, James (Augustine Aloysius)** 1882-1941 **TCLC 3, 8, 16, 35, 52; DA; DAB; DAC; DAM MST, NOV, POET; PC 22; SSC 3, 26; WLC**
See also CA 104; 126; CDBLB 1914-1945; DLB 10, 19, 36, 162; MTCW 1, 2

**Jozsef, Attila** 1905-1937 ...................... **TCLC 22**
See also CA 116

**Juana Ines de la Cruz** 1651(?)-1695**LC 5; HLCS 1; PC 24**

**Judd, Cyril**
See Kornbluth, C(yril) M.; Pohl, Frederik

**Julian of Norwich** 1342(?)-1416(?) ............. **LC 6**
See also DLB 146

**Junger, Sebastian** 1962- ..................... **CLC 109**
See also AAYA 28; CA 165

**Juniper, Alex**
See Hospital, Janette Turner

**Junius**
See Luxemburg, Rosa

**Just, Ward (Swift)** 1935- ..................... **CLC 4, 27**
See also CA 25-28R; CANR 32; INT CANR-32

**Justice, Donald (Rodney)** 1925- CLC **6, 19, 102; DAM POET**
See also CA 5-8R; CANR 26, 54, 74; DLBY 83; INT CANR-26; MTCW 2

**Juvenal** c. 60-c. 13 .............................. **CMLC 8**
See also Juvenalis, Decimus Junius
See also DLB 211

**Juvenalis, Decimus Junius** 55(?)-c. 127(?)
See Juvenal

**Juvenis**
See Bourne, Randolph S(illiman)

**Kacew, Romain** 1914-1980
See Gary, Romain
See also CA 108; 102

**Kadare, Ismail** 1936- .......................... **CLC 52**
See also CA 161

**Kadohata, Cynthia** ............................. **CLC 59**
See also CA 140

**Kafka, Franz** 1883-1924**TCLC 2, 6, 13, 29, 47, 53; DA; DAB; DAC; DAM MST, NOV; SSC 5, 29, 35; WLC**
See also CA 105; 126; DLB 81; MTCW 1, 2

**Kahanovitsch, Pinkhes**
See Der Nister

**Kahn, Roger** 1927- .............................. **CLC 30**
See also CA 25-28R; CANR 44, 69; DLB 171; SATA 37

**Kain, Saul**
See Sassoon, Siegfried (Lorraine)

**Kaiser, Georg** 1878-1945 ....................... **TCLC 9**
See also CA 106; DLB 124

**Kaletski, Alexander** 1946- .................... **CLC 39**
See also CA 118; 143

**Kalidasa** fl. c. 400- ..................... **CMLC 9; PC 22**

**Kallman, Chester (Simon)** 1921-1975 ..... **CLC 2**
See also CA 45-48; 53-56; CANR 3

**Kaminsky, Melvin** 1926-
See Brooks, Mel
See also CA 65-68; CANR 16

**Kaminsky, Stuart M(elvin)** 1934- ......... **CLC 59**
See also CA 73-76; CANR 29, 53

**Kandinsky, Wassily** 1866-1944 ........... **TCLC 92**
See also CA 118; 155

**Kane, Francis**
See Robbins, Harold

**Kane, Paul**
See Simon, Paul (Frederick)

**Kane, Wilson**
See Bloch, Robert (Albert)

**Kanin, Garson** 1912-1999 ..................... **CLC 22**
See also AITN 1; CA 5-8R; 177; CANR 7, 78; DLB 7

**Kaniuk, Yoram** 1930- ........................... **CLC 19**
See also CA 134

**Kant, Immanuel** 1724-1804 ............ **NCLC 27, 67**
See also DLB 94

**Kantor, MacKinlay** 1904-1977 ................ **CLC 7**
See also CA 61-64; 73-76; CANR 60, 63; DLB 9, 102; MTCW 2

**Kaplan, David Michael** 1946- ................ **CLC 50**

**Kaplan, James** 1951- ............................ **CLC 59**
See also CA 135

**Karageorge, Michael**
See Anderson, Poul (William)

**Karamzin, Nikolai Mikhailovich** 1766-1826 **NCLC 3**
See also DLB 150

**Karapanou, Margarita** 1946- ................ **CLC 13**
See also CA 101

**Karinthy, Frigyes** 1887-1938 ............... **TCLC 47**
See also CA 170

**Karl, Frederick R(obert)** 1927- ........... **CLC 34**
See also CA 5-8R; CANR 3, 44

**Kastel, Warren**
See Silverberg, Robert

**Kataev, Evgeny Petrovich** 1903-1942
See Petrov, Evgeny
See also CA 120

**Kataphusin**
See Ruskin, John

**Katz, Steve** 1935- .................................. **CLC 47**
See also CA 25-28R; CAAS 14, 64; CANR 12; DLBY 83

**Kauffman, Janet** 1945- .......................... **CLC 42**

See also CA 117; CANR 43; DLBY 86

**Kaufman, Bob (Garnell)** 1925-1986 ....... **CLC 49**
See also BW 1; CA 41-44R; 118; CANR 22; DLB 16, 41

**Kaufman, George S.** 1889-1961 ...**CLC 38; DAM DRAM**
See also CA 108; 93-96; DLB 7; INT 108; MTCW 2

**Kaufman, Sue** ..................................... **CLC 3, 8**
See also Barondess, Sue K(aufman)

**Kavafis, Konstantinos Petrou** 1863-1933
See Cavafy, C(onstantine) P(eter)
See also CA 104

**Kavan, Anna** 1901-1968 ................ **CLC 5, 13, 82**
See also CA 5-8R; CANR 6, 57; MTCW 1

**Kavanagh, Dan**
See Barnes, Julian (Patrick)

**Kavanagh, Julie** 1952- ......................... **CLC 119**
See also CA 163

**Kavanagh, Patrick (Joseph)** 1904-1967 **CLC 22**
See also CA 123; 25-28R; DLB 15, 20; MTCW 1

**Kawabata, Yasunari** 1899-1972 . **CLC 2, 5, 9, 18, 107; DAM MULT; SSC 17**
See also CA 93-96; 33-36R; DLB 180; MTCW 2

**Kaye, M(ary) M(argaret)** 1909- ............. **CLC 28**
See also CA 89-92; CANR 24, 60; MTCW 1, 2; SATA 62

**Kaye, Mollie**
See Kaye, M(ary) M(argaret)

**Kaye-Smith, Sheila** 1887-1956 ........... **TCLC 20**
See also CA 118; DLB 36

**Kaymor, Patrice Maguilene**
See Senghor, Leopold Sedar

**Kazan, Elia** 1909- ......................... **CLC 6, 16, 63**
See also CA 21-24R; CANR 32, 78

**Kazantzakis, Nikos** 1883(?)-1957 **TCLC 2, 5, 33**
See also CA 105; 132; MTCW 1, 2

**Kazin, Alfred** 1915-1998 .......... **CLC 34, 38, 119**
See also CA 1-4R; CAAS 7; CANR 1, 45, 79; DLB 67

**Keane, Mary Nesta (Skrine)** 1904-1996
See Keane, Molly
See also CA 108; 114; 151

**Keane, Molly** ........................................ **CLC 31**
See also Keane, Mary Nesta (Skrine)
See also INT 114

**Keates, Jonathan** 1946(?)- ..................... **CLC 34**
See also CA 163

**Keaton, Buster** 1895-1966 ..................... **CLC 20**

**Keats, John** 1795-1821 ..**NCLC 8, 73; DA; DAB; DAC; DAM MST, POET; PC 1; WLC**
See also CDBLB 1789-1832; DLB 96, 110

**Keene, Donald** 1922- ............................. **CLC 34**
See also CA 1-4R; CANR 5

**Keillor, Garrison** ........................... **CLC 40, 115**
See also Keillor, Gary (Edward)
See also AAYA 2; BEST 89:3; DLBY 87; SATA 58

**Keillor, Gary (Edward)** 1942-
See Keillor, Garrison
See also CA 111; 117; CANR 36, 59; DAM POP; MTCW 1, 2

**Keith, Michael**
See Hubbard, L(afayette) Ron(ald)

**Keller, Gottfried** 1819-1890 .... **NCLC 2; SSC 26**
See also DLB 129

**Keller, Nora Okja** ............................... **CLC 109**

**Kellerman, Jonathan** 1949- **CLC 44; DAM POP**
See also BEST 90:1; CA 106; CANR 29, 51; INT CANR-29

**Kelley, William Melvin** 1937- ............... **CLC 22**
See also BW 1; CA 77-80; CANR 27; DLB 33

**Kellogg, Marjorie** 1922- ........................ **CLC 2**
See also CA 81-84

**Kellow, Kathleen**
See Hibbert, Eleanor Alice Burford

**Kelly, M(ilton) T(erry)** 1947- ............... **CLC 55**

See also CA 97-100; CAAS 22; CANR 19, 43
**Kelman, James** 1946- ...................... **CLC 58, 86**
See also CA 148; DLB 194
**Kemal, Yashar** 1923- ........................ **CLC 14, 29**
See also CA 89-92; CANR 44
**Kemble, Fanny** 1809-1893 .................... **NCLC 18**
See also DLB 32
**Kemelman, Harry** 1908-1996 .................. **CLC 2**
See also AITN 1; CA 9-12R; 155; CANR 6, 71;
DLB 28
**Kempe, Margery** 1373(?)-1440(?) .......... **LC 6**
See also DLB 146
**Kempis, Thomas a** 1380-1471 ................. **LC 11**
**Kendall, Henry** 1839-1882 ................... **NCLC 12**
**Keneally, Thomas (Michael)** 1935- **CLC 5, 8, 10,
14, 19, 27, 43, 117; DAM NOV**
See also CA 85-88; CANR 10, 50, 74; MTCW 1, 2
**Kennedy, Adrienne (Lita)** 1931- **CLC 66; BLC 2;
DAM MULT; DC 5**
See also BW 2, 3; CA 103; CAAS 20; CABS 3;
CANR 26, 53; DLB 38
**Kennedy, John Pendleton** 1795-1870 ..... **NCLC 2**
See also DLB 3
**Kennedy, Joseph Charles** 1929-
See Kennedy, X. J.
See also CA 1-4R; CANR 4, 30, 40; SATA 14, 86
**Kennedy, William** 1928- **CLC 6, 28, 34, 53; DAM
NOV**
See also AAYA 1; CA 85-88; CANR 14, 31, 76;
DLB 143; DLBY 85; INT CANR-31; MTCW 1,
2; SATA 57
**Kennedy, X. J.** ................................ **CLC 8, 42**
See also Kennedy, Joseph Charles
See also CAAS 9; CLR 27; DLB 5; SAAS 22
**Kenny, Maurice (Francis)** 1929- . **CLC 87; DAM
MULT**
See also CA 144; CAAS 22; DLB 175; NNAL
**Kent, Kelvin**
See Kuttner, Henry
**Kenton, Maxwell**
See Southern, Terry
**Kenyon, Robert O.**
See Kuttner, Henry
**Kepler, Johannes** 1571-1630 ................... **LC 45**
**Kerouac, Jack** ........... **CLC 1, 2, 3, 5, 14, 29, 61**
See also Kerouac, Jean-Louis Lebris de
See also AAYA 25; CDALB 1941-1968; DLB 2,
16; DLBD 3; DLBY 95; MTCW 2
**Kerouac, Jean-Louis Lebris de** 1922-1969
See Kerouac, Jack
See also AITN 1; CA 5-8R; 25-28R; CANR 26,
54; DA; DAB; DAC; DAM MST, NOV, POET,
POP; MTCW 1, 2; WLC
**Kerr, Jean** 1923- ............................. **CLC 22**
See also CA 5-8R; CANR 7; INT CANR-7
**Kerr, M. E.** ........................................ **CLC 12, 35**
See also Meaker, Marijane (Agnes)
See also AAYA 2, 23; CLR 29; SAAS 1
**Kerr, Robert** ........................................ **CLC 55**
**Kerrigan, (Thomas) Anthony** 1918- .... **CLC 4, 6**
See also CA 49-52; CAAS 11; CANR 4
**Kerry, Lois**
See Duncan, Lois
**Kesey, Ken (Elton)** 1935- **CLC 1, 3, 6, 11, 46, 64;
DA; DAB; DAC; DAM MST, NOV, POP;
WLC**
See also AAYA 25; CA 1-4R; CANR 22, 38, 66;
CDALB 1968-1988; DLB 2, 16, 206; MTCW 1,
2; SATA 66
**Kesselring, Joseph (Otto)** 1902-1967 .. **CLC 45;
DAM DRAM, MST**
See also CA 150
**Kessler, Jascha (Frederick)** 1929- ......... **CLC 4**
See also CA 17-20R; CANR 8, 48
**Kettelkamp, Larry (Dale)** 1933- ........... **CLC 12**
See also CA 29-32R; CANR 16; SAAS 3; SATA 2
**Key, Ellen** 1849-1926 ........................... **TCLC 65**

**Keyber, Conny**
See Fielding, Henry
**Keyes, Daniel** 1927- .. **CLC 80; DA; DAC; DAM
MST, NOV**
See also AAYA 23; CA 17-20R; CANR 10, 26, 54,
74; MTCW 2; SATA 37
**Keynes, John Maynard** 1883-1946 ...... **TCLC 64**
See also CA 114; 162, 163; DLBD 10; MTCW 2
**Khanshendel, Chiron**
See Rose, Wendy
**Khayyam, Omar** 1048-1131 **CMLC 11; DAM
POET; PC 8**
**Kherdian, David** 1931- .......................... **CLC 6, 9**
See also CA 21-24R; CAAS 2; CANR 39, 78; CLR
24; JRDA; MAICYA; SATA 16, 74
**Khlebnikov, Velimir** ............................ **TCLC 20**
See also Khlebnikov, Viktor Vladimirovich
**Khlebnikov, Viktor Vladimirovich** 1885-1922
See Khlebnikov, Velimir
See also CA 117
**Khodasevich, Vladislav (Felitsianovich)** 1886-1939
**TCLC 15**
See also CA 115
**Kielland, Alexander Lange** 1849-1906 .. **TCLC 5**
See also CA 104
**Kiely, Benedict** 1919- ...................... **CLC 23, 43**
See also CA 1-4R; CANR 2; DLB 15
**Kienzle, William X(avier)** 1928- . **CLC 25; DAM
POP**
See also CA 93-96; CAAS 1; CANR 9, 31, 59;
INT CANR-31; MTCW 1, 2
**Kierkegaard, Soren** 1813-1855 ..... **NCLC 34, 78**
**Kieslowski, Krzysztof** 1941-1996 ....... **CLC 120**
See also CA 147; 151
**Killens, John Oliver** 1916-1987 ........... **CLC 10**
See also BW 2; CA 77-80; 123; CAAS 2; CANR
26; DLB 33
**Killigrew, Anne** 1660-1685 ....................... **LC 4**
See also DLB 131
**Kim**
See Simenon, Georges (Jacques Christian)
**Kincaid, Jamaica** 1949- **CLC 43, 68; BLC 2; DAM
MULT, NOV**
See also AAYA 13; BW 2, 3; CA 125; CANR 47,
59; CDALBS; DLB 157; MTCW 2
**King, Francis (Henry)** 1923- .. **CLC 8, 53; DAM
NOV**
See also CA 1-4R; CANR 1, 33; DLB 15, 139;
MTCW 1
**King, Kennedy**
See Brown, George Douglas
**King, Martin Luther, Jr.** 1929-1968 **CLC 83; BLC
2; DA; DAB; DAC; DAM MST, MULT;
WLCS**
See also BW 2, 3; CA 25-28; CANR 27, 44; CAP
2; MTCW 1, 2; SATA 14
**King, Stephen (Edwin)** 1947- **CLC 12, 26, 37, 61,
113; DAM NOV, POP; SSC 17**
See also AAYA 1, 17; BEST 90:1; CA 61-64;
CANR 1, 30, 52, 76; DLB 143; DLBY 80; JRDA;
MTCW 1, 2; SATA 9, 55
**King, Steve**
See King, Stephen (Edwin)
**King, Thomas** 1943- **CLC 89; DAC; DAM MULT**
See also CA 144; DLB 175; NNAL; SATA 96
**Kingman, Lee** ........................................ **CLC 17**
See also Natti, (Mary) Lee
See also SAAS 3; SATA 1, 67
**Kingsley, Charles** 1819-1875 .............. **NCLC 35**
See also DLB 21, 32, 163, 190; YABC 2
**Kingsley, Sidney** 1906-1995 ................. **CLC 44**
See also CA 85-88; 147; DLB 7
**Kingsolver, Barbara** 1955- **CLC 55, 81; DAM POP**
See also AAYA 15; CA 129; 134; CANR 60;
CDALBS; DLB 206; INT 134; MTCW 2
**Kingston, Maxine (Ting Ting) Hong** 1940- **C L C
12, 19, 58, 121; DAM MULT, NOV; WLCS**

See also AAYA 8; CA 69-72; CANR 13, 38,
74; CDALBS; DLB 173, 212; DLBY 80; INT
CANR-13; MTCW 1, 2; SATA 53
**Kinnell, Galway** 1927- **CLC 1, 2, 3, 5, 13, 29; PC
26**
See also CA 9-12R; CANR 10, 34, 66; DLB 5;
DLBY 87; INT CANR-34; MTCW 1, 2
**Kinsella, Thomas** 1928- ...................... **CLC 4, 19**
See also CA 17-20R; CANR 15; DLB 27; MTCW
1, 2
**Kinsella, W(illiam) P(atrick)** 1935- . **CLC 27,
43; DAC; DAM NOV, POP**
See also AAYA 7; CA 97-100; CAAS 7; CANR
21, 35, 66, 75; INT CANR-21; MTCW 1, 2
**Kinsey, Alfred C(harles)** 1894-1956 ... **TCLC 91**
See also CA 115; 170; MTCW 2
**Kipling, (Joseph) Rudyard** 1865-1936 **TCLC 8, 17;
DA; DAB; DAC; DAM MST, POET; PC 3;
SSC 5; WLC**
See also CA 105; 120; CANR 33; CDBLB 1890-
1914; CLR 39; DLB 19, 34, 141, 156; MAICYA;
MTCW 1, 2; SATA 100; YABC 2
**Kirkup, James** 1918- .............................. **CLC 1**
See also CA 1-4R; CAAS 4; CANR 2; DLB 27;
SATA 12
**Kirkwood, James** 1930(?)-1989 ............... **CLC 9**
See also AITN 2; CA 1-4R; 128; CANR 6, 40
**Kirshner, Sidney**
See Kingsley, Sidney
**Kis, Danilo** 1935-1989 ........................... **CLC 57**
See also CA 109; 118; 129; CANR 61; DLB 181;
MTCW 1
**Kivi, Aleksis** 1834-1872 ...................... **NCLC 30**
**Kizer, Carolyn (Ashley)** 1925- . **CLC 15, 39, 80;
DAM POET**
See also CA 65-68; CAAS 5; CANR 24, 70; DLB
5, 169; MTCW 2
**Klabund** 1890-1928 ............................ **TCLC 44**
See also CA 162; DLB 66
**Klappert, Peter** 1942- ......................... **CLC 57**
See also CA 33-36R; DLB 5
**Klein, A(braham) M(oses)** 1909-1972 .. **CLC 19;
DAB; DAC; DAM MST**
See also CA 101; 37-40R; DLB 68
**Klein, Norma** 1938-1989 ...................... **CLC 30**
See also AAYA 2; CA 41-44R; 128; CANR 15,
37; CLR 2, 19; INT CANR-15; JRDA;
MAICYA; SAAS 1; SATA 7, 57
**Klein, T(heodore) E(ibon) D(onald)** 1947- **CLC 34**
See also CA 119; CANR 44, 75
**Kleist, Heinrich von** 1777-1811 **NCLC 2, 37; DAM
DRAM; SSC 22**
See also DLB 90
**Klima, Ivan** 1931- ............... **CLC 56; DAM NOV**
See also CA 25-28R; CANR 17, 50
**Klimentov, Andrei Platonovich** 1899-1951
See Platonov, Andrei
See also CA 108
**Klinger, Friedrich Maximilian von** 1752-1831
**NCLC 1**
See also DLB 94
**Klingsor the Magician**
See Hartmann, Sadakichi
**Klopstock, Friedrich Gottlieb** 1724-1803 **NCLC 11**
See also DLB 97
**Knapp, Caroline** 1959- ........................ **CLC 99**
See also CA 154
**Knebel, Fletcher** 1911-1993 .................. **CLC 14**
See also AITN 1; CA 1-4R; 140; CAAS 3; CANR
1, 36; SATA 36; SATA-Obit 75
**Knickerbocker, Diedrich**
See Irving, Washington
**Knight, Etheridge** 1931-1991 ... **CLC 40; BLC 2;
DAM POET; PC 14**
See also BW 1, 3; CA 21-24R; 133; CANR 23;
DLB 41; MTCW 2
**Knight, Sarah Kemble** 1666-1727 ............. **LC 7**

**Loxsmith, John**
  See Brunner, John (Kilian Houston)
**Loy, Mina** .............. **CLC 28; DAM POET; PC 16**
  See also Lowry, Mina Gertrude
  See also DLB 4, 54
**Loyson-Bridet**
  See Schwob, Marcel (Mayer Andre)
**Lucan** 39-65 ........................................ **CMLC 33**
  See also DLB 211
**Lucas, Craig** 1951- ............................... **CLC 64**
  See also CA 137; CANR 71
**Lucas, E(dward) V(errall)** 1868-1938 **T C L C
  73**
  See also CA 176; DLB 98, 149, 153; SATA 20
**Lucas, George** 1944- ............................. **CLC 16**
  See also AAYA 1, 23; CA 77-80; CANR 30; SATA
  56
**Lucas, Hans**
  See Godard, Jean-Luc
**Lucas, Victoria**
  See Plath, Sylvia
**Lucian** c. 120-c. 180 ........................... **CMLC 32**
  See also DLB 176
**Ludlam, Charles** 1943-1987 ............ **CLC 46, 50**
  See also CA 85-88; 122; CANR 72
**Ludlum, Robert** 1927- . **CLC 22, 43; DAM NOV,
  POP**
  See also AAYA 10; BEST 89:1, 90:3; CA 33-36R;
  CANR 25, 41, 68; DLBY 82; MTCW 1, 2
**Ludwig, Ken** .......................................... **CLC 60**
**Ludwig, Otto** 1813-1865 ........................ **NCLC 4**
  See also DLB 129
**Lugones, Leopoldo** 1874-1938**TCLC 15; HLCS 2**
  See also CA 116; 131; HW 1
**Lu Hsun** 1881-1936 ................. **TCLC 3; SSC 20**
  See also Shu-Jen, Chou
**Lukacs, George** ...................................... **CLC 24**
  See also Lukacs, Gyorgy (Szegeny von)
**Lukacs, Gyorgy (Szegeny von)** 1885-1971
  See Lukacs, George
  See also CA 101; 29-32R; CANR 62; MTCW 2
**Luke, Peter (Ambrose Cyprian)** 1919-1995 **C L C
  38**
  See also CA 81-84; 147; CANR 72; DLB 13
**Lunar, Dennis**
  See Mungo, Raymond
**Lurie, Alison** 1926- ................. **CLC 4, 5, 18, 39**
  See also CA 1-4R; CANR 2, 17, 50; DLB 2; MTCW
  1; SATA 46
**Lustig, Arnost** 1926- ............................. **CLC 56**
  See also AAYA 3; CA 69-72; CANR 47; SATA 56
**Luther, Martin** 1483-1546 .................... **LC 9, 37**
  See also DLB 179
**Luxemburg, Rosa** 1870(?)-1919 .......... **TCLC 63**
  See also CA 118
**Luzi, Mario** 1914- ................................. **CLC 13**
  See also CA 61-64; CANR 9, 70; DLB 128
**Lyly, John** 1554(?)-1606**LC 41; DAM DRAM; DC
  7**
  See also DLB 62, 167
**L'Ymagier**
  See Gourmont, Remy (-Marie-Charles) de
**Lynch, B. Suarez**
  See Bioy Casares, Adolfo; Borges, Jorge Luis
**Lynch, B. Suarez**
  See Bioy Casares, Adolfo
**Lynch, David (K.)** 1946- ........................ **CLC 66**
  See also CA 124; 129
**Lynch, James**
  See Andreyev, Leonid (Nikolaevich)
**Lynch Davis, B.**
  See Bioy Casares, Adolfo; Borges, Jorge Luis
**Lyndsay, Sir David** 1490-1555 .................. **LC 20**
**Lynn, Kenneth S(chuyler)** 1923- ........... **CLC 50**
  See also CA 1-4R; CANR 3, 27, 65
**Lynx**
  See West, Rebecca

**Lyons, Marcus**
  See Blish, James (Benjamin)
**Lyre, Pinchbeck**
  See Sassoon, Siegfried (Lorraine)
**Lytle, Andrew (Nelson)** 1902-1995 ........ **CLC 22**
  See also CA 9-12R; 150; CANR 70; DLB 6; DLBY
  95
**Lyttelton, George** 1709-1773 ................... **LC 10**
**Maas, Peter** 1929- ................................... **CLC 29**
  See also CA 93-96; INT 93-96; MTCW 2
**Macaulay, Rose** 1881-1958 ............. **TCLC 7, 44**
  See also CA 104; DLB 36
**Macaulay, Thomas Babington** 1800-1859
  **NCLC 42**
  See also CDBLB 1832-1890; DLB 32, 55
**MacBeth, George (Mann)** 1932-1992**CLC 2, 5, 9**
  See also CA 25-28R; 136; CANR 61, 66; DLB 40;
  MTCW 1; SATA 4; SATA-Obit 70
**MacCaig, Norman (Alexander)** 1910- . **CLC 36;
  DAB; DAM POET**
  See also CA 9-12R; CANR 3, 34; DLB 27
**MacCarthy, Sir(Charles Otto) Desmond** 1877-1952
  **TCLC 36**
  See also CA 167
**MacDiarmid, Hugh** .. **CLC 2, 4, 11, 19, 63; PC 9**
  See also Grieve, C(hristopher) M(urray)
  See also CDBLB 1945-1960; DLB 20
**MacDonald, Anson**
  See Heinlein, Robert A(nson)
**Macdonald, Cynthia** 1928- ................. **CLC 13, 19**
  See also CA 49-52; CANR 4, 44; DLB 105
**MacDonald, George** 1824-1905 .............. **TCLC 9**
  See also CA 106; 137; CANR 80; DLB 18, 163,
  178; MAICYA; SATA 33, 100
**Macdonald, John**
  See Millar, Kenneth
**MacDonald, John D(ann)** 1916-1986 . **CLC 3, 27,
  44; DAM NOV, POP**
  See also CA 1-4R; 121; CANR 1, 19, 60; DLB 8;
  DLBY 86; MTCW 1, 2
**Macdonald, John Ross**
  See Millar, Kenneth
**Macdonald, Ross** ............ **CLC 1, 2, 3, 14, 34, 41**
  See also Millar, Kenneth
  See also DLBD 6
**MacDougal, John**
  See Blish, James (Benjamin)
**MacEwen, Gwendolyn (Margaret)** 1941-1987**CLC
  13, 55**
  See also CA 9-12R; 124; CANR 7, 22; DLB 53;
  SATA 50; SATA-Obit 55
**Macha, Karel Hynek** 1810-1846 .......... **NCLC 46**
**Machado (y Ruiz), Antonio** 1875-1939 .. **TCLC 3**
  See also CA 104; 174; DLB 108; HW 2
**Machado de Assis, Joaquim Maria** 1839-1908
  **TCLC 10; BLC 2; HLCS 2; SSC 24**
  See also CA 107; 153
**Machen, Arthur** ...................... **TCLC 4; SSC 20**
  See also Jones, Arthur Llewellyn
  See also DLB 36, 156, 178
**Machiavelli, Niccolo** 1469-1527 .. **LC 8, 36; DA;
  DAB; DAC; DAM MST; WLCS**
**MacInnes, Colin** 1914-1976 ................. **CLC 4, 23**
  See also CA 69-72; 65-68; CANR 21; DLB 14;
  MTCW 1, 2
**MacInnes, Helen (Clark)** 1907-1985**CLC 27, 39;
  DAM POP**
  See also CA 1-4R; 117; CANR 1, 28, 58; DLB 87;
  MTCW 1, 2; SATA 22; SATA-Obit 44
**Mackenzie, Compton (Edward Montague)** 1883-
  1972 ................................................ **CLC 18**
  See also CA 21-22; 37-40R; CAP 2; DLB 34, 100
**Mackenzie, Henry** 1745-1831 .............. **NCLC 41**
  See also DLB 39
**Mackintosh, Elizabeth** 1896(?)-1952
  See Tey, Josephine
  See also CA 110

**MacLaren, James**
  See Grieve, C(hristopher) M(urray)
**Mac Laverty, Bernard** 1942- ................. **CLC 31**
  See also CA 116; 118; CANR 43; INT 118
**MacLean, Alistair (Stuart)** 1922(?)-1987 **CLC 3,
  13, 50, 63; DAM POP**
  See also CA 57-60; 121; CANR 28, 61; MTCW 1;
  SATA 23; SATA-Obit 50
**Maclean, Norman (Fitzroy)** 1902-1990 . **CLC 78;
  DAM POP; SSC 13**
  See also CA 102; 132; CANR 49; DLB 206
**MacLeish, Archibald** 1892-1982**CLC 3, 8, 14, 68;
  DAM POET**
  See also CA 9-12R; 106; CANR 33, 63;
  CDALBS; DLB 4, 7, 45; DLBY 82; MTCW
  1, 2
**MacLennan, (John) Hugh** 1907-1990 **CLC 2, 14,
  92; DAC; DAM MST**
  See also CA 5-8R; 142; CANR 33; DLB 68;
  MTCW 1, 2
**MacLeod, Alistair** 1936- .. **CLC 56; DAC; DAM
  MST**
  See also CA 123; DLB 60; MTCW 2
**Macleod, Fiona**
  See Sharp, William
**MacNeice, (Frederick) Louis** 1907-1963**CLC 1, 4,
  10, 53; DAB; DAM POET**
  See also CA 85-88; CANR 61; DLB 10, 20;
  MTCW 1, 2
**MacNeill, Dand**
  See Fraser, George MacDonald
**Macpherson, James** 1736-1796 ................. **LC 29**
  See also Ossian
  See also DLB 109
**Macpherson, (Jean) Jay** 1931- .............. **CLC 14**
  See also CA 5-8R; DLB 53
**MacShane, Frank** 1927- ......................... **CLC 39**
  See also CA 9-12R; CANR 3, 33; DLB 111
**Macumber, Mari**
  See Sandoz, Mari(e Susette)
**Madach, Imre** 1823-1864 ...................... **NCLC 19**
**Madden, (Jerry) David** 1933- ............. **CLC 5, 15**
  See also CA 1-4R; CAAS 3; CANR 4, 45; DLB 6;
  MTCW 1
**Maddern, Al(an)**
  See Ellison, Harlan (Jay)
**Madhubuti, Haki R.** 1942- ... **CLC 6, 73; BLC 2;
  DAM MULT, POET; PC 5**
  See also Lee, Don L.
  See also BW 2, 3; CA 73-76; CANR 24, 51, 73;
  DLB 5, 41; DLBD 8; MTCW 2
**Maepenn, Hugh**
  See Kuttner, Henry
**Maepenn, K. H.**
  See Kuttner, Henry
**Maeterlinck, Maurice** 1862-1949 **TCLC 3; DAM
  DRAM**
  See also CA 104; 136; CANR 80; DLB 192; SATA
  66
**Maginn, William** 1794-1842 .................. **NCLC 8**
  See also DLB 110, 159
**Mahapatra, Jayanta** 1928- **CLC 33; DAM MULT**
  See also CA 73-76; CAAS 9; CANR 15, 33, 66
**Mahfouz, Naguib (Abdel Aziz Al-Sabilgi)** 1911(?)-
  See Mahfuz, Najib
  See also BEST 89:2; CA 128; CANR 55; DAM
  NOV; MTCW 1, 2
**Mahfuz, Najib** ..................................... **CLC 52, 55**
  See also Mahfouz, Naguib (Abdel Aziz Al-
  Sabilgi)
  See also DLBY 88
**Mahon, Derek** 1941- ............................. **CLC 27**
  See also CA 113; 128; DLB 40
**Mailer, Norman** 1923-**CLC 1, 2, 3, 4, 5, 8, 11, 14,
  28, 39, 74, 111; DA; DAB; DAC; DAM MST,
  NOV, POP**
  See also AITN 2; CA 9-12R; CABS 1; CANR 28,

**Martines, Julia**
See O'Faolain, Julia
**Martinez, Enrique Gonzalez**
See Gonzalez Martinez, Enrique
**Martinez, Jacinto Benavente y**
See Benavente (y Martinez), Jacinto
**Martinez Ruiz, Jose** 1873-1967
See Azorin; Ruiz, Jose Martinez
See also CA 93-96; HW 1
**Martinez Sierra, Gregorio** 1881-1947 .. **TCLC 6**
See also CA 115
**Martinez Sierra, Maria (de la O'LeJarraga)** 1874-1974 ................................................ **TCLC 6**
See also CA 115
**Martinsen, Martin**
See Follett, Ken(neth Martin)
**Martinson, Harry (Edmund)** 1904-1978  **CLC 14**
See also CA 77-80; CANR 34
**Marut, Ret**
See Traven, B.
**Marut, Robert**
See Traven, B.
**Marvell, Andrew** 1621-1678 **LC 4, 43; DA; DAB; DAC; DAM MST, POET; PC 10; WLC**
See also CDBLB 1660-1789; DLB 131
**Marx, Karl (Heinrich)** 1818-1883 ....... **NCLC 17**
See also DLB 129
**Masaoka Shiki** ................................... **TCLC 18**
See also Masaoka Tsunenori
**Masaoka Tsunenori** 1867-1902
See Masaoka Shiki
See also CA 117
**Masefield, John (Edward)** 1878-1967**CLC 11, 47; DAM POET**
See also CA 19-20; 25-28R; CANR 33; CAP 2; CDBLB 1890-1914; DLB 10, 19, 153, 160; MTCW 1, 2; SATA 19
**Maso, Carole** 19(?)- ............................... **CLC 44**
See also CA 170
**Mason, Bobbie Ann** 1940-**CLC 28, 43, 82; SSC 4**
See also AAYA 5; CA 53-56; CANR 11, 31, 58; CDALBS; DLB 173; DLBY 87; INT CANR-31; MTCW 1, 2
**Mason, Ernst**
See Pohl, Frederik
**Mason, Lee W.**
See Malzberg, Barry N(athaniel)
**Mason, Nick** 1945- ................................. **CLC 35**
**Mason, Tally**
See Derleth, August (William)
**Mass, William**
See Gibson, William
**Master Lao**
See Lao Tzu
**Masters, Edgar Lee** 1868-1950 **TCLC 2, 25; DA; DAC; DAM MST, POET; PC 1; WLCS**
See also CA 104; 133; CDALB 1865-1917; DLB 54; MTCW 1, 2
**Masters, Hilary** 1928- .......................... **CLC 48**
See also CA 25-28R; CANR 13, 47
**Mastrosimone, William** 19(?)- ............. **CLC 36**
**Mathe, Albert**
See Camus, Albert
**Mather, Cotton** 1663-1728 ....................... **LC 38**
See also CDALB 1640-1865; DLB 24, 30, 140
**Mather, Increase** 1639-1723 .................... **LC 38**
See also DLB 24
**Matheson, Richard Burton** 1926- ......... **CLC 37**
See also CA 97-100; DLB 8, 44; INT 97-100
**Mathews, Harry** 1930- ....................... **CLC 6, 52**
See also CA 21-24R; CAAS 6; CANR 18, 40
**Mathews, John Joseph** 1894-1979**CLC 84; DAM MULT**
See also CA 19-20; 142; CANR 45; CAP 2; DLB 175; NNAL
**Mathias, Roland (Glyn)** 1915- .............. **CLC 45**
See also CA 97-100; CANR 19, 41; DLB 27

**Matsuo Basho** 1644-1694 ....................... **PC 3**
See also DAM POET
**Mattheson, Rodney**
See Creasey, John
**Matthews, Brander** 1852-1929 ............ **TCLC 95**
See also DLB 71, 78; DLBD 13
**Matthews, Greg** 1949- .......................... **CLC 45**
See also CA 135
**Matthews, William (Procter, III)** 1942-1997 **C L C 40**
See also CA 29-32R; 162; CAAS 18; CANR 12, 57; DLB 5
**Matthias, John (Edward)** 1941- ............... **CLC 9**
See also CA 33-36R; CANR 56
**Matthiessen, Peter** 1927-**CLC 5, 7, 11, 32, 64; DAM NOV**
See also AAYA 6; BEST 90:4; CA 9-12R; CANR 21, 50, 73; DLB 6, 173; MTCW 1, 2; SATA 27
**Maturin, Charles Robert** 1780(?)-1824 **NCLC 6**
See also DLB 178
**Matute (Ausejo), Ana Maria** 1925- ........ **CLC 11**
See also CA 89-92; MTCW 1
**Maugham, W. S.**
See Maugham, W(illiam) Somerset
**Maugham, W(illiam) Somerset** 1874-1965**CLC 1, 11, 15, 67, 93; DA; DAB; DAC; DAM DRAM, MST, NOV; SSC 8; WLC**
See also CA 5-8R; 25-28R; CANR 40; CDBLB 1914-1945; DLB 10, 36, 77, 100, 162, 195; MTCW 1, 2; SATA 54
**Maugham, William Somerset**
See Maugham, W(illiam) Somerset
**Maupassant, (Henri Rene Albert) Guy de** 1850-1893 .. **NCLC 1, 42; DA; DAB; DAC; DAM MST; SSC 1; WLC**
See also DLB 123
**Maupin, Armistead** 1944- ... **CLC 95; DAM POP**
See also CA 125; 130; CANR 58; INT 130; MTCW 2
**Maurhut, Richard**
See Traven, B.
**Mauriac, Claude** 1914-1996 ..................... **CLC 9**
See also CA 89-92; 152; DLB 83
**Mauriac, Francois (Charles)** 1885-1970**CLC 4, 9, 56; SSC 24**
See also CA 25-28; CAP 2; DLB 65; MTCW 1, 2
**Mavor, Osborne Henry** 1888-1951
See Bridie, James
See also CA 104
**Maxwell, William (Keepers, Jr.)** 1908- **CLC 19**
See also CA 93-96; CANR 54; DLBY 80; INT 93-96
**May, Elaine** 1932- ................................. **CLC 16**
See also CA 124; 142; DLB 44
**Mayakovski, Vladimir (Vladimirovich)** 1893-1930 **TCLC 4, 18**
See also CA 104; 158; MTCW 2
**Mayhew, Henry** 1812-1887 ................... **NCLC 31**
See also DLB 18, 55, 190
**Mayle, Peter** 1939(?)- .......................... **CLC 89**
See also CA 139; CANR 64
**Maynard, Joyce** 1953- .......................... **CLC 23**
See also CA 111; 129; CANR 64
**Mayne, William (James Carter)** 1928- **CLC 12**
See also AAYA 20; CA 9-12R; CANR 37, 80; CLR 25; JRDA; MAICYA; SAAS 11; SATA 6, 68
**Mayo, Jim**
See L'Amour, Louis (Dearborn)
**Maysles, Albert** 1926- .......................... **CLC 16**
See also CA 29-32R
**Maysles, David** 1932- ........................... **CLC 16**
**Mazer, Norma Fox** 1931- ....................... **CLC 26**
See also AAYA 5; CA 69-72; CANR 12, 32, 66; CLR 23; JRDA; MAICYA; SAAS 1; SATA 24, 67, 105
**Mazzini, Guiseppe** 1805-1872 .............. **NCLC 34**
**McAuley, James Phillip** 1917-1976 ....... **CLC 45**

See also CA 97-100
**McBain, Ed**
See Hunter, Evan
**McBrien, William Augustine** 1930- ..... **CLC 44**
See also CA 107
**McCaffrey, Anne (Inez)** 1926- ..... **CLC 17; DAM NOV, POP**
See also AAYA 6; AITN 2; BEST 89:2; CA 25-28R; CANR 15, 35, 55; CLR 49; DLB 8; JRDA; MAICYA; MTCW 1, 2; SAAS 11; SATA 8, 70
**McCall, Nathan** 1955(?)- ....................... **CLC 86**
See also BW 3; CA 146
**McCann, Arthur**
See Campbell, John W(ood, Jr.)
**McCann, Edson**
See Pohl, Frederik
**McCarthy, Charles, Jr.** 1933-
See McCarthy, Cormac
See also CANR 42, 69; DAM POP; MTCW 2
**McCarthy, Cormac** 1933- .... **CLC 4, 57, 59, 101**
See also McCarthy, Charles, Jr.
See also DLB 6, 143; MTCW 2
**McCarthy, Mary (Therese)** 1912-1989**CLC 1, 3, 5, 14, 24, 39, 59; SSC 24**
See also CA 5-8R; 129; CANR 16, 50, 64; DLB 2; DLBY 81; INT CANR-16; MTCW 1, 2
**McCartney, (James) Paul** 1942- ..... **CLC 12, 35**
See also CA 146
**McCauley, Stephen (D.)** 1955- .............. **CLC 50**
See also CA 141
**McClure, Michael (Thomas)** 1932- ... **CLC 6, 10**
See also CA 21-24R; CANR 17, 46, 77; DLB 16
**McCorkle, Jill (Collins)** 1958- ............. **CLC 51**
See also CA 121; DLBY 87
**McCourt, Frank** 1930- ....................... **CLC 109**
See also CA 157
**McCourt, James** 1941- ............................. **CLC 5**
See also CA 57-60
**McCourt, Malachy** 1932- ..................... **CLC 119**
**McCoy, Horace (Stanley)** 1897-1955 ... **TCLC 28**
See also CA 108; 155; DLB 9
**McCrae, John** 1872-1918 ...................... **TCLC 12**
See also CA 109; DLB 92
**McCreigh, James**
See Pohl, Frederik
**McCullers, (Lula) Carson (Smith)** 1917-1967 **CLC 1, 4, 10, 12, 48, 100; DA; DAB; DAC; DAM MST, NOV; SSC 9, 24; WLC**
See also AAYA 21; CA 5-8R; 25-28R; CABS 1, 3; CANR 18; CDALB 1941-1968; DLB 2, 7, 173; MTCW 1, 2; SATA 27
**McCulloch, John Tyler**
See Burroughs, Edgar Rice
**McCullough, Colleen** 1938(?)-**CLC 27, 107; DAM NOV, POP**
See also CA 81-84; CANR 17, 46, 67; MTCW 1, 2
**McDermott, Alice** 1953- ....................... **CLC 90**
See also CA 109; CANR 40
**McElroy, Joseph** 1930- ...................... **CLC 5, 47**
See also CA 17-20R
**McEwan, Ian (Russell)** 1948- **CLC 13, 66; DAM NOV**
See also BEST 90:4; CA 61-64; CANR 14, 41, 69; DLB 14, 194; MTCW 1, 2
**McFadden, David** 1940- ........................ **CLC 48**
See also CA 104; DLB 60; INT 104
**McFarland, Dennis** 1950- ..................... **CLC 65**
See also CA 165
**McGahern, John** 1934- .... **CLC 5, 9, 48; SSC 17**
See also CA 17-20R; CANR 29, 68; DLB 14; MTCW 1
**McGinley, Patrick (Anthony)** 1937- ..... **CLC 41**
See also CA 120; 127; CANR 56; INT 127
**McGinley, Phyllis** 1905-1978 ................. **CLC 14**
See also CA 9-12R; 77-80; CANR 19; DLB 11, 48; SATA 2, 44; SATA-Obit 24
**McGinniss, Joe** 1942- ........................... **CLC 32**

See also AITN 2; BEST 89:2; CA 25-28R; CANR 26, 70; DLB 185; INT CANR-26
**McGivern, Maureen Daly**
See Daly, Maureen
**McGrath, Patrick** 1950- ........................ **CLC 55**
See also CA 136; CANR 65
**McGrath, Thomas (Matthew)** 1916-1990 **CLC 28, 59; DAM POET**
See also CA 9-12R; 132; CANR 6, 33; MTCW 1; SATA 41; SATA-Obit 66
**McGuane, Thomas (Francis III)** 1939- **CLC 3, 7, 18, 45**
See also AITN 2; CA 49-52; CANR 5, 24, 49; DLB 2, 212; DLBY 80; INT CANR-24; MTCW 1
**McGuckian, Medbh** 1950- ..... **CLC 48; DAM POET**
See also CA 143; DLB 40
**McHale, Tom** 1942(?)-1982 ................... **CLC 3, 5**
See also CA 1; CA 77-80; 106
**McIlvanney, William** 1936- ................... **CLC 42**
See also CA 25-28R; CANR 61; DLB 14, 207
**McIlwraith, Maureen Mollie Hunter**
See Hunter, Mollie
See also SATA 2
**McInerney, Jay** 1955- . **CLC 34, 112; DAM POP**
See also AAYA 18; CA 116; 123; CANR 45, 68; INT 123; MTCW 2
**McIntyre, Vonda N(eel)** 1948- ............... **CLC 18**
See also CA 81-84; CANR 17, 34, 69; MTCW 1
**McKay, Claude** TCLC **7, 41; BLC 3; DAB; PC 2**
See also McKay, Festus Claudius
See also DLB 4, 45, 51, 117
**McKay, Festus Claudius** 1889-1948
See McKay, Claude
See also BW 1, 3; CA 104; 124; CANR 73; DA; DAC; DAM MST, MULT, NOV, POET; MTCW 1, 2; WLC
**McKuen, Rod** 1933- ............................. **CLC 1, 3**
See also AITN 1; CA 41-44R; CANR 40
**McLoughlin, R. B.**
See Mencken, H(enry) L(ouis)
**McLuhan, (Herbert) Marshall** 1911-1980 **CLC 37, 83**
See also CA 9-12R; 102; CANR 12, 34, 61; DLB 88; INT CANR-12; MTCW 1, 2
**McMillan, Terry (L.)** 1951- .... **CLC 50, 61, 112; BLCS; DAM MULT, NOV, POP**
See also AAYA 21; BW 2, 3; CA 140; CANR 60; MTCW 2
**McMurtry, Larry (Jeff)** 1936- **CLC 2, 3, 7, 11, 27, 44; DAM NOV, POP**
See also AAYA 15; AITN 2; BEST 89:2; CA 5-8R; CANR 19, 43, 64; CDALB 1968-1988; DLB 2, 143; DLBY 80, 87; MTCW 1, 2
**McNally, T. M.** 1961- ............................. **CLC 82**
**McNally, Terrence** 1939- **CLC 4, 7, 41, 91; DAM DRAM**
See also CA 45-48; CANR 2, 56; DLB 7; MTCW 2
**McNamer, Deirdre** 1950- ....................... **CLC 70**
**McNeal, Tom** ........................................ **CLC 119**
**McNeile, Herman Cyril** 1888-1937
See Sapper
See also DLB 77
**McNickle, (William) D'Arcy** 1904-1977 **CLC 89; DAM MULT**
See also CA 9-12R; 85-88; CANR 5, 45; DLB 175, 212; NNAL; SATA-Obit 22
**McPhee, John (Angus)** 1931- ............... **CLC 36**
See also BEST 90:1; CA 65-68; CANR 20, 46, 64, 69; DLB 185; MTCW 1, 2
**McPherson, James Alan** 1943- ...... **CLC 19, 77; BLCS**
See also BW 1, 3; CA 25-28R; CAAS 17; CANR 24, 74; DLB 38; MTCW 1, 2
**McPherson, William (Alexander)** 1933- **CLC 34**

See also CA 69-72; CANR 28; INT CANR-28
**Mead, George Herbert** 1873-1958 ....... **TCLC 89**
**Mead, Margaret** 1901-1978 ................... **CLC 37**
See also AITN 1; CA 1-4R; 81-84; CANR 4; MTCW 1, 2; SATA-Obit 20
**Meaker, Marijane (Agnes)** 1927-
See Kerr, M. E.
See also CA 107; CANR 37, 63; INT 107; JRDA; MAICYA; MTCW 1; SATA 20, 61, 99
**Medoff, Mark (Howard)** 1940- **CLC 6, 23; DAM DRAM**
See also AITN 1; CA 53-56; CANR 5; DLB 7; INT CANR-5
**Medvedev, P. N.**
See Bakhtin, Mikhail Mikhailovich
**Meged, Aharon**
See Megged, Aharon
**Meged, Aron**
See Megged, Aharon
**Megged, Aharon** 1920- ........................... **CLC 9**
See also CA 49-52; CAAS 13; CANR 1
**Mehta, Ved (Parkash)** 1934- ................. **CLC 37**
See also CA 1-4R; CANR 2, 23, 69; MTCW 1
**Melanter**
See Blackmore, R(ichard) D(oddridge)
**Melies, Georges** 1861-1938 ................. **TCLC 81**
**Melikow, Loris**
See Hofmannsthal, Hugo von
**Melmoth, Sebastian**
See Wilde, Oscar
**Meltzer, Milton** 1915- ........................... **CLC 26**
See also AAYA 8; CA 13-16R; CANR 38; CLR 13; DLB 61; JRDA; MAICYA; SAAS 1; SATA 1, 50, 80
**Melville, Herman** 1819-1891 **NCLC 3, 12, 29, 45, 49; DA; DAB; DAC; DAM MST, NOV; SSC 1, 17; WLC**
See also AAYA 25; CDALB 1640-1865; DLB 3, 74; SATA 59
**Menander** c. 342B.C.-c. 292B.C. **CMLC 9; DAM DRAM; DC 3**
See also DLB 176
**Mencken, H(enry) L(ouis)** 1880-1956 . **TCLC 13**
See also CA 105; 125; CDALB 1917-1929; DLB 11, 29, 63, 137; MTCW 1, 2
**Mendelsohn, Jane** 1965(?)- ................... **CLC 99**
See also CA 154
**Mercer, David** 1928-1980 .. **CLC 5; DAM DRAM**
See also CA 9-12R; 102; CANR 23; DLB 13; MTCW 1
**Merchant, Paul**
See Ellison, Harlan (Jay)
**Meredith, George** 1828-1909 **TCLC 17, 43; DAM POET**
See also CA 117; 153; CANR 80; CDBLB 1832-1890; DLB 18, 35, 57, 159
**Meredith, William (Morris)** 1919- **CLC 4, 13, 22, 55; DAM POET**
See also CA 9-12R; CAAS 14; CANR 6, 40; DLB 5
**Merezhkovsky, Dmitry Sergeyevich** 1865-1941 **TCLC 29**
See also CA 169
**Merimee, Prosper** 1803-1870 **NCLC 6, 65; SSC 7**
See also DLB 119, 192
**Merkin, Daphne** 1954- ........................... **CLC 44**
See also CA 123
**Merlin, Arthur**
See Blish, James (Benjamin)
**Merrill, James (Ingram)** 1926-1995 **CLC 2, 3, 6, 8, 13, 18, 34, 91; DAM POET**
See also CA 13-16R; 147; CANR 10, 49, 63; DLB 5, 165; DLBY 85; INT CANR-10; MTCW 1, 2
**Merriman, Alex**
See Silverberg, Robert
**Merriman, Brian** 1747-1805 ............... **NCLC 70**
**Merritt, E. B.**

See Waddington, Miriam
**Merton, Thomas** 1915-1968 **CLC 1, 3, 11, 34, 83; PC 10**
See also CA 5-8R; 25-28R; CANR 22, 53; DLB 48; DLBY 81; MTCW 1, 2
**Merwin, W(illiam) S(tanley)** 1927- **CLC 1, 2, 3, 5, 8, 13, 18, 45, 88; DAM POET**
See also CA 13-16R; CANR 15, 51; DLB 5, 169; INT CANR-15; MTCW 1, 2
**Metcalf, John** 1938- ............................... **CLC 37**
See also CA 113; DLB 60
**Metcalf, Suzanne**
See Baum, L(yman) Frank
**Mew, Charlotte (Mary)** 1870-1928 ........ **TCLC 8**
See also CA 105; DLB 19, 135
**Mewshaw, Michael** 1943- ...................... **CLC 9**
See also CA 53-56; CANR 7, 47; DLBY 80
**Meyer, June**
See Jordan, June
**Meyer, Lynn**
See Slavitt, David R(ytman)
**Meyer-Meyrink, Gustav** 1868-1932
See Meyrink, Gustav
See also CA 117
**Meyers, Jeffrey** 1939- ............................. **CLC 39**
See also CA 73-76; CANR 54; DLB 111
**Meynell, Alice (Christina Gertrude Thompson)** 1847-1922 ...................................... **TCLC 6**
See also CA 104; 177; DLB 19, 98
**Meyrink, Gustav** ................................... **TCLC 21**
See also Meyer-Meyrink, Gustav
See also DLB 81
**Michaels, Leonard** 1933- .... **CLC 6, 25; SSC 16**
See also CA 61-64; CANR 21, 62; DLB 130; MTCW 1
**Michaux, Henri** 1899-1984 ................ **CLC 8, 19**
See also CA 85-88; 114
**Micheaux, Oscar (Devereaux)** 1884-1951 **TCLC 76**
See also BW 3; CA 174; DLB 50
**Michelangelo** 1475-1564 ......................... **LC 12**
**Michelet, Jules** 1798-1874 .................... **NCLC 31**
**Michels, Robert** 1876-1936 ................... **TCLC 88**
**Michener, James A(lbert)** 1907(?)-1997 **CLC 1, 5, 11, 29, 60, 109; DAM NOV, POP**
See also AAYA 27; AITN 1; BEST 90:1; CA 5-8R; 161; CANR 21, 45, 68; DLB 6; MTCW 1, 2
**Mickiewicz, Adam** 1798-1855 ................ **NCLC 3**
**Middleton, Christopher** 1926- .............. **CLC 13**
See also CA 13-16R; CANR 29, 54; DLB 40
**Middleton, Richard (Barham)** 1882-1911 **TCLC 56**
See also DLB 156
**Middleton, Stanley** 1919- ...................... **CLC 7, 38**
See also CA 25-28R; CAAS 23; CANR 21, 46, 81; DLB 14
**Middleton, Thomas** 1580-1627 ....... **LC 33; DAM DRAM, MST; DC 5**
See also DLB 58
**Migueis, Jose Rodrigues** 1901- ............ **CLC 10**
**Mikszath, Kalman** 1847-1910 .............. **TCLC 31**
See also CA 170
**Miles, Jack** ........................................ **CLC 100**
**Miles, Josephine (Louise)** 1911-1985 . **CLC 1, 2, 14, 34, 39; DAM POET**
See also CA 1-4R; 116; CANR 2, 55; DLB 48
**Militant**
See Sandburg, Carl (August)
**Mill, John Stuart** 1806-1873 ......... **NCLC 11, 58**
See also CDBLB 1832-1890; DLB 55, 190
**Millar, Kenneth** 1915-1983 . **CLC 14; DAM POP**
See also Macdonald, Ross
See also CA 9-12R; 110; CANR 16, 63; DLB 2; DLBD 6; DLBY 83; MTCW 1, 2
**Millay, E. Vincent**
See Millay, Edna St. Vincent
**Millay, Edna St. Vincent** 1892-1950 **TCLC 4, 49; DA; DAB; DAC; DAM MST, POET; PC 6;**

WLCS
See also CA 104; 130; CDALB 1917-1929; DLB 45, MTCW 1, 2

**Miller, Arthur** 1915-**CLC 1, 2, 6, 10, 15, 26, 47, 78; DA; DAB; DAC; DAM DRAM, MST, DC 1; WLC**
See also AAYA 15; AITN 1; CA 1-4R; CABS 3; CANR 2, 30, 54, 76; CDALB 1941-1968; DLB 7; MTCW 1, 2

**Miller, Henry (Valentine)** 1891-1980**CLC 1, 2, 4, 9, 14, 43, 84; DA; DAB; DAC; DAM MST, NOV; WLC**
See also CA 9-12R; 97-100; CANR 33, 64; CDALB 1929-1941; DLB 4, 9; DLBY 80; MTCW 1, 2

**Miller, Jason** 1939(?)- ............................. **CLC 2**
See also AITN 1; CA 73-76; DLB 7

**Miller, Sue** 1943- ........... **CLC 44; DAM POP**
See also BEST 90:3; CA 139; CANR 59; DLB 143

**Miller, Walter M(ichael, Jr.)** 1923-**CLC 4, 30**
See also CA 85-88; DLB 8

**Millett, Kate** 1934- ................................. **CLC 67**
See also AITN 1; CA 73-76; CANR 32, 53, 76; MTCW 1, 2

**Millhauser, Steven (Lewis)** 1943-**CLC 21, 54, 109**
See also CA 110; 111; CANR 63; DLB 2; INT 111; MTCW 2

**Millin, Sarah Gertrude** 1889-1968 ........ **CLC 49**
See also CA 102; 93-96

**Milne, A(lan) A(lexander)** 1882-1956**TCLC 6, 88; DAB; DAC; DAM MST**
See also CA 104; 133; CLR 1, 26; DLB 10, 77, 100, 160; MAICYA; MTCW 1, 2; SATA 100; YABC 1

**Milner, Ron(ald)** 1938- .. **CLC 56; BLC 3; DAM MULT**
See also AITN 1; BW 1; CA 73-76; CANR 24, 81; DLB 38; MTCW 1

**Milnes, Richard Monckton** 1809-1885 **NCLC 61**
See also DLB 32, 184

**Milosz, Czeslaw** 1911-**CLC 5, 11, 22, 31, 56, 82; DAM MST, POET; PC 8; WLCS**
See also CA 81-84; CANR 23, 51; MTCW 1, 2

**Milton, John** 1608-1674**LC 9, 43; DA; DAB; DAC; DAM MST, POET; PC 19; WLC**
See also CDBLB 1660-1789; DLB 131, 151

**Min, Anchee** 1957- ................................. **CLC 86**
See also CA 146

**Minehaha, Cornelius**
See Wedekind, (Benjamin) Frank(lin)

**Miner, Valerie** 1947- ............................. **CLC 40**
See also CA 97-100; CANR 59

**Minimo, Duca**
See D'Annunzio, Gabriele

**Minot, Susan** 1956- ................................. **CLC 44**
See also CA 134

**Minus, Ed** 1938- ...................................... **CLC 39**

**Miranda, Javier**
See Bioy Casares, Adolfo

**Miranda, Javier**
See Bioy Casares, Adolfo

**Mirbeau, Octave** 1848-1917 ................. **TCLC 55**
See also DLB 123, 192

**Miro (Ferrer), Gabriel (Francisco Victor)** 1879-1930 ................................................... **TCLC 5**
See also CA 104

**Mishima, Yukio** 1925-1970**CLC 2, 4, 6, 9, 27; DC 1; SSC 4**
See also Hiraoka, Kimitake
See also DLB 182; MTCW 2

**Mistral, Frederic** 1830-1914 ............... **TCLC 51**
See also CA 122

**Mistral, Gabriela** .......................... **TCLC 2; HLC**
See also Godoy Alcayaga, Lucila
See also MTCW 2

**Mistry, Rohinton** 1952- .............. **CLC 71; DAC**
See also CA 141

**Mitchell, Clyde**
See Ellison, Harlan (Jay); Silverberg, Robert

**Mitchell, James Leslie** 1901-1935
See Gibbon, Lewis Grassic
See also CA 104; DLB 15

**Mitchell, Joni** 1943- ............................. **CLC 12**
See also CA 112

**Mitchell, Joseph (Quincy)** 1908-1996 ... **CLC 98**
See also CA 77-80; 152; CANR 69; DLB 185; DLBY 96

**Mitchell, Margaret (Munnerlyn)** 1900-1949 **TCLC 11; DAM NOV, POP**
See also AAYA 23; CA 109; 125; CANR 55; CDALBS; DLB 9; MTCW 1, 2

**Mitchell, Peggy**
See Mitchell, Margaret (Munnerlyn)

**Mitchell, S(ilas) Weir** 1829-1914 ... **TCLC 36**
See also CA 165; DLB 202

**Mitchell, W(illiam) O(rmond)** 1914-1998**CLC 25; DAC; DAM MST**
See also CA 77-80; 165; CANR 15, 43; DLB 88

**Mitchell, William** 1879-1936 ............... **TCLC 81**

**Mitford, Mary Russell** 1787-1855 ......... **NCLC 4**
See also DLB 110, 116

**Mitford, Nancy** 1904-1973 ..................... **CLC 44**
See also CA 9-12R; DLB 191

**Miyamoto, (Chujo) Yuriko** 1899-1951 . **TCLC 37**
See also CA 170, 174; DLB 180

**Miyazawa, Kenji** 1896-1933 ................. **TCLC 76**
See also CA 157

**Mizoguchi, Kenji** 1898-1956 ............... **TCLC 72**
See also CA 167

**Mo, Timothy (Peter)** 1950(?)- ................ **CLC 46**
See also CA 117; DLB 194; MTCW 1

**Modarressi, Taghi (M.)** 1931- ............... **CLC 44**
See also CA 121; 134; INT 134

**Modiano, Patrick (Jean)** 1945- ............... **CLC 18**
See also CA 85-88; CANR 17, 40; DLB 83

**Moerck, Paal**
See Roelvaag, O(le) E(dvart)

**Mofolo, Thomas (Mokopu)** 1875(?)-1948**TCLC 22; BLC 3; DAM MULT**
See also CA 121; 153; MTCW 2

**Mohr, Nicholasa** 1938-**CLC 12; DAM MULT; HLC**
See also AAYA 8; CA 49-52; CANR 1, 32, 64; CLR 22; DLB 145; HW 1, 2; JRDA; SAAS 8; SATA 8, 97

**Mojtabai, A(nn) G(race)** 1938- **CLC 5, 9, 15, 29**
See also CA 85-88

**Moliere** 1622-1673 **LC 10, 28; DA; DAB; DAC; DAM DRAM, MST; WLC**

**Molin, Charles**
See Mayne, William (James Carter)

**Molnar, Ferenc** 1878-1952**TCLC 20; DAM DRAM**
See also CA 109; 153

**Momaday, N(avarre) Scott** 1934- **CLC 2, 19, 85, 95; DA; DAB; DAC; DAM MST, MULT, NOV, POP; PC 25; WLCS**
See also AAYA 11; CA 25-28R; CANR 14, 34, 68; CDALBS; DLB 143, 175; INT CANR-14; MTCW 1, 2; NNAL; SATA 48; SATA-Brief 30

**Monette, Paul** 1945-1995 ....................... **CLC 82**
See also CA 139; 147

**Monroe, Harriet** 1860-1936 ................. **TCLC 12**
See also CA 109; DLB 54, 91

**Monroe, Lyle**
See Heinlein, Robert A(nson)

**Montagu, Elizabeth** 1720-1800 ............. **NCLC 7**

**Montagu, Mary (Pierrepont) Wortley** 1689-1762 **LC 9; PC 16**
See also DLB 95, 101

**Montagu, W. H.**
See Coleridge, Samuel Taylor

**Montague, John (Patrick)** 1929- ..... **CLC 13, 46**
See also CA 9-12R; CANR 9, 69; DLB 40; MTCW 1

**Montaigne, Michel (Eyquem) de** 1533-1592**LC 8;**

DA; DAB; DAC; DAM MST; WLC

**Montale, Eugenio** 1896-1981**CLC 7, 9, 18; PC 13**
See also CA 17-20R; 104; CANR 30; DLB 114; MTCW 1

**Montesquieu, Charles-Louis de Secondat** 1689-1755 ................................................... **LC 7**

**Montgomery, (Robert) Bruce** 1921-1978
See Crispin, Edmund
See also CA 104

**Montgomery, L(ucy) M(aud)** 1874-1942**TCLC 51; DAC; DAM MST**
See also AAYA 12; CA 108; 137; CLR 8; DLB 92; DLBD 14; JRDA; MAICYA; MTCW 2; SATA 100; YABC 1

**Montgomery, Marion H., Jr.** 1925- .......... **CLC 7**
See also AITN 1; CA 1-4R; CANR 3, 48; DLB 6

**Montgomery, Max**
See Davenport, Guy (Mattison, Jr.)

**Montherlant, Henry (Milon) de** 1896-1972**CLC 8, 19; DAM DRAM**
See also CA 85-88; 37-40R; DLB 72; MTCW 1

**Monty Python**
See Chapman, Graham; Cleese, John (Marwood); Gilliam, Terry (Vance); Idle, Eric; Jones, Terence Graham Parry; Palin, Michael (Edward)
See also AAYA 7

**Moodie, Susanna (Strickland)** 1803-1885 **NCLC 14**
See also DLB 99

**Mooney, Edward** 1951-
See Mooney, Ted
See also CA 130

**Mooney, Ted** ............................................. **CLC 25**
See also Mooney, Edward

**Moorcock, Michael (John)** 1939- **CLC 5, 27, 58**
See also Bradbury, Edward P.
See also AAYA 26; CA 45-48; CAAS 5; CANR 2, 17, 38, 64; DLB 14; MTCW 1, 2; SATA 93

**Moore, Brian** 1921-1999**CLC 1, 3, 5, 7, 8, 19, 32, 90; DAB; DAC; DAM MST**
See also CA 1-4R; 174; CANR 1, 25, 42, 63; MTCW 1, 2

**Moore, Edward**
See Muir, Edwin

**Moore, G. E.** 1873-1958 ......................... **TCLC 89**

**Moore, George Augustus** 1852-1933**TCLC 7; SSC 19**
See also CA 104; 177; DLB 10, 18, 57, 135

**Moore, Lorrie** ........................... **CLC 39, 45, 68**
See also Moore, Marie Lorena

**Moore, Marianne (Craig)** 1887-1972**CLC 1, 2, 4, 8, 10, 13, 19, 47; DA; DAB; DAC; DAM MST, POET; PC 4; WLCS**
See also CA 1-4R; 33-36R; CANR 3, 61; CDALB 1929-1941; DLB 45; DLBD 7; MTCW 1, 2; SATA 20

**Moore, Marie Lorena** 1957-
See Moore, Lorrie
See also CA 116; CANR 39

**Moore, Thomas** 1779-1852 ..................... **NCLC 6**
See also DLB 96, 144

**Morand, Paul** 1888-1976 ......... **CLC 41; SSC 22**
See also CA 69-72; DLB 65

**Morante, Elsa** 1918-1985 .................. **CLC 8, 47**
See also CA 85-88; 117; CANR 35; DLB 177; MTCW 1, 2

**Moravia, Alberto** 1907-1990**CLC 2, 7, 11, 27, 46; SSC 26**
See also Pincherle, Alberto
See also DLB 177; MTCW 2

**More, Hannah** 1745-1833 ..................... **NCLC 27**
See also DLB 107, 109, 116, 158

**More, Henry** 1614-1687 ............................. **LC 9**
See also DLB 126

**More, Sir Thomas** 1478-1535 ............. **LC 10, 32**

**Moreas, Jean** ....................................... **TCLC 18**

See also CA 140

**Ouida** ...................................................... **TCLC 43**
See also De La Ramee, (Marie) Louise
See also DLB 18, 156

**Ousmane, Sembene** 1923- ........ **CLC 66; BLC 3**
See also BW 1, 3; CA 117; 125; CANR 81; MTCW 1

**Ovid** 43B.C.-17 ...... **CMLC 7; DAM POET; PC 2**
See also DLB 211

**Owen, Hugh**
See Faust, Frederick (Schiller)

**Owen, Wilfred (Edward Salter)** 1893-1918 **TCLC 5, 27; DA; DAB; DAC; DAM MST, POET; PC 19; WLC**
See also CA 104; 141; CDBLB 1914-1945; DLB 20; MTCW 2

**Owens, Rochelle** 1936- ............................ **CLC 8**
See also CA 17-20R; CAAS 2; CANR 39

**Oz, Amos** 1939-**CLC 5, 8, 11, 27, 33, 54; DAM NOV**
See also CA 53-56; CANR 27, 47, 65; MTCW 1, 2

**Ozick, Cynthia** 1928-**CLC 3, 7, 28, 62; DAM NOV, POP; SSC 15**
See also BEST 90:1; CA 17-20R; CANR 23, 58; DLB 28, 152; DLBY 82; INT CANR-23; MTCW 1, 2

**Ozu, Yasujiro** 1903-1963 ........................ **CLC 16**
See also CA 112

**Pacheco, C.**
See Pessoa, Fernando (Antonio Nogueira)

**Pa Chin** ................................................... **CLC 18**
See also Li Fei-kan

**Pack, Robert** 1929- ................................... **CLC 13**
See also CA 1-4R; CANR 3, 44; DLB 5

**Padgett, Lewis**
See Kuttner, Henry

**Padilla (Lorenzo), Heberto** 1932- .......... **CLC 38**
See also AITN 1; CA 123; 131; HW 1

**Page, Jimmy** 1944- ................................... **CLC 12**

**Page, Louise** 1955- ................................... **CLC 40**
See also CA 140; CANR 76

**Page, P(atricia) K(athleen)** 1916- .... **CLC 7, 18; DAC; DAM MST; PC 12**
See also CA 53-56; CANR 4, 22, 65; DLB 68; MTCW 1

**Page, Thomas Nelson** 1853-1922 ............ **SSC 23**
See also CA 118; 177; DLB 12, 78; DLBD 13

**Pagels, Elaine Hiesey** 1943- .............. **CLC 104**
See also CA 45-48; CANR 2, 24, 51

**Paget, Violet** 1856-1935
See Lee, Vernon
See also CA 104; 166

**Paget-Lowe, Henry**
See Lovecraft, H(oward) P(hillips)

**Paglia, Camille (Anna)** 1947- .............. **CLC 68**
See also CA 140; CANR 72; MTCW 2

**Paige, Richard**
See Koontz, Dean R(ay)

**Paine, Thomas** 1737-1809 .................... **NCLC 62**
See also CDALB 1640-1865; DLB 31, 43, 73, 158

**Pakenham, Antonia**
See Fraser, (Lady) Antonia (Pakenham)

**Palamas, Kostes** 1859-1943 .................... **TCLC 5**
See also CA 105

**Palazzeschi, Aldo** 1885-1974 .................. **CLC 11**
See also CA 89-92; 53-56; DLB 114

**Paley, Grace** 1922-**CLC 4, 6, 37; DAM POP; SSC 8**
See also CA 25-28R; CANR 13, 46, 74; DLB 28; INT CANR-13; MTCW 1, 2

**Palin, Michael (Edward)** 1943- .............. **CLC 21**
See also Monty Python
See also CA 107; CANR 35; SATA 67

**Palliser, Charles** 1947- ........................... **CLC 65**
See also CA 136; CANR 76

**Palma, Ricardo** 1833-1919 ................... **TCLC 29**
See also CA 168

**Pancake, Breece Dexter** 1952-1979
See Pancake, Breece D'J
See also CA 123; 109

**Pancake, Breece D'J** ............................. **CLC 29**
See also Pancake, Breece Dexter
See also DLB 130

**Panko, Rudy**
See Gogol, Nikolai (Vasilyevich)

**Papadiamantis, Alexandros** 1851-1911 **TCLC 29**
See also CA 168

**Papadiamantopoulos, Johannes** 1856-1910
See Moreas, Jean
See also CA 117

**Papini, Giovanni** 1881-1956 .................. **TCLC 22**
See also CA 121

**Paracelsus** 1493-1541 .............................. **LC 14**
See also DLB 179

**Parasol, Peter**
See Stevens, Wallace

**Pardo Bazan, Emilia** 1851-1921 ........ **SSC 30**

**Pareto, Vilfredo** 1848-1923 ............. **TCLC 69**
See also CA 175

**Parfenie, Maria**
See Codrescu, Andrei

**Parini, Jay (Lee)** 1948- .......................... **CLC 54**
See also CA 97-100; CAAS 16; CANR 32

**Park, Jordan**
See Kornbluth, C(yril) M.; Pohl, Frederik

**Park, Robert E(zra)** 1864-1944 ............ **TCLC 73**
See also CA 122; 165

**Parker, Bert**
See Ellison, Harlan (Jay)

**Parker, Dorothy (Rothschild)** 1893-1967**CLC 15, 68; DAM POET; SSC 2**
See also CA 19-20; 25-28R; CAP 2; DLB 11, 45, 86; MTCW 1, 2

**Parker, Robert B(rown)** 1932- .... **CLC 27; DAM NOV, POP**
See also AAYA 28; BEST 89:4; CA 49-52; CANR 1, 26, 52; INT CANR-26; MTCW 1

**Parkin, Frank** 1940- .............................. **CLC 43**
See also CA 147

**Parkman, Francis, Jr.** 1823-1893 ....... **NCLC 12**
See also DLB 1, 30, 186

**Parks, Gordon (Alexander Buchanan)** 1912-**CLC 1, 16; BLC 3; DAM MULT**
See also AITN 2; BW 2, 3; CA 41-44R; CANR 26, 66; DLB 33; MTCW 2; SATA 8, 108

**Parmenides** c. 515B.C.-c. 450B.C. ...... **CMLC 22**
See also DLB 176

**Parnell, Thomas** 1679-1718 ....................... **LC 3**
See also DLB 94

**Parra, Nicanor** 1914- **CLC 2, 102; DAM MULT; HLC**
See also CA 85-88; CANR 32; HW 1; MTCW 1

**Parrish, Mary Frances**
See Fisher, M(ary) F(rances) K(ennedy)

**Parson**
See Coleridge, Samuel Taylor

**Parson Lot**
See Kingsley, Charles

**Partridge, Anthony**
See Oppenheim, E(dward) Phillips

**Pascal, Blaise** 1623-1662 ......................... **LC 35**

**Pascoli, Giovanni** 1855-1912 ............... **TCLC 45**
See also CA 170

**Pasolini, Pier Paolo** 1922-1975**CLC 20, 37, 106; PC 17**
See also CA 93-96; 61-64; CANR 63; DLB 128, 177; MTCW 1

**Pasquini**
See Silone, Ignazio

**Pastan, Linda (Olenik)** 1932- ..... **CLC 27; DAM POET**
See also CA 61-64; CANR 18, 40, 61; DLB 5

**Pasternak, Boris (Leonidovich)** 1890-1960 **CLC 7, 10, 18, 63; DA; DAB; DAC; DAM MST, NOV, POET; PC 6; SSC 31; WLC**
See also CA 127; 116; MTCW 1, 2

**Patchen, Kenneth** 1911-1972**CLC 1, 2, 18; DAM POET**
See also CA 1-4R; 33-36R; CANR 3, 35; DLB 16, 48; MTCW 1

**Pater, Walter (Horatio)** 1839-1894 ........ **NCLC 7**
See also CDBLB 1832-1890; DLB 57, 156

**Paterson, A(ndrew) B(arton)** 1864-1941**TCLC 32**
See also CA 155; SATA 97

**Paterson, Katherine (Womeldorf)** 1932-**CLC 12, 30**
See also AAYA 1; CA 21-24R; CANR 28, 59; CLR 7, 50; DLB 52; JRDA; MAICYA; MTCW 1; SATA 13, 53, 92

**Patmore, Coventry Kersey Dighton** 1823-1896 **NCLC 9**
See also DLB 35, 98

**Paton, Alan (Stewart)** 1903-1988 **CLC 4, 10, 25, 55, 106; DA; DAB; DAC; DAM MST, NOV; WLC**
See also AAYA 26; CA 13-16; 125; CANR 22; CAP 1; DLBD 17; MTCW 1, 2; SATA 11; SATA-Obit 56

**Paton Walsh, Gillian** 1937-
See Walsh, Jill Paton
See also CANR 38; JRDA; MAICYA; SAAS 3; SATA 4, 72, 109

**Patton, George S.** 1885-1945 ............... **TCLC 79**

**Paulding, James Kirke** 1778-1860 ........ **NCLC 2**
See also DLB 3, 59, 74

**Paulin, Thomas Neilson** 1949-
See Paulin, Tom
See also CA 123; 128

**Paulin, Tom** .............................................. **CLC 37**
See also Paulin, Thomas Neilson
See also DLB 40

**Paustovsky, Konstantin (Georgievich)** 1892-1968 **CLC 40**
See also CA 93-96; 25-28R

**Pavese, Cesare** 1908-1950**TCLC 3; PC 13; SSC 19**
See also CA 104; 169; DLB 128, 177

**Pavic, Milorad** 1929- .............................. **CLC 60**
See also CA 136; DLB 181

**Pavlov, Ivan Petrovich** 1849-1936 ......... **TCLC 91**
See also CA 118

**Payne, Alan**
See Jakes, John (William)

**Paz, Gil**
See Lugones, Leopoldo

**Paz, Octavio** 1914-1998**CLC 3, 4, 6, 10, 19, 51, 65, 119; DA; DAB; DAC; DAM MST, MULT, POET; HLC; PC 1; WLC**
See also CA 73-76; 165; CANR 32, 65; DLBY 90, 98; HW 1, 2; MTCW 1, 2

**p'Bitek, Okot** 1931-1982 **CLC 96; BLC 3; DAM MULT**
See also BW 2, 3; CA 124; 107; DLB 125; MTCW 1, 2

**Peacock, Molly** 1947- ............................. **CLC 60**
See also CA 103; CAAS 21; CANR 52; DLB 120

**Peacock, Thomas Love** 1785-1866 ...... **NCLC 22**
See also DLB 96, 116

**Peake, Mervyn** 1911-1968 ................ **CLC 7, 54**
See also CA 5-8R; 25-28R; CANR 3; DLB 15, 160; MTCW 1; SATA 23

**Pearce, Philippa** ..................................... **CLC 21**
See also Christie, (Ann) Philippa
See also CLR 9; DLB 161; MAICYA; SATA 1, 67

**Pearl, Eric**
See Elman, Richard (Martin)

**Pearson, T(homas) R(eid)** 1956- .......... **CLC 39**
See also CA 120; 130; INT 130

**Peck, Dale** 1967- .................................... **CLC 81**
See also CA 146; CANR 72

**Peck, John** 1941- ...................................... **CLC 3**
See also CA 49-52; CANR 3

**Peck, Richard (Wayne)** 1934- .......... **CLC 21**
 See also AAYA 1, 24; CA 85-88; CANR 19,
  38; CLR 15; INT CANR-19; JRDA;
  MAICYA; SAAS 2; SATA 18, 55, 97
**Peck, Robert Newton** 1928- **CLC 17; DA; DAC;**
  **DAM MST**
 See also AAYA 3; CA 81-84; CANR 31, 63; CLR
  45; JRDA; MAICYA; SAAS 1; SATA 21, 62;
  SATA-Essay 108
**Peckinpah, (David) Sam(uel)** 1925-1984 **CLC 20**
 See also CA 109; 114
**Pedersen, Knut** 1859-1952
 See Hamsun, Knut
 See also CA 104; 119; CANR 63; MTCW 1, 2
**Peeslake, Gaffer**
 See Durrell, Lawrence (George)
**Peguy, Charles Pierre** 1873-1914 ....... **TCLC 10**
 See also CA 107
**Peirce, Charles Sanders** 1839-1914 **TCLC 81**
**Pena, Ramon del Valle y**
 See Valle-Inclan, Ramon (Maria) del
**Pendennis, Arthur Esquir**
 See Thackeray, William Makepeace
**Penn, William** 1644-1718 ......................... **LC 25**
 See also DLB 24
**Pepece**
 See Prado (Calvo), Pedro
**Pepys, Samuel** 1633-1703 **LC 11; DA; DAB; DAC;**
  **DAM MST; WLC**
 See also CDBLB 1660-1789; DLB 101
**Percy, Walker** 1916-1990 **CLC 2, 3, 6, 8, 14, 18,**
  **47, 65; DAM NOV, POP**
 See also CA 1-4R; 131; CANR 1, 23, 64; DLB 2;
  DLBY 80, 90; MTCW 1, 2
**Percy, William Alexander** 1885-1942 . **TCLC 84**
 See also CA 163; MTCW 2
**Perec, Georges** 1936-1982 ............. **CLC 56, 116**
 See also CA 141; DLB 83
**Pereda (y Sanchez de Porrua), Jose Maria de** 1833-
  1906 .............................................. **TCLC 16**
 See also CA 117
**Pereda y Porrua, Jose Maria de**
 See Pereda (y Sanchez de Porrua), Jose Maria de
**Peregoy, George Weems**
 See Mencken, H(enry) L(ouis)
**Perelman, S(idney) J(oseph)** 1904-1979 **CLC 3, 5,**
  **9, 15, 23, 44, 49; DAM DRAM; SSC 32**
 See also AITN 1, 2; CA 73-76; 89-92; CANR 18;
  DLB 11, 44; MTCW 1, 2
**Peret, Benjamin** 1899-1959 ................. **TCLC 20**
 See also CA 117
**Peretz, Isaac Loeb** 1851(?)-1915 **TCLC 16; SSC 26**
 See also CA 109
**Peretz, Yitzhok Leibush**
 See Peretz, Isaac Loeb
**Perez Galdos, Benito** 1843-1920 **TCLC 27; HLCS**
  **2**
 See also CA 125; 153; HW 1
**Perrault, Charles** 1628-1703 ...................... **LC 2**
 See also MAICYA; SATA 25
**Perry, Brighton**
 See Sherwood, Robert E(mmet)
**Perse, St.-John**
 See Leger, (Marie-Rene Auguste) Alexis Saint-
  Leger
**Perutz, Leo(pold)** 1882-1957 ............... **TCLC 60**
 See also CA 147; DLB 81
**Peseenz, Tulio F.**
 See Lopez y Fuentes, Gregorio
**Pesetsky, Bette** 1932- ............................. **CLC 28**
 See also CA 133; DLB 130
**Peshkov, Alexei Maximovich** 1868-1936
 See Gorky, Maxim
 See also CA 105; 141; DA; DAC; DAM DRAM,
  MST, NOV; MTCW 2
**Pessoa, Fernando (Antonio Nogueira)** 1888-1935
  **TCLC 27; DAM MULT; HLC; PC 20**

 See also CA 125
**Peterkin, Julia Mood** 1880-1961 ........... **CLC 31**
 See also CA 102; DLB 9
**Peters, Joan K(aren)** 1945- ................... **CLC 39**
 See also CA 158
**Peters, Robert L(ouis)** 1924- ................... **CLC 7**
 See also CA 13-16R; CAAS 8; DLB 105
**Petofi, Sandor** 1823-1849 ..................... **NCLC 21**
**Petrakis, Harry Mark** 1923- ................... **CLC 3**
 See also CA 9-12R; CANR 4, 30
**Petrarch** 1304-1374 **CMLC 20; DAM POET; PC 8**
**Petrov, Evgeny** ..................................... **TCLC 21**
 See also Kataev, Evgeny Petrovich
**Petry, Ann (Lane)** 1908-1997 ......... **CLC 1, 7, 18**
 See also BW 1, 3; CA 5-8R; 157; CAAS 6; CANR
  4, 46; CLR 12; DLB 76; JRDA; MAICYA;
  MTCW 1; SATA 5; SATA-Obit 94
**Petursson, Halligrimur** 1614-1674 ............ **LC 8**
**Peychinovich**
 See Vazov, Ivan (Minchov)
**Phaedrus** c. 18B.C.-c. 50 ..................... **CMLC 25**
 See also DLB 211
**Philips, Katherine** 1632-1664 .................. **LC 30**
 See also DLB 131
**Philipson, Morris H.** 1926- ................... **CLC 53**
 See also CA 1-4R; CANR 4
**Phillips, Caryl** 1958- **CLC 96; BLCS; DAM MULT**
 See also BW 2; CA 141; CANR 63; DLB 157;
  MTCW 2
**Phillips, David Graham** 1867-1911 ...... **TCLC 44**
 See also CA 108; 176; DLB 9, 12
**Phillips, Jack**
 See Sandburg, Carl (August)
**Phillips, Jayne Anne** 1952- **CLC 15, 33; SSC 16**
 See also CA 101; CANR 24, 50; DLBY 80; INT
  CANR-24; MTCW 1, 2
**Phillips, Richard**
 See Dick, Philip K(indred)
**Phillips, Robert (Schaeffer)** 1938- ....... **CLC 28**
 See also CA 17-20R; CAAS 13; CANR 8; DLB
  105
**Phillips, Ward**
 See Lovecraft, H(oward) P(hillips)
**Piccolo, Lucio** 1901-1969 ....................... **CLC 13**
 See also CA 97-100; DLB 114
**Pickthall, Marjorie L(owry) C(hristie)** 1883-1922
  **TCLC 21**
 See also CA 107; DLB 92
**Pico della Mirandola, Giovanni** 1463-1494 **LC 15**
**Piercy, Marge** 1936- .... **CLC 3, 6, 14, 18, 27, 62**
 See also CA 21-24R; CAAS 1; CANR 13, 43, 66;
  DLB 120; MTCW 1, 2
**Piers, Robert**
 See Anthony, Piers
**Pieyre de Mandiargues, Andre** 1909-1991
 See Mandiargues, Andre Pieyre de
 See also CA 103; 136; CANR 22
**Pilnyak, Boris** ..................................... **TCLC 23**
 See also Vogau, Boris Andreyevich
**Pincherle, Alberto** 1907-1990 **CLC 11, 18; DAM**
  **NOV**
 See also Moravia, Alberto
 See also CA 25-28R; 132; CANR 33, 63; MTCW
  1
**Pinckney, Darryl** 1953- ......................... **CLC 76**
 See also BW 2, 3; CA 143; CANR 79
**Pindar** 518B.C.-446B.C. ......... **CMLC 12; PC 19**
 See also DLB 176
**Pineda, Cecile** 1942- ............................. **CLC 39**
 See also CA 118
**Pinero, Arthur Wing** 1855-1934 **TCLC 32; DAM**
  **DRAM**
 See also CA 110; 153; DLB 10
**Pinero, Miguel (Antonio Gomez)** 1946-1988 **CLC**
  **4, 55**
 See also CA 61-64; 125; CANR 29; HW 1
**Pinget, Robert** 1919-1997 ........... **CLC 7, 13, 37**

 See also CA 85-88; 160; DLB 83
**Pink Floyd**
 See Barrett, (Roger) Syd; Gilmour, David; Ma-
  son, Nick; Waters, Roger; Wright, Rick
**Pinkney, Edward** 1802-1828 ................. **NCLC 31**
**Pinkwater, Daniel Manus** 1941- ........... **CLC 35**
 See also Pinkwater, Manus
 See also AAYA 1; CA 29-32R; CANR 12, 38; CLR
  4; JRDA; MAICYA; SAAS 3; SATA 46, 76
**Pinkwater, Manus**
 See Pinkwater, Daniel Manus
 See also SATA 8
**Pinsky, Robert** 1940- **CLC 9, 19, 38, 94, 121; DAM**
  **POET**
 See also CA 29-32R; CAAS 4; CANR 58; DLBY
  82, 98; MTCW 2
**Pinta, Harold**
 See Pinter, Harold
**Pinter, Harold** 1930- **CLC 1, 3, 6, 9, 11, 15, 27,**
  **58, 73; DA; DAB; DAC; DAM DRAM,**
  **MST; WLC**
 See also CA 5-8R; CANR 33, 65; CDBLB 1960 to
  Present; DLB 13; MTCW 1, 2
**Piozzi, Hester Lynch (Thrale)** 1741-1821 **NCLC**
  **57**
 See also DLB 104, 142
**Pirandello, Luigi** 1867-1936 ... **TCLC 4, 29; DA;**
  **DAB; DAC; DAM DRAM, MST; DC 5; SSC**
  **22; WLC**
 See also CA 104; 153; MTCW 2
**Pirsig, Robert M(aynard)** 1928- .. **CLC 4, 6, 73;**
  **DAM POP**
 See also CA 53-56; CANR 42, 74; MTCW 1, 2;
  SATA 39
**Pisarev, Dmitry Ivanovich** 1840-1868 .. **NCLC 25**
**Pix, Mary (Griffith)** 1666-1709 .................. **LC 8**
 See also DLB 80
**Pixerecourt, (Rene Charles) Guilbert de** 1773-1844
  **NCLC 39**
 See also DLB 192
**Plaatje, Sol(omon) T(shekisho)** 1876-1932 **TCLC**
  **73; BLCS**
 See also BW 2, 3; CA 141; CANR 79
**Plaidy, Jean**
 See Hibbert, Eleanor Alice Burford
**Planche, James Robinson** 1796-1880 .. **NCLC 42**
**Plant, Robert** 1948- ............................... **CLC 12**
**Plante, David (Robert)** 1940- **CLC 7, 23, 38; DAM**
  **NOV**
 See also CA 37-40R; CANR 12, 36, 58; DLBY 83;
  INT CANR-12; MTCW 1
**Plath, Sylvia** 1932-1963 **CLC 1, 2, 3, 5, 9, 11, 14,**
  **17, 50, 51, 62, 111; DA; DAB; DAC; DAM**
  **MST, POET; PC 1; WLC**
 See also AAYA 13; CA 19-20; CANR 34; CAP 2;
  CDALB 1941-1968; DLB 5, 6, 152; MTCW 1,
  2; SATA 96
**Plato** 428(?)B.C.-348(?)B.C. **CMLC 8; DA; DAB;**
  **DAC; DAM MST; WLCS**
 See also DLB 176
**Platonov, Andrei** ................................... **TCLC 14**
 See also Klimentov, Andrei Platonovich
**Platt, Kin** 1911- ..................................... **CLC 26**
 See also AAYA 11; CA 17-20R; CANR 11; JRDA;
  SAAS 17; SATA 21, 86
**Plautus** c. 251B.C.-184B.C. ...... **CMLC 24; DC 6**
 See also DLB 211
**Plick et Plock**
 See Simenon, Georges (Jacques Christian)
**Plimpton, George (Ames)** 1927- ........... **CLC 36**
 See also AITN 1; CA 21-24R; CANR 32, 70; DLB
  185; MTCW 1, 2; SATA 10
**Pliny the Elder** c. 23-79 ..................... **CMLC 23**
 See also DLB 211
**Plomer, William Charles Franklin** 1903-1973
  **CLC 4, 8**
 See also CA 21-22; CANR 34; CAP 2; DLB 20,

**Putnam, Arthur Lee**
See Alger, Horatio, Jr.
**Puzo, Mario** 1920-1999 **CLC 1, 2, 6, 36, 107; DAM NOV, POP**
See also CA 65-68; CANR 4, 42, 65; DLB 6; MTCW 1, 2
**Pygge, Edward**
See Barnes, Julian (Patrick)
**Pyle, Ernest Taylor** 1900-1945
See Pyle, Ernie
See also CA 115; 160
**Pyle, Ernie** 1900-1945 ......................... **TCLC 75**
See also Pyle, Ernest Taylor
See also DLB 29; MTCW 2
**Pyle, Howard** 1853-1911 ...................... **TCLC 81**
See also CA 109; 137; CLR 22; DLB 42, 188; DLBD 13; MAICYA; SATA 16, 100
**Pym, Barbara (Mary Crampton)** 1913-1980 **C L C 13, 19, 37, 111**
See also CA 13-14; 97-100; CANR 13, 34; CAP 1; DLB 14, 207; DLBY 87; MTCW 1, 2
**Pynchon, Thomas (Ruggles, Jr.)** 1937- **CLC 2, 3, 6, 9, 11, 18, 33, 62, 72; DA; DAB; DAC; DAM MST, NOV, POP; SSC 14; WLC**
See also BEST 90:2; CA 17-20R; CANR 22, 46, 73; DLB 2, 173; MTCW 1, 2
**Pythagoras** c. 570B.C.-c. 500B.C. ....... **CMLC 22**
See also DLB 176
**Q**
See Quiller-Couch, SirArthur (Thomas)
**Qian Zhongshu**
See Ch'ien Chung-shu
**Qroll**
See Dagerman, Stig (Halvard)
**Quarrington, Paul (Lewis)** 1953- ......... **CLC 65**
See also CA 129; CANR 62
**Quasimodo, Salvatore** 1901-1968 ......... **CLC 10**
See also CA 13-16; 25-28R; CAP 1; DLB 114; MTCW 1
**Quay, Stephen** 1947- ............................. **CLC 95**
**Quay, Timothy** 1947- ............................. **CLC 95**
**Queen, Ellery** ...................................... **CLC 3, 11**
See also Dannay, Frederic; Davidson, Avram (James); Lee, Manfred B(ennington); Marlowe, Stephen; Sturgeon, Theodore (Hamilton); Vance, John Holbrook
**Queen, Ellery, Jr.**
See Dannay, Frederic; Lee, Manfred B(ennington)
**Queneau, Raymond** 1903-1976 **CLC 2, 5, 10, 42**
See also CA 77-80; 69-72; CANR 32; DLB 72; MTCW 1, 2
**Quevedo, Francisco de** 1580-1645 ............ **LC 23**
**Quiller-Couch, SirArthur (Thomas)** 1863-1944 **TCLC 53**
See also CA 118; 166; DLB 135, 153, 190
**Quin, Ann (Marie)** 1936-1973 ................. **CLC 6**
See also CA 9-12R; 45-48; DLB 14
**Quinn, Martin**
See Smith, Martin Cruz
**Quinn, Peter** 1947- ............................... **CLC 91**
**Quinn, Simon**
See Smith, Martin Cruz
**Quiroga, Horacio (Sylvestre)** 1878-1937 . **T C L C 20; DAM MULT; HLC**
See also CA 117; 131; HW 1; MTCW 1
**Quoirez, Francoise** 1935- ...................... **CLC 9**
See also Sagan, Francoise
See also CA 49-52; CANR 6, 39, 73; MTCW 1, 2
**Raabe, Wilhelm (Karl)** 1831-1910 ...... **TCLC 45**
See also CA 167; DLB 129
**Rabe, David (William)** 1940- **CLC 4, 8, 33; DAM DRAM**
See also CA 85-88; CABS 3; CANR 59; DLB 7
**Rabelais, Francois** 1483-1553 . **LC 5; DA; DAB; DAC; DAM MST; WLC**
**Rabinovitch, Sholem** 1859-1916

See Aleichem, Sholom
See also CA 104
**Rabinyan, Dorit** 1972- ......................... **CLC 119**
See also CA 170
**Rachilde** 1860-1953 ............................. **TCLC 67**
See also DLB 123, 192
**Racine, Jean** 1639-1699 **LC 28; DAB; DAM MST**
**Radcliffe, Ann (Ward)** 1764-1823 .... **NCLC 6, 55**
See also DLB 39, 178
**Radiguet, Raymond** 1903-1923 ............ **TCLC 29**
See also CA 162; DLB 65
**Radnoti, Miklos** 1909-1944 ................. **TCLC 16**
See also CA 118
**Rado, James** 1939- ............................. **CLC 17**
See also CA 105
**Radvanyi, Netty** 1900-1983
See Seghers, Anna
See also CA 85-88; 110
**Rae, Ben**
See Griffiths, Trevor
**Raeburn, John (Hay)** 1941- ............... **CLC 34**
See also CA 57-60
**Ragni, Gerome** 1942-1991 .................... **CLC 17**
See also CA 105; 134
**Rahv, Philip** 1908-1973 ........................ **CLC 24**
See also Greenberg, Ivan
See also DLB 137
**Raimund, Ferdinand Jakob** 1790-1836 **NCLC 69**
See also DLB 90
**Raine, Craig** 1944- ......................... **CLC 32, 103**
See also CA 108; CANR 29, 51; DLB 40
**Raine, Kathleen (Jessie)** 1908- ......... **CLC 7, 45**
See also CA 85-88; CANR 46; DLB 20; MTCW 1
**Rainis, Janis** 1865-1929 ...................... **TCLC 29**
See also CA 170
**Rakosi, Carl** 1903- .............................. **CLC 47**
See also Rawley, Callman
See also CAAS 5; DLB 193
**Raleigh, Richard**
See Lovecraft, H(oward) P(hillips)
**Raleigh, Sir Walter** 1554(?)-1618 ...... **LC 31, 39**
See also CDBLB Before 1660; DLB 172
**Rallentando, H. P.**
See Sayers, Dorothy L(eigh)
**Ramal, Walter**
See de la Mare, Walter (John)
**Ramana Maharshi** 1879-1950 ............. **TCLC 84**
**Ramoacn y Cajal, Santiago** 1852-1934 **TCLC 93**
**Ramon, Juan**
See Jimenez (Mantecon), Juan Ramon
**Ramos, Graciliano** 1892-1953 ............. **TCLC 32**
See also CA 167; HW 2
**Rampersad, Arnold** 1941- ..................... **CLC 44**
See also BW 2, 3; CA 127; 133; CANR 81; DLB 111; INT 133
**Rampling, Anne**
See Rice, Anne
**Ramsay, Allan** 1684(?)-1758 ..................... **LC 29**
See also DLB 95
**Ramuz, Charles-Ferdinand** 1878-1947 **TCLC 33**
See also CA 165
**Rand, Ayn** 1905-1982 **CLC 3, 30, 44, 79; DA; DAC; DAM MST, NOV, POP; WLC**
See also AAYA 10; CA 13-16R; 105; CANR 27, 73; CDALBS; MTCW 1, 2
**Randall, Dudley (Felker)** 1914- **CLC 1; BLC 3; DAM MULT**
See also BW 1, 3; CA 25-28R; CANR 23; DLB 41
**Randall, Robert**
See Silverberg, Robert
**Ranger, Ken**
See Creasey, John
**Ransom, John Crowe** 1888-1974 **CLC 2, 4, 5, 11, 24; DAM POET**
See also CA 5-8R; 49-52; CANR 6, 34; CDALBS; DLB 45, 63; MTCW 1, 2
**Rao, Raja** 1909- ............ **CLC 25, 56; DAM NOV**

See also CA 73-76; CANR 51; MTCW 1, 2
**Raphael, Frederic (Michael)** 1931- ... **CLC 2, 14**
See also CA 1-4R; CANR 1; DLB 14
**Ratcliffe, James P.**
See Mencken, H(enry) L(ouis)
**Rathbone, Julian** 1935- ........................ **CLC 41**
See also CA 101; CANR 34, 73
**Rattigan, Terence (Mervyn)** 1911-1977 .. **CLC 7; DAM DRAM**
See also CA 85-88; 73-76; CDBLB 1945-1960; DLB 13; MTCW 1, 2
**Ratushinskaya, Irina** 1954- ................. **CLC 54**
See also CA 129; CANR 68
**Raven, Simon (Arthur Noel)** 1927- ....... **CLC 14**
See also CA 81-84
**Ravenna, Michael**
See Welty, Eudora
**Rawley, Callman** 1903-
See Rakosi, Carl
See also CA 21-24R; CANR 12, 32
**Rawlings, Marjorie Kinnan** 1896-1953 **T C L C 4**
See also AAYA 20; CA 104; 137; CANR 74; DLB 9, 22, 102; DLBD 17; JRDA; MAICYA; MTCW 2; SATA 100; YABC 1
**Ray, Satyajit** 1921-1992 **CLC 16, 76; DAM MULT**
See also CA 114; 137
**Read, Herbert Edward** 1893-1968 ............ **CLC 4**
See also CA 85-88; 25-28R; DLB 20, 149
**Read, Piers Paul** 1941- ................. **CLC 4, 10, 25**
See also CA 21-24R; CANR 38; DLB 14; SATA 21
**Reade, Charles** 1814-1884 ............... **NCLC 2, 74**
See also DLB 21
**Reade, Hamish**
See Gray, Simon (James Holliday)
**Reading, Peter** 1946- ........................... **CLC 47**
See also CA 103; CANR 46; DLB 40
**Reaney, James** 1926- **CLC 13; DAC; DAM MST**
See also CA 41-44R; CAAS 15; CANR 42; DLB 68; SATA 43
**Rebreanu, Liviu** 1885-1944 ................. **TCLC 28**
See also CA 165
**Rechy, John (Francisco)** 1934- **CLC 1, 7, 14, 18, 107; DAM MULT; HLC**
See also CA 5-8R; CAAS 4; CANR 6, 32, 64; DLB 122; DLBY 82; HW 1, 2; INT CANR-6
**Redcam, Tom** 1870-1933 ...................... **TCLC 25**
**Reddin, Keith** ......................................... **CLC 67**
**Redgrove, Peter (William)** 1932- ...... **CLC 6, 41**
See also CA 1-4R; CANR 3, 39, 77; DLB 40
**Redmon, Anne** .................................... **CLC 22**
See also Nightingale, Anne Redmon
See also DLBY 86
**Reed, Eliot**
See Ambler, Eric
**Reed, Ishmael** 1938- . **CLC 2, 3, 5, 6, 13, 32, 60; BLC 3; DAM MULT**
See also BW 2, 3; CA 21-24R; CANR 25, 48, 74; DLB 2, 5, 33, 169; DLBD 8; MTCW 1, 2
**Reed, John (Silas)** 1887-1920 ................ **TCLC 9**
See also CA 106
**Reed, Lou** ............................................. **CLC 21**
See also Firbank, Louis
**Reeve, Clara** 1729-1807 ....................... **NCLC 19**
See also DLB 39
**Reich, Wilhelm** 1897-1957 ................... **TCLC 57**
**Reid, Christopher (John)** 1949- ........... **CLC 33**
See also CA 140; DLB 40
**Reid, Desmond**
See Moorcock, Michael (John)
**Reid Banks, Lynne** 1929-
See Banks, Lynne Reid
See also CA 1-4R; CANR 6, 22, 38; CLR 24; JRDA; MAICYA; SATA 22, 75
**Reilly, William K.**
See Creasey, John

POET

**Russell, (Henry) Ken(neth Alfred)** 1927-**CLC 16**
See also CA 105
**Russell, William Martin** 1947- ............ **CLC 60**
See also CA 164
**Rutherford, Mark** ................................ **TCLC 25**
See also White, William Hale
See also DLB 18
**Ruyslinck, Ward** 1929- .......................... **CLC 14**
See also Belser, Reimond Karel Maria de
**Ryan, Cornelius (John)** 1920-1974 ......... **CLC 7**
See also CA 69-72; 53-56; CANR 38
**Ryan, Michael** 1946- .............................. **CLC 65**
See also CA 49-52; DLBY 82
**Ryan, Tim**
See Dent, Lester
**Rybakov, Anatoli (Naumovich)** 1911-1998**CLC 23,
53**
See also CA 126; 135; 172; SATA 79; SATA-Obit
108
**Ryder, Jonathan**
See Ludlum, Robert
**Ryga, George** 1932-1987 .. **CLC 14; DAC; DAM
MST**
See also CA 101; 124; CANR 43; DLB 60
**S. H.**
See Hartmann, Sadakichi
**S. S.**
See Sassoon, Siegfried (Lorraine)
**Saba, Umberto** 1883-1957 ..................... **TCLC 33**
See also CA 144; CANR 79; DLB 114
**Sabatini, Rafael** 1875-1950 ................... **TCLC 47**
See also CA 162
**Sabato, Ernesto (R.)** 1911- ... **CLC 10, 23; DAM
MULT; HLC**
See also CA 97-100; CANR 32, 65; DLB 145; HW
1, 2; MTCW 1, 2
**Sa-Carniero, Mario de** 1890-1916 ....... **TCLC 83**
**Sacastru, Martin**
See Bioy Casares, Adolfo
**Sacastru, Martin**
See Bioy Casares, Adolfo
**Sacher-Masoch, Leopold von** 1836(?)-1895**NCLC
31**
**Sachs, Marilyn (Stickle)** 1927- ............ **CLC 35**
See also AAYA 2; CA 17-20R; CANR 13, 47; CLR
2; JRDA; MAICYA; SAAS 2; SATA 3, 68
**Sachs, Nelly** 1891-1970 ................... **CLC 14, 98**
See also CA 17-18; 25-28R; CAP 2; MTCW 2
**Sackler, Howard (Oliver)** 1929-1982 ..... **CLC 14**
See also CA 61-64; 108; CANR 30; DLB 7
**Sacks, Oliver (Wolf)** 1933- .................. **CLC 67**
See also CA 53-56; CANR 28, 50, 76; INT CANR-
28; MTCW 1, 2
**Sadakichi**
See Hartmann, Sadakichi
**Sade, Donatien Alphonse Francois, Comte de** 1740-
1814 .................................................. **NCLC 47**
**Sadoff, Ira** 1945- ...................................... **CLC 9**
See also CA 53-56; CANR 5, 21; DLB 120
**Saetone**
See Camus, Albert
**Safire, William** 1929- ............................ **CLC 10**
See also CA 17-20R; CANR 31, 54
**Sagan, Carl (Edward)** 1934-1996 .... **CLC 30, 112**
See also AAYA 2; CA 25-28R; 155; CANR 11, 36,
74; MTCW 1, 2; SATA 58; SATA-Obit 94
**Sagan, Francoise** ................. **CLC 3, 6, 9, 17, 36**
See also Quoirez, Francoise
See also DLB 83; MTCW 2
**Sahgal, Nayantara (Pandit)** 1927- ......... **CLC 41**
See also CA 9-12R; CANR 11
**Saint, H(arry) F.** 1941- .......................... **CLC 50**
See also CA 127
**St. Aubin de Teran, Lisa** 1953-
See Teran, Lisa St. Aubin de
See also CA 118; 126; INT 126

**Saint Birgitta of Sweden** c. 1303-1373**C M L C
24**
**Sainte-Beuve, Charles Augustin** 1804-1869
**NCLC 5**
**Saint-Exupery, Antoine (Jean Baptiste Marie
Roger) de** 1900-1944**TCLC 2, 56; DAM NOV;
WLC**
See also CA 108; 132; CLR 10; DLB 72; MAICYA;
MTCW 1, 2; SATA 20
**St. John, David**
See Hunt, E(verette) Howard, (Jr.)
**Saint-John Perse**
See Leger, (Marie-Rene Auguste) Alexis Saint-
Leger
**Saintsbury, George (Edward Bateman)** 1845-1933
**TCLC 31**
See also CA 160; DLB 57, 149
**Sait Faik** ................................................ **TCLC 23**
See also Abasiyanik, Sait Faik
**Saki** ......................................... **TCLC 3; SSC 12**
See also Munro, H(ector) H(ugh)
See also MTCW 2
**Sala, George Augustus** ..................... **NCLC 46**
**Salama, Hannu** 1936- .......................... **CLC 18**
**Salamanca, J(ack) R(ichard)** 1922-**CLC 4, 15**
See also CA 25-28R
**Sale, J. Kirkpatrick**
See Sale, Kirkpatrick
**Sale, Kirkpatrick** 1937- ......................... **CLC 68**
See also CA 13-16R; CANR 10
**Salinas, Luis Omar** 1937-**CLC 90; DAM MULT;
HLC**
See also CA 131; CANR 81; DLB 82; HW 1, 2
**Salinas (y Serrano), Pedro** 1891(?)-1951**TCLC 17**
See also CA 117; DLB 134
**Salinger, J(erome) D(avid)** 1919-**CLC 1, 3, 8, 12,
55, 56; DA; DAB; DAC; DAM MST, NOV,
POP; SSC 2, 28; WLC**
See also AAYA 2; CA 5-8R; CANR 39; CDALB
1941-1968; CLR 18; DLB 2, 102, 173; MAICYA;
MTCW 1, 2; SATA 67
**Salisbury, John**
See Caute, (John) David
**Salter, James** 1925- ..................... **CLC 7, 52, 59**
See also CA 73-76; DLB 130
**Saltus, Edgar (Everton)** 1855-1921 ........ **TCLC 8**
See also CA 105; DLB 202
**Saltykov, Mikhail Evgrafovich** 1826-1889 **N C L C
16**
**Samarakis, Antonis** 1919- ....................... **CLC 5**
See also CA 25-28R; CAAS 16; CANR 36
**Sanchez, Florencio** 1875-1910 ............ **TCLC 37**
See also CA 153; HW 1
**Sanchez, Luis Rafael** 1936- .................. **CLC 23**
See also CA 128; DLB 145; HW 1
**Sanchez, Sonia** 1934-**CLC 5, 116; BLC 3; DAM
MULT; PC 9**
See also BW 2, 3; CA 33-36R; CANR 24, 49, 74;
CLR 18; DLB 41; DLBD 8; MAICYA; MTCW
1, 2; SATA 22
**Sand, George** 1804-1876 ... **NCLC 2, 42, 57; DA;
DAB; DAC; DAM MST, NOV; WLC**
See also DLB 119, 192
**Sandburg, Carl (August)** 1878-1967**CLC 1, 4, 10,
15, 35; DA; DAB; DAC; DAM MST, POET;
PC 2; WLC**
See also AAYA 24; CA 5-8R; 25-28R; CANR 35;
CDALB 1865-1917; DLB 17, 54; MAICYA;
MTCW 1, 2; SATA 8
**Sandburg, Charles**
See Sandburg, Carl (August)
**Sandburg, Charles A.**
See Sandburg, Carl (August)
**Sanders, (James) Ed(ward)** 1939- **CLC 53; DAM
POET**
See also CA 13-16R; CAAS 21; CANR 13, 44, 78;
DLB 16

**Sanders, Lawrence** 1920-1998**CLC 41; DAM
POP**
See also BEST 89:4; CA 81-84; 165; CANR
33, 62; MTCW 1
**Sanders, Noah**
See Blount, Roy (Alton), Jr.
**Sanders, Winston P.**
See Anderson, Poul (William)
**Sandoz, Mari(e Susette)** 1896-1966 ...... **CLC 28**
See also CA 1-4R; 25-28R; CANR 17, 64; DLB 9,
212; MTCW 1, 2; SATA 5
**Saner, Reg(inald Anthony)** 1931- ........... **CLC 9**
See also CA 65-68
**Sankara** 788-820 ................................. **CMLC 32**
**Sannazaro, Jacopo** 1456(?)-1530 ................ **LC 8**
**Sansom, William** 1912-1976**CLC 2, 6; DAM NOV;
SSC 21**
See also CA 5-8R; 65-68; CANR 42; DLB 139;
MTCW 1
**Santayana, George** 1863-1952 ............. **TCLC 40**
See also CA 115; DLB 54, 71; DLBD 13
**Santiago, Danny** ..................................... **CLC 33**
See also James, Daniel (Lewis)
See also DLB 122
**Santmyer, Helen Hoover** 1895-1986 ...... **CLC 33**
See also CA 1-4R; 118; CANR 15, 33; DLBY 84;
MTCW 1
**Santoka, Taneda** 1882-1940 ................. **TCLC 72**
**Santos, Bienvenido N(uqui)** 1911-1996 **CLC 22;
DAM MULT**
See also CA 101; 151; CANR 19, 46
**Sapper** .................................................... **TCLC 44**
See also McNeile, Herman Cyril
**Sapphire**
See Sapphire, Brenda
**Sapphire, Brenda** 1950- ......................... **CLC 99**
**Sappho** fl. 6th cent. B.C.- **CMLC 3; DAM POET;
PC 5**
See also DLB 176
**Saramago, Jose** 1922- .......... **CLC 119; HLCS 1**
See also CA 153
**Sarduy, Severo** 1937-1993 .. **CLC 6, 97; HLCS 1**
See also CA 89-92; 142; CANR 58, 81; DLB 113;
HW 1, 2
**Sargeson, Frank** 1903-1982 .................. **CLC 31**
See also CA 25-28R; 106; CANR 38, 79
**Sarmiento, Felix Ruben Garcia**
See Dario, Ruben
**Saro-Wiwa, Ken(ule Beeson)** 1941-1995**CLC 114**
See also BW 2; CA 142; 150; CANR 60; DLB 157
**Saroyan, William** 1908-1981**CLC 1, 8, 10, 29, 34,
56; DA; DAB; DAC; DAM DRAM, MST,
NOV; SSC 21; WLC**
See also CA 5-8R; 103; CANR 30; CDALBS; DLB
7, 9, 86; DLBY 81; MTCW 1, 2; SATA 23;
SATA-Obit 24
**Sarraute, Nathalie** 1900-**CLC 1, 2, 4, 8, 10, 31, 80**
See also CA 9-12R; CANR 23, 66; DLB 83;
MTCW 1, 2
**Sarton, (Eleanor) May** 1912-1995 **CLC 4, 14, 49,
91; DAM POET**
See also CA 1-4R; 149; CANR 1, 34, 55; DLB 48;
DLBY 81; INT CANR-34; MTCW 1, 2; SATA
36; SATA-Obit 86
**Sartre, Jean-Paul** 1905-1980 . **CLC 1, 4, 7, 9, 13,
18, 24, 44, 50, 52; DA; DAB; DAC; DAM
DRAM, MST, NOV; DC 3; SSC 32; WLC**
See also CA 9-12R; 97-100; CANR 21; DLB 72;
MTCW 1, 2
**Sassoon, Siegfried (Lorraine)** 1886-1967 .. **C L C
36; DAB; DAM MST, NOV, POET; PC 12**
See also CA 104; 25-28R; CANR 36; DLB 20, 191;
DLBD 18; MTCW 1, 2
**Satterfield, Charles**
See Pohl, Frederik
**Saul, John (W. III)** 1942- ... **CLC 46; DAM NOV,
POP**

See also AAYA 10; BEST 90:4; CA 81-84;
CANR 16, 40, 81; SATA 98

**Saunders, Caleb**
See Heinlein, Robert A(nson)

**Saura (Atares), Carlos** 1932- ............... **CLC 20**
See also CA 114; 131; CANR 79; HW 1

**Sauser-Hall, Frederic** 1887-1961 .......... **CLC 18**
See also Cendrars, Blaise
See also CA 102; 93-96; CANR 36, 62; MTCW 1

**Saussure, Ferdinand de** 1857-1913 ..... **TCLC 49**

**Savage, Catharine**
See Brosman, Catharine Savage

**Savage, Thomas** 1915- ........................... **CLC 40**
See also CA 126; 132; CAAS 15; INT 132

**Savan, Glenn** 19(?)- ................................. **CLC 50**

**Sayers, Dorothy L(eigh)** 1893-1957 **TCLC 2, 15;
DAM POP**
See also CA 104; 119; CANR 60; CDBLB 1914-
1945; DLB 10, 36, 77, 100; MTCW 1, 2

**Sayers, Valerie** 1952- ........................... **CLC 50**
See also CA 134; CANR 61

**Sayles, John (Thomas)** 1950- ...... **CLC 7, 10, 14**
See also CA 57-60; CANR 41; DLB 44

**Scammell, Michael** 1935- ................... **CLC 34**
See also CA 156

**Scannell, Vernon** 1922- ......................... **CLC 49**
See also CA 5-8R; CANR 8, 24, 57; DLB 27; SATA
59

**Scarlett, Susan**
See Streatfeild, (Mary) Noel

**Scarron**
See Mikszath, Kalman

**Schaeffer, Susan Fromberg** 1941- **CLC 6, 11, 22**
See also CA 49-52; CANR 18, 65; DLB 28;
MTCW 1, 2; SATA 22

**Schary, Jill**
See Robinson, Jill

**Schell, Jonathan** 1943- ........................... **CLC 35**
See also CA 73-76; CANR 12

**Schelling, Friedrich Wilhelm Joseph von** 1775-
1854 ................................................. **NCLC 30**
See also DLB 90

**Schendel, Arthur van** 1874-1946 ......... **TCLC 56**

**Scherer, Jean-Marie Maurice** 1920-
See Rohmer, Eric
See also CA 110

**Schevill, James (Erwin)** 1920- ............... **CLC 7**
See also CA 5-8R; CAAS 12

**Schiller, Friedrich** 1759-1805 **NCLC 39, 69; DAM
DRAM**
See also DLB 94

**Schisgal, Murray (Joseph)** 1926- ........... **CLC 6**
See also CA 21-24R; CANR 48

**Schlee, Ann** 1934- ................................. **CLC 35**
See also CA 101; CANR 29; SATA 44; SATA-
Brief 36

**Schlegel, August Wilhelm von** 1767-1845 **NCLC
15**
See also DLB 94

**Schlegel, Friedrich** 1772-1829 ............ **NCLC 45**
See also DLB 90

**Schlegel, Johann Elias (von)** 1719(?)-1749 **LC 5**

**Schlesinger, Arthur M(eier), Jr.** 1917- **CLC 84**
See also AITN 1; CA 1-4R; CANR 1, 28, 58; DLB
17; INT CANR-28; MTCW 1, 2; SATA 61

**Schmidt, Arno (Otto)** 1914-1979 .......... **CLC 56**
See also CA 128; 109; DLB 69

**Schmitz, Aron Hector** 1861-1928
See Svevo, Italo
See also CA 104; 122; MTCW 1

**Schnackenberg, Gjertrud** 1953- ........... **CLC 40**
See also CA 116; DLB 120

**Schneider, Leonard Alfred** 1925-1966
See Bruce, Lenny
See also CA 89-92

**Schnitzler, Arthur** 1862-1931 **TCLC 4; SSC 15**
See also CA 104; DLB 81, 118

**Schoenberg, Arnold** 1874-1951 ...... **TCLC 75**
See also CA 109

**Schonberg, Arnold**
See Schoenberg, Arnold

**Schopenhauer, Arthur** 1788-1860 ....... **NCLC 51**
See also DLB 90

**Schor, Sandra (M.)** 1932(?)-1990 ........... **CLC 65**
See also CA 132

**Schorer, Mark** 1908-1977 ...................... **CLC 9**
See also CA 5-8R; 73-76; CANR 7; DLB 103

**Schrader, Paul (Joseph)** 1946- ............. **CLC 26**
See also CA 37-40R; CANR 41; DLB 44

**Schreiner, Olive (Emilie Albertina)** 1855-1920
**TCLC 9**
See also CA 105; 154; DLB 18, 156, 190

**Schulberg, Budd (Wilson)** 1914- ...... **CLC 7, 48**
See also CA 25-28R; CANR 19; DLB 6, 26, 28;
DLBY 81

**Schulz, Bruno** 1892-1942 . **TCLC 5, 51; SSC 13**
See also CA 115; 123; MTCW 2

**Schulz, Charles M(onroe)** 1922- .......... **CLC 12**
See also CA 9-12R; CANR 6; INT CANR-6;
SATA 10

**Schumacher, E(rnst) F(riedrich)** 1911-1977
**CLC 80**
See also CA 81-84; 73-76; CANR 34

**Schuyler, James Marcus** 1923-1991 **CLC 5, 23;
DAM POET**
See also CA 101; 134; DLB 5, 169; INT 101

**Schwartz, Delmore (David)** 1913-1966 **CLC 2, 4,
10, 45, 87; PC 8**
See also CA 17-18; 25-28R; CANR 35; CAP 2;
DLB 28, 48; MTCW 1, 2

**Schwartz, Ernst**
See Ozu, Yasujiro

**Schwartz, John Burnham** 1965- ........... **CLC 59**
See also CA 132

**Schwartz, Lynne Sharon** 1939- ............. **CLC 31**
See also CA 103; CANR 44; MTCW 2

**Schwartz, Muriel A.**
See Eliot, T(homas) S(tearns)

**Schwarz-Bart, Andre** 1928- ................. **CLC 2, 4**
See also CA 89-92

**Schwarz-Bart, Simone** 1938- ...... **CLC 7; BLCS**
See also BW 2; CA 97-100

**Schwitters, Kurt (Hermann Edward Karl Julius)**
1887-1948 ...................................... **TCLC 95**
See also CA 158

**Schwob, Marcel (Mayer Andre)** 1867-1905 **T CLC
20**
See also CA 117; 168; DLB 123

**Sciascia, Leonardo** 1921-1989 ........ **CLC 8, 9, 41**
See also CA 85-88; 130; CANR 35; DLB 177;
MTCW 1

**Scoppettone, Sandra** 1936- .................... **CLC 26**
See also AAYA 11; CA 5-8R; CANR 41, 73; SATA
9, 92

**Scorsese, Martin** 1942- .................... **CLC 20, 89**
See also CA 110; 114; CANR 46

**Scotland, Jay**
See Jakes, John (William)

**Scott, Duncan Campbell** 1862-1947 **TCLC 6; DAC**
See also CA 104; 153; DLB 92

**Scott, Evelyn** 1893-1963 ........................ **CLC 43**
See also CA 104; 112; CANR 64; DLB 9, 48

**Scott, F(rancis) R(eginald)** 1899-1985 .. **CLC 22**
See also CA 101; 114; DLB 88; INT 101

**Scott, Frank**
See Scott, F(rancis) R(eginald)

**Scott, Joanna** 1960- ............................... **CLC 50**
See also CA 126; CANR 53

**Scott, Paul (Mark)** 1920-1978 ........... **CLC 9, 60**
See also CA 81-84; 77-80; CANR 33; DLB 14,
207; MTCW 1

**Scott, Sarah** 1723-1795 ........................... **LC 44**
See also DLB 39

**Scott, Walter** 1771-1832 **NCLC 15, 69; DA; DAB;**

DAC; DAM MST, NOV, POET; PC 13;
SSC 32; WLC
See also AAYA 22; CDBLB 1789-1832; DLB 93,
107, 116, 144, 159; YABC 2

**Scribe, (Augustin) Eugene** 1791-1861 **NCLC 16;
DAM DRAM; DC 5**
See also DLB 192

**Scrum, R.**
See Crumb, R(obert)

**Scudery, Madeleine de** 1607-1701 ............. **LC 2**

**Scum**
See Crumb, R(obert)

**Scumbag, Little Bobby**
See Crumb, R(obert)

**Seabrook, John**
See Hubbard, L(afayette) Ron(ald)

**Sealy, I. Allan** 1951- ............................. **CLC 55**

**Search, Alexander**
See Pessoa, Fernando (Antonio Nogueira)

**Sebastian, Lee**
See Silverberg, Robert

**Sebastian Owl**
See Thompson, Hunter S(tockton)

**Sebestyen, Ouida** 1924- ...................... **CLC 30**
See also AAYA 8; CA 107; CANR 40; CLR 17;
JRDA; MAICYA; SAAS 10; SATA 39

**Secundus, H. Scriblerus**
See Fielding, Henry

**Sedges, John**
See Buck, Pearl S(ydenstricker)

**Sedgwick, Catharine Maria** 1789-1867 **NCLC 19**
See also DLB 1, 74

**Seelye, John (Douglas)** 1931- ................. **CLC 7**
See also CA 97-100; CANR 70; INT 97-100

**Seferiades, Giorgos Stylianou** 1900-1971
See Seferis, George
See also CA 5-8R; 33-36R; CANR 5, 36; MTCW
1

**Seferis, George** ................................... **CLC 5, 11**
See also Seferiades, Giorgos Stylianou

**Segal, Erich (Wolf)** 1937- **CLC 3, 10; DAM POP**
See also BEST 89:1; CA 25-28R; CANR 20, 36,
65; DLBY 86; INT CANR-20; MTCW 1

**Seger, Bob** 1945- ................................... **CLC 35**

**Seghers, Anna** ........................................ **CLC 7**
See also Radvanyi, Netty
See also DLB 69

**Seidel, Frederick (Lewis)** 1936- ........... **CLC 18**
See also CA 13-16R; CANR 8; DLBY 84

**Seifert, Jaroslav** 1901-1986 ....... **CLC 34, 44, 93**
See also CA 127; MTCW 1, 2

**Sei Shonagon** c. 966-1017(?) ............... **CMLC 6**

**Séjour, Victor** 1817-1874 ......................... **DC 10**
See also DLB 50

**Sejour Marcou et Ferrand, Juan Victor**
See Séjour, Victor

**Selby, Hubert, Jr.** 1928- **CLC 1, 2, 4, 8; SSC 20**
See also CA 13-16R; CANR 33; DLB 2

**Selzer, Richard** 1928- ............................. **CLC 74**
See also CA 65-68; CANR 14

**Sembene, Ousmane**
See Ousmane, Sembene

**Senancour, Etienne Pivert de** 1770-1846 **NCLC 16**
See also DLB 119

**Sender, Ramon (Jose)** 1902-1982 .. **CLC 8; DAM
MULT; HLC**
See also CA 5-8R; 105; CANR 8; HW 1; MTCW
1

**Seneca, Lucius Annaeus** c. 1-c. 65 **CMLC 6; DAM
DRAM; DC 5**
See also DLB 211

**Senghor, Leopold Sedar** 1906- **CLC 54; BLC 3;
DAM MULT, POET; PC 25**
See also BW 2, 3; CA 116; 125; CANR 47, 74;
MTCW 1, 2

**Senna, Danzy** 1970- ............................. **CLC 119**
See also CA 169

**Silkin, Jon** 1930- ..................... **CLC 2, 6, 43**
See also CA 5-8R; CAAS 5; DLB 27

**Silko, Leslie (Marmon)** 1948- **CLC 23, 74, 114;**
**DA; DAC; DAM MST, MULT, POP; WLCS**
See also AAYA 14; CA 115; 122; CANR 45, 65;
DLB 143, 175; MTCW 2; NNAL

**Sillanpaa, Frans Eemil** 1888-1964 ........ **CLC 19**
See also CA 129; 93-96; MTCW 1

**Sillitoe, Alan** 1928- .... **CLC 1, 3, 6, 10, 19, 57**
See also AITN 1; CA 9-12R; CAAS 2; CANR 8,
26, 55; CDBLB 1960 to Present; DLB 14, 139;
MTCW 1, 2; SATA 61

**Silone, Ignazio** 1900-1978 ...................... **CLC 4**
See also CA 25-28; 81-84; CANR 34; CAP 2;
MTCW 1

**Silver, Joan Micklin** 1935- ................... **CLC 20**
See also CA 114; 121; INT 121

**Silver, Nicholas**
See Faust, Frederick (Schiller)

**Silverberg, Robert** 1935- ...... **CLC 7; DAM POP**
See also AAYA 24; CA 1-4R; CAAS 3; CANR 1,
20, 36; CLR 59; DLB 8; INT CANR-20;
MAICYA; MTCW 1, 2; SATA 13, 91; SATA-
Essay 104

**Silverstein, Alvin** 1933- ...................... **CLC 17**
See also CA 49-52; CANR 2; CLR 25; JRDA;
MAICYA; SATA 8, 69

**Silverstein, Virginia B(arbara Opshelor)** 1937-
**CLC 17**
See also CA 49-52; CANR 2; CLR 25; JRDA;
MAICYA; SATA 8, 69

**Sim, Georges**
See Simenon, Georges (Jacques Christian)

**Simak, Clifford D(onald)** 1904-1988 . **CLC 1, 55**
See also CA 1-4R; 125; CANR 1, 35; DLB 8;
MTCW 1; SATA-Obit 56

**Simenon, Georges (Jacques Christian)** 1903-1989
**CLC 1, 2, 3, 8, 18, 47; DAM POP**
See also CA 85-88; 129; CANR 35; DLB 72; DLBY
89; MTCW 1, 2

**Simic, Charles** 1938- **CLC 6, 9, 22, 49, 68; DAM**
**POET**
See also CA 29-32R; CAAS 4; CANR 12, 33, 52,
61; DLB 105; MTCW 2

**Simmel, Georg** 1858-1918 ................... **TCLC 64**
See also CA 157

**Simmons, Charles (Paul)** 1924- .......... **CLC 57**
See also CA 89-92; INT 89-92

**Simmons, Dan** 1948- ......... **CLC 44; DAM POP**
See also AAYA 16; CA 138; CANR 53, 81

**Simmons, James (Stewart Alexander)** 1933-**CLC**
**43**
See also CA 105; CAAS 21; DLB 40

**Simms, William Gilmore** 1806-1870 .... **NCLC 3**
See also DLB 3, 30, 59, 73

**Simon, Carly** 1945- ............................... **CLC 26**
See also CA 105

**Simon, Claude** 1913-1984**CLC 4, 9, 15, 39; DAM**
**NOV**
See also CA 89-92; CANR 33; DLB 83; MTCW 1

**Simon, (Marvin) Neil** 1927-**CLC 6, 11, 31, 39, 70;**
**DAM DRAM**
See also AITN 1; CA 21-24R; CANR 26, 54; DLB
7; MTCW 1, 2

**Simon, Paul (Frederick)** 1941(?)- ......... **CLC 17**
See also CA 116; 153

**Simonon, Paul** 1956(?)- ......................... **CLC 30**

**Simpson, Harriette**
See Arnow, Harriette (Louisa) Simpson

**Simpson, Louis (Aston Marantz)** 1923-**CLC 4, 7,**
**9, 32; DAM POET**
See also CA 1-4R; CAAS 4; CANR 1, 61; DLB 5;
MTCW 1, 2

**Simpson, Mona (Elizabeth)** 1957- ......... **CLC 44**
See also CA 122; 135; CANR 68

**Simpson, N(orman) F(rederick)** 1919- . **CLC 29**
See also CA 13-16R; DLB 13

**Sinclair, Andrew (Annandale)** 1935-. **CLC 2,**
**14**
See also CA 9-12R; CAAS 5; CANR 14, 38;
DLB 14; MTCW 1

**Sinclair, Emil**
See Hesse, Hermann

**Sinclair, Iain** 1943- ............................... **CLC 76**
See also CA 132; CANR 81

**Sinclair, Iain MacGregor**
See Sinclair, Iain

**Sinclair, Irene**
See Griffith, D(avid Lewelyn) W(ark)

**Sinclair, Mary Amelia St. Clair** 1865(?)-1946
See Sinclair, May
See also CA 104

**Sinclair, May** 1863-1946 ................... **TCLC 3, 11**
See also Sinclair, Mary Amelia St. Clair
See also CA 166; DLB 36, 135

**Sinclair, Roy**
See Griffith, D(avid Lewelyn) W(ark)

**Sinclair, Upton (Beall)** 1878-1968**CLC 1, 11, 15,**
**63; DA; DAB; DAC; DAM MST, NOV; WLC**
See also CA 5-8R; 25-28R; CANR 7; CDALB 1929-
1941; DLB 9; INT CANR-7; MTCW 1, 2;
SATA 9

**Singer, Isaac**
See Singer, Isaac Bashevis

**Singer, Isaac Bashevis** 1904-1991**CLC 1, 3, 6, 9,**
**11, 15, 23, 38, 69, 111; DA; DAB; DAC; DAM**
**MST, NOV; SSC 3; WLC**
See also AITN 1, 2; CA 1-4R; 134; CANR 1, 39;
CDALB 1941-1968; CLR 1; DLB 6, 28, 52;
DLBY 91; JRDA; MAICYA; MTCW 1, 2;
SATA 3, 27; SATA-Obit 68

**Singer, Israel Joshua** 1893-1944 ........ **TCLC 33**
See also CA 169

**Singh, Khushwant** 1915- ....................... **CLC 11**
See also CA 9-12R; CAAS 9; CANR 6

**Singleton, Ann**
See Benedict, Ruth (Fulton)

**Sinjohn, John**
See Galsworthy, John

**Sinyavsky, Andrei (Donatevich)** 1925-1997**CLC 8**
See also CA 85-88; 159

**Sirin, V.**
See Nabokov, Vladimir (Vladimirovich)

**Sissman, L(ouis) E(dward)** 1928-1976 **CLC 9, 18**
See also CA 21-24R; 65-68; CANR 13; DLB 5

**Sisson, C(harles) H(ubert)** 1914- .......... **CLC 8**
See also CA 1-4R; CAAS 3; CANR 3, 48; DLB 27

**Sitwell, Dame Edith** 1887-1964**CLC 2, 9, 67; DAM**
**POET; PC 3**
See also CA 9-12R; CANR 35; CDBLB 1945-1960;
DLB 20; MTCW 1, 2

**Siwaarmill, H. P.**
See Sharp, William

**Sjoewall, Maj** 1935- ............................... **CLC 7**
See also CA 65-68; CANR 73

**Sjowall, Maj**
See Sjoewall, Maj

**Skelton, John** 1463-1529 ......................... **PC 25**

**Skelton, Robin** 1925-1997 ..................... **CLC 13**
See also AITN 2; CA 5-8R; 160; CAAS 5; CANR
28; DLB 27, 53

**Skolimowski, Jerzy** 1938- .................... **CLC 20**
See also CA 128

**Skram, Amalie (Bertha)** 1847-1905 .... **TCLC 25**
See also CA 165

**Skvorecky, Josef (Vaclav)** 1924-**CLC 15, 39, 69;**
**DAC; DAM NOV**
See also CA 61-64; CAAS 1; CANR 10, 34, 63;
MTCW 1, 2

**Slade, Bernard** ................................. **CLC 11, 46**
See also Newbound, Bernard Slade
See also CAAS 9; DLB 53

**Slaughter, Carolyn** 1946- ..................... **CLC 56**
See also CA 85-88

**Slaughter, Frank G(ill)** 1908- ........... **CLC 29**
See also AITN 2; CA 5-8R; CANR 5; INT
CANR-5

**Slavitt, David R(ytman)** 1935- ........... **CLC 5, 14**
See also CA 21-24R; CAAS 3; CANR 41; DLB 5,
6

**Slesinger, Tess** 1905-1945 ................... **TCLC 10**
See also CA 107; DLB 102

**Slessor, Kenneth** 1901-1971 ................. **CLC 14**
See also CA 102; 89-92

**Slowacki, Juliusz** 1809-1849 ............... **NCLC 15**

**Smart, Christopher** 1722-1771**LC 3; DAM POET;**
**PC 13**
See also DLB 109

**Smart, Elizabeth** 1913-1986 ................ **CLC 54**
See also CA 81-84; 118; DLB 88

**Smiley, Jane (Graves)** 1949- **CLC 53, 76; DAM**
**POP**
See also CA 104; CANR 30, 50, 74; INT CANR-
30

**Smith, A(rthur) J(ames) M(arshall)** 1902-1980
**CLC 15; DAC**
See also CA 1-4R; 102; CANR 4; DLB 88

**Smith, Adam** 1723-1790 ........................ **LC 36**
See also DLB 104

**Smith, Alexander** 1829-1867 .......... **NCLC 59**
See also DLB 32, 55

**Smith, Anna Deavere** 1950- ................. **CLC 86**
See also CA 133

**Smith, Betty (Wehner)** 1896-1972 ........ **CLC 19**
See also CA 5-8R; 33-36R; DLBY 82; SATA 6

**Smith, Charlotte (Turner)** 1749-1806 . **NCLC 23**
See also DLB 39, 109

**Smith, Clark Ashton** 1893-1961 .......... **CLC 43**
See also CA 143; CANR 81; MTCW 2

**Smith, Dave** ..................................... **CLC 22, 42**
See also Smith, David (Jeddie)
See also CAAS 7; DLB 5

**Smith, David (Jeddie)** 1942-
See Smith, Dave
See also CA 49-52; CANR 1, 59; DAM POET

**Smith, Florence Margaret** 1902-1971
See Smith, Stevie
See also CA 17-18; 29-32R; CANR 35; CAP 2;
DAM POET; MTCW 1, 2

**Smith, Iain Crichton** 1928-1998 ........... **CLC 64**
See also CA 21-24R; 171; DLB 40, 139

**Smith, John** 1580(?)-1631 ...................... **LC 9**
See also DLB 24, 30

**Smith, Johnston**
See Crane, Stephen (Townley)

**Smith, Joseph, Jr.** 1805-1844 ............. **NCLC 53**

**Smith, Lee** 1944- ............................. **CLC 25, 73**
See also CA 114; 119; CANR 46; DLB 143; DLBY
83; INT 119

**Smith, Martin**
See Smith, Martin Cruz

**Smith, Martin Cruz** 1942-**CLC 25; DAM MULT,**
**POP**
See also BEST 89:4; CA 85-88; CANR 6, 23, 43,
65; INT CANR-23; MTCW 2; NNAL

**Smith, Mary-Ann Tirone** 1944- ........... **CLC 39**
See also CA 118; 136

**Smith, Patti** 1946- ............................... **CLC 12**
See also CA 93-96; CANR 63

**Smith, Pauline (Urmson)** 1882-1959 ... **TCLC 25**

**Smith, Rosamond**
See Oates, Joyce Carol

**Smith, Sheila Kaye**
See Kaye-Smith, Sheila

**Smith, Stevie** ................ **CLC 3, 8, 25, 44; PC 12**
See also Smith, Florence Margaret
See also DLB 20; MTCW 2

**Smith, Wilbur (Addison)** 1933- ........... **CLC 33**
See also CA 13-16R; CANR 7, 46, 66; MTCW 1, 2

**Smith, William Jay** 1918- ...................... **CLC 6**
See also CA 5-8R; CANR 44; DLB 5; MAICYA;

SAAS 22; SATA 2, 68

**Smith, Woodrow Wilson**
See Kuttner, Henry

**Smolenskin, Peretz** 1842-1885 .......... **NCLC 30**

**Smollett, Tobias (George)** 1721-1771 ... **LC 2, 46**
See also CDBLB 1660-1789; DLB 39, 104

**Snodgrass, W(illiam) D(e Witt)** 1926- **CLC 2, 6, 10, 18, 68; DAM POET**
See also CA 1-4R; CANR 6, 36, 65; DLB 5; MTCW 1, 2

**Snow, C(harles) P(ercy)** 1905-1980**CLC 1, 4, 6, 9, 13, 19; DAM NOV**
See also CA 5-8R; 101; CANR 28; CDBLB 1945-1960; DLB 15, 77; DLBD 17; MTCW 1, 2

**Snow, Frances Compton**
See Adams, Henry (Brooks)

**Snyder, Gary (Sherman)** 1930-**CLC 1, 2, 5, 9, 32, 120; DAM POET; PC 21**
See also CA 17-20R; CANR 30, 60; DLB 5, 16, 165, 212; MTCW 2

**Snyder, Zilpha Keatley** 1927- ................ **CLC 17**
See also AAYA 15; CA 9-12R; CANR 38; CLR 31; JRDA; MAICYA; SAAS 2; SATA 1, 28, 75

**Soares, Bernardo**
See Pessoa, Fernando (Antonio Nogueira)

**Sobh, A.**
See Shamlu, Ahmad

**Sobol, Joshua** ......................................... **CLC 60**

**Socrates** 469B.C.-399B.C. .................... **CMLC 27**

**Soderberg, Hjalmar** 1869-1941 .......... **TCLC 39**

**Sodergran, Edith (Irene)**
See Soedergran, Edith (Irene)

**Soedergran, Edith (Irene)** 1892-1923 .. **TCLC 31**

**Softly, Edgar**
See Lovecraft, H(oward) P(hillips)

**Softly, Edward**
See Lovecraft, H(oward) P(hillips)

**Sokolov, Raymond** 1941- ......................... **CLC 7**
See also CA 85-88

**Solo, Jay**
See Ellison, Harlan (Jay)

**Sologub, Fyodor** ..................................... **TCLC 9**
See also Teternikov, Fyodor Kuzmich

**Solomons, Ikey Esquir**
See Thackeray, William Makepeace

**Solomos, Dionysios** 1798-1857 ............ **NCLC 15**

**Solwoska, Mara**
See French, Marilyn

**Solzhenitsyn, Aleksandr I(sayevich)** 1918- **C L C 1, 2, 4, 7, 9, 10, 18, 26, 34, 78; DA; DAB; DAC; DAM MST, NOV; SSC 32; WLC**
See also AITN 1; CA 69-72; CANR 40, 65; MTCW 1, 2

**Somers, Jane**
See Lessing, Doris (May)

**Somerville, Edith** 1858-1949 ................ **TCLC 51**
See also DLB 135

**Somerville & Ross**
See Martin, Violet Florence; Somerville, Edith

**Sommer, Scott** 1951- ............................. **CLC 25**
See also CA 106

**Sondheim, Stephen (Joshua)** 1930- **CLC 30, 39; DAM DRAM**
See also AAYA 11; CA 103; CANR 47, 68

**Song, Cathy** 1955- .................................... **PC 21**
See also CA 154; DLB 169

**Sontag, Susan** 1933- **CLC 1, 2, 10, 13, 31, 105; DAM POP**
See also CA 17-20R; CANR 25, 51, 74; DLB 2, 67; MTCW 1, 2

**Sophocles** 496(?)B.C.-406(?)B.C. .. **CMLC 2; DA; DAB; DAC; DAM DRAM, MST; DC 1; WLCS**
See also DLB 176

**Sordello** 1189-1269 ............................. **CMLC 15**

**Sorel, Georges** 1847-1922 ................... **TCLC 91**
See also CA 118

**Sorel, Julia**

See Drexler, Rosalyn

**Sorrentino, Gilbert** 1929- . **CLC 3, 7, 14, 22, 40**
See also CA 77-80; CANR 14, 33; DLB 5, 173; DLBY 80; INT CANR-14

**Soto, Gary** 1952-**CLC 32, 80; DAM MULT; HLC**
See also AAYA 10; CA 119; 125; CANR 50, 74; CLR 38; DLB 82; HW 1, 2; INT 125; JRDA; MTCW 2; SATA 80

**Soupault, Philippe** 1897-1990 ................ **CLC 68**
See also CA 116; 147; 131

**Souster, (Holmes) Raymond** 1921- ... **CLC 5, 14; DAC; DAM POET**
See also CA 13-16R; CAAS 14; CANR 13, 29, 53; DLB 88; SATA 63

**Southern, Terry** 1924(?)-1995 ................ **CLC 7**
See also CA 1-4R; 150; CANR 1, 55; DLB 2

**Southey, Robert** 1774-1843 ................... **NCLC 8**
See also DLB 93, 107, 142; SATA 54

**Southworth, Emma Dorothy Eliza Nevitte** 1819-1899 ............................................. **NCLC 26**

**Souza, Ernest**
See Scott, Evelyn

**Soyinka, Wole** 1934-**CLC 3, 5, 14, 36, 44; BLC 3; DA; DAB; DAC; DAM DRAM, MST, MULT; DC 2; WLC**
See also BW 2, 3; CA 13-16R; CANR 27, 39; DLB 125; MTCW 1, 2

**Spackman, W(illiam) M(ode)** 1905-1990**C L C 46**
See also CA 81-84; 132

**Spacks, Barry (Bernard)** 1931- ............ **CLC 14**
See also CA 154; CANR 33; DLB 105

**Spanidou, Irini** 1946- ............................. **CLC 44**

**Spark, Muriel (Sarah)** 1918- **CLC 2, 3, 5, 8, 13, 18, 40, 94; DAB; DAC; DAM MST, NOV; SSC 10**
See also CA 5-8R; CANR 12, 36, 76; CDBLB 1945-1960; DLB 15, 139; INT CANR-12; MTCW 1, 2

**Spaulding, Douglas**
See Bradbury, Ray (Douglas)

**Spaulding, Leonard**
See Bradbury, Ray (Douglas)

**Spence, J. A. D.**
See Eliot, T(homas) S(tearns)

**Spencer, Elizabeth** 1921- ....................... **CLC 22**
See also CA 13-16R; CANR 32, 65; DLB 6; MTCW 1; SATA 14

**Spencer, Leonard G.**
See Silverberg, Robert

**Spencer, Scott** 1945- ............................. **CLC 30**
See also CA 113; CANR 51; DLBY 86

**Spender, Stephen (Harold)** 1909-1995**CLC 1, 2, 5, 10, 41, 91; DAM POET**
See also CA 9-12R; 149; CANR 31, 54; CDBLB 1945-1960; DLB 20; MTCW 1, 2

**Spengler, Oswald (Arnold Gottfried)** 1880-1936 **TCLC 25**
See also CA 118

**Spenser, Edmund** 1552(?)-1599 ... **LC 5, 39; DA; DAB; DAC; DAM MST, POET; PC 8; WLC**
See also CDBLB Before 1660; DLB 167

**Spicer, Jack** 1925-1965 .... **CLC 8, 18, 72; DAM POET**
See also CA 85-88; DLB 5, 16, 193

**Spiegelman, Art** 1948- ......................... **CLC 76**
See also AAYA 10; CA 125; CANR 41, 55, 74; MTCW 2; SATA 109

**Spielberg, Peter** 1929- ............................. **CLC 6**
See also CA 5-8R; CANR 4, 48; DLBY 81

**Spielberg, Steven** 1947- ......................... **CLC 20**
See also AAYA 8, 24; CA 77-80; CANR 32; SATA 32

**Spillane, Frank Morrison** 1918-
See Spillane, Mickey
See also CA 25-28R; CANR 28, 63; MTCW 1, 2; SATA 66

**Spillane, Mickey** ............................... **CLC 3, 13**
See also Spillane, Frank Morrison
See also MTCW 2

**Spinoza, Benedictus de** 1632-1677 ............. **LC 9**

**Spinrad, Norman (Richard)** 1940- ......... **CLC 46**
See also CA 37-40R; CAAS 19; CANR 20; DLB 8; INT CANR-20

**Spitteler, Carl (Friedrich Georg)** 1845-1924 **TCLC 12**
See also CA 109; DLB 129

**Spivack, Kathleen (Romola Drucker)** 1938-**C L C 6**
See also CA 49-52

**Spoto, Donald** 1941- ............................. **CLC 39**
See also CA 65-68; CANR 11, 57

**Springsteen, Bruce (F.)** 1949- .............. **CLC 17**
See also CA 111

**Spurling, Hilary** 1940- ......................... **CLC 34**
See also CA 104; CANR 25, 52

**Spyker, John Howland**
See Elman, Richard (Martin)

**Squires, (James) Radcliffe** 1917-1993 .. **CLC 51**
See also CA 1-4R; 140; CANR 6, 21

**Srivastava, Dhanpat Rai** 1880(?)-1936
See Premchand
See also CA 118

**Stacy, Donald**
See Pohl, Frederik

**Stael, Germaine de** 1766-1817
See Stael-Holstein, Anne Louise Germaine Necker Baronn
See also DLB 119

**Stael-Holstein, Anne Louise Germaine Necker Baronn** 1766-1817 ........................ **NCLC 3**
See also Stael, Germaine de
See also DLB 192

**Stafford, Jean** 1915-1979**CLC 4, 7, 19, 68; SSC 26**
See also CA 1-4R; 85-88; CANR 3, 65; DLB 2, 173; MTCW 1, 2; SATA-Obit 22

**Stafford, William (Edgar)** 1914-1993 .. **CLC 4, 7, 29; DAM POET**
See also CA 5-8R; !42; CAAS 3; CANR 5, 22; DLB 5, 206; INT CANR-22

**Stagnelius, Eric Johan** 1793-1823 ...... **NCLC 61**

**Staines, Trevor**
See Brunner, John (Kilian Houston)

**Stairs, Gordon**
See Austin, Mary (Hunter)

**Stalin, Joseph** 1879-1953 .................... **TCLC 92**

**Stannard, Martin** 1947- ......................... **CLC 44**
See also CA 142; DLB 155

**Stanton, Elizabeth Cady** 1815-1902 ..... **TCLC 73**
See also CA 171; DLB 79

**Stanton, Maura** 1946- .............................. **CLC 9**
See also CA 89-92; CANR 15; DLB 120

**Stanton, Schuyler**
See Baum, L(yman) Frank

**Stapledon, (William) Olaf** 1886-1950 .. **TCLC 22**
See also CA 111; 162; DLB 15

**Starbuck, George (Edwin)** 1931-1996 .. **CLC 53; DAM POET**
See also CA 21-24R; 153; CANR 23

**Stark, Richard**
See Westlake, Donald E(dwin)

**Staunton, Schuyler**
See Baum, L(yman) Frank

**Stead, Christina (Ellen)** 1902-1983 . **CLC 2, 5, 8, 32, 80**
See also CA 13-16R; 109; CANR 33, 40; MTCW 1, 2

**Stead, William Thomas** 1849-1912 ..... **TCLC 48**
See also CA 167

**Steele, Richard** 1672-1729 ..................... **LC 18**
See also CDBLB 1660-1789; DLB 84, 101

**Steele, Timothy (Reid)** 1948- ................ **CLC 45**
See also CA 93-96; CANR 16, 50; DLB 120

**Steffens, (Joseph) Lincoln** 1866-1936 . **TCLC 20**

See also CA 117

**Stegner, Wallace (Earle)** 1909-1993 . **CLC 9, 49, 81; DAM NOV; SSC 27**

See also AITN 1; BEST 90:3; CA 1-4R; 141; CAAS 9; CANR 1, 21, 46; DLB 9, 206; DLBY 93; MTCW 1, 2

**Stein, Gertrude** 1874-1946**TCLC 1, 6, 28, 48; DA; DAB; DAC; DAM MST, NOV, POET; PC 18; WLC**

See also CA 104; 132; CDALB 1917-1929; DLB 4, 54, 86; DLBD 15; MTCW 1, 2

**Steinbeck, John (Ernst)** 1902-1968 . **CLC 1, 5, 9, 13, 21, 34, 45, 75; DA; DAB; DAC; DAM DRAM, MST, NOV; SSC 11; WLC**

See also AAYA 12; CA 1-4R; 25-28R; CANR 1, 35; CDALB 1929-1941; DLB 7, 9, 212; DLBD 2; MTCW 1, 2; SATA 9

**Steinem, Gloria** 1934- ............................ **CLC 63**

See also CA 53-56; CANR 28, 51; MTCW 1, 2

**Steiner, George** 1929- ....... **CLC 24; DAM NOV**

See also CA 73-76; CANR 31, 67; DLB 67; MTCW 1, 2; SATA 62

**Steiner, K. Leslie**

See Delany, Samuel R(ay, Jr.)

**Steiner, Rudolf** 1861-1925 ................... **TCLC 13**

See also CA 107

**Stendhal** 1783-1842**NCLC 23, 46; DA; DAB; DAC; DAM MST, NOV; SSC 27; WLC**

See also DLB 119

**Stephen, Adeline Virginia**

See Woolf, (Adeline) Virginia

**Stephen, SirLeslie** 1832-1904 ............. **TCLC 23**

See also CA 123; DLB 57, 144, 190

**Stephen, Sir Leslie**

See Stephen, SirLeslie

**Stephen, Virginia**

See Woolf, (Adeline) Virginia

**Stephens, James** 1882(?)-1950 .............. **TCLC 4**

See also CA 104; DLB 19, 153, 162

**Stephens, Reed**

See Donaldson, Stephen R.

**Steptoe, Lydia**

See Barnes, Djuna

**Sterchi, Beat** 1949- ............................... **CLC 65**

**Sterling, Brett**

See Bradbury, Ray (Douglas); Hamilton, Edmond

**Sterling, Bruce** 1954- ........................... **CLC 72**

See also CA 119; CANR 44

**Sterling, George** 1869-1926 ................ **TCLC 20**

See also CA 117; 165; DLB 54

**Stern, Gerald** 1925- ..................... **CLC 40, 100**

See also CA 81-84; CANR 28; DLB 105

**Stern, Richard (Gustave)** 1928- ........ **CLC 4, 39**

See also CA 1-4R; CANR 1, 25, 52; DLBY 87; INT CANR-25

**Sternberg, Josef von** 1894-1969 ........... **CLC 20**

See also CA 81-84

**Sterne, Laurence** 1713-1768**LC 2, 48; DA; DAB; DAC; DAM MST, NOV; WLC**

See also CDBLB 1660-1789; DLB 39

**Sternheim, (William Adolf) Carl** 1878-1942 **TCLC 8**

See also CA 105; DLB 56, 118

**Stevens, Mark** 1951- ............................. **CLC 34**

See also CA 122

**Stevens, Wallace** 1879-1955**TCLC 3, 12, 45; DA; DAB; DAC; DAM MST, POET; PC 6; WLC**

See also CA 104; 124; CDALB 1929-1941; DLB 54; MTCW 1, 2

**Stevenson, Anne (Katharine)** 1933- . **CLC 7, 33**

See also CA 17-20R; CAAS 9; CANR 9, 33; DLB 40; MTCW 1

**Stevenson, Robert Louis (Balfour)** 1850-1894 **NCLC 5, 14, 63; DA; DAB; DAC; DAM MST, NOV; SSC 11; WLC**

See also AAYA 24; CDBLB 1890-1914; CLR 10, 11; DLB 18, 57, 141, 156, 174; DLBD 13; JRDA;

MAICYA; SATA 100; YABC 2

**Stewart, J(ohn) I(nnes) M(ackintosh)** 1906-1994 **CLC 7, 14, 32**

See also CA 85-88; 147; CAAS 3; CANR 47; MTCW 1, 2

**Stewart, Mary (Florence Elinor)** 1916-**CLC 7, 35, 117; DAB**

See also AAYA 29; CA 1-4R; CANR 1, 59; SATA 12

**Stewart, Mary Rainbow**

See Stewart, Mary (Florence Elinor)

**Stifle, June**

See Campbell, Maria

**Stifter, Adalbert** 1805-1868 ..**NCLC 41; SSC 28**

See also DLB 133

**Still, James** 1906- ................................. **CLC 49**

See also CA 65-68; CAAS 17; CANR 10, 26; DLB 9; SATA 29

**Sting** 1951-

See Sumner, Gordon Matthew

See also CA 167

**Stirling, Arthur**

See Sinclair, Upton (Beall)

**Stitt, Milan** 1941- ................................. **CLC 29**

See also CA 69-72

**Stockton, Francis Richard** 1834-1902

See Stockton, Frank R.

See also CA 108; 137; MAICYA; SATA 44

**Stockton, Frank R.** ............................... **TCLC 47**

See also Stockton, Francis Richard

See also DLB 42, 74; DLBD 13; SATA-Brief 32

**Stoddard, Charles**

See Kuttner, Henry

**Stoker, Abraham** 1847-1912

See Stoker, Bram

See also CA 105; 150; DA; DAC; DAM MST, NOV; SATA 29

**Stoker, Bram** 1847-1912 . **TCLC 8; DAB; WLC**

See also Stoker, Abraham

See also AAYA 23; CDBLB 1890-1914; DLB 36, 70, 178

**Stolz, Mary (Slattery)** 1920- ................ **CLC 12**

See also AAYA 8; AITN 1; CA 5-8R; CANR 13, 41; JRDA; MAICYA; SAAS 3; SATA 10, 71

**Stone, Irving** 1903-1989 ........ **CLC 7; DAM POP**

See also AITN 1; CA 1-4R; 129; CAAS 3; CANR 1, 23; INT CANR-23; MTCW 1, 2; SATA 3; SATA-Obit 64

**Stone, Oliver (William)** 1946- .............. **CLC 73**

See also AAYA 15; CA 110; CANR 55

**Stone, Robert (Anthony)** 1937- ... **CLC 5, 23, 42**

See also CA 85-88; CANR 23, 66; DLB 152; INT CANR-23; MTCW 1

**Stone, Zachary**

See Follett, Ken(neth Martin)

**Stoppard, Tom** 1937-**CLC 1, 3, 4, 5, 8, 15, 29, 34, 63, 91; DA; DAB; DAC; DAM DRAM, MST; DC 6; WLC**

See also CA 81-84; CANR 39, 67; CDBLB 1960 to Present; DLB 13; DLBY 85; MTCW 1, 2

**Storey, David (Malcolm)** 1933- ... **CLC 2, 4, 5, 8; DAM DRAM**

See also CA 81-84; CANR 36; DLB 13, 14, 207; MTCW 1

**Storm, Hyemeyohsts** 1935- **CLC 3; DAM MULT**

See also CA 81-84; CANR 45; NNAL

**Storm, Theodor** 1817-1888 .................... **SSC 27**

**Storm, (Hans) Theodor (Woldsen)** 1817-1888 **NCLC 1; SSC 27**

See also DLB 129

**Storni, Alfonsina** 1892-1938**TCLC 5; DAM MULT; HLC**

See also CA 104; 131; HW 1

**Stoughton, William** 1631-1701 ................ **LC 38**

See also DLB 24

**Stout, Rex (Todhunter)** 1886-1975 .......... **CLC 3**

See also AITN 2; CA 61-64; CANR 71

**Stow, (Julian) Randolph** 1935- .. **CLC 23, 48**

See also CA 13-16R; CANR 33; MTCW 1

**Stowe, Harriet (Elizabeth) Beecher** 1811-1896 **NCLC 3, 50; DA; DAB; DAC; DAM MST, NOV; WLC**

See also CDALB 1865-1917; DLB 1, 12, 42, 74, 189; JRDA; MAICYA; YABC 1

**Strachey, (Giles) Lytton** 1880-1932 ..... **TCLC 12**

See also CA 110; DLB 149; DLBY 10; MTCW 2

**Strand, Mark** 1934- .... **CLC 6, 18, 41, 71; DAM POET**

See also CA 21-24R; CANR 40, 65; DLB 5; SATA 41

**Straub, Peter (Francis)** 1943-**CLC 28, 107; DAM POP**

See also BEST 89:1; CA 85-88; CANR 28, 65; DLBY 84; MTCW 1, 2

**Strauss, Botho** 1944- ............................. **CLC 22**

See also CA 157; DLB 124

**Streatfeild, (Mary) Noel** 1895(?)-1986 .. **CLC 21**

See also CA 81-84; 120; CANR 31; CLR 17; DLB 160; MAICYA; SATA 20; SATA-Obit 48

**Stribling, T(homas) S(igismund)** 1881-1965**CLC 23**

See also CA 107; DLB 9

**Strindberg, (Johan) August** 1849-1912**TCLC 1, 8, 21, 47; DA; DAB; DAC; DAM DRAM, MST; WLC**

See also CA 104; 135; MTCW 2

**Stringer, Arthur** 1874-1950 ................ **TCLC 37**

See also CA 161; DLB 92

**Stringer, David**

See Roberts, Keith (John Kingston)

**Stroheim, Erich von** 1885-1957 .......... **TCLC 71**

**Strugatskii, Arkadii (Natanovich)** 1925-1991 **CLC 27**

See also CA 106; 135

**Strugatskii, Boris (Natanovich)** 1933- . **CLC 27**

See also CA 106

**Strummer, Joe** 1953(?)- ........................ **CLC 30**

**Strunk, William, Jr.** 1869-1946 .......... **TCLC 92**

See also CA 118; 164

**Stuart, Don A.**

See Campbell, John W(ood, Jr.)

**Stuart, Ian**

See MacLean, Alistair (Stuart)

**Stuart, Jesse (Hilton)** 1906-1984**CLC 1, 8, 11, 14, 34; SSC 31**

See also CA 5-8R; 112; CANR 31; DLB 9, 48, 102; DLBY 84; SATA 2; SATA-Obit 36

**Sturgeon, Theodore (Hamilton)** 1918-1985 **CLC 22, 39**

See also Queen, Ellery

See also CA 81-84; 116; CANR 32; DLB 8; DLBY 85; MTCW 1, 2

**Sturges, Preston** 1898-1959 ................ **TCLC 48**

See also CA 114; 149; DLB 26

**Styron, William** 1925- . **CLC 1, 3, 5, 11, 15, 60; DAM NOV, POP; SSC 25**

See also BEST 90:4; CA 5-8R; CANR 6, 33, 74; CDALB 1968-1988; DLB 2, 143; DLBY 80; INT CANR-6; MTCW 1, 2

**Su, Chien** 1884-1918

See Su Man-shu

See also CA 123

**Suarez Lynch, B.**

See Bioy Casares, Adolfo; Borges, Jorge Luis

**Suckow, Ruth** 1892-1960 ....................... **SSC 18**

See also CA 113; DLB 9, 102

**Sudermann, Hermann** 1857-1928 ........ **TCLC 15**

See also CA 107; DLB 118

**Sue, Eugene** 1804-1857 ......................... **NCLC 1**

See also DLB 119

**Sueskind, Patrick** 1949- ........................ **CLC 44**

See also Suskind, Patrick

**Sukenick, Ronald** 1932- ........... **CLC 3, 4, 6, 48**

See also CA 25-28R; CAAS 8; CANR 32; DLB

Trevanian ................................. **CLC 29**
    See also Whitaker, Rod(ney)
Trevor, Glen
    See Hilton, James
Trevor, William 1928-**CLC 7, 9, 14, 25, 71, 116;**
    **SSC 21**
    See also Cox, William Trevor
    See also DLB 14, 139; MTCW 2
Trifonov, Yuri (Valentinovich) 1925-1981**CLC 45**
    See also CA 126; 103; MTCW 1
Trilling, Lionel 1905-1975 .......... **CLC 9, 11, 24**
    See also CA 9-12R; 61-64; CANR 10; DLB 28, 63;
    INT CANR-10; MTCW 1, 2
Trimball, W. H.
    See Mencken, H(enry) L(ouis)
Tristan
    See Gomez de la Serna, Ramon
Tristram
    See Housman, A(lfred) E(dward)
Trogdon, William (Lewis) 1939-
    See Heat-Moon, William Least
    See also CA 115; 119; CANR 47; INT 119
Trollope, Anthony 1815-1882 .. **NCLC 6, 33; DA;**
    **DAB; DAC; DAM MST, NOV; SSC 28; WLC**
    See also CDBLB 1832-1890; DLB 21, 57, 159;
    SATA 22
Trollope, Frances 1779-1863 .......... **NCLC 30**
    See also DLB 21, 166
Trotsky, Leon 1879-1940 ..................... **TCLC 22**
    See also CA 118; 167
Trotter (Cockburn), Catharine 1679-1749 **LC 8**
    See also DLB 84
Trout, Kilgore
    See Farmer, Philip Jose
Trow, George W. S. 1943- ...................... **CLC 52**
    See also CA 126
Troyat, Henri 1911- ............................... **CLC 23**
    See also CA 45-48; CANR 2, 33, 67; MTCW 1
Trudeau, G(arretson) B(eekman) 1948-
    See Trudeau, Garry B.
    See also CA 81-84; CANR 31; SATA 35
Trudeau, Garry B. .................................. **CLC 12**
    See also Trudeau, G(arretson) B(eekman)
    See also AAYA 10; AITN 2
Truffaut, Francois 1932-1984 ........ **CLC 20, 101**
    See also CA 81-84; 113; CANR 34
Trumbo, Dalton 1905-1976 .................... **CLC 19**
    See also CA 21-24R; 69-72; CANR 10; DLB 26
Trumbull, John 1750-1831 ................. **NCLC 30**
    See also DLB 31
Trundlett, Helen B.
    See Eliot, T(homas) S(tearns)
Tryon, Thomas 1926-1991 **CLC 3, 11; DAM POP**
    See also AITN 1; CA 29-32R; 135; CANR 32, 77;
    MTCW 1
Tryon, Tom
    See Tryon, Thomas
Ts'ao Hsueh-ch'in 1715(?)-1763 ................. **LC 1**
Tsushima, Shuji 1909-1948
    See Dazai Osamu
    See also CA 107
Tsvetaeva (Efron), Marina (Ivanovna) 1892-1941
    **TCLC 7, 35; PC 14**
    See also CA 104; 128; CANR 73; MTCW 1, 2
Tuck, Lily 1938- .................................. **CLC 70**
    See also CA 139
Tu Fu 712-770 ............................................ **PC 9**
    See also DAM MULT
Tunis, John R(oberts) 1889-1975 .......... **CLC 12**
    See also CA 61-64; CANR 62; DLB 22, 171;
    JRDA; MAICYA; SATA 37; SATA-Brief 30
Tuohy, Frank .......................................... **CLC 37**
    See also Tuohy, John Francis
    See also DLB 14, 139
Tuohy, John Francis 1925-
    See Tuohy, Frank
    See also CA 5-8R; CANR 3, 47

Turco, Lewis (Putnam) 1934- ...... **CLC 11, 63**
    See also CA 13-16R; CAAS 22; CANR 24, 51;
    DLBY 84
Turgenev, Ivan 1818-1883 **NCLC 21; DA; DAB;**
    **DAC; DAM MST, NOV; DC 7; SSC 7; WLC**
Turgot, Anne-Robert-Jacques 1727-1781 **LC 26**
Turner, Frederick 1943- ......................... **CLC 48**
    See also CA 73-76; CAAS 10; CANR 12, 30, 56;
    DLB 40
Tutu, Desmond M(pilo) 1931- .. **CLC 80; BLC 3;**
    **DAM MULT**
    See also BW 1, 3; CA 125; CANR 67, 81
Tutuola, Amos 1920-1997**CLC 5, 14, 29; BLC 3;**
    **DAM MULT**
    See also BW 2, 3; CA 9-12R; 159; CANR 27, 66;
    DLB 125; MTCW 1, 2
Twain, Mark**TCLC 6, 12, 19, 36, 48, 59; SSC 34;**
    **WLC**
    See also Clemens, Samuel Langhorne
    See also AAYA 20; CLR 58; DLB 11, 12, 23, 64, 74
Tyler, Anne 1941-**CLC 7, 11, 18, 28, 44, 59, 103;**
    **DAM NOV, POP**
    See also AAYA 18; BEST 89:1; CA 9-12R; CANR
    11, 33, 53; CDALBS; DLB 6, 143; DLBY 82;
    MTCW 1, 2; SATA 7, 90
Tyler, Royall 1757-1826 .......................... **NCLC 3**
    See also DLB 37
Tynan, Katharine 1861-1931 ........... **TCLC 3**
    See also CA 104; 167; DLB 153
Tyutchev, Fyodor 1803-1873 ................. **NCLC 34**
Tzara, Tristan 1896-1963 **CLC 47; DAM POET**
    See also CA 153; 89-92; MTCW 2
Uhry, Alfred 1936- **CLC 55; DAM DRAM, POP**
    See also CA 127; 133; INT 133
Ulf, Haerved
    See Strindberg, (Johan) August
Ulf, Harved
    See Strindberg, (Johan) August
Ulibarri, Sabine R(eyes) 1919- ... **CLC 83; DAM**
    **MULT; HLCS 2**
    See also CA 131; CANR 81; DLB 82; HW 1, 2
Unamuno (y Jugo), Miguel de 1864-1936**TCLC 2,**
    **9; DAM MULT, NOV; HLC; SSC 11**
    See also CA 104; 131; CANR 81; DLB 108; HW
    1, 2; MTCW 1, 2
Undercliffe, Errol
    See Campbell, (John) Ramsey
Underwood, Miles
    See Glassco, John
Undset, Sigrid 1882-1949 ... **TCLC 3; DA; DAB;**
    **DAC; DAM MST, NOV; WLC**
    See also CA 104; 129; MTCW 1, 2
Ungaretti, Giuseppe 1888-1970 ... **CLC 7, 11, 15**
    See also CA 19-20; 25-28R; CAP 2; DLB 114
Unger, Douglas 1952- ........................... **CLC 34**
    See also CA 130
Unsworth, Barry (Forster) 1930- .......... **CLC 76**
    See also CA 25-28R; CANR 30, 54; DLB 194
Updike, John (Hoyer) 1932- **CLC 1, 2, 3, 5, 7, 9,**
    **13, 15, 23, 34, 43, 70; DA; DAB; DAC; DAM**
    **MST, NOV, POET, POP; SSC 13, 27; WLC**
    See also CA 1-4R; CABS 1; CANR 4, 33, 51;
    CDALB 1968-1988; DLB 2, 5, 143; DLBD 3;
    DLBY 80, 82, 97; MTCW 1, 2
Upshaw, Margaret Mitchell
    See Mitchell, Margaret (Munnerlyn)
Upton, Mark
    See Sanders, Lawrence
Upward, Allen 1863-1926 ..................... **TCLC 85**
    See also CA 117; DLB 36
Urdang, Constance (Henriette) 1922- .. **CLC 47**
    See also CA 21-24R; CANR 9, 24
Uriel, Henry
    See Faust, Frederick (Schiller)
Uris, Leon (Marcus) 1924-**CLC 7, 32; DAM NOV,**
    **POP**
    See also AITN 1, 2; BEST 89:2; CA 1-4R; CANR

1, 40, 65; MTCW 1, 2; SATA 49
Urmuz
    See Codrescu, Andrei
Urquhart, Jane 1949- ................. **CLC 90; DAC**
    See also CA 113; CANR 32, 68
Ustinov, Peter (Alexander) 1921- ........... **CLC 1**
    See also AITN 1; CA 13-16R; CANR 25, 51; DLB
    13; MTCW 2
U Tam'si, Gerald Felix Tchicaya
    See Tchicaya, Gerald Felix
U Tam'si, Tchicaya
    See Tchicaya, Gerald Felix
Vachss, Andrew (Henry) 1942- ........... **CLC 106**
    See also CA 118; CANR 44
Vachss, Andrew H.
    See Vachss, Andrew (Henry)
Vaculik, Ludvik 1926- ............................ **CLC 7**
    See also CA 53-56; CANR 72
Vaihinger, Hans 1852-1933 ................. **TCLC 71**
    See also CA 116; 166
Valdez, Luis (Miguel) 1940-**CLC 84; DAM MULT;**
    **DC 10; HLC**
    See also CA 101; CANR 32, 81; DLB 122; HW 1
Valenzuela, Luisa 1938- ..... **CLC 31, 104; DAM**
    **MULT; HLCS 2; SSC 14**
    See also CA 101; CANR 32, 65; DLB 113; HW 1,
    2
Valera y Alcala-Galiano, Juan 1824-1905
    **TCLC 10**
    See also CA 106
Valery, (Ambroise) Paul (Toussaint Jules) 1871-
    1945 .......... **TCLC 4, 15; DAM POET; PC 9**
    See also CA 104; 122; MTCW 1, 2
Valle-Inclan, Ramon (Maria) del 1866-1936**TCLC**
    **5; DAM MULT; HLC**
    See also CA 106; 153; CANR 80; DLB 134; HW 2
Vallejo, Antonio Buero
    See Buero Vallejo, Antonio
Vallejo, Cesar (Abraham) 1892-1938**TCLC 3, 56;**
    **DAM MULT; HLC**
    See also CA 105; 153; HW 1
Valles, Jules 1832-1885 ....................... **NCLC 71**
    See also DLB 123
Vallette, Marguerite Eymery
    See Rachilde
Valle Y Pena, Ramon del
    See Valle-Inclan, Ramon (Maria) del
Van Ash, Cay 1918- ............................... **CLC 34**
Vanbrugh, Sir John 1664-1726 ..... **LC 21; DAM**
    **DRAM**
    See also DLB 80
Van Campen, Karl
    See Campbell, John W(ood, Jr.)
Vance, Gerald
    See Silverberg, Robert
Vance, Jack .......................................... **CLC 35**
    See also Kuttner, Henry; Vance, John Holbrook
    See also DLB 8
Vance, John Holbrook 1916-
    See Queen, Ellery; Vance, Jack
    See also CA 29-32R; CANR 17, 65; MTCW 1
Van Den Bogarde, Derek Jules Gaspard Ulric
    Niven 1921-
    See Bogarde, Dirk
    See also CA 77-80
Vandenburgh, Jane ................................ **CLC 59**
    See also CA 168
Vanderhaeghe, Guy 1951- ..................... **CLC 41**
    See also CA 113; CANR 72
van der Post, Laurens (Jan) 1906-1996 .. **CLC 5**
    See also CA 5-8R; 155; CANR 35; DLB 204
van de Wetering, Janwillem 1931- ........ **CLC 47**
    See also CA 49-52; CANR 4, 62
Van Dine, S. S. ..................................... **TCLC 23**
    See also Wright, Willard Huntington
Van Doren, Carl (Clinton) 1885-1950 . **TCLC 18**
    See also CA 111; 168

Williams, Ben Ames 1889-1953 ..... **TCLC 89**
See also DLB 102
Williams, C(harles) K(enneth) 1936-**CLC 33, 56;**
**DAM POET**
See also CA 37-40R; CAAS 26; CANR 57; DLB 5
Williams, Charles
See Collier, James L(incoln)
Williams, Charles (Walter Stansby) 1886-1945
**TCLC 1, 11**
See also CA 104; 163; DLB 100, 153
Williams, (George) Emlyn 1905-1987 .. **CLC 15;**
**DAM DRAM**
See also CA 104; 123; CANR 36; DLB 10, 77;
MTCW 1
Williams, Hank 1923-1953 .................. **TCLC 81**
Williams, Hugo 1942- ........................... **CLC 42**
See also CA 17-20R; CANR 45; DLB 40
Williams, J. Walker
See Wodehouse, P(elham) G(renville)
Williams, John A(lfred) 1925-**CLC 5, 13; BLC 3;**
**DAM MULT**
See also BW 2, 3; CA 53-56; CAAS 3; CANR 6,
26, 51; DLB 2, 33; INT CANR-6
Williams, Jonathan (Chamberlain) 1929-**CLC 13**
See also CA 9-12R; CAAS 12; CANR 8; DLB 5
Williams, Joy 1944- ............................ **CLC 31**
See also CA 41-44R; CANR 22, 48
Williams, Norman 1952- .................... **CLC 39**
See also CA 118
Williams, Sherley Anne 1944- **CLC 89; BLC 3;**
**DAM MULT, POET**
See also BW 2, 3; CA 73-76; CANR 25; DLB 41;
INT CANR-25; SATA 78
Williams, Shirley
See Williams, Sherley Anne
Williams, Tennessee 1911-1983**CLC 1, 2, 5, 7, 8,**
**11, 15, 19, 30, 39, 45, 71, 111; DA; DAB;**
**DAC; DAM DRAM, MST; DC 4; WLC**
See also AITN 1, 2; CA 5-8R; 108; CABS 3;
CANR 31; CDALB 1941-1968; DLB 7; DLBD
4; DLBY 83; MTCW 1, 2
Williams, Thomas (Alonzo) 1926-1990 . **CLC 14**
See also CA 1-4R; 132; CANR 2
Williams, William C.
See Williams, William Carlos
Williams, William Carlos 1883-1963**CLC 1, 2, 5,**
**9, 13, 22, 42, 67; DA; DAB; DAC; DAM MST,**
**POET; PC 7; SSC 31**
See also CA 89-92; CANR 34; CDALB 1917-1929;
DLB 4, 16, 54, 86; MTCW 1, 2
Williamson, David (Keith) 1942- ......... **CLC 56**
See also CA 103; CANR 41
Williamson, Ellen Douglas 1905-1984
See Douglas, Ellen
See also CA 17-20R; 114; CANR 39
Williamson, Jack ................................ **CLC 29**
See also Williamson, John Stewart
See also CAAS 8; DLB 8
Williamson, John Stewart 1908-
See Williamson, Jack
See also CA 17-20R; CANR 23, 70
Willie, Frederick
See Lovecraft, H(oward) P(hillips)
Willingham, Calder (Baynard, Jr.) 1922-1995
**CLC 5, 51**
See also CA 5-8R; 147; CANR 3; DLB 2, 44;
MTCW 1
Willis, Charles
See Clarke, Arthur C(harles)
Willis, Fingal O'Flahertie
See Wilde, Oscar
Willy
See Colette, (Sidonie-Gabrielle)
Willy, Colette
See Colette, (Sidonie-Gabrielle)
Wilson, A(ndrew) N(orman) 1950- ....... **CLC 33**
See also CA 112; 122; DLB 14, 155, 194; MTCW

2
Wilson, Angus (Frank Johnstone) 1913-1991
**CLC 2, 3, 5, 25, 34; SSC 21**
See also CA 5-8R; 134; CANR 21; DLB 15, 139,
155; MTCW 1, 2
Wilson, August 1945-**CLC 39, 50, 63, 118; BLC**
**3; DA; DAB; DAC; DAM DRAM, MST,**
**MULT; DC 2; WLCS**
See also AAYA 16; BW 2, 3; CA 115; 122; CANR
42, 54, 76; MTCW 1, 2
Wilson, Brian 1942- ........................... **CLC 12**
Wilson, Colin 1931- ....................... **CLC 3, 14**
See also CA 1-4R; CAAS 5; CANR 1, 22, 33, 77;
DLB 14, 194; MTCW 1
Wilson, Dirk
See Pohl, Frederik
Wilson, Edmund 1895-1972 ... **CLC 1, 2, 3, 8, 24**
See also CA 1-4R; 37-40R; CANR 1, 46; DLB 63;
MTCW 1, 2
Wilson, Ethel Davis (Bryant) 1888(?)-1980 **C L C**
**13; DAC; DAM POET**
See also CA 102; DLB 68; MTCW 1
Wilson, John 1785-1854 ....................... **NCLC 5**
Wilson, John (Anthony) Burgess 1917-1993
See Burgess, Anthony
See also CA 1-4R; 143; CANR 2, 46; DAC; DAM
NOV; MTCW 1, 2
Wilson, Lanford 1937- **CLC 7, 14, 36; DAM**
**DRAM**
See also CA 17-20R; CABS 3; CANR 45; DLB 7
Wilson, Robert M. 1944- ........................**CLC 7, 9**
See also CA 49-52; CANR 2, 41; MTCW 1
Wilson, Robert McLiam 1964- ............. **CLC 59**
See also CA 132
Wilson, Sloan 1920- ........................... **CLC 32**
See also CA 1-4R; CANR 1, 44
Wilson, Snoo 1948- .............................. **CLC 33**
See also CA 69-72
Wilson, William S(mith) 1932- ............ **CLC 49**
See also CA 81-84
Wilson, (Thomas) Woodrow 1856-1924**TCLC 79**
See also CA 166; DLB 47
Winchilsea, Anne (Kingsmill) Finch Counte 1661-
1720
See Finch, Anne
Windham, Basil
See Wodehouse, P(elham) G(renville)
Wingrove, David (John) 1954- .............. **CLC 68**
See also CA 133
Winnemucca, Sarah 1844-1891 .......... **NCLC 79**
Wintergreen, Jane
See Duncan, Sara Jeannette
Winters, Janet Lewis ............................ **CLC 41**
See also Lewis, Janet
See also DLBY 87
Winters, (Arthur) Yvor 1900-1968 . **CLC 4, 8, 32**
See also CA 11-12; 25-28R; CAP 1; DLB 48;
MTCW 1
Winterson, Jeanette 1959- . **CLC 64; DAM POP**
See also CA 136; CANR 58; DLB 207; MTCW 2
Winthrop, John 1588-1649 ..................... **LC 31**
See also DLB 24, 30
Wirth, Louis 1897-1952 ...................... **TCLC 92**
Wiseman, Frederick 1930- ................... **CLC 20**
See also CA 159
Wister, Owen 1860-1938 .................... **TCLC 21**
See also CA 108; 162; DLB 9, 78, 186; SATA 62
Witkacy
See Witkiewicz, Stanislaw Ignacy
Witkiewicz, Stanislaw Ignacy 1885-1939**TCLC 8**
See also CA 105; 162
Wittgenstein, Ludwig (Josef Johann) 1889-1951
**TCLC 59**
See also CA 113; 164; MTCW 2
Wittig, Monique 1935(?)- ..................... **CLC 22**
See also CA 116; 135; DLB 83
Wittlin, Jozef 1896-1976 ...................... **CLC 25**

See also CA 49-52; 65-68; CANR 3
Wodehouse, P(elham) G(renville) 1881-1975**CLC**
**1, 2, 5, 10, 22; DAB; DAC; DAM NOV; SSC**
**2**
See also AITN 2; CA 45-48; 57-60; CANR 3, 33;
CDBLB 1914-1945; DLB 34, 162; MTCW 1, 2;
SATA 22
Woiwode, L.
See Woiwode, Larry (Alfred)
Woiwode, Larry (Alfred) 1941- ......... **CLC 6, 10**
See also CA 73-76; CANR 16; DLB 6; INT CANR-
16
Wojciechowska, Maia (Teresa) 1927- .. **CLC 26**
See also AAYA 8; CA 9-12R; CANR 4, 41; CLR
1; JRDA; MAICYA; SAAS 1; SATA 1, 28, 83;
SATA-Essay 104
Wolf, Christa 1929- .................. **CLC 14, 29, 58**
See also CA 85-88; CANR 45; DLB 75; MTCW 1
Wolfe, Gene (Rodman) 1931-**CLC 25; DAM POP**
See also CA 57-60; CAAS 9; CANR 6, 32, 60;
DLB 8; MTCW 2
Wolfe, George C. 1954- ............. **CLC 49; BLCS**
See also CA 149
Wolfe, Thomas (Clayton) 1900-1938**TCLC 4, 13,**
**29, 61; DA; DAB; DAC; DAM MST, NOV;**
**SSC 33; WLC**
See also CA 104; 132; CDALB 1929-1941;
DLB 9, 102; DLBD 2, 16; DLBY 85, 97;
MTCW 1, 2
Wolfe, Thomas Kennerly, Jr. 1930-
See Wolfe, Tom
See also CA 13-16R; CANR 9, 33, 70; DAM POP;
DLB 185; INT CANR-9; MTCW 1, 2
Wolfe, Tom ...................... **CLC 1, 2, 9, 15, 35, 51**
See also Wolfe, Thomas Kennerly, Jr.
See also AAYA 8; AITN 2; BEST 89:1; DLB 152
Wolff, Geoffrey (Ansell) 1937- .............. **CLC 41**
See also CA 29-32R; CANR 29, 43, 78
Wolff, Sonia
See Levitin, Sonia (Wolff)
Wolff, Tobias (Jonathan Ansell) 1945-**CLC 39, 64**
See also AAYA 16; BEST 90:2; CA 114; 117;
CAAS 22; CANR 54, 76; DLB 130; INT 117;
MTCW 2
Wolfram von Eschenbach c. 1170-c. 1220**CMLC 5**
See also DLB 138
Wolitzer, Hilma 1930- ........................... **CLC 17**
See also CA 65-68; CANR 18, 40; INT CANR-18;
SATA 31
Wollstonecraft, Mary 1759-1797 .......... **LC 5, 50**
See also CDBLB 1789-1832; DLB 39, 104, 158
Wonder, Stevie ...................................... **CLC 12**
See also Morris, Steveland Judkins
Wong, Jade Snow 1922- ........................ **CLC 17**
See also CA 109
Woodberry, George Edward 1855-1930 **TCLC 73**
See also CA 165; DLB 71, 103
Woodcott, Keith
See Brunner, John (Kilian Houston)
Woodruff, Robert W.
See Mencken, H(enry) L(ouis)
Woolf, (Adeline) Virginia 1882-1941 **TCLC 1, 5,**
**20, 43, 56; DA; DAB; DAC; DAM MST,**
**NOV; SSC 7; WLC**
See also Woolf, Virginia Adeline
See also CA 104; 130; CANR 64; CDBLB 1914-
1945; DLB 36, 100, 162; DLBD 10; MTCW 1
Woolf, Virginia Adeline
See Woolf, (Adeline) Virginia
See also MTCW 2
Woollcott, Alexander (Humphreys) 1887-1943
**TCLC 5**
See also CA 105; 161; DLB 29
Woolrich, Cornell 1903-1968 ................ **CLC 77**
See also Hopley-Woolrich, Cornell George
Wordsworth, Dorothy 1771-1855 ......... **NCLC 25**
See also DLB 107

# Literary Criticism Series
# Cumulative Topic Index

This index lists all topic entries in Gale's *Classical and Medieval Literature Criticism, Contemporary Literary Criticism, Literature Criticism from 1400 to 1800, Nineteenth-Century Literature Criticism,* and *Twentieth-Century Literary Criticism.*

**Topic Index**

Topic Index

# Twentieth-Century Literary Criticism
## Cumulative Nationality Index

Nationality Index

Housman, Laurence  **7**
Hudson, W(illiam) H(enry)  **29**
Hulme, T(homas) E(rnest)  **21**
Hunt, Violet  **53**
Jacobs, W(illiam) W(ymark)  **22**
James, Montague (Rhodes)  **6**
Jerome, Jerome K(lapka)  **23**
Johnson, Lionel (Pigot)  **19**
Kaye-Smith, Sheila  **20**
Keynes, John Maynard  **64**
Kipling, (Joseph) Rudyard  **8, 17**
Laski, Harold  **79**
Lawrence, D(avid) H(erbert Richards)  **2, 9,
    16, 33, 48, 61, 93**
Lawrence, T(homas) E(dward)  **18**
Lee, Vernon  **5**
Lee-Hamilton, Eugene (Jacob)  **22**
Leverson, Ada  **18**
Lewis, (Percy) Wyndham  **2, 9**
Lindsay, David  **15**
Lowndes, Marie Adelaide (Belloc)  **12**
Lowry, (Clarence) Malcolm  **6, 40**
Lucas, E(dward) V(errall)  **73**
Macaulay, Rose  **7, 44**
MacCarthy, (Charles Otto) Desmond  **36**
Maitland, Frederic  **65**
Manning, Frederic  **25**
Meredith, George  **17, 43**
Mew, Charlotte (Mary)  **8**
Meynell, Alice (Christina Gertrude Thompson)
    **6**
Middleton, Richard (Barham)  **56**
Milne, A(lan) A(lexander)  **6, 88**
Moore, G. E.  **89**
Morrison, Arthur  **72**
Murry, John Middleton  **16**
Nightingale, Florence  **85**
Noyes, Alfred  **7**
Oppenheim, E(dward) Phillips  **45**
Orwell, George  **2, 6, 15, 31, 51**
Ouida  **43**
Owen, Wilfred (Edward Salter)  **5, 27**
Pinero, Arthur Wing  **32**
Powys, T(heodore) F(rancis)  **9**
Quiller-Couch, Arthur (Thomas)  **53**
Richardson, Dorothy Miller  **3**
Rohmer, Sax  **28**
Rolfe, Frederick (William Serafino Austin Lewis
    Mary)  **12**
Rosenberg, Isaac  **12**
Ruskin, John  **20**
Rutherford, Mark  **25**
Sabatini, Rafael  **47**
Saintsbury, George (Edward Bateman)  **31**
Saki  **3**
Sapper  **44**
Sayers, Dorothy L(eigh)  **2, 15**
Shiel, M(atthew) P(hipps)  **8**
Sinclair, May  **3, 11**
Stapledon, (William) Olaf  **22**
Stead, William Thomas  **48**
Stephen, Leslie  **23**
Strachey, (Giles) Lytton  **12**
Summers, (Alphonsus Joseph-Mary Augustus)
    Montague  **16**
Sutro, Alfred  **6**
Swinburne, Algernon Charles  **8, 36**
Symons, Arthur  **11**
Thomas, (Philip) Edward  **10**
Thompson, Francis Joseph  **4**
Tomlinson, H(enry) M(ajor)  **71**
Upward, Allen  **85**
Van Druten, John (William)  **2**

Wallace, (Richard Horatio) Edgar  **57**
Wallas, Graham  **91**
Walpole, Hugh (Seymour)  **5**
Ward, Mrs. Humphry  **55**
Warung, Price  **45**
Webb, (Martha) Beatrice (Potter)  **22**
Webb, Mary (Gladys Meredith)  **24**
Webb, Sidney (James)  **22**
Welch, (Maurice) Denton  **22**
Wells, H(erbert) G(eorge)  **6, 12, 19**
Williams, Charles (Walter Stansby)  **1, 11**
Woolf, (Adeline) Virginia  **1, 5, 20, 43, 56**
Yonge, Charlotte (Mary)  **48**
Zangwill, Israel  **16**

## ESTONIAN
Talvik, Heiti  **87**
Tammsaare, A(nton) H(ansen)  **27**

## FINNISH
Leino, Eino  **24**
Soedergran, Edith (Irene)  **31**
Westermarck, Edward  **87**

## FRENCH
Alain  **41**
Alain-Fournier  **6**
Apollinaire, Guillaume  **3, 8, 51**
Artaud, Antonin (Marie Joseph)  **3, 36**
Barbusse, Henri  **5**
Barres, (Auguste-) Maurice  **47**
Benda, Julien  **60**
Bergson, Henri(-Louis)  **32**
Bernanos, (Paul Louis) Georges  **3**
Bernhardt, Sarah (Henriette Rosine)  **75**
Bloy, Leon  **22**
Bourget, Paul (Charles Joseph)  **12**
Claudel, Paul (Louis Charles Marie)  **2, 10**
Colette, (Sidonie-Gabrielle)  **1, 5, 16**
Coppee, Francois  **25**
Daumal, Rene  **14**
Desnos, Robert  **22**
Drieu la Rochelle, Pierre(-Eugene)  **21**
Dujardin, Edouard (Emile Louis)  **13**
Durkheim, Emile  **55**
Eluard, Paul  **7, 41**
Epstein, Jean  **92**
Fargue, Leon-Paul  **11**
Feydeau, Georges (Leon Jules Marie)  **22**
France, Anatole  **9**
Gide, Andre (Paul Guillaume)  **5, 12, 36**
Giraudoux, (Hippolyte) Jean  **2, 7**
Gourmont, Remy (-Marie-Charles) de  **17**
Huysmans, Joris-Karl  **7, 69**
Jacob, (Cyprien-)Max  **6**
Jammes, Francis  **75**
Jarry, Alfred  **2, 14**
Larbaud, Valery (Nicolas)  **9**
Leautaud, Paul  **83**
Leblanc, Maurice (Marie Emile)  **49**
Leroux, Gaston  **25**
Loti, Pierre  **11**
Martin du Gard, Roger  **24**
Melies, Georges  **81**
Mirbeau, Octave  **55**
Mistral, Frederic  **51**
Moreas, Jean  **18**
Nizan, Paul  **40**
Peguy, Charles Pierre  **10**
Peret, Benjamin  **20**
Proust, (Valentin-Louis-George-Eugene-)
    Marcel  **7, 13, 33**
Rachilde  **67**

Radiguet, Raymond  **29**
Renard, Jules  **17**
Rolland, Romain  **23**
Rostand, Edmond (Eugene Alexis)  **6, 37**
Roussel, Raymond  **20**
Saint-Exupery, Antoine (Jean Baptiste Marie
    Roger) de  **2, 56**
Schwob, Marcel (Mayer Andre)  **20**
Sorel, Georges  **91**
Sully Prudhomme  **31**
Teilhard de Chardin, (Marie Joseph) Pierre  **9**
Valery, (Ambroise) Paul (Toussaint Jules)  **4,
    15**
Verne, Jules (Gabriel)  **6, 52**
Vian, Boris  **9**
Weil, Simone (Adolphine)  **23**
Zola, Emile (Edouard Charles Antoine)  **1, 6,
    21, 41**

## GERMAN
Andreas-Salome, Lou  **56**
Auerbach, Erich  **43**
Barlach, Ernst  **84**
Benjamin, Walter  **39**
Benn, Gottfried  **3**
Borchert, Wolfgang  **5**
Brecht, (Eugen) Bertolt (Friedrich)  **1, 6, 13,
    35**
Carossa, Hans  **48**
Cassirer, Ernst  **61**
Doblin, Alfred  **13**
Doeblin, Alfred  **13**
Einstein, Albert  **65**
Ewers, Hanns Heinz  **12**
Feuchtwanger, Lion  **3**
Frank, Bruno  **81**
George, Stefan (Anton)  **2, 14**
Goebbels, (Paul) Joseph  **68**
Haeckel, Ernst Heinrich (Philipp August)  **83**
Hauptmann, Gerhart (Johann Robert)  **4**
Heym, Georg (Theodor Franz Arthur)  **9**
Heyse, Paul (Johann Ludwig von)  **8**
Hitler, Adolf  **53**
Horney, Karen (Clementine Theodore
    Danielsen)  **71**
Huch, Ricarda (Octavia)  **13**
Kaiser, Georg  **9**
Klabund  **44**
Kolmar, Gertrud  **40**
Lasker-Schueler, Else  **57**
Liliencron, (Friedrich Adolf Axel) Detlev von
    **18**
Luxemburg, Rosa  **63**
Mann, (Luiz) Heinrich  **9**
Mann, (Paul) Thomas  **2, 8, 14, 21, 35, 44, 60**
Mannheim, Karl  **65**
Michels, Robert  **88**
Morgenstern, Christian  **8**
Nietzsche, Friedrich (Wilhelm)  **10, 18, 55**
Ophuls, Max  **79**
Otto, Rudolf  **85**
Plumpe, Friedrich Wilhelm  **53**
Raabe, Wilhelm (Karl)  **45**
Rilke, Rainer Maria  **1, 6, 19**
Schwitters, Kurt (Hermann Edward Karl Julius)
    **95**
Simmel, Georg  **64**
Spengler, Oswald (Arnold Gottfried)  **25**
Sternheim, (William Adolf) Carl  **8**
Sudermann, Hermann  **15**
Toller, Ernst  **10**
Vaihinger, Hans  **71**
Wassermann, (Karl) Jakob  **6**

Weber, Max **69**
Wedekind, (Benjamin) Frank(lin) **7**
Wiene, Robert **56**

**GHANIAN**
Casely-Hayford, J(oseph) E(phraim) **24**

**GREEK**
Cavafy, C(onstantine) P(eter) **2, 7**
Kazantzakis, Nikos **2, 5, 33**
Palamas, Kostes **5**
Papadiamantis, Alexandros **29**
Sikelianos, Angelos **39**

**HAITIAN**
Roumain, Jacques (Jean Baptiste) **19**

**HUNGARIAN**
Ady, Endre **11**
Babits, Mihaly **14**
Csath, Geza **13**
Herzl, Theodor **36**
Horvath, Oedoen von **45**
Jozsef, Attila **22**
Karinthy, Frigyes **47**
Mikszath, Kalman **31**
Molnar, Ferenc **20**
Moricz, Zsigmond **33**
Radnoti, Miklos **16**

**ICELANDIC**
Sigurjonsson, Johann **27**

**INDIAN**
Chatterji, Saratchandra **13**
Dasgupta, Surendranath **81**
Gandhi, Mohandas Karamchand **59**
Ghose, Aurabinda **63**
Iqbal, Muhammad **28**
Naidu, Sarojini **80**
Premchand **21**
Ramana Maharshi **84**
Tagore, Rabindranath **3, 53**
Vivekananda, Swami **88**

**INDONESIAN**
Anwar, Chairil **22**

**IRANIAN**
Hedayat, Sadeq **21**

**IRISH**
A.E. **3, 10**
Baker, Jean H. **3, 10**
Cary, (Arthur) Joyce (Lunel) **1, 29**
Dunsany, Lord **2, 59**
Gogarty, Oliver St. John **15**
Gregory, Isabella Augusta (Persse) **1**
Harris, Frank **24**
Joyce, James (Augustine Aloysius) **3, 8, 16, 35, 52**
Ledwidge, Francis **23**
Martin, Violet Florence **51**
Moore, George Augustus **7**
O'Grady, Standish (James) **5**
Shaw, Bernard **45**
Shaw, George Bernard **3, 9, 21**
Somerville, Edith **51**
Stephens, James **4**
Stoker, Bram **8**
Synge, (Edmund) J(ohn) M(illington) **6, 37**
Tynan, Katharine **3**
Wilde, Oscar **1, 8, 23, 41**

Yeats, William Butler **1, 11, 18, 31, 93**

**ITALIAN**
Alvaro, Corrado **60**
Betti, Ugo **5**
Brancati, Vitaliano **12**
Campana, Dino **20**
Carducci, Giosue (Alessandro Giuseppe) **32**
Croce, Benedetto **37**
D'Annunzio, Gabriele **6, 40**
Deledda, Grazia (Cosima) **23**
Giacosa, Giuseppe **7**
Jovine, Francesco **79**
Lampedusa, Giuseppe (Tomasi) di **13**
Malaparte, Curzio **52**
Marinetti, Filippo Tommaso **10**
Mosca, Gaetano **75**
Papini, Giovanni **22**
Pareto, Vilfredo **69**
Pascoli, Giovanni **45**
Pavese, Cesare **3**
Pirandello, Luigi **4, 29**
Saba, Umberto **33**
Svevo, Italo **2, 35**
Tozzi, Federigo **31**
Verga, Giovanni (Carmelo) **3**

**JAMAICAN**
De Lisser, H(erbert) G(eorge) **12**
Garvey, Marcus (Moziah Jr.) **41**
Mais, Roger **8**
McKay, Claude **7, 41**
Redcam, Tom **25**

**JAPANESE**
Akutagawa, Ryunosuke **16**
Dazai Osamu **11**
Futabatei, Shimei **44**
Hagiwara Sakutaro **60**
Hayashi, Fumiko **27**
Ishikawa, Takuboku **15**
Masaoka Shiki **18**
Miyamoto, (Chujo) Yuriko **37**
Miyazawa, Kenji **76**
Mizoguchi, Kenji **72**
Nagai Kafu **51**
Natsume, Soseki **2, 10**
Nishida, Kitaro **83**
Noguchi, Yone **80**
Rohan, Koda **22**
Santoka, Taneda **72**
Shimazaki Toson **5**
Yokomitsu Riichi **47**
Yosano Akiko **59**

**LATVIAN**
Rainis, Janis **29**

**LEBANESE**
Gibran, Kahlil **1, 9**

**LESOTHAN**
Mofolo, Thomas (Mokopu) **22**

**LITHUANIAN**
Kreve (Mickevicius), Vincas **27**

**MEXICAN**
Azuela, Mariano **3**
Gamboa, Federico **36**
Gonzalez Martinez, Enrique **72**
Nervo, (Jose) Amado (Ruiz de) **11**
Reyes, Alfonso **33**

Romero, Jose Ruben **14**
Villaurrutia, Xavier **80**

**NEPALI**
Devkota, Laxmiprasad **23**

**NEW ZEALANDER**
Mander, (Mary) Jane **31**
Mansfield, Katherine **2, 8, 39**

**NICARAGUAN**
Dario, Ruben **4**

**NORWEGIAN**
Bjoernson, Bjoernstjerne (Martinius) **7, 37**
Bojer, Johan **64**
Grieg, (Johan) Nordahl (Brun) **10**
Hamsun, Knut **2, 14, 49**
Ibsen, Henrik (Johan) **2, 8, 16, 37, 52**
Kielland, Alexander Lange **5**
Lie, Jonas (Lauritz Idemil) **5**
Obstfelder, Sigbjoern **23**
Skram, Amalie (Bertha) **25**
Undset, Sigrid **3**

**PAKISTANI**
Iqbal, Muhammad **28**

**PERUVIAN**
Palma, Ricardo **29**
Vallejo, Cesar (Abraham) **3, 56**

**POLISH**
Asch, Sholem **3**
Borowski, Tadeusz **9**
Conrad, Joseph **1, 6, 13, 25, 43, 57**
Peretz, Isaac Loeb **16**
Prus, Boleslaw **48**
Przybyszewski, Stanislaw **36**
Reymont, Wladyslaw (Stanislaw) **5**
Schulz, Bruno **5, 51**
Sienkiewicz, Henryk (Adam Alexander Pius) **3**
Singer, Israel Joshua **33**
Witkiewicz, Stanislaw Ignacy **8**

**PORTUGUESE**
Pessoa, Fernando (Antonio Nogueira) **27**
Sa-Carniero, Mario de **83**

**PUERTO RICAN**
Hostos (y Bonilla), Eugenio Maria de **24**

**ROMANIAN**
Bacovia, George **24**
Caragiale, Ion Luca **76**
Rebreanu, Liviu **28**

**RUSSIAN**
Aldanov, Mark (Alexandrovich) **23**
Andreyev, Leonid (Nikolaevich) **3**
Annensky, Innokenty (Fyodorovich) **14**
Artsybashev, Mikhail (Petrovich) **31**
Babel, Isaak (Emmanuilovich) **2, 13**
Bagritsky, Eduard **60**
Balmont, Konstantin (Dmitriyevich) **11**
Bely, Andrey **7**
Berdyaev, Nikolai (Aleksandrovich) **67**
Bergelson, David **81**
Blok, Alexander (Alexandrovich) **5**
Bryusov, Valery Yakovlevich **10**
Bulgakov, Mikhail (Afanas'evich) **2, 16**
Bulgya, Alexander Alexandrovich **53**
Bunin, Ivan Alexeyevich **6**